W9-BSH-588

BLEAK HOUSE

AN AUTHORITATIVE AND ANNOTATED TEXT
ILLUSTRATIONS
A NOTE ON THE TEXT
GENESIS AND COMPOSITION
BACKGROUNDS
CRITICISM

A NORTON CRITICAL EDITION

CHARLES DICKENS

BLEAK HOUSE

AN AUTHORITATIVE AND
ANNOTATED TEXT
ILLUSTRATIONS
A NOTE ON THE TEXT
GENESIS AND COMPOSITION
BACKGROUNDS
CRITICISM

Edited by

GEORGE FORD
UNIVERSITY OF ROCHESTER

SYLVÈRE MONOD
UNIVERSITY OF PARIS-III (SORBONNE)

W · W · NORTON & COMPANY
New York · London

W. W. Norton & Company, Inc., 500 Fifth Avenue, New York, N.Y. 10110

Library of Congress Cataloging in Publication Data

Dickens, Charles, 1812–1870.
Bleak house.

(A Norton critical edition)
Bibliography: p.
I. Ford, George Harry, 1914– II. Monod,
Sylvère, 1921– III. Title.
PZ3.D55Bl73 [PR4556] 823'.8 77-7783
ISBN 0-393-04374-6
ISBN 0-393-09332-8 pbk.

PRINTED IN THE UNITED STATES OF AMERICA

6 7 8 9 0

Contents

List of Illustrations

Introduction

Critical assessments of *Bleak House* have been remarkable in their variety. In 1853, a review in the *Spectator* (included in the Criticism section of the present volume) treated the novel as if it were a kind of clumsy bungle. More than a hundred years later, in his 1964 edition of *Bleak House*, Geoffrey Tillotson described it as "the finest literary work the nineteenth century produced in England." And in 1970, not quite so hyperbolically, Mrs. Q. D. Leavis concluded her chapter in *Dickens the Novelist* by contending that *Bleak House* is certainly "the most impressive and rewarding of all Dickens's novels." Dickens himself ranked it only a little below the novel which preceded it, *David Copperfield*. The strikingly popular success of *Bleak House* from the moment its first monthly installment was published in March, 1852 (for despite the *Spectator* review it began a best seller and remained one), gave him great satisfaction, even though *Copperfield* was to remain, among all his writings, his favorite.

Between the two novels was a gap of thirteen months, a period in which the thirty-eight-year-old author elected to take a rest from novel writing. The final number of *Copperfield* was published in October, 1850, and it was not until November, 1851, that the writing of *Bleak House* commenced. During the rest period between the novels Dickens did not abstain from other kinds of prose. For his highly successful magazine, *Household Words*, he contributed a number of articles and also dictated a book, *A Child's History of England*, which appeared in installments from January, 1851, to September, 1853. Nevertheless most of his energies during this interval were expended in areas other than literary. In particular he was keenly involved in directing a touring troupe of amateur actors in a play by his friend, Bulwer-Lytton, the proceeds from the performances being donated to a fund in aid of artists. Also public-spirited, and of greater significance in the shaping of *Bleak House*, was the assistance he provided for his wealthy friend, Angela Burdett-Coutts, in her projects for slum clearance and the building of model housing. This activity, together with what he witnessed while preparing articles on the role of the police in London slum areas, reinforced his awareness that behind the impressively solid front of mid-Victorian prosperity, the urban poor were living in a deplorable state of wretchedness and ignorance.

Pollution was another related problem that engaged Dickens' energies at this time, an issue which since the ravages of cholera in 1848–49 had become of pressing importance. His active interest in the reforms needed for urban sanitation led to his being a speaker at meetings of the Metropolitan Sanitary Association. An extract from one of these speeches, of May, 1851, is included below in the section called Backgrounds. In this section, consisting of a compilation of documents from the period, the topic of pollution is most prominently featured. We have made it prominent partly because it seems to have provided the controlling metaphor for *Bleak House*, but also because of the clear indications of the intensity of Dickens' involvement with the issue, both as a citizen and as a writer. The other two topics, under which we have also grouped some contemporary documents, are less often referred to by Dickens in 1851–53. One is the Court of Chancery, accounts of which he must have read in *The Times* during this period (accounts which confirmed his own earlier formed impressions), and the other is government itself. His interest in the latter subject could have been stimulated likewise by newspaper accounts of the rise and fall of political parties, especially the collapse of Lord Russell's government in February, 1852; and his interest may have been further intensified by his having been asked to stand for Parliament in February, 1852, and again in June. In view of his active involvement in contemporary issues, it was almost inevitable that these requests would be made, but despite the attractions of political power for Dickens his response was always to decline. On February 28, 1852, he commented:

> In the Parliamentary matter—it is impossible that I could go into it with the new book in hand. . . . And I don't know but I am far more useful (and certainly far more happy) in my own sphere of service than among the bellowers and prosers of St. Stephen's.

His satisfaction in having chosen to make novels rather than legislation must have been reinforced later when what seemed to him the chaos of the Parliamentary scene became intensified. The Doodle-Foodle parliamentary shuffles of 1852–53 as pictured in his novel led on, in the world outside his novel, to the blunders of war in Crimea in 1853–54.

In sketching Dickens' experiences and interests in 1851–53, we have emphasized public issues rather than his private life. The emphasis is appropriate enough, for one of the principal differences between *David Copperfield* and *Bleak House* resides in the distinctive preoccupation, in the earlier novel, with the lives of private individuals and families. In David's life history, public issues are of subordinate importance. *Bleak House,* by contrast, seems predominantly topical. Yet it is misleading to overlook the role of the private worlds in *Bleak House,* the worlds of the mutual interaction of individual characters and of the household (there are at least twenty-four different households pictured in the story). It would be equally misleading to overlook the importance of private family life for Dickens himself at this time. His letters show that he was as much preoccupied with household concerns as with major public issues. In the interval between the two novels, his father died painfully, an event followed two weeks later by the death of his infant daughter, Dora. And more pressing, perhaps, than an awareness of familial mortality was a realization of impending familial responsibilities. As the father of a large number of children, Dickens was confronting the prospect of their eventually having to choose appropriate careers for themselves. His letters refer several times to his eldest son, Charles, who did not flourish on the Latin courses at Eton and who proposed a career in the army before electing to try his hand at business. Richard Carstone in the novel was probably not modeled on Dickens' son, yet the account of his wavering essays into different professions may have been affected by his creator's preoccupation, as a father, with the virtues of energetic decisiveness and the capacity for self-help.

The letters of the period also clearly bring out Dickens' role as a householder. During the course of composing *Bleak House,* he moved his family from a large house in London, Devonshire Terrace, to a larger establishment on Tavistock Square (where the redecorating held up the writing for several weeks). In the summers of 1851 and 1852, he settled in houses on the English seacoast, and in 1853 was at Boulogne in France. At times none of these establishments satisfied him, and he expressed a restless urge to find some other ideal country retreat in which he could write in isolation.

These experiences, like the very title of the novel, can provide a corrective reminder that *Bleak House* is concerned with houses and households, in the countryside as well as in cities, and not exclusively with public issues such as Chancery iniquities, London slums, bungling philanthropy, political ineptitudes, and other such topics, however arresting these may appear to us, especially on a first reading.

As indicated in our note on the text, the present edition of *Bleak House,* like our edition of *Hard Times,* seems to be the first in which the text has been established by a comparative study of all the editions of the novel published during the author's lifetime and explicitly or implicitly sanctioned by him. For making available to us the original manuscript and corrected proofs of *Bleak*

House, we wish to acknowledge the assistance of the Keeper of Printed Books at the Victoria and Albert Museum. We are also grateful to Dr. Peter Sharratt for his princely gift of a first edition of *Bleak House* to one of the editors, and to Dr. Michael Slater for helpful advice and in particular for making available to us a copy of *Bleak House* in which the running headlines were inserted in Dickens' own handwriting.

For assistance in annotations, our debts are perhaps more extensive. Some preliminary studies on the allusions in the novel have been made, in particular by T. W. Hill, Tadao Yamamoto, and Stephen C. Gill, and we have appreciated the lead-ins they have offered even when our readings differ from theirs.[1] Our more ambitious objective has been to provide, for the first time so far as we know, a full-scale set of notes to enable today's readers to follow up allusions that have become obscure after 120 years. As a supplement to these footnotes we also include a separate Introductory Note on Law Courts and Colleges, which aims to explain some of the legal procedures referred to in the opening chapter in particular but throughout the novel as well.

In the preparation of these annotations it became evident that *Bleak House* is one of the most richly and diversely allusive of novels, and we have therefore had to call for advice from experts in a variety of fields. Our consultants on legal history included Mr. Justice Foster of the Court of Chancery, Professor Henry Manne, and Mr. Douglas Hamer; on the history of medicine, Mr. Eric Gaskell of the Wellcome Institute; on nineteenth-century technology, Mr. Richard Altick, the late Sir Arthur Elton, and Mr. Robert Patterson of the Castle Museum, York; on law enforcement, Dr. J. J. Tobias of the Police College of London; and on London topography, Mrs. Hazel Shepherd and Mr. Leslie Staples. Other helpful consultants included historians of costume and, most extensively, religion (Dickens' abundant references to the Book of Common Prayer are a significant aspect of his style in *Bleak House*). Perhaps most illuminating has been the identification of songs, such as the one sung by Krook on the night of his drunken death, or Skimpole's song about "The Peasant Boy," and here we were aided by several historians of music including Dr. Lillian Ruff. To all of these consultants, named and unnamed, we wish to express our warm sense of gratitude.

Because of the very long period during which we have been intermittently engaged with this project, we must also acknowledge a special debt to fellow editors and scholars who have recently pub-

1. T. W. Hill, "Notes on *Bleak House*," *Dickensian*, 40 (1943–44), 39–44, 65–70, 133–41; Tadao Yamamoto, *Growth and System of the Language of Dickens* (Osaka, 1952); Stephen C. Gill, "Allusion in *Bleak House*," *Nineteenth-Century Fiction*, 22 (1967), 145–54.

lished editions or studies of *Bleak House*. Some five years ago, after compiling some 460 notes, we had overconfidently assumed that no more tracking down of references would be required, but in this seemingly inexhaustible text we ourselves kept turning up new references, and, as other annotators subsequently appeared on the scene, we discovered that there were about a dozen allusions we had overlooked. All of these scholars have generously allowed us to include such overlooked items (which are acknowledged in the notes). We are grateful to Norman Page for two such notes from his 1971 edition of the novel, and to Grahame Smith for three others in his *Bleak House* of 1974. Most especially we appreciate the permission given by Susan Shatto to incorporate six notes from her two articles published in *Dickens Studies Newsletter* in 1975. Our only regret is that we had not known earlier of her fellow labors in the vineyard and of her impressive searchings for elusive allusions.

To an even greater extent than in the case of our edition of *Hard Times*, it may be remarked here that although the principal responsibility for preparing the text of the novel fell to the editor in France, while preparing the annotations and selecting the background documents were the task of the editor in America, the preparation of this edition has been a joint effort involving constant mutual consultation and advice about every aspect of the work.

George Ford
Rochester, New York

Sylvère Monod
Paris, France

British Museum
Bloomsbury Square
Red Lion Square
Bedford Row
Lincolns Inn
Lincolns Inn Fields
Hart Street
Long Acre
Bow Street
Covent Garden
King Street
Strand
Somerset Place
Savoy

HOLBORN
WEST
SMITHFIELD
FLEET
STREET
LUDGATE HILL
LUDGATE
STREET
NEW BRIDGE STREET
TEMPLE
GARDENS
BLACK FRIARS BRIDGE
T H A M E S

Introductory Note on Law Courts and Colleges

Although not formally qualified as a lawyer, Dickens had acquired an extraordinarily rich knowledge of the world of lawyers and law practice, and *Bleak House* bristles with references to the technicalities of a legal system that may sometimes prove baffling. A professor of the history of law at Oxford, William Holdsworth, hailed Dickens as an outstanding legal historian. The compliment is well deserved, and the novelist's special knowledge is certainly one of the assets of his storytelling, but it is a quality that can also cut in opposite directions. Consider, for example, the opening sentence:

> London. Michaelmas Term lately over, and the Lord Chancellor sitting in Lincoln's Inn Hall.

What, we may ask, is Michaelmas Term? Why is the Court therefore sitting in Lincoln's Inn Hall? What sort of inn are we supposed to visualize? And what is a Lord Chancellor?

To answer such questions and to follow out the legal allusions in the opening chapter, it is necessary only to allow the novelist his assumptions that his readers have some rudimentary understanding of how a mid-nineteenth-century court functioned and how the lawyers practicing in that court were trained for their roles.

The Court of Chancery

During the period in which *Bleak House* is set, several different kinds of courts existed in England. To simplify the account, these can be grouped under two categories. The first, the *Courts of Common Law,* were concerned with cases of theft, robbery, murder, and other such crimes or misdemeanors. Thus in *Bleak House,* when a murder is committed, the police detectives arrest a suspect, who is committed to jail and will be tried and sentenced in a common-law court by a judge and jury. Such courts were also responsible for conducting inquests, the *coroner* being an officer of one of these Courts of Common Law. Again, in *Bleak House,* when a suspected suicide occurs, a coroner, assisted by a jury from the locality, conducts an on-the-spot investigation of the incident.

The second type of court, the *Court of Chancery,* existed to settle cases involving such issues as disputes about legacies, trusts, mortgages, in which the remedy sought by the contestants would be decided on the principles of *Equity* rather than on the rules of Common Law. These principles of Equity, as Douglas Hamer explains, are unwritten; each case in a court of Equity is treated as unique and "not determinable by the fixed and universal rules of Common Law." The difference can be nicely illustrated, as Hamer says, by *The Merchant of Venice,* in which Portia pleads her case on the basis of Equity, whereas Shylock pleads his on the basis of Law.[1]

1. Douglas Hamer, "Dickens, The Old Court of Chancery," *Notes and Queries* (Sept. 1970), 342.

Thus, as originally established in earlier centuries, the Court of Chancery served to protect the rights of individuals and to compensate for the rigidities of Law. By Dickens' time, however, what had once been a humane and flexible institution had developed rigidities of its own.

The presiding judge of this Court, which plays such a large role in *Bleak House*, was the *Lord Chancellor*, a member of the Prime Minister's cabinet and President (*ex officio*) of the House of Lords. His office was the highest in the legal profession of England. Assisting him in his duties were other Chancery Court officers, the Master of the Rolls and three Vice Chancellors.

The traditional procedures of the Court of Chancery differed from those practiced in the Courts of Common Law. There was no jury in this court; all cases were decided by the presiding judge, whose verdict was arrived at after sifting evidence submitted by the contesting parties in the form of lengthy affidavits read aloud in court by lawyers. It should also be noted that in the court itself witnesses never appeared as such; if they had evidence to offer, it would have been gathered, in written form, previous to the court hearings. It is this practice that explains why in Dickens' novel Miss Flite, Gridley, and Richard Carstone "all go to court to listen to the proceedings but never give evidence."[2]

Until the Court of Chancery was reformed, in the second half of the nineteenth century, obtaining a decision was likely to be frustratingly slow and also expensive, as Dickens himself had discovered in 1844 when he launched suits against five piratical publishers for breach of copyright. As he complained in a letter: "I was really treated as if I were the robber instead of the robbed." Although the Vice Chancellor's ruling was emphatically in Dickens' favor, the suit cost him more than any damages he was able to collect, and he resolved never again to become involved in dealings with Chancery, remarking bitterly, in 1846, that "it is better to suffer a great wrong than to have recourse to the much greater wrong of the law."

An example can illustrate why there could be such delays and expenses. Let us suppose a wealthy property owner dies and leaves most of his estate to a nephew, with also a few bequests to his servants. Another nephew contends that the will is invalid, and that an earlier will, leaving part of the estate to the second nephew, is the proper one. Employing a solicitor, this second nephew (the plaintiff) has a *bill* drawn up to state his claims against the first nephew (the defendant), and this opening transaction is filed in the Court of Chancery.

Once such procedures were initiated, the heirs could not draw on the estates they had inherited, for all property was taken over by the Court and held until a decision was reached—hence the expression that a house is "*in Chancery*." Such an arrangement assured the Court that expenses involved in the case would be covered. If settlement were long delayed, it also meant that some of the heirs would have a very long wait or would never receive the legacies assigned to them. As *The Times* commented (March 28, 1851): "Butlers, and housekeepers, and gardeners of the kindest master in the world, in spite of ample legacies in his will, are rotting on parish pay [i.e., on welfare payments]."

These proceedings having been launched, the first nephew would be obliged to employ a solicitor and a staff of clerks to gather evidence from

2. Ibid.

witnesses at a hearing held under the auspices of commissioners appointed by the Court. All the living and travel expenses of these officials and witnesses had to be paid for by the litigants. Copies of all the evidence presented at these proceedings had to be made for the participants in the case and at their expense. These documents made up what Dickens, in his opening scene, calls the "bills, cross-bills, answers, rejoinders, injunctions, affidavits, issues, references to masters, masters' reports, mountains of costly nonsense." The reference here to the "masters' reports" pertains to the second stage of presenting a case in the Court of Chancery. After the solicitors had gathered the written evidence for their cases, court officials (or their deputies) called *Masters* reviewed the assembled evidence and reported on whether it was in satisfactory order to present before the Lord Chancellor. These well-paid Chancery officials seem to have played a large role in delaying the settlement of cases. In an article in *Household Words* (March 19, 1853), Dickens spoke witheringly of a Chancery Master as "a sufficiently absurd monster for human reason to reflect upon."

Another group of court officials who had to be paid to funnel the case into the hands of the Lord Chancellor was known as the *Six Clerks.* Such lawyers had at one time acted as solicitors for contestants in the courtroom, and although no longer functioning in that role, the office of the Six Clerks continued to collect fees.

A further obstacle to arriving at decisions would occur when disagreements developed about which of the two types of courts should have jurisdiction in such a case. As one of the characters in *Bleak House* remarks: "Equity sends questions to Law; Law sends questions back to Equity" (chapter VIII).

That Chancery decisions were often delayed is therefore understandable. Even more conducive to delays, however, was what happened when some party to the suit died before a decision had been arrived at and the whole case had, in effect, to be re-prepared. In the present example, if the first nephew died first, his heir would have to pay expenses for re-preparing what was called a *Bill of Revivor.* No doubt many cases were equitably settled by the Court of Chancery without such extensive delays or expenses, but there were others that dragged on interminably. One of these, the William Jennings case, was initiated in 1798. In 1852, when Dickens began writing his novel, it was still unsettled, and he seems to have made it his model for his Jarndyce and Jarndyce suit. Another Chancery suit which also served as a model was, as he states in his Preface, a case of more recent occurrence. A third case, which he had asked one of his assistants to investigate, was the Day case; it had opened in 1834, and by 1853, after expenditures of more than £70,000, its prospects of settlement were "as far off as ever." In response to his inquiry about how many lawyers participated when the case was to be heard in Court, his informant reported: "Formerly always 17, sometimes 30 or 40; it used to be said the Bar [*i.e.,* all the barristers of England]. The number has been reduced." It was cases such as these that prompted an editorial in Dickens' *Household Words* (December 25, 1852) to describe the High Court of Chancery as "High, as we say also of venison or pheasant, when it gets into very bad odour."

Whether Dickens' picture of Chancery cases was historically accurate and representative has been extensively debated. Some of his contemporaries, such as Lord Denman (a former Chancellor), contended that he was wasting his breath in exposing the shortcomings of Chancery practices, because in the very year in which he began his novel, 1852, Parliament had passed legislation (as recommended by a commission reporting on Chancery in 1850) that markedly reformed the Court. These reforms were to be followed by others later in the century, in 1858, 1862, and 1873. Yet it is hard to imagine that the pains of the law's delay, as Hamlet styled them, were eliminated overnight. And for the period in which the novel appears to be set, it has been demonstrated by the legal historian William Holdsworth that the account of Jarndyce and Jarndyce was historically accurate.[3] The exact time of the action of the novel cannot be readily pinpointed, for, like D. H. Lawrence in *Women in Love*, Dickens preferred not to specify precisely when his story takes place. Most readers agree that the settings correspond to the late 1830's, but in any event, the action certainly occurs well before the reforms established by the Court of Chancery Acts of 1852.

Law Schools and Residences: The Inns

When we read of *Lincoln's Inn* and conjure up a hostelry that provides lodging and dining facilities, we are not off the track, but we are overlooking some of the many other functions served by this anciently founded sort of Inn. Such an establishment combines some of the functions of a law school and a dining club, with rooms and dining hall for students and other residents, and usually a chapel. Its blocks of buildings, often situated round a square or park, included offices for lawyers such as those occupied by Mr. Vholes in Symond's Inn. An Inn is also a kind of society or fraternity, with officers supervising its endowments and the expenditure of fees paid by student-members, and also regulating the requirements to qualify for admission to the Bar. Such officers, chosen from among the senior members of the society, were called *benchers*. Some Inns were named after their original founders (Thavies Inn and Symond's Inn); others for their locality, in particular Middle Temple and Inner Temple, whose buildings are located on property once held by the Knights Templars in the early medieval period, property which was leased to the students of law in 1326.

Four of these Inns were classified as *Inns of Court* (Lincoln's Inn, Inner Temple, Middle Temple, and Gray's Inn). These four Inns of Court had the exclusive right to admit candidates to practice law as barristers. Most of the other Inns were classified as Inns of Chancery and were attached to one of the Inns of Court in a kind of "satellite" relationship. The Inns of Chancery, unlike the Inns of Court, have not survived in the twentieth century. Some of the buildings, such as Staple Inn, still stand but have been taken over for offices.

As a map of central London can show, most of the law colleges, offices, and residences were within easy walking distance of each other, and the same area also included facilities for storing legal records, such as the *Rolls Office*, and courtrooms, such as Lincoln's Inn Hall. Also at hand were, of course, dealers in legal supplies, stationers such as Mr. Snagsby, as well as

3. See William S. Holdsworth, *Charles Dickens as Legal Historian* (New Haven, 1928). See also Trevor Blount, "The Documentary Symbolism of Chancery in *Bleak House*," *Dickensian* (1966), 47–52, 106–11, 167–74.

the copyists employed by them for transcribing documents. A potential barrister preparing to practice in the courtrooms, or a law-office clerk preparing to become a solicitor, would have all the facilities for training and practice conveniently clustered for him in a small area, less than a square mile in size—a city within a city.

To speak of barristers and solicitors is to touch on one of the distinctive features of the English legal system: the division of functions performed by lawyers. A *solicitor*, such as Mr. Kenge or Mr. Tulkinghorn in Dickens' novel, would have been trained by working in a lawyer's office. Having bound himself to his employer by articles (the contract for his apprenticeship), he was called an *articled clerk*. After qualifying as a solicitor, he would advise clients on legal matters and prepare cases on their behalf, but he would not ordinarily plead his client's case in court. For this function he would employ a *barrister*, a member of the Bar who had graduated, in effect, from one of the Inns of Court, to present the case before the judge. As the opening chapter of *Bleak House* indicates, the barristers were of several ranks. A senior barrister, appointed to the rank of Queen's Counsellor, sat in a special row of benches in the court and wore a black silk gown (Mr. Blowers, in the opening chapter, is described as "the eminent silk gown"). Such counsellors also wore, like the judges, wigs of goat hair (junior lawyers wore wigs of coarser horse hair). The highest order of barrister was called *Serjeant*. Until the rank was abolished in the late nineteenth century, the Serjeants had an Inn of their own, to which Dickens refers in Chapter XIX.

The Terms and Vacation

The amount of activity in this law pocket of London varied with the seasons. During the long four-month summer vacation (July through October), this section of London was considerably depopulated, with only a few of the junior clerks (such as Mr. Guppy in *Bleak House*) continuing to work at their offices. Dickens makes fun of the fact that the country managed to continue functioning during this *Long Vacation*, even though the law courts have virtually suspended their activities. During the rest of the year, there were four "terms" in which the courts were in session, during which those preparing to become barristers were required to eat dinner in the halls of their Inns. These four terms were: Hilary Term (January 11–31); Easter Term (April 15–May 8); Trinity Term (May 22–June 12); Michaelmas Term (November 2–25). Between these terms, courts might continue in session. For the Court of Chancery, it was customary, at such times, to change the place of meeting from Westminster Hall to Lincoln's Inn Hall, as in the late November scene, following Michaelmas Term, with which *Bleak House* opens.

The Text of
Bleak House

FRONTISPIECE.

BY

CHARLES DICKENS.

LONDON:
BRADBURY & EVANS, BOUVERIE STREET.
1853.

Contents of *Bleak House*

Preface

A Chancery Judge once had the kindness to inform me, as one of a company of some hundred and fifty men and women not labouring under any suspicions of lunacy, that the Court of Chancery, though the shining subject of much popular prejudice (at which point I thought the Judge's eye had a cast in my direction), was almost immaculate. There had been, he admitted, a trivial blemish or so in its rate of progress, but this was exaggerated, and had been entirely owing to the "parsimony of the public"; which guilty public, it appeared, had been until lately bent in the most determined manner on by no means enlarging the number of Chancery Judges appointed—I believe by Richard the Second, but any other King will do as well.

This seemed to me too profound a joke to be inserted in the body of this book, or I should have restored it to Conversation Kenge or to Mr. Vholes, with one or other of whom I think it must have originated. In such mouths I might have coupled it with an apt quotation from one of Shakespeare's Sonnets.

> My nature is subdued
> To what it works in, like the dyer's hand:
> Pity me then, and wish I were renew'd!

But as it is wholesome that the parsimonious public should know what has been doing, and still is doing, in this connexion, I mention here that everything set forth in these pages concerning the Court of Chancery is substantially true, and within the truth. The case of Gridley is in no essential altered from one of actual occurrence, made public by a disinterested person who was professionally acquainted with the whole of the monstrous wrong from beginning to end. At the present moment[1] there is a suit before the Court which was commenced nearly twenty years ago; in which from thirty to forty counsel have been known to appear at one time; in which costs have been incurred to the amount of seventy thousand pounds; which is a *friendly suit*; and which is (I am assured) no nearer to its termination now than when it was begun. There is another well-known suit in Chancery, not yet decided, which was commenced before the close of the last century, and in which more than double the amount of seventy thousand pounds has been swallowed up in costs. If I wanted other authorities for Jarndyce and Jarndyce, I could rain them on these pages, to the shame of—a parsimonious public.

There is only one other point on which I offer a word of remark.

1. In August 1853. [Dickens' note].

The possibility of what is called Spontaneous Combustion has been denied since the death of Mr. Krook; and my good friend Mr. Lewes (quite mistaken, as he soon found, in supposing the thing to have been abandoned by all authorities) published some ingenious letters to me at the time when that event was chronicled, arguing that Spontaneous Combustion could not possibly be. I have no need to observe that I do not wilfully or negligently mislead my readers, and that before I wrote that description I took pains to investigate the subject. There are about thirty cases on record, of which the most famous, that of the Countess Cornelia de Baudi Cesenate, was minutely investigated and described by Giuseppe Bianchini, a prebendary of Verona, otherwise distinguished in letters, who published an account of it at Verona, in 1731, which he afterwards republished at Rome. The appearances beyond all rational doubt observed in that case, are the appearances observed in Mr. Krook's case. The next most famous instance happened at Rheims, six years earlier; and the historian in that case is Le Cat, one of the most renowned surgeons produced by France. The subject was a woman, whose husband was ignorantly convicted of having murdered her; but, on solemn appeal to a higher court, he was acquitted, because it was shown upon the evidence that she had died the death to which this name of Spontaneous Combustion is given. I do not think it necessary to add to these notable facts, and that general reference to the authorities which will be found at page 413,[2] the recorded opinions and experiences of distinguished medical professors, French, English, and Scotch, in more modern days; contenting myself with observing, that I shall not abandon the facts until there shall have been a considerable Spontaneous Combustion of the testimony on which human occurrences are usually received.

In Bleak House, I have purposely dwelt upon the romantic side of familiar things.

2. Another case, very clearly described by a dentist, occurred at the town of Columbus, in the United States of America, quite recently. The subject was a German, who kept a liquor-shop, and was an inveterate drunkard. [Dickens' note.]

Chapter I

IN CHANCERY

London. Michaelmas Term lately over, and the Lord Chancellor sitting in Lincoln's Inn Hall. Implacable November weather. As much mud in the streets, as if the waters had but newly retired from the face of the earth, and it would not be wonderful to meet a Megalosaurus, forty feet long or so, waddling like an elephantine lizard up Holborn Hill. Smoke lowering down from chimney-pots, making a soft black drizzle, with flakes of soot in it as big as full-grown snow-flakes—gone into mourning, one might imagine, for the death of the sun. Dogs, undistinguishable in mire. Horses, scarcely better; splashed to their very blinkers. Foot passengers, jostling one another's umbrellas, in a general infection of ill-temper, and losing their foot-hold at street-corners, where tens of thousands of other foot passengers have been slipping and sliding since the day broke (if the day ever broke), adding new deposits to the crust upon crust of mud, sticking at those points tenaciously to the pavement, and accumulating at compound interest.

Fog everywhere. Fog up the river, where it flows among green aits[1] and meadows; fog down the river, where it rolls defiled among the tiers of shipping and the waterside pollutions of a great (and dirty) city. Fog on the Essex marshes, fog on the Kentish heights. Fog creeping into the cabooses of collier-brigs, fog lying out on the yards, and hovering in the rigging of great ships; fog drooping on the gunwales of barges and small boats. Fog in the eyes and throats of ancient Greenwich pensioners,[2] wheezing by the firesides of their wards; fog in the stem and bowl of the afternoon pipe of the wrathful skipper, down in his close cabin; fog cruelly pinching the toes and fingers of his shivering little 'prentice boy on deck. Chance people on the bridges peeping over the parapets into a nether sky of fog, with fog all round them, as if they were up in a balloon, and hanging in the misty clouds.

Gas looming through the fog in divers places in the streets, much as the sun may, from the spongey fields, be seen to loom by husbandman and ploughboy. Most of the shops lighted two hours before their time—as the gas seems to know, for it has a haggard and unwilling look.

The raw afternoon is rawest, and the dense fog is densest, and the muddy streets are muddiest, near that leaden-headed old obstruction, appropriate ornament for the threshold of a leaden-

1. Small islands in the River Thames above London.

2. Retired sailors in the Naval hospital at Greenwich.

headed old corporation: Temple Bar.[3] And hard by Temple Bar, in Lincoln's Inn Hall, at the very heart of the fog, sits the Lord High Chancellor in his High Court of Chancery.[4]

Never can there come fog too thick, never can there come mud and mire too deep, to assort with the groping and floundering condition which this High Court of Chancery, most pestilent of hoary sinners, holds, this day, in the sight of heaven and earth.

On such an afternoon, if ever, the Lord High Chancellor ought to be sitting here—as here he is—with a foggy glory round his head, softly fenced in with crimson cloth and curtains, addressed by a large advocate with great whiskers, a little voice, and an interminable brief, and outwardly directing his contemplation to the lantern in the roof, where he can see nothing but fog. On such an afternoon, some score of members of the High Court of Chancery bar ought to be—as here they are—mistily engaged in one of the ten thousand stages of an endless cause, tripping one another up on slippery precedents, groping knee-deep in technicalities, running their goat-hair and horse-hair warded heads against walls of words, and making a pretence of equity with serious faces, as players might. On such an afternoon, the various solicitors in the cause, some two or three of whom have inherited it from their fathers, who made a fortune by it, ought to be—as are they not?—ranged in a line, in a long matted well[5] (but you might look in vain for Truth at the bottom of it), between the registrar's red table and the silk gowns, with bills, cross-bills, answers, rejoinders, injunctions, affidavits, issues, references to masters, masters' reports, mountains of costly nonsense, piled before them. Well may the court be dim, with wasting candles here and there; well may the fog hang heavy in it, as if it would never get out; well may the stained glass windows lose their colour, and admit no light of day into the place; well may the uninitiated from the streets, who peep in through the glass panes in the door, be deterred from entrance by its owlish aspect, and by the drawl languidly echoing to the roof from the padded dais where the Lord High Chancellor looks into the lantern that has no light in it,[6] and where the attendant wigs are all stuck in a fog-bank! This is the Court of Chancery; which has its decaying houses and its blighted lands in every shire; which has its worn-out lunatic in every madhouse,[7] and its dead in every churchyard;

3. One of the outer barrier-archways spanning a street that led to the old walled city of London. This "obstruction," with its leaden ornaments on top, was rebuilt by Christopher Wren in 1672, but because it created traffic jams, it was removed in 1878.

4. Concerning the various legal terms in this chapter, see the Introductory Note on Law Courts and Colleges, pp. xvi–xx.

5. Coconut matting was used to cover the courtroom floor.

6. A louver, i.e., a lantern-shaped structure surmounting the roof, designed to provide ventilation.

7. Chancery jurisdiction included deciding whether a person was to be declared insane and also assigning such persons to custody in asylums.

which has its ruined suitor, with his slipshod heels and threadbare dress, borrowing and begging through the round of every man's acquaintance; which gives to monied might, the means abundantly of wearying out the right; which so exhausts finances, patience, courage, hope; so overthrows the brain and breaks the heart;[8] that there is not an honourable man among its practitioners who would not give—who does not often give—the warning, "Suffer any wrong that can be done you, rather than come here!"

Who happen to be in the Lord Chancellor's court this murky afternoon besides the Lord Chancellor, the counsel in the cause, two or three counsel who are never in any cause, and the well of solicitors before mentioned? There is the registrar below the Judge, in wig and gown; and there are two or three maces, or petty-bags, or privy purses, or whatever they may be, in legal court suits. These are all yawning; for no crumb of amusement ever falls from JARNDYCE AND JARNDYCE (the cause in hand), which was squeezed dry years upon years ago. The short-hand writers, the reporters of the court, and the reporters of the newspapers, invariably decamp with the rest of the regulars when Jarndyce and Jarndyce comes on. Their places are a blank. Standing on a seat at the side of the hall, the better to peer into the curtained sanctuary,[9] is a little mad old woman in a squeezed bonnet, who is always in court, from its sitting to its rising, and always expecting some incomprehensible judgment to be given in her favour. Some say she really is, or was, a party to a suit; but no one knows for certain, because no one cares. She carries some small litter in her reticule which she calls her documents; principally consisting of paper matches and dry lavender. A sallow prisoner has come up, in custody, for the half-dozenth time, to make a personal application "to purge himself of his contempt"; which, being a solitary surviving executor who has fallen into a state of conglomeration about accounts of which it is not pretended that he had ever any knowledge, he is not at all likely ever to do. In the meantime his prospects in life are ended. Another ruined suitor, who periodically appears from Shropshire, and breaks out into efforts to address the Chancellor at the close of the day's business, and who can by no means be made to understand that the Chancellor is legally ignorant of his existence after making it desolate for a quarter of a century, plants himself in a good place and keeps an eye on the Judge, ready to call out "My Lord!" in a voice of sonorous complaint, on the instant of his rising. A few lawyers' clerks and others who know this suitor by sight, linger, on the chance of his furnishing some fun, and enlivening the dismal weather a little.

Jarndyce and Jarndyce drones on. This scarecrow of a suit has, in course of time, become so complicated, that no man alive knows what it means. The parties to it understand it least; but it has been

8. Cf. Wordsworth's *Michael*, l. 450: "Would overset the brain, or break the heart."
9. The raised platform on which the Chancellor sat had curtains on three sides.

observed that no two Chancery lawyers can talk about it for five minutes, without coming to a total disagreement as to all the premises. Innumerable children have been born into the cause; innumerable young people have married into it; innumerable old people have died out of it. Scores of persons have deliriously found themselves made parties in Jarndyce and Jarndyce, without knowing how or why; whole families have inherited legendary hatreds with the suit. The little plaintiff or defendant, who was promised a new rocking-horse when Jarndyce and Jarndyce should be settled, has grown up, possessed himself of a real horse, and trotted away into the other world. Fair wards of court[1] have faded into mothers and grandmothers; a long procession of Chancellors has come in and gone out; the legion of bills in the suit have been transformed into mere bills of mortality; there are not three Jarndyces left upon the earth perhaps, since old Tom Jarndyce in despair blew his brains out at a coffee-house in Chancery Lane; but Jarndyce and Jarndyce still drags its dreary length before the Court,[2] perennially hopeless.

Jarndyce and Jarndyce has passed into a joke. That is the only good that has ever come of it. It has been death to many, but it is a joke in the profession. Every master in Chancery has had a reference out of it. Every Chancellor was "in it," for somebody or other, when he was counsel at the bar. Good things have been said about it by blue-nosed, bulbous-shoed old benchers, in select port-wine committee after dinner in hall. Articled clerks have been in the habit of fleshing their legal wit upon it. The last Lord Chancellor handled it neatly when, correcting Mr. Blowers, the eminent silk gown who said that such a thing might happen when the sky rained potatoes, he observed, "or when we get through Jarndyce and Jarndyce, Mr. Blowers";—a pleasantry that particularly tickled the maces, bags, and purses.

How many people out of the suit, Jarndyce and Jarndyce has stretched forth its unwholesome hand to spoil and corrupt, would be a very wide question. From the master, upon whose impaling files reams of dusty warrants in Jarndyce and Jarndyce have grimly writhed into many shapes; down to the copying-clerk in the Six Clerks' Office, who has copied his tens of thousands of Chancery-folio-pages under that eternal heading; no man's nature has been made better by it. In trickery, evasion, procrastination, spoliation, botheration, under false pretences of all sorts, there are influences that can never come to good. The very solicitors' boys who have kept the wretched suitors at bay, by protesting time out of mind that Mr. Chizzle, Mizzle, or otherwise, was particularly engaged and had appointments until dinner, may have got an extra moral twist

1. Minors, for whom guardians were appointed by the Court of Chancery.

2. Cf. Pope's *Essay on Criticism*, 1.357: "That, like a wounded snake, drags its slow length along." (Noted by Susan Shatto, 1975.)

and shuffle into themselves out of Jarndyce and Jarndyce. The receiver in the cause has acquired a goodly sum of money by it, but has acquired too a distrust of his own mother, and a contempt for his own kind. Chizzle, Mizzle, and otherwise, have lapsed into a habit of vaguely promising themselves that they will look into that outstanding little matter, and see what can be done for Drizzle—who was not well used—when Jarndyce and Jarndyce shall be got out of the office. Shirking and sharking,[3] in all their many varieties, have been sown broadcast by the ill-fated cause; and even those who have contemplated its history from the outermost circle of such evil, have been insensibly tempted into a loose way of letting bad things alone to take their own bad course, and a loose belief that if the world go wrong, it was, in some off-hand manner, never meant to go right.

Thus, in the midst of the mud and at the heart of the fog, sits the Lord High Chancellor in his High Court of Chancery.

"Mr. Tangle," says the Lord High Chancellor, latterly something restless under the eloquence of that learned gentleman.

"Mlud," says Mr. Tangle. Mr. Tangle knows more of Jarndyce and Jarndyce than anybody. He is famous for it—supposed never to have read anything else since he left school.

"Have you nearly concluded your argument?"

"Mlud, no—variety of points—feel it my duty tsubmit—ludship," is the reply that slides out of Mr. Tangle.

"Several members of the bar are still to be heard, I believe?" says the Chancellor, with a slight smile.

Eighteen of Mr. Tangle's learned friends, each armed with a little summary of eighteen hundred sheets, bob up like eighteen hammers in a piano-forte, make eighteen bows, and drop into their eighteen places of obscurity.

"We will proceed with the hearing on Wednesday fortnight," says the Chancellor. For the question at issue is only a question of costs, a mere bud on the forest tree of the parent suit, and really will come to a settlement one of these days.

The Chancellor rises; the bar rises; the prisoner is brought forward in a hurry; the man from Shropshire cries, "My lord!" Maces, bags, and purses, indignantly proclaim silence, and frown at the man from Shropshire.

"In reference," proceeds the Chancellor, still on Jarndyce and Jarndyce, "to the young girl——"

"Begludship's pardon—boy," says Mr. Tangle, prematurely.

"In reference," proceeds the Chancellor, with extra distinctness, "to the young girl and boy, the two young people,"

(Mr. Tangle crushed.)

3. Cheating and swindling.

"Whom I directed to be in attendance to-day, and who are now in my private room, I will see them and satisfy myself as to the expediency of making the order for their residing with their uncle."

Mr. Tangle on his legs again.

"Begludship's pardon—dead."

"With their," Chancellor looking through his double eye-glass at the papers on his desk, "grandfather."

"Begludship's pardon—victim of rash action—brains."

Suddenly a very little counsel, with a terrific bass voice, arises, fully inflated, in the back settlements of the fog, and says, "Will you lordship allow me? I appear for him. He is a cousin, several times removed. I am not at the moment prepared to inform the Court in what exact remove he is a cousin; but he *is* a cousin."

Leaving this address (delivered like a sepulchral message) ringing in the rafters of the roof, the very little counsel drops, and the fog knows him no more. Everybody looks for him. Nobody can see him.[4]

"I will speak with both the young people," says the Chancellor anew, "and satisfy myself on the subject of their residing with their cousin. I will mention the matter to-morrow morning when I take my seat."

The Chancellor is about to bow to the bar, when the prisoner is presented. Nothing can possibly come of the prisoner's conglomeration, but his being sent back to prison; which is soon done. The man from Shropshire ventures another demonstrative "My lord!" but the Chancellor, being aware of him, has dexterously vanished. Everybody else quickly vanishes too. A battery of blue bags is loaded with heavy charges of papers and carried off by clerks; the little mad old woman marches off with her documents; the empty court is locked up. If all the injustice it has committed, and all the misery it has caused, could only be locked up with it, and the whole burnt away in a great funeral pyre—why so much the better for other parties than the parties in Jarndyce and Jarndyce!

Chapter II

IN FASHION

It is but a glimpse of the world of fashion that we want on this same miry afternoon. It is not so unlike the Court of Chancery, but that we may pass from the one scene to the other, as the crow flies. Both the world of fashion and the Court of Chancery are things of precedent and usage; oversleeping Rip Van Winkles, who have played at strange games through a deal of thundery weather;[1] sleep-

4. See Job 7:8–10.

1. In Irving's *Rip Van Winkle,* the sound of a game of ninepins played on a mountaintop seemed like thunder to the hero.

ing beauties, whom the Knight will wake one day, when all the stopped spits in the kitchen shall begin to turn prodigiously!

It is not a large world. Relatively even to this world of ours, which has its limits too (as your Highness shall find when you have made the tour of it, and are come to the brink of the void beyond), it is a very little speck. There is much good in it; there are many good and true people in it; it has its appointed place. But the evil of it is, that it is a world wrapped up in too much jeweller's cotton[2] and fine wool, and cannot hear the rushing of the larger worlds, and cannot see them as they circle round the sun. It is a deadened world, and its growth is sometimes unhealthy for want of air.

My Lady Dedlock has returned to her house in town for a few days previous to her departure for Paris, where her ladyship intends to stay some weeks; after which her movements are uncertain. The fashionable intelligence says so, for the comfort of the Parisians, and it knows all fashionable things. To know things otherwise, were to be unfashionable. My Lady Dedlock has been down at what she calls, in familiar conversation, her "place" in Lincolnshire. The waters are out in Lincolnshire. An arch of the bridge in the park has been sapped and sopped away. The adjacent low-lying ground, for half a mile in breadth, is a stagnant river, with melancholy trees for islands in it, and a surface punctured all over, all day long, with falling rain. My Lady Dedlock's "place" has been extremely dreary. The weather, for many a day and night, has been so wet that the trees seem wet through, and the soft loppings and prunings of the woodman's axe can make no crash or crackle as they fall. The deer, looking soaked, leave quagmires, where they pass. The shot of a rifle loses its sharpness in the moist air, and its smoke moves in a tardy little cloud towards the green rise, coppice-topped, that makes a background for the falling rain. The view from my Lady Dedlock's own windows is alternately a lead-coloured view, and a view in Indian ink. The vases on the stone terrace in the foreground catch the rain all day; and the heavy drops fall, drip, drip, drip, upon the broad flagged pavement, called, from old time, the Ghost's Walk, all night. On Sundays, the little church in the park is mouldy; the oaken pulpit breaks out into a cold sweat; and there is a general smell and taste as of the ancient Dedlocks in their graves. My Lady Dedlock (who is childless), looking out in the early twilight from her boudoir at a keeper's lodge, and seeing the light of a fire upon the latticed panes, and smoke rising from the chimney, and a child, chased by a woman, running out into the rain to meet the shining figure of a wrapped-up man coming through the gate, has been put quite out of temper. My Lady Dedlock says she has been "bored to death."

2. Layers of fluffy cotton used as wrapping to protect fragile jewelry.

Therefore my Lady Dedlock has come away from the place in Lincolnshire, and has left it to the rain, and the crows, and the rabbits, and the deer, and the partridges and pheasants. The pictures of the Dedlocks past and gone have seemed to vanish into the damp walls in mere lowness of spirits, as the housekeeper has passed along the old rooms, shutting up the shutters. And when they will next come forth again, the fashionable intelligence—which, like the fiend, is omniscient of the past and present, but not the future—cannot yet undertake to say.

Sir Leicester Dedlock is only a baronet,[3] but there is no mightier baronet than he. His family is as old as the hills, and infinitely more respectable. He has a general opinion that the world might get on without hills, but would be done up without Dedlocks. He would on the whole admit Nature to be a good idea (a little low, perhaps, when not enclosed with a park-fence), but an idea dependent for its execution on your great county families. He is a gentleman of strict conscience, disdainful of all littleness and meanness, and ready, on the shortest notice, to die any death you may please to mention rather than give occasion for the least impeachment of his integrity. He is an honourable, obstinate, truthful, high-spirited, intensely prejudiced, perfectly unreasonable man.

Sir Leicester is twenty years, full measure, older than my Lady. He will never see sixty-five again, nor perhaps sixty-six, nor yet sixty-seven. He has a twist of the gout now and then, and walks a little stiffly. He is of a worthy presence, with his light grey hair and whiskers, his fine shirt-frill, his pure white waistcoat, and his blue coat with bright buttons always buttoned. He is ceremonious, stately, most polite on every occasion to my Lady, and holds her personal attractions in the highest estimation. His gallantry to my Lady, which has never changed since he courted her, is the one little touch of romantic fancy in him.

Indeed, he married her for love. A whisper still goes about, that she had not even family; howbeit, Sir Leicester had so much family that perhaps he had enough, and could dispense with any more. But she had beauty, pride, ambition, insolent resolve, and sense enough to portion out a legion of fine ladies. Wealth and station, added to these, soon floated her upward; and for years, now, my Lady Dedlock has been at the centre of the fashionable intelligence, and at the top of the fashionable tree.

How Alexander wept when he had no more worlds to conquer,[4] everybody knows—or has some reason to know by this time, the

3. A knight whose title is hereditary (and often very old and prestigious) but who is not a member of the House of Lords and thus ranks below a Baron, the lowest grade of the peerage.

4. According to Plutarch's *On the Tranquility of Mind,* when Alexander the Great was told of the existence of an infinite number of worlds, he wept because "where there is such a vast multitude of them we have not yet conquered one."

matter having been rather frequently mentioned. My Lady Dedlock, having conquered *her* world, fell, not into the melting,[5] but rather into the freezing mood. An exhausted composure, a worn-out placidity, an equanimity of fatigue not to be ruffled by interest or satisfaction, are the trophies of her victory. She is perfectly well-bred. If she could be translated to Heaven to-morrow, she might be expected to ascend without any rapture.

She has beauty still, and, if it be not in its heyday, it is not yet in its autumn. She has a fine face—originally of a character that would be rather called very pretty than handsome, but improved into classicality by the acquired expression of her fashionable state. Her figure is elegant, and has the effect of being tall. Not that she is so, but that "the most is made," as the Honourable Bob Stables has frequently asserted upon oath, "of all her points." The same authority observes that she is perfectly got up; and remarks, in commendation of her hair especially, that she is the best-groomed woman in the whole stud.

With all her perfections on her head,[6] my Lady Dedlock has come up from her place in Lincolnshire (hotly pursued by the fashionable intelligence), to pass a few days at her house in town previous to her departure for Paris, where her ladyship intends to stay some weeks, after which her movements are uncertain. And at her house in town, upon this muddy, murky afternoon, presents himself an old-fashioned old gentleman, attorney-at-law, and eke solicitor of the High Court of Chancery, who has the honour of acting as legal adviser of the Dedlocks, and has as many cast-iron boxes in his office with that name outside, as if the present baronet were the coin of the conjurer's trick, and were constantly being juggled through the whole set.[7] Across the hall, and up the stairs, and along the passages, and through the rooms, which are very brilliant in the season[8] and very dismal out of it—Fairyland to visit but a desert to live in—the old gentleman is conducted, by a Mercury in powder,[9] to my Lady's presence.

The old gentleman is rusty to look at, but is reputed to have made good thrift out of aristocratic marriage settlements and aristocratic wills, and to be very rich. He is surrounded by a mysterious halo of family confidences; of which he is known to be the silent

5. Tearful. Cf. Othello, who is finally moved to tears: "Albeit unused to the melting mood." (*Othello*, V.ii.349.)

6. In *Hamlet* (I.v.78–79) the Ghost speaks of being "sent to my account / With all my imperfections on my head." (Noted by Grahame Smith.)

7. Variation of a conjuring trick devised by Robert-Houdin in 1845, in which a coin, contributed by a member of an audience, is first made to disappear and is afterwards discovered inside a locked iron box, this box being the smallest of a nest of locked boxes. The coin seems, by magic, to have passed through several layers of iron containers.

8. Chiefly the months of May, June, and July, when country gentry visited London to take part in social events.

9. A footman whose hair has been powdered. One of the roles of the god Mercury was to conduct the souls of the dead to Hades.

depository. There are noble Mausoleums rooted for centuries in retired glades of parks, among the growing timber and the fern, which perhaps hold fewer noble secrets than walk abroad among men, shut up in the breast of Mr. Tulkinghorn. He is of what is called the old school—a phrase generally meaning any school that seems never to have been young—and wears knee breeches[1] tied with ribbons, and gaiters or stockings. One peculiarity of his black clothes, and of his black stockings, be they silk or worsted, is, that they never shine. Mute, close, irresponsive to any glancing light, his dress is like himself. He never converses, when not professionally consulted. He is found sometimes, speechless but quite at home, at corners of dinner-tables in great country houses, and near doors of drawing-rooms, concerning which the fashionable intelligence is eloquent; where everybody knows him, and where half the Peerage stops to say, "How do you do, Mr. Tulkinghorn?" he receives these salutations with gravity, and buries them along with the rest of his knowledge.

Sir Leicester Dedlock is with my Lady, and is happy to see Mr. Tulkinghorn. There is an air of prescription about him which is always agreeable to Sir Leicester; he receives it as a kind of tribute. He likes Mr. Tulkinghorn's dress; there is a kind of tribute in that too. It is eminently respectable, and likewise, in a general way, retainer-like. It expresses, as it were, the steward of the legal mysteries, the butler of the legal cellar, of the Dedlocks.

Has Mr. Tulkinghorn any idea of this himself? It may be so, or it may not; but there is this remarkable circumstance to be noted in everything associated with my Lady Dedlock as one of a class—as one of the leaders and representatives of her little world. She supposes herself to be an inscrutable Being, quite out of the reach and ken of ordinary mortals—seeing herself in her glass, where indeed she looks so. Yet, every dim little star revolving about her, from her maid to the manager of the Italian Opera, knows her weaknesses, prejudices, follies, haughtinesses, and caprices; and lives upon as accurate a calculation and as nice a measure of her moral nature, as her dressmaker takes of her physical proportions. Is a new dress, a new custom, a new singer, a new dancer, a new form of jewellery, a new dwarf or giant, a new chapel, a new anything, to be set up? There are deferential people, in a dozen callings, whom my Lady Dedlock suspects of nothing but prostration before her, who can tell you how to manage her as if she were a baby; who do nothing but nurse her all their lives; who, humbly affecting to follow with profound subservience, lead her and her whole troop after them; who, in hooking one, hook all and bear them off, as Lemuel Gul-

1. Knee-breeches went out of fashion in the early nineteenth century, being displaced by trousers.

liver bore away the stately fleet of the majestic Lilliput. "If you want to address our people, sir," say Blaze and Sparkle the jewellers —meaning by our people, Lady Dedlock and the rest—"you must remember that you are not dealing with the general public; you must hit our people in their weakest place, and their weakest place is such a place." "To make this article go down, gentlemen," say Sheen and Gloss the mercers,[2] to their friends the manufacturers, "you must come to us, because we know where to have the fashionable people, and we can make it fashionable." "If you want to get this print upon the tables of my high connexion, sir," says Mr. Sladdery the librarian,[3] "or if you want to get this dwarf or giant[4] into the houses of my high connexion, sir, or if you want to secure to this entertainment, the patronage of my high connexion, sir, you must leave it, if you please, to me; for I have been accustomed to study the leaders of my high connexion, sir; and I may tell you, without vanity, that I can turn them round my finger,"—in which Mr. Sladdery, who is an honest man, does not exaggerate at all.

Therefore, while Mr. Tulkinghorn may not know what is passing in the Dedlock mind at present, it is very possible that he may.

"My Lady's cause has been again before the Chancellor, has it, Mr. Tulkinghorn?" says Sir Leicester, giving him his hand.

"Yes. It has been on again to-day," Mr. Tulkinghorn replies; making one of his quiet bows to my Lady, who is on a sofa near the fire, shading her face with a hand-screen.[5]

"It would be useless to ask," says my Lady, with the dreariness of the place in Lincolnshire still upon her, "whether anything has been done."

"Nothing that *you* would call anything, has been done to-day," replies Mr. Tulkinghorn.

"Nor ever will be," says my Lady.

Sir Leicester has no objection to an interminable Chancery suit. It is a slow, expensive, British, constitutional kind of thing. To be sure, he has not a vital interest in the suit in question, her part in which was the only property my Lady brought him; and he has a shadowy impression that for his name—the name of Dedlock—to be in a cause, and not in the title of that cause, is a most ridiculous accident. But he regards the Court of Chancery, even if it should involve an occasional delay of justice and a trifling amount of confusion, as a something, devised in conjunction with a variety of other somethings, by the perfection of human wisdom, for the eternal set-

2. Dealers in fine fabrics for clothes.

3. Bookseller. Such men also sometimes served as agents for theatrical entertainments and exhibitions.

4. Entertainments at high society parties might feature dwarfs or giants as exhibits. The American dwarf General Tom Thumb (whose promoter was P. T. Barnum) had been strikingly successful in his appearances in England in the 1840's.

5. A fan-like object held so as to shield the face from the heat of a fireplace.

tlement (humanly speaking) of everything. And he is upon the whole of a fixed opinion, that to give the sanction of his countenance to any complaints respecting it, would be to encourage some person in the lower classes to rise up somewhere—like Wat Tyler.[6]

"As a few fresh affidavits have been put upon the file" says Mr. Tulkinghorn, "and as they are short, and as I proceed upon the troublesome principle of begging leave to possess my clients with any new proceedings in a cause"; cautious man Mr. Tulkinghorn, taking no more responsibility than necessary; "and further, as I see you are going to Paris; I have brought them in my pocket."

(Sir Leicester was going to Paris too, by-the-bye, but the delight of the fashionable intelligence was in his Lady.)

Mr. Tulkinghorn takes out his papers, asks permission to place them on a golden talisman of a table at my Lady's elbow, puts on his spectacles, and begins to read by the light of a shaded lamp.

" 'In Chancery. Between John Jarndyce——' "

My Lady interrupts, requesting him to miss as many of the formal horrors as he can.

Mr. Tulkinghorn glances over his spectacles, and begins again lower down. My Lady carelessly and scornfully abstracts her attention. Sir Leicester in a great chair looks at the fire, and appears to have a stately liking for the legal repetitions and prolixities, as ranging among the national bulwarks. It happens that the fire is hot, where my Lady sits; and that the hand-screen is more beautiful than useful, being priceless but small. My Lady, changing her position, sees the papers on the table—looks at them nearer—looks at them nearer still—asks impulsively:

"Who copied that?"

Mr. Tulkinghorn stops short, surprised by my Lady's animation and her unusual tone.

"Is it what you people call law-hand?" she asks, looking full at him in her careless way again, and toying with her screen.

"Not quite. Probably"—Mr. Tulkinghorn examines it as he speaks—"the legal character it has, was acquired after the original hand was formed. Why do you ask?"

"Anything to vary this detestable monotony. O, go on, do!"

Mr. Tulkinghorn reads again. The heat is greater, my Lady screens her face. Sir Leicester doses, starts up suddenly, and cries "Eh? what do you say?"

"I say I am afraid," says Mr. Tulkinghorn, who has risen hastily, "that Lady Dedlock is ill."

"Faint," my Lady murmurs, with white lips, "only that; but it is like the faintness of death. Don't speak to me. Ring, and take me to my room!"

6. Leader of the Peasants' Revolt of 1381.

Mr. Tulkinghorn retires into another chamber; bells ring, feet shuffle and patter, silence ensues. Mercury at last begs Mr. Tulkinghorn to return.

"Better now," quoth Sir Leicester, motioning the lawyer to sit down and read to him alone. "I have been quite alarmed. I never knew my Lady swoon before. But the weather is extremely trying—and she really has been bored to death down at our place in Lincolnshire."

Chapter III

A PROGRESS

I have a great deal of difficulty in beginning to write my portion of these pages, for I know I am not clever. I always knew that. I can remember, when I was a very little girl indeed, I used to say to my doll, when we were alone together, "Now, Dolly, I am not clever, you know very well, and you must be patient with me, like a dear!" And so she used to sit propped up in a great arm-chair, with her beautiful complexion and rosy lips, staring at me—or not so much at me, I think, as at nothing—while I busily stitched away, and told her every one of my secrets.

My dear old doll! I was such a shy little thing that I seldom dared to open my lips, and never dared to open my heart, to anybody else. It almost makes me cry to think what a relief it used to be to me, when I came home from school of a day, to run up-stairs to my room, and say, "O you dear faithful Dolly, I knew you would be expecting me!" and then to sit down on the floor, leaning on the elbow of her great chair, and tell her all I had noticed since we parted. I had always rather a noticing way—not a quick way, O no!—a silent way of noticing what passed before me, and thinking I should like to understand it better. I have not by any means a quick understanding. When I love a person very tenderly indeed, it seems to brighten. But even that may be my vanity.

I was brought up, from my earliest remembrance—like some of the princesses in the fairy stories, only I was not charming—by my godmother. At least I only knew her as such. She was a good, good woman! She went to church three times every Sunday, and to morning prayers on Wednesdays and Fridays, and to lectures whenever there were lectures; and never missed. She was handsome; and if she had ever smiled, would have been (I used to think) like an angel—but she never smiled. She was always grave, and strict. She was so very good herself, I thought, that the badness of other people made her frown all her life. I felt so different from her, even making every allowance for the differences between a child and a woman; I felt so poor, so trifling, and so far off; that I never could be unrestrained with her—no, could never even love her as I wished. It made me very sorry to consider how good she was, and how unworthy of her I was; and I used ardently to hope that I might have a better heart; and I talked it over very often with the dear old doll; but I never loved my godmother as I ought to have loved her, and as I felt I must have loved her if I had been a better girl.

This made me, I dare say, more timid and retiring than I naturally was, and cast me upon Dolly as the only friend with whom I felt at ease. But something happened when I was still quite a little thing, that helped it very much.

I had never heard my mama spoken of. I had never heard of my papa either, but I felt more interested about my mama. I had never worn a black frock, that I could recollect. I had never been shown my mama's grave. I had never been told where it was. Yet I had never been taught to pray for any relation but my godmother. I had more than once approached this subject of my thoughts with Mrs. Rachael, our only servant, who took my light away when I was in bed (another very good woman, but austere to me), and she had only said, "Esther, good night!" and gone away and left me.

Although there were seven girls at the neighbouring school where I was a day boarder, and although they called me little Esther Summerson, I knew none of them at home. All of them were older than I, to be sure (I was the youngest there by a good deal), but there seemed to be some other separation between us besides that, and besides their being far more clever than I was, and knowing much more than I did. One of them, in the first week of my going to the school (I remember it very well), invited me home to a little party, to my great joy. But my godmother wrote a stiff letter declining for me, and I never went. I never went out at all.

It was my birthday. There were holidays at school on other birthdays—none on mine. There were rejoicings at home on other birthdays, as I knew from what I heard the girls relate to one another—there were none on mine. My birthday was the most melancholy day at home, in the whole year.

I have mentioned that, unless my vanity should deceive me (as I know it may, for I may be very vain, without suspecting it—though indeed I don't), my comprehension is quickened when my affection is. My disposition is very affectionate; and perhaps I might still feel such a wound, if such a wound could be received more than once, with the quickness of that birthday.

Dinner was over, and my godmother and I were sitting at the table before the fire. The clock ticked, the fire clicked; not another sound had been heard in the room, or in the house, for I don't know how long. I happened to look timidly up from my stitching, across the table, at my godmother, and I saw in her face, looking gloomily at me, "It would have been far better, little Esther, that you had had no birthday; that you had never been born!"

I broke out crying and sobbing, and I said, "O, dear godmother, tell me, pray do tell me, did mama die on my birthday?"

"No," she returned. "Ask me no more, child!"

"O, do pray tell me something of her. Do now, at last, dear godmother, if you please! What did I do to her? How did I lose her? Why am I so different from other children, and why is it my fault, dear godmother? No, no, no, don't go away. O, speak to me!"

I was in a kind of fright beyond my grief; and I had caught hold of her dress, and was kneeling to her. She had been saying all the while, "Let me go!" But now she stood still.

Her darkened face had such power over me, that it stopped me in the midst of my vehemence. I put up my trembling little hand to clasp hers, or to beg her pardon with what earnestness I might, but withdrew it as she looked at me, and laid it on my fluttering heart. She raised me, sat in her chair, and standing me before her, said, slowly, in a cold, low voice—I see her knitted brow, and pointed finger:

"Your mother, Esther, is your disgrace, and you were hers. The time will come—and soon enough—when you will understand this better, and will feel it too, as no one save a woman can. I have forgiven her"; but her face did not relent; "the wrong she did to me, and I say no more of it, though it was greater than you will ever know—than any one will ever know, but I, the sufferer. For yourself, unfortunate girl, orphaned and degraded from the first of these evil anniversaries, pray daily that the sins of others be not visited upon your head, according to what is written.[1] Forget your mother, and leave all other people to forget her who will do her unhappy child that greatest kindness. Now, go!"

She checked me, however, as I was about to depart from her—so frozen as I was!—and added this:

"Submission, self-denial, diligent work, are the preparations for a life begun with such a shadow on it. You are different from other children, Esther, because you were not born, like them, in common sinfulness and wrath. You are set apart."

I went up to my room, and crept to bed, and laid my doll's cheek against mine wet with tears; and holding that solitary friend upon my bosom, cried myself to sleep. Imperfect as my understanding of my sorrow was, I knew that I had brought no joy, at any time, to anybody's heart, and that I was to no one upon earth what Dolly was to me.

1. See Numbers 14:18: "visiting the iniquity of the fathers upon the children unto the third and fourth generation."

Dear, dear, to think how much time we passed alone together afterwards, and how often I repeated to the doll the story of my birthday, and confided to her that I would try, as hard as ever I could, to repair the fault I had been born with (of which I confusedly felt guilty and yet innocent), and would strive as I grew up to be industrious, contented, and kind-hearted, and to do some good to some one, and win some love to myself if I could. I hope it is not self-indulgent to shed these tears as I think of it. I am very thankful, I am very cheerful, but I cannot quite help their coming to my eyes.

There! I have wiped them away now, and can go on again properly.

I felt the distance between my godmother and myself so much more after the birthday, and felt so sensible of filling a place in her house which ought to have been empty, that I found her more difficult of approach, though I was fervently grateful to her in my heart, than ever. I felt in the same way towards my school companions; I felt in the same way towards Mrs. Rachael, who was a widow; and oh, towards her daughter, of whom she was proud, who came to see her once a fortnight! I was very retired and quiet, and tried to be very diligent.

One sunny afternoon, when I had come home from school with my books and portfolio, watching my long shadow at my side, and as I was gliding up-stairs to my room as usual, my godmother looked out of the parlour door, and called me back. Sitting with her, I found—which was very unusual indeed—a stranger. A portly important-looking gentleman, dressed all in black, with a white cravat, large gold watch seals, a pair of gold eye-glasses, and a large seal-ring upon his little finger.

"This," said my godmother in an undertone, "is the child." Then she said, in her naturally stern way of speaking, "This is Esther, sir."

The gentleman put up his eye-glasses to look at me, and said, "Come here, my dear!" He shook hands with me, and asked me to take off my bonnet—looking at me all the while. When I had complied, he said, "Ah!" and afterwards "Yes!" And then, taking off his eye-glasses, and folding them in a red case, and leaning back in his arm-chair, turning the case about in his two hands he gave my godmother a nod. Upon that, my godmother said, "You may go upstairs, Esther!" and I made him my curtsey and left him.

It must have been two years afterwards, and I was almost fourteen, when one dreadful night my godmother and I sat at the fireside. I was reading aloud, and she was listening. I had come down at nine o'clock, as I always did, to read the Bible to her; and was reading, from St. John, how our Saviour stooped down, writing with his finger in the dust, when they brought the sinful woman to him.

" 'So when they continued asking him, he lifted up himself and said unto them, He that is without sin among you, let him first cast a stone at her!' "[2]

I was stopped by my godmother's rising, putting her hand to her head, and crying out, in an awful voice, from quite another part of the book:

" 'Watch ye therefore! lest coming suddenly he find you sleeping. And what I say unto you, I say unto all, Watch!' "[3]

In an instant, while she stood before me repeating these words, she fell down on the floor. I had no need to cry out; her voice had sounded through the house, and been heard in the street.

She was laid upon her bed. For more than a week she lay there, little altered outwardly; with her old handsome resolute frown that I so well knew, carved upon her face. Many and many a time, in the day and in the night, with my head upon the pillow by her that my whispers might be plainer to her, I kissed her, thanked her, prayed for her, asked her for her blessing and forgiveness, entreated her to give me the least sign that she knew or heard me. No, no, no. Her face was immoveable. To the very last, and even afterwards, her frown remained unsoftened.

On the day after my poor good godmother was buried, the gentleman in black with the white neckcloth reappeared. I was sent for by Mrs. Rachel, and found him in the same place, as if he had never gone away.

"My name is Kenge," he said; "you may remember it, my child; Kenge and Carboy, Lincoln's Inn."

I replied that I remembered to have seen him once before.

"Pray be seated—here near me. Don't distress yourself; it's of no use. Mrs. Rachael, I needn't inform you, who were acquainted with the late Miss Barbary's affairs, that her means die with her; and that this young lady, now her aunt is dead——"

"My aunt, sir!"

"It really is of no use carrying on a deception when no object is to be gained by it," said Mr. Kenge, smoothly. "Aunt in fact, though not in law. Don't distress yourself! Don't weep! Don't tremble! Mrs. Rachael, our young friend has no doubt heard of—the—a—Jarndyce and Jarndyce."

"Never," said Mrs. Rachael.

"Is it possible," pursued Mr. Kenge, putting up his eye-glasses, "that our young friend—I *beg* you won't distress yourself!—never heard of Jarndyce and Jarndyce!"

I shook my head, wondering even what it was.

"Not of Jarndyce and Jarndyce?" said Mr. Kenge, looking over his glasses at me, and softly turning the case about and about, as if

2. John 8:7.
3. Mark 13:35–37, alluding to the second coming of Christ.

he were petting something. "Not of one of the greatest Chancery suits known? Not of Jarndyce and Jarndyce—the—a—in itself a monument of Chancery practice. In which (I would say) every difficulty, every contingency, every masterly fiction, every form of procedure known in that court, is represented over and over again? It is a cause that could not exist, out of this free and great country. I should say that the aggregate of costs in Jarndyce and Jarndyce, Mrs. Rachael"; I was afraid he addressed himself to her, because I appeared inattentive; "amounts at the present hour to from SIX-ty to SEVEN-ty THOUSAND POUNDS!" said Mr. Kenge, leaning back in his chair.

I felt very ignorant, but what could I do? I was so entirely unacquainted with the subject, that I understood nothing about it even then.

"And she really never heard of the cause!" said Mr. Kenge. "Surprising!"

"Miss Barbary, sir," returned Mrs. Rachael, "who is now among the Seraphim——"

("I hope so, I am sure," said Mr. Kenge politely.)

"— Wished Esther only to know what would be serviceable to her. And she knows, from any teaching she has had here, nothing more."

"Well!" said Mr. Kenge. "Upon the whole, very proper. Now to the point," addressing me. "Miss Barbary, your sole relation (in fact, that is; for I am bound to observe that in law you had none), being deceased, and it naturally not being to be expected that Mrs. Rachael——"

"O dear no!" said Mrs. Rachael, quickly.

"Quite so," assented Mr. Kenge;—"that Mrs. Rachael should charge herself with your maintenance and support (I beg you won't distress yourself), you are in a position to receive the renewal of an offer which I was instructed to make to Miss Barbary some two years ago, and which, though rejected then, was understood to be renewable under the lamentable circumstances that have since occurred. Now, if I avow, that I represent, in Jarndyce and Jarndyce, and otherwise, a highly humane, but at the same time singular man, shall I compromise myself by any stretch of my professional caution?" said Mr. Kenge, leaning back in his chair again, and looking calmly at us both.

He appeared to enjoy beyond everything the sound of his own voice. I couldn't wonder at that, for it was mellow and full, and gave great importance to every word he uttered. He listened to himself with obvious satisfaction, and sometimes gently beat time to his own music with his head, or rounded a sentence with his hand. I was very much impressed by him—even then, before I knew that he formed himself on the model of a great lord who was his client, and that he was generally called Conversation Kenge.

"Mr. Jarndyce," he pursued, "being aware of the—I would say, desolate—position of our young friend, offers to place her at a first-rate establishment; where her education shall be completed, where her comfort shall be secured, where her reasonable wants shall be anticipated, where she shall be eminently qualified to discharge her duty in that station of life unto which it has pleased—shall I say Providence?—to call her."

My heart was filled so full, both by what he said, and by his affecting manner of saying it, that I was not able to speak, though I tried.

"Mr. Jarndyce," he went on, "makes no condition, beyond expressing his expectation that our young friend will not at any time remove herself from the establishment in question without his knowledge and concurrence. That she will faithfully apply herself to the acquisition of those accomplishments, upon the exercise of which she will be ultimately dependent. That she will tread in the paths of virtue and honour, and—the—a——so forth."

I was still less able to speak than before.

"Now, what does our young friend say?" proceeded Mr. Kenge. "Take time, take time! I pause for her reply. But take time!"

What the destitute subject of such an offer tried to say, I need not repeat. What she did say, I could more easily tell, if it were worth the telling. What she felt, and will feel to her dying hour, I could never relate.

This interview took place at Windsor, where I had passed (as far as I knew) my whole life. On that day week, amply provided with all necessaries, I left it, inside the stage-coach, for Reading.

Mrs. Rachael was too good to feel any emotion at parting, but I was not so good, and wept bitterly. I thought that I ought to have known her better after so many years, and ought to have made myself enough of a favourite with her to make her sorry then. When she gave me one cold parting kiss upon my forehead, like a thaw-drop from the stone porch—it was a very frosty day—I felt so miserable and self-reproachful, that I clung to her and told her it was my fault, I knew, that she could say good-bye so easily!

"No, Esther!" she returned. "It is your misfortune!"

The coach was at the little lawn-gate—we had not come out until we heard the wheels—and thus I left her, with a sorrowful heart. She went in before my boxes were lifted to the coach-roof, and shut the door. As long as I could see the house, I looked back at it from the window, through my tears. My godmother had left Mrs. Rachael all the little property she possessed; and there was to be a sale; and an old hearthrug with roses on it, which always seemed to me the first thing in the world I had ever seen, was hanging outside in the frost and snow. A day or two before, I had wrapped the dear old doll in her own shawl, and quietly laid her—I am half ashamed to tell it—in the garden-earth, under the tree that shaded my old window. I had no companion left but my bird, and him I carried with me in his cage.

When the house was out of sight, I sat, with my bird-cage in the straw at my feet, forward on the low seat, to look out of the high window; watching the frosty trees, that were like beautiful pieces of spar; and the fields all smooth and white with last night's snow; and the sun, so red but yielding so little heat; and the ice, dark like metal, where the skaters and sliders had brushed the snow away. There was a gentleman in the coach who sat on the opposite seat and looked very large in a quantity of wrappings; but he sat gazing out of the other window, and took no notice of me.

I thought of my dead godmother; of the night when I read to her; of her frowning so fixedly and sternly in her bed; of the strange place I was going to; of the people I should find there, and what they would be like, and what they would say to me; when a voice in the coach gave me a terrible start.

It said, "What the de-vil are you crying for?"

I was so frightened that I lost my voice, and could only answer in a whisper. "Me, sir?" For of course I knew it must have been the gentleman in the quantity of wrappings, though he was still looking out of his window.

"Yes, you," he said, turning round.

"I didn't know I was crying, sir," I faltered.

"But you are!" said the gentleman. "Look here!" He came quite opposite to me from the other corner of the coach, brushed one of his large furry cuffs across my eyes (but without hurting me), and showed me that it was wet.

"There! Now you know you are," he said. "Don't you?"

"Yes, sir," I said.

"And what are you crying for?" said the gentleman. "Don't you want to go there?"

"Where, sir?"

"Where? Why, wherever you are going," said the gentleman.

"I am very glad to go there, sir," I answered.

"Well then! Look glad!" said the gentleman.

I thought he was very strange; or at least that what I could see of him was very strange, for he was wrapped up to the chin, and his face was almost hidden in a fur cap, with broad fur straps at the side of his head, fastened under his chin; but I was composed again, and not afraid of him. So I told him that I thought I must have been crying, because of my godmother's death, and because of Mrs. Rachael's not being sorry to part with me.

"Con-found Mrs. Rachael!" said the gentleman. "Let her fly away in a high wind on a broomstick!"

I began to be really afraid of him now, and looked at him with the greatest astonishment. But I thought that he had pleasant eyes, although he kept on muttering to himself in an angry manner, and calling Mrs. Rachael names.

After a little while, he opened his outer wrapper, which appeared to me large enough to wrap up the whole coach, and put his arm down into a deep pocket in the side.

"Now, look here!" he said. "In this paper," which was nicely folded, "is a piece of the best plum-cake that can be got for money—sugar on the outside an inch thick, like fat on mutton chops. Here's a little pie (a gem this is, both for size and quality), made in France. And what do you suppose it's made of? Livers of fat geese. There's a pie! Now let's see you eat 'em."

"Thank you, sir," I replied, "thank you very much indeed, but I hope you won't be offended; they are too rich for me."

"Floored again!" said the gentleman, which I didn't at all understand, and threw them both out of window.

He did not speak to me any more, until he got out of the coach a little way short of Reading, when he advised me to be a good girl, and to be studious; and shook hands with me. I must say I was relieved by his departure. We left him at a milestone. I often walked past it afterwards, and never for a long time, without thinking of him, and half expecting to meet him. But I never did; and so, as time went on, he passed out of my mind.

When the coach stopped, a very neat lady looked up at the window, and said:

"Miss Donny."

"No, ma'am, Esther Summerson."

"That is quite right," said the lady, "Miss Donny."

I now understood that she introduced herself by that name, and begged Miss Donny's pardon for my mistake, and pointed out my boxes at her request. Under the direction of a very neat maid, they were put outside a very small green carriage; and then Miss Donny, the maid, and I, got inside, and were driven away.

"Everything is ready for you, Esther," said Miss Donny; "and the scheme of your pursuits has been arranged in exact accordance with the wishes of your guardian, Mr. Jarndyce."

"Of——did you say, ma'am?"

"Of your guardian, Mr. Jarndyce," said Miss Donny.

I was so bewildered that Miss Donny thought the cold had been too severe for me, and lent me her smelling-bottle.

"Do you know my—guardian, Mr. Jarndyce, ma'am?" I asked, after a good deal of hesitation.

"Not personally, Esther," said Miss Donny; "merely through his solicitors, Messrs. Kenge and Carboy, of London. A very superior gentleman, Mr. Kenge. Truly eloquent indeed. Some of his periods[4] quite majestic!"

I felt this to be very true, but was too confused to attend to it. Our speedy arrival at our destination, before I had time to recover myself, increased my confusion; and I never shall forget the uncertain and unreal air of everything at Greenleaf (Miss Donny's house), that afternoon!

But I soon became used to it. I was so adapted to the routine of Greenleaf before long, that I seemed to have been there a great while: and almost to have dreamed rather than to have really lived, my old life at my godmother's. Nothing could be more precise, exact, and orderly, than Greenleaf. There was a time for everything all round the dial of the clock, and everything was done at its appointed moment.

We were twelve boarders, and there were two Miss Donnys, twins. It was understood that I would have to depend, by-and-bye, on my qualifications as a governess; and I was not only instructed in everything that was taught at Greenleaf, but was very soon engaged in helping to instruct others. Although I was treated in every other respect like the rest of the school, this single difference was made in my case from the first. As I began to know more, I taught more, and so in course of time I had plenty to do, which I was very fond of doing, because it made the dear girls fond of me. At last, whenever a new pupil came who was a little downcast and unhappy, she was so sure—indeed I don't know why—to make a friend of me, that all newcomers were confided to my care. They said I was so gentle; but I am sure *they* were! I often thought of the resolution I had made on my birthday, to try to be industrious, contented, and truehearted, and to do some good to some one, and win some love if I could; and indeed, indeed, I felt almost ashamed to have done so little and have won so much.

I passed at Greenleaf six happy, quiet years. I never saw in any face there, thank Heaven, on my birthday, that it would have been better if I had never been born. When the day came round, it brought me so many tokens of affectionate remembrance that my room was beautiful with them from New Year's Day to Christmas.

In those six years I had never been away, except on visits at holiday time in the neighbourhood. After the first six months or so, I had taken Miss Donny's advice in reference to the propriety of writing to Mr. Kenge, to say that I was happy and grateful; and with her approval I had written such a letter. I had received a formal answer acknowledging its receipt, and saying, "We note the contents thereof, which shall be duly communicated to our client." After

4. Highly elaborate sentences.

that, I sometimes heard Miss Donny and her sister mention how regularly my accounts were paid; and about twice a year I ventured to write a similar letter. I always received by return of post exactly the same answer, in the same round hand; with the signature of Kenge and Carboy in another writing, which I supposed to be Mr. Kenge's.

It seems so curious to me to be obliged to write all this about myself! As if this narrative were the narrative of *my* life! But my little body will soon fall into the background now.

Six quiet years (I find I am saying it for the second time) I had passed at Greenleaf, seeing in those around me, as it might be in a looking-glass, every stage of my own growth and change there, when, one November morning, I received this letter. I omit the date.

Old Square, Lincoln's Inn.

Madam,

Jarndyce and Jarndyce.

Our clt Mr. Jarndyce being abt to rece into his house, under an Order of the Ct of Chy, a Ward of the Ct in this cause, for whom he wishes to secure an elgble compn, directs us to inform you that he will be glad of your serces in the afsd capacity.

We have arrngd for your being forded, carriage free, p^{r} eight o'clock coach from Reading, on Monday morning next, to White Horse Cellar, Piccadilly, London, where one of our clks will be in waiting to convey you to our offe as above.

We are, Madam, Your obed^{t} Serv^{ts},

Kenge and Carboy.

Miss Esther Summerson.

O, never, never, never shall I forget the emotion this letter caused in the house! It was so tender in them to care so much for me; it was so gracious in that Father who had not forgotten me, to have made my orphan way so smooth and easy, and to have inclined so many youthful natures towards me; that I could hardly bear it. Not that I would have had them less sorry—I am afraid not; but the pleasure of it, and the pain of it, and the pride and joy of it, and the humble regret of it, were so blended, that my heart seemed almost breaking while it was full of rapture.

The letter gave me only five days' notice of my removal. When every minute added to the proofs of love and kindness that were given me in those five days; and when at last the morning came, and when they took me through all the rooms that I might see them for the last time; and when some cried, "Esther, dear, say good-bye to me here, at my bedside, where you first spoke so kindly to me!" and when others asked me only to write their names, "With Esther's love"; and when they all surrounded me with their parting presents, and clung to me weeping, and cried, "What shall we do when dear, dear Esther's gone!" and when I tried to tell them how forbearing, and how good they had all been to me, and how I blessed, and thanked them every one; what a heart I had!

And when the two Miss Donnys grieved as much to part with me, as the least among them; and when the maids said, "Bless you, miss, wherever you go!" and when the ugly lame old gardener, who I thought had hardly noticed me in all those years, came panting after the coach to give me a little nosegay of geraniums, and told me I had been the light of his eyes—indeed the old man said so!—what a heart I had then!

And could I help it, if with all this, and the coming to the little school, and the unexpected sight of the poor children outside waving their hats and bonnets to me, and of a grey-haired gentleman and lady, whose daughter I had helped to teach and at whose house I had visited (who were said to be the proudest people in all that country), caring for nothing but calling out, "Good-bye, Esther. May you be very happy!"—could I help it if I was quite bowed down in the coach by myself, and said, "O, I am so thankful, I am so thankful!" many times over!

But of course I soon considered that I must not take tears where I was going, after all that had been done for me. Therefore, of course, I made myself sob less, and persuaded myself to be quiet by saying very often, "Esther, now you really must! This *will not* do!" I cheered myself up pretty well at last, though I am afraid I was longer about it than I ought to have been; and when I had cooled my eyes with lavender water, it was time to watch for London.

I was quite persuaded that we were there, when we were ten miles off; and when we really were there, that we should never get there. However, when we began to jolt upon a stone pavement, and particularly when every other conveyance seemed to be running into us, and we seemed to be running into every other conveyance, I began to believe that we really were approaching the end of our journey. Very soon afterwards we stopped.

A young gentleman who had inked himself by accident, addressed me from the pavement, and said, "I am from Kenge and Carboy's, miss, of Lincoln's Inn."

"If you please, sir," said I.

He was very obliging; and as he handed me into a fly,[5] after

5. A light one-horse carriage or cab.

superintending the removal of my boxes, I asked him whether there was a great fire anywhere? For the streets were so full of dense brown smoke that scarcely anything was to be seen.

"Oh dear no, miss," he said. "This is a London particular."[6]

I had never heard of such a thing.

"A fog, miss," said the young gentleman.

"O indeed!" said I.

We drove slowly through the dirtiest and darkest streets that ever were seen in the world (I thought), and in such a distracting state of confusion that I wondered how the people kept their senses, until we passed into sudden quietude under an old gateway, and drove on through a silent square until we came to an odd nook in a corner, where there was an entrance up a steep, broad flight of stairs, like an entrance to a church. And there really was a churchyard, outside under some cloisters, for I saw the gravestones from the staircase window.[7]

This was Kenge and Carboy's. The young gentleman showed me through an outer office into Mr. Kenge's room—there was no one in it—and politely put an arm-chair for me by the fire. He then called my attention to a little looking-glass, hanging from a nail on one side of the chimney-piece.

"In case you should wish to look at yourself, miss, after the journey, as you're going before the Chancellor. Not that it's requisite, I am sure," said the young gentleman civilly.

"Going before the Chancellor?" I said, startled for a moment.

"Only a matter of form, miss," returned the young gentleman. "Mr. Kenge is in Court now. He left his compliments, and would you partake of some refreshment"; there were biscuits and a decanter of wine on a small table; "and look over the paper"; which the young gentleman gave me as he spoke. He then stirred the fire, and left me.

Everything was so strange—the stranger for its being night in the day-time, the candles burning with a white flame, and looking raw and cold—that I read the words in the newspaper without knowing what they meant, and found myself reading the same words repeatedly. As it was of no use going on in that way, I put the paper down, took a peep at my bonnet in the glass to see if it was neat, and looked at the room which was not half lighted, and at the shabby

6. Cf. John Timbs, *Curiosities of London* (1855), on fog: "This phenomenon is caused by the half million of blazing coal-fires in the metropolis contributing a vast quantity of fuliginous matter, which, mingling with the vapour, partly arising from imperfect drainage, produces that foggy darkness. . . . Sometimes it is of a bottle-green colour but . . . at other times it is of a pea-soup yellow; in the midst of which the street gas-lights appear like the pin-head lamps of old. The latter is the genuine 'London Fog.' "

7. A burial ground under the foundation-arches of Lincoln's Inn Chapel.

dusty tables, and at the piles of writings, and at a bookcase full of the most inexpressive-looking books that ever had anything to say for themselves. Then I went on, thinking, thinking, thinking; and the fire went on, burning, burning, burning; and the candles went on flickering and guttering, and there were no snuffers—until the young gentleman by-and-bye brought a very dirty pair; for two hours.

At last Mr. Kenge came. *He* was not altered; but he was surprised to see how altered I was; and appeared quite pleased. "As you are going to be the companion of the young lady who is now in the Chancellor's private room, Miss Summerson," he said, "we thought it well that you should be in attendance also. You will not be discomposed by the Lord Chancellor, I dare say?"

"No, sir," I said, "I don't think I shall." Really not seeing, on consideration, why I should be.

So Mr. Kenge gave me his arm, and we went round the corner, under a colonnade, and in at a side door. And so we came, along a passage, into a comfortable sort of room, where a young lady and a young gentleman were standing near a great, loud-roaring fire. A screen was interposed between them and it, and they were leaning on the screen, talking.

They both looked up when I came in, and I saw in the young lady, with the fire shining upon her, such a beautiful girl! With such rich golden hair, such soft blue eyes, and such a bright, innocent trusting face!

"Miss Ada," said Mr. Kenge, "this is Miss Summerson."

She came to meet me with a smile of welcome and her hand extended, but seemed to change her mind in a moment, and kissed me. In short, she had such a natural, captivating, winning manner, that in a few minutes we were sitting in the window-seat, with the light of the fire upon us, talking together, as free and happy as could be.

What a load off my mind! It was so delightful to know that she could confide in me, and like me! it was so good of her, and so encouraging to me!

The young gentleman was her distant cousin, she told me, and his name Richard Carstone. He was a handsome youth, with an ingenuous face, and a most engaging laugh; and after she had called him up to where we sat, he stood by us, in the light of the fire too, talking gaily, like a light-hearted boy. He was very young; not more than nineteen then, if quite so much, but nearly two years older than she was. They were both orphans, and (what was very unexpected and curious to me) had never met before that day. Our all three coming together for the first time, in such an unusual place, was a thing to talk about; and we talked about it; and the fire, which had left off roaring, winked its red eyes at us—as Richard said—like a drowsy old Chancery lion.

We conversed in a low tone, because a full-dressed gentleman in a bag wig[8] frequently came in and out and when he did so, we could hear a drawling sound in the distance, which he said was one of the counsel in our case addressing the Lord Chancellor. He told Mr. Kenge that the Chancellor would be up in five minutes; and presently we heard a bustle, and a tread of feet, and Mr. Kenge said that the Court had risen, and his lordship was in the next room.

The gentleman in the bag wig opened the door almost directly, and requested Mr. Kenge to come in. Upon that, we all went into the next room; Mr. Kenge first, with my darling—it is so natural to me now, that I can't help writing it; and there, plainly dressed in black, and sitting in an arm-chair at a table near the fire, was his lordship, whose robe, trimmed with beautiful gold-lace, was thrown upon another chair. He gave us a searching look as we entered, but his manner was both courtly and kind.

The gentleman in the bag wig laid bundles of papers on his lordship's table and his lordship silently selected one, and turned over the leaves.

"Miss Clare," said the Lord Chancellor. "Miss Ada Clare?"

Mr. Kenge presented her, and his lordship begged her to sit down near him. That he admired her, and was interested by her, even *I* could see in a moment. It touched me, that the home of such a beautiful young creature should be represented by that dry official place. The Lord High Chancellor, at his best, appeared so poor a substitute for the love and pride of parents.

"The Jarndyce in question," said the Lord Chancellor, still turning over leaves, "is Jarndyce of Bleak House."

"Jarndyce of Bleak House, my lord," said Mr. Kenge.

"A dreary name," said the Lord Chancellor.

"But not a dreary place at present, my Lord," said Mr. Kenge.

"And Bleak House," said his lordship, "is in——"

"Hertfordshire, my lord."

"Mr. Jarndyce of Bleak House is not married?" said his lordship.

"He is not, my lord," said Mr. Kenge.

A pause.

"Young Mr. Richard Carstone is present?" said the Lord Chancellor, glancing towards him.

Richard bowed and stepped forward.

"Hum!" said the Lord Chancellor, turning over more leaves.

"Mr. Jarndyce of Bleak House, my lord," Mr. Kenge observed, in

8. An eighteenth-century style of wig in which the back hair was held in a silk pouch or bag.

a low voice, "if I may venture to remind your lordship, provides a suitable companion for——"

"For Mr. Richard Carstone?" I thought (but I am not quite sure) I heard his lordship say, in an equally low voice, and with a smile.

"For Miss Ada Clare. This is the young lady. Miss Summerson."

His lordship gave me an indulgent look, and acknowledged my curtsey very graciously.

"Miss Summerson is not related to any party in the cause, I think?"

"No, my lord."

Mr. Kenge leant over before it was quite said, and whispered. His lordship, with his eyes upon his papers, listened, nodded twice or thrice, turned over more leaves, and did not look towards me again, until we were going away.

Mr. Kenge now retired and Richard with him, to where I was, near the door, leaving my pet (it is so natural to me that again I can't help it!) sitting near the Lord Chancellor; with whom his lordship spoke a little apart; asking her, as she told me afterwards, whether she had well reflected on the proposed arrangement, and if she thought she would be happy under the roof of Mr. Jarndyce of Bleak House, and why she thought so? Presently he rose courteously and released her, and then he spoke for a minute or two with Richard Carstone; not seated, but standing, and altogether with more ease and less ceremony—as if he still knew, though he *was* Lord Chancellor, how to go straight to the candour of a boy.

"Very well!" said his lordship aloud. "I shall make the order. Mr. Jarndyce of Bleak House has chosen, so far as I may judge," and this was when he looked at me, "a very good companion for the young lady, and the arrangement altogether seems the best of which the circumstances admit."

He dismissed us pleasantly, and we all went out, very much obliged to him for being so affable and polite; by which he had certainly lost no dignity, but seemed to us to have gained some.

When we got under the colonnade, Mr. Kenge remembered that he must go back for a moment, to ask a question; and left us in the fog, with the Lord Chancellor's carriage and servants waiting for him to come out.

"Well!" said Richard Carstone, "*that's* over! And where do we go next, Miss Summerson?"

"Don't you know?" I said.

"Not in the least," said he.

"And don't *you* know, my love?" I asked Ada.

"No!" said she. "Don't you?"

"Not at all!" said I.

The little old Lady.

We looked at one another, half laughing at our being like the children in the wood,[9] when a curious little old woman in a squeezed bonnet, and carrying a reticule, came curtseying and smiling up to us, with an air of great ceremony.

"Oh!" said she. "The wards in Jarndyce! Ve-ry happy, I am sure, to have the honour! It is a good omen for youth, and hope, and beauty, when they find themselves in this place, and don't know what's to come of it."

"Mad!" whispered Richard, not thinking she could hear him.

"Right! Mad, young gentleman," she returned so quickly that he was quite abashed. "I was a ward myself. I was not mad at that time," curtseying low, and smiling between every little sentence. "I had youth and hope. I believe, beauty. It matters very little now. Neither of the three served, or saved me. I have the honour to attend Court regularly. With my documents. I expect a judgment. Shortly. On the Day of Judgment. I have discovered that the sixth seal mentioned in the Revelations is the Great Seal.[1] It has been open a long time! Pray accept my blessing."

As Ada was a little frightened, I said, to humour the poor old lady, that we were much obliged to her.

"Ye-es!" she said mincingly. "I imagine so. And here is Conversation Kenge. With *his* documents! How does your honourable worship do?"

"Quite well, quite well! Now don't be troublesome, that's a good soul!" said Mr. Kenge, leading the way back.

"By no means," said the poor old lady, keeping up with Ada and me. "Anything but troublesome. I shall confer estates on both—which is not being troublesome, I trust? I expect a judgment. Shortly. On the Day of Judgment. This is a good omen for you. Accept my blessing!"

She stopped at the bottom of the steep, broad flight of stairs; but we looked back as we went up, and she was still there, saying, still with a curtsey and a smile between every little sentence. "Youth. And hope. And beauty. And Chancery. And Conversation Kenge! Ha! Pray accept my blessing!"

Chapter IV

TELESCOPIC PHILANTHROPHY

We were to pass the night, Mr. Kenge told us when we arrived in his room, at Mrs. Jellyby's; and then he turned to me, and said he took it for granted I knew who Mrs. Jellyby was?

9. See "The Children in the Wood," an old ballad about an orphaned brother and sister who were abandoned in a forest.

1. The opening of the sixth seal was to be followed by a series of terrible calamities on earth (see Revelations 6:12–17). The speaker equates this seal with the Lord Chancellor's Great Seal used for stamping state documents.

"I really don't, sir," I returned. "Perhaps Mr. Carstone—or Miss Clare——"

But no, they knew nothing whatever about Mrs. Jellyby.

"In-deed! Mrs. Jellyby," said Mr. Kenge, standing with his back to the fire, and casting his eyes over the dusty hearth-rug as if it were Mrs. Jellyby's biography, "is a lady of very remarkable strength of character, who devotes herself entirely to the public. She has devoted herself to an extensive variety of public subjects, at various times, and is at present (until something else attracts her) devoted to the subject of Africa; with a view to the general cultivation of the coffee berry—*and* the natives—and the happy settlement, on the banks of the African rivers, of our superabundant home population. Mr. Jarndyce, who is desirous to aid any work that is considered likely to be a good work, and who is much sought after by philanthropists, has, I believe, a very high opinion of Mrs. Jellyby."

Mr. Kenge, adjusting his cravat, then looked at us.

"And Mr. Jellyby, sir?" suggested Richard.

"Ah! Mr. Jellyby," said Mr. Kenge, "is—a—I don't know that I can describe him to you better than by saying that he is the husband of Mrs. Jellyby."

"A nonentity, sir?" said Richard, with a droll look.

"I don't say that," returned Mr. Kenge, gravely. "I can't say that, indeed, for I know nothing whatever *of* Mr. Jellyby. I never, to my knowledge, had the pleasure of seeing Mr. Jellyby. He may be a very superior man; but he is, so to speak, merged—Merged—in the more shining qualities of his wife." Mr. Kenge proceeded to tell us that as the road to Bleak House would have been very long, dark, and tedious, on such an evening, and as we had been travelling already, Mr. Jarndyce had himself proposed this arrangement. A carriage would be at Mrs. Jellyby's to convey us out of town, early in the forenoon of to-morrow.

He then rang a little bell, and the young gentleman came in. Addressing him by the name of Guppy, Mr. Kenge inquired whether Miss Summerson's boxes and the rest of the baggage had been "sent round." Mr. Guppy said yes, they had been sent round, and a coach was waiting to take us round too, as soon as we pleased.

"Then it only remains," said Mr. Kenge, shaking hands with us, "for me to express my lively satisfaction in (good day, Miss Clare!) the arrangement this day concluded, and my (*good-bye* to you, Miss Summerson!) lively hope that it will conduce to the happiness, the (glad to have had the honour of making your acquaintance, Mr. Carstone!) welfare, the advantage in all points of view, of all concerned! Guppy, see the party safely there."

"Where *is* 'there,' Mr. Guppy?" said Richard, as we went downstairs.

"No distance," said Mr. Guppy; "round in Thavies Inn, you know."

"I can't say I know where it is, for I come from Winchester,[1] and am strange in London."

"Only round the corner," said Mr. Guppy. "We just twist up Chancery Lane, and cut along Holborn, and there we are in four minutes' time, as near as a toucher.[2] This is about a London particular *now*, ain't it, miss?" He seemed quite delighted with it on my account.

"The fog is very dense, indeed!" said I.

"Not that it affects you, though, I'm sure," said Mr. Guppy, putting up the steps. "On the contrary, it seems to do you good, miss, judging from your appearance."

I knew he meant well in paying me this compliment, so I laughed at myself for blushing at it, when he had shut the door and got upon the box; and we all three laughed, and chatted about our inexperience, and the strangeness of London, until we turned up under an archway to our destination: a narrow street of high houses, like an oblong cistern to hold the fog. There was a confused little crowd of people, principally children, gathered about the house at which we stopped, which had a tarnished brass plate on the door, with the inscription, JELLYBY.

"Don't be frightened!" said Mr. Guppy, looking in at the coach-window. "One of the young Jellybys been and got his head through the area railings!"

"O poor child," said I, "let me out, if you please!"

"Pray be careful of yourself, miss. The young Jellybys are always up to something," said Mr. Guppy.

I made my way to the poor child, who was one of the dirtiest little unfortunates I ever saw, and found him very hot and frightened, and crying loudly, fixed by the neck between two iron railings, while a milkman and a beadle,[3] with the kindest intentions possible, were endeavouring to drag him back by the legs, under a general impression that his skull was compressible by those means. As I found (after pacifying him), that he was a little boy, with a naturally large head, I thought that, perhaps, where his head could go, his body could follow, and mentioned that the best mode of extrication might be to push him forward. This was so favourably received by the milkman and beadle, that he would immediately have been pushed into the area,[4] if I had not held his pinafore, while Richard and Mr. Guppy ran down through the kitchen, to catch him when

1. Site of one of England's oldest schools.
2. A *toucher* in lawn-bowling is a bowl that touches the jack or scoring-pin. *As near as a toucher* means here "as close as possible to four minutes."
3. A parish officer, a kind of policeman.
4. Pit between sidewalk and housefront (guarded by railings) with steps providing access to basement.

he should be released. At last he was happily got down without any accident, and then he began to beat Mr. Guppy with a hoop-stick in quite a frantic manner.

Nobody had appeared belonging to the house, except a person in pattens,[5] who had been poking at the child from below with a broom; I don't know with what object, and I don't think she did. I therefore supposed that Mrs. Jellyby was not at home; and was quite surprised when the person appeared in the passage without the pattens, and going up to the back room on the first floor, before Ada and me, announced us as, "Them two young ladies, Missis Jellyby!" We passed several more children on the way up, whom it was difficult to avoid treading on in the dark; and as we came into Mrs. Jellyby's presence, one of the poor little things fell downstairs—down a whole flight (as it sounded to me), with a great noise.

Mrs. Jellyby, whose face reflected none of the uneasiness which we could not help showing in our own faces, as the dear child's head recorded its passage with a bump on every stair—Richard afterwards said he counted seven, besides one for the landing—received us with perfect equanimity. She was a pretty, very diminutive, plump woman, of from forty to fifty, with handsome eyes, though they had a curious habit of seeming to look a long way off. As if—I am quoting Richard again—they could see nothing nearer than Africa!

"I am very glad indeed," said Mrs. Jellyby, in an agreeable voice, "to have the pleasure of receiving you. I have a great respect for Mr. Jarndyce; and no one in whom he is interested can be an object of indifference to me."

We expressed our acknowledgements, and sat down behind the door where there was a lame invalid of a sofa. Mrs. Jellyby had very good hair, but was too much occupied with her African duties to brush it. The shawl in which she had been loosely muffled, dropped on to her chair when she advanced to us; and as she turned to resume her seat, we could not help noticing that her dress didn't nearly meet up the back, and that the open space was railed across with a lattice-work of stay-lace[6]—like a summerhouse.

The room, which was strewn with papers and nearly filled by a great writing-table covered with similar litter, was, I must say, not only very untidy, but very dirty. We were obliged to take notice of that with our sense of sight, even while, with our sense of hearing, we followed the poor child who had tumbled downstairs: I think into the back kitchen, where somebody seemed to stifle him.

But what principally struck us was a jaded and unhealthy-looking, though by no means plain girl, at the writing-table, who sat biting

5. Overshoes with wooden soles and iron skates, designed for walking through mud.

6. Strings for tightening a corset.

the feather of her pen, and staring at us. I suppose nobody ever was in such a state of ink. And, from her tumbled hair to her pretty feet, which were disfigured with frayed and broken satin slippers trodden down at heel, she really seemed to have no article of dress upon her, from a pin upwards, that was in its proper condition or its right place.

"You find me, my dears," said Mrs. Jellyby, snuffing the two great office candles in tin candlesticks which made the room taste strongly of hot tallow (the fire had gone out, and there was nothing in the grate but ashes, a bundle of wood, and a poker), "you find me, my dears, as usual, very busy; but that you will excuse. The African project at present employs my whole time. It involves me in correspondence with public bodies, and with private individuals anxious for the welfare of their species all over the country. I am happy to say it is advancing. We hope by this time next year to have from a hundred and fifty to two hundred healthy families cultivating coffee and educating the natives of Borrioboola-Gha, on the left bank of the Niger."

As Ada said nothing, but looked at me, I said it must be very gratifying.

"It *is* gratifying," said Mrs. Jellyby. "It involves the devotion of all my energies, such as they are; but that is nothing, so that it succeeds; and I am more confident of success every day. Do you know, Miss Summerson, I almost wonder that *you* never turned your thoughts to Africa."

This application of the subject was really so unexpected to me, that I was quite at a loss how to receive it. I hinted that the climate——

"The finest climate in the world!" said Mrs. Jellyby.

"Indeed, ma'am?"

"Certainly. With precaution," said Mrs. Jellyby. "You may go into Holborn, without precaution, and be run over. You may go into Holborn, with precaution, and never be run over. Just so with Africa."

I said, "No doubt."—I meant as to Holborn.

"If you would like," said Mrs. Jellyby, putting a number of papers towards us, "to look over some remarks on that head, and on the general subject (which have been extensively circulated), while I finish a letter I am now dictating—to my eldest daughter, who is my amanuensis——"

The girl at the table left off biting her pen, and made a return to our recognition, which was half bashful and half sulky.

"—I shall then have finished for the present," proceeded Mrs. Jellyby, with a sweet smile; "though my work is never done. Where are you, Caddy?"

" 'Presents her compliments to Mr. Swallow and begs——' " said Caddy.

" 'And begs,' " said Mrs. Jellyby, dictating, " 'to inform him, in reference to his letter of inquiry on the African project.'—No, Peepy! Not on any account!"

Peepy (so self-named) was the unfortunate child who had fallen down-stairs, who now interrupted the correspondence by presenting himself, with a strip of plaister on his forehead, to exhibit his wounded knees, in which Ada and I did not know which to pity most—the bruises or the dirt. Mrs. Jellyby merely added, with the serene composure with which she said everything, "Go along, you naughty Peepy!" and fixed her fine eyes on Africa again.

However, as she at once proceeded with her dictation, and as I interrupted nothing by doing it, I ventured quietly to stop poor Peepy as he was going out, and to take him up to nurse. He looked very much astonished at it, and at Ada's kissing him; but soon fell fast asleep in my arms, sobbing at longer and longer intervals, until he was quiet. I was so occupied with Peepy that I lost the letter in detail, though I derived such a general impression from it of the momentous importance of Africa, and the utter insignificance of all other places and things, that I felt quite ashamed to have thought so little about it.

"Six o'clock!" said Mrs. Jellyby. "And our dinner hour is nominally (for we dine at all hours) five! Caddy, show Miss Clare and Miss Summerson their rooms. You will like to make some change, perhaps? You will excuse me, I know, being so much occupied. O, that very bad child! Pray put him down, Miss Summerson!"

I begged permission to retain him, truly saying that he was not at all troublesome; and carried him up-stairs and laid him on my bed. Ada and I had two upper rooms, with a door of communication between. They were excessively bare and disorderly, and the curtain to my window was fastened up with a fork.

"You would like some hot water, wouldn't you?" said Miss Jellyby, looking round for a jug with a handle to it, but looking in vain.

"If it is not being troublesome," said we.

"Oh, it's not the trouble," returned Miss Jellyby; "the question is, if there *is* any."

The evening was so very cold, and the rooms had such a marshy smell, that I must confess it was a little miserable; and Ada was half crying. We soon laughed, however, and were busily unpacking, when Miss Jellyby came back to say that she was sorry there was no hot water; but they couldn't find the kettle, and the boiler was out of order.

We begged her not to mention it, and made all the haste we

could to get down to the fire again. But all the little children had come up to the landing outside, to look at the phenomenon of Peepy lying on my bed; and our attention was distracted by the constant apparition of noses and fingers, in situations of danger between the hinges of the doors. It was impossible to shut the door of either room; for my lock, with no knob to it, looked as if it wanted to be wound up; and though the handle of Ada's went round and round with the greatest smoothness, it was attended with no effect whatever on the door. Therefore I proposed to the children that they should come in and be very good at my table, and I would tell them the story of Little Red Riding Hood while I dressed; which they did, and were as quiet as mice, including Peepy, who awoke opportunely before the appearance of the wolf.

When we went down-stairs we found a mug, with "A Present from Tunbridge Wells" on it, lighted up in the staircase window with a floating wick;[7] and a young woman, with a swelled face bound up in a flannel bandage, blowing the fire of the drawing-room (now connected by an open door with Mrs. Jellyby's room), and choaking dreadfully. It smoked to that degree in short, that we all sat coughing and crying with the windows open for half an hour; during which Mrs. Jellyby, with the same sweetness of temper, directed letters about Africa. Her being so employed was, I must say, a great relief to me; for Richard told us that he had washed his hands in a pie-dish, and that they had found the kettle on his dressing-table; and he made Ada laugh so, that they made me laugh in the most ridiculous manner.

Soon after seven o'clock we went down to dinner; carefully, by Mrs. Jellyby's advice; for the stair-carpets, besides being very deficient in stair-wires,[8] were so torn as to be absolute traps. We had a fine cod-fish, a piece of roast beef, a dish of cutlets, and a pudding; an excellent dinner, if it had had any cooking to speak of, but it was almost raw. The young woman with the flannel bandage waited, and dropped everything on the table wherever it happened to go, and never moved it again until she put it on the stairs. The person I had seen in pattens (who I suppose to have been the cook), frequently came and skirmished with her at the door, and there appeared to be ill-will between them.

All through dinner; which was long, in consequence of such accidents as the dish of potatoes being mislaid in the coal scuttle, and the handle of the corkscrew coming off, and striking the young woman in the chin; Mrs. Jellyby preserved the evenness of her disposition. She told us a great deal that was interesting about Borrioboola-Gha and the natives; and received so many letters that

7. Improvised lamp with the wick floating in the oil.

8. Metal rods to keep carpets snug with stairs.

Richard, who sat by her, saw four envelopes in the gravy at once. Some of the letters were proceedings of ladies' committees, or resolutions of ladies' meetings, which she read to us; others were applications from people excited in various ways about the cultivation of coffee, and natives; others required answers, and these she sent her eldest daughter from the table three or four times to write. She was full of business, and undoubtedly was, as she had told us, devoted to the cause.

I was a little curious to know who a mild bald gentleman in spectacles was, who dropped into a vacant chair (there was no top or bottom in particular) after the fish was taken away, and seemed passively to submit himself to Borrioboola-Gha, but not to be actively interested in that settlement. As he never spoke a word, he might have been a native, but for his complexion. It was not until we left the table, and he remained alone with Richard, that the possibility of his being Mr. Jellyby ever entered my head. But he *was* Mr. Jellyby; and a loquacious young man called Mr. Quale, with large shining knobs for temples, and his hair all brushed to the back of his head, who came in the evening, and told Ada he was a philanthropist, also informed her that he called the matrimonial alliance of Mrs. Jellyby with Mr. Jellyby the union of mind and matter.

This young man, besides having a great deal to say for himself about Africa, and a project of his for teaching the coffee colonists to teach the natives to turn piano-forte legs and establish an export trade, delighted in drawing Mrs. Jellyby out by saying, "I believe now, Mrs. Jellyby, you have received as many as from one hundred and fifty to two hundred letters respecting Africa in a single day, have you not?" or, "If my memory does not deceive me, Mrs. Jellyby, you once mentioned that you had sent off five thousand circulars from one post-office at one time?"—always repeating Mrs. Jellyby's answer to us like an interpreter. During the whole evening, Mr. Jellyby sat in a corner with his head against the wall, as if he were subject to low spirits. It seemed that he had several times opened his mouth when alone with Richard, after dinner, as if he had something on his mind; but had always shut it again, to Richard's extreme confusion, without saying anything.

Mrs. Jellyby, sitting in quite a nest of wastepaper, drank coffee all the evening and dictated at intervals to her eldest daughter. She also held a discussion with Mr. Quale; of which the subject seemed to be—if I understood it—the Brotherhood of Humanity; and gave utterance to some beautiful sentiments. I was not so attentive an auditor as I might have wished to be, however, for Peepy and the other children came flocking about Ada and me in a corner of the drawing-room to ask for another story; so we sat down among them, and told them in whispers Puss in Boots and I don't know what else, until Mrs. Jellyby accidentally remembering them, sent them to bed. As Peepy cried for me to take him to bed, I carried him up-stairs, where the young woman with the flannel bandage charged into the midst of the little family like a dragoon, and overturned them into cribs.

After that, I occupied myself in making our room a little tidy, and in coaxing a very cross fire that had been lighted, to burn; which at last it did, quite brightly. On my return down-stairs, I felt that Mrs. Jellyby looked down upon me rather, for being so frivolous; and I was sorry for it; though at the same time I knew that I had no higher pretensions.

It was nearly midnight before we found an opportunity of going to bed; and even then we left Mrs. Jellyby among her papers drinking coffee, and Miss Jellyby biting the feather of her pen.

"What a strange house!" said Ada, when we got up-stairs. "How curious of my cousin Jarndyce to send us here!"

"My love," said I, "it quite confuses me. I want to understand it, and I can't understand it at all."

"What?" asked Ada, with her pretty smile.

"All this, my dear," said I. "It *must* be very good of Mrs. Jellyby to take such pains about a scheme for the benefit of Natives—and yet—Peepy and the housekeeping!"

Ada laughed; and put her arm about my neck, as I stood looking at the fire; and told me I was a quiet, dear, good creature, and had won her heart. "You are so thoughtful, Esther," she said, "and yet so cheerful! and you do so much, so unpretendingly! You would make a home out of even this house."

My simple darling! She was quite unconscious that she only praised herself, and that it was in the goodness of her own heart that she made so much of me!

"May I ask you a question?" said I, when we had sat before the fire a little while.

"Five hundred," said Ada.

"Your cousin, Mr. Jarndyce. I owe so much to him. Would you mind describing him to me?"

Shaking back her golden hair, Ada turned her eyes upon me with such laughing wonder, that I was full of wonder too—partly at her beauty, partly at her surprise.

"Esther!" she cried.

"My dear!"

"You want a description of my cousin Jarndyce?"

"My dear, I never saw him."

"And *I* never saw him!" returned Ada.

Well, to be sure!

No, she had never seen him. Young as she was when her mama

died, she remembered how the tears would come into her eyes when she spoke of him, and of the noble generosity of his character, which she had said was to be trusted above all earthly things; and Ada trusted it. Her cousin Jarndyce had written to her a few months ago,—"a plain, honest letter," Ada said—proposing the arrangement we were now to enter on, and telling her that, "in time it might heal some of the wounds made by the miserable Chancery suit." She had replied, gratefully accepting his proposal. Richard had received a similar letter, and had made a similar response. He *had* seen Mr. Jarndyce once, but only once, five years ago, at Winchester school. He had told Ada, when they were leaning on the screen before the fire where I found them, that he recollected him as "a bluff, rosy fellow." This was the utmost description Ada could give me.

It set me thinking so, that when Ada was asleep, I still remained before the fire, wondering and wondering about Bleak House, and wondering and wondering that yesterday morning should seem so long ago. I don't know where my thoughts had wandered, when they were recalled by a tap at the door.

I opened it softly, and found Miss Jellyby shivering there, with a broken candle in a broken candlestick in one hand, and an egg-cup in the other.

"Good night!" she said, very sulkily.

"Good night!" said I.

"May I come in?" she shortly and unexpectedly asked me in the same sulky way.

"Certainly," said I. "Don't wake Miss Clare."

She would not sit down, but stood by the fire, dipping her inky middle finger in the egg-cup, which contained vinegar, and smearing it over the ink stains on her face; frowning the whole time, and looking very gloomy.

"I wish Africa was dead!" she said, on a sudden.

I was going to remonstrate.

"I do!" she said. "Don't talk to me, Miss Summerson. I hate it and detest it. It's a beast!"

I told her she was tired, and I was sorry. I put my hand upon her head, and touched her forehead, and said it was hot now, but would be cool to-morrow. She still stood, pouting and frowning at me; but presently put down her egg-cup, and turned softly towards the bed where Ada lay.

"She is very pretty!" she said, with the same knitted brow, and in the same uncivil manner.

I assented with a smile.

"An orphan. Ain't she?"

"Yes."

"But knows a quantity, I suppose? Can dance, and play music, and sing? She can talk French, I suppose, and do geography, and globes, and needlework, and everything?"

"No doubt," said I.

"*I* can't," she returned. "I can't do anything hardly, except write. I'm always writing for Ma. I wonder you two were not ashamed of yourselves to come in this afternoon, and see me able to do nothing else. It was like your ill-nature. Yet you think yourselves very fine, I dare say!"

I could see that the poor girl was near crying, and I resumed my chair without speaking, and looked at her (I hope) as mildly as I felt towards her.

"It's disgraceful," she said. "You know it is. The whole house is disgraceful. The children are disgraceful. *I'm* disgraceful. Pa's miserable, and no wonder! Priscilla drinks—she's always drinking. It's a great shame and a great story of you, if you say you didn't smell her to-day. It was as bad as a public-house, waiting at dinner; you know it was!"

"My dear, I don't know it," said I.

"You do," she said, very shortly. "You shan't say you don't. You do!"

"O, my dear!" said I, "if you won't let me speak——,

"You're speaking now. You know you are. Don't tell stories, Miss Summerson."

"My dear," said I, "as long as you won't hear me out——,

"I don't want to hear you out."

"O yes, I think you do," said I, "because that would be so very unreasonable. I did not know what you tell me, because the servant did not come near me at dinner; but I don't doubt what you tell me, and I am sorry to hear it."

"You needn't make a merit of that," said she.

"No, my dear," said I. "That would be very foolish."

She was still standing by the bed, and now stooped down (but still with the same discontented face) and kissed Ada. That done, she came softly back, and stood by the side of my chair. Her bosom was heaving in a distressful manner that I greatly pitied; but I thought it better not to speak.

"I wish I was dead!" she broke out. "I wish we were all dead. It would be a great deal better for us."

In a moment afterwards, she knelt on the ground at my side, hid her face in my dress, passionately begged my pardon, and wept. I comforted her, and would have raised her, but she cried, No, no; she wanted to stay there!

"You used to teach girls," she said. "If you could only have taught me, I could have learnt from you! I am so very miserable, and I like you so much!"

I could not persuade her to sit by me, or to do anything but move a ragged stool to where she was kneeling, and take that, and still hold my dress in the same manner. By degrees, the poor tired girl fell asleep; and then I contrived to raise her head so that it should rest on my lap, and to cover us both with shawls. The fire went out, and all night long she slumbered thus before the ashy grate. At first I was painfully awake, and vainly tried to lose myself, with my eyes closed, among the scenes of the day. At length, by slow degrees, they became indistinct and mingled. I began to lose the identity of the sleeper resting on me. Now it was Ada; now, one of my old Reading friends from whom I could not believe I had so recently parted. Now it was the little mad woman worn out with curtseying and smiling; now, some one in authority at Bleak House. Lastly, it was no one, and I was no one.

The purblind day was feebly struggling with the fog, when I opened my eyes to encounter those of a dirty-faced little spectre fixed upon me. Peepy had scaled his crib, and crept down in his bedgown and cap, and was so cold that his teeth were chattering as if he had cut them all.

Chapter V

A MORNING ADVENTURE

Although the morning was raw, and although the fog still seemed heavy—I say seemed, for the windows were so encrusted with dirt, that they would have made Midsummer sunshine dim—I was sufficiently forewarned of the discomfort within doors at that early hour, and sufficiently curious about London, to think it a good idea on the part of Miss Jellyby when she proposed that we should go out for a walk.

"Ma won't be down for ever so long," she said, "and then it's a chance if breakfast's ready for an hour afterwards, they dawdle so. As to Pa, he gets what he can, and goes to the office. He never has what you would call a regular breakfast. Priscilla leaves him out the loaf and some milk, when there is any, overnight. Sometimes there isn't any milk, and sometimes the cat drinks it. But I'm afraid you must be tired, Miss Summerson; and perhaps you would rather go to bed."

"I am not at all tired, my dear," said I, "and would much prefer to go out."

"If you're sure you would," returned Miss Jellyby, "I'll get my things on."

Ada said she would go too, and was soon astir. I made a proposal to Peepy, in default of being able to do anything better for him, that he should let me wash him, and afterwards lay him down on my bed again. To this he submitted with the best grace possible; staring at me during the whole operation, as if he never had been, and never could again be, so astonished in his life—looking very miserable also, certainly, but making no complaint, and going snugly to sleep as soon as it was over. At first I was in two minds about taking such a liberty, but I soon reflected that nobody in the house was likely to notice it.

What with the bustle of despatching Peepy, and the bustle of getting myself ready, and helping Ada, I was soon quite in a glow. We found Miss Jellyby trying to warm herself at the fire in the writing-room, which Priscilla was then lighting with a smutty parlour candlestick—throwing the candle in to make it burn better. Everything was just as we had left it last night, and was evidently intended to remain so. Below-stairs the dinner-cloth had not been taken away, but had been left ready for breakfast. Crumbs, dust, and wastepaper were all over the house. Some pewter-pots[1] and a milk-can hung on the area railings; the door stood open; and we met the cook round the corner coming out of a public-house, wiping her mouth. She mentioned, as she passed us, that she had been to see what o'clock it was.[2]

But before we met the cook, we met Richard, who was dancing up and down Thavies Inn to warm his feet. He was agreeably surprised to see us stirring so soon, and said he would gladly share our walk. So he took care of Ada, and Miss Jellyby and I went first. I may mention that Miss Jellyby had relapsed into her sulky manner, and that I really should not have thought she liked me much, unless she had told me so.

"Where would you wish to go?" she asked.

"Anywhere, my dear," I replied.

"Anywhere's nowhere," said Miss Jellyby, stopping perversely.

"Let us go somewhere at any rate," said I.

She then walked me on very fast.

"I don't care!" she said. "Now, you are my witness, Miss Summerson, I say I don't care—but if he was to come to our house, with his great shining lumpy forehead, night after night, till he was as old as Methuselah, I wouldn't have anything to say to him. Such ASSES as he and Ma make of themselves!"

"My dear!" I remonstrated, in allusion to the epithet, and the vigorous emphasis Miss Jellyby set upon it. "Your duty as a child ——"

"O! don't talk of duty as a child, Miss Summerson; where's Ma's

1. Beer-mugs, brought home in the evening from the neighborhood bar, were left hanging on an outside railing (after they had been emptied) to be collected in the morning by a potboy.

2. A euphemism current after 1798 when Parliament passed a tax on clocks in households. Because public houses were required by this law to display clocks (called "Parliamentaries"), anyone could justify visiting a barroom by saying he was just finding out what time it was.

duty as a parent? All made over to the public and Africa, I suppose! Then let the public and Africa show duty as a child; it's much more their affair than mine. You are shocked, I dare say! Very well, so am I shocked too; so we are both shocked, and there's an end of it!"

She walked me on faster yet.

"But for all that, I say again, he may come, and come, and come, and I won't have anything to say to him. I can't bear him. If there's any stuff in the world that I hate and detest, it's the stuff he and Ma talk. I wonder the very paving-stones opposite our house can have the patience to stay there, and be a witness of such inconsistencies and contradictions as all that sounding nonsense, and Ma's management!"

I could not but understand her to refer to Mr. Quale, the young gentleman who had appeared after dinner yesterday. I was saved the disagreeable necessity of pursuing the subject, by Richard and Ada coming up at a round pace, laughing, and asking us if we meant to run a race? Thus interrupted, Miss Jellyby became silent, and walked moodily on at my side; while I admired the long successions and varieties of streets, the quantity of people already going to and fro, the number of vehicles passing and repassing, the busy preparations in the setting forth of shop windows and the sweeping out of shops, and the extraordinary creatures in rags, secretly groping among the swept-out rubbish for pins and other refuse.

"So, cousin," said the cheerful voice of Richard to Ada, behind me. "We are never to get out of Chancery! We have come by another way to our place of meeting yesterday, and—by the Great Seal, here's the old lady again!"

Truly, there she was, immediately in front of us, curtseying, and smiling, and saying, with her yesterday's air of patronage:

"The wards in Jarndyce! Ve-ry happy, I am sure!"

"You are out early, ma'am," said I, as she curtseyed to me.

"Ye-es! I usually walk here early. Before the Court sits. It's retired. I collect my thoughts here for the business of the day," said the old lady, mincingly. "The business of the day requires a great deal of thought. Chancery justice is so ve-ry difficult to follow."

"Who's this, Miss Summerson?" whispered Miss Jellyby, drawing my arm tighter through her own.

The little old lady's hearing was remarkably quick. She answered for herself directly.

"A suitor, my child. At your service. I have the honour to attend court regularly. With my documents. Have I the pleasure of addressing another of the youthful parties in Jarndyce?" said the old lady, recovering herself, with her head on one side, from a very low curtsey.

Richard, anxious to atone for his thoughtlessness of yesterday, good-naturedly explained that Miss Jellyby was not connected with the suit.

"Ha!" said the old lady. "She does not expect a judgment? She will still grow old. But not so old. O dear, no! This is the garden of Lincoln's Inn. I call it my garden. It is quite a bower in the summer-time. Where the birds sing melodiously. I pass the greater part of the long vacation[3] here. In contemplation. You find the long vacation exceedingly long, don't you?"

We said yes, as she seemed to expect us to say so.

"When the leaves are falling from the trees, and there are no more flowers in bloom to make up into nosegays[4] for the Lord Chancellor's court," said the old lady, "the vacation is fulfilled; and the sixth seal, mentioned in the Revelations, again prevails. Pray come and see my lodging. It will be a good omen for me. Youth, and hope, and beauty, are very seldom there. It is a long long time since I had a visit from either."

She had taken my hand, and, leading me and Miss Jellyby away, beckoned Richard and Ada to come too. I did not know how to excuse myself, and looked to Richard for aid. As he was half amused and half curious, and all in doubt how to get rid of the old lady without offence, she continued to lead us away, and he and Ada continued to follow; our strange conductress informing us all the time, with much smiling condescension, that she lived close by.

It was quite true, as it soon appeared. She lived so close by, that we had not time to have done humouring her for a few moments, before she was at home. Slipping us out at a little side gate, the old lady stopped most unexpectedly in a narrow back street, part of some courts and lanes immediately outside the wall of the Inn, and said, "This is my lodging. Pray walk up!"

She had stopped at a shop, over which was written KROOK, RAG AND BOTTLE WAREHOUSE. Also, in long thin letters, KROOK, DEALER IN MARINE STORES. In one part of the window was a picture of a red paper mill, at which a cart was unloading a quantity of sacks of old rags. In another, was the inscription, BONES BOUGHT. In another, KITCHEN-STUFF BOUGHT. In another, OLD IRON BOUGHT. In another, WASTE PAPER BOUGHT. In another, LADIES' AND GENTLEMEN'S WARDROBES BOUGHT. Everything seemed to be bought, and nothing to be sold there. In all parts of the window were quantities of dirty bottles: blacking bottles, medicine bottles, ginger-beer and soda-water bottles, pickle bottles, wine bottles, ink bottles: I am reminded by mentioning the latter, that the shop had,

3. See Introductory Note on Law Courts, p. xx.

4. Bunches of flowers, on the desk of a judge. Their fragrance was supposed to offset the bad air of a courtroom.

in several little particulars, the air of being in a legal neighbourhood, and of being, as it were, a dirty hanger-on and disowned relation of the law. There were a great many ink bottles. There was a little tottering bench of shabby old volumes, outside the door, labelled "Law Books, all at 9*d*." Some of the inscriptions I have enumerated were written in law-hand, like the papers I had seen in Kenge and Carboy's office, and the letters I had so long received from the firm. Among them was one, in the same writing, having nothing to do with the business of the shop, but announcing that a respectable man aged forty-five wanted engrossing[5] or copying to execute with neatness and despatch: Address to Nemo, care of Mr. Krook within. There were several second-hand bags, blue and red,[6] hanging up. A little way within the shop-door, lay heaps of old crackled parchment scrolls, and discoloured and dog's-eared law-papers. I could have fancied that all the rusty keys, of which there must have been hundreds huddled together as old iron, had once belonged to doors of rooms or strong chests in lawyers' offices. The litter of rags tumbled partly into and partly out of a one-legged wooden scale, hanging without any counterpoise from a beam, might have been counsellors' bands[7] and gowns torn up. One had only to fancy, as Richard whispered to Ada and me while we all stood looking in, that yonder bones in a corner, piled together and picked very clean, were the bones of clients, to make the picture complete.

As it was still foggy and dark, and as the shop was blinded besides by the wall of Lincoln's Inn, intercepting the light within a couple of yards, we should not have seen so much but for a lighted lantern that an old man in spectacles and a hairy cap was carrying about in the shop. Turning towards the door, he now caught sight of us. He was short, cadaverous, and withered; with his head sunk sideways between his shoulders, and the breath issuing in visible smoke from his mouth, as if he were on fire within. His throat, chin, and eyebrows were so frosted with white hairs, and so gnarled with veins and puckered skin, that he looked, from his breast upward, like some old root in a fall of snow.

"Hi hi!" said the old man coming to the door. "Have you anything to sell?"

We naturally drew back and glanced at our conductress, who had been trying to open the house-door with a key she had taken from her pocket, and to whom Richard now said that, as we had had the pleasure of seeing where she lived, we would leave her, being pressed for time. But she was not to be so easily left. She became so fantastically and pressingly earnest in her entreaties that we would

5. Transcribing legal documents in large, clear handwriting.
6. Cloth book-bags for carrying documents, blue used by junior lawyers and red by senior lawyers.
7. A starched white tab, like a tie, worn by lawyers.

walk up, and see her apartment for an instant; and was so bent, in her harmless way, on leading me in, as part of the good omen she desired; that I (whatever the others might do) saw nothing for it but to comply. I suppose we were all more or less curious;—at any rate, when the old man added his persuasions to hers, and said, "Aye, aye! Please her! It won't take a minute! Come in, come in! Come in through the shop, if t'other door's out of order!" we all went in, stimulated by Richard's laughing encouragement, and relying on his protection.

"My landlord, Krook," said the little old lady, condescending to him from her lofty station, as she presented him to us. "He is called among the neighbours the Lord Chancellor. His shop is called the Court of Chancery. He is a very eccentric person. He is very odd. Oh, I assure you he is very odd!"

She shook her head a great many times, and tapped her forehead with her finger, to express to us that we must have the goodness to excuse him, "For he is a little—you know!—M—!" said the old lady, with great stateliness. The old man overheard, and laughed.

"It's true enough," he said, going before us with the lantern, "that they call me the Lord Chancellor, and call my shop Chancery. And why do you think they call me the Lord Chancellor, and my shop Chancery?"

"I don't know, I am sure!" said Richard, rather carelessly.

"You see," said the old man, stopping and turning round, "they —Hi! Here's lovely hair! I have got three sacks of ladies' hair below, but none so beautiful and fine as this. What colour, and what texture!"

"That'll do, my good friend!" said Richard, strongly disapproving of his having drawn one of Ada's tresses through his yellow hand. "You can admire as the rest of us do, without taking that liberty."

The old man darted at him a sudden look, which even called my attention from Ada, who, startled and blushing, was so remarkably beautiful that she seemed to fix the wandering attention of the little old lady herself. But as Ada interposed, and laughingly said she could only feel proud of such genuine admiration, Mr. Krook shrunk into his former self as suddenly as he had leaped out of it.

"You see I have so many things here," he resumed, holding up the lantern, "of so many kinds, and all, as the neighbours think (but *they* know nothing), wasting away and going to rack and ruin, that that's why they have given me and my place a christening. And I have so many old parchmentses and papers in my stock. And I have a liking for rust and must and cobwebs. And all's fish that comes to my net. And I can't abear to part with anything I once lay hold of (or so my neighbours think, but what do *they* know?) or to alter anything, or to have any sweeping, nor scouring, nor cleaning, nor repairing going on about me. That's the way I've got the ill name of Chancery. *I* don't mind. I go to see my noble and learned brother pretty well every day, when he sits in the Inn. He don't notice me, but I notice him. There's no great odds betwixt us. We both grub on in a muddle. Hi, Lady Jane!"[8]

A large grey cat leaped from some neighbouring shelf on his shoulder, and startled us all.

"Hi! show 'em how you scratch. Hi! Tear, my lady!" said her master.

The cat leaped down, and ripped at a bundle of rags with her tigerish claws, with a sound that it set my teeth on edge to hear.

"She'd do as much for any one I was to set her on," said the old man. "I deal in cat-skins among other general matters, and hers was offered to me. It's a very fine skin, as you may see, but I didn't have it stripped off! *That* warn't like Chancery practice though, says you!"

He had by this time led us across the shop, and now opened a door in the back part of it, leading to the house-entry. As he stood with his hand upon the lock, the little old lady graciously observed to him before passing out:

"That will do, Krook. You mean well, but are tiresome. My young friends are pressed for time. I have none to spare myself, having to attend court very soon. My young friends are the wards in Jarndyce."

"Jarndyce!" said the old man with a start.

"Jarndyce and Jarndyce. The great suit, Krook," returned his lodger.

"Hi!" exclaimed the old man, in a tone of thoughtful amazement, and with a wider stare than before. "Think of it!"

He seemed so rapt all in a moment, and looked so curiously at us, that Richard said:

"Why you appear to trouble yourself a good deal about the causes before your noble and learned brother, the other Chancellor!"

"Yes," said the old man abstractedly. "Sure! *Your* name now will be——"

"Richard Carstone."

"Carstone," he repeated, slowly checking off that name upon his forefinger; and each of the others he went on to mention, upon a separate finger. "Yes. There was the name of Barbary, and the name of Clare, and the name of Dedlock, too, I think."

"He knows as much of the cause as the real salaried Chancellor!" said Richard, quite astonished, to Ada and me.

8. Presumably named after Lady Jane Grey (1537–54), whose execution for suspected treason is described in Dickens' *A Child's History of England*, ch. XXX.

"Aye!" said the old man, coming slowly out of his abstraction. "Yes! Tom Jarndyce—you'll excuse me, being related; but he was never known about court by any other name, and was as well known there, as—she is now"; nodding slightly at his lodger; "Tom Jarndyce was often in here. He got into a restless habit of strolling about when the cause was on, or expected, talking to the little shop-keepers, and telling 'em to keep out of Chancery, whatever they did. 'For,' says he, 'it's being ground to bits in a slow mill; it's being roasted at a slow fire; it's being stung to death by single bees; it's being drowned by drops; it's going mad by grains.' He was as near making away with himself, just where the young lady stands, as near could be."

We listened with horror.

"He came in at the door," said the old man, slowly pointing an imaginary track along the shop, "on the day he did it—the whole neighbourhood had said for months before, that he would do it, of a certainty, sooner or later—he come in at the door that day, and walked along there, and sat himself on a bench that stood there, and asked me (you'll judge I was a mortal sight younger then) to fetch him a pint of wine. 'For,' says he, 'Krook, I am much depressed; my cause is on again, and I think I'm nearer Judgment than I ever was.' I hadn't a mind to leave him alone; and I persuaded him to go to the tavern over the way there, t'other side my lane (I mean Chancery Lane); and I followed and looked in at the window, and saw him, comfortable as I thought, in the arm-chair by the fire, and company with him. I hadn't hardly got back here, when I heard a shot go echoing and rattling right away into the inn. I ran out—neighbours ran out—twenty of us cried at once, 'Tom Jarndyce!' "

The old man stopped, looked hard at us, looked down into the lantern, blew the light out, and shut the lantern up.

"We were right, I needn't tell the present hearers. Hi! To be sure, how the neighbourhood poured into court that afternoon while the cause was on! How my noble and learned brother, and all the rest of 'em, grubbed and muddled away as usual, and tried to look as if they hadn't heard a word of the last fact in the case; or as if they had—O dear me!—nothing at all to do with it, if they had heard of it by any chance!"

Ada's colour had entirely left her, and Richard was scarcely less pale. Nor could I wonder, judging even from my emotions, and I was no party in the suit, that to hearts so untried and fresh, it was a shock to come into the inheritance of a protracted misery, attended in the minds of many people with such dreadful recollections. I had another uneasiness, in the application of the painful story to the poor half-witted creature who had brought us there; but, to my surprise, she seemed perfectly unconscious of that, and only led the way up-stairs again; informing us, with the toleration of a superior creature for the infirmities of a common mortal, that her landlord was "a little—M—, you know!"

She lived at the top of the house, in a pretty large room, from which she had a glimpse of the roof of Lincoln's Inn Hall. This seemed to have been her principal inducement, originally, for taking up her residence there. She could look at it, she said, in the night: especially in the moonshine. Her room was clean, but very, very bare. I noticed the scantiest necessaries in the way of furniture; a few old prints from books, of Chancellors and barristers, wafered against the wall; and some half-dozen reticules and work-bags, "containing documents," as she informed us. There were neither coals nor ashes in the grate, and I saw no articles of clothing anywhere, nor any kind of food. Upon a shelf in an open cupboard were a plate or two, a cup or two, and so forth; but all dry and empty. There was a more affecting meaning in her pinched appearance, I thought as I looked round, than I had understood before.

"Extremely honoured, I am sure," said our poor hostess, with the greatest suavity, "by this visit from the wards in Jarndyce. And very much indebted for the omen. It is a retired situation. Considering. I am limited as to situation. In consequence of the necessity of attending on the Chancellor. I have lived here many years. I pass my days in court; my evenings and my nights here. I find the nights long, for I sleep but little, and think much. That is, of course, unavoidable; being in Chancery. I am sorry I cannot offer chocolate. I expect a judgment shortly, and shall then place my establishment on a superior footing. At present, I don't mind confessing to the wards in Jarndyce (in strict confidence), that I sometimes find it difficult to keep up a genteel appearance. I have felt the cold here. I have felt something sharper than cold. It matters very little. Pray excuse the introduction of such mean topics."

She partly drew aside the curtain of the long low garret-window, and called our attention to a number of bird-cages hanging there: some containing several birds. There were larks, linnets, and goldfinches—I should think at least twenty.

"I began to keep the little creatures," she said, "with an object that the wards will readily comprehend. With the intention of restoring them to liberty. When my judgment should be given. Ye-es! They die in prison, though. Their lives, poor silly things, are so short in comparison with Chancery proceedings, that, one by one, the whole collection has died over and over again. I doubt, do you know, whether one of these, though they are all young, will live to be free! Ve-ry mortifying, is it not?"

Although she sometimes asked a question, she never seemed to expect a reply; but rambled on as if she were in the habit of doing so, when no one but herself was present.

"Indeed," she pursued, "I positively doubt sometimes, I do assure you, whether while matters are still unsettled, and the sixth or Great Seal still prevails, *I* may not one day be found lying stark and senseless here, as I have found so many birds!"

Richard, answering what he saw in Ada's compassionate eyes, took the opportunity of laying some money, softly and unobserved, on the chimney-piece. We all drew nearer to the cages, feigning to examine the birds.

"I can't allow them to sing much," said the little old lady, "for (you'll think this curious) I find my mind confused by the idea that they are singing, while I am following the arguments in Court. And my mind requires to be so very clear, you know! Another time, I'll tell you their names. Not at present. On a day of such good omen, they shall sing as much as they like. In honour of youth," a smile and curtsey; "hope," a smile and curtsey; "and beauty," a smile and curtsey. "There! We'll let in the full light."

The birds began to stir and chirp.

"I cannot admit the air freely," said the little old lady; the room was close, and would have been the better for it; "because the cat you saw down-stairs—called Lady Jane—is greedy for their lives. She crouches on the parapet outside for hours and hours. I have discovered," whispering mysteriously, "that her natural cruelty is sharpened by a jealous fear of their regaining their liberty. In consequence of the judgment I expect being shortly given. She is sly, and full of malice. I half believe, sometimes, that she is no cat, but the wolf of the old saying. It is so very difficult to keep her from the door."

Some neighbouring bells, reminding the poor soul that it was half-past nine, did more for us in the way of bringing our visit to an end, than we could easily have done for ourselves. She hurriedly took up her little bag of documents, which she had laid upon the table on coming in, and asked if we were also going into Court? On our answering no, and that we would on no account detain her, she opened the door to attend us down-stairs.

"With such an omen, it is even more necessary than usual that I should be there before the Chancellor comes in," said she, "for he might mention my case the first thing. I have a presentiment that he *will* mention it the first thing this morning."

She stopped to tell us, in a whisper, as we were going down, that the whole house was filled with strange lumber which her landlord had bought piecemeal, and had no wish to sell—in consequence of being a little—M—. This was on the first floor. But she had made a previous stoppage on the second floor, and had silently pointed at a dark door there.

"The only other lodger," she now whispered, in explanation; "a law-writer. The children in the lanes here, say he has sold himself to the devil. I don't know what he can have done with the money. Hush!"

She appeared to mistrust that the lodger might hear her, even there; and repeating "Hush!" went before us on tiptoe, as though even the sound of her footsteps might reveal to him what she had said.

Passing through the shop on our way out, as we had passed through it on our way in, we found the old man storing a quantity of packets of waste paper, in a kind of well in the floor. He seemed to be working hard, with the perspiration standing on his forehead, and had a piece of chalk by him; with which, as he put each separate package or bundle down, he made a crooked mark on the panelling of the wall.

Richard and Ada, and Miss Jellyby, and the little old lady, had gone by him, and I was going, when he touched me on the arm to stay me, and chalked the letter J upon the wall—in a very curious manner, beginning with the end of the letter, and shaping it backward. It was a capital letter, not a printed one, but just such a letter as any clerk in Messrs. Kenge and Carboy's office would have made.[9]

"Can you read it?" he asked me with a keen glance.

"Surely," said I. "It's very plain."

"What is it?"

"J."

With another glance at me, and a glance at the door, he rubbed it out, and turned an a in its place (not a capital letter this time), and said, "What's that?"

I told him. He then rubbed that out, and turned the letter r, and asked me the same question. He went on quickly, until he had formed, in the same curious manner, beginning at the ends and bottoms of the letters, the word JARNDYCE, without once leaving two letters on the wall together.

"What does that spell?" he asked me.

When I told him, he laughed. In the same odd way, yet with the same rapidity, he then produced singly, and rubbed out singly, the letters forming the two words BLEAK HOUSE. These, in some astonishment, I also read; and he laughed again.

"Hi!" said the old man, laying aside the chalk, "I have a turn for

9. Although written by reversing the usual direction of forming a letter, the completed "J" is of normal shape and not itself "backward."

copying from memory, you see, miss, though I can neither read nor write."

He looked so disagreeable, and his cat looked so wickedly at me, as if I were a blood-relation of the birds up-stairs, that I was quite relieved by Richard's appearing at the door and saying:

"Miss Summerson, I hope you are not bargaining for the sale of your hair. Don't be tempted. Three sacks below are quite enough for Mr. Krook!"

I lost no time in wishing Mr. Krook good morning, and joining my friends outside, where we parted with the little old lady, who gave us her blessing with great ceremony, and renewed her assurance of yesterday in reference to her intention of settling estates on Ada and me. Before we finally turned out of those lanes, we looked back, and saw Mr. Krook standing at his shop-door, in his spectacles, looking after us, with his cat upon his shoulder, and her tail sticking up on one side of his hairy cap, like a tall feather.

"Quite an adventure for a morning in London!" said Richard, with a sigh. "Ah, cousin, cousin, it's a weary word this Chancery!"

"It is to me, and has been ever since I can remember," returned Ada. "I am grieved that I should be the enemy—as I suppose I am—of a great number of relations and others; and that they should be my enemies—as I suppose they are; and that we should all be ruining one another, without knowing how or why, and be in constant doubt and discord all our lives. It seems very strange, as there must be right somewhere, that an honest judge in real earnest has not been able to find out through all these years where it is."

"Ah, cousin!" said Richard. "Strange, indeed! all this wasteful wanton chess-playing *is* very strange. To see that composed Court yesterday jogging on so serenely, and to think of the wretchedness of the pieces on the board, gave me the headache and the heartache both together. My head ached with wondering how it happened, if men were neither fools nor rascals; and my heart ached to think they could possibly be either. But at all events, Ada—I may call you Ada?"

"Of course you may, cousin Richard."

"At all events, Ada, Chancery will work none of its bad influence on *us*. We have happily been brought together, thanks to our good kinsman, and it can't divide us now!"

"Never, I hope, cousin Richard!" said Ada, gently.

Miss Jellyby gave my arm a squeeze, and me a very significant look. I smiled in return, and we made the rest of the way back very pleasantly.

In half an hour after our arrival, Mrs. Jellyby appeared; and in the course of an hour the various things necessary for breakfast straggled one by one into the dining-room. I do not doubt that Mrs.

Jellyby had gone to bed, and got up in the usual manner, but she presented no appearance of having changed her dress. She was greatly occupied during breakfast; for the morning's post brought a heavy correspondence relative to Borrioboola-Gha, which would occasion her (she said) to pass a busy day. The children tumbled about, and notched memoranda of their accidents in their legs, which were perfect little calendars of distress; and Peepy was lost for an hour and a half, and brought home from Newgate market by a policeman. The equable manner in which Mrs. Jellyby sustained both his absence, and his restoration to the family circle, surprised us all.

She was by that time perseveringly dictating to Caddy, and Caddy was fast relapsing into the inky condition in which we had found her. At one o'clock an open carriage arrived for us, and a cart for our luggage. Mrs. Jellyby charged us with many remembrances to her good friend, Mr. Jarndyce; Caddy left her desk to see us depart, kissed me in the passage, and stood biting her pen, and sobbing on the steps; Peepy, I am happy to say, was asleep, and spared the pain of separation (I was not without misgivings that he had gone to Newgate market in search of me); and all the other children got up behind the barouche and fell off, and we saw them with great concern, scattered over the surface of Thavies Inn, as we rolled out of its precincts.

Chapter VI

QUITE AT HOME

The day had brightened very much, and still brightened as we went westward. We went our way through the sunshine and the fresh air, wondering more and more at the extent of the streets, the brilliancy of the shops, the great traffic, and the crowds of people whom the pleasanter weather seemed to have brought out like many-coloured flowers. By-and-by we began to leave the wonderful city, and to proceed through suburbs which, of themselves, would have made a pretty large town, in my eyes; and at last we got into a real country road again, with windmills, rick-yards, milestones, farmers' waggons, scents of old hay, swinging signs and horse troughs: trees, fields, and hedgerows. It was delightful to see the green landscape before us, and the immense metropolis behind; and when a waggon with a train of beautiful horses, furnished with red trappings and clear-sounding bells, came by us with its music, I believe we could all three have sung to the bells, so cheerful were the influences around.

"The whole road has been reminding me of my namesake

Whittington,"[1] said Richard, "and that waggon is the finishing touch. Halloa! what's the matter?"

We had stopped, and the waggon had stopped too. Its music changed as the horses came to a stand, and subsided to a gentle tinkling, except when a horse tossed his head, or shook himself, and sprinkled off a little shower of bell-ringing.

"Our postillion is looking after the waggoner," said Richard; "and the waggoner is coming back after us. Why, here's an extraordinary thing!" added Richard, looking closely at the man. "He has got your name, Ada, in his hat!"

He had all our names in his hat. Tucked within the band were three small notes; one, addressed to Ada; one, to Richard; one, to me. These the waggoner delivered to each of us respectively, reading the name aloud first. In answer to Richard's inquiry from whom they came, he briefly answered, "Master, sir, if you please"; and putting on his hat again (which was like a soft bowl), cracked his whip, reawakened his music, and went melodiously away.

"Is that Mr. Jarndyce's waggon?" said Richard, calling to our post-boy.

"Yes, sir," he replied. "Going to London."

We opened the notes. Each was a counterpart of the other, and contained these words, in a solid, plain hand.

> I look forward, my dear, to our meeting easily, and without constraint on either side. I therefore have to propose that we meet as old friends, and take the past for granted. It will be a relief to you possibly, and to me certainly, and so my love to you.
>
> JOHN JARNDYCE.

I had perhaps less reason to be surprised than either of my companions, having never yet enjoyed an opportunity of thanking one who had been my benefactor and sole earthly dependence through so many years. I had not considered how I could thank him, my gratitude lying too deep in my heart for that; but I now began to consider how I could meet him without thanking him, and felt it would be very difficult indeed.

The notes revived, in Richard and Ada, a general impression that they both had, without quite knowing how they came by it, that their cousin Jarndyce could never bear acknowledgments for any kindness he performed, and that, sooner than receive any, he would resort to the most singular expedients and evasions, or would even run away. Ada dimly remembered to have heard her mother tell, when she was a very little child, that he had once done her an act of uncommon generosity, and that on her going to his house to

1. Richard Whittington, a poor boy who was summoned by the sound of bells, on a road near London, to try his fortune in the city. His later financial success led to his becoming Lord Mayor.

thank him, he happened to see her through a window coming to the door, and immediately escaped by the back gate, and was not heard of for three months. This discourse led to a great deal more on the same theme, and indeed it lasted us all day, and we talked of scarcely anything else. If we did, by any chance, diverge into another subject, we soon returned to this; and wondered what the house would be like, and when we should get there, and whether we should see Mr. Jarndyce as soon as we arrived, or after a delay, and what he would say to us, and what we should say to him. All of which we wondered about, over and over again.

The roads were very heavy for the horses, but the pathway was generally good; so we alighted and walked up all the hills, and liked it so well that we prolonged our walk on the level ground when we got to the top. At Barnet there were other horses waiting for us; but as they had only just been fed, we had to wait for them too, and got a long fresh walk, over a common and an old battle-field,[2] before the carriage came up. These delays so protracted the journey, that the short day was spent, and the long night had closed in, before we came to St. Albans; near to which town Bleak House was, we knew.

By that time we were so anxious and nervous, that even Richard confessed, as we rattled over the stones of the old street, to feeling an irrational desire to drive back again. As to Ada and me, whom he had wrapped up with great care, the night being sharp and frosty, we trembled from head to foot. When we turned out of the town, round a corner, and Richard told us that the post-boy, who had for a long time sympathised with our heightened expectation, was looking back and nodding, we both stood up in the carriage (Richard holding Ada, lest she should be jolted down), and gazed round upon the open country and the starlight night, for our destination. There was a light sparkling on the top of a hill before us, and the driver, pointing to it with his whip, and crying, "That's Bleak House!" put his horses into a canter, and took us forward at such a rate, uphill though it was, that the wheels sent the road drift flying about our heads like spray from a water-mill. Presently we lost the light, presently saw it, presently lost it, presently saw it, and turned into an avenue of trees, and cantered up towards where it was beaming brightly. It was in a window of what seemed to be an old-fashioned house, with three peaks in the roof in front, and a broad circular sweep leading to the porch. A bell was rung as we drew up, and amidst the sound of its deep voice in the still air, and the distant barking of some dogs, and a gush of light from the opened door, and the smoking and steaming of the heated horses, and the

2. Site of the Battle of Barnet during the Wars of the Roses where, in 1471, the Yorkists under Edward IV defeated the Lancastrians.

quickened beating of our own hearts, we alighted in no inconsiderable confusion.

"Ada, my love, Esther, my dear, you are welcome. I rejoice to see you! Rick, if I had a hand to spare at present, I would give it you!"

The gentleman who said these words in a clear, bright, hospitable voice, had one of his arms round Ada's waist, and the other round mine, and kissed us both in a fatherly way, and bore us across the hall into a ruddy little room, all in a glow with a blazing fire. Here he kissed us again, and, opening his arms, made us sit down side by side, on a sofa ready drawn out near the hearth. I felt that if we had been at all demonstrative, he would have run away in a moment.

"Now, Rick!" said he, "I have a hand at liberty. A word in earnest is as good as a speech. I am heartily glad to see you. You are at home. Warm yourself!"

Richard shook him by both hands with an intuitive mixture of respect and frankness, and only saying (though with an earnestness that rather alarmed me, I was so afraid of Mr. Jarndyce's suddenly disappearing), "You are very kind, sir! We are very much obliged to you!" laid aside his hat and coat, and came up to the fire.

"And how did you like the ride? And how did you like Mrs. Jellyby, my dear?" said Mr. Jarndyce to Ada.

While Ada was speaking to him in reply, I glanced (I need not say with how much interest) at his face. It was a handsome, lively, quick face, full of change and motion; and his hair was a silvered iron-grey. I took him to be nearer sixty than fifty, but he was upright, hearty, and robust. From the moment of his first speaking to us, his voice had connected itself with an association in my mind that I could not define; but now, all at once, a something sudden in his manner, and a pleasant expression in his eyes, recalled the gentleman in the stage-coach, six years ago, on the memorable day of my journey to Reading. I was certain it was he. I never was so frightened in my life as when I made the discovery, for he caught my glance, and appearing to read my thoughts, gave such a look at the door that I thought we had lost him.

However, I am happy to say he remained where he was, and asked me what *I* thought of Mrs. Jellyby?

"She exerts herself very much for Africa, sir," I said.

"Nobly!" returned Mr. Jarndyce. "But you answer like Ada." Whom I had not heard. "You all think something else, I see."

"We rather thought," said I, glancing at Richard and Ada, who entreated me with their eyes to speak, "that perhaps she was a little unmindful of her home."

"Floored!" cried Mr. Jarndyce.

I was rather alarmed again.

"Well! I want to know your real thoughts, my dear. I may have sent you there on purpose."

"We thought that, perhaps," said I, hesitating, "it is right to begin with the obligations of home, sir; and that, perhaps, while those are overlooked and neglected, no other duties can possibly be substituted for them."

"The little Jellybys," said Richard, coming to my relief, "are really—I can't help expressing myself strongly, sir—in a devil of a state."

"She means well," said Mr. Jarndyce, hastily. "The wind's in the east."[3]

"It was in the north, sir, as we came down," observed Richard.

"My dear Rick," said Mr. Jarndyce, poking the fire; "I'll take an oath it's either in the east, or going to be. I am always conscious of an uncomfortable sensation now and then when the wind is blowing in the east."

"Rheumatism, sir?" said Richard.

"I dare say it is, Rick. I believe it is. And so the little Jell—I had my doubts about 'em—are in a—oh, Lord, yes, it's easterly!" said Mr. Jarndyce.

He had taken two or three undecided turns up and down while uttering these broken sentences, retaining the poker in one hand and rubbing his hair with the other, with a good-natured vexation, at once so whimsical and so loveable, that I am sure we were more delighted with him than we could possibly have expressed in any words. He gave an arm to Ada and an arm to me, and bidding Richard bring a candle, was leading the way out, when he suddenly turned us all back again.

"Those little Jellybys. Couldn't you—didn't you—now, if it had rained sugar-plums, or three-cornered raspberry tarts, or anything of that sort!" said Mr. Jarndyce.

"O, cousin—!" Ada hastily began.

"Good, my pretty pet. I like cousin. Cousin John, perhaps, is better."

"Then, cousin John!—" Ada laughingly began again.

"Ha, ha! Very good indeed!" said Mr. Jarndyce, with great enjoyment. "Sounds uncommonly natural. Yes, my dear?"

"It did better than that. It rained Esther."

"Ay?" said Mr. Jarndyce. "What did Esther do?"

"Why, cousin John," said Ada, clasping her hands upon his arm, and shaking her head at me across him—for I wanted her to be

3. The east wind, bringing inclement weather, is popularly supposed to be injurious to health and spirits. In Victorian times, according to F. S. Schwarzbach (1975), an east wind had especially unpleasant properties because it could bring with it the smells and pollution of London's East End. See Dickens' speech of May 10, 1851 (pp. 915–916), in which he notes: "The air from Gin Lane will be carried, when the wind is Easterly, into May Fair."

quiet: "Esther was their friend directly. Esther nursed them, coaxed them to sleep, washed and dressed them, told them stories, kept them quiet, bought them keepsakes"—My dear girl! I had only gone out with Peepy, after he was found, and given him a little, tiny horse!—"and, cousin John, she softened poor Caroline, the eldest one, so much, and was so thoughtful for me and so amiable! —No, no, I won't be contradicted, Esther dear! You know, you know, it's true!"

The warm-hearted darling leaned across her cousin John, and kissed me; and then looking up in his face, boldly said, "At all events, cousin John, I *will* thank you for the companion you have given me." I felt as if she challenged him to run away. But he didn't.

"Where did you say the wind was, Rick?" asked Mr. Jarndyce.

"In the north, as we came down, sir."

"You are right. There's no east in it. A mistake of mine. Come, girls, come and see your home!"

It was one of those delightfully irregular houses where you go up and down steps out of one room into another, and where you come upon more rooms when you think you have seen all there are, and where there is a bountiful provision of little halls and passages, and where you find still older cottage-rooms in unexpected places, with lattice windows and green growth pressing through them. Mine, which we entered first, was of this kind, with an up-and-down roof, that had more corners in it than I ever counted afterwards, and a chimney (there was a wood-fire on the hearth) paved all round with pure white tiles, in every one of which a bright miniature of the fire was blazing. Out of this room, you went down two steps, into a charming little sitting-room, looking down upon a flower-garden, which room was henceforth to belong to Ada and me. Out of this you went up three steps, into Ada's bedroom, which had a fine broad window, commanding a beautiful view (we saw a great expanse of darkness lying underneath the stars), to which there was a hollow window-seat, in which, with a spring-lock, three dear Adas might have been lost at once. Out of this room, you passed into a little gallery, with which the other best rooms (only two) communicated, and so, by a little staircase of shallow steps, with a number of corner stairs in it, considering its length, down into the hall. But if, instead of going out at Ada's door, you came back into my room, and went out at the door by which you had entered it, and turned up a few crooked steps that branched off in an unexpected manner from the stairs, you lost yourself in passages, with mangles in them, and three-cornered tables, and a Native-Hindoo chair, which was also a sofa, a box, and a bedstead, and looked in every form, something between a bamboo skeleton and a great bird-cage, and had been brought from India nobody knew by whom or when. From these, you came on Richard's room, which was part library, part sitting-room, part bedroom, and seemed indeed a comfortable compound of many rooms. Out of that, you went straight, with a little interval of passage, to the plain room where Mr. Jarndyce slept, all the year round, with his window open, his bedstead without any furniture standing in the middle of the floor for more air, and his cold-bath gaping for him in a smaller room adjoining. Out of that, you came into another passage, where there were back-stairs, and where you could hear the horses being rubbed down, outside the stable, and being told to Hold up, and Get over, as they slipped about very much on the uneven stones. Or you might, if you came out at another door (every room had at least two doors), go straight down to the hall again by half-a-dozen steps and a low archway, wondering how you got back there, or had ever got out of it.

The furniture, old-fashioned rather than old, like the house, was as pleasantly irregular. Ada's sleeping-room was all flowers—in chintz and paper, in velvet, in needlework, in the brocade of two stiff courtly chairs, which stood, each attended by a little page of a stool for greater state, on either side of the fireplace. Our sitting-room was green; and had, framed and glazed, upon the walls, numbers of surprising and surprised birds, staring out of pictures at a real trout in a case, as brown and shining as if it had been served with gravy; at the death of Captain Cook;[4] and at the whole process of preparing tea in China, as depicted by Chinese artists.[5] In my room there were oval engravings of the months—ladies haymaking, in short waists,[6] and large hats tied under the chin, for June—smooth-legged noblemen, pointing, with cocked-hats, to village steeples, for October. Half-length portraits, in crayons, abounded all through the house; but were so dispersed that I found the brother of a youthful officer of mine in the china-closet, and the grey old age of my pretty young bride, with a flower in her boddice, in the breakfast-room. As substitutes, I had four angels, of Queen Anne's reign, taking a complacent gentleman to heaven, in festoons,[7] with some difficulty; and a composition in needlework, representing fruit, a kettle, and an alphabet. All the moveables, from the wardrobes to the chairs and tables, hangings, glasses, even to the pin-cushions and scent-bottles on the dressing-tables, displayed the same quaint variety. They agreed in nothing but their perfect neatness, their display of the whitest linen, and their stor-

4. The massacre in 1779 of the explorer James Cook by Hawaiian natives was the subject of a painting by George Carter (exhibited 1785) which was reproduced as a popular engraving.

5. As noted by T. W. Hill, prints on rice paper, imported from China, were an early nineteenth-century vogue.

6. Dresses in which the waistline is high on the body, a style which became fashionable in the late eighteenth century.

7. Ropes made of flowers and leaves. Queen Anne's reign was 1702–14.

ing-up, wheresoever the existence of a drawer, small or large, rendered it possible, of quantities of rose-leaves and sweet lavender. Such, with its illuminated windows, softened here and there by shadows of curtains, shining out upon the star-light night; with its light, and warmth, and comfort; with its hospitable jingle, at a distance, of preparations for dinner; with the face of its generous master brightening everything we saw; and just wind enough without to sound a low accompaniment to everything we heard; were our first impressions of Bleak House.

"I am glad you like it," said Mr. Jarndyce, when he had brought us round again to Ada's sitting-room. "It makes no pretensions; but it is a comfortable little place, I hope, and will be more so with such bright young looks in it. You have barely half an hour before dinner. There's no one here but the finest creature upon earth—a child."

"More children, Esther!" said Ada.

"I don't mean literally a child," pursued Mr. Jarndyce; "not a child in years. He is grown up—he is at least as old as I am—but in simplicity, and freshness, and enthusiasm, and a fine guileless inaptitude for all worldly affairs, he is a perfect child."

We felt that he must be very interesting.

"He knows Mrs. Jellyby," said Mr. Jarndyce. "He is a musical man; an Amateur, but might have been a Professional. He is an Artist, too; an Amateur, but might have been a Professional. He is a man of attainments and of captivating manners. He has been unfortunate in his affairs, and unfortunate in his pursuits, and unfortunate in his family; but he don't care—he's a child!"

"Did you imply that he has children of his own, sir?" inquired Richard.

"Yes, Rick! Half-a-dozen. More! Nearer a dozen, I should think. But he has never looked after them. How could he? He wanted somebody to look after *him*. He is a child, you know!" said Mr. Jarndyce.

"And have the children looked after themselves at all, sir?" inquired Richard.

"Why, just as you may suppose," said Mr. Jarndyce: his countenance suddenly falling. "It is said that the children of the very poor are not brought up, but dragged up. Harold Skimpole's children have tumbled up somehow or other.—The wind's getting round again, I am afraid. I feel it rather!"

Richard observed that the situation was exposed on a sharp night.

"It *is* exposed," said Mr. Jarndyce. "No doubt that's the cause. Bleak House has an exposed sound. But you are coming my way. Come along!"

Our luggage having arrived, and being all at hand, I was dressed in a few minutes, and engaged in putting my worldly goods away, when a maid (not the one in attendance upon Ada, but another, whom I had not seen) brought a basket into my room, with two bunches of keys in it, all labelled.

"For you, miss, if you please," said she.

"For me?" said I.

"The housekeeping keys, miss."

I showed my surprise; for she added with some little surprise on her own part: "I was told to bring them as soon as you was alone, miss. Miss Summerson, if I don't deceive myself?"

"Yes," said I. "That is my name."

"The large bunch is the housekeeping, and the little bunch is the cellars, miss. Any time you was pleased to appoint to-morrow morning, I was to show you the presses[8] and things they belong to."

I said I would be ready at half-past six; and, after she was gone, stood looking at the basket, quite lost in the magnitude of my trust. Ada found me thus; and had such a delightful confidence in me when I showed her the keys and told her about them, that it would have been insensibility and ingratitude not to feel encouraged. I knew, to be sure, that it was the dear girl's kindness; but I liked to be so pleasantly cheated.

When we went downstairs, we were presented to Mr. Skimpole, who was standing before the fire, telling Richard how fond he used to be, in his school-time, of football. He was a little bright creature, with a rather large head; but a delicate face, and a sweet voice, and there was a perfect charm in him. All he said was so free from effort and spontaneous, and was said with such a captivating gaiety, that it was fascinating to hear him talk. Being of a more slender figure than Mr. Jarndyce, and having a richer complexion, with browner hair, he looked younger. Indeed, he had more the appearance, in all respects, of a damaged young man, than a well-preserved elderly one. There was an easy negligence in his manner, and even in his dress (his hair carelessly disposed, and his neck-kerchief loose and flowing, as I have seen artists paint their own portraits), which I could not separate from the idea of a romantic youth who had undergone some unique process of depreciation. It struck me as being not at all like the manner or appearance of a man who had advanced in life by the usual road of years, cares, and experiences.

I gathered from the conversation, that Mr. Skimpole had been educated for the medical profession, and had once lived, in his professional capacity, in the household of a German prince. He told us, however, that as he had always been a mere child in point of weights and measures, and had never known anything about them (except that they disgusted him), he had never been able to pre-

8. Cupboards for clothes and linens.

scribe with the requisite accuracy of detail. In fact, he said, he had no head for detail. And he told us, with great humour, that when he was wanted to bleed the prince, or physic any of his people, he was generally found lying on his back, in bed, reading the newspapers, or making fancy sketches in pencil, and couldn't come. The prince, at last objecting to this, "in which," said Mr. Skimpole, in the frankest manner, "he was perfectly right," the engagement terminated, and Mr. Skimpole having (as he added with delightful gaiety) "nothing to live upon but love, fell in love, and married, and surrounded himself with rosy cheeks." His good friend Jarndyce and some other of his good friends then helped him, in quicker or slower succession, to several openings in life; but to no purpose, for he must confess to two of the oddest infirmities in the world: one was, that he had no idea of time; the other, that he had no idea of money. In consequence of which he never kept an appointment, never could transact any business, and never knew the value of anything! Well! So he had got on in life, and here he was! He was very fond of reading the papers, very fond of making fancy sketches with a pencil, very fond of nature, very fond of art. All he asked of society was, to let him live. *That* wasn't much. His wants were few. Give him the papers, conversation, music, mutton, coffee, landscape, fruit in the season, a few sheets of Bristol-board,[9] and a little claret, and he asked no more. He was a mere child in the world, but he didn't cry for the moon. He said to the world, "Go your several ways in peace! Wear red coats, blue coats, lawn sleeves,[1] put pens behind your ears, wear aprons;[2] go after glory, holiness, commerce, trade, any object you prefer; only—let Harold Skimpole live!"

All this, and a great deal more, he told us, not only with the utmost brilliancy and enjoyment, but with a certain vivacious candour—speaking of himself as if he were not at all his own affair, as if Skimpole were a third person, as if he knew that Skimpole had his singularities, but still had his claims too, which were the general business of the community and must not be slighted. He was quite enchanting. If I felt at all confused at that early time, in endeavouring to reconcile anything he said with anything I had thought about the duties and accountabilities of life (which I am far from sure of), I was confused by not exactly understanding why he was free of them. That he *was* free of them, I scarcely doubted; he was so very clear about it himself.

"I covet nothing," said Mr. Skimpole, in the same light way. "Possession is nothing to me. Here is my friend Jarndyce's excellent house. I feel obliged to him for possessing it. I can sketch it, and

9. Stiff paper, like thin cardboard, used for drawing and painting.
1. Linen sleeves worn by bishops.
2. In the nineteenth century, aprons were worn by shopkeepers and salesmen in all retail trades.

alter it. I can set it to music. When I am here, I have sufficient possession of it, and have neither trouble, cost, nor responsibility. My steward's name, in short, is Jarndyce, and he can't cheat me. We have been mentioning Mrs. Jellyby. There is a bright-eyed woman, of a strong will and immense power of business detail, who throws herself into objects with surprising ardour! I don't regret that *I* have not a strong will and an immense power of business-detail to throw myself into objects with surprising ardour. I can admire her without envy. I can sympathise with the objects. I can dream of them. I can lie down on the grass—in fine weather—and float along an African river, embracing all the natives I meet, as sensible of the deep silence, and sketching the dense overhanging tropical growth as accurately as if I were there. I don't know that it's of any direct use my doing so, but it's all I can do, and I do it thoroughly. Then, for Heaven's sake, having Harold Skimpole, a confiding child, petitioning you, the world, an agglomeration of practical people of business habits, to let him live and admire the human family, do it somehow or other, like good souls, and suffer him to ride his rocking-horse!"

It was plain enough that Mr. Jarndyce had not been neglectful of the adjuration. Mr. Skimpole's general position there would have rendered it so, without the addition of what he presently said.

"It's only you, the generous creatures, whom I envy," said Mr. Skimpole, addressing us, his new friends, in an impersonal manner. "I envy you your power of doing what you do. It is what I should revel in, myself. I don't feel any vulgar gratitude to you. I almost feel as if *you* ought to be grateful to *me*, for giving you the opportunity of enjoying the luxury of generosity. I know you like it. For anything I can tell, I may have come into the world expressly for the purpose of increasing your stock of happiness. I may have been born to be a benefactor to you, by sometimes giving you an opportunity of assisting me in my little perplexities. Why should I regret my incapacity for details and worldly affairs, when it leads to such pleasant consequences? I don't regret it therefore."

Of all his playful speeches (playful, yet always fully meaning what they expressed) none seemed to be more to the taste of Mr. Jarndyce than this. I had often new temptations, afterwards, to wonder whether it was really singular, or only singular to me, that he, who was probably the most grateful of mankind upon the least occasion, should so desire to escape the gratitude of others.

We were all enchanted. I felt it a merited tribute to the engaging qualities of Ada and Richard, that Mr. Skimpole, seeing them for the first time, should be so unreserved, and should lay himself out to be so exquisitely agreeable. They (and especially Richard) were naturally pleased for similar reasons, and considered it no common privilege to be so freely confided in by such an attractive man. The more we listened, the more gaily Mr. Skimpole talked. And what with his fine hilarious manner, and his engaging candour, and his genial ways of lightly tossing his own weaknesses about, as if he had said, "I am a child, you know! You are designing people compared with me," (he really made me consider myself in that light); "but I am gay and innocent; forget your worldly arts and play with me!"—the effect was absolutely dazzling.

He was so full of feeling too, and had such a delicate sentiment for what was beautiful or tender, that he could have won a heart by that alone. In the evening, when I was preparing to make tea, and Ada was touching the piano in the adjoining room and softly humming a tune to her cousin Richard, which they had happened to mention, he came and sat down on the sofa near me, and so spoke of Ada that I almost loved him.

"She is like the morning," he said. "With that golden hair, those blue eyes, and that fresh bloom on her cheek, she is like the summer morning. The birds here will mistake her for it. We will not call such a lovely young creature as that, who is a joy to all mankind, an orphan. She is the child of the universe."

Mr. Jarndyce, I found, was standing near us, with his hands behind him, and an attentive smile upon his face.

"The universe," he observed, "makes rather an indifferent parent, I am afraid."

"O! I don't know!" cried Mr. Skimpole, buoyantly.

"I think I do know," said Mr. Jarndyce.

"Well!" cried Mr. Skimpole, "you know the world (which in your sense is the universe), and I know nothing of it, so you shall have your way. But if I had mine," glancing at the cousins, "there should be no brambles of sordid realities in such a path as that. It should be strewn with roses; it should lie through bowers, where there was no spring, autumn, nor winter, but perpetual summer. Age or change should never wither it.[3] The base word money should never be breathed near it!"

Mr. Jarndyce patted him on the head with a smile, as if he had been really a child; and passing a step or two on, and stopping a moment, glanced at the young cousins. His look was thoughtful, but had a benignant expression in it which I often (how often!) saw again: which has long been engraven on my heart. The room in which they were, communicating with that in which he stood, was only lighted by the fire. Ada sat at the piano; Richard stood beside her, bending down. Upon the wall, their shadows blended together, surrounded by strange forms, not without a ghostly motion caught from the unsteady fire, though reflecting from motionless objects.

3. Cf. Enobarbus's tribute to Cleopatra: "Age cannot wither her nor custom stale/ Her infinite variety." (*Antony and Cleopatra*, II.ii.240–41.)

Ada touched the notes so softly, and sang so low, that the wind, sighing away to the distant hills, was as audible as the music. The mystery of the future, and the little clue afforded to it by the voice of the present, seemed expressed in the whole picture.

But it is not to recall this fancy, well as I remember it, that I recall the scene. First, I was not quite unconscious of the contrast in respect of meaning and intention, between the silent look directed that way, and the flow of words that had preceded it. Secondly, though Mr. Jarndyce's glance, as he withdrew it, rested for but a moment on me, I felt as if, in that moment, he confided to me—and knew that he confided to me, and that I received the confidence—his hope that Ada and Richard might one day enter on a dearer relationship.

Mr. Skimpole could play on the piano and the violoncello; and he was a composer—had composed half an opera once, but got tired of it—and played what he composed, with taste. After tea we had quite a little concert, in which Richard—who was enthralled by Ada's singing, and told me that she seemed to know all the songs that ever were written—and Mr. Jarndyce, and I, were the audience. After a little while I missed, first Mr. Skimpole, and afterwards Richard; and while I was thinking how could Richard stay away so long, and lose so much, the maid who had given me the keys looked in at the door, saying, "If you please, miss, could you spare a minute!"

When I was shut out with her in the hall, she said, holding up her hands, "Oh if you please, miss, Mr. Carstone says would you come up-stairs to Mr. Skimpole's room. He has been took, miss!"

"Took?" said I.

"Took, miss. Sudden," said the maid.

I was apprehensive that his illness might be of a dangerous kind; but of course I begged her to be quiet and not disturb any one; and collected myself, as I followed her quickly up-stairs, sufficiently to consider what were the best remedies to be applied if it should prove to be a fit. She threw open a door, and I went into a chamber; where, to my unspeakable surprise, instead of finding Mr. Skimpole stretched upon the bed, or prostrate on the floor, I found him standing before the fire smiling at Richard, while Richard, with a face of great embarrassment, looked at a person on a sofa, in a white great-coat, with smooth hair upon his head and not much of it, which he was wiping smoother, and making less of, with a pocket-handkerchief.

"Miss Summerson," said Richard, hurriedly, "I am glad you are come. You will be able to advise us. Our friend, Mr. Skimpole—don't be alarmed!—is arrested for debt."

"And, really, my dear Miss Summerson," said Mr. Skimpole,

with his agreeable candour, "I never was in a situation, in which that excellent sense, and quiet habit of method and usefulness, which anybody must observe in you who has the happiness of being a quarter of an hour in your society, was more needed."

The person on the sofa, who appeared to have a cold in his head, gave such a very loud snort, that he startled me.

"Are you arrested for much, sir?" I inquired of Mr. Skimpole.

"My dear Miss Summerson," said he, shaking his head pleasantly, "I don't know. Some pounds, odd shillings, and halfpence, I think, were mentioned."

"It's twenty-four pound, sixteen, and seven-pence ha'penny," observed the stranger. "That's wot it is."

"And it sounds—somehow it sounds," said Mr. Skimpole, "like a small sum?"

The strange man said nothing, but made another snort. It was such a powerful one that it seemed quite to lift him up out of his seat.

"Mr. Skimpole," said Richard to me, "has a delicacy in applying to my cousin Jarndyce, because he has lately—I think, sir, I understood you that you had lately——"

"Oh, yes!" returned Mr. Skimpole, smiling. "Though I forgot how much it was, and when it was. Jarndyce would readily do it again; but I have the epicure-like feeling that I would prefer a novelty in help; that I would rather," and he looked at Richard and me, "develop generosity in a new soil, and in a new form of flower."

"What do you think will be best, Miss Summerson?" said Richard, aside.

I ventured to inquire, generally, before replying, what would happen if the money were not produced.

"Jail," said the strange man, coolly putting his handkerchief into his hat, which was on the floor at his feet. "Or Coavinses."

"May I ask, sir, what is——"

"Coavinses?" said the strange man. "A 'ouse."[4]

Richard and I looked at one another again. It was a most singular thing that the arrest was our embarrassment, and not Mr. Skimpole's. He observed us with a genial interest; but there seemed, if I may venture on such a contradiction, nothing selfish in it. He had entirely washed his hands of the difficulty, and it had become ours.

"I thought," he suggested, as if good-naturedly to help us out, "that being parties in a Chancery suit concerning (as people say) a large amount of property, Mr. Richard or his beautiful cousin, or both, could sign something, or make over something, or give some sort of undertaking, or pledge, or bond? I don't know what the

4. A so-called lock-up house, named after its proprietor, which combined features of a jail and a hotel. In such establishments debtors were detained until someone paid for their release (as in Thackeray's *Vanity Fair*, LIII) or until they were transferred to a debtors' prison.

business name of it may be, but I suppose there is some instrument within their power that would settle this?"

"Not a bit on it," said the strange man.

"Really?" returned Mr. Skimpole. "That seems odd, now, to one who is no judge of these things!"

"Odd or even," said the stranger, gruffly, "I can tell you, not a bit on it!"

"Keep your temper, my good fellow, keep your temper!" Mr. Skimpole gently reasoned with him, as he made a little drawing of his head on the fly-leaf of a book. "Don't be ruffled by your occupation. We can separate you from your office; we can separate the individual from the pursuit. We are not so prejudiced as to suppose that in private life you are otherwise than a very estimable man, with a great deal of poetry in your nature, of which you may not be conscious."

The stranger only answered with another violent snort; whether in acceptance of the poetry-tribute, or in disdainful rejection of it, he did not express to me.

"Now, my dear Miss Summerson, and my dear Mr. Richard," said Mr. Skimpole, gaily, innocently, and confidingly, as he looked at his drawing with his head on one side; "here you see me utterly incapable of helping myself, and entirely in your hands! I only ask to be free. The butterflies are free. Mankind will surely not deny to Harold Skimpole what it concedes to the butterflies!"

"My dear Miss Summerson," said Richard, in a whisper, "I have ten pounds that I received from Mr. Kenge. I must try what that will do."

I possessed fifteen pounds, odd shillings, which I had saved from my quarterly allowance during several years. I had always thought that some accident might happen which would throw me suddenly, without any relation, or any property, on the world; and had always tried to keep some little money by me, that I might not be quite penniless. I told Richard of my having this little store, and having no present need of it; and I asked him delicately to inform Mr. Skimpole, while I should be gone to fetch it, that we would have the pleasure of paying his debt.

When I came back, Mr. Skimpole kissed my hand, and seemed quite touched. Not on his own account (I was again aware of that perplexing and extraordinary contradiction), but on ours; as if personal considerations were impossible with him, and the contemplation of our happiness alone affected him. Richard, begging me, for the greater grace of the transaction, as he said, to settle with Coavinses (as Mr. Skimpole now jocularly called him), I counted out the money and received the necessary acknowledgment. This, too, delighted Mr. Skimpole.

His compliments were so delicately administered that I blushed less than I might have done; and settled with the stranger in the white coat without making any mistakes. He put the money in his pocket, and shortly said, "Well, then, I'll wish you a good evening, miss."

"My friend," said Mr. Skimpole, standing with his back to the fire, after giving up the sketch when it was half finished, "I should like to ask you something without offence."

I think the reply was, "Cut away, then!"

"Did you know this morning, now, that you were coming out on this errand?" said Mr. Skimpole.

"Know'd it yes'day aft'noon at tea-time," said Coavinses.

"It didn't affect your appetite? Didn't make you at all uneasy?"

"Not a bit," said Coavinses. "I know'd if you wos missed to-day, you wouldn't be missed to-morrow. A day makes no such odds."

"But when you came down here," proceeded Mr. Skimpole, "it was a fine day. The sun was shining, the wind was blowing, the lights and shadows were passing across the fields, the birds were singing."

"Nobody said they warn't, in *my* hearing," returned Coavinses.

"No," observed Mr. Skimpole. "But what did you think upon the road?"

"Wot do you mean?" growled Coavinses, with an appearance of strong resentment. "Think! I've got enough to do, and little enough to get for it, without thinking. Thinking!" (with profound contempt).

"Then you didn't think, at all events," proceeded Mr. Skimpole, "to this effect. 'Harold Skimpole loves to see the sun shine; loves to hear the wind blow; loves to watch the changing lights and shadows; loves to hear the birds, those choristers in Nature's great cathedral.[5] And does it seem to me that I am about to deprive Harold Skimpole of his share in such possessions, which are his only birthright!' You thought nothing to that effect?"

"I—certainly—did—NOT," said Coavinses, whose doggedness in utterly renouncing the idea was of that intense kind, that he could only give adequate expression to it by putting a long interval between each word, and accompanying the last with a jerk that might have dislocated his neck.

"Very odd and very curious, the mental process is, in you men of business!" said Mr. Skimpole, thoughtfully. "Thank you, my friend. Good night."

As our absence had been long enough already to seem strange down-stairs, I returned at once, and found Ada sitting at work by the fireside talking to her cousin John. Mr. Skimpole presently

5. Cf. Shakespeare's comparing a forest, in winter, to the ruins of a gothic monastery church: "Bare ruin'd choirs where late the sweet birds sang." (*Sonnets*, LXXIII.)

appeared, and Richard shortly after him. I was sufficiently engaged, during the remainder of the evening, in taking my first lesson in backgammon from Mr. Jarndyce, who was very fond of the game, and from whom I wished, of course, to learn it as quickly as I could, in order that I might be of the very small use of being able to play when he had no better adversary. But I thought, occasionally when Mr. Skimpole played some fragments of his own composition; or when, both at the piano and the violoncello, and at our table, he preserved, with an absence of all effort, his delightful spirits and his easy flow of conversation; that Richard and I seemed to retain the transferred impression of having been arrested since dinner, and that it was very curious altogether.

It was late before we separated: for when Ada was going at eleven o'clock, Mr. Skimpole went to the piano, and rattled, hilariously, that the best of all ways, to lengthen our days, was to steal a few hours from Night, my dear![6] It was past twelve before he took his candle and his radiant face out of the room; and I think he might have kept us there, if he had seen fit, until daybreak. Ada and Richard were lingering for a few moments by the fire, wondering whether Mrs. Jellyby had yet finished her dictation for the day, when Mr. Jarndyce, who had been out of the room, returned.

"Oh, dear me, what's this, what's this!" he said, rubbing his head and walking about with his good-humoured vexation. "What's this they tell me? Rick, my boy, Esther, my dear, what have you been doing? Why did you do it? How could you do it? How much apiece was it?—The wind's round again. I feel it all over me!"

We neither of us quite knew what to answer.

"Come, Rick, come! I must settle this before I sleep. How much are you out of pocket? You two made the money up, you know! Why did you? How could you?—O Lord, yes, it's due east—must be!"

"Really, sir," said Richard, "I don't think it would be honourable in me to tell you. Mr. Skimpole relied upon us——"

"Lord bless you, my dear boy! He relies upon everybody!" said Mr. Jarndyce, giving his head a great rub, and stopping short.

"Indeed, sir?"

"Everybody! And he'll be in the same scrape again next week!" said Mr. Jarndyce, walking again at a great pace, with a candle in his hand that had gone out. "He's always in the same scrape. He was born in the same scrape. I verily believe that the announcement in the newspapers when his mother was confined was, 'On Tuesday last, at her residence in Botheration Buildings, Mrs. Skimpole of a son in difficulties.' "

6. From the song by Thomas Moore (1779–1851) "The Young May Moon": "And the best of all ways to lengthen our days,/ Is to steal a few hours from the night, my dear."

Richard laughed heartily, but added, "Still, sir, I don't want to shake his confidence, or to break his confidence; and if I submit to your better knowledge again, that I ought to keep his secret, I hope you will consider before you press me any more. Of course, if you do press me, sir, I shall know I am wrong, and will tell you."

"Well!" cried Mr. Jarndyce, stopping again, and making several absent endeavours to put his candlestick in his pocket. "I—here! Take it away, my dear. I don't know what I am about with it; it's all the wind—invariably has that effect—I won't press you, Rick; you may be right. But really—to get hold of you and Esther—and to squeeze you like a couple of tender young Saint Michael's oranges![7]—It'll blow a gale in the course of the night!"

He was now alternately putting his hands into his pockets, as if he were going to keep them there a long time; and taking them out again, and vehemently rubbing them all over his head.

I ventured to take this opportunity of hinting that Mr. Skimpole, being in all such matters, quite a child—

"Eh, my dear?" said Mr. Jarndyce, catching at the word.

"—Being quite a child, sir," said I, "and so different from other people——"

"You are right!" said Mr. Jarndyce, brightening. "Your woman's wit hits the mark. He is a child—an absolute child. I told you he was a child, you know, when I first mentioned him."

Certainly! certainly! we said.

"And he *is* a child. Now, isn't he?" asked Mr. Jarndyce, brightening more and more.

He was indeed, we said.

"When you come to think of it, it's the height of childishness in you—I mean me—" said Mr. Jarndyce, "to regard him for a moment as a man. You can't make *him* responsible. The idea of Harold Skimpole with designs or plans, or knowledge of consequences! Ha, ha, ha!"

It was so delicious to see the clouds about his bright face clear away, and to see him so heartily pleased, and to know, as it was impossible not to know, that the source of his pleasure was the goodness which was tortured by condemning, or mistrusting, or secretly accusing any one, that I saw the tears in Ada's eyes, while she echoed his laugh, and felt them in my own.

"Why, what a cod's head and shoulders I am,"[8] said Mr. Jarndyce, "to require reminding of it! The whole business shows the child from beginning to end. Nobody but a child would have thought of singling *you* two out for parties in the affair! Nobody

7. High quality oranges from St. Michael's island in the Azores.

8. In effect, "How idiotic I am"—alluding to the idiotic expression of a codfish on display in a fish market.

but a child would have thought of *your* having the money! If it had been a thousand pounds, it would have been just the same!" said Mr. Jarndyce, with his whole face in a glow.

We all confirmed it from our night's experience.

"To be sure, to be sure!" said Mr. Jarndyce. "However, Rick, Esther, and you too, Ada, for I don't know that even your little purse is safe from his inexperience—I must have a promise all round, that nothing of this sort shall ever be done any more. No advance! Not even sixpences."

We all promised faithfully; Richard, with a merry glance at me, touching his pocket, as if to remind me that there was no danger of *our* transgressing.

"As to Skimpole," said Mr. Jarndyce, "a habitable doll's house, with good board, and a few tin people[9] to get into debt with and borrow money of, would set the boy up in life. He is in a child's sleep by this time, I suppose; it's time I should take my craftier head to my more worldly pillow. Good night, my dears. God bless you!"

He peeped in again, with a smiling face, before we had lighted our candles, and said, "O! I have been looking at the weathercock. I find it was a false alarm about the wind. It's in the south!" And went away singing to himself.

Ada and I agreed, as we talked together for a little while upstairs, that this caprice about the wind was a fiction; and that he used the pretence to account for any disappointment he could not conceal, rather than he would blame the real cause of it, or disparage or depreciate any one. We thought this very characteristic of his eccentric gentleness; and of the difference between him and those petulant people who make the weather and the winds (particularly that unlucky wind which he had chosen for such a different purpose) the stalking-horse of their splenetic and gloomy humours.

Indeed, so much affection for him had been added in this one evening to my gratitude, that I hoped I already began to understand him through that mingled feeling. Any seeming inconsistencies in Mr. Skimpole, or in Mrs. Jellyby, I could not expect to be able to reconcile; having so little experience or practical knowledge. Neither did I try; for my thoughts were busy, when I was alone, with Ada and Richard, and with the confidence I had seemed to receive concerning them. My fancy, made a little wild by the wind perhaps, would not consent to be all unselfish, either, though I would have persuaded it to be so if I could. It wandered back to my godmother's house, and came along the intervening track, raising up shadowy speculations which had sometimes trembled there in the dark,

9. Probably toy people, as in the expression *tin soldiers.*

as to what knowledge Mr. Jarndyce had of my earliest history—even as to the possibility of his being my father—though that idle dream was quite gone now.

It was all gone now, I remembered, getting up from the fire. It was not for me to muse over bygones, but to act with a cheerful spirit and a grateful heart. So I said to myself, "Esther, Esther, Esther! Duty, my dear!" and gave my little basket of housekeeping keys such a shake, that they sounded like little bells, and rang me hopefully to bed.

Chapter VII

THE GHOST'S WALK

While Esther sleeps, and while Esther wakes, it is still wet weather down at the place in Lincolnshire. The rain is ever falling, drip, drip, drip, by day and night, upon the broad flagged terrace-pavement, The Ghost's Walk. The weather is so very bad, down in Lincolnshire, that the liveliest imagination can scarcely apprehend its ever being fine again. Not that there is any superabundant life of imagination on the spot, for Sir Leicester is not here (and, truly, even if he were, would not do much for it in that particular), but is in Paris, with my Lady; and solitude, with dusky wings, sits brooding upon Chesney Wold.[1]

There may be some motions of fancy among the lower animals at Chesney Wold. The horses in the stables—the long stables in a barren, red-brick courtyard, where there is a great bell in a turret, and a clock with a large face, which the pigeons who live near it, and who love to perch upon its shoulders, seem to be always consulting—*they* may contemplate some mental pictures of fine weather on occasions, and may be better artists at them than the grooms. The old roan, so famous for cross-country work, turning his large eyeball to the grated window near his rack, may remember the fresh leaves that glisten there at other times, and the scents that stream in, and may have a fine run with the hounds, while the human helper, clearing out the next stall, never stirs beyond his pitchfork and birch-broom. The grey, whose place is opposite the door, and who, with an impatient rattle of his halter, pricks his ears and turns his head so wistfully when it is opened, and to whom the opener says, "Woa grey, then, steady! Noabody wants you to-day!" may know it quite as well as the man. The whole seemingly monotonous and uncompanionable half-dozen, stabled together, may pass the long wet hours, when the door is shut, in livelier communication

1. Cf. Milton's address to the Spirit that presided over the creation of the world: "with mighty wings outspread,/ Dove-like sat'st brooding on the vast abyss." ***Paradise Lost,*** **I, 20–21. (Noted by Susan Shatto, 1975.)**

than is held in the servants' hall, or at the Dedlock Arms;—or may even beguile the time by improving (perhaps corrupting) the pony in the loose-box in the corner.

So the mastiff, dozing in his kennel, in the courtyard, with his large head on his paws, may think of the hot sunshine, when the shadows of the stable-buildings tire his patience out by changing, and leave him, at one time of the day, no broader refuge than the shadow of his own house, where he sits on end, panting and growling short, and very much wanting something to worry, besides himself and his chain. So, now, half-waking and all-winking, he may recall the house full of company, the coach-houses full of vehicles, the stables full of horses, and the outbuildings full of attendants upon horses, until he is undecided about the present, and comes forth to see how it is. Then, with the impatient shake of himself, he may growl in the spirit, "Rain, rain, rain! Nothing but rain—and no family here!" as he goes in again, and lies down with a gloomy yawn.

So with the dogs in the kennel-buildings across the park, who have their restless fits, and whose doleful voices, when the wind has been very obstinate, have even made it known in the house itself: up-stairs, down-stairs, and in my lady's chamber.[2] They may hunt the whole country-side, while the raindrops are pattering round their inactivity. So the rabbits with their self-betraying tails, frisking in and out of holes at roots of trees, may be lively with ideas of the breezy days when their ears are blown about, or of those seasons of interest when there are sweet young plants to gnaw. The turkey in the poultry-yard, always troubled with a class-grievance (probably Christmas), may be reminiscent of that summer morning wrongfully taken from him, when he got into the lane among the felled trees, where there was a barn and barley. The discontented goose, who stoops to pass under the old gateway, twenty feet high, may gabble out, if we only knew it, a waddling preference for weather when the gateway casts its shadow on the ground.

Be this as it may, there is not much fancy otherwise stirring at Chesney Wold. If there be a little at any odd moment, it goes, like a little noise in that old echoing place, a long way, and usually leads off to ghosts and mystery.

It has rained so hard and rained so long, down in Lincolnshire, that Mrs. Rouncewell, the old housekeeper at Chesney Wold, has several times taken off her spectacles and cleaned them, to make certain that the drops were not upon the glasses. Mrs. Rouncewell might have been sufficiently assured by hearing the rain, but that she is rather deaf, which nothing will induce her to believe. She is a

2. From the nursery rhyme: "Goosey, Goosey, Gander,/ Whither do you wander?/ Upstairs, downstairs,/ And in my Lady's Chamber."

fine old lady, handsome, stately, wonderfully neat, and has such a back and such a stomacher,[3] that if her stays should turn out when she dies to have been a broad old-fashioned family fire-grate, nobody who knows her would have cause to be surprised. Weather affects Mrs. Rouncewell little. The house is there in all weathers, and the house, as she expresses it, "is what she looks at." She sits in her room (in a side passage on the ground floor, with an arched window commanding a smooth quadrangle, adorned at regular intervals with smooth round trees and smooth round blocks of stone, as if the trees were going to play at bowls with the stones), and the whole house reposes on her mind. She can open it on occasion, and be busy and fluttered; but it is shut-up now, and lies on the breadth of Mrs. Rouncewell's iron-bound bosom, in a majestic sleep.

It is the next difficult thing to an impossibility to imagine Chesney Wold without Mrs. Rouncewell, but she has only been here fifty years. Ask her how long, this rainy day, and she shall answer "fifty year three months and a fortnight, by the blessing of Heaven, if I live till Tuesday." Mr. Rouncewell died some time before the decease of the pretty fashion of pig-tails, and modestly hid his own (if he took it with him) in the corner of the churchyard in the park, near the mouldy porch. He was born in the market-town, and so was his young widow. Her progress in the family began in the time of the last Sir Leicester, and originated in the still-room.[4]

The present representative of the Dedlocks is an excellent master. He supposes all his dependents to be utterly bereft of individual characters, intentions, or opinions, and is persuaded that he was born to supersede the necessity of their having any. If he were to make a discovery to the contrary, he would be simply stunned—would never recover himself, most likely, except to gasp and die. But he is an excellent master still, holding it a part of his state to be so. He has a great liking for Mrs. Rouncewell; he says she is a most respectable, creditable woman. He always shakes hands with her, when he comes down to Chesney Wold, and when he goes away; and if he were very ill, or if he were knocked down by accident, or run over, or placed in any situation expressive of a Dedlock at a disadvantage, he would say, if he could speak, "Leave me, and send Mrs. Rouncewell here!" feeling his dignity, at such a pass, safer with her than with anybody else.

Mrs. Rouncewell has known trouble. She has had two sons, of whom the younger ran wild, and went for a soldier, and never came back. Even to this hour, Mrs. Rouncewell's calm hands lose their

3. A vest covering chest and stomach, usually ornamented with jewels or embroidery, fashionable as an article of dress for women in the seventeenth century.

4. A room in large-scale domestic establishments where homemade liqueurs were distilled and tea and coffee prepared. The servant in charge was called the still-room maid.

composure when she speaks of him, and unfolding themselves from her stomacher, hover about her in an agitated manner, as she says, what a likely lad, what a fine lad, what a gay, good-humoured, clever lad he was! Her second son[5] would have been provided for at Chesney Wold, and would have been made steward in due season; but he took, when he was a schoolboy, to constructing steam-engines out of saucepans, and setting birds to draw their own water, with the least possible amount of labour; so assisting them with artful contrivance[6] of hydraulic pressure, that a thirsty canary had only, in a literal sense, to put his shoulder to the wheel, and the job was done. This propensity gave Mrs. Rouncewell great uneasiness. She felt it, with a mother's anguish, to be a move in the Wat Tyler[7] direction: well knowing that Sir Leicester had that general impression of an aptitude for any art to which smoke and a tall chimney might be considered essential. But the doomed young rebel (otherwise a mild youth, and very persevering), showing no sign of grace as he got older; but, on the contrary, constructing a model of a power-loom, she was fain, with many tears, to mention his backslidings to the baronet. "Mrs. Rouncewell," said Sir Leicester, "I can never consent to argue, as you know, with any one on any subject. You had better get rid of your boy; you had better get him into some Works. The iron country farther north is, I suppose, the congenial direction for a boy with these tendencies." Farther north he went, and farther north he grew up; and if Sir Leicester Dedlock ever saw him, when he came to Chesney Wold to visit his mother, or ever thought of him afterwards, it is certain that he only regarded him as one of a body of some odd thousand conspirators, swarthy and grim, who were in the habit of turning out by torchlight, two or three nights in the week, for unlawful purposes.

Nevertheless Mrs. Rouncewell's son has, in the course of nature and art, grown up, and established himself, and married, and called unto him Mrs. Rouncewell's grandson: who, being out of his apprenticeship, and home from a journey in far countries,[8] whither he was sent to enlarge his knowledge and complete his preparation for the venture of this life, stands leaning against the chimney-piece this very day, in Mrs. Rouncewell's room at Chesney Wold.

"And, again and again, I am glad to see you, Watt![9] And, once again, I am glad to see you, Watt!" says Mrs. Rouncewell. "You are a fine young fellow. You are like your poor uncle George. Ah!" Mrs. Rouncewell's hands unquiet, as usual, on this reference.

5. Her other son, an industrialist, was the elder of the two brothers.

6. Device for trained songbirds enabling them to raise tiny buckets of drinking water up to the perch in their cage.

7. Leader of a mob of peasants which attacked London in 1381. Tyler was reputed to have been prompted to his revolutionary role after a tax-collecting official (whom he later killed) had made advances to his daughter. See also Dickens' *A Child's History of England*, ch. XIX.

8. Cf. Luke 15:13. (Allusion noted by Stephen Gill.)

9. Named after James Watt (1736–1819), inventor of the steam engine.

"They say I am like my father, grandmother."

"Like him also, my dear—but most like your poor uncle George! And your dear father." Mrs. Rouncewell folds her hands again. "He is well?"

"Thriving, grandmother, in every way."

"I am thankful!" Mrs. Rouncewell is fond of her son, but has a plaintive feeling towards him—much as if he were a very honourable soldier, who had gone over to the enemy.

"He is quite happy?" says she.

"Quite."

"I am thankful! So he has brought you up to follow in his ways, and has sent you into foreign countries and the like? Well, he knows best. There may be a world beyond Chesney Wold that I don't understand. Though I am not young, either. And I have seen a quantity of good company too!"

"Grandmother," says the young man, changing the subject, "what a very pretty girl that was, I found with you just now. You called her Rosa?"

"Yes, child. Daughter of a widow in the village. Maids are so hard to teach, now-a-days, that I have put her about me young. She's an apt scholar, and will do well. She shows the house already, very pretty. She lives with me at my table here."

"I hope I have not driven her away?"

"She supposes we have family affairs to speak about, I dare say. She is very modest. It is a fine quality in a young woman. And scarcer," says Mrs. Rouncewell, expanding her stomacher to its utmost limits, "than it formerly was!"

The young man inclines his head, in acknowledgment of the precepts of experience. Mrs. Rouncewell listens.

"Wheels!" says she. They have long been audible to the younger ears of her companion. "What wheels on such a day as this, for gracious sake?"

After a short interval a tap at the door. "Come in!" A dark-eyed, dark-haired, shy, village beauty comes in—so fresh in her rosy and yet delicate bloom that the drops of rain, which have beaten on her hair, look like the dew upon a flower fresh gathered.

"What company is this, Rosa?" says Mrs. Rouncewell.

"It's two young men in a gig, ma'am, who want to see the house—yes, and if you please, I told them so!" in quick reply to a gesture of dissent from the housekeeper. "I went to the hall-door, and told them it was the wrong day, and the wrong hour; but the young man who was driving took off his hat in the wet, and begged me to bring this card to you."

"Read it, my dear Watt," says the housekeeper.

Rosa is so shy as she gives it to him, that they drop it between them, and almost knock their foreheads together as they pick it up. Rosa is shyer than before.

"Mr. Guppy" is all the information the card yields.

"Guppy!" repeats Mrs. Rouncewell. "Mr. Guppy! Nonsense, I never heard of him!"

"If you please, he told *me* that!" says Rosa. "But he said that he and the other young gentleman came from London only last night by the mail, on business at the magistrates' meeting, ten miles off, this morning; and that as their business was soon over, and they had heard a great deal said of Chesney Wold, and really didn't know what to do with themselves, they had come through the wet to see it. They are lawyers. He says he is not in Mr. Tulkinghorn's office, but he is sure he may make use of Mr. Tulkinghorn's name, if necessary." Finding, now she leaves off, that she has been making quite a long speech, Rosa is shyer then ever.

Now, Mr. Tulkinghorn is, in a manner, part and parcel of the place; and, besides, is supposed to have made Mrs. Rouncewell's will. The old lady relaxes, consents to the admission of the visitors as a favour, and dismisses Rosa. The grandson, however, being smitten by a sudden wish to see the house himself, proposes to join the party. The grandmother, who is pleased that he should have that interest, accompanies him—though to do him justice, he is exceedingly unwilling to trouble her.

"Much obliged to you, ma'am!" says Mr. Guppy, divesting himself of his wet dreadnought[1] in the hall. "Us London lawyers don't often get an out;[2] and when we do, we like to make the most of it, you know."

The old housekeeper, with a gracious severity of deportment, waves her hand towards the great staircase. Mr. Guppy and his friend follow Rosa, Mrs. Rouncewell and her grandson follow them, a young gardener goes before to open the shutters.

As is usually the case with people who go over houses, Mr. Guppy and his friend are dead beat before they have well begun. They straggle about in wrong places, look at wrong things, don't care for the right things, gape when more rooms are opened, exhibit forlorn depression of spirits, and are clearly knocked up. In each successive chamber that they enter, Mrs. Rouncewell, who is as upright as the house itself, rests apart in a window-seat, or other such nook, and listens with stately approval to Rosa's exposition. Her grandson is so attentive to it that Rosa is shyer than ever—and prettier. Thus they pass on from room to room, raising the pictured Dedlocks for a few brief minutes as the young gardener admits the light, and reconsigning them to their graves as he shuts it out again.

1. Weather-resistant overcoat.

2. Excursion or outing.

It appears to the afflicted Mr. Guppy and his inconsolable friend, that there is no end to the Dedlocks, whose family greatness seems to consist in their never having done anything to distinguish themselves, for seven hundred years.

Even the long drawing-room of Chesney Wold cannot revive Mr. Guppy's spirits. He is so low that he droops on the threshold, and has hardly strength of mind to enter. But a portrait over the chimney-piece, painted by the fashionable artist of the day, acts upon him like a charm. He recovers in a moment. He stares at it with uncommon interest; he seems to be fixed and fascinated by it.

"Dear me!" says Mr. Guppy. "Who's that?"

"The picture over the fire-place," says Rosa, "is the portrait of the present Lady Dedlock. It is considered a perfect likeness, and the best work of the master."

" 'Blest!" says Mr. Guppy, staring in a kind of dismay at his friend, "if I can ever have seen her. Yet I know her! Has the picture been engraved, miss?"

"The picture has never been engraved. Sir Leicester has always refused permission."

"Well!" says Mr. Guppy in a low voice, "I'll be shot if it ain't very curious how well I know that picture! So that's Lady Dedlock, is it!"

"The picture on the right is the present Sir Leicester Dedlock. The picture on the left is his father, the late Sir Leicester."

Mr. Guppy has no eyes for either of those magnates. "It's unaccountable to me," he says, still staring at the portrait, "how well I know that picture! I'm dashed!" adds Mr. Guppy, looking round, "if I don't think I must have had a dream of that picture, you know!"

As no one present takes any especial interest in Mr. Guppy's dreams, the probability is not pursued. But he still remains so absorbed by the portrait that he stands immoveable before it until the young gardener has closed the shutters; when he comes out of the room in a dazed state, that is an odd though a sufficient substitute for interest, and follows into the succeeding rooms with a confused stare, as if he were looking everywhere for Lady Dedlock again.

He sees no more of her. He sees her rooms, which are the last shown, as being very elegant, and he looks out of the windows from which she looked out, not long ago, upon the weather that bored her to death. All things have an end—even houses that people take infinite pains to see, and are tired of before they begin to see them. He has come to the end of the sight, and the fresh village beauty to the end of her description; which is always this:

"The terrace below is much admired. It is called, from an old story in the family, The Ghost's Walk."

"No?" says Mr. Guppy, greedily curious; "what's the story, miss? Is it anything about a picture?"

"Pray, tell us the story," says Watt, in a half whisper.

"I don't know it, sir." Rosa is shyer than ever.

"It is not related to visitors; it is almost forgotten," says the housekeeper, advancing. "It has never been more than a family anecdote."

"You'll excuse my asking again if it has anything to do with a picture, ma'am," observes Mr. Guppy, "because I do assure you that the more I think of that picture the better I know it, without knowing how I know it!"

The story has nothing to do with a picture; the housekeeper can guarantee that. Mr. Guppy is obliged to her for the information; and is, moreover, generally obliged. He retires with his friend, guided down another staircase by the young gardener; and presently is heard to drive away. It is now dusk. Mrs. Rouncewell can trust to the discretion of her two young hearers, and may tell *them* how the terrace came to have that ghostly name. She seats herself in a large chair by the fast-darkening window, and tells them:

"In the wicked days, my dears, of King Charles the First—I mean, of course, in the wicked days of the rebels who leagued themselves against that excellent King—Sir Morbury Dedlock was the owner of Chesney Wold. Whether there was any account of a ghost in the family before those days, I can't say. I should think it very likely indeed."

Mrs. Rouncewell holds this opinion, because she considers that a family of such antiquity and importance has a right to a ghost. She regards a ghost as one of the privileges of the upper classes; a genteel distinction to which the common people have no claim.

"Sir Morbury Dedlock," says Mrs. Rouncewell, "was, I have no occasion to say, on the side of the blessed martyr.[3] But it *is* supposed that his Lady, who had none of the family blood in her veins, favoured the bad cause. It is said that she had relations among King Charles's enemies; that she was in correspondence with them; and that she gave them information. When any of the country gentlemen who followed His Majesty's cause met here, it is said that my Lady was always nearer to the door of their council-room than they supposed. Do you hear a sound like a footstep passing along the terrace, Watt?"

Rosa draws nearer to the housekeeper.

"I heard the rain-drip on the stones," replies the young man, "and I hear a curious echo—I suppose an echo—which is very like a halting step."

The housekeeper gravely nods and continues:

3. King Charles I was styled a martyr by Royalists after his execution in 1649.

"Partly on account of this division between them, and partly on other accounts, Sir Morbury and his Lady led a troubled life. She was a lady of a haughty temper. They were not well suited to each other in age or character, and they had no children to moderate between them. After her favourite brother, a young gentleman, was killed in the civil wars (by Sir Morbury's near kinsman), her feeling was so violent that she hated the race into which she had married. When the Dedlocks were about to ride out from Chesney Wold in the King's cause, she is supposed to have more than once stolen down into the stables in the dead of night, and lamed their horses; and the story is, that once, at such an hour, her husband saw her gliding down the stairs and followed her into the stall where his own favourite horse stood. There he seized her by the wrist; and in a struggle or in a fall, or through the horse being frightened and lashing out, she was lamed in the hip, and from that hour began to pine away."

The housekeeper has dropped her voice to little more than a whisper.

"She had been a lady of a handsome figure and a noble carriage. She never complained of the change; she never spoke to any one of being crippled, or of being in pain; but, day by day, she tried to walk upon the terrace; and with the help of the stone balustrade and with the help of a stick, went up and down, up and down, up and down, in sun and shadow, with greater difficulty every day. At last, one afternoon, her husband (to whom she had never, on any persuasion, opened her lips since that night), standing at the great south window, saw her drop upon the pavement. He hastened down to raise her, but she repulsed him as he bent over her, and looking at him fixedly and coldly, said, 'I will die here where I have walked. And I will walk here, though I am in my grave. I will walk here, until the pride of this house is humbled. And when calamity, or when disgrace is coming to it, let the Dedlocks listen for my step!' "

Watt looks at Rosa. Rosa in the deepening gloom looks down upon the ground, half frightened and half shy.

"There and then she died. And from those days," says Mrs. Rouncewell, "the name has come down—The Ghost's Walk. If the tread is an echo, it is an echo that is only heard after dark, and is often unheard for a long while together. But it comes back, from time to time; and so sure as there is sickness or death in the family, it will be heard then."

"—And disgrace, grandmother—" says Watt.

"Disgrace never comes to Chesney Wold," returns the housekeeper.

Her grandson apologises, with "True. True."

"That is the story. Whatever the sound is, it is a worrying

sound," says Mrs. Rouncewell, getting up from her chair, "and what is to be noticed in it, is, that it *must be heard*. My Lady, who is afraid of nothing, admits that when it is there, it must be heard. You cannot shut it out. Watt, there is a tall French clock behind you (placed there, 'a purpose) that has a loud beat when it is in motion, and can play music. You understand how those things are managed?"

"Pretty well, grandmother, I think."

"Set it a going."

Watt sets it a going—music and all.

"Now, come hither," says the housekeeper. "Hither, child, towards my Lady's pillow. I am not sure that it is dark enough yet, but listen! Can you hear the sound upon the terrace, through the music, and the beat, and everything?"

"I certainly can!"

"So my Lady says."

Chapter VIII

COVERING A MULTITUDE OF SINS[1]

It was interesting when I dressed before daylight, to peep out of window, where my candles were reflected in the black panes like two beacons, and, finding all beyond still enshrouded in the indistinctness of last night, to watch how it turned out when the day came on. As the prospect gradually revealed itself, and disclosed the scene over which the wind had wandered in the dark, like my memory over my life, I had a pleasure in discovering the unknown objects that had been around me in my sleep. At first they were faintly discernible in the mist, and above them the later stars still glimmered. That pale interval over, the picture began to enlarge and fill up so fast, that, at every new peep, I could have found enough to look at for an hour. Imperceptibly, my candles became the only incongruous part of the morning, the dark places in my room all melted away, and the day shone bright upon a cheerful landscape, prominent in which the old Abbey Church, with its massive tower, threw a softer train of shadow on the view than seemed compatible with its rugged character. But so from rough outsides (I hope I have learnt), serene and gentle influences often proceed.

Every part of the house was in such order, and every one was so attentive to me, that I had no trouble with my two bunches of keys: though what with trying to remember the contents of each little store-room drawer, and cupboard; and what with making notes on a slate about jams, and pickles, and preserves, and bottles, and glass, and china, and a great many other things; and what with being generally a methodical, old-maidish sort of foolish little person; I was so

1. See I Peter 4:8.

busy that I could not believe it was breakfast-time when I heard the bell ring. Away I ran, however, and made tea, as I had already been installed into the responsibility of the teapot; and then, as they were all rather late, and nobody was down yet, I thought I would take a peep at the garden and get some knowledge of that too. I found it quite a delightful place; in front, the pretty avenue and drive by which we had approached (and where, by-the-bye, we had cut up the gravel so terribly with our wheels that I asked the gardener to roll it); at the back, the flower-garden, with my darling at her window up there, throwing it open to smile out at me, as if she would have kissed me from that distance. Beyond the flower-garden was a kitchen-garden, and then a paddock, and then a snug little rick-yard,[2] and then a dear little farm-yard. As to the House itself, with its three peaks in the roof; its various-shaped windows, some so large, some so small, and all so pretty; its trellis-work, against the south-front for roses and honey-suckle, and its homely, comfortable, welcoming look: it was, as Ada said, when she came out to meet me with her arm through that of its master, worthy of her cousin John —a bold thing to say, though he only pinched her dear cheek for it.

Mr. Skimpole was as agreeable at breakfast, as he had been overnight. There was honey on the table, and it led him into a discourse about Bees. He had no objection to honey, he said (and I should think he had not, for he seemed to like it), but he protested against the overweening assumptions of Bees. He didn't at all see why the busy Bee should be proposed as a model to him; he supposed the Bee liked to make honey, or he wouldn't do it—nobody asked him. It was not necessary for the Bee to make such a merit of his tastes. If every confectioner went buzzing about the world, banging against everything that came in his way, and egotistically calling upon everybody to take notice that he was going to his work and must not be interrupted, the world would be quite an insupportable place. Then, after all, it was a ridiculous position, to be smoked out of your fortune with brimstone,[3] as soon as you had made it. You would have a very mean opinion of a Manchester man,[4] if he spun cotton for no other purpose. He must say he thought a Drone the embodiment of a pleasanter and wiser idea. The Drone said, unaffectedly, "You will excuse me; I really cannot attend to the shop! I find myself in a world in which there is so much to see, and so short a time to see it in, that I must take the liberty of looking about me, and begging to be provided for by somebody who doesn't want to look about him." This appeared to Mr. Skimpole to be the Drone philosophy, and he thought it a very good philosophy—al-

2. Farm-yard for storing hay in stacks (ricks).

3. In earlier times honey was garnered from hives by suffocating the bees with sulphur fumes (*brimstone*) thus depriving them of their "fortune." See Thomas Hardy's *Under the Greenwood Tree* IV, 2.

4. A businessman from Manchester, one of the chief centers for manufacturing cotton.

ways supposing the Drone to be willing to be on good terms with the Bee; which, so far as he knew, the easy fellow always was, if the consequential creature would only let him, and not be so conceited about his honey![5]

He pursued this fancy with the lightest foot over a variety of ground, and made us all merry; though again he seemed to have as serious a meaning in what he said as he was capable of having. I left them still listening to him, when I withdrew to attend to my new duties. They had occupied me for some time, and I was passing through the passages on my return with my basket of keys on my arm, when Mr. Jarndyce called me into a small room next his bed-chamber, which I found to be in part a little library of books and papers, and in part quite a little museum of his boots and shoes, and hat-boxes.

"Sit down, my dear," said Mr. Jarndyce. "This, you must know, is the Growlery. When I am out of humour, I come and growl here."

"You must be here very seldom, sir," said I.

"O, you don't know me!" he returned. "When I am deceived or disappointed in—the wind, and it's Easterly, I take refuge here. The Growlery is the best-used room in the house. You are not aware of half my humours yet. My dear, how you are trembling!"

I could not help it: I tried very hard; but being alone with that benevolent presence, and meeting his kind eyes, and feeling so happy, and so honoured there, and my heart so full——

I kissed his hand. I don't know what I said, or even that I spoke. He was disconcerted, and walked to the window; I almost believed with an intention of jumping out, until he turned, and I was reassured by seeing in his eyes what he had gone there to hide. He gently patted me on the head, and I sat down.

"There! There!" he said. "That's over. Pooh! Don't be foolish."

"It shall not happen again, sir," I returned; "but at first it is difficult——"

"Nonsense!" he said, "it's easy, easy. Why not? I hear of a good little orphan girl without a protector, and I take it into my head to be that protector. She grows up, and more than justifies my good opinion, and I remain her guardian and her friend. What is there in all this? So, so! Now, we have cleared off old scores, and I have before me thy pleasant, trusting, trusty face again."

I said to myself, "Esther, my dear, you surprise me! This really is not what I expected of you!" and it had such a good effect that I folded my hands upon my basket and quite recovered myself. Mr.

5. In *A Jar of Honey from Mount Hybla* (1848) Leigh Hunt offers his own "discourse about Bees" which includes his lamenting the massacre of drones by working bees: "Every year those gentlemen [the drones] have to pay for their idle and luxurious lives by one great pang of abolition. They are all stung and swept away into nothingness! Truly a circumstance to 'give us pause,' and perplex us with our wax and honey" (ch. XI).

Jarndyce, expressing his approval in his face, began to talk to me as confidentially as if I had been in the habit of conversing with him every morning for I don't know how long. I almost felt as if I had.

"Of course, Esther," he said, "you don't understand this Chancery business?"

And of course I shook my head.

"I don't know who does," he returned. "The Lawyers have twisted it into such a state of bedevilment that the original merits of the case have long disappeared from the face of the earth. It's about a Will, and the trusts under a Will—or it was, once. It's about nothing but Costs, now. We are always appearing, and disappearing, and swearing, and interrogating, and filing, and cross-filing, and arguing, and sealing, and motioning, and referring, and reporting, and revolving about the Lord Chancellor and all his satellites, and equitably waltzing ourselves off to dusty death,[6] about Costs. That's the great question. All the rest, by some extraordinary means, has melted away."

"But it was, sir," said I, to bring him back, for he began to rub his head, "about a Will?"

"Why, yes, it was about a Will when it was about anything," he returned. "A certain Jarndyce, in an evil hour, made a great fortune, and made a great Will. In the question how the trusts under that Will are to be administered, the fortune left by the Will is squandered away; the legatees under the Will are reduced to such a miserable condition that they would be sufficiently punished if they had committed an enormous crime in having money left them; and the Will itself is made a dead letter. All through the deplorable cause, everything that everybody in it, except one man, knows already, is referred to that only one man who don't know it, to find out—all through the deplorable cause, everybody must have copies, over and over again, of everything that has accumulated about it in the way of cartloads of papers (or must pay for them without having them, which is the usual course, for nobody wants them); and must go down the middle and up again, through such an infernal country-dance of costs and fees and nonsense and corruption, as was never dreamed of in the wildest visions of a Witch's Sabbath. Equity sends questions to Law, Law sends questions back to Equity; Law finds it can't do this, Equity finds it can't do that; neither can so much as say it can't do anything, without this solicitor instructing and this counsel appearing for A, and that solicitor instructing and that counsel appearing for B; and so on through the whole alphabet, like the history of the Apple Pie.[7] And thus, through years and years, and lives and lives, everything goes on, constantly

6. See *Macbeth*, V.v.23.

7. Mother Goose story designed to teach children the alphabet from A to Z: A stood for Apple Pie; and B bit it; C cut it; O opened it, etc.

beginning over and over again, and nothing ever ends. And we can't get out of the suit on any terms, for we are made parties to it, and *must be* parties to it, whether we like it or not. But it won't do to think of it! When my great uncle, poor Tom Jarndyce, began to think of it, it was the beginning of the end!"

"The Mr. Jarndyce, sir, whose story I have heard?"

He nodded gravely. "I was his heir, and this was his house, Esther. When I came here, it was bleak indeed. He had left the signs of his misery upon it."

"How changed it must be now!" I said.

"It had been called, before his time, the Peaks. He gave it its present name, and lived here shut up: day and night poring over the wicked heaps of papers in the suit and hoping against hope to disentangle it from its mystification and bring it to a close. In the meantime the place became dilapidated, the wind whistled through the cracked walls, the rain fell through the broken roof, the weeds choked the passage to the rotting door. When I brought what remained of him home here, the brains seemed to me to have been blown out of the house too; it was so shattered and ruined."

He walked a little to and fro, after saying this to himself with a shudder, and then looked at me, and brightened, and came and sat down again with his hands in his pockets.

"I told you this was the Growlery, my dear. Where was I?"

I reminded him, at the hopeful change he had made in Bleak house.

"Bleak House: true. There is, in that city of London there, some property of ours, which is much at this day what Bleak House was then,—I say property of ours, meaning of the Suit's, but I ought to call it the property of Costs; for Costs is the only power on earth that will ever get anything out of it now, or will ever know it for anything but an eyesore and a heartsore. It is a street of perishing blind houses, with their eyes stoned out; without a pane of glass, without so much as a window-frame, with the bare blank shutters tumbling from their hinges and falling asunder; the iron rails peeling away in flakes of rust; the chimneys sinking in; the stone steps to every door (and every door might be Death's Door) turning stagnant green; the very crutches on which the ruins are propped, decaying. Although Bleak House was not in Chancery, its master was, and it was stamped with the same seal. These are the Great Seal's impressions, my dear, all over England—the children know them!"

"How changed it is!" I said again.

"Why, so it is," he answered much more cheerfully; "and it is wisdom in you to keep me to the bright side of the picture." (The idea of my wisdom!) "These are things I never talk about, or even think about, excepting in the Growlery here. If you consider it right to mention them to Rick and Ada," looking seriously at me, "you can. I leave it to your discretion, Esther."

"I hope, sir"—said I.

"I think you had better call me Guardian, my dear."

I felt that I was choking again—I taxed myself with it, "Esther, now, you know you are!"—when he feigned to say this slightly, as if it were a whim, instead of a thoughtful tenderness. But I gave the housekeeping keys the least shake in the world as a reminder to myself, and folding my hands in a still more determined manner on the basket, looked at him quietly.

"I hope, Guardian," said I, "that you may not trust too much to my discretion. I hope you may not mistake me. I am afraid it will be a disappointment to you to know that I am not clever—but it really is the truth; and you would soon find it out if I had not the honesty to confess it."

He did not seem at all disappointed: quite the contrary. He told me, with a smile all over his face, that he knew me very well indeed, and that I was quite clever enough for him.

"I hope I may turn out so," said I, "but I am much afraid of it, Guardian."

"You are clever enough to be the good little woman of our lives here, my dear," he returned, playfully; "the little old woman of the Child's (I don't mean Skimpole's) Rhyme

" 'Little old woman, and whither so high?'—
'To sweep the cobwebs out of the sky.'

You will sweep them so neatly out of *our* sky, in the course of your housekeeping, Esther, that one of these days we shall have to abandon the Growlery, and nail up the door."

This was the beginning of my being called Old Woman, and Little Old Woman, and Cobweb, and Mrs. Shipton, and Mother Hubbard, and Dame Durden,[8] and so many names of that sort, that my own name soon became quite lost among them.

"However," said Mr. Jarndyce, "to return to our gossip. Here's Rick, a fine young fellow full of promise. What's to be done with him?"

8. Nicknames referring to folklore mother-figures. In an old nursery rhyme, "The Little Old Woman," a housekeeper, who carried a broom, was tossed high into the sky. When asked, "Where are you going to up so high?" she replied, "To brush the cobwebs off the sky." *Cobweb,* in Shakespeare's *A Midsummer Night's Dream,* is one of the fairies whose task is to look after the needs of others. *Mrs. Shipton,* usually called Mother Shipton, was a Welsh prophetess whose predictions were popular in the early nineteenth century. *Mother Hubbard,* who attended to the needs of her dog, was the subject of the well-known nursery rhyme. *Dame Durden* was the heroine of a song about a countrywoman who employed five menservants who mated with her five maidservants on St. Valentine's Day.

O my goodness, the idea of asking my advice on such a point!

"Here he is, Esther," said Mr. Jarndyce, comfortably putting his hands in his pockets and stretching out his legs. "He must have a profession; he must make some choice for himself. There will be a world more Wiglomeration[9] about it, I suppose, but it must be done."

"More what, Guardian?" said I.

"More Wiglomeration," said he. "It's the only name I know for the thing. He is a ward in Chancery, my dear. Kenge and Carboy will have something to say about it; Master Somebody—a sort of ridiculous Sexton, digging graves for the merits of causes in a back room at the end of Quality Court, Chancery Lane—will have something to say about it; Counsel will have something to say about it; the Chancellor will have something to say about it; the Satellites[1] will have something to say about it; they will all have to be handsomely fee'd, all round, about it; the whole thing will be vastly ceremonious, wordy, unsatisfactory, and expensive, and I call it, in general, Wiglomeration. How mankind ever came to be afflicted with Wiglomeration, or for whose sins these young people ever fell into a pit of it, I don't know; so it is."

He began to rub his head again, and to hint that he felt the wind. But it was a delightful instance of his kindness towards me, that whether he rubbed his head, or walked about, or did both, his face was sure to recover its benignant expression as it looked at mine; and he was sure to turn comfortable again, and put his hands in his pockets and stretch out his legs.

"Perhaps it would be best, first of all," said I, "to ask Mr. Richard what he inclines to himself."

"Exactly so," he returned. "That's what I mean! You know, just accustom yourself to talk it over, with your tact and in your quiet way, with him and Ada, and see what you all make of it. We are sure to come at the heart of the matter by your means, little woman."

I really was frightened at the thought of the importance I was attaining, and the number of things that were being confided to me. I had not meant this at all; I had meant that he should speak to Richard. But of course I said nothing in reply, except that I would do my best, though I feared (I really felt it necessary to repeat this) that he thought me much more sagacious than I was. At which my guardian only laughed the pleasantest laugh I ever heard.

9. A portmanteau word seemingly coined by Mr. Jarndyce. See p. 7 regarding the Chancery prisoner "who has fallen into a state of conglomeration about accounts" and pp. xx and 6 regarding the wigs of the Chancery lawyers.

1. The eighteen lawyers who assist Mr. Tangle in the Jarndyce case. See p. 9. Concerning *Master*, see the Introductory Note on Law Courts, p. xviii.

"Come!" he said, rising and pushing back his chair. "I think we may have done with the Growlery for one day! Only a concluding word. Esther, my dear, do you wish to ask me anything?"

He looked so attentively at me, that I looked attentively at him, and felt sure I understood him.

"About myself, sir?" said I.

"Yes."

"Guardian," said I, venturing to put my hand, which was suddenly colder than I could have wished, in his, "nothing! I am quite sure that if there were anything I ought to know, or had any need to know, I should not have to ask you to tell it to me. If my whole reliance and confidence were not placed in you, I must have a hard heart indeed. I have nothing to ask you; nothing in the world."

He drew my hand through his arm, and we went away to look for Ada. From that hour I felt quite easy with him, quite unreserved, quite content to know no more, quite happy.

We lived, at first, rather a busy life at Bleak House; for we had to become acquainted with many residents in and out of the neighbourhood who knew Mr. Jarndyce. It seemed to Ada and me that everybody knew him, who wanted to do anything with anybody else's money. It amazed us, when we began to sort his letters, and to answer some of them for him in the Growlery of a morning, to find how the great object of the lives of nearly all his correspondents appeared to be to form themselves into committees for getting in and laying out money. The ladies were as desperate as the gentlemen; indeed, I think they were even more so. They threw themselves into committees in the most impassioned manner, and collected subscriptions with a vehemence quite extraordinary. It appeared to us that some of them must pass their whole lives in dealing out subscription-cards to the whole Post-office Directory—shilling cards, half-crown cards, half-sovereign cards, penny cards. They wanted everything. They wanted wearing apparel, they wanted linen rags, they wanted money, they wanted coals, they wanted soup, they wanted interest, they wanted autographs, they wanted flannel, they wanted whatever Mr. Jarndyce had—or had not. Their objects were as various as their demands. They were going to raise new buildings, they were going to pay off debts on old buildings, they were going to establish in a picturesque building (engraving of proposed West Elevation attached) the Sisterhood of Mediæval Marys;[2] they were going to give a testimonial to Mrs. Jellyby; they were going to have their Secretary's portrait painted, and presented to his mother-in-law, whose deep devotion to him was well known; they were going to get up everything, I really

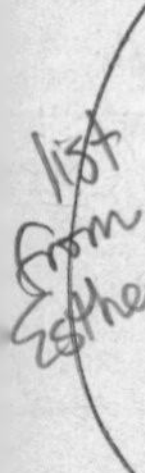

2. The High Church revival at Oxford inspired the founding of Sisterhoods in the Anglican church in the 1840's.

believe, from five hundred thousand tracts to an annuity, and from a marble monument to a silver teapot. They took a multitude of titles. They were the women of England, the Daughters of Britain, the Sisters of all the Cardinal Virtues separately, the Females of America, the Ladies of a hundred denominations. They appeared to be always excited about canvassing and electing. They seemed to our poor wits, and according to their own accounts, to be constantly polling people by tens of thousands, yet never bringing their candidates in for anything. It made our heads ache to think, on the whole, what feverish lives they must lead.

Among the ladies who were most distinguished for this rapacious benevolence (if I may use the expression), was a Mrs. Pardiggle, who seemed, as I judged from the number of her letters to Mr. Jarndyce, to be almost as powerful a correspondent as Mrs. Jellyby herself. We observed that the wind always changed when Mrs. Pardiggle became the subject of conversation; and that it invariably interrupted Mr. Jarndyce, and prevented his going any farther, when he had remarked that there were two classes of charitable people: one, the people who did a little and made a great deal of noise; the other, the people who did a great deal and made no noise at all. We were therefore curious to see Mrs. Pardiggle, suspecting her to be a type of the former class; and were glad when she called one day with her five young sons.

She was a formidable style of lady, with spectacles, a prominent nose, and a loud voice, who had the effect of wanting a great deal of room. And she really did, for she knocked down little chairs with her skirts that were quite a great way off. As only Ada and I were at home, we received her timidly; for she seemed to come in like cold weather, and to make the little Pardiggles blue as they followed.

"These, young ladies," said Mrs. Pardiggle, with great volubility, after the first salutations, "are my five boys. You may have seen their names in a printed subscription list (perhaps more than one), in the possession of our esteemed friend, Mr. Jarndyce. Egbert, my eldest (twelve), is the boy who sent out his pocket-money, to the amount of five-and-threepence, to the Tockahoopo Indians. Oswald, my second (ten-and-a-half), is the child who contributed two-and-ninepence to the Great National Smithers Testimonial. Francis, my third (nine), one-and-sixpence-halfpenny; Felix, my fourth (seven), eightpence to the Superannuated Widows; Alfred, my youngest (five), has voluntarily enrolled himself in the Infant Bonds of Joy, and is pledged never, through life, to use tobacco in any form."[3]

3. Beginning in 1847, children who were persuaded into signing pledges to abstain from alcohol and tobacco for the rest of their lives were organized into groups known as Bands of Hope. In North America the organization was more commonly called the Loyal Temperance Legion.

We had never seen such dissatisfied children. It was not merely that they were weazen and shrivelled—though they were certainly that too—but they looked absolutely ferocious with discontent. At the mention of the Tockahoopo Indians,[4] I could really have supposed Egbert to be one of the most baleful members of that tribe, he gave me such a savage frown. The face of each child, as the amount of his contribution was mentioned, darkened in a peculiarly vindictive manner, but his was by far the worst. I must except, however, the little recruit into the Infant Bonds of Joy, who was stolidly and evenly miserable.

"You have been visiting, I understand," said Mrs. Pardiggle, "at Mrs. Jellyby's?"

We said yes, we had passed one night there.

"Mrs. Jellyby," pursued the lady, always speaking in the same demonstrative, loud, hard tone, so that her voice impressed my fancy as if it had a sort of spectacles on too—and I may take the opportunity of remarking that her spectacles were made the less engaging by her eyes being what Ada called "choking eyes," meaning very prominent: "Mrs. Jellyby is a benefactor to society, and deserves a helping hand. My boys have contributed to the African project—Egbert, one-and-six, being the entire allowance of nine weeks; Oswald, one-and-a-penny-halfpenny, being the same; the rest, according to their little means. Nevertheless, I do not go with Mrs. Jellyby in all things. I do not go with Mrs. Jellyby in her treatment of her young family. It has been noticed. It has been observed that her young family are excluded from participation in the objects to which she is devoted. She may be right, she may be wrong; but, right or wrong, this is not my course with *my* young family. I take them everywhere."

I was afterwards convinced (and so was Ada) that from the ill-conditioned eldest child, these words extorted a sharp yell. He turned it off into a yawn, but it began as a yell.

"They attend Matins with me (very prettily done), at half-past six o'clock in the morning all the year round, including of course the depth of winter," said Mrs. Pardiggle rapidly, "and they are with me during the revolving duties of the day. I am a School lady, I am a Visiting lady, I am a Reading lady, I am a Distributing lady; I am on the local Linen Box Committee, and many general Committees; and my canvassing alone is very extensive—perhaps no one's more so. But they are my companions everywhere; and by these means they acquire that knowledge of the poor, and that capacity of doing charitable business in general—in short, that taste for the sort of

4. Egbert and his four brothers were all named after saints or heroes who were admired by leaders of the High Church movement, as noted by Butt and Tillotson. The Indian name *Tuckahoo*, applied to inhabitants in parts of Virginia, may have inspired the name of the tribe to which Egbert contributed.

thing—which will render them in after life a service to their neighbours, and a satisfaction to themselves. My young family are not frivolous; they expend the entire amount of their allowance, in subscriptions, under my direction; and they have attended as many public meetings, and listened to as many lectures, orations, and discussions, as generally fall to the lot of few grown people. Alfred (five), who, as I mentioned, has of his own election joined the Infant Bonds of Joy, was one of the very few children who manifested consciousness on that occasion, after a fervid address of two hours from the chairman of the evening."

Alfred glowered at us as if he never could, or would, forgive the injury of that night.

"You may have observed, Miss Summerson," said Mrs. Pardiggle, "in some of the lists to which I have referred, in the possession of our esteemed friend Mr. Jarndyce, that the names of my young family are concluded with the name of O. A. Pardiggle, F.R.S.,[5] one pound. That is their father. We usually observe the same routine. I put down my mite first; then my young family enrol their contributions, according to their ages and their little means; and then Mr. Pardiggle brings up the rear. Mr. Pardiggle is happy to throw in his limited donation, under my direction; and thus things are made, not only pleasant to ourselves, but, we trust, improving to others."

Suppose Mr. Pardiggle were to dine with Mr. Jellyby, and suppose Mr. Jellyby were to relieve his mind after dinner to Mr. Pardiggle, would Mr. Pardiggle, in return, make any confidential communication to Mr. Jellyby? I was quite confused to find myself thinking this, but it came into my head.

"You are very pleasantly situated here!" said Mrs. Pardiggle.

We were glad to change the subject; and going to the window, pointed out the beauties of the prospect, on which the spectacles appeared to me to rest with curious indifference.

"You know Mr. Gusher?" said our visitor.

We were obliged to say that we had not the pleasure of Mr. Gusher's acquaintance.

"The loss is yours, I assure you," said Mrs. Pardiggle, with her commanding deportment. "He is a very fervid impassioned speaker—full of fire! Stationed in a waggon on this lawn, now, which, from the shape of the land, is naturally adapted to a public meeting, he would improve almost any occasion you could mention for hours and hours! By this time, young ladies," said Mrs. Pardiggle, moving back to her chair, and overturning, as if by invisible agency, a little round table at a considerable distance with my work-basket on it, "by this time you have found me out, I dare say?"

5. Fellow of the Royal Society.

This was really such a confusing question that Ada looked at me in perfect dismay. As to the guilty nature of my own consciousness, after what I had been thinking, it must have been expressed in the colour of my cheeks.

"Found out, I mean," said Mrs. Pardiggle, "the prominent point in my character. I am aware that it is so prominent as to be discoverable immediately. I lay myself open to detection, I know. Well! I freely admit, I am a woman of business. I love hard work; I enjoy hard work. The excitement does me good. I am so accustomed and inured to hard work that I don't know what fatigue is."

We murmured that it was very astonishing and very gratifying; or something to that effect. I don't think we knew why it was either, but this was what our politeness expressed.

"I do not understand what it is to be tired; you cannot tire me if you try!" said Mrs. Pardiggle. "The quantity of exertion (which is no exertion to me), the amount of business (which I regard as nothing), that I go through, sometimes astonishes myself. I have seen my young family, and Mr. Pardiggle, quite worn out with witnessing it, when I may truly say I have been as fresh as a lark!"

If that dark-visaged eldest boy could look more malicious than he had already looked, this was the time when he did it. I observed that he doubled his right fist, and delivered a secret blow into the crown of his cap, which was under his left arm.

"This gives me a great advantage when I am making my rounds," said Mrs. Pardiggle. "If I find a person unwilling to hear what I have to say, I tell that person directly, 'I am incapable of fatigue, my good friend, I am never tired, and I mean to go on until I have done.' It answers admirably! Miss Summerson, I hope I shall have your assistance in my visiting rounds immediately, and Miss Clare's very soon?"

At first I tried to excuse myself, for the present, on the general ground of having occupations to attend to, which I must not neglect. But as this was an ineffectual protest, I then said, more particularly, that I was not sure of my qualifications. That I was inexperienced in the art of adapting my mind to minds very differently situated, and addressing them from suitable points of view. That I had not that delicate knowledge of the heart which must be essential to such a work. That I had much to learn, myself, before I could teach others, and that I could not confide in my good intentions alone. For these reasons, I thought it best to be as useful as I could, and to render what kind services I could, to those immediately about me; and to try to let that circle of duty gradually and naturally expand itself. All this I said, with anything but confidence, because Mrs. Pardiggle was much older than I, and had great experience, and was so very military in her manners.

"You are wrong, Miss Summerson," said she: "but perhaps you are not equal to hard work, or the excitement of it; and that makes a vast difference. If you would like to see how I go through my work, I am now about—with my young family—to visit a brick-maker in the neighbourhood (a very bad character), and shall be glad to take you with me. Miss Clare also, if she will do me the favour."

Ada and I interchanged looks, and, as we were going out in any case, accepted the offer. When we hastily returned from putting on our bonnets, we found the young family languishing in a corner, and Mrs. Pardiggle sweeping about the room, knocking down nearly all the light objects it contained. Mrs. Pardiggle took possession of Ada, and I followed with the family.

Ada told me afterwards that Mrs. Pardiggle talked in the same loud tone (that, indeed, I overheard), all the way to the brickmaker's, about an exciting contest which she had for two or three years waged against another lady, relative to the bringing in of their rival candidates for a pension somewhere. There had been a quantity of printing, and promising, and proxying, and polling; and it appeared to have imparted great liveliness to all concerned, except the pensioners—who were not elected yet.

I am very fond of being confided in by children, and am happy in being usually favoured in that respect, but on this occasion it gave me great uneasiness. As soon as we were out of doors, Egbert, with the manner of a little footpad, demanded a shilling of me, on the ground that his pocket-money was "boned"[6] from him. On my pointing out the great impropriety of the word, especially in connexion with his parent (for he added sulkily "By her!"), he pinched me and said, "O then! Now! Who are you? *You* wouldn't like it, I think? What does she make a sham for, and pretend to give me money, and take it away again? Why do you call it *my* allowance, and never let me spend it?" These exasperating questions so inflamed his mind, and the minds of Oswald and Francis, that they all pinched me at once, and in a dreadfully expert way: screwing up such little pieces of my arms that I could hardly forbear crying out. Felix, at the same time, stamped upon my toes. And the Bond of Joy, who, on account of always having the whole of his little income anticipated, stood in fact pledged to abstain from cakes as well as tobacco, so swelled with grief and rage when we passed a pastry-cook's shop, that he terrified me by becoming purple. I never underwent so much, both in body and mind, in the course of a walk with young people, as from these unnaturally constrained children, when they paid me the compliment of being natural.

6. Stolen.

I was glad when we came to the brickmaker's house; though it was one of a cluster of wretched hovels in a brickfield, with pigsties close to the broken windows, and miserable little gardens before the doors, growing nothing but stagnant pools. Here and there, an old tub was put to catch the droppings of rain-water from a roof, or they were banked up with mud into a little pond like a large dirt-pie. At the doors and windows, some men and women lounged or prowled about, and took little notice of us, except to laugh to one another, or to say something as we passed, about gentlefolks minding their own business, and not troubling their heads and muddying their shoes with coming to look after other people's.

Mrs. Pardiggle, leading the way with a great show of moral determination, and talking with much volubility about the untidy habits of the people (though I doubted if the best of us could have been tidy in such a place), conducted us into a cottage at the farthest corner, the ground-floor room of which we nearly filled. Besides ourselves, there were in this damp offensive room—a woman with a black eye, nursing a poor little gasping baby by the fire; a man, all stained with clay and mud, and looking very dissipated, lying at full length on the ground, smoking a pipe; a powerful young man, fastening a collar on a dog; and a bold girl, doing some kind of washing in very dirty water. They all looked up at us as we came in, and the woman seemed to turn her face towards the fire, as if to hide her bruised eye; nobody gave us any welcome.

"Well, my friends," said Mrs. Pardiggle; but her voice had not a friendly sound, I thought; it was much too business-like and systematic. "How do you do, all of you? I am here again. I told you, you couldn't tire me, you know. I am fond of hard work, and am true to my word."

"There an't," growled the man on the floor, whose head rested on his hand as he stared at us, "any more on you to come in, is there?"

"No, my friend," said Mrs. Pardiggle, seating herself on one stool, and knocking down another. "We are all here."

"Because I thought there warn't enough of you, perhaps?" said the man, with his pipe between his lips, as he looked round upon us.

The young man and the girl both laughed. Two friends of the young man whom we had attracted to the doorway, and who stood there with their hands in their pockets, echoed the laugh noisily.

"You can't tire me, good people," said Mrs. Pardiggle to these latter. "I enjoy hard work; and the harder you make mine, the better I like it."

"Then make it easy for her!" growled the man upon the floor. "I wants it done, and over. I wants a end of these liberties took with my place. I wants a end of being drawed like a badger. Now you're a-going to poll-pry[7] and question according to custom—I know what you're a-going to be up to. Well! You haven't got no occasion to be up to it. I'll save you the trouble. Is my daughter a-washin? Yes, she *is* a-washin. Look at the water. Smell it! That's wot we drinks. How do you like it, and what do you think of gin, instead! An't my place dirty? Yes, it is dirty—it's nat'rally dirty, and it's nat'rally onwholesome; and we've had five dirty and onwholesome children, as is all dead infants, and so much the better for them, and for us besides. Have I read the little book wot you left? No, I an't read the little book wot you left. There an't nobody here as knows how to read it; and if there wos, it wouldn't be suitable to me. It's a book fit for a babby, and I'm not a babby. If you was to leave me a doll, I shouldn't nuss it. How have I been conducting of myself? Why, I've been drunk for three days; and I'd a been drunk four, if I'd a had the money. Don't I never mean for to go to church? No, I don't never mean for to go to church. I shouldn't be expected there, if I did; the beadle's too gen-teel for me.[8] And how did my wife get that black eye? Why, I giv' it her; and if she says I didn't, she's a Lie!"

He had pulled his pipe out of his mouth to say all this, and he now turned over on his other side, and smoked again. Mrs. Pardiggle, who had been regarding him through her spectacles with a forcible composure, calculated, I could not help thinking, to increase his antagonism, pulled out a good book, as if it were a constable's staff, and took the whole family into custody. I mean into religious custody, of course; but she really did it, as if she were an inexorable moral Policeman carrying them all off to a station-house.

Ada and I were very uncomfortable. We both felt intrusive and out of place; and we both thought that Mrs. Pardiggle would have got on infinitely better, if she had not had such a mechanical way of taking possession of people. The children sulked and stared; the family took no notice of us whatever, except when the young man made the dog bark: which he usually did when Mrs. Pardiggle was most emphatic. We both felt painfully sensible that between us and these people there was an iron barrier, which could not be removed by our new friend. By whom, or how, it could be removed, we did not know; but we knew that. Even what she read and said, seemed to us to be ill chosen for such auditors, if it had been imparted ever so modestly and with ever so much tact. As to the little book to which the man on the floor had referred, we acquired a knowledge of it afterwards; and Mr. Jarndyce said he doubted if Robinson

7. To ask impertinent questions like Paul Pry, the title character in a comic play of 1825 by John Poole (later a friend of Dickens).

8. Beadles were responsible for maintaining order during church services by ejecting anyone considered to be behaving unrespectably.

Crusoe could have read it, though he had had no other on his desolate island.

We were much relieved, under these circumstances, when Mrs. Pardiggle left off. The man on the floor then turning his head round again, said morosely,

"Well! You've done, have you?"

"For to-day, I have, my friend. But I am never fatigued. I shall come to you again, in your regular order," returned Mrs. Pardiggle, with demonstrative cheerfulness.

"So long as you goes now," said he, folding his arms and shutting his eyes with an oath, "you may do wot you like!"

Mrs. Pardiggle accordingly rose, and made a little vortex in the confined room from which the pipe itself very narrowly escaped. Taking one of her young family in each hand, and telling the others to follow closely, and expressing her hope that the brickmaker and all his house would be improved when she saw them next, she then proceeded to another cottage. I hope it is not unkind in me to say that she certainly did make, in this, as in everything else, a show that was not conciliatory, of doing charity by wholesale, and of dealing in it to a large extent.

She supposed that we were following her; but as soon as the space was left clear, we approached the woman sitting by the fire, to ask if the baby were ill.

She only looked at it as it lay on her lap. We had observed before, that when she looked at it she covered her discoloured eye with her hand, as though she wished to separate any association with noise and violence and ill-treatment, from the poor little child.

Ada, whose gentle heart was moved by its appearance, bent down to touch its little face. As she did so, I saw what happened and drew her back. The child died.

"O Esther!" cried Ada, sinking on her knees beside it. "Look here! O Esther, my love, the little thing! The suffering, quiet, pretty little thing! I am so sorry for it. I am so sorry for the mother. I never saw a sight so pitiful as this before! O baby, baby!"

Such compassion, such gentleness, as that with which she bent down weeping, and put her hand upon the mother's, might have softened any mother's heart that ever beat. The woman at first gazed at her in astonishment, and then burst into tears.

Presently I took the light burden from her lap; did what I could to make the baby's rest the prettier and gentler; laid it on a shelf, and covered it with my own handkerchief. We tried to comfort the mother, and we whispered to her what Our Saviour said of children.[9] She answered nothing, but sat weeping—weeping very much.

9. See Mark 10:14: "Suffer the little children to come unto me."

When I turned, I found that the young man had taken out the dog, and was standing at the door looking in upon us; with dry eyes, but quiet. The girl was quiet too, and sat in a corner looking on the ground. The man had risen. He still smoked his pipe with an air of defiance, but he was silent.

An ugly woman, very poorly clothed, hurried in while I was glancing at them, and coming straight up to the mother, said, "Jenny! Jenny!" The mother rose on being so addressed, and fell upon the woman's neck.

She also had upon her face and arms the marks of ill-usage. She had no kind of grace about her, but the grace of sympathy; but when she condoled with the woman, and her own tears fell, she wanted no beauty. I say condoled, but her only words were "Jenny! Jenny!" All the rest was in the tone in which she said them.

I thought it very touching to see these two women, coarse and shabby and beaten, so united; to see what they could be to one another; to see how they felt for one another; how the heart of each to each was softened by the hard trials of their lives. I think the best side of such people is almost hidden from us. What the poor are to the poor is little known, excepting to themselves and God.

We felt it better to withdraw and leave them uninterrupted. We stole out quietly, and without notice from any one except the man. He was leaning against the wall near the door; and finding that there was scarcely room for us to pass, went out before us. He seemed to want to hide that he did this on our account, but we perceived that he did, and thanked him. He made no answer.

Ada was so full of grief all the way home, and Richard, whom we found at home, was so distressed to see her in tears (though he said to me when she was not present, how beautiful it was too!) that we arranged to return at night with some little comforts, and repeat our visit at the brickmaker's house. We said as little as we could to Mr. Jarndyce, but the wind changed directly.

Richard accompanied us at night to the scene of our morning expedition. On our way there, we had to pass a noisy drinking-house, where a number of men were flocking about the door. Among them, and prominent in some dispute, was the father of the little child. At a short distance, we passed the young man and the dog, in congenial company. The sister was standing laughing and talking with some other young women, at the corner of the row of cottages; but she seemed ashamed, and turned away as we went by.

We left our escort within sight of the brickmaker's dwelling, and proceeded by ourselves. When we came to the door, we found the woman who had brought such consolation with her, standing there, looking anxiously out.

"It's you, young ladies, is it?" she said in a whisper. "I'm a-watching for my master. My heart's in my mouth. If he was to catch me away from home, he'd pretty near murder me."

"Do you mean your husband?" said I.

"Yes, miss, my master. Jenny's asleep, quite worn out. She's scarcely had the child off her lap, poor thing, these seven days and nights, except when I've been able to take it for a minute or two."

As she gave way for us, we went softly in, and put what we had brought, near the miserable bed on which the mother slept. No effort had been made to clean the room—it seemed in its nature almost hopeless of being clean; but the small waxen form, from which so much solemnity diffused itself, had been composed afresh, and washed, and neatly dressed in some fragments of white linen; and on my handerchief, which still covered the poor baby, a little bunch of sweet herbs had been laid by the same rough scarred hands, so lightly, so tenderly!

"May Heaven reward you!" we said to her. "You are a good woman."

"Me, young ladies?" she returned with surprise. "Hush! Jenny, Jenny!"

The mother had moaned in her sleep, and moved. The sound of the familiar voice seemed to calm her again. She was quiet once more.

How little I thought, when I raised my handkerchief to look upon the tiny sleeper underneath, and seemed to see a halo shine around the child through Ada's drooping hair as her pity bent her head—how little I thought in whose unquiet bosom that handkerchief would come to lie, after covering the motionless and peaceful breast! I only thought that perhaps the Angel of the child might not be all unconscious of the woman who replaced it with so compassionate a hand; not all unconscious of her presently, when we had taken leave, and left her at the door, by turns looking, and listening in terror for herself, and saying in her old soothing manner, "Jenny, Jenny!"

Chapter IX

SIGNS AND TOKENS

I don't know how it is, I seem to be always writing about myself. I mean all the time to write about other people, and I try to think about myself as little as possible, and I am sure, when I find myself coming into the story again, I am really vexed and say, "Dear, dear, you tiresome little creature, I wish you wouldn't!" but it is all of no use. I hope any one who may read what I write, will understand that if these pages contain a great deal about me, I can only suppose it must be because I have really something to do with them, and can't be kept out.

My darling and I read together, and worked, and practised; and found so much employment for our time, that the winter days flew by us like bright-winged birds. Generally in the afternoons, and always in the evenings, Richard gave us his company. Although he was one of the most restless creatures in the world, he certainly was very fond of our society.

He was very, very, very fond of Ada. I mean it, and I had better say it at once. I had never seen any young people falling in love before, but I found them out quite soon. I could not say so, of course, or show that I knew anything about it. On the contrary, I was so demure, and used to seem so unconscious, that sometimes I considered within myself while I was sitting at work, whether I was not growing quite deceitful.

But there was no help for it. All I had to do was to be quiet, and I was as quiet as a mouse. They were as quiet as mice, too, so far as any words were concerned; but the innocent manner in which they relied more and more upon me, as they took more and more to one another, was so charming, that I had great difficulty in not showing how it interested me.

"Our dear little old woman is such a capital old woman," Richard would say, coming up to meet me in the garden early, with his pleasant laugh and perhaps the least tinge of a blush, "that I can't get on without her. Before I begin my harum-scarum day—grinding away at these books and instruments, and then galloping up hill and down dale, all the country round, like a highwayman—it does me so much good to come and have a steady walk with our comfortable friend, that here I am again!"

"You know, Dame Durden, dear," Ada would say at night, with her head upon my shoulder, and the firelight shining in her thoughtful eyes, "I don't want to talk when we come up-stairs here. Only to sit a little while, thinking, with your dear face for company; and to hear the wind, and remember the poor sailors at sea——"

Ah! Perhaps Richard was going to be a sailor. We had talked it over very often, now, and there was some talk of gratifying the inclination of his childhood for the sea. Mr. Jarndyce had written to a relation of the family, a great Sir Leicester Dedlock, for his interest in Richard's favour, generally; and Sir Leicester had replied in a gracious manner, "that he would be happy to advance the prospects of the young gentleman if it should ever prove to be within his power, which was not at all probable—and that my Lady sent her compliments to the young gentleman (to whom she perfectly remembered that she was allied by remote consanguinity), and trusted that he would ever do his duty in any honourable profession to which he might devote himself."

"So I apprehend it's pretty clear," said Richard to me, "that I shall have to work my own way. Never mind! Plenty of people have had to do that before now, and have done it. I only wish I had the command of a clipping privateer, to begin with, and could carry off the Chancellor and keep him on short allowance until he gave judgment in our cause. He'd find himself growing thin, if he didn't look sharp!"

With a buoyancy and hopefulness and a gaiety that hardly ever flagged, Richard had a carelessness in his character that quite perplexed me—principally because he mistook it in such a very odd way, for prudence. It entered into all his calculations about money, in a singular manner, which I don't think I can better explain than by reverting for a moment to our loan to Mr. Skimpole.

Mr. Jarndyce had ascertained the amount, either from Mr. Skimpole himself or from Coavinses, and had placed the money in my hands with instructions to me to retain my own part of it and hand the rest to Richard. The number of little acts of thoughtless expenditure which Richard justified by the recovery of his ten pounds, and the number of times he talked to me as if he had saved or realised that amount, would form a sum in simple addition.

"My prudent Mother Hubbard, why not?" he said to me, when he wanted, without the least consideration, to bestow five pounds on the brickmaker. "I made ten pounds, clear, out of Coavinses' business."

"How was that?" said I.

"Why, I got rid of ten pounds which I was quite content to get rid of, and never expected to see any more. You don't deny that?"

"No," said I.

"Very well! then I came into possession of ten pounds—"

"The same ten pounds," I hinted.

"That has nothing to do with it!" returned Richard. "I have got ten pounds more than I expected to have, and consequently I can afford to spend it without being particular."

In exactly the same way, when he was persuaded out of the sacrifice of these five pounds by being convinced that it would do no good, he carried that sum to his credit and drew upon it.

"Let me see!" he would say. "I saved five pounds out of the brickmaker's affair; so, if I have a good rattle to London and back in a post-chaise, and put that down at four pounds, I shall have saved one. And it's a very good thing to save one, let me tell you: a penny saved, is a penny got!"

I believe Richard's was as frank and generous a nature as there possibly can be. He was ardent and brave, and, in the midst of all his wild restlessness, was so gentle, that I knew him like a brother in a few weeks. His gentleness was natural to him, and would have shown itself abundantly, even without Ada's influence; but, with it, he became one of the most winning of companions, always so ready to be interested, and always so happy, sanguine, and light-hearted. I am sure that I, sitting with them, and walking with them, and talking with them, and noticing from day to day how they went on, falling deeper and deeper in love, and saying nothing about it, and each shyly thinking that this love was the greatest of secrets, perhaps not yet suspected even by the other—I am sure that I was scarcely less enchanted than they were, and scarcely less pleased with the pretty dream.

We were going on in this way, when one morning at breakfast Mr. Jarndyce received a letter, and looking at the superscription said, "From Boythorn? Aye, aye!" and opened and read it with evident pleasure, announcing to us, in a parenthesis, when he was about half-way through, that Boythorn was "coming down" on a visit. Now, who was Boythorn? we all thought. And I dare say we all thought, too—I am sure I did, for one—would Boythorn at all interfere with what was going forward?

"I went to school with this fellow, Lawrence Boythorn," said Mr. Jarndyce, tapping the letter as he laid it on the table, "more than five-and-forty years ago. He was then the most impetuous boy in the world, and he is now the most impetuous man. He was then the loudest boy in the world, and he is now the loudest man. He was then the heartiest and sturdiest boy in the world, and he is now the heartiest and sturdiest man. He is a tremendous fellow."

"In stature, sir?" asked Richard.

"Pretty well, Rick, in that respect," said Mr. Jarndyce; "being some ten years older than I, and a couple of inches taller, with his head thrown back like an old soldier, his stalwart chest squared, his hands like a clean blacksmith's, and his lungs!—there's no simile for his lungs. Talking, laughing, or snoring, they make the beams of the house shake."

As Mr. Jarndyce sat enjoying the image of his friend Boythorn, we observed the favourable omen that there was not the least indication of any change in the wind.

"But it's the inside of the man, the warm heart of the man, the passion of the man, the fresh blood of the man, Rick—and Ada, and little Cobweb too, for you are all interested in a visitor!—that I speak of," he pursued. "His language is as sounding as his voice. He is always in extremes; perpetually in the superlative degree. In his condemnation he is all ferocity. You might suppose him to be an Ogre, from what he says; and I believe he has the reputation of one with some people. There! I tell you no more of him beforehand. You must not be surprised to see him take me under his protection; for he has never forgotten that I was a low boy at school, and that our friendship began in his knocking two of my head tyrant's teeth out (he says six) before breakfast. Boythorn and his man," to me, "will be here this afternoon, my dear."

I took care that the necessary preparations were made for Mr. Boythorn's reception, and we looked forward to his arrival with some curiosity. The afternoon wore away, however, and he did not appear. The dinner-hour arrived, and still he did not appear. The dinner was put back an hour, and we were sitting round the fire with no light but the blaze, when the hall-door suddenly burst open, and the hall resounded with these words, uttered with the greatest vehemence and in a stentorian tone:

"We have been misdirected, Jarndyce, by a most abandoned ruffian, who told us to take the turning to the right instead of to the left. He is the most intolerable scoundrel on the face of the earth. His father must have been a most consummate villain, ever to have had such a son. I would have that fellow shot without the least remorse!"

"Did he do it on purpose?" Mr. Jarndyce inquired.

"I have not the slightest doubt that the scoundrel has passed his whole existence in misdirecting travellers!" returned the other. "By my soul, I thought him the worst-looking dog I had ever beheld, when he was telling me to take the turning to the right. And yet I stood before that fellow face to face, and didn't knock his brains out!"

"Teeth, you mean?" said Mr. Jarndyce.

"Ha, ha, ha!" laughed Mr. Lawrence Boythorn, really making the whole house vibrate. "What, you have not forgotten it yet! Ha, ha, ha!—And that was another most consummate vagabond! By my soul, the countenance of that fellow, when he was a boy, was the blackest image of perfidy, cowardice, and cruelty ever set up as a scarecrow in a field of scoundrels. If I were to meet that most unparalleled despot in the streets to-morrow, I would fell him like a rotten tree!"

"I have no doubt of it," said Mr. Jarndyce. "Now, will you come up-stairs?"

"By my soul, Jarndyce," returned his guest, who seemed to refer to his watch, "if you had been married, I would have turned back at the garden-gate, and gone away to the remotest summits of the Himalaya Mountains, sooner than I would have presented myself at this unseasonable hour."

"Not quite so far, I hope?" said Mr. Jarndyce.

"By my life and honour, yes!" cried the visitor. "I wouldn't be guilty of the audacious insolence of keeping a lady of the house waiting all this time, for any earthly consideration. I would infinitely rather destroy myself—infinitely rather!"

Talking thus, they went up-stairs; and presently we heard him in his bedroom thundering "Ha, ha, ha!" and again "Ha, ha, ha!" until the flattest echo in the neighbourhood seemed to catch the contagion, and to laugh as enjoyingly as he did, or as we did when we heard him laugh.

We all conceived a prepossession in his favour; for there was a sterling quality in this laugh, and in his vigorous healthy voice, and in the roundness and fulness with which he uttered every word he spoke, and in the very fury of his superlatives, which seemed to go off like blank cannons and hurt nothing. But we were hardly prepared to have it so confirmed by his appearance, when Mr. Jarndyce presented him. He was not only a very handsome old gentleman—upright and stalwart as he had been described to us—with a massive grey head, a fine composure of face when silent, a figure that might have become corpulent but for his being so continually in earnest that he gave it no rest, and a chin that might have subsided into a double chin but for the vehement emphasis in which it was constantly required to assist; but he was such a true gentleman in his manner, so chivalrously polite, his face was lighted by a smile of so much sweetness and tenderness, and it seemed so plain that he had nothing to hide, but showed himself exactly as he was—incapable (as Richard said) of anything on a limited scale, and firing away with those blank great guns, because he carried no small arms whatever—that really I could not help looking at him with equal pleasure as he sat at dinner, whether he smilingly conversed with Ada and me, or was led by Mr. Jarndyce into some great volley of superlatives, or threw up his head like a blood-hound, and gave out that tremendous, Ha, ha, ha!

"You have brought your bird with you, I suppose?" said Mr. Jarndyce.

"By Heaven, he is the most astonishing bird in Europe!" replied the other. "He *is* the most wonderful creature! I wouldn't take ten thousand guineas for that bird. I have left an annuity for his sole support, in case he should outlive me. He is, in sense and attachment, a phenomenon. And his father before him was one of the most astonishing birds that ever lived!"

The subject of this laudation was a very little canary, who was so tame that he was brought down by Mr. Boythorn's man, on his forefinger, and, after taking a gentle flight round the room, alighted on his master's head. To hear Mr. Boythorn presently expressing the most implacable and passionate sentiments, with this fragile mite of a creature quietly perched on his forehead, was to have a good illustration of his character, I thought.

"By my soul, Jarndyce," he said, very gently holding up a bit of bread to the canary to peck at, "if I were in your place, I would seize every Master in Chancery by the throat to-morrow morning, and shake him until his money rolled out of his pockets, and his bones rattled in his skin. I would have a settlement out of somebody, by fair means or by foul. If you would empower me to do it, I would do it for you with the greatest satisfaction!" (All this time the very small canary was eating out of his hand.)

"I thank you, Lawrence, but the suit is hardly at such a point at present," returned Mr. Jarndyce, laughing, "that it would be greatly advanced, even by the legal process of shaking the Bench and the whole Bar."

"There never was such an infernal cauldron as that Chancery, on the face of the earth!" said Mr. Boythorn. "Nothing but a mine below it on a busy day in term time, with all its records, rules, and precedents collected in it, and every functionary belonging to it also, high and low, upward and downward, from its son the Accountant-General to its father the Devil, and the whole blown to atoms with ten thousand hundredweight of gunpowder, would reform it in the least!"

It was impossible not to laugh at the energetic gravity with which he recommended this strong measure of reform. When we laughed, he threw up his head, and shook his broad chest, and again the whole country seemed to echo to his Ha, ha, ha! It had not the least effect in disturbing the bird, whose sense of security was complete; and who hopped about the table with its quick head now on this side and now on that, turning its bright sudden eye on its master, as if he were no more than another bird.

"But how do you and your neighbour get on about the disputed right of way?" said Mr. Jarndyce. "You are not free from the toils of the law yourself!"

"The fellow has brought actions against *me* for trespass, and I have brought actions against *him* for trespass," returned Mr. Boythorn. "By Heaven, he is the proudest fellow breathing. It is morally impossible that his name can be Sir Leicester. It must be Sir Lucifer."

"Complimentary to our distant relation!" said my Guardian laughingly, to Ada and Richard.

"I would beg Miss Clare's pardon and Mr. Carstone's pardon," resumed our visitor, "if I were not reassured by seeing in the fair face of the lady, and the smile of the gentleman, that it is quite unnecessary, and that they keep their distant relation at a comfortable distance."

"Or he keeps us," suggested Richard.

"By my soul!" exclaimed Mr. Boythorn, suddenly firing another volley, "that fellow is, and his father was, and his grandfather was, the most stiff-necked, arrogant, imbecile, pig-headed numskull, ever, by some inexplicable mistake of Nature, born in any station of life but a walking-stick's! The whole of that family are the most solemnly conceited and consummate blockheads!—But it's no matter; he should not shut up my path if he were fifty baronets melted into one, and living in a hundred Chesney Wolds, one within another, like the ivory balls in a Chinese carving.[1] The fellow, by his agent, or secretary, or somebody, writes to me, 'Sir Leicester Dedlock, Baronet, presents his compliments to Mr. Lawrence Boythorn, and has to call his attention to the fact that the green pathway by the old parsonage-house, now the property of Mr. Lawrence Boythorn, is Sir Leicester's right of way, being in fact a portion of the park of Chesney Wold; and that Sir Leicester finds it convenient to close up the same.' I write to the fellow, 'Mr. Lawrence Boythorn presents his compliments to Sir Leicester Dedlock, Baronet, and has to call *his* attention to the fact that he totally denies the whole of Sir Leicester Dedlock's positions on every possible subject, and has to add, in reference to closing up the pathway, that he will be glad to see the man who may undertake to do it.' The fellow sends a most abandoned villain with one eye, to construct a gateway. I play upon that execrable scoundrel with a fire-engine, until the breath is nearly driven out of his body. The fellow erects a gate in the night. I chop it down and burn it in the morning. He sends his myrmidons to come over the fence, and pass and repass. I catch them in humane man traps, fire split peas at their legs, play upon them with the engine—resolve to free mankind from the insupportable burden of the existence of those lurking ruffians. He brings actions for trespass; I bring actions for trespass. He brings actions for assault and battery; I defend them, and continue to assault and batter. Ha, ha, ha!"

To hear him say all this with unimaginable energy, one might have thought him the angriest of mankind. To see him at the very same time, looking at the bird now perched upon his thumb, and softly smoothing its feathers with his forefinger, one might have thought him the gentlest. To hear him laugh, and see the broad good nature of his face then, one might have supposed that he had not a care in the world, or a dispute, or a dislike, but that his whole existence was a summer joke.

"No, no," he said, "no closing up of my paths, by any Dedlock! Though I willingly confess," here he softened in a moment, "that Lady Dedlock is the most accomplished lady in the world, to whom I would do any homage that a plain gentleman, and no baronet

1. Cf. Dickens' description of Chinese art in *Household Words* (July 5, 1851): "the laboriously-carved ivory balls of the flowery Empire, ball within ball and circle within circle, which have made no advance and been of no earthly use for thousands of years."

with a head seven hundred years thick, may. A man who joined his regiment at twenty, and, within a week, challenged the most imperious and presumptuous coxcomb of a commanding officer that ever drew the breath of life through a tight waist—and got broke for it[2]—is not the man to be walked over, by all the Sir Lucifers, dead or alive, locked or unlocked. Ha, ha, ha!"

"Nor the man to allow his junior to be walked over, either?" said my Guardian.

"Most assuredly not!" said Mr. Boythorn, clapping him on the shoulder with an air of protection, that had something serious in it, though he laughed. "He will stand by the low boy, always. Jarndyce, you may rely upon him! But, speaking of this trespass—with apologies to Miss Clare and Miss Summerson for the length at which I have pursued so dry a subject—is there nothing for me from your men, Kenge and Carboy?"

"I think not, Esther?" said Mr. Jarndyce.

"Nothing, Guardian."

"Much obliged!" said Mr. Boythorn. "Had no need to ask, after even my slight experience of Miss Summerson's forethought for every one about her." (They all encouraged me; they were determined to do it.) "I inquired because, coming from Lincolnshire, I of course have not yet been in town, and I thought some letters might have been sent down here. I dare say they will report progress to-morrow morning."

I saw him so often, in the course of the evening, which passed very pleasantly, contemplate Richard and Ada with an interest and a satisfaction that made his fine face remarkably agreeable as he sat at a little distance from the piano listening to the music—and he had small occasion to tell us that he was passionately fond of music, for his face showed it—that I asked my Guardian, as we sat at the backgammon board, whether Mr. Boythorn had ever been married.

"No," said he. "No."

"But he meant to be!" said I.

"How did you find out that?" he returned, with a smile.

"Why, Guardian," I exclaimed, not without reddening a little at hazarding what was in my thoughts, "there is something so tender in his manner, after all, and he is so very courtly and gentle to us, and——"

Mr. Jarndyce directed his eyes to where he was sitting, as I have just described him.

I said no more.

"You are right, little woman," he answered. "He was all but married, once. Long ago. And once."

"Did the lady die?"

2. Dismissed from his rank as an officer.

"No—but she died to him. That time has had its influence on all his later life. Would you suppose him to have a head and a heart full of romance yet?"

"I think, Guardian, I might have supposed so. But it is easy to say that, when you have told me so."

"He has never since been what he might have been," said Mr. Jarndyce, "and now you see him in his age with no one near him but his servant, and his little yellow friend.—It's your throw, my dear!"

I felt, from my Guardian's manner, that beyond this point I could not pursue the subject without changing the wind. I therefore forbore to ask any further questions. I was interested, but not curious. I thought a little while about this old love-story in the night, when I was awakened by Mr. Boythorn's lusty snoring; and I tried to do that very difficult thing, imagine old people young again, and invested with the graces of youth. But I fell asleep before I had succeeded, and dreamed of the days when I lived in my godmother's house. I am not sufficiently acquainted with such subjects to know whether it is at all remarkable that I almost always dreamed of that period of my life.

With the morning, there came a letter from Messrs. Kenge and Carboy to Mr. Boythorn, informing him that one of their clerks would wait upon him at noon. As it was the day of the week on which I paid the bills, and added up my books, and made all the household affairs as compact as possible, I remained at home while Mr. Jarndyce, Ada, and Richard, took advantage of a very fine day to make a little excursion. Mr. Boythorn was to wait for Kenge and Carboy's clerk, and then was to go on foot to meet them on their return.

Well! I was full of business, examining tradesmen's books, adding up columns, paying money, filing receipts, and I dare say making a great bustle about it, when Mr. Guppy was announced and shown in. I had had some idea that the clerk who was to be sent down, might be the young gentleman who had met me at the coach-office; and I was glad to see him, because he was associated with my present happiness.

I scarcely knew him again, he was so uncommonly smart. He had an entirely new suit of glossy clothes on, a shining hat, lilac-kid gloves, a neckerchief of a variety of colours, a large hot-house flower in his button-hole, and a thick gold ring on his little finger. Besides which, he quite scented the dining-room with bear's-grease and other perfumery. He looked at me with an attention that quite confused me, when I begged him to take a seat until the servant should return; and as he sat there, crossing and uncrossing his legs in a corner, and I asked him if he had had a pleasant ride, and hoped that Mr. Kenge was well, I never looked at him, but I found him looking at me, in the same scrutinising and curious way.

When the request was brought to him that he would go up-stairs to Mr. Boythorn's room, I mentioned that he would find lunch prepared for him when he came down, of which Mr. Jarndyce hoped he would partake. He said with some embarrassment, holding the handle of the door, "Shall I have the honour of finding you here, miss?" I replied yes, I should be there; and he went out with a bow and another look.

I thought him only awkward and shy, for he was evidently much embarrassed; and I fancied that the best thing I could do, would be to wait until I saw that he had everything he wanted, and then to leave him to himself. The lunch was soon brought, but it remained for some time on the table. The interview with Mr. Boythorn was a long one—and a stormy one too, I should think; for although his room was at some distance, I heard his loud voice every now and then like a high wind, and evidently blowing perfect broadsides of denunciation.

At last Mr. Guppy came back, looking something the worse for the conference. "My eye, miss," he said in a low voice, "he's a Tartar!"

"Pray take some refreshment, sir," said I.

Mr. Guppy sat down at the table, and began nervously sharpening the carving-knife on the carving-fork; still looking at me (as I felt quite sure without looking at him), in the same unusual manner. The sharpening lasted so long, that at last I felt a kind of obligation on me to raise my eyes, in order that I might break the spell under which he seemed to labour, of not being able to leave off.

He immediately looked at the dish, and began to carve.

"What will you take yourself, miss? You'll take a morsel of something?"

"No, thank you," said I.

"Shan't I give you a piece of anything at all, miss?" said Mr. Guppy, hurriedly drinking off a glass of wine.

"Nothing, thank you," said I. "I have only waited to see that you have everything you want. Is there anything I can order for you?"

"No, I am much obliged to you, miss, I'm sure. I've everything I can require to make me comfortable—at least I—not comfortable —I'm never that": he drank off two more glasses of wine, one after another.

I thought I had better go.

"I beg your pardon, miss!" said Mr. Guppy, rising , when he saw me rise. "But would you allow me the favour of a minute's private conversation?"

Not knowing what to say, I sat down again.

"What follows is without prejudice, miss?" said Mr. Guppy, anxiously, bringing a chair towards my table.

"I don't understand what you mean," said I, wondering.

"It's one of our law terms, miss. You won't make any use of it to my detriment, at Kenge and Carboy's, or elsewhere. If our conversation shouldn't lead to anything, I am to be as I was, and am not to be prejudiced in my situation or worldly prospects. In short, it's in total confidence."

"I am at a loss, sir," said I, "to imagine what you can have to communicate in total confidence to me, whom you have never seen but once; but I should be very sorry to do you any injury."

"Thank you, miss. I'm sure of it—that's quite sufficient." All this time Mr. Guppy was either planing his forehead with his handkerchief, or tightly rubbing the palm of his left hand with the palm of his right. "If you would excuse my taking another glass of wine, miss, I think it might assist me in getting on, without a continual choke that cannot fail to be mutually unpleasant."

He did so, and came back again. I took the opportunity of moving well behind my table.

"You wouldn't allow me to offer you one, would you, miss?" said Mr. Guppy, apparently refreshed.

"Not any," said I.

"Not half a glass?" said Mr. Guppy; "quarter? No! Then, to proceed. My present salary, Miss Summerson, at Kenge and Carboy's, is two pound a week. When I first had the happiness of looking upon you, it was one-fifteen, and had stood at that figure for a lengthened period. A rise of five has since taken place, and a further rise of five is guaranteed at the expiration of a term not exceeding twelve months from the present date. My mother has a little property, which takes the form of a small life annuity; upon which she lives in an independent though unassuming manner, in the Old Street Road. She is eminently calculated for a mother-in-law. She never interferes, is all for peace, and her disposition easy. She has her failings—as who has not?—but I never knew her do it when company was present; at which time you may freely trust her with wines, spirits, or malt liquors. My own abode is lodgings at Penton Place, Pentonville. It is lowly, but airy, open at the back, and considered one of the 'ealthiest outlets. Miss Summerson! In the mildest language, I adore you. Would you be so kind as to allow me (as I may say) to file a declaration—to make an offer!"

Mr. Guppy went down on his knees. I was well behind my table, and not much frightened. I said, "Get up from that ridiculous position immediately, sir, or you will oblige me to break my implied promise and ring the bell!"

"Hear me out, miss!" said Mr. Guppy, folding his hands.

"I cannot consent to hear another word, sir," I returned, "unless you get up from the carpet directly, and go and sit down at the table, as you ought to do if you have any sense at all."

He looked piteously, but slowly rose and did so.

"Yet what a mockery it is, miss," he said, with his hand upon his heart, and shaking his head at me in a melancholy manner over the tray, "to be stationed behind food at such a moment. The soul recoils from food at such a moment, miss."

"I beg you to conclude," said I; "you have asked me to hear you out, and I beg you to conclude."

"I will, miss," said Mr. Guppy. "As I love and honour, so likewise I obey.[3] Would that I could make Thee the subject of that vow, before the shrine!"

"That is quite impossible," said I, "and entirely out of the question."

"I am aware," said Mr. Guppy, leaning forward over the tray, and regarding me, as I again strangely felt, though my eyes were not directed to him, with his late intent look, "I am aware that in a worldly point of view, according to all appearances, my offer is a poor one. But, Miss Summerson! Angel!—No, don't ring—I have been brought up in a sharp school, and am accustomed to a variety of general practice. Though a young man, I have ferreted out evidence, got up cases, and seen lots of life. Blest with your hand, what means might I not find of advancing your interests, and pushing your fortunes! What might I not get to know, nearly concerning you? I know nothing now, certainly; but what *might* I not, if I had your confidence, and you set me on?"

I told him that he addressed my interest, or what he supposed to be my interest, quite as unsuccessfully as he addressed my inclination; and he would now understand that I requested him, if he pleased, to go away immediately.

"Cruel miss," said Mr. Guppy "hear but another word! I think you must have seen that I was struck with those charms, on the day when I waited at the Whytorseller. I think you must have remarked that I could not forbear a tribute to those charms when I put up the steps of the 'ackney-coach. It was a feeble tribute to Thee, but it was well meant. Thy image has ever since been fixed in my breast. I have walked up and down, of an evening, opposite Jellyby's house, only to look upon the bricks that once contained Thee. This out of to-day, quite an unnecessary out so far as the attendance, which was its pretended object, went, was planned by me alone for Thee alone. If I speak of interest, it is only to recommend myself and my respectful wretchedness. Love was before it, and is before it."

3. See the bride's vow in "The Order of Matrimony" in *The Book of Common Prayer*: "wilt thou obey him, and serve him, love, honour and keep him . . ."

"I should be pained, Mr. Guppy," said I, rising and putting my hand upon the bell-rope, "to do you, or any one who was sincere, the injustice of slighting any honest feeling, however disagreeably expressed. If you have really meant to give me a proof of your good opinion, though ill-timed and misplaced, I feel that I ought to thank you. I have very little reason to be proud, and I am not proud. I hope," I think I added, without very well knowing what I said, "that you will now go away as if you had never been so exceedingly foolish, and attend to Messrs. Kenge and Carboy's business."

"Half a minute, miss!" cried Mr. Guppy, checking me as I was about to ring. "This has been without prejudice?"

"I will never mention it," said I, "unless you should give me future occasion to do so."

"A quarter of a minute, miss! In case you should think better—at any time, however distant, *that's* no consequence, for my feelings can never alter—of anything I have said, particularly what might I not do—Mr. William Guppy, eighty-seven, Penton Place, or if removed, or dead (of blighted hopes or anything of that sort), care of Mrs. Guppy, three hundred and two, Old Street Road, will be sufficient."

I rang the bell, the servant came, and Mr. Guppy, laying his written card upon the table, and making a dejected bow, departed. Raising my eyes as he went out, I once more saw him looking at me after he had passed the door.

I sat there for another hour or more, finishing my books and payments, and getting through plenty of business. Then, I arranged my desk, and put everything away, and was so composed and cheerful that I thought I had quite dismissed this unexpected incident. But, when I went up-stairs to my own room, I surprised myself by beginning to laugh about it, and then surprised myself still more by beginning to cry about it. In short, I was in a flutter for a little while; and felt as if an old chord had been more coarsely touched than it ever had been since the days of the dear old doll, long buried in the garden.

Chapter X

THE LAW-WRITER

On the eastern borders of Chancery Lane, that is to say, more particularly in Cook's Court, Cursitor Street, Mr. Snagsby, Law-Stationer, pursues his lawful calling. In the shade of Cook's Court, at most times a shady place, Mr. Snagsby has dealt in all sorts of blank forms of legal process; in skins and rolls of parchment; in paper—foolscap, brief, draft, brown, white, whitey-brown, and blotting; in stamps; in office-quills, pens, ink, India-rubber, pounce, pins, pencils, sealing-wax, and wafers; in red tape and green ferret; in pocket-books, almanacks, diaries, and law lists; in string boxes, rulers, ink-stands—glass and leaden, penknives, scissors, bodkins, and other small office-cutlery;[1] in short, in articles too numerous to mention; ever since he was out of his time,[2] and went into partnership with Peffer. On that occasion, Cook's Court was in a manner revolutionised by the new inscription in fresh paint, Peffer and Snagsby, displacing the time-honoured and not easily to be deciphered legend, Peffer, only. For smoke, which is the London ivy, had so wreathed itself round Peffer's name, and clung to his dwelling-place, that the affectionate parasite quite overpowered the parent tree.

Peffer is never seen in Cook's Court now. He is not expected there, for he has been recumbent this quarter of a century in the churchyard of St. Andrew's, Holborn, with the waggons and hackney-coaches roaring past him, all the day and half the night, like one great dragon. If he ever steal forth when the dragon is at rest, to air himself again in Cook's Court, until admonished to return by the crowing of the sanguine cock in the cellar at the little dairy in Cursitor Street, whose ideas of daylight it would be curious to ascertain, since he knows from his personal observation next to nothing about it—if Peffer ever do revisit the pale glimpses of Cook's Court, which no law-stationer in the trade can positively deny, he comes invisibly, and no one is the worse or wiser.

In his lifetime, and likewise in the period of Snagsby's "time" of seven long years, there dwelt with Peffer, in the same law-stationering premises, a niece—a short, shrewd niece, something too violently compressed about the waist, and with a sharp nose like a sharp autumn evening, inclining to be frosty towards the end. The Cook's-Courtiers had a rumour flying among them, that the mother of this niece did, in her daughter's childhood, moved by too jealous a solicitude that her figure should approach perfection, lace her up every morning with her maternal foot against the bed-post for a stronger hold and purchase; and further, that she exhibited internally pints of vinegar and lemon-juice; which acids, they held, had mounted to the nose and temper of the patient. With whichsoever of the many tongues of Rumour this frothy report originated, it either never reached, or never influenced, the ears of young Snagsby; who, having wooed and won its fair subject on his arrival at man's estate, entered into two partnerships at once. So now, in Cook's Court, Cursitor Street, Mr. Snagsby and the niece are one; and the niece still cherishes her figure—which, however tastes may

1. ***Pounce***: a fine pumice-stone powder sprinkled on parchment or paper to prevent ink blots. ***Wafers***: paper discs used as seals for documents or letters. ***Ferret***: silk tape used on legal documents. ***Bodkins:*** small pointed tools for piercing holes.

2. Since completing his apprenticeship as a law-stationer.

differ, is unquestionably so far precious, that there is mighty little of it.

Mr. and Mrs. Snagsby are not only one bone and one flesh but, to the neighbours' thinking, one voice too. That voice, appearing to proceed from Mrs. Snagsby alone, is heard in Cook's Court very often. Mr. Snagsby, otherwise than as he finds expression through these dulcet tones, is rarely heard. He is a mild, bald, timid man, with a shining head, and a scrubby clump of black hair sticking out at the back. He tends to meekness and obesity. As he stands at his door in Cook's Court, in his grey shop-coat and black calico sleeves, looking up at the clouds; or stands behind a desk in his dark shop, with a heavy flat ruler, snipping and slicing at sheepskin, in company with his two 'prentices; he is emphatically a retiring and unassuming man. From beneath his feet, at such times, as from a shrill ghost unquiet in its grave, there frequently arise complainings and lamentations in the voice already mentioned; and haply, on some occasions, when these reach a sharper pitch than usual, Mr. Snagsby mentions to the 'prentices, "I think my little woman is a-giving it to Guster!"

This proper name, so used by Mr. Snagsby, has before now sharpened the wit of the Cook's-Courtiers to remark that it ought to be the name of Mrs. Snagsby; seeing that she might with great force and expression be termed a Guster, in compliment to her stormy character. It is, however, the possession, and the only possession, except fifty shillings per annum and a very small box indifferently filled with clothing, of a lean young woman from a workhouse (by some supposed to have been christened Augusta); who, although she was farmed or contracted for, during her growing time, by an amiable benefactor of his species resident at Tooting,[3] and cannot fail to have been developed under the most favourable circumstances, "has fits"—which the parish can't account for.

Guster, really aged three or four and twenty, but looking a round ten years older, goes cheap with this unaccountable drawback of fits; and is so apprehensive of being returned on the hands of her patron saint, that except when she is found with her head in the pail, or the sink, or the copper,[4] or the dinner, or anything else that happens to be near her at the time of her seizure, she is always at work. She is a satisfaction to the parents and guardians of the 'prentices, who feel that there is little danger of her inspiring tender emotions in the breast of youth; she is a satisfaction to Mrs.

3. Site of an orphanage-farm south of London where children were boarded for a small fee paid by their parishes. The establishment was notorious for its maltreatment of the inmates, who suffered from overcrowding and lack of food and sanitation. In 1849 a severe outbreak of cholera, in which 150 children died, led to criminal charges being brought against the proprietor, Drouet, the "amiable benefactor of his species."

4. Large pot used for cooking or for boiling laundry.

Snagsby, who can always find fault with her; she is a satisfaction to Mr. Snagsby, who thinks it a charity to keep her. The law-stationer's establishment is, in Guster's eyes, a Temple of plenty and splendour. She believes the little drawing-room up-stairs, always kept, as one may say, with its hair in papers and its pinafore on, to be the most elegant apartment in Christendom. The view it commands of Cook's Court at one end (not to mention a squint into Cursitor Street), and of Coavinses' the sheriff's officer's backyard at the other, she regards as a prospect of unequalled beauty. The portraits it displays in oil—and plenty of it too—of Mr. Snagsby looking at Mrs. Snagsby and of Mrs. Snagsby looking at Mr. Snagsby, are in her eyes as achievements of Raphael or Titian. Guster has some recompenses for her many privations.

Mr. Snagsby refers everything not in the practical mysteries of the business to Mrs. Snagsby. She manages the money, reproaches the Tax-gatherers, appoints the times and places of devotion on Sundays, licenses Mr. Snagsby's entertainments, and acknowledges no responsibility as to what she thinks fit to provide for dinner; insomuch that she is the high standard of comparison among the neighbouring wives, a long way down Chancery Lane on both sides, and even out in Holborn, who, in any domestic passages of arms, habitually call upon their husbands to look at the difference between their (the wives') position and Mrs. Snagsby's, and their (the husbands') behaviour and Mr. Snagsby's. Rumour, always flying, bat-like, about Cook's Court, and skimming in and out at everybody's windows, does say that Mrs. Snagsby is jealous and inquisitive; and that Mr. Snagsby is sometimes worried out of house and home, and that if he had the spirit of a mouse he wouldn't stand it. It is even observed, that the wives who quote him to their self-willed husbands as a shining example, in reality look down upon him; and that nobody does so with greater superciliousness than one particular lady, whose lord is more than suspected of laying his umbrella on her as an instrument of correction. But these vague whisperings may arise from Mr. Snagsby's being, in his way, rather a meditative and poetical man; loving to walk in Staple Inn in the summer time, and to observe how countrified the sparrows and the leaves are; also to lounge about the Rolls Yard[5] of a Sunday afternoon, and to remark (if in good spirits) that there were old times once, and that you'd find a stone coffin or two, now, under that chapel, he'll be bound, if you was to dig for it. He solaces his imagination, too, by thinking of the many Chancellors and Vices, and Masters of the Rolls, who are deceased; and he gets such a flavour of the country out of telling the two 'prentices how he *has* heard

5. Courtyard adjacent to the Rolls' House and its chapel off Chancery Lane, where Chancery records (originally written on rolls) had been stored since 1377.

say that a brook "as clear as crystial"[6] once ran right down the middle of Holborn, when Turnstile really was a turnstile,[7] leading slap away into the meadows—gets such a flavour of the country out of this, that he never wants to go there.

The day is closing in and the gas is lighted, but is not yet fully effective, for it is not quite dark. Mr. Snagsby standing at his shop-door looking up at the clouds, sees a crow, who is out late, skim westward over the leaden slice of sky belonging to Cook's Court. The crow flies straight across Chancery Lane and Lincoln's Inn Garden, into Lincoln's Inn Fields.

Here, in a large house, formerly a house of state, lives Mr. Tulkinghorn. It is let off in sets of chambers now; and in those shrunken fragments of its greatness, lawyers lie like maggots in nuts. But its roomy staircases, passages, and antechambers still remain; and even its painted ceilings, where Allegory, in Roman helmet and celestial linen, sprawls among balustrades and pillars, flowers, clouds, and big-legged boys, and makes the head ache—as would seem to be Allegory's object always, more or less.[8] Here, among his many boxes labelled with transcendent names, lives Mr. Tulkinghorn, when not speechlessly at home in country-houses where the great ones of the earth are bored to death. Here he is to-day, quiet at his table. An Oyster of the old school, whom nobody can open.

Like as he is to look at, so is his apartment in the dusk of the present afternoon. Rusty, out of date, withdrawing from attention, able to afford it. Heavy broad-backed old-fashioned mahogany and horsehair chairs, not easily lifted, obsolete tables with spindle-legs and dusty baize covers, presentation prints of the holders of great titles in the last generation, or the last but one, environ him. A thick and dingy Turkey-carpet muffles the floor where he sits, attended by two candles in old-fashioned silver candlesticks, that give a very insufficient light to his large room. The titles on the backs of his books have retired into the binding; everything that can have a lock has got one; no key is visible. Very few loose papers are about. He has some manuscript near him, but is not referring to it. With the round top of an inkstand, and two broken bits of sealing-wax, he is silently and slowly working out whatever train of indeci-

6. See Revelation 22:1: "And he shewed me a pure river of water of life, clear as crystal; proceeding out of the throne of God."

7. *Holborn*: a street named after a brook (bourne), which formerly ran through it. A chronicle of 1502 records that the brook "broke out of the ground . . . and ran down the whole street till the Old-bourne bridge." It was later covered over by the street and converted into a sewer flowing into the Fleet River. *Turnstile*: a street in what had become a highly built-up section of London. In earlier times it was a footpath leading into Lincoln's Inn Fields through a turnstile installed to prevent sheep from straying into the city.

8. Early eighteenth-century painted ceilings featured scenes of personified abstractions such as Virtue or Charity. The figure of Allegory, with his pointing finger suggesting lessons to be learned from him (see Chapters XVI, XXII, XLVIII), is dressed in Roman costume in accord with Neo-Classical fashions in vogue at the time the mansion had been a "house of state."

sion is in his mind. Now, the inkstand top is in the middle: now, the red bit of sealing-wax, now the black bit. That's not it. Mr. Tulkinghorn must gather them all up and begin again.

Here, beneath the painted ceiling, with foreshortened Allegory staring down at his intrusion as if it meant to swoop upon him, and he cutting it dead, Mr. Tulkinghorn has at once his house and office. He keeps no staff; only one middle-aged man, usually a little out at elbows, who sits in a high Pew in the hall, and is rarely over-burdened with business. Mr. Tulkinghorn is not in a common way. He wants no clerks. He is a great reservoir of confidences, not to be so tapped. His clients want *him*; he is all in all. Drafts that he requires to be drawn, are drawn by special-pleaders in the Temple on mysterious instructions; fair copies that he requires to be made, are made at the stationer's, expense being no consideration. The middle-aged man in the Pew, knows scarcely more of the affairs of the Peerage, than any crossing-sweeper in Holborn.

The red bit, the black bit, the inkstand top, the other inkstand top, the little sand-box.[9] So! You to the middle, you to the right, you to the left. This train of indecision must surely be worked out now or never.—Now! Mr. Tulkinghorn gets up, adjusts his spectacles, puts on his hat, puts the manuscript in his pocket, goes out, tells the middle-aged man out at elbows, "I shall be back presently." Very rarely tells him anything more explicit.

Mr. Tulkinghorn goes, as the crow came—not quite so straight, but nearly—to Cook's Court, Cursitor Street. To Snagsby's, Law-Stationer's, Deeds engrossed and copied, Law-Writing executed in all its branches, &c., &c., &c.

It is somewhere about five or six o'clock in the afternoon, and a balmy fragrance of warm tea hovers in Cook's Court. It hovers about Snagsby's door. The hours are early there; dinner at half-past one, and supper at half-past nine. Mr. Snagsby was about to descend into the subterranean regions to take tea, when he looked out of his door just now, and saw the crow who was out late.

"Master at home?"

Guster is minding the shop, for the 'prentices take tea in the kitchen, with Mr. and Mrs. Snagsby; consequently, the robe-maker's two daughters, combing their curls at the two glasses in the two second-floor windows of the opposite house, are not driving the two 'prentices to distraction, as they fondly suppose, but are merely awakening the unprofitable admiration of Guster, whose hair won't grow, and never would, and, it is confidently thought, never will.

"Master at home?" says Mr. Tulkinghorn.

Master is at home, and Guster will fetch him. Guster disappears, glad to get out of the shop, which she regards with mingled dread

9. Sand was sprinkled on writing-paper for purposes of blotting.

and veneration as a storehouse of awful implements of the great torture of the law: a place not to be entered after the gas is turned off.

Mr. Snagsby appears: greasy, warm, herbaceous, and chewing. Bolts a bit of bread and butter. Says, "Bless my soul, sir! Mr. Tulkinghorn!"

"I want half a word with you, Snagsby."

"Certainly, sir! Dear me, sir, why didn't you send your young man round for me? Pray walk into the back shop, sir." Snagsby has brightened in a moment.

The confined room, strong of parchment-grease, is warehouse, counting-house, and copying-office. Mr. Tulkinghorn sits, facing round, on a stool at the desk.

"Jarndyce and Jarndyce, Snagsby."

"Yes, sir." Mr. Snagsby turns up the gas, and coughs behind his hand, modestly anticipating profit. Mr. Snagsby, as a timid man, is accustomed to cough with a variety of expressions, and so to save words.

"You copied some affidavits in that cause for me lately."

"Yes, sir, we did."

"There was one of them," says Mr. Tulkinghorn, carelessly feeling—tight, unopenable Oyster of the old school!—in the wrong coat-pocket, "the handwriting of which is peculiar, and I rather like. As I happened to be passing, and thought I had it about me, I looked in to ask you—but I haven't got it. No matter, any other time will do—Ah! here it is!—I looked in to ask you who copied this?"

"Who copied this, sir?" says Mr. Snagsby, taking it, laying it flat on the desk, and separating all the sheets at once with a twirl and a twist of the left hand peculiar to law-stationers. "We gave this out, sir. We were giving out rather a large quantity of work just at that time. I can tell you in a moment who copied it, sir, by referring to my Book."

Mr. Snagsby takes his Book down from the safe, makes another bolt of the bit of bread and butter which seems to have stopped short, eyes the affidavit aside, and brings his right forefinger travelling down a page of the Book. "Jewby—Packer—Jarndyce."

"Jarndyce! Here we are, sir," says Mr. Snagsby. "To be sure! I might have remembered it. This was given out, sir, to a Writer who lodges just over on the opposite side of the lane."

Mr. Tulkinghorn has seen the entry, found it before the Law-stationer, read it while the forefinger was coming down the hill.

"*What* do you call him? Nemo?" says Mr. Tulkinghorn.

"Nemo, sir. Here it is. Forty-two folio. Given out on the Wednesday night, at eight o'clock; brought in on the Thursday morning, at half after nine."

"Nemo!" repeats Mr. Tulkinghorn. "Nemo is Latin for no one."

"It must be English for some one, sir, I think," Mr. Snagsby submits, with his deferential cough. That's the person's name. Here it is, you see, sir! Forty-two folio.[1] Given out Wednesday night, eight o'clock; brought in Thursday morning, half after nine."

The tail of Mr. Snagsby's eye becomes conscious of the head of Mrs. Snagsby looking in at the shop-door to know what he means by deserting his tea. Mr. Snagsby addresses an explanatory cough to Mrs. Snagsby, as who should say, "My dear, a customer!"

"Half after nine, sir," repeats Mr. Snagsby. "Our law-writers, who live by job-work, are a queer lot; and this may not be his name, but it's the name he goes by. I remember now, sir, that he gives it in a written advertisement he sticks up down at the Rule Office, and the King's Bench Office, and the Judges' Chambers, and so forth. You know the kind of document, sir—wanting employ?"

Mr. Tulkinghorn glances through the little window at the back of Coavinses', the sheriff's officer's, where lights shine in Coavinses' windows. Coavinses' coffee-room is at the back, and the shadows of several gentlemen under a cloud loom cloudily upon the blinds. Mr. Snagsby takes the opportunity of slightly turning his head, to glance over his shoulder at his little woman, and to make apologetic motions with his mouth to this effect: "Tul-king-horn—rich—in-flu-en-tial!"

"Have you given this man work before?" asks Mr. Tulkinghorn.

"O dear, yes, sir! Work of yours."

"Thinking of more important matters, I forget where you said he lived?"

"Across the lane, sir. In fact he lodges at a—" Mr. Snagsby makes another bolt, as if the bit of bread and butter were insurmountable—"at a rag and bottle shop."

"Can you show me the place as I go back?"

"With the greatest pleasure, sir!"

Mr. Snagsby pulls off his sleeves and his grey coat, pulls on his black coat, takes his hat from its peg. "Oh! here is my little woman!" he says aloud. "My dear, will you be so kind as to tell one of the lads to look after the shop, while I step across the lane with Mr. Tulkinghorn? Mrs. Snagsby, sir—I shan't be two minutes, my love!"

Mrs. Snagsby bends to the lawyer, retires behind the counter, peeps at them through the window-blind, goes softly into the back office, refers to the entries in the book still lying open. Is evidently curious.

"You will find that the place is rough, sir," says Mr. Snagsby, walking deferentially in the road, and leaving the narrow pavement

1. *Folio* refers to a quantity of words to be copied rather than to the size of a page. A *Chancery folio* consisted of ninety words. *Forty-two folio* would thus be 3,780 words of manuscript.

to the lawyer; "and the party is very rough. But they're a wild lot in general, sir. The advantage of this particular man is, that he never wants sleep. He'll go at it right on end, if you want him to, as long as ever you like."

It is quite dark now, and the gas-lamps have acquired their full effect. Jostling against clerks going to post the day's letters, and against counsel and attorneys going home to dinner, and against plaintiffs and defendants, and suitors of all sorts, and against the general crowd, in whose way the forensic wisdom of ages has interposed a million of obstacles to the transaction of the commonest business of life—diving through law and equity, and through that kindred mystery, the street mud, which is made of nobody knows what, and collects about us nobody knows whence or how: we only knowing in general that when there is too much of it, we find it necessary to shovel it away—the lawyer and the law-stationer come to a Rag and Bottle shop, and general emporium of much disregarded merchandise, lying and being in the shadow of the wall of Lincoln's Inn, and kept, as is announced in paint, to all whom it may concern, by one Krook.

"This is where he lives, sir," says the law-stationer.

"This is where he lives, is it?" says the lawyer unconcernedly. "Thank you."

"Are you not going in, sir?"

"No, thank you, no; I am going on to the Fields at present. Good evening. Thank you!" Mr. Snagsby lifts his hat, and returns to his little woman and his tea.

But Mr. Tulkinghorn does not go on to the Fields at present. He goes a short way, turns back, comes again to the shop of Mr. Krook, and enters it straight. It is dim enough, with a blot-headed candle or so in the windows, and an old man and a cat sitting in the back part by a fire. The old man rises and comes forward, with another blot-headed candle[2] in his hand.

"Pray is your lodger within?"

"Male or female, sir?" says Mr. Krook.

"Male. The person who does copying."

Mr. Krook has eyed his man narrowly. Knows him by sight. Has an indistinct impression of his aristocratic repute.

"Did you wish to see him, sir?"

"Yes."

"It's what I seldom do myself," says Mr. Krook, with a grin. "Shall I call him down? But it's a weak chance if he'd come, sir!"

"I'll go up to him, then," says Mr. Tulkinghorn.

"Second floor, sir. Take the candle. Up there!" Mr. Krook, with his cat beside him, stands at the bottom of the staircase, looking

2. Unidentified but perhaps (like *cabbage head*, p. 396) a candle which has a large lump of charred soot at the end of its untrimmed wick.

after Mr. Tulkinghorn. "Hi—hi!" he says, when Mr. Tulkinghorn has nearly disappeared. The lawyer looks down over the hand-rail. The cat expands her wicked mouth, and snarls at him.

"Order, Lady Jane! Behave yourself to visitors, my lady! You know what they say of my lodger?" whispers Krook, going up a step or two.

"What do they say of him?"

"They say he has sold himself to the Enemy; but you and I know better—he don't buy. I'll tell you what, though; my lodger is so black-humoured and gloomy, that I believe he'd as soon make that bargain as any other. Don't put him out, sir. That's my advice!"

Mr. Tulkinghorn with a nod goes on his way. He comes to the dark door on the second floor. He knocks, receives no answer, opens it, and accidentally extinguishes his candle in doing so.

The air of the room is almost bad enough to have extinguished it, if he had not. It is a small room, nearly black with soot, and grease, and dirt. In the rusty skeleton of a grate, pinched at the middle as if Poverty had gripped it, a red coke fire burns low. In the corner by the chimney, stand a deal table and a broken desk; a wilderness marked with a rain of ink. In another corner, a ragged old portmanteau on one of the two chairs, serves for cabinet or wardrobe; no larger one is needed, for it collapses like the cheeks of a starved man. The floor is bare; except that one old mat, trodden to shreds of rope-yarn, lies perishing upon the hearth. No curtain veils the darkness of the night, but the discoloured shutters are drawn together; and through the two gaunt holes pierced in them, famine might be staring in—the Banshee[3] of the man upon the bed.

For, on a low bed opposite the fire, a confusion of dirty patchwork, lean-ribbed ticking, and coarse sacking, the lawyer, hesitating just within the doorway, sees a man. He lies there, dressed in shirt and trousers, with bare feet. He has a yellow look in the spectral darkness of a candle that has guttered down, until the whole length of its wick (still burning) has doubled over, and left a tower of winding-sheet[4] above it. His hair is ragged, mingling with his whiskers and his beard—the latter, ragged too, and grown, like the scum and mist around him, in neglect. Foul and filthy as the room is, foul and filthy as the air, it is not easy to perceive what fumes those are which most oppress the senses in it; but through the general sickness and faintness, and the odour of stale tobacco, there comes into the lawyer's mouth the bitter, vapid taste of opium.

"Hallo, my friend!" he cries, and strikes his iron candlestick against the door.

3. "A supernatural being supposed by the peasantry of Ireland and the Scottish Highlands to wail under the windows of a house where one of the inmates is about to die." (*NED*)

4. "A mass of solidified drippings of grease clinging to the side of a candle, resembling a sheet folded in creases, and regarded in popular superstition as an omen of death." (*NED*)

He thinks he has awakened his friend. He lies a little turned away, but his eyes are surely open.

"Hallo, my friend!" he cries again. "Hallo! Hallo!"

As he rattles on the door, the candle which has drooped so long, goes out, and leaves him in the dark; with the gaunt eyes in the shutters staring down upon the bed.

Chapter XI

OUR DEAR BROTHER

A touch on the lawyer's wrinkled hand, as he stands in the dark room, irresolute, makes him start and say, "What's that?"

"It's me," returns the old man of the house, whose breath is in his ear. "Can't you wake him?"

"No."

"What have you done with your candle?"

"It's gone out. Here it is."

Krook takes it, goes to the fire, stoops over the red embers, and tries to get a light. The dying ashes have no light to spare, and his endeavours are vain. Muttering after an ineffectual call to his lodger, that he will go down-stairs and bring a lighted candle from the shop, the old man departs. Mr. Tulkinghorn, for some new reason that he has, does not await his return in the room, but on the stairs outside.

The welcome light soon shines upon the wall, as Krook comes slowly up, with his green-eyed cat following at his heels. "Does the man generally sleep like this?" inquires the lawyer, in a low voice. "Hi! I don't know," says Krook, shaking his head and lifting his eyebrows. "I know next to nothing of his habits, except that he keeps himself very close."

Thus whispering, they both go in together. As the light goes in, the great eyes in the shutters, darkening, seem to close. Not so the eyes upon the bed.

"God save us!" exclaims Mr. Tulkinghorn. "He is dead!"

Krook drops the heavy hand he has taken up, so suddenly that the arm swings over the bedside.

They look at one another for a moment.

"Send for some doctor! Call for Miss Flite up the stairs, sir. Here's poison by the bed! Call out for Flite, will you?" says Krook, with his lean hands spread out above the body like a vampire's wings.

Mr. Tulkinghorn hurries to the landing, and calls "Miss Flite! Flite! Make haste, here, whoever you are! Flite!" Krook follows him with his eyes, and, while he is calling, finds opportunity to steal to the old portmanteau, and steal back again.

"Run, Flite, run! The nearest doctor! Run!" So Mr. Krook addresses a crazy little woman, who is his female lodger: who appears and vanishes in a breath; who soon returns, accompanied by a testy medical man, brought from his dinner—with a broad snuffy upper lip, and a broad Scotch tongue.

"Ey! Bless the hearts o' ye," says the medical man, looking up at them after a moment's examination. "He's just as dead as Phairy!"[1]

Mr. Tulkinghorn (standing by the old portmanteau) inquires if he has been dead any time?

"Any time, sir?" says the medical gentleman. "It's probable he wull have been dead aboot three hours."

"About that time, I should say," observes a dark young man, on the other side of the bed.

"Air you in the maydickle prayfession yourself, sir?" inquires the first.

The dark young man says yes.

"Then I'll just tak' my depairture," replies the other; "for I'm nae gude here!" With which remark he finishes his brief attendance, and returns to finish his dinner.

The dark young surgeon passes the candle across and across the face, and carefully examines the law-writer, who has established his pretensions to his name by becoming indeed No one.

"I knew this person by sight, very well," says he. "He has purchased opium of me for the last year and a half. Was anybody present related to him?" glancing round upon the three bystanders.

"I was his landlord," grimly answers Krook, taking the candle from the surgeon's outstretched hand. "He told me once, I was the nearest relation he had."

"He has died," says the surgeon, "of an over-dose of opium, there is no doubt. The room is strongly flavoured with it. There is enough here now," taking an old teapot from Mr. Krook, "to kill a dozen people."

"Do you think he did it on purpose?" asks Krook.

"Took the over-dose?"

"Yes!" Krook almost smacks his lips with the unction of a horrible interest.

"I can't say. I should think it unlikely, as he has been in the habit of taking so much. But nobody can tell. He was very poor, I suppose?"

"I suppose he was. His room—don't look rich," says Krook, who might have changed eyes with his cat, as he casts his sharp glance around. "But I have never been in it since he had it, and he was too close to name his circumstarnces to me."

"Did he owe you any rent?"

"Six weeks."

1. As dead as Pharaoh.

"He will never pay it!" says the young man, resuming his examination. "It is beyond a doubt that he is indeed as dead as Pharaoh; and to judge from his appearance and condition, I should think it a happy release. Yet he must have been a good figure when a youth, and I dare say, good-looking." He says this, not unfeelingly, while sitting on the bedstead's edge, with his face towards that other face, and his hand upon the region of the heart. "I recollect once thinking there was something in his manner, uncouth as it was, that denoted a fall in life. Was that so?" he continues, looking round.

Krook replies, "You might as well ask me to describe the ladies whose heads of hair I have got in sacks down-stairs. Than that he was my lodger for a year and a half, and lived—or didn't live—by law-writing, I know no more of him."

During this dialogue, Mr. Tulkinghorn has stood aloof by the old portmanteau, with his hands behind him, equally removed, to all appearance, from all three kinds of interest exhibited near the bed—from the young surgeon's professional interest in death, noticeable as being quite apart from his remarks on the deceased as an individual; from the old man's unction; and the little crazy woman's awe. His imperturbable face has been as inexpressive as his rusty clothes. One could not even say he has been thinking all this while. He has shown neither patience nor impatience, nor attention nor abstraction. He has shown nothing but his shell. As easily might the tone of a delicate musical instrument be inferred from its case, as the tone of Mr. Tulkinghorn from *his* case.

He now interposes; addressing the young surgeon, in his unmoved, professional way.

"I looked in here," he observes, "just before you, with the intention of giving this deceased man, whom I never saw alive, some employment at his trade of copying. I had heard of him from my stationer—Snagsby of Cook's Court. Since no one here knows anything about him, it might be as well to send for Snagsby. Ah!" to the little crazy woman, who has often seen him in Court, and whom he has often seen, and who proposes, in frightened dumb-show, to go for the law-stationer. "Suppose you do!"

While she is gone, the surgeon abandons his hopeless investigation, and covers its subject with the patchwork counterpane. Mr. Krook and he interchange a word or two. Mr. Tulkinghorn says nothing; but stands, ever, near the old portmanteau.

Mr. Snagsby arrives hastily in his grey coat and his black sleeves. "Dear me, dear me," he says; "and it has come to this, has it! Bless my soul!"

"Can you give the person of the house any information about this unfortunate creature, Snagsby?" inquires Mr. Tulkinghorn. "He was in arrears with his rent, it seems. And he must be buried, you know."

"Well, sir," says Mr. Snagsby, coughing his apologetic cough behind his hand; "I really don't know what advice I could offer, except sending for the beadle."

"I don't speak of advice," returns Mr. Tulkinghorn. "*I* could advise——"

("No one better, sir, I am sure," says Mr. Snagsby, with his deferential cough.)

"I speak of affording some clue to his connexions, or to where he came from, or to anything concerning him."

"I assure you, sir," says Mr. Snagsby, after prefacing his reply with his cough of general propitiation, "that I no more know where he came from than I know——"

"Where he has gone to, perhaps," suggests the surgeon, to help him out.

A pause. Mr. Tulkinghorn looking at the law-stationer. Mr. Krook, with his mouth open, looking for somebody to speak next.

"As to his connexions, sir," says Mr. Snagsby, "if a person was to say to me, 'Snagsby, here's twenty thousand pound down, ready for you in the Bank of England, if you'll only name one of 'em,' I couldn't do it, sir! About a year and a half ago—to the best of my belief at the time when he first came to lodge at the present rag and bottle shop——"

"That was the time!" says Krook, with a nod.

"About a year and a half ago," says Mr. Snagsby, strengthened, "he came into our place one morning after breakfast, and finding my little woman (which I name Mrs. Snagsby when I use that appellation) in our shop, produced a specimen of his handwriting, and gave her to understand that he was in wants of copying work to do, and was—not to put too fine a point upon it—" a favourite apology for plain-speaking with Mr. Snagsby, which he always offers with a sort of argumentative frankness, "hard up! My little woman is not in general partial to strangers, particular—not to put too fine a point upon it—when they want anything. But she was rather took by something about this person; whether by his being unshaved, or by his hair being in want of attention, or by what other ladies' reasons, I leave you to judge; and she accepted of the specimen, and likewise of the address. My little woman hasn't a good ear for names," proceeds Mr. Snagsby, after consulting his cough of consideration behind his hand, "and she considered Nemo equally the same as Nimrod. In consequence of which, she got into the habit of saying to me at meals, 'Mr. Snagsby, you haven't found Nimrod any work yet!' or 'Mr. Snagsby, why didn't you give that eight-and-thirty Chancery folio[2] in Jarndyce, to Nimrod?' or such like. And that is the way he gradually fell into job-work at

2. See p. 122, note 1.

our place; and that is the most I know of him, except that he was a quick hand, and a hand not sparing of night-work; and that if you gave him out, say five-and-forty folio on the Wednesday night, you would have it brought in on the Thursday morning. All of which—" Mr. Snagsby concludes by politely motioning with his hat towards the bed, as much as to add, "I have no doubt my honourable friend would confirm, if he were in a condition to do it."

"Hadn't you better see," says Mr. Tulkinghorn to Krook, "whether he had any papers that may enlighten you? There will be an Inquest, and you will be asked the question. You can read?"

"No, I can't," returns the old man, with a sudden grin.

"Snagsby," says Mr. Tulkinghorn, "look over the room for him. He will get into some trouble or difficulty, otherwise. Being here, I'll wait, if you make haste; and then I can testify on his behalf, if it should ever be necessary, that all was fair and right. If you will hold the candle for Mr. Snagsby, my friend, he'll soon see whether there is anything to help you."

"In the first place, here's an old portmanteau, sir," says Snagsby.

Ah, to be sure, so there is! Mr. Tulkinghorn does not appear to have seen it before, though he is standing so close to it, and though there is very little else, Heavens knows.

The marine-store merchant holds the light, and the law-stationer conducts the search. The surgeon leans against the corner of the chimney-piece; Miss Flite peeps and trembles just within the door. The apt old scholar of the old school, with his dull black breeches tied with ribbons at the knees, his large black waistcoat, his long-sleeved black coat, and his wisp of limp white neckerchief tied in the bow the Peerage knows so well, stands in exactly the same place and attitude.

There are some worthless articles of clothing in the old portmanteau; there is a bundle of pawnbrokers' duplicates, those turnpike tickets on the road of Poverty; there is a crumpled paper, smelling of opium, on which are scrawled rough memoranda—as, took, such a day, so many grains; took, such another day, so many more—begun some time ago, as if with the intention of being regularly continued, but soon left off. There are a few dirty scraps of newspapers, all referring to Coroners' Inquests; there is nothing else. They search the cupboard, and the drawer of the ink-splashed table. There is not a morsel of an old letter, or of any other writing, in either. The young surgeon examines the dress on the law-writer. A knife and some odd halfpence are all he finds. Mr. Snagsby's suggestion is the practical suggestion after all, and the beadle must be called in.

So the little crazy lodger goes for the beadle, and the rest come out of the room. "Don't leave the cat there!" says the surgeon;

"that won't do!" Mr. Krook therefore drives her out before him; and she goes furtively down-stairs, winding her lithe tail and licking her lips.

"Good night!" says Mr. Tulkinghorn; and goes home to Allegory and meditation.

By this time the news has got into the court. Groups of its inhabitants assemble to discuss the thing; and the outposts of the army of observation (principally boys) are pushed forward to Mr. Krook's window, which they closely invest. A policeman has already walked up to the room, and walked down again to the door, where he stands like a tower, only condescending to see the boys at his base occasionally; but whenever he does see them, they quail and fall back. Mrs. Perkins, who has not been for some weeks on speaking terms with Mrs. Piper, in consequence of an unpleasantness originating in young Perkins having "fetched" young Piper "a crack," renews her friendly intercourse on this auspicious occasion. The potboy[3] at the corner, who is a privileged amateur, as possessing official knowledge of life, and having to deal with drunken men occasionally, exchanges confidential communications with the policeman, and has the appearance of an impregnable youth, unassailable by truncheons and unconfinable in station-houses. People talk across the court out of window, and bare-headed scouts come hurrying in from Chancery Lane to know what's the matter. The general feeling seems to be that it's a blessing Mr. Krook warn't made away with first, mingled with a little natural disappointment that he was not. In the midst of this sensation, the beadle arrives.

The beadle, though generally understood in the neighbourhood to be a ridiculous institution, is not without a certain popularity for the moment, if it were only as a man who is going to see the body. The policeman considers him an imbecile civilian, a remnant of the barbarous watchmen-times; but gives him admission, as something that must be borne with until Government shall abolish him.[4] The sensation is heightened, as the tidings spread from mouth to mouth that the beadle is on the ground, and has gone in.

By-and-by the beadle comes out, once more intensifying the sensation, which has rather languished in the interval. He is understood to be in want of witnesses, for the Inquest to-morrow, who can tell the Coroner and Jury anything whatever respecting the deceased. Is immediately referred to innumerable people who can tell nothing whatever. Is made more imbecile by being constantly

3. Bar-keeper's assistant, responsible for delivering and collecting beer-pots. See p. 46, note 1.

4. Following the passing of a Police Act by Parliament in 1829, the newly established Metropolitan Police and City Police gradually took over duties previously handled by the beadles, in particular their function as parish night watchmen which they had exercised in "the barbarous watchmen-times."

informed that Mrs. Green's son "was a law-writer his-self, and knowed him better than anybody"—which son of Mrs. Green's appears, on inquiry, to be at the present time aboard a vessel bound for China, three months out, but considered accessible by telegraph, on application to the Lords of the Admiralty. Beadle goes into various shops and parlours, examining the inhabitants; always shutting the door first, and by exclusion, delay, and general idiotcy, exasperating the public. Policeman seen to smile to potboy. Public loses interest, and undergoes reaction. Taunts the beadle, in shrill youthful voices, with having boiled a boy; choruses fragments of a popular song to that effect, and importing that the boy was made into soup for the workhouse.[5] Policeman at last finds it necessary to support the law, and seize a vocalist; who is released upon the flight of the rest, on condition of his getting out of this then, come! and cutting it—a condition he immediately observes. So the sensation dies off for the time; and the unmoved policeman (to whom a little opium, more or less, is nothing), with his shining hat, stiff stock, inflexible great-coat, stout belt and bracelet, and all things fitting, pursues his lounging way with a heavy tread: beating the palms of his white gloves one against the other, and stopping now and then, at a street-corner, to look casually about for anything between a lost child and a murder.

Under cover of the night, the feeble-minded beadle comes flitting about Chancery Lane with his summonses, in which every Juror's name is wrongly spelt, and nothing is rightly spelt but the beadle's own name, which nobody can read or wants to know. The summonses served, and his witnesses forewarned, the beadle goes to Mr. Krook's, to keep a small appointment he has made with certain paupers; who, presently arriving, are conducted up-stairs, where they leave the great eyes in the shutter something new to stare at, in that last shape which earthly lodgings take for No one—and for Every one.

And, all that night, the coffin stands ready by the old portmanteau; and the lonely figure on the bed, whose path in life has lain through five-and-forty years, lies there, with no more track behind him, that any one can trace, than a deserted infant.

Next day the court is all alive—is like a fair, as Mrs. Perkins, more than reconciled to Mrs. Piper, says, in amicable conversation with that excellent woman. The Coroner is to sit in the first-floor

5. "The Workhouse Boy," a grimly comic song about a boy having been cooked to death in a workhouse soup-pot: "At length the soup copper repairs did need,/ The Coppersmith came, and there he seed,/ A dollop of bones lay a grizzling there,/ In the leg of the breeches the poor boy did vear!/ To gain his fill the boy did stoop,/ And, dreadful to tell, he vos boil'd in the soup,!/ And ve all of us say, and ve say it sincere,/ That he vos push'd in there by an Overseer." (Identified by Harry Stone in 1963.)

room at the Sol's Arms, where the Harmonic Meetings take place twice a week, and where the chair is filled by a gentleman of professional celebrity, faced by Little Swills, the comic vocalist, who hopes (according to the bill in the window) that his friends will rally round him, and support first-rate talent. The Sol's Arms does a brisk stroke of business all the morning. Even children so require sustaining, under the general excitement, that a pieman who has established himself for the occasion at the corner of the court, says his brandy-balls[6] go off like smoke. What time the beadle, hovering between the door of Mr. Krook's establishment and the door of the Sol's Arms, shows the curiosity in his keeping to a few discreet spirits, and accepts the compliment of a glass of ale or so in return.

At the appointed hour arrives the Coroner, for whom the Jurymen are waiting, and who is received with a salute of skittles,[7] from the good dry skittle-ground attached to the Sol's Arms. The Coroner frequents more public-houses than any man alive. The smell of sawdust, beer, tobacco-smoke, and spirits, is inseparable in his vocation from death in its most awful shapes. He is conducted by the beadle and the landlord to the Harmonic Meeting Room, where he puts his hat on the piano, and takes a Windsor-chair at the head of a long table, formed of several short tables put together, and ornamented with glutinous rings in endless involutions, made by pots and glasses. As many of the Jury as can crowd together at the table sit there. The rest get among the spittoons and pipes, or lean against the piano. Over the Coroner's head is a small iron garland, the pendant handle of a bell, which rather gives the Majesty of the Court the appearance of going to be hanged presently.

Call over and swear the Jury! While the ceremony is in progress, sensation is created by the entrance of a chubby little man in a large shirt-collar, with a moist eye, and an inflamed nose, who modestly takes a position near the door as one of the general public, but seems familiar with the room too. A whisper circulates that this is Little Swills. It is considered not unlikely that he will get up an imitation of the Coroner, and make it the principal feature of the Harmonic Meeting in the evening.

"Well, gentlemen—" the Coroner begins.

"Silence there, will you!" says the beadle. Not to the Coroner, though it might appear so.

"Well, gentlemen," resumes the Coroner. "You are impanelled here, to inquire into the death of a certain man. Evidence will be given before you, as to the circumstances attending that death, and you will give your verdict according to the—skittles; they must be

6. Brandy-colored confections.
7. A noisy bowling-game played with ninepins.

stopped, you know, beadle!—evidence, and not according to anything else. The first thing to be done is to view the body."

"Make way there!" cries the beadle.

So they go out in a loose procession, something after the manner of a straggling funeral, and make their inspection in Mr. Krook's back second floor, from which a few of the Jurymen retire pale and precipitately. The beadle is very careful that two gentlemen not very neat about the cuffs and buttons (for whose accommodation he has provided a special little table near the Coroner, in the Harmonic Meeting Room) should see all that is to be seen. For they are the public chroniclers of such inquiries, by the line; and he is not superior to the universal human infirmity, but hopes to read in print what "Mooney, the active and intelligent beadle of the district," said and did; and even aspires to see the name of Mooney as familiarly and patronisingly mentioned as the name of the Hangman is, according to the latest examples.

Little Swills is waiting for the Coroner and Jury on their return. Mr. Tulkinghorn, also. Mr. Tulkinghorn is received with distinction, and seated near the Coroner; between that high judicial officer, a bagatelle-board,[8] and the coal-box. The inquiry proceeds. The Jury learn how the subject of their inquiry died, and learn no more about him. "A very eminent solicitor is in attendance, gentlemen," says the Coroner, "who, I am informed, was accidentally present, when discovery of the death was made; but he could only repeat the evidence you have already heard from the surgeon, the landlord, the lodger, and the law-stationer; and it is not necessary to trouble him. Is anybody in attendance who knows anything more?"

Mrs. Piper pushed forward by Mrs. Perkins. Mrs. Piper sworn.

Anastasia Piper, gentlemen. Married woman. Now, Mrs. Piper—what have you got to say about this?

Why, Mrs. Piper has a good deal to say, chiefly in parenthesis and without punctuation, but not much to tell. Mrs. Piper lives in the court (which her husband is a cabinet-maker), and it has long been well beknown among the neighbours (counting from the day next but one before the half-baptising of Alexander James Piper aged eighteen months and four days old on accounts of not being expected to live such was the sufferings gentlemen of that child in his gums)[9] as the Plaintive—so Mrs. Piper insists on calling the deceased—was reported to have sold himself. Thinks it was the Plaintive's air in which that report originatinin. See the Plaintive

8. A kind of billiard table with nine holes at one end through which balls are sunk.

9. Children too sick to be brought to church for public baptism could be baptised privately. Because such ceremonies were sometimes imperfectly performed, and had to be later completed by public baptism, they were called half-baptisms.

often and considered as his air was feariocious and not to be allowed to go about some children being timid (and if doubted hoping Mrs. Perkins may be brought forward for she is here and will do credit to her husband and herself and family). Has seen the Plaintive wexed and worrited by the children (for children they will ever be and you cannot expect them specially if of playful dispositions to be Methoozellers which you was not yourself). On accounts of this and his dark looks has often dreamed as she see him take a pick-axe from his pocket and split Johnny's head (which the child knows not fear and has repeatually called after him close at his eels). Never however see the Plaintive take a pick-axe or any other wepping far from it. Has seen him hurry away when run and called after as if not partial to children and never see him speak to neither child nor grown person at any time (excepting the boy that sweeps the crossing down the lane over the way round the corner which if he was here would tell you that he has been seen a-speaking to him frequent).

Says the Coroner, is that boy here? Says the beadle, no, sir, he is not here. Says the Coroner, go and fetch him then. In the absence of the active and intelligent, the Coroner converses with Mr. Tulkinghorn.

O! Here's the boy, gentlemen!

Here he is, very muddy, very hoarse, very ragged. Now, boy!—But stop a minute. Caution. This boy must be put through a few preliminary paces.

Name, Jo. Nothing else that he knows on. Don't know that everybody has two names. Never heerd of sich a think. Don't know that Jo is short for a longer name. Thinks it long enough for *him*. *He* don't find no fault with it. Spell it? No. *He* can't spell it. No father, no mother, no friends. Never been to school. What's home? Knows a broom's a broom, and knows it's wicked to tell a lie. Don't recollect who told him about the broom, or about the lie, but knows both. Can't exactly say what'll be done to him arter he's dead if he tells a lie to the gentlemen here, but believes it'll be something wery bad to punish him, and serve him right—and so he'll tell the truth.

"This won't do, gentlemen!" says the Coroner, with a melancholy shake of the head.

"Don't you think you can receive his evidence, sir?" asks an attentive Juryman.

"Out of the question," says the Coroner. "You have heard the boy. 'Can't exactly say' won't do, you know. We can't take *that*, in a Court of Justice, gentlemen. It's terrible depravity. Put the boy aside."

Boy put aside; to the great edification of the audience;—especially of Little Swills, the Comic Vocalist.

Now. Is there any other witness? No other witness.

Very well, gentlemen! Here's a man unknown, proved to have been in the habit of taking opium in large quantities for a year and a half; found dead of too much opium. If you think you have any evidence to lead you to the conclusion that he committed suicide, you will come to that conclusion. If you think it is a case of accidental death, you will find a verdict accordingly.

Verdict accordingly. Accidental death. No doubt. Gentlemen, you are discharged. Good afternoon.

While the Coroner buttons his great-coat, Mr. Tulkinghorn and he give private audience to the rejected witness in a corner.

That graceless creature only knows that the dead man (whom he recognised just now by his yellow face and black hair) was sometimes hooted and pursued about the streets. That one cold winter night, when he, the boy, was shivering in a doorway near his crossing, the man turned to look at him, and came back, and, having questioned him and found that he had not a friend in the world, said, "Neither have I. Not one!" and gave him the price of a supper and a night's lodging. That the man had often spoken to him since; and asked him whether he slept sound at night, and how he bore cold and hunger, and whether he ever wished to die; and similar strange questions. That when the man had no money, he would say in passing, "I am as poor as you to-day, Jo"; but that when he had any, he had always (as the boy most heartily believes) been glad to give him some.

"He was wery good to me," says the boy, wiping his eyes with his wretched sleeve. "Wen I see him a-layin' so stritched out just now, I wished he could have heerd me tell him so. He wos wery good to me, he wos!"

As he shuffles down-stairs, Mr. Snagsby, lying in wait for him, puts a half-crown in his hand. "If you ever see me coming past your crossing with my little woman—I mean a lady—" says Mr. Snagsby, with his finger on his nose, "don't allude to it!"

For some little time the Jurymen hang about the Sol's Arms colloquially. In the sequel, half-a-dozen are caught up in a cloud of pipe-smoke that pervades the parlour of the Sol's Arms; two stroll to Hampstead; and four engage to go half-price to the play at night, and top up with oysters. Little Swills is treated on several hands. Being asked what he thinks of the proceedings, characterises them (his strength lying in a slangular direction) as "a rummy start."[1] The landlord of the Sol's Arms, finding Little Swills so popular,

1. A queer and surprising incident.

commends him highly to the Jurymen and public; observing that, for a song in character, he don't know his equal, and that that man's character-wardrobe would fill a cart.

Thus, gradually the Sol's Arms melts into the shadowy night, and then flares out of it strong in gas. The Harmonic Meeting hour arriving, the gentleman of professional celebrity takes the chair; is faced (red-faced) by Little Swills; their friends rally round them, and support first-rate talent. In the zenith of the evening, Little Swills says, Gentlemen, if you'll permit me, I'll attempt a short description of a scene of real life that came off here to-day. Is much applauded and encouraged; goes out of the room as Swills; comes in as the Coroner (not the least in the world like him); describes the Inquest, with recreative intervals of piano-forte accompaniment to the refrain—With his (the Coroner's) tippy tol li doll, tippy tol lo doll, tippy tol li doll, Dee!

The jingling piano at last is silent, and the Harmonic friends rally round their pillows. Then there is rest around the lonely figure, now laid in its last earthly habitation; and it is watched by the gaunt eyes in the shutters through some quiet hours of night. If this forlorn man could have been prophetically seen lying here, by the mother at whose breast he nestled, a little child, with eyes upraised to her loving face, and soft hand scarcely knowing how to close upon the neck to which it crept, what an impossibility the vision would have seemed! O, if, in brighter days, the now-extinguished fire within him ever burned for one woman who held him in her heart, where is she, while these ashes are above the ground!

It is anything but a night of rest at Mr. Snagsby's, in Cook's Court; where Guster murders sleep,[2] by going, as Mr. Snagsby himself allows—not to put too fine a point upon it—out of one fit into twenty. The occasion of this seizure is, that Guster has a tender heart, and a susceptible something that possibly might have been imagination, but for Tooting and her patron saint.[3] Be it what it may, now, it was so direfully impressed at tea-time by Mr. Snagsby's account of the inquiry at which he had assisted, that at supper-time she projected herself into the kitchen, preceded by a flying Dutch-cheese, and fell into a fit of unusual duration: which she only came out of to go into another, and another, and so on through a chain of fits, with short intervals between, of which she has pathetically availed herself by consuming them in entreaties to Mrs. Snagsby not to give her warning "when she quite comes to"; and also in appeals to the whole establishment to lay her down on the stones, and go to bed. Hence, Mr. Snagsby, at last hearing the cock at the little dairy in Cursitor Street go into that disinterested ecstasy of his

2. Cf. "Methought I heard a voice cry 'Sleep no more!/ Macbeth does murther sleep.' " (*Macbeth,* II.ii.35.)

3. On Drouet's orphanage see p. 117, note 3.

on the subject of daylight, says, drawing a long breath, though the most patient of men, "I thought you was dead, I am sure!"

What question this enthusiastic fowl supposes he settles when he strains himself to such an extent, or why he should thus crow (so men crow on various triumphant public occasions, however) about what cannot be of any moment to him, is his affair. It is enough that daylight comes, morning comes, noon comes.

Then the active and intelligent, who has got into the morning papers as such, comes with his pauper company to Mr. Krook's, and bears off the body of our dear brother here departed,[4] to a hemmed-in churchyard, pestiferous and obscene, whence malignant diseases are communicated to the bodies of our dear brothers and sisters who have not departed; while our dear brothers and sisters who hang about official backstairs—would to Heaven they *had* departed!—are very complacent and agreeable. Into a beastly scrap of ground which a Turk would reject as a savage abomination, and a Caffre[5] would shudder at, they bring our dear brother here departed, to receive Christian burial.

With houses looking on, on every side, save where a reeking little tunnel of a court gives access to the iron gate—with every villainy of life in action close on death, and every poisonous element of death in action close on life—here, they lower our dear brother down a foot or two: here, sow him in corruption, to be raised in corruption:[6] an avenging ghost at many a sick-bedside: a shameful testimony to future ages, how civilisation and barbarism walked this boastful island together.

Come night, come darkness,[7] for you cannot come too soon, or stay too long, by such a place as this! Come, straggling lights into the windows of the ugly houses; and you who do iniquity therein, do it at least with this dread scene shut out! Come, flame of gas, burning so sullenly above the iron gate, on which the poisoned air deposits its witch-ointment slimy to the touch! It is well that you should call to every passer-by, "Look here!"

With the night, comes a slouching figure through the tunnel-court, to the outside of the iron gate. It holds the gate with its hands, and looks in between the bars; stands looking in for a little while.

It then, with an old broom it carries, softly sweeps the step, and makes the archway clean. It does so very busily and trimly; looks in again, a little while; and so departs.

4. See in *The Book of Common Prayer*: "Forasmuch as it hath pleased Almighty God . . . to take unto himself the soul of our dear brother here departed, we therefore commit his body to the ground."

5. South African native of the Bantu family.

6. Cf. I Corinthians 15–42: "So also is the resurrection of the dead. It is sown in corruption, it is raised in incorruption."

7. Cf. *Macbeth* (III.ii.46–47): "Come, seeling night,/ Scarf up the tender eye of pitiful day" (noted by Grahame Smith).

Jo, is it thou? Well, well! Though a rejected witness, who "can't exactly say" what will be done to him in greater hands than men's, thou art not quite in outer darkness.[8] There is something like a distant ray of light thy muttered reason for this:

"He wos wery good to me, he wos!"

Chapter XII

ON THE WATCH

It has left off raining down in Lincolnshire, at last, and Chesney Wold has taken heart. Mrs. Rouncewell is full of hospitable cares, for Sir Leicester and my Lady are coming home from Paris. The fashionable intelligence has found it out, and communicates the glad tidings to benighted England. It has also found out that they will entertain a brilliant and distinguished circle of the *élite* of the *beau monde* (the fashionable intelligence is weak in English, but a giant refreshed[1] in French), at the ancient and hospitable family seat in Lincolnshire.

For the greater honour of the brilliant and distinguished circle, and of Chesney Wold into the bargain, the broken arch of the bridge in the park is mended; and the water, now retired within its proper limits and again spanned gracefully, makes a figure in the prospect from the house. The clear cold sunshine glances into the brittle woods, and approvingly beholds the sharp wind scattering the leaves and drying the moss. It glides over the park after the moving shadows of the clouds, and chases them, and never catches them, all day. It looks in at the windows, and touches the ancestral portraits with bars and patches of brightness, never contemplated by the painters. Athwart the picture of my Lady, over the great chimney-piece, it throws a broad bend-sinister[2] of light that strikes down crookedly into the hearth, and seems to rend it.

Through the same cold sunshine, and the same sharp wind, my Lady and Sir Leicester, in their travelling chariot (my Lady's woman, and Sir Leicester's man affectionate in the rumble), start for home. With a considerable amount of jingling and whip-cracking, and many plunging demonstrations on the part of two bare-backed horses, and two Centaurs[3] with glazed hats, jackboots, and flowing manes and tails, they rattle out of the yard of the Hotel Bristol in the Place Vendôme, and canter between the sun-and-

8. See Matthew 22:13: "Then said the king to his servants, Bind him hand and foot, and . . . cast him into outer darkness."

1. Cf. Psalms 78:66: "So the Lord awaked as one out of sleep: and like a giant refreshed with wine." (Noted by Susan Shatto, 1975.)

2. A narrow stripe on a coat of arms extending diagonally from the top left side (called, in heraldry, the *sinister*) to the base of the shield. Such a band indicated illegitimacy in the bearer's ancestry.

3. The two lead horses, ridden by grooms, seem half horse and half man, whereas the other two horses are "bare-backed" and without riders.

shadow-chequered colonnade of the Rue de Rivoli, and the garden of the ill-fated palace of a headless king and queen,[4] off by the Place of Concord, and the Elysian Fields, and the Gate of the Star, out of Paris.

Sooth to say, they cannot go away too fast; for, even here, my Lady Dedlock has been bored to death. Concert, assembly, opera, theatre, drive, nothing is new to my Lady, under the worn-out heavens. Only last Sunday, when poor wretches were gay—within the walls, playing with children among the clipped trees and the statues in the Palace Garden; walking, a score abreast, in the Elysian Fields, made more Elysian by performing dogs and wooden horses; between whiles filtering (a few) through the gloomy Cathedral of our Lady, to say a word or two at the base of a pillar, within flare of a rusty little gridiron-full of gusty little tapers—without the walls,[5] encompassing Paris with dancing, love-making, wine-drinking, tobacco-smoking, tomb-visiting, billiard card and domino playing, quack-doctoring, and much murderous refuse, animate and inanimate—only last Sunday, my Lady, in the desolation of Boredom and the clutch of Giant Despair,[6] almost hated her own maid for being in spirits.

She cannot, therefore, go too fast from Paris. Weariness of soul lies before her, as it lies behind—her Ariel has put a girdle of it round the whole earth,[7] and it cannot be unclasped—but the imperfect remedy is always to fly, from the last place where it has been experienced. Fling Paris back into the distance, then, exchanging it for endless avenues and cross-avenues of wintry trees! And, when next beheld, let it be some leagues away, with the Gate of the Star a white speck glittering in the sun, and the city a mere mound in a plain: two dark square towers rising out of it, and light and shadow descending on it aslant, like the angels in Jacob's dream![8]

Sir Leicester is generally in a complacent state, and rarely bored. When he has nothing else to do, he can always contemplate his own greatness. It is a considerable advantage to a man, to have so inexhaustible a subject. After reading his letters, he leans back in his corner of the carriage, and generally reviews his importance to society.

"You have an unusual amount of correspondence this morning?" says my Lady, after a long time. She is fatigued with reading. Has almost read a page in twenty miles.

"Nothing in it, though. Nothing whatever."

"I saw one of Mr. Tulkinghorn's long effusions, I think?"

4. The Tuileries, a palace of Louis XVI and Queen Marie Antoinette, who were guillotined in 1793.

5. Neighborhoods of Paris outside the old walled section of the city.

6. Allegorical figure in John Bunyan's *Pilgrim's Progress* (1678).

7. Cf. *A Midsummer Night's Dream* (II.i.175): "I'll put a girdle round about the earth." The speaker is Puck, whom Dickens has confused here with Ariel in *The Tempest*.

8. Genesis 28:12.

"You see everything," says Sir Leicester, with admiration.

"Ha!" sighs my Lady. "He is the most tiresome of men!"

"He sends—I really beg your pardon—he sends," says Sir Leicester, selecting the letter, and unfolding it, "a message to you. Our stopping to change horses, as I came to his postscript, drove it out of my memory. I beg you'll excuse me. He says—" Sir Leicester is so long in taking out his eye-glass and adjusting it, that my Lady looks a little irritated. "He says 'In the matter of the right of way —' I beg your pardon, that's not the place. He says—yes! Here I have it! He says 'I beg my respectful compliments to my Lady, who, I hope, has benefited by the change. Will you do me the favour to mention (as it may interest her), that I have something to tell her on her return, in reference to the person who copied the affidavit in the Chancery suit, which so powerfully stimulated her curiosity. I have seen him.' "

My Lady, leaning forward, looks out of her window.

"That's the message," observes Sir Leicester.

"I should like to walk a little," says my Lady, still looking out of her window.

"Walk!" repeats Sir Leicester, in a tone of surprise.

"I should like to walk a little," says my Lady, with unmistakable distinctness. "Please to stop the carriage."

The carriage is stopped, the affectionate man alights from the rumble, opens the door, and lets down the steps, obedient to an impatient motion of my Lady's hand. My Lady alights so quickly and walks away so quickly, that Sir Leicester, for all his scrupulous politeness, is unable to assist her, and is left behind. A space of a minute or two has elapsed before he comes up with her. She smiles, looks very handsome, takes his arm, lounges with him for a quarter of a mile, is very much bored, and resumes her seat in the carriage.

The rattle and clatter continue through the greater part of three days, with more or less of bell-jingling and whip-cracking, and more or less plunging of Centaurs and bare-backed horses. Their courtly politeness to each other, at the Hotels where they tarry, is the theme of general admiration. Though my Lord *is* a little aged for my Lady, says Madame, the hostess of the Golden Ape, and though he might be her amiable father, one can see at a glance that they love each other. One observes my Lord with his white hair, standing, hat in hand, to help my Lady to and from the carriage. One observes my Lady, how recognisant of my Lord's politeness, with an inclination of her gracious head, and the concession of her so-genteel fingers! It is ravishing!

The sea has no appreciation of great men, but knocks them about like the small fry. It is habitually hard upon Sir Leicester, whose countenance it greenly mottles in the manner of sage-cheese, and in whose aristocratic system it effects a dismal revolution. It is the

Radical of Nature to him. Nevertheless, his dignity gets over it, after stopping to refit; and he goes on with my Lady for Chesney Wold, lying only one night in London on the way to Lincolnshire.

Through the same cold sunlight—colder as the day declines,—and through the same sharp wind—sharper as the separate shadows of bare trees gloom together in the woods, and as the Ghost's Walk, touched at the western corner by a pile of fire in the sky, resigns itself to coming night,—they drive into the park. The Rooks, swinging in their lofty houses in the elm-tree avenue, seem to discuss the question of the occupancy of the carriage as it passes underneath; some agreeing that Sir Leicester and my Lady are come down; some arguing with malcontents who won't admit it; now, all consenting to consider the question disposed of; now, all breaking out again in violent debate, incited by one obstinate and drowsy bird, who will persist in putting in a last contradictory croak. Leaving them to swing and caw, the travelling chariot rolls on to the house: where fires gleam warmly through some of the windows, though not through so many as to give an inhabited expression to the darkening mass of front. But the brilliant and distinguished circle will soon do that.

Mrs. Rouncewell is in attendance, and receives Sir Leicester's customary shake of the hand with a profound curtsey.

"How do you do, Mrs. Rouncewell? I am glad to see you."

"I hope I have the honour of welcoming you in good health, Sir Leicester?"

"In excellent health, Mrs. Rouncewell."

"My Lady is looking charmingly well," says Mrs. Rouncewell, with another curtsey.

My Lady signifies, without profuse expenditure of words, that she is as wearily well as she can hope to be.

But Rosa is in the distance, behind the housekeeper; and my Lady, who has not subdued the quickness of her observation, whatever else she may have conquered, asks:

"Who is that girl?"

"A young scholar of mine, my Lady. Rosa."

"Come here, Rosa!" Lady Dedlock beckons her, with even an appearance of interest. "Why, do you know how pretty you are, child?" she says, touching her shoulder with her two forefingers.

Rosa, very much abashed, says, "No, if you please, my Lady!" and glances up, and glances down, and don't know where to look, but looks all the prettier.

"How old are you?"

"Nineteen, my Lady."

"Nineteen," repeats my Lady thoughtfully. "Take care they don't spoil you by flattery."

"Yes, my Lady."

My Lady taps her dimpled cheek with the same delicate gloved fingers, and goes on to the foot of the oak staircase, where Sir Leicester pauses for her as her knightly escort. A staring old Dedlock in a panel, as large as life and as dull, looks as if he didn't know what to make of it—which was probably his general state of mind in the days of Queen Elizabeth.

That evening, in the housekeeper's room, Rosa can do nothing but murmur Lady Dedlock's praises. She is so affable, so graceful, so beautiful, so elegant; has such a sweet voice and such a thrilling touch, that Rosa can feel it yet! Mrs. Rouncewell confirms all this, not without personal pride, reserving only the one point of affability. Mrs. Rouncewell is not quite sure as to that. Heaven forbid that she should say a syllable in dispraise of any member of that excellent family; above all, of my Lady, whom the whole world admires; but if my Lady would only be "a little more free," not quite so cold and distant, Mrs. Rouncewell thinks she would be more affable.

" 'Tis almost a pity," Mrs. Rouncewell adds—only "almost," because it borders on impiety to suppose that anything could be better than it is, in such an express dispensation as the Dedlock affairs; "that my Lady has no family. If she had had a daughter now, a grown young lady, to interest her, I think she would have had the only kind of excellence she wants."

"Might not that have made her still more proud, grandmother?" says Watt; who has been home and come back again, he is such a good grandson.

"More and most, my dear," returns the housekeeper with dignity, "are words it's not my place to use—nor so much as to hear—applied to any drawback on my Lady."

"I beg your pardon, grandmother. But she *is* proud, is she not?"

"If she is, she has reason to be. The Dedlock family have always reason to be."

"Well!" says Watt, "it's to be hoped they line out of their Prayer-Books a certain passage for the common people about pride and vainglory.[9] Forgive me, grandmother! Only a joke!"

"Sir Leicester and Lady Dedlock, my dear, are not fit subjects for joking."

"Sir Leicester is no joke by any means," says Watt; "and I humbly ask his pardon. I suppose, grandmother, that even with the family and their guests down here, there is no objection to my prolonging my stay at the Dedlock Arms for a day or two, as any other traveller might?"

"Surely, none in the world, child."

9. See the "Litany" in *The Book of Common Prayer:* "From blindness of heart, from pride, vainglory . . . and all uncharitableness: Good Lord, deliver us."

"I am glad of that," says Watt, "because I—because I have an inexpressible desire to extend my knowledge of this beautiful neighbourhood."

He happens to glance at Rosa, who looks down, and is very shy, indeed. But according to the old superstition, it should be Rosa's ears that burn, and not her fresh bright cheeks; for my Lady's maid is holding forth about her at this moment, with surpassing energy.

My Lady's maid is a Frenchwoman of two-and-thirty, from somewhere in the southern country about Avignon and Marseilles—a large-eyed brown woman with black hair; who would be handsome, but for a certain feline mouth, and general uncomfortable tightness of face, rendering the jaws too eager, and the skull too prominent. There is something indefinably keen and wan about her anatomy; and she has a watchful way of looking out of the corners of her eyes without turning her head, which could be pleasantly dispensed with —especially when she is in an ill-humour and near knives. Through all the good taste of her dress and little adornments, these objections so express themselves, that she seems to go about like a very neat She-Wolf imperfectly tamed. Besides being accomplished in all the knowledge appertaining to her post, she is almost an Englishwoman in her acquaintance with the language—consequently she is in no want of words to shower upon Rosa for having attracted my Lady's attention; and she pours them out with such grim ridicule as she sits at dinner, that her companion, the affectionate man, is rather relieved when she arrives at the spoon stage of that performance.

Ha, ha, ha! She, Hortense, been in my Lady's service since five years, and always kept at the distance, and this doll, this puppet, caressed—absolutely caressed—by my Lady on the moment of her arriving at the house! Ha, ha, ha! "And do you know how pretty you are child?"—"No, my Lady."—You are right there! "And how old are you, child? And take care they do not spoil you by flattery, child!" O how droll! It is the *best* thing altogether.

In short, it is such an admirable thing, that Mademoiselle Hortense can't forget it; but at meals for days afterwards, even among her countrywomen and others attached in like capacity to the troop of visitors, relapses into silent enjoyment of the joke—an enjoyment expressed, in her own convivial manner, by an additional tightness of face, thin elongation of compressed lips, and sidewise look: which intense appreciation of humour is frequently reflected in my Lady's mirrors, when my Lady is not among them.

All the mirrors in the house are brought into action now: many of them after a long blank. They reflect handsome faces, simpering faces, youthful faces, faces of threescore-and-ten that will not submit to be old; the entire collection of faces that have come to pass a January week or two at Chesney Wold, and which the fashionable intelligence, a mighty hunter before the Lord,[1] hunts with a keen scent, from their breaking cover[2] at the Court of St. James's to their being run down to Death. The place in Lincolnshire is all alive. By day, guns and voices are heard ringing in the woods, horsemen and carriages enliven the park roads, servants and hangers-on pervade the Village and the Dedlock Arms. Seen by night, from distant openings in the trees, the row of windows in the long drawing-room, where my Lady's picture hangs over the great chimney-piece, is like a row of jewels set in a black frame. On Sunday, the chill little church is almost warmed by so much gallant company, and the general flavour of the Dedlock dust is quenched in delicate perfumes.

The brilliant and distinguished circle comprehends within it, no contracted amount of education, sense, courage, honour, beauty, and virtue. Yet there is something a little wrong about it, in despite of its immense advantages. What can it be?

Dandyism? There is no King George the Fourth now (more's the pity!) to set the dandy fashion; there are no clear-starched, jack-towel[3] neckcloths, no short-waisted coats, no false calves,[4] no stays. There are no caricatures, now, of effeminate Exquisites so arrayed, swooning in opera-boxes with excess of delight, and being revived by other dainty creatures, poking long-necked scent-bottles at their noses. There is no beau whom it takes four men at once to shake into his buckskins,[5] or who goes to see all the executions, or who is troubled with the self-reproach of having once consumed a pea.[6] But is there Dandyism in the brilliant and distinguished circle notwithstanding, Dandyism of a more mischievous sort, that has got below the surface and is doing less harmless things than jack-towelling itself and stopping its own digestion, to which no rational person need particularly object?

Why, yes. It cannot be disguised. There *are*, at Chesney Wold this January week, some ladies and gentlemen of the newest fashion, who have set up a Dandyism—in Religion, for instance. Who, in mere lackadaisical want of an emotion, have agreed upon a little dandy talk about the Vulgar wanting faith in things in general;

1. Nimrod. See Genesis 10:8–9.
2. Being introduced into society at a ceremony, held at St. James's Palace, in which persons are presented to the Monarch. This presentation is likened to a fox leaving a place of concealment (cover) and coming out into the open where hunters will pursue him until he is run down to his death.
3. Cloth shaped like a roller-towel, wound round the neck so as to resemble a high stiff collar.
4. Padding worn under stockings by men seeking to disguise the thinness of their lower legs.
5. Tight-fitting breeches.
6. Beau Brummell (1778–1840), the eminent dandy, was asked by a lady if he never tasted vegetables. "Madame," he replied, "I once ate a pea!"

meaning, in the things that have been tried and found wanting, as though a low fellow should unaccountably lose faith in a bad shilling, after finding it out! Who would make the Vulgar very picturesque and faithful, by putting back the hands upon the Clock of Time, and cancelling a few hundred years of history.

There are also ladies and gentlemen of another fashion, not so new, but very elegant who have agreed to put a smooth glaze on the world, and to keep down all its realities. For whom everything must be languid and pretty. Who have found out the perpetual stoppage. Who are to rejoice at nothing, and be sorry for nothing. Who are not to be disturbed by ideas. On whom even the Fine Arts, attending in powder[7] and walking backward like the Lord Chamberlain, must array themselves in the milliners' and tailors' patterns of past generations, and be particularly careful not to be in earnest, or to receive any impress from the moving age.

Then there is my Lord Boodle, of considerable reputation with his party, who has known what office is, and who tells Sir Leicester Dedlock with much gravity, after dinner, that he really does not see to what the present age is tending. A debate is not what a debate used to be; the House is not what the House used to be; even a Cabinet is not what it formerly was. He perceives with astonishment, that supposing the present Government to be overthrown, the limited choice of the Crown, in the formation of a new Ministry, would lie between Lord Coodle and Sir Thomas Doodle—supposing it to be impossible for the Duke of Foodle to act with Goodle, which may be assumed to be the case in consequence of the breach arising out of that affair with Hoodle. Then, giving the Home Department and the Leadership of the House of Commons to Joodle, the Exchequer to Koodle, the Colonies to Loodle, and the Foreign Office to Moodle, what are you to do with Noodle? You can't offer him the Presidency of the Council; that is reserved for Poodle. You can't put him in the Woods and Forests; that is hardly good enough for Quoodle. What follows? That the country is shipwrecked, lost, and gone to pieces (as is made manifest to the patriotism of Sir Leicester Dedlock), because you can provide for Noodle!

On the other hand, the Right Honourable William Buffy, M.P., contends across the table with some one else, that the shipwreck of the country—about which there is no doubt; it is only the manner of it that is in question—is attributable to Cuffy. If you had done with Cuffy what you ought to have done when he first came into Parliament, and had prevented him from going over to Duffy, you would have got him into alliance with Fuffy, you would have had

7. I.e., like the old-fashioned wearing of powdered wigs.

with you the weight attaching as a smart debater to Guffy, you would have brought to bear upon the elections the wealth of Huffy, you would have got in for three counties Juffy, Kuffy, and Luffy, and you would have strengthened your administration by the official knowledge and the business habits of Muffy. All this, instead of being as you now are, dependent on the mere caprice of Puffy!

As to this point, and as to some minor topics, there are differences of opinion; but it is perfectly clear to the brilliant and distinguished circle, all round, that nobody is in question but Boodle and his retinue, and Buffy and *his* retinue. These are the great actors for whom the stage is reserved. A People there are, no doubt—a certain large number of supernumeraries, who are to be occasionally addressed, and relied upon for shouts and choruses, as on the theatrical stage; but Boodle and Buffy, their followers and families, their heirs, executors, administrators, and assigns, are the born first-actors, managers, and leaders, and no others can appear upon the scene for ever and ever.

In this, too, there is perhaps more Dandyism at Chesney Wold than the brilliant and distinguished circle will find good for itself in the long run. For it is, even with the stillest and politest circles, as with the circle the necromancer draws around him—very strange appearances may be seen in active motion outside.[8] With this difference; that, being realities and not phantoms, there is the greater danger of their breaking in.

Chesney Wold is quite full, anyhow; so full, that a burning sense of injury arises in the breasts of ill-lodged ladies'-maids, and is not to be extinguished. Only one room is empty. It is a turret chamber of the third order of merit, plainly but comfortably furnished, and having an old-fashioned business air. It is Mr. Tulkinghorn's room, and is never bestowed on anybody else, for he may come at any time. He is not come yet. It is his quiet habit to walk across the park from the village, in fine weather; to drop into this room, as if he had never been out of it since he was last seen there; to request a servant to inform Sir Leicester that he is arrived, in case he should be wanted; and to appear ten minutes before dinner, in the shadow of the library door. He sleeps in his turret with a complaining flagstaff over his head; and has some leads[9] outside, on which, any fine morning when he is down here, his black figure may be seen walking before breakfast like a larger species of rook.

Every day before dinner, my Lady looks for him in the dusk of the library, but he is not there. Every day at dinner, my Lady glances down the table for the vacant place, that would be waiting

8. A *necromancr*–i.e., a sorcerer who summons the spirits of the dead–protects himself from these *strange appearances* or *phantoms* by surrounding himself with a magic circle to prevent their *breaking in.* Cf. Coleridge, "Kubla Khan": "Weave a circle round him thrice."

9. A flat lead roof.

to receive him if he had just arrived; but there is no vacant place. Every night, my Lady casually asks her maid:

"Is Mr. Tulkinghorn come?"

Every night the answer is, "No, my Lady, not yet."

One night, while having her hair undressed, my Lady loses herself in deep thought after this reply, until she sees her own brooding face in the opposite glass, and a pair of black eyes curiously observing her.

"Be so good as to attend," says my Lady then, addressing the reflection of Hortense, "to your business. You can contemplate your beauty at another time."

"Pardon! It was your Ladyship's beauty."

"That," says my Lady, "you needn't contemplate at all."

At length one afternoon a little before sunset, when the bright groups of figures, which have for the last hour or two enlivened the Ghost's Walk, are all dispersed, and only Sir Leicester and my Lady remain upon the terrace, Mr. Tulkinghorn appears. He comes towards them at his usual methodical pace, which is never quickened, never slackened. He wears his usual expressionless mask—if it be a mask—and carries family secrets in every limb of his body, and every crease of his dress. Whether his whole soul is devoted to the great, or whether he yields them nothing beyond the services he sells, is his personal secret. He keeps it, as he keeps the secrets of his clients; he is his own client in that matter, and will never betray himself.

"How do you do, Mr. Tulkinghorn?" says Sir Leicester, giving him his hand.

Mr. Tulkinghorn is quite well. Sir Leicester is quite well. My Lady is quite well. All highly satisfactory. The lawyer, with his hands behind him, walks, at Sir Leicester's side, along the terrace. My Lady walks upon the other side.

"We expected you before," says Sir Leicester. A gracious observation. As much as to say, "Mr. Tulkinghorn, we remember your existence when you are not here to remind us of it by your presence. We bestow a fragment of our minds upon you, sir, you see!"

Mr. Tulkinghorn, comprehending it, inclines his head, and says he is much obliged.

"I should have come down sooner," he explains, "but that I have been much engaged with those matters in the several suits between yourself and Boythorn."

"A man of a very ill-regulated mind," observes Sir Leicester, with severity. "An extremely dangerous person in any community. A man of a very low character of mind."

"He is obstinate," says Mr. Tulkinghorn.

"It is natural to such a man to be so," says Sir Leicester, looking most profoundly obstinate himself. "I am not at all surprised to hear it."

"The only question is," pursues the lawyer, "whether you will give up anything."

"No, sir," replies Sir Leicester. "Nothing. *I* give up?"

"I don't mean anything of importance. That, of course, I know you would not abandon. I mean any minor point."

"Mr. Tulkinghorn," returns Sir Leicester, "there can be no minor point between myself and Mr. Boythorn. If I go farther, and observe that I cannot readily conceive how *any* right of mine can be a minor point, I speak not so much in reference to myself as an individual, as in reference to the family position I have it in charge to maintain."

Mr. Tulkinghorn inclines his head again. "I have now my instructions," he says. "Mr. Boythorn will give us a great deal of trouble ——"

"It is the character of such a mind, Mr. Tulkinghorn," Sir Leicester interrupts him, "*to* give trouble. An exceedingly ill-conditioned, levelling person. A person who, fifty years ago, would probably have been tried at the Old Bailey for some demagogue proceeding, and severely punished—if not," adds Sir Leicester, after a moment's pause, "if not hanged, drawn, and quartered."

Sir Leicester appears to discharge his stately breast of a burden, in passing this capital sentence; as if it were the next satisfactory thing to having the sentence executed.

"But night is coming on," said he, "and my Lady will take cold. My dear, let us go in."

As they turn towards the hall-door, Lady Dedlock addresses Mr. Tulkinghorn for the first time.

"You sent me a message respecting the person whose writing I happened to inquire about. It was like you to remember the circumstance; I had quite forgotten it. Your message reminded me of it again. I can't imagine what association I had, with a hand like that; but I surely had some."

"You had some?" Mr. Tulkinghorn repeats.

"O yes!" returns my Lady, carelessly. "I think I must have had some. And did you really take the trouble to find out the writer of that actual thing—what was it!—Affidavit?"

"Yes."

"How very odd!"

They pass into a sombre breakfast-room on the ground floor, lighted in the day by two deep windows. It is now twilight. The fire glows brightly on the panelled wall, and palely on the window-glass, where, through the cold reflection of the blaze, the colder landscape shudders in the wind, and a grey mist creeps along: the only traveller besides the waste of clouds.

My Lady lounges in a great chair in the chimney-corner, and Sir Leicester takes another great chair opposite. The lawyer stands before the fire, with his hand out at arm's length, shading his face. He looks across his arm at my Lady.

"Yes," he says, "I inquired about the man, and found him. And what is very strange, I found him——"

"Not to be any out-of-the-way person, I am afraid!" Lady Dedlock languidly anticipates.

"I found him dead."

"O dear me!" remonstrates Sir Leicester. Not so much shocked by the fact, as by the fact of the fact being mentioned.

"I was directed to his lodging—a miserable, poverty-stricken place—and I found him dead."

"You will excuse me, Mr. Tulkinghorn," observes Sir Leicester. "I think the less said——"

"Pray, Sir Leicester, let me hear the story out" (it is my Lady speaking). "It is quite a story for twilight. How very shocking! Dead?"

Mr. Tulkinghorn re-asserts it by another inclination of his head. "Whether by his own hand——"

"Upon my honour!" cries Sir Leicester. "Really!"

"Do let me hear the story!" says my Lady.

"Whatever you desire, my dear. But I must say——"

"No, you mustn't say! Go on, Mr. Tulkinghorn."

Sir Leicester's gallantry concedes the point; though he still feels that to bring this sort of squalor among the upper classes is really—really——

"I was about to say," resumes the lawyer, with undisturbed calmness, "that whether he had died by his own hand or not, it was beyond my power to tell you. I should amend that phrase, however, by saying that he had unquestionably died of his own act; though whether by his own deliberate intention, or by mischance, can never certainly be known. The Coroner's jury found that he took the poison accidentally."

"And what kind of man," my Lady asks, "was this deplorable creature?"

"Very difficult to say," returns the lawyer, shaking his head. "He had lived so wretchedly, and was so neglected, with his gipsy colour, and his wild black hair and beard, that I should have considered him the commonest of the common. The surgeon had a notion that he had once been something better, both in appearance and condition."

"What did they call the wretched being?"

"They called him what he had called himself, but no one knew his name."

"Not even any one who had attended on him?"

"No one had attended on him. He was found dead. In fact, I found him."

"Without any clue to anything more?"

"Without any; there was," says the lawyer meditatively, "an old portmanteau; but—No, there were no papers."

During the utterance of every word of this short dialogue, Lady Dedlock and Mr. Tulkinghorn, without any other alteration in their customary deportment, have looked very steadily at one another—as was natural, perhaps, in the discussion of so unusual a subject. Sir Leicester has looked at the fire, with the general expression of the Dedlock on the staircase. The story being told, he renews his stately protest, saying, that as it is quite clear that no association in my Lady's mind can possibly be traceable to this poor wretch (unless he was a begging-letter writer); he trusts to hear no more about a subject so far removed from my Lady's station.

"Certainly, a collection of horrors," says my Lady, gathering up her mantles and furs; "but they interest one for the moment! Have the kindness, Mr. Tulkinghorn, to open the door for me."

Mr. Tulkinghorn does so with deference, and holds it open while she passes out. She passes close to him, with her usual fatigued manner, and insolent grace. They meet again at dinner—again, next day—again, for many days in succession. Lady Dedlock is always the same exhausted deity, surrounded by worshippers, and terribly liable to be bored to death, even when presiding at her own shrine. Mr. Tulkinghorn is always the same speechless repository of noble confidences; so oddly out of place, and yet so perfectly at home. They appear to take as little note of one another, as any two people, enclosed within the same walls, could. But whether each evermore watches and suspects the other, evermore mistrustful of some great reservation; whether each is evermore prepared at all points for the other, and never to be taken unawares; what each would give to know how much the other knows—all this is hidden, for the time, in their own hearts.

Chapter XIII

ESTHER'S NARRATIVE

We held many consultations about what Richard was to be; first, without Mr. Jarndyce, as he had requested, and afterwards with him; but it was a long time before we seemed to make progress. Richard said he was ready for anything. When Mr. Jarndyce doubted whether he might not already be too old to enter the Navy, Richard said he had thought of that, and perhaps he was.

When Mr. Jarndyce asked him what he thought of the Army, Richard said he had thought of that too, and it wasn't a bad idea. When Mr. Jarndyce advised him to try and decide within himself, whether his old preference for the sea was an ordinary boyish inclination, or a strong impulse, Richard answered, Well, he really *had* tried very often, and he couldn't make out.

"How much of this indecision of character," Mr. Jarndyce said to me, "is chargeable on that incomprehensible heap of uncertainty and procrastination on which he has been thrown from his birth, I don't pretend to say; but that Chancery, among its other sins, is responsible for some of it, I can plainly see. It has engendered or confirmed in him a habit of putting off—and trusting to this, that, and the other chance, without knowing what chance—and dismissing everything as unsettled, uncertain, and confused. The character of much older and steadier people may be even changed by the circumstances surrounding them. It would be too much to expect that a boy's, in its formation, should be the subject of such influences, and escape them."

I felt this to be true; though, if I may venture to mention what I thought besides, I thought it much to be regretted that Richard's education had not counteracted those influences, or directed his character. He had been eight years at a public school,[1] and had learnt, I understood, to make Latin Verses of several sorts, in the most admirable manner. But I never heard that it had been anybody's business to find out what his natural bent was, or where his failings lay, or to adapt any kind of knowledge to *him*. He had been adapted to the Verses, and had learnt the art of making them to such perfection, that if he had remained at school until he was of age, I suppose he could only have gone on making them over and over again, unless he had enlarged his education by forgetting how to do it. Still, although I had no doubt that they were very beautiful, and very improving, and very sufficient for a great many purposes of life, and always remembered all through life, I did doubt whether Richard would not have profited by some one studying him a little, instead of his studying them quite so much.

To be sure, I knew nothing of the subject, and do not even now know whether the young gentlemen of classic Rome or Greece made verses to the same extent—or whether the young gentlemen of any country ever did.

"I haven't the least idea," said Richard, musing, "what I had better be. Except that I am quite sure I don't want to go into the Church, it's a toss-up."

"You have no inclination in Mr. Kenge's way?" suggested Mr. Jarndyce.

"I don't know that, sir!" replied Richard. "I am fond of boating.

1. Winchester, a private school in which classical studies were stressed.

Articled clerks go a good deal on the water. It's a capital profession!"

"Surgeon—" suggested Mr. Jarndyce.

"That's the thing, sir!" cried Richard.

I doubt if he had ever once thought of it before.

"That's the thing, sir!" repeated Richard, with the greatest enthusiasm. "We have got it at last. M.R.C.S.!"[2]

He was not to be laughed out of it, though he laughed at it heartily. He said he had chosen his profession, and the more he thought of it, the more he felt that his destiny was clear; the art of healing was the art of all others for him. Mistrusting that he only came to this conclusion, because, having never had much chance of finding out for himself what he was fitted for, and having never been guided to the discovery, he was taken by the newest idea, and was glad to get rid of the trouble of consideration, I wondered whether the Latin Verses often ended in this, or whether Richard's was a solitary case.

Mr. Jarndyce took great pains to talk with him, seriously, and to put it to his good sense not to deceive himself in so important a matter. Richard was a little grave after these interviews; but invariably told Ada and me "that it was all right," and then began to talk about something else.

"By Heaven!" cried Mr. Boythorn, who interested himself strongly in the subject—though I need not say that, for he could do nothing weakly; "I rejoice to find a young gentleman of spirit and gallantry devoting himself to that noble profession! The more spirit there is in it, the better for mankind, and the worse for those mercenary task-masters and low tricksters who delight in putting that illustrious art at a disadvantage in the world. By all that is base and despicable," cried Mr. Boythorn, "the treatment of Surgeons aboard ship is such, that I would submit the legs—both legs—of every member of the Admiralty Board to a compound fracture, and render it a transportable offence in any qualified practitioner to set them, if the system were not wholly changed in eight-and-forty hours!"

"Wouldn't you give them a week?" asked Mr. Jarndyce.

"No!" cried Mr. Boythorn, firmly. "Not on any consideration! Eight-and-forty hours! As to Corporations, Parishes, Vestry-Boards, and similar gatherings of jolter-headed clods, who assemble to exchange such speeches that, by Heaven! they ought to be worked in quicksilver mines for the short remainder of their miserable existence, if it were only to prevent their detestable English from contaminating a language spoken in the presence of the Sun—as to those fellows, who meanly take advantage of the ardour of gentle-

2. Member of the Royal College of Surgeons.

men in the pursuit of knowledge, to recompense the inestimable services of the best years of their lives, their long study, and their expensive education, with pittances too small for the acceptance of clerks, I would have the necks of every one of them wrung, and their skulls arranged in Surgeons' Hall[3] for the contemplation of the whole profession—in order that its younger members might understand from actual measurement, in early life, *how* thick skulls may become!"

He wound up this vehement declaration by looking round upon us with a most agreeable smile, and suddenly thundering, Ha, ha, ha! over and over again, until anybody else might have been expected to be quite subdued by the exertion.

As Richard still continued to say that he was fixed in his choice, after repeated periods for consideration had been recommended by Mr. Jarndyce, and had expired; and as he still continued to assure Ada and me, in the same final manner, that it was "all right"; it became advisable to take Mr. Kenge into council. Mr. Kenge, therefore, came down to dinner one day, and leaned back in his chair, and turned his eye-glasses over and over, and spoke in a sonorous voice, and did exactly what I remembered to have seen him do when I was a little girl.

"Ah!" said Mr. Kenge. "Yes. Well! A very good profession, Mr. Jarndyce; a very good profession."

"The course of study and preparation requires to be diligently pursued," observed my Guardian, with a glance at Richard.

"O, no doubt," said Mr. Kenge. "Diligently."

"But that being the case, more or less, with all pursuits, that are worth much," said Mr. Jarndyce, "it is not a special consideration which another choice would be likely to escape."

"Truly," said Mr. Kenge. "And Mr. Richard Carstone, who has so meritoriously acquitted himself in the—shall I say the classic shades?—in which his youth has been passed, will, no doubt, apply the habits, if not the principles and practice, of versification in that tongue in which a poet was said (unless I mistake) to be born, not made,[4] to the more eminently practical field of action on which he enters."

"You may rely upon it," said Richard, in his off-hand manner, "that I shall go at it and do my best."

"Very well, Mr. Jarndyce!" said Mr. Kenge, gently nodding his head. "Really, when we are assured by Mr. Richard that he means to go at it, and to do his best," nodding feelingly and smoothly over

3. A building occupied by the Company of Surgeons in the eighteenth century. In the nineteenth century the name continued to be loosely used to refer to a new building, completed in 1837, occupied by the Royal College of Surgeons, located in Lincoln's Inn Fields. It included a museum displaying a collection of skulls.

4. "*Poeta nascitur non fit*"—from the fragmentary writings of Florus, a second-century Roman poet.

those expressions; "I would submit to you, that we have only to inquire into the best mode of carrying out the object of his ambition. Now, with reference to placing Mr. Richard with some sufficiently eminent practitioner. Is there any one in view at present?"

"No one, Rick, I think?" said my Guardian.

"No one, sir," said Richard.

"Quite so!" observed Mr. Kenge. "As to situation, now. Is there any particular feeling on that head?"

"N—no," said Richard.

"Quite so!" observed Mr. Kenge again.

"I should like a little variety," said Richard; "—I mean a good range of experience."

"Very requisite, no doubt," returned Mr. Kenge. "I think this may be easily arranged, Mr. Jarndyce? We have only, in the first place, to discover a sufficiently eligible practitioner; and, as soon as we make our want—and, shall I add, our ability to pay a premium?—known, our only difficulty will be in the selection of one from a large number. We have only, in the second place, to observe those little formalities which are rendered necessary by our time of life, and our being under the guardianship of the Court. We shall soon be—shall I say, in Mr. Richard's own light-hearted manner, 'going at it'—to our heart's content. It is a coincidence," said Mr. Kenge, with a tinge of melancholy in his smile, "one of those coincidences which may or may not require an explanation beyond our present limited faculties, that I have a cousin in the medical profession. He might be deemed eligible by you, and might be disposed to respond to this proposal. I can answer for him as little as for you; but he *might!*"

As this was an opening in the prospect, it was arranged that Mr. Kenge should see his cousin. And as Mr. Jarndyce had before proposed to take us to London for a few weeks, it was settled next day that we should make our visit at once, and combine Richard's business with it.

Mr. Boythorn leaving us within a week, we took up our abode at a cheerful lodging near Oxford Street, over an upholsterer's shop. London was a great wonder to us, and we were out for hours and hours at a time; seeing the sights; which appeared to be less capable of exhaustion than we were. We made the round of the principal theatres, too, with great delight, and saw all the plays that were worth seeing. I mention this, because it was at the theatre that I began to be made uncomfortable again, by Mr. Guppy.

I was sitting in front of the box one night with Ada; and Richard was in the place he liked best, behind Ada's chair; when, happening to look down into the pit, I saw Mr. Guppy, with his hair flattened down upon his head, and woe depicted in his face, looking up at me. I felt, all through the performance, that he never looked at the actors, but constantly looked at me, and always with a carefully prepared expression of the deepest misery and the profoundest dejection.

It quite spoiled my pleasure for that night, because it was so very embarrassing and so very ridiculous. But, from that time forth, we never went to the play without my seeing Mr. Guppy in the pit, always with his hair straight and flat, his shirt-collar turned down, and a general feebleness about him. If he were not there when we went in, and I began to hope he would not come, and yielded myself for a little while to the interest of the scene, I was certain to encounter his languishing eyes when I least expected it, and, from that time, to be quite sure that they were fixed upon me all the evening.

I really cannot express how uneasy this made me. If he would only have brushed up his hair, or turned up his collar, it would have been bad enough; but to know that that absurd figure was always gazing at me, and always in that demonstrative state of despondency, put such a constraint upon me that I did not like to laugh at the play, or to cry at it, or to move or to speak. I seemed able to do nothing naturally. As to escaping Mr. Guppy by going to the back of the box, I could not bear to do that; because I knew Richard and Ada relied on having me next them, and that they could never have talked together so happily if anybody else had been in my place. So there I sat, not knowing where to look—for wherever I looked, I knew Mr. Guppy's eyes were following me—and thinking of the dreadful expense to which this young man was putting himself on my account.

Sometimes, I thought of telling Mr. Jarndyce. Then I feared that the young man would lose his situation, and that I might ruin him. Sometimes, I thought of confiding in Richard; but was deterred by the possibility of his fighting Mr. Guppy, and giving him black eyes. Sometimes, I thought, should I frown at him, or shake my head. Then I felt I could not do it. Sometimes I considered whether I should write to his mother, but that ended in my being convinced that to open a correspondence would be to make the matter worse. I always came to the conclusion, finally, that I could do nothing. Mr. Guppy's perseverance, all this time, not only produced him regularly at any theatre to which we went, but caused him to appear in the crowd as we were coming out, and even to get up behind our fly—where I am sure I saw him, two or three times, struggling among the most dreadful spikes.[5] After we got home, he

5. Spikes attached to the rear axle of a carriage to discourage anyone seeking a free ride.

haunted a post opposite our house. The upholsterer's where we lodged, being at the corner of two streets, and my bedroom window being opposite the post, I was afraid to go near the window when I went up-stairs, lest I should see him (as I did one moonlight night) leaning against the post, and evidently catching cold. If Mr. Guppy had not been, fortunately for me, engaged in the day-time, I really should have had no rest from him.

While we were making this round of gaieties, in which Mr. Guppy so extraordinarily participated, the business which had helped to bring us to town was not neglected. Mr. Kenge's cousin was a Mr. Bayham Badger,[6] who had a good practice at Chelsea, and attended a large public Institution besides. He was quite willing to receive Richard into his house, and to superintend his studies; and as it seemed that those could be pursued advantageously under Mr. Badger's roof, and Mr. Badger liked Richard, and as Richard said he liked Mr. Badger "well enough," an agreement was made, the Lord Chancellor's consent was obtained, and it was all settled.

On the day when matters were concluded between Richard and Mr. Badger, we were all under engagement to dine at Mr. Badger's house. We were to be "merely a family party," Mrs. Badger's note said; and we found no lady there but Mrs. Badger herself. She was surrounded in the drawing-room by various objects, indicative of her painting a little, playing the piano a little, playing the guitar a little, playing the harp a little, singing a little, working a little, reading a little, writing poetry a little, and botanising a little. She was a lady of about fifty, I should think, youthfully dressed, and of a very fine complexion. If I add, to the little list of her accomplishments, that she rouged a little, I do not mean that there was any harm in it.

Mr. Bayham Badger himself was a pink, fresh-faced, crisp-looking gentleman, with a weak voice, white teeth, light hair, and surprised eyes; some years younger, I should say, than Mrs. Bayham Badger. He admired her exceedingly, but principally, and to begin with, on the curious ground (as it seemed to us) of her having had three husbands. We had barely taken our seats, when he said to Mr. Jarndyce quite triumphantly,

"You would hardly suppose that I am Mrs. Bayham Badger's third!"

"Indeed?" said Mr. Jarndyce.

"Her third!" said Mr. Badger. "Mrs. Bayham Badger has not the appearance, Miss Summerson, of a lady who has had two former husbands?"

I said "Not at all!"

"And most remarkable men!" said Mr. Badger, in a tone of confidence. "Captain Swosser of the Royal Navy, who was Mrs. Badger's

6. Surgeons in England were addressed as *Mr.* rather than *Dr.*

first husband, was a very distinguished officer indeed. The name of Professor Dingo, my immediate predecessor, is one of European reputation."

Mrs. Badger overheard him, and smiled.

"Yes, my dear!" Mr. Badger replied to the smile, "I was observing to Mr. Jarndyce and Miss Summerson, that you had had two former husbands—both very distinguished men. And they found it, as people generally do, difficult to believe."

"I was barely twenty," said Mrs. Badger, "when I married Captain Swosser of the Royal Navy. I was in the Mediterranean with him; I am quite a Sailor. On the twelfth anniversary of my wedding-day, I became the wife of Professor Dingo."

("Of European reputation," added Mr. Badger, in an undertone.)

"And when Mr. Badger and myself were married," pursued Mrs. Badger, "we were married on the same day of the year. I had become attached to the day."

"So that Mrs. Badger has been married to three husbands—two of them highly distinguished men," said Mr. Badger, summing up the facts; "and, each time, upon the twenty-first of March at Eleven in the forenoon!"

We all expressed our admiration.

"But for Mr. Badger's modesty," said Mr. Jarndyce, "I would take leave to correct him, and say three distinguished men."

"Thank you, Mr. Jarndyce! What I always tell him!" observed Mrs. Badger.

"And, my dear," said Mr. Badger, "what do *I* always tell you? That without any affectation of disparaging such professional distinction as I may have attained (which our friend Mr. Carstone will have many opportunities of estimating), I am not so weak—no really," said Mr. Badger to us generally, "so unreasonable—as to put my reputation on the same footing with such first-rate men as Captain Swosser and Professor Dingo. Perhaps you may be interested, Mr. Jarndyce," continued Mr. Bayham Badger, leading the way into the next drawing-room, "in this portrait of Captain Swosser. It was taken on his return home from the African Station, where he had suffered from the fever of the country. Mrs. Badger considers it too yellow. But it's a very fine head. A very fine head!"

We all echoed "A very fine head!"

"I feel when I look at it," said Mr. Badger, " 'that's a man I should like to have seen!' It strikingly bespeaks the first-class man that Captain Swosser pre-eminently was. On the other side, Professor Dingo. I knew him well—attended him in his last illness—a speaking likeness! Over the piano, Mrs. Bayham Badger when Mrs. Swosser. Over the sofa, Mrs. Bayham Badger when Mrs. Dingo. Of

Mrs. Bayham Badger *in esse*, I possess the original, and have no copy."

Dinner was now announced, and we went down-stairs. It was a very genteel entertainment, very handsomely served. But the Captain and the Professor still ran in Mr. Badger's head, and, as Ada and I had the honour of being under his particular care, we had the full benefit of them.

"Water, Miss Summerson? Allow me! Not in that tumbler, pray. Bring me the Professor's goblet, James!"

Ada very much admired some artificial flowers, under a glass.

"Astonishing how they keep!" said Mr. Badger. "They were presented to Mrs. Bayham Badger when she was in the Mediterranean."

He invited Mr. Jarndyce to take a glass of claret.

"Not that claret!" he said. "Excuse me. This is an occasion, and *on* an occasion I produce some very special claret I happen to have. (James, Captain Swosser's wine!) Mr. Jarndyce, this is a wine that was imported by the Captain, we will not say how many years ago. You will find it very curious. My dear, I shall be happy to take some of this wine with you. (Captain Swosser's claret to your mistress, James!) My love, your health!"

After dinner, when we ladies retired, we took Mrs. Badger's first and second husband with us. Mrs. Badger gave us, in the drawing-room, a Biographical sketch of the life and services of Captain Swosser before his marriage, and a more minute account of him dating from the time when he fell in love with her, at a ball on board the Crippler, given to the officers of that ship when she lay in Plymouth Harbour.

"The dear old Crippler!" said Mrs. Badger, shaking her head. "She was a noble vessel. Trim, ship-shape, all a taunto,[7] as Captain Swosser used to say. You must excuse me if I occasionally introduce a nautical expression; I was quite a sailor once. Captain Swosser loved that craft for my sake. When she was no longer in commission, he frequently said that if he were rich enough to buy her old hulk, he would have an inscription let into the timbers of the quarter-deck where we stood as partners in the dance, to mark the spot where he fell—raked fore and aft (Captain Swosser used to say) by the fire from my tops. It was his naval way of mentioning my eyes."

Mrs. Badger shook her head, sighed, and looked in the glass.

"It was a great change from Captain Swosser to Professor Dingo," she resumed, with a plaintive smile. "I felt it a good deal at first. Such an entire revolution in my mode of life! But custom, combined with science—particularly science—inured me to it. Being the Professor's sole companion in his botanical excursions, I

7. With all sails hoisted.

almost forgot that I had ever been afloat, and became quite learned. It is singular that the Professor was the Antipodes of Captain Swosser, and that Mr. Badger is not in the least like either!"

We then passed into a narrative of the deaths of Captain Swosser and Professor Dingo, both of whom seemed to have had very bad complaints. In the course of it, Mrs. Badger signified to us that she had never madly loved but once; and that the object of that wild affection, never to be recalled in its fresh enthusiasm, was Captain Swosser. The Professor was yet dying by inches in the most dismal manner, and Mrs. Badger was giving us imitations of his way of saying, with great difficulty, "Where is Laura? Let Laura give me my toast and water!" when the entrance of the gentlemen consigned him to the tomb.

Now, I observed that evening, as I had observed for some days past, that Ada and Richard were more than ever attached to each other's society; which was but natural, seeing that they were going to be separated so soon. I was therefore not very much surprised, when we got home, and Ada and I retired up-stairs, to find Ada more silent than usual; though I was not quite prepared for her coming into my arms, and beginning to speak to me, with her face hidden.

"My darling Esther!" murmured Ada. "I have a great secret to tell you!"

A mighty secret, my pretty one, no doubt!

"What is it, Ada?"

"O Esther, you would never guess!"

"Shall I try to guess?" said I.

"O no! Don't! Pray don't!" cried Ada, very much startled by the idea of my doing so.

"Now, I wonder who it can be about?" said I, pretending to consider.

"It's about," said Ada, in a whisper. "It's about—my cousin Richard!"

"Well, my own!" said I, kissing her bright hair, which was all I could see. "And what about him?"

"O Esther, you would never guess!"

It was so pretty to have her clinging to me in that way, hiding her face; and to know that she was not crying in sorrow, but in a little glow of joy, and pride, and hope; that I would not help her just yet.

"He says—I know it's very foolish, we are both so young—but he says," with a burst of tears, "that he loves me dearly, Esther."

"Does he indeed?" said I. "I never heard of such a thing! Why, my pet of pets, I could have told you that weeks and weeks ago!"

To see Ada lift up her flushed face in joyful surprise, and hold me round the neck, and laugh, and cry, and blush, and laugh, was so pleasant!

"Why, my darling!" said I, "what a goose you must take me for! Your cousin Richard has been loving you as plainly as he could, for I don't know how long!"

"And yet you never said a word about it!" cried Ada, kissing me.

"No, my love," said I. "I waited to be told."

"But now I have told you, you don't think it wrong of me; do you?" returned Ada. She might have coaxed me to say No, if I had been the hardest-hearted Duenna in the world. Not being that yet, I said No, very freely.

"And now," said I, "I know the worst of it."

"O, that's not quite the worst of it, Esther dear!" cried Ada, holding me tighter, and laying down her face again upon my breast.

"No?" said I. "Not even that?"

"No, not even that!" said Ada, shaking her head.

"Why, you never mean to say—!" I was beginning in joke.

But Ada, looking up, and smiling through her tears, cried, "Yes, I do! You know, you know I do!" and then sobbed out, "With all my heart I do! With all my whole heart, Esther!"

I told her, laughing, why I had known that, too, just as well as I had known the other! And we sat before the fire, and I had all the talking to myself for a little while (though there was not much of it); and Ada was soon quiet and happy.

"Do you think my cousin John knows, dear Dame Durden?" she asked.

"Unless my cousin John is blind, my pet," said I, "I should think my cousin John knows pretty well as much as we know."

"We want to speak to him before Richard goes," said Ada, timidly, "and we wanted you to advise us, and to tell him so. Perhaps you wouldn't mind Richard's coming in, Dame Durden?"

"O! Richard is outside, is he, my dear?" said I.

"I am not quite certain," returned Ada, with a bashful simplicity that would have won my heart, if she had not won it long before; "but I think he's waiting at the door."

There he was, of course. They brought a chair on either side of me, and put me between them, and really seemed to have fallen in love with me, instead of one another; they were so confiding, and so trustful, and so fond of me. They went on in their own wild way for a little while—*I* never stopped them; I enjoyed it too much myself—and then we gradually fell to considering how young they were, and how there must be a lapse of several years before this early love could come to anything, and how it could come to happiness only if it were real and lasting, and inspired them with a steady resolution to do their duty to each other, with constancy, fortitude, and perseverance: each always for the other's sake. Well! Richard said that he would work his fingers to the bone for Ada, and Ada said that she would work her fingers to the bone for Richard, and they called me all sorts of endearing and sensible names, and we sat there, advising and talking, half the night. Finally, before we parted, I gave them my promise to speak to their cousin John to-morrow.

So, when to-morrow came, I went to my guardian after breakfast, in the room that was our town-substitute for the Growlery, and told him that I had it in trust to tell him something.

"Well, little woman," said he, shutting up his book, "if you have accepted the trust, there can be no harm in it."

"I hope not, Guardian," said I. "I can guarantee that there is no secrecy in it. For it only happened yesterday."

"Aye? And what is it, Esther?"

"Guardian," said I, "you remember the happy night when we first came down to Bleak House? When Ada was singing in the dark room?"

I wished to call to his remembrance the look he had given me then. Unless I am much mistaken, I saw that I did so.

"Because," said I, with a little hesitation.

"Yes, my dear!" said he. "Don't hurry."

"Because," said I, "Ada and Richard have fallen in love. And have told each other so."

"Already!" cried my guardian, quite astonished.

"Yes!" said I, "and to tell you the truth, Guardian, I rather expected it."

"The deuce you did!" said he.

He sat considering for a minute or two; with his smile, at once so handsome and so kind, upon his changing face; and then requested me to let them know that he wished to see them. When they came, he encircled Ada with one arm, in his fatherly way, and addressed himself to Richard with a cheerful gravity.

"Rick," said Mr. Jarndyce, "I am glad to have won your confidence. I hope to preserve it. When I contemplated these relations between us four which have so brightened my life, and so invested it with new interests and pleasures, I certainly did contemplate, afar off, the possibility of you and your pretty cousin here (don't be shy, Ada, don't be shy, my dear!) being in a mind to go through life together. I saw, and do see, many reasons to make it desirable. But that was afar off, Rick, afar off!"

"We look afar off, sir," returned Richard.

"Well!" said Mr. Jarndyce. "That's rational. Now, hear me, my dears! I might tell you that you don't know your own minds yet; that a thousand things may happen to divert you from one another;

that it is well this chain of flowers you have taken up is very easily broken, or it might become a chain of lead. But I will not do that. Such wisdom will come soon enough, I dare say, if it is to come at all. I will assume that, a few years hence, you will be in your hearts to one another, what you are to-day. All I say before speaking to you according to that assumption is, if you *do* change—if you *do* come to find that you are more commonplace cousins to each other as man and woman, than you were as boy and girl (your manhood will excuse me, Rick!)—don't be ashamed still to confide in me, for there will be nothing monstrous or uncommon in it. I am only your friend and distant kinsman. I have no power over you whatever. But I wish and hope to retain your confidence, if I do nothing to forfeit it."

"I am very sure, sir," returned Richard, "that I speak for Ada, too, when I say that you have the strongest power over us both—rooted in respect, gratitude, and affection—strengthening every day."

"Dear cousin John," said Ada, on his shoulder, "my father's place can never be empty again. All the love and duty I could ever have rendered to him, is transferred to you."

"Come!" said Mr. Jarndyce. "Now for our assumption. Now we lift our eyes up, and look hopefully at the distance! Rick, the world is before you; and it is most probable that as you enter it, so it will receive you. Trust in nothing but in Providence and your own efforts. Never separate the two, like the heathen waggoner.[8] Constancy in love is a good thing; but it means nothing, and is nothing, without constancy in every kind of effort. If you had the abilities of all the great men, past and present, you could do nothing well, without sincerely meaning it, and setting about it. If you entertain the supposition that any real success, in great things or in small, ever was or could be, ever will or can be, wrested from Fortune by fits and starts, leave that wrong idea here, or leave your cousin Ada here."

"I will leave *it* here, sir," replied Richard, smiling, "if I brought it here just now (but I hope I did not), and will work my way on to my cousin Ada in the hopeful distance."

"Right!" said Mr. Jarndyce. "If you are not to make her happy, why should you pursue her?"

"I wouldn't make her unhappy—no, not even for her love," retorted Richard, proudly.

"Well said!" cried Mr. Jarndyce; "that's well said! She remains here, in her home with me. Love her, Rick, in your active life, no less than in her home when you revisit it, and all will go well. Oth-

8. In Aesop's *Fables*, a wagon-driver prayed to the god, Hercules, to extricate his wagon from a mud-hole. Hercules replied that instead of calling upon the gods for help he ought first to put his own shoulder to the wheel.

erwise, all will go ill. That's the end of my preaching. I think you and Ada had better take a walk."

Ada tenderly embraced him, and Richard heartily shook hands with him, and then the cousins went out of the room—looking back again directly, though, to say that they would wait for me.

The door stood open, and we both followed them with our eyes, as they passed down the adjoining room on which the sun was shining, and out at its farther end. Richard with his head bent, and her hand drawn through his arm, was talking to her very earnestly; and she looked up in his face, listening, and seemed to see nothing else. So young, so beautiful, so full of hope and promise, they went on lightly through the sunlight, as their own happy thoughts might then be traversing the years to some, and making them all years of brightness. So they passed away into the shadow, and were gone. It was only a burst of light that had been so radiant. The room darkened as they went out, and the sun was clouded over.

"Am I right, Esther?" said my Guardian, when they were gone. He who was so good and wise, to ask *me* whether he was right!

"Rick may gain, out of this, the quality he wants. Wants, at the core of so much that is good!" said Mr. Jarndyce, shaking his head. "I have said nothing to Ada, Esther. She has her friend and counsellor always near." And he laid his hand lovingly upon my head.

I could not help showing that I was a little moved, though I did all I could to conceal it.

"Tut, tut!" said he. "But we must take care, too, that our little woman's life is not all consumed in care for others."

"Care? My dear Guardian, I believe I am the happiest creature in the world!"

"I believe so, too," said he. "But some one may find out, what Esther never will,—that the little woman is to be held in remembrance above all other people!"

I have omitted to mention in its place, that there was some one else at the family dinner party. It was not a lady. It was a gentleman. It was a gentleman of a dark complexion—a young surgeon. He was rather reserved, but I thought him very sensible and agreeable. At least, Ada asked me if I did not, and I said yes.

Chapter XIV

DEPORTMENT

Richard left us on the very next evening, to begin his new career, and committed Ada to my charge with great love for her, and great trust in me. It touched me then to reflect, and it touches me now, more nearly, to remember (having what I have to tell) how they both thought of me, even at that engrossing time. I was a part of all their plans, for the present and the future. I was to write to Richard once a week, making my faithful report of Ada, who was to write to him every alternate day. I was to be informed, under his own hand, of all his labours and successes; I was to observe how resolute and persevering he would be; I was to be Ada's bridesmaid when they were married; I was to live with them afterwards; I was to keep all the keys of their house; I was to be made happy for ever and a day.

"And if the suit *should* make us rich, Esther—which it may, you know!" said Richard, to crown all.

A shade crossed Ada's face.

"My dearest Ada," asked Richard, pausing, "why not?"

"It had better declare us poor at once," said Ada.

"O! I don't know about that," returned Richard; "but, at all events, it won't declare anything at once. It hasn't declared anything in Heaven knows how many years."

"Too true," said Ada.

"Yes, but," urged Richard, answering what her look suggested rather than her words, "the longer it goes on, dear cousin, the nearer it must be to a settlement one way or other. Now, is not that reasonable?"

"You know best, Richard. But I am afraid if we trust to it, it will make us unhappy."

"But, my Ada, we are not going to trust to it!" cried Richard gaily. "We know it better than to trust to it. We only say that if it *should* make us rich, we have no constitutional objection to being rich. The Court is, by solemn settlement of law, our grim old guardian, and we are to suppose that what it gives us (when it gives us anything) is our right. It is not necessary to quarrel with our right."

"No," said Ada, "But it may be better to forget all about it."

"Well, well!" cried Richard, "then we will forget all about it! We consign the whole thing to oblivion. Dame Durden puts on her approving face, and it's done!"

"Dame Durden's approving face," said I, looking out of the box in which I was packing his books, "was not very visible when you called it by that name; but it does approve, and she thinks you can't do better."

So Richard said there was an end of it,—and immediately began, on no other foundation, to build as many castles in the air as would man the great wall of China. He went away in high spirits. Ada and I, prepared to miss him very much, commenced our quieter career.

On our arrival in London, we had called with Mr. Jarndyce at Mrs. Jellyby's, but had not been so fortunate as to find her at home. It appeared that she had gone somewhere, to a tea-drinking, and had taken Miss Jellyby with her. Besides the tea-drinking, there was to be some considerable speech-making and letter-writing on the general merits of the cultivation of coffee, conjointly with natives, at the Settlement of Borrioboola Gha. All this involved, no doubt, sufficient active exercise of pen and ink, to make her daughter's part in the proceedings anything but a holiday.

It being, now, beyond the time appointed for Mrs. Jellyby's return, we called again. She was in town, but not at home, having gone to Mile End, directly after breakfast, on some Borrioboolan business, arising out of a Society called the East London Branch Aid Ramification. As I had not seen Peepy on the occasion of our last call (when he was not to be found anywhere, and when the cook rather thought he must have strolled away with the dustman's cart), I now inquired for him again. The oyster-shells he had been building a house with, were still in the passage, but he was nowhere discoverable, and the cook supposed that he had "gone after the sheep." When we repeated, with some surprise, "The sheep?" she said, O yes, on market days he sometimes followed them quite out of town, and came back in such a state as never was!

I was sitting at the window with my guardian, on the following morning, and Ada was busy writing—of course to Richard—when Miss Jellyby was announced, and entered, leading the identical Peepy, whom she had made some endeavours to render presentable, by wiping the dirt into corners of his face and hands, and making his hair very wet and then violently frizzling it with her fingers. Everything the dear child wore, was either too large for him or too small. Among his other contradictory decorations he had the hat of a Bishop, and the little gloves of a baby. His boots were, on a small scale, the boots of a ploughman: while his legs, so crossed and recrossed with scratches that they looked like maps, were bare, below a very short pair of plaid drawers finished off with two frills of perfectly different patterns. The deficient buttons on his plaid frock had evidently been supplied from one of Mr. Jellyby's coats, they were so extremely brazen and so much too large. Most extraordinary specimens of needlework appeared on several parts of his dress, where it had been hastily mended; and I recognized the same hand on Miss Jellyby's. She was, however, unaccountably improved in her appearance, and looked very pretty. She was conscious of poor little Peepy being but a failure after all her trouble, and she showed it as she came in, by the way in which she glanced, first at him and then at us.

"O dear me!" said my guardian. "Due East!"

Ada and I gave her a cordial welcome, and presented her to Mr. Jarndyce; to whom she said, as she sat down:

"Ma's compliments, and she hopes you'll excuse her, because she's correcting proofs of the plan. She's going to put out five thousand new circulars, and she knows you'll be interested to hear that.

I have brought one of them with me. Ma's compliments." With which she presented it sulkily enough.

"Thank you," said my guardian. "I am much obliged to Mrs. Jellyby. O dear me! This is a very trying wind!"

We were busy with Peepy; taking off his clerical hat; asking him if he remembered us; and so on. Peepy retired behind his elbow at first, but relented at the sight of sponge-cake, and allowed me to take him on my lap, where he sat munching quietly. Mr. Jarndyce then withdrawing into the temporary Growlery, Miss Jellyby opened a conversation with her usual abruptness.

"We are going on just as bad as ever in Thavies Inn," said she. "I have no peace of my life. Talk of Africa! I couldn't be worse off if I was a what-'s-his-name—man and a brother!"[1]

I tried to say something soothing.

"O, it's of no use, Miss Summerson," exclaimed Miss Jellyby, "though I thank you for the kind intention all the same. I know how I am used, and I am not to be talked over. *You* wouldn't be talked over, if you were used so. Peepy, go and play at Wild Beasts under the piano!"

"I shan't!" said Peepy.

"Very well, you ungrateful, naughty, hard-hearted boy!" returned Miss Jellyby, with tears in her eyes. "I'll never take pains to dress you any more."

"Yes, I will go, Caddy!" cried Peepy, who was really a good child, and who was so moved by his sister's vexation that he went at once.

"It seems a little thing to cry about," said poor Miss Jellyby, apologetically, "but I am quite worn out. I was directing the new circulars till two this morning. I detest the whole thing so, that that alone makes my head ache till I can't see out of my eyes. And look at that poor unfortunate child! Was there ever such a fright as he is!"

Peepy, happily unconscious of the defects in his appearance, sat on the carpet behind one of the legs of the piano, looking calmly out of his den at us, while he ate his cake.

"I have sent him to the other end of the room," observed Miss Jellyby, drawing her chair nearer ours, "because I don't want him to hear the conversation. Those little things are so sharp! I was going to say, we really are going on worse than ever. Pa will be a bankrupt before long, and then I hope Ma will be satisfied. There'll be nobody but Ma to thank for it."

We said we hoped Mr. Jellyby's affairs were not in so bad a state as that.

"It's of no use hoping, though it's very kind of you," returned

1. In propaganda pamphlets against the slave trade a picture of a slave being lashed had the inscription: "Am I not a man and a brother?"

Miss Jellyby, shaking her head. "Pa told me, only yesterday morning (and dreadfully unhappy he is), that he couldn't weather the storm. I should be surprised if he could. When all our tradesmen send into our house any stuff they like, and the servants do what they like with it, and I have no time to improve things if I knew how, and Ma don't care about anything, I should like to make out how Pa *is* to weather the storm. I declare if I was Pa, I'd run away."

"My dear!" said I, smiling. "Your papa, no doubt, considers his family."

"O yes, his family is all very fine, Miss Summerson," replied Miss Jellyby; "but what comfort is his family to him? His family is nothing but bills, dirt, waste, noise, tumbles down-stairs, confusion, and wretchedness. His scrambling home, from week's-end to week's-end, is like one great washing-day—only nothing's washed!"

Miss Jellyby tapped her foot upon the floor, and wiped her eyes.

"I am sure I pity Pa to that degree," she said, "and am so angry with Ma, that I can't find words to express myself! However, I am not going to bear it, I am determined. I won't be a slave all my life, and I won't submit to be proposed to by Mr. Quale. A pretty thing, indeed, to marry a Philanthropist. As if I hadn't had enough of *that*!" said poor Miss Jellyby.

I must confess that I could not help feeling rather angry with Mrs. Jellyby myself; seeing and hearing this neglected girl, and knowing how much of bitterly satirical truth there was in what she said.

"If it wasn't that we had been intimate when you stopped at our house," pursued Miss Jellyby, "I should have been ashamed to come here to-day, for I know what a figure I must seem to you two. But, as it is, I made up my mind to call: especially as I am not likely to see you again, the next time you come to town."

She said this with such great significance that Ada and I glanced at one another, foreseeing something more.

"No!" said Miss Jellyby, shaking her head. "Not at all likely! I know I may trust you two. I am sure you won't betray me. I am engaged."

"Without their knowledge at home?" said I.

"Why, good gracious me, Miss Summerson," she returned, justifying herself in a fretful but not angry manner, "how can it be otherwise? You know what Ma is—and I needn't make poor Pa more miserable by telling *him*."

"But would it not be adding to his unhappiness, to marry without his knowledge or consent, my dear?" said I.

"No," said Miss Jellyby, softening. "I hope not. I should try to make him happy and comfortable when he came to see me; and

Peepy and the others should take it in turns to come and stay with me; and they should have some care taken of them, then."

There was a good deal of affection in poor Caddy. She softened more and more while saying this, and cried so much over the unwonted little home-picture she had raised in her mind, that Peepy, in his cave under the piano, was touched, and turned himself over on his back with loud lamentations. It was not until I had brought him to kiss his sister, and had restored him to his place in my lap, and had shown him that Caddy was laughing (she laughed expressly for the purpose), that we could recall his peace of mind; even then, it was for some time conditional on his taking us in turns by the chin, and smoothing our faces all over with his hand. At last, as his spirits were not yet equal to the piano, we put him on a chair to look out of the window; and Miss Jellyby, holding him by one leg, resumed her confidence.

"It began in your coming to our house," she said.

We naturally asked how?

"I felt I was so awkward," she replied, "that I made up my mind to be improved in that respect, at all events, and to learn to dance. I told Ma I was ashamed of myself, and I must be taught to dance. Ma looked at me in that provoking way of hers as if I wasn't in sight; but I was quite determined to be taught to dance, and so I went to Mr. Turveydrop's Academy in Newman Street."

"And was it there, my dear——" I began.

"Yes, it was there," said Caddy, "and I am engaged to Mr. Turveydrop. There are two Mr. Turveydrops, father and son. My Mr. Turveydrop is the son, of course. I only wish I had been better brought up, and was likely to make him a better wife; for I am very fond of him."

"I am sorry to hear this," said I, "I must confess."

"I don't know why you should be sorry," she retorted a little anxiously, "but I am engaged to Mr. Turveydrop, whether or no, and he is very fond of me. It's a secret as yet, even on his side, because old Mr. Turveydrop has a share in the connexion, and it might break his heart, or give him some other shock, if he was told of it abruptly. Old Mr. Turveydrop is a very gentlemanly man indeed—very gentlemanly."

"Does his wife know of it?" asked Ada.

"Old Mr. Turveydrop's wife, Miss Clare?" returned Miss Jellyby, opening her eyes. "There's no such person. He is a widower."

We were here interrupted by Peepy, whose leg had undergone so much on account of his sister's unconsciously jerking it like a bell-rope whenever she was emphatic, that the afflicted child now bemoaned his sufferings with a very low-spirited noise. As he appealed to me for compassion, and as I was only a listener, I undertook to hold him. Miss Jellyby proceeded, after begging Peepy's pardon with a kiss, and assuring him that she hadn't meant to do it.

"That's the state of the case," said Caddy. "If I ever blame myself, I still think it's Ma's fault. We are to be married whenever we can, and then I shall go to Pa at the office and write to Ma. It won't much agitate Ma; I am only pen and ink to *her*. One great comfort is," said Caddy, with a sob, "that I shall never hear of Africa after I am married. Young Mr. Turveydrop hates it for my sake; and if old Mr. Turveydrop knows there is such a place, it's as much as he does."

"It was he who was very gentlemanly, I think!" said I.

"Very gentlemanly, indeed," said Caddy. "He is celebrated, almost everywhere, for his Deportment."

"Does he teach?" asked Ada.

"No, he don't teach anything in particular," replied Caddy. "But his Deportment is beautiful."

Caddy went on to say, with considerable hesitation and reluctance, that there was one thing more she wished us to know, and felt we ought to know, and which she hoped would not offend us. It was, that she had improved her acquaintance with Miss Flite, the little crazy old lady; and that she frequently went there early in the morning, and met her lover for a few minutes before breakfast—only for a few minutes. "I go there, at other times," said Caddy, "but Prince does not come then. Young Mr. Turveydrop's name is Prince; I wish it wasn't, because it sounds like a dog, but of course he didn't christen himself. Old Mr. Turveydrop had him christened Prince, in remembrance of the Prince Regent. Old Mr. Turveydrop adored the Prince Regent on account of his Deportment. I hope you won't think the worse of me for having made these little appointments at Miss Flite's, where I first went with you; because I like the poor thing for her own sake, and I believe she likes me. If you could see young Mr. Turveydrop, I am sure you would think well of him—at least, I am sure you couldn't possibly think any ill of him. I am going there now, for my lesson. I couldn't ask you to go with me, Miss Summerson; but if you would," said Caddy, who had said all this, earnestly and tremblingly, "I should be very glad —very glad."

It happened that we had arranged with my Guardian to go to Miss Flite's that day. We had told him of our former visit, and our account had interested him; but something had always happened to prevent our going there again. As I trusted that I might have sufficient influence with Miss Jellyby to prevent her taking any very rash step, if I fully accepted the confidence she was so willing to place in me, poor girl, I proposed that she and I and Peepy should go to the Academy, and afterwards meet my Guardian and Ada at Miss Flite's—whose name I now learnt for the first time. This was on condition that Miss Jellyby and Peepy should come back with us to dinner. The last article of the agreement being joyfully acceded to by both, we smartened Peepy up a little, with the assistance of a few pins, some soap and water, and a hair-brush; and went out: bending our steps towards Newman Street, which was very near.

I found the Academy established in a sufficiently dingy house at the corner of an archway, with busts in all the staircase windows. In the same house there were also established, as I gathered from the plates on the door, a drawing-master, a coal-merchant (there was, certainly, no room for his coals), and a lithographic artist. On the plate which, in size and situation, took precedence of all the rest, I read, MR. TURVEYDROP. The door was open, and the hall was blocked up by a grand piano, a harp, and several other musical instruments in cases, all in progress of removal, and all looking rakish in the daylight. Miss Jellyby informed me that the Academy had been lent, last night, for a concert.

We went upstairs—it had been quite a fine house once, when it was anybody's business to keep it clean and fresh, and nobody's business to smoke in it all day—and into Mr. Turveydrop's great room, which was built out into a mews at the back, and was lighted by a skylight. It was a bare, resounding room, smelling of stables; with cane forms[2] along the walls; and the walls ornamental at regular intervals with painted lyres, and little cut-glass branches for candles, which seemed to be shedding their old-fashioned drops as other branches might shed autumn leaves. Several young lady pupils, ranging from thirteen or fourteen years of age to two or three and twenty, were assembled; and I was looking among them for their instructor, when Caddy, pinching my arm, repeated the ceremony of introduction. "Miss Summerson, Mr. Prince Turveydrop!"

I curtseyed to a little blue-eyed fair man of youthful appearance, with flaxen hair parted in the middle, and curling at the ends all round his head. He had a little fiddle, which we used to call at school a kit, under his left arm, and its little bow in the same hand. His little dancing-shoes were particularly diminutive, and he had a little innocent, feminine manner, which not only appealed to me in an amiable way, but made this singular effect upon me: that I received the impression that he was like his mother, and that his mother had not been much considered or well used.

"I am very happy to see Miss Jellyby's friend," he said, bowing low to me. "I began to fear," with timid tenderness, "as it was past the usual time, that Miss Jellyby was not coming."

2. Benches.

"I beg you will have the goodness to attribute that to me, who have detained her, and to receive my excuses, sir," said I.

"O dear!" said he.

"And pray," I entreated, "do not allow me to be the cause of any more delay."

With that apology I withdrew to a seat between Peepy (who, being well used to it, had already climbed into a corner place) and an old lady of a censorious countenance, whose two nieces were in the class, and who was very indignant with Peepy's boots. Prince Turveydrop then tinkled the strings of his kit with his fingers, and the young ladies stood up to dance. Just then, there appeared from a side door, old Mr. Turveydrop, in the full lustre of his Deportment.

He was a fat old gentleman with a false complexion, false teeth, false whiskers, and a wig. He had a fur collar, and he had a padded breast to his coat, which only wanted a star or a broad blue ribbon to be complete. He was pinched in, and swelled out, and got up, and strapped down, as much as he could possibly bear. He had such a neckcloth on (puffing his very eyes out of their natural shape), and his chin and even his ears so sunk into it, that it seemed as though he must inevitably double up, if it were cast loose. He had, under his arm, a hat of great size and weight, shelving downward from the crown to the brim; and in his hand a pair of white gloves, with which he flapped it, as he stood poised on one leg, in a high-shouldered, round-elbowed state of elegance not to be surpassed. He had a cane, he had an eye-glass, he had a snuff-box, he had rings, he had wristbands, he had everything but any touch of nature; he was not like youth, he was not like age, he was not like anything in the world but a model of Deportment.

"Father! A visitor. Miss Jellyby's friend, Miss Summerson."

"Distinguished," said Mr. Turveydrop, "by Miss Summerson's presence." As he bowed to me in that tight state, I almost believed I saw creases come into the whites of his eyes.

"My father," said the son, aside, to me, with quite an affecting belief in him, "is a celebrated character. My father is greatly admired."

"Go on, Prince! Go on!" said Mr. Turveydrop, standing with his back to the fire, and waving his gloves condescendingly. "Go on, my son!"

At this command, or by this gracious permission, the lesson went on. Prince Turveydrop sometimes played the kit, dancing; sometimes played the piano, standing; sometimes hummed the tune with what little breath he could spare, while he set a pupil right; always conscientiously moved with the least proficient through every step and every part of the figure; and never rested for an instant. His dis-

The Dancing-School.

tinguished father did nothing whatever, but stand before the fire, a model of Deportment.

"And he never does anything else," said the old lady of the censorious countenance. "Yet would you believe that it's *his* name on the door-plate?"

"His son's name is the same, you know," said I.

"He wouldn't let his son have any name, if he could take it from him," returned the old lady. "Look at the son's dress!" It certainly was plain—threadbare—almost shabby. "Yet the father must be garnished and tricked out," said the old lady, "because of his Deportment. I'd deport him! Transport him would be better!"

I felt curious to know more concerning this person. I asked, "Does he give lessons in Deportment, now?"

"Now!" returned the old lady, shortly. "Never did."

After a moment's consideration, I suggested that perhaps fencing had been his accomplishment?

"I don't believe he can fence at all, ma'am," said the old lady.

I looked surprised and inquisitive. The old lady, becoming more and more incensed against the Master of Deportment as she dwelt upon the subject, gave me some particulars of his career, with strong assurances that they were mildly stated.

He had married a meek dancing-mistress, with a tolerable connexion (having never in his life before done anything but deport himself), and had worked her to death, or had, at the best, suffered her to work herself to death, to maintain him in those expenses which were indispensable to his position. At once to exhibit his Deportment to the best models, and to keep the best models constantly before himself, he had found it necessary to frequent all public places of fashionable and lounging resort; to be seen at Brighton and elsewhere at fashionable times; and to lead an idle life in the very best clothes. To enable him to do this, the affectionate little dancing-mistress had toiled and laboured, and would have toiled and laboured to that hour, if her strength had lasted so long. For the mainspring of the story was that, in spite of the man's absorbing selfishness, his wife (overpowered by his Deportment) had, to the last, believed in him, and had, on her death-bed, in the most moving terms, confided him to their son as one who had an inextinguishable claim upon him, and whom he could never regard with too much pride and deference. The son, inheriting his mother's belief, and having the Deportment always before him, had lived and grown in the same faith, and now, at thirty years of age, worked for his father twelve hours a-day, and looked up to him with veneration on the old imaginary pinnacle.

"The airs the fellow gives himself!" said my informant, shaking her head at old Mr. Turveydrop with speechless indignation as he drew on his tight gloves: of course unconscious of the homage she was rendering. "He fully believes he is one of the aristocracy! And he is so condescending to the son he so egregiously deludes, that you might suppose him the most virtuous of parents. O!" said the old lady, apostrophising him with infinite vehemence, "I could bite you!"

I could not help being amused, though I heard the old lady out with feelings of real concern. It was difficult to doubt her, with the father and son before me. What I might have thought of them without the old lady's account, or what I might have thought of the old lady's account without them, I cannot say. There was a fitness of things in the whole that carried conviction with it.

My eyes were yet wandering, from young Mr. Turveydrop working so hard, to old Mr. Turveydrop deporting himself so beautifully, when the latter came ambling up to me, and entered into conversation.

He asked me, first of all, whether I conferred a charm and a distinction on London by residing in it? I did not think it necessary to reply that I was perfectly aware I should not do that, in any case, but merely told him where I did reside.

"A lady so graceful and accomplished," he said, kissing his right glove, and afterwards extending it towards the pupils, "will look leniently on the deficiencies here. We do our best to polish—polish—polish!"

He sat down beside me; taking some pains to sit on the form, I thought, in imitation of the print of his illustrious model on the sofa.[3] And really he did look very like it.

"To polish—polish—polish!" he repeated, taking a pinch of snuff and gently fluttering his fingers. "But we are not—if I may say so, to one formed to be graceful both by Nature and Art"; with the high-shouldered bow, which it seemed impossible for him to make without lifting up his eyebrows and shutting his eyes—"we are not what we used to be in point of Deportment."

"Are we not, sir?" said I.

"We have degenerated," he returned, shaking his head, which he could do, to a very limited extent, in his cravat. "A levelling age is not favourable to Deportment. It develops vulgarity. Perhaps I speak with some little partiality. It may not be for me to say that I have been called, for some years now, Gentleman Turveydrop; or that His Royal Highness the Prince Regent did me the honour to inquire, on my removing my hat as he drove out of the Pavilion at Brighton (that fine building). 'Who is he? Who the Devil is he? Why don't I know him? Why hasn't he thirty thousand a year?'

3. Copy of a portrait painted in 1822 by Sir Thomas Lawrence (1769–1830), of George IV posed in a seated position.

But these are little matters of anecdote—the general property, ma'am,—still repeated, occasionally, among the upper classes."

"Indeed?" said I.

He replied with the high-shouldered bow. "Where what is left among us of Deportment," he added, "still lingers, England—alas, my country!—has degenerated very much, and is degenerating every day. She has not many gentlemen left. We are few. I see nothing to succeed us, but a race of weavers."

"One might hope that the race of gentlemen would be perpetuated here," said I.

"You are very good," he smiled, with the high-shouldered bow again. "You flatter me. But, no—no! I have never been able to imbue my poor boy with that part of his art. Heaven forbid that I should disparage my dear child, but he has—no Deportment."

"He appears to be an excellent master," I observed.

"Understand me, my dear madam, he *is* an excellent master. All that can be acquired, he has acquired. All that can be imparted, he can impart. But there *are* things"—he took another pinch of snuff and made the bow again, as if to add, "this kind of thing, for instance."

I glanced towards the centre of the room, where Miss Jellyby's lover, now engaged with single pupils, was undergoing greater drudgery than ever.

"My amiable child," murmured Mr. Turveydrop, adjusting his cravat.

"Your son is indefatigable," said I.

"It is my reward," said Mr. Turveydrop, "to hear you say so. In some respects, he treads in the footsteps of his sainted mother. She was a devoted creature. But Wooman, lovely Wooman,"[4] said Mr. Turveydrop, with very disagreeable gallantry, "what a sex you are!"

I rose and joined Miss Jellyby, who was, by this time, putting on her bonnet. The time allotted to a lesson having fully elapsed, there was a general putting on of bonnets. When Miss Jellyby and the unfortunate Prince found an opportunity to become betrothed I don't know, but they certainly found none, on this occasion, to exchange a dozen words.

"My dear," said Mr. Turveydrop benignly to his son, "do you know the hour?"

"No, father." The son had no watch. The father had a handsome gold one, which he pulled out, with an air that was an example to mankind.

"My son," said he, "it's two o'clock. Recollect your school at Kensington at three."

4. Cf. Byron's poem, "I would I were a Careless Child" (1807): "And woman, lovely woman! thou,/ My hope, my comforter, my all!" (Noted by Susan Shatto, 1975.)

VS Sir D. – unnecessary to society used people to detriment

"That's time enough for me, father," said Prince. "I can take a morsel of dinner, standing, and be off."

"My dear boy," returned his father, "you must be very quick. You will find the cold mutton on the table."

"Thank you, father. Are *you* off now, father?"

"Yes, my dear. I suppose," said Mr. Turveydrop, shutting his eyes and lifting up his shoulders, with modest consciousness, "that I must show myself, as usual, about town."

"You had better dine out comfortably, somewhere," said his son.

"My dear child, I intend to. I shall take my little meal, I think, at the French house, in the Opera Colonnade."

"That's right. Good-bye, father!" said Prince, shaking hands.

"Good-bye, my son. Bless you!"

Mr. Turveydrop said this in quite a pious manner, and it seemed to do his son good; who, in parting from him, was so pleased with him, so dutiful to him, and so proud of him, that I almost felt as if it were an unkindness to the younger man not to be able to believe implicitly in the elder. The few moments that were occupied by Prince in taking leave of us (and particularly of one of us, as I saw, being in the secret), enhanced my favourable impression of his almost childish character. I felt a liking for him, and a compassion for him, as he put his little kit in his pocket—and with it his desire to stay a little while with Caddy—and went away good-humouredly to his cold mutton and his school at Kensington, that made me scarcely less irate with his father than the censorious old lady.

The father opened the room-door for us, and bowed us out, in a manner, I must acknowledge, worthy of his shining original. In the same style he presently passed us on the other side of the street, on his way to the aristocratic part of the town, where he was going to show himself among the few other gentlemen left. For some moments, I was so lost in reconsidering what I had heard and seen in Newman Street, that I was quite unable to talk to Caddy, or even to fix my attention on what she said to me: especially when I began to inquire in my mind whether there were, or ever had been, any other gentlemen, not in the dancing profession, who lived and founded a reputation entirely on their Deportment. This became so bewildering, and suggested the possibility of so many Mr. Turveydrops, that I said, "Esther, you must make up your mind to abandon this subject altogether, and attend to Caddy." I accordingly did so, and we chatted all the rest of the way to Lincoln's Inn.

Caddy told me that her lover's education had been so neglected, that it was not always easy to read his notes. She said, if he were not so anxious about his spelling, and took less pains to make it clear, he would do better; but he put so many unnecessary letters into short words, that they sometimes quite lost their English appearance. "He does it with the best intentions" observed Caddy, "but it hasn't the effect he means, poor fellow!" Caddy then went on to reason, how could he be expected to be a scholar, when he had passed his whole life in the dancing-school, and had done nothing but teach and fag, fag and teach, morning, noon, and night! And what did it matter? She could write letters enough for both, as she knew to her cost, and it was far better for him to be amiable than learned. "Besides, it's not as if I was an accomplished girl, who had any right to give herself airs," said Caddy. "I know little enough, I am sure, thanks to Ma!"

"There's another thing I want to tell you, now we are alone," continued Caddy, "which I should not have liked to mention unless you had seen Prince, Miss Summerson. You know what a house ours is. It's of no use my trying to learn anything that it would be useful for Prince's wife to know, in *our* house. We live in such a state of muddle that it's impossible, and I have only been more disheartened whenever I have tried. So I get a little practice with—who do you think? Poor Miss Flite! Early in the morning, I help her to tidy her room, and clean her birds; and I make her cup of coffee for her (of course she taught me), and I have learnt to make it so well that Prince says it's the very best coffee he ever tasted, and would quite delight old Mr. Turveydrop, who is very particular indeed about his coffee. I can make little puddings too; and I know how to buy neck of mutton, and tea, and sugar, and butter, and a good many housekeeping things. I am not clever at my needle, yet," said Caddy, glancing at the repairs on Peepy's frock, "but perhaps I shall improve, and since I have been engaged to Prince, and have been doing all this, I have felt better-tempered, I hope, and more forgiving to Ma. It rather put me out, at first this morning, to see you and Miss Clare looking so neat and pretty, and to feel ashamed of Peepy and myself too; but, on the whole, I hope I am better-tempered than I was, and more forgiving to Ma."

The poor girl, trying so hard, said it from her heart, and touched mine. "Caddy, my love," I replied, "I begin to have a great affection for you, and I hope we shall become friends." "Oh, do you?" cried Caddy; "how happy that would make me!" "My dear Caddy," said I, "let us be friends from this time, and let us often have a chat about these matters, and try to find the right way through them." Caddy was overjoyed. I said everything I could, in my old-fashioned way, to comfort and encourage her; and I would not have objected to old Mr. Turveydrop, that day, for any smaller consideration than a settlement on his daughter-in-law.

By this time, we were come to Mr. Krook's, whose private door stood open. There was a bill, pasted on the door-post, announcing a room to let on the second floor. It reminded Caddy to tell me as we proceeded upstairs, that there had been a sudden death there, and an inquest; and that our little friend had been ill of the fright. The door and window of the vacant room being open, we looked in. It was the room with the dark door, to which Miss Flite had secretly directed my attention when I was last in the house. A sad and desolate place it was; a gloomy, sorrowful place, that gave me a strange sensation of mournfulness and even dread. "You look pale," said Caddy, when we came out, "and cold!" I felt as if the room had chilled me.

We had walked slowly, while we were talking; and my guardian and Ada were here before us. We found them in Miss Flite's garret. They were looking at the birds, while a medical gentleman who was so good as to attend Miss Flite with much solicitude and compassion, spoke with her cheerfully by the fire.

"I have finished my professional visit," he said, coming forward. "Miss Flite is much better, and may appear in Court (as her mind is set upon it) to-morrow. She has been greatly missed there, I understand."

Miss Flite received the compliment with complacency, and dropped a general curtsey to us.

"Honoured, indeed," said she, "by another visit from the wards in Jarndyce! Ve-ry happy to receive Jarndyce of Bleak House beneath my humble roof!" with a special curtsey. "Fitz-Jarndyce, my dear"; she had bestowed that name on Caddy, it appeared, and always called her by it; "a double welcome!"

"Has she been very ill?" asked Mr. Jarndyce of the gentleman whom we had found in attendance on her. She answered for herself directly, though he had put the question in a whisper.

"O decidedly unwell! O very unwell indeed," she said, confidentially. "Not pain, you know—trouble. Not bodily so much as nervous, nervous! The truth is," in a subdued voice and trembling, "we have had death here. There was poison in the house. I am very susceptible to such horrid things. It frightened me. Only Mr. Woodcourt knows how much. My physician, Mr. Woodcourt!" with great stateliness. "The wards in Jarndyce—Jarndyce of Bleak House—Fitz-Jarndyce!"

"Miss Flite," said Mr. Woodcourt, in a grave kind voice, as if he were appealing to her while speaking to us; and laying his hand gently on her arm; "Miss Flite describes her illness with her usual accuracy. She was alarmed by an occurrence in the house which might have alarmed a stronger person, and was made ill by the distress and agitation. She brought me here, in the first hurry of the discovery, though too late for me to be of any use to the unfortunate man. I have compensated myself for that disappointment by coming here since, and being of some small use to her."

"The kindest physician in the college," whispered Miss Flite to me. "I expect a Judgment. On the day of Judgment. And shall then confer estates."

"She will be as well, in a day or two," said Mr. Woodcourt, looking at her with an observant smile, "as she ever will be. In other words, quite well of course. Have you heard of her good fortune?"

"Most extraordinary!" said Miss Flite, smiling brightly. "You never heard of such a thing, my dear! Every Saturday, Conversation Kenge, or Guppy (clerk to Conversation K.), places in my hand a paper of shillings. Shillings. I assure you! Always the same number in the paper. Always one for every day in the week. Now you know, really! So well-timed, is it not? Ye-es! From whence do these papers come, you say? That is the great question. Naturally. Shall I tell you what *I* think? *I* think," said Miss Flite, drawing herself back with a very shrewd look, and shaking her right forefinger in a most significant manner, "that the Lord Chancellor, aware of the length of time during which the Great Seal has been open (for it has been open a long time!), forwards them. Until the Judgment I expect, is given. Now that's very creditable, you know. To confess in that way that he *is* a little slow for human life. So delicate! Attending Court the other day—I attend it regularly—with my documents—I taxed him with it, and he almost confessed. That is, I smiled at him from my bench, and *he* smiled at me from his bench. But it's great good fortune, is it not? And Fitz-Jarndyce lays the money out for me to great advantage. O, I assure you to the greatest advantage!"

I congratulated her (as she addressed herself to me) upon this fortunate addition to her income, and wished her a long continuance of it. I did not speculate upon the source from which it came, or wonder whose humanity was so considerate. My Guardian stood before me, contemplating the birds, and I had no need to look beyond him.

"And what do you call these little fellows, ma'am?" said he in his pleasant voice. "Have they any names?"

"I can answer for Miss Flite that they have," said I, "for she promised to tell us what they were. Ada remembers?"

Ada remembered very well.

"Did I?" said Miss Flite—"Who's that at my door? What are you listening at my door for, Krook?"

The old man of the house, pushing it open before him, appeared there with his fur-cap in his hand, and his cat at his heels.

"I warn't listening, Miss Flite," he said. "I was going to give a rap with my knuckles, only you're so quick!"

"Make your cat go down. Drive her away!" the old lady angrily exclaimed.

"Bah, bah!—there ain't no danger, gentlefolks," said Mr. Krook, looking slowly and sharply from one to another, until he had looked at all of us; "she'd never offer at the birds when I was here, unless I told her to it."

"You will excuse my landlord," said the old lady, with a dignified air. "M, quite M! What do you want, Krook, when I have company?"

"Hi!" said the old man. "You know I am the Chancellor."

"Well?" returned Miss Flite. "What of that?"

"For the Chancellor," said the old man, with a chuckle, "not to be acquainted with a Jarndyce is queer, ain't it, Miss Flite? Mightn't I take the liberty?—Your servant, sir. I know Jarndyce and Jarndyce a'most as well as you do, sir. I knowed old Squire Tom, sir. I never to my knowledge see you afore though, not even in Court. Yet, I go there a mortal sight of times in the course of the year, taking one day with another."

"I never go there," said Mr. Jarndyce (which he never did on any consideration). "I would sooner go—somewhere else."

"Would you though?" returned Krook, grinning. "You're bearing hard upon my noble and learned brother in your meaning, sir; though, perhaps, it is but nat'ral in a Jarndyce. The burnt child, sir! What, you're looking at my lodger's birds, Mr. Jarndyce?" The old man had come by little and little into the room, until he now touched my Guardian with his elbow, and looked close up into his face with his spectacled eyes. "It's one of her strange ways, that she'll never tell the names of these birds if she can help it, though she named 'em all." This was in a whisper. "Shall I run 'em over, Flite?" he asked aloud, winking at us and pointing at her as she turned away, affecting to sweep the grate.

"If you like," she answered hurriedly.

The old man, looking up at the cages, after another look at us, went through the list.

"Hope, Joy, Youth, Peace, Rest, Life, Dust, Ashes, Waste, Want, Ruin, Despair, Madness, Death, Cunning, Folly, Words, Wigs, Rags, Sheepskin, Plunder, Precedent, Jargon, Gammon, and Spinach.[5] That's the whole collection," said the old man, "all cooped up together, by my noble and learned brother."

"This is a bitter wind!" muttered my Guardian.

"When my noble and learned brother gives his Judgment, they're to be let go free," said Krook, winking at us again. "And then," he added, whispering and grinning, "if that ever was to happen—which it won't—the birds that have never been caged would kill 'em."

5. Ham (*gammon*) and *spinach*, a dish, but here quoted from the nursery rhyme "A Frog He Would A-Wooing Go": "With a rowley, powley, gammon and spinach." Gammon also means a seemingly nonsensical style of talk that may mislead a listener.

"If ever the wind was in the east," said my Guardian, pretending to look out of the window for a weathercock, "I think it's there to-day!"

We found it very difficult to get away from the house. It was not Miss Flite who detained us; she was as reasonable a little creature in consulting the convenience of others, as there possibly could be. It was Mr. Krook. He seemed unable to detach himself from Mr. Jarndyce. If he had been linked to him, he could hardly have attended him more closely. He proposed to show us his Court of Chancery, and all the strange medley it contained; during the whole of our inspection (prolonged by himself) he kept close to Mr. Jarndyce, and sometimes detained him, under one pretence or other, until we had passed on, as if he were tormented by an inclination to enter upon some secret subject, which he could not make up his mind to approach. I cannot imagine a countenance and manner more singularly expressive of caution and indecision, and a perpetual impulse to do something he could not resolve to venture on, than Mr. Krook's was, that day. His watchfulness of my Guardian was incessant. He rarely removed his eyes from his face. If he went on beside him, he observed him with the slyness of an old white fox. If he went before, he looked back. When we stood still, he got opposite to him, and drawing his hand across and across his open mouth with a curious expression of a sense of power, and turning up his eyes, and lowering his grey eyebrows until they appeared to be shut, seemed to scan every lineament of his face.

At last, having been (always attended by the cat) all over the house, and having seen the whole stock of miscellaneous lumber, which was certainly curious, we came into the back part of the shop. Here, on the head of an empty barrel stood on end, were an ink-bottle, some old stumps of pens, and some dirty playbills; and, against the wall, were pasted several large printed alphabets in several plain hands.

"What are you doing here?" asked my Guardian.

"Trying to learn myself to read and write," said Krook.

"And how do you get on?"

"Slow. Bad," returned the old man, impatiently. "It's hard at my time of life."

"It would be easier to be taught by some one," said my Guardian.

"Aye, but they might teach me wrong!" returned the old man, with a wonderfully suspicious flash of his eye. "I don't know what I may have lost, by not being learnd afore. I wouldn't like to lose anything by being learnd wrong now."

"Wrong?" said my Guardian, with his good-humoured smile. "Who do you suppose would teach you wrong?"

"I don't know, Mr. Jarndyce of Bleak House!" replied the old man, turning up his spectacles on his forehead, and rubbing his hands. "I don't suppose as anybody would—but I'd rather trust my own self than another!"

These answers, and his manner, were strange enough to cause my Guardian to inquire of Mr. Woodcourt, as we all walked across Lincoln's Inn together, whether Mr. Krook were really, as his lodger represented him, deranged? The young surgeon replied no, he had seen no reason to think so. He was exceedingly distrustful, as ignorance usually was, and he was always more or less under the influence of raw gin: of which he drank great quantities, and of which he and his back-shop, as we might have observed, smelt strongly; but he did not think him mad, as yet.

On our way home, I so conciliated Peepy's affections by buying him a windmill and two flour-sacks, that he would suffer nobody else to take off his hat and gloves, and would sit nowhere at dinner but at my side. Caddy sat upon the other side of me, next to Ada, to whom we imparted the whole history of the engagement as soon as we got back. We made much of Caddy, and Peepy too; and Caddy brightened exceedingly; and my Guardian was as merry as we were; and we were all very happy indeed; until Caddy went home at night in a hackney-coach, with Peepy fast asleep, but holding tight to the windmill.

I have forgotten to mention—at least I have not mentioned—that Mr. Woodcourt was the same dark young surgeon whom we had met at Mr. Badger's. Or, that Mr. Jarndyce invited him to dinner that day. Or, that he came. Or, that when they were all gone, and I said to Ada, "Now, my darling, let us have a little talk about Richard!" Ada laughed and said——

But, I don't think it matters what my darling said. She was always merry.

Chapter XV

BELL YARD

While we were in London, Mr. Jarndyce was constantly beset by the crowd of excitable ladies and gentlemen whose proceedings had so much astonished us. Mr. Quale, who presented himself soon after our arrival, was in all such excitements. He seemed to project those two shining knobs of temples of his into everything that went on, and to brush his hair farther and farther back, until the very roots were almost ready to fly out of his head in inappeasable philanthropy. All objects were alike to him, but he was always particularly ready for anything in the way of a testimonial to any one. His great power seemed to be his power of indiscriminate admiration. He would sit, for any length of time, with the utmost enjoyment, bathing his temples in the light of any order of luminary. Having first seen him perfectly swallowed up in admiration of Mrs. Jellyby, I had supposed her to be the absorbing object of his devotion. I soon discovered my mistake, and found him to be train-bearer and organ-blower to a whole procession of people.

Mrs. Pardiggle came one day for a subscription to something—and with her, Mr. Quale. Whatever Mrs. Pardiggle said, Mr. Quale repeated to us; and just as he had drawn Mrs. Jellyby out, he drew Mrs. Pardiggle out. Mrs. Pardiggle wrote a letter of introduction to my Guardian, in behalf of her eloquent friend, Mr. Gusher. With Mr. Gusher, appeared Mr. Quale again. Mr. Gusher, being a flabby gentleman with a moist surface, and eyes so much too small for his moon of a face that they seemed to have been originally made for somebody else, was not at first sight prepossessing; yet he was scarcely seated, before Mr. Quale asked Ada and me, not inaudibly, whether he was not a great creature—which he certainly was, flabbily speaking; though Mr. Quale meant in intellectual beauty—and whether we were not struck by his massive configuration of brow? In short, we heard of a great many Missions of various sorts, among this set of people; but nothing respecting them was half so clear to us, as that it was Mr. Quale's mission to be in ecstasies with everybody else's mission, and that it was the most popular mission of all.

Mr. Jarndyce had fallen into this company, in the tenderness of his heart and his earnest desire to do all the good in his power; but that he felt it to be too often an unsatisfactory company, where benevolence took spasmodic forms; where charity was assumed, as a regular uniform, by loud professors and speculators in cheap notoriety, vehement in profession, restless and vain in action, servile in the last degree of meanness to the great, adulatory of one another, and intolerable to those who were anxious quietly to help the weak from falling, rather than with a great deal of bluster and self-laudation to raise them up a little way when they were down; he plainly told us. When a testimonial was originated to Mr. Quale, by Mr. Gusher (who had already got one, originated by Mr. Quale), and when Mr. Gusher spoke for an hour and a half on the subject to a meeting, including two charity schools of small boys and girls, who were specially reminded of the widow's mite,[1] and requested to come forward with halfpence and be acceptable sacrifices; I think the wind was in the east for three whole weeks.

I mention this because I am coming to Mr. Skimpole again. It seemed to me that his off-hand professions of childishness and care-

1. A farthing contributed to the treasury by a poor widow, representing for her a major financial sacrifice. See Mark 12:42.

lessness were a great relief to my guardian, by contrast with such things, and were the more readily believed in; since, to find one perfectly undesigning and candid man, among many opposites, could not fail to give him pleasure. I should be sorry to imply that Mr. Skimpole divined this, and was politic: I really never understood him well enough to know. What he was to my Guardian, he certainly was to the rest of the world.

He had not been very well; and thus, though he lived in London, we had seen nothing of him until now. He appeared one morning, in his usual agreeable way, and as full of pleasant spirits as ever.

Well, he said, here he was! He had been bilious, but rich men were often bilious, and therefore he had been persuading himself that he was a man of property. So he was, in a certain point of view—in his expansive intentions. He had been enriching his medical attendant in the most lavish manner. He had always doubled, and sometimes quadrupled, his fees. He had said to the doctor, "Now, my dear doctor, it is quite a delusion on your part to suppose that you attend me for nothing. I am overwhelming you with money—in my expansive intentions—if you only knew it!" And really (he said) he meant it to that degree, that he thought it much the same as doing it. If he had had those bits of metal or thin paper, to which mankind attached so much importance, to put in the doctor's hand, he would have put them in the doctor's hand. Not having them, he substituted the will for the deed. Very well! If he really meant it—if his will were genuine and real; which it was—it appeared to him that it was the same as coin, and cancelled the obligation.

"It may be, partly, because I know nothing of the value of money," said Mr. Skimpole, "but I often feel this. It seems so reasonable! My butcher says to me, he wants that little bill. It's a part of the pleasant unconscious poetry of the man's nature, that he always calls it a 'little' bill—to make the payment appear easy to both of us. I reply to the butcher, My good friend, if you knew it you are paid. You haven't had the trouble of coming to ask for the little bill. You are paid. I mean it."

"But, suppose," said my Guardian, laughing, "he had meant the meat in the bill, instead of providing it?"

"My dear Jarndyce," he returned, "you surprise me. You take the butcher's position. A butcher I once dealt with occupied that very ground. Says he, 'Sir, why did you eat spring lamb at eighteen-pence a pound?' 'Why did I eat spring lamb at eighteen-pence a pound, my honest friend?' said I, naturally amazed by the question, 'I like spring lamb!' This was so far convincing. 'Well, sir,' says he, 'I wish I had meant the lamb as you mean the money!' 'My good fellow,' said I, 'pray let us reason like intellectual beings. How could that be? It was impossible. You *had* got the lamb, and I have *not* got the money. You couldn't really mean the lamb without sending it in, whereas I can, and do, really mean the money without paying it!' He had not a word. There was an end of the subject."

"Did he take no legal proceedings?" inquired my guardian.

"Yes, he took legal proceedings," said Mr. Skimpole. "But, in that, he was influenced by passion; not by reason. Passion reminds me of Boythorn. He writes me that you and the ladies have promised him a short visit at his bachelor-house in Lincolnshire."

"He is a great favourite with my girls," said Mr. Jarndyce, "and I have promised for them."

"Nature forgot to shade him off, I think?" observed Mr. Skimpole to Ada and me. "A little too boisterous, like the sea? A little too vehement—like a bull, who has made up his mind to consider every colour scarlet? But, I grant a sledge-hammering sort of merit in him!"

I should have been surprised if those two could have thought very highly of one another; Mr. Boythorn attaching so much importance to many things, and Mr. Skimpole caring so little for anything. Besides which, I had noticed Mr. Boythorn more than once on the point of breaking out into some strong opinion, when Mr. Skimpole was referred to. Of course I merely joined Ada in saying that we had been greatly pleased with him.

"He has invited me," said Mr. Skimpole; "and if a child may trust himself in such hands: which the present child is encouraged to do, with the united tenderness of two angels to guard him; I shall go. He proposes to frank me down and back again.[2] I suppose it will cost money? Shillings perhaps? Or pounds? Or something of that sort? By-the-bye. Coavinses. You remember our friend Coavinses, Miss Summerson?"

He asked me, as the subject arose in his mind, in his graceful light-hearted manner, and without the least embarrassment.

"O yes!" said I.

"Coavinses has been arrested by the great Bailiff," said Mr. Skimpole. "He will never do violence to the sunshine any more."

It quite shocked me to hear it; for I had already recalled, with anything but a serious association, the image of the man sitting on the sofa that night, wiping his head.

"His successor informed me of it yesterday," said Mr. Skimpole. "His successor is in my house now—in possession, I think he calls it. He came yesterday, on my blue-eyed daughter's birthday. I put it to him, 'This is unreasonable and inconvenient. If you had a blue-eyed daughter, you wouldn't like *me* to come, uninvited, on *her* birthday?' But he stayed."

2. To pay for my expenses, round trip.

Mr. Skimpole laughed at the pleasant absurdity, and lightly touched the piano by which he was seated.

"And he told me," he said, playing little chords where I shall put full stops, "That Coavinses had left. Three children. No mother. And that Coavinses' profession. Being unpopular. The rising Coavinses. Were at a considerable disadvantage."

Mr. Jarndyce got up, rubbing his head, and began to walk about. Mr. Skimpole played the melody of one of Ada's favourite songs. Ada and I both looked at Mr. Jarndyce, thinking that we knew what was passing in his mind.

After walking and stopping, and several times leaving off rubbing his head, and beginning again, my Guardian put his hand upon the keys and stopped Mr. Skimpole's playing. "I don't like this, Skimpole," he said thoughtfully.

Mr. Skimpole, who had quite forgotten the subject, looked up surprised.

"The man was necessary," pursued my guardian, walking backward and forward in the very short space between the piano and the end of the room, and rubbing his hair up from the back of his head as if a high east wind had blown it into that form. "If we make such men necessary by our faults and follies, or by our want of worldly knowledge, or by our misfortunes, we must not revenge ourselves upon them. There was no harm in his trade. He maintained his children. One would like to know more about this."

"O! Coavinses?" cried Mr. Skimpole, at length perceiving what he meant. "Nothing easier. A walk to Coavinses' headquarters, and you can know what you will."

Mr. Jarndyce nodded to us, who were only waiting for the signal. "Come! We will walk that way, my dears. Why not that way, as soon as another!" We were quickly ready, and went out. Mr. Skimpole went with us, and quite enjoyed the expedition. It was so new and so refreshing, he said, for him to want Coavinses, instead of Coavinses wanting him!

He took us, first, to Cursitor Street, Chancery Lane, where there was a house with barred windows, which he called Coavinses' Castle. On our going into the entry and ringing a bell, a very hideous boy came out of a sort of office, and looked at us over a spiked wicket.

"Who did you want?" said the boy, fitting two of the spikes into his chin.

"There was a follower, or an officer, or something, here," said Mr. Jarndyce, "who is dead."

"Yes?" said the boy. "Well?"

"I want to know his name, if you please?"

"Name of Neckett," said the boy.

"And his address?"

"Bell Yard," said the boy. "Chandler's shop, left hand side, name of Blinder."

"Was he—I don't know how to shape the question," murmured my guardian—"industrious?"

"Was Neckett?" said the boy. "Yes, wery much so. He was never tired of watching. He'd set upon a post at a street corner, eight or ten hours at a stretch, if he undertook to do it."

"He might have done worse," I heard my Guardian soliloquize. "He might have undertaken to do it, and not done it. Thank you. That's all I want."

We left the boy, with his head on one side, and his arms on the gate, fondling and sucking the spikes; and went back to Lincoln's Inn, where Mr. Skimpole, who had not cared to remain nearer Coavinses, awaited us. Then, we all went to Bell Yard: a narrow alley, at a very short distance. We soon found the chandler's shop. In it, was a good-natured-looking old woman, with a dropsy, or an asthma, or perhaps both.

"Neckett's children?" said she, in reply to my inquiry. "Yes, surely, miss. Three pair,[3] if you please. Door right opposite the top of the stairs." And she handed me a key across the counter.

I glanced at the key and glanced at her; but she took it for granted that I knew what to do with it. As it could only be intended for the children's door, I came out, without asking any more questions, and led the way up the dark stairs. We went as quietly as we could, but four of us made some noise on the aged boards; and when we came to the second story, we found we had disturbed a man who was standing there, looking out of his room.

"Is it Gridley that's wanted?" he said, fixing his eyes on me with an angry stare.

"No sir," said I, "I am going higher up."

He looked at Ada, and at Mr. Jarndyce, and at Mr. Skimpole: fixing the same angry stare on each in succession, as they passed and followed me. Mr. Jarndyce gave him good day. "Good day!" he said, abruptly and fiercely. He was a tall sallow man, with a care-worn head, on which but little hair remained, a deeply lined face, and prominent eyes. He had a combative look; and a chafing, irritable manner, which, associated with his figure—still large and powerful, though evidently in its decline—rather alarmed me. He had a pen in his hand, and, in the glimpse I caught of his room in passing, I saw that it was covered with a litter of papers.

Leaving him standing there, we went up to the top room. I tapped at the door, and a little shrill voice inside said, "We are locked in. Mrs. Blinder's got the key!"

I applied the key on hearing this, and opened the door. In a poor room, with a sloping ceiling, and containing very little furniture,

3. Three flights of stairs.

was a mite of a boy, some five or six years old, nursing and hushing a heavy child of eighteen months. There was no fire, though the weather was cold; both children were wrapped in some poor shawls and tippets, as a substitute. Their clothing was not so warm, however, but that their noses looked red and pinched, and their small figures shrunken, as the boy walked up and down, nursing and hushing the child with its head on his shoulder.

"Who has locked you up here alone?" we naturally asked.

"Charley," said the boy, standing still to gaze at us.

"Is Charley your brother?"

"No. She's my sister, Charlotte. Father called her Charley."

"Are there any more of you besides Charley?"

"Me," said the boy, "and Emma," patting the limp bonnet of the child he was nursing. "And Charley."

"Where is Charley now?"

"Out a-washing," said the boy, beginning to walk up and down again, and taking the nankeen bonnet much too near the bedstead, by trying to gaze at us at the same time.

We were looking at one another, and at these two children, when there came into the room a very little girl, childish in figure but shrewd and older-looking in the face—pretty-faced too—wearing a womanly sort of bonnet much too large for her, and drying her bare arms on a womanly sort of apron. Her fingers were white and wrinkled with washing, and the soap-suds were yet smoking which she wiped off her arms. But for this, she might have been a child, playing at washing, and imitating a poor working-woman with a quick observation of the truth.

She had come running from some place in the neighbourhood, and had made all the haste she could. Consequently, though she was very light, she was out of breath, and could not speak at first, as she stood panting, and wiping her arms, and looking quietly at us.

"O, here's Charley!" said the boy.

The child he was nursing, stretched forth its arms, and cried out to be taken by Charley. The little girl took it, in a womanly sort of manner belonging to the apron and the bonnet, and stood looking at us over the burden that clung to her most affectionately.

"Is it possible," whispered my Guardian, as we put a chair for the little creature, and got her to sit down with her load: the boy keeping close to her, holding to her apron, "that this child works for the rest? Look at this! For God's sake look at this!"

It was a thing to look at. The three children close together, and two of them relying solely on the third, and the third so young and yet with an air of age and steadiness that sat so strangely on the childish figure.

"Charley, Charley!" said my guardian. "How old are you?"

"Over thirteen, sir," replied the child.

"O! What a great age!" said my Guardian. "What a great age, Charley!"

I cannot describe the tenderness with which he spoke to her; half playfully, yet all the more compassionately and mournfully.

"And do you live alone here with these babies, Charley?" said my Guardian.

"Yes, sir," returned the child, looking up into his face with perfect confidence, "since father died."

"And how do you live, Charley? O! Charley," said my Guardian, turning his face away for a moment, "how do you live?"

"Since father died, sir, I've gone out to work. I'm out washing to-day."

"God help you, Charley!" said my Guardian. "You're not tall enough to reach the tub!"

"In pattens I am, sir," she said, quickly. "I've got a high pair as belonged to mother."

"And when did mother die? Poor mother!"

"Mother died just after Emma was born," said the child, glancing at the face upon her bosom. "Then father said I was to be as good a mother to her as I could. And so I tried. And so I worked at home, and did cleaning and nursing and washing, for a long time before I began to go out. And that's how I know how; don't you see, sir?"

"And do you often go out?"

"As often as I can," said Charley, opening her eyes and smiling, "because of earning sixpences and shillings!"

"And do you always lock the babies up when you go out?"

"To keep 'em safe, sir, don't you see?" said Charley. "Mrs. Blinder comes up now and then, and Mr. Gridley comes up sometimes, and perhaps I can run in sometimes, and they can play, you know, and Tom an't afraid of being locked up, are you, Tom?"

"No-o!" said Tom, stoutly.

"When it comes on dark the lamps are lighted down in the court, and they show up here quite bright—almost quite bright. Don't they, Tom?"

"Yes, Charley," said Tom, "almost quite bright."

"Then he's as good as gold," said the little creature—O! in such a motherly, womanly way! "And when Emma's tired he puts her to bed. And when he's tired he goes to bed himself. And when I come home and light the candle, and has a bit of supper, he sits up again and has it with me. Don't you, Tom?"

"O yes, Charley!" said Tom. "That I do!" And either in this glimpse of the great pleasure of his life, or in gratitude and love for Charley, who was all in all to him, he laid his face among the scanty folds of her frock, and passed from laughing into crying.

It was the first time since our entry that a tear had been shed among these children. The little orphan girl had spoken of their father and their mother, as if all that sorrow were subdued by the necessity of taking courage, and by her childish importance in being able to work, and by her bustling, busy way. But now, when Tom cried; although she sat quite tranquil, looking quietly at us, and did not by any movement disturb a hair of the head of either of her little charges; I saw two silent tears fall down her face.

I stood at the window with Ada, pretending to look at the house-tops, and the blackened stacks of chimneys, and the poor plants, and the birds in little cages belonging to the neighbours, when I found that Mrs. Blinder, from the shop below, had come in (perhaps it had taken her all this time to get up-stairs) and was talking to my Guardian.

"It's not much to forgive 'em the rent, sir," she said; "who could take it from them!"

"Well, well!" said my Guardian to us two. "It is enough that the time will come when this good woman will find that it *was* much, and that forasmuch as she did it unto the least of these—![4] This child," he added, after a few moments, "could she possibly continue this?"

"Really, sir, I think she might," said Mrs. Blinder, getting her heavy breath by painful degrees. "She's as handy as it's possible to be. Bless you, sir, the way she tended them two children, after the mother died, was the talk of the yard! And it was a wonder to see her with him after he was took ill, it really was! 'Mrs. Blinder,' he said to me the very last he spoke—he was lying there—'Mrs. Blinder, whatever my calling may have been, I see a Angel sitting in this room last night along with my child, and I trust her to our Father!' "

"He had no other calling?" said my Guardian.

"No, sir," returned Mrs. Blinder, "he was nothing but a follerer. When he first came to lodge here, I didn't know what he was, and I confess that when I found out I gave him notice. It wasn't liked in the yard. It wasn't approved by the other lodgers. It is *not* a genteel calling," said Mrs. Blinder, "and most people do object to it. Mr. Gridley objected to it, very strong, and he is a good lodger, though his temper has been hard tried."

"So you gave him notice?" said my Guardian.

"So I gave him notice," said Mrs. Blinder. "But really when the time came, and I knew no other ill of him, I was in doubts. He was punctual and diligent; he did what he had to do, sir," said Mrs. Blinder, unconsciously fixing Mr. Skimpole with her eye; "and it's something in this world even to do that."

"So you kept him after all?"

4. In Matthew 25:40–45, Christ speaks of those who help the helpless: "Inasmuch as ye have done it unto one of the least of these my brethren, ye have done it unto me."

"Why, I said that if he could arrange with Mr. Gridley, I could arrange it with the other lodgers, and should not so much mind its being liked or disliked in the yard. Mr. Gridley gave his consent gruff—but gave it. He was always gruff with him, but he has been kind to the children since. A person is never known till a person is proved."

"Have many people been kind to the children?" asked Mr. Jarndyce.

"Upon the whole, not so bad, sir," said Mrs. Blinder; "but certainly not so many as would have been if their father's calling had been different. Mr. Coavins gave a guinea, and the follerers made up a little purse. Some neighbours in the yard, that had always joked and tapped their shoulders when he went by, came forward with a little subscription, and—in general—not so bad. Similarly with Charlotte. Some people won't employ her because she was a follerer's child; some people that do employ her cast it at her; some make a merit of having her to work for them, with that and all her drawbacks upon her, and perhaps pay her less and put upon her more. But she's patienter than others would be, and is clever too, and always willing, up to the full mark of her strength and over. So I should say, in general, not so bad, sir, but might be better."

Mrs. Blinder sat down to give herself a more favourable opportunity of recovering her breath, exhausted anew by so much talking before it was fully restored. Mr. Jarndyce was turning to speak to us, when his attention was attracted by the abrupt entrance into the room of the Mr. Gridley who had been mentioned, and whom we had seen on our way up.

"I don't know what you may be doing here, ladies and gentlemen," he said, as if he resented our presence, "but you'll excuse my coming in. I don't come in to stare about me. Well, Charley! Well, Tom! Well, little one! How is it with us all to-day?"

He bent over the group, in a caressing way, and clearly was regarded as a friend by the children, though his face retained its stern character, and his manner to us was as rude as it could be. My Guardian noticed it, and respected it.

"No one, surely, would come here to stare about him," he said mildly.

"May be so, sir, may be so," returned the other, taking Tom upon his knee, and waving him off impatiently. "I don't want to argue with ladies and gentlemen. I have had enough of arguing to last one man his life."

"You have sufficient reason, I dare say," said Mr. Jarndyce, "for being chafed and irritated——"

"There again!" exclaimed the man, becoming violently angry. "I am of a quarrelsome temper. I am irascible. I am not polite!"

"Not very, I think."

"Sir," said Gridley, putting down the child, and going up to him as if he meant to strike him. "Do you know anything of Courts of Equity?"

"Perhaps I do, to my sorrow."

"To your sorrow?" said the man, pausing in his wrath. "If so, I beg your pardon. I am not polite, I know. I beg your pardon! Sir," with renewed violence, "I have been dragged for five-and-twenty years over burning iron, and I have lost the habit of treading upon velvet. Go into the Court of Chancery yonder, and ask what is one of the standing jokes that brighten up their business sometimes, and they will tell you that the best joke they have is the man from Shropshire. I," he said, beating one hand on the other, passionately, "am the man from Shropshire."

"I believe I and my family have also had the honour of furnishing some entertainment in the same grave place," said my Guardian composedly. "You may have heard my name—Jarndyce."

"Mr. Jarndyce," said Gridley, with a rough sort of salutation, "you bear your wrongs more quietly than I can bear mine. More than that, I tell you—and I tell this gentleman, and these young ladies, if they are friends of yours—that if I took my wrongs in any other way, I should be driven mad! It is only by resenting them, and by revenging them in my mind, and by angrily demanding the justice I never get, that I am able to keep my wits together. It is only that," he said, speaking in a homely, rustic way, and with great vehemence. "You may tell me that I over-excite myself. I answer that it's in my nature to do it, under wrong, and I must do it. There's nothing between doing it, and sinking into the smiling state of the poor little mad woman that haunts the Court. If I was once to sit down under it, I should become imbecile."

The passion and heat in which he was, and the manner in which his face worked, and the violent gestures with which he accompanied what he said, were most painful to see.

"Mr. Jarndyce," he said, "consider my case. As true as there is a Heaven above us, this is my case. I am one of two brothers. My father (a farmer) made a will, and left his farm and stock, and so forth, to my mother, for her life. After my mother's death all was to come to me, except a legacy of three hundred pounds that I was then to pay my brother. My mother died. My brother, some time afterwards, claimed his legacy. I, and some of my relations, said that he had had a part of it already, in board and lodging, and some other things. Now mind! That was the question, and nothing else. No one disputed the will; no one disputed anything but whether part of that three hundred pounds had been already paid or not. To settle that question, my brother filing a bill, I was obliged to go into this accursed Chancery; I was forced there, because the law forced me, and would let me go nowhere else. Seventeen people were made defendants to that simple suit! It first came on, after two years. It was then stopped for another two years, while the Master (may his head rot off!) inquired whether I was my father's son—about which there was no dispute at all with any mortal creature. He then found out that there were not defendants enough—remember, there were only seventeen as yet!—but that we must have another who had been left out; and must begin all over again. The costs at that time—before the thing was begun!—were three times the legacy. My brother would have given up the legacy, and joyful, to escape more costs. My whole estate, left to me in that will of my father's, has gone in costs. The suit, still undecided, has fallen into rack, and ruin, and despair, with everything else—and here I stand, this day! Now, Mr. Jarndyce, in your suit there are thousands and thousands involved where in mine there are hundreds. Is mine less hard to bear, or is it harder to bear, when my whole living was in it, and has been thus shamefully sucked away?"

Mr. Jarndyce said that he condoled with him with all his heart, and that he set up no monopoly, himself, in being unjustly treated by this monstrous system.

"There again!" said Mr. Gridley, with no diminution of his rage. "The system! I am told, on all hands, it's the system. I mustn't look to individuals. It's the system. I mustn't go into Court, and say, 'My Lord, I beg to know this from you—is this right or wrong? Have you the face to tell me I have received justice, and therefore am dismissed?' My Lord knows nothing of it. He sits there to administer the system. I mustn't go to Mr. Tulkinghorn, the solicitor in Lincoln's Inn Fields, and say to him when he makes me furious, by being so cool and satisfied—as they all do; for I know they gain by it while I lose, don't I?—I mustn't say to him, I will have something out of some one for my ruin, by fair means or foul! *He* is not responsible. It's the system. But if I do no violence to any of them, here—I may! I don't know what may happen if I am carried beyond myself at last!—I will accuse the individual workers of that system against me, face to face, before the great eternal bar!"

His passion was fearful. I could not have believed in such rage without seeing it.

"I have done!" he said, sitting down and wiping his face. "Mr. Jarndyce, I have done! I am violent, I know. I ought to know it. I have been in prison for contempt of Court. I have been in prison for threatening the solicitor. I have been in this trouble, and that trouble, and shall be again. I am the man from Shropshire, and I sometimes go beyond amusing them—though they have found it amusing, too, to see me committed into custody, and brought up in custody, and all that. It would be better for me, they tell me, if I restrained myself. I tell them, that if I did restrain myself, I should become imbecile. I was a good-enough-tempered man once, I believe. People in my part of the country say they remember me so; but, now, I must have this vent under my sense of injury, or nothing could hold my wits together. 'It would be far better for you, Mr. Gridley,' the Lord Chancellor told me last week, 'not to waste your time here, and to stay, usefully employed, down in Shropshire.' 'My Lord, my Lord, I know it would,' said I to him, 'and it would have been far better for me never to have heard the name of your high office; but, unhappily for me, I can't undo the past, and the past drives me here!'—Besides," he added, breaking fiercely out, "I'll shame them. To the last, I'll show myself in that Court to its shame. If I knew when I was going to die, and could be carried there, and had a voice to speak with, I would die there, saying, 'You have brought me here, and sent me from here, many and many a time. Now send me out, feet foremost!' "

His countenance had, perhaps for years, become so set in its contentious expression that it did not soften, even now when he was quiet.

"I came to take these babies down to my room for an hour," he said, going to them again, "and let them play about. I didn't mean to say all this, but it don't much signify. You're not afraid of me, Tom; are you?"

"No!" said Tom. "You ain't angry with *me*."

"You are right, my child. You're going back, Charley? Aye? Come then, little one!" He took the youngest child on his arm, where she was willing enough to be carried. "I shouldn't wonder if we found a ginger-bread soldier down-stairs. Let's go and look for him!"

He made his former rough salutation, which was not deficient in a certain respect, to Mr. Jarndyce; and bowing slightly to us, went down-stairs to his room.

Upon that, Mr. Skimpole began to talk, for the first time since our arrival, in his usual gay strain. He said, Well, it was really very pleasant to see how things lazily adapted themselves to purposes. Here was this Mr. Gridley, a man of a robust will, and surprising energy—intellectually speaking, a sort of inharmonious blacksmith[5]—and he could easily imagine that there Gridley was, years ago, wandering about in life for something to expend his superfluous combativeness upon—a sort of Young Love among the thorns[6]—when the Court of Chancery came in his way, and accommodated

5. Alluding to "The Harmonious Blacksmith," an air for harpsichord (1720) by G. F. Handel.

6. Perhaps alluding to a song by Thomas Moore (1779–1852): "Young Love liv'd once in an humble shed,/ Where roses breathing,/ And woodbines wreathing,/ Around the lattice their tendrils spread,/ As wild and sweet as the life he led."

him with the exact thing he wanted. There they were, matched, ever afterwards! Otherwise he might have been a great general, blowing up all sorts of towns, or he might have been a great politician, dealing in all sorts of parliamentary rhetoric; but, as it was, he and the Court of Chancery had fallen upon each other in the pleasantest way, and nobody was much the worse, and Gridley was, so to speak, from that hour provided for. Then look at Coavinses! How delightfully poor Coavinses (father of these charming children) illustrated the same principle! He, Mr. Skimpole, himself, had sometimes repined at the existence of Coavinses. He had found Coavinses in his way. He could have dispensed with Coavinses. There had been times when, if he had been a Sultan, and his Grand Vizier had said one morning, "What does the Commander of the Faithful require at the hands of his slave?" he might have even gone so far as to reply, "The head of Coavinses!" But what turned out to be the case? That, all that time, he had been giving employment to a most deserving man; that he had been a benefactor to Coavinses; that he had actually been enabling Coavinses to bring up these charming children in this agreeable way, developing these social virtues! Insomuch that his heart had just now swelled, and the tears had come into his eyes, when he had looked round the room, and thought, "I was the great patron of Coavinses, and his little comforts were *my* work!"

There was something so captivating in his light way of touching these fantastic strings, and he was such a mirthful child by the side of the graver childhood we had seen, that he made my Guardian smile even as he turned towards us from a little private talk with Mrs. Blinder. We kissed Charley, and took her down-stairs with us, and stopped outside the house to see her run away to her work. I don't know where she was going, but we saw her run, such a little, little creature, in her womanly bonnet and apron, through a covered way at the bottom of the court; and melt into the city's strife and sound, like a dewdrop in an ocean.

Chapter XVI

TOM-ALL-ALONE'S

My Lady Dedlock is restless, very restless. The astonished fashionable intelligence hardly knows where to have her. To-day, she is at Chesney Wold; yesterday, she was at her house in town; tomorrow, she may be abroad, for anything the fashionable intelligence can with confidence predict. Even Sir Leicester's gallantry has some trouble to keep pace with her. It would have more, but that his other faithful ally, for better and for worse—the gout—darts into the old oak bed-chamber at Chesney Wold, and grips him by both legs.

Sir Leicester receives the gout as a troublesome demon, but still a demon of the patrician order. All the Dedlocks, in the direct male line, through a course of time during and beyond which the memory of man goeth not to the contrary,[1] have had the gout. It can be proved, sir. Other men's fathers may have died of the rheumatism, or may have taken base contagion from the tainted blood of the sick vulgar, but the Dedlock family have communicated something exclusive, even to the levelling process of dying, by dying of their own family gout. It has come down, through the illustrious line, like the plate, or the pictures, or the place in Lincolnshire. It is among their dignities. Sir Leicester is, perhaps, not wholly without an impression, though he has never resolved it into words, that the angel of death in the discharge of his necessary duties may observe to the shades of the aristocracy, "My lords and gentlemen, I have the honour to present to you another Dedlock certified to have arrived per the family gout."

Hence, Sir Leicester yields up his family legs to the family disorder, as if he held his name and fortune on that feudal tenure. He feels, that for a Dedlock to be laid upon his back and spasmodically twitched and stabbed in his extremities, is a liberty taken somewhere; but, he thinks, "We have all yielded to this; it belongs to us; it has, for some hundreds of years, been understood that we are not to make the vaults in the park interesting on more ignoble terms; and I submit myself to the compromise."

And a goodly show he makes, lying in a flush of crimson and gold, in the midst of the great drawing-room, before his favourite picture of my Lady, with broad strips of sunlight shining in, down the long perspective, through the long line of windows, and alternating with soft reliefs of shadow. Outside, the stately oaks, rooted for ages in the green ground which has never known ploughshare, but was still a Chase when kings rode to battle with sword and shield, and rode a-hunting with bow and arrow; bear witness to his greatness. Inside, his forefathers, looking on him from the walls, say, "Each of us was a passing reality, here, and left this coloured shadow of himself, and melted into remembrance as dreamy as the distant voices of the rooks now lulling you to rest"; and bear their testimony to his greatness, too. And he is very great, this day. And woe to Boythorn, or other daring wight, who shall presumptuously contest an inch with him!

1. Phrase used by lawyers signifying from time immemorial. As noted by T. W. Hill, it appears in *Blackstone's Commentaries on the Laws of England* (1765–69): "Time whereof the memory of man runneth not to the contrary."

My Lady is at present represented, near Sir Leicester, by her portrait. She has flitted away to town, with no intention of remaining there, and will soon flit hither again, to the confusion of the fashionable intelligence. The house in town is not prepared for her reception. It is muffled and dreary. Only one Mercury in powder,[2] gapes disconsolate at the hall-window; and he mentioned last night to another Mercury of his acquaintance also accustomed to good society, that if that sort of thing was to last—which it couldn't, for a man of his spirits couldn't bear it, and a man of his figure couldn't be expected to bear it—there would be no resource for him, upon his honour, but to cut his throat!

What connexion can there be, between the place in Lincolnshire, the house in town, the Mercury in powder, and the whereabout of Jo the outlaw with the broom, who had that distant ray of light upon him when he swept the churchyard step? What connexion can there have been between many people in the innumerable histories of this world, who, from opposite sides of great gulfs, have, nevertheless, been very curiously brought together!

Jo sweeps his crossing all day long, unconscious of the link, if any link there be. He sums up his mental condition, when asked a question, by replying that he "don't know nothink." He knows that it's hard to keep the mud off the crossing in dirty weather, and harder still to live by doing it. Nobody taught him, even that much; he found it out.

Jo lives—that is to say, Jo has not yet died—in a ruinous place, known to the like of him by the name of Tom-all-Alone's. It is a black, dilapidated street, avoided by all decent people; where the crazy houses were seized upon, when their decay was far advanced, by some bold vagrants, who, after establishing their own possession, took to letting them out in lodgings. Now, these tumbling tenements contain, by night, a swarm of misery. As, on the ruined human wretch, vermin parasites appear, so these ruined shelters have bred a crowd of foul existence that crawls in and out of gaps in walls and boards; and coils itself to sleep, in maggot numbers, where the rain drips in; and comes and goes, fetching and carrying fever, and sowing more evil in its every footprint than Lord Coodle, and Sir Thomas Doodle, and the Duke of Foodle, and all the fine gentlemen in office, down to Zoodle, shall set right in five hundred years—though born expressly to do it.

Twice, lately, there has been a crash and a cloud of dust, like the springing of a mine, in Tom-all-Alone's; and, each time, a house has fallen. These accidents have made a paragraph in the newspapers, and have filled a bed or two in the nearest hospital. The gaps

2. See p. 13, note 9.

remain, and there are not unpopular lodgings among the rubbish. As several more houses are nearly ready to go, the next crash in Tom-all-Alone's may be expected to be a good one.

This desirable property is in Chancery, of course. It would be an insult to the discernment of any man with half an eye, to tell him so. Whether "Tom" is the popular representative of the original plaintiff or defendant in Jarndyce and Jarndyce; or whether Tom lived here when the suit had laid the street waste, all alone, until other settlers came to join him; or whether the traditional title is a comprehensive name for a retreat cut off from honest company and put out of the pale of hope; perhaps nobody knows. Certainly, Jo don't know.

"For *I* don't," says Jo, "*I* don't know nothink."

It must be a strange state to be like Jo! To shuffle through the streets, unfamiliar with the shapes, and in utter darkness as to the meaning, of those mysterious symbols, so abundant over the shops, and at the corners of streets, and on the doors, and in the windows! To see people read, and to see people write, and to see the postmen deliver letters, and not to have the least idea of all that language—to be, to every scrap of it, stone blind and dumb! It must be very puzzling to see the good company going to the churches on Sundays, with their books in their hands, and to think (for perhaps Jo *does* think, at odd times) what does it all mean, and if it means anything to anybody, how comes it that it means nothing to me? To be hustled, and jostled, and moved on; and really to feel that it would appear to be perfectly true that I have no business, here, or there, or anywhere; and yet to be perplexed by the consideration that I *am* here somehow, too, and everybody overlooked me until I became the creature that I am! It must be a strange state, not merely to be told that I am scarcely human (as in the case of my offering myself for a witness), but to feel it of my own knowledge all my life! To see the horses, dogs, and cattle, go by me, and to know that in ignorance I belong to them, and not to the superior beings in my shape, whose delicacy I offend! Jo's ideas of a Criminal Trial, or a Judge, or a Bishop, or a Government, or that inestimable jewel to him (if he only knew it) the Constitution, should be strange! His whole material and immaterial life is wonderfully strange; his death, the strangest thing of all.

Jo comes out of Tom-all-Alone's, meeting the tardy morning which is always late in getting down there, and munches his dirty bit of bread as he comes along. His way lying through many streets, and the houses not yet being open, he sits down to breakfast on the door-step of the Society for the Propagation of the Gospel in Foreign Parts, and gives it a brush when he has finished, as an acknowledgment of the accommodation. He admires the size of the edifice, and wonders what it's all about. He has no idea, poor wretch, of the spiritual destitution of a coral reef in the Pacific, or what it costs to look up the precious souls among the cocoa-nuts and bread-fruit.

He goes to his crossing, and begins to lay it out for the day. The town awakes; the great tee-totum[3] is set up for its daily spin and whirl; all that unaccountable reading and writing, which has been suspended for a few hours, recommences. Jo, and the other lower animals, get on in the unintelligible mess as they can. It is market-day. The blinded oxen, over-goaded, over-driven, never guided, run into wrong places and are beaten out; and plunge, red-eyed and foaming, at stone walls; and often sorely hurt the innocent, and often sorely hurt themselves. Very like Jo and his order; very, very like!

A band of music comes and plays. Jo listens to it. So does a dog—a drover's dog, waiting for his master outside a butcher's shop, and evidently thinking about those sheep he has had upon his mind for some hours, and is happily rid of. He seems perplexed respecting three or four; can't remember where he left them; looks up and down the street, as half expecting to see them astray; suddenly pricks up his ears and remembers all about it. A thoroughly vagabond dog, accustomed to low company and public-houses; a terrific dog to sheep; ready at a whistle to scamper over their backs, and tear out mouthfuls of their wool; but an educated, improved, developed dog, who has been taught his duties, and knows how to discharge them. He and Jo listen to the music, probably with much the same amount of animal satisfaction; likewise, as to awakened association, aspiration or regret, melancholy or joyful reference to things beyond the senses, they are probably upon a par. But, otherwise, how far above the human listener is the brute!

Turn that dog's descendants wild, like Jo, and in a very few years they will so degenerate that they will lose even their bark—but not their bite.

The day changes as it wears itself away, and becomes dark and drizzly. Jo fights it out, at his crossing, among the mud and wheels, the horses, whips, and umbrellas, and gets but a scanty sum to pay for the unsavoury shelter of Tom-all-Alone's. Twilight comes on; gas begins to start up in the shops; the lamplighter, with his ladder, runs along the margin of the pavement. A wretched evening is beginning to close in.

In his chambers, Mr. Tulkinghorn sits meditating an application to the nearest magistrate to-morrow morning for a warrant. Gridley, a disappointed suitor, has been here to-day, and has been alarming. We are not to be put in bodily fear, and that ill-conditioned fellow shall be held to bail again. From the ceiling, foreshortened Allegory,

3. A toy top with four sides inscribed with letters.

in the person of one impossible Roman upside down, points with the arm of Samson (out of joint, and an odd one) obtrusively toward the window. Why should Mr. Tulkinghorn, for such no reason, look out of window! Is the hand not always pointing there? So he does not look out of window.

And if he did, what would it be to see a woman going by? There are women enough in the world, Mr. Tulkinghorn thinks—too many; they are at the bottom of all that goes wrong in it, though, for the matter of that, they create business for lawyers. What would it be to see a woman going by, even though she were going secretly? They are all secret. Mr. Tulkinghorn knows that, very well.

But they are not all like the woman who now leaves him and his house behind; between whose plain dress, and her refined manner, there is something exceedingly inconsistent. She should be an upper servant by her attire, yet, in her air and step, though both are hurried and assumed—as far as she can assume in the muddy streets, which she treads with an unaccustomed foot—she is a lady. Her face is veiled, and still she sufficiently betrays herself to make more than one of those who pass her look round sharply.

She never turns her head. Lady or servant, she has a purpose in her, and can follow it. She never turns her head, until she comes to the crossing where Jo plies with his broom. He crosses with her, and begs. Still, she does not turn her head until she has landed on the other side. Then, she slightly beckons to him, and says, "Come here!"

Jo follows her, a pace or two, into a quiet court.

"Are you the boy I've read of in the papers?" she asks behind her veil.

"I don't know," says Jo, staring moodily at the veil, "nothink about no papers. I don't know nothink about nothink at all."

"Were you examined at an Inquest?"

"I don't know nothink about no—where I was took by the beadle, do you mean?" says Jo. "Was the boy's name at the Inkwhich, Jo?"

"Yes."

"That's me!" says Jo.

"Come farther up."

"You mean about the man?" says Jo, following. "Him as wos dead?"

"Hush! Speak in a whisper! Yes. Did he look, when he was living, so very ill and poor?"

"O jist!" says Jo.

"Did he look like—not like *you*?" says the woman with abhorrence.

"O, not so bad as me," says Jo. "I'm a regular one, *I* am! You didn't know him, did you?"

"How dare you ask me if I knew him?"

"No offence, my lady," says Jo, with much humility; for even he has got at the suspicion of her being a lady.

"I am not a lady. I am a servant."

"You are a jolly servant!" says Jo; without the least idea of saying anything offensive; merely as a tribute of admiration.

"Listen and be silent. Don't talk to me, and stand farther from me! Can you show me all those places that were spoken of in the account I read? The place he wrote for, the place he died at, the place where you were taken to, and the place where he was buried? Do you know the place where he was buried?"

Jo answers with a nod; having also nodded as each other place was mentioned.

"Go before me, and show me all those dreadful places. Stop opposite to each, and don't speak to me unless I speak to you. Don't look back. Do what I want, and I will pay you well."

Jo attends closely while the words are being spoken; tells them off on his broom-handle, finding them rather hard; pauses to consider their meaning; considers it satisfactory, and nods his ragged head.

"I am fly," says Jo. "But fen larks, you know! Stow hooking it!"[4]

"What does the horrible creature mean?" exclaims the servant, recoiling from him.

"Stow cutting away, you know!" says Jo.

"I don't understand you. Go on before! I will give you more money than you ever had in your life."

Jo screws up his mouth into a whistle, gives his ragged head a rub, takes his broom under his arm, and leads the way; passing deftly, with his bare feet, over the hard stones, and through the mud and mire.

Cook's Court. Jo stops. A pause.

"Who lives here?"

"Him wot give him his writing, and give me half a bull,"[5] says Jo, in a whisper, without looking over his shoulder.

"Go on to the next."

Krook's house. Jo stops again. A longer pause.

"Who lives here?"

"*He* lived here," Jo answers as before.

After a silence he is asked, "In which room?"

"In the back room up there. You can see the winder from this

4. *I am fly*: (in effect) I know what you want. *Fen larks*: No tricks allowed. *Stow hooking it!*: Don't try running away!

5. Half a crown (two shillings and six pence)—originally half a *bull's eye*.

corner. Up there! That's where I see him stritched out. This is the public ouse where I was took to."

"Go on to the next!"

It is a longer walk to the next; but Jo, relieved of his first suspicions, sticks to the terms imposed upon him, and does not look round. By many devious ways, reeking with offence of many kinds, they come to the little tunnel of a court, and to the gas-lamp (lighted now), and to the iron gate.

"He was put there," says Jo, holding to the bars and looking in.

"Where? O, what a scene of horror!"

"There!" says Jo, pointing. "Over yinder. Among them piles of bones, and close to that there kitchin winder! They put him wery nigh the top. They was obliged to stamp upon it to git it in. I could unkiver it for you with my broom, if the gate wos open. That's why they locks it, I s'pose," giving it a shake. "It's always locked. Look at the rat!" cries Jo, excited. "Hi! Look! There he goes! Ho! Into the ground!"

The servant skrinks into a corner—into a corner of that hideous archway, with its deadly stains contaminating her dress; and putting out her two hands, and passionately telling him to keep away from her, for he is loathsome to her, so remains for some moments. Jo stands staring, and is still staring when she recovers herself.

"Is this place of abomination, consecrated ground?"

"I don't know nothink of consequential ground," says Jo, still staring.

"Is it blessed?"

"WHICH?" says Jo, in the last degree amazed.

"Is it blessed?"

"I'm blest if I know," says Jo, staring more than ever; "but I shouldn't think it warn't. Blest?" repeats Jo, something troubled in his mind. "It an't done it much good if it is. Blest? I should think it was t'othered myself. But I don't know nothink!"

The servant takes as little heed of what he says, as she seems to take of what she has said herself. She draws off her glove, to get some money from her purse. Jo silently notices how white and small her hand is, and what a jolly servant she must be to wear such sparkling rings.

She drops a piece of money in his hand, without touching it, and shuddering as their hands approach. "Now," she adds, "show me the spot again!"

Jo thrusts the handle of his broom between the bars of the gate, and, with his utmost power of elaboration, points it out. At length, looking aside to see if he has made himself intelligible, he finds that he is alone.

His first proceeding is, to hold the piece of money to the gas-light,

Consecrated ground.

and to be overpowered at finding that it is yellow—gold. His next is, to give it a one-sided bite at the edge, as a test of its quality. His next to put it in his mouth for safety, and to sweep the step and passage with great care. His job done, he sets off for Tom-all-Alone's; stopping in the light of innumerable gas-lamps to produce the piece of gold, and give it another one-sided bite, as a re-assurance of its being genuine.

The Mercury in powder is in no want of society to-night, for my Lady goes to a grand dinner, and three or four balls. Sir Leicester is fidgety, down at Chesney Wold, with no better company than the gout; he complains to Mrs. Rouncewell that the rain makes such a monotonous pattering on the terrace, that he can't read the paper, even by the fireside in his own snug dressing-room.

"Sir Leicester would have done better to try the other side of the house, my dear," says Mrs. Rouncewell to Rosa. "His dressing-room is on my Lady's side. And in all these years I never heard the step upon the Ghost's Walk, more distinct than it is to-night!"

Chapter XVII

ESTHER'S NARRATIVE

Richard very often came to see us while we remained in London (though he soon failed in his letter-writing), and with his quick abilities, his good spirits, his good temper, his gaiety and freshness, was always delightful. But, though I liked him more and more, the better I knew him, I still felt more and more, how much it was to be regretted that he had been educated in no habits of application and concentration. The system which had addressed him in exactly the same manner as it had addressed hundreds of other boys, all varying in character and capacity, had enabled him to dash through his tasks, always with fair credit, and often with distinction; but in a fitful, dazzling way that had confirmed his reliance on those very qualities in himself, which it had been most desirable to direct and train. They were great qualities, without which no high place can be meritoriously won; but, like fire and water, though excellent servants, they were very bad masters. If they had been under Richard's direction, they would have been his friends; but Richard being under their direction, they became his enemies.

I write down these opinions, not because I believe that this or any other thing was so, because I thought so; but only because I did think so, and I want to be quite candid about all I thought and did. These were my thoughts about Richard. I thought I often observed besides, how right my guardian was in what he had said; and that the uncertainties and delays of the Chancery suit had imparted to his nature something of the careless spirit of a gamester, who felt that he was part of a great gaming system.

Mr. and Mrs. Bayham Badger coming one afternoon, when my guardian was not at home, in the course of conversation I naturally inquired after Richard.

"Why, Mr. Carstone," said Mrs. Badger, "is very well, and is, I assure you, a great acquisition to our society. Captain Swosser used to say of me that I was always better than land a-head and a breeze a-starn to the midshipmen's mess when the purser's junk[1] had become as tough as the fore-topsel weather earings.[2] It was his naval way of mentioning generally that I was an acquisition to any society. I may render the same tribute, I am sure, to Mr. Carstone. But I—you won't think me premature if I mention it?"

I said no, as Mrs. Badger's insinuating tone seemed to require such an answer.

"Nor Miss Clare?" said Mrs. Bayham Badger, sweetly.

Ada said no, too, and looked uneasy.

"Why, you see, my dears," said Mrs. Badger—"you'll excuse my calling you my dears?"

We entreated Mrs. Badger not to mention it.

"Because you really are, if I may take the liberty of saying so," pursued Mrs. Badger, "so perfectly charming. You see, my dears, that although I am still young—or Mr. Bayham Badger pays me the compliment of saying so—"

"No," Mr. Badger called out, like some one contradicting at a public meeting. "Not at all!"

"Very well," smiled Mrs. Badger, "we will say still young."

("Undoubtedly," said Mr. Badger.)

"My dears, though still young, I have had many opportunities of observing young men. There were many such on board the dear old Crippler, I assure you. After that, when I was with Captain Swosser in the Mediterranean, I embraced every opportunity of knowing and befriending the midshipmen under Captain Swosser's command. *You* never heard them called the young gentlemen, my dears, and probably would not understand allusions to their pipe-claying their weekly accounts;[3] but it is otherwise with me, for blue water has been a second home to me, and I have been quite a sailor. Again, with Professor Dingo."

("A man of European reputation," murmured Mr. Badger.)

"When I lost my dear first, and became the wife of my dear second," said Mrs. Badger, speaking of her former husbands as if they were parts of a charade, "I still enjoyed opportunities of observing youth. The class attendant on Professor Dingo's lectures

1. Salt meat used on long sea voyages.
2. Short ropes that fasten the corners (ears) of a sail to the yard.
3. Bills for the bar in the officers' mess. *Pipe-claying* was the applying of a fine clay used by sailors for erasing stains from their white uniforms.

was a large one, and it became my pride, as the wife of an eminent scientific man seeking herself in science the utmost consolation it could impart, to throw our house open to the students, as a kind of Scientific Exchange. Every Tuesday evening there was lemonade and a mixed biscuit, for all who chose to partake of those refreshments. And there was science to an unlimited extent."

("Remarkable assemblies those, Miss Summerson," said Mr. Badger, reverentially. "There must have been great intellectual friction going on there, under the auspices of such a man!")

"And now," pursued Mrs. Badger, "now that I am the wife of my dear third, Mr. Badger, I still pursue those habits of observation which were formed during the lifetime of Captain Swosser, and adapted to new and unexpected purposes during the lifetime of Professor Dingo. I therefore have not come to the consideration of Mr. Carstone as a Neophyte. And yet I am very much of the opinion, my dears, that he has not chosen his profession advisedly."

Ada looked so very anxious now, that I asked Mrs. Badger on what she founded her supposition?

"My dear Miss Summerson," she replied, "on Mr. Carstone's character and conduct. He is of such a very easy disposition, that probably he would never think it worth while to mention how he really feels; but he feels languid about the profession. He has not that positive interest in it which makes it his vocation. If he has any decided impression in reference to it, I should say it was that it is a tiresome pursuit. Now, this is not promising. Young men, like Mr. Allan Woodcourt, who take to it from a strong interest in all that it can do, will find some reward in it through a great deal of work for a very little money, and through years of considerable endurance and disappointment. But I am quite convinced that this would never be the case with Mr. Carstone."

"Does Mr. Badger think so too?" asked Ada, timidly.

"Why," said Mr. Badger, "to tell the truth, Miss Clare, this view of the matter had not occurred to me until Mrs. Badger mentioned it. But when Mrs. Badger put it in that light, I naturally gave great consideration to it; knowing that Mrs. Badger's mind, in addition to its natural advantages, has had the rare advantage of being formed by two such very distinguished (I will even say illustrious) public men as Captain Swosser of the Royal Navy and Professor Dingo. The conclusion at which I have arrived is—in short, is Mrs. Badger's conclusion."

"It was a maxim of Captain Swosser's," said Mrs. Badger, "speaking in his figurative naval manner, that when you make pitch hot, you cannot make it too hot; and that if you only have to swab a plank, you should swab it as if Davy Jones were after you. It appears to me that this maxim is applicable to the medical, as well as to the nautical profession."

"To all professions," observed Mr. Badger. "It was admirably said by Captain Swosser. Beautifully said."

"People objected to Professor Dingo, when we were staying in the North of Devon, after our marriage," said Mrs. Badger, "that he disfigured some of the houses and other buildings, by chipping off fragments of those edifices with his little geological hammer. But the Professor replied, that he knew of no building, save the Temple of Science. The principle is the same, I think?"

"Precisely the same," said Mr. Badger. "Finely expressed! The Professor made the same remark, Miss Summerson, in his last illness; when (his mind wandering) he insisted on keeping his little hammer under the pillow, and chipping at the countenances of the attendants. The ruling passion!"[4]

Although we could have dispensed with the length at which Mr. and Mrs. Badger pursued the conversation, we both felt that it was disinterested in them to express the opinion they had communicated to us, and that there was a great probability of its being sound. We agreed to say nothing to Mr. Jarndyce until we had spoken to Richard; and, as he was coming next evening, we resolved to have a very serious talk with him.

So, after he had been a little while with Ada, I went in and found my darling (as I knew she would be) prepared to consider him thoroughly right in whatever he said.

"And how do you get on, Richard?" said I. I always sat down on the other side of him. He made quite a sister of me.

"O! well enough!" said Richard.

"He can't say better than that, Esther, can he?" cried my pet, triumphantly.

I tried to look at my pet in the wisest manner, but of course I couldn't.

"Well enough?" I repeated.

"Yes," said Richard, "well enough. It's rather jog-trotty and humdrum. But it'll do as well as anything else!"

"O! my dear Richard!" I remonstrated.

"What's the matter?" said Richard.

"Do as well as anything else!"

"I don't think there's any harm in that, Dame Durden," said Ada, looking so confidingly at me across him; "because if it will do as well as anything else, it will do very well, I hope."

"O yes, I hope so," returned Richard, carelessly tossing his hair from his forehead. "After all, it may be only a kind of probation till our suit is—I forgot though. I am not to mention the suit. Forbid-

4. Alexander Pope wrote, in *Epistles to Several Persons*, Ep. iii, To Lord Bathurst (1733), I, 153:

> The ruling passion, be it what it will,
> The ruling passion conquers reason still.

den ground! O yes, it's all right enough. Let us talk about something else."

Ada would have done so, willingly, and with a full persuasion that we had brought the question to a most satisfactory state. But I thought it would be useless to stop there, so I began again.

"No, but, Richard," said I, "and my dear Ada! Consider how important it is to you both, and what a point of honour it is towards your cousin, that you, Richard, should be quite in earnest without any reservation. I think we had better talk about this, really, Ada. It will be too late, very soon."

"O yes! We must talk about it!" said Ada. "But I think Richard is right."

What was the use of my trying to look wise, when she was so pretty, and so engaging, and so fond of him!

"Mr. and Mrs. Badger were here yesterday, Richard," said I, "and they seemed disposed to think that you had no great liking for the profession."

"Did they though?" said Richard. "O! Well, that rather alters the case, because I had no idea that they thought so, and I should not have liked to disappoint or inconvenience them. The fact is, I don't care much about it. But O, it don't matter! It'll do as well as anything else!"

"You hear him, Ada!" said I.

"The fact is," Richard proceeded, half thoughtfully and half jocosely, "it is not quite in my way. I don't take to it. And I get too much of Mrs. Bayham Badger's first and second."

"I am sure *that's* very natural!" cried Ada, quite delighted. "The very thing we both said yesterday, Esther!"

"Then," pursued Richard, "it's monotonous, and to-day is too like yesterday, and to-morrow is too like to-day."

"But I am afraid," said I, "this is an objection to all kinds of application—to life itself, except under some very uncommon circumstances."

"Do you think so?" returned Richard, still considering. "Perhaps! Ha! Why, then, you know," he added, suddenly becoming gay again, "we travel outside a circle, to what I said just now. It'll do as well as anything else. O, it's all right enough! Let us talk about something else."

But even Ada, with her loving face—and if it had seemed innocent and trusting, when I first saw it in that memorable November fog, how much more so did it seem now, when I knew her innocent and trusting heart—even Ada shook her head at this, and looked serious. So I thought it a good opportunity to hint to Richard, that if he were sometimes a little careless of himself, I was very sure he never meant to be careless of Ada; and that it was a part of his affectionate consideration for her, not to slight the importance of a step that might influence both their lives. This made him almost grave.

"My dear Mother Hubbard," he said, "that's the very thing! I have thought of that, several times; and have been quite angry with myself for meaning to be so much in earnest, and—somehow—not exactly being so. I don't know how it is; I seem to want something or other to stand by. Even you have no idea how fond I am of Ada (my darling cousin, I love you, so much!), but I don't settle down to constancy in other things. It's such uphill work, and it takes such a time!" said Richard, with an air of vexation.

"That may be," I suggested, "because you don't like what you have chosen."

"Poor fellow!" said Ada. "I am sure I don't wonder at it!"

No. It was not of the least use my trying to look wise. I tried again; but how could I do it, or how could it have any effect if I could, while Ada rested her clasped hands upon his shoulder, and while he looked at her tender blue eyes, and while they looked at him!

"You see, my precious girl," said Richard, passing her golden curls through and through his hand, "I was a little hasty, perhaps; or I misunderstood my own inclinations, perhaps. They don't seem to lie in that direction. I couldn't tell, till I tried. Now the question is, whether it's worth while to undo all that has been done. It seems like making a great disturbance about nothing particular."

"My dear Richard," said I, "how *can* you say about nothing particular?"

"I don't mean absolutely that," he returned. "I mean that it *may* be nothing particular, because I may never want it."

Both Ada and I urged, in reply, not only that it was decidedly worth while to undo what had been done, but that it must be undone. I then asked Richard whether he had thought of any more congenial pursuit?

"There, my dear Mrs. Shipton," said Richard, "you touch me home. Yes, I have. I have been thinking that the law is the boy for me."

"The law!" repeated Ada, as if she were afraid of the name.

"If I went into Kenge's office," said Richard, "and if I were placed under articles to Kenge, I should have my eye on the—hum! —the forbidden ground—and should be able to study it, and master it, and to satisfy myself that it was not neglected, and was being properly conducted. I should be able to look after Ada's interests, and my own interests (the same thing!); and I should peg away at Blackstone[5] and all those fellows with the most tremendous ardour."

I was not by any means so sure of that; and I saw how his hankering after the vague things yet to come of those long-deferred hopes, cast a shade on Ada's face. But I thought it best to encourage him in any project of continuous exertion, and only advised him to be quite sure that his mind was made up now.

"My dear Minerva," said Richard, "I am as steady as you are. I made a mistake; we are all liable to mistakes; I won't do so any more, and I'll become such a lawyer as is not often seen. That is, you know," said Richard, relapsing into doubt, "if it really is worth while, after all, to make such a disturbance about nothing particular!"

This led to our saying again, with a great deal of gravity, all that we had said already, and to our coming to much the same conclusion afterwards. But we so strongly advised Richard to be frank and open with Mr. Jarndyce, without a moment's delay; and his disposition was naturally so opposed to concealment, that he sought him out at once (taking us with him), and made a full avowal. "Rick," said my Guardian, after hearing him attentively, "we can retreat with honour, and we will. But we must be careful—for our cousin's sake, Rick, for our cousin's sake—that we make no more such mistakes. Therefore, in the matter of the law, we will have a good trial before we decide. We will look before we leap, and take plenty of time about it."

Richard's energy was of such an impatient and fitful kind, that he would have liked nothing better than to have gone to Mr. Kenge's office in that hour, and to have entered into articles with him on the spot. Submitting, however, with a good grace to the caution that we had shown to be so necessary, he contented himself with sitting down among us in his lightest spirits, and talking as if his one unvarying purpose in life from childhood had been that one which now held possession of him. My guardian was very kind and cordial with him, but rather grave; enough so to cause Ada, when he had departed and we were going up-stairs to bed, to say:

"Cousin John, I hope you don't think the worse of Richard?"

"No, my love," said he.

"Because it was very natural that Richard should be mistaken in such a difficult case. It is not uncommon."

"No, no, my love," said he. "Don't look unhappy."

"O, I am not unhappy, cousin John!" said Ada, smiling cheerfully, with her hand upon his shoulder, where she had put it in bid-

5. Sir William Blackstone's *Commentaries on the Laws of England* (1765–69) was the basic textbook for law students.

ding him good night. "But I should be a little so, if you thought at all the worse of Richard."

"My dear," said Mr. Jarndyce, "I should think the worse of him only if you were ever in the least unhappy through his means. I should be more disposed to quarrel with myself, even then, than with poor Rick, for I brought you together. But, tut, all this is nothing! He has time before him, and the race to run. *I* think the worse of him? Not I, my loving cousin! And not you, I swear!"

"No, indeed, cousin John," said Ada, "I am sure I could not—I am sure I would not—think any ill of Richard, if the whole world did. I could, and I would, think better of him then, than at any other time!"

So quietly and honestly she said it, with her hands upon his shoulders—both hands now—and looking up into his face, like the picture of Truth!

"I think," said my guardian, thoughtfully regarding her, "I think it must be somewhere written that the virtues of the mothers shall, occasionally, be visited on the children, as well as the sins of the fathers.[6] Good night, my rosebud. Good night, little woman. Pleasant slumbers! Happy dreams!"

This was the first time I ever saw him follow Ada with his eyes, with something of a shadow on their benevolent expression. I well remembered the look with which he had contemplated her and Richard, when she was singing in the fire-light; it was but a very little while since he had watched them passing down the room in which the sun was shining, and away into the shade; but his glance was changed, and even the silent look of confidence in me which now followed it once more, was not quite so hopeful and untroubled as it had originally been.

Ada praised Richard more to me, that night, than ever she had praised him yet. She went to sleep with a little bracelet he had given her clasped upon her arm. I fancied she was dreaming of him when I kissed her cheek after she had slept an hour, and saw how tranquil and happy she looked.

For I was so little inclined to sleep, myself, that night, that I sat up working. It would not be worth mentioning for its own sake, but I was wakeful and rather low-spirited. I don't know why. At least, I don't think I know why. At least, perhaps I do, but I don't think it matters.

At any rate, I made up my mind to be so dreadfully industrious that I would leave myself not a moment's leisure to be low-spirited. For I naturally said, "Esther! You to be low-spirited. *You!*" And it really was time to say so, for I—yes, I really did see myself in the

6. See Numbers 14:18.

glass, almost crying. "As if you had anything to make you unhappy, instead of everything to make you happy, you ungrateful heart!" said I.

If I could have made myself go to sleep, I would have done it directly; but, not being able to do that, I took out of my basket some ornamental work for our house (I mean Bleak House) that I was busy with at that time, and sat down to it with great determination. It was necessary to count all the stitches in that work, and I resolved to go on with it until I couldn't keep my eyes open, and then to go to bed.

I soon found myself very busy. But I had left some silk downstairs in a work-table drawer in the temporary Growlery; and coming to a stop for want of it, I took my candle and went softly down to get it. To my great surprise, on going in, I found my guardian still there, and sitting looking at the ashes. He was lost in thought, his book lay unheeded by his side, his silvered iron-grey hair was scattered confusedly upon his forehead as though his hand had been wandering among it while his thoughts were elsewhere, and his face looked worn. Almost frightened by coming upon him so unexpectedly, I stood still for a moment; and should have retired without speaking, had he not, in again passing his hand abstractedly through his hair, seen me and started.

"Esther!"

I told him what I had come for.

"At work so late, my dear?"

"I am working late to-night," said I, "because I couldn't sleep, and wished to tire myself. But, dear Guardian, you are late too, and look weary. You have no trouble, I hope, to keep you waking?"

"None, little woman, that *you* would readily understand," said he.

He spoke in a regretful tone so new to me, that I inwardly repeated, as if that would help me to his meaning. "That *I* could readily understand!"

"Remain a moment, Esther," said he. "You were in my thoughts."

"I hope I was not the trouble, Guardian?"

He slightly waved his hand, and fell into his usual manner. The change was so remarkable, and he appeared to make it by dint of so much self-command, that I found myself again inwardly repeating, "None that *I* could understand!"

"Little woman," said my guardian, "I was thinking—that is, I have been thinking since I have been sitting here—that you ought to know, of your own history, all I know. It is very little. Next to nothing."

"Dear Guardian," I replied, "when you spoke to me before on that subject——"

"But since then," he gravely interposed, anticipating what I meant to say, "I have reflected that your having anything to ask me, and my having anything to tell you, are different considerations, Esther. It is perhaps my duty to impart to you the little I know."

"If you think so, Guardian, it is right."

"I think so," he returned, very gently, and kindly, and very distinctly. "My dear, I think so now. If any real disadvantage can attach to your position, in the mind of any man or woman worth a thought, it is right that you, at least, of all the world should not magnify it to yourself, by having vague impressions of its nature."

I sat down; and said, after a little effort to be as calm as I ought to be, "One of my earliest remembrances, Guardian, is of these words: 'Your mother, Esther, is your disgrace, and you were hers. The time will come, and soon enough, when you will understand this better, and will feel it too, as no one save a woman can.'" I had covered my face with my hands, in repeating the words; but I took them away now with a better kind of shame, I hope, and told him, that to him I owed the blessing that I had from my childhood to that hour never, never, never felt it. He put up his hand as if to stop me. I well knew that he was never to be thanked, and said no more.

"Nine years, my dear," he said, after thinking for a little while, "have passed since I received a letter from a lady living in seclusion, written with a stern passion and power that rendered it unlike all other letters I have ever read. It was written to me (as it told me in so many words), perhaps, because it was the writer's idiosyncrasy to put that trust in me: perhaps, because it was mine to justify it. It told me of a child, an orphan girl then twelve years old, in some such cruel words as those which live in your remembrance. It told me that the writer had bred her in secrecy from her birth, had blotted out all trace of her existence, and that if the writer were to die before the child became a woman, she would be left entirely friendless, nameless, and unknown. It asked me to consider if I would, in that case, finish what the writer had begun?"

I listened in silence, and looked attentively at him.

"Your early recollection, my dear, will supply the gloomy medium through which all this was seen and expressed by the writer, and the distorted religion which clouded her mind with impressions of the need there was for the child to expiate an offence of which she was quite innocent. I felt concerned for the little creature, in her darkened life; and replied to the letter."

I took his hand and kissed it.

"It laid the injunction on me that I should never propose to see the writer, who had long been estranged from all intercourse with the world, but who would see a confidential agent if I would appoint one. I accredited Mr. Kenge. To him, the lady said, of her own accord, and not of his seeking, that her name was an assumed one. That she was, if there were any ties of blood in such a case, the child's aunt. That more than this she would never (and he was well persuaded of the steadfastness of her resolution), for any human consideration, disclose. My dear, I have told you all."

I held his hand for a little while in mine.

"I saw my ward oftener than she saw me," he added, cheerily making light of it, "and I always knew she was beloved, useful, and happy. She repays me twenty-thousand-fold, and twenty more to that, every hour in every day!"

"And oftener still," said I, "she blesses the Guardian who is a Father to her!"

At the word Father, I saw his former trouble come into his face. He subdued it as before, and it was gone in an instant; but it had been there, and it had come so swiftly upon my words that I felt as if they had given him a shock. I again inwardly repeated, wondering, "That *I* could readily understand. None that *I* could readily understand!" No, it was true. I did not understand it. Not for many and many a day.

"Take a fatherly good night, my dear," said he, kissing me on the forehead, "and so to rest. These are late hours for working and thinking. You do that for all of us, all day long, little housekeeper!"

I neither worked nor thought, any more, that night. I opened my grateful heart to Heaven in thankfulness for its Providence to me and its care of me, and fell alseep.

We had a visitor next day. Mr. Allan Woodcourt came. He came to take leave of us; he had settled to do so beforehand. He was going to China, and to India, as a surgeon on board ship. He was to be away a long, long time.

I believe—at least I know—that he was not rich. All his widowed mother could spare had been spent in qualifying him for his profession. It was not lucrative to a young practitioner, with very little influence in London; and although he was, night and day, at the service of numbers of poor people, and did wonders of gentleness and skill for them, he gained very little by it in money. He was seven years older than I. Not that I need mention it, for it hardly seems to belong to anything.

I think—I mean, he told us—that he had been in practice three or four years, and that if he could have hoped to contend through three or four more, he would not have made the voyage on which he was bound. But he had no fortune or private means, and so he was going away. He had been to see us several times altogether. We thought it a pity he should go away. Because he was distinguished in his art among those who knew it best, and some of the greatest men belonging to it had a high opinion of him.

When he came to bid us good-bye, he brought his mother with him for the first time. She was a pretty old lady, with bright black eyes, but she seemed proud. She came from Wales; and had had, a long time go, an eminent person for an ancestor, of the name of Morgan ap-Kerrig[7]—of some place that sounded like Gimlet—who was the most illustrious person that ever was known, and all of whose relations were a sort of Royal Family. He appeared to have passed his life in always getting up into mountains, and fighting somebody, and a Bard whose name sounded like Crumlinwallinwer had sung his praises, in a piece which was called, as nearly as I could catch it, Mewlinnwillinwodd.

Mrs. Woodcourt, after expatiating to us on the fame of her great kinsman, said that no doubt, wherever her son Allan went, he would remember his pedigree, and would on no account form an alliance below it. She told him that there were many handsome English ladies in India who went out on speculation, and that there were some to be picked up with property; but that neither charms nor wealth would suffice for the descendant from such a line, without birth: which must ever be the first consideration. She talked so much about birth, that, for a moment, I half fancied, and with pain—but what an idle fancy to suppose that she could think or care what *mine* was!

Mr. Woodcourt seemed a little distressed by her prolixity, but he was too considerate to let her see it, and contrived delicately to bring the conversation round to making his acknowledgments to my guardian for his hospitality, and for the very happy hours—he called them the very happy hours—he had passed with us. The recollection of them, he said, would go with him wherever he went, and would be always treasured. And so we gave him our hands, one after another—at least, they did—and I did; and so he put his lips to Ada's hand—and to mine; and so he went away upon his long, long voyage!

I was very busy indeed, all day, and wrote directions home to the servants, and wrote notes for my guardian, and dusted his books and papers, and jingled my housekeeping keys a good deal, one way and another. I was still busy between the lights, singing and working by the window, when who should come in but Caddy, whom I had no expectation of seeing!

7. Among others, the eighth-century Welsh King Morgan of Morgannwg may be alluded to. *ap-Kerrig* (more correctly *ap-Cerrig*) means "Son of Stones." The other Welsh names in the paragraph seem to have been Dickens' own coinages, and no specific bard or poem has been identified as the original.

"Why, Caddy, my dear," said I, "what beautiful flowers!"

She had such an exquisite little nosegay in her hand.

"Indeed, I think so, Esther," replied Caddy. "They are the loveliest I ever saw."

"Prince, my dear?" said I, in a whisper.

"No," answered Caddy, shaking her head, and holding them to me to smell. "Not Prince."

"Well, to be sure, Caddy!" said I. "You must have two lovers!"

"What? Do they look like that sort of thing?" said Caddy.

"Do they look like that sort of thing?" I repeated, pinching her cheek.

Caddy only laughed in return; and telling me that she had come for half-an-hour, at the expiration of which time Prince would be waiting for her at the corner, sat chatting with me and Ada in the window: every now and then, handing me the flowers again, or trying how they looked against my hair. At last, when she was going, she took me into my room, and put them in my dress.

"For me?" said I, surprised.

"For you," said Caddy, with a kiss. "They were left behind by Somebody."

"Left behind?"

"At poor Miss Flite's" said Caddy. "Somebody who has been very good to her, was hurrying away an hour ago, to join a ship, and left these flowers behind. No, no! Don't take them out. Let the pretty little things lie here!" said Caddy, adjusting them with a careful hand, "because I was present myself, and I shouldn't wonder if Somebody left them on purpose!"

"Do they look like that sort of thing?" said Ada, coming laughingly behind me, and clasping me merrily round the waist. "O, yes, indeed they do, Dame Durden! They look very, very like that sort of thing. O, very like it indeed, my dear!"

Chapter XVIII

LADY DEDLOCK

It was not so easy as it had appeared at first, to arrange for Richard's making a trial of Mr. Kenge's office. Richard himself was the chief impediment. As soon as he had it in his power to leave Mr. Badger at any moment, he began to doubt whether he wanted to leave him at all. He didn't know, he said, really. It wasn't a bad profession; he couldn't assert that he disliked it; perhaps he liked it as well as he liked any other—suppose he gave it one more chance! Upon that, he shut himself up, for a few weeks, with some books and some bones, and seemed to acquire a considerable fund of information with great rapidity. His fervour, after lasting about a month, began to cool; and when it was quite cooled, began to grow warm again. His vacillations between law and medicine lasted so long, that Midsummer arrived before he finally separated from Mr. Badger, and entered on an experimental course of Messrs. Kenge and Carboy. For all his waywardness, he took great credit to himself as being determined to be in earnest "this time." And he was so good-natured throughout, and in such high spirits, and so fond of Ada, that it was very difficult indeed to be otherwise than pleased with him.

"As to Mr. Jarndyce," who, I may mention, found the wind much given, during this period, to sticking in the east; "As to Mr. Jarndyce," Richard would say to me, "he is the finest fellow in the world, Esther! I must be particularly careful, if it were only for his satisfaction, to take myself well to task, and have a regular wind-up of this business now."

The idea of his taking himself well to task, with that laughing face and heedless manner, and with a fancy that everything could catch and nothing could hold, was ludicrously anomalous. However, he told us between-whiles, that he was doing it to such an extent, that he wondered his hair didn't turn grey. His regular wind-up of the business was (as I have said), that he went to Mr. Kenge's about Midsummer, to try how he liked it.

All this time he was, in money affairs, what I have described him in a former illustration: generous, profuse, wildly careless, but fully persuaded that he was rather calculating and prudent. I happened to say to Ada, in his presence, half-jestingly, half-seriously, about the time of his going to Mr. Kenge's, that he needed to have Fortunatus's[1] purse, he made so light of money, which he answered in this way;

"My jewel of a dear cousin, you hear this old woman! Why does she say that? Because I gave eight pounds odd (or whatever it was) for a certain neat waistcoat and buttons a few days ago. Now, if I had stayed at Badger's I should have been obliged to spend twelve pounds at a blow, for some heart-breaking lecture-fees. So I make four pounds—in a lump—by the transaction!"

It was a question much discussed between him and my guardian what arrangements should be made for his living in London, while he experimented on the law; for we had long since gone back to Bleak House, and it was too far off to admit of his coming there oftener than once a week. My guardian told me that if Richard were to settle down at Mr. Kenge's he would take some apartments

1. This hero of a Renaissance period romance acquired a magic purse containing inexhaustible supplies of money.

or chambers, where we, too, could occasionally stay for a few days at a time; "but, little woman," he added, rubbing his head very significantly, "he hasn't settled down there yet!" The discussions ended in our hiring for him, by the month, a neat little furnished lodging in a quiet old house near Queen Square. He immediately began to spend all the money he had, in buying the oddest little ornaments and luxuries for this lodging; and as often as Ada and I dissuaded him from making any purchase that he had in contemplation which was particularly unnecessary and expensive, he took credit for what it would have cost, and made out that to spend anything less on something else was to save the difference.

While these affairs were in abeyance, our visit to Mr. Boythorn's was postponed. At length, Richard having taken possession of his lodging, there was nothing to prevent our departure. He could have gone with us at that time of the year, very well; but he was in the full novelty of his new position, and was making most energetic attempts to unravel the mysteries of the fatal suit. Consequently we went without him; and my darling was delighted to praise him for being so busy.

We made a pleasant journey down into Lincolnshire by the coach, and had an entertaining companion in Mr. Skimpole. His furniture had been all cleared off, it appeared, by the person who took possession of it on his blue-eyed daughter's birthday; but he seemed quite relieved to think that it was gone. Chairs and tables, he said, were wearisome objects; they were monotonous ideas, they had no variety of expression, they looked you out of countenance, and you looked them out of countenance. How pleasant, then, to be bound to no particular chairs and tables, but to sport like a butterfly among all the furniture on hire, and to flit from rosewood to mahogany, and from mahogany to walnut, and from this shape to that, as the humour took one!

"The oddity of the thing is," said Mr. Skimpole, with a quickened sense of the ludicrous, "that my chairs and tables were not paid for, and yet my landlord walks off with them as composedly as possible. Now, that seems droll! There is something grotesque in it. The chair and table merchant never engaged to pay my landlord my rent. Why should my landlord quarrel with *him*? If I have a pimple on my nose which is disagreeable to my landlord's peculiar ideas of beauty, my landlord has no business to scratch my chair and table merchant's nose, which has no pimple on it. His reasoning seems defective!"

"Well," said my guardian, good-humouredly, "it's pretty clear that whoever became security for those chairs and tables will have to pay for them."

"Exactly!" returned Mr. Skimpole. "That's the crowning point of unreason in the business! I said to my landlord, 'My good man, you are not aware that my excellent friend Jarndyce will have to pay for those things that you are sweeping off in that indelicate manner. Have you no consideration for *his* property?' He hadn't the least."

"And refused all proposals," said my guardian.

"Refused all proposals," returned Mr. Skimpole. "I made him business proposals. I had him into my room. I said, 'You are a man of business, I believe?' He replied, 'I am.' 'Very well,' said I, 'now let us be business-like. Here is an inkstand, here are pens and paper, here are wafers.[2] What do you want? I have occupied your house for a considerable period, I believe to our mutual satisfaction until this unpleasant misunderstanding arose; let us be at once friendly and business-like. What do you want?' In reply to this, he made use of the figurative expression—which has something Eastern about it—that he had never seen the colour of my money. 'My amiable friend,' said I, 'I never have any money. I never know anything about money.' 'Well, sir, said he, 'what do you offer if I give you time?' 'My good fellow,' said I, 'I have no idea of time; but you say you are a man of business, and whatever you can suggest to be done in a business-like way with pen, and ink, and paper —and wafers—I am ready to do. Don't pay yourself at another man's expense (which is foolish), but be business-like!' However, he wouldn't be, and there was an end of it."

If these were some of the inconveniences of Mr. Skimpole's childhood, it assuredly possessed its advantages too. On the journey he had a very good appetite for such refreshment as came in our way (including a basket of choice hot-house peaches), but never thought of paying for anything. So when the coachman came round for his fee, he pleasantly asked him what he considered a very good fee indeed, now—a liberal one—and, on his replying, half-a-crown for a single passenger, said it was little enough too, all things considered; and left Mr. Jarndyce to give it him.

It was delightful weather. The green corn waved so beautifully, the larks sang so joyfully, the hedges were so full of wild flowers, the trees were so thickly out in leaf, the bean-fields, with a light wind blowing over them, filled the air with such a delicious fragrance! Late in the afternoon we came to the market-town where we were to alight from the coach—a dull little town, with a church-spire, and a market-place, and a market-cross, and one intensely sunny street, and a pond with an old horse cooling his legs in it, and a very few men sleepily lying and standing about in narrow little bits of shade. After the rustling of the leaves and the waving of the corn all along the road, it looked as still, as hot, as motionless a little town as England could produce.

2. Paper discs used as seals for documents or letters.

At the inn, we found Mr. Boythorn on horseback, waiting with an open carriage, to take us to his house, which was a few miles off. He was overjoyed to see us, and dismounted with great alacrity.

"By Heaven!" said he, after giving us a courteous greeting, "this is a most infamous coach. It is the most flagrant example of an abominable public vehicle that ever encumbered the face of the earth. It is twenty-five minutes after its time, this afternoon. The coachman ought to be put to death!"

"*Is* he after his time?" said Mr. Skimpole, to whom he happened to address himself. "You know my infirmity."

"Twenty-five minutes! Twenty-six minutes!" replied Mr. Boythorn, referring to his watch. "With two ladies in the coach, this scoundrel has deliberately delayed his arrival six-and-twenty minutes. Deliberately! It is impossible that it can be accidental! But his father—and his uncle—were the most profligate coachmen that ever sat upon a box."

While he said this in tones of the greatest indignation, he handed us into the little phaeton with the utmost gentleness, and was all smiles and pleasure.

"I am sorry, ladies," he said, standing bare-headed at the carriage-door, when all was ready, "that I am obliged to conduct you nearly two miles out of the way. But our direct road lies through Sir Leicester Dedlock's park; and, in that fellow's property, I have sworn never to set foot of mine, or horse's foot of mine, pending the present relations between us, while I breathe the breath of life!" And here, catching my guardian's eye, he broke into one of his tremendous laughs, which seemed to shake even the motionless little market-town.

"Are the Dedlocks down here, Lawrence?" said my guardian as we drove along, and Mr. Boythorn trotted on the green turf by the roadside.

"Sir Arrogant Numskull is here," replied Mr. Boythorn. "Ha ha ha! Sir Arrogant is here, and I am glad to say, has been laid by the heels here. My Lady," in naming whom he always made a courtly gesture as if particularly to exclude her from any part in the quarrel, "is expected, I believe, daily. I am not in the least surprised that she postpones her appearance as long as possible. Whatever can have induced that transcendant woman to marry that effigy and figure-head of a baronet, is one of the most impenetrable mysteries that ever baffled human inquiry. Ha ha ha ha!"

"I suppose," said my guardian, laughing, "*we* may set foot in the park while we are here? The prohibition does not extend to us, does it?"

"I can lay no prohibition on my guests," he said, bending his head to Ada and me, with the smiling politeness which sat so gracefully upon him, "except in the matter of their departure. I am only sorry that I cannot have the happiness of being their escort about Chesney Wold, which is a very fine place! But, by the light of this summer day, Jarndyce, if you call upon the owner, while you stay with me, you are likely to have but a cool reception. He carries himself like an eight-day clock at all times; like one of a race of eight-day clocks[3] in gorgeous cases that never go and never went—Ha ha ha!—but he will have some extra stiffness, I can promise you, for the friends of his friend and neighbour, Boythorn!"

"I shall not put him to the proof," said my guardian. "He is as indifferent to the honour of knowing me, I dare say, as I am to the honour of knowing him. The air of the grounds, and perhaps such a view of the house as any other sight-seer might get, are quite enough for me."

"Well," said Mr. Boythorn, "I am glad of it on the whole. It's in better keeping. I am looked upon, about here, as a second Ajax defying the lightning.[4] Ha ha ha ha! When I go into our little church on a Sunday, a considerable part of the inconsiderable congregation expect to see me drop, scorched and withered, on the pavement under the Dedlock displeasure. Ha ha ha ha! I have no doubt he is surprised that I don't. For he is, by Heaven! the most self-satisfied, and the shallowest, and the most coxcombical and utterly brainless ass!"

Our coming to the ridge of a hill we had been ascending, enabled our friend to point out Chesney Wold itself to us, and diverted his attention from its master.

It was a picturesque old house, in a fine park richly wooded. Among the trees, and not far from the residence, he pointed out the spire of the little church of which he had spoken. O, the solemn woods over which the light and shadow travelled swiftly, as if Heavenly wings were sweeping on benignant errands through the summer air; the smooth green slopes, the glittering water, the garden where the flowers were so symmetrically arranged in clusters of the richest colours, how beautiful they looked! The house, with gable and chimney, and tower, and turret, and dark doorway, and broad terrace-walk, twining among the balustrades of which, and lying heaped upon the vases, there was one great flush of roses,

3. Usually grandfather clocks, in elaborately decorated cases. The mechanism, invented in the seventeenth century, required winding only once a week (as illustrated in Laurence Sterne's *Tristram Shandy*). Such clocks do not seem to have had any special reputation for not working, and the "race" of them here would hence be an imaginary breed.

4. Greek leader at the siege of Troy. On his return voyage to Greece, Ajax angered the gods by boasting about his prowess in surviving a shipwreck, and he perished when Poseidon's trident split the rock on which he had thought to save himself.

seemed scarcely real in its light solidity, and in the serene and peaceful hush that rested all around it. To Ada and to me, that, above all, appeared the pervading influence. On everything, house, garden, terrace, green slopes, water, old oaks, fern, moss, woods again, and far away across the openings in the prospect, to the distance lying wide before us with a purple bloom upon it, there seemed to be such undisturbed repose.

When we came into the little village, and passed a small inn with the sign of the Dedlock Arms swinging over the road in front, Mr. Boythorn interchanged greetings with a young gentleman sitting on a bench outside the inn-door, who had some fishing-tackle lying beside him.

"That's the housekeeper's grandson, Mr. Rouncewell by name," said he; "and he is in love with a pretty girl up at the House. Lady Dedlock has taken a fancy to the pretty girl, and is going to keep her about her own fair person—an honour which my young friend himself does not at all appreciate. However, he can't marry just yet, even if his Rosebud were willing; so he is fain to make the best of it. In the meanwhile, he comes here pretty often, for a day or two at a time, to—fish. Ha ha ha ha!"

"Are he and the pretty girl engaged, Mr. Boythorn?" asked Ada.

"Why, my dear Miss Clare," he returned, "I think they may perhaps understand each other; but you will see them soon, I dare say, and I must learn from you on such a point—not you from me."

Ada blushed; and Mr. Boythorn, trotting forward on his comely grey horse, dismounted at his own door, and stood ready, with extended arm and uncovered head, to welcome us when we arrived.

He lived in a pretty house, formerly the Parsonage-house, with a lawn in front, a bright flower-garden at the side, and a well-stocked orchard and kitchen-garden in the rear, enclosed with a venerable wall that had of itself a ripened ruddy look. But, indeed, everything about the place wore an aspect of maturity and abundance. The old lime-tree walk was like green cloisters, the very shadows of the cherry-trees and apple-trees were heavy with fruit, the gooseberry-bushes were so laden that their branches arched and rested on the earth, the strawberries and raspberries grew in like profusion, and the peaches basked by the hundred on the wall. Tumbled about among the spread nets and the glass frames sparkling and winking in the sun, there were such heaps of drooping pods, and marrows, and cucumbers, that every foot of ground appeared a vegetable treasury, while the smell of sweet herbs and all kinds of wholesome growth (to say nothing of the neighbouring meadows where the hay was carrying) made the whole air a great nosegay. Such stillness and composure reigned within the orderly precincts of the old red wall, that even the feathers hung in garlands to scare the birds hardly stirred; and the wall had such a ripening influence that where, here and there high up, a disused nail and scrap of list[5] still clung to it, it was easier to fancy that they had mellowed with the changing seasons, than that they had rusted and decayed according to the common fate.

The house, though a little disorderly in comparison with the garden, was a real old house, with settles in the chimney of the brick-floored kitchen, and great beams across the ceilings. On one side of it was the terrible piece of ground in dispute, where Mr. Boythorn maintained a sentry in a smock-frock, day and night, whose duty was supposed to be, in cases of aggression, immediately to ring a large bell hung up there for the purpose, to unchain a great bull-dog established in a kennel as his ally, and generally to deal destruction on the enemy. Not content with these precautions, Mr. Boythorn had himself composed and posted there, on painted boards to which his name was attached in large letters, the following solemn warnings: "Beware of the Bull-dog. He is most ferocious. Lawrence Boythorn." "The blunderbuss is loaded with slugs. Lawrence Boythorn." "Man-traps and spring-guns are set here at all times of the day and night. Lawrence Boythorn." "Take notice. That any person or persons audaciously presuming to trespass on this property, will be punished with the utmost severity of private chastisement, and prosecuted with the utmost rigour of the law. Lawrence Boythorn." These he showed us, from the drawing-room window, while his bird was hopping about his head; and he laughed, "Ha ha ha ha! Ha ha ha ha!" to that extent as he pointed them out, that I really thought he would have hurt himself.

"But this is taking a good deal of trouble," said Mr. Skimpole, in his light way, "when you are not in earnest after all?"

"Not in earnest!" returned Mr. Boythorn, with unspeakable warmth. "Not in earnest! If I could have hoped to train him, I would have bought a Lion instead of that dog, and would have turned him loose upon the first intolerable robber who should dare to make an encroachment on my rights. Let Sir Leicester Dedlock consent to come out and decide this question by single combat, and I will meet him with any weapon known to mankind in any age or country. I am that much in earnest. Not more!"

We arrived at his house on a Saturday. On the Sunday morning we all set forth to walk to the little church in the park. Entering the park, almost immediately by the disputed ground, we pursued a pleasant footpath winding among the verdant turf and the beautiful trees, until it brought us to the church-porch.

5. Cloth.

The congregation was extremely small and quite a rustic one, with the exception of a large muster of servants from the House, some of whom were already in their seats, while others were yet dropping in. There were some stately footmen; and there was a perfect picture of an old coachman, who looked as if he were the official representative of all the pomps and vanities[6] that had ever been put into his coach. There was a very pretty show of young women; and above them, the handsome old face and fine responsible portly figure of the housekeeper, towered pre-eminent. The pretty girl, of whom Mr. Boythorn had told us, was close by her. She was so very pretty, that I might have known her by her beauty, even if I had not seen how blushingly conscious she was of the eyes of the young fisherman, whom I discovered not far off. One face, and not an agreeable one, though it was handsome, seemed maliciously watchful of this pretty girl, and indeed of every one and everything there. It was a Frenchwoman's.

As the bell was yet ringing and the great people were not yet come, I had leisure to glance over the church, which smelt as earthy as a grave, and to think what a shady, ancient, solemn little church it was. The windows, heavily shaded by trees, admitted a subdued light that made the faces around me pale, and darkened the old brasses in the pavement, and the time and damp-worn monuments, and rendered the sunshine in the little porch, where a monotonous ringer was working at the bell, inestimably bright. But a stir in that direction, a gathering of reverential awe in the rustic faces, and a blandly-ferocious assumption on the part of Mr. Boythorn of being resolutely unconscious of somebody's existence, forewarned me that the great people were come, and that the service was going to begin.

" 'Enter not into judgment with thy servant, O Lord, for in thy sight——' "[7]

Shall I ever forget the rapid beating at my heart, occasioned by the look I met, as I stood up! Shall I ever forget the manner in which those handsome proud eyes seemed to spring out of their languor, and to hold mine! It was only a moment before I cast mine down—released again, if I may say so—on my book; but I knew the beautiful face quite well, in that short space of time.

And, very strangely, there was something quickened within me, associated with the lonely days at my godmother's; yes, away even to the days when I had stood on tiptoe to dress myself at my little glass, after dressing my doll. And this, although I had never seen

6. See "A Catechism" in *The Book of Common Prayer*: "I should renounce the devil and all his works, the pomps and vanity of this wicked world."

7. "Enter not into judgment with thy servant, O Lord: for in thy sight shall no man living be justified" (Psalms 143). An opening recitation for Sunday services.

this lady's face before in all my life—I was quite sure of it—absolutely certain.

It was easy to know that the ceremonious, gouty, grey-haired gentleman, the only other occupant of the great pew, was Sir Leicester Dedlock; and that the lady was Lady Dedlock. But why her face should be, in a confused way, like a broken glass to me, in which I saw scraps of old remembrances; and why I should be so fluttered and troubled (for I was still), by having casually met her eyes; I could not think.

I felt it to be an unmeaning weakness in me, and tried to overcome it by attending to the words I heard. Then, very strangely, I seemed to hear them, not in the reader's voice, but in the well-remembered voice of my godmother. This made me think, did Lady Dedlock's face accidentally resemble my godmother's? It might be that it did, a little; but the expression was so different, and the stern decision which had worn into my godmother's face, like weather into rocks, was so completely wanting in the face before me, that it could not be that resemblance which had struck me. Neither did I know the loftiness and haughtiness of Lady Dedlock's face at all, in any one. And yet *I*—*I*, little Esther Summerson, the child who lived a life apart, and on whose birthday there was no rejoicing—seemed to arise before my own eyes, evoked out of the past by some power in this fashionable lady, whom I not only entertained no fancy that I had ever seen, but whom I perfectly well knew I had never seen until that hour.

It made me tremble so, to be thrown into this unaccountable agitation, that I was conscious of being distressed even by the observation of the French maid, though I knew she had been looking watchfully here, and there, and everywhere, from the moment of her coming into the church. By degrees, though very slowly, I at last overcame my strange emotion. After a long time, I looked towards Lady Dedlock again. It was while they were preparing to sing, before the sermon. She took no heed of me, and the beating at my heart was gone. Neither did it revive for more than a few moments, when she once or twice afterwards glanced at Ada or at me through her glass.

The service being concluded, Sir Leicester gave his arm with much state and gallantry to Lady Dedlock—though he was obliged to walk by the help of a thick stick—and escorted her out of church to the pony carriage in which they had come. The servants then dispersed, and so did the congregation; whom Sir Leicester had contemplated all along (Mr. Skimpole said to Mr. Boythorn's infinite delight), as if he were a considerable landed proprietor in Heaven.

"He believes he is!" said Mr. Boythorn. "He firmly believes it. So did his father, and his grandfather, and his great-grandfather!"

"Do you know," pursued Mr. Skimpole, very unexpectedly, to Mr. Boythorn, "it's agreeable to me to see a man of that sort."

"*Is* it!" said Mr. Boythorn.

"Say that he wants to patronise me," pursued Mr. Skimpole. "Very well! I don't object."

"*I* do," said Mr. Boythorn, with great vigour.

"Do you really?" returned Mr. Skimpole, in his easy light vein. "But that's taking trouble, surely. And why should you take trouble? Here am I, content to receive things childishly, as they fall out: and I never take trouble! I come down here, for instance, and I find a mighty potentate, exacting homage. Very well! I say, 'Mighty potentate, here *is* my homage! It's easier to give it, than to withhold it. Here it is. If you have anything of an agreeable nature to show me, I shall be happy to see it; if you have anything of an agreeable nature to give me, I shall be happy to accept it.' Mighty potentate replies in effect, 'This is a sensible fellow. I find him accord with my digestion and my bilious system. He doesn't impose upon me the necessity of rolling myself up like a hedgehog with my points outward. I expand, I open, I turn my silver lining outward like Milton's cloud,[8] and it's more agreeable to both of us.' That's my view of such things: speaking as a child!"

"But suppose you went down somewhere else to-morrow," said Mr. Boythorn, "where there was the opposite of that fellow—or of this fellow—How then?"

"How then?" said Mr. Skimpole, with an appearance of the utmost simplicity and candour. "Just the same then! I should say, 'My esteemed Boythorn'—to make you the personification of our imaginary friend—'my esteemed Boythorn, you object to the mighty potentate? Very good. So do I. I take it that my business in the social system is to be agreeable. I take it that everybody's business in the social system is to be agreeable. It's a system of harmony, in short. Therefore if you object, I object. Now, excellent Boythorn, let us go to dinner!' "

"But excellent Boythorn might say," returned our host, swelling and growing very red, "I'll be——"

"I understand," said Mr. Skimpole. "Very likely he would."

"—— if I *will* go to dinner!" cried Mr. Boythorn, in a violent burst, and stopping to strike his stick upon the ground. "And he would probably add, 'Is there such a thing as principle, Mr. Harold Skimpole?' "

"To which Harold Skimpole would reply, you know," he returned in his gayest manner, and with his most ingenuous smile,

8. See *Comus* (223–24): "There does a sable cloud/ Turn forth her silver lining on the night."

" 'Upon my life I have not the least idea! I don't know what it is you call by that name, or where it is, or who possesses it. If you possess it, and find it comfortable, I am quite delighted, and congratulate you heartily. But I know nothing about it, I assure you; for I am a mere child, and I lay no claim to it, and I don't want it!' So, you see, excellent Boythorn and I would go to dinner after all!"

This was one of many little dialogues between them, which I always expected to end, and which I dare say would have ended under other circumstances, in some violent explosion on the part of our host. But he had so high a sense of his hospitable and responsible position as our entertainer, and my guardian laughed so sincerely at and with Mr. Skimpole, as a child who blew bubbles and broke them all day long, that matters never went beyond this point. Mr. Skimpole, who always seemed quite unconscious of having been on delicate ground, then betook himself to beginning some sketch in the park which he never finished, or to playing fragments of airs on the piano, or to singing scraps of songs, or to lying down on his back under a tree, and looking at the sky—which he couldn't help thinking, he said, was what he was meant for; it suited him so exactly.

"Enterprise and effort," he would say to us (on his back), "are delightful to me. I believe I am truly cosmopolitan. I have the deepest sympathy with them. I lie in a shady place like this, and think of adventurous spirits going to the North Pole, or penetrating to the heart of the Torrid Zone, with admiration. Mercenary creatures may ask, 'What is the use of a man's going to the North Pole! What good does it do?' I can't say; but, for anything I *can* say, he may go for the purpose—though he don't know it—of employing my thoughts as I lie here. Take an extreme case. Take the case of the Slaves on American plantations. I dare say they are worked hard, I dare say they don't altogether like it, I dare say theirs is an unpleasant experience on the whole; but they people the landscape for me, they give it a poetry for me, and perhaps that is one of the pleasanter objects of their existence. I am very sensible of it, if it be, and I shouldn't wonder if it were!"

I always wondered on these occasions whether he ever thought of Mrs. Skimpole and the children, and in what point of view they presented themselves to his cosmopolitan mind. So far as I could understand, they rarely presented themselves at all.

The week had gone round to the Saturday following that beating of my heart in the church; and every day had been so bright and blue, that to ramble in the woods, and to see the light striking down among the transparent leaves, and sparkling in the beautiful interlacings of the shadows of the trees, while the birds poured out their songs, and the air was drowsy with the hum of insects, had been most delightful. We had one favourite spot, deep in moss and last year's leaves, where there were some felled trees from which the bark was all stripped off. Seated among these, we looked through a green vista supported by thousands of natural columns, the whitened stems of trees, upon a distant prospect made so radiant by its contrast with the shade in which we sat, and made so precious by the arched perspective through which we saw it, that it was like a glimpse of the better land. Upon the Saturday we sat here, Mr. Jarndyce, Ada, and I, until we heard thunder muttering in the distance, and felt the large rain-drops rattle through the leaves.

The weather had been all the week extremely sultry; but, the storm broke so suddenly—upon us, at least, in that sheltered spot—that before we reached the outskirts of the wood, the thunder and lightning were frequent, and the rain came plunging through the leaves, as if every drop were a great leaden bead. As it was not a time for standing among trees, we ran out of the wood, and up and down the moss-grown steps which crossed the plantation-fence like two broad-staved ladders placed back to back, and made for a keeper's lodge which was close at hand. We had often noticed the dark beauty of this lodge standing in a deep twilight of trees, and how the ivy clustered over it, and how there was a steep hollow near, where we had once seen the keeper's dog dive down into the fern as if it were water.

The lodge was so dark within, now the sky was overcast, that we only clearly saw the man who came to the door when we took shelter there, and put two chairs for Ada and me. The lattice windows were all thrown open, and we sat, just within the doorway, watching the storm. It was grand to see how the wind awoke, and bent the trees, and drove the rain before it like a cloud of smoke; and to hear the solemn thunder, and to see the lightning; and while thinking with awe of the tremendous powers by which our little lives are encompassed, to consider how beneficent they are, and how upon the smallest flower and leaf there was already a freshness poured from all this seeming rage, which seemed to make creation new again.

"Is it not dangerous to sit in so exposed a place?"

"O no, Esther dear!" said Ada, quietly.

Ada said it to me, but, *I* had not spoken.

The beating of my heart came back again. I had never heard the voice, as I had never seen the face, but it affected me in the same strange way. Again, in a moment, there arose before my mind innumerable pictures of myself.

Lady Dedlock had taken shelter in the lodge, before our arrival there, and had come out of the gloom within. She stood behind my chair, with her hand upon it. I saw her with her hand close to my shoulder, when I turned my head.

"I have frightened you?" she said.

No. It was not fright. Why should I be frightened!

"I believe," said Lady Dedlock to my guardian, "I have the pleasure of speaking to Mr. Jarndyce."

"Your remembrance does me more honour than I had supposed it would, Lady Dedlock," he returned.

"I recognized you in church on Sunday. I am sorry that any local disputes of Sir Leicester's—they are not of his seeking, however, I believe—should render it a matter of some absurd difficulty to show you any attention here."

"I am aware of the circumstances," returned my guardian with a smile, "and am sufficiently obliged."

She had given him her hand, in an indifferent way that seemed habitual to her, and spoke in a correspondingly indifferent manner, though in a very pleasant voice. She was as graceful as she was beautiful; perfectly self-possessed; and had the air, I thought, of being able to attract and interest any one, if she had thought it worth her while. The keeper had brought her a chair, on which she sat, in the middle of the porch between us.

"Is the young gentleman disposed of, whom you wrote to Sir Leicester about, and whose wishes Sir Leicester was sorry not to have it in his power to advance in any way?" she said, over her shoulder, to my guardian.

"I hope so," said he.

She seemed to respect him, and even to wish to conciliate him. There was something very winning in her haughty manner; and it became more familiar—I was going to say more easy, but that could hardly be—as she spoke to him over her shoulder.

"I presume this is your other ward, Miss Clare?"

He presented Ada, in form.

"You will lose the disinterested part of your Don Quixote character," said Lady Dedlock to Mr. Jarndyce, over her shoulder again, "if you only redress the wrongs of beauty like this. But present me," and she turned full upon me, "to this young lady too!"

"Miss Summerson really is my ward," said Mr. Jarndyce. "I am responsible to no Lord Chancellor in her case."

"Has Miss Summerson lost both her parents?" said my Lady.

"Yes."

"She is very fortunate in her guardian."

Lady Dedlock looked at me, and I looked at her, and said I was indeed. All at once she turned from me with a hasty air almost expressive of displeasure or dislike, and spoke to him over her shoulder again.

"Ages have passed since we were in the habit of meeting, Mr. Jarndyce."

"A long time. At least I thought it was a long time, until I saw you last Sunday," he returned.

"What! Even you are a courtier, or think it necessary to become one to me!" she said, with some disdain. "I have achieved that reputation, I suppose."

"You have achieved so much, Lady Dedlock," said my guardian, "that you pay some little penalty, I dare say. But none to me."

"So much!" she repeated, slightly laughing. "Yes!"

With her air of superiority, and power, and fascination, and I know not what, she seemed to regard Ada and me as little more than children. So, as she slightly laughed, and afterwards sat looking at the rain, she was as self-possessed, and as free to occupy herself with her own thoughts, as if she had been alone.

"I think you knew my sister, when we were abroad together, better than you knew me?" she said, looking at him again.

"Yes, we happened to meet oftener," he returned.

"We went our several ways," said Lady Dedlock, "and had little in common even before we agreed to differ. It is to be regretted, I suppose, but it could not be helped."

Lady Dedlock again sat looking at the rain. The storm soon began to pass upon its way. The shower greatly abated, the lightning ceased, the thunder rolled among the distant hills, and the sun began to glisten on the wet leaves and the falling rain. As we sat there, silently, we saw a little pony phaeton coming towards us at a merry pace.

"The messenger is coming back, my Lady," said the keeper, "with the carriage."

As it drove up, we saw that there were two people inside. There alighted from it, with some cloaks and wrappers, first the Frenchwoman whom I had seen in church, and secondly the pretty girl; the Frenchwoman, with a defiant confidence; the pretty girl confused and hesitating.

"What now?" said Lady Dedlock. "Two!"

"I am your maid, my Lady, at the present," said the Frenchwoman. "The message was for the attendant."

"I was afraid you might mean me, my Lady," said the pretty girl.

"I did mean you, child," replied her mistress calmly. "Put that shawl on me."

She slightly stooped her shoulders to receive it, and the pretty girl lightly dropped it in its place. The Frenchwoman stood unnoticed, looking on with her lips very tightly set.

"I am sorry," said Lady Dedlock to Mr. Jarndyce, "that we are not likely to renew our former acquaintance. You will allow me to send the carriage back for your two wards. It shall be here directly."

But as he would on no account accept this offer, she took a graceful leave of Ada—none of me—and put her hand upon his proffered arm, and got into the carriage; which was a little, low, park carriage, with a hood.

"Come in, child," she said to the pretty girl, "I shall want you. Go on!"

The carriage rolled away; and the Frenchwoman, with the wrappers she had brought hanging over her arm, remained standing where she had alighted.

I supposed there is nothing Pride can so little bear with as Pride itself, and that she was punished for her imperious manner. Her retaliation was the most singular I could have imagined. She remained perfectly still until the carriage had turned into the drive, and then, without the least discomposure of countenance, slipped off her shoes, left them on the ground, and walked deliberately in the same direction, through the wettest of the wet grass.

"Is that young woman mad?" said my guardian.

"O no sir!" said the keeper, who, with his wife, was looking after her. "Hortense is not one of that sort. She has as good a head-piece as the best. But she's mortal high and passionate—powerful high and passionate; and what with having notice to leave, and having others put above her, she don't take kindly to it."

"But why should she walk shoeless, through all that water?" said my guardian.

"Why, indeed, sir, unless it is to cool her down!" said the man.

"Or unless she fancies it's blood,"[9] said the woman. "She'd as soon walk through that as anything else, I think, when her own's up!"

We passed not far from the House, a few minutes afterwards. Peaceful as it had looked when we first saw it, it looked even more so now, with a diamond spray glittering all about it, a light wind blowing, the birds no longer hushed but singing strongly, everything refreshed by the late rain, and the little carriage shining at the doorway like a fairy carriage made of silver. Still, very steadfastly and quietly walking towards it, a peaceful figure too in the landscape, went Mademoiselle Hortense, shoeless, through the wet grass.

Chapter XIX

MOVING ON

It is the long vacation in the regions of Chancery Lane. The good ships Law and Equity, those teak-built, copper-bottomed, iron-fastened, brazened-faced, and not by any means fast-sailing Clippers,

9. Cf. *Macbeth* (III.iv.126–28): "I am in blood/ Stepp'd in so far that, should I wade no more,/ Returning were as tedious as to go o'er."

are laid up in ordinary.[1] The Flying Dutchman,[2] with a crew of ghostly clients imploring all whom they may encounter to peruse their papers, has drifted, for the time being, Heaven knows where. The Courts are all shut up; the public offices lie in a hot sleep; Westminster Hall itself is a shady solitude where nightingales might sing, and a tenderer class of suitors than is usually found there, walk.

The Temple, Chancery Lane, Serjeants' Inn,[3] and Lincoln's Inn even unto the Fields,[4] are like tidal harbours at low water; where stranded proceedings, offices at anchor, idle clerks lounging on lop-sided stools that will not recover their perpendicular until the current of Term sets in, lie high and dry upon the ooze of the long vacation. Outer doors of chambers are shut up by the score, messages and parcels are to be left at the Porter's Lodge by the bushel. A crop of grass would grow in the chinks of the stone pavement outside Lincoln's Inn Hall, but that the ticket-porters, who have nothing to do beyond sitting in the shade there, with their white aprons over their heads to keep the flies off, grub it up and eat it thoughtfully.

There is only one Judge in town. Even he only comes twice a-week to sit in chambers. If the country folks of those assize towns on his circuit could only see him now! No full-bottomed wig, no red petticoats, no fur, no javelin-men, no white wands.[5] Merely a close-shaved gentleman in white trousers and a white hat, with sea-bronze on the judicial countenance, and a strip of bark peeled by the solar rays from the judicial nose, who calls in at the shell-fish shop as he comes along, and drinks iced ginger-beer!

The bar of England is scattered over the face of the earth. How England can get on through four long summer months without its bar—which is its acknowledged refuge in adversity, and its only legitimate triumph in prosperity—is beside the question; assuredly that shield and buckler of Britannia are not in present wear. The learned gentleman who is always so tremendously indignant at the unprecedented outrage committed on the feelings of his client by the opposite party, that he never seems likely to recover it, is doing infinitely better than might be expected, in Switzerland. The learned gentleman who does the withering business, and who blights all opponents with his gloomy sarcasm, is as merry as a grig[6] at a French watering-place. The learned gentleman who weeps by the pint on the smallest provocation has not shed a tear these six

1. A ship that is laid up and out of commission although still afloat.
2. Legendary ship doomed to drift forever and barred from entering ports.
3. An Inn for high-ranking lawyers, demolished after the office of Serjeants was abolished in the 1870's.
4. Cf. Wordsworth's sonnet "Upon Westminster Bridge": "Ships, towers, domes, theatres, and temples lie/ Open unto the fields . . ."
5. Officers carrying white staves who attended a judge in ceremonial processions, as did the *javelin-men* (spear bearers).
6. Extremely animated (perhaps originally meaning "merry as a cricket").

weeks. The very learned gentleman who has cooled the natural heat of his gingery complexion in pools and fountains of law, until he has become great in knotty arguments for term-time, when he poses the drowsy Bench with legal "chaff", inexplicable to the uninitiated and to most of the initiated too, is roaming, with a characteristic delight in aridity and dust, about Constantinople. Other dispersed fragments of the same great Palladium[7] are to be found on the canals of Venice, at the second cataract of the Nile, in the baths of Germany, and sprinkled on the sea-sand all over the English coast. Scarcely one is to be encountered in the deserted region of Chancery Lane. If such a lonely member of the bar do flit across the waste, and come upon a prowling suitor who is unable to leave off haunting the scenes of his anxiety, they frighten one another, and retreat into opposite shades.

It is the hottest long vacation known for many years. All the young clerks are madly in love, and, according to their various degrees, pine for bliss with the beloved object, at Margate, Ramsgate, or Gravesend.[8] All the middle-aged clerks think their families too large. All the unowned dogs who stray into the Inns of Court, and pant about staircases and other dry places, seeking water, give short howls of aggravation. All the blind men's dogs in the streets draw their masters against pumps, or trip them over buckets. A shop with a sun-blind and a watered pavement, and a bowl of gold and silver fish in the window, is a sanctuary. Temple Bar gets so hot, that it is, to the adjacent Strand and Fleet Street, what a heater is in an urn, and keeps them simmering all night.

There are offices about the Inns of Court in which a man might be cool, if any coolness were worth purchasing at such a price in dulness; but the little thoroughfares immediately outside those retirements seem to blaze. In Mr. Krook's court, it is so hot that the people turn their houses inside out, and sit in chairs upon the pavement—Mr. Krook included, who there pursues his studies, with his cat (who never is too hot) by his side. The Sol's Arms has discontinued the harmonic meetings for the season, and Little Swills is engaged at the Pastoral Gardens down the river, where he comes out in quite an innocent manner, and sings comic ditties of a juvenile complexion, calculated (as the bill says) not to wound the feelings of the most fastidious mind.

Over all the legal neighbourhood, there hangs, like some great veil of rust, or gigantic cobweb, the idleness and pensiveness of the long vacation. Mr. Snagsby, law-stationer of Cook's Court, Cursitor

7. At Troy, an ancient statue of the goddess Pallas Athena (to which here the Bar of England is likened). The safety of Troy was thought to depend upon the statue's being retained intact in the city.

8. Margate and Ramsgate are seaside resort towns. (A painting of 1854, "Ramsgate Sands," by William Frith, records what they were like in midsummer.) Gravesend, on the Thames estuary, was a popular site for excursions from London.

Street, is sensible of the influence; not only in his mind as a sympathetic and contemplative man, but also in his business as a law-stationer aforesaid. He has more leisure for musing in Staple Inn and in the Rolls Yard, during the long vacation, than at other seasons; and he says to the two 'prentices, what a thing it is in such hot weather to think that you live in an island, with the sea a-rolling and a-bowling right round you.

Guster is busy in the little drawing-room, on this present afternoon in the long vacation, when Mr. and Mrs. Snagsby have it in contemplation to receive company. The expected guests are rather select than numerous, being Mr. and Mrs. Chadband, and no more. From Mr. Chadband's being much given to describe himself, both verbally and in writing, as a vessel, he is occasionally mistaken by strangers for a gentleman connected with navigation; but he is, as he expresses it, "in the ministry." Mr. Chadband is attached to no particular denomination; and is considered by his persecutors to have nothing so very remarkable to say on the greatest of subjects as to render his volunteering, on his own account, at all incumbent on his conscience; but he has his followers, and Mrs. Snagsby is of the number. Mrs. Snagsby has but recently taken a passage upward by the vessel, Chadband; and her attention was attracted to that Bark A 1,[9] when she was something flushed by the hot weather.

"My little woman," says Mr. Snagsby to the sparrows in Staple Inn, "likes to have her religion rather sharp, you see!"

So Guster, much impressed by regarding herself for the time as the handmaid of Chadband, whom she knows to be endowed with the gift of holding forth for four hours at a stretch, prepares the little drawing-room for tea. All the furniture is shaken and dusted, the portraits of Mr. and Mrs. Snagsby are touched up with a wet cloth, the best tea-service is set forth, and there is excellent provision made of dainty new bread, crusty twists, cool fresh butter, thin slices of ham, tongue, and German sausage, and delicate little rows of anchovies nestling in parsley; not to mention new-laid eggs, to be brought up warm in a napkin, and hot buttered toast. For Chadband is rather a consuming vessel—the persecutors say a gorging vessel; and can wield such weapons of the flesh as a knife and fork, remarkably well.

Mr. Snagsby in his best coat, looking at all the preparations when they are completed and coughing his cough of deference behind his hand, says to Mrs. Snagsby, "At what time did you expect Mr. and Mrs. Chadband, my love?"

"At six," says Mrs. Snagsby.

Mr. Snagsby observes in a mild and casual way, that "it's gone that."

9. Sailing ship registered as in the category of first-class vessel.

"Perhaps you'd like to begin without them," is Mrs. Snagsby's reproachful remark.

Mr. Snagsby does look as if he would like it very much, but he says, with his cough of mildness, "No, my dear, no. I merely named the time."

"What's time," says Mrs. Snagsby, "to eternity?"

"Very true, my dear," says Mr. Snagsby. "Only when a person lays in victuals for tea, a person does it with a view—perhaps—more to time. And when a time is named for having tea, it's better to come up to it."

"To come up to it!"[1] Mrs. Snagsby repeats with severity. "Up to it! As if Mr. Chadband was a fighter!"

"Not at all, my dear," says Mr. Snagsby.

Here Guster, who has been looking out of the bedroom window, comes rustling and scratching down the little staircase like a popular ghost, and, falling flushed into the drawing-room, announces that Mr. and Mrs. Chadband have appeared in the court. The bell at the inner door in the passage immediately thereafter tinkling, she is admonished by Mrs. Snagsby, on pain of instant reconsignment to her patron saint, not to omit the ceremony of announcement. Much discomposed in her nerves (which were previously in the best order) by this threat, she so fearfully mutilates that point of state as to announce "Mr. and Mrs. Cheeseming, least which, Imeantersay, whatsername!" and retires conscience-stricken from the presence.

Mr. Chadband is a large yellow man, with a fat smile, and a general appearance of having a good deal of train oil[2] in his system. Mrs. Chadband is a stern, severe-looking, silent woman. Mr. Chadband moves softly and cumbrously, not unlike a bear who has been taught to walk upright. He is very much embarrassed about the arms, as if they were inconvenient to him, and he wanted to grovel; is very much in a perspiration about the head; and never speaks without first putting up his great hand, as delivering a token to his hearers that he is going to edify them.

"My friends," says Mr. Chadband, "Peace be on this house! On the master thereof, on the mistress thereof, on the young maidens, and on the young men! My friends, why do I wish for peace? What is peace? Is it war? No. Is it strife? No. Is it lovely, and gentle, and

1. Up to scratch: a reference to a line drawn across the center of the ring in the early days of prize-fighting. Contestants would commence a match by stepping up to opposite sides of this line, and the match would end when one of the two could no longer come up to the scratch line at the beginning of a new round.

2. A whale oil, chiefly used as an illuminant for lamps, obtained by boiling blubber on board whaling vessels or in factories ("Oil Mills") ashore. The term *train,* derived from a Dutch word, has no connection with railway trains or machinery. According to the *National Encyclopedia* (1873), train oil "is of a brownish colour, rather viscid, and has a disagreeable smell and taste."

beautiful, and pleasant, and serene, and joyful? O yes! Therefore, my friends, I wish for peace, upon you and upon yours."

In consequence of Mrs. Snagsby looking deeply edified, Mr. Snagsby thinks it expedient on the whole to say Amen, which is well received.

"Now, my friends," proceeds Mr. Chadband, "since I am upon this theme——"

Guster presents herself. Mrs. Snagsby, in a spectral bass voice, and without removing her eyes from Chadband, says, with dread distinctness, "Go away!"

"Now, my friends," says Chadband, "since I am upon this theme, and in my lowly path improving it——"

Guster is heard unaccountably to murmur "one thousing seven hunderd and eighty-two." The spectral voice repeats more solemnly, "Go away!"

"Now, my friends," says Mr. Chadband, "we will inquire in a spirit of love——"

Still Guster reiterates "one thousing seven hunderd and eighty-two."

Mr. Chadband, pausing with the resignation of a man accustomed to be persecuted, and languidly folding up his chin into his fat smile, says, "Let us hear the maiden! Speak, maiden!"

"One thousing seven hunderd and eighty-two,[3] if you please, sir. Which he wish to know what the shilling ware for," says Guster, breathless.

"For?" returns Mrs. Chadband. "For his fare!"

Guster replies that "he insistes on one and eightpence, or on summonsizzing the party." Mrs. Snagsby and Mrs. Chadband are proceeding to grow shrill in indignation, when Mr. Chadband quiets the tumult by lifting up his hand.

"My friends," says he, "I remember a duty unfulfilled yesterday. It is right that I should be chastened in some penalty. I ought not to murmur. Rachael, pay the eightpence!"

While Mrs. Snagsby, drawing her breath, looks hard at Mr. Snagsby, as who should say, "You hear this Apostle!" and while Mr. Chadband glows with humility and train oil, Mrs. Chadband pays the money. It is Mr. Chadband's habit—it is the head and front of his pretensions indeed—to keep this sort of debtor and creditor account in the smallest items, and to post it publicly on the most trivial occasions.

"My friends," says Chadband, "eightpence is not much; it might justly have been one and fourpence; it might justly have been half-a-crown. O let us be joyful, joyful! O let us be joyful!"

With which remark, which appears from its sound to be an

3. Number inscribed on the cab-driver's badge.

extract in verse, Mr. Chadband stalks to the table, and, before taking a chair, lifts up his admonitory hand.

"My friends," says he, "what is this which we now behold as being spread before us? Refreshment. Do we need refreshment then, my friends? We do. And why do we need refreshment, my friends? Because we are but mortal, because we are but sinful, because we are but of the earth, because we are not of the air. Can we fly, my friends? We cannot. Why can we not fly, my friends?"

Mr. Snagsby, presuming on the success of the last point, ventures to observe in a cheerful and rather knowing tone, "No wings." But, is immediately frowned down by Mrs. Snagsby.

"I say, my friends," pursues Mr. Chadband, utterly rejecting and obliterating Mr. Snagsby's suggestion, "why can we not fly? Is it because we are calculated to walk? It is. Could we walk, my friends, without strength? We could not. What should we do without strength, my friends? Our legs would refuse to bear us, our knees would double up, our ankles would turn over, and we should come to the ground. Then from whence, my friends, in a human point of view, do we derive the strength that is necessary to our limbs? Is it," says Chadband, glancing over the table, "from bread in various forms, from butter which is churned from the milk which is yielded untoe us by the cow, from the eggs which are laid by the fowl, from ham, from tongue, from sausage, and from such like? It is. Then let us partake of the good things which are set before us!"

The persecutors denied that there was any particular gift in Mr. Chadband's piling verbose flights of stairs, one upon another, after this fashion. But this can only be received as a proof of their determination to persecute, since it must be within everybody's experience, that the Chadband style of oratory is widely received and much admired.

Mr. Chadband, however, having concluded for the present, sits down at Mrs. Snagsby's table, and lays about him prodigiously. The conversion of nutriment of any sort into oil of the quality already mentioned, appears to be a process so inseparable from the constitution of this exemplary vessel, that in beginning to eat and drink, he may be described as always becoming a kind of considerable Oil Mills, or other large factory for the production of that article on a wholesale scale. On the present evening of the long vacation, in Cook's Court, Cursitor Street, he does such a powerful stroke of business, that the warehouse appears to be quite full when the works cease.

At this period of the entertainment, Guster, who has never recovered her first failure, but has neglected no possible or impossible means of bringing the establishment and herself into contempt —among which may be briefly enumerated her unexpectedly performing clashing military music on Mr. Chadband's head with plates, and afterwards crowning that gentleman with muffins—at this period of the entertainment, Guster whispers Mr. Snagsby that he is wanted.

"And being wanted in the—not to put too fine a point upon it —in the shop!" says Mr. Snagsby, rising, "perhaps this good company will excuse me for half a minute."

Mr. Snagsby descends, and find the two 'prentices intently contemplating a police constable, who holds a ragged boy by the arm.

"Why, bless my heart," says Mr. Snagsby, "what's the matter!"

"This boy," says the constable, "although he's repeatedly told to, won't move on—"

"I'm always a-moving on, sir," cries the boy, wiping away his grimy tears with his arm. "I've always been a-moving and a-moving on, ever since I was born. Where can I possible move to, sir, more nor I do move!"

"He won't move on," says the constable, calmly, with a slight professional hitch of his neck involving its better settlement in his stiff stock, "although he has been repeatedly cautioned, and therefore I am obliged to take him into custody.[4] He's as obstinate a young gonoph[5] as I know. He WON'T move on."

"O my eye! Where can I move to!" cries the boy, clutching quite desperately at his hair, and beating his bare feet upon the floor of Mr. Snagsby's passage.

"Don't you come none of that, or I shall make blessed short work of you!" says the constable, giving him a passionless shake. "My instructions are, that you are to move on. I have told you so five hundred times."

"But where?" cries the boy.

"Well! Really, constable, you know," says Mr. Snagsby wistfully, and coughing behind his hand his cough of great perplexity and doubt; "really that does seem a question. Where, you know?"

"My instructions don't go to that," replies the constable. "My instructions are that this boy is to move on."

Do you hear, Jo? It is nothing to you or to any one else, that the great lights of the parliamentary sky have failed for some few years, in this business, to set you the example of moving on. The one grand recipe remains for you—the profound philosophical prescription—the be-all and the end-all[6] of your strange existence upon earth. Move on! You are by no means to move off, Jo, for the great lights can't at all agree about that. Move on!

Mr. Snagsby says nothing to this effect; says nothing at all,

4. In accord with the Metropolitan Police Acts of 1829 and 1839, police constables were empowered to require loiterers to "move on." Cf. *Household Words* (September 6, 1851), p. 569.
5. Pickpocket.
6. *Macbeth* (I.vii.5).

indeed; but coughs his forlornest cough, expressive of no thoroughfare in any direction. By this time Mr. and Mrs. Chadband, and Mrs. Snagsby, hearing the altercation, have appeared upon the stairs. Guster having never left the end of the passage, the whole household are assembled.

"The simple question is, sir," says the constable, "whether you know this boy. He says you do."

Mrs. Snagsby, from her elevation, instantly cries out, "No he don't!"

"My lit-tle woman!" says Mr. Snagsby, looking up the staircase. "My love, permit me! Pray have a moment's patience, my dear. I do know something of this lad, and in what I know of him, I can't say that there's any harm; perhaps on the contrary, constable." To whom the law-stationer relates his Joful and woful experience, suppressing the half-crown fact.

"Well!" says the constable, "so far, it seems, he had grounds for what he said. When I took him into custody up in Holborn, he said you knew him. Upon that, a young man who was in the crowd said he was acquainted with you, and you were a respectable housekeeper, and if I'd call and make the inquiry, he'd appear. The young man don't seem inclined to keep his word, but—Oh! Here *is* the young man!"

Enter Mr. Guppy, who nods to Mr. Snagsby, and touches his hat with the chivalry of clerkship to the ladies on the stairs.

"I was strolling away from the office just now, when I found this row going on," says Mr. Guppy to the law-stationer; "and as your name was mentioned, I thought it was right the thing should be looked into."

"It was very good-natured of you, sir," says Mr. Snagsby, "and I am obliged to you." And Mr. Snagsby again relates his experience, again suppressing the half-crown fact.

"Now, I know where you live," says the constable, then, to Jo. "You live down in Tom-all-Alone's. That's a nice innocent place to live in, ain't it?"

"I can't go and live in no nicer place, sir, " replies Jo. "They wouldn't have nothink to say to me if I wos to go to a nice innocent place fur to live. Who ud go and let a nice innocent lodging to such a reg'lar one as me!"

"You are very poor, ain't you?" says the constable.

"Yes, I am indeed, sir, wery poor in gin'ral," replies Jo.

"I leave you to judge now! I shook these two-half-crowns out of him," says the constable, producing them to the company, "in only putting my hand upon him!"

"They're wot's left, Mr. Sangsby," says Jo, "out of a sov'ring as wos give me by a lady in a wale as sed she wos a servant and as come to my crossin one night and asked to be showd this 'ere ouse and the ouse wot him as you give the writin to died at, and the berrin-ground wot he's berrid in. She ses to me, she ses, 'are you the boy at the Inkwhich?' she ses. I ses, 'yes,' I ses. She ses to me, she ses, 'can you show me all them places?' I ses, 'yes, I can,' I ses. And she ses to me 'do it,' and I dun it, and she giv me a sov'ring and hooked it. And I an't had much of the sov'ring neither," says Jo, with dirty tears, "fur I had to pay five bob, down in Tom-all-Alone's, afore they'd square it fur to give me change, and then a young man he thieved another five while I was asleep, and another boy he thieved ninepence, and the landlord he stood drains[7] round with a lot more on it."

"You don't expect anybody to believe this, about the lady and the sovereign, do you?" says the constable, eyeing him aside with ineffable disdain.

"I don't know as I do, sir," replies Jo. "I don't expect nothink at all, sir, much, but that's the true hist'ry on it."

"You see what he is!" the constable observes to the audience. "Well, Mr. Snagsby, if I don't lock him up this time, will you engage for his moving on?"

"No!" cries Mrs. Snagsby from the stairs.

"My little woman!" pleads her husband. "Constable, I have no doubt he'll move on. You know you really must do it," says Mr. Snagsby.

"I'm everyways agreeable, sir," says the hapless Jo.

"Do it, then," observes the constable. "You know what you have got to do. Do it! And recollect you won't get off so easy next time. Catch hold of your money. Now, the sooner you're five mile off, the better for all parties."

With this farewell hint, and pointing generally to the setting sun, as a likely place to move on to, the constable bids his auditors good afternoon; and makes the echoes of Cook's Court perform slow music for him as he walks away on the shady side, carrying his iron-bound hat in his hand for a little ventilation.

Now, Jo's improbable story concerning the lady and the sovereign has awakened more or less the curiosity of all the company. Mr. Guppy, who has an inquiring mind in matters of evidence, and who has been suffering severely from the lassitude of the long vacation, takes that interest in the case, that he enters on a regular cross-examination of the witness, which is found so interesting by the ladies that Mrs. Snagsby politely invites him to step up-stairs, and drink a cup of tea, if he will excuse the disarranged state of the tea-table, consequent on their previous exertions. Mr. Guppy yielding his

7. Drinks.

assent to this proposal, Jo is requested to follow into the drawing-room doorway, where Mr. Guppy takes him in hand as a witness, patting him into this shape, that shape, and the other shape, like a butter-man dealing with so much butter, and worrying him according to the best models. Nor is the examination unlike many such model displays, both in respect of its eliciting nothing, and of its being lengthy; for Mr. Guppy is sensible of his talent, and Mrs. Snagsby feels, not only that it gratifies her inquisitive disposition, but that it lifts her husband's establishment higher up in the law. During the progress of this keen encounter, the vessel Chadband, being merely engaged in the oil trade, gets aground, and waits to be floated off.

"Well!" says Mr. Guppy, "either this boy sticks to it like cobbler's-wax, or there is something out of the common here that beats anything that ever came into my way at Kenge and Carboy's."

Mrs. Chadband whispers Mrs. Snagsby, who exclaims, "You don't say so!"

"For years!" replies Mrs. Chadband.

"Has known Kenge and Carboy's office for years," Mrs. Snagsby triumphantly explains to Mr. Guppy. "Mrs. Chadband—this gentleman's wife—Reverend Mr. Chadband."

"Oh, indeed!" says Mr. Guppy.

"Before I married my present husband," says Mrs. Chadband.

"Was you a party in anything, ma'am?" says Mr. Guppy, transferring his cross-examination.

"No."

"*Not* a party in anything, ma'am?" says Mr. Guppy.

Mrs. Chadband shakes her head.

"Perhaps you were acquainted with somebody who was a party in something, ma'am?" says Mr. Guppy, who likes nothing better than to model his conversation on forensic principles.

"Not exactly that, either!" replies Mrs. Chadband, humouring the joke with a hard-favoured smile.

"Not exactly that, either!" repeats Mr. Guppy. "Very good. Pray, ma'am, was it a lady of your acquaintance who had some transactions (we will not at present say what transactions) with Kenge and Carboy's office, or was it a gentleman of your acquaintance? Take time, ma'am. We shall come to it presently. Man or woman, ma'am?"

"Neither," says Mrs. Chadband, as before.

"Oh! A child!" says Mr. Guppy, throwing on the admiring Mrs. Snagsby the regular acute professional eye which is thrown on British jurymen. "Now, ma'am, perhaps you'll have the kindness to tell us *what* child."

"You have got it at last, sir," says Mrs. Chadband, with another hard-favoured smile. "Well, sir, it was before your time, most likely, judging from your appearance. I was left in charge of a child named Esther Summerson, who was put out in life by Messrs Kenge and Carboy."

"Miss Summerson, ma'am!" cries Mr. Guppy, excited.

"*I* call her Esther Summerson," says Mrs. Chadband, with austerity. "There was no Miss-ing of the girl in my time. It was Esther. 'Esther, do this! Esther, do that!' and she was made to do it."

"My dear ma'am," returns Mr. Guppy, moving across the small apartment, "the humble individual who now addresses you received that young lady in London, when she first came here from the establishment to which you have alluded. Allow me to have the pleasure of taking you by the hand."

Mr. Chadband, at last seeing his opportunity, makes his accustomed signal, and rises with a smoking head, which he dabs with his pocket-handkerchief. Mrs. Snagsby whispers "Hush!"

"My friends," says Chadband, "we have partaken in moderation" (which was certainly not the case so far as he was concerned), "of the comforts which have been provided for us. May this house live upon the fatness of the land;[8] may corn and wine be plentiful therein; may it grow, may it thrive, may it prosper, may it advance, may it proceed, may it press forward! But, my friends, have we partaken of anything else? We have. My friends, of what else have we partaken? Of spiritual profit? Yes. From whence have we derived that spiritual profit? My young friend, stand forth!"

Jo, thus apostrophised, gives a slouch backward, and another slouch forward, and another slouch to each side, and confronts the eloquent Chadband, with evident doubts of his intentions.

"My young friend," says Chadband, "you are to us a pearl, you are to us a diamond, you are to us a gem, you are to us a jewel. And why, my young friend?"

"*I* don't know," replies Jo. "I don't know nothink."

"My young friend," says Chadband, "it is because you know nothing that you are to us a gem and jewel. For what are you, my young friend? Are you a beast of the field? No. A bird of the air? No. A fish of the sea or river? No. You are a human boy, my young friend. A human boy. O glorious to be a human boy! And why glorious, my young friend? Because you are capable of receiving the lessons of wisdom, because you are capable of profiting by this discourse, which I now deliver for your good, because you are not a stick, or a staff, or a stock, or a stone, or a post, or a pillar.

O running stream of sparkling joy
To be a soaring human boy![9]

8. See Genesis 27:28.

9. Although bearing a remote resemblance to Blake's *Songs of Innocence*, these verses seem to have been Mr. Chadband's own invention.

And do you cool yourself in that stream now, my young friend? No. Why do you not cool yourself in that stream now? Because you are in a state of darkness, because you are in a state of obscurity, because you are in a state of sinfulness, because you are in a state of bondage. My young friend, what *is* bondage? Let us, in a spirit of love, inquire."

At this threatening stage of the discourse, Jo, who seems to have been gradually going out of his mind, smears his right arm over his face, and gives a terrible yawn. Mrs. Snagsby indignantly expresses her belief that he is a limb of the arch-fiend.

"My friends," says Mr. Chadband, with his persecuted chin folding itself up into its fat smile again as he looks round, "it is right that I should be humbled, it is right that I should be tried, it is right that I should be mortified, it is right that I should be corrected. I stumbled, on Sabbath last, when I thought with pride of my three hours' improving. The account is now favourably balanced: my creditor has accepted a composition. O let us be joyful, joyful! O let us be joyful!"

Great sensation on the part of Mrs. Snagsby.

"My friends," says Chadband, looking round him in conclusion, "I will not proceed with my young friend now. Will you come tomorrow, my young friend, and inquire of this good lady where I am to be found to deliver a discourse untoe you, and will you come like the thirsty swallow[1] upon the next day, and upon the day after that, and upon the day after that, and upon many pleasant days, to hear discourses?" (This, with a cow-like lightness.)

Jo, whose immediate object seems to be to get away on any terms, gives a shuffling nod. Mr. Guppy then throws him a penny, and Mrs. Snagsby calls to Guster to see him safely out of the house. But, before he goes down-stairs, Mr. Snagsby loads him with some broken meats from the table, which he carries away, hugging in his arms.

So Mr. Chadband—of whom the persecutors say that it is no wonder he should go on for any length of time uttering such abominable nonsense, but that the wonder rather is that he should ever leave off, having once the audacity to begin—retires into private life until he invests a little capital of supper in the oil-trade. Jo moves on, through the long vacation, down to Blackfriars Bridge, where he finds a baking stony corner, wherein to settle to his repast.

And there he sits, munching and gnawing, and looking up at the great Cross on the summit of St. Paul's Cathedral, glittering above a red and violet-tinted cloud of smoke. From the boy's face one might suppose that sacred emblem to be, in his eyes, the crowning confusion of the great, confused city; so golden, so high up, so far

1. Unidentified.

out of his reach. There he sits, the sun going down, the river running fast, the crowd flowing by him in two streams—everything moving on to some purpose and to one end—until he is stirred up, and told to "move on" too.

Chapter XX

A NEW LODGER

The long vacation saunters on towards term-time, like an idle river very leisurely strolling down a flat country to the sea. Mr. Guppy saunters along with it congenially. He has blunted the blade of his penknife, and broken the point off, by sticking that instrument into his desk in every direction. Not that he bears the desk any ill-will, but he must do something, and it must be something of an unexciting nature, which will lay neither his physical nor his intellectual energies under too heavy contribution. He finds that nothing agrees with him so well, as to make little gyrations on one leg of his stool, and stab his desk, and gape.

Kenge and Carboy are out of town, and the articled clerk has taken out a shooting license, and gone down to his father's, and Mr. Guppy's two fellow-stipendiaries are away on leave. Mr. Guppy, and Mr. Richard Carstone, divide the dignity of the office. But Mr. Carstone is for the time being established in Kenge's room, whereat Mr. Guppy chafes. So exceedingly, that he with biting sarcasm informs his mother, in the confidential moments when he sups with her off a lobster and lettuce, in the Old Street Road, that he is afraid the office is hardly good enough for swells, and that if he had known there was a swell[1] coming, he would have got it painted.

Mr. Guppy suspects everybody who enters on the occupation of a stool in Kenge and Carboy's office, of entertaining, as a matter of course, sinister designs upon him. He is clear that every such person wants to depose him. If he be ever asked how, why, when, or wherefore, he shuts up one eye and shakes his head. On the strength of these profound views, he in the most ingenious manner takes infinite pains to counterplot, when there is no plot; and plays the deepest games of chess without any adversary.

It is a source of much gratification to Mr. Guppy, therefore, to find the new-comer constantly poring over the papers in Jarndyce and Jarndyce; for he well knows that nothing but confusion and failure can come of that. His satisfaction communicates itself to a third saunterer through the long vacation in Kenge and Carboy's office; to wit, Young Smallweed.

Whether Young Smallweed (metaphorically called Small and eke

1. Stylishly dressed person. A swell was usually of high social station, and according to John Bee's *Slang: A Dictionary* (1823), no one who worked for his living could be a "real swell" except a lawyer, clergyman, or doctor.

Chick Weed, as it were jocularly to express a fledgling) was ever a boy is much doubted in Lincoln's Inn. He is now something under fifteen, and an old limb of the law. He is facetiously understood to entertain a passion for a lady at a cigar-shop, in the neighbourhood of Chancery Lane, and for her sake to have broken off a contract with another lady, to whom he had been engaged some years. He is a town-made article, of small stature and weazen features; but may be perceived from a considerable distance by means of his very tall hat. To become a Guppy is the object of his ambition. He dresses at that gentleman (by whom he is patronized), talks at him, walks at him, founds himself entirely on him. He is honoured with Mr. Guppy's particular confidence, and occasionally advises him, from the deep wells of his experience, on difficult points in private life.

Mr. Guppy has been lolling out of window all the morning, after trying all the stools in succession and finding none of them easy, and after several times putting his head into the iron safe with a notion of cooling it. Mr. Smallweed has been twice dispatched for effervescent drinks, and has twice mixed them in the two official tumblers and stirred them up with the ruler. Mr. Guppy propounds, for Mr. Smallweed's consideration, the paradox that the more you drink the thirstier you are; and reclines his head upon the window-sill in a state of hopeless languor.

While thus looking out into the shade of Old Square, Lincoln's Inn, surveying the intolerable bricks and mortar, Mr. Guppy becomes conscious of a manly whisker emerging from the cloistered walk below, and turning itself up in the direction of his face. At the same time, a low whistle is wafted through the Inn, and a suppressed voice cries, "Hip! Gup-py!"

"Why, you don't mean it?" says Mr. Guppy, aroused. "Small! Here's Jobling!" Small's head looks out of window too, and nods to Jobling.

"Where have you sprung up from?" inquires Mr. Guppy.

"From the market-gardens down by Deptford. I can't stand it any longer. I must enlist. I say! I wish you'd lend me half-a-crown. Upon my soul I'm hungry."

Jobling looks hungry, and also has the appearance of having run to seed in the market-gardens down by Deptford.

"I say! Just throw out half-a-crown, if you have got one to spare. I want to get some dinner."

"Will you come and dine with me?" says Mr. Guppy, throwing out the coin, which Mr. Jobling catches neatly.

"How long should I have to hold out?" say Jobling.

"Not half an hour. I am only waiting here till the enemy goes," returns Mr. Guppy, butting inward with his head.

"What enemy?"

"A new one. Going to be articled. Will you wait?"

"Can you give a fellow anything to read in the meantime?" says Mr. Jobling.

Smallweed suggests the Law List.[2] But Mr. Jobling declares, with much earnestness, that he "can't stand it."

"You shall have the paper," says Mr. Guppy. "He shall bring it down. But you had better not be seen about here. Sit on our staircase and read. It's a quiet place."

Jobling nods intelligence and acquiescence. The sagacious Smallweed supplies him with the newspaper, and occasionally drops his eye upon him from the landing as a precaution against his becoming disgusted with waiting, and making an untimely departure. At last the enemy retreats, and then Smallweed fetches Mr. Jobling up.

"Well, and how are you?" says Mr. Guppy, shaking hands with him.

"So, so. How are you?"

Mr. Guppy replying that he is not much to boast of, Mr. Jobling ventures on the question, "How is *she*?" This Mr. Guppy resents as a liberty; retorting, "Jobling, there *are* chords in the human mind—" Jobling begs pardon.

"Any subject but that!" says Mr. Guppy, with a gloomy enjoyment of his injury. "For there *are* chords, Jobling——"

Mr. Jobling begs pardon again.

During this short colloquy, the active Smallweed, who is of the dinner party, has written in legal characters on a slip of paper, "Return immediately." This notification to all whom it may concern, he inserts in the letter-box; and then putting on the tall hat, at the angle of inclination at which Mr. Guppy wears his, informs his patron that they may now make themselves scarce.

Accordingly they betake themselves to a neighbouring dining-house, of the class known among its frequenters by the denomination Slap-Bang[3] where the waitress, a bouncing young female of forty, is supposed to have made some impression on the susceptible Smallweed; of whom it may be remarked that he is a weird changeling, to whom years are nothing. He stands precociously possessed of centuries of owlish wisdom. If he ever lay in a cradle, it seems as if he must have lain there in a tail-coat. He has an old, old eye, has Smallweed: and he drinks and smokes, in a monkeyish way; and his neck is stiff in his collar; and he is never to be taken in; and

2. "An annual English publication of a *quasi* official character, comprising various statistics of interest in connection with the legal profession" (H. M. Mozley and G. C. Whiteley, *Law Dictionary*).

3. Slam-Bang shops or Slap-Bangs were eating houses, "so called from the maladroit manner of serving up the viands to their customers" (John Bee, *Slang: A Dictionary*, 1823). Earlier the expression had meant that no credit was given in these establishments and that customers had to pay cash "slam bang," i.e., immediately.

he knows all about it, whatever it is. In short, in his bringing up, he has been so nursed by Law and Equity that he has become a kind of fossil Imp, to account for whose terrestrial existence it is reported at the public offices that his father was John Doe, and his mother the only female member of the Roe family:[4] also that his first long-clothes were made from a blue bag.[5]

Into the dining-house, unaffected by the seductive show in the window, of artificially whitened cauliflowers and poultry, verdant baskets of peas, coolly blooming cucumbers, and joints ready for the spit, Mr. Smallweed leads the way. They know him there, and defer to him. He has his favourite box, he bespeaks all the papers, he is down upon bald patriarchs, who keep them more than ten minutes afterwards.[6] It is of no use trying him with anything less than a full-sized "bread," or proposing to him any joint in cut, unless it is in the very best cut. In the matter of gravy he is adamant.

Conscious of his elfin power, and submitting to his dread experience, Mr. Guppy consults him in the choice of that day's banquet; turning an appealing look towards him as the waitress repeats the catalogue of viands, and saying "What do *you* take, Chick?" Chick, out of the profoundity of his artfulness, preferring "veal and ham and French beans—And don't you forget the stuffing, Polly" (with an unearthly cock of his venerable eye); Mr. Guppy and Mr. Jobling give the like order. Three pint pots of half-and-half[7] are superadded. Quickly the waitress returns, bearing what is apparently a model of the tower of Babel, but what is really a pile of plates and flat tin dish-covers. Mr. Smallweed, approving of what is set before him, conveys intelligent benignity into his ancient eye, and winks upon her. Then, amid a constant coming in, and going out, and running about, and a clatter of crockery, and a rumbling up and down of the machine which brings the nice cuts from the kitchen, and a shrill crying for more nice cuts down the speaking-pipe, and a shrill reckoning of the cost of nice cuts that have been disposed of, and a general flush and steam of hot joints, cut and uncut, and a considerably heated atmosphere in which the soiled knives and tablecloths seem to break out spontaneously into eruptions of grease and blotches of beer, the legal triumvirate appease their appetites.

Mr. Jobling is buttoned up closer than mere adornment might require. His hat presents at the rims a peculiar appearance of a glis-

4. John Doe and Richard Roe, fictitious names used by lawyers to refer to plaintiffs and defendants.

5. Cloth bags used by lawyers for carrying documents.

6. Copies of the latest newspapers, provided for circulating among restaurant customers on a variable priority basis, were impatiently awaited by those next in line.

7. Mixture of light and dark ales.

tening nature, as if it had been a favourite snail-promenade. The same phenomenon is visible on some parts of his coat, and particularly at the seams. He has the faded appearance of a gentleman in embarrassed circumstances; even his light whiskers droop with something of a shabby air.

His appetite is so vigorous, that it suggests spare living for some little time back. He makes such a speedy end of his plate of veal and ham, bringing it to a close while his companions are yet midway in theirs, that Mr. Guppy proposes another. "Thank you, Guppy," says Mr. Jobling, "I really don't know but what I *will* take another."

Another being brought, he falls to with great good will.

Mr. Guppy takes silent notice of him at intervals, until he is half way through this second plate, and stops to take an enjoying pull at his pint pot of half-and-half (also renewed), and stretches out his legs and rubs his hands. Beholding him in which glow of contentment, Mr. Guppy says:

"You are a man again, Tony!"

"Well, not quite yet," says Mr. Jobling. "Say, just born."

"Will you take any other vegetables? Grass?[8] Peas? Summer cabbage?"

"Thank you, Guppy," says Mr. Jobling. "I really don't know but what I *will* take summer cabbage."

Order given; with the sarcastic addition (from Mr. Smallweed) of "Without slugs, Polly!" And cabbage produced.

"I am growing up, Guppy," says Mr. Jobling, plying his knife and fork with a relishing steadiness.

"Glad to hear it."

"In fact, I have just turned into my teens," says Mr. Jobling.

He says no more until he has performed his task, which he achieves as Messrs Guppy and Smallweed finish theirs; thus getting over the ground in excellent style, and beating those two gentlemen easily by a veal and ham and a cabbage.

"Now, Small," says Mr. Guppy, "what would you recommend about pastry?"

"Marrow puddings," says Mr. Smallweed, instantly.

"Aye, aye!" cries Mr. Jobling, with an arch look. "You're there, are you? Thank you, Guppy, I don't know but what I *will* take a marrow pudding."

Three marrow puddings being produced, Mr. Jobling adds, in a pleasant humour, that he is coming of age fast. To these succeed, by command of Mr. Smallweed, "three Cheshires";[9] and to those, "three small rums." This apex of the entertainment happily

8. Sparrow-grass (asparagus).

9. A cheese resembling a mild cheddar.

reached, Mr. Jobling puts up his legs on the carpeted seat (having his own side of the box to himself), leans against the wall, and says, "I am grown up, now, Guppy. I have arrived at maturity."

"What do you think, now," says Mr. Guppy, "about—you don't mind Smallweed?"

"Not the least in the world. I have the pleasure of drinking his good health."

"Sir, to you!" says Mr. Smallweed.

"I was saying, what do you think *now*," pursues Mr. Guppy, "of enlisting?"

"Why, what I may think after dinner," returns Mr. Jobling, "is one thing, my dear Guppy, and what I may think before dinner is another thing. Still, even after dinner, I ask myself the question, What am I to do? How am I to live? Ill fo manger, you know," says Mr. Jobling, pronouncing that word as if he meant a necessary fixture in an English stable. "Ill fo manger.[1] That's the French saying, and mangering is as necessary to me as it is to a Frenchman. Or more so."

Mr. Smallweed is decidedly of opinion "much more so."

"If any man had told me," pursues Jobling, "even so lately as when you and I had the frisk down in Lincolnshire, Guppy, and drove over to see that house at Castle Wold——"

Mr. Smallweed corrects him—Chesney Wold.

"Chesney Wold. (I thank my honourable friend for that cheer.) If any man had told me, then, that I should be as hard up at the present time as I literally find myself, I should have—well, I should have pitched into him," says Mr. Jobling, taking a little rum-and-water with an air of desperate resignation; "I should have let fly at his head."

"Still, Tony, you were on the wrong side of the post[2] then," remonstrates Mr. Guppy. "You were talking about nothing else in the gig."

"Guppy," says Mr. Jobling, "I will not deny it. I was on the wrong side of the post. But I trusted to things coming round."

That very popular trust in flat things coming round! Not in their being beaten round, or worked round, but in their "coming" round! As though a lunatic should trust in the world's "coming" triangular!

"I had confident expectations that things would come round and be all square," says Mr. Jobling, with some vagueness of expression, and perhaps of meaning, too. "But I was disappointed. They never did. And when it came to creditors making rows at the office, and to people that the office dealt with making complaints about dirty

1. Fractured French version of a speech in Molière's *L'Avare* (III.i): "il faut manger pour vivre" ("one must eat in order to live").

2. Betting on losing horses, i.e., those on the wrong side of the winning post.

trifles of borrowed money, why there was an end of that connexion. And of any new professional connexion, too; for if I was to give a reference to-morrow, it would be mentioned, and would sew me up. Then, what's a fellow to do? I have been keeping out of the way, and living cheap, down about the market gardens; but what's the use of living cheap when you have got no money? You might as well live dear."

"Better," Mr. Smallweed thinks.

"Certainly. It's the fashionable way; and fashion and whiskers have been my weaknesses, and I don't care who knows it," says Mr. Jobling. "They are great weaknesses—Damme, sir, they are great. Well!" proceeds Mr. Jobling, after a defiant visit to his rum-and-water, "what can a fellow do, I ask you, *but* enlist?"

Mr. Guppy comes more fully into the conversation, to state what, in his opinion, a fellow can do. His manner is the gravely impressive manner of a man who has not committed himself in life, otherwise than as he has become the victim of a tender sorrow of the heart.

"Jobling," says Mr. Guppy, "myself and our mutual friend Smallweed——"

(Mr. Smallweed modestly observes "Gentlemen both!" and drinks).

"Have had a little conversation on this matter more than once, since you——"

"Say, got the sack!" cries Mr. Jobling, bitterly. "Say it, Guppy. You mean it."

"N-o-o! Left the Inn," Mr. Smallweed delicately suggests.

"Since you left the Inn, Jobling," says Mr. Guppy; "and I have mentioned, to our mutual friend Smallweed, a plan I have lately thought of proposing. You know Snagsby the stationer?"

"I know there is such a stationer," returns Mr. Jobling. "He was not ours, and I am not acquainted with him."

"He *is* ours, Jobling, and I *am* acquainted with him," Mr. Guppy retorts. "Well, sir! I have lately become better acquainted with him, through some accidental circumstances that have made me a visitor of his in private life. Those circumstances it is not necessary to offer in argument. They may—or they may not—have some reference to a subject, which may—or may not—have cast its shadow on my existence."

As it is Mr. Guppy's perplexing way, with boastful misery to tempt his particular friends into this subject, and the moment they touch it, to turn on them with that trenchant severity about the chords in the human mind; both Mr. Jobling and Mr. Smallweed decline the pitfall, by remaining silent.

"Such things may be," repeats Mr. Guppy, "or they may not be. They are no part of the case. It is enough to mention, that both

Mr. and Mrs. Snagsby are very willing to oblige me; and that Snagsby has, in busy times, a good deal of copying work to give out. He has all Tulkinghorn's, and an excellent business besides. I believe, if our mutual friend Smallweed were put into the box, he could prove this?"

Mr. Smallweed nods, and appears greedy to be sworn.

"Now, gentlemen of the jury," says Mr. Guppy—"I mean, now Jobling—you may say this is a poor prospect of a living. Granted. But it's better than nothing, and better than enlistment. You want time. There must be time for these late affairs to blow over. You might live through it on much worse terms than by writing for Snagsby."

Mr. Jobling is about to interrupt, when the sagacious Smallweed checks him with a dry cough, and the words, "Hem! Shakespeare!"[3]

"There are two branches to this subject, Jobling," says Mr. Guppy. "That is the first. I come to the second. You know Krook, the Chancellor, across the lane. Come, Jobling," says Mr. Guppy, in his encouraging cross-examination-tone, "I think you know Krook, the Chancellor, across the lane?"

"I know him by sight," says Mr. Jobling.

"You know him by sight. Very well. And you know little Flite?"

"Everybody knows her," says Mr. Jobling.

"Everybody knows her. *Very* well. Now it has been one of my duties of late, to pay Flite a certain weekly allowance, deducting from it the amount of her weekly rent: which I have paid (in consequence of instructions I have received) to Krook himself, regularly in her presence. This has brought me into communication with Krook, and into a knowledge of his house and his habits. I know he has a room to let. You may live there at a very low charge, under any name you like; as quietly as if you were a hundred miles off. He'll ask no questions; and would accept you as a tenant, at a word from me—before the clock strikes, if you chose. And I'll tell you another thing, Jobling," says Mr. Guppy, who has suddenly lowered his voice, and become familiar again, "he's an extraordinary old chap—always rummaging among a litter of papers and grubbing away at teaching himself to read and write; without getting on a bit, as it seems to me. He is a most extraordinary old chap, sir. I don't know but what it might be worth a fellow's while to look him up a bit."

"You don't mean—?" Mr. Jobling begins.

"I mean," returns Mr. Guppy, shrugging his shoulders with becoming modesty, "that *I* can't make him out. I appeal to our

3. No quotation from Shakespeare has been identified in Guppy's speech. Perhaps Smallweed merely intends to compliment his friend by likening his eloquence to Shakespeare's. According to Susan Shatto (1975) the expression means "Be silent!" It is similarly used in *Pickwick Papers* (ch. XLI).

mutual friend Smallweed whether he has or has not heard me remark, that I can't make him out."

Mr. Smallweed bears the concise testimony, "A few!"

"I have seen something of the profession, and something of life, Tony," says Mr. Guppy, "and it's seldom I can't make a man out, more or less. But such an old card as this; so deep, so sly, and secret (though I don't believe he is ever sober), I never came across. Now, he must be precious old, you know, and he has not a soul about him, and he is reported to be immensely rich; and whether he is a smuggler, or a receiver, or an unlicensed pawnbroker, or a money-lender—all of which I have thought likely at different times—it might pay you to knock up a sort of a knowledge of him. I don't see why you shouldn't go in for it, when everything else suits."

Mr. Jobling, Mr. Guppy, and Mr. Smallweed, all lean their elbows on the table, and their chins upon their hands, and look at the ceiling. After a time, they all drink, slowly lean back, put their hands in their pockets, and look at one another.

"If I had the energy I once possessed, Tony!" says Mr. Guppy, with a sigh. "But there are chords in the human mind——"

Expressing the remainder of the desolate sentiment in rum-and-water, Mr. Guppy concludes by resigning the adventure to Tony Jobling, and informing him that during the vacation and while things are slack, his purse, "as far as three or four or even five pound goes," will be at his disposal. "For never shall it be said," Mr. Guppy adds with emphasis, "that William Guppy turned his back upon his friend!"

The latter part of the proposal is so directly to the purpose, that Mr. Jobling says with emotion, "Guppy, my trump, your fist!" Mr. Guppy presents it, saying, "Jobling, my boy, there it is!" Mr. Jobling returns, "Guppy, we have been pals now for some years!" Mr. Guppy replies, "Jobling, we have." They then shake hands, and Mr. Jobling adds in a feeling manner, "Thank you, Guppy, I don't know but what I *will* take another glass for old acquaintance sake."

"Krook's last lodger died there," observes Mr. Guppy, in an incidental way.

"Did he though!" says Mr. Jobling.

"There was a verdict. Accidental death. You don't mind that?"

"No," says Mr. Jobling, "I don't mind it; but he might as well have died somewhere else. It's devilish odd that he need go and die at *my* place!" Mr. Jobling quite resents this liberty; several times returning to it with such remarks as, "There are places enough to die in, I should think!" or, "He wouldn't have liked my dying at *his* place, I dare say!"

However, the compact being virtually made, Mr. Guppy proposes to dispatch the trusty Smallweed to ascertain if Mr. Krook is at home, as in that case they may complete the negotiations, without delay. Mr. Jobling approving, Smallweed puts himself under the tall hat and conveys it out of the dining-rooms in the Guppy manner. He soon returns with the intelligence that Mr. Krook is at home, and that he has seen him through the shop-door, sitting in the back premises, sleeping, "like one o'clock."[4]

"Then I'll pay," says Mr. Guppy, "and we'll go and see him. Small, what will it be?"

Mr. Smallweed, compelling the attendance of the waitress with one hitch of his eyelash, instantly replies as follows: "Four veals and hams is three, and four potatoes is three and four, and one summer cabbage is three and six, and three marrows is four and six, and six breads is five, and three Cheshires is five and three, and four pints of half-and-half is six and three, and four small rums is eight and three, and three Pollys is eight and six. Eight and six in half a sovereign, Polly, and eighteenpence out!"

Not at all excited by these stupendous calculations, Smallweed dismisses his friends with a cool nod, and remains behind to take a little admiring notice of Polly, as opportunity may serve, and to read the daily papers; which are so very large in proportion to himself, shorn of his hat, that when he holds up The Times to run his eye over the columns, he seems to have retired for the night, and to have disappeared under the bedclothes.

Mr. Guppy and Mr. Jobling repair to the rag and bottle shop, where they find Krook still sleeping like one o'clock; that is to say, breathing stertorously with his chin upon his breast, and quite insensible to any external sounds, or even to gentle shaking. On the table beside him, among the usual lumber, stand an empty gin-bottle and a glass. The unwholesome air is so stained with this liquor, that even the green eyes of the cat upon her shelf, as they open and shut and glimmer on the visitors, look drunk.

"Hold up here!" says Mr. Guppy, giving the relaxed figure of the old man another shake. "Mr. Krook! Halloa, sir!"

But it would seem as easy to wake a bundle of old clothes, with a spirituous heat smouldering in it. "Did you ever see such a stupor as he falls into, between drink and sleep?" says Mr. Guppy.

"If this is his regular sleep," returns Jobling, rather alarmed, "it'll last a long time one of these days, I am thinking."

"It's always more like a fit than a nap," says Mr. Guppy, shaking

4. An expression of disputed origin usually applied to an activity in which time seems to fly as during a workman's midday meal-time break which terminates in the clock's striking one. It was most commonly applied to any fast and smooth action like the running of a race horse. Mr. Dorrit's playing the piano is described as "like one o'clock—beautiful!" (*Little Dorrit*, ch. VI).

him again. "Halloa, your lordship! Why he might be robbed, fifty times over! Open your eyes!"

After much ado, he opens them, but without appearing to see his visitors, or any other objects. Though he crosses one leg on another, and folds his hands, and several times closes and opens his parched lips, he seems to all intents and purposes as insensible as before.

"He is alive, at any rate," says Mr. Guppy. "How are you, my Lord Chancellor? I have brought a friend of mine, sir, on a little matter of business."

The old man still sits, often smacking his dry lips without the least consciousness. After some minutes, he makes an attempt to rise. They help him up, and he staggers against the wall, and stares at them.

"How do you do, Mr. Krook?" says Mr. Guppy, in some discomfiture. "How do you do, sir? You are looking charming, Mr. Krook. I hope you are pretty well?"

The old man, in aiming a purposeless blow at Mr. Guppy, or at nothing, feebly swings himself round, and comes with his face against the wall. So he remains for a minute or two, heaped up against it; and then staggers down the shop to the front door. The air, the movement in the court, the lapse of time, or the combination of these things, recovers him. He comes back pretty steadily, adjusting his fur-cap on his head, and looking keenly at them.

"Your servant, gentlemen; I've been dozing. Hi! I am hard to wake, odd times."

"Rather so, indeed, sir," responds Mr. Guppy.

"What? You've been a-trying to do it, have you?" says the suspicious Krook.

"Only a little," Mr. Guppy explains.

The old man's eye resting on the empty bottle, he takes it up, examines it, and slowly tilts it upside down.

"I say!" he cries, like the Hobgoblin in the story.[5] "Somebody's been making free here!"

"I assure you we found it so," says Mr. Guppy. "Would you allow me to get it filled for you?"

"Yes, certainly I would!" cries Krook, in high glee. "Certainly I would! Don't mention it! Get it filled next door—Sol's Arms—the Lord Chancellor's fourteenpenny. Bless you, they know *me*!"

He so presses the empty bottle upon Mr. Guppy, that that gen-

5. Cf. Robert Southey's story *The Three Bears*, 1837 (later called *Goldilocks and the Three Bears*), in which the bears exclaim that someone has made free with their food. Dickens' version, involving hobgoblins instead of bears, has not been identified by folklorists. Cf. Katherine M. Briggs, *A Dictionary of Folk Tales* (1970), II, p. 566. As noted by Susan Shatto (1975), Dickens refers to *The Three Hobgoblins* again in *Our Mutual Friend*, III, ch. 13.

tleman, with a nod to his friend, accepts the trust, and hurries out and hurries in again with the bottle filled. The old man receives it in his arms like a beloved grandchild, and pats it tenderly.

"But, I say!" he whispers, with his eyes screwed up, after tasting it, "this ain't the Lord Chancellor's fourteenpenny. This is eighteenpenny!"

"I thought you might like that better," says Mr. Guppy.

"You're a nobleman, sir," returns Krook, with another taste—and his hot breath seems to come towards them like a flame. "You're a baron of the land."

Taking advantage of this auspicious moment, Mr. Guppy presents his friend under the impromptu name of Mr. Weevle, and states the object of their visit. Krook with his bottle under his arm (he never gets beyond a certain point of either drunkenness or sobriety), takes time to survey his proposed lodger, and seems to approve of him. "You'd like to see the room, young man?" he says. "Ah! It's a good room! Been whitewashed. Been cleaned down with soft soap and soda. Hi! It's worth twice the rent; letting alone my company when you want it, and such a cat to keep the mice away."

Commending the room after this manner, the old man takes them up-stairs, where indeed they do find it cleaner than it used to be, and also containing some old articles of furniture which he has dug up from his inexhaustible stores. The terms are easily concluded—for the Lord Chancellor cannot be hard on Mr. Guppy, associated as he is with Kenge and Carboy, Jarndyce and Jarndyce, and other famous claims on his professional consideration—and it is agreed that Mr. Weevle shall take possession on the morrow. Mr. Weevle and Mr. Guppy then repair to Cook's Court, Cursitor Street, where the personal introduction of the former to Mr. Snagsby is effected, and (more important) the vote and interest of Mrs. Snagsby are secured. They then report progress to the eminent Smallweed, waiting at the office in his tall hat for that purpose, and separate; Mr. Guppy explaining that he would terminate his little entertainment by standing treat at the play, but that there are chords in the human mind which would render it a hollow mockery.

On the morrow, in the dusk of evening, Mr. Weevle modestly appears at Krook's, by no means incommoded with luggage, and establishes himself in his new lodging; where the two eyes in the shutters stare at him in his sleep, as if they were full of wonder. On the following day Mr. Weevle, who is a handy good-for-nothing kind of young fellow, borrows a needle and thread of Miss Flite, and a hammer of his landlord, and goes to work devising apologies for window-curtains, and knocking up apologies for shelves, and hanging up his two teacups, milkpot, and crockery sundries on a pennyworth of little hooks, like a shipwrecked sailor making the best of it.

But what Mr. Weevle prizes most, of all his few possessions (next after his light whiskers, for which he has an attachment that only whiskers can awaken in the breast of man), is a choice collection of copper-plate impressions from that truly national work, The Divinities of Albion, or Galaxy Gallery of British Beauty,[6] representing ladies of title and fashion in every variety of smirk that art, combined with capital, is capable of producing. With these magnificent portraits, unworthily confined in a bandbox during his seclusion among the market-gardens, he decorates his apartment; and as the Galaxy Gallery of British Beauty wears every variety of fancy dress, plays every variety of musical instrument, fondles every variety of dog, ogles every variety of prospect and is backed up by every variety of flower-pot and balustrade, the result is very imposing.

But fashion is Mr. Weevle's, as it was Tony Jobling's weakness. To borrow yesterday's paper from the Sol's Arms of an evening, and read about the brilliant and distinguished meteors that are shooting across the fashionable sky in every direction, is unspeakable consolation to him. To know what member of what brilliant and distinguished circle accomplished the brilliant and distinguished feat of joining it yesterday, or contemplates the no less brilliant and distinguished feat of leaving it to-morrow, gives him a thrill of joy. To be informed what the Galaxy Gallery of British Beauty is about, and means to be about, and what Galaxy marriages are on the tapis,[7] and what Galaxy rumours are in circulation, is to become acquainted with the most glorious destinies of mankind. Mr. Weevle reverts from this intelligence, to the Galaxy portraits implicated; and seems to know the originals, and to be known of them.

For the rest he is a quiet lodger, full of handy shifts and devices as before mentioned, able to cook and clean for himself as well as to carpenter, and developing social inclinations after the shades of evening have fallen on the court. At those times, when he is not visited by Mr. Guppy, or by a small light in his likeness quenched in a dark hat, he comes out of his dull room—where he has inherited the deal wilderness of desk bespattered with a rain of ink—and talks to Krook, or is "very free," as they call it in the court, commendingly, with any one disposed for conversation. Wherefore Mrs. Piper, who leads the court, is impelled to offer two remarks to Mrs. Perkins: Firstly, that if her Johnny was to have whiskers, she could

6. Annuals, featuring portraits of ladies of fashion, were popular publications in the Victorian period. One of these, edited by the Countess of Blessington in 1848–49, bore the title *The Book of Beauty, or Regal Gallery*. (Noted by Michael Wilkins in *Dickensian*, 1976.)

7. Under consideration.

wish 'em to be identically like that young man's; and secondly, Mark my words, Mrs. Perkins, ma'am, and don't you be surprised, Lord bless you, if that young man comes in at last for old Krook's money!

Chapter XXI

THE SMALLWEED FAMILY

In a rather ill-favoured and ill-savoured neighbourhood, though one of its rising grounds bears the name of Mount Pleasant, the Elfin Smallweed, christened Bartholomew, and known to the domestic hearth as Bart, passes that limited portion of his time on which the office and its contingencies have no claim. He dwells in a little narrow street, always solitary, shady, and sad, closely bricked in on all sides like a tomb, but where there yet lingers the stump of an old forest tree, whose flavour is about as fresh and natural as the Smallweed smack of youth.

There has been only one child in the Smallweed family for several generations. Little old men and women there have been, but no child, until Mr. Smallweed's grandmother, now living, became weak in her intellect, and fell (for the first time) into a childish state. With such infantine graces as a total want of observation, memory, understanding and interest, and an eternal disposition to fall asleep over the fire and into it, Mr. Smallweed's grandmother has undoubtedly brightened the family.

Mr. Smallweed's grandfather is likewise of the party. He is in a helpless condition as to his lower, and nearly so as to his upper limbs; but his mind is unimpaired. It holds, as well as it ever held, the first four rules of arithmetic, and a certain small collection of the hardest facts. In respect of ideality, reverence, wonder, and other such phrenological attributes,[1] it is no worse off than it used to be. Everything that Mr. Smallweed's grandfather ever put away in his mind was a grub at first, and is a grub at last. In all his life he has never bred a single butterfly.

The father of this pleasant grandfather, of the neighbourhood of Mount Pleasant, was a horny-skinned, two-legged, money-getting species of spider, who spun webs to catch unwary flies, and retired into holes until they were entrapped. The name of this old pagan's God was Compound Interest. He lived for it, married it, died of it. Meeting with a heavy loss in an honest little enterprise in which all the loss was intended to have been on the other side, he broke something—something necessary to his existence; therefore it

1. According to the theories of phrenology, the size of different areas of the surface of the brain provides clues to an individual's moral qualities ("ideality, reverence, wonder") as well as to his intellectual capacities.

couldn't have been his heart—and made an end of his career. As his character was not good, and he had been bred at a Charity School, in a complete course, according to question and answer, of those ancient people the Amorites and Hittites,[2] he was frequently quoted as an example of the failure of education.

His spirit shone through his son, to whom he had always preached of "going out" early in life, and whom he made a clerk in a sharp scrivener's office at twelve years old. There, the young gentleman improved his mind, which was of a lean and anxious character; and developing the family gifts, gradually elevated himself into the discounting profession. Going out early in life, and marrying late, as his father had done before him, he too begat a lean and anxious-minded son; who, in his turn, going out early in life and marrying late, became the father of Bartholomew and Judith Smallweed, twins. During the whole time consumed in the slow growth of this family tree, the house of Smallweed, always early to go out and late to marry, has strengthened itself in its practical character, has discarded all amusements, discountenanced all story-books, fairy tales, fictions, and fables, and banished all levities whatsoever. Hence the gratifying fact, that it has had no child born to it, and that the complete little men and women whom it has produced, have been observed to bear a likeness to old monkeys with something depressing on their minds.

At the present time, in the dark little parlour certain feet below the level of the street—a grim, hard, uncouth parlour, only ornamented with the coarsest of baize table-covers, and the hardest of sheet-iron tea-trays, and offering in its decorative character no bad allegorical representation of Grandfather Smallweed's mind—seated in two black horse-hair porter's chairs,[3] one on each side of the fireplace, the superannuated Mr. and Mrs. Smallweed wile away the rosy hours. On the stove are a couple of trivets for the pots and kettles which it is Grandfather Smallweed's usual occupation to watch, and projecting from the chimney-piece between them is a sort of brass gallows for roasting, which he also superintends when it is in action. Under the venerable Mr. Smallweed's seat, and guarded by his spindle legs, is a drawer in his chair, reported to contain property to a fabulous amount. Beside him is a spare cushion, with which he is always provided, in order that he may have something to throw at the venerable partner of his respected age whenever she makes an allusion to money—a subject on which he is particularly sensitive.

2. Pupils at the Charity School would be required to memorize information from the Bible about the peoples who had been enemies of Israel. See, e.g., Joshua 12:8.

3. Chairs encased by a hood shaped like a nutshell to protect the sitter from drafts (porters were often stationed in drafty lobbies).

"And where's Bart?" Grandfather Smallweed inquires of Judy, Bart's twin-sister.

"He an't come in yet," says Judy.

"It's his tea-time, isn't it?"

"No."

"How much do you mean to say it wants then?"

"Ten minutes."

"Hey?"

"Ten minutes."—(Loud on the part of Judy.)

"Ho!" says Grandfather Smallweed. "Ten minutes."

Grandmother Smallweed, who has been mumbling and shaking her head at the trivets, hearing figures mentioned, connects them with money, and screeches, like a horrible old parrot without any plumage, "Ten ten-pound notes!"

Grandfather Smallweed immediately throws the cushion at her.

"Drat you, be quiet!" says the good old man.

The effect of this act of jaculation is twofold. It not only doubles up Mrs. Smallweed's head against the side of her porter's chair, and causes her to present, when extricated by her grand-daughter, a highly unbecoming state of cap, but the necessary exertion recoils on Mr. Smallweed himself, whom it throws back into *his* porter's chair, like a broken puppet. The excellent old gentleman being, at these times, a mere clothes-bag with a black skull-cap on the top of it, does not present a very animated appearance, until he has undergone the two operations at the hands of his grand-daughter, of being shaken up like a great bottle, and poked and punched like a great bolster. Some indication of a neck being developed in him by these means, he and the sharer of his life's evening again sit fronting one another in their two porter's chairs, like a couple of sentinels long forgotten on their post by the Black Serjeant, Death.

Judy the twin is worthy company for these associates. She is so indubitably sister to Mr. Smallweed the younger, that the two kneaded into one would hardly make a young person of average proportions; while she so happily exemplifies the before-mentioned family likeness to the monkey tribe, that, attired in a spangled robe and cap, she might walk about the table-land on the top of a barrel-organ without exciting much remark as an unusual specimen. Under existing circumstances, however, she is dressed in a plain, spare gown of brown stuff.

Judy never owned a doll, never heard of Cinderella, never played at any game. She once or twice fell into children's company when she was about ten years old, but the children couldn't get on with Judy, and Judy couldn't get on with them. She seemed like an animal of another species, and there was instinctive repugnance on both sides. It is very doubtful whether Judy knows how to laugh. She has so rarely seen the thing done that the probabilities are strong the other way. Of anything like a youthful laugh, she certainly can have no conception. If she were to try one, she would find her teeth in her way; modelling that action of her face, as she has unconsciously modelled all its other expressions, on her pattern of sordid age. Such is Judy.

And her twin-brother couldn't wind up a top for his life. He knows no more of Jack the Giant Killer, or of Sinbad the Sailor, than he knows of the people in the stars. He could as soon play at leap-frog, or at cricket, as change into a cricket or a frog himself. But he is so much the better off than his sister, that on his narrow world of fact an opening has dawned, into such broader regions as lie within the ken of Mr. Guppy. Hence, his admiration and his emulation of that shining enchanter.

Judy, with a gong-like clash and clatter, sets one of the sheet-iron tea-trays on the table, and arranges cups and saucers. The bread she puts on in an iron basket; and the butter (and not much of it) in a small pewter plate. Grandfather Smallweed looks hard after the tea as it is served out, and asks Judy where the girl is?

"Charley, do you mean?" says Judy.

"Hey?" from Grandfather Smallweed.

"Charley, do you mean?"

This touches a spring in Grandmother Smallweed, who, chuckling, as usual, at the trivets, cries—"Over the water! Charley over the water, Charley over the water, over the water to Charley, Charley over the water, over the water to Charley!"[4] and becomes quite energetic about it. Grandfather looks at the cushion, but has not sufficiently recovered his late exertion.

"Ha!" he says, when there is silence—"if that's her name. She eats a deal. It would be better to allow her for her keep."

Judy, with her brother's wink, shakes her head, and purses up her mouth into No, without saying it.

"No?" returns the old man. "Why not?"

"She'd want sixpence a day, and we can do it for less," says Judy.

"Sure?"

Judy answers with a nod of deepest meaning, and calls, as she scrapes the butter on the loaf with every precaution against waste, and cuts it into slices, "You Charley, where are you?" Timidly obe-

4. Prince Charles Stuart (1720–88), leader of the Stuart faction and later a claimant for the English throne, lived in exile on the continent. At private gatherings his followers in England used to sing songs honoring their King across the water ("We'll o'er the water to Charlie"), and, at public dinners, they would toast him secretly by passing their wine glasses over the water in their finger-bowls.

dient to the summons, a little girl in a rough apron and a large bonnet, with her hands covered with soap and water, and a scrubbing-brush in one of them, appears, and curtseys.

"What work are you about now?" says Judy, making an ancient snap at her, like a very sharp old beldame.

"I'm a-cleaning the up-stairs back room, miss," replies Charley.

"Mind you do it thoroughly, and don't loiter. Shirking won't do for me. Make haste! Go along!" cries Judy, with a stamp upon the ground. "You girls are more trouble than you're worth, by half."

On this severe matron, as she returns to her task of scraping the butter and cutting the bread, falls the shadow of her brother, looking in at the window. For whom, knife and loaf in hand, she opens the street door.

"Ay, ay, Bart!" says Grandfather Smallweed. "Here you are, hey?"

"Here I am," says Bart.

"Been along with your friend again, Bart?"

Small nods.

"Dining at his expense, Bart?"

Small nods again.

"That's right. Live at his expense as much as you can, and take warning by his foolish example. That's the use of such a friend. The only use you can put him to," says the venerable sage.

His grandson, without receiving this good counsel as dutifully as he might, honours it with all such acceptance as may lie in a slight wink and a nod, and takes a chair at the tea-table. The four old faces then hover over teacups, like a company of ghastly cherubim;[5] Mrs. Smallweed perpetually twitching her head and chattering at the trivets, and Mr. Smallweed requiring to be repeatedly shaken up like a large black draught.[6]

"Yes, yes," says the good old gentleman, reverting to his lesson of wisdom. "That's such advice as your father would have given you, Bart. You never saw your father. More's the pity. He was my true son." Whether it is intended to be conveyed that he was particularly pleasant to look at, on that account, does not appear.

"He was my true son," repeats the old gentleman, folding his bread-and-butter on his knee; "a good accountant, and died fifteen years ago."

Mrs. Smallweed, following her usual instinct, breaks out with "Fifteen hundred pound. Fifteen hundred pound in a black box,

5. Alluding to *A Study of Heads* by Sir Joshua Reynolds (1723–92), a painting of five bodiless heads of an angelic-looking girl, ranged in a circle.

6. An unpleasant-tasting laxative lavishly administered to hospital patients in the nineteenth century. Consisting of a mixture of senna powder, licorice, and magnesium sulphate, it had to be thoroughly shaken before being taken.

fifteen hundred pound locked up, fifteen hundred pound put away and hid!" Her worthy husband, setting aside his bread-and-butter, immediately discharges the cushion at her, crushes her against the side of her chair, and falls back in his own, overpowered. His appearance after visiting Mrs. Smallweed with one of these admonitions, is particularly impressive and not wholly prepossessing; firstly, because the exertion generally twists his black skull-cap over one eye and gives him an air of goblin rakishness; secondly, because he mutters violent imprecations against Mrs. Smallweed; and thirdly, because the contrast between those powerful expressions and his powerless figure is suggestive of a baleful old malignant, who would be very wicked if he could. All this, however, is so common in the Smallweed family circle, that it produces no impression. The old gentleman is merely shaken, and has his internal feathers beaten up; the cushion is restored to its usual place beside him; and the old lady, perhaps with her cap adjusted, and perhaps not, is planted in her chair again, ready to be bowled down like a ninepin.

Some time elapses, in the present instance, before the old gentleman is sufficiently cool to resume his discourse; and even then he mixes it up with several edifying expletives addressed to the unconscious partner of his bosom, who holds communication with nothing on earth but the trivets. As thus:

"If your father, Bart, had lived longer, he might have been worth a deal of money—you brimstone chatterer!—but just as he was beginning to build up the house that he had been making the foundations for, through many a year—you jade of a magpie, jackdaw, and poll-parrot, what do you mean!—he took ill and died of a low fever, always being a sparing and a spare man, full of business care —I should like to throw a cat at you instead of a cushion, and I will too if you make such a confounded fool of yourself!—and your mother, who was a prudent woman as dry as a chip, just dwindled away like touchwood[7] after you and Judy were born—You are an old pig. You are a brimstone pig. You're a head of swine!"

Judy, not interested in what she has often heard, begins to collect in a basin various tributary streams of tea, from the bottom of cups and saucers and from the bottom of the teapot, for the little charwoman's evening meal. In like manner she gets together, in the iron bread-basket, as many outside fragments and worn-down heels of loaves as the rigid economy of the house has left in existence.

"But your father and me were partners, Bart," says the old gentleman; "and when I am gone, you and Judy will have all there is. It's rare for you both, that you went out early in life—Judy to the flower business, and you to the law. You won't want to spend it. You'll get your living without it, and put more to it. When I am

7. Wood transformed by fungi into a soft, white substance.

gone, Judy will go back to the flower business, and you'll still stick to the law."

One might infer, from Judy's appearance, that her business rather lay with the thorns than the flowers; but she has, in her time, been apprenticed to the art and mystery of artificial flower-making. A close observer might perhaps detect, both in her eye and her brother's, when their venerable grandsire anticipates his being gone, some little impatience to know when he may be going, and some resentful opinion that it is time he went.

"Now, if everybody has done," says Judy, completing her preparations, "I'll have that girl in to her tea. She would never leave off, if she took it by herself in the kitchen."

Charley is accordingly introduced, and, under a heavy fire of eyes, sits down to her basin and a Druidical ruin[8] of bread-and-butter. In the active superintendence of this young person, Judy Smallweed appears to attain a perfectly geological age, and to date from the remotest periods. Her systematic manner of flying at her and pouncing on her, with or without pretence, whether or no, is wonderful; evincing an accomplishment in the art of girl-driving, seldom reached by the oldest practitioners.

"Now, don't stare about you all the afternoon," cries Judy, shaking her head and stamping her foot as she happens to catch the glance which has been previously sounding the basin of tea, "but take your victuals and get back to your work."

"Yes, miss," says Charley.

"Don't say yes," returns Miss Smallweed, "for I know what you girls are. Do it without saying it, and then I may begin to believe you."

Charley swallows a great gulp of tea in token of submission, and so disperses the Druidical ruins that Miss Smallweed charges her not to gormandize, which, "in you girls," she observes, is disgusting. Charley might find some more difficulty in meeting her views on the general subject of girls, but for a knock at the door.

"See who it is, and don't chew when you open it!" cries Judy.

The object of her attentions withdrawing for the purpose, Miss Smallweed takes that opportunity of jumbling the remainder of the bread-and-butter together, and launching two or three dirty teacups into the ebb-tide of the basin of tea; as a hint that she considers the eating and drinking terminated.

"Now! Who is it, and what's wanted?" says the snappish Judy.

It is one "Mr. George," it appears. Without other announcement or ceremony, Mr. George walks in.

8. The scraps of bread-crusts look like ruined Druidical monuments such as those at Stonehenge. Cf. the servant-girl's meal in *The Old Curiosity Shop* (ch. XXXVI): "a dreary waste of cold potatoes looking as eatable as Stonehenge."

"Whew!" says Mr. George. "You are hot here. Always a fire, eh? Well! Perhaps you do right to get used to one." Mr. George makes the latter remark to himself, as he nods to Grandfather Smallweed.

"Ho! It's you!" cries the old gentleman. "How de do? How de do?"

"Middling," replies Mr. George, taking a chair. "Your granddaughter I have had the honour of seeing before; my service to you, miss."

"This is my grandson," says Grandfather Smallweed. "You ha'n't seen him before. He is in the law, and not much at home."

"My service to him, too! He is like his sister. He is very like his sister. He is devilish like his sister," says Mr. George, laying a great and not altogether complimentary stress on his last adjective.

"And how does the world use you, Mr. George?" Grandfather Smallweed inquires, slowly rubbing his legs.

"Pretty much as usual. Like a football."

He is a swarthy browned man of fifty; well-made, and good-looking; with crisp dark hair, bright eyes, and a broad chest. His sinewy and powerful hands, as sunburnt as his face, have evidently been used to a pretty rough life. What is curious about him is, that he sits forward on his chair as if he were, from long habit, allowing space for some dress or accoutrements that he has altogether laid aside. His step too is measured and heavy, and would go well with a weighty clash and jingle of spurs. He is close-shaved now, but his mouth is set as if his upper lip had been for years familiar with a great moustache; and his manner of occasionally laying the open palm of his broad brown hand upon it, is to the same effect. Altogether, one might guess Mr. George to have been a trooper once upon a time.

A special contrast Mr. George makes to the Smallweed family. Trooper was never yet billeted upon a household more unlike him. It is a broadsword to an oyster-knife. His developed figure, and their stunted forms; his large manner, filling any amount of room, and their little narrow pinched ways; his sounding voice, and their sharp spare tones; are in the strongest and the strangest opposition. As he sits in the middle of the grim parlour, leaning a little forward, with his hands upon his thighs and his elbows squared, he looks as though, if he remained there long, he would absorb into himself the whole family and the whole four-roomed house, extra little back-kitchen and all.

"Do you rub your legs to rub life into 'em?" he asks of Grandfather Smallweed after looking round the room.

"Why, it's partly a habit, Mr. George, and—yes—it partly helps the circulation," he replies.

"The cir-cu-la-tion!" repeats Mr. George, folding his arms upon his chest, and seeming to become two sizes larger. "Not much of that, I should think."

"Truly, I'm old, Mr. George," says Grandfather Smallweed. "But I can carry my years. I'm older than *her,*" nodding at his wife, "and see what she is!—You're a brimstone chatterer!" with a sudden revival of his late hostility.

"Unlucky old soul!" says Mr. George, turning his head in that direction. "Don't scold the old lady. Look at her here, with her poor cap half off her head, and her poor hair all in a muddle. Hold up, ma'am. That's better. There we are! Think of your mother, Mr. Smallweed," says Mr. George, coming back to his seat from assisting her, "if your wife an't enough."

"I suppose you were an excellent son, Mr. George?" the old man hints, with a leer.

The colour of Mr. George's face rather deepens, as he replies: "Why no. I wasn't."

"I am astonished at it."

"So am I. I ought to have been a good son, and I think I meant to have been one. But I wasn't. I was a thundering bad son, that's the long and the short of it, and never was a credit to anybody."

"Surprising!" cries the old man.

"However," Mr. George resumes, "the less said about it, the better now. Come! You know the agreement. Always a pipe out of the two months' interest! (Bosh! It's all correct. You needn't be afraid to order the pipe. Here's the new bill, and here's the two months' interest-money, and a devil-and-all of a scrape it is to get it together in my business)."

Mr. George sits, with his arms folded, consuming the family and the parlour while Grandfather Smallweed is assisted by Judy to two black leathern cases out of a locked bureau; in one of which he secures the document he has just received, and from the other takes another similar document which he hands to Mr. George, who twists it up for a pipe-light. As the old man inspects, through his glasses, every up-stroke and down-stroke of both documents, before he releases them from their leathern prison; and as he counts the money three times over, and requires Judy to say every word she utters at least twice, and is as tremulously slow of speech and action as it is possible to be; this business is a long time in progress. When it is quite concluded, and not before, he disengages his ravenous eyes and fingers from it, and answers Mr. George's last remark by saying, "Afraid to order the pipe? We are not so mercenary as that, sir. Judy, see directly to the pipe and the glass of cold brandy-and-water for Mr. George."

The sportive twins, who have been looking straight before them all this time, except when they have been engrossed by the black leathern cases, retire together, generally disdainful of the visitor, but leaving him to the old man, as two young cubs might leave a traveller to the parental bear.

"And there you sit, I suppose, all the day long, eh?" says Mr. George, with folded arms.

"Just so, just so," the old man nods.

"And don't you occupy yourself at all?"

"I watch the fire—and the boiling and the roasting—"

"When there is any," says Mr. George, with great expression.

"Just so. When there is any."

"Don't you read, or get read to?"

The old man shakes his head with sharp sly triumph. "No, no. We have never been readers in our family. It don't pay. Stuff. Idleness. Folly. No no!"

"There's not much to choose between your two states," says the visitor, in a key too low for the old man's dull hearing, as he looks from him to the old woman and back again. "I say!" in a louder voice.

"I hear you."

"You'll sell me up at last, I suppose, when I am a day in arrear."

"My dear friend!" cries Grandfather Smallweed, stretching out both hands to embrace him. "Never! Never, my dear friend! But my friend in the city that I got to lend you the money—*he* might!"

"O! you can't answer for him?" says Mr. George, finishing the inquiry, in his lower key, with the words, "you lying old rascal!"

"My dear friend, he is not to be depended on. I wouldn't trust him. He will have his bond, my dear friend."

"Devil doubt him," says Mr. George. Charley appearing with a tray, on which are the pipe, a small paper of tobacco, and the brandy-and-water, he asks her, "How do you come here! you haven't got the family face."

"I goes out to work, sir," returns Charley.

The trooper (if trooper he be or have been) takes her bonnet off, with a light touch for so strong a hand, and pats her on the head. "You give the house almost a wholesome look. It wants a bit of youth as much as it wants fresh air." Then he dismisses her, lights his pipe, and drinks to Mr. Smallweed's friend in the city—the one solitary flight of that esteemed old gentleman's imagination.

"So you think he might be hard upon me, eh?"

"I think he might—I am afraid he would. I have known him do it," says Grandfather Smallweed, incautiously, "twenty times."

Incautiously, because his stricken better-half, who has been dozing over the fire for some time, is instantly aroused and jabbers, "Twenty thousand pounds, twenty twenty-pound notes in a money-box, twenty guineas, twenty million twenty per cent, twenty—" and is then cut short by the flying cushion, which the visitor, to whom this singular experiment appears to be a novelty, snatches from her face as it crushes her in the usual manner.

"You're a brimstone idiot. You're a scorpion—a brimstone scorpion! You're a sweltering toad. You're a chattering clattering broomstick witch, that ought to be burnt!" gasps the old man, prostrate in his chair. "My dear friend, will you shake me up a little?"

Mr. George, who has been looking first at one of them and then at the other, as if he were demented, takes his venerable acquaintance by the throat on receiving this request, and dragging him upright in his chair as easily as if he were a doll, appears in two minds whether or no to shake all future power of cushioning out of him, and shake him into his grave. Resisting the temptation, but agitating him violently enough to make his head roll like a harlequin's, he puts him smartly down in his chair again, and adjusts his skull cap with such a rub, that the old man winks with both eyes for a minute afterwards.

"O Lord!" gasps Mr. Smallweed. "That'll do. Thank you, my dear friend, that'll do. O dear me, I'm out of breath. O Lord!" And Mr. Smallweed says it, not without evident apprehensions of his dear friend, who still stands over him, looming larger than ever.

The alarming presence, however, gradually subsides into its chair, and falls to smoking in long puffs; consoling itself with the philosophical reflection, "The name of your friend in the city begins with a D, comrade, and you're about right respecting the bond."

"Did you speak, Mr. George?" inquires the old man.

The trooper shakes his head; and leaning forward with his right elbow on his right knee and his pipe supported in that hand, while his other hand, resting on his left leg, squares his left elbow in a martial manner, continues to smoke. Meanwhile he looks at Mr. Smallweed with grave attention, and now and then fans the cloud of smoke away, in order that he may see him the more clearly.

"I take it," he says, making just as much and as little change in his position as will enable him to reach the glass to his lips, with a round, full action, "that I am the only man alive (or dead either), that gets the value of a pipe out of *you*?"

"Well!" returns the old man, "it's true that I don't see company, Mr. George, and that I don't treat. I can't afford to do it. But as you, in your pleasant way, made your pipe a condition——"

"Why, it's not for the value of it; that's no great thing. It was a fancy to get it out of you. To have something in for my money."

"Ha! You're prudent, prudent, sir!" cries Grandfather Smallweed, rubbing his legs.

"Very. I always was." Puff. "It's a sure sign of my prudence, that I ever found the way here." Puff. "Also, that I am what I am." Puff. "I am well known to be prudent," says Mr. George, composedly smoking. "I rose in life, that way."

"Don't be down-hearted sir. You may rise yet."

Mr. George laughs and drinks.

"Ha'n't you no relations, now," asks Grandfather Smallweed, with a twinkle in his eyes, "who would pay off this little principal, or who would lend you a good name or two that I could persuade my friend in the city to make you a further advance upon? Two good names would be sufficient for my friend in the city. Ha'n't you no such relations, Mr. George?"

Mr. George, still composedly smoking, replies, "If I had, I shouldn't trouble them. I have been trouble enough to my belongings in my day. It *may* be a very good sort of penitence in a vagabond, who has wasted the best time of his life, to go back then to decent people that he never was a credit to, and live upon them; but it's not my sort. The best kind of amends then, for having gone away, is to keep away, in my opinion."

"But natural affection, Mr. George," hints Grandfather Smallweed.

"For two good names, hey?" says Mr. George, shaking his head, and still composedly smoking. "No. That's not my sort, either."

Grandfather Smallweed has been gradually sliding down in his chair since his last adjustment, and is now a bundle of clothes, with a voice in it calling for Judy. That Houri[9] appearing, shakes him up in the usual manner, and is charged by the old gentleman to remain near him. For he seems chary of putting his visitor to the trouble of repeating his late attentions.

"Ha!" he observes, when he is in trim again. "If you could have traced out the Captain, Mr. George, it would have been the making of you. If, when you first came here, in consequence of our advertisements in the newspaper—when I say 'our,' I'm alluding to the advertisements of my friend in the city, and one or two others who embark their capital in the same way, and are so friendly towards me as sometimes to give me a lift with my little pittance—if, at that time, you could have helped us, Mr. George, it would have been the making of you."

"I was willing enough to be 'made,' as you call it," says Mr. George, smoking not quite so placidly as before, for since the entrance of Judy he has been in some measure disturbed by a fasci-

9. A beautiful nymph in the Mohammedan Paradise.

nation, not of the admiring kind, which obliges him to look at her as she stands by her grandfather's chair; "but, on the whole, I am glad I wasn't now."

"Why, Mr. George? In the name of—of Brimstone, why?" says Grandfather Smallweed, with a plain appearance of exasperation. (Brimstone apparently suggested by his eye lighting on Mrs. Smallweed in her slumber.)

"For two reasons, comrade."

"And what two reasons, Mr. George? In the name of the——"

"Of our friend in the city?" suggests Mr. George, composedly drinking.

"Ay, if you like. What two reasons?"

"In the first place," returns Mr. George; but still looking at Judy, as if, she being so old and so like her grandfather, it is indifferent which of the two he addresses; "you gentlemen took me in. You advertised that Mr. Hawdon (Captain Hawdon, if you hold to the saying, Once a captain always a captain) was to hear of something to his advantage."

"Well?" returns the old man, shrilly and sharply.

"Well!" says Mr. George, smoking on. "It wouldn't have been much to his advantage to have been clapped into prison by the whole bill and judgment trade of London."

"How do you know that? Some of his rich relations might have paid his debts, or compounded for 'em. Besides, he had taken *us* in. He owed us immense sums, all round. I would sooner have strangled him than had no return. If I sit here thinking of him," snarls the old man, holding up his impotent ten fingers, "I want to strangle him now." And in a sudden access of fury, he throws the cushion at the unoffending Mrs. Smallweed, but it passes harmlessly on one side of her chair.

"I don't need to be told," returns the trooper, taking his pipe from his lips for a moment, and carrying his eyes back from following the progress of the cushion, to the pipe-bowl which is burning low, "that he carried on heavily and went to ruin. I have been at his right hand many a day, when he was charging upon ruin full-gallop. I was with him, when he was sick and well, rich and poor. I laid this hand upon him, after he had run through everything and broken down everything beneath him—when he held a pistol to his head."

"I wish he had let it off!" says the benevolent old man, "and blown his head into as many pieces as he owed pounds!"

"That would have been a smash indeed," returns the trooper coolly; "any way, he had been young, hopeful, and handsome in the days gone by; and I am glad I never found him, when he was neither, to lead to a result so much to his advantage. That's reason number one."

"I hope number two's as good?" snarls the old man.

"Why no. It's more of a selfish reason. If I had found him, I must have gone to the other world to look. He was there."

"How do you know he was there?"

"He wasn't here."

"How do you know he wasn't here?"

"Don't lose your temper as well as your money," says Mr. George, calmly knocking the ashes out of his pipe. "He was drowned long before. I am convinced of it. He went over a ship's side. Whether intentionally or accidentally, I don't know. Perhaps your friend in the city does. Do you know what that tune is, Mr. Smallweed?" he adds, after breaking off to whistle one, accompanied on the table with the empty pipe.

"Tune!" replies the old man. "No. We never have tunes here."

"That's the Dead March in Saul.[1] They bury soldiers to it; so it's the natural end of the subject. Now, if your pretty granddaughter —excuse me, miss—will condescend to take care of this pipe for two months, we shall save the cost of one next time. Good evening, Mr. Smallweed!"

"My dear friend!" The old man gives him both his hands.

"So you think your friend in the city will be hard upon me, if I fail in a payment?" says the trooper, looking down upon him like a giant.

"My dear friend, I am afraid he will," returns the old man, looking up at him like a pigmy.

Mr. George laughs; and with a glance at Mr. Smallweed, and a parting salutation to the scornful Judy, strides out of the parlour, clashing imaginary sabres and other metallic appurtenances as he goes.

"You're a damned rogue," says the old gentleman, making a hideous grimace at the door as he shuts it. "But I'll lime[2] you, you dog, I'll lime you!"

After this amiable remark, his spirit soars into those enchanting regions of reflection which its education and pursuits have opened to it; and again he and Mrs. Smallweed wile away the rosy hours, two unrelieved sentinels forgotten as aforesaid by the Black Serjeant.

While the twain are faithful to their post, Mr. George strides through the streets with a massive kind of swagger and a grave enough face. It is eight o'clock now, and the day is fast drawing in. He stops hard by Waterloo Bridge, and reads a playbill; decides to

1. Funeral march in Handel's oratorio, *Saul* (1738).

2. Catch you as birds are trapped by bird-lime.

go to Astley's Theatre.[3] Being there, is much delighted with the horses and the feats of strength; looks at the weapons with a critical eye; disapproves of the combats, as giving evidences of unskilful swordsmanship; but is touched home by the sentiments. In the last scene, when the Emperor of Tartary gets up into a cart and condescends to bless the united lovers by hovering over them with the Union-Jack, his eye-lashes are moistened with emotion.

The theatre over, Mr. George comes across the water again, and makes his way to that curious region lying about the Haymarket and Leicester Square, which is a centre of attraction to indifferent foreign hotels and indifferent foreigners, racket-courts, fighting-men, swordsmen, footguards, old china, gaming-houses, exhibitions, and a large medley of shabbiness and shrinking out of sight. Penetrating to the heart of this region, he arrives, by a court and a long white-washed passage, at a great brick building, composed of bare walls, floors, roof-rafters, and skylights; on the front of which, if it can be said to have any front, is painted GEORGE'S SHOOTING GALLERY, &c.

Into George's Shooting Gallery, &c., he goes; and in it there are gas-lights (partly turned off now), and two whitened targets for rifle-shooting, and archery accommodation, and fencing appliances, and all necessaries for the British art of boxing. None of these sports or exercises are being pursued in George's Shooting Gallery to-night; which is so devoid of company, that a little grotesque man, with a large head, has it all to himself, and lies asleep upon the floor.

The little man is dressed something like a gunsmith, in a green baize apron and cap; and his face and hands are dirty with gunpowder, and begrimed with the loading of guns. As he lies in the light, before a glaring white target, the black upon him shines again. Not far off, is the strong, rough, primitive table, with a vice upon it, at which he has been working. He is a little man with a face all crushed together, who appears, from a certain blue and speckled appearance that one of his cheeks presents, to have been blown up, in the way of business, at some odd time or times.

"Phil!" says the trooper, in a quiet voice.

"All right!" cries Phil, scrambling to his feet.

"Anything been doing?"

"Flat as ever so much swipes,"[4] says Phil. "Five dozen rifle and a dozen pistol. As to aim!" Phil gives a howl at the recollection.

"Shut up shop, Phil!"

As Phil moves about to execute this order, it appears that he is lame, though able to move very quickly. On the speckled side of his

3. A popular theater featuring circus-style spectacles and melodramas.

4. Weak beer.

face he has no eyebrow, and on the other side he has a bushy black one, which want of uniformity gives him a very singular and rather sinister appearance. Everything seems to have happened to his hands that could possibly take place, consistently with the retention of all the fingers; for they are notched, and seamed, and crumpled all over. He appears to be very strong, and lifts heavy benches about as if he had no idea what weight was. He has a curious way of limping round the gallery with his shoulder against the wall, and tacking off at objects he wants to lay hold of, instead of going straight to them, which has left a smear all round the four walls, conventionally called "Phil's mark."

This custodian of George's Gallery in George's absence concludes his proceedings, when he has locked the great doors, and turned out all the lights but one, which he leaves to glimmer, by dragging out from a wooden cabin in a corner two mattresses and bedding. These being drawn to opposite ends of the gallery, the trooper makes his own bed, and Phil makes his.

"Phil!" says the master, walking towards him without his coat and waistcoat, and looking more soldierly than ever in his braces. "You were found in a doorway, weren't you?"

"Gutter," says Phil. "Watchman tumbled over me."

"Then, vagabondizing came natural to *you*, from the beginning."

"As nat'ral as possible," says Phil.

"Good night!"

"Good night, guv'ner."

Phil cannot even go straight to bed, but finds it necessary to shoulder round two sides of the gallery and then tack off at his mattress. The trooper, after taking a turn or two in the rifle-distance, and looking up at the moon now shining through the skylights, strides to his own mattress by a shorter route, and goes to bed too.

Chapter XXII

MR. BUCKET

Allegory looks pretty cool in Lincoln's Inn Fields, though the evening is hot; for both Mr. Tulkinghorn's windows are wide open, and the room is lofty, gusty, and gloomy. These may not be desirable characteristics when November comes with fog and sleet, or January with ice and snow; but they have their merits in the sultry long vacation weather. They enable Allegory, though it has cheeks like peaches, and knees like bunches of blossoms, and rosy swellings for calves to its legs and muscles to its arms, to look tolerably cool to-night.

Plenty of dust comes in at Mr. Tulkinghorn's windows, and plenty more has generated among his furniture and papers. It lies thick everywhere. When a breeze from the country that has lost its way, takes fright, and makes a blind hurry to rush out again, it flings as much dust in the eyes of Allegory as the law—or Mr. Tulkinghorn, one of its trustiest representatives—may scatter, on occasion, in the eyes of the laity.

In his lowering magazine of dust, the universal article into which his papers and himself, and all his clients, and all things of earth, animate and inanimate, are resolving, Mr. Tulkinghorn sits at one of the open windows, enjoying a bottle of old port. Though a hard-grained man, close, dry, and silent, he can enjoy old wine with the best. He has a priceless binn of port in some artful cellar under the Fields, which is one of his many secrets. When he dines alone in chambers, as he has dined to-day, and has his bit of fish and his steak or chicken brought in from the coffee-house, he descends with a candle to the echoing regions below the deserted mansion, and, heralded by a remote reverberation of thundering doors, comes gravely back, encircled by an earthy atmosphere, and carrying a bottle from which he pours a radiant nectar, two score and ten years old, that blushes in the glass to find itself so famous,[1] and fills the whole room with the fragrance of southern grapes.

Mr. Tulkinghorn, sitting in the twilight by the open window, enjoys his wine. As if it whispered to him of its fifty years of silence and seclusion, it shuts him up the closer. More impenetrable than ever, he sits, and drinks, and mellows as it were, in secrecy; pondering, at that twilight hour, on all the mysteries he knows, associated with darkening woods in the country, and vast blank shut-up houses in town: and perhaps sparing a thought or two for himself, and his family history, and his money, and his will—all a mystery to every one—and that one bachelor friend of his, a man of the same mould and a lawyer too, who lived the same kind of life until he was seventy-five years old, and then, suddenly conceiving (as it is supposed) an impression that it was too monotonous, gave his gold watch to his hairdresser one summer evening, and walked leisurely home to the Temple, and hanged himself.

But Mr. Tulkinghorn is not alone to-night, to ponder at his usual length. Seated at the same table, though with his chair modestly and uncomfortably drawn a little away from it, sits a bald, mild, shining man, who coughs respectfully behind his hand when the lawyer bids him fill his glass.

1. According to T. W. Hill, an allusion to Byron's saying after the publication of *Childe Harold*: "I awoke one morning and found myself famous" (cited by Thomas Moore in his *Life of Lord Byron*, ch. 14).

"Now, Snagsby," says Mr. Tulkinghorn, "to go over this odd story again."

"If you please, sir."

"You told me when you were so good as to step round here, last night——"

"For which I must ask you to excuse me if it was a liberty, sir; but I remembered that you had taken a sort of an interest in that person, and I thought it possible that you might—just—wish—to——"

Mr. Tulkinghorn is not the man to help him to any conclusion, or to admit anything as to any possibility concerning himself. So Mr. Snagsby trails off into saying, with an awkward cough, "I must ask you to excuse the liberty, sir, I am sure."

"Not at all," says Mr. Tulkinghorn. "You told me, Snagsby, that you put on your hat and came round without mentioning your intention to your wife. That was prudent, I think, because it's not a matter of such importance that it requires to be mentioned."

"Well, sir," returns Mr. Snagsby, "you see my little woman is—not to put too fine a point upon it—inquisitive. She's inquisitive. Poor little thing, she's liable to spasms, and it's good for her to have her mind employed. In consequence of which she employs it—I should say upon every individual thing she can lay hold of, whether it concerns her or not—especially not. My little woman has a very active mind, sir."

Mr. Snagsby drinks, and murmurs with an admiring cough behind his hand, "Dear me, very fine wine indeed!"

"Therefore you kept your visit to yourself, last night?" says Mr. Tulkinghorn. "And to-night, too?"

"Yes, sir, and to-night, too. My little woman is at present in—not to put too fine a point upon it—in a pious state, or in what she considers such, and attends the Evening Exertions (which is the name they go by) of a reverend party of the name of Chadband. He has a great deal of eloquence at his command, undoubtedly, but I am not quite favourable to his style myself. That's neither here nor there. My little woman being engaged in that way, made it easier for me to step round in a quiet manner."

Mr. Tulkinghorn assents. "Fill your glass, Snagsby."

"Thank you, sir, I am sure," returns the stationer, with his cough of deference. "This is wonderfully fine wine, sir!"

"It is a rare wine now," says Mr. Tulkinghorn. "It is fifty years old."

"Is it indeed, sir? But I am not surprised to hear it, I am sure. It might be—any age almost." After rendering this general tribute to the port, Mr. Snagsby in his modesty coughs an apology behind his hand for drinking anything so precious.

"Will you run over, once again, what the boy said?" asks Mr. Tulkinghorn, putting his hands into the pockets of his rusty small-clothes[2] and leaning quietly back in his chair.

"With pleasure, sir."

Then, with fidelity, though with some prolixity, the law-stationer repeats Jo's statement made to the assembled guests at his house. On coming to the end of his narrative, he gives a great start, and breaks off with—"Dear me, sir, I wasn't aware there was any other gentleman present!"

Mr. Snagsby is dismayed to see, standing with an attentive face between himself and the lawyer, at a little distance from the table, a person with a hat and stick in his hands, who was not there when he himself came in, and has not since entered by the door or by either of the windows. There is a press in the room, but its hinges have not creaked, nor has a step been audible upon the floor. Yet this third person stands there, with his attentive face, and his hat and stick in his hands, and his hands behind him, a composed and quiet listener. He is a stoutly built, steady-looking, sharp-eyed man in black, of about the middle age. Except that he looks at Mr. Snagsby as if he were going to take his portrait, there is nothing remarkable about him at first sight but his ghostly manner of appearing.

"Don't mind this gentleman," says Mr. Tulkinghorn, in his quiet way. "This is only Mr. Bucket."

"O indeed, sir?" returns the stationer, expressing by a cough that he is quite in the dark as to who Mr. Bucket may be.

"I wanted him to hear this story," says the lawyer, "because I have half a mind (for a reason) to know more of it, and he is very intelligent in such things. What do you say to this, Bucket?"

"It's very plain, sir. Since our people have moved this boy on, and he's not to be found on his old lay,[3] if Mr. Snagsby don't object to go down with me to Tom-all-Alone's and point him out, we can have him here in less than a couple of hours' time. I can do it without Mr. Snagsby, of course; but this is the shortest way."

"Mr. Bucket is a detective officer, Snagsby," says the lawyer in explanation.

"Is he, indeed, sir?" says Mr. Snagsby, with a strong tendency in his clump of hair to stand on end.

"And if you have no real objection to accompany Mr. Bucket to the place in question," pursues the lawyer, "I shall feel obliged to you if you will do so."

In a moment's hesitation on the part of Mr. Snagsby, Bucket dips down to the bottom of his mind.

"Don't you be afraid of hurting the boy," he says. "You won't do

2. Knee-breeches.

3. Place of work (as crossing-sweeper).

that. It's all right as far as the boy's concerned. We shall only bring him here to ask him a question or so I want to put to him, and he'll be paid for his trouble, and sent away again. It'll be a good job for him. I promise you, as a man, that you shall see the boy sent away all right. Don't you be afraid of hurting him; you an't going to do that."

"Very well, Mr. Tulkinghorn!" cries Mr. Snagsby cheerfully, and reassured, "since that's the case——"

"Yes! and lookee here, Mr. Snagsby," resumes Bucket, taking him aside by the arm, tapping him familiarly on the breast, and speaking in a confidential tone. "You're a man of the world, you know, and a man of business, and a man of sense. That's what you are."

"I am sure I am much obliged to you for your good opinion," returns the stationer, with his cough of modesty, "but——"

"That's what you *are*, you know," says Bucket. "Now it an't necessary to say to a man like you, engaged in your business, which is a business of trust and requires a person to be wide awake and have his senses about him, and his head screwed on tight (I had an uncle in your business once)—it an't necessary to say to a man like you, that it's the best and wisest way to keep little matters like this quiet. Don't you see? Quiet!"

"Certainly, certainly," returns the other.

"I don't mind telling *you*," says Bucket, with an engaging appearance of frankness, "that as far as I can understand it, there seems to be a doubt whether this dead person wasn't entitled to a little property, and whether this female hasn't been up to some games respecting that property, don't you see?"

"O!" says Mr. Snagsby, but not appearing to see quite distinctly.

"Now, what *you* want," pursues Bucket, again tapping Mr. Snagsby on the breast in a comfortable and soothing manner, "is, that every person should have their rights according to justice. That's what *you* want."

"To be sure," returns Mr. Snagsby with a nod.

"On account of which, and at the same time to oblige a—do you call it, in your business, customer or client? I forget how my uncle used to call it."

"Why, I generally say customer myself," replies Mr. Snagsby.

"You're right!" returns Mr. Bucket, shaking hands with him quite affectionately,—"on account of which, and at the same time to oblige a real good customer, you mean to go down with me, in confidence, to Tom-all-Alone's, and to keep the whole thing quiet ever afterwards and never mention it to any one. That's about your intentions, if I understand you?"

"You are right, sir. You are right," says Mr. Snagsby.

"Then here's your hat," returns his new friend, quite as intimate with it as if he had made it; "and if you're ready, I am."

They leave Mr. Tulkinghorn, without a ruffle on the surface of his unfathomable depths, drinking his old wine, and go down into the streets.

"You don't happen to know a very good sort of person of the name of Gridley, do you?" says Bucket, in friendly converse as they descend the stairs.

"No," says Mr. Snagsby, considering, "I don't know anybody of that name. Why?"

"Nothing particular," says Bucket; "only, having allowed his temper to get a little the better of him, and having been threatening some respectable people, he is keeping out of the way of a warrant I have got against him—which it's a pity that a man of sense should do."

As they walk along, Mr. Snagsby observes, as a novelty, that, however quick their pace may be, his companion still seems in some undefinable manner to lurk and lounge; also, that whenever he is going to turn to the right or left, he pretends to have a fixed purpose in his mind of going straight ahead, and wheels off, sharply, at the very last moment. Now and then, when they pass a police-constable on his beat, Mr. Snagsby notices that both the constable and his guide fall into a deep abstraction as they come towards each other, and appear entirely to overlook each other, and to gaze into space. In a few instances, Mr. Bucket, coming behind some undersized young man with a shining hat on, and his sleek hair twisted into one flat curl on each side of his head, almost without glancing at him touches him with his stick; upon which the young man, looking round, instantly evaporates. For the most part Mr. Bucket notices things in general, with a face as unchanging as the great mourning ring[4] on his little finger, or the brooch, composed of not much diamond and a good deal of setting, which he wears in his shirt.

When they come at last to Tom-all-Alone's, Mr. Bucket stops for a moment at the corner, and takes a lighted bull's-eye[5] from the constable on duty there, who then accompanies him with his own particular bull's-eye at his waist. Between his two conductors, Mr. Snagsby passes along the middle of a villainous street, undrained, unventilated, deep in black mud and corrupt water—though the roads are dry elsewhere—and reeking with such smells and sights that he, who has lived in London all his life, can scarce believe his senses. Branching from this street and its heaps of ruins, are other streets and courts so infamous that Mr. Snagsby sickens in body and mind, and feels as if he were going, every moment deeper down, into the infernal gulf.

"Draw off a bit here, Mr. Snagsby," says Bucket, as a kind of

4. Ring worn as a memorial of a person's death, usually inscribed with designs or mottoes or with the initials of the deceased and the date of death.

5. An oil lantern with a lens providing a beam of light like a flashlight or electric torch.

shabby palanquin[6] is borne towards them, surrounded by a noisy crowd. "Here's the fever coming up the street!"

As the unseen wretch goes by, the crowd, leaving the object of attraction, hovers round the three visitors, like a dream of horrible faces, and fades away up alleys and into ruins, and behind walls; and with occasional cries and shrill whistles of warning, thenceforth flits about them until they leave the place.

"Are those the fever-houses, Darby?"[7] Mr. Bucket coolly asks, as he turns his bull's eye on a line of stinking ruins.

Darby replies that "all them are,'" and further that in all, for months and months, the people "have been down by dozens," and have been carried out, dead and dying, "like sheep with the rot." Bucket observing to Mr. Snagsby as they go on again, that he looks a little poorly, Mr. Snagsby answers that he feels as if he couldn't breathe the dreadful air.

There is inquiry made, at various houses, for a boy named Jo. As few people are known in Tom-all-Alone's by any Christian sign, there is much reference to Mr. Snagsby whether he means Carrots, or the Colonel, or Gallows, or Young Chisel, or Terrier Tip, or Lanky, or the Brick. Mr. Snagsby describes over and over again. There are conflicting opinions respecting the original of his picture. Some think it must be Carrots; some say the Brick. The Colonel is produced, but is not at all near the thing. Whenever Mr. Snagsby and his conductors are stationary, the crowd flows round, and from its squalid depths obsequious advice heaves up to Mr. Bucket. Whenever they move, and the angry bull's-eyes glare, it fades away, and flits about them up the alleys, and in the ruins, and behind the walls, as before.

At last there is a lair found out where Toughy, or the Tough Subject, lays him down at night; and it is thought that the tough subject may be Jo. Comparison of notes between Mr. Snagsby and the proprietress of the house—a drunken face tied up in a black bundle, and flaring out of a heap of rags on the floor of a dog-hutch which is her private apartment—leads to the establishment of this conclusion. Toughy has gone to the Doctor's to get a bottle of stuff for a sick woman, but will be here anon.

"And who have we got here to-night?" says Mr. Bucket, opening another door and glaring in with his bull's-eye. "Two drunken men, eh? And two women? The men are sound enough," turning back each sleeper's arm from his face to look at him. "Are these your good men, my dears?"

6. Vehicle used in India resembling a stretcher but with side-curtains enabling the person being carried to remain unseen.

7. The policeman's name may be associated with the term *darbies*, meaning *handcuffs*.

"Yes, sir," returns one of the women. "They are our husbands."

"Brickmakers, eh?"

"Yes, sir."

"What are you doing here? You don't belong to London."

"No sir. We belong to Hertfordshire."

"Whereabouts in Hertfordshire?"

"Saint Albans."

"Come up on the tramp?"

"We walked up yesterday. There's no work down with us at present, but we have done no good by coming here, and shall do none, I expect."

"That's not the way to do much good," says Mr. Bucket, turning his head in the direction of the unconscious figures on the ground.

"It an't indeed," replies the woman, with a sigh. "Jenny and me knows it full well."

The room, though two or three feet higher than the door, is so low that the head of the tallest of the visitors would touch the blackened ceiling if he stood upright. It is offensive to every sense; even the gross candle burns pale and sickly in the polluted air. There are a couple of benches, and a higher bench by way of table. The men lie asleep where they stumbled down, but the women sit by the candle. Lying in the arms of the woman who has spoken, is a very young child.

"Why, what age do you call that little creature?" says Bucket. "It looks as if it was born yesterday." He is not at all rough about it; and as he turns his light gently on the infant, Mr. Snagsby is strangely reminded of another infant, encircled with light, that he has seen in pictures.

"He is not three weeks old yet, sir," says the woman.

"Is he your child?"

"Mine."

The other woman, who was bending over it when they came in, stoops down again, and kisses it as it lies asleep.

"You seem as fond of it as if you were the mother yourself," says Mr. Bucket.

"I was the mother of one like it, master, and it died."

"Ah, Jenny, Jenny!" says the other woman to her; "better so. Much better to think of dead than alive, Jenny! Much better!"

"Why, you an't such an unnatural woman, I hope," returns Bucket, sternly, "as to wish your own child dead?"

"God knows you are right, master," she returns. "I am not. I'd stand between it and death, with my own life if I could, as true as any pretty lady."

"Then don't talk in that wrong manner," says Mr. Bucket, mollified again. "Why do you do it?"

"It's brought into my head, master," returns the woman, her eyes filling with tears, "when I look down at the child lying so. If it was never to wake no more, you'd think me mad, I should take on so. I know that very well. I was with Jenny when she lost hers—warn't I, Jenny?—and I know how she grieved. But look round you, at this place. Look at them"; glancing at the sleepers on the ground. "Look at the boy you're waiting for, who's gone out to do me a good turn. Think of the children that your business lays with often and often, and that *you* see grow up!"

"Well, well," says Mr. Bucket, "you train him respectable and he'll be a comfort to you, and look after you in your old age, you know."

"I mean to try hard," she answers, wiping her eyes. "But I have been a-thinking, being over-tired to-night, and not well with the ague, of all the many things that'll come in his way. My master will be against it, and he'll be beat, and see me beat, and made to fear his home, and perhaps to stray wild. If I work for him ever so much, and ever so hard, there's no one to help me; and if he should be turned bad, 'spite of all I could do, and the time should come when I should sit by him in his sleep, made hard and changed, an't it likely I should think of him as he lies in my lap now, and wish he had died as Jenny's child died!"

"There, there!" says Jenny. "Liz, you're tired and ill. Let me take him."

In doing so, she displaces the mother's dress, but quickly readjusts it over the wounded and bruised bosom where the baby has been lying.

"It's my dead child," says Jenny, walking up and down as she nurses, "that makes me love this child so dear, and it's my dead child that makes her love it so dear too, as even to think of its being taken away from her now. While she thinks that, *I* think what fortune would I give to have my darling back. But we mean the same thing, if we knew how to say it, us two mothers does in our poor hearts!"

As Mr. Snagsby blows his nose, and coughs his cough of sympathy, a step is heard without. Mr. Bucket throws his light into the doorway, and says to Mr. Snagsby, "Now what do you say to Toughy? Will *he* do?"

"That's Jo," says Mr. Snagsby.

Jo stands amazed in the disc of light, like a ragged figure in a magic-lanthorn,[8] trembling to think that he has offended against

8. Magic lanterns, invented in the seventeenth century, were popularly used to project horror shows (called phantasmagorias) featuring images of spectres and monsters. The spelling of *lanthorn* is seemingly derived from folk etymology because early lanterns were made of horn rather than glass.

the law in not having moved on far enough. Mr. Snagsby, however, giving him the consolatory assurance, "It's only a job you will be paid for, Jo," he recovers; and on being taken outside by Mr. Bucket for a little private confabulation, tells his tale satisfactorily, though out of breath.

"I have squared it with the lad," says Mr. Bucket, returning, "and it's all right. Now, Mr. Snagsby, we're ready for you."

First, Jo has to complete his errand of good-nature by handing over the physic he has been to get, which he delivers with the laconic verbal direction that "it's to be all took d'rectly." Secondly, Mr. Snagsby has to lay upon the table half-a-crown, his usual panacea for an immense variety of afflictions. Thirdly, Mr. Bucket has to take Jo by the arm a little above the elbow and walk him on before him; without which observance, neither the Tough Subject nor any other Subject could be professionally conducted to Lincoln's Inn Fields. These arrangements completed, they give the women good night, and come out once more into black and foul Tom-all-Alone's.

By the noisome ways through which they descended into that pit, they gradually emerge from it; the crowd flitting, and whistling, and skulking about them, until they come to the verge, where restoration of the bull's-eyes is made to Darby. Here, the crowd, like a concourse of imprisoned demons, turns back, yelling, and is seen no more. Through the clearer and fresher streets, never so clear and fresh to Mr. Snagsby's mind as now, they walk and ride, until they come to Mr. Tulkinghorn's gate.

As they ascend the dim stairs (Mr. Tulkinghorn's chambers being on the first floor), Mr. Bucket mentions that he has the key of the outer door in his pocket, and that there is no need to ring. For a man so expert in most things of that kind, Bucket takes time to open the door, and makes some noise too. It may be that he sounds a note of preparation.[9]

Howbeit, they come at last into the hall, where a lamp is burning and so into Mr. Tulkinghorn's usual room—the room where he drank his old wine to-night. He is not there, but his two old-fashioned candlesticks are; and the room is tolerably light.

Mr. Bucket, still having his professional hold of Jo, and appearing to Mr. Snagsby to possess an unlimited number of eyes, makes a little way into this room, when Jo starts and stops.

"What's the matter?" says Bucket in a whisper.

"There she is!" cries Jo.

"Who?"

"The lady!"

A female figure, closely veiled, stands in the middle of the room,

9. See *Henry V*, IV (chorus), 14.

where the light falls upon it. It is quite still and silent. The front of the figure is towards them, but it takes no notice of their entrance, and remains like a statue.

"Now, tell me," says Bucket aloud, "how you know that to be the lady."

"I know the wale," replies Jo, staring, "and the bonnet, and the gownd."

"Be quite sure of what you say, Tough," returns Bucket, narrowly observant of him. "Look again."

"I am a-looking as hard as ever I can look," says Jo, with starting eyes, "and that there's the wale, the bonnet, and the gownd."

"What about those rings you told me of?" asks Bucket.

"A-sparkling all over here," says Jo, rubbing the fingers of his left hand on the knuckles of his right, without taking his eyes from the figure.

The figure removes the right-hand glove, and shows the hand.

"Now what do you say to that?" asks Bucket.

Jo shakes his head. "Not rings a bit like them. Not a hand like that."

"What are you talking of?" says Bucket; evidently pleased though, and well pleased too.

"Hand was a deal whiter, a deal delicater, and a deal smaller," returns Jo.

"Why, you'll tell me I'm my own mother next," says Mr. Bucket. "Do you recollect the lady's voice?"

"I think I does," says Jo.

The figure speaks. "Was it at all like this? I will speak as long as you like if you are not sure. Was it this voice, or at all like this voice?"

Jo looks aghast at Mr. Bucket. "Not a bit!"

"Then, what," retorts that worthy, pointing to the figure, "did you say it was the lady for?"

"Cos," says Jo, with a perplexed stare, but without being at all shaken in his certainty, "Cos that there's the wale, the bonnet, and the gownd. It is her and it an't her. It an't her hand, nor yit her rings, nor yit her woice. But that there's the wale, the bonnet, and the gownd, and they're wore the same way wot she wore 'em and it's her heigth wot she wos, and she giv me a sov'ring and hooked it."[1]

"Well!" says Mr. Bucket, slightly, "we haven't got much good out of *you*. But, however, here's five shillings for you. Take care how you spend it, and don't get yourself into trouble." Bucket stealthily tells the coins from one hand into the other like counters

1. Ran away.

—which is a way he has, his principal use of them being in these games of skill—and then puts them, in a little pile, into the boy's hand, and takes him out to the door; leaving Mr. Snagsby, not by any means comfortable under these mysterious circumstances, alone with the veiled figure. But on Mr. Tulkinghorn's coming into the room, the veil is raised, and a sufficiently good-looking Frenchwoman is revealed, though her expression is something of the intensest.

"Thank you, Mademoiselle Hortense," says Mr. Tulkinghorn, with his usual equanimity. "I will give you no further trouble about this little wager."

"You will do me the kindness to remember, sir, that I am not at present placed?" says Mademoiselle.

"Certainly, certainly!"

"And to confer upon me the favour of your distinguished recommendation?"

"By all means, Mademoiselle Hortense."

"A word from Mr. Tulkinghorn is so powerful."—"It shall not be wanting, Mademoiselle."—"Receive the assurance of my devoted gratitude, dear sir."—"Good night." Mademoiselle goes out with an air of native gentility; and Mr. Bucket, to whom it is, on an emergency, as natural to be groom of the ceremonies, as it is to be anything else, shows her down-stairs, not without gallantry.

"Well, Bucket?" quoth Mr. Tulkinghorn, on his return.

"It's all squared, you see, as I squared it myself, sir. There an't a doubt that it was the other one with this one's dress on. The boy was exact respecting colours and everything. Mr. Snagsby, I promised you as a man that he should be sent away all right. Don't say it wasn't done!"

"You have kept your word, sir," returns the stationer; "and if I can be of no further use, Mr. Tulkinghorn, I think, as my little woman will be getting anxious——"

"Thank you, Snagsby, no further use," says Mr. Tulkinghorn. "I am quite indebted to you for the trouble you have taken already."

"Not at all, sir. I wish you good night."

"You see, Mr. Snagsby," says Mr. Bucket, accompanying him to the door, and shaking hands with him over and over again, "what I like in you is, that you're a man it's of no use pumping; that's what *you* are. When you know you have done a right thing, you put it away, and it's done with and gone, and there's an end of it. That's what *you* do."

"That is certainly what I endeavour to do, sir," returns Mr. Snagsby.

"No, you don't do yourself justice. It an't what you endeavour to do," says Mr. Bucket, shaking hands with him and blessing him in the tenderest manner, "it's what you *do*. That's what I estimate in a man in your way of business."

Mr. Snagsby makes a suitable response; and goes homeward so confused by the events of the evening, that he is doubtful of his being awake and out—doubtful of the reality of the streets through which he goes—doubtful of the reality of the moon that shines above him. He is presently reassured on these subjects, by the unchallengeable reality of Mrs. Snagsby, sitting up with her head in a perfect beehive of curl-papers and nightcap: who has despatched Guster to the police-station with official intelligence of her husband's being made away with, and who, within the last two hours, has passed through every stage of swooning with the greatest decorum. But, as the little woman feelingly says, many thanks she gets for it!

Chapter XXIII

ESTHER'S NARRATIVE

We came home from Mr. Boythorn's after six pleasant weeks. We were often in the park, and in the woods, and seldom passed the Lodge where we had taken shelter without looking in to speak to the keeper's wife; but we saw no more of Lady Dedlock, except at church on Sundays. There was company at Chesney Wold; and although several beautiful faces surrounded her, her face retained the same influence on me as at first. I do not quite know, even now, whether it was painful or pleasurable; whether it drew me towards her, or made me shrink from her. I think I admired her with a kind of fear; and I know that in her presence my thoughts always wandered back, as they had done at first, to that old time of my life.

I had a fancy, on more than one of these Sundays, that what this lady so curiously was to me, I was to her—I mean that I disturbed her thoughts as she influenced mine, though in some different way. But when I stole a glance at her, and saw her so composed and distant and unapproachable, I felt this to be a foolish weakness. Indeed, I felt the whole state of my mind in reference to her to be weak and unreasonable; and I remonstrated with myself about it as much as I could.

One incident that occurred before we quitted Mr. Boythorn's house, I had better mention in this place.

I was walking in the garden with Ada, when I was told that some one wished to see me. Going into the breakfast-room, where this person was waiting, I found it to be the French maid who had cast off her shoes and walked through the wet grass, on the day when it thundered and lightened.

"Mademoiselle," she began, looking fixedly at me with her too-eager eyes, though otherwise presenting an agreeable appearance, and speaking neither with boldness nor servility, "I have taken a great liberty in coming here, but you know how to excuse it, being so amiable, mademoiselle."

"No excuse is necessary," I returned, "if you wish to speak to me."

"That is my desire, mademoiselle. A thousand thanks for the permission. I have your leave to speak. Is it not?" she said, in a quick, natural way.

"Certainly," said I.

"Mademoiselle, you are so amiable! Listen, then, if you please. I have left my Lady. We could not agree. My Lady is so high; so very high. Pardon! Mademoiselle, you are right!" Her quickness anticipated what I might have said presently, but as yet had only thought. "It is not for me to come here to complain of my Lady. But I say she is so high, so very high. I will say not a word more. All the world knows that."

"Go on, if you please," said I.

"Assuredly; mademoiselle, I am thankful for your politeness. Mademoiselle, I have an inexpressible desire to find service with a young lady who is good, accomplished, beautiful. You are good, accomplished, and beautiful as an angel. Ah, could I have the honour of being your domestic!"

"I am sorry——" I began.

"Do not dismiss me so soon, mademoiselle!" she said, with an involuntary contraction of her fine black eyebrows. "Let me hope, a moment! Mademoiselle, I know this service would be more retired than that which I have quitted. Well! I wish that. I know this service would be less distinguished than that which I have quitted. Well! I wish that. I know that I should win less, as to wages, here. Good. I am content."

"I assure you," said I, quite embarrassed by the mere idea of having such an attendant, "that I keep no maid——"

"Ah, mademoiselle, but why not? Why not, when you can have one so devoted to you! Who would be enchanted to serve you; who would be so true, so zealous, and so faithful, every day! Mademoiselle, I wish with all my heart to serve you. Do not speak of money at present. Take me as I am. For nothing!"

She was so singularly earnest that I drew back, almost afraid of her. Without appearing to notice it, in her ardour she still pressed herself upon me; speaking in a rapid subdued voice, though always with a certain grace and propriety.

"Mademoiselle, I come from the South country, where we are quick, and where we like and dislike very strong. My Lady was too high for me; I was too high for her. It is done—past—finished! Receive me as your domestic, and I will serve you well. I will do more for you, than you figure to yourself now. Chut! mademoiselle, I will—no matter, I will do my utmost possible, in all things. If you accept my service, you will not repent it. Mademoiselle, you will not repent it, and I will serve you well. You don't know how well!"

There was a lowering energy in her face, as she stood looking at me while I explained the impossibility of my engaging her (without thinking it necessary to say how very little I desired to do so), which seemed to bring visibly before me some woman from the streets of Paris in the reign of terror. She heard me out without interruption; and then said, with her pretty accent, and in her mildest voice;

"Hey, mademoiselle, I have received my answer! I am sorry of it. But I must go elsewhere, and seek what I have not found here. Will you graciously let me kiss your hand?"

She looked at me more intently as she took it, and seemed to take note, with her momentary touch, of every vein in it. "I fear I surprised you, mademoiselle, on the day of the storm?" she said, with a parting curtsey.

I confessed that she had surprised us all.

"I took an oath, mademoiselle," she said, smiling, "and I wanted to stamp it on my mind, so that I might keep it faithfully. And I will! Adieu, mademoiselle!"

So ended our conference, which I was very glad to bring to a close. I supposed she went away from the village, for I saw her no more; and nothing else occurred to disturb our tranquil summer pleasures, until six weeks were out, and we returned home as I began just now by saying.

At that time, and for a good many weeks after that time, Richard was constant in his visits. Besides coming every Saturday or Sunday, and remaining with us until Monday morning, he sometimes rode out on horseback unexpectedly, and passed the evening with us, and rode back again early next day. He was as vivacious as ever, and told us he was very industrious; but I was not easy in my mind about him. It appeared to me that his industry was all misdirected. I could not find that it led to anything but the formation of delusive hopes in connexion with the suit already the pernicious cause of so much sorrow and ruin. He had got at the core of that mystery now, he told us; and nothing could be plainer than that the will under which he and Ada were to take, I don't know how many thousands of pounds, must be finally established, if there were any sense or justice in the Court of Chancery—but O what a great *if* that sounded in my ears—and that this happy conclusion could not be much longer delayed. He proved this to himself by all the weary arguments on that side he had read, and every one of them sunk him deeper in the infatuation. He had even begun to haunt the Court. He told us how he saw Miss Flite there daily; how they talked together, and how he did her little kindnesses; and how, while he laughed at her, he pitied her from his heart. But he never thought—never, my poor, dear, sanguine Richard, capable of so much happiness then, and with such better things before him!—what a fatal link was riveting between his fresh youth and her faded age; between his free hopes and her caged birds, and her hungry garret, and her wandering mind.

Ada loved him too well, to mistrust him much in anything he said or did, and my guardian, though he frequently complained of the east wind and read more than usual in the Growlery, preserved a strict silence on the subject. So I thought, one day when I went to London to meet Caddy Jellyby, at her solicitation, I would ask Richard to be in waiting for me at the coach-office, that we might have a little talk together. I found him there when I arrived, and we walked away arm in arm.

"Well, Richard," said I, as soon as I could begin to be grave with him, "are you beginning to feel more settled now?"

"O yes, my dear!" returned Richard. "I am all right enough."

"But settled?" said I.

"How do you mean, settled?" returned Richard, with his gay laugh.

"Settled in the law," said I.

"O aye," replied Richard, "I'm all right enough."

"You said that before, my dear Richard."

"And you don't think it's an answer, eh? Well! Perhaps it's not. Settled? You mean, do I feel as if I were settling down?"

"Yes."

"Why, no, I can't say I am settling down," said Richard, strongly emphasising "down," as if that expressed the difficulty; "because one can't settle down while this business remains in such an unsettled state. When I say this business, of course I mean the—forbidden subject."

"Do you think it will ever be in a settled state?" said I.

"Not the least doubt of it," answered Richard.

We walked a little way without speaking; and presently Richard addressed me in his frankest and most feeling manner, thus:

"My dear Esther, I understand you, and I wish to Heaven I were a more constant sort of fellow. I don't mean constant to Ada, for I love her dearly—better and better every day—but constant to myself. (Somehow, I mean something that I can't very well express, but you'll make it out.) If I were a more constant sort of fellow, I should have held on, either to Badger, or to Kenge and Carboy, like grim Death; and should have begun to be steady and systematic by this time, and shouldn't be in debt, and——"

"*Are* you in debt, Richard?"

"Yes," said Richard, "I am a little so, my dear. Also, I have taken rather too much to billiards, and that sort of thing. Now the murder's out; you despise me, Esther, don't you?"

"You know I don't," said I.

"You are kinder to me than I often am to myself," he returned. "My dear Esther, I am a very unfortunate dog not to be more settled, but how *can* I be more settled? If you lived in an unfinished house, you couldn't settle down in it; if you were condemned to leave everything you undertook, unfinished, you would find it hard to apply yourself to anything; and yet that's my unhappy case. I was born into this unfinished contention with all its chances and changes, and it began to unsettle me before I quite knew the difference between a suit at law and a suit of clothes; and it has gone on unsettling me every since; and here I am now, conscious sometimes that I am but a worthless fellow to love my confiding cousin Ada."

We were in a solitary place, and he put his hands before his eyes and sobbed as he said the words.

"O Richard!" said I, "do not be so moved. You have a noble nature, and Ada's love may make you worthier every day."

"I know, my dear," he replied, pressing my arm, "I know all that. You mustn't mind my being a little soft now, for I have had all this upon my mind for a long time; and have often meant to speak to you, and have sometimes wanted opportunity and sometimes courage. I know what the thought of Ada ought to do for me, but it doesn't do it. I am too unsettled even for that. I love her most devotedly; and yet I do her wrong, in doing myself wrong, every day and hour. But it can't last for ever. We shall come on for a final hearing, and get judgment in our favour; and then you and Ada shall see what I can really be!"

It had given me a pang to hear him sob, and see the tears start out between his fingers; but that was infinitely less affecting to me than the hopeful animation with which he said these words.

"I have looked well into the papers, Esther—I have been deep in them for months"—he continued, recovering his cheerfulness in a moment, "and you may rely upon it that we shall come out triumphant. As to years of delay, there has been no want of them, Heaven knows! and there is the greater probability of our bringing the matter to a speedy close; in fact, it's on the paper[1] now. It will be all right at last, and then you shall see!"

Recalling how he had just now placed Messrs. Kenge and Carboy

1. I.e., it is among cases slated to be considered by the Lord Chancellor on the day assigned.

in the same category with Mr. Badger, I asked him when he intended to be articled in Lincoln's Inn?

"There again! I think not at all, Esther," he returned with an effort. "I fancy I have had enough of it. Having worked at Jarndyce and Jarndyce like a galley slave, I have slaked my thirst for the law, and satisfied myself that I shouldn't like it. Besides, I find it unsettles me more and more to be so constantly upon the scene of action. So what," continued Richard, confident again by this time, "do I naturally turn my thoughts to?"

"I can't imagine," said I.

"Don't look so serious," returned Richard, "because it's the best thing I can do, my dear Esther, I am certain. It's not as if I wanted a profession for life. These proceedings will come to a termination, and then I am provided for. No. I look upon it as a pursuit which is in its nature more or less unsettled, and therefore suited to my temporary condition—I may say, precisely suited. What is it that I naturally turn my thoughts to?"

I looked at him, and shook my head.

"What," said Richard, in a tone of perfect conviction, "but the army!"

"The army?" said I.

"The army, of course. What I have to do, is, to get a commission; and—there I am, you know!" said Richard.

And then he showed me, proved by elaborate calculations in his pocket-book, that supposing he had contracted, say two hundred pounds of debt in six months, out of the army; and that he contracted no debt at all within a corresponding period, in the army—as to which he had quite made up his mind; this step must involve a saving of four hundred pounds in a year, or two thousand pounds in five years—which was a considerable sum. And then he spoke so ingenuously and sincerely, of the sacrifice he made in withdrawing himself for a time from Ada, and of the earnestness with which he aspired—as in thought he always did, I know full well—to repay her love, and to ensure her happiness, and to conquer what was amiss in himself, and to acquire the very soul of decision, that he made my heart ache keenly, sorely. For I thought how would this end, how could this end, when so soon and so surely all his manly qualities were touched by the fatal blight that ruined everything it rested on!

I spoke to Richard with all the earnestness I felt, and all the hope I could not quite feel then; and implored him, for Ada's sake, not to put any trust in Chancery. To all I said, Richard readily assented; riding over the Court and everything else in his easy way, and drawing the brightest pictures of the character he was to settle into—alas, when the grievous suit should loose its hold upon him!

We had a long talk, but it always came back to that, in substance.

At last, we came to Soho Square, where Caddy Jellyby had appointed to wait for me, at a quiet place in the neighbourhood of Newman Street. Caddy was in the garden in the centre, and hurried out as soon as I appeared. After a few cheerful words, Richard left us together.

"Prince has a pupil over the way, Esther," said Caddy, "and got the key[2] for us. So if you will walk round and round here with me, we can lock ourselves in, and I can tell you comfortably what I wanted to see your dear good face about."

"Very well, my dear," said I. "Nothing could be better." So Caddy, after affectionately squeezing the dear good face as she called it, locked the gate, and took my arm, and we began to walk round the garden very cosily.

"You see, Esther," said Caddy, who thoroughly enjoyed a little confidence, "after you spoke to me about its being wrong to marry without Ma's knowledge, or even to keep Ma long in the dark respecting our engagement—though I don't believe Ma cares much for me, I must say—I thought it right to mention your opinions to Prince. In the first place, because I want to profit by everything you tell me; and in the second place, because I have no secrets from Prince."

"I hope he approved, Caddy?"

"O, my dear! I assure you he would approve of anything you could say. You have no idea what an opinion he has of you!"

"Indeed!"

"Esther, it's enough to make anybody but me jealous," said Caddy, laughing and shaking her head; "but it only makes me joyful, for you are the first friend I ever had, and the best friend I ever can have, and nobody can respect and love you too much to please me."

"Upon my word, Caddy," said I, "you are in the general conspiracy to keep me in a good humour. Well, my dear?"

"Well! I am going to tell you," replied Caddy, crossing her hands confidentially upon my arm. "So we talked a good deal about it, and so I said to Prince, 'Prince, as Miss Summerson——' "

"I hope you didn't say 'Miss Summerson'?"

"No. I didn't!" cried Caddy, greatly pleased, and with the brightest of faces. "I said, 'Esther.' I said to Prince, 'As Esther is decidedly of that opinion, Prince, and has expressed it to me, and always hints it when she writes those kind notes, which you are so fond of hearing me read to you, I am prepared to disclose the truth to Ma whenever you think proper. And I think, Prince,' said I, 'that

2. Keys provided for residents in the vicinity to allow exclusive access to the garden in the center of the Square. The garden was fenced and had locked gates.

Esther thinks that I should be in a better, and truer, and more honourable position altogether, if you did the same to your Papa.'"

"Yes, my dear," said I, "Esther certainly does think so."

"So I was right, you see!" exclaimed Caddy. "Well! this troubled Prince a good deal; not because he had the least doubt about it, but because he is so considerate of the feelings of old Mr. Turveydrop; and he had his apprehensions that old Mr. Turveydrop might break his heart, or faint away, or be very much overcome in some affecting manner or other, if he made such an announcement. He feared old Mr. Turveydrop might consider it undutiful, and might receive too great a shock. For old Mr. Turveydrop's deportment is very beautiful you know, Esther," said Caddy; "and his feelings are extremely sensitive."

"Are they, my dear?"

"O, extremely sensitive. Prince says so. Now, this has caused my darling child—I didn't mean to use the expression to you, Esther," Caddy apologised, her face suffused with blushes, "but I generally call Prince my darling child."

I laughed; and Caddy laughed and blushed, and went on.

"This has caused him, Esther——"

"Caused whom, my dear?"

"O, you tiresome thing!" said Caddy, laughing, with her pretty face on fire. "My darling child, if you insist upon it!—This has caused him weeks of uneasiness, and has made him delay, from day to day, in a very anxious manner. At last he said to me, 'Caddy, if Miss Summerson, who is a great favourite with my father, could be prevailed upon to be present when I broke the subject, I think I could do it.' So I promised I would ask you. And I made up my mind, besides," said Caddy, looking at me hopefully, but timidly, "that if you consented, I would ask you afterwards to come with me to Ma. This is what I meant, when I said in my note that I had a great favour and a great assistance to beg of you. And if you thought you could grant it, Esther, we should both be very grateful."

"Let me see, Caddy," said I, pretending to consider. "Really, I think I could do a greater thing than that, if the need were pressing. I am at your service and the darling child's, my dear, whenever you like."

Caddy was quite transported by this reply of mine; being, I believe, as susceptible to the least kindness or encouragement as any tender heart that ever beat in this world; and after another turn or two round the garden, during which she put on an entirely new pair of gloves, and made herself as resplendent as possible that she might do no avoidable discredit to the Master of Deportment, we went to Newman Street direct.

Prince was teaching, of course. We found him engaged with a not very hopeful pupil—a stubborn little girl with a sulky forehead, a deep voice, and an inanimate dissatisfied mamma—whose case was certainly not rendered more hopeful by the confusion into which we threw her preceptor. The lesson at last came to an end, after proceeding as discordantly as possible; and when the little girl had changed her shoes, and had had her white muslin extinguished in shawls, she was taken away. After a few words of preparation, we then went in search of Mr. Turveydrop; whom we found, grouped with his hat and gloves, as a model of Deportment, on the sofa in his private apartment—the only comfortable room in the house. He appeared to have dressed at his leisure, in the intervals of a light collation; and his dressing-case, brushes, and so forth, all of quite an elegant kind, lay about.

"Father, Miss Summerson; Miss Jellyby.",

"Charmed! Enchanted!" said Mr. Turveydrop, rising with his high-shouldered bow. "Permit me!" handing chairs. "Be seated!" kissing the tips of his left fingers. "Overjoyed!" shutting his eyes and rolling. "My little retreat is made a Paradise." Re-composing himself on the sofa, like the second gentleman in Europe.[3]

"Again you find us, Miss Summerson," said he, "using our little arts to polish, polish! Again the sex stimulates us, and rewards us, by the condescension of its lovely presence. It is much in these times (and we have made an awfully degenerating business of it since the days of His Royal Highness the Prince Regent—my patron, if I may presume to say so) to experience that Deportment is not wholly trodden under foot by mechanics. That it can bask in the smile of Beauty, my dear madam."

I said nothing, which I thought a suitable reply; and he took a pinch of snuff.

"My dear son," said Mr. Turveydrop, "you have four schools this afternoon. I would recommend a hasty sandwich."

"Thank you, father," returned Prince, "I will be sure to be punctual. My dear father, may I beg you to prepare your mind for what I am going to say!"

"Good Heaven!" exclaimed the model, pale and aghast, as Prince and Caddy, hand in hand, bent down before him. "What is this? Is this lunacy! Or what is this?"

"Father," returned Prince, with great submission, "I love this young lady, and we are engaged."

"Engaged!" cried Mr. Turveydrop, reclining on the sofa, and shutting out the sight with his hand. "An arrow launched at my brain, by my own child!"

3. The Prince Regent, Turveydrop's "illustrious model" (later George IV, 1820–30), was known as "the first gentleman in Europe."

"We have been engaged for some time, father," faltered Prince; "and Miss Summerson, hearing of it, advised that we should declare the fact to you, and was so very kind as to attend on the present occasion. Miss Jellyby is a young lady who deeply respects you, father."

Mr. Turveydrop uttered a groan.

"No, pray don't! Pray don't, father," urged his son. "Miss Jellyby is a young lady who deeply respects you, and our first desire is to consider your comfort."

Mr. Turveydrop sobbed.

"No pray don't, father!" cried his son.

"Boy," said Mr. Turveydrop, "it is well that your sainted mother is spared this pang. Strike deep, and spare not.[4] Strike home, sir, strike home!"

"Pray, don't say so, father," implored Prince, in tears. "It goes to my heart. I do assure you, father, that our first wish and intention is to consider your comfort. Caroline and I do not forget our duty—what is my duty is Caroline's, as we have often said together—and, with your approval and consent, father, we will devote ourselves to making your life agreeable."

"Strike home," murmured Mr. Turveydrop. "Strike home!"

But he seemed to listen, I thought, too.

"My dear father," returned Prince, "we well know what little comforts you are accustomed to, and have a right to; and it will always be our study, and our pride, to provide those before anything. If you will bless us with your approval and consent, father, we shall not think of being married until it is quite agreeable to you; and when we *are* married, we shall always make you—of course—our first consideration. You must ever be the Head and Master here, father; and we feel how truly unnatural it would be in us, if we failed to know it, or if we failed to exert ourselves in every possible way to please you."

Mr. Turveydrop underwent a severe internal struggle, and came upright on the sofa again, with his cheeks puffing over his stiff cravat: a perfect model of parental deportment.

"My son!" said Mr. Turveydrop. "My children! I cannot resist your prayer. Be happy!"

His benignity, as he raised his future daughter-in-law and stretched out his hand to his son (who kissed it with affectionate respect and gratitude), was the most confusing sight I ever saw.

"My children," said Mr. Turveydrop, paternally encircling Caddy with his left arm as she sat beside him, and putting his right hand gracefully on his hip. "My son and daughter, your happiness shall

4. See God's words to Saul, I Samuel 15:3: "Smite Amalek . . . and spare them not."

be my care. I will watch over you. You shall always live with me"; meaning, of course, I will always live with you; "this house is henceforth as much yours as mine; consider it your home. May you long live to share it with me!"

The power of his Deportment was such, that they really were as much overcome with thankfulness as if, instead of quartering himself upon them for the rest of his life, he were making some munificent sacrifice in their favour.

"For myself, my children," said Mr. Turveydrop, "I am falling into the sear and yellow leaf,[5] and it is impossible to say how long the last feeble traces of gentlemanly Deportment may linger in this weaving and spinning age. But, so long, I will do my duty to society, and will show myself, as usual, about town. My wants are few and simple. My little apartment here, my few essentials for the toilet, my frugal morning meal, and my little dinner, will suffice. I charge your dutiful affection with the supply of these requirements, and I charge myself with all the rest."

They were overpowered afresh by his uncommon generosity.

"My son," said Mr. Turveydrop, "for those little points in which you are deficient—points of Deportment which are born with a man—which may be improved by cultivation, but can never be originated—you may still rely on me. I have been faithful to my post, since the days of His Royal Highness the Prince Regent; and I will not desert it now. No, my son. If you have ever contemplated your father's poor position with a feeling of pride, you may rest assured that he will do nothing to tarnish it. For yourself, Prince, whose character is different (we cannot be all alike, nor is it advisable that we should), work, be industrious, earn money, and extend the connexion as much as possible."

"That you may depend I will do, dear father, with all my heart," replied Prince.

"I have no doubt of it," said Mr. Turveydrop. "Your qualities are not shining, my dear child, but they are steady and useful. And to both of you, my dear children, I would merely observe, in the spirit of a sainted Wooman on whose path I had the happiness of casting, I believe, *some* ray of light,—take care of the establishment, take care of my simple wants, and bless you both!"

Old Mr. Turveydrop then became so very gallant, in honour of the occasion, that I told Caddy we must really go to Thavies Inn at once if we were to go at all that day. So we took our departure, after a very loving farewell between Caddy and her betrothed: and during our walk she was so happy, and so full of old Mr. Turveydrop's praises, that I would not have said a word in his disparagement for any consideration.

5. See *Macbeth* (V.iii.23).

The house in Thavies Inn had bills in the windows announcing that it was to let, and it looked dirtier and gloomier and ghastlier than ever. The name of poor Mr. Jellyby had appeared in the list of Bankrupts, but a day or two before; and he was shut up in the dining-room with two gentlemen, and a heap of blue bags, account-books, and papers, making the most desperate endeavours to understand his affairs. They appeared to me to be quite beyond his comprehension; for when Caddy took me into the dining-room by mistake, and we came upon Mr. Jellyby in his spectacles, forlornly fenced into a corner by the great dining-table and the two gentlemen, he seemed to have given up the whole thing, and to be speechless and insensible.

Going up-stairs to Mrs. Jellyby's room (the children were all screaming in the kitchen, and there was no servant to be seen), we found that lady in the midst of a voluminous correspondence, opening, reading, and sorting letters, with a great accumulation of torn covers on the floor. She was so preoccupied that at first she did not know me, though she sat looking at me with that curious, bright-eyed, far-off look of hers.

"Ah! Miss Summerson!" she said at last. "I was thinking of something so different! I hope you are well. I am happy to see you. Mr. Jarndyce and Miss Clare quite well?"

I hoped in return that Mr. Jellyby was quite well.

"Why, not quite, my dear," said Mrs. Jellyby, in the calmest manner. "He has been unfortunate in his affairs, and is a little out of spirits. Happily for me, I am so much engaged that I have no time to think about it. We have, at the present moment, one hundred and seventy families, Miss Summerson, averaging five persons in each, either gone or going to the left bank of the Niger."

I thought of the one family so near us, who were neither gone nor going to the left bank of the Niger, and wondered how she could be so placid.

"You have brought Caddy back, I see," observed Mrs. Jellyby, with a glance at her daughter. "It has become quite a novelty to see her here. She has almost deserted her old employment and in fact obliges me to employ a boy."

"I am sure, Ma—" began Caddy.

"Now you know, Caddy," her mother mildly interposed, "that I *do* employ a boy, who is now at his dinner. What is the use of your contradicting?"

"I was not going to contradict, Ma," returned Caddy. "I was only going to say, that surely you wouldn't have me be a mere drudge all my life?"

"I believe, my dear," said Mrs. Jellyby, still opening her letters, casting her bright eyes smilingly over them, and sorting them as she spoke, "that you have a business example before you in your mother. Besides. A mere drudge? If you had any sympathy with the destinies of the human race, it would raise you high above any such idea. But you have none. I have often told you, Caddy, you have no such sympathy."

"Not if it's Africa, Ma, I have not."

"Of course you have not. Now, if I were not happily so much engaged, Miss Summerson," said Mrs. Jellyby, sweetly casting her eyes for a moment on me, and considering where to put the particular letter she had just opened, "this would distress and disappoint me. But I have so much to think of, in connexion with Borrioboola-Gha, and it is so necessary I should concentrate myself, that there is my remedy, you see."

As Caddy gave me a glance of entreaty, and as Mrs. Jellyby was looking far away into Africa straight through my bonnet and head, I thought it a good opportunity to come to the subject of my visit, and to attract Mrs. Jellyby's attention.

"Perhaps," I began, "you will wonder what has brought me here to interrupt you."

"I am always delighted to see Miss Summerson," said Mrs. Jellyby, pursuing her employment with a placid smile. "Though I wish," and she shook her head, "she was more interested in the Borrioboolan project."

"I have come with Caddy," said I, "because Caddy justly thinks she ought not to have a secret from her mother; and fancies I shall encourage and aid her (though I am sure I don't know how), in imparting one."

"Caddy," said Mrs. Jellyby, pausing for a moment in her occupation, and then serenely pursuing it after shaking her head "you are going to tell me some nonsense."

Caddy untied the strings of her bonnet, took her bonnet off, and letting it dangle on the floor by the strings, and crying heartily, said, "Ma, I am engaged."

"O, you ridiculous child!" observed Mrs. Jellyby, with an abstracted air, as she looked over the dispatch last opened; "what a goose you are!"

"I am engaged, Ma," sobbed Caddy, "to young Mr. Turveydrop, at the Academy; and old Mr. Turveydrop (who is a very gentlemanly man indeed) has given his consent, and I beg and pray you'll give us yours, Ma, because I never could be happy without it. I never, never could!" sobbed Caddy, quite forgetful of her general complainings, and of everything but her natural affection.

"You see again, Miss Summerson," observed Mrs. Jellyby, serenely, "what a happiness it is to be so much occupied as I am, and to have this necessity for self-concentration that I have. Here is Caddy engaged to a dancing-master's son—mixed up with people who have no more sympathy with the destinies of the human race than she has herself! This, too, when Mr. Quale, one of the first philanthropists of our time, has mentioned to me that he was really disposed to be interested in her!"

"Ma, I always hated and detested Mr. Quale!" sobbed Caddy.

"Caddy, Caddy!" returned Mrs. Jellyby, opening another letter with the greatest complacency. "I have no doubt you did. How could you do otherwise, being totally destitute of the sympathies with which he overflows! Now, if my public duties were not a favourite child to me, if I were not occupied with large measures on a vast scale, these petty details might grieve me very much, Miss Summerson. But can I permit the film of a silly proceeding on the part of Caddy (from whom I expect nothing else), to interpose between me and the great African continent? No. No," repeated Mrs. Jellyby, in a calm clear voice, and with an agreeable smile, as she opened more letters and sorted them. "No, indeed."

I was so unprepared for the perfect coolness of this reception, though I might have expected it, that I did not know what to say. Caddy seemed equally at a loss. Mrs. Jellyby continued to open and sort letters; and to repeat occasionally, in quite a charming tone of voice, and with a smile of perfect composure, "No, indeed."

"I hope, Ma," sobbed poor Caddy at last, "you are not angry?"

"O Caddy, you really are an absurd girl," returned Mrs. Jellyby, "to ask such questions, after what I have said of the preoccupation of my mind."

"And I hope, Ma, you give us your consent, and wish us well?" said Caddy.

"You are a nonsensical child to have done anything of this kind," said Mrs. Jellyby; "and a degenerate child, when you might have devoted yourself to the great public measure. But the step is taken, and I have engaged a boy, and there is no more to be said. Now, pray, Caddy," said Mrs. Jellyby—for Caddy was kissing her—"don't delay me in my work, but let me clear off this heavy batch of papers before the afternoon post comes in!"

I thought I could not do better than take my leave; I was detained for a moment by Caddy's saying,

"You won't object to my bringing him to see you, Ma?"

"O dear me, Caddy," cried Mrs. Jellyby, who had relapsed into that distant contemplation, "have you begun again? Bring whom?"

"Him, Ma."

"Caddy, Caddy!" said Mrs. Jellyby, quite weary of such little matters. "Then you must bring him some evening which is not a Parent Society night, or a Branch night, or a Ramification night. You must accommodate the visit to the demands upon my time.

My dear Miss Summerson, it was very kind of you to come here to help out this silly chit. Good-bye! When I tell you that I have fifty-eight new letters from manufacturing families anxious to understand the details of the Native and Coffee Cultivation question, this morning, I need not apologize for having very little leisure."

I was not surprised by Caddy's being in low spirits, when we went down-stairs; or by her sobbing afresh on my neck, or by her saying she would far rather have been scolded than treated with such indifference, or by her confiding to me that she was so poor in clothes, that how she was ever to be married creditably she didn't know. I gradually cheered her up, by dwelling on the many things she would do for her unfortunate father, and for Peepy, when she had a home of her own; and finally we went down-stairs into the damp dark kitchen, where Peepy and his little brothers and sisters were grovelling on the stone floor, and where we had such a game of play with them, that to prevent myself from being quite torn to pieces I was obliged to fall back on my fairy tales. From time to time, I heard loud voices in the parlour overhead; and occasionally a violent tumbling about of the furniture. The last effect I am afraid was caused by poor Mr. Jellyby's breaking away from the dining-table, and making rushes at the window, with the intention of throwing himself into the area, whenever he made any new attempt to understand his affairs.

As I rode quietly home at night after the day's bustle, I thought a good deal of Caddy's engagement, and felt confirmed in my hopes (in spite of the elder Mr. Turveydrop) that she would be the happier and better for it. And if there seemed to be but a slender chance of her and her husband ever finding out what the model of Deportment really was, why that was all for the best too, and who would wish them to be wiser? I did not wish them to be any wiser, and indeed was half ashamed of not entirely believing in him myself. And I looked up at the stars, and thought about travellers in distant countries and the stars *they* saw, and hoped I might always be so blest and happy as to be useful to some one in my small way.

They were so glad to see me when I got home, as they always were, that I could have sat down and cried for joy, if that had not been a method of making myself disagreeable. Everybody in the house, from the lowest to the highest, showed me such a bright face of welcome, and spoke so cheerily, and was so happy to do anything for me, that I suppose there never was such a fortunate little creature in the world.

We got into such a chatty state that night, through Ada and my guardian drawing me out to tell them all about Caddy, that I went on prose, prose, prosing, for a length of time. At last I got up to my room, quite red to think how I had been holding forth; and then I heard a soft tap at my door. So I said, "Come in!" and there came in a pretty little girl, neatly dressed in mourning, who dropped a curtsey.

"If you please, miss," said the little girl, in a soft voice, "I am Charley."

"Why, so you are," said I, stooping down in astonishment, and giving her a kiss. "How glad I am to see you, Charley!"

"If you please, miss," pursued Charley, in the same soft voice, "I'm your maid."

"Charley?"

"If you please, miss, I'm a present to you, with Mr. Jarndyce's love."

I sat down with my hand on Charley's neck, and looked at Charley.

"And O, miss," says Charley, clapping her hands, with the tears starting down her dimpled cheeks, "Tom's at school, if you please, and learning so good! And little Emma, she's with Mrs. Blinder, miss, a being took such care of! And Tom, he would have been at school—and Emma, she would have been left with Mrs. Blinder—and me, I should have been here—all a deal sooner, miss; only Mr. Jarndyce thought that Tom and Emma and me had better get a little used to parting first, we was so small. Don't cry, if you please, miss!"

"I can't help it, Charley."

"No, miss, nor I can't help it," says Charley. "And if you please, miss, Mr. Jarndyce's love, and he thinks you'll like to teach me now and then. And if you please, Tom and Emma and me is to see each other once a month. And I'm so happy and so thankful, miss," cried Charley, with a heaving heart, "and I'll try to be such a good maid!"

"O Charley dear, never forget who did all this!"

"No, miss, I never will. Nor Tom won't. Nor yet Emma. It was all you, miss."

"I have known nothing of it. It was Mr. Jarndyce, Charley."

"Yes, miss, but it was all done for the love of you, and that you might be my mistress. If you please, miss, I am a little present with his love, and it was all done for the love of you. Me and Tom was to be sure to remember it."

Charley dried her eyes, and entered on her functions: going in her matronly little way about and about the room, and folding up everything she could lay her hands upon. Presently, Charley came creeping back to my side, and said:

"O, don't cry, if you please, miss."

And I said again, "I can't help it, Charley."

And Charley said again, "No, miss, nor I can't help it." And so, after all, I did cry for joy indeed, and so did she.

Chapter XXIV

AN APPEAL CASE

As soon as Richard and I had held the conversation of which I have given an account, Richard communicated the state of his mind to Mr. Jarndyce. I doubt if my guardian were altogether taken by surprise, when he received the representation; though it caused him much uneasiness and disappointment. He and Richard were often closeted together, late at night and early in the morning, and passed whole days in London, and had innumerable appointments with Mr. Kenge, and laboured through a quantity of disagreeable business. While they were thus employed, my guardian, though he underwent considerable inconvenience from the state of the wind, and rubbed his head so constantly that not a single hair upon it ever rested in its right place, was as genial with Ada and me as at any other time, but maintained a steady reserve on these matters. And as our utmost endeavours could only elicit from Richard himself sweeping assurances that everything was going on capitally, and that it really was all right at last, our anxiety was not much relieved by him.

We learnt, however, as the time went on, that a new application was made to the Lord Chancellor on Richard's behalf, as an Infant and a Ward, and I don't know what; and that there was a quantity of talking; and that the Lord Chancellor described him, in open court, as a vexatious and capricious infant; and that the matter was adjourned and readjourned, and referred, and reported on, and petitioned about, until Richard began to doubt (as he told us) whether, if he entered the army at all, it would not be as veteran of seventy or eighty years of age. At last an appointment was made for him to see the Lord Chancellor again in his private room, and there the Lord Chancellor very seriously reproved him for trifling with time, and not knowing his mind—"a pretty good joke, I think," said Richard, "from that quarter!"— and at last it was settled that his application should be granted. His name was entered at the Horse Guards, as an applicant for an Ensign's commission; the purchase-money[1] was deposited at an Agent's; and Richard, in his usual characteristic way, plunged into a violent course of military study, and got up at five o'clock every morning to practise the broadsword exercise.

Thus vacation succeeded term, and term succeeded vacation. We sometimes heard of Jarndyce and Jarndyce, as being in the paper or out of the paper, or as being to be mentioned, or as being to be

1. Money to pay for a commission in the army. Such transactions of buying and selling were done away with in 1871.

spoken to; and it came on, and it went off. Richard, who was now in a Professor's house in London, was able to be with us less frequently than before; my guardian still maintained the same reserve; and so time passed until the commission was obtained, and Richard received directions with it to join a regiment in Ireland.

He arrived post-haste with the intelligence one evening, and had a long conference with my guardian. Upwards of an hour elapsed before my guardian put his head into the room where Ada and I were sitting, and said, "Come in, my dears!" We went in, and found Richard, whom we had last seen in high spirits, leaning on the chimney-piece, looking mortified and angry.

"Rick and I, Ada," said Mr. Jarndyce, "are not quite of one mind. Come, come, Rick, put a brighter face upon it!"

"You are very hard with me, sir," said Richard. "The harder, because you have been so considerate to me in all other respects, and have done me kindnesses that I can never acknowledge. I never could have been set right without you, sir."

"Well, well!" said Mr. Jarndyce, "I want to set you more right yet. I want to set you more right with yourself."

"I hope you will excuse my saying, sir," returned Richard in a fiery way, but yet respectfully, "that I think I am the best judge about myself."

"I hope you will excuse my saying, my dear Rick," observed Mr. Jarndyce with the sweetest cheerfulness and good humour, "that it's quite natural in you to think so, but I don't think so. I must do my duty, Rick, or you could never care for me in cool blood; and I hope you will always care for me, cool and hot."

Ada had turned so pale, that he made her sit down in his reading-chair, and sat beside her.

"It's nothing, my dear," he said, "it's nothing. Rick and I have only had a friendly difference, which we must state to you, for you are the theme. Now you are afraid of what's coming."

"I am not indeed, cousin John," replied Ada, with a smile, "if it is to come from you."

"Thank you, my dear. Do you give me a minute's calm attention, without looking at Rick. And, little woman, do you likewise. My dear girl," putting his hands on hers, as it lay on the side of the easy-chair, "you recollect the talk we had, we four, when the little woman told me of a little love affair?"

"It is not likely that either Richard or I can ever forget your kindness, that day, cousin John."

"I can never forget it," said Richard.

"And I can never forget it," said Ada.

"So much the easier what I have to say, and so much the easier for us to agree," returned my guardian, his face irradiated by the gentleness and honour of his heart. "Ada, my bird, you should know that Rick has now chosen his profession for the last time. All that he has of certainty will be expended when he is fully equipped. He has exhausted his resources, and is bound henceforward to the tree he has planted."

"Quite true that I have exhausted my present resources, and I am quite content to know it. But what I have of certainty, sir," said Richard, "is not all I have."

"Rick, Rick!" cried my guardian, with a sudden terror in his manner, and in an altered voice, and putting up his hands as if he would have stopped his ears, "for the love of God, don't found a hope or expectation on the family curse! Whatever you do on this side the grave, never give one lingering glance towards the horrible phantom that has haunted us so many years. Better to borrow, better to beg, better to die!"

We were all startled by the fervour of this warning. Richard bit his lip and held his breath, and glanced at me, as if he felt, and knew that I felt too, how much he needed it.

"Ada, my dear," said Mr. Jarndyce, recovering his cheerfulness, "these are strong words of advice; but I live in Bleak House, and have seen a sight here. Enough of that. All Richard had, to start him in the race of life, is ventured. I recommend to him and you, for his sake and your own, that he should depart from us with the understanding that there is no sort of contract between you. I must go further. I will be plain with you both. You were to confide freely in me, and I will confide freely in you. I ask you wholly to relinquish, for the present, any tie but your relationship."

"Better to say at once, sir," returned Richard, "that you renounce all confidence in me, and that you advise Ada to do the same."

"Better to say nothing of the sort, Rick, because I don't mean it."

"You think I have begun ill, sir," retorted Richard. "I *have*, I know."

"How I hoped you would begin, and how go on, I told you when we spoke of these things last," said Mr. Jarndyce, in a cordial and encouraging manner. "You have not made that beginning yet; but there is a time for all things, and yours is not gone by—rather, it is just now fully come. Make a clear beginning altogether. You two (very young, my dears) are cousins. As yet, you are nothing more. What more may come, must come of being worked out, Rick; and no sooner."

"You are very hard with me, sir," said Richard. "Harder than I could have supposed you would be."

"My dear boy," said Mr. Jarndyce, "I am harder with myself when I do anything that gives you pain. You have your remedy in your own hands. Ada, it is better for him that he should be free, and that there should be no youthful engagement between you. Rick, it is better for her, much better; you owe it to her. Come! Each of you will do what is best for the other, if not what is best for yourselves."

"Why is it best, sir?" returned Richard, hastily. "It was not, when we opened our hearts to you. You did not say so, then."

"I have had experience since. I don't blame you, Rick—but I have had experience since."

"You mean of me, sir."

"Well! Yes, of both of you," said Mr. Jarndyce, kindly. "The time is not come for your standing pledged to one another. It is not right, and I must not recognize it. Come, come, my young cousins, begin afresh! Bygones shall be bygones, and a new page turned for you to write your lives in."

Richard gave an anxious glance at Ada, but said nothing.

"I have avoided saying one word to either of you, or to Esther," said Mr. Jarndyce, "until now, in order that we might be open as the day, and all on equal terms. I now affectionately advise, I now most earnestly entreat, you two, to part as you came here. Leave all else to time, truth, and steadfastness. If you do otherwise, you will do wrong; and you will have made me do wrong, in ever bringing you together."

A long silence succeeded.

"Cousin Richard," said Ada, then, raising her blue eyes tenderly to his face, "after what our cousin John has said, I think no choice is left us. Your mind may be quite at ease about me; for you will leave me here under his care, and will be sure that I can have nothing to wish for; quite sure, if I guide myself by his advice. I—I don't doubt, cousin Richard," said Ada, a little confused, "that you are very fond of me, and I—I don't think you will fall in love with anybody else. But I should like you to consider well about it, too; as I should like you to be in all things very happy. You may trust in me, cousin Richard. I am not at all changeable; but I am not unreasonable, and should never blame you. Even cousins may be sorry to part; and in truth I am very, very sorry, Richard, though I know it's for your welfare. I shall always think of you affectionately, and often talk of you with Esther, and—and perhaps you will sometimes think a little of me, cousin Richard. So now," said Ada, going up to him and giving him her trembling hand, "we are only cousins again, Richard—for the time perhaps—and I pray for a blessing on my dear cousin, wherever he goes!"

It was strange to me that Richard should not be able to forgive my guardian, for entertaining the very same opinion of him which he himself had expressed of himself in much stronger terms to me.

But, it was certainly the case. I observed, with great regret, that from this hour he never was as free and open with Mr. Jarndyce as he had been before. He had every reason given him to be so, but he was not; and, solely on his side, an estrangement began to arise between them.

In the business of preparation and equipment he soon lost himself, and even his grief at parting from Ada, who remained in Hertfordshire, while he, Mr. Jarndyce, and I went up to London for a week. He remembered her by fits and starts, even with bursts of tears; and at such times would confide to me the heaviest self-reproaches. But in a few minutes he would recklessly conjure up some undefinable means by which they were both to be made rich and happy for ever, and would become as gay as possible.

It was a busy time, and I trotted about with him all day long, buying a variety of things, of which he stood in need. Of the things he would have bought, if he had been left to his own ways, I say nothing. He was perfectly confidential with me, and often talked so sensibly and feelingly about his faults and his vigorous resolutions, and dwelt so much upon the encouragement he derived from these conversations, that I could never have been tired if I had tried.

There used, in that week, to come backward and forward to our lodging, to fence with Richard, a person who had formerly been a cavalry soldier; he was a fine bluff-looking man, of a frank free bearing, with whom Richard had practised for some months. I heard so much about him, not only from Richard, but from my guardian too, that I was purposely in the room, with my work, one morning after breakfast when he came.

"Good morning, Mr. George," said my guardian, who happened to be alone with me. "Mr. Carstone will be here directly. Meanwhile, Miss Summerson is very happy to see you, I know. Sit down."

He sat down, a little disconcerted by my presence, I thought; and, without looking at me, drew his heavy sunburnt hand across and across his upper lip.

"You are as punctual as the sun," said Mr. Jarndyce.

"Military time, sir," he replied. "Force of habit. A mere habit in me, sir. I am not at all business-like."

"Yet you have a large establishment, too, I am told?" said Mr. Jarndyce.

"Not much of a one, sir. I keep a shooting gallery, but not much of a one."

"And what kind of a shot, and what kind of a swordsman, do you make of Mr. Carstone?" said my guardian.

"Pretty good, sir," he replied, folding his arms upon his broad chest, and looking very large. "If Mr. Carstone was to give his full mind to it, he would come out very good."

"But he don't, I suppose?" said my guardian.

"He did at first, sir, but not afterwards. Not his full mind. Perhaps he has something else upon it—some young lady, perhaps." His bright dark eyes glanced at me for the first time.

"He has not me upon his mind, I assure you, Mr. George," said I, laughing, "though you seem to suspect me."

He reddened a little through his brown, and made me a trooper's bow. "No offence, I hope, miss. I am one of the Roughs."

"Not at all," said I. "I take it as a compliment."

If he had not looked at me before, he looked at me now, in three or four quick successive glances. "I beg your pardon, sir," he said to my guardian, with a manly kind of diffidence, "but you did me the honour to mention the young lady's name——"

"Miss Summerson."

"Miss Summerson," he repeated, and looked at me again.

"Do you know the name?" I asked.

"No, miss. To my knowledge, I never heard it. I thought I had seen you somewhere."

"I think not," I returned, raising my head from my work to look at him; and there was something so genuine in his speech and manner that I was glad of the opportunity. "I remember faces very well."

"So do I, miss!" he returned, meeting my look with the fulness of his dark eyes and broad forehead. "Humph! What set me off, now, upon that!"

His once more reddening through his brown, and being disconcerted by his efforts to remember the association, brought my guardian to his relief.

"Have you many pupils, Mr. George?"

"They vary in their number, sir. Mostly, they're but a small lot to live by."

"And what classes of chance people come to practise at your gallery?"

"All sorts, sir. Natives and foreigners. From gentlemen to 'prentices. I have had French women come, before now, and show themselves dabs[2] at pistol-shooting. Mad people out of number, of course—but *they* go everywhere, where the doors stand open."

"People don't come with grudges, and schemes of finishing their practice with live targets, I hope?" said my guardian, smiling.

"Not much of that, sir, though that *has* happened. Mostly they

2. Experts.

come for skill—or idleness. Six of one, and half-a-dozen of the other. I beg your pardon," said Mr. George, sitting stiffly upright, and squaring an elbow on each knee, "but I believe you're a Chancery suitor, if I have heard correct?"

"I am sorry to say I am."

"I have had one of *your* compatriots in my time, sir."

"A Chancery suitor?" returned my guardian. "How was that?"

"Why, the man was so badgered, and worried, and tortured, by being knocked about from post to pillar, and from pillar to post," said Mr. George, "that he got out of sorts. I don't believe he had any idea of taking aim at anybody; but he was in that condition of resentment and violence, that he would come and pay for fifty shots, and fire away till he was red hot. One day I said to him when there was nobody by, and he had been talking to me angrily about his wrongs, 'If this practice is a safety-valve, comrade, well and good; but I don't altogether like your being so bent upon it, in your present state of mind; I'd rather you took to something else.' I was on my guard for a blow, he was that passionate; but he received it in very good part, and left off directly. We shook hands and struck up a sort of a friendship."

"What was that man?" asked my guardian, in a new tone of interest.

"Why, he began by being a small Shropshire farmer, before they made a baited bull of him," said Mr. George.

"Was his name Gridley?"

"It was, sir."

Mr. George directed another succession of quick bright glances at me, as my guardian and I exchanged a word or two of surprise at the coincidence; and I therefore explained to him how we knew the name. He made me another of his soldierly bows, in acknowledgment of what he called my condescension.

"I don't know," he said, as he looked at me, "what it is that sets me off again—but—bosh! what's my head running against!" He passed one of his heavy hands over his crisp dark hair, as if to sweep the broken thoughts out of his mind; and sat a little forward, with one arm akimbo and the other resting on his leg, looking in a brown study at the ground.

"I am sorry to learn that the same state of mind has got this Gridley into new troubles, and that he is in hiding," said my guardian.

"So I am told, sir," returned Mr. George, still musing and looking on the ground. "So I am told."

"You don't know where?"

"No, sir," returned the trooper, lifting up his eyes and coming out of his reverie. "I can't say anything about him. He will be worn out soon, I expect. You may file a strong man's heart away for a good many years, but it will tell all of a sudden at last."

Richard's entrance stopped the conversation. Mr. George rose, made me another of his soldierly bows, wished my guardian a good day, and strode heavily out of the room.

This was the morning of the day appointed for Richard's departure. We had no more purchases to make now; I had completed all his packing early in the afternoon; and our time was disengaged until night, when he was to go to Liverpool for Holyhead. Jarndyce and Jarndyce being again expected to come on that day, Richard proposed to me that we should go down to the Court and hear what passed. As it was his last day, and he was eager to go, and I had never been there, I gave my consent, and we walked down to Westminster, where the Court was then sitting. We beguiled the way with arrangements concerning the letters that Richard was to write to me, and the letters that I was to write to him; and with a great many hopeful projects. My guardian knew where we were going, and therefore was not with us.

When we came to the Court, there was the Lord Chancellor—the same whom I had seen in his private room in Lincoln's Inn—sitting in great state and gravity, on the bench; with the mace and seals on a red table below him, and an immense flat nosegay, like a little garden, which scented the whole Court. Below the table, again, was a long row of solicitors, with bundles of papers on the matting at their feet; and then there were the gentlemen of the bar in wigs and gowns—some awake and some asleep, and one talking, and nobody paying much attention to what he said. The Lord Chancellor leaned back in his very easy chair, with his elbow on the cushioned arm, and his forehead resting on his hand; some of those who were present, dozed; some read the newspapers; some walked about, or whispered in groups: all seemed perfectly at their ease, by no means in a hurry, very unconcerned, and extremely comfortable.

To see everything going on so smoothly, and to think of the roughness of the suitors' lives and deaths; to see all that full dress and ceremony, and to think of the waste, and want, and beggared misery it represented; to consider that, while the sickness of hope deferred[3] was raging in so many hearts, this polite show went calmly on from day to day, and year to year, in such good order and composure; to behold the Lord Chancellor, and the whole array of practitioners under him, looking at one another and at the spectators, as if nobody had ever heard that all over England the name in which they were assembled was a bitter jest: was held in universal horror, contempt, and indignation: was known for something so

3. Cf. Proverbs 13:12.

flagrant and bad, that little short of a miracle could bring any good out of it to any one: this was so curious and self-contradictory to me, who had no experience of it, that it was at first incredible, and I could not comprehend it. I sat where Richard put me, and tried to listen, and looked about me; but there seemed to be no reality in the whole scene, except poor little Miss Flite, the madwoman, standing on a bench, and nodding at it.

Miss Flite soon espied us, and came to where we sat. She gave me a gracious welcome to her domain, and indicated, with much gratification and pride, its principal attractions. Mr. Kenge also came to speak to us, and did the honours of the place in much the same way; with the bland modesty of a proprietor. It was not a very good day for a visit, he said; he would have preferred the first day of term; but it was imposing, it was imposing.

When we had been there half an hour or so, the case in progress —if I may use a phrase so ridiculous in such a connexion—seemed to die out of its own vapidity, without coming, or being by anybody expected to come, to any result. The Lord Chancellor then threw down a bundle of papers from his desk to the gentlemen below him, and somebody said, "JARNDYCE AND JARNDYCE." Upon this there was a buzz, and a laugh, and a general withdrawal of the bystanders, and a bringing in of great heaps, and piles, and bags and bags-full of papers.

I think it came on "for further directions,"—about some bill of costs, to the best of my understanding, which was confused enough. But I counted twenty-three gentlemen in wigs, who said they were "in it"; and none of them appeared to understand it much better than I. They chatted about it with the Lord Chancellor, and contradicted and explained among themselves, and some of them said it was this way, and some of them said it was that way, and some of them jocosely proposed to read huge volumes of affidavits, and there was more buzzing and laughing, and everybody concerned was in a state of idle entertainment, and nothing could be made of it by anybody. After an hour or so of this, and a good many speeches being begun and cut short, it was "referred back for the present," as Mr. Kenge said, and the papers were bundled up again, before the clerks had finished bringing them in.

I glanced at Richard, on the termination of these hopeless proceedings, and was shocked to see the worn look of his handsome young face. "It can't last for ever, Dame Durden. Better luck next time!" was all he said.

I had seen Mr. Guppy bringing in papers, and arranging them for Mr. Kenge; and he had seen me and made me a forlorn bow, which rendered me desirous to get out of the Court. Richard had given me his arm, and was taking me away, when Mr. Guppy came up.

"I beg your pardon, Mr. Carstone," said he in a whisper, "and Miss Summerson's also; but there's a lady here, a friend of mine, who knows her, and wishes to have the pleasure of shaking hands." As he spoke, I saw before me, as if she had started into bodily shape from my remembrance, Mrs. Rachael of my godmother's house.

"How do you do, Esther?" said she. "Do you recollect me?"

I gave her my hand, and told her yes, and that she was very little altered.

"I wonder you remember those times, Esther," she returned with her old asperity. "They are changed now. Well! I am glad to see you, and glad you are not too proud to know me." But, indeed she seemed disappointed that I was not.

"Proud, Mrs. Rachael!" I remonstrated.

"I am married, Esther," she returned, coldly correcting me, "and am Mrs. Chadband. Well! I wish you good day, and I hope you'll do well."

Mr. Guppy, who had been attentive to this short dialogue, heaved a sigh in my ear, and elbowed his own and Mrs. Rachael's way through the confused little crowd of people coming in and going out, which we were in the midst of, and which the change in the business has brought together. Richard and I were making our own way through it, and I was yet in the first chill of the late unexpected recognition, when I saw, coming towards us, but not seeing us, no less a person than Mr. George. He made nothing of the people about him as he tramped on, staring over their heads into the body of the Court.

"George!" said Richard, as I called his attention to him.

"You are well met, sir," he returned. "And you, miss. Could you point a person out for me, I want? I don't understand these places."

Turning as he spoke, and making an easy way for us, he stopped when we were out of the press, in a corner behind a great red curtain.

"There's a little cracked old woman," he began, "that ——"

I put up my finger, for Miss Flite was close by me; having kept beside me all the time, and having called the attention of several of her legal acquaintance to me (as I had overheard to my confusion), by whispering in their ears, "Hush! Fitz-Jarndyce on my left!"

"Hem!" said Mr. George. "You remember, miss, that we passed some conversation on a certain man this morning?—Gridley," in a low whisper behind his hand.

"Yes," said I.

"He is hiding at my place. I couldn't mention it. Hadn't his authority. He is on his last march, miss, and has a whim to see her. He says they can feel for one another, and she has been almost as good as a friend to him here. I came down to look for her; for when

I sat by Gridley this afternoon, I seemed to hear the roll of the muffled drums."

"Shall I tell her?" said I.

"Would you be so good?" he returned, with a glance of something like apprehension at Miss Flite. "It's a Providence I met you, miss; I doubt if I should have known how to get on with that lady." And he put one hand in his breast, and stood upright in a martial attitude, as I informed little Miss Flite, in her ear, of the purport of his kind errand.

"My angry friend from Shropshire! Almost as celebrated as myself!" she exclaimed. "Now really! My dear, I will wait upon him with the greatest pleasure."

"He is living concealed at Mr. George's," said I. "Hush! This is Mr. George."

"In—deed!" returned Miss Flite. "Very proud to have the honour! A military man, my dear. You know, a perfect General!" she whispered to me.

Poor Miss Flite deemed it necessary to be so courtly and polite, as a mark of her respect for the army, and to curtsey so very often, that it was no easy matter to get her out of the Court. When this was at last done, and addressing Mr. George, as "General," she gave him her arm, to the great entertainment of some idlers who were looking on, he was so discomposed, and begged me so respectfully "not to desert him," that I could not make up my mind to do it; especially as Miss Flite was always tractable with me, and as she too said, "Fitz-Jarndyce, my dear, you will accompany us, of course." As Richard seemed quite willing, and even anxious, that we should see them safely to their destination, we agreed to do so. And as Mr. George informed us that Gridley's mind had run on Mr. Jarndyce all the afternoon, after hearing of their interview in the morning, I wrote a hasty note in pencil to my guardian to say where we were gone, and why. Mr. George sealed it at a coffee-house, that it might lead to no discovery, and we sent it off by a ticket-porter.[4]

We then took a hackney-coach, and drove away to the neighbourhood of Leicester Square. We walked through some narrow courts, for which Mr. George apologised, and soon came to the Shooting Gallery, the door of which was closed. As he pulled a bell-handle which hung by a chain to the door-post, a very respectable old gentleman, with grey hair, wearing spectacles, and dressed in a black spencer[5] and gaiters and a broad-brimmed hat, and carrying a large gold-headed cane, addressed him.

"I ask your pardon, my good friend," said he; "but is this George's Shooting Gallery?"

4. A carrier licensed to deliver parcels and messages.

5. A short double-breasted overcoat popularized by Earl Spencer (1758–1834).

"It is, sir," returned Mr. George, glancing up at the great letters in which that inscription was painted on the whitewashed wall.

"Oh! To be sure!" said the old gentleman, following his eyes. "Thank you. Have you rung the bell?"

"My name is George, sir, and I have rung the bell."

"Oh, indeed?" said the old gentleman. "Your name is George? Then I am here as soon as you, you see. You came for me, no doubt?"

"No, sir. You have the advantage of me."

"Oh, indeed?" said the old gentleman. "Then it was your young man who came for me. I am a physician, and was requested—five minutes ago—to come and visit a sick man, at George's Shooting Gallery."

"The muffled drums," said Mr. George, turning to Richard and me, and gravely shaking his head. "It's quite correct, sir. Will you please to walk in?"

The door being at that moment opened, by a very singular-looking little man in a green baize cap and apron, whose face, and hands, and dress, were blackened all over, we passed along a dreary passage into a large building with bare brick walls; where there were targets, and guns, and swords, and other things of that kind. When we had all arrived here, the physician stopped, and, taking off his hat, appeared to vanish by magic, and to leave another and quite a different man in his place.

"Now look'ee here, George," said the man, turning quickly round upon him, and tapping him on the breast with a large forefinger. "You know me, and I know you. You're a man of the world, and I'm a man of the world. My name's Bucket, as you are aware, and I have got a peace-warrant[6] against Gridley. You have kept him out of the way a long time, and you have been artful in it, and it does you credit."

Mr. George, looking hard at him, bit his lip and shook his head.

"Now, George," said the other, keeping close to him, "you're a sensible man, and a well-conducted man; that's what *you* are, beyond a doubt. And mind you, I don't talk to you as a common character, because you have served your country, and you know that when duty calls we must obey. Consequently, you're very far from wanting to give trouble. If I required assistance, you'd assist me; that's what *you'd* do. Phil Squod, don't you go a-sidling round this gallery like that"; the dirty little man was shuffling about with his shoulder against the wall, and his eyes on the intruder, in a manner that looked threatening: "because I know you, and won't have it."

"Phil!" said Mr. George.

"Yes, guv'ner."

6. Arrest-warrant issued by a Justice of the Peace.

"Be quiet."

The little man, with a low growl, stood still.

"Ladies and gentlemen," said Mr. Bucket, "you'll excuse anything that may appear to be disagreeable in this, for my name's Inspector Bucket of the Detective, and I have a duty to perform. George, I know where my man is, because I was on the roof last night, and saw him through the skylight, and you along with him. He is in there, you know," pointing; "that's where *he* is—on a sofy. Now I must see my man, and I must tell my man to consider himself in custody; but you know me, and you know I don't want to take any uncomfortable measures. You give me your word, as from one man to another (and an old soldier, mind you, likewise!), that it's honourable between us two, and I'll accommodate you to the utmost of my power."

"I give it," was the reply. "But it wasn't handsome in you, Mr. Bucket."

"Gammon,[7] George! Not handsome?" said Mr. Bucket, tapping him on his broad breast again, and shaking hands with him. "I don't say it wasn't handsome in you to keep my man so close, do I? Be equally good-tempered to me, old boy! Old William Tell, Old Shaw, the Life Guardsman![8] Why, he's a model of the whole British army in himself, ladies and gentlemen. I'd give a fifty-pun' note to be such a figure of a man!"

The affair being brought to this head, Mr. George, after a little consideration, proposed to go in first to his comrade (as he called him), taking Miss Flite with him. Mr. Bucket agreeing, they went away to the further end of the gallery, leaving us sitting and standing by a table covered with guns. Mr. Bucket took this opportunity of entering into a little light conversation: asking me if I were afraid of fire-arms, as most young ladies were; asking Richard if he were a good shot; asking Phil Squod which he considered the best of those rifles, and what it might be worth, first-hand; telling him, in return, that it was a pity he ever gave way to his temper, for he was naturally so amiable, that he might have been a young woman; and making himself generally agreeable.

After a time he followed us to the further end of the gallery, and Richard and I were going quietly away, when Mr. George came after us. He said that if we had no objection to see his comrade, he would take a visit from us very kindly. The words had hardly passed his lips, when the bell was rung, and my guardian appeared; "on the

7. According to John Bee's *Slang: A Dictionary* (1823), gammon was "deceitful talk, between fun and falsehood."

8. William Tell was a legendary Swiss hero, famous as a marksman. Lance-Corporal John Shaw (1789–1815) was a prize-fighter whose "Herculean" physique made him a favorite model for painters such as B. R. Haydon and William Etty. After enlisting in the Life Guards in 1807, Shaw became famous for his exploits at Waterloo where he reputedly killed ten French lancers with his sword, dying himself at the close of the battle from a multiplicity of wounds.

chance," he slightly observed, "of being able to do any little thing for a poor fellow involved in the same misfortune as himself." We all four went back together, and went into the place where Gridley was.

It was a bare room, partitioned off from the gallery with unpainted wood. As the screening was not more than eight or ten feet high, and only enclosed the sides, not the top, the rafters of the high gallery roof were overhead, and the skylight through which Mr. Bucket had looked down. The sun was low—near setting—and its light came redly in above, without descending to the ground. Upon a plain canvas-covered sofa lay the man from Shropshire—dressed much as we had seen him last, but so changed, that at first I recognised no likeness in his colourless face to what I recollected.

He had been still writing in his hiding-place, and still dwelling on his grievances, hour after hour. A table and some shelves were covered with manuscript papers, and with worn pens, and a medley of such tokens. Touchingly and awfully drawn together, he and the little mad woman were side by side, and, as it were, alone. She sat on a chair holding his hand, and none of us went close to them.

His voice had faded, with the old expression of his face, with his strength, with his anger, with his resistance to the wrongs that had at last subdued him. The faintest shadow of an object full of form and colour, is such a picture of it, as he was of the man from Shropshire whom we had spoken with before.

He inclined his head to Richard and me, and spoke to my guardian.

"Mr. Jarndyce, it is very kind of you to come to see me. I am not long to be seen, I think. I am very glad to take your hand, sir. You are a good man, superior to injustice, and God knows I honour you."

They shook hands earnestly, and my guardian said some words of comfort to him.

"It may seem strange to you, sir," returned Gridley; "I should not have liked to see you, if this had been the first time of our meeting. But you know I made a fight for it, you know I stood up with my single hand against them all, you know I told them the truth to the last, and told them what they were, and what they had done to me; so I don't mind your seeing me, this wreck."

"You have been courageous with them, many and many a time," returned my guardian.

"Sir, I have been"; with a faint smile. "I told you what would come of it, when I ceased to be so; and, see here! Look at us—look at us!" He drew the hand Miss Flite held, through her arm, and brought her something nearer to him.

"This ends it. Of all my old associations, of all my old pursuits and hopes, of all the living and the dead world, this one poor soul alone comes natural to me, and I am fit for. There is a tie of many suffering years between us two, and it is the only tie I ever had on earth that Chancery has not broken."

"Accept my blessing, Gridley," said Miss Flite, in tears, "Accept my blessing!"

"I thought, boastfully, that they never could break my heart, Mr. Jarndyce. I was resolved that they should not. I did believe that I could, and would, charge them with being the mockery they were, until I died of some bodily disorder. But I am worn out. How long I have been wearing out, I don't know; I seemed to break down in an hour. I hope they may never come to hear of it. I hope everybody, here, will lead them to believe that I died defying them, consistently and perseveringly, as I did through so many years."

Here Mr. Bucket, who was sitting in a corner, by the door, good-naturedly offered such consolation as he could administer.

"Come, come!" he said from his corner. "Don't go on in that way, Mr. Gridley. You are only a little low. We are all of us a little low, sometimes. *I* am. Hold up, hold up! You'll lose your temper with the whole round of 'em, again and again; and I shall take you on a score of warrants yet, if I have luck."

He only shook his head.

"Don't shake your head," said Mr. Bucket. "Nod it; that's what I want to see you do. Why, Lord bless your soul, what times we have had together! Haven't I seen you in the Fleet[9] over and over again, for contempt? Haven't I come into Court, twen-ty afternoons, for no other purpose than to see you pin the Chancellor like a bull-dog? Don't you remember, when you first began to threaten the lawyers, and the peace was sworn against you two or three times a week? Ask the little old lady there; she has been always present. Hold up, Mr. Gridley, hold up, sir!"

"What are you going to do about him?" asked George, in a low voice.

"I don't know yet," said Bucket, in the same tone. Then resuming his encouragement, he pursued aloud;

"Worn out, Mr. Gridley? After dodging me for all these weeks, and forcing me to climb the roof here like a Tom Cat, and to come to see you as a Doctor? That ain't like being worn out. *I* should think not! Now I tell you what you want. You want excitement, you know, to keep *you* up; that's what *you* want. You're used to it, and you can't do without it. I couldn't myself. Very well, then; here's this warrant got by Mr. Tulkinghorn of Lincoln's Inn Fields, and backed into half-a-dozen counties since. What do you say to coming along with me, upon this warrant, and having a good angry argument before the Magistrates? It'll do you good; it'll freshen you up, and get you into training for another turn at the Chancellor.

9. Until 1842 a prison for debtors.

Give in? Why, I am surprised to hear a man of your energy talk of giving in. You mustn't do that. You're half the fun of the fair, in the Court of Chancery. George, you lend Mr. Gridley a hand, and let's see now whether he won't be better up than down."

"He is very weak," said the trooper, in a low voice.

"Is he?" returned Bucket, anxiously. "I only want to rouse him. I don't like to see an old acquaintance giving in like this. It would cheer him up more than anything, if I could make him a little waxy with me. He's welcome to drop into me, right and left, if he likes, I shall never take advantage of it."

The roof rang with a scream from Miss Flite, which still rings in my ears.

"O no, Gridley!" she cried, as he fell heavily and calmly back from before her, "not without my blessing. After so many years!"

The sun was down, the light had gradually stolen from the roof, and the shadow had crept upward. But, to me, the shadow of that pair, one living and one dead, fell heavier on Richard's departure, than the darkness of the darkest night. And through Richard's farewell words I heard it echoed:

"Of all my old associations, of all my old pursuits and hopes, of all the living and the dead world, this one poor soul alone comes natural to me, and I am fit for. There is a tie of many suffering years between us two, and it is the only tie I ever had on earth that Chancery has not broken!"

Chapter XXV

MRS. SNAGSBY SEES IT ALL

There is disquietude in Cook's Court, Cursitor Street. Black suspicion hides in that peaceful region. The mass of Cook's-Courtiers are in their usual state of mind, no better and no worse; but, Mr. Snagsby is changed, and his little woman knows it.

For Tom-all-Alone's and Lincoln's Inn Fields persist in harnessing themselves, a pair of ungovernable coursers, to the chariot of Mr. Snagsby's imagination; and Mr. Bucket drives; and the passengers are Jo and Mr. Tulkinghorn; and the complete equipage whirls through the Law Stationery business at wild speed, all round the clock. Even in the little front kitchen where the family meals are taken, it rattles away at a smoking pace from the dinner-table, when Mr. Snagsby pauses in carving the first slice of the leg of mutton baked with potatoes, and stares at the kitchen wall.

Mr. Snagsby cannot make out what it is that he has had to do with. Something is wrong, somewhere; but what something, what may come of it, to whom, when, and from which unthought of and unheard of quarter, is the puzzle of his life. His remote impressions of the robes and coronets, the stars and garters, that sparkle through the surface-dust of Mr. Tulkinghorn's chambers; his veneration for the mysteries presided over by that best and closest of his customers, whom all the Inns of Court, all Chancery Lane, and all the legal neighbourhood agree to hold in awe; his remembrance of Detective Mr. Bucket with his fore-finger, and his confidential manner impossible to be evaded or declined; persuade him that he is a party to some dangerous secret, without knowing what it is. And it is the fearful peculiarity of this condition that, at any hour of his daily life, at any opening of the shop-door, at any pull of the bell, at any entrance of a messenger, or any delivery of a letter, the secret may take air and fire, explode, and blow up—Mr. Bucket only knows whom.

For which reason, whenever a man unknown comes into the shop (as many men unknown do), and says, "Is Mr. Snagsby in?" or words to that innocent effect, Mr. Snagsby's heart knocks hard at his guilty breast. He undergoes so much from such inquiries, that when they are made by boys he revenges himself by flipping at their ears over the counter, and asking the young dogs what they mean by it, and why they can't speak out at once? More impracticable men and boys persist in walking into Mr. Snagsby's sleep, and terrifying him with unaccountable questions; so that often, when the cock at the little dairy in Cursitor Street breaks out in his usual absurd way about the morning, Mr. Snagsby finds himself in a crisis of nightmare, with his little woman shaking him, and saying, "What's the matter with the man!"

The little woman herself is not the least item in his difficulty. To know that he is always keeping a secret from her; that he has, under all circumstances, to conceal and hold fast a tender double tooth, which her sharpness is ever ready to twist out of his head; gives Mr. Snagsby, in her dentistical presence, much of the air of a dog who has a reservation from his master, and will look anywhere rather than meet his eye.

These various signs and tokens, marked by the little woman, are not lost upon her. They impel her to say, "Snagsby has something on his mind!" And thus suspicion gets into Cook's Court, Cursitor Street. From suspicion to jealousy, Mrs. Snagsby finds the road as natural and short as from Cook's Court to Chancery Lane. And thus jealousy gets into Cook's Court, Cursitor Street. Once there (and it was always lurking thereabout), it is very active and nimble in Mrs. Snagsby's breast—prompting her to nocturnal examinations of Mr. Snagsby's pockets; to secret perusals of Mr. Snagsby's letters; to private researches in the Day Book and Ledger, till, cash-box, and iron safe; to watchings at windows, listenings behind doors, and a general putting of this and that together by the wrong end.

Mrs. Snagsby is so perpetually on the alert, that the house becomes ghostly with creaking boards and rustling garments. The 'prentices think somebody may have been murdered there, in bygone times. Guster holds certain loose atoms of an idea (picked up at Tooting,[1] where they were found floating among the orphans), that there is buried money underneath the cellar, guarded by an old man with a white beard, who cannot get out for seven thousand years, because he said the Lord's Prayer backwards.

"Who was Nimrod?"[2] Mrs. Snagsby repeatedly inquires of herself. "What was that lady—that creature? And who is that boy?" Now, Nimrod being as dead as the mighty hunter whose name Mrs. Snagsby has appropriated, and the lady being unproducible, she directs her mental eye, for the present, with redoubled vigilance, to the boy. "And who," quoth Mrs. Snagsby, for the thousand and first time, "is that boy? Who is that——!" And there Mrs. Snagsby is seized with an inspiration.

He has no respect for Mr. Chadband. No, to be sure, and he wouldn't have, of course. Naturally he wouldn't, under those contagious circumstances. He was invited and appointed by Mr. Chadband—why, Mrs. Snagsby heard it herself with her own ears!—to come back, and be told where he was to go, to be addressed by Mr. Chadband; and he never came! Why did he never come? Because he was told not to come. Who told him not to come? Who? Ha, ha! Mrs. Snagsby sees it all.

But happily (and Mrs. Snagsby tightly shakes her head and tightly smiles), that boy was met by Mr. Chadband yesterday in the streets; and that boy, as affording a subject which Mr. Chadband desires to improve for the spiritual delight of a select congregation, was seized by Mr. Chadband and threatened with being delivered over to the police, unless he showed the reverend gentleman where he lived, and unless he entered into, and fulfilled, an undertaking to appear in Cook's Court to-morrow night—"to—mor—row—night," Mrs. Snagsby repeats for mere emphasis, with another tight smile, and another tight shake of her head; and to-morrow night that boy will be here, and to-morrow night Mrs. Snagsby will have her eye upon him and upon some one else; and O you may walk a long while in your secret ways (says Mrs. Snagsby, with haughtiness and scorn), but you can't blind ME!

Mrs. Snagsby sounds no timbrel[3] in anybody's ears, but holds her purpose quietly, and keeps her counsel. To-morrow comes, the savoury preparations for the Oil Trade come, the evening comes.

1. Concerning the orphanage, see p. 117, note 3.

2. On Mrs. Snagsby's not having "a good ear for names" and her considering "Nemo equally the same as Nimrod," see p. 128.

3. See "Sound the Loud Timbrel" in *Sacred Songs*, by Thomas Moore (1779–1852).

Comes, Mr. Snagsby in his black coat; come, the Chadbands; come (when the gorging vessel is replete), the 'prentices and Guster, to be edified; comes, at last, with his slouching head, and his shuffle backward, and his shuffle forward, and his shuffle to the right, and his shuffle to the left, and his bit of fur cap in his muddy hand, which he picks as if it were some mangy bird he had caught, and was plucking before eating raw, Jo, the very, very tough subject Mr. Chadband is to improve.

Mrs. Snagsby screws a watchful glance on Jo, as he is brought into the little drawing-room by Guster. He looks at Mr. Snagsby the moment he comes in. Aha! Why does he look at Mr. Snagsby? Mr. Snagsby looks at him. Why should he do that, but that Mrs. Snagsby sees it all? Why else should that look pass between them, why else should Mr. Snagsby be confused, and cough a signal cough behind his hand? It is as clear as crystal that Mr. Snagsby is that boy's father.

"Peace, my friends," says Chadband, rising and wiping the oily exudations from his reverend visage. "Peace be with us! My friends, why with us? Because," with his fat smile, "it cannot be against us, because it must be for us: because it is not hardening, because it is softening; because it does not make war like the hawk, but comes home untoe us like the dove. Therefore, my friends, peace be with us! My human boy, come forward!"

Stretching forth his flabby paw, Mr. Chadband lays the same on Jo's arm, and considers where to station him. Jo, very doubtful of his reverend friend's intentions, and not at all clear but that something practical and painful is going to be done to him, mutters, "You let me alone. I never said nothink to you. You let me alone."

"No, my young friend," says Chadband, smoothly, "I will not let you alone. And why? Because I am a harvest-labourer, because I am a toiler and a moiler, because you are delivered over untoe me, and are become as a precious instrument in my hands. My friends, may I so employ this instrument as to use it toe your advantage, toe your profit, toe your gain, toe your welfare, toe your enrichment! My young friend, sit upon this stool."

Jo, apparently possessed by an impression that the reverend gentleman wants to cut his hair, shields his head with both arms, and is got into the required position with great difficulty, and every possible manifestation of reluctance.

When he is at last adjusted like a lay-figure,[4] Mr. Chadband, retiring behind the table, holds up his bear's-paw, and says, "My friends!" This is the signal for a general settlement of the audience. The 'prentices giggle internally, and nudge each other. Guster falls into a staring and vacant state, compounded of a stunned admira-

4. Jointed wooden dummy of the human body used by artists for poses and arrangements of draperies.

Mr. Chadband "improving" a tough subject.

tion of Mr. Chadband and pity for the friendless outcast whose condition touches her nearly. Mrs. Snagsby silently lays trains of gunpowder. Mrs. Chadband composes herself grimly by the fire, and warms her knees: finding that sensation favourable to the reception of eloquence.

It happens that Mr. Chadband has a pulpit habit of fixing some member of his congregation with his eye, and fatly arguing his points with that particular person; who is understood to be expected to be moved to an occasional grunt, groan, gasp, or other audible expression of inward working; which expression of inward working, being echoed by some elderly lady in the next pew, and so communicated, like a game of forfeits, through a circle of the more fermentable sinners present, serves the purpose of parliamentary cheering, and gets Mr. Chadband's steam up. From mere force of habit, Mr. Chadband in saying "My friends!" has rested his eye on Mr. Snagsby; and proceeds to make that ill-starred stationer, already sufficiently confused, the immediate recipient of his discourse.

"We have here among us, my friends," says Chadband, "a Gentile and a Heathen, a dweller in the tents[5] of Tom-all-Alone's and a mover-on upon the surface of the earth. We have here among us, my friends," and Mr. Chadband, untwisting the point with his dirty thumb-nail, bestows an oily smile on Mr. Snagsby, signifying that he will throw him an argumentative back-fall presently if he be not already down, "a brother and a boy. Devoid of parents, devoid of relations, devoid of flocks and herds, devoid of gold and silver, and of precious stones. Now, my friends, why do I say he is devoid of these possessions? Why? Why is he?" Mr. Chadband states the question as if he were propounding an entirely new riddle, of much ingenuity and merit, to Mr. Snagsby, and entreating him not to give it up.

Mr. Snagsby, greatly perplexed by the mysterious look he received just now from his little woman—at about the period when Mr. Chadband mentioned the word parents—is tempted into modestly remarking, "I don't know, I'm sure, sir." On which interruption, Mrs. Chadband glares, and Mrs. Snagsby says, "For shame!"

"I hear a voice," says Chadband; "is it a still small voice,[6] my friends? I fear not, though I fain would hope so——"

("Ah—h!" from Mrs. Snagsby.)

"Which says, I don't know. Then I will tell you why. I say this brother, present here among us, is devoid of parents, devoid of relations, devoid of flocks and herds, devoid of gold, of silver, and of precious stones, because he is devoid of the light that shines in upon some of us. What is that light? What is it? I ask you what is that light?"

Mr. Chadband draws back his head and pauses, but Mr. Snagsby

5. Cf. Psalms 84:10 and 120:5.

6. I Kings 19:12.

is not to be lured on to his destruction again. Mr. Chadband, leaning forward over the table, pierces what he has got to follow, directly into Mr. Snagsby, with the thumb-nail already mentioned.

"It is," says Chadband, "the ray of rays, the sun of suns, the moon of moons, the star of stars. It is the light of Terewth."

Mr. Chadband draws himself up again, and looks triumphantly at Mr. Snagsby, as if he would be glad to know how he feels after that.

"Of Terewth," says Mr. Chadband, hitting him again. "Say not to me it is *not* the lamp of lamps. I say to you, it is. I say to you, a million of times over, it is. It is! I say to you that I will proclaim it to you, whether you like it or not; nay, that the less you like it, the more I will proclaim it to you. With a speaking-trumpet! I say to you that if you rear yourself against it, you shall fall, you shall be bruised, you shall be battered, you shall be flawed, you shall be smashed."

The present effect of this flight of oratory—much admired for its general power by Mr. Chadband's followers—being not only to make Mr. Chadband unpleasantly warm, but to represent the innocent Mr. Snagsby in the light of a determined enemy to virtue, with a forehead of brass and a heart of adamant,[7] that unfortunate tradesman becomes yet more disconcerted; and is in a very advanced state of low spirits and false position, when Mr. Chadband accidentally finishes him.

"My friends," he resumes, after dabbing his fat head for some time—and it smokes to such an extent that he seems to light his pocket-handkerchief at it, which smokes, too, after every dab—"to pursue the subject we are endeavouring with our lowly gifts to improve, let us in a spirit of love inquire what is that Terewth to which I have alluded. For, my young friends," suddenly addressing the 'prentices and Guster, to their consternation, "if I am told by the doctor that calomel or castor-oil is good for me, I may naturally ask what is calomel, and what is castor-oil. I may wish to be informed of that, before I dose myself with either or with both. Now, my young friends, what is this Terewth, then? Firstly (in a spirit of love), what is the common sort of Terewth—the working clothes—the every-day wear, my young friends? Is it deception?"

("Ah—h!" from Mrs. Snagsby.)

"Is it suppression?"

(A shiver in the negative from Mrs. Snagsby.)

"Is it reservation?"

(A shake of the head from Mrs. Snagsby—very long and very tight.)

"No, my friends, it is neither of these. Neither of these names

7. Biblical references to people who obstinately ignore the wishes of God. See Isaiah 48:4 and also Zechariah 7:12: "Yea, they made their hearts as an adamant stone, lest they should hear the law."

belongs to it. When this young Heathen now among us—who is now, my friends, asleep, the seal of indifference and perdition being set upon his eyelids; but do not wake him, for it is right that I should have to wrestle, and to combat and to struggle, and to conquer, for his sake—when this young hardened Heathen told us a story of a Cock, and of a Bull, and of a lady, and of a sovereign, was *that* the Terewth? No. Or, if it was partly, was it wholly and entirely? No, my friends, no!"

If Mr. Snagsby could withstand his little woman's look, as it enters at his eyes, the windows of his soul, and searches the whole tenement, he were other than the man he is. He cowers and droops.

"Or, my juvenile friends," says Chadband, descending to the level of their comprehension, with a very obtrusive demonstration, in his greasily meek smile, of coming a long way down-stairs for the purpose, "if the master of this house was to go forth into the city and there see an eel, and was to come back, and was to call untoe him the mistress of this house, and was to say, "Sarah, rejoice with me, for I have seen an elephant!" would *that* be Terewth?"

Mrs. Snagsby in tears.

"Or put it, my juvenile friends, that he saw an elephant, and returning said, "Lo, the city is barren, I have seen but an eel," would *that* be Terewth?"

Mrs. Snagsby sobbing loudly.

"Or put it, my juvenile friends," says Chadband, stimulated by the sound, "that the unnatural parents of this slumbering Heathen—for parents he had, my juvenile friends, beyond a doubt—after casting him forth to the wolves and the vultures, and the wild dogs and the young gazelles, and the serpents, went back to their dwellings and had their pipes, and their pots, and their flutings and their dancings, and their malt liquors, and their butcher's meat and poultry, would *that* be Terewth?"

Mrs. Snagsby replies by delivering herself a prey to spasms; not an unresisting prey, but a crying and a tearing one, so that Cook's Court re-echoes with her shrieks. Finally, becoming cataleptic, she has to be carried up the narrow staircase like a grand piano. After unspeakable suffering, productive of the utmost consternation, she is pronounced, by expresses from the bedroom, free from pain, though much exhausted; in which state of affairs Mr. Snagsby, trampled and crushed in the piano-forte removal, and extremely timid and feeble, ventures to come out from behind the door in the drawing-room.

All this time, Jo has been standing on the spot where he woke up, ever picking his cap, and putting bits of fur in his mouth. He spits them out with a remorseful air, for he feels that it is in his nature to be an unimprovable reprobate, and that it's no good *his* trying to keep awake, for *he* won't never know nothink. Though it may be, Jo, that there is a history so interesting and affecting even to minds as near the brutes as thine, recording deeds done on this earth for common men, that if the Chadbands, removing their own persons from the light, would but show it thee in simple reverence, would but leave it unimproved, would but regard it as being eloquent enough without their modest aid—it might hold thee awake, and thou might learn from it yet!

Jo never heard of any such book. Its compilers, and the Reverend Chadband, are all one to him—except that he knows the Reverend Chadband, and would rather run away from him for an hour than hear him talk for five minutes. "It an't no good my waiting here no longer," thinks Jo. "Mr. Sangsby an't a-going to say nothink to me to-night." And down-stairs he shuffles.

But down-stairs is the charitable Guster, holding by the hand-rail of the kitchen stairs, and warding off a fit, as yet doubtfully, the same having been induced by Mrs. Snagsby's screaming. She has her own supper of bread and cheese to hand to Jo; with whom she ventures to interchange a word or so, for the first time.

"Here's something to eat, poor boy," says Guster.

"Thank'ee, mum," says Jo.

"Are you hungry?"

"Jist!" says Jo.

"What's gone of your father and your mother, eh?"

Jo stops in the middle of a bite, and looks petrified. For this orphan charge of the Christian saint whose shrine was at Tooting,[8] has patted him on the shoulder; and it is the first time in his life that any decent hand has been so laid upon him.

"I never know'd nothink about 'em," says Jo.

"No more didn't I of mine," cries Guster. She is repressing symptoms favourable to the fit, when she seems to take alarm at something, and vanishes down the stairs.

"Jo," whispers the law-stationer softly, as the boy lingers on the step.

"Here I am, Mr. Sangsby!"

"I didn't know you were gone—there's another half-crown, Jo. It was quite right of you to say nothing about the lady the other night when we were out together. It would breed trouble. You can't be too quiet, Jo."

"I am fly,[9] master!"

And so, good night.

A ghostly shade, frilled and night-capped, follows the law-stationer to the room he came from, and glides higher up. And henceforth he begins, go where he will, to be attended by another

8. See p. 117, note 3.

9. I understand (see p. 201, note 4).

shadow than his own, hardly less constant than his own, hardly less quiet than his own. And into whatsoever atmosphere of secrecy his own shadow may pass, let all concerned in the secrecy beware! For the watchful Mrs. Snagsby is there too—bone of his bone, flesh of his flesh,[1] shadow of his shadow.

Chapter XXVI

SHARPSHOOTERS

Wintry morning, looking with dull eyes and sallow face upon the neighbourhood of Leicester Square, finds its inhabitants unwilling to get out of bed. Many of them are not early risers at the brightest of times, being birds of night who roost when the sun is high, and are wide awake and keen for prey when the stars shine out. Behind dingy blind and curtain, in upper story and garret, skulking more or less under false names, false hair, false titles, false jewellery, and false histories, a colony of brigands lie in their first sleep. Gentlemen of the green baize road[1] who could discourse, from personal experience, of foreign galleys and home treadmills;[2] spies of strong governments that eternally quake with weakness and miserable fear, broken traitors, cowards, bullies, gamesters, shufflers, swindlers, and false witnesses; some not unmarked by the branding-iron, beneath their dirty braid;[3] all with more cruelty in them than was in Nero, and more crime than is in Newgate.[4] For, howsoever bad the devil can be in fustian or smock-frock (and he can be very bad in both), he is a more designing, callous, and intolerable devil when he sticks a pin in his shirt-front, calls himself a gentleman, backs a card or colour, plays a game or so of billiards, and knows a little about bills and promissory notes, than in any other form he wears. And in such form Mr. Bucket shall find him, when he will, still pervading the tributary channels of Leicester Square.

But the wintry morning wants him not and wakes him not. It wakes Mr. George of the Shooting Gallery, and his Familiar. They arise, roll up and stow away their mattresses. Mr. George, having shaved himself before a looking-glass of minute proportions, then marches out, bare-headed and bare-chested, to the Pump, in the little yard, and anon comes back shining with yellow soap, friction, drifting rain, and exceedingly cold water. As he rubs himself upon a

1. See Genesis 2:23: "And Adam said, this is now bone of my bones, and flesh of my flesh."

1. Card-sharpers. ("Gentlemen of the road" is a euphemism for highwaymen, and "green baize" refers to covers for card tables in gambling establishments.)

2. Criminals whose punishments included forced labor in galleys abroad and toiling in treadmills in English prisons.

3. Presumably a coat ornamented with braid, a costume giving a pseudo-military appearance. In his sketch, "A Flight," Dickens described a "Tobacco-smoky Frenchman" as "dressed entirely in dirt and braid."

4. A prison in London.

large jack-towel, blowing like a military sort of diver just come up: his crisp hair curling tighter and tighter on his sunburnt temples, the more he rubs it, so that it looks as if it never could be loosened by any less coercive instrument than an iron rake or a curry-comb—as he rubs, and puffs, and polishes, and blows, turning his head from side to side, the more conveniently to excoriate his throat, and standing with his body well bent forward, to keep the wet from his martial legs—Phil, on his knees lighting a fire, looks round as if it were enough washing for him to see all that done, and sufficient renovation, for one day, to take in the superfluous health his master throws off.

When Mr. George is dry, he goes to work to brush his head with two hard brushes at once, to that unmerciful degree that Phil, shouldering his way round the gallery in the act of sweeping it, winks with sympathy. This chafing over, the ornamental part of Mr. George's toilet is soon performed. He fills his pipe, lights it, and marches up and down smoking, as his custom is, while Phil, raising a powerful odour of hot rolls and coffee, prepares breakfast. He smokes gravely, and marches in slow time. Perhaps this morning's pipe is devoted to the memory of Gridley in his grave.

"And so, Phil," says George of the Shooting Gallery, after several turns in silence; "you were dreaming of the country last night?"

Phil, by-the-bye, said as much, in a tone of surprise, as he scrambled out of bed.

"Yes, guv'ner."

"What was it like?"

"I hardly know what it was like, guv'ner," says Phil, considering.

"How did you know it was the country?"

"On accounts of the grass, I think. And the swans upon it," says Phil, after further consideration.

"What were the swans doing on the grass?"

"They was a-eating of it, I expect," says Phil.

The master resumes his march, and the man resumes his preparation of breakfast. It is not necessarily a lengthened preparation, being limited to the setting forth of very simple breakfast requisites for two, and the broiling of a rasher of bacon at the fire in the rusty grate; but as Phil has to sidle round a considerable part of the gallery for every object he wants, and never brings two objects at once, it takes time under the circumstances. At length the breakfast is ready. Phil announcing it, Mr. George knocks the ashes out of his pipe on the hob, stands his pipe itself in the chimney corner, and sits down to the meal. When he has helped himself, Phil follows suit; sitting at the extreme end of the little oblong table, and taking his plate on his knees. Either in humility, or to hide his blackened hands, or because it is his natural manner of eating.

"The country," says Mr. George, plying his knife and fork; "why, I suppose you never clapped your eyes on the country, Phil?"

"I see the marshes once," says Phil, contentedly eating his breakfast.

"What marshes?"

"*The* marshes, commander," returns Phil.

"Where are they?"

"I don't know where they are," says Phil; "but I see 'em, guv'ner. They was flat. And miste."

Governor and Commander are interchangeable terms with Phil, expressive of the same respect and deference, and applicable to nobody but Mr. George.

"I was born in the country, Phil."

"Was you indeed, commander?"

"Yes. And bred there."

Phil elevates his one eyebrow, and, after respectfully staring at his master to express interest, swallows a great gulp of coffee, still staring at him.

"There's not a bird's note that I don't know," says Mr. George. "Not many an English leaf or berry that I couldn't name. Not many a tree that I couldn't climb yet, if I was put to it. I was a real country boy, once. My good mother lived in the country."

"She must have been a fine old lady, guv'ner," Phil observes.

"Ay! and not so old either, five-and-thirty years ago," says Mr. George. "But I'll wager that at ninety she would be near as upright as me, and near as broad across the shoulders."

"Did she die at ninety, guv'ner?" inquires Phil.

"No. Bosh! Let her rest in peace, God Bless her!" says the trooper. "What set me on about country boys, and runaways, and good-for-nothings? You, to be sure! So you never clapped your eyes upon the country—marshes and dreams excepted. Eh?"

Phil shakes his head.

"Do you want to see it?"

"N-no, I don't know as I do, particular," says Phil.

"The town's enough for you, eh?"

"Why, you see, commander," says Phil, "I ain't acquainted with anythink else, and I doubt if I ain't a-getting too old to take to novelties."

"How old *are* you, Phil?" asks the trooper, pausing as he conveys his smoking saucer to his lips.

"I'm something with a eight in it," says Phil. "It can't be eighty. Nor yet eighteen. It's betwixt 'em, somewheres."

Mr. George, slowly putting down his saucer without tasting its contents, is laughingly beginning, "Why, what the deuce, Phil,"—when he stops, seeing that Phil is counting on his dirty fingers.

"I was just eight," says Phil, "agreeable to the parish calculation, when I went with the tinker. I was sent on a errand, and I see him a sittin under a old buildin with a fire all to himself wery comfortable, and he says, 'Would you like to come along a me, my man?' I says 'Yes,' and him and me and the fire goes home to Clerkenwell together. That was April Fool Day. I was able to count up to ten; and when April Fool Day come round again, I says to myself, 'Now, old chap, you're one and a eight in it.' April Fool Day after that, 'Now, old chap, you're two and a eight in it.' In course of time, I come to ten and a eight in it; two tens and a eight in it. When it got so high, it got the upper hand of me; but this is how I always know there's a eight in it."

"Ah!" says Mr. George, resuming his breakfast. "And where's the tinker?"

"Drink put him in the hospital, guv'ner, and the hospital put him—in a glass case, I *have* heerd," Phil replies mysteriously.

"By that means you got promotion? Took the business, Phil?"

"Yes, commander, I took the business. Such as it was. It wasn't much of a beat—round Saffron Hill, Hatton Garden, Clerkenwell, Smiffeld, and there—poor neighbourhood, where they uses up the kettles till they're past mending. Most of the tramping tinkers used to come and lodge at our place; that was the best part of my master's earnings. But they didn't come to me. I warn't like him. He could sing 'em a good song. *I* couldn't! He could play 'em a tune on any sort of pot you please, so as it was iron or block tin. I never could do nothing with a pot, but mend it or bile it—never had a note of music in me. Besides, I was too ill-looking, and their wives complained of me."

"They were mighty particular. You would pass muster in a crowd, Phil!" says the trooper, with a pleasant smile.

"No, guv'ner," returns Phil, shaking his head. "No, I shouldn't. I was passable enough when I went with the tinker, though nothing to boast of then: but what with blowing the fire with my mouth when I was young, and spileing my complexion, and singeing my hair off, and swallering the smoke; and what with being nat'rally unfort'nate in the way of running against hot metal, and marking myself by sich means; and what with having turn-ups[5] with the tinker as I got older, almost whenever he was too far gone in drink—which was almost always—my beauty was queer, wery queer, even at that time. As to since; what with a dozen years in a dark forge, where the men was given to larking; and what with being scorched in a accident at a gas-works; and what with being blowed out of winder, case-filling at the firework business; I am ugly enough to be made a show on!"

5. Fist-fights.

Resigning himself to which condition with a perfectly satisfied manner, Phil begs the favour of another cup of coffee. While drinking it, he says:

"It was after the case-filling blow-up, when I first see you, commander. You remember?"

"I remember, Phil. You were walking along in the sun."

"Crawling, guv'ner, again a wall——"

"True, Phil—shouldering your way on——"

"In a nightcap!" exclaims Phil, excited.

"In a nightcap——"

"And hobbling with a couple of sticks!" cries Phil, still more excited.

"With a couple of sticks. When——"

"When you stops, you know," cries Phil, putting down his cup and saucer, and hastily removing his plate from his knees, "and says to me, 'What, comrade! You have been in the wars!' I didn't say much to you, commander, then, for I was took by surprise, that a person so strong and healthy and bold as you was, should stop to speak to such a limping bag of bones as I was. But you says to me, says you, delivering it out of your chest as hearty as possible, so that it was like a glass of something hot, 'What accident have you met with? You have been badly hurt. What's amiss, old boy? Cheer up, and tell us about it!' Cheer up! I was cheered already! I says as much to you, you says more to me, I says more to you, you says more to me, and here I am, commander! Here I am, commander!" cries Phil, who has started from his chair and unaccountably begun to sidle away. "If a mark's wanted, or if it will improve the business, let the customers take aim at me. They can't spoil *my* beauty. *I*'m all right. Come on! If they want a man to box at, let 'em box at me. Let 'em knock me well about the head. *I* don't mind! If they want a light-weight, to be throwed for practice, Cornwall, Devonshire, or Lancashire,[6] let 'em throw *me*. They won't hurt me. I have been throwed, all sorts of styles, all my life!"

With this unexpected speech, energetically delivered, and accompanied by action illustrative of the various exercises referred to, Phil Squod shoulders his way round three sides of the gallery, and abruptly tacking off at his commander, makes a butt at him with his head, intended to express devotion to his service. He then begins to clear away the breakfast.

Mr. George, after laughing cheerfully, and clapping him on the shoulder, assists in these arrangements, and helps to get the gallery into business order. That done, he takes a turn at the dumb-bells;

6. Regional names for different sets of rules for wrestling matches.

and afterwards weighing himself, and opining that he is getting "too fleshy," engages with great gravity in solitary broadsword practice. Meanwhile, Phil has fallen to work at his usual table, where he screws and unscrews, and cleans, and files, and whistles into small apertures, and blackens himself more and more, and seems to do and undo everything that can be done and undone about a gun. Master and man are at length disturbed by footsteps in the passage, where they make an unusual sound, denoting the arrival of unusual company. These steps, advancing nearer and nearer to the gallery, bring into it a group, at first sight scarcely reconcilable with any day in the year but the fifth of November.[7]

It consists of a limp and ugly figure carried in a chair by two bearers, and attended by a lean female with a face like a pinched mask, who might be expected immediately to recite the popular verses, commemorative of the time when they did contrive to blow Old England up alive, but for her keeping her lips tightly and defiantly closed as the chair is put down. At which point, the figure in it gasping, "O Lord! O dear me! I am shaken!" adds, "How de do, my dear friend, how de do?" Mr. George then descries, in the procession, the venerable Mr. Smallweed out for an airing, attended by his grand-daughter Judy as body-guard.

"Mr. George, my dear friend," says Grandfather Smallweed, removing his right arm from the neck of one of his bearers, whom he has nearly throttled coming along, "how de do? You're surprised to see me, my dear friend."

"I should hardly have been more surprised to have seen your friend in the city," returns Mr. George.

"I am very seldom out," pants Mr. Smallweed. "I haven't been out for many months. It's inconvenient—and it comes expensive. But I longed so much to see you, my dear Mr. George. How de do, sir?"

"I am well enough," says Mr. George. "I hope you are the same."

"You can't be too well, my dear friend." Mr. Smallweed takes him by both hands. "I have brought my grand-daughter Judy. I couldn't keep her away. She longed so much to see you."

"Hum! She bears it calmly!" mutters Mr. George.

"So we got a hackney-cab, and put a chair in it, and just round the corner they lifted me out of the cab and into the chair, and car-

7. Annual festival celebrating the capture of Guy Fawkes, a conspirator in the plot to blow up the Houses of Parliament, on November 5, 1605. Grotesque scarecrow-like effigies (guys) are carried through the streets by children who recite the "popular verses": "Please to remember/ The Fifth of November,/ Gunpowder treason and plot;/ I see no reason/ Why gunpowder treason/ Should ever be forgot."

ried me here, that I might see my dear friend in his own establishment! This," says Grandfather Smallweed, alluding to the bearer, who has been in danger of strangulation, and who withdraws adjusting his windpipe, "is the driver of the cab. He has nothing extra. It is by agreement included in his fare. This person," the other bearer, "we engaged in the street outside for a pint of beer. Which is twopence. Judy, give the person twopence. I was not sure you had a workman of your own here, my dear friend, or we needn't have employed this person."

Grandfather Smallweed refers to Phil, with a glance of considerable terror, and a half-subdued "O Lord! O dear me!" Nor is his apprehension, on the surface of things, without some reason; for Phil, who has never beheld the apparition in the black velvet cap before, has stopped short with a gun in his hand, with much of the air of a dead shot, intent on picking Mr. Smallweed off as an ugly old bird of the crow species.

"Judy, my child," says Grandfather Smallweed, "give the person his twopence. It's a great deal for what he has done."

The person, who is one of those extraordinary specimens of human fungus that spring up spontaneously in the western streets of London, ready dressed in an old red jacket, with a "Mission" for holding horses and calling coaches, receives his twopence with anything but transport, tosses the money into the air, catches it overhanded, and retires.

"My dear Mr. George," says Grandfather Smallweed, "would you be so kind as help to carry me to the fire? I am accustomed to a fire, and I am an old man, and I soon chill. O dear me!"

His closing exclamation is jerked out of the venerable gentleman by the suddenness with which Mr. Squod, like a genie, catches him up, chair and all, and deposits him on the hearthstone.

"O Lord!" says Mr. Smallweed, panting. "O dear me! O my stars! My dear friend, your workman is very strong—and very prompt, O Lord, he is very prompt! Judy, draw me back a little. I'm being scorched in the legs"; which indeed is testified to the noses of all present by the smell of his worsted stockings.

The gentle Judy, having backed her grandfather a little way from the fire, and having shaken him up as usual, and having released his overshadowed eye from its black velvet extinguisher, Mr. Smallweed again says, "O dear me! O Lord!" and looking about, and meeting Mr. George's glance, again stretches out both hands.

"My dear friend! So happy in this meeting! And this is your establishment? It's a delightful place. It's a picture! You never find that anything goes off here, accidentally; do you, my dear friend?" adds Grandfather Smallweed, very ill at ease.

"No, no. No fear of that."

"And your workman. He—O dear me!—he never lets anything off without meaning it; does he, my dear friend?"

"He has never hurt anybody but himself," says Mr. George, smiling.

"But he might, you know. He seems to have hurt himself a good deal, and he might hurt somebody else," the old gentleman returns. "He mightn't mean it—or he even might. Mr. George, will you order him to leave his infernal fire-arms alone, and go away?"

Obedient to a nod from the trooper, Phil retires, empty-handed, to the other end of the gallery. Mr. Smallweed, reassured, falls to rubbing his legs.

"And you're doing well, Mr. George?" he says to the trooper, squarely standing faced-about towards him with his broadsword in his hand. "You are prospering, please the Powers?"

Mr. George answers with a cool nod, adding, "Go on. You have not come to say that, I know."

"You are so sprightly, Mr. George," returns the venerable grandfather. "You are such good company."

"Ha ha! Go on!" says Mr. George.

"My dear friend!—But that sword looks awful gleaming and sharp. It might cut somebody, by accident. It makes me shiver, Mr. George—Curse him!" says the excellent old gentleman apart to Judy, as the trooper takes a step or two away to lay it aside. "He owes me money, and might think of paying off all scores in this murdering place. I wish your brimstone grandmother was here, and he'd shave her head off."

Mr. George, returning, folds his arms and looking down at the old man, sliding every moment lower and lower in his chair, says quietly, "Now for it!"

"Ho!" cries Mr. Smallweed, rubbing his hands with an artful chuckle. "Yes. Now for it. Now for what, my dear friend?"

"For a pipe," says Mr. George; who with great composure sets his chair in the chimney-corner, takes his pipe from the grate, fills it and lights it, and falls to smoking peacefully.

This tends to the discomfiture of Mr. Smallweed, who finds it so difficult to resume his object, whatever it may be, that he becomes exasperated, and secretly claws the air with an impotent vindictiveness expressive of an intense desire to tear and rend the visage of Mr. George. As the excellent old gentleman's nails are long and leaden, and his hands lean and veinous, and his eyes green and watery; and, over and above this, as he continues, while he claws, to slide down in his chair and to collapse into a shapeless bundle; he becomes such a ghastly spectacle, even in the accustomed eyes of Judy, that that young virgin pounces at him with something more than the ardour of affection, and so shakes him up, and pats and pokes him in divers parts of his body, but particularly in that part which the science of self-defence would call his wind, that in his grievous distress he utters enforced sounds like a paviour's rammer.[8]

When Judy has by these means set him up again in his chair, with a white face and a frosty nose (but still clawing), she stretches out her weazen forefinger, and gives Mr. George one poke in the back. The trooper raising his head, she makes another poke at her esteemed grandfather; and, having thus brought them together, stares rigidly at the fire.

"Aye, aye! Ho, ho! U—u—u—ugh!" chatters Grandfather Smallweed, swallowing his rage. "My dear friend!" (still clawing).

"I tell you what," says Mr. George. "If you want to converse with me, you must speak out. I am one of the Roughs, and I can't go about and about. I haven't the art to do it. I am not clever enough. It don't suit me. When you go winding round and round me," says the trooper, putting his pipe between his lips again, "damme, if I don't feel as if I was being smothered!"

And he inflates his broad chest to its utmost extent, as if to assure himself that he is not smothered yet.

"If you have come to give me a friendly call," continues Mr. George, "I am obliged to you; how are you? If you have come to see whether there's any property on the premises, look about you; you are welcome. If you want to out with something, out with it!"

The blooming Judy, without removing her gaze from the fire, gives her grandfather one ghostly poke.

"You see! It's her opinion, too. And why the devil that young woman won't sit down like a Christian," says Mr. George, with his eyes musingly fixed on Judy, "*I* can't comprehend."

"She keeps at my side to attend to me, sir," says Grandfather Smallweed. "I am an old man, my dear Mr. George, and I need some attention. I can carry my years; I am not a Brimstone pollparrot"; (snarling and looking unconsciously for the cushion;) "but I need attention, my dear friend."

"Well!" returns the trooper, wheeling his chair to face the old man. "Now then?"

"My friend in the city, Mr. George, has done a little business with a pupil of yours."

"Has he?" says Mr. George. "I am sorry to hear it."

"Yes, sir." Grandfather Smallweed rubs his legs. "He is a fine young soldier now, Mr. George, by the name of Carstone. Friends came forward, and paid it all up, honourable."

"Did they?" returns Mr. George. "Do you think your friend in the city would like a piece of advice?"

8. Device used by pavement-makers (pavers) for ramming stones into the ground.

"I think he would, my dear friend. From you."

"I advise him, then, to do no more business in that quarter. There's no more to be got by it. The young gentleman, to my knowledge, is brought to a dead halt."

"No, no, my dear friend. No, no, Mr. George. No, no, no, sir," remonstrates Grandfather Smallweed, cunningly rubbing his spare legs. "Not quite a dead halt, I think. He has good friends, and he is good for his pay, and he is good for the selling price of his commission, and he is good for his chance in a law-suit, and he is good for his chance in a wife, and—oh, do you know, Mr. George, I think my friend would consider the young gentleman good for something yet?" says Grandfather Smallweed, turning up his velvet cap, and scratching his ear like a monkey.

Mr. George, who has put aside his pipe and sits with an arm on his chair-back, beats a tattoo on the ground with his right foot, as if he were not particularly pleased with the turn the conversation has taken.

"But to pass from one subject to another," resumes Mr. Smallweed. "To promote the conversation, as a joker might say. To pass, Mr. George, from the ensign to the captain."

"What are you up to, now?" asks Mr. George, pausing with a frown in stroking the recollection of his moustache. "What captain?"

"Our captain. The captain we know of. Captain Hawdon."

"O! that's it, is it?" says Mr. George, with a low whistle, as he sees both grandfather and grand-daughter looking hard at him; "You are there? Well, what about it? Come, I won't be smothered any more. Speak!"

"My dear friend," returns the old man, "I was applied—Judy, shake me up a little!—I was applied to, yesterday, about the captain; and my opinion still is, that the captain is not dead."

"Bosh!" observes Mr. George.

"What was your remark, my dear friend?" inquires the old man with his hand to his ear.

"Bosh!"

"Ho!" says Grandfather Smallweed. "Mr. George, of my opinion you can judge for yourself, according to the questions asked of me, and the reasons given for asking 'em. Now, what do you think the lawyer making the inquiries wants?"

"A job," says Mr. George.

"Nothing of the kind!"

"Can't be a lawyer, then," says Mr. George, folding his arms with an air of confirmed resolution.

"My dear friend, he is a lawyer, and a famous one. He wants to see some fragment in Captain Hawdon's writing. He don't want to keep it. He only wants to see it, and compare it with a writing in his possession."

"Well?"

"Well, Mr. George. Happening to remember the advertisement concerning Captain Hawdon, and any information that could be given respecting him, he looked it up and came to me—just as you did, my dear friend. *Will* you shake hands? So glad you came that day! I should have missed forming such a friendship, if you hadn't come!"

"Well, Mr. Smallweed?" says Mr. George again, after going through the ceremony with some stiffness.

"I had no such thing. I have nothing but his signature. Plague pestilence and famine, battle murder and sudden death upon him," says the old man, making a curse out of one of his few remembrances of a prayer,[9] and squeezing up his velvet cap between his angry hands, "I have half a million of his signatures, I think! But you," breathlessly recovering his mildness of speech, as Judy re-adjusts the cap on his skittle-ball of a head; "you, my dear Mr. George, are likely to have some letter or paper that would suit the purpose. Anything would suit the purpose, written in the hand."

"Some writing in that hand," says the trooper, pondering, "may be, I have."

"My dearest friend!"

"May be, I have not."

"Ho!" says Grandfather Smallweed, crest-fallen.

"But if I had bushels of it, I would not show as much as would make a cartridge, without knowing why."

"Sir, I have told you why. My dear Mr. George, I have told you why."

"Not enough," says the trooper, shaking his head. "I must know more, and approve it."

"Then, will you come to the lawyer? My dear friend, will you come and see the gentleman?" urges Grandfather Smallweed, pulling out a lean old silver watch, with hands like the legs of a skeleton. "I told him it was probable I might call upon him, between ten and eleven this forenoon; and it's now half after ten. Will you come and see the gentleman, Mr. George?"

"Hum!" says he, gravely. "I don't mind that. Though why this should concern you so much, I don't know."

"Everything concerns me, that has a chance in it of bringing anything to light about him. Didn't he take us all in? Didn't he owe us immense sums, all round? Concern me? Who can anything about

9. See the "Litany" in *The Book of Common Prayer*: "from plague, pestilence, and famine; from battle, and murder, and from sudden death, Good Lord, deliver us."

him concern, more than me? Not, my dear friend," says Grandfather Smallweed, lowering his tone, "that I want *you* to betray anything. Far from it. Are you ready to come, my dear friend?"

"Ay! I'll come in a moment. I promise nothing, you know."

"No, my dear Mr. George; no."

"And you mean to say you're going to give me a lift to this place, wherever it is, without charging for it?" Mr. George inquires, getting his hat, and thick wash-leather gloves.

This pleasantry so tickles Mr. Smallweed, that he laughs, long and low, before the fire. But ever while he laughs, he glances over his paralytic shoulder at Mr. George, and eagerly watches him as he unlocks the padlock of a homely cupboard at the distant end of the gallery, looks here and there upon the higher shelves, and ultimately takes something out with a rustling of paper, folds it, and puts it in his breast. Then Judy pokes Mr. Smallweed once, and Mr. Smallweed pokes Judy once.

"I am ready," says the trooper, coming back. "Phil, you can carry this old gentleman to his coach, and make nothing of him."

"O dear me! O Lord! Stop a moment!" says Mr. Smallweed. "He's so very prompt! Are you sure you can do it carefully, my worthy man?"

Phil makes no reply; but, seizing the chair and its load, sidles away, tightly hugged by the now speechless Mr. Smallweed, and bolts along the passage, as if he had an acceptable commission to carry the old gentleman to the nearest volcano. His shorter trust, however, terminating at the cab, he deposits him there; and the fair Judy takes her place beside him, and the chair embellishes the roof, and Mr. George takes the vacant place upon the box.

Mr. George is quite confounded by the spectacle he beholds from time to time as he peeps into the cab, through the window behind him; where the grim Judy is always motionless, and the old gentleman with his cap over one eye is always sliding off the seat into the straw,[1] and looking upward at him, out of his other eye, with a helpless expression of being jolted in the back.

Chapter XXVII

MORE OLD SOLDIERS THAN ONE

Mr. George has not far to ride with folded arms upon the box, for their destination is Lincoln's Inn Fields. When the driver stops his horses, Mr. George alights, and looking in at the window, says:

"What, Mr. Tulkinghorn's your man, is he?"

"Yes, my dear friend. Do you know him, Mr. George?"

1. Straw was strewn on the floor of the cab to keep the passengers' feet warm.

"Why, I have heard of him—seen him too, I think. But I don't know him, and he don't know me."

There ensues the carrying of Mr. Smallweed up-stairs; which is done to perfection with the trooper's help. He is borne into Mr. Tulkinghorn's great room, and deposited on the Turkey rug before the fire. Mr. Tulkinghorn is not within at the present moment, but will be back directly. The occupant of the pew in the hall, having said thus much, stirs the fire, and leaves the triumvirate to warm themselves.

Mr. George is mightily curious in respect of the room. He looks up at the painted ceiling, looks round at the old law-books, contemplates the portraits of the great clients, reads aloud the names on the boxes.

" 'Sir Leicester Dedlock, Baronet,' " Mr. George reads thoughtfully. "Ha! 'Manor of Chesney Wold.' Humph!" Mr. George stands looking at these boxes a long while—as if they were pictures—and comes back to the fire repeating, "Sir Leicester Dedlock, Baronet, and Manor of Chesney Wold, hey?"

"Worth a mint of money, Mr. George!" whispers Grandfather Smallweed, rubbing his legs. "Powerfully rich!"

"Who do you mean? This old gentleman, or the Baronet?"

"This gentleman, this gentleman."

"So I have heard; and knows a thing a two, I'll hold a wager. Not bad quarters, either," says Mr. George, looking round again. "See the strong box, yonder!"

This reply is cut short by Mr. Tulkinghorn's arrival. There is no change in him, of course. Rustily drest, with his spectacles in his hand, and their very case worn threadbare. In manner, close and dry. In voice, husky and low. In face, watchful behind a blind; habitually not uncensorious and contemptuous perhaps. The peerage may have warmer worshippers and faithfuller believers than Mr. Tulkinghorn, after all, if everything were known.

"Good morning, Mr. Smallweed, good morning!" he says as he comes in. "You have brought the serjeant, I see. Sit down, serjeant."

As Mr. Tulkinghorn takes off his gloves and puts them in his hat, he looks with half-closed eyes across the room to where the trooper stands, and says within himself perchance, "You'll do, my friend!"

"Sit down, serjeant," he repeats, as he comes to his table, which is set on one side of the fire, and takes his easy-chair. "Cold and raw this morning, cold and raw!" Mr. Tulkinghorn warms before the bars, alternately, the palms and knuckles of his hands, and looks (from behind that blind which is always down) at the trio sitting in a little semicircle before him.

"Now, I can feel what I am about!" (as perhaps he can in two senses) "Mr. Smallweed." The old gentleman is newly shaken up by Judy, to bear his part in the conversation. "You have brought our good friend the serjeant, I see."

"Yes, sir," returns Mr. Smallweed, very servile to the lawyer's wealth and influence.

"And what does the serjeant say about this business?"

"Mr. George," says Grandfather Smallweed, with a tremulous wave of his shrivelled hand, "this is the gentleman, sir."

Mr. George salutes the gentleman; but otherwise sits bolt upright and profoundly silent—very forward in his chair, as if the full complement of regulation appendages[1] for a field-day hung about him.

Mr. Tulkinghorn proceeds: "Well, George?—I believe your name is George?"

"It is so, sir."

"What do you say, George?"

"I ask your pardon, sir," returns the trooper, "but I should wish to know what *you* say?"

"Do you mean in point of reward?"

"I mean in point of everything, sir."

This is so very trying to Mr. Smallweed's temper, that he suddenly breaks out with "You're a Brimstone beast!" and as suddenly asks pardon of Mr. Tulkinghorn; excusing himself for this slip of the tongue, by saying to Judy, "I was thinking of your grandmother, my dear."

"I supposed, serjeant," Mr. Tulkinghorn resumes, as he leans on one side of his chair and crosses his legs, "that Mr. Smallweed might have sufficiently explained the matter. It lies in the smallest compass, however. You served under Captain Hawdon at one time, and were his attendant in illness, and rendered him many little services, and were rather in his confidence, I am told. That is so, is it not?"

"Yes, sir, that is so," says Mr. George, with military brevity.

"Therefore you may happen to have in your possession something—anything, no matter what—accounts, instructions, orders, a letter, anything—in Captain Hawdon's writing. I wish to compare his writing with some that I have. If you can give me the opportunity, you shall be rewarded for your trouble. Three, four, five, guineas, you would consider handsome, I dare say."

"Noble, my dear friend!" cries Grandfather Smallweed, screwing up his eyes.

"If not, say how much more, in your conscience as a soldier, you can demand. There is no need for you to part with the writing, against your inclination—though I should prefer to have it."

Mr. George sits squared in exactly the same attitude, looks at the

1. Full-scale outfit of weapons and other equipment carried slung by a soldier participating in a military display.

ground, looks at the painted ceiling, and says never a word. The irascible Mr. Smallweed scratches the air.

"The question is," says Mr. Tulkinghorn in his methodical, subdued, uninterested way, "first, whether you have any of Captain Hawdon's writing?"

"First, whether I have any of Captain Hawdon's writing, sir," repeats Mr. George.

"Secondly, what will satisfy you for the trouble of producing it?"

"Secondly, what will satisfy me for the trouble of producing it, sir," repeats Mr. George.

"Thirdly, you can judge for yourself whether it is at all like that," says Mr. Tulkinghorn, suddenly handing him some sheets of written paper tied together.

"Whether it is at all like that, sir. Just so," repeats Mr. George.

All three repetitions Mr. George pronounces in a mechanical manner, looking straight at Mr. Tulkinghorn; nor does he so much as glance at the affidavit in Jarndyce and Jarndyce, that has been given to him for his inspection (though he still holds it in his hand), but continues to look at the lawyer with an air of troubled meditation.

"Well?" says Mr. Tulkinghorn. "What do you say?"

"Well, sir," replies Mr. George, rising erect and looking immense, "I would rather, if you'll excuse me, have nothing to do with this."

Mr. Tulkinghorn, outwardly quite undisturbed, demands "Why not?"

"Why, sir," returns the trooper. "Except on military compulsion, I am not a man of business. Among civilians I am what they call in Scotland a ne'er-do-weel. I have no head for papers, sir. I can stand any fire better than a fire of cross questions. I mentioned to Mr. Smallweed, only an hour or so ago, that when I come into things of this kind I feel as if I was being smothered. And that is my sensation," says Mr. George, looking round upon the company, "at the present moment."

With that, he takes three strides forward to replace the papers on the lawyer's table, and three strides backward to resume his former station: where he stands perfectly upright, now looking at the ground, and now at the painted ceiling, with his hands behind him as if to prevent himself from accepting any other document whatever.

Under this provocation, Mr. Smallweed's favourite adjective of disparagement is so close to his tongue, that he begins the words "my dear friend" with the monosyllable "Brim"; thus converting the possessive pronoun into Brimmy, and appearing to have an impediment in his speech. Once past this difficulty, however, he exhorts his dear friend in the tenderest manner not to be rash, but to do what so eminent a gentleman requires, and to do it with a good grace: confident that it must be unobjectionable as well as profitable. Mr. Tulkinghorn merely utters such occasional sentences as "You are the best judge of your own interest, serjeant." "Take care you do no harm by this." "Please yourself, please yourself." "If you know what you mean, that's quite enough." These he utters with an appearance of perfect indifference, as he looks over the papers on his table, and prepares to write a letter.

Mr. George looks distrustfully from the painted ceiling to the ground, from the ground to Mr. Smallweed, from Mr. Smallweed to Mr. Tulkinghorn, and from Mr. Tulkinghorn to the painted ceiling again; often in his perplexity changing the leg on which he rests.

"I do assure you, sir," says Mr. George, "not to say it offensively, that between you and Mr. Smallweed here, I really am being smothered fifty times over. I really am, sir. I am not a match for you gentlemen. Will you allow me to ask, why you want to see the captain's hand, in the case that I could find any specimen of it?"

Mr. Tulkinghorn quietly shakes his head. "No. If you were a man of business, serjeant, you would not need to be informed, that there are confidential reasons, very harmless in themselves, for many such wants, in the profession to which I belong. But if you are afraid of doing any injury to Captain Hawdon, you may set your mind at rest about that."

"Ay! he is dead, sir."

"*Is* he?" Mr. Tulkinghorn quietly sits down to write.

"Well, sir," says the trooper, looking into his hat after another disconcerted pause; "I am sorry not to have given you more satisfaction. If it would be any satisfaction to any one, that I should be confirmed in my judgment that I would rather have nothing to do with this, by a friend of mine, who has a better head for business than I have, and who is an old soldier, I am willing to consult with him. I—I really am so completely smothered myself at present," says Mr. George, passing his hand hopelessly across his brow, "that I don't know but what it might be a satisfaction to me."

Mr. Smallweed, hearing that this authority is an old soldier, so strongly inculcates the expediency of the trooper's taking counsel with him, and particularly informing him of its being a question of five guineas or more, that Mr. George engages to go and see him. Mr. Tulkinghorn says nothing either way.

"I'll consult my friend, then, by your leave, sir," says the trooper, "and I'll take the liberty of looking in again with a final answer in the course of the day. Mr. Smallweed, if you wish to be carried down-stairs——"

"In a moment, my dear friend, in a moment. Will you first let me speak half a word with this gentleman, in private?"

"Certainly, sir. Don't hurry yourself on my account." The

trooper retires to a distant part of the room, and resumes his curious inspection of the boxes; strong and otherwise.

"If I wasn't as weak as a Brimstone Baby, sir," whispers Grandfather Smallweed, drawing the lawyer down to his level by the lappel of his coat, and flashing some half-quenched green fire out of his angry eyes, "I'd tear the writing away from him. He's got it buttoned in his breast. I saw him put it there. Judy saw him put it there. Speak up, you crabbed image for the sign of a walking-stick shop,[2] and say you saw him put it there!"

This vehement conjuration the old gentleman accompanies with such a thrust at his grand-daughter, that it is too much for his strength, and he slips away out of his chair, drawing Mr. Tulkinghorn with him, until he is arrested by Judy, and well shaken.

"Violence will not do for me, my friend," Mr. Tulkinghorn then remarks coolly.

"No, no, I know, I know, sir. But it's chafing and galling—it's—it's worse than your smattering chattering Magpie of a grandmother," to the imperturbable Judy, who only looks at the fire, "to know he has got what's wanted, and won't give it up. He, not to give it up! *He!* A vagabond! But never mind, sir, never mind. At the most, he has only his own way for a little while. I have him periodically in a vice. I'll twist him, sir. I'll screw him, sir. If he won't do it with a good grace, I'll make him do it with a bad one, sir!—Now, my dear Mr. George," says Grandfather Smallweed, winking at the lawyer hideously, as he releases him, "I am ready for your kind assistance, my excellent friend!"

Mr. Tulkinghorn, with some shadowy sign of amusement manifesting itself through his self-possession, stands on the hearth-rug with his back to the fire, watching the disappearance of Mr. Smallweed, and acknowledging the trooper's parting salute with one slight nod.

It is more difficult to get rid of the old gentleman, Mr. George finds, than to bear a hand in carrying him down-stairs; for, when he is replaced in his conveyance, he is so loquacious on the subject of the guineas, and retains such an affectionate hold of his button—having, in truth, a secret longing to rip his coat open, and rob him—that some degree of force is necessary on the trooper's part to effect a separation. It is accomplished at last, and he proceeds alone in quest of his adviser.

By the cloisterly Temple, and by Whitefriars (there, not without a glance at Hanging-Sword Alley, which would seem to be something in his way), and by Blackfriars Bridge, and Blackfriars Road,

2. A London shop which had a sign featuring two wooden walking sticks with grotesque carved heads of an old woman and old man. (Allusion identified by C. F. Tufnell in 1924.)

Mr. George sedately marches to a street of little shops lying somewhere in that ganglion of roads from Kent and Surrey, and of streets from the bridges of London, centering in the far-famed Elephant who has lost his castle formed of a thousand four-horse coaches, to a stronger iron monster than he, ready to chop him into mince-meat any day he dares.[3] To one of the little shops in this street, which is a musician's shop, having a few fiddles in the window, and some Pan's pipes and a tambourine, and a triangle, and certain elongated scraps of music, Mr. George directs his massive tread. And halting at a few paces from it, as he sees a soldierly-looking woman, with her outer skirts tucked up, come forth with a small wooden tub, and in that tub commence a whisking and a splashing on the margin of the pavement, Mr. George says to himself, "She's as usual, washing greens. I never saw her, except upon a baggage-waggon, when she wasn't washing greens!"

The subject of this reflection is at all events so occupied in washing greens at present, that she remains unsuspicious of Mr. George's approach; until, lifting up herself and her tub together, when she has poured the water off into the gutter, she finds him standing near her. Her reception of him is not flattering.

"George, I never see you but I wish you was a hundred mile away!"

The trooper, without remarking on this welcome, follows into the musical instrument shop, where the lady places her tub of greens upon the counter, and having shaken hands with him, rests her arms upon it.

"I never," she says, "George, consider Matthew Bagnet safe a minute when you're near him. You are that restless and that roving ——"

"Yes, I know I am, Mrs. Bagnet. I know I am."

"You know you are!" says Mrs. Bagnet. "What's the use of that? W*hy* are you?"

"The nature of the animal, I suppose," returns the trooper good-humouredly.

"Ah!" cries Mrs. Bagnet, something shrilly, "but what satisfaction will the nature of the animal be to me, when the animal shall have tempted my Mat away from the musical business to New Zealand or Australey?"

Mrs. Bagnet is not at all an ill-looking woman. Rather large-boned, a little coarse in the grain, and freckled by the sun and wind which have tanned her hair upon the forehead; but healthy, wholesome, and bright-eyed. A strong, busy, active, honest-faced woman of from forty-five to fifty. Clean, hardy, and so economically dressed

3. Elephant and Castle, a district of London, had formerly been a center for stagecoaches but had now been taken over by railways.

(though substantially), that the only article of ornament of which she stands possessed appears to be her wedding-ring; around which her finger has grown to be so large since it was put on, that it will never come off again until it shall mingle with Mrs. Bagnet's dust.

"Mrs. Bagnet," says the trooper, "I am on my parole with you. Mat will get no harm from me. You may trust me so far."

"Well, I think I may. But the very looks of you are unsettling," Mrs. Bagnet rejoins. "Ah, George, George! If you had only settled down, and married Joe Pouch's widow when he died in North America, *she*'d have combed your hair for you."

"It was a chance for me, certainly," returns the trooper, half-laughingly, half-seriously, "but I shall never settle down into a respectable man now. Joe Pouch's widow might have done me good —there was something in her—and something of her—but I couldn't make up my mind to it. If I had had the luck to meet with such a wife as Mat found!"

Mrs. Bagnet, who seems in a virtuous way to be under little reserve with a good sort of fellow, but to be another good sort of fellow herself for that matter, receives this compliment by flicking Mr. George in the face with a head of greens, and taking her tub into the little room behind the shop.

"Why, Quebec, my poppet," says George, following, on invitation, into that apartment. "And little Malta, too! Come and kiss your Bluffy!"

These young ladies—not supposed to have been actually christened by the names applied to them, though always so called in the family, from the places of their birth in barracks—are respectively employed on three-legged stools: the younger (some five or six years old), in learning her letters out of a penny primer; the elder (eight or nine perhaps), in teaching her, and sewing with great assiduity. Both hail Mr. George with acclamations as an old friend, and after some kissing and romping plant their stools beside him.

"And how's young Woolwich?"[4] says Mr. George.

"Ah! There now!" cries Mrs. Bagnet, turning about from her saucepans (for she is cooking dinner), with a bright flush on her face. "Would you believe it? Got an engagement at the Theayter, with his father, to play the fife in a military piece."

"Well done, my godson!" cries Mr. George, slapping his thigh.

"I believe you!" says Mrs. Bagnet. "He's a Briton. That's what Woolwich is. A Briton!"

"And Mat blows away at his bassoon, and you're respectable civilians one and all," says Mr. George. "Family people. Children growing up. Mat's old mother in Scotland, and your old father somewhere else, corresponded with; and helped a little; and—well, well!

4. A training center for the Royal Artillery on the outskirts of London. Bagnet was presumably stationed there before his regiment was sent out to garrisons at Quebec and Malta, each location providing a name for one of his children.

To be sure, I don't know why I shouldn't be wished a hundred mile away, for I have not much to do with all this!"

Mr. George is becoming thoughtful; sitting before the fire in the whitewashed room, which has a sanded floor, and a barrack smell, and contains nothing superfluous, and has not a visible speck of dirt or dust in it, from the faces of Quebec and Malta to the bright tin pots and pannikins upon the dresser shelves;—Mr. George is becoming thoughtful, sitting here while Mrs. Bagnet is busy, when Mr. Bagnet and young Woolwich opportunely come home. Mr. Bagnet is an ex-artilleryman, tall and upright, with shaggy eyebrows, and whiskers like the fibres of a cocoa-nut, not a hair upon his head, and a torrid complexion. His voice, short, deep, and resonant, is not at all unlike the tones of the instrument to which he is devoted. Indeed there may be generally observed in him an unbending, unyielding, brass-bound air,[5] as if he were himself the bassoon of the human orchestra. Young Woolwich is the type and model of a young drummer.

Both father and son salute the trooper heartily. He saying, in due season, that he has come to advise with Mr. Bagnet, Mr. Bagnet hospitably declares that he will hear of no business until after dinner; and that his friend shall not partake of his counsel, without first partaking of boiled pork and greens. The trooper yielding to this invitation, he and Mr. Bagnet, not to embarrass the domestic preparations, go forth and take a turn up and down the little street, which they promenade with measured tread and folded arms, as if it were a rampart.

"George," says Mr. Bagnet. "You know me. It's my old girl that advises. She has the head. But I never own to it before her. Discipline must be maintained. Wait till the greens is off her mind. Then, we'll consult. Whatever the old girl says, do—do it!"

"I intend to, Mat," replies the other. "I would sooner take her opinion than that of a college."

"College," returns Mr. Bagnet, in short sentences, bassoon-like. "What college could you leave—in another quarter of the world—with nothing but a grey cloak and an umbrella—to make its way home to Europe? The old girl would do it to-morrow. Did it once!"

"You are right," says Mr. George.

"What college," pursues Bagnet, "could you set up in life—with two penn'orth of white lime—a penn'orth of fuller's earth—a ha'porth of sand—and the rest of the change out of sixpence, in money? That's what the old girl started on. In the present business."

"I am rejoiced to hear it's thriving, Mat."

"The old girl," says Mr. Bagnet, acquiescing, "saves. Has a stock-

5. As Dickens explained in a letter (November 3, 1852), the adjective *brass-bound* "applies to the man [Bagnet] not the instrument."

ing somewhere. With money in it. I never saw it. But I know she's got it. Wait till the greens is off her mind. Then she'll set you up."

"She is a treasure!" exclaims Mr. George.

"She's more. But I never own to it before her. Discipline must be maintained. It was the old girl that brought out my musical abilities. I should have been in the artillery now, but for the old girl. Six years I hammered at the fiddle. Ten at the flute. The old girl said it wouldn't do; intention good, but want of flexibility; try the bassoon. The old girl borrowed a bassoon from the bandmaster of the Rifle Regiment. I practised in the trenches. Got on, got another, get a living by it!"

George remarks that she looks as fresh as a rose, and as sound as an apple.

"The old girl," says Mr. Bagnet in reply, "is a thoroughly fine woman. Consequently, she is like a thoroughly fine day. Gets finer as she gets on. I never saw the old girl's equal. But I never own to it before her. Discipline must be maintained!"

Proceeding to converse on indifferent matters, they walk up and down the little street, keeping step and time, until summoned by Quebec and Malta to do justice to the pork and greens; over which Mrs. Bagnet, like a military chaplain, says a short grace. In the distribution of these comestibles, as in every other household duty, Mrs. Bagnet developes an exact system; sitting with every dish before her; allotting to every portion of pork its own portion of pot-liquor, greens, potatoes, and even mustard; and serving it out complete. Having likewise served out the beer from a can, and thus supplied the mess with all things necessary, Mrs. Bagnet proceeds to satisfy her own hunger, which is in a healthy state. The kit of the mess, if the table furniture may be so denominated, is chiefly composed of utensils of horn and tin, that have done duty in several parts of the world. Young Woolwich's knife in particular, which is of the oyster kind, with the additional feature of a strong shutting-up movement which frequently balks the appetite of that young musician, is mentioned as having gone in various hands the complete round of foreign service.

The dinner done, Mrs. Bagnet, assisted by the younger branches (who polish their own cups and platters, knives and forks), makes all the dinner garniture shine as brightly as before, and puts it all away; first sweeping the hearth, to the end that Mr. Bagnet and the visitor may not be retarded in the smoking of their pipes. These household cares involve much pattening[6] and counter-pattening in the back yard, and considerable use of a pail, which is finally so happy as to assist in the ablutions of Mrs. Bagnet herself. That old

6. Pattens are shoes with skate-like attachments designed for walking through mud.

girl reappearing by-and-by, quite fresh, and sitting down to her needlework, then and only then—the greens being only then to be considered as entirely off her mind—Mr. Bagnet requests the trooper to state his case.

This, Mr. George does with great discretion; appearing to address himself to Mr. Bagnet, but having an eye solely on the old girl all the time, as Bagnet has himself. She, equally discreet, busies herself with her needlework. The case fully stated, Mr. Bagnet resorts to his standard artifice for the maintenance of discipline.

"That's the whole of it, is it, George?" says he.

"That's the whole of it."

"You act according to my opinion?"

"I shall be guided," replies George, "entirely by it."

"Old girl," says Mr. Bagnet, "give him my opinion. You know it. Tell him what it is."

It is, that he cannot have too little to do with people who are too deep for him, and cannot be too careful of interference with matters he does not understand; that the plain rule, is to do nothing in the dark, to be a party to nothing under-handed or mysterious, and never to put his foot where he cannot see the ground. This, in effect, is Mr. Bagnet's opinion, as delivered through the old girl; and it so relieves Mr. George's mind, by confirming his own opinion and banishing his doubts, that he composes himself to smoke another pipe on that exceptional occasion, and to have a talk over old times with the whole Bagnet family, according to their various ranges of experience.

Through these means it comes to pass, that Mr. George does not again rise to his full height in that parlour until the time is drawing on when the bassoon and fife are expected by a British public at the theatre; and as it takes time even then for Mr. George, in his domestic character of Bluffy, to take leave of Quebec and Malta, and insinuate a sponsorial shilling into the pocket of his godson, with felicitations on his success in life, it is dark when Mr. George again turns his face towards Lincoln's Inn Fields.

"A family home," he ruminates, as he marches along, "however small it is, makes a man like me look lonely. But it's well I never made that evolution of matrimony. I shouldn't have been fit for it. I am such a vagabond still, even at my present time of life, that I couldn't hold to the gallery a month together, if it was a regular pursuit, or if I didn't camp there, gipsy fashion. Come! I disgrace nobody and cumber nobody; that's something. I have not done that for many a long year!"

So he whistles it off, and marches on.

Arrived in Lincoln's Inn Fields, and mounting Mr. Tulkinghorn's stair, he finds the outer door closed, and the chambers shut; but the trooper not knowing much about outer doors, and the staircase being dark besides, he is yet fumbling and groping about, hoping to discover a bell-handle or to open the door for himself, when Mr. Tulkinghorn comes up the stairs (quietly, of course), and angrily asks:

"Who is that? What are you doing there?"

"I ask your pardon, sir. It's George. The serjeant."

"And couldn't George, the serjeant, see that my door was locked?"

"Why, no, sir, I couldn't. At any rate, I didn't," says the trooper, rather nettled.

"Have you changed your mind? or are you in the same mind?" Mr. Tulkinghorn demands. But he knows well enough at a glance.

"In the same mind, sir."

"I thought so. That's sufficient. You can go. So you are the man," says Mr. Tulkinghorn, opening his door with the key, "in whose hiding-place Mr. Gridley was found?"

"Yes, I *am* the man," says the trooper, stopping two or three stairs down. "What then, sir?"

"What then? I don't like your associates. You should not have seen the inside of my door this morning, if I had thought of your being that man. Gridley? A threatening, murderous, dangerous fellow."

With these words, spoken in an unusually high tone for him, the lawyer goes into his rooms, and shuts the door with a thundering noise.

Mr. George takes his dismissal in great dudgeon; the greater, because a clerk coming up the stairs has heard the last words of all, and evidently applies them to him. "A pretty character to bear," the trooper growls with a hasty oath, as he strides down-stairs. "A threatening, murderous, dangerous fellow!" and looking up, he sees the clerk looking down at him, and marking him as he passes the lamp. This so intensifies his dudgeon, that for five minutes he is in an ill-humour. But he whistles that off, like the rest of it; and marches home to the Shooting Gallery.

Chapter XXVIII

THE IRONMASTER

Sir Leicester Dedlock has got the better, for the time being, of the family gout; and is once more, in a literal no less than in a figurative point of view, upon his legs. He is at his place in Lincolnshire; but the waters are out again on the low-lying grounds, and the cold and damp steal into Chesney Wold, though well defended, and eke into Sir Leicester's bones. The blazing fires of faggot and coal—

Dedlock timber and antediluvian forest—that blaze upon the broad wide hearths, and wink in the twilight on the frowning woods, sullen to see how trees are sacrificed, do not exclude the enemy. The hot-water pipes that trail themselves all over the house, the cushioned doors and windows, and the screens and curtains, fail to supply the fires' deficiencies, and to satisfy Sir Leicester's need. Hence the fashionable intelligence proclaims one morning to the listening earth,[1] that Lady Dedlock is expected shortly to return to town for a few weeks.

It is a melancholy truth that even great men have their poor relations. Indeed great men have often more than their fair share of poor relations; inasmuch as very red blood of the superior quality, like inferior blood unlawfully shed, *will* cry aloud, and *will* be heard. Sir Leicester's cousins, in the remotest degree, are so many Murders, in the respect that they "will out."[2] Among whom there are cousins who are so poor, that one might almost dare to think it would have been the happier for them never to have been plated links upon the Dedlock chain of gold, but to have been made of common iron at first, and done base service.

Service, however (with a few limited reservations; genteel but not profitable), they may not do, being of the Dedlock dignity. So they visit their richer cousins, and get into debt when they can, and live but shabbily when they can't, and find—the women no husbands, and the men no wives—and ride in borrowed carriages, and sit at feasts that are never of their own making, and so go through high life. The rich family sum has been divided by so many figures, and they are the something over that nobody knows what to do with.

Everybody on Sir Leicester Dedlock's side of the question, and of his way of thinking, would appear to be his cousin more or less. From my Lord Boodle, through the Duke of Foodle, down to Noodle, Sir Leicester, like a glorious spider, stretches his threads of relationship. But while he is stately in the cousinship of the Everybodys, he is a kind and generous man, according to his dignified way, in the cousinship of the Nobodys; and at the present time, in despite of the damp, he stays out the visit of several such cousins at Chesney Wold, with the constancy of a martyr.

Of these, foremost in the front rank stands Volumnia Dedlock, a young lady (of sixty) who is doubly highly related; having the honour to be a poor relation, by the mother's side, to another great family. Miss Volumnia, displaying in early life a pretty talent for

1. In Addison's ode, "The Spacious Firmament on High," the skies acknowledge their Creator ("Their great Original proclaim") as likewise does the moon: "And nightly to the listening Earth/ Repeats the story of her birth."

2. The expression "Murder will out" occurs in Chaucer's "Nun's Priest's Tale," line 4242, but for the overall idea of blood that "*will* cry aloud" see *Hamlet* (II.ii.621–22) and *Macbeth* (III.iv.122–23).

cutting ornaments out of coloured paper, and also for singing to the guitar in the Spanish tongue, and propounding French conundrums in country houses, passed the twenty years of her existence between twenty and forty in a sufficiently agreeable manner. Lapsing then out of date, and being considered to bore mankind by her vocal performances in the Spanish language, she retired to Bath; where she lives slenderly on an annual present from Sir Leicester, and whence she makes occasional resurrections in the country houses of her cousins. She has an extensive acquaintance at Bath among appalling old gentlemen with thin legs and nankeen trousers, and is of high standing in that dreary city. But she is a little dreaded elsewhere, in consequence of an indiscreet profusion in the article of rouge, and persistency in an obsolete pearl necklace like a rosary of little bird's-eggs.

In any country in a wholesome state, Volumnia would be a clear case for the pension list. Efforts have been made to get her on it; and when William Buffy came in, it was fully expected that her name would be put down for a couple of hundred a-year. But William Buffy somehow discovered, contrary to all expectation, that these were not times when it could be done; and this was the first clear indication Sir Leicester Dedlock had conveyed to him, that the country was going to pieces.

There is likewise the Honourable Bob Stables, who can make warm mashes[3] with the skill of a veterinary surgeon, and is a better shot than most gamekeepers. He has been for some time particularly desirous to serve his country in a post of good emoluments, unaccompanied by any trouble or responsibility. In a well-regulated body politic, this natural desire on the part of a spirited young gentleman so highly connected, would be speedily recognised; but somehow William Buffy found, when he came in, that these were not times in which he could manage that little matter, either;[4] and this was the second indication Sir Leicester Dedlock had conveyed to him, that the country was going to pieces.

The rest of the cousins are ladies and gentlemen of various ages and capacities; the major part, amiable and sensible, and likely to have done well enough in life if they could have overcome their cousinship; as it is, they are almost all a little worsted by it, and lounge in purposeless and listless paths, and seem to be quite as much at a loss how to dispose of themselves, as anybody else can be how to dispose of them.

In this society, and where not, my Lady Dedlock reigns supreme.

3. Mixture of grain or bran and hot water as feed for horses and cattle.

4. In the early 1850's, reforms of the Civil Service were being recommended (following reforms already introduced in the Indian Civil Service) whereby candidates for government posts were to be appointed on the basis of their performance in competitive examinations rather than by their being "highly connected."

Beautiful, elegant, accomplished, and powerful in her little world (for the world of fashion does not stretch *all* the way from pole to pole), her influence in Sir Leicester's house, however haughty and indifferent her manner, is greatly to improve it and refine it. The cousins, even those older cousins who were paralysed when Sir Leicester married her, do her feudal homage; and the Honourable Bob Stables daily repeats to some chosen person, between breakfast and lunch, his favourite original remark, that she is the best-groomed woman in the whole stud.

Such the guests in the long drawing-room at Chesney Wold this dismal night, when the step on the Ghost's Walk (inaudible here, however) might be the step of a deceased cousin shut out in the cold. It is near bed-time. Bedroom fires blaze brightly all over the house, raising ghosts of grim furniture on wall and ceiling. Bedroom candlesticks[5] bristle on the distant table by the door, and cousins yawn on ottomans. Cousins at the piano, cousins at the soda-water tray, cousins rising from the card-table, cousins gathered round the fire. Standing on one side of his own peculiar fire (for there are two), Sir Leicester. On the opposite side of the broad hearth, my Lady at her table. Volumnia, as one of the more privileged cousins, in a luxurious chair between them. Sir Leicester glancing, with magnificent displeasure, at the rouge and the pearl necklace.

"I occasionally meet on my staircase here," drawls Volumnia, whose thoughts perhaps are already hopping up it to bed, after a long evening of very desultory talk, "one of the prettiest girls, I think, that I ever saw in my life."

"A *protegée* of my Lady's," observes Sir Leicester.

"I thought so. I felt sure that some uncommon eye must have picked that girl out. She really is a marvel. A dolly sort of beauty, perhaps," says Miss Volumnia, reserving her own sort, "but in its way, perfect; such bloom I never saw!"

Sir Leicester, with his magnificent glance of displeasure at the rouge, appears to say so too.

"Indeed," remarks my Lady, languidly, "if there is any uncommon eye in the case, it is Mrs. Rouncewell's, and not mine. Rosa is her discovery."

"Your maid, I suppose?"

"No. My anything; pet—secretary—messenger—I don't know what."

"You like to have her about you, as you would like to have a flower, or a bird, or a picture, or a poodle—no, not a poodle, though—or anything else that was equally pretty?" says Volumnia, sympathising. "Yes, how charming now! and how well that delight-

5. A candlestick with a short stem mounted on a broad flat tray. Each guest was supplied with one to take to his bedroom.

ful old soul Mrs. Rouncewell is looking. She must be an immense age, and yet she is as active and handsome!—She is the dearest friend I have, positively!"

Sir Leicester feels it to be right and fitting that the housekeeper of Chesney Wold should be a remarkable person. Apart from that, he has a real regard for Mrs. Rouncewell, and likes to hear her praised. So he says, "You are right, Volumnia"; which Volumnia is extremely glad to hear.

"She has no daughter of her own, has she?"

"Mrs. Rouncewell? No, Volumnia. She has a son. Indeed, she had two."

My Lady, whose chronic malady of boredom has been sadly aggravated by Volumnia this evening, glances wearily towards the candlesticks and heaves a noiseless sigh.

"And it is a remarkable example of the confusion into which the present age has fallen; of the obliteration of landmarks, the opening of floodgates, and the uprooting of distinctions," says Sir Leicester with stately gloom; "that I have been informed, by Mr. Tulkinghorn, that Mrs. Rouncewell's son has been invited to go into Parliament."

Miss Volumnia utters a little sharp scream.

"Yes, indeed," repeats Sir Leicester. "Into Parliament."

"I ne-ver heard of such a thing! Good gracious, what is the man?" exclaims Volumnia.

"He is called, I believe—an—Ironmaster." Sir Leicester says it slowly, and with gravity and doubt, as not being sure but that he is called a Lead-mistress; or that the right word may be some other word expressive of some other relationship to some other metal.

Volumnia utters another little scream.

"He has declined the proposal, if my information from Mr. Tulkinghorn be correct, as I have no doubt it is, Mr. Tulkinghorn being always correct and exact; still that does not," says Sir Leicester, "that does not lessen the anomaly; which is fraught with strange considerations—startling considerations, as it appears to me."

Miss Volumnia rising with a look candlestick-wards, Sir Leicester politely performs the grand tour of the drawing-room, brings one, and lights it at my Lady's shaded lamp.

"I must beg you, my Lady," he says while doing so, "to remain a few moments; for this individual of whom I speak, arrived this evening shortly before dinner, and requested—in a very becoming note"; Sir Leicester, with his habitual regard to truth, dwells upon it; "I am bound to say, in a very becoming and well-expressed note—the favour of a short interview with yourself and *my*self, on the subject of this young girl. As it appeared that he wished to depart tonight, I replied that we would see him before retiring."

Miss Volumnia with a third little scream takes flight, wishing her hosts—O Lud!—well rid of the—what is it?—Ironmaster!

The other cousins soon disperse, to the last cousin there. Sir Leicester rings the bell. "Make my compliments to Mr. Rouncewell, in the housekeeper's apartments, and say I can receive him now."

My Lady, who has heard all this with slight attention outwardly, looks towards Mr. Rouncewell as he comes in. He is a little over fifty perhaps, of a good figure, like his mother; and has a clear voice, a broad forehead from which his dark hair has retired, and a shrewd, though open face. He is a responsible-looking gentleman dressed in black, portly enough, but strong and active. Has a perfectly natural and easy air, and is not in the least embarrassed by the great presence into which he comes.

"Sir Leicester and Lady Dedlock, as I have already apologised for intruding on you, I cannot do better than be very brief. I thank you, Sir Leicester."

The head of the Dedlocks has motioned towards a sofa between himself and my Lady. Mr. Rouncewell quietly takes his seat there.

"In these busy times, when so many great undertakings are in progress, people like myself have so many workmen in so many places, that we are always on the flight."

Sir Leicester is content enough that the ironmaster should feel that there is no hurry there; there, in that ancient house, rooted in that quiet park, where the ivy and the moss have had time to mature, and the gnarled and warted elms, and the umbrageous oaks, stand deep in the fern and leaves of a hundred years; and where the sun-dial on the terrace has dumbly recorded for centuries that Time, which was as much the property of every Dedlock—while he lasted—as the house and lands. Sir Leicester sits down in an easy-chair, opposing his repose and that of Chesney Wold to the restless flights of ironmasters.

"Lady Dedlock has been so kind," proceeds Mr. Rouncewell, with a respectful glance and a bow that way, "as to place near her a young beauty of the name of Rosa. Now, my son has fallen in love with Rosa; and has asked my consent to his proposing marriage to her, and to their becoming engaged if she will take him—which I suppose she will. I have never seen Rosa until to-day, but I have some confidence in my son's good sense—even in love. I find her what he represents her, to the best of my judgment; and my mother speaks of her with great commendation."

"She in all respects deserves it," says my Lady.

"I am happy, Lady Dedlock, that you say so; and I need not comment on the value to me of your kind opinion of her."

"That," observes Sir Leicester, with unspeakable grandeur; for he thinks the ironmaster a little too glib; "must be quite unnecessary."

"Quite unnecessary, Sir Leicester. Now, my son is a very young man, and Rosa is a very young woman. As I made my way, so my son must make his; and his being married at present is out of the question. But supposing I gave my consent to his engaging himself to this pretty girl, if this pretty girl will engage herself to him, I think it a piece of candour to say at once—I am sure, Sir Leicester and Lady Dedlock, you will understand and excuse me—I should make it a condition that she did not remain at Chesney Wold. Therefore, before communicating further with my son, I take the liberty of saying that if her removal would be in any way inconvenient or objectionable, I will hold the matter over with him for any reasonable time, and leave it precisely where it is."

Not remain at Chesney Wold! Make it a condition! All Sir Leicester's old misgivings relative to Wat Tyler,[6] and the people in the iron districts who do nothing but turn out by torchlight, come in a shower upon his head: the fine grey hair of which, as well as of his whiskers, actually stirs with indignation.

"Am I to understand, sir," says Sir Leicester, "and is my Lady to understand"; he brings her in thus specially, first as a point of gallantry, and next as a point of prudence, having great reliance on her sense; "am I to understand, Mr. Rouncewell, and is my Lady to understand, sir, that you consider this young woman too good for Chesney Wold, or likely to be injured by remaining here?"

"Certainly not, Sir Leicester."

"I am glad to hear it." Sir Leicester very lofty indeed.

"Pray, Mr. Rouncewell," says my Lady, warning Sir Leicester off with the slightest gesture of her pretty hand, as if he were a fly, "explain to me what you mean."

"Willingly, Lady Dedlock. There is nothing I could desire more."

Addressing her composed face, whose intelligence, however, is too quick and active to be concealed by any studied impassiveness, however habitual, to the strong Saxon face of the visitor, a picture of resolution and perseverance, my Lady listens with attention, occasionally slightly bending her head.

"I am the son of your housekeeper, Lady Dedlock, and passed my childhood about this house. My mother has lived here half a century, and will die here I have no doubt. She is one of those examples—perhaps as good a one as there is—of love, and attachment, and fidelity in such a station, which England may well be proud of; but of which no order can appropriate the whole pride or the whole merit; because such an instance bespeaks high worth on two sides; on the great side assuredly; on the small one, no less assuredly."

Sir Leicester snorts a little to hear the law laid down in this way;

6. Leader of the Peasants' Revolt in 1381. (See p. 79, note 7.)

but in his honour and his love of truth, he freely, though silently, admits the justice of the ironmaster's proposition.

"Pardon me for saying what is so obvious, but I wouldn't have it hastily supposed," with the least turn of his eyes towards Sir Leicester, "that I am ashamed of my mother's position here, or wanting in all just respect for Chesney Wold and the family. I certainly may have desired—I certainly have desired, Lady Dedlock—that my mother should retire after so many years, and end her days with me. But as I have found that to sever this strong bond would be to break her heart, I have long abandoned that idea."

Sir Leicester very magnificent again, at the notion of Mrs. Rouncewell being spirited off from her natural home, to end her days with an ironmaster.

"I have been," proceeds the visitor, in a modest clear way, "an apprentice, and a workman. I have lived on workman's wages, years and years, and beyond a certain point have had to educate myself. My wife was a foreman's daughter, and plainly brought up. We have three daughters, besides this son of whom I have spoken; and being fortunately able to give them greater advantages than we had ourselves, we have educated them well; very well. It has been one of our great cares and pleasures to make them worthy of any station."

A little boastfulness in his fatherly tone here, as if he added in his heart, "even of the Chesney Wold station." Not a little more magnificence, therefore, on the part of Sir Leicester.

"All this is so frequent, Lady Dedlock, where I live, and among the class to which I belong, that what would be generally called unequal marriages are not of such rare occurrence with us as elsewhere. A son will sometimes make it known to his father that he has fallen in love, say with a young woman in the factory. The father, who once worked in a factory himself, will be a little disappointed at first, very possibly. It may be that he had other views for his son. However, the chances are, that having ascertained the young woman to be of unblemished character, he will say to his son, 'I must be quite sure that you are in earnest here. This is a serious matter for both of you. Therefore I shall have this girl educated for two years'—or, it may be, 'I shall place this girl at the same school with your sisters for such a time, during which you will give me your word and honour to see her only so often. If, at the expiration of that time, when she has so far profited by her advantages as that you may be upon a fair equality, you are both in the same mind, I will do my part to make you happy.' I know of several cases such as I describe, my Lady, and I think they indicate to me my own course now."

Sir Leicester's magnificence explodes. Calmly, but terribly.

"Mr. Rouncewell," says Sir Leicester, with his right hand in the breast of his blue coat—the attitude of state in which he is painted in the gallery: "do you draw a parallel between Chesney Wold, and a—" here he resists a disposition to choke—"a factory?"

"I need not reply, Sir Leicester, that the two places are very different; but, for the purposes of this case, I think a parallel may be justly drawn between them."

Sir Leicester directs his majestic glance down one side of the long drawing-room, and up the other, before he can believe that he is awake.

"Are you aware, sir, that this young woman whom my Lady—my Lady—has placed near her person, was brought up at the village school outside the gates?"

"Sir Leicester, I am quite aware of it. A very good school it is, and handsomely supported by this family."

"Then, Mr. Rouncewell," returns Sir Leicester, "the application of what you have said is, to me, incomprehensible."

"Will it be more comprehensible, Sir Leicester, if I say," the ironmaster is reddening a little, "that I do not regard the village school as teaching everything desirable to be known by my son's wife?"

From the village school of Chesney Wold, intact as it is this minute, to the whole framework of society: from the whole framework of society, to the aforesaid framework receiving tremendous cracks in consequence of people (ironmasters, lead-mistresses, and what not) not minding their catechism, and getting out of the station unto which they are called[7]—necessarily and for ever, according to Sir Leicester's rapid logic, the first station in which they happen to find themselves; and from that, to their educating other people out of *their* stations, and so obliterating the landmarks, and opening the floodgates, and all the rest of it; this is the swift progress of the Dedlock mind.

"My Lady, I beg your pardon. Permit me, for one moment." She has given a faint indication of intending to speak. "Mr. Rouncewell, our views of duty, and our views of station, and our views of education, and our views of—in short, *all* our views—are so diametrically opposed, that to prolong this discussion must be repellant to your feelings, and repellant to my own. This young woman is honoured with my Lady's notice and favour. If she wishes to withdraw herself from that notice and favour, or if she chooses to place herself under the influence of any one who may in his peculiar opinions—you will allow me to say, in his peculiar opinions—though I readily admit that he is not accountable for them to me—who may, in his peculiar opinions, withdraw her from that notice

7. See "A Catechism" in *The Book of Common Prayer*: "My duty towards my neighbour is . . . to submit myself to all my governours . . . and masters . . . and do my duty in that state of life, unto which it shall please God to call me."

and favour, she is at any time at liberty to do so. We are obliged to you for the plainness with which you have spoken. It will have no effect of itself, one way or other, on the young woman's position here. Beyond this we can make no terms; and here we beg—if you will be so good—to leave the subject."

The visitor pauses a moment to give my Lady an opportunity, but she says nothing. He then rises and replies:

"Sir Leicester and Lady Dedlock, allow me to thank you for your attention, and only to observe that I shall very seriously recommend my son to conquer his present inclinations. Good night!"

"Mr. Rouncewell," says Sir Leicester, with all the nature of a gentleman shining in him, "it is late, and the roads are dark. I hope your time is not so precious but that you will allow my Lady and myself to offer you the hospitality of Chesney Wold for to-night at least."

"I hope so," adds my Lady.

"I am much obliged to you, but I have to travel all night, in order to reach a distant part of the country, punctually at an appointed time in the morning."

Therewith the ironmaster takes his departure; Sir Leicester ringing the bell, and my Lady rising as he leaves the room.

When my Lady goes to her boudoir, she sits down thoughtfully by the fire; and, inattentive to the Ghost's Walk, looks at Rosa, writing in an inner room. Presently my Lady calls her.

"Come to me, child. Tell me the truth. Are you in love?"

"Oh! My Lady!"

My Lady, looking at the downcast and blushing face, says smiling:

"Who is it? Is it Mrs. Rouncewell's grandson?"

"Yes, if you please, my Lady. But I don't know that I am in love with him—yet."

"Yet, you silly little thing! Do you know that he loves *you*, yet?"

"I think he likes me a little, my Lady." And Rosa bursts into tears.

Is this Lady Dedlock standing beside the village beauty, smoothing her dark hair with that motherly touch, and watching her with eyes so full of musing interest? Aye, indeed it is!

"Listen to me, child. You are young and true, and I believe you are attached to me."

"Indeed I am, my Lady. Indeed there is nothing in the world I wouldn't do, to show how much."

"And I don't think you would wish to leave me just yet, Rosa, even for a lover?"

"No, my Lady! O no!" Rosa looks up for the first time, quite frightened at the thought.

"Confide in me, my child. Don't fear me. I wish you to be

happy, and will make you so—if I can make anybody happy on this earth."

Rosa, with fresh tears, kneels at her feet and kisses her hand. My Lady takes the hand with which she has caught it, and, standing with her eyes fixed on the fire, puts it about and about between her own two hands, and gradually lets it fall. Seeing her so absorbed, Rosa softly withdraws; but still my Lady's eyes are on the fire.

In search of what? Of any hand that is no more, of any hand that never was, of any touch that might have magically changed her life? Or does she listen to the Ghost's Walk, and think what step does it most resemble? A man's? A woman's? The pattering of a little child's feet, ever coming on—on—on? Some melancholy influence is upon her; or why should so proud a lady close the doors, and sit alone upon the hearth so desolate?

Volumnia is away next day, and all the cousins are scattered before dinner. Not a cousin of the batch but is amazed to hear from Sir Leicester, at breakfast-time, of the obliteration of landmarks, and opening of floodgates, and cracking of the framework of society, manifested through Mrs. Rouncewell's son. Not a cousin of the batch but is really indignant, and connects it with the feebleness of William Buffy when in office, and really does feel deprived of a stake in the country—or the pension list—or something—by fraud and wrong. As to Volumnia, she is handed down the great staircase by Sir Leicester, as eloquent upon the theme, as if there were a general rising in the North of England to obtain her rouge-pot and pearl necklace. And thus, with a clatter of maids and valets—for it is one appurtenance of their cousinship, that, however difficult they may find it to keep themselves, they *must* keep maids and valets—the cousins disperse to the four winds of heaven; and the one wintry wind that blows to-day shakes a shower from the trees near the deserted house, as if all the cousins had been changed into leaves.

Chapter XXIX

THE YOUNG MAN

Chesney Wold is shut up, carpets are rolled into scrolls in corners of comfortless rooms, bright damask does penance in brown holland,[1] carving and gilding puts on mortification, and the Dedlock ancestors retire from the light of day again. Around and around the house the leaves fall thick—but never fast, for they come circling down with a dead lightness that is sombre and slow. Let the gardener sweep and sweep the turf as he will, and press the leaves into full barrows, and wheel them off, still they lie ankle-

1. Plain linen slipcovers for furniture not in use.

deep. Howls the shrill wind around Chesney Wold; the sharp rain beats, the windows rattle, and the chimneys growl. Mists hide in the avenues, veil the points of view, and move in funeral-wise across the rising grounds. On all the house there is a cold, blank smell, like the smell of the little church, though something dryer: suggesting that the dead and buried Dedlocks walk there, in the long nights, and leave the flavour of their graves behind them.

But the house in town, which is rarely in the same mind as Chesney Wold at the same time; seldom rejoicing when it rejoices, or mourning when it mourns, excepting when a Dedlock dies; the house in town shines out awakened. As warm and bright as so much state may be, as delicately redolent of pleasant scents that bear no trace of winter as hothouse flowers can make it; soft and hushed, so that the ticking of the clocks and the crisp burning of the fires alone disturb the stillness in the rooms; it seems to wrap those chilled bones of Sir Leicester's in rainbow-coloured wool. And Sir Leicester is glad to repose in dignified contentment before the great fire in the library, condescendingly perusing the backs of his books; or honouring the fine arts with a glance of approbation. For he has his pictures, ancient and modern. Some of the Fancy Ball School[2] in which Art occasionally condescends to become a master, which would be best catalogued like the miscellaneous articles in a sale. As, "Three high-backed chairs, a table and cover, long-necked bottle (containing wine), one flask, one Spanish female's costume, three-quarter face portrait of Miss Jogg the model, and a suit of armour containing Don Quixote." Or, "One stone terrace (cracked), one gondola in distance, one Venetian senator's dress complete, richly embroidered white satin costume with profile portrait of Miss Jogg the model, one scimetar superbly mounted in gold with jewelled handle, elaborate Moorish dress (very rare) and Othello."

Mr. Tulkinghorn comes and goes pretty often; there being estate business to do, leases to be renewed, and so on. He sees my Lady pretty often, too; and he and she are as composed, and as indifferent, and take as little heed of one another, as ever. Yet it may be that my Lady fears this Mr. Tulkinghorn, and that he knows it. It may be that he pursues her doggedly and steadily, with no touch of compunction, remorse, or pity. It may be that her beauty, and all the state and brilliancy surrounding her, only give him the greater zest for what he is set upon, and make him the more inflexible in it. Whether he be cold and cruel, whether immovable in what he has made his duty, whether absorbed in love of power, whether determined to have nothing hidden from him in ground where he has burrowed among secrets all his life, whether he in his heart despises the splendour of which he is a distant beam, whether he is always

2. Academy-style paintings in which the principal subjects wear historic or exotic costumes and accouterments such as might be worn at a Fancy Dress Ball.

treasuring up slights and offences in the affability of his gorgeous clients—whether he be any of this, or all of this, it may be that my Lady had better have five thousand pairs of fashionable eyes upon her, in distrustful vigilance, than the two eyes of this rusty lawyer, with his wisp of neckcloth and his dull black breeches tied with ribbons at the knees.

Sir Leicester sits in my Lady's room—that room in which Mr. Tulkinghorn read the affidavit in Jarndyce and Jarndyce—particularly complacent. My Lady—as on that day—sits before the fire with her screen in her hand. Sir Leicester is particularly complacent, because he has found in his newspaper some congenial remarks bearing directly on the floodgates and the framework of society. They apply so happily to the late case, that Sir Leicester has come from the library to my Lady's room expressly to read them aloud. "The man who wrote this article," he observes by way of preface, nodding at the fire as if he were nodding down at the man from a Mount,[3] "has a well-balanced mind."

The man's mind is not so well balanced but that he bores my Lady, who, after a languid effort to listen, or rather a languid resignation of herself to a show of listening, becomes distraught, and falls into a contemplation of the fire as if it were her fire at Chesney Wold, and she had never left it. Sir Leicester, quite unconscious, reads on through his double eye-glass, occasionally stopping to remove his glass and express approval, as "Very true indeed," "Very properly put," "I have frequently made the same remark myself"; invariably losing his place after each observation, and going up and down the column to find it again.

Sir Leicester is reading, with infinite gravity and state, when the door opens, and the Mercury in powder makes this strange announcement:

"The young man, my Lady, of the name of Guppy."

Sir Leicester pauses, stares, repeats in a killing voice:

"The young man of the name of Guppy?"

Looking round, he beholds the young man of the name of Guppy, much discomfited, and not presenting a very impressive letter of introduction in his manner and appearance.

"Pray," says Sir Leicester to Mercury, "what do you mean by announcing with this abruptness a young man of the name of Guppy?"

"I beg your pardon, Sir Leicester, but my Lady said she would see the young man whenever he called. I was not aware that you were here, Sir Leicester."

With this apology, Mercury directs a scornful and indignant look at the young man of the name of Guppy, which plainly says,

3. Probably Mount Olympus (referred to at the end of the chapter), although Mount Sinai would also fit the passage.

"What do you come calling here for, and getting *me* into a row?"

"It is quite right. I gave him those directions," says my Lady. "Let the young man wait."

"By no means, my Lady. Since he has your orders to come, I will not interrupt you." Sir Leicester in his gallantry retires, rather declining to accept a bow from the young man as he goes out, and majestically supposing him to be some shoemaker of intrusive appearance.

Lady Dedlock looks imperiously at her visitor, when the servant has left the room; casting her eyes over him from head to foot. She suffers him to stand by the door, and asks him what he wants?

"That your ladyship would have the kindness to oblige me with a little conversation," returns Mr. Guppy, embarrassed.

"You are, of course, the person who has written me so many letters?"

"Several, your ladyship. Several, before your ladyship condescended to favour me with an answer."

"And could you not take the same means of rendering a conversation unnecessary? Can you not still?"

Mr. Guppy screws his mouth into a silent "No!" and shakes his head.

"You have been strangely importunate. If it should appear, after all, that what you have to say does not concern me—and I don't know how it can, and don't expect that it will—you will allow me to cut you short with but little ceremony. Say what you have to say, if you please."

My Lady, with a careless toss of her screen, turns herself towards the fire again, sitting almost with her back to the young man of the name of Guppy.

"With your ladyship's permission, then," says the young man, "I will now enter on my business. Hem! I am, as I told your ladyship in my first letter, in the law. Being in the law, I have learnt the habit of not committing myself in writing, and therefore I did not mention to your ladyship the name of the firm with which I am connected, and in which my standing—and I may add income—is tolerably good. I may now state to your ladyship, in confidence, that the name of that firm is Kenge and Carboy, of Lincoln's Inn; which may not be altogether unknown to your ladyship in connexion with the case in Chancery of Jarndyce and Jarndyce."

My Lady's figure begins to be expressive of some attention. She has ceased to toss the screen, and holds it as if she were listening.

"Now, I may say to your ladyship at once," says Mr. Guppy, a little emboldened, "it is no matter arising out of Jarndyce and Jarndyce that made me so desirous to speak to your ladyship, which conduct I have no doubt did appear, and does appear, obtrusive—in fact, almost blackguardly." After waiting for a moment to receive some assurance to the contrary, and not receiving any, Mr. Guppy proceeds. "If it had been Jarndyce and Jarndyce, I should have gone at once to your ladyship's solicitor, Mr. Tulkinghorn of the Fields. I have the pleasure of being acquainted with Mr. Tulkinghorn—at least we move when we meet one another—and if it had been any business of that sort, I should have gone to him."

My Lady turns a little round, and says, "You had better sit down."

"Thank your ladyship." Mr. Guppy does so. "Now, your ladyship"; Mr. Guppy refers to a little slip of paper on which he has made small notes of his line of argument, and which seems to involve him in the densest obscurity whenever he looks at it; "I—O yes!—I place myself entirely in your ladyship's hands. If your ladyship was to make any complaint to Kenge and Carboy, or to Mr. Tulkinghorn, of the present visit, I should be placed in a very disagreeable situation. That, I openly admit. Consequently, I rely upon your ladyship's honour."

My Lady, with a disdainful gesture of the hand that holds the screen, assures him of his being worth no complaint from her.

"Thank your ladyship," says Mr. Guppy, "quite satisfactory. Now —I—dash it!—The fact is, that I put down a head or two here of the order of the points I thought of touching upon, and they're written short, and I can't quite make out what they mean. If your ladyship will excuse me taking it to the window half a moment, I——"

Mr. Guppy going to the window, tumbles into a pair of lovebirds, to whom he says in his confusion, "I beg your pardon, I am sure." This does not tend to the greater legibility of his notes. He murmurs, growing warm and red, and holding the slip of paper now close to his eyes, now a long way off, "C.S. What's C.S. for? O! 'E.S.!' O, I know! Yes, to be sure!" And comes back enlightened.

"I am not aware," says Mr. Guppy, standing midway between my Lady and his chair, "whether your ladyship ever happened to hear of, or to see, a young lady of the name of Miss Esther Summerson."

My Lady's eyes look at him full. "I saw a young lady of that name not long ago. This past autumn."

"Now, did it strike your ladyship that she was like anybody?" asks Mr. Guppy, crossing his arms, holding his head on one side, and scratching the corner of his mouth with his memoranda.

My Lady removes her eyes from him no more.

"No."

"Not like your ladyship's family?"

"No."

"I think your ladyship," says Mr. Guppy, "can hardly remember Miss Summerson's face?"

"I remember the young lady very well. What has this to do with me?"

"Your ladyship, I do assure you, that having Miss Summerson's image imprinted on my art—which I mention in confidence—I found, when I had the honour of going over your ladyship's mansion of Chesney Wold, while on a short out in the county of Lincolnshire with a friend, such a resemblance between Miss Esther Summerson and your ladyship's own portrait, that it completely knocked me over; so much so, that I didn't at the moment even know what it *was* that knocked me over. And now I have the honour of beholding your ladyship near, (I have often, since that, taken the liberty of looking at your ladyship in your carriage in the park, when I dare say you was not aware of me, but I never saw your ladyship so near,) it's really more surprising than I thought it."

Young man of the name of Guppy! There have been times, when ladies lived in strongholds, and had unscrupulous attendants within call, when that poor life of yours would not have been worth a minute's purchase, with those beautiful eyes looking at you as they look at this moment.

My Lady, slowly using her little hand-screen as a fan, asks him again, what he supposes that his taste for likenesses has to do with her?

"Your ladyship," replies Mr. Guppy, again referring to his paper, "I am coming to that. Dash these notes! O! 'Mrs. Chadband.' Yes." Mr. Guppy draws his chair a little forward, and seats himself again. My Lady reclines in her chair composedly, though with a trifle less of graceful ease than usual, perhaps; and never falters in her steady gaze. "A—stop a minute, though!" Mr. Guppy refers again. "E. S. twice? O yes! yes, I see my way now, right on."

Rolling up the slip of paper as an instrument to point his speech with, Mr. Guppy proceeds.

"Your ladyship, there is a mystery about Miss Esther Summerson's birth and bringing up. I am informed of that fact, because—which I mention in confidence—I know it in the way of my profession at Kenge and Carboy's. Now, as I have already mentioned to your ladyship, Miss Summerson's image is imprinted on my art. If I could clear this mystery for her, or prove her to be well related, or find that having the honour to be a remote branch of your ladyship's family she had a right to be made a party in Jarndyce and Jarndyce, why, I might make a sort of a claim upon Miss Summerson to look with an eye of more decided favour on my proposals than she has exactly done as yet. In fact, as yet she hasn't favoured them at all."

A kind of angry smile just dawns upon my Lady's face.

"Now, it's a very singular circumstance, your ladyship," says Mr. Guppy, "though one of those circumstances that do fall in the way of us professional men—which I may call myself, for though not admitted, yet I have had a present of my articles made to me by Kenge and Carboy, on my mother's advancing from the principal of her little income the money for the stamp,[4] which comes heavy—that I have encountered the person who lived as servant with the lady who brought Miss Summerson up, before Mr. Jarndyce took charge of her. That lady was a Miss Barbary, your ladyship."

Is the dead colour on my Lady's face, reflected from the screen which has a green silk ground, and which she holds in her raised hand as if she had forgotten it; or is it a dreadful paleness that has fallen on her?

"Did your ladyship," says Mr. Guppy, "ever happen to hear of Miss Barbary?"

"I don't know. I think so. Yes."

"Was Miss Barbary at all connected with your ladyship's family?"

My Lady's lips move, but they utter nothing. She shakes her head.

"*Not* connected?" says Mr. Guppy. "O! Not to your ladyship's knowledge, perhaps? Ah! But might be? Yes." After each of these interrogatories, she has inclined her head. "Very good! Now, this Miss Barbary was extremely close—seems to have been extraordinarily close for a female, females being generally (in common life at least) rather given to conversation—and my witness never had an idea whether she possessed a single relative. On one occasion, and only one, she seems to have been confidential to my witness, on a single point; and she then told her that the little girl's real name was not Esther Summerson, but Esther Hawdon."

"My God!"

Mr. Guppy stares. Lady Dedlock sits before him, looking him through, with the same dark shade upon her face, in the same attitude even to the holding of the screen, with her lips a little apart, her brow a little contracted, but, for the moment, dead. He sees her consciousness return, sees a tremor pass across her frame like a ripple over water, sees her lips shake, sees her compose them by a great effort, sees her force herself back to the knowledge of his presence, and of what he has said. All this, so quickly, that her exclamation and her dead condition seem to have passed away like the features of those long-preserved dead bodies sometimes opened up in tombs, which, struck by the air like lightning, vanish in a breath.

"Your ladyship is acquainted with the name of Hawdon?"

"I have heard it before."

4. The contract (articles) concerning terms of apprenticeship in a law office required paying for an official stamp to make the agreement binding.

"Name of any collateral, or remote, branch of your ladyship's family?"

"No."

"Now, your ladyship," says Mr. Guppy, "I come to the last point of the case, so far as I have got it up. It's going on, and I shall gather it up closer and closer as it goes on. Your ladyship must know—if your ladyship don't happen, by any chance, to know already—that there was found dead at the house of a person named Krook, near Chancery Lane, some time ago, a law-writer in great distress. Upon which law-writer there was an inquest, and which law-writer was an anonymous character, his name being unknown. But, your ladyship, I have discovered very lately, that that law-writer's name was Hawdon."

"And what is *that* to me?"

"Aye, your ladyship, that's the question! Now, your ladyship, a queer thing happened after that man's death. A lady started up; a disguised lady, your ladyship, who went to look at the scene of action, and went to look at his grave. She hired a crossing-sweeping boy to show it her. If your ladyship would wish to have the boy produced in corroboration of this statement, I can lay my hand upon him at any time."

The wretched boy is nothing to my Lady, and she does *not* wish to have him produced.

"Oh, I assure your ladyship it's a very queer start[5] indeed," says Mr. Guppy. "If you was to hear him tell about the rings that sparkled on her fingers when she took her glove off, you'd think it quite romantic."

There are diamonds glittering on the hand that holds the screen. My Lady trifles with the screen, and makes them glitter more; again with that expression which in other times might have been so dangerous to the young man of the name of Guppy.

"It was supposed, your ladyship, that he left no rag or scrap behind him by which he could possibly be identified. But he did. He left a bundle of old letters."

The screen still goes, as before. All this time, her eyes never once release him.

"They were taken and secreted. And to-morrow night, your ladyship, they will come into my possession."

"Still I ask you, what is this to me?"

"Your ladyship, I conclude with that." Mr. Guppy rises. "If you think there's enough, in this chain of circumstances put together—in the undoubted strong likeness of this young lady to your ladyship, which is a positive fact for a jury—in her having been brought up by Miss Barbary—in Miss Barbary stating Miss Summerson's

5. Surprising incident.

real name to be Hawdon—in your ladyship's knowing both those names *very well*—and in Hawdon's dying as he did—to give your ladyship a family interest in going further into the case, I will bring those papers here. I don't know what they are, except that they are old letters: I have never had them in my possession yet. I will bring those papers here, as soon as I get them; and go over them for the first time with your ladyship. I have told your ladyship my object. I have told your ladyship that I should be placed in a very disagreeable situation, if any complaint was made; and all is in strict confidence."

Is this the full purpose of the young man of the name of Guppy, or has he any other? Do his words disclose the length, breadth, depth, of his object and suspicion in coming here; or, if not, what do they hide? He is a match for my Lady there. She may look at him, but he can look at the table, and keep that witness-box face of his from telling anything.

"You may bring the letters," says my Lady, "if you choose."

"Your ladyship is not very encouraging, upon my word and honour," says Mr. Guppy, a little injured.

"You may bring the letters," she repeats, in the same tone, "if you——please."

"It shall be done. I wish your ladyship good day."

On a table near her is a rich bauble of a casket, barred and clasped like an old strong chest. She, looking at him still, takes it to her and unlocks it.

"Oh! I assure your ladyship I am not actuated by any motives of that sort," says Mr. Guppy; "and I couldn't accept of anything of the kind. I wish your ladyship good day, and am much obliged to you all the same."

So the young man makes his bow, and goes down-stairs; where the supercilious Mercury does not consider himself called upon to leave his Olympus[6] by the hall-fire, to let the young man out.

As Sir Leicester basks in his library, and dozes over his newspaper, is there no influence in the house to startle him; not to say, to make the very trees at Chesney Wold fling up their knotted arms, the very portraits frown, the very armour stir?

No. Words, sobs, and cries, are but air; and air is so shut in and shut out throughout the house in town, that sounds need be uttered trumpet-tongued[7] indeed by my Lady in her chamber, to carry any faint vibration to Sir Leicester's ears; and yet this cry is in the house, going upward from a wild figure on its knees.

"O my child, my child! Not dead in the first hours of her life, as my cruel sister told me; but sternly nurtured by her, after she had renounced me and my name! O my child, O my child!"

6. Mountain on which the Greek gods resided. Mercury, the Roman equivalent to Hermes, was their messenger.

7. *Macbeth* (I.vii.19).

Chapter XXX

ESTHER'S NARRATIVE

Richard had been gone away some time, when a visitor came to pass a few days with us. It was an elderly lady. It was Mrs. Woodcourt, who, having come from Wales to stay with Mrs. Bayham Badger, and having written to my guardian, "by her son Allan's desire," to report that she had heard from him and that he was well, "and sent his kind remembrances to all of us," had been invited by my guardian to make a visit to Bleak House. She stayed with us nearly three weeks. She took very kindly to me, and was extremely confidential; so much so that sometimes she almost made me uncomfortable. I had no right, I knew very well, to be uncomfortable because she confided in me, and I felt it was unreasonable; still, with all I could do, I could not quite help it.

She was such a sharp little lady, and used to sit with her hands folded in each other, looking so very watchful while she talked to me, that perhaps I found that rather irksome. Or perhaps it was her being so upright and trim; though I don't think it was that, because I thought that quaintly pleasant. Nor can it have been the general expression of her face, which was very sparkling and pretty for an old lady. I don't know what it was. Or at least if I do, now, I thought I did not then. Or at least—but it don't matter.

Of a night when I was going up-stairs to bed, she would invite me into her room, where she sat before the fire in a great chair; and, dear me, she would tell me about Morgan ap Kerrig until I was quite low-spirited! Sometimes she recited a few verses from Crumlinwallinwer and the Mewlinwillinwodd (if those are the right names, which I dare say they are not), and would become quite fiery with the sentiments they expressed. Though I never knew what they were (being in Welsh), further than that they were highly eulogistic of the lineage of Morgan ap Kerrig.

"So, Miss Summerson," she would say to me with stately triumph, "this, you see, is the fortune inherited by my son. Wherever my son goes, he can claim kindred with Ap Kerrig. He may not have money, but he always has what is much better—family, my dear."

I had my doubts of their caring so very much for Morgan ap Kerrig, in India and China: but of course I never expressed them. I used to say it was a great thing to be so highly connected.

"It *is*, my dear, a great thing," Mrs. Woodcourt would reply. "It has its disadvantages; my son's choice of a wife, for instance, is limited by it; but the matrimonial choice of the Royal family is limited, in much the same manner."

Then she would pat me on the arm and smooth my dress, as

much as to assure me that she had a good opinion of me, the distance between us notwithstanding.

"Poor Mr. Woodcourt, my dear," she would say, and always with some emotion, for with her lofty pedigree she had a very affectionate heart, "was descended from a great Highland family, the Mac Coorts of Mac Coort. He served his king and country as an officer in the Royal Highlanders, and he died on the field. My son is one of the last representatives of two old families. With the blessing of Heaven he will set them up again, and unite them with another old family."

It was in vain for me to try to change the subject, as I used to try—only for the sake of novelty—or perhaps because—but I need not be so particular. Mrs. Woodcourt never would let me change it.

"My dear," she said one night, "you have so much sense, and you look at the world in a quiet manner so superior to your time of life, that it is a comfort to me to talk to you about these family matters of mine. You don't know much of my son, my dear; but you know enough of him, I dare say, to recollect him?"

"Yes, ma'am. I recollect him."

"Yes, my dear. Now, my dear, I think you are a judge of character, and I should like to have your opinion of him?"

"O, Mrs. Woodcourt!" said I, "that is so difficult."

"Why is it so difficult, my dear?" she returned. "I don't see it myself."

"To give an opinion——"

"On so slight an acquaintance, my dear. *That's* true."

I didn't mean that; because Mr. Woodcourt had been at our house a good deal altogether, and had become quite intimate with my guardian. I said so, and added that he seemed to be very clever in his profession—we thought—and that his kindness and gentleness to Miss Flite were above all praise.

"You do him justice!" said Mrs. Woodcourt, pressing my hand. "You define him exactly. Allan is a dear fellow, and in his profession faultless. I say it, though I am his mother. Still, I must confess he is not without faults, love."

"None of us are," said I.

"Ah! But his really are faults that he might correct, and ought to correct," returned the sharp old lady, sharply shaking her head. "I am so much attached to you, that I may confide in you, my dear, as a third party wholly disinterested, that he is fickleness itself."

I said, I should have thought it hardly possible that he could have been otherwise than constant to his profession, and zealous in the pursuit of it, judging from the reputation he had earned.

"You are right again, my dear," the old lady retorted; "but I don't refer to his profession, look you."

"O!" said I.

"No," said she. "I refer, my dear, to his social conduct. He is always paying trivial attentions to young ladies, and always has been, ever since he was eighteen. Now, my dear, he has never really cared for any one of them, and has never meant in doing this to do any harm, or to express anything but politeness and good nature. Still, it's not right, you know; is it?"

"No," said I, as she seemed to wait for me.

"And it might lead to mistaken notions, you see, my dear."

I supposed it might.

"Therefore, I have told him, many times, that he really should be more careful, both in justice to himself and in justice to others. And he has always said, 'Mother, I will be; but you know me better than anybody else does, and you know I mean no harm—in short, mean nothing.' All of which is very true, my dear, but is no justification. However, as he is now gone so far away, and for an indefinite time, and as he will have good opportunities and introductions, we may consider this past and gone. And you, my dear," said the old lady, who was now all nods and smiles; "regarding your dear self, my love?"

"Me, Mrs. Woodcourt?"

"Not to be always selfish, talking of my son, who has gone to seek his fortune, and to find a wife—when do you mean to seek *your* fortune and to find a husband, Miss Summerson? Hey, look you! Now you blush!"

I don't think I did blush—at all events, it was not important if I did—and I said, my present fortune perfectly contented me, and I had no wish to change it.

"Shall I tell you what I always think of you, and the fortune yet to come for you, my love?" said Mrs. Woodcourt.

"If you believe you are a good prophet," said I.

"Why, then, it is that you will marry some one, very rich and very worthy, much older—five-and-twenty years, perhaps—than yourself. And you will be an excellent wife, and much beloved, and very happy."

"That is a good fortune," said I. "But why is it to be mine?"

"My dear," she returned, "there's suitability in it—you are so busy, and so neat, and so peculiarly situated altogether, that there's suitability in it, and it will come to pass. And nobody, my love, will congratulate you more sincerely on such a marriage than I shall."

It was curious that this should make me uncomfortable, but I think it did. I know it did. It made me for some part of that night quite uncomfortable. I was so ashamed of my folly, that I did not like to confess it even to Ada; and that made me more uncomfortable still. I would have given anything not to have been so much in the bright old lady's confidence, if I could have possibly declined it. It gave me the most inconsistent opinions of her. At one time I thought she was a story-teller, and at another that she was the pink of truth. Now, I suspected that she was very cunning; next moment, I believed her honest Welsh heart to be perfectly innocent and simple. And, after all, what did it matter to me, and why did it matter to me? Why could not I, going up to bed with my basket of keys, stop to sit down by her fire, and accommodate myself for a little while to her, at least as well as to anybody else; and not trouble myself about the harmless things she said to me? Impelled towards her, as I certainly was, for I was very anxious that she should like me, and was very glad indeed that she did, why should I harp afterwards, with actual distress and pain, on every word she said, and weigh it over and over again in twenty scales? Why was it so worrying to me to have her in our house, and confidential to me every night, when I yet felt that it was better and safer, somehow, that she should be there than anywhere else? These were perplexities and contradictions that I could not account for. At least, if I could—but I shall come to all that by and by, and it is mere idleness to go on about it now.

So when Mrs. Woodcourt went away, I was sorry to lose her, but was relieved too. And then Caddy Jellyby came down; and Caddy brought such a packet of domestic news, that it gave us abundant occupation.

First, Caddy declared (and would at first declare nothing else) that I was the best adviser that ever was known. This, my pet said, was no news at all; and this, *I* said, of course, was nonsense. Then Caddy told us that she was going to be married in a month; and that if Ada and I would be her bridesmaids, she was the happiest girl in the world. To be sure, this was news indeed; and I thought we never should have done talking about it, we had so much to say to Caddy, and Caddy had so much to say to us.

It seemed that Caddy's unfortunate papa had got over his bankruptcy—"gone through the Gazette,"[1] was the expression Caddy used, as if it were a tunnel,—with the general clemency and commiseration of his creditors; and had got rid of his affairs in some blessed manner, without succeeding in understanding them; and had given up everything he possessed (which was not worth much, I should think, to judge from the state of the furniture), and had satisfied every one concerned that he could do no more, poor man. So he had been honourably dismissed to "the office," to begin the world again. What he did at the office, I never knew: Caddy said he was a "Custom-House and General Agent," and the only thing I ever understood about that business was, that when he wanted money more than usual he went to the Docks to look for it, and hardly ever found it.

1. An official publication which included reports of bankruptcies.

As soon as her papa had tranquillised his mind by becoming this shorn lamb, and they had removed to a furnished lodging in Hatton Garden (where I found the children, when I afterwards went there, cutting the horsehair out of the seats of the chairs, and choking themselves with it), Caddy had brought about a meeting between him and old Mr. Turveydrop; and poor Mr. Jellyby, being very humble and meek, had deferred to Mr. Turveydrop's Deportment so submissively, that they had become excellent friends. By degrees, old Mr. Turveydrop, thus familiarised with the idea of his son's marriage, had worked up his parental feelings to the height of contemplating that event as being near at hand; and had given his gracious consent to the young couple commencing housekeeping at the Academy in Newman Street, when they would.

"And your papa, Caddy. What did he say?"

"O! poor Pa," said Caddy, "only cried, and said he hoped we might get on better than he and Ma had got on. He didn't say so before Prince, he only said so to me. And he said, 'My poor girl, you have not been very well taught how to make a home for your husband; but unless you mean with all your heart to strive to do it, you had better murder him than marry him—if you really love him.' "

"And how did you reassure him, Caddy?"

"Why, it was very distressing, you know, to see poor Pa so low, and hear him say such terrible things, and I couldn't help crying myself. But I told him that I *did* mean it with all my heart; and that I hoped our house would be a place for him to come and find some comfort in, of an evening; and that I hoped and thought I could be a better daughter to him there, than at home. Then I mentioned Peepy's coming to stay with me; and then Pa began to cry again, and said the children were Indians."

"Indians, Caddy?"

"Yes," said Caddy, "Wild Indians. And Pa said,"—(here she began to sob, poor girl, not at all like the happiest girl in the world)—"that he was sensible the best thing that could happen to them was, their being all Tomahawked together."

Ada suggested that it was comfortable to know that Mr. Jellyby did not mean these destructive sentiments.,

"No, of course I know Pa wouldn't like his family to be weltering in their blood," said Caddy; "but he means that they are very unfortunate in being Ma's children, and that he is very unfortunate in being Ma's husband; and I am sure that's true, though it seems unnatural to say so."

I asked Caddy if Mrs. Jellyby knew that her wedding-day was fixed.

"O! you know what Ma is, Esther," she returned. "It's impossible to say whether she knows it or not. She had been told it often enough; and when she *is* told it, she only gives me a placid look, as if I was I don't know what—a steeple in the distance," said Caddy, with a sudden idea; "and then she shakes her head, and says 'O Caddy, Caddy, what a teaze you are!' and goes on with the Borrioboola letters."

"And about your wardrobe, Caddy?" said I. For she was under no restraint with us.

"Well, my dear Esther," she returned, drying her eyes, "I must do the best I can, and trust to my dear Prince never to have an unkind remembrance of my coming so shabbily to him. If the question concerned an outfit for Borrioboola, Ma would know all about it, and would be quite excited. Being what it is, she neither knows nor cares."

Caddy was not at all deficient in natural affection for her mother, but mentioned this with tears, as an undeniable fact: which I am afraid it was. We were sorry for the poor dear girl and found so much to admire in the good disposition which had survived under such discouragement, that we both at once (I mean Ada and I) proposed a little scheme, that made her perfectly joyful. This was, her staying with us for three weeks; my staying with her for one; and our all three contriving and cutting out, and repairing, and sewing, and saving, and doing the very best we could think of, to make the most of her stock. My guardian being as pleased with the idea as Caddy was, we took her home next day to arrange the matter; and brought her out again in triumph, with her boxes, and all the purchases that could be squeezed out of a ten-pound note, which Mr. Jellyby had found in the Docks I suppose, but which he at all events gave her. What my guardian would not have given her, if we had encouraged him, it would be difficult to say; but we thought it right to compound for no more than her wedding-dress and bonnet. He agreed to this compromise; and if Caddy had ever been happy in her life, she was happy when we sat down to work.

She was clumsy enough with her needle, poor girl, and pricked her fingers as much as she had been used to ink them. She could not help reddening a little, now and then: partly with the smart, and partly with vexation at being able to do no better; but she soon got over that, and began to improve rapidly. So day after day, she, and my darling, and my little maid Charley, and a milliner out of the town, and I, sat hard at work, as pleasantly as possible.

Over and above this, Caddy was very anxious "to learn housekeeping," as she said. Now, Mercy upon us! the idea of her learning housekeeping of a person of my vast experience was such a joke, that I laughed, and coloured up, and fell into a comical confusion when she proposed it. However, I said, "Caddy, I am sure you are very welcome to learn anything that you can learn of *me*, my dear"; and I showed her all my books and methods, and all my fidgety ways. You would have supposed that I was showing her some wonderful inventions, by her study of them; and if you had seen her, whenever I jingled my housekeeping keys, get up and attend me, certainly you might have thought that there never was a greater impostor than I, with a blinder follower than Caddy Jellyby.

So, what with working and housekeeping, and lessons to Charley, and backgammon in the evening with my guardian, and duets with Ada, the three weeks slipped fast away. Then I went home with Caddy, to see what could be done there; and Ada and Charley remained behind, to take care of my guardian.

When I say I went home with Caddy, I mean to the furnished lodging in Hatton Garden. We went to Newman Street two or three times, where preparations were in progress too; a good many, I observed, for enhancing the comforts of old Mr. Turveydrop, and a few for putting the newly-married couple away cheaply at the top of the house; but our great point was to make the furnished lodging decent for the wedding-breakfast, and to imbue Mrs. Jellyby beforehand with some faint sense of the occasion.

The latter was the more difficult thing of the two, because Mrs. Jellyby and an unwholesome boy occupied the front sitting-room (the back one was a mere closet), and it was littered down with waste-paper and Borrioboolan documents, as an untidy stable might be littered with straw. Mrs. Jellyby sat there all day, drinking strong coffee, dictating, and holding Borrioboolan interviews by appointment. The unwholesome boy, who seemed to me to be going into a decline, took his meals out of the house. When Mr. Jellyby came home, he usually groaned and went down into the kitchen. There he got something to eat, if the servant would give him anything; and then, feeling that he was in the way, went out and walked about Hatton Garden in the wet. The poor children scrambled up and tumbled down the house, as they had always been accustomed to do.

The production of these devoted little sacrifices, in any presentable condition, being quite out of the question at a week's notice, I proposed to Caddy that we should make them as happy as we could, on her marriage morning, in the attic where they all slept; and should confine our greatest efforts to her mama and her mama's room, and a clean breakfast. In truth Mrs. Jellyby required a good deal of attention, the lattice-work up her back having widened considerably since I first knew her, and her hair looking like the mane of a dustman's[2] horse.

Thinking that the display of Caddy's wardrobe would be the best

2. Employed to remove trash and garbage.

means of approaching the subject, I invited Mrs. Jellyby to come and look at it spread out on Caddy's bed, in the evening after the unwholesome boy was gone.

"My dear Miss Summerson," said she, rising from her desk, with her usual sweetness of temper, "these are really ridiculous preparations, though your assisting them is a proof of your kindness. There is something so inexpressibly absurd to me, in the idea of Caddy being married! O Caddy, you silly, silly, silly puss!"

She came up-stairs with us notwithstanding, and looked at the clothes in her customary far-off manner. They suggested one distinct idea to her; for she said, with her placid smile, and shaking her head, "My good Miss Summerson, at half the cost, this weak child might have been equipped for Africa!"

On our going down-stairs again, Mrs. Jellyby asked me whether this troublesome business was really to take place next Wednesday? And on my replying yes, she said, "Will my room be required, my dear Miss Summerson? For it's quite impossible that I can put my papers away."

I took the liberty of saying that the room would certainly be wanted, and that I thought we must put the papers away somewhere. "Well, my dear Miss Summerson," said Mrs. Jellyby, "you know best, I dare say. But by obliging me to employ a boy, Caddy has embarrassed me to that extent, overwhelmed as I am with public business, that I don't know which way to turn. We have a Ramification meeting, too, on Wednesday afternoon, and the inconvenience is very serious."

"It is not likely to occur again," said I, smiling. "Caddy will be married but once, probably."

"That's true," Mrs. Jellyby replied, "that's true, my dear. I suppose we must make the best of it!"

The next question was, how Mrs. Jellyby should be dressed on the occasion. I thought it very curious to see her looking on serenely from her writing-table, while Caddy and I discussed it; occasionally shaking her head at us with a half-reproachful smile, like a superior spirit who could just bear with our trifling.

The state in which her dresses were, and the extraordinary confusion in which she kept them, added not a little to our difficulty; but at length we devised something not very unlike what a commonplace mother might wear on such an occasion. The abstracted manner in which Mrs. Jellyby would deliver herself up to having this attire tried on by the dressmaker, and the sweetness with which she would then observe to me how sorry she was that I had not turned my thoughts to Africa, were consistent with the rest of her behaviour.

The lodging was rather confined as to space, but I fancied that if

Mrs. Jellyby's household had been the only lodgers in Saint Paul's or Saint Peter's, the sole advantage they would have found in the size of the building would have been its affording a great deal of room to be dirty in. I believe that nothing belonging to the family, which it had been possible to break, was unbroken at the time of those preparations for Caddy's marriage; that nothing which it had been possible to spoil in any way was unspoilt; and that no domestic object which was capable of collecting dirt, from a dear child's knee to the door-plate, was without as much dirt as could well accumulate upon it.

Poor Mr. Jellyby, who very seldom spoke, and almost always sat when he was at home with his head against the wall, became interested when he saw that Caddy and I were attempting to establish some order among all this waste and ruin, and took off his coat to help. But such wonderful things came tumbling out of the closets when they were opened—bits of mouldy pie, sour bottles, Mrs. Jellyby's caps, letters, tea, forks, odd boots and shoes of children, firewood, wafers, saucepan-lids, damp sugar in odds and ends of paper bags, foot-stools, blacklead brushes, bread, Mrs. Jellyby's bonnets, books with butter sticking to the binding, guttered candle-ends put out by being turned upside down in broken candlesticks, nut-shells, heads and tails of shrimps, dinner-mats, gloves, coffee-grounds, umbrellas—that he looked frightened, and left off again. But he came in regularly every evening, and sat without his coat, with his head against the wall; as though he would have helped us, if he had known how.

"Poor Pa!" said Caddy to me, on the night before the great day, when we really had got things a little to rights. "It seems unkind to leave him, Esther. But what could I do, if I stayed! Since I first knew you, I have tidied and tidied over and over again; but it's useless. Ma and Africa, together, upset the whole house directly. We never have a servant who don't drink. Ma's ruinous to everything."

Mr. Jellyby could not hear what she said, but he seemed very low indeed, and shed tears, I thought.

"My heart aches for him; that it does!" sobbed Caddy. "I can't help thinking, to-night, Esther, how dearly I hope to be happy with Prince, and how dearly Pa hoped, I dare say, to be happy with Ma. What a disappointed life!"

"My dear Caddy!" said Mr. Jellyby, looking slowly round from the wall. It was the first time, I think, I ever heard him say three words together.

"Yes, Pa!" cried Caddy, going to him and embracing him affectionately.

"My dear Caddy," said Mr. Jellyby. "Never have——"

"Not Prince, Pa?" faltered Caddy. "Not have Prince?"

"Yes, my dear," said Mr. Jellyby. "Have him, certainly. But, never have——"

I mentioned, in my account of our first visit in Thavies Inn, that Richard described Mr. Jellyby as frequently opening his mouth after dinner without saying anything. It was a habit of his. He opened his mouth now, a great many times, and shook his head in a melancholy manner.

"What do you wish me not to have? Don't have what, dear Pa?" asked Caddy, coaxing him, with her arms round his neck.

"Never have a Mission, my dear child."

Mr. Jellyby groaned, and laid his head against the wall again; and this was the only time I ever heard him make an approach to expressing his sentiments on the Borrioboolan question. I suppose he had been more talkative and lively, once; but he seemed to have been completely exhausted long before I knew him.

I thought Mrs. Jellyby never would have left off serenely looking over her papers, and drinking coffee, that night. It was twelve o'clock before we could obtain possession of the room; and the clearance it required then, was so discouraging, that Caddy, who was almost tired out, sat down in the middle of the dust, and cried. But she soon cheered up, and we did wonders with it before we went to bed.

In the morning it looked, by the aid of a few flowers and a quantity of soap and water, and a little arrangement, quite gay. The plain breakfast made a cheerful show, and Caddy was perfectly charming. But when my darling came, I thought—and I think now—that I never had seen such a dear face as my beautiful pet's.

We made a little feast for the children up-stairs, and we put Peepy at the head of the table, and we showed them Caddy in her bridal dress, and they clapped their hands and hurrahed, and Caddy cried to think that she was going away from them, and hugged them over and over again, until we brought Prince up to fetch her away—when, I am sorry to say, Peepy bit him. Then there was old Mr. Turveydrop down-stairs in a state of Deportment not to be expressed, benignly blessing Caddy, and giving my guardian to understand, that his son's happiness was his own parental work, and that he sacrificed personal considerations to ensure it. "My dear sir," said Mr. Turveydrop, "these young people will live with me; my house is large enough for their accommodation, and they shall not want the shelter of my roof. I could have wished—you will understand the allusion, Mr. Jarndyce, for you remember my illustrious patron the Prince Regent—I could have wished that my son had married into a family where there was more Deportment; but the will of Heaven be done!"

Mr. and Mrs. Pardiggle were of the party—Mr. Pardiggle, an obstinate-looking man with a large waistcoat and stubbly hair, who was always talking in a loud bass voice about his mite, or Mrs. Pardiggle's mite, or their five boys' mites. Mr. Quale, with his hair brushed back as usual, and his knobs of temples shining very much, was also there; not in the character of a disappointed lover, but as the Accepted of a young—at least, an unmarried—lady, a Miss Wisk, who was also there. Miss Wisk's mission, my guardian said, was to show the world that woman's mission was man's mission; and that the only genuine mission, of both man and woman, was to be always moving declaratory resolutions about things in general at public meetings. The guests were few; but were, as one might expect at Mrs. Jellyby's, all devoted to public objects only. Besides those I have mentioned, there was an extremely dirty lady, with her bonnet all awry, and the ticketed price of her dress still sticking on it, whose neglected home, Caddy told me, was like a filthy wilderness, but whose church was like a fancy fair. A very contentious gentleman, who said it was his mission to be everybody's brother, but who appeared to be on terms of coolness with the whole of his large family, completed the party.

A party, having less in common with such an occasion, could hardly have been got together by any ingenuity. Such a mean mission as the domestic mission, was the very last thing to be endured among them; indeed, Miss Wisk informed us, with great indignation, before we sat down to breakfast, that the idea of woman's mission lying chiefly in the narrow sphere of Home was an outrageous slander on the part of her Tyrant, Man. One other singularity was, that nobody with a mission—except Mr. Quale, whose mission, as I think I have formerly said, was to be in ecstasies with everybody's mission—cared at all for anybody's mission. Mrs. Pardiggle being as clear that the only one infallible course was her course of pouncing upon the poor, and applying benevolence to them like a strait-waistcoat; as Miss Wisk was that the only practical thing for the world was the emancipation of Woman from the thraldom of her Tyrant, Man. Mrs. Jellyby, all the while, sat smiling at the limited vision that could see anything but Borrioboola-Gha.

But I am anticipating now the purport of our conversation on the ride home, instead of first marrying Caddy. We all went to church, and Mr. Jellyby gave her away. Of the air with which old Mr. Turveydrop, with his hat under his left arm, (the inside presented at the clergyman like a cannon,) and his eyes creasing themselves up into his wig, stood, stiff and high-shouldered, behind us bridesmaids during the ceremony, and afterwards saluted us, I could never say enough to do it justice. Miss Wisk, whom I cannot report as prepossessing in appearance, and whose manner was grim, listened to the proceedings, as part of Woman's wrongs, with a disdainful face. Mrs. Jellyby, with her calm smile and her bright eyes, looked the least concerned of all the company.

We duly came back to breakfast, and Mrs. Jellyby sat at the head of the table, and Mr. Jellyby at the foot. Caddy had previously stolen up-stairs, to hug the children again, and tell them that her name was Turveydrop. But this piece of information, instead of being an agreeable surprise to Peepy, threw him on his back in such transports of kicking grief, that I could do nothing on being sent for, but accede to the proposal that he should be admitted to the breakfast table. So he came down, and sat in my lap; and Mrs. Jellyby, after saying, in reference to the state of his pinafore, "O you naughty Peepy, what a shocking little pig you are!" was not at all discomposed. He was very good, except that he brought down Noah with him (out of an ark I had given him before we went to church), and *would* dip him head first into the wine-glasses, and then put him in his mouth.

My guardian, with his sweet temper and his quick perception and his amiable face, made something agreeable even out of the ungenial company. None of them seemed able to talk about anything but his, or her, own one subject, and none of them seemed able to talk about even that, as part of a world in which there was anything else; but my guardian turned it all to the merry encouragement of Caddy, and the honour of the occasion, and brought us through the breakfast nobly. What we should have done without him, I am afraid to think: for all the company despising the bride and bridegroom, and old Mr. Turveydrop—and old Mr. Turveydrop, in virtue of his Deportment, considering himself vastly superior to all the company—it was a very unpromising case.

At last the time came when poor Caddy was to go, and when all her property was packed on the hired coach and pair that was to take her and her husband to Gravesend. It affected us to see Caddy clinging, then, to her deplorable home, and hanging on her mother's neck with the greatest tenderness.

"I am sorry I couldn't go on writing from dictation, Ma," sobbed Caddy. "I hope you forgive me now?"

"O Caddy, Caddy!" said Mrs. Jellyby, "I have told you over and over again that I have engaged a boy, and there's an end of it."

"You are sure you are not in the least angry with me, Ma? Say you are sure before I go away, Ma?"

"You foolish Caddy," returned Mrs. Jellyby, "do I look angry, or have I inclination to be angry, or time to be angry? How *can* you?"

"Take a little care of Pa while I am gone, mama!"

Mrs. Jellyby positively laughed at the fancy. "You romantic child," said she, lightly patting Caddy's back. "Go along. I am excellent friends with you. Now, good-bye, Caddy, and be very happy!"

Then Caddy hung upon her father, and nursed his cheek against hers as if he were some poor dull child in pain. All this took place in the hall. Her father released her, took out his pocket-handkerchief, and sat down on the stairs with his head against the wall. I hope he found some consolation in walls. I almost think he did.

And then Prince took her arm in his, and turned with great emotion and respect to his father, whose Deportment at that moment was overwhelming.

"Thank you over and over again, father!" said Prince, kissing his hand. "I am very grateful for all your kindness and consideration regarding our marriage, and so, I can assure you, is Caddy."

"Very," sobbed Caddy. "Ve-ry!"

"My dear son," said Mr. Turveydrop, "and dear daughter, I have done my duty. If the spirit of a sainted Wooman hovers above us, and looks down on the occasion, that, and your constant affection, will be my recompense. You will not fail in *your* duty, my son and daughter, I believe?"

"Dear father, never!" cried Prince.

"Never, never, dear Mr. Turveydrop!" said Caddy.

"This," returned Mr. Turveydrop, "is as it should be. My children, my home is yours, my heart is yours, my all is yours. I will never leave you; nothing but Death shall part us. My dear son, you contemplate an absence of a week, I think?"

"A week, dear father. We shall return home this day week."

"My dear child," said Mr. Turveydrop, "let me, even under the present exceptional circumstances, recommend strict punctuality. It is highly important to keep the connexion together; and schools, if at all neglected, are apt to take offence."

"This day week, father, we shall be sure to be home to dinner."

"Good!" said Mr. Turveydrop. "You will find fires, my dear Caroline, in your own bedroom, and dinner prepared in my apartment. Yes, yes, Prince!" anticipating some self-denying objection on his son's part with a great air. "You and our Caroline will be strange in the upper part of the premises, and will, therefore, dine that day in my apartment. Now, bless ye!"

They drove away; and whether I wondered most at Mrs. Jellyby, or at Mr. Turveydrop, I did not know. Ada and my guardian were in the same condition when we came to talk it over. But before we drove away, too, I received a most unexpected and eloquent compliment from Mr. Jellyby. He came up to me in the hall, took both my hands, pressed them earnestly, and opened his mouth twice. I was so sure of his meaning, that I said, quite flurried, "You are very welcome, sir. Pray don't mention it!"

"I hope this marriage is for the best, guardian?" said I, when we three were on our road home.

"I hope it is, little woman. Patience. We shall see."

"Is the wind in the East to-day?" I ventured to ask him.

He laughed heartily, and answered "No."

"But it must have been this morning, I think," said I.

He answered, "No," again; and this time my dear girl confidently answered "No," too, and shook the lovely head which, with its blooming flowers against the golden hair, was like the very Spring. "Much *you* know of East winds, my ugly darling," said I, kissing her in my admiration—I couldn't help it.

Well! It was only their love for me, I know very well, and it is a long time ago. I must write it, even if I rub it out again, because it gives me so much pleasure. They said there could be no East wind where Somebody was; they said that wherever Dame Durden went, there was sunshine and summer air.

Chapter XXXI

NURSE AND PATIENT

I had not been at home again many days, when one evening I went up-stairs into my own room to take a peep over Charley's shoulder, and see how she was getting on with her copy-book. Writing was a trying business to Charley, who seemed to have no natural power over a pen, but in whose hand every pen appeared to become perversely animated, and to go wrong and crooked, and to stop, and splash, and sidle into corners, like a saddle-donkey. It was very odd, to see what old letters Charley's young hand made; they, so wrinkled, and shrivelled, and tottering; it, so plump and round. Yet Charley was uncommonly expert at other things, and had as nimble little fingers as I ever watched.

"Well, Charley," said I, looking over a copy of the letter O in which it was represented as square, triangular, pear-shaped, and collapsed in all kinds of ways, "we are improving. If we only get to make it round, we shall be perfect, Charley."

Then I made one, and Charley made one, and the pen wouldn't join Charley's neatly, but twisted it up into a knot.

"Never mind, Charley. We shall do it in time."

Charley laid down her pen, the copy being finished; opened and shut her cramped little hand; looked gravely at the page, half in pride and half in doubt; and got up, and dropped me a curtsey.

"Thank you, miss. If you please, miss, did you know a poor person of the name of Jenny?"

"A brickmaker's wife, Charley? Yes."

"She came and spoke to me when I was out a little while ago, and said you knew her, miss. She asked me if I wasn't the young lady's little maid—meaning you for the young lady, miss—and I said yes, miss."

"I thought she had left this neighbourhood altogether, Charley."

"So she had, miss, but she's come back again to where she used to live—she and Liz. Did you know another poor person of the name of Liz, miss?"

"I think I do, Charley, though not by name."

"That's what she said!" returned Charley. "They have both come back, miss, and have been tramping high and low."

"Tramping high and low, have they, Charley?"

"Yes, miss." If Charley could only have made the letters in her copy as round as the eyes with which she looked into my face, they would have been excellent. "And this poor person came about the house three or four days, hoping to get a glimpse of you, miss—all she wanted, she said—but you were away. That was when she saw me. She saw me a-going about, miss," said Charley, with a short laugh of the greatest delight and pride, "and she thought I looked like your maid!"

"Did she though, really, Charley?"

"Yes, miss!" said Charley, "really and truly." And Charley, with another short laugh of the purest glee, made her eyes very round again, and looked as serious as became my maid. I was never tired of seeing Charley in the full enjoyment of that great dignity, standing before me with her youthful face and figure, and her steady manner, and her childish exultation breaking through it now and then in the pleasantest way.

"And where did you see her, Charley?" said I.

My little maid's countenance fell, as she replied, "By the doctor's shop, miss." For Charley wore her black frock yet.

I asked if the brickmaker's wife were ill, but Charley said No. It was some one else. Some one in her cottage who had tramped down to Saint Albans, and was tramping he didn't know where. A poor boy, Charley said. No father, no mother, no any one. "Like as Tom might have been, miss, if Emma and me had died after father," said Charley, her round eyes filling with tears.

"And she was getting medicine for him, Charley?"

"She said, miss," returned Charley, "how that he had once done as much for her."

My little maid's face was so eager, and her quiet hands were folded so closely in one another as she stood looking at me, that I had no great difficulty in reading her thoughts. "Well, Charley," said I, "it appears to me that you and I can do no better than go round to Jenny's and see what's the matter."

The alacrity with which Charley brought my bonnet and veil, and, having dressed me, quaintly pinned herself into her warm shawl and made herself look like a little old woman, sufficiently expressed her readiness. So Charley and I, without saying anything to any one, went out.

It was a cold, wild night, and the trees shuddered in the wind. The rain had been thick and heavy all day, and with little intermission for many days. None was falling just then, however. The sky had partly cleared, but was very gloomy—even above us, where a few stars were shining. In the north and north-west, where the sun had set three hours before, there was a pale dead light both beautiful and awful; and into it long sullen lines of cloud waved up, like a sea stricken immoveable as it was heaving. Towards London, a lurid glare overhung the whole dark waste; and the contrast between these two lights, and the fancy which the redder light engendered of an unearthly fire, gleaming on all the unseen buildings of the city, and on all the faces of its many thousands of wondering inhabitants, was as solemn as might be.

I had no thought, that night—none, I am quite sure—of what was soon to happen to me. But I have always remembered since, that when we had stopped at the garden-gate to look up at the sky, and when we went upon our way, I had for a moment an undefinable impression of myself as being something different from what I then was. I know it was then, and there, that I had it. I have ever since connected the feeling with that spot and time, and with everything associated with that spot and time, to the distant voices in the town, the barking of a dog, and the sound of wheels coming down the miry hill.

It was Saturday night; and most of the people belonging to the place where we were going, were drinking elsewhere. We found it quieter than I had previously seen it, though quite as miserable. The kilns were burning, and a stifling vapour set towards us with a pale blue glare.

We came to the cottage, where there was a feeble candle in the patched window. We tapped at the door, and went in. The mother of the little child who had died, was sitting in a chair on one side of the poor fire by the bed; and opposite to her, a wretched boy, supported by the chimney-piece, was cowering on the floor. He held under his arm like a little bundle, a fragment of a fur cap; and as he tried to warm himself, he shook until the crazy door and window shook. The place was closer than before, and had an unhealthy, and a very peculiar smell.

I had not lifted my veil when I first spoke to the woman, which was at the moment of our going in. The boy staggered up instantly, and stared at me with a remarkable expression of surprise and terror.

His action was so quick, and my being the cause of it was so evident that I stood still, instead of advancing nearer.

"I won't go no more to the berryin ground," muttered the boy; "I ain't a-going there, so I tell you!"

I lifted my veil and spoke to the woman. She said to me in a low voice, "Don't mind him, ma'am. He'll soon come back to his head;" and said to him, "Jo, Jo, what's the matter?"

"I know wot she's come for?" cried the boy.

"Who?"

"The lady there. She's come to get me to go along with her to the berryin ground. I won't go to the berryin ground. I don't like the name of it. She might go a berryin *me*." His shivering came on again, and as he leaned against the wall, he shook the hovel.

"He has been talking off and on about such like, all day, ma'am," said Jenny, softly. "Why, how you stare! This is *my* lady, Jo."

"Is it?" returned the boy, doubtfully, and surveying me with his arm held out above his burning eyes. "She looks to me the t'other one. It ain't the bonnet, nor yet it ain't the gownd, but she looks to me the t'other one."

My little Charley, with her premature experience of illness and trouble, had pulled off her bonnet and shawl, and now went quietly up to him with a chair, and sat him down in it like an old sick nurse. Except that no such attendant could have shown him Charley's youthful face, which seemed to engage his confidence.

"I say!" said the boy. "*You* tell me. Ain't the lady the t'other lady?"

Charley shook her head, as she methodically drew his rags about him and made him as warm as she could.

"O!" the boy muttered. "Then I s'pose she ain't."

"I came to see if I could do you any good," said I. "What is the matter with you?"

"I'm a being froze," returned the boy, hoarsely, with his haggard gaze wandering about me, "and then burnt up, and then froze, and then burnt up, ever so many times in a hour. And my head's all sleepy, and all a going made like—and I'm so dry—and my bones isn't half so much bones as pain."

"When did he come here?" I asked the woman.

"This morning, ma'am, I found him at the corner of the town. I had known him up in London yonder. Hadn't I, Jo?"

"Tom-all-Alone's," the boy replied.

Whenever he fixed his attention or his eyes, it was only for a very little while. He soon began to droop his head again, and roll it heavily, and speak as if he were half awake.

"When did he come from London?" I asked.

"I come from London yes'day," said the boy himself, now flushed and hot. "I'm a going somewheres."

"Where is he going?" I asked.

"Somewheres," repeated the boy, in a louder tone. "I have been moved on, and moved on, more nor ever I was afore, since the t'other one giv' me the sov'ring. Mrs. Sangsby, she's always a watching and a driving of me—what have I done to her?—and they're all a watching and a driving of me. Every one of 'em's doing of it, from the time when I don't get up, to the time when I don't go to bed. And I'm a going somewheres. That's where I'm a going. She told me, down in Tom-all-Alone's, as she came from Stolbuns, and so I took the Stolbuns Road. It's as good as another."

He always concluded by addressing Charley.

"What is to be done with him?" said I, taking the woman aside. "He could not travel in this state, even if he had a purpose, and knew where he was going!"

"I know no more, ma'am, than the dead," she replied, glancing compassionately at him. "Perhaps the dead know better, if they could only tell us. I've kept him here all day for pity's sake, and I've given him broth and physic, and Liz has gone to try if any one will take him in (here's my pretty in the bed—her child, but I call it mine); but I can't keep him long, for if my husband was to come home and find him here, he'd be rough in putting him out, and might do him a hurt. Hark! Here comes Liz back!"

The other woman came hurriedly in as she spoke, and the boy got up with a half obscured sense that he was expected to be going. When the little child awoke, and when and how Charley got at it, took it out of bed, and began to walk about hushing it, I don't know. There she was, doing all this, in a quiet motherly manner, as if she were living in Mrs. Blinder's attic with Tom and Emma again.

The friend had been here and there, and had been played about from hand to hand, and had come back as she went. At first it was too early for the boy to be received into the proper refuge, and at last it was too late. One official sent her to another, and the other sent her back again to the first, and so backward and forward; until it appeared to me as if both must have been appointed for their skill in evading their duties, instead of performing them. And now, after all, she said, breathing quickly, for she had been running, and was frightened too, "Jenny, your master's on the road home, and mine's not far behind, and the Lord help the boy, for we can do no more for him!" They put a few halfpence together, and hurried them into his hand, and so, in an oblivious, half-thankful, half-insensible way, he shuffled out of the house.

"Give me the child, my dear!" said its mother to Charley, "and thank you kindly too! Jenny, woman dear, good night! Young lady, if my master don't fall out with me, I'll look down by the kiln by and by, where the boy will be most like, and again in the morning!" She hurried off; and presently we passed her hushing and singing to her child at her own door, and looking anxiously along the road for her drunken husband.

I was afraid of staying then, to speak to either woman, lest I should bring her into trouble. But I said to Charley that we must not leave the boy to die. Charley, who knew what to do much better than I did, and whose quickness equalled her presence of mind, glided on before me, and presently we came up with Jo, just short of the brick-kiln.

I think he must have begun his journey with some small bundle under his arm, and must have had it stolen, or lost it. For he still carried his wretched fragment of fur cap like a bundle, though he went bare-headed through the rain, which now fell fast. He stopped when we called to him, and again showed a dread of me when I came up; standing with his lustrous eyes fixed upon me, and even arrested in his shivering fit.

I asked him to come with us, and we would take care that he had some shelter for the night.

"I don't want no shelter," he said; "I can lay amongst the warm bricks."

"But don't you know that people die there?" replied Charley.

"They dies everywheres," said the boy. They dies in their lodgings—she knows where; I showed her—and they dies down in Tom-all-Alone's in heaps. They dies more than they lives, according to what *I* see." Then he hoarsely whispered Charley. "If she ain't the t'other one, she ain't the forrenner. Is there *three* of 'em then?"

Charley looked at me a little frightened. I felt half frightened at myself when the boy glared on me so.

But he turned and followed, when I beckoned to him; and finding that he acknowledged that influence in me, I led the way straight home. It was not far; only at the summit of the hill. We passed but one man. I doubted if we should have got home without assistance; the boy's steps were so uncertain and tremulous. He made no complaint, however, and was strangely unconcerned about himself, if I may say so strange a thing.

Leaving him in the hall for a moment, shrunk into a corner of the window-seat, and staring with an indifference that could scarcely be called wonder, at the comfort and brightness about him, I went into the drawing-room to speak to my guardian. There I found Mr. Skimpole, who had come down by the coach, as he frequently did without notice, and never bringing any clothes with him, but always borrowing everything he wanted.

They came out with me directly, to look at the boy. The servants had gathered in the hall, too; and he shivered in the window-seat with Charley standing by him, like some wounded animal that had been found in a ditch.

"This is a sorrowful case," said my guardian, after asking him a question or two, and touching him, and examining his eyes. "What do you say, Harold?"

"You had better turn him out," said Mr. Skimpole.

"What do you mean?" inquired my guardian, almost sternly.

"My dear Jarndyce," said Skimpole, "you know what I am: I am a child. Be cross to me, if I deserve it. But I have a constitutional objection to this sort of thing. I always had, when I was a medical man. He's not safe, you know. There's a very bad sort of fever about him."

Mr. Skimpole had retreated from the hall to the drawing-room again, and said this in his airy way, seated on the music-stool as we stood by.

"You'll say it's childish," observed Mr. Skimpole, looking gaily at us. "Well, I dare say it may be; but I *am* a child and I never pretend to be anything else. If you put him out in the road, you only put him where he was before. He will be no worse off than he was, you know. Even make him better off, if you like. Give him sixpence, or five shillings, or five pound ten—you are arithmeticians, and I am not—and get rid of him!"

"And what is he to do then?" asked my guardian.

"Upon my life," said Mr. Skimpole, shrugging his shoulders with his engaging smile, "I have not the least idea what he is to do then. But I have no doubt he'll do it."

"Now, is it not a horrible reflection," said my guardian, to whom I had hastily explained the unavailing efforts of the two women, "is it not a horrible reflection," walking up and down and rumpling his hair, "that if this wretched creature were a convicted prisoner, his hospital would be wide open to him, and he would be as well taken care of as any sick boy in the kingdom?"

"My dear Jarndyce," returned Mr. Skimpole, "you'll pardon the simplicity of the question, coming as it does from a creature who is perfectly simple in worldly matters—but why *isn't* he a prisoner then?"

My guardian stopped and looked at him with a whimsical mixture of amusement and indignation in his face.

"Our young friend is not to be suspected of any delicacy, I should imagine," said Mr. Skimpole, unabashed and candid. "It seems to me that it would be wiser, as well as in a certain kind of way more respectable, if he showed some misdirected energy that got him into prison. There would be more of an adventurous spirit in it, and consequently more of a certain sort of poetry."

"I believe," returned my guardian, resuming his uneasy walk, "that there is not such another child on earth as you are."

"Do you really?" said Mr. Skimpole; "I dare say! But I confess I don't see why our young friend, in his degree, should not seek to invest himself with such poetry as is open to him. He is no doubt born with an appetite—probably, when he is in a safer state of health, he has an excellent appetite. Very well. At our young friend's natural dinner hour, most likely about noon, our young friend says in effect to society, 'I am hungry; will you have the goodness to produce your spoon, and feed me?' Society, which has taken upon itself the general arrangement of the whole system of spoons, and professes to have a spoon for our young friend, does *not* produce that spoon; and our young friend, therefore, says, 'You really must excuse me if I seize it.' Now, this appears to me a case of misdirected energy, which has a certain amount of reason in it, and a certain amount of romance; and I don't know but what I should be more interested in our young friend, as an illustration of such a case, than merely as a poor vagabond—which any one can be."

"In the meantime," I ventured to observe, "he is getting worse."

"In the meantime," said Mr. Skimpole, cheerfully, "as Miss Summerson, with her practical good sense, observes, he is getting worse. Therefore I recommend your turning him out before he gets still worse."

The amiable face with which he said it, I think I shall never forget.

"Of course, little woman," observed my guardian, turning to me, "I can ensure his admission into the proper place by merely going there to enforce it, though it's a bad state of things when, in his condition, that is necessary. But it's growing late, and is a very bad night, and the boy is worn out already. There is a bed in the wholesome loft-room by the stable; we had better keep him there till morning, when he can be wrapped up and removed. We'll do that."

"O!" said Mr. Skimpole, with his hands upon the keys of the piano as we moved away. "Are you going back to our young friend?"

"Yes," said my guardian.

"How I envy you your constitution, Jarndyce!" returned Mr. Skimpole, with playful admiration. "You don't mind these things, neither does Miss Summerson. You are ready at all times to go anywhere, and do anything. Such is Will! I have no Will at all—and no Won't—simply Can't."

"You can't recommend anything for the boy, I suppose?" said

my guardian, looking back over his shoulder, half angrily; only half angrily, for he never seemed to consider Mr. Skimpole an accountable being.

"My dear Jarndyce, I observed a bottle of cooling medicine in his pocket, and it's impossible for him to do better than take it. You can tell them to sprinkle a little vinegar[1] about the place where he sleeps and to keep it moderately cool, and him moderately warm. But it is mere impertinence in me to offer any recommendation. Miss Summerson has such a knowledge of detail, and such a capacity for the administration of detail, that she knows all about it."

We went back into the hall, and explained to Jo what we proposed to do, which Charley explained to him again, and which he received with the languid unconcern I had already noticed, wearily looking on at what was done, as if it were for somebody else. The servants compassionating his miserable state, and being very anxious to help, we soon got the loft-room ready; and some of the men about the house carried him across the wet yard, well wrapped up. It was pleasant to observe how kind they were to him, and how there appeared to be a general impression among them that frequently calling him "Old Chap" was likely to revive his spirits. Charley directed the operations, and went to and fro between the loft-room and the house with such little stimulants and comforts as we thought it safe to give him. My guardian himself saw him before he was left for the night, and reported to me, when he returned to the Growlery to write a letter on the boy's behalf, which a messenger was charged to deliver at daylight in the morning, that he seemed easier, and inclined to sleep. They had fastened his door on the outside, he said, in case of his being delirious; but had so arranged that he could not make any noise without being heard.

Ada being in our room with a cold, Mr. Skimpole was left alone all this time, and entertained himself by playing snatches of pathetic airs, and sometimes singing to them (as we heard at a distance) with great expression and feeling. When we rejoined him in the drawing-room he said he would give us a little ballad, which had come into his head, "apropos of our young friend"; and he sang one about a Peasant boy,

> "Thrown on the wide world, doom'd to wander and roam,
> Bereft of his parents, bereft of a home."[2]

—quite exquisitely. It was a song that always made him cry, he told us.

1. Commonly used as a disinfectant in sick-rooms.

2. "The Peasant Boy," a song (1825) by John Parry (1776–1851): "Thrown on the wide world, doom'd to wander and roam,/ Bereft of his parents, bereft of a home,/ A stranger to pleasure, to comfort and joy,/ Behold little Edmund, the poor Peasant boy!/ Oh pity oh pity the poor Peasant boy!"

He was extremely gay all the rest of the evening: "for he absolutely chirped," those were his delighted words, "when he thought by what a happy talent for business he was surrounded." He gave us, in his glass of negus,[3] "Better health to our young friend!" and supposed, and gaily pursued, the case of his being reserved like Whittington[4] to become Lord Mayor of London. In that event, no doubt, he would establish the Jarndyce Institution and the Summerson Alms-houses, and a little annual Corporation Pilgrimage to St. Albans. He had no doubt, he said, that our young friend was an excellent boy in his way, but his way was not the Harold Skimpole way; what Harold Skimpole was, Harold Skimpole had found himself, to his considerable surprise, when he first made his own acquaintance; he had accepted himself with all his failings, and had thought it sound philosophy to make the best of the bargain; and he hoped we would do the same.

Charley's last report was, that the boy was quiet. I could see, from my window, the lantern they had left him burning quietly; and I went to bed very happy to think that he was sheltered.

There was more movement and more talking than usual a little before day-break, and it awoke me. As I was dressing, I looked out of my window, and asked one of our men who had been among the active sympathisers last night, whether there was anything wrong about the house. The lantern was still burning in the loft-window.

"It's the boy, miss," said he.

"Is he worse?" I inquired.

"Gone, miss."

"Dead!"

"Dead, miss? No. Gone clean off."

At what time of the night he had gone, or how, or why, it seemed hopeless ever to divine. The door remaining as it had been left, and the lantern standing in the window, it could only be supposed that he had got out by a trap in the floor which communicated with an empty cart-house below. But he had shut it down again, if that were so; and it looked as if it had not been raised. Nothing of any kind was missing. On this fact being clearly ascertained, we all yielded to the painful belief that delirium had come upon him in the night, and that, allured by some imaginary object, or pursued by some imaginary horror, he had strayed away in that worse than helpless state;—all of us, that is to say, but Mr. Skimpole who repeatedly suggested, in his usual easy light style, that it had occurred to our young friend that he was not a safe inmate, having a bad kind of fever upon him; and that he had, with great natural politeness, taken himself off.

3. Mixture of port wine, boiling water, and sliced lemons.

4. See p. 58, note 1.

Every possible inquiry was made, and every place was searched. The brick-kilns were examined, the cottages were visited, the two women were particularly questioned, but they knew nothing of him, and nobody could doubt that their wonder was genuine. The weather had for some time been too wet, and the night itself had been too wet, to admit of any tracing by footsteps. Hedge and ditch, and wall, and rick and stack, were examined by our men for a long distance round, lest the boy should be lying in such a place insensible or dead; but nothing was seen to indicate that he had ever been near. From the time when he was left in the loft-room. he vanished.

The search continued for five days. I do not mean that it ceased, even then; but that my attention was then diverted into a current very memorable to me.

As Charley was at her writing again in my room in the evening, and as I sat opposite to her at work, I felt the table tremble. Looking up, I saw my little maid shivering from head to foot.

"Charley," said I, "are you so cold?"

"I think I am, miss," she replied. "I don't know what it is. I can't hold myself still. I felt so, yesterday; at about this same time, miss. Don't be uneasy, I think I am ill."

I heard Ada's voice outside, and I hurried to the door of communication between my room and our pretty sitting-room, and locked it. Just in time, for she tapped at it while my hand was yet upon the key.

Ada called to me to let her in; but I said, "Not now, my dearest. Go away. There's nothing the matter; I will come to you presently." Ah! it was a long, long time, before my darling girl and I were companions again.

Charley fell ill. In twelve hours she was very ill. I moved her to my room, and laid her in my bed, and sat down quietly to nurse her. I told my guardian all about it, and why I felt it was necessary that I should seclude myself, and my reason for not seeing my darling above all. At first she came very often to the door, and called to me, and even reproached me with sobs and tears; but I wrote her a long letter, saying that she made me anxious and unhappy, and imploring her, as she loved me, and wished my mind to be at peace, to come no nearer than the garden. After that, she came beneath the window, even oftener than she had come to the door; and, if I had learnt to love her dear sweet voice before when we were hardly ever apart, how did I learn to love it then, when I stood behind the window-curtain listening and replying, but not so much as looking out! How did I learn to love it afterwards, when the harder time came!

They put a bed for me in our sitting-room; and by keeping the door wide open, I turned the two rooms into one, now that Ada had vacated that part of the house, and kept them always fresh and airy. There was not a servant, in or about the house, but was so good that they would all most gladly have come to me at any hour of the day or night, without the least fear or unwillingness; but I thought it best to choose one worthy woman who was never to see Ada, and whom I could trust to come and go with all precaution. Through her means, I got out to take the air with my guardian, when there was no fear of meeting Ada; and wanted for nothing in the way of attendance, any more than in any other respect.

And thus poor Charley sickened and grew worse, and fell into heavy danger of death, and lay severely ill for many a long round of day and night. So patient she was, so uncomplaining, and inspired by such a gentle fortitude, that very often as I sat by Charley, holding her head in my arms—repose would come to her, so, when it would come to her in no other attitude—I silently prayed to our Father in heaven that I might not forget the lesson which this little sister taught me.

I was very sorrowful to think that Charley's pretty looks would change and be disfigured, even if she recovered—she was such a child with her dimpled face—but that thought was, for the greater part, lost in her greater peril. When she was at the worst, and her mind rambled again to the cares of her father's sick-bed, and the little children, she still knew me so far as that she would lie quiet in my arms when she could lie quiet nowhere else, and murmur out the wanderings of her mind less restlessly. At those times I used to think, how should I ever tell the two remaining babies that the baby who had learned of her faithful heart to be a mother to them in their need, was dead!

There were other times when Charley knew me well, and talked to me; telling me that she sent her love to Tom and Emma, and that she was sure Tom would grow up to be a good man. At those times Charley would speak to me of what she had read to her father as well as she could, to comfort him; of that young man carried out to be buried, who was the only son of his mother and she was a widow; of the ruler's daughter raised up by the gracious hand upon her bed of death. And Charley told me that when her father died, she had kneeled down and prayed in her first sorrow that he likewise might be raised up, and given back to his poor children; and that if she should never get better, and should die too, she thought it likely that it might come into Tom's mind to offer the same prayer for her.[5] Then would I show Tom how these people of old days had been brought back to life on earth, only that we might know our hope to be restored in Heaven!

But of all the various times there were in Charley's illness, there

5. See Matthew 9:25-26.

was not one when she lost the gentle qualities I have spoken of. And there were many, many, when I thought in the night of the last high belief in the watching Angel, and the last higher trust in God, on the part of her poor despised father.

And Charley did not die. She flutteringly and slowly turned the dangerous point, after long lingering there, and then began to mend. The hope that never had been given, from the first, of Charley being in outward appearance Charley any more, soon began to be encouraged; and even that prospered, and I saw her growing into her old childish likeness again.

It was a great morning, when I could tell Ada all this as she stood out in the garden; and it was a great evening, when Charley and I at last took tea together in the next room. But, on that same evening, I felt that I was stricken cold.

Happily for both of us, it was not until Charley was safe in bed again and placidly asleep, that I began to think the contagion of her illness was upon me. I had been able easily to hide what I had felt at tea-time, but I was past that already now, and I knew that I was rapidly following in Charley's steps.

I was well enough, however, to be up early in the morning, and to return my darling's cheerful blessing from the garden, and to talk with her as long as usual. But I was not free from an impression that I had been walking about the two rooms in the night, a little beside myself, though knowing where I was; and I felt confused at times—with a curious sense of fulness, as if I were becoming too large altogether.

In the evening I was so much worse, that I resolved to prepare Charley; with which view, I said, "You're getting quite strong, Charley, are you not?"

"O quite!" said Charley.

"Strong enough to be told a secret, I think, Charley?"

"Quite strong enough for that, miss!" cried Charley. But Charley's face fell in the height of her delight, for she saw the secret in *my* face; and she came out of the great chair, and fell upon my bosom, and said, "O miss, it's my doing! It's my doing!" and a great deal more, out of the fulness of her grateful heart.

"Now, Charley," said I, after letting her go on for a little while, "if I am to be ill, my great trust, humanly speaking, is in you. And unless you are as quiet and composed for me, as you always were for yourself, you can never fulfil it, Charley."

"If you'll let me cry a little longer, miss," said Charley. "O my dear, my dear! if you'll only let me cry a little longer, O my dear!" —how affectionately and devotedly she poured this out, as she clung to my neck, I never can remember without tears—"I'll be good."

So I let Charley cry a little longer, and it did us both good.

"Trust in me now, if you please, miss," said Charley, quietly. "I am listening to everything you say."

"It is very little at present, Charley. I shall tell your doctor tonight that I don't think I am well, and that you are going to nurse me."

For that the poor child thanked me with her whole heart.

"And in the morning, when you hear Miss Ada in the garden, if I should not be quite able to go to the window-curtain as usual, do you go, Charley, and say I am asleep—that I have rather tired myself, and am asleep. At all times keep the room as I have kept it, Charley, and let no one come."

Charley promised, and I lay down, for I was very heavy. I saw the doctor that night, and asked the favour of him that I wished to ask, relative to his saying nothing of my illness in the house as yet. I have a very indistinct remembrance of that night melting into day, and of day melting into night again; but I was just able, on the first morning, to get to the window, and speak to my darling.

On the second morning I heard her dear voice—O how dear now!—outside; and I asked Charley, with some difficulty (speech being painful to me), to go and say I was asleep. I heard her answer softly, "Don't disturb her, Charley, for the world!"

"How does my own Pride look, Charley?" I inquired.

"Disappointed, miss," said Charley, peeping through the curtain.

"But I know she is very beautiful this morning."

"She is indeed, miss," answered Charley, peeping. "Still looking up at the window."

With her blue clear eyes, God bless them, always loveliest when raised like that!

I called Charley to me, and gave her her last charge.

"Now, Charley, when she knows I am ill, she will try to make her way into the room. Keep her out, Charley, if you love me truly, to the last! Charley, if you let her in but once, only to look upon me for one moment as I lie here, I shall die."

"I never will! I never will!" she promised me.

"I believe it, my dear Charley. And now come and sit beside me for a little while, and touch me with your hand. For I cannot see you, Charley; I am blind."

Chapter XXXII

THE APPOINTED TIME[1]

It is night in Lincoln's Inn—perplexed and troublous valley of the shadow[2] of the law, where suitors generally find but little day—and fat candles are snuffed out in offices, and clerks have rattled

1. See Job 7:1: "Is there not an appointed time to man upon earth?"

2. Cf. Psalms 23:4.

down the crazy wooden stairs, and dispersed. The bell that rings at nine o'clock, has ceased its doleful clangour about nothing; the gates are shut; and the night-porter, a solemn warder with a mighty power of sleep, keeps guard in his lodge. From tiers of staircase windows, clogged lamps[3] like the eyes of Equity, bleared Argus[4] with a fathomless pocket for every eye and an eye upon it, dimly blink at the stars. In dirty upper casements, here and there, hazy little patches of candle-light reveal where some wise draughtsman and conveyancer yet toils for the entanglement of real estate in meshes of sheepskin, in the average ratio of about a dozen of sheep to an acre of land. Over which bee-like industry, these benefactors of their species linger yet, though office-hours be past; that they may give, for every day, some good account at last.[5]

In the neighbouring court, where the Lord Chancellor of the Rag and Bottle shop dwells, there is a general tendency towards beer and supper. Mrs. Piper and Mrs. Perkins, whose respective sons, engaged with a circle of acquaintance in the game of hide and seek, have been lying in ambush about the by-ways of Chancery Lane for some hours, and scouring the plain of the same thoroughfare to the confusion of passengers—Mrs. Piper and Mrs. Perkins have but now exchanged congratulations on the children being abed; and they still linger on a door-step over a few parting words. Mr. Krook and his lodger, and the fact of Mr. Krook's being "continual in liquor," and the testamentary prospects of the young man are, as usual, the staple of their conversation. But they have something to say, likewise, of the Harmonic Meeting at the Sol's Arms; where the sound of the piano through the partly-opened windows jingles out into the court, and where Little Swills, after keeping the lovers of harmony in a roar like a very Yorick,[6] may now be heard taking the gruff line in a concerted piece,[7] and sentimentally adjuring his friends and patrons to Listen, listen, listen, Tew the wa-ter-Fall![8] Mrs. Perkins and Mrs. Piper compare opinions on the subject of the young lady of professional celebrity who assists at the Harmonic Meetings, and who has a space to herself in the manuscript announcement in the window; Mrs. Perkins possessing information that she has been married a year and a half, though announced as Miss M. Melvilleson, the noted syren, and that her baby is clandestinely conveyed to the

3. Long after gas lighting ("upstart gas" as it is called in ch. XLVII) was in common use, the law colleges clung to using dim oil lamps on the stairways of their inns.

4. A herdsman with a hundred eyes appointed by Hera to watch her rival, Io.

5. See the hymn by Isaac Watts (1674–1748): "How doth the little busy bee/ Improve each shining hour." The final stanza reads: "In books or work, or healthful play/ Let my first years be past;/ That I may give for every day/ A good account at last."

6. See Hamlet's address to the skull of Yorick, the king's jester: "Your flashes of merriment that were wont to set the table on a roar" (V.i.211).

7. Singing the bass part in a duet or a quartet.

8. "Listen, listen, listen, listen to the wa-ter-fall"—chorus line for a glee, "Here in Cool Grot," by the Irish composer (and father of the Duke of Wellington) the Earl of Mornington (1735–81).

Sol's Arms every night to receive its natural nourishment during the entertainments. "Sooner than which, myself," says Mrs. Perkins, "I would get my living by selling lucifers." Mrs. Piper, as in duty bound, is of the same opinion; holding that a private station is better than public applause, and thanking Heaven for her own (and, by implication, Mrs. Perkins's) respectability. By this time, the potboy of the Sol's Arms appearing with her supper-pint well frothed, Mrs. Piper accepts that tankard and retires in-doors, first giving a fair good night to Mrs. Perkins, who has had her own pint in her hand ever since it was fetched from the same hostelry by young Perkins before he was sent to bed. Now there is a sound of putting up shop-shutters in the court, and a smell as of the smoking of pipes; and shooting stars are seen in upper windows, further indicating retirement to rest. Now, too, the policeman begins to push at doors; to try fastenings; to be suspicious of bundles; and to administer his beat, on the hypothesis that every one is either robbing, or being robbed.

It is a close night, though the damp cold is searching too; and there is a laggard mist a little way up in the air. It is a fine steaming night to turn the slaughter-houses, the unwholesome trades, the sewerage, bad water, and burial-grounds to account, and give the Registrar of Deaths some extra business. It may be something in the air—there is plenty in it—or it may be something in himself that is in fault; but Mr. Weevle, otherwise Jobling, is very ill at ease. He comes and goes, between his own room and the open street door, twenty times an hour. He has been doing so ever since it fell dark. Since the Chancellor shut up his shop, which he did very early to-night, Mr. Weevle has been down and up, and down and up (with a cheap tight velvet skull-cap on his head, making his whiskers look out of all proportion), oftener than before.

It is no phenomenon that Mr. Snagsby should be ill at ease too; for he always is so, more or less, under the oppressive influence of the secret that is upon him. Impelled by the mystery, of which he is a partaker, and yet in which he is not a sharer, Mr. Snagsby haunts what seems to be its fountain-head—the rag and bottle shop in the court. It has an irresistible attraction for him. Even now, coming round by the Sol's Arms with the intention of passing down the court, and out at the Chancery Lane end, and so terminating his unpremeditated after-supper stroll of ten minutes long from his own door and back again, Mr. Snagsby approaches.

"What, Mr. Weevle?" says the stationer, stopping to speak. "Are *you* there?"

"Ay!" says Weevle. "Here I am, Mr. Snagsby."

"Airing yourself, as I am doing, before you go to bed?" the stationer inquires.

"Why, there's not much air to be got here; and what there is, is not very freshening," Weevle answers, glancing up and down the court.

"Very true, sir. Don't you observe," says Mr. Snagsby, pausing to sniff and taste the air a little; "don't you observe, Mr. Weevle, that you're—not to put too fine a point upon it—that you're rather greasy here, sir?"

"Why, I have noticed myself that there is a queer kind of flavour in the place to-night," Mr. Weevle rejoins. "I suppose it's chops at the Sol's Arms."

"Chops, do you think? Oh!—Chops, eh?" Mr. Snagsby sniffs and tastes again. "Well, sir, I suppose it is. But I should say their cook at the Sol wanted a little looking after. She has been burning 'em, sir? And I don't think"; Mr. Snagsby sniffs and tastes again, and then spits and wipes his mouth; "I don't think—not to put too fine a point upon it—that they were quite fresh, when they were shown the gridiron."

"That's very likely. It's a tainting sort of weather."

"It *is* a tainting sort of weather," says Mr. Snagsby, "and I find it sinking to the spirits."

"By George! *I* find it gives me the horrors," returns Mr. Weevle.

"Then, you see, you live in a lonesome way, and in a lonesome room, with a black circumstance hanging over it," says Mr. Snagsby, looking in past the other's shoulder along the dark passage, and then falling back a step to look up at the house. "*I* couldn't live in that room alone, as you do, sir. I should get so fidgety and worried of an evening, sometimes, that I should be driven to come to the door, and stand here, sooner than sit there. But then it's very true that you didn't see, in your room, what *I* saw there. That makes a difference."

"I know quite enough about it," returns Tony.

"It's not agreeable, is it?" pursues Mr. Snagsby, coughing his cough of mild persuasion behind his hand. "Mr. Krook ought to consider it in the rent. I hope he does, I am sure."

"I hope he does," says Tony. "But I doubt it."

"You find the rent high, do you, sir?" returns the stationer. "Rents *are* high about here. I don't know how it is exactly, but the law seems to put things up in price. Not," adds Mr. Snagsby, with his apologetic cough, "that I mean to say a word against the profession I get my living by."

Mr. Weevle again glances up and down the court, and then looks at the stationer. Mr. Snagsby, blankly catching his eye, looks upward for a star or so, and coughs a cough expressive of not exactly seeing his way out of this conversation.

"It is a curious fact, sir," he observes, slowly rubbing his hands, "that he should have been——"

"Who's he?" interrupts Mr. Weevle.

"The deceased, you know," says Mr. Snagsby, twitching his head and right eyebrow towards the staircase, and tapping his acquaintance on the button.

"Ah, to be sure!" returns the other, as if he were not over-fond of the subject. "I thought we had done with him."

"I was only going to say it's a curious fact, sir, that he should have come and lived here, and been one of my writers, and then that you should come and live here, and be one of my writers, too. Which there is nothing derogatory, but far from it in the appellation," says Mr. Snagsby, breaking off with a mistrust that he may have unpolitely asserted a kind of proprietorship in Mr. Weevle, "because I have known writers that have gone into Brewers' houses and done really very respectable indeed. Eminently respectable, sir," adds Mr. Snagsby, with a misgiving that he has not improved the matter.

"It's a curious coincidence, as you say," answers Weevle, once more glancing up and down the court.

"Seems a Fate in it, don't there?" suggests the stationer.

"There does."

"Just so," observes the stationer, with his confirmatory cough. "Quite a Fate in it. Quite a Fate. Well, Mr. Weevle, I am afraid I must bid you good night"; Mr. Snagsby speaks as if it made him desolate to go, though he has been casting about for any means of escape ever since he stopped to speak; "my little woman will be looking for me else. Good night, sir!"

If Mr. Snagsby hastens home to save his little woman the trouble of looking for him, he might set his mind at rest on that score. His little woman has had her eye upon him round the Sol's Arms all this time, and now glides after him with a pocket handkerchief wrapped over her head; honouring Mr. Weevle and his doorway with a searching glance as she goes past.

"You'll know me again, ma'am, at all events" says Mr. Weevle to himself; "and I can't compliment you on your appearance, whoever you are, with your head tied up in a bundle. Is this fellow *never* coming!"

This fellow approaches as he speaks. Mr. Weevle softly holds up his finger, and draws him into the passage, and closes the street door. Then they go up-stairs; Mr. Weevle heavily, and Mr. Guppy (for it is he) very lightly indeed. When they are shut into the back room, they speak low.

"I thought you had gone to Jericho at least, instead of coming here," says Tony.

"Why, I said about ten."

"You said about ten," Tony repeats. "Yes, so you did say about ten. But according to my count, it's ten times ten—it's a hundred o'clock. I never had such a night in my life!"

"What has been the matter?"

"That's it!" says Tony. "Nothing has been the matter. But here have I been stewing and fuming in this jolly old crib, till I have had the horrors falling on me as thick as hail. *There*'s a blessed-looking candle!" says Tony, pointing to the heavily burning taper on his table with a great cabbage head and a long winding-sheet.[9]

"That's easily improved," Mr. Guppy observes, as he takes the snuffers in hand.

"*Is* it?" returns his friend. "Not so easily as you think. It has been smouldering like that ever since it was lighted."[1]

"Why, what's the matter with you, Tony?" inquires Mr. Guppy, looking at him, snuffers in hand, as he sits down with his elbow on the table.

"William Guppy," replies the other, "I am in the Downs.[2] It's this unbearably dull, suicidal room—and old Boguey down-stairs, I suppose." Mr. Weevle moodily pushes the snuffer-tray from him with his elbow, leans his head on his hand, puts his feet on the fender, and looks at the fire. Mr. Guppy, observing him, slightly tosses his head, and sits down on the other side of the table in an easy attitude.

"Wasn't that Snagsby talking to you, Tony?"

"Yes, and be——yes, it was Snagsby," says Mr. Weevle, altering the construction of his sentence.

"On business?"

"No. No business. He was only sauntering by, and stopped to prose."

"I thought it was Snagsby," says Mr. Guppy, "and thought it as well that he shouldn't see me, so I waited till he was gone."

"There we go again, William G.!" cries Tony, looking up for an instant. "So mysterious and secret! By George, if we were going to commit a murder, we couldn't have more mystery about it!"

Mr. Guppy affects to smile; and with the view of changing the conversation, looks with an admiration, real or pretended, round the room at the Galaxy Gallery of British Beauty; terminating his survey with the portrait of Lady Dedlock over the mantel-shelf, in which she is represented on a terrace, with a pedestal upon the terrace, and a vase upon the pedestal, and her shawl upon the vase, and a prodigious piece of fur upon the shawl, and her arm on the prodigious piece of fur, and a bracelet on her arm.

"That's very like Lady Dedlock," says Mr. Guppy. "It's a speaking likeness."

9. A cabbage head is presumably the large lump of charred soot that accumulates at the end of an untrimmed wick. On *winding-sheet*, see p. 124, note 4.

1. I.e., clipping (snuffing) the used wick will not fix this candle.

2. Despondent.

"I wish it was," growls Tony, without changing his position. "I should have some fashionable conversation here, then."

Finding, by this time, that his friend is not to be wheedled into a more sociable humour, Mr. Guppy puts about upon the ill-used tack, and remonstrates with him.

"Tony," says he, "I can make allowances for lowness of spirits, for no man knows what it is when it does come upon a man, better than I do; and no man perhaps has a better right to know it, than a man who has an unrequited image imprinted on his art. But there are bounds to these things when an unoffending party is in question, and I will acknowledge to you, Tony, that I don't think your manner on the present occasion is hospitable or quite gentlemanly."

"This is strong language, William Guppy," returns Mr. Weevle.

"Sir, it may be," retorts Mr. William Guppy, "but I feel strongly when I use it."

Mr. Weevle admits that he has been wrong, and begs Mr. William Guppy to think no more about it. Mr. William Guppy, however, having got the advantage, cannot quite release it without a little more injured remonstrance.

"No! Dash it, Tony," says that gentleman, "you really ought to be careful how you wound the feelings of a man, who has an unrequited image imprinted on his art, and who is *not* altogether happy in those chords which vibrate to the tenderest emotions. You, Tony, possess in yourself all that is calculated to charm the eye, and allure the taste. It is not—happily for you, perhaps, and I may wish that I could say the same—it is not your character to hover around one flower.[3] The ole garden is open to you, and your airy pinions carry you through it. Still, Tony, far be it from me, I am sure, to wound even your feelings without a cause!"

Tony again entreats that the subject may be no longer pursued, saying emphatically, "William Guppy, drop it!" Mr. Guppy acquiesces, with the reply, "I never should have taken it up, Tony, of my own accord."

"And now," says Tony, stirring the fire, "touching this same bundle of letters. Isn't it an extraordinary thing of Krook to have appointed twelve o'clock to-night to hand 'em over to me?"

"Very. What did he do it for?"

"What does he do anything for? *He* don't know. Said, to-day was his birthday, and he'd hand 'em over to-night at twelve o'clock. He'll have drunk himself blind by that time. He has been at it all day."

"He hasn't forgotten the appointment, I hope?"

"Forgotten? Trust him for that. He never forgets anything. I saw

3. Cf. Macheath's song: "My heart was so free,/ It rov'd like the Bee,/ 'Till Polly my Passion requited;/ I sipt each Flower,/ I chang'd ev'ry Hour,/ But here ev'ry Flow'r is united." *The Beggar's Opera*, I.xiii.

him to-night, about eight—helped him to shut up his shop—and he had got the letters then in his hairy cap. He pulled it off, and showed 'em me. When the shop was closed, he took them out of this cap, hung his cap on the chair-back, and stood turning them over before the fire. I heard him a little while afterwards through the floor here, humming, like the wind, the only song he knows—about Bibo, and old Charon, and Bibo being drunk when he died,[4] or something or other. He has been as quiet, since, as an old rat asleep in his hole."

"And you are to go down at twelve?"

"At twelve. And, as I tell you, when you came it seemed to me a hundred."

"Tony," says Mr. Guppy, after considering a little with his legs crossed, "he can't read yet, can he?"

"Read! He'll never read. He can make all the letters separately, and he knows most of them separately when he sees them; he has got on that much, under me; but he can't put them together. He's too old to acquire the knack of it now—and too drunk."

"Tony," says Mr. Guppy, uncrossing and recrossing his legs; "how do you suppose he spelt out that name of Hawdon?"

"He never spelt it out. You know what a curious power of eye he has, and how he has been used to employ himself in copying things by eye alone. He imitated it—evidently from the direction of a letter; and asked me what it meant."

"Tony," says Mr. Guppy, uncrossing and recrossing his legs again; "should you say that the original was a man's writing or a woman's?"

"A woman's. Fifty to one a lady's—slopes a good deal, and the end of the letter 'n,' long and hasty."

Mr. Guppy has been biting his thumb-nail during this dialogue, generally changing the thumb when he has changed the cross leg. As he is going to do so again, he happens to look at his coat-sleeve. It takes his attention. He stares at it, aghast.

"Why, Tony, what on earth is going on in this house to-night? Is there a chimney on fire?"

"Chimney on fire!"

"Ah!" returns Mr. Guppy. "See how the soot's falling. See here, on my arm! See again, on the table here! Con-found the stuff, it won't blow off—smears, like black fat!"

They look at one another, and Tony goes listening to the door,

4. In a song by John Travers (ca. 1703–58), a drunkard talks with Charon, the ferryman who rowed the shades of the dead across the River Styx. "When Bibo thought fit from the world to retreat,/ As full of Champagne as an egg's full of meat./ He wak'd in the boat; And to Charon he said,/ He would be row'd back, for he was not yet dead./ 'Trim the boat, and sit quiet,' stern Charon replied,/ 'You may have forgot you were drunk when you died.' "

and a little way up-stairs, and a little way down-stairs. Comes back, and says it's all right, and all quiet; and quotes the remark he lately made to Mr. Snagsby, about their cooking chops at the Sol's Arms.

"And it was then," resumes Mr. Guppy, still glancing with remarkable aversion at his coat-sleeve, as they pursue their conversation before the fire, leaning on opposite sides of the table, with their heads very near together, "that he told you of his having taken the bundle of letters from his lodger's portmanteau?"

"That was the time, sir," answers Tony, faintly adjusting his whiskers. "Whereupon I wrote a line to my dear boy, the Honourable William Guppy, informing him of the appointment for to-night, and advising him not to call before: Boguey being a Sly-boots."

The light vivacious tone of fashionable life which is usually assumed by Mr. Weevle, sits so ill upon him to-night, that he abandons that and his whiskers together; and, after looking over his shoulder, appears to yield himself up, a prey to the horrors again.

"You are to bring the letters to your room to read and compare, and to get yourself into a position to tell him all about them. That's the arrangement, isn't it, Tony?" asks Mr. Guppy, anxiously biting his thumb-nail.

"You can't speak too low. Yes. That's what he and I agreed."

"I tell you what, Tony——"

"You can't speak too low," says Tony once more. Mr. Guppy nods his sagacious head, advances it yet closer, and drops into a whisper.

"I tell you what. The first thing to be done is, to make another packet, like the real one; so that, if he should ask to see the real one while it's in my possession, you can show him the dummy."

"And suppose he detects the dummy as soon as he sees it—which with his biting screw of an eye is about five hundred times more likely than not," suggests Tony.

"Then we'll face it out. They don't belong to him, and they never did. You found that; and you placed them in my hands—a legal friend of yours—for security. If he forces us to it, they'll be producible, won't they?"

"Ye-es," is Mr. Weevle's reluctant admission.

"Why, Tony," remonstrates his friend, "how you look! You don't doubt William Guppy? You don't suspect any harm?"

"I don't suspect anything more than I know, William," returns the other, gravely.

"And what do you know?" urges Mr. Guppy, raising his voice a little; but on his friend's once more warning him. "I tell you, you can't speak too low," he repeats his question without any sound at all; forming with his lips only the words, "What do you know?"

"I know three things. First, I know that here we are whispering in secrecy; a pair of conspirators."

"Well!" says Mr. Guppy, "and we had better be that than a pair of noodles, which we should be, if we were doing anything else, for it's the only way of doing what we want to do. Secondly?"

"Secondly, it's not made out to me how it's likely to be profitable, after all."

Mr. Guppy casts up his eyes at the portrait of Lady Dedlock over the mantel-shelf, and replies, "Tony, you are asked to leave that to the honour of your friend. Besides its being calculated to serve that friend, in those chords of the human mind which—which need not be called into agonising vibration on the present occasion—your friend is no fool. What's that?"

"It's eleven o'clock striking by the bell of St. Paul's. Listen, and you'll hear all the bells in the city jangling."

Both sit silent, listening to the metal voices, near and distant, resounding from towers of various heights, in tones more various than their situations. When these at length cease, all seems more mysterious and quiet than before. One disagreeable result of whispering is, that it seems to evoke an atmosphere of silence, haunted by the ghosts of sound—strange cracks and tickings, the rustling of garments that have no substance in them, and the tread of dreadful feet that would leave no mark on the sea-sand or the winter snow. So sensitive the two friends happen to be, that the air is full of these phantoms; and the two look over their shoulders by one consent, to see that the door is shut.

"Yes, Tony?" says Mr. Guppy, drawing nearer to the fire, and biting his unsteady thumb-nail. "You were going to say, thirdly?"

"It's far from a pleasant thing to be plotting about a dead man in the room where he died, especially when you happen to live in it."

"But we are plotting nothing against him, Tony."

"May be not, still I don't like it. Live here by yourself, and see how *you* like it."

"As to dead men, Tony," proceeds Mr. Guppy, evading this proposal, "there have been dead men in most rooms."

"I know there have; but in most rooms you let them alone, and —and they let you alone," Tony answers.

The two look at each other again. Mr. Guppy makes a hurried remark to the effect that they may be doing the deceased a service; that he hopes so. There is an oppressive blank, until Mr. Weevle, by stirring the fire suddenly, makes Mr. Guppy start as if his heart had been stirred instead.

"Fah! Here's more of this hateful soot hanging about," says he. "Let us open the window a bit, and get a mouthful of air. It's too close."

He raises the sash, and they both rest on the window-sill, half in and half out of the room. The neighbouring houses are too near, to admit of their seeing any sky without craning their necks and looking up; but lights in frowsy windows here and there, and the rolling of distant carriages, and the new expression that there is of the stir of men, they find to be comfortable. Mr. Guppy, noiselessly tapping on the window-sill, resumes his whispering in quite a light-comedy tone.

"By-the-bye, Tony, don't forget old Smallweed"; meaning the Younger of that name. "I have not let him into this, you know. That grandfather of his is too keen by half. It runs in the family."

"I remember," says Tony. "I am up to all that."

"And as to Krook," resumes Mr. Guppy. "Now, do you suppose he really has got hold of any other papers of importance, as he has boasted to you, since you have been such allies?"

Tony shakes his head. "I don't know. Can't imagine. If we get through this business without rousing his suspicions, I shall be better informed no doubt. How can I know without seeing them, when he don't know himself? He is always spelling out words from them, and chalking them over the table and the shop-wall, and asking what this is, and what that is; but his whole stock from beginning to end, may easily be the waste paper he bought it as, for anything I can say. It's a monomania with him, to think he is possessed of documents. He has been going to learn to read them this last quarter of a century, I should judge, from what he tells me."

"How did he first come by that idea, though? that's the question," Mr. Guppy suggests with one eye shut, after a little forensic meditation. "He may have found papers in something he bought, where papers were not supposed to be; and may have got it into his shrewd head, from the manner and place of their concealment, that they are worth something."

"Or he may have been taken in, in some pretended bargain. Or he may have been muddled altogether, by long staring at whatever he *has* got, and by drink, and by hanging about the Lord Chancellor's Court and hearing of documents for ever," returns Mr. Weevle.

Mr. Guppy sitting on the window-sill, nodding his head and balancing all these possibilities in his mind, continues thoughtfully to tap it, and clasp it, and measure it with his hand, until he hastily draws his hand away.

"What in the Devil's name," he said, "is this! Look at my fingers!"

A thick yellow liquor defiles them, which is offensive to the touch and sight and more offensive to the smell. A stagnant, sickening oil, with some natural repulsion in it that makes them both shudder.

"What have you been doing here? What have you been pouring out of window?"

"I pouring out of window? Nothing, I swear. Never, since I have been here!" cries the lodger.

And yet look here—and look here! When he brings the candle, here, from the corner of the window-sill, it slowly drips, and creeps away down the bricks; here, lies in a little thick nauseous pool.

"This is a horrible house," says Mr. Guppy, shutting down the window. "Give me some water, or I shall cut my hand off."

He so washes, and rubs, and scrubs, and smells and washes, that he has not long restored himself with a glass of brandy, and stood silently before the fire, when Saint Paul's bell strikes twelve, and all those other bells strike twelve from their towers of various heights in the dark air, and in their many tones. When all is quiet again, the lodger says:

"It's the appointed time at last. Shall I go?"

Mr. Guppy nods, and gives him a "lucky touch" on the back; but not with the washed hand, though it is his right hand.

He goes down-stairs; and Mr. Guppy tries to compose himself, before the fire, for waiting a long time. But in no more than a minute or two the stairs creak, and Tony comes swiftly back.

"Have you got them?"

"Got them! No. The old man's not there."

He has been so horribly frightened in the short interval, that his terror seizes the other, who makes a rush at him, and asks loudly, "What's the matter?"

"I couldn't make him hear, and I softly opened the door and looked in. And the burning smell is there—and the soot is there, and the oil is there—and he is *not* there!"—Tony ends this with a groan.

Mr. Guppy takes the light. They go down, more dead than alive, and holding one another, push open the door of the back shop. The cat has retreated close to it, and stands snarling—not at them; at something on the ground, before the fire. There is very little fire left in the grate, but there is a smouldering suffocating vapour in the room, and a dark greasy coating on the walls and ceiling. The chairs and table, and the bottle so rarely absent from the table, all stand as usual. On one chair-back, hang the old man's hairy cap and coat.

"Look!" whispers the lodger, pointing his friend's attention to these objects with a trembling finger. "I told you so. When I saw him last, he took his cap off, took out the little bundle of old letters, hung his cap on the back of the chair—his coat was there already, for he had pulled that off, before he went to put the shutters up, and I left him turning the letters over in his hand, standing just where that crumbled black thing is upon the floor."

Is he hanging somewhere? They look up. No.

"See!" whispers Tony. "At the foot of the same chair, there lies a dirty bit of thin red cord that they tie up pens with. That went round the letters. He undid it slowly, leering and laughing at me, before he began to turn them over, and threw it there. I saw it fall."

"What's the matter with the cat?" says Mr. Guppy. "Look at her!"

"Mad, I think. And no wonder in this evil place."

They advance slowly, looking at all these things. The cat remains where they found her, still snarling at the something on the ground, before the fire and between the two chairs. What is it? Hold up the light.

Here is a small burnt patch of flooring; here is the tinder from a little bundle of burnt paper, but not so light as usual, seeming to be steeped in something; and here is—is it the cinder of a small charred and broken log of wood sprinkled with white ashes, or is it coal? O Horror, he IS here! and this from which we run away, striking out the light and overturning one another into the street, is all that represents him.

Help, help, help! come into this house for Heaven's sake!

Plenty will come in, but none can help. The Lord Chancellor of that Court, true to his title in his last act, has died the death of all Lord Chancellors in all Courts, and of all authorities in all places under all names soever, where false pretences are made, and where injustice is done. Call the death by any name Your Highness will, attribute it to whom you will, or say it might have been prevented how you will, it is the same death eternally—inborn, inbred, engendered in the corrupted humours of the vicious body itself, and that only—Spontaneous Combustion, and none other of all the deaths that can be died.

Chapter XXXIII

INTERLOPERS

Now do those two gentlemen not very neat about the cuffs and buttons who attended the last Coroner's Inquest at the Sol's Arms, reappear in the precincts with surprising swiftness (being, in fact, breathlessly fetched by the active and intelligent beadle), and institute perquisitions through the court, and dive into the Sol's parlour, and write with ravenous little pens on tissue-paper.[1] Now do they note down, in the watches of the night, how the neighbourhood of Chancery Lane was yesterday, at about midnight, thrown into a state of the most intense agitation and excitement by the following alarming and horrible discovery. Now do they set forth how it will

1. Thin paper (called *flimsy*) backed with copying paper, used by journalists to make multiple copies of their reports for newspapers.

doubtless be remembered, that some time back a painful sensation was created in the public mind, by a case of mysterious death from opium occurring in the first floor of the house occupied as a rag, bottle, and general marine store shop, by an eccentric individual of intemperate habits, far advanced in life, named Krook; and how, by a remarkable coincidence, Krook was examined at the Inquest, which it may be recollected was held on that occasion at the Sol's Arms, a well-conducted tavern, immediately adjoining the premises in question, on the west side, and licensed by a highly respectable landlord, Mr. James George Bogsby. Now do they show (in as many words as possible), how during some hours of yesterday evening a very peculiar smell was observed by the inhabitants of the court in which the tragical occurrence which forms the subject of that present account transpired; and which odour was at one time so powerful, that Mr. Swills, a comic vocalist, professionally engaged by Mr. J. G. Bogsby, has himself stated to our reporter that he mentioned to Miss M. Melvilleson, a lady of some pretensions to musical ability, likewise engaged by Mr. J. G. Bogsby to sing at a series of concerts called Harmonic Assemblies or Meetings, which it would appear are held at the Sol's Arms, under Mr. Bogsby's direction, pursuant to the Act of George the Second, that he (Mr. Swills) found his voice seriously affected by the impure state of the atmosphere; his jocose expression at the time, being, "that he was like an empty post-office, for he hadn't a single note in him." How this account of Mr. Swills is entirely corroborated by two intelligent married females residing in the same court, and known respectively by the names of Mrs. Piper and Mrs. Perkins; both of whom observed the foetid effluvia, and regarded them as being emitted from the premises in the occupation of Krook, the unfortunate deceased. All this and a great deal more, the two gentlemen, who have formed an amicable partnership in the melancholy catastrophe, write down on the spot; and the boy population of the court (out of bed in a moment) swarm up the shutters of the Sol's Arms parlour, to behold the tops of their heads while they are about it.

The whole court, adult as well as boy, is sleepless for that night, and can do nothing but wrap up its many heads, and talk of the ill-fated house, and look at it. Miss Flite has been bravely rescued from her chamber, as if it were in flames, and accommodated with a bed at the Sol's Arms. The Sol neither turns off its gas nor shuts its door, all night; for any kind of public excitement makes good for the Sol, and causes the court to stand in need of comfort. The house has not done so much in the stomachic article of cloves,[2] or in brandy-and-water warm, since the Inquest. The moment the

2. Something good for the stomach, probably a hot punch spiced with cloves.

potboy heard what had happened, he rolled up his shirt-sleeves tight to his shoulders, and said, "There'll be a run upon us!" In the first outcry, young Piper dashed off for the fire-engines; and returned in triumph at a jolting gallop, perched up aloft on the Phoenix,[3] and holding on to that fabulous creature with all his might, in the midst of helmets and torches. One helmet remains behind, after careful investigation of all chinks and crannies, and slowly paces up and down before the house, in company with one of the two policemen who have been likewise left in charge thereof. To this trio, everybody in the court, possessed of sixpence, has an insatiate desire to exhibit hospitality in a liquid form.

Mr. Weevle and his friend Mr. Guppy are within the bar at the Sol, and are worth anything to the Sol that the bar contains if they will only stay there. "This is not a time," says Mr. Bogsby, "to haggle about money," though he looks something sharply after it, over the counter; "give your orders, you two gentlemen, and you're welcome to whatever you put a name to."

Thus entreated, the two gentlemen (Mr. Weevle especially) put names to so many things that in course of time they find it difficult to put a name to anything quite distinctly; though they still relate, to all new comers, some version of the night they have had of it, and of what they said, and what they thought, and what they saw. Meanwhile, one or other of the policemen often flits about the door, and pushing it open a little way at the full length of his arm, looks in from outer gloom. Not that he has any suspicions, but that he may as well know what they are up to, in there.

Thus, night pursues its leaden course; finding the court still out of bed through the unwonted hours, still treating and being treated, still conducting itself similarly to a court that has had a little money left it unexpectedly. Thus, night at length with slow-retreating steps departs, and the lamplighter going his rounds, like an executioner to a despotic king, strikes off the little heads of fire that have aspired to lessen the darkness. Thus, the day cometh, whether or no.

And the day may discern, even with its dim London eye, that the court has been up all night. Over and above the faces that have fallen drowsily on tables, and the heels that lie prone on hard floors instead of beds, the brick and mortar physiognomy of the very court itself looks worn and jaded. And now the neighbourhood waking up, and beginning to hear of what has happened, comes streaming in, half-dressed, to ask questions; and the two policemen and the helmet (who are far less impressible externally than the court) have enough to do to keep the door.

3. Emblem of a fire-insurance company which maintained its own fire-fighting equipment.

"Good gracious, gentlemen!" says Mr. Snagsby, coming up. "What's this I hear?"

"Why, it's true," returns one of the policemen. "That's what it is. Now move on here, come!"

"Why, good gracious, gentlemen," says Mr. Snagsby, somewhat promptly backed away, "I was at this door last night betwixt ten and eleven o'clock, in conversation with the young man who lodges here."

"Indeed?" returns the policeman. "You will find the young man next door then. Now move on here, some of you."

"Not hurt, I hope?" says Mr. Snagsby.

"Hurt? No. What's to hurt him?"

Mr. Snagsby, wholly unable to answer this, or any question, in his troubled mind, repairs to the Sol's Arms, and finds Mr. Weevle languishing over tea and toast; with a considerable expression on him of exhausted excitement, and exhausted tobacco-smoke.

"And Mr. Guppy likewise!" quoth Mr. Snagsby. "Dear, dear, dear! What a fate there seems in all this! And my lit——"

Mr. Snagsby's power of speech deserts him in the formation of the words "my little woman." For to see that injured female walk into the Sol's Arms at that hour of the morning and stand before the beer engine, with her eyes fixed upon him like an accusing spirit, strikes him dumb.

"My dear," says Mr. Snagsby, when his tongue is loosened, "will you take anything? A little—not to put too fine a point upon it—drop of shrub?"[4]

"No," says Mrs. Snagsby.

"My love, you know these two gentlemen?"

"Yes!" says Mrs. Snagsby; and in a rigid manner acknowledges their presence, still fixing Mr. Snagsby with her eye.

The devoted Mr. Snagsby cannot bear this treatment. He takes Mrs. Snagsby by the hand, and leads her aside to an adjacent cask.

"My little woman, why do you look at me in that way? Pray don't do it."

"I can't help my looks," says Mrs. Snagsby, "and if I could I wouldn't."

Mr. Snagsby, with his cough of meekness, rejoins,—"Wouldn't you really, my dear?" and meditates. Then coughs his cough of trouble, and says, "This is a dreadful mystery, my love!" still fearfully disconcerted by Mrs. Snagsby's eye.

"It *is*," returns Mrs. Snagsby, shaking her head, "a dreadful mystery."

"My little woman," urges Mr. Snagsby, in a piteous manner, "don't for goodness' sake speak to me with that bitter expression,

4. Punch made of rum, lemon peel, and oranges.

and look at me in that searching way! I beg and entreat of you not to do it. Good Lord, you don't suppose that I would go spontaneously combusting any person, my dear?"

"I can't say," returns Mrs. Snagsby.

On a hasty review of his unfortunate position, Mr. Snagsby "can't say," either. He is not prepared positively to deny that he may have had something to do with it. He has had something—he don't know what—to do with so much in this connexion that is mysterious, that it is possible he may even be implicated, without knowing it, in the present transaction. He faintly wipes his forehead with his handkerchief, and gasps.

"My life," says the unhappy stationer, "would you have any objections to mention why, being in general so delicately circumspect in your conduct, you come into a Wine Vaults before breakfast?"

"Why do *you* come here?" inquires Mrs. Snagsby.

"My dear, merely to know the rights of the fatal accident which has happened to the venerable party who has been—combusted." Mr. Snagsby has made a pause to suppress a groan. "I should then have related them to you, my love, over your French roll."

"I dare say you would! You relate everything to me, Mr. Snagsby."

"Every—my lit——?"

"I should be glad," says Mrs. Snagsby, after contemplating his increased confusion with a severe and sinister smile, "if you would come home with me; I think you may be safer there, Mr. Snagsby, than anywhere else."

"My love, I don't know but what I may be, I am sure. I am ready to go."

Mr. Snagsby casts his eye forlornly round the bar, gives Messrs. Weevle and Guppy good morning, assures them of the satisfaction with which he sees them uninjured, and accompanies Mrs. Snagsby from the Sol's Arms. Before night, his doubt whether he may not be responsible for some inconceivable part in the catastrophe which is the talk of the whole neighbourhood, is almost resolved into certainty by Mrs. Snagsby's pertinacity in that fixed gaze. His mental sufferings are so great, that he entertains wandering ideas of delivering himself up to justice, and requiring to be cleared, if innocent, and punished with the utmost rigour of the law, if guilty.

Mr. Weevle and Mr. Guppy, having taken their breakfast, step into Lincoln's Inn to take a little walk about the square, and clear as many of the dark cobwebs out of their brains as a little walk may.

"There can be no more favourable time than the present, Tony," says Mr. Guppy, after they have broodingly made out the four sides of the square, "for a word or two between us, upon a point on which we must, with very little delay, come to an understanding."

"Now, I tell you what, William G!" returns the other, eyeing his companion with a bloodshot eye. "If it's a point of conspiracy, you needn't take the trouble to mention it. I have had enough of that, and I ain't going to have any more. We shall have *you* taking fire next, or blowing up with a bang."

This supposititious phenomenon is so very disagreeable to Mr. Guppy that his voice quakes, as he says in a moral way, "Tony, I should have thought that what we went through last night, would have been a lesson to you never to be personal any more as long as you lived." To which Mr. Weevle returns, "William, I should have thought it would have been a lesson to *you* never to conspire any more as long as you lived." To which Mr. Guppy says, "Who's conspiring?" To which Mr. Jobling replies, "Why, *you* are!" To which Mr. Guppy retorts, "No, I am not." To which Mr. Jobling retorts again, "Yes, you are!" To which Mr. Guppy retorts, "Who says so?" To which Mr. Jobling retorts, "*I* say so!" To which Mr. Guppy retorts, "Oh, indeed?" To which Mr. Jobling retorts, "Yes, indeed!" And both being now in a heated state, they walk on silently for a while, to cool down again.

"Tony," says Mr. Guppy, then, "if you heard your friend out instead of flying at him, you wouldn't fall into mistakes. But your temper is hasty, and you are not considerate. Possessing in yourself, Tony, all that is calculated to charm the eye——"

"Oh! Blow the eye!" cries Mr. Weevle, cutting him short. "Say what you have got to say!"

Finding his friend in this morose and material condition, Mr. Guppy only expresses the finer feelings of his soul through the tone of injury in which he recommences:

"Tony, when I say there is a point on which we must come to an understanding pretty soon, I say so quite apart from any kind of conspiring, however innocent. You know it is professionally arranged beforehand, in all cases that are tried, what facts the witnesses are to prove. Is it, or is it not, desirable that we should know what facts we are to prove, on the inquiry into the death of this unfortunate old Mo—— gentleman?" (Mr. Guppy was going to say, Mogul, but thinks gentleman better suited to the circumstances.)

"What facts? *The* facts."

"The facts bearing on that inquiry. Those are—" Mr. Guppy tells them off on his fingers—"what we knew of his habits; when you saw him last; what his condition was then; the discovery that we made, and how we made it."

"Yes," says Mr. Weevle. "Those are about the facts."

"We made the discovery, in consequence of his having, in his eccentric way, an appointment with you for twelve o'clock at night, when you were to explain some writing to him, as you had often done before, on account of his not being able to read. I, spending the evening with you, was called down—and so forth. The inquiry being only into the circumstances touching the death of the deceased, it's not necessary to go beyond these facts, I suppose you'll agree?"

"No!" returns Mr. Weevle. "I suppose not."

"And this is not a conspiracy, perhaps?" says the injured Guppy.

"No," returns his friend; "if it's nothing worse than this, I withdraw the observation."

"Now, Tony," says Mr. Guppy, taking his arm again, and walking him slowly on, "I should like to know, in a friendly way, whether you have yet thought over the many advantages of your continuing to live at that place?"

"What do you mean?" says Tony, stopping.

"Whether you have yet thought over the many advantages of your continuing to live at that place?" repeats Mr. Guppy, walking him on again.

"At what place? *That* place?" pointing in the direction of the rag and bottle shop.

Mr. Guppy nods.

"Why, I wouldn't pass another night there, for any consideration that you could offer me," says Mr. Weevle, haggardly staring.

"Do you mean it though, Tony?"

"Mean it! Do I look as if I mean it? I feel as if I do; I know that," says Mr. Weevle, with a very genuine shudder.

"Then the possibility, or probability—for such it must be considered—of your never being disturbed in possession of those effects, lately belonging to a lone old man who seemed to have no relation in the world; and the certainty of your being able to find out what he really had got stored up there; don't weigh with you at all against last night, Tony, if I understand you?" says Mr. Guppy, biting his thumb with the appetite of vexation.

"Certainly not. Talk in that cool way of a fellow's living there?" cries Mr. Weevle, indignantly. "Go and live there yourself."

"O! I, Tony!" says Mr. Guppy, soothing him. "I have never lived there, and couldn't get a lodging there now; whereas you have got one."

"You are welcome to it," rejoins his friend, "and—ugh!—you may make yourself at home in it."

"Then you really and truly at this point," says Mr. Guppy, "give up the whole thing, if I understand you, Tony?"

"You never," returns Tony, with a most convincing steadfastness, "said a truer word in all your life. I do!"

While they are so conversing, a hackney-coach drives into the square, on the box of which vehicle a very tall hat makes itself manifest to the public. Inside the coach, and consequently not so manifest to the multitude, though sufficiently so to the two friends, for the coach stops almost at their feet, are the venerable Mr. Smallweed and Mrs. Smallweed, accompanied by their grand-daughter Judy. An air of haste and excitement pervades the party; and as the tall hat (surmounting Mr. Smallweed the younger) alights, Mr. Smallweed the elder pokes his head out of window, and bawls to Mr. Guppy, "How de do, sir! How de do!"

"What do Chick and his family want here at this time of the morning, I wonder!" says Mr. Guppy, nodding to his familiar.

"My dear sir," cries Grandfather Smallweed, "would you do me a favour? Would you and your friend be so very obleeging as to carry me into the public-house in the court, while Bart and his sister bring their grandmother along? Would you do an old man that good turn, sir?"

Mr. Guppy looks at his friend, repeating inquiringly, "the public-house in the court?" And they prepare to bear the venerable burden to the Sol's Arms.

"There's your fare!" says the Patriarch to the coachman with a fierce grin, and shaking his incapable fist at him. "Ask me for a penny more, and I'll have my lawful revenge upon you. My dear young men, be easy with me, if you please. Allow me to catch you round the neck. I won't squeeze you tighter than I can help. O Lord! O dear me! O my bones!"

It is well that the Sol is not far off, for Mr. Weevle presents an apoplectic appearance before half the distance is accomplished. With no worse aggravation of his symptoms, however, than the utterance of divers croaking sounds, expressive of obstructed respiration, he fulfils his share of the porterage, and the benevolent old gentleman is deposited by his own desire in the parlour of the Sol's Arms.

"O Lord!" gasps Mr. Smallweed, looking about him, breathless, from an arm-chair. "O dear me! O my bones and back! O my aches and pains! Sit down, you dancing, prancing, shambling, scrambling poll-parrot! sit down!"

This little apostrophe to Mrs. Smallweed is occasioned by a propensity on the part of that unlucky old lady, whenever she finds herself on her feet, to amble about, and "set"[5] to inanimate objects, accompanying herself with a chattering noise, as in a witch dance. A nervous affection has probably as much to do with these demonstrations, as any imbecile intention in the poor old woman; but on the present occasion they are so particularly lively in connex-

5. To point as a hunting dog points at game.

ion with the Windsor arm-chair,[6] fellow to that in which Mr. Smallweed is seated, that she only quite desists when her grandchildren have held her down in it: her lord in the meanwhile bestowing upon her, with great volubility, the endearing epithet of "a pig-headed Jackdaw," repeated a surprising number of times.

"My dear sir," Grandfather Smallweed then proceeds, addressing Mr. Guppy, "there has been a calamity here. Have you heard of it, either of you?"

"Heard of it, sir! Why, we discovered it."

"You discovered it! You two discovered it! Bart, *they* discovered it!"

The two discoverers stare at the Smallweeds, who return the compliment.

"My dear friends," whines Grandfather Smallweed, putting out both his hands, "I owe you a thousand thanks for discharging the melancholy office of discovering the ashes of Mrs. Smallweed's brother."

"Eh?" says Mr. Guppy.

"Mrs. Smallweed's brother, my dear friend—her only relation. We were not on terms, which is to be deplored now, but he never *would* be on terms. He was not fond of us. He was eccentric—he was very eccentric. Unless he has left a will (which is not at all likely) I shall take out letters of administration. I have come down to look after the property; it must be sealed up, it must be protected. I have come down," repeats Grandfather Smallweed, hooking the air towards him with all his ten fingers at once, "to look after the property."

"I think, Small," says the disconsolate Mr. Guppy, "you might have mentioned that the old man was your uncle."

"You two were so close about him that I thought you would like me to be the same," returns that old bird, with a secretly glistening eye. "Besides, I wasn't proud of him."

"Besides which, it was nothing to you, you know, whether he was or not," says Judy. Also with a secretly glistening eye.

"He never saw me in his life, to know me," observes Small; "I don't know why I should introduce *him*, I am sure!"

"No, he never communicated with us—which is to be deplored," the old gentleman strikes in; "but I have come to look after the property—to look over the papers, and to look after the property. We shall make good our title. It is in the hands of my solicitor. Mr. Tulkinghorn, of Lincoln's Inn Fields, over the way there, is so good as to act as my solicitor; and grass don't grow under *his* feet, I can tell ye. Krook was Mrs. Smallweed's only brother; she had no relation but Krook, and Krook had no relation but Mrs. Smallweed. I

6. Wooden chair with a high back made of long slender spokes.

am speaking of your brother, you brimstone black-beetle, that was seventy-six years of age."

Mrs. Smallweed instantly begins to shake her head, and pipe up, "Seventy-six pound seven and sevenpence! Seventy-six thousand bags of money! Seventy-six hundred thousand million of parcels of bank notes!"

"Will somebody give me a quart pot?" exclaims her exasperated husband, looking helplessly about him, and finding no missile within his reach. "Will somebody obleege me with a spittoon? Will somebody hand me anything hard and bruising to pelt at her? You hag, you cat, you dog, you brimstone barker!" Here Mr. Smallweed, wrought up to the highest pitch by his own eloquence, actually throws Judy at her grandmother in default of anything else, by butting that young virgin at the old lady with such force as he can muster, and then dropping into his chair in a heap.

"Shake me up, somebody, if you'll be so good," says the voice from within the faintly struggling bundle into which he has collapsed. "I have come to look after the property. Shake me up; and call in the police on duty at the next house, to be explained to about the property. My solicitor will be here presently to protect the property. Transportation or the gallows for anybody who shall touch the property!" As his dutiful grandchildren set him up, panting, and putting him through the usual restorative process of shaking and punching, he still repeats like an echo, "the—the property! The property!—property!"

Mr. Weevle and Mr. Guppy look at each other; the former as having relinquished the whole affair; the latter with a discomfited countenance, as having entertained some lingering expectations yet. But there is nothing to be done in opposition to the Smallweed interest. Mr. Tulkinghorn's clerk comes down from his official pew in the chambers, to mention to the police that Mr. Tulkinghorn is answerable for its being all correct about the next of kin, and that the papers and effects will be formally taken possession of in due time and course. Mr. Smallweed is at once permitted so far to assert his supremacy as to be carried on a visit of sentiment into the next house, and up-stairs into Miss Flite's deserted room, where he looks like a hideous bird of prey newly added to her aviary.

The arrival of this unexpected heir soon taking wind in the court, still makes good for the Sol, and keeps the court upon its mettle. Mrs. Piper and Mrs. Perkins think it hard upon the young man if there really is no will, and consider that a handsome present ought to be made him out of the estate. Young Piper and young Perkins, as members of that restless juvenile circle which is the terror of the foot-passengers in Chancery Lane, crumble into ashes behind the pump and under the archway, all day long; where wild yells and hootings take place over their remains. Little Swills and Miss M. Melvilleson enter into affable conversation with their patrons, feeling that these unusual occurrences level the barriers between professionals and non-professionals. Mr. Bogsby puts up "The popular song of King Death![7] with chorus by the whole strength of the company," as the great Harmonic feature of the week; and announces in the bill that "J. G. B. is induced to do so at a considerable extra expense, in consequence of a wish which has been very generally expressed at the bar by a large body of respectable individuals and in homage to a late melancholy event which has aroused so much sensation." There is one point connected with the deceased, upon which the court is particularly anxious; namely, that the fiction of a full-sized coffin should be preserved, though there is so little to put in it. Upon the undertaker's stating in the Sol's bar, in the course of the day, that he has received orders to construct "a six-footer," the general solicitude is much relieved, and it is considered that Mr. Smallweed's conduct does him great honour.

Out of the court, and a long way out of it, there is considerable excitement too; for men of science and philosophy come to look, and carriages set down doctors at the corner who arrive with the same intent, and there is more learned talk about inflammable gases and phosphuretted hydrogen than the court has ever imagined. Some of these authorities (of course the wisest) hold with indignation that the deceased had no business to die in the alleged manner; and being reminded by other authorities of a certain inquiry into the evidence for such deaths, reprinted in the sixth volume of the Philosophical Transactions;[8] and also of a book not quite unknown, on English Medical Jurisprudence; and likewise of the Italian case of the Countess Cornelia Baudi as set forth in detail by one Bianchini,[9] prebendary of Verona, who wrote a scholarly work or so, and was occasionally heard of in his time as having gleams of reason in him; and also of the testimony of Messrs. Foderé and Mere,[1] two pestilent Frenchmen who *would* investigate the subject; and further, of the corroborative testimony of Monsieur Le Cat, a rather celebrated French surgeon once upon a time, who had the unpoliteness to live in a house where such a case occurred, and even to write an account of it;—still they regard the late Mr. Krook's

7. A song by Barry Cornwall (1787–1874): "King Death was a rare old fellow,/ He sat where no sun could shine,/ And he lifted his hand so yellow,/ And poured out his coal-black wine. . . . There came to him many a maiden,/ Whose eyes had forgot to shine,/ And widows with grief o'er laden/ For a draught of his sleepy Wine!"

8. Published collections of reports presented to the Royal Society of London for Improving Natural Knowledge.

9. Cf. Dickens' list of authorities in his Preface (para. 4).

1. The French doctor's name was Charles Marc. His name was similarly misspelled (as noted by Mr. E. Gaskell) in a work probably consulted by Dickens: *Curiosities of Medical Experience* (London, 1839), by John Gideon Millingen.

obstinacy, in going out of the world by any such byeway, as wholly unjustifiable and personally offensive. The less the court understands of all this, the more the court likes it; and the greater enjoyment it has in the stock in trade of the Sol's Arms. Then, there comes the artist of a picture newspaper, with a foreground and figures ready drawn for anything, from a wreck on the Cornish coast to a review in Hyde Park, or a meeting at Manchester,—and in Mrs. Perkins's own room, memorable evermore, he then and there throws in upon the block, Mr. Krook's house as large as life; in fact, considerably larger, making a very Temple of it. Similarly, being permitted to look in at the door of the fatal chamber, he depicts that apartment as three-quarters of a mile long, by fifty yards high; at which the court is particularly charmed. All this time, the two gentlemen before mentioned pop in and out of every house, and assist at the philosophical disputations,—go everywhere, and listen to everybody,—and yet are always diving into the Sol's parlour, and writing with the ravenous little pens on the tissue paper.

At last come the Coroner and his inquiry, like as before, except that the Coroner cherishes this case as being out of the common way, and tells the gentlemen of the Jury, in his private capacity, that "that would seem to be an unlucky house next door, gentlemen, a destined house; but so we sometimes find it; and these are mysteries we can't account for!" After which the six-footer[2] comes into action, and is much admired.

In all these proceedings Mr. Guppy has so slight a part, except when he gives his evidence, that he is moved on like a private individual, and can only haunt the secret house on the outside; where he has the mortification of seeing Mr. Smallweed padlocking the door, and of bitterly knowing himself to be shut out. But before these proceedings draw to a close, that is to say, on the night next after the catastrophe, Mr. Guppy has a thing to say that must be said to Lady Dedlock.

For which reason, with a sinking heart, and with that hangdog sense of guilt upon him, which dread and watching, enfolded in the Sol's Arms, have produced, the young man of the name of Guppy presents himself at the town mansion at about seven o'clock in the evening, and requests to see her ladyship. Mercury replies that she is going out to dinner; don't he see the carriage at the door? Yes, he does see the carriage at the door; but he wants to see my Lady too.

Mercury is disposed, as he will presently declare to a fellow gentleman in waiting, "to pitch into the young man"; but his instructions are positive. Therefore he sulkily supposes that the young man must come up into the library. There he leaves the young man in a large room, not over-light, while he makes report of him.

2. Krook's coffin.

Mr. Guppy looks into the shade in all directions, discovering everywhere a certain charred and whitened little heap of coal or wood. Presently he hears a rustling. Is it—? No, it's no ghost; but fair flesh and blood, most brilliantly dressed.

"I have to beg your ladyship's pardon," Mr. Guppy stammers, very downcast. "This is an inconvenient time——"

"I told you, you could come at any time." She takes a chair, looking straight at him as on the last occasion.

"Thank your ladyship. Your ladyship is very affable."

"You can sit down." There is not much affability in her tone.

"I don't know, your ladyship, that it's worth while my sitting down and detaining you, for I—I have not got the letters that I mentioned when I had the honour of waiting on your ladyship."

"Have you come merely to say so?"

"Merely to say so, your ladyship." Mr. Guppy, besides being depressed, disappointed, and uneasy, is put at a further disadvantage by the splendour and beauty of her appearance. She knows its influence perfectly; has studied it too well to miss a grain of its effect on any one. As she looks at him so steadily and coldly, he not only feels conscious that he has no guide, in the least perception of what is really the complexion of her thoughts; but also that he is being every moment, as it were, removed further and further from her.

She will not speak, it is plain. So he must.

"In short, your ladyship," says Mr. Guppy, like a meanly penitent thief, "the person I was to have had the letters of, has come to a sudden end, and—" He stops. Lady Dedlock calmly finishes the sentence.

"And the letters are destroyed with the person?"

Mr. Guppy would say no, if he could—as he is unable to hide.

"I believe so, your ladyship."

If he could see the least sparkle of relief in her face now? No, he could see no such thing, even if that brave outside did not utterly put him away, and he were not looking beyond it and about it.

He falters an awkward excuse or two for his failure.

"Is this all you have to say?" inquires Lady Dedlock, having heard him out—or as nearly out as he can stumble.

Mr. Guppy thinks that's all.

"You had better be sure that you wish to say nothing more to me; this being the last time you will have the opportunity."

Mr. Guppy is quite sure. And indeed he has no such wish at present, by any means.

"That is enough. I will dispense with excuses. Good evening to you!" and she rings for Mercury to show the young man of the name of Guppy out.

But in that house, in that same moment, there happens to be an old man of the name of Tulkinghorn. And that old man, coming with his quiet footstep to the library, has his hand at that moment on the handle of the door—comes in—and comes face to face with the young man as he is leaving the room.

One glance between the old man and the lady; and for an instant the blind that is always down flies up. Suspicion, eager and sharp, looks out. Another instant; close again.

"I beg your pardon, Lady Dedlock. I beg your pardon a thousand times. It is so very unusual to find you here at this hour. I supposed the room was empty. I beg your pardon!"

"Stay!" She negligently calls him back. "Remain here, I beg. I am going out to dinner. I have nothing more to say to this young man!"

The disconcerted young man bows, as he goes out, and cringingly hopes that Mr. Tulkinghorn of the Fields is well.

"Aye, aye?" says the lawyer, looking at him from under his bent brows; though he has no need to look again—not he. "From Kenge and Carboy's, surely?"

"Kenge and Carboy's, Mr. Tulkinghorn. Name of Guppy, sir."

"To be sure. Why, thank you, Mr. Guppy, I am very well!"

"Happy to hear it, sir. You can't be too well, sir, for the credit of the profession."

"Thank you, Mr. Guppy!"

Mr. Guppy sneaks away. Mr. Tulkinghorn, such a foil in his old-fashioned rusty black to Lady Dedlock's brightness, hands her down the staircase to her carriage. He returns rubbing his chin, and rubs it a good deal in the course of the evening.

Chapter XXXIV

A TURN OF THE SCREW

"Now, what," says Mr. George, "may this be? Is it blank cartridge, or ball? A flash in the pan, or a shot?"

An open letter is the subject of the trooper's speculations, and it seems to perplex him mightily. He looks at it at arm's length, brings it close to him, holds it in his right hand, holds it in his left hand, reads it with his head on this side, with his head on that side, contracts his eyebrows, elevates them; still, cannot satisfy himself. He smooths it out upon the table with his heavy palm, and thoughtfully walking up and down the gallery, makes a halt before it every now and then, to come upon it with a fresh eye. Even that won't do. "Is it," Mr. George still muses, "blank cartridge or ball?"

Phil Squod, with the aid of a brush and paint-pot, is employed in the distance whitening the targets; softly whistling, in quick-march time, and in drum-and-fife manner, that he must and will go back again to the girl he left behind him.[1]

"Phil!" The trooper beckons as he calls him.

Phil approaches in his usual way; sidling off at first as if he were going anywhere else, and then bearing down upon his commander like a bayonet-charge. Certain splashes of white show in high relief upon his dirty face, and he scrapes his one eyebrow with the handle of his brush.

"Attention, Phil! Listen to this."

"Steady, commander, steady."

" 'Sir. Allow me to remind you (though there is no legal necessity for my doing so, as you are aware) that the bill at two months' date drawn on yourself by Mr. Matthew Bagnet, and by you accepted, for the sum of ninety-seven pounds four shillings and ninepence, will become due to-morrow, when you will please be prepared to take up the same on presentation. Yours, JOSHUA SMALLWEED.'—What do you make of that, Phil?"

"Mischief, guv'ner."

"Why?"

"I think," replies Phil, after pensively tracing out a cross-wrinkle in his forehead with the brush-handle, "that mischeevious consequences is always meant when money's asked for."

"Lookye, Phil," says the trooper, sitting on the table. "First and last, I have paid, I may say, half as much again as this principal, in interest and one thing and another."

Phil intimates, by sidling back a pace or two, with a very unaccountable wrench of his wry face, that he does not regard the transaction as being made more promising by this incident.

"And lookye further, Phil," says the trooper, staying his premature conclusions with a wave of his hand. "There has always been an understanding that this bill was to be what they call Renewed. And it has been renewed, no end of times. What do you say now?"

"I say that I think the times is come to a end at last."

"You do? Humph! I am much of the same mind myself."

"Joshua Smallweed is him that was brought here in a chair?"

"The same."

"Guv'ner," says Phil, with exceeding gravity, "he's a leech in his dispositions, he's a screw and a wice in his actions, a snake in his twistings, and a lobster in his claws."

Having thus expressively uttered his sentiments, Mr. Squod, after waiting a little to ascertain if any further remark be expected of him, gets back, by his usual series of movements, to the target he

1. Lines from a song (sung by a soldier): "Kind Heaven send me back again/ To the girl I've left behind me." As a march this piece has been long a favorite with military bands.

has in hand; and vigorously signifies, through his former musical medium, that he must and he will return to that ideal young lady. George having folded the letter, walks in that direction.

"There *is* a way, commander," says Phil, looking cunningly at him, "of settling this."

"Paying the money, I suppose? I wish I could."

Phil shakes his head. "No, guv'ner, no; not so bad as that. There *is* a way," says Phil, with a highly artistic turn of his brush—"what I'm a doing at present."

"Whitewashing."[2]

Phil nods.

"A pretty way that would be! Do you know what would become of the Bagnets in that case? Do you know they would be ruined to pay off my old scores? *You're* a moral character," says the trooper, eyeing him in his large way with no small indignation, "upon my life you are, Phil!"

Phil, on one knee at the target, is in course of protesting earnestly, though not without many allegorical scoops of his brush, and smoothings of the white surface round the rim with his thumb, that he had forgotten the Bagnet responsibility, and would not so much as injure a hair of the head of any member of that worthy family, when steps are audible in the long passage without, and a cheerful voice is heard to wonder whether George is at home. Phil, with a look at his master, hobbles up, saying, "Here's the guv'ner, Mrs. Bagnet! Here he is!" and the old girl herself, accompanied by Mr. Bagnet, appears.

The old girl never appears in walking trim, in any season of the year, without a grey cloth cloak, coarse and much worn but very clean, which is, undoubtedly, the identical garment rendered so interesting to Mr. Bagnet by having made its way home to Europe from another quarter of the globe, in company with Mrs. Bagnet and an umbrella. The latter faithful appendage is also invariably a part of the old girl's presence out of doors. It is of no colour known in this life, and has a corrugated wooden crook for a handle, with a metallic object let into its prow or beak, resembling a little model of a fan-light over a street door, or one of the oval glasses out of a pair of spectacles: which ornamental object has not that tenacious capacity of sticking to its post that might be desired in an article long associated with the British army. The old girl's umbrella is of a flabby habit of waist, and seems to be in need of stays—an appearance that is possibly referable to its having served, through a series of years, at home as a cupboard, and on journeys as a carpet bag. She never puts it up, having the greatest reliance on her well-proved cloak with its capacious hood; but generally uses the instrument as a

2. Declaring himself bankrupt.

wand with which to point out joints of meat or bunches of greens in marketing, or to arrest the attention of tradesmen by a friendly poke. Without her market-basket, which is a sort of wicker well with two flapping lids, she never stirs abroad. Attended by these her trusty companions, therefore, her honest sunburnt face looking cheerily out of a rough straw bonnet, Mrs. Bagnet now arrives, fresh-coloured and bright, in George's Shooting Gallery.

"Well, George, old fellow," says she, "and how do *you* do, this sunshiny morning?"

Giving him a friendly shake of the hand, Mrs. Bagnet draws a long breath after her walk, and sits down to enjoy a rest. Having a faculty, matured on the tops of baggage-waggons, and in other such positions, of resting easily anywhere, she perches on a rough bench, unties her bonnet-strings, pushes back her bonnet, crosses her arms, and looks perfectly comfortable.

Mr. Bagnet, in the meantime, has shaken hands with his old comrade, and with Phil: on whom Mrs. Bagnet likewise bestows a good-humoured nod and smile.

"Now, George," says Mrs. Bagnet, briskly, "here we are, Lignum and myself"; she often speaks of her husband by this appellation, on account, as it is supposed, of Lignum Vitae[3] having been his old regimental nickname when they first became acquainted, in compliment to the extreme hardness and toughness of his physiognomy; "just looked in, we have, to make it all correct as usual about that security. Give him the new bill to sign, George, and he'll sign it like a man."

"I was coming to you this morning," observes the trooper, reluctantly.

"Yes, we thought you'd come to us this morning, but we turned out early, and left Woolwich, the best of boys, to mind his sisters, and came to you instead—as you see! For Lignum, he's tied so close now, and gets so little exercise, that a walk does him good. But what's the matter, George?" asks Mrs. Bagnet, stopping in her cheerful talk. "You don't look yourself."

"I am not quite myself," returns the trooper; "I have been a little put out, Mrs. Bagnet."

Her quick bright eye catches the truth directly. "George!" holding up her forefinger. "Don't tell me there's anything wrong about that security of Lignum's! Don't do it, George, on account of the children."

The trooper looks at her with a troubled visage.

"George," says Mrs. Bagnet, using both her arms for emphasis, and occasionally bringing down her open hands upon her knees. "If

3. A dense hardwood from the West Indies used for making mallets, ships' pulleys, and other durable articles.

you have allowed anything wrong to come to that security of Lignum's, and if you have let him in for it, and if you have put us in danger of being sold up—and I see sold up in your face, George, as plain as print—you have done a shameful action, and have deceived us cruelly. I tell you, cruelly, George. There!"

Mr. Bagnet, otherwise as immoveable as a pump or a lamp-post, puts his large right hand on the top of his bald head, as if to defend it from a shower-bath, and looks with great uneasiness at Mrs. Bagnet.

"George!" says that old girl, "I wonder at you! George, I am ashamed of you! George, I couldn't have believed you would have done it! I always knew you to be a rolling stone that gathered no moss; but I never thought you would have taken away what little moss there was for Bagnet and the children to lie upon. You know what a hard-working, steady-going chap he is. You know what Quebec and Malta and Woolwich are—and I never did think you would, or could, have had the heart to serve us so. O George!" Mrs. Bagnet gathers up her cloak to wipe her eyes on, in a very genuine manner. "How could you do it?"

Mrs. Bagnet ceasing, Mr. Bagnet removes his hand from his head, as if the shower-bath were over, and looks disconsolately at Mr. George; who has turned quite white, and looks distressfully at the grey cloak and straw bonnet.

"Mat," says the trooper, in a subdued voice, addressing him, but still looking at his wife; "I am sorry you take it so much to heart, because I do hope it's not so bad as that comes to. I certainly have, this morning, received this letter"; which he reads aloud; "but I hope it may be set right yet. As to a rolling stone, why, what you say is true. I *am* a rolling stone; and I never rolled in anybody's way, I fully believe, that I rolled the least good to. But it's impossible for an old vagabond comrade to like your wife and family better than *I* like 'em, Mat, and I trust you'll look upon me as forgivingly as you can. Don't think I've kept anything from you. I haven't had the letter more than a quarter of an hour."

"Old girl!" murmurs Mr. Bagnet, after a short silence, "will you tell him my opinion?"

"Oh! Why didn't he marry," Mrs. Bagnet answers, half laughing and half crying, "Joe Pouch's widder in North America? Then he wouldn't have got himself into these troubles."

"The old girl," says Mr. Bagnet, "puts it correct—why didn't you?"

"Well, she has a better husband by this time, I hope," returns the trooper. "Anyhow, here I stand, this present day, *not* married to Joe Pouch's widder. What shall I do? You see all I have got about me. It's not mine; it's yours. Give the word, and I'll sell off every morsel. If I could have hoped it would have brought in nearly the sum wanted, I'd have sold all long ago. Don't believe that I'll leave you or yours in the lurch, Mat. I'd sell myself first. I only wish," says the trooper, giving himself a disparaging blow in the chest, "that I knew of any one who'd buy such a second-hand piece of old stores."

"Old girl," murmurs Mr. Bagnet, "give him another bit of my mind."

"George," says the old girl, "you are not so much to be blamed, on full consideration, except for ever taking this business without the means."

"And that was like me!" observes the penitent trooper, shaking his head. "Like me, I know."

"Silence! The old girl," says Mr. Bagnet, "is correct—in her way of giving my opinions—hear me out!"

"That was when you never ought to have asked for the security, George, and when you never ought to have got it, all things considered. But what's done, can't be undone. You are always an honourable and straightforward fellow, as far as lays in your power, though a little flighty. On the other hand, you can't admit but what it's natural in us to be anxious, with such a thing hanging over our heads. So forget and forgive all round, George. Come! Forget and forgive all round!"

Mrs. Bagnet, giving him one of her honest hands, and giving her husband the other, Mr. George gives each of them one of his, and holds them while he speaks.

"I do assure you both, there's nothing I wouldn't do to discharge this obligation. But whatever I have been able to scrape together, has gone every two months in keeping it up. We have lived plainly enough here, Phil and I. But the Gallery don't quite do what was expected of it, and it's not—in short, it's not the Mint. It was wrong in me to take it? Well, so it was. But I was in a manner drawn into that step, and I thought it might steady me, and set me up, and you'll try to overlook my having such expectations, and upon my soul, I am very much obliged to you, and very much ashamed of myself." With these concluding words, Mr. George gives a shake to each of the hands he holds, and, relinquishing them, backs a pace or two, in a broad-chested upright attitude, as if he had made a final confession, and were immediately going to be shot with all military honours.

"George, hear me out!" says Mr. Bagnet, glancing at his wife. "Old girl, go on!"

Mr. Bagnet, being in this singular manner heard out, has merely to observe that the letter must be attended to without any delay; that it is advisable that George and he should immediately wait on

Mr. Smallweed in person; and that the primary object is to save and hold harmless Mr. Bagnet, who had none of the money. Mr. George entirely assenting, puts on his hat, and prepares to march with Mr. Bagnet to the enemy's camp.

"Don't you mind a woman's hasty word, George," says Mrs. Bagnet, patting him on the shoulder. "I trust my old Lignum to you, and I am sure you'll bring him through it."

The trooper returns that this is kindly said, and that he *will* bring Lignum through it somehow. Upon which Mrs. Bagnet, with her cloak, basket, and umbrella, goes home, bright-eyed again, to the rest of her family, and the comrades sally forth on the hopeful errand of mollifying Mr. Smallweed.

Whether there are two people in England less likely to come satisfactorily out of any negotiation with Mr. Smallweed than Mr. George and Mr. Matthew Bagnet, may be very reasonably questioned. Also, notwithstanding their martial appearance, broad shoulders, and heavy tread, whether there are, within the same limits, two more simple and unaccustomed children, in all the Smallweedy affairs of life. As they proceed with great gravity through the streets towards the region of Mount Pleasant, Mr. Bagnet, observing his companion to be thoughtful, considers it a friendly part to refer to Mrs. Bagnet's late sally.

"George, you know the old girl—she's as sweet and as mild as milk. But touch her on the children—or myself—and she's off like gunpowder."

"It does her credit, Mat!"

"George," says Mr. Bagnet, looking straight before him, "the old girl—can't do anything—that don't do her credit. More or less. I never say so. Discipline must be maintained."

"She's worth her weight in gold," returns the trooper.

"In gold?" says Mr. Bagnet. "I'll tell you what. The old girl's weight—is twelve stone six. Would I take that weight—in any metal—*for* the old girl? No. Why not? Because the old girl's metal is far more precious—than the preciousest metal. And she's *all* metal!"

"You are right, Mat!"

"When she took me—and accepted of the ring—she 'listed under me and the children—heart and head; for life. She's that earnest," says Mr. Bagnet, "and that true to her colours—that, touch us with a finger—and she turns out—and stands to her arms. If the old girl fires wide—once in a way—at the call of duty—look over it, George. For she's loyal!"

"Why, bless her, Mat!" returns the trooper, "I think the higher of her for it!"

"You are right!" says Mr. Bagnet, with the warmest enthusiasm, though without relaxing the rigidity of a single muscle. "Think as high of the old girl—as the rock of Gibraltar—and still you'll be thinking low—of such merits. But I never own to it before her. Discipline must be maintained."

These encomiums bring them to Mount Pleasant, and to Grandfather Smallweed's house. The door is opened by the perennial Judy, who having surveyed them from top to toe, with no particular favour, but indeed with a malignant sneer, leaves them standing there, while she consults the oracle as to their admission. The oracle may be inferred to give consent, from the circumstance of her returning with the words on her honey lips "that they can come in if they want to it." Thus privileged they come in, and find Mr. Smallweed with his feet in the drawer of his chair as if it were a paper foot-bath, and Mrs. Smallweed obscured with the cushion like a bird that is not to sing.

"My dear friend," says Grandfather Smallweed, with those two lean affectionate arms of his stretched forth. "How de do? How de do? Who is our friend, my dear friend?"

"Why, this," returns George, not able to be very conciliatory at first, "is Matthew Bagnet, who has obliged me in that matter of ours, you know."

"Oh! Mr. Bagnet? Surely!" The old man looks at him under his hand.

"Hope you're well, Mr. Bagnet? Fine man, Mr. George! Military air, sir!"

No chairs being offered, Mr. George brings one forward for Bagnet, and one for himself. They sit down; Mr. Bagnet as if he had no power of bending himself, except at the hips, for that purpose.

"Judy," says Mr. Smallweed, "bring the pipe."

"Why, I don't know," Mr. George interposes, "that the young woman need give herself that trouble, for to tell you the truth, I am not inclined to smoke it to-day."

"Ain't you?" returns the old man. "Judy, bring the pipe."

"The fact is, Mr. Smallweed," proceeds George, "that I find myself in rather an unpleasant state of mind. It appears to me, sir, that your friend in the city has been playing tricks."

"O dear no!" says Grandfather Smallweed. "He never does that!"

"Don't he? Well, I am glad to hear it, because I thought it might be *his* doing. This, you know, I am speaking of. This letter."

Grandfather Smallweed smiles in a very ugly way, in recognition of the letter.

"What does it mean?" asks Mr. George.

"Judy," says the old man. "Have you got the pipe? Give it to me. Did you say what does it mean, my good friend?"

"Aye! Now, come, come, you know, Mr. Smallweed," urges the trooper, constraining himself to speak as smoothly and confidentially as he can, holding the open letter in one hand, and resting the broad knuckles of the other on his thigh; "a good lot of money has passed between us, and we are face to face at the present moment, and are both well aware of the understanding there has always been. I am prepared to do the usual thing which I have done regularly, and to keep this matter going. I never got a letter like this from you before, and I have been a little put about by it this morning; because here's my friend Matthew Bagnet, who, you know, had none of the money——"

"I *don't* know it, you know," says the old man, quietly.

"Why, con-found you—it, I mean—I tell you so; don't I?"

"Oh, yes, you tell me so," returns Grandfather Smallweed. "But I don't know it."

"Well!" says the trooper, swallowing his fire. "*I* know it.'

Mr. Smallweed replies with excellent temper, "Ah, that's quite another thing!" And adds, "but it don't matter. Mr. Bagnet's situation is all one, whether or no."

The unfortunate George makes a great effort to arrange the affair comfortably, and to propitiate Mr. Smallweed by taking him upon his own terms.

"That's just what I mean. As you say, Mr. Smallweed, here's Matthew Bagnet liable to be fixed whether or no. Now, you see, that makes his good lady very uneasy in her mind, and me too; for, whereas I'm a harum-scarum sort of a good-for-nought, that more kicks than halfpence come natural to, why he's a steady family man, don't you see? Now, Mr. Smallweed," says the trooper, gaining confidence as he proceeds in this soldierly mode of doing business; "although you and I are good friends enough in a certain sort of a way, I am well aware that I can't ask you to let my friend Bagnet off entirely."

"O dear, you are too modest. You can *ask* me anything, Mr. George." (There is an Ogreish kind of jocularity in Grandfather Smallweed to-day.)

"And you can refuse, you mean, eh? Or not you so much, perhaps, as your friend in the city? Ha ha ha!"

"Ha ha ha!" echoes Grandfather Smallweed. In such a very hard manner, and with eyes so particularly green, that Mr. Bagnet's natural gravity is much deepened by the contemplation of that venerable man.

"Come!" says the sanguine George, "I am glad to find we can be pleasant, because I want to arrange this pleasantly. Here's my friend Bagnet, and here am I. We'll settle the matter on the spot, if you please, Mr. Smallweed, in the usual way. And you'll ease my friend

Mr. Smallweed breaks the pipe of peace.

Bagnet's mind, and his family's mind, a good deal, if you'll just mention to him what our understanding is."

Here some shrill spectre cries out in a mocking manner, "O good gracious! O!"—unless, indeed, it be the sportive Judy, who is found to be silent when the startled visitors look round, but whose chin has received a recent toss, expressive of derision and contempt. Mr. Bagnet's gravity becomes yet more profound.

"But I think you asked me, Mr. George"; old Smallweed, who all this time has had the pipe in his hand, is the speaker now; "I think you asked me, what did the letter mean?"

"Why, yes, I did," returns the trooper, in his off-hand way: "but I don't care to know particularly, if it's all correct and pleasant."

Mr. Smallweed, purposely balking himself in an aim at the trooper's head, throws the pipe on the ground and breaks it to pieces.

"That's what it means, my dear friend. I'll smash you. I'll crumble you. I'll powder you. Go to the devil!"

The two friends rise and look at one another. Mr. Bagnet's gravity has now attained its profoundest point.

"Go to the devil!" repeats the old man. "I'll have no more of your pipe-smokings and swaggerings. What? You're an independent dragoon too! Go to my lawyer (you remember where; you have been there before), and show your independence now, will you? Come, my dear friend, there's a chance for you. Open the street door, Judy; put these blusterers out! Call in help if they don't go. Put 'em out!"

He vociferates this so loudly, that Mr. Bagnet, laying his hands on the shoulders of his comrade, before the latter can recover from his amazement, gets him on the outside of the street door; which is instantly slammed by the triumphant Judy. Utterly confounded, Mr. George awhile stands looking at the knocker. Mr. Bagnet, in a perfect abyss of gravity, walks up and down before the little parlour window, like a sentry, and looks in every time he passes; apparently revolving something in his mind.

"Come, Mat!" says Mr. George, when he has recovered himself, "we must try the lawyer. Now, what do you think of this rascal?"

Mr. Bagnet, stopping to take a farewell look into the parlour, replies, with one shake of his head directed at the interior, "If my old girl had been here—I'd have told him!" Having so discharged himself of the subject of his cogitations, he falls into step, and marches off with the trooper, shoulder to shoulder.

When they present themselves in Lincoln's Inn Fields, Mr. Tulkinghorn is engaged, and not to be seen. He is not at all willing to see them; for when they have waited a full hour, and the clerk, on his bell being rung, takes the opportunity of mentioning as much, he brings forth no more encouraging message than that Mr. Tulkinghorn has nothing to say to them, and they had better not wait. They do wait, however, with the perseverance of military tactics; and at last the bell rings again, and the client in possession comes out of Mr. Tulkinghorn's room.

The client is a handsome old lady; no other than Mrs. Rouncewell, housekeeper at Chesney Wold. She comes out of the sanctuary with a fair old-fashioned curtsey, and softly shuts the door. She is treated with some distinction there; for the clerk steps out of his pew to show her through the outer office, and to let her out. The old lady is thanking him for his attention, when she observes the comrades in waiting.

"I beg your pardon, sir, but I think those gentlemen are military?"

The clerk referring the question to them with his eye, and Mr. George not turning round from the almanack over the fire-place, Mr. Bagnet takes upon himself to reply, "Yes, ma'am. Formerly."

"I thought so. I was sure of it. My heart warms, gentlemen, at the sight of you. It always does at the sight of such. God bless you, gentlemen! You'll excuse an old woman; but I had a son once who went for a soldier. A fine handsome youth he was, and good in his bold way, though some people did disparage him to his poor mother. I ask your pardon for troubling you, sir. God bless you, gentlemen!"

"Same to you, ma'am!" returns Mr. Bagnet, with right good will.

There is something very touching in the earnestness of the old lady's voice, and in the tremble that goes through her quaint old figure. But Mr. George is so occupied with the almanack over the fire-place (calculating the coming months by it perhaps), that he does not look round until she has gone away, and the door is closed upon her.

"George," Mr. Bagnet gruffly whispers, when he does turn from the almanack at last. "Don't be cast down! 'Why, soldiers, why—should we be melancholly boys?'[4] Cheer up, my hearty!"

The clerk having now again gone in to say that they are still there, and Mr. Tulkinghorn being heard to return with some irascibility, "Let 'em come in then!" they pass into the great room with the painted ceiling, and find him standing before the fire.

"Now, you men, what do you want? Serjeant, I told you the last time I saw you that I don't desire your company here."

Serjeant replies—dashed within the last few minutes as to his usual manner of speech, or even as to his usual carriage—that he has received this letter, has been to Mr. Smallweed about it, and has been referred there.

4. From an early eighteenth-century song, of disputed authorship, "How Stands the Glass Around?": "Why, soldiers, why/ Should we be melancholy, boys?/ Why, soldiers, why?/ Whose business 'tis to die?/ What, sighing? fie!/ Don't fear; drink on; be jolly, boys!"

"I have nothing to say to you," rejoins Mr. Tulkinghorn. "If you get into debt, you must pay your debts, or take the consequences. You have no occasion to come here to learn that, I suppose?"

Serjeant is sorry to say that he is not prepared with the money.

"Very well! Then the other man—this man, if this is he—must pay it for you."

Serjeant is sorry to add that the other man is not prepared with the money either.

"Very well! Then you must pay it between you, or you must both be sued for it, and both suffer. You have had the money and must refund it. You are not to pocket other people's pounds, shillings, and pence, and escape scot free."

The lawyer sits down in his easy-chair and stirs the fire. Mr. George hopes he will have the goodness to——

"I tell you, Serjeant, I have nothing to say to you. I don't like your associates, and don't want you here. This matter is not at all in my course of practice, and is not in my office. Mr. Smallweed is good enough to offer these affairs to me, but they are not in my way. You must go to Melchisedech's in Clifford's Inn."

"I must make an apology to you, sir," says Mr. George, "for pressing myself upon you with so little encouragement—which is almost as unpleasant to me as it can be to you; but would you let me say a private word to you?"

Mr. Tulkinghorn rises with his hands in his pockets, and walks into one of the window recesses. "Now! I have no time to waste." In the midst of his perfect assumption of indifference, he directs a sharp look at the trooper; taking care to stand with his own back to the light, and to have the other with his face towards it.

"Well, sir," says Mr. George, "this man with me is the other party implicated in this unfortunate affair—nominally, only nominally—and my sole object is to prevent his getting into trouble on my account. He is a most respectable man with a wife and family; formerly in the Royal Artillery—"

"My friend, I don't care a pinch of snuff for the whole Royal Artillery establishment—officers, men, tumbrils, waggons, horses, guns, and ammunition."

" 'Tis likely, sir. But I care a good deal for Bagnet and his wife and family being injured on my account. And if I could bring them through this matter, I should have no help for it but to give up without any other consideration, what you wanted of me the other day."

"Have you got it here?"

"I have got it here, sir."

"Serjeant," the lawyer proceeds in his dry, passionless manner, far more hopeless in the dealing with, than any amount of vehemence, "make up your mind while I speak to you, for this is final. After I have finished speaking I have closed the subject, and I won't re-open it. Understand that. You can leave here, for a few days, what you say you have brought here, if you choose; you can take it away at once, if you choose. In case you choose to leave it here, I can do this for you—I can replace this matter on its old footing, and I can go so far besides as to give you a written undertaking that this man Bagnet shall never be troubled in any way until you have been proceeded against to the utmost—that your means shall be exhausted before the creditor looks to his. This is in fact all but freeing him. Have you decided?"

The trooper puts his hand into his breast, and answers with a long breath, "I must do it, sir."

So Mr. Tulkinghorn, putting on his spectacles, sits down and writes the undertaking; which he slowly reads and explains to Bagnet, who has all this time been staring at the ceiling, and who now puts his hand on his bald head again, under this new verbal shower-bath, and seems exceedingly in need of the old girl through whom to express his sentiments. The trooper then takes from his breast-pocket a folded paper, which he lays with an unwilling hand at the lawyer's elbow. " 'Tis only a letter of instructions, sir. The last I ever had from him."

Look at a millstone, Mr. George, for some change in its expression, and you will find it quite as soon as in the face of Mr. Tulkinghorn when he opens and reads the letter! He refolds it, and lays it in his desk, with a countenance as imperturbable as Death.

Nor has he anything more to say or do, but to nod once in the same frigid and discourteous manner, and to say briefly, "You can go. Show these men out, there!" Being shown out, they repair to Mr. Bagnet's residence to dine.

Boiled beef and greens constitute the day's variety on the former repast of boiled pork and greens; and Mrs. Bagnet serves out the meal in the same way, and seasons it with the best of temper; being that rare sort of old girl that she receives Good to her arms without a hint that it might be Better; and catches light from any little spot of darkness near her. The spot on this occasion is the darkened brow of Mr. George; he is unusually thoughtful and depressed. At first Mrs. Bagnet trusts to the combined endearments of Quebec and Malta to restore him; but finding those young ladies sensible that their existing Bluffy[5] is not the Bluffy of their usual frolicsome acquaintance, she winks off the light infantry, and leaves him to deploy at leisure on the open ground of the domestic hearth.

But he does not. He remains in close order,[6] clouded and depressed. During the lengthy cleaning up and pattening process,

5. George's nickname "in his domestic character" among the Bagnets. See pp. 342 and 345.

6. Closed up like the ranks of a military unit operating in "close order" formation.

when he and Mr. Bagnet are supplied with their pipes, he is no better than he was at dinner. He forgets to smoke, looks at the fire and ponders, lets his pipe out, fills the breast of Mr. Bagnet with perturbation and dismay, by showing that he has no enjoyment of tobacco.

Therefore when Mrs. Bagnet at last appears, rosy from the invigorating pail, and sits down to her work, Mr. Bagnet growls, "Old girl!" and winks monitions to her to find out what's the matter.

"Why, George!" says Mrs. Bagnet, quietly threading her needle. "How low you are!"

"Am I? Not good company? Well, I am afraid I am not."

"He ain't at all like Bluffy, mother!" cries little Malta.

"Because he ain't well, *I* think, mother," adds Quebec.

"Sure that's a bad sign not to be like Bluffy, too!" returns the trooper, kissing the young damsels. "But it's true," with a sigh—"true, I am afraid. These little ones are always right!"

"George," says Mrs. Bagnet, working busily, "if I thought you cross enough to think of anything that a shrill old soldier's wife—who could have bitten her tongue off afterwards, and ought to have done it almost—said this morning, I don't know what I shouldn't say to you now."

"My kind soul of a darling," returns the trooper. "Not a morsel of it."

"Because really and truly, George, what I said and meant to say, was that I trusted Lignum to you, and was sure you'd bring him through it. And you *have* brought him through it, noble!"

"Thank'ee, my dear!" says George. "I am glad of your good opinion."

In giving Mrs. Bagnet's hand, with her work in it, a friendly shake—for she took her seat beside him—the trooper's attention is attracted to her face. After looking at it for a little while as she plies her needle, he looks to young Woolwich, sitting on his stool in the corner, and beckons that fifer to him.

"See there, my boy," says George, very gently smoothing the mother's hair with his hand, "there's a good loving forehead for you! All bright with love of you, my boy. A little touched by the sun and the weather through following your father about and taking care of you, but as fresh and wholesome as a ripe apple on a tree."

Mr. Bagnet's face expresses, so far as in its wooden material lies, the highest approbation and acquiescence.

"The time will come, my boy," pursues the trooper, "when this hair of your mother's will be grey, and this forehead all crossed and re-crossed with wrinkles—and a fine old lady she'll be then. Take care, while you are young, that you can think in those days, '*I* never whitened a hair of her dear head—*I* never marked a sorrowful line in her face!' For of all the many things that you can think of when you are a man, you had better have *that* by you, Woolwich!"

Mr. George concludes by rising from his chair, seating the boy beside his mother in it, and saying, with something of a hurry about him, that he'll smoke his pipe in the street a bit.

Chapter XXXV

ESTHER'S NARRATIVE

I lay ill through several weeks, and the usual tenor of my life became like an old remembrance. But this was not the effect of time, so much as of the change in all my habits, made by the helplessness and inaction of a sick room. Before I had been confined to it many days, everything else seemed to have retired into a remote distance, where there was little or no separation between the various stages of my life which had been really divided by years. In falling ill, I seemed to have crossed a dark lake, and to have left all my experiences, mingled together by the great distance, on the healthy shore.

My housekeeping duties, though at first it caused me great anxiety to think that they were unperformed, were soon as far off as the oldest of the old duties at Greenleaf, or the summer afternoons when I went home from school with my portfolio under my arm, and my childish shadow at my side, to my godmother's house. I had never known before how short life really was, and into how small a space the mind could put it.

While I was very ill, the way in which these divisions of time became confused with one another, distressed my mind exceedingly. At once a child, an elder girl, and the little woman I had been so happy as, I was not only oppressed by cares and difficulties adapted to each station, but by the great perplexity of endlessly trying to reconcile them. I suppose that few who have not been in such a condition can quite understand what I mean, or what painful unrest arose from this source.

For the same reason I am almost afraid to hint at that time in my disorder—it seemed one long night, but I believe there were both nights and days in it—when I laboured up colossal staircases, ever striving to reach the top, and ever turned, as I have seen a worm in a garden path, by some obstruction, and labouring again. I knew perfectly at intervals, and I think vaguely at most times, that I was in my bed; and I talked with Charley, and felt her touch, and knew her very well; yet I would find myself complaining, "O more of these never-ending stairs, Charley,—more and more—piled up to the sky, I think!" and labouring on again.

Dare I hint at that worse time when, strung together somewhere in great black space, there was a flaming necklace, or ring, or starry circle of some kind, of which *I* was one of the beads! And when my only prayer was to be taken off from the rest, and when it was such inexplicable agony and misery to be a part of the dreadful thing?

Perhaps the less I say of these sick experiences, the less tedious and the more intelligible I shall be. I do not recall them to make others unhappy, or because I am now the least unhappy in remembering them. It may be that if we knew more of such strange afflictions, we might be better able to alleviate their intensity.

The repose that succeeded, the long delicious sleep, the blissful rest, when in my weakness I was too calm to have any care for myself, and could have heard (or so I think now) that I was dying; with no other emotion than with a pitying love for those I left behind—this state can be perhaps more widely understood. I was in this state when I first shrunk from the light as it twinkled on me once more, and knew with a boundless joy for which no words are rapturous enough, that I should see again.

I had heard my Ada crying at the door, day and night; I had heard her calling to me that I was cruel and did not love her; I had heard her praying and imploring to be let in to nurse and comfort me, and to leave my bedside no more; but I had only said, when I could speak, "Never, my sweet girl, never!" and I had over and over again reminded Charley that she was to keep my darling from the room, whether I lived or died. Charley had been true to me in that time of need, and with her little hand and her great heart had kept the door fast.

But now, my sight strengthening, and the glorious light coming every day more fully and brightly on me, I could read the letters that my dear wrote to me every morning and evening, and could put them to my lips and lay my cheek upon them with no fear of hurting her. I could see my little maid, so tender and so careful, going about the two rooms setting everything in order, and speaking cheerfully to Ada from the open window again. I could understand the stillness in the house, and the thoughtfulness it expressed on the part of all those who had always been so good to me. I could weep in the exquisite felicity of my heart, and be as happy in my weakness as ever I had been in my strength.

By and by, my strength began to be restored. Instead of lying, with so strange a calmness, watching what was done for me, as if it were done for some one else whom I was quietly sorry for, I helped it a little, and so on to a little more and much more, until I became useful to myself, and interested, and attached to life again.

How well I remember the pleasant afternoon when I was raised in bed with pillows for the first time, to enjoy a great tea-drinking with Charley! The little creature—sent into the world, surely, to minister to the weak and sick—was so happy, and so busy, and stopped so often in her preparations to lay her head upon my bosom, and fondle me, and cry with joyful tears she was so glad, she was so glad! that I was obliged to say, "Charley, if you go on in this way, I must lie down again, my darling, for I am weaker than I thought I was!" So Charley became as quiet as a mouse, and took her bright face here and there, across and across the two rooms, out of the shade into the divine sunshine, and out of the sunshine into the shade, while I watched her peacefully. When all her preparations were concluded and the pretty tea-table with its little delicacies to tempt me, and its white cloth, and its flowers, and everything so lovingly and beautifully arranged for me by Ada down-stairs, was ready at the bedside, I felt sure I was steady enough to say something to Charley that was not new to my thoughts.

First, I complimented Charley on the room; and indeed, it was so fresh and airy, so spotless and neat, that I could scarce believe I had been lying there so long. This delighted Charley, and her face was brighter than before.

"Yet, Charley," said I, looking round, "I miss something, surely, that I am accustomed to?"

Poor little Charley looked round too, and pretended to shake her head, as if there were nothing absent.

"Are the pictures all as they used to be?" I asked her.

"Every one of them, miss," said Charley.

"And the furniture, Charley?"

"Except where I have moved it about, to make more room, miss."

"And yet," said I, "I miss some familiar object. Ah, I know what it is, Charley! It's the looking-glass."

Charley got up from the table, making as if she had forgotten something, and went into the next room; and I heard her sob there.

I had thought of this very often. I was now certain of it. I could thank God that it was not a shock to me now. I called Charley back; and when she came—at first pretending to smile, but as she drew nearer to me, looking grieved—I took her in my arms, and said, "It matters very little, Charley. I hope I can do without my old face very well."

I was presently so far advanced as to be able to sit up in a great chair, and even giddily to walk into the adjoining room, leaning on Charley. The mirror was gone from its usual place in that room too; but what I had to bear, was none the harder to bear for that.

My guardian had throughout been earnest to visit me, and there was now no good reason why I should deny myself that happiness. He came one morning; and when he first came in, could only hold me in his embrace, and say, "My dear, dear girl!" I had long known —who could know better?—what a deep fountain of affection and generosity his heart was; and was it not worth my trivial suffering and change to fill such a place in it? "O yes!" I thought. "He has seen me, and he loves me better than he did; he has seen me, and is even fonder of me than he was before; and what have I to mourn for!"

He sat down by me on the sofa, supporting me with his arm. For a little while he sat with his hand over his face, but when he removed it, fell into his usual manner. There never can have been, there never can be, a pleasanter manner.

"My little woman," said he, "what a sad time this has been. Such an inflexible little woman, too, through all!"

"Only for the best, guardian," said I.

"For the best?" he repeated, tenderly. "Of course, for the best. But here have Ada and I been perfectly forlorn and miserable; here has your friend Caddy been coming and going late and early; here has every one about the house been utterly lost and dejected; here has even poor Rick been writing—to *me* too—in his anxiety for you!"

I had read of Caddy in Ada's letters, but not of Richard. I told him so.

"Why, no, my dear," he replied. "I have thought it better not to mention it to her."

"And you speak of his writing to *you*," said I, repeating his emphasis. "As if it were not natural for him to do so, guardian; as if he could write to a better friend!"

"He thinks he could, my love," returned my guardian, "and to many a better. The truth is, he wrote to me under a sort of protest, while unable to write to you with any hope of an answer—wrote coldly, haughtily, distantly, resentfully. Well, dearest little woman, we must look forbearingly on it. He is not to blame. Jarndyce and Jarndyce has warped him out of himself, and perverted me in his eyes. I have known it do as bad deeds, and worse, many a time. If two angels could be concerned in it, I believe it would change their nature."

"It has not changed yours, guardian."

"Oh yes, it has, my dear," he said, laughingly. "It has made the south wind easterly, I don't know how often. Rick mistrusts and suspects me—goes to lawyers, and is taught to mistrust and suspect me. Hears I have conflicting interests; claims clashing against his, and what not. Whereas, Heaven knows that if I could get out of the mountains of Wiglomeration[1] on which my unfortunate name has been so long bestowed (which I can't), or could level them by

1. See p. 91, note 9.

the extinction of my own original right (which I can't either, and no human power ever can, anyhow, I believe, to such a pass have we got), I would do it this hour. I would rather restore to poor Rick his proper nature, than be endowed with all the money that dead suitors, broken, heart and soul, upon the wheel of Chancery, have left unclaimed with the Accountant-General—and that's money enough, my dear, to be cast into a pyramid, in memory of Chancery's transcendant wickedness."

"Is it possible, guardian," I asked, amazed, "that Richard can be suspicious of you?"

"Ah, my love, my love," he said, "it is in the subtle poison of such abuses to breed such diseases. His blood is infected, and objects lose their natural aspects in his sight. It is not *his* fault."

"But it is a terrible misfortune, guardian."

"It is a terrible misfortune, little woman, to be ever drawn within the influences of Jarndyce and Jarndyce. I know none greater. By little and little he has been induced to trust in that rotten reed, and it communicates some portion of its rottenness to everything around him. But again, I say, with all my soul, we must be patient with poor Rick, and not blame him. What a troop of fine fresh hearts, like his, have I seen in my time turned by the same means!"

I could not help expressing something of my wonder and regret that his benevolent disinterested intentions had prospered so little.

"We must not say so, Dame Durden," he cheerfully replied; "Ada is the happier, I hope; and that is much. I did think that I and both these young creatures might be friends, instead of distrustful foes, and that we might so far counteract the suit, and prove too strong for it. But it was too much to expect. Jarndyce and Jarndyce was the curtain of Rick's cradle."

"But, guardian, may we not hope that a little experience will teach him what a false and wretched thing it is?"

"We *will* hope so, my Esther," said Mr. Jarndyce, "and that it may not teach him so too late. In any case we must not be hard on him. There are not many grown and matured men living while we speak, good men too, who, if they were thrown into this same court as suitors, would not be vitally changed and depreciated within three years—within two—within one. How can we stand amazed at poor Rick? A young man so unfortunate," here he fell into a lower tone, as if he were thinking aloud, "cannot at first believe (who could?) that Chancery is what it is. He looks to it, flushed and fitfully, to do something with his interests, and bring them to some settlement. It procrastinates, disappoints, tries, tortures him; wears out his sanguine hopes and patience, thread by thread; but he still looks to it, and hankers after it, and finds his whole world treacherous and hollow. Well, well, well! Enough of this, my dear!"

He had supported me, as at first, all this time; and his tenderness was so precious to me, that I leaned my head upon his shoulder and loved him as if he had been my father. I resolved in my own mind in this little pause, by some means, to see Richard when I grew strong, and try to set him right.

"There are better subjects than these," said my guardian, "for such a joyful time as the time of our dear girl's recovery. And I had a commission to broach one of them, as soon as I should begin to talk. When shall Ada come to see you, my love?"

I had been thinking of that too. A little in connexion with the absent mirrors, but not much; for I knew my loving girl would be changed by no change in my looks.

"Dear guardian," said I, "as I have shut her out so long—though indeed, indeed, she is like the light to me——"

"I know it well, Dame Durden, well."

He was so good, his touch expressed such endearing compassion and affection, and the tone of his voice carried such comfort into my heart, that I stopped for a little while, quite unable to go on. "Yes, yes, you are tired," said he. "Rest a little."

"As I have kept Ada out so long," I began afresh after a short while, "I think I should like to have my own way a little longer, guardian. It would be best to be away from here before I see her. If Charley and I were to go to some country lodging as soon as I can move, and if I had a week there, in which to grow stronger and to be revived by the sweet air, and to look forward to the happiness of having Ada with me again, I think it would be better for us."

I hope it was not a poor thing in me to wish to be a little more used to my altered self, before I met the eyes of the dear girl I longed so ardently to see; but it is the truth. I did. He understood me, I was sure; but I was not afraid of that. If it were a poor thing, I knew he would pass it over.

"Our spoilt little woman," said my guardian, "shall have her own way even in her inflexibility, though at the price, I know, of tears down-stairs. And see here! Here is Boythorn, heart of chivalry, breathing such ferocious vows as never were breathed on paper before, that if you don't go and occupy his whole house, he having already turned out of it expressly for that purpose, by Heaven and by earth he'll put it down, and not leave one brick standing on another!"

And my guardian put a letter in my hand; without any ordinary beginning such as "My dear Jarndyce," but rushing at once into the words, "I swear if Miss Summerson do not come down and take possession of my house, which I vacate for her this day at one o'clock, p.m.," and then with the utmost seriousness, and in the most emphatic terms, going on to make the extraordinary declaration he had quoted. We did not appreciate the writer the less for laughing heartily over it; and we settled that I should send him a letter of thanks on the morrow, and accept his offer. It was a most agreeable one to me; for of all the places I could have thought of, I should have liked to go to none so well as Chesney Wold.

"Now, little housewife," said my guardian, looking at his watch, "I was strictly timed before I came up-stairs, for you must not be tired too soon; and my time has waned away to the last minute. I have one other petition. Little Miss Flite, hearing a rumour that you were ill, made nothing of walking down here—twenty miles, poor soul, in a pair of dancing shoes—to inquire. It was Heaven's mercy we were at home, or she would have walked back again."

The old conspiracy to make me happy! Everybody seemed to be in it!

"Now, pet," said my guardian, "if it would not be irksome to you to admit the harmless little creature one afternoon, before you save Boythorn's otherwise devoted house from demolition, I believe you would make her prouder and better pleased with herself than I—though my eminent name *is* Jarndyce—could do in a lifetime."

I have no doubt he knew there would be something in the simple image of the poor afflicted creature, that would fall like a gentle lesson on my mind at that time. I felt it as he spoke to me. I could not tell him heartily enough how ready I was to receive her. I had always pitied her; never so much as now. I had always been glad of my little power to soothe her under her calamity; but never, never, half so glad before.

We arranged a time for Miss Flite to come out by the coach, and share my early dinner. When my guardian left me, I turned my face away upon my couch, and prayed to be forgiven if I, surrounded by such blessings, had magnified to myself the little trial that I had to undergo. The childish prayer of that old birthday, when I had aspired to be industrious, contented, and true-hearted, and to do some good to some one, and win some love to myself if I could, came back into my mind with a reproachful sense of all the happiness I had since enjoyed, and all the affectionate hearts that had been turned towards me. If I were weak now, what had I profited by those mercies? I repeated the old childish prayer in its old childish words, and found that its old peace had not departed from it.

My guardian now came every day. In a week or so more, I could walk about our rooms, and hold long talks with Ada, from behind the window-curtain. Yet I never saw her; for I had not as yet the courage to look at the dear face, though I could have done so easily without her seeing me.

On the appointed day Miss Flite arrived. The poor little creature ran into my room quite forgetful of her usual dignity, and, crying from her very heart of hearts, "My dear Fitz-Jarndyce!" fell upon my neck and kissed me twenty times.

"Dear me!" said she, putting her hand into her reticule, "I have nothing here but documents, my dear Fitz-Jarndyce: I must borrow a pocket-handkerchief."

Charley gave her one, and the good creature certainly made use of it, for she held it to her eyes with both hands, and sat so, shedding tears for the next ten minutes.

"With pleasure, my dear Fitz-Jarndyce," she was careful to explain. "Not the least pain. Pleasure to see you well again. Pleasure at having the honour of being admitted to see you. I am so much fonder of you, my love, than of the Chancellor. Though I *do* attend Court regularly. By the by, my dear, mentioning pocket-handkerchiefs——"

Miss Flite here looked at Charley, who had been to meet her at the place where the coach stopped. Charley glanced at me, and looked unwilling to pursue the suggestion.

"Ve-ry right!" said Miss Flite, "ve-ry correct. Truly! Highly indiscreet of me to mention it; but, my dear Miss Fitz-Jarndyce, I am afraid I am at times (between ourselves, you wouldn't think it) a little—rambling, you know," said Miss Flite, touching her forehead. "Nothing more."

"What were you going to tell me?" said I, smiling, for I saw she wanted to go on. "You have roused my curiosity, and now you must gratify it."

Miss Flite looked at Charley for advice in this important crisis, who said, "If you please, ma'am, you had better tell then," and therein gratified Miss Flite beyond measure.

"So sagacious, our young friend," said she to me, in her mysterious way. "Diminutive. But ve-ry sagacious! Well, my dear, it's a pretty anecdote. Nothing more. Still I think it charming. Who should follow us down the road from the coach, my dear, but a poor person in a very ungenteel bonnet——"

"Jenny, if you please, miss," said Charley.

"Just so!" Miss Flite acquiesced with the greatest suavity. "Jenny. Ye-es! And what does she tell our young friend, but that there has been a lady with a veil inquiring at her cottage after my dear Fitz-Jarndyce's health, and taking a handkerchief away with her as a little keepsake, merely because it was my amiable Fitz-Jarndyce's! Now, you know, so very prepossessing in the lady with the veil!"

"If you please, miss," said Charley, to whom I looked in some astonishment, "Jenny says that when her baby died, you left a handkerchief there, and that she put it away and kept it with the baby's little things. I think, if you please, partly because it was yours, miss, and partly because it had covered the baby."

"Diminutive," whispered Miss Flite, making a variety of motions about her own forehead to express intellect in Charley. "But ex-ceedingly sagacious! And so clear! My love, she's clearer than any Counsel I ever heard!"

"Yes, Charley," I returned. "I remember it. Well?"

"Well, miss," said Charley, "and that's the handkerchief the lady took. And Jenny wants you to know that she wouldn't have made away with it herself for a heap of money, but that the lady took it, and left some money instead. Jenny don't know her at all, if you please, miss."

"Why, who can she be?" said I.

"My love," Miss Flite suggested, advancing her lips to my ear, with her most mysterious look, "in *my* opinion—don't mention this to our diminutive friend—she's the Lord Chancellor's wife. He's married, you know. And I understand she leads him a terrible life. Throws his lordship's papers into the fire, my dear, if he won't pay the jeweller!"

I did not think very much about this lady then, for I had an impression that it might be Caddy. Besides, my attention was diverted by my visitor, who was cold after her ride, and looked hungry; and who, our dinner being brought in, required some little assistance in arraying herself with great satisfaction in a pitiable old scarf and a much-worn and often-mended pair of gloves, which she had brought down in a paper parcel. I had to preside, too, over the entertainment, consisting of a dish of fish, a roast fowl, a sweet-bread, vegetables, pudding, and Madeira; and it was so pleasant to see how she enjoyed it, and with what state and ceremony she did honour to it, that I was soon thinking of nothing else.

When we had finished, and had our little dessert before us, embellished by the hands of my dear, who would yield the superintendence of everything prepared for me to no one; Miss Flite was so very chatty and happy, that I thought I would lead her to her own history, as she was always pleased to talk about herself. I began by saying, "You have attended on the Lord Chancellor many years, Miss Flite?"

"O many, many, many years, my dear. But I expect a Judgment. Shortly."

There was an anxiety even in her hopefulness, that made me doubtful if I had done right in approaching the subject. I thought I would say no more about it.

"My father expected a Judgment," said Miss Flite. "My brother.

My sister. They all expected a Judgment. The same that I expect."

"They are all——"

"Ye-es. Dead, of course, my dear," said she.

As I saw she would go on, I thought it best to try to be serviceable to her by meeting the theme, rather than avoiding it.

"Would it not be wiser," said I, "to expect this Judgment no more?"

"Why, my dear," she answered promptly, "of course it would!"

"And to attend the Court no more?"

"Equally of course," said she. "Very wearing to be always in expectation of what never comes, my dear Fitz-Jarndyce. Wearing, I assure you, to the bone!"

She slightly showed me her arm, and it was fearfully thin indeed.

"But, my dear," she went on, in her mysterious way, "there's a dreadful attraction in the place. Hush! Don't mention it to our diminutive friend when she comes in. Or it may frighten her. With good reason. There's a cruel attraction in the place. You *can't* leave it. And you *must* expect."

I tried to assure her that this was not so. She heard me patiently and smilingly, but was ready with her own answer.

"Aye, aye, aye! You think so, because I am a little rambling. Ve-ry absurd, to be a little rambling, is it not? Ve-ry confusing, too. To the head. I find it so. But, my dear, I have been there many years, and I have noticed. It's the Mace and Seal upon the table."

What could they do, did she think? I mildly asked her.

"Draw," returned Miss Flite. "Draw people on, my dear. Draw peace out of them. Sense out of them. Good looks out of them. Good qualities out of them. I have felt them even drawing my rest away in the night. Cold and glittering devils!"

She tapped me several times upon the arm, and nodded good-humouredly, as if she were anxious I should understand that I had no cause to fear her, though she spoke so gloomily, and confided these awful secrets to me.

"Let me see," said she. "I'll tell you my own case. Before they ever drew me—before I had ever seen them—what was it I used to do? Tambourine playing? No, Tambour work.[2] I and my sister worked at tambour work. Our father and our brother had a builder's business. We all lived together. Ve-ry respectably, my dear! First, our father was drawn—slowly. Home was drawn with him. In a few years, he was a fierce, sour, angry bankrupt, without a kind word or a kind look for any one. He had been so different, Fitz-Jarndyce. He was drawn to a debtors' prison. There he died. Then our brother was drawn—swiftly—to drunkenness. And rags. And death. Then my sister was drawn. Hush! Never ask to what! Then I was ill, and

2. Embroidery stitched on cloth which has been stretched on a round, drum-like frame.

in misery; and heard, as I had often heard before, that this was all the work of Chancery. When I got better, I went to look at the Monster. And then I found out how it was, and I was drawn to stay there."

Having got over her own short narrative, in the delivery of which she had spoken in a low, strained voice, as if the shock were fresh upon her, she gradually resumed her usual air of amiable importance.

"You don't quite credit me, my dear! Well well! You will, some day. I am a little rambling. But I have noticed. I have seen many new faces come, unsuspicious, within the influence of the Mace and Seal, in these many years. As my father's came there. As my brother's. As my sister's. As my own. I hear Conversation Kenge, and the rest of them, say to the new faces, 'Here's little Miss Flite. O you are new here; and you must come and be presented to little Miss Flite!' Ve-ry good. Proud I am sure to have the honour! And we all laugh. But, Fitz-Jarndyce, I know what will happen. I know, far better than they do, when the attraction has begun. I know the signs, my dear. I saw them begin in Gridley. And I saw them end. Fitz-Jarndyce, my love," speaking low again, "I saw them beginning in our friend the Ward in Jarndyce. Let some one hold him back. Or he'll be drawn to ruin."

She looked at me in silence for some moments, with her face gradually softening into a smile. Seeming to fear that she had been too gloomy, and seeming also to lose the connexion in her mind, she said, politely, as she sipped her glass of wine, "Yes, my dear, as I was saying, I expect a Judgment. Shortly. Then I shall release my birds, you know, and confer estates."

I was much impressed by her allusion to Richard, and by the sad meaning, so sadly illustrated in her poor pinched form, that made its way through all her incoherence. But happily for her, she was quite complacent again now, and beamed with nods and smiles.

"But, my dear," she said, gaily, reaching out her hand to put it upon mine. "You have not congratulated me on my physician. Positively not once, yet!"

I was obliged to confess that I did not quite know what she meant.

"My physician, Mr. Woodcourt, my dear, who was so exceedingly attentive to me. Though his services were rendered quite gratuitously. Until the Day of Judgment. I mean *the* judgment that will dissolve the spell upon me of the Mace and Seal."

"Mr. Woodcourt is so far away, now," said I, "that I thought the time for such congratulation was past, Miss Flite."

"But, my child," she returned, "is it possible that you don't know what has happened?"

"No," said I.

"Not what everybody has been talking of, my beloved Fitz-Jarndyce!"

"No," said I. "You forget how long I have been here."

"True! My dear, for the moment—true. I blame myself. But my memory has been drawn out of me, with everything else, by what I mentioned. Ve-ry strong influence, is it not? Well, my dear, there has been a terrible shipwreck over in those East-Indian seas."

"Mr. Woodcourt shipwrecked!"

"Don't be agitated, my dear. He is safe. An awful scene. Death in all shapes. Hundreds of dead and dying. Fire, storm, and darkness. Numbers of the drowning thrown upon a rock. There, and through it all, my dear physician was a hero. Calm and brave, through everything. Saved many lives, never complained in hunger and thirst, wrapped naked people in his spare clothes, took the lead, showed them what to do, governed them, tended the sick, buried the dead, and brought the poor survivors safely off at last! My dear, the poor emaciated creatures all but worshipped him. They fell down at his feet, when they got to the land, and blessed him. The whole country rings with it. Stay! Where's my bag of documents? I have got it there, and you shall read it, you shall read it!"

And I *did* read all the noble history; though very slowly and imperfectly then, for my eyes were so dimmed that I could not see the words, and I cried so much that I was many times obliged to lay down the long account she had cut out of the newspaper. I felt so triumphant ever to have known the man who had done such generous and gallant deeds; I felt such glowing exultation in his renown; I so admired and loved what he had done; that I envied the storm-worn people who had fallen at his feet and blessed him as their preserver. I could myself have kneeled down then, so far away, and blessed him, in my rapture that he should be so truly good and brave. I felt that no one—mother, sister, wife—could honour him more than I. I did, indeed!

My poor little visitor made me a present of the account, and when, as the evening began to close in, she rose to take her leave, lest she should miss the coach by which she was to return, she was still full of the shipwreck, which I had not yet sufficiently composed myself to understand in all its details.

"My dear," said she, as she carefully folded up her scarf and gloves, "my brave physician ought to have a Title bestowed upon him. And no doubt he will. You are of that opinion?"

That he well deserved one, yes. That he would ever have one, no.

"Why not, Fitz-Jarndyce?" she asked, rather sharply.

I said it was not the custom in England to confer titles on men distinguished by peaceful services, however good and great; unless occasionally, when they consisted of the accumulation of some very large amount of money.

"Why good gracious," said Miss Flite, "how can you say that? Surely you know, my dear, that all the greatest ornaments of England in knowledge, imagination, active humanity, and improvement of every sort, are added to its nobility! Look round you, my dear, and consider. *You* must be rambling a little now, I think, if you don't know that this is the great reason why titles will always last in the land!"

I am afraid she believed what she said; for there were moments when she was very mad indeed.

And now I must part with the little secret I have thus far tried to keep. I had thought, sometimes, that Mr. Woodcourt loved me; and that if he had been richer, he would perhaps have told me that he loved me, before he went away. I had thought, sometimes, that if he had done so, I should have been glad of it. But how much better it was now, that this had never happened! What should I have suffered, if I had had to write to him, and tell him that the poor face he had known as mine was quite gone from me, and that I freely released him from his bondage to one whom he had never seen!

O, it was so much better, as it was! With a great pang mercifully spared me, I could take back to my heart my childish prayer to be all he had so brightly shown himself; and there was nothing to be undone: no chain for me to break, or for him to drag; and I could go, please God, my lowly way along the path of duty, and he could go his nobler way upon its broader road; and though we were apart upon the journey, I might aspire to meet him, unselfishly, innocently, better far than he had thought me when I found some favour in his eyes, at the journey's end.

Chapter XXXVI

CHESNEY WOLD

Charley and I did not set off alone upon our expedition into Lincolnshire. My guardian had made up his mind not to lose sight of me until I was safe in Mr. Boythorn's house; so he accompanied us, and we were two days upon the road. I found every breath of air, and every scent, and every flower and leaf and blade of grass, and every passing cloud, and everything in nature, more beautiful and wonderful to me than I had ever found it yet. This was my first gain from my illness. How little I had lost, when the wide world was so full of delight for me.

My guardian intending to go back immediately, we appointed, on our way down, a day when my dear girl should come. I wrote her a letter, of which he took charge; and he left us within half an hour of our arrival at our destination, on a delightful evening in the early summer time.

If a good fairy had built the house for me with a wave of her wand, and I had been a princess and her favoured godchild, I could not have been more considered in it. So many preparations were made for me, and such an endearing remembrance was shown of all my little tastes and likings, that I could have sat down, overcome, a dozen times, before I had revisited half the rooms. I did better than that, however, by showing them all to Charley instead. Charley's delight calmed mine; and after we had had a walk in the garden, and Charley had exhausted her whole vocabulary of admiring expressions, I was as tranquilly happy as I ought to have been. It was a great comfort to be able to say to myself after tea, "Esther, my dear, I think you are quite sensible enough to sit down now, and write a note of thanks to your host." He had left a note of welcome for me, as sunny as his own face, and had confided his bird to my care, which I knew to be his highest mark of confidence. Accordingly I wrote a little note to him in London, telling him how all his favourite plants and trees were looking, and how the most astonishing of birds had chirped the honours of the house to me in the most hospitable manner, and how, after singing on my shoulder, to the inconceivable rapture of my little maid, he was then at roost in the usual corner of his cage, but whether dreaming or no I could not report. My note finished and sent off to the post, I made myself very busy in unpacking and arranging; and I sent Charley to bed in good time, and told her I should want her no more that night.

For I had not yet looked in the glass, and had never asked to have my own restored to me. I knew this to be a weakness which must be overcome; but I had always said to myself that I would begin afresh, when I got to where I now was. Therefore I had wanted to be alone, and therefore I said, now alone, in my own room, "Esther, if you are to be happy, if you are to have any right to pray to be true-hearted, you must keep your word, my dear." I was quite resolved to keep it; but I sat down for a little while first, to reflect upon all my blessings. And then I said my prayers, and thought a little more.

My hair had not been cut off, though it had been in danger more than once. It was long and thick. I let it down, and shook it out, and went up to the glass upon the dressing-table. There was a little muslin curtain drawn across it. I drew it back: and stood for a moment looking through such a veil of my own hair, that I could see nothing else. Then I put my hair aside, and looked at the reflection in the mirror; encouraged by seeing how placidly it looked at me. I was very much changed—O very, very much. At first, my face was so strange to me, that I think I should have put my hands before it and started back, but for the encouragement I have mentioned. Very soon it became more familiar, and then I knew the extent of the alteration in it even better than I had done at first. It was not like what I had expected; but I had expected nothing definite, and I dare say anything definite would have surprised me.

I had never been a beauty, and had never thought myself one; but I had been very different from this. It was all gone now. Heaven was so good to me, that I could let it go with a few not bitter tears, and could stand there arranging my hair for the night quite thankfully.

One thing troubled me, and I considered it for a long time before I went to sleep. I had kept Mr. Woodcourt's flowers. When they were withered I had dried them, and put them in a book that I was fond of. Nobody knew this, not even Ada. I was doubtful whether I had a right to preserve what he had sent to one so different—whether it was generous towards him to do it. I wished to be generous to him, even in the secret depths of my heart, which he would never know, because I could have loved him—could have been devoted to him. At last I came to the conclusion that I might keep them; if I treasured them only as a remembrance of what was irrevocably past and gone, never to be looked back on any more, in any other light. I hope this may not seem trivial. I was very much in earnest.

I took care to be up early in the morning, and to be before the glass when Charley came in on tiptoe.

"Dear, dear, miss!" cried Charley, starting. "Is that you?"

"Yes, Charley," said I, quietly putting up my hair. "And I am very well indeed, and very happy."

I saw it was a weight off Charley's mind, but it was a greater weight off mine. I knew the worst now, and was composed to it. I shall not conceal, as I go on, the weaknesses I could not quite conquer; but they always passed from me soon, and the happier frame of mind stayed by me faithfully.

Wishing to be fully re-established in my strength and my good spirits before Ada came, I now laid down a little series of plans with Charley for being in the fresh air all day long. We were to be out before breakfast, and were to dine early, and were to be out again before and after dinner, and were to walk in the garden after tea, and were to go to rest betimes, and were to climb every hill and explore every road, land, and field in the neighbourhood. As to restoratives and strengthening delicacies, Mr. Boythorn's good housekeeper was for ever trotting about with something to eat or drink in her hand; I could not even be heard of as resting in the park, but she would come trotting after me with a basket, her cheerful face shining with a lecture on the importance of frequent nourishment.

Then there was a pony expressly for my riding, a chubby pony, with a short neck and a mane all over his eyes, who could canter—when he would—so easily and quietly, that he was a treasure. In a very few days, he would come to me in the paddock when I called him, and eat out of my hand, and follow me about. We arrived at such a capital understanding, that when he was jogging with me lazily, and rather obstinately, down some shady lane, if I patted his neck, and said, "Stubbs, I am surprised you don't canter when you know how much I like it; and I think you might oblige me, for you are only getting stupid and going to sleep," he would give his head a comical shake or two, and set off directly; while Charley would stand still and laugh with such enjoyment, that her laughter was like music. I don't know who had given Stubbs his name, but it seemed to belong to him as naturally as his rough coat. Once we put him in a little chaise, and drove him triumphantly through the green lanes for five miles; but all at once, as we were extolling him to the skies, he seemed to take it ill that he should have been accompanied so far by the circle of tantalizing little gnats, that had been hovering round and round his ears the whole way without appearing to advance an inch; and stopped to think about it. I suppose he came to the decision that it was not to be borne; for he steadily refused to move, until I gave the reins to Charley and got out and walked; when he followed me with a sturdy sort of good humour, putting his head under my arm, and rubbing his ear against my sleeve. It was in vain for me to say, "Now, Stubbs, I feel quite sure from what I know of you, that you will go on if I ride a little while"; for the moment I left him, he stood stock still again. Consequently I was obliged to lead the way, as before; and in this order we returned home, to the great delight of the village.

Charley and I had reason to call it the most friendly of villages, I am sure; for in a week's time the people were so glad to see us go by, though ever so frequently in the course of a day, that there were faces of greeting in every cottage. I had known many of the grown people before, and almost all the children; but now the very steeple began to wear a familiar and affectionate look. Among my new friends was an old woman who lived in such a little thatched and whitewashed dwelling, that when the outside shutter was turned up on its hinges, it shut up the whole house-front. This old lady had a grandson who was a sailor; and I wrote a letter to him for her, and drew at the top of it the chimney-corner in which she had brought him up, and where his old stool yet occupied its old place. This was considered by the whole village the most wonderful achievement in the world; but when an answer came back all the way from Plymouth, in which he mentioned that he was going to take the picture all the way to America, and from America would write again, I got all the credit that ought to have been given to the Post-office, and was invested with the merit of the whole system.

Thus, what with being so much in the air, playing with so many children, gossiping with so many people, sitting on invitation in so many cottages, going on with Charley's education, and writing long letters to Ada every day, I had scarcely any time to think about that little loss of mine, and was almost always cheerful. If I did think of it at odd moments now and then, I had only to be busy and forget it. I felt it more than I had hoped I should, once, when a child said, "Mother, why is the lady not a pretty lady now, like she used to be?" But when I found the child was not less fond of me, and drew its soft hand over my face with a kind of pitying protection in its touch, that soon set me up again. There were many little occurrences which suggested to me, with great consolation, how natural it is to gentle hearts to be considerate and delicate towards any inferiority. One of these particularly touched me. I happened to stroll into the little church when a marriage was just concluded, and the young couple had to sign the register. The bridegroom, to whom the pen was handed first, made a rude cross for his mark; the bride, who came next, did the same. Now, I had known the bride when I was last there, not only as the prettiest girl in the place, but as having quite distinguished herself in the school; and I could not help looking at her with some surprise. She came aside and whispered to me, while tears of honest love and admiration stood in her bright eyes, "He's a dear good fellow, miss; but he can't write yet —he's going to learn of me—and I wouldn't shame him for the world!" Why, what had I to fear, I thought, when there was this nobility in the soul of a labouring man's daughter!

The air blew as freshly and revivingly upon me as it had ever blown, and the healthy colour came into my new face as it had come into my old one. Charley was wonderful to see, she was so radiant and so rosy; and we both enjoyed the whole day, and slept soundly the whole night.

There was a favourite spot of mine in the park-woods of Chesney Wold, where a seat had been erected commanding a lovely view. The wood had been cleared and opened, to improve this point of sight; and the bright sunny landscape beyond, was so beautiful that I rested there at least once every day. A picturesque part of the Hall, called the Ghost's Walk, was seen to advantage from this higher ground; and the startling name, and the old legend in the Dedlock family which I had heard from Mr. Boythorn, accounting for it, mingled with the view and gave it something of a mysterious interest, in addition to its real charms. There was a bank here, too, which was a famous one for violets; and as it was a daily delight of Charley's to gather wild flowers, she took as much to the spot as I did.

It would be idle to inquire now why I never went close to the house, or never went inside it. The family were not there, I had heard on my arrival, and were not expected. I was far from being incurious or uninterested about the building; on the contrary, I often sat in this place, wondering how the rooms ranged, and whether any echo like a footstep really did resound at times, as the story said, upon the lonely Ghost's Walk. The indefinable feeling with which Lady Dedlock had impressed me, may have had some influence in keeping me from the house even when she was absent. I am not sure. Her face and figure were associated with it, naturally; but I cannot say that they repelled me from it, though something did. For whatever reason or no reason, I had never once gone near it, down to the day at which my story now arrives.

I was resting at my favourite point, after a long ramble, and Charley was gathering violets at a little distance from me. I had been looking at the Ghost's Walk lying in a deep shade of masonry afar off, and picturing to myself the female shape that was said to haunt it, when I became aware of a figure approaching through the wood. The perspective was so long, and so darkened by leaves, and the shadows of the branches on the ground made it so much more intricate to the eye, that at first I could not discern what figure it was. By little and little, it revealed itself to be a woman's—a lady's—Lady Dedlock's. She was alone, and coming to where I sat with a much quicker step, I observed to my surprise, than was usual with her.

I was fluttered by her being unexpectedly so near (she was almost within speaking distance before I knew her), and would have risen to continue my walk. But I could not. I was rendered motionless. Not so much by her hurried gesture of entreaty, not so much by her quick advance and outstretched hands, not so much by the great change in her manner, and the absence of her haughty self-restraint, as by a something in her face that I had pined for and dreamed of when I was a little child; something I had never seen in any face; something I had never seen in hers before.

A dread and faintness fell upon me, and I called to Charley. Lady Dedlock stopped, upon the instant, and changed back almost to what I had known her.

"Miss Summerson, I am afraid I have startled you," she said, now advancing slowly. "You can scarcely be strong yet. You have been very ill, I know. I have been much concerned to hear it."

I could no more have removed my eyes from her pale face, than I could have stirred from the bench on which I sat. She gave me her hand; and its deadly coldness, so at variance with the enforced composure of her features, deepened the fascination that overpowered me. I cannot say what was in my whirling thoughts.

"You are recovering again?" she asked kindly.

"I was quite well but a moment ago, Lady Dedlock."

"Is this your young attendant?"

"Yes."

"Will you send her on before, and walk towards your house with me?"

"Charley," said I, "take your flowers home, and I will follow you directly."

Charley, with her best curtsey, blushingly tied on her bonnet, and went her way. When she was gone, Lady Dedlock sat down on the seat beside me.

I cannot tell in any words what the state of my mind was, when I saw in her hand my handkerchief, with which I had covered the dead baby.

I looked at her; but I could not see her, I could not hear her, I could not draw my breath. The beating of my heart was so violent and wild, that I felt as if my life were breaking from me. But when she caught me to her breast, kissed me, wept over me, compassionated me, and called me back to myself; when she fell down on her knees and cried to me, "O my child, my child, I am your wicked and unhappy mother! O try to forgive me!"—when I saw her at my feet on the bare earth in her great agony of mind, I felt, through all my tumult of emotion, a burst of gratitude to the providence of God that I was so changed as that I never could disgrace her by any trace of likeness; as that nobody could ever now look at me, and look at her, and remotely think of any near tie between us.

I raised my mother up, praying and beseeching her not to stoop before me in such affliction and humiliation. I did so in broken incoherent words; for, besides the trouble I was in, it frightened me to see her at *my* feet. I told her—or I tried to tell her—that if it were for me, her child, under any circumstances to take upon me to forgive her, I did it, and had done it, many, many years. I told her that my heart overflowed with love for her; that it was natural love, which nothing in the past had changed, or could change. That it was not for me, then resting for the first time on my mother's bosom, to take her to account for having given me life; but that my duty was to bless her and receive her, though the whole world turned from her, and that I only asked her leave to do it. I held my mother in my embrace, and she held me in hers; and among the still woods in the silence of the summer day, there seemed to be nothing but our two troubled minds that was not at peace.

"To bless and receive me," groaned my mother, "it is far too late.

I must travel my dark road alone, and it will lead me where it will. From day to day, sometimes from hour to hour, I do not see the way before my guilty feet. This is the earthly punishment I have brought upon myself. I bear it, and I hide it."

Even in the thinking of her endurance, she drew her habitual air of proud indifference about her like a veil, though she soon cast it off again.

"I must keep this secret, if by any means it can be kept, not wholly for myself. I have a husband, wretched and dishonouring creature that I am!"

These words she uttered with a suppressed cry of despair, more terrible in its sound than any shriek. Covering her face with her hands, she shrunk down in my embrace as if she were unwilling that I should touch her; nor could I, by my utmost persuasions, or by any endearments I could use, prevail upon her to rise. She said, No, no, no, she could only speak to me so; she must be proud and disdainful everywhere else; she would be humbled and ashamed there, in the only natural moments of her life.

My unhappy mother told me that in my illness she had been nearly frantic. She had but then known that her child was living. She could not have suspected me to be that child before. She had followed me down here, to speak to me but once in all her life. We never could associate, never could communicate, never probably from that time forth could interchange another word, on earth. She put into my hands a letter she had written for my reading only; and said, when I had read it, and destroyed it—but not so much for her sake, since she asked nothing, as for her husband's and my own—I must evermore consider her as dead. If I could believe that she loved me, in this agony in which I saw her, with a mother's love, she asked me to do that; for then I might think of her with a greater pity, imagining what she suffered. She had put herself beyond all hope, and beyond all help. Whether she preserved her secret until death, or it came to be discovered and she brought dishonour and disgrace upon the name she had taken, it was her solitary struggle always; and no affection could come near her, and no human creature could render her any aid.

"But is the secret safe so far?" I asked. "Is it safe now, dearest mother?"

"No," replied my mother. "It has been very near discovery. It was saved by an accident. It may be lost by another accident—to-morrow, any day."

"Do you dread a particular person?"

"Hush! Do not tremble and cry so much for me. I am not worthy of these tears," said my mother, kissing my hands. "I dread one person very much."

"An enemy?"

"Not a friend. One who is too passionless to be either. He is Sir Leicester Dedlock's lawyer; mechanically faithful without attachment, and very jealous of the profit, privilege, and reputation of being master of the mysteries of great houses."

"Has he any suspicions?"

"Many."

"Not of you?" I said alarmed.

"Yes! He is always vigilant, and always near me. I may keep him at a standstill, but I can never shake him off."

"Has he so little pity or compunction?"

"He has none, and no anger. He is indifferent to everything but his calling. His calling is the acquisition of secrets, and the holding possession of such power as they give him, with no sharer or opponent in it."

"Could you trust in him?"

"I shall never try. The dark road I have trodden for so many years will end where it will. I follow it alone to the end, whatever the end be. It may be near, it may be distant; while the road lasts, nothing turns me."

"Dear mother, are you so resolved?"

"I *am* resolved. I have long outbidden folly with folly, pride with pride, scorn with scorn, insolence with insolence, and have outlived many vanities with many more. I will outlive this danger, and outdie it, if I can. It has closed around me, almost as awfully as if these woods of Chesney Wold had closed around the house; but my course through it is the same. I have but one: I can have but one."

"Mr. Jarndyce——" I was beginning, when my mother hurriedly inquired:

"Does *he* suspect?"

"No," said I. "No, indeed! Be assured that he does not!" And I told her what he had related to me as his knowledge of my story. "But he is so good and sensible," said I, "that perhaps if he knew——"

My mother, who until this time had made no change in her position, raised her hand up to my lips, and stopped me.

"Confide fully in him," she said, after a little while. "You have my free consent—a small gift from such a mother to her injured child!—but do not tell me of it. Some pride is left in me, even yet."

I explained, as nearly as I could then, or can recall now—for my agitation and distress throughout were so great that I scarcely understood myself, though every word that was uttered in the mother's voice, so unfamiliar and so melancholy to me; which in my childhood I had never learned to love and recognise, had never been sung to sleep with, had never heard a blessing from, had never had a hope inspired by; made an enduring impression on my memory—I say I explained, or tried to do it, how I had only hoped that Mr. Jarndyce, who had been the best of fathers to me, might be able to afford some counsel and support to her. But my mother answered no, it was impossible; no one could help her. Through the desert that lay before her, she must go alone.

"My child, my child!" she said. "For the last time! These kisses for the last time! These arms upon my neck for the last time! We shall meet no more. To hope to do what I seek to do, I must be what I have been so long. Such is my reward and doom. If you hear of Lady Dedlock, brilliant, prosperous, and flattered; think of your wretched mother, conscience-stricken, underneath that mask! Think that the reality is in her suffering, in her useless remorse, in her murdering within her breast the only love and truth of which it is capable! And then forgive her, if you can; and cry to Heaven to forgive her, which it never can!"

We held one another for a little space yet, but she was so firm, that she took my hands away, and put them back against my breast, and, with a last kiss as she held them there, released them and went from me into the wood. I was alone; and, calm and quiet below me in the sun and shade, lay the old house, with its terraces and turrets, on which there had seemed to me to be such complete repose when I first saw it, but which now looked like the obdurate and unpitying watcher of my mother's misery.

Stunned as I was, as weak and helpless at first as I had ever been in my sick chamber, the necessity of guarding against the danger of discovery, or even of the remotest suspicion, did me service. I took such precautions as I could to hide from Charley that I had been crying; and I constrained myself to think of every sacred obligation that there was upon me to be careful and collected. It was not a little while before I could succeed, or could even restrain bursts of grief; but after an hour or so, I was better, and felt that I might return. I went home very slowly, and told Charley, whom I found at the gate looking for me, that I had been tempted to extend my walk after Lady Dedlock had left me, and that I was over-tired, and would lie down. Safe in my own room, I read the letter. I clearly derived from it—and that was much then—that I had not been abandoned by my mother. Her elder and only sister, the godmother of my childhood, discovering signs of life in me when I had been laid aside as dead, had in her stern sense of duty, with no desire or willingness that I should live, reared me in rigid secrecy, and had never again beheld my mother's face from within a few hours of my birth. So strangely did I hold my place in this world, that, until within a short time back, I had never, to my own mother's knowledge, breathed—had been buried—had never been endowed with life—had never borne a name. When she had first seen me in the church, she had been startled; and had thought of what would have been like me, if it had ever lived, and had lived on; but that was all, then.

What more the letter told me, needs not to be repeated here. It has its own times and places in my story.

My first care was to burn what my mother had written, and to consume even its ashes. I hope it may not appear very unnatural or bad in me, that I then became heavily sorrowful to think I had ever been reared. That I felt as if I knew it would have been better and happier for many people, if indeed I had never breathed. That I had a terror of myself, as the danger and the possible disgrace of my own mother and of a proud family name. That I was so confused and shaken, as to be possessed by a belief that it was right, and had been intended, that I should die in my birth; and that it was wrong, and not intended, that I should be then alive.

These are the real feelings that I had. I fell asleep, worn out; and when I awoke, I cried afresh to think I was back in the world, with my load of trouble for others. I was more than ever frightened of myself, thinking anew of her, against whom I was a witness; of the owner of Chesney Wold; of the new and terrible meaning of the old words, now moaning in my ear like a surge upon the shore, "Your mother, Esther, was your disgrace, and you are hers. The time will come—and soon enough—when you will understand this better, and will feel it too, as no one save a woman can." With them, those other words returned, "Pray daily that the sins of others be not visited upon your head." I could not disentangle all that was about me; and I felt as if the blame and the shame were all in me, and the visitation had come down.

The day waned into a gloomy evening, overcast and sad, and I still contended with the same distress. I went out alone, and, after walking a little in the park, watching the dark shades falling on the trees, and the fitful flight of the bats, which sometimes almost touched me, was attracted to the house for the first time. Perhaps I might not have gone near it, if I had been in a stronger frame of mind. As it was, I took the path that led close by it.

I did not dare to linger or to look up, but I passed before the terrace garden with its fragrant odours, and its broad walks, and its well-kept beds and smooth turf; and I saw how beautiful and grave it was, and how the old stone balustrades and parapets, and wide flights of shallow steps, were seamed by time and weather; and how the trained moss and ivy grew about them, and around the old stone pedestal of the sun-dial; and I heard the fountain falling. Then the way went by long lines of dark windows, diversified by turreted towers, and porches, of eccentric shapes, where old stone lions and grotesque monsters bristled outside dens of shadow, and snarled at the evening gloom over the escutcheons they held in their grip. Thence the path wound underneath a gateway, and through a court-yard where the principal entrance was (I hurried quickly on), and by the stables where none but deep voices seemed to be, whether in the murmuring of the wind through the strong mass of ivy holding to a high red wall, or in the low complaining of the weathercock, or in the barking of the dogs, or in the slow striking of a clock. So, encountering presently a sweet smell of limes, whose rustling I could hear, I turned with the turning of the path, to the south front; and there, above me, were the balustrades of the Ghost's Walk, and one lighted window that might be my mother's.

The way was paved here, like the terrace overhead, and my footsteps from being noiseless made an echoing sound upon the flags. Stopping to look at nothing, but seeing all I did see as I went, I was passing quickly on, and in a few moments should have passed the lighted window, when my echoing footsteps brought it suddenly into my mind that there was a dreadful truth in the legend of the Ghost's Walk; that it was I, who was to bring calamity upon the stately house; and that my warning feet were haunting it even then. Seized with an augmented terror of myself which turned me cold, I ran from myself and everything, retraced the way by which I had come, and never paused until I had gained the lodge-gate, and the park lay sullen and black behind me.

Not before I was alone in my own room for the night, and had again been dejected and unhappy there, did I begin to know how wrong and thankless this state was. But from my darling who was coming on the morrow, I found a joyful letter, full of such loving anticipation that I must have been of marble if it had not moved me; from my guardian, too, I found another letter, asking me to tell Dame Durden, if I should see that little woman anywhere, that they had moped most pitiably without her, that the housekeeping was going to rack and ruin, that nobody else could manage the keys, and that everybody in and about the house declared it was not the same house, and was becoming rebellious for her return. Two such letters together made me think how far beyond my deserts I was beloved, and how happy I ought to be. That made me think of all my past life; and that brought me, as it ought to have done before, into a better condition.

For, I saw very well that I could not have been intended to die, or I should never have lived; not to say should never have been reserved for such a happy life. I saw very well how many things had worked together, for my welfare; and that if the sins of the fathers were sometimes visited upon the children, the phrase did not mean what I had in the morning feared it meant. I knew I was as innocent of my birth as a queen of hers; and that before my Heavenly Father

I should not be punished for birth, nor a queen rewarded for it. I had had experience, in the shock of that very day, that I could, even thus soon, find comforting reconcilements to the change that had fallen on me. I renewed my resolutions, and prayed to be strengthened in them; pouring out my heart for myself, and for my unhappy mother, and feeling that the darkness of the morning was passing away. It was not upon my sleep; and when the next day's light awoke me, it was gone.

My dear girl was to arrive at five o'clock in the afternoon. How to help myself through the intermediate time better than by taking a long walk along the road by which she was to come, I did not know; so Charley and I and Stubbs—Stubbs, saddled, for we never drove him after the one great occasion—made a long expedition along that road, and back. On our return, we held a great review of the house and garden; and saw that everything was in its prettiest condition, and had the bird out ready as an important part of the establishment.

There were more than two full hours yet to elapse, before she could come; and in that interval, which seemed a long one, I must confess I was nervously anxious about my altered looks. I loved my darling so well that I was more concerned for their effect on her than on any one. I was not in this slight distress because I at all repined—I am quite certain I did not, that day—but, I thought, would she be wholly prepared? When she first saw me, might she not be a little shocked and disappointed? Might it not prove a little worse than she expected? Might she not look for her old Esther, and not find her? Might she not have to grow used to me, and to begin all over again?

I knew the various expressions of my sweet girl's face so well and it was such an honest face in its loveliness, that I was sure, beforehand, she could not hide that first look from me. And I considered whether, if it should signify any one of these meanings, which was so very likely, could I quite answer for myself?

Well, I thought I could. After last night, I thought I could. But to wait and wait, and expect and expect, and think and think, was such bad preparation, that I resolved to go along the road again, and meet her.

So, I said to Charley, "Charley, I will go by myself and walk along the road until she comes." Charley highly approving of anything that pleased me, I went, and left her at home.

But before I got to the second milestone, I had been in so many palpitations from seeing dust in the distance (though I knew it was not, and could not, be the coach yet), that I resolved to turn back and go home again. And when I had turned, I was in such fear of the coach coming up behind me (though I still knew that it neither would, nor could, do any such thing), that I ran the greater part of the way, to avoid being overtaken.

Then, I considered, when I had got safe back again, this was a nice thing to have done! Now I was hot, and had made the worst of it, instead of the best.

At last, when I believed there was at least a quarter of an hour more yet, Charley all at once cried out to me as I was trembling in the garden, "Here she comes, miss! Here she is!"

I did not mean to do it, but I ran up-stairs into my room, and hid myself behind the door. There I stood trembling, even when I heard my darling calling as she came up-stairs, "Esther, my dear, my love, where are you? Little woman, dear Dame Durden!"

She ran in, and was running out again when she saw me. Ah, my angel girl! the old dear look, all love, all fondness, all affection. Nothing else in it—no, nothing, nothing!

O how happy I was, down upon the floor, with my sweet beautiful girl down upon the floor too, holding my scarred face to her lovely cheek, bathing it with tears and kisses, rocking me to and fro like a child, calling me by every tender name that she could think of, and pressing me to her faithful heart.

Chapter XXXVII

JARNDYCE AND JARNDYCE

If the secret I had to keep had been mine, I must have confided it to Ada before we had been long together. But it was not mine; and I did not feel that I had a right to tell it, even to my guardian, unless some great emergency arose. It was a weight to bear alone; still my present duty appeared to be plain, and blest in the attachment of my dear, I did not want an impulse and encouragement to do it. Though often when she was asleep, and all was quiet, the remembrance of my mother kept me waking, and made the night sorrowful, I did not yield to it at another time; and Ada found me what I used to be—except, of course, in that particular of which I have said enough, and which I have no intention of mentioning any more, just now, if I can help it.

The difficulty that I felt in being quite composed that first evening, when Ada asked me, over our work, if the family were at the house, and when I was obliged to answer yes, I believed so, for Lady Dedlock had spoken to me in the woods the day before yesterday, was great. Greater still, when Ada asked me what she had said, and when I replied that she had been kind and interested; and when Ada, while admitting her beauty and elegance, remarked upon her proud manner, and her imperious chilling air. But Charley helped me through unconsciously, by telling us that Lady Dedlock had only stayed at the House two nights, on her way from London to visit at some other great house in the next county; and that she had left early on the morning after we had seen her at our view, as we called it. Charley verified the adage about little pitchers,[1] I am sure; for she heard of more sayings and doings, in a day, than would have come to my ears in a month.

We were to stay a month at Mr. Boythorn's. My pet had scarcely been there a bright week, as I recollect the time, when one evening after we had finished helping the gardener in watering his flowers, and just as the candles were lighted, Charley, appearing with a very important air behind Ada's chair, beckoned me mysteriously out of the room.

"Oh! if you please, miss," said Charley in a whisper, with her eyes at their roundest and largest. "You're wanted at the Dedlock Arms."

"Why, Charley," said I, "who can possibly want me at the public-house?"

"I don't know, miss," returned Charley, putting her head forward, and folding her hands tight upon the band of her little apron; which she always did, in the enjoyment of anything mysterious or confidential, "but it's a gentleman, miss, and his compliments, and will you please to come without saying anything about it."

"Whose compliments, Charley?"

"His'n, miss," returned Charley; whose grammatical education was advancing, but not very rapidly.

"And how do you come to be the messenger, Charley?"

"I am not the messenger, if you please, miss," returned my little maid. "It was W. Grubble, miss."

"And who is W. Grubble, Charley?"

"Mister Grubble, miss," returned Charley. "Don't you know, miss? The Dedlock Arms, by W. Grubble," which Charley delivered as if she were slowly spelling out the sign.

"Aye? The landlord, Charley?"

"Yes, miss. If you please, miss, his wife is a beau-tiful woman, but she broke her ankle, and it never joined. And her brother's the sawyer, that was put in the cage,[2] miss, and they expect he'll drink himself to death entirely on beer," said Charley.

Not knowing what might be the matter, and being easily apprehensive now, I thought it best to go to this place by myself. I bade Charley be quick with my bonnet and veil, and my shawl; and having put them on, went away down the little hilly street, where I was as much at home as in Mr. Boythorn's garden.

Mr. Grubble was standing in his shirt sleeves at the door of his

1. "Little pitchers have great ears"—meaning that children have acute hearing, the analogy derived from the proportionately large handles on small earthenware vessels.
2. Prisoner's cage.

very clean little tavern, waiting for me. He lifted off his hat with both hands when he saw me coming, and carrying it so, as if it were an iron vessel (it looked as heavy), preceded me along the sanded passage to his best parlour: a neat carpeted room, with more plants in it than were quite convenient, a coloured print of Queen Caroline,[3] several shells, a good many tea-trays, two stuffed and dried fish in glass cases, and either a curious egg or a curious pumpkin (but I don't know which, and I doubt if many people did) hanging from the ceiling. I knew Mr. Grubble very well by sight, from his often standing at his door. A pleasant-looking, stoutish, middle-aged man, who never seemed to consider himself cosily dressed for his own fireside without his hat and top-boots, but who never wore a coat except at church.

He snuffed the candle, and backing away a little to see how it looked, backed out of the room—unexpectedly to me, for I was going to ask him by whom he had been sent. The door of the opposite parlour being then opened, I heard some voices, familiar in my ears, I thought, which stopped. A quick light step approached the room in which I was, and who should stand before me, but Richard!

"My dear Esther!" he said, "my best friend!" and he really was so warm-hearted and earnest, that in the first surprise and pleasure of his brotherly greeting, I could scarcely find breath to tell him that Ada was well.

"Answering my very thoughts—always the same dear girl!" said Richard, leading me to a chair, and seating himself beside me.

I put my veil up, but not quite.

"Always the same dear girl!" said Richard, just as heartily as before.

I put up my veil altogether, and laying my hand on Richard's sleeve, and looking in his face, told him how much I thanked him for his kind welcome, and how greatly I rejoiced to see him; the more so, because of the determination I had made in my illness, which I now conveyed to him.

"My love," said Richard, "there is no one with whom I have a greater wish to talk, than you, for I want you to understand me."

"And I want you, Richard," said I, shaking my head, "to understand some one else.'

"Since you refer so immediately to John Jarndyce," said Richard—"I suppose you mean him?"

"Of course I do."

"Then, I may say at once that I am glad of it, because it is on that subject that I am anxious to be understood. By you, mind—you, my dear! I am not accountable to Mr. Jarndyce, or Mr. Anybody."

3. **Wife of George IV (1768–1821), or wife of George II (1683–1737).**

I was pained to find him taking this tone, and he observed it.

"Well, well, my dear," said Richard, "we won't go into that now. I want to appear quietly in your country house here, with you under my arm, and give my charming cousin a surprise. I suppose your loyalty to John Jarndyce will allow that?"

"My dear Richard," I returned, "you know you would be heartily welcome at his house—your home, if you will but consider it so; and you are as heartily welcome here!"

"Spoken like the best of little women!" cried Richard, gaily.

I asked him how he liked his profession?

"Oh, I like it well enough!" said Richard. "It's all right. It does as well as anything else, for a time. I don't know that I shall care about it when I come to be settled; but I can sell out then, and—however, never mind all that botheration at present."

So young and handsome, and in all respects so perfectly the opposite of Miss Flite! And yet, in the clouded, eager, seeking look that passed over him, so dreadfully like her!

"I am in town on leave, just now," said Richard.

"Indeed?"

"Yes. I have run over to look after my—my Chancery interests, before the long vacation," said Richard, forcing a careless laugh. "We are beginning to spin along with that old suit at last, I promise you."

No wonder that I shook my head!

"As you say, it's not a pleasant subject." Richard spoke with the same shade crossing his face as before. "Let it go to the four winds for to-night.—Puff! Gone!—Who do you suppose is with me?"

"Was it Mr. Skimpole's voice I heard?"

"That's the man! He does me more good than anybody. What a fascinating child it is!"

I asked Richard if any one knew of their coming down together. He answered, No, nobody. He had been to call upon the dear old infant—so he called Mr. Skimpole—and the dear old infant had told him where we were, and he had told the dear old infant he was bent on coming to see us, and the dear old infant had directly wanted to come too; and so he had brought him. "And he is worth—not to say his sordid expenses—but thrice his weight in gold," said Richard. "He is such a cheery fellow. No worldliness about him. Fresh and green-hearted!"

I certainly did not see the proof of Mr. Skimpole's unworldliness in his having his expenses paid by Richard; but I made no remark about that. Indeed, he came in, and turned our conversation. He was charmed to see me; said he had been shedding delicious tears of joy and sympathy, at intervals for six weeks, on my account; had never been so happy as in hearing of my progress; began to understand the mixture of good and evil in the world now; felt that he appreciated health the more, when somebody else was ill; didn't know but what it might be in the scheme of things that A should squint to make B happier in looking straight; or that C should carry a wooden leg, to make D better satisfied with his flesh and blood in a silk stocking.

"My dear Miss Summerson, here is our friend Richard," said Mr. Skimpole, "full of the brightest visions of the future, which he evokes out of the darkness of Chancery. Now that's delightful, that's inspiriting, that's full of poetry! In old times, the woods and solitudes were made joyous to the shepherd by the imaginary piping and dancing of Pan and the Nymphs. This present shepherd, our pastoral Richard, brightens the dull Inns of Court by making Fortune and her train sport through them to the melodious notes of a judgment from the bench. That's very pleasant, you know! Some ill-conditioned growling fellow may say to me, 'What's the use of these legal and equitable abuses? How do you defend them?' I reply, 'My growling friend, I *don't* defend them, but they are very agreeable to me. There is a shepherd-youth, a friend of mine, who transmutes them into something highly fascinating to my simplicity. I don't say it is for this that they exist—for I am a child among you worldly grumblers, and not called upon to account to you or myself for anything—but it may be so.' "

I began seriously to think that Richard could scarcely have found a worse friend than this. It made me uneasy that at such a time, when he most required some right principle and purpose, he should have this captivating looseness and putting-off of everything, this airy dispensing with all principle and purpose, at his elbow. I thought I could understand how such a nature as my guardian's, experienced in the world, and forced to contemplate the miserable evasions and contentions of the family misfortune, found an immense relief in Mr. Skimpole's avowal of his weaknesses and display of guileless candour; but I could not satisfy myself that it was as artless as it seemed; or that it did not serve Mr. Skimpole's idle turn quite as well as any other part, and with less trouble.

They both walked back with me; and Mr. Skimpole leaving us at the gate, I walked softly in with Richard, and said, "Ada, my love, I have brought a gentleman to visit you." It was not difficult to read the blushing, startled face. She loved him dearly, and he knew it, and I knew it. It was a very transparent business, that meeting as cousins only.

I almost mistrusted myself, as growing quite wicked in my suspicions, but I was not so sure that Richard loved her dearly. He admired her very much—any one must have done that—and I dare say, would have renewed their youthful engagement with great pride and ardour, but that he knew how she would respect her promise to my guardian. Still, I had a tormenting idea that the influence upon him extended even here: that he was postponing his best truth and earnestness, in this as in all things, until Jarndyce and Jarndyce should be off his mind. Ah me! what Richard would have been without that blight, I never shall know now!

He told Ada, in his most ingenuous way, that he had not come to make any secret inroad on the terms she had accepted (rather too implicitly and confidingly, he thought) from Mr. Jarndyce; that he had come openly to see her, and to see me, and to justify himself for the present terms on which he stood with Mr. Jarndyce. As the dear old infant would be with us directly, he begged that I would make an appointment for the morning, when he might set himself right, through the means of an unreserved conversation with me. I proposed to walk with him in the park at seven o'clock, and this was arranged. Mr. Skimpole soon afterwards appeared, and made us merry for an hour. He particularly requested to see Little Coavinses (meaning Charley), and told her, with a patriarchal air, that he had given her late father all the business in his power; and that if one of her little brothers would make haste to get set-up in the same profession, he hoped he should still be able to put a good deal of employment in his way.

"For I am constantly being taken in these nets," said Mr. Skimpole, looking beamingly at us over a glass of wine-and-water, "and am constantly being bailed out—like a boat. Or paid off—like a ship's company. Somebody always does it for me. I can't do it, you know, for I never have any money. But Somebody does it. I get out by Somebody's means; I am not like the starling;[4] I get out. If you were to ask me who Somebody is, upon my word I couldn't tell you. Let us drink to Somebody. God bless him!"

Richard was a little late in the morning, but I had not to wait for him long, and we turned into the park. The air was bright and dewy, and the sky without a cloud. The birds sang delightfully; the sparkles in the fern, the grass, and trees, were exquisite to see; the richness of the woods seemed to have increased twenty-fold since yesterday, as if, in the still night when they had looked so massively hushed in sleep, Nature, through all the minute details of every wonderful leaf, had been more wakeful than usual for the glory of that day.

"This is a lovely place," said Richard, looking around. "None of the jar and discord of law-suits here!"

But there was other trouble.

"I tell you what, my dear girl," said Richard, "when I get affairs in general settled, I shall come down here, I think, and rest."

4. "I can't get out" is the song of a caged starling in Sterne's *A Sentimental Journey*.

"Would it not be better to rest now?" I asked.

"Oh, as to resting *now*," said Richard, "or as to doing anything very definite *now*, that's not easy. In short, it can't be done; *I* can't do it at least."

"Why not?" said I.

"You know why not, Esther. If you were living in an unfinished house, liable to have the roof put on or taken off—to be from top to bottom pulled down or built up—to-morrow, next day, next week, next month, next year—you would find it hard to rest or settle. So do I. Now? There's no now for us suitors."

I could almost have believed in the attraction on which my poor little wandering friend had expatiated, when I saw again the darkened look of last night. Terrible to think, it had in it also, a shade of that unfortunate man who had died.

"My dear Richard," said I, "this is a bad beginning of our conversation."

"I knew you would tell me so, Dame Durden."

"And not I alone, dear Richard. It was not I who cautioned you once, never to found a hope or expectation on the family curse."

"There you come back to John Jarndyce!" said Richard, impatiently. "Well! We must approach him sooner or later, for he is the staple of what I have to say; and it's as well at once. My dear Esther, how can you be so blind? Don't you see that he is an interested party, and that it may be very well for him to wish me to know nothing of the suit, and care nothing about it, but that it may not be quite so well for me?"

"O Richard," I remonstrated, "is it possible that you can ever have seen him and heard him, that you can ever have lived under his roof and known him, and can yet breathe, even to me in this solitary place where there is no one to hear us, such unworthy suspicions?"

He reddened deeply, as if his natural generosity felt a pang of reproach. He was silent for a little while, before he replied in a subdued voice:

"Esther, I am sure you know that I am not a mean fellow, and that I have some sense of suspicion and distrust being poor qualities in one of my years."

"I know it very well," said I. "I am not more sure of anything."

"That's a dear girl!" retorted Richard, "and like you, because it gives me comfort. I had need to get some scrap of comfort out of all this business, for it's a bad one at the best, as I have no occasion to tell you."

"I know perfectly," said I. "I know as well, Richard—what shall I say? as well as you do—that such misconstructions are foreign to your nature. And I know, as well as you know, what so changes it."

"Come, sister, come," said Richard, a little more gaily, "you will be fair with me at all events. If I have the misfortune to be under that influence, so has he. If it has a little twisted me, it may have a little twisted him, too. I don't say that he is not an honourable man, out of all this complication and uncertainty; I am sure he is. But it taints everybody. You know it taints everybody. You have heard him say so fifty times. Then why should *he* escape?"

"Because," said I, "his is an uncommon character, and he has resolutely kept himself outside the circle, Richard."

"Oh, because and because!" replied Richard, in his vivacious way. "I am not sure, my dear girl, but that it may be wise and specious to preserve that outward indifference. It may cause other parties interested to become lax about their interests; and people may die off, and points may drag themselves out of memory, and many things may smoothly happen that are convenient enough."

I was so touched with pity for Richard, that I could not reproach him any more, even by a look. I remembered my guardian's gentleness towards his errors, and with what perfect freedom from resentment he had spoken of them.

"Esther," Richard resumed, "you are not to suppose that I have come here to make under-handed charges against John Jarndyce. I have only come to justify myself. What I say is, it was all very well, and we got on very well, while I was a boy, utterly regardless of this same suit; but as soon as I began to take an interest in it, and to look into it, then it was quite another thing. Then John Jarndyce discovers that Ada and I must break off, and that if I don't amend that very objectionable course, I am not fit for her. Now, Esther, I don't mean to amend that very objectionable course: I will not hold John Jarndyce's favour on those unfair terms of compromise, which he has no right to dictate. Whether it pleases him or displeases him, I must maintain my rights, and Ada's. I have been thinking about it a good deal, and this is the conclusion I have come to."

Poor dear Richard! He had indeed been thinking about it a good deal. His face, his voice, his manner all showed that, too plainly.

"So I tell him honourably (you are to know I have written to him about all this) that we are at issue, and that we had better be at issue openly than covertly. I thank him for his good-will and his protection, and he goes his road, and I go mine. The fact is, our roads are not the same. Under one of the wills in dispute, I should take much more than he. I don't mean to say that it is the one to be established; but there it is, and it has its chance."

"I have not to learn from you, my dear Richard," said I, "of your letter. I have heard of it already, without an offended or angry word."

"Indeed?" replied Richard, softening. "I am glad I said he was an honourable man, out of all this wretched affair. But I always say that, and have never doubted it. Now, my dear Esther, I know these views of mine appear extremely harsh to you, and will to Ada when you tell her what has passed between us. But if you had gone into the case as I have, if you had only applied yourself to the papers as I did when I was at Kenge's, if you only knew what an accumulation of charges and counter-charges, and suspicions and cross-suspicions, they involve, you would think me moderate in comparison."

"Perhaps so," said I. "But do you think that, among those many papers, there is much truth and justice, Richard?"

"There is truth and justice somewhere in the case, Esther——"

"Or was once, long ago," said I.

"Is—is—must be somewhere," pursued Richard, impetuously, "and must be brought out. To allow Ada to be made a bribe and hush-money of, is not the way to bring it out. You say the suit is changing me; John Jarndyce says it changes, has changed, and will change, everybody who has any share in it. Then the greater right I have on my side, when I resolve to do all I can to bring it to an end."

"All you can, Richard! Do you think that in these many years no others have done all they could? Has the difficulty grown easier because of so many failures?"

"It can't last for ever," returned Richard, with a fierceness kindling in him which again presented to me that last sad reminder. "I am young and earnest; and energy and determination have done wonders many a time. Others have only half thrown themselves into it. I devote myself to it. I make it the object of my life."

"O Richard, my dear, so much the worse, so much the worse!"

"No, no, no, don't you be afraid for me," he returned, affectionately. "You're a dear, good, wise, quiet, blessed girl; but you have your prepossessions. So I come round to John Jarndyce. I tell you, my good Esther, when he and I were on those terms which he found so convenient, we were not on natural terms."

"Are division and animosity your natural terms, Richard?"

"No, I don't say that. I mean that all this business puts us on unnatural terms, with which natural relations are incompatible. See another reason for urging it on! I may find out, when it's over, that I have been mistaken in John Jarndyce. My head may be clearer when I am free of it, and I may then agree with what you say today. Very well. Then I shall acknowledge it, and make him reparation."

Everything postponed to that imaginary time! Everything held in confusion and indecision until then!

"Now, my best of confidantes," said Richard, "I want my cousin, Ada, to understand that I am not captious, fickle, and willful, about

John Jarndyce; but that I have this purpose and reason at my back. I wish to represent myself to her through you, because she has a great esteem and respect for her cousin John; and I know you will soften the course I take, even though you disapprove of it; and—and in short," said Richard, who had been hesitating through these words, "I—I don't like to represent myself in this litigious, contentious, doubting character, to a confiding girl like Ada."

I told him that he was more like himself in those latter words, than in anything he had said yet.

"Why," acknowledged Richard, "that may be true enough, my love. I rather feel it to be so. But I shall be able to give myself fair-play by and by. I shall come all right again, then, don't you be afraid."

I asked him if this were all he wished me to tell Ada?

"Not quite," said Richard. "I am bound not to withhold from her that John Jarndyce answered my letter in his usual manner, addressing me as 'My dear Rick,' trying to argue me out of my opinions, and telling me that they should make no difference in him. (All very well of course, but not altering the case.) I also want Ada to know, that if I see her seldom just now, I am looking after her interests as well as my own—we two being in the same boat exactly—and that I hope she will not suppose, from any flying rumours she may hear, that I am at all light-headed or imprudent; on the contrary, I am always looking forward to the termination of the suit, and always planning in that direction. Being of age now, and having taken the step I have taken, I consider myself free from any accountability to John Jarndyce; but Ada being still a ward of the Court, I don't yet ask her to renew our engagement. When she is free to act for herself, I shall be myself once more, and we shall both be in very different worldly circumstances, I believe. If you tell her all this with the advantage of your considerate way, you will do me a very great and a very kind service, my dear Esther; and I shall knock Jarndyce and Jarndyce on the head with greater vigour. Of course I ask for no secrecy at Bleak House."

"Richard," said I, "you place great confidence in me, but I fear you will not take advice from me?"

"It's impossible that I can on this subject, my dear girl. On any other, readily."

As if there were any other in his life! As if his whole career and character were not being dyed one colour!

"But I may ask you a question, Richard?"

"I think so," said he, laughing. "I don't know who may not, if you may not."

"You say, yourself, you are not leading a very settled life."

"How can I, my dear Esther, with nothing settled?"

"Are you in debt again?"

"Why, of course I am," said Richard, astonished at my simplicity.

"Is it of course?"

"My dear child, certainly. I can't throw myself into an object so completely, without expense. You forget, or perhaps you don't know, that under either of the wills Ada and I take something. It's only a question between the larger sum and the smaller. I shall be within the mark any way. Bless your heart, my excellent girl," said Richard, quite amused with me, "I shall be all right! I shall pull through, my dear!"

I felt so deeply sensible of the danger in which he stood, that I tried, in Ada's name, in my guardian's, in my own, by every fervent means that I could think of, to warn him of it, and to show him some of his mistakes. He received everything I said with patience and gentleness, but it all rebounded from him without taking the least effect. I could not wonder at this, after the reception his preoccupied mind had given to my guardian's letter; but I determined to try Ada's influence yet.

So, when our walk brought us round to the village again, and I went home to breakfast, I prepared Ada for the account I was going to give her, and told her exactly what reason we had to dread that Richard was losing himself, and scattering his whole life to the winds. It made her very unhappy, of course; though she had a far, far greater reliance on his correcting his errors than I could have—which was so natural and loving in my dear!—and she presently wrote him this little letter:

"My dearest Cousin,—Esther has told me all you said to her this morning. I write this, to repeat most earnestly for myself all that she said to you, and to let you know how sure I am that you will sooner or later find our cousin John a pattern of truth, sincerity and goodness, when you will deeply deeply grieve to have done him (without intending it) so much wrong.

"I do not quite know how to write what I wish to say next, but I trust you will understand it as I mean it. I have some fears, my dearest cousin, that it may be partly for my sake you are now laying up so much unhappiness for yourself—and, if for yourself, for me. In case this should be so, or in case you should entertain much thought of me in what you are doing, I most earnestly entreat and beg you to desist. You can do nothing for my sake that will make me half so happy, as for ever turning your back upon the shadow in which we both were born. Do not be angry with me for saying this. Pray, pray, dear Richard, for my sake, and for your own, and in a natural repugnance for that source of trouble which had its share in making us both orphans when we were very young, pray, pray, let it go for ever. We have reason to know, by this time, that there is no good in it, and no hope; that there is nothing to be got from it but sorrow.

"My dearest cousin, it is needless for me to say that you are quite free, and that it is very likely you may find some one whom you will love much better than your first fancy. I am quite sure, if you will let me say so, that the object of your choice would greatly prefer to follow your fortunes far and wide, however moderate or poor, and see you happy, doing your duty and pursuing your chosen way; than to have the hope of being, or even to be, very rich with you (if such a thing were possible), at the cost of dragging years of procrastination and anxiety, and of your indifference to other aims. You may wonder at my saying this so confidently with so little knowledge or experience, but I know it for a certainty from my own heart.—Ever, my dearest cousin, your most affectionate, ADA."

This note brought Richard to us very soon; but it made little change in him, if any. We would fairly try, he said, who was right and who was wrong—he would show us—we should see! He was animated and glowing, as if Ada's tenderness had gratified him; but I could only hope, with a sigh, that the letter might have some stronger effect upon his mind on re-perusal, than it assuredly had then.

As they were to remain with us that day, and had taken their places to return by the coach next morning, I sought an opportunity of speaking to Mr. Skimpole. Our out-of-door life easily threw one in my way; and I delicately said, that there was a responsibility in encouraging Richard.

"Responsibility, my dear Miss Summerson?" he repeated, catching at the word with the pleasantest smile. "I am the last man in the world for such a thing. I never was responsible in my life—I can't be."

"I am afraid everybody is obliged to be," said I, timidly enough: he being so much older and more clever than I.

"No, really?" said Mr. Skimpole, receiving this new light with a most agreeable jocularity of surprise. "But every man's not obliged to be solvent? I am not. I never was. See, my dear Miss Summerson," he took a handful of loose silver and halfpence from his pocket, "there's so much money. I have not an idea how much. I have not the power of counting. Call it four and ninepence—call it four pound nine. They tell me I owe more than that. I dare say I do. I dare say I owe as much as good-natured people will let me owe. If they don't stop, why should I? There you have Harold Skimpole in little. If that's responsibility, I am responsible."

The perfect ease of manner with which he put the money up again, and looked at me with a smile on his refined face, as if he had been mentioning a curious little fact about somebody else, almost made me feel as if he really had nothing to do with it.

"Now when you mention responsibility," he resumed, "I am disposed to say, that I never had the happiness of knowing any one whom I should consider so refreshingly responsible as yourself. You appear to me to be the very touchstone of responsibility. When I see you, my dear Miss Summerson, intent upon the perfect working of the whole little orderly system of which you are the centre, I feel inclined to say to myself—in fact I do say to myself, very often—*that's* responsibility!"

It was difficult, after this, to explain what I meant, but I persisted so far as to say that we all hoped he would check and not confirm Richard in the sanguine views he entertained just then.

"Most willingly," he retorted, "if I could. But, my dear Miss Summerson, I have no art, no disguise. If he takes me by the hand, and leads me through Westminster Hall in an airy procession after Fortune, I must go. If he says, 'Skimpole, join the dance!' I must join it. Common sense wouldn't, I know; but I have *no* common sense."

It was very unfortunate for Richard, I said.

"Do you think so!" returned Mr. Skimpole. "Don't say that, don't say that. Let us suppose him keeping company with Common Sense—an excellent man—a good deal wrinkled—dreadfully practical—change for a ten-pound note in every pocket—ruled account-book in his hand—say, upon the whole, resembling a tax-gatherer. Our dear Richard, sanguine, ardent, overleaping obstacles, bursting with poetry like a young bud, says to this highly respectable companion, 'I see a golden prospect before me; it's very bright, it's very beautiful, it's very joyous; here I go, bounding over the landscape to come at it!' The respectable companion instantly knocks him down with the ruled account-book; tells him, in a literal prosaic way, that he sees no such thing; shows him it's nothing but fees, fraud, horsehair wigs, and black gowns. Now you know that's a painful change; —sensible in the last degree, I have no doubt, but disagreeable. *I* can't do it. I haven't got the ruled account-book. I have none of the tax-gathering elements in my composition, I am not at all respectable, and I don't want to be. Odd perhaps, but so it is!"

It was idle to say more; so I proposed that we should join Ada and Richard, who were a little in advance, and I gave up Mr. Skimpole in despair. He had been over the Hall in the course of the morning, and whimsically described the family pictures as we walked. There were such portentous shepherdesses among the Ladies Dedlock dead and gone, he told us, that peaceful crooks became weapons of assault in their hands. They tended their flocks severely in buckram and powder, and put their sticking-plaster patches on to terrify commoners, as the chiefs of some other tribes put on their war-paint. There was a Sir Somebody Dedlock, with a battle, a sprung-mine, volumes of smoke, flashes of lightning, a town on fire, and a stormed fort, all in full action between his horse's two hind legs: showing, he supposed, how little a Dedlock made of such trifles. The whole race he represented as having evidently been, in life, what he called "stuffed people,"—a large collection, glassy eyed, set up in the most approved manner on their various twigs and perches, very correct, perfectly free from animation, and always in glass cases.

I was not so easy now, during any reference to the name, but that I felt it a relief when Richard, with an exclamation of surprise, hurried away to meet a stranger, whom he first descried coming slowly towards us.

"Dear me!" said Mr. Skimpole. "Vholes!"

We asked if that were a friend of Richard's?

"Friend and legal adviser," said Mr. Skimpole. "Now, my dear Miss Summerson, if you want common sense, responsibility, and respectability, all united—if you want an exemplary man—Vholes is *the* man."

We had not known, we said, that Richard was assisted by any gentleman of that name.

"When he emerged from legal infancy," returned Mr. Skimpole, "he parted from our conversational friend Kenge, and took up, I believe, with Vholes. Indeed, I know he did, because I introduced him to Vholes."

"Had you known him long?" asked Ada.

"Vholes? My dear Miss Clare, I had had that kind of acquaintance with him which I have had with several gentlemen of his profession. He had done something or other, in a very agreeable, civil manner—taken proceedings, I think, is the expression—which ended in the proceeding of his taking *me*. Somebody was so good as to step in and pay the money—something and fourpence was the amount; I forget the pounds and shillings, but I know it ended with fourpence, because it struck me at the time as being so odd that I could owe anybody fourpence—and after that, I brought them together. Vholes asked me for the introduction, and I gave it. Now I come to think of it," he looked inquiringly at us with his frankest smile as he made the discovery, "Vholes bribed me, perhaps? He gave me something, and called it commission. Was it a five-pound note? Do you know, I think it *must* have been a five-pound note!"

His further consideration of the point was prevented by Richard's coming back to us in an excited state, and hastily presenting Mr. Vholes—a sallow man with pinched lips that looked as if they were cold, a red eruption here and there upon his face, tall and thin, about fifty years of age, high-shouldered, and stooping. Dressed in black, black-gloved, and buttoned to the chin, there was nothing so remarkable in him as a lifeless manner, and a slow fixed way he had of looking at Richard.

"I hope I don't disturb you, ladies," said Mr. Vholes; and now I observed that he was further remarkable for an inward manner of speaking. "I arranged with Mr. Carstone that he should always know when his cause was in the Chancellor's paper,[5] and being informed by one of my clerks last night after post time that it stood, rather unexpectedly, in the paper for to-morrow, I put myself into the coach early this morning and came down to confer with him."

"Yes," said Richard, flushed, and looking triumphantly at Ada and me, "we don't do these things in the old slow way, now. We spin along, now! Mr. Vholes, we must hire something to get over to the post town in, and catch the mail to-night, and go by it!"

"Anything you please, sir," returned Mr. Vholes. "I am quite at your service."

"Let me see," said Richard, looking at his watch. "If I run down to the Dedlock, and get my portmanteau fastened up, and order a gig, or a chaise, or whatever's to be got, we shall have an hour then before starting. I'll come back to tea. Cousin Ada, will you and Esther take care of Mr. Vholes while I am gone?"

He was away directly, in his heat and hurry, and was soon lost in the dusk of evening. We who were left walked on towards the house.

"Is Mr. Carstone's presence necessary to-morrow, sir?" said I. "Can it do any good?"

"No, miss," Mr. Vholes replied. "I am not aware that it can."

Both Ada and I expressed our regret that he should go, then, only to be disappointed.

"Mr. Carstone has laid down the principle of watching his own interests," said Mr. Vholes, "and when a client lays down his own principle, and it is not immoral, it devolves upon me to carry it out. I wish in business to be exact and open. I am a widower with three daughters—Emma, Jane, and Caroline—and my desire is so to discharge the duties of life as to leave them a good name. This appears to be a pleasant spot, miss."

The remark being made to me, in consequence of my being next him as we walked, I assented, and enumerated its chief attractions.

"Indeed?" said Mr. Vholes. "I have the privilege of supporting an aged father in the Vale of Taunton—his native place—and I admire that country very much. I had no idea there was anything so attractive here."

To keep up the conversation, I asked Mr. Vholes if he would like to live altogether in the country?

"There, miss," said he, "you touch me on a tender string. My health is not good (my digestion being much impaired), and if I

5. I.e., when it is among cases slated to be considered by the Lord Chancellor on the day assigned.

had only myself to consider, I should take refuge in rural habits; especially as the cares of business have prevented me from ever coming much into contact with general society, and particularly with ladies' society, which I have most wished to mix in. But with my three daughters, Emma, Jane, and Caroline—and my aged father—I cannot afford to be selfish. It is true, I have no longer to maintain a dear grandmother who died in her hundred-and-second year; but enough remains to render it indispensable that the mill should be always going."

It required some attention to hear him, on account of his inward speaking and his lifeless manner.

"You will excuse my having mentioned my daughters," he said. "They are my weak point. I wish to leave the poor girls some little independence, as well as a good name."

We now arrived at Mr. Boythorn's house, where the tea-table, all prepared, was awaiting us. Richard came in restless and hurried, shortly afterwards, and leaning over Mr. Vholes's chair, whispered something in his ear. Mr. Vholes replied aloud—or as nearly aloud I suppose as he ever replied to anything—"You will drive me, will you, sir? It is all the same to me, sir. Anything you please. I am quite at your service."

We understood from what followed that Mr. Skimpole was to be left until the morning to occupy the two places which had been already paid for. As Ada and I were both in low spirits concerning Richard, and very sorry so to part with him, we made it as plain as we politely could that we should leave Mr. Skimpole to the Dedlock Arms, and retire when the night-travellers were gone.

Richard's high spirits carrying everything before them, we all went out together to the top of the hill above the village, where he had ordered a gig to wait; and where we found a man with a lantern standing at the head of the gaunt pale horse[6] that had been harnessed to it.

I never shall forget those two seated side by side in the lantern's light; Richard, all flush and fire and laughter, with the reins in his hand; Mr. Vholes, quite still, black-gloved, and buttoned up, looking at him as if he were looking at his prey and charming it. I have before me the whole picture of the warm dark night, the summer lightning, the dusty track of road closed in by hedgerows and high trees, the gaunt pale horse with his ears pricked up, and the driving away at speed to Jarndyce and Jarndyce.

My dear girl told me, that night, how Richard's being thereafter prosperous or ruined, befriended or deserted, could only make this difference to her, that the more he needed love from one unchang-

6. "And I looked, and beheld a pale horse: and his name that sat on him was Death" (Revelation 6:8).

ing heart, the more love that unchanging heart would have to give him; how he thought of her through his present errors, and she would think of him at all times: never of herself, if she could devote herself to him: never of her own delights, if she could minister to his.

And she kept her word?

I look along the road before me, where the distance already shortens and the journey's end is growing visible; and, true and good above the dead sea of the Chancery suit, and all the ashey fruit it casts ashore,[7] I think I see my darling.

Chapter XXXVIII

A STRUGGLE

When our time came for returning to Bleak House again, we were punctual to the day, and were received with an overpowering welcome. I was perfectly restored to health and strength; and finding my housekeeping keys laid ready for me in my room, rang myself in as if I had been a new year, with a merry little peal. "Once more, duty, duty, Esther," said I; "and if you are not overjoyed to do it, more than cheerfully and contentedly, through anything and everything, you ought to be. That's all I have to say to *you*, my dear!"

The first few mornings were mornings of so much bustle and business, devoted to such settlements of accounts, such repeated journeys to and fro between the Growlery and all other parts of the house, so many re-arrangements of drawers and presses, and such a general new beginning altogether, that I had not a moment's leisure. But when these arrangements were completed, and everything was in order, I paid a visit of a few hours to London, which something in the letter I had destroyed at Chesney Wold had induced me to decide upon in my own mind.

I made Caddy Jellyby—her maiden name was so natural to me that I always called her by it—the pretext for this visit; and wrote her a note previously, asking the favour of her company on a little business expedition. Leaving home very early in the morning, I got to London by stage-coach in such good time, that I got to Newman Street with the day before me.

Caddy, who had not seen me since her wedding-day, was so glad and so affectionate that I was half-inclined to fear I should make

7. Alluding to the legend of the Apples of Sodom which grew on the shores of the Dead Sea. The fruit was of luscious appearance but ashy to taste. The legend was given currency by Thomas Moore's "The Fire Worshippers" in his *Lalla Rookh* (1817) and by Byron's *Childe Harold* (III.xxxiv). See also Deuteronomy 32:32.

her husband jealous. But he was, in his way, just as bad—I mean as good; and in short it was the old story, and nobody would leave me any possibility of doing anything meritorious.

The elder Mr. Turveydrop was in bed, I found, and Caddy was milling his chocolate, which a melancholy little boy who was an apprentice—it seemed such a curious thing to be apprenticed to the trade of dancing—was waiting to carry upstairs. Her father-in-law was extremely kind and considerate, Caddy told me, and they lived most happily together. (When she spoke of their living together, she meant that the old gentleman had all the good things and all the good lodging, while she and her husband had what they could get, and were poked into two corner rooms over the Mews.)[1]

"And how is your mama, Caddy?" said I.

"Why, I hear of her, Esther," replied Caddy, "through Pa; but I see very little of her. We are good friends, I am glad to say; but Ma thinks there is something absurd in my having married a dancing-master, and she is rather afraid of its extending to her."

It struck me that if Mrs. Jellyby had discharged her own natural duties and obligations, before she swept the horizon with a telescope in search of others, she would have taken the best precautions against becoming absurd; but I need scarcely observe that I kept this to myself.

"And your papa, Caddy?"

"He comes here every evening," returned Caddy, "and is so fond of sitting in the corner there, that it's a treat to see him."

Looking at the corner, I plainly perceived the mark of Mr. Jellyby's head against the wall. It was consolatory to know that he had found such a resting-place for it.

"And you, Caddy," said I, "you are always busy, I'll be bound?"

"Well, my dear," returned Caddy, "I am indeed; for to tell you a grand secret, I am qualifying myself to give lessons. Prince's health is not strong, and I want to be able to assist him. What with schools, and classes here, and private pupils, *and* the apprentices, he really has too much to do, poor fellow!"

The notion of the apprentices was still so odd to me, that I asked Caddy if there were many of them?

"Four," said Caddy. "One in-door, and three out. They are very good children, only when they get together they *will* play—children-like—instead of attending to their work. So the little boy you saw just now waltzes by himself in the empty kitchen, and we distribute the others over the house as well as we can."

"That is only for their steps, of course?" said I.

"Only for their steps," said Caddy. "In that way they practise, so many hours at a time, whatever steps they happen to be upon. They

1. Stables.

dance in the academy; and at this time of year we do Figures at five every morning."

"Why, what a laborious life!" I exclaimed.

"I assure you, my dear," returned Caddy, smiling, "when the out-door apprentices ring us up in the morning (the bell rings into our room, not to disturb old Mr. Turveydrop), and when I put up the window, and see them standing on the door-step with their little pumps under their arms, I am actually reminded of the Sweeps."[2]

All this presented the art to me in a singular light, to be sure. Caddy enjoyed the effect of her communication, and cheerfully recounted the particulars of her own studies.

"You see, my dear, to save expense, I ought to know something of the Piano, and I ought to know something of the Kit[3] too, and consequently I have to practise those two instruments as well as the details of our profession. If Ma had been like anybody else, I might have had some little musical knowledge to begin upon. However, I hadn't any; and that part of the work is, at first, a little discouraging, I must allow. But I have a very good ear, and I am used to drudgery—I have to thank Ma for that, at all events—and where there's a will there's a way, you know, Esther, the world over." Saying these words, Caddy laughingly sat down at a little jingling square piano, and really rattled off a quadrille with great spirit. Then she good-humouredly and blushingly got up again, and while she still laughed herself, said, "Don't laugh at me, please; that's a dear girl!"

I would sooner have cried, but I did neither. I encouraged her and praised her with all my heart. For I conscientiously believed, dancing-master's wife though she was, and dancing-mistress though in her limited ambition she aspired to be, she had struck out a natural, wholesome, loving course of industry and perseverance that was quite as good as a Mission.

"My dear," said Caddy, delighted, "you can't think how you cheer me. I shall owe you, you don't know how much. What changes, Esther, even in my small world! You recollect that first night, when I was so unpolite and inky? Who would have thought, then, of my ever teaching people to dance, of all other possibilities and impossibilities!"

Her husband, who had left us while we had this chat, now coming back, preparatory to exercising the apprentices in the ballroom, Caddy informed me she was quite at my disposal. But it was not my time yet, I was glad to tell her; for I should have been vexed

2. Small boys whose work of cleaning chimneys began very early in the morning.

3. Small fiddle used in dance studios. See p. 170.

to take her away then. Therefore we three adjourned to the apprentices together, and I made one in the dance.

The apprentices were the queerest little people. Besides the melancholy boy, who, I hoped, had not been made so by waltzing alone in the empty kitchen, there were two other boys, and one dirty little limp girl in a gauzy dress. Such a precocious little girl, with such a dowdy bonnet on (that, too, of a gauzy texture), who brought her sandalled shoes in an old threadbare velvet reticule. Such mean little boys, when they were not dancing, with string, and marbles, and cramp-bones[4] in their pockets, and the most untidy legs and feet—and heels particularly. I asked Caddy what had made their parents choose this profession for them? Caddy said she didn't know; perhaps they were designed for teachers; perhaps for the stage. They were all people in humble circumstances, and the melancholy boy's mother kept a ginger-beer shop.

We danced for an hour with great gravity; the melancholy child doing wonders with his lower extremities, in which there appeared to be some sense of enjoyment though it never rose above his waist. Caddy, while she was observant of her husband, and was evidently founded upon him, had acquired a grace and self-possession of her own, which, united to her pretty face and figure, was uncommonly agreeable. She already relieved him of much of the instruction of these young people; and he seldom interfered, except to walk his part in the figure if he had anything to do in it. He always played the tune. The affectation of the gauzy child, and her condescension to the boys, was a sight. And thus we danced an hour by the clock.

When the practice was concluded, Caddy's husband made himself ready to go out of town to a school, and Caddy ran away to get ready to go out with me. I sat in the ball-room in the interval, contemplating the apprentices. The two out-door boys went upon the staircase to put on their half-boots, and pull the in-door boy's hair: as I judged from the nature of his objections. Returning with their jackets buttoned, and their pumps stuck in them, they then produced packets of cold bread and meat, and bivouacked under a painted lyre on the wall. The little gauzy child, having whisked her sandals into the reticule and put on a trodden down pair of shoes, shook her head into the dowdy bonnet at one shake; and answering my inquiry whether she liked dancing, by replying, "Not with boys," tied it across her chin and went home contemptuous.

"Old Mr. Turveydrop is so sorry," said Caddy, "that he has not finished dressing yet, and cannot have the pleasure of seeing you before you go. You are such a favourite of his, Esther."

4. Bones from the leg of a sheep, reputed to be a charm against cramps, and also used in children's games.

I expressed myself much obliged to him, but did not think it necessary to add that I readily dispensed with this attention.

"It takes him a long time to dress," said Caddy, "because he is very much looked up to in such things, you know, and has a reputation to support. You can't think how kind he is to Pa. He talks to Pa, of an evening, about the Prince Regent, and I never saw Pa so interested."

There was something in the picture of Mr. Turveydrop bestowing his Deportment on Mr. Jellyby, that quite took my fancy. I asked Caddy, if he brought her papa out much?

"No," said Caddy, "I don't know that he does that; but he talks to Pa, and Pa greatly admires him, and listens, and likes it. Of course I am aware that Pa has hardly any claims to Deportment, but they get on together delightfully. You can't think what good companions they make. I never saw Pa take snuff before in my life; but he takes one pinch out of Mr. Turveydrop's box regularly, and keeps putting it to his nose and taking it away again, all the evening."

That old Mr. Turveydrop should ever, in the chances and changes of life, have come to the rescue of Mr. Jellyby from Borrioboola-Gha, appeared to me to be one of the pleasantest of oddities.

"As to Peepy," said Caddy, with a little hesitation, "whom I was most afraid of—next to having any family of my own, Esther—as an inconvenience to Mr. Turveydrop, the kindness of the old gentleman to that child is beyond everything. He asks to see him, my dear! He lets him take the newspaper up to him in bed; he gives him the crusts of his toast to eat; he sends him on little errands about the house; he tells him to come to me for sixpences. In short," said Caddy, cheerily, "and not to prose, I am a very fortunate girl, and ought to be very grateful. Where are we going, Esther?"

"To the Old Street Road," said I; "where I have a few words to say to the solicitor's clerk, who was sent to greet me at the coach-office on the very day when I came to London, and first saw you, my dear. Now I think of it, the gentleman who brought us to your house."

"Then, indeed, I seem to be naturally the person to go with you," returned Caddy.

To the Old Street Road we went, and there inquired at Mrs. Guppy's residence for Mrs. Guppy. Mrs. Guppy, occupying the parlours, and having indeed been visibly in danger of cracking herself like a nut in the front parlour-door by peeping out before she was asked for, immediately presented herself, and requested us to walk in. She was an old lady in a large cap, with rather a red nose and rather an unsteady eye, but smiling all over. Her close little sitting-room was prepared for a visit; and there was a portrait of her son in it, which, I had almost written here, was more like than life: it insisted upon him with such obstinacy, and was so determined not to let him off.

Not only was the portrait there, but we found the original there too. He was dressed in a great many colours, and was discovered at a table reading law-papers with his forefinger to his forehead.

"Miss Summerson," said Mr. Guppy, rising, "this is indeed an Oasis. Mother, will you be so good as to put a chair for the other lady, and get out of the gangway?"

Mrs. Guppy, whose incessant smiling gave her quite a waggish appearance, did as her son requested; and then sat down in a corner, holding her pocket-handkerchief to her chest, like a fomentation, with both hands.

I presented Caddy, and Mr. Guppy said that any friend of mine was more than welcome. I then proceeded to the object of my visit.

"I took the liberty of sending you a note, sir," said I.

Mr. Guppy acknowledged its receipt by taking it out of his breast-pocket, putting it to his lips, and returning it to his pocket with a bow. Mr. Guppy's mother was so diverted that she rolled her head as she smiled, and made a silent appeal to Caddy with her elbow.

"Could I speak to you alone for a moment?" said I.

Anything like the jocoseness of Mr. Guppy's mother now, I think I never saw. She made no sound of laughter; but she rolled her head, and shook it and put her handkerchief to her mouth, and appealed to Caddy with her elbow, and her hand, and her shoulder, and was so unspeakably entertained altogether that it was with some difficulty she could marshal Caddy through the little folding-door into her bedroom adjoining.

"Miss Summerson," said Mr. Guppy, "you will excuse the waywardness of a parent ever mindful of a son's appiness. My mother, though highly exasperating to the feelings, is actuated by maternal dictates."

I could hardly have believed that anybody could in a moment have turned so red, or changed so much, as Mr. Guppy did when I now put up my veil.

"I asked the favour of seeing you for a few minutes here," said I, "in preference to calling at Mr. Kenge's, because, remembering what you said on an occasion when you spoke to me in confidence, I feared I might otherwise cause you some embarrassment, Mr. Guppy."

I caused him embarrassment enough as it was, I am sure. I never saw such faltering, such confusion, such amazement and apprehension.

"Miss Summerson," stammered Mr. Guppy, "I—I—beg your pardon, but in our profession—we—we—find it necessary to be explicit. You have referred to an occasion, miss, when I—when I did myself the honour of making a declaration which——"

Something seemed to rise in his throat that he could not possibly swallow. He put his hand there, coughed, made faces, tried again to swallow it, coughed again, made faces again, looked all round the room, and fluttered his papers.

"A kind of a giddy sensation has come upon me, miss," he explained, "which rather knocks me over. I—er—a little subject to this sort of thing—er—By George!"

I gave him a little time to recover. He consumed it in putting his hand to his forehead and taking it away again, and in backing his chair into the corner behind him.

"My intention was to remark, miss," said Mr. Guppy, "—dear me—something bronchial, I think—hem!—to remark that you was so good on that occasion as to repel and repudiate that declaration. You—you wouldn't perhaps object to admit that? Though no witnesses are present, it might be a satisfaction to—to your mind—if you was to put in that admission."

"There can be no doubt," said I, "that I declined your proposal without any reservation or qualification whatever, Mr. Guppy."

"Thank you, miss," he returned, measuring the table with his troubled hands. "So far that's satisfactory, and it does you credit. Er—this is certainly bronchial!—must be in the tubes—er—you wouldn't perhaps be offended if I was to mention—not that it's necessary, for your own good sense or any person's sense must show 'em that—if I was to mention that such declaration on my part was final, and there terminated?"

"I quite understand that," said I.

"Perhaps—er—it may not be worth the form, but it might be a satisfaction to your mind—perhaps you wouldn't object to admit that, miss?" said Mr. Guppy.

"I admit it most fully and freely," said I.

"Thank you," returned Mr. Guppy. "Very honourable, I am sure. I regret that my arrangements in life, combined with circumstances over which I have no control, will put it out of my power ever to fall back upon that offer, or to renew it in any shape or form whatever; but it will ever be a retrospect entwined—er—with friendship's bowers." Mr. Guppy's bronchitis came to his relief, and stopped his measurement of the table.

"I may now perhaps mention what I wished to say to you?" I began.

"I shall be honoured, I am sure," said Mr. Guppy. "I am so persuaded that your own good sense and right feeling, miss, will—will keep you as square as possible—that I can have nothing but pleasure, I am sure, in hearing any observation you may wish to offer."

"You were so good as to imply, on that occasion——"

"Excuse me, miss," said Mr. Guppy, "but we had better not travel out of the record into implication. I cannot admit that I implied anything."

"You said on that occasion," I recommenced, "that you might possibly have the means of advancing my interests, and promoting my fortunes, by making discoveries of which I should be the subject. I presume that you founded that belief upon your general knowledge of my being an orphan girl, indebted for everything to the benevolence of Mr. Jarndyce. Now, the beginning and the end of what I have come to beg of you is, Mr. Guppy, that you will have the kindness to relinquish all idea of so serving me. I have thought of this sometimes, and I have thought of it most, lately—since I have been ill. At length I have decided, in case you should at any time recall that purpose, and act upon it in any way, to come to you, and assure you that you are altogether mistaken. You could make no discovery in reference to me that would do me the least service, or give me the least pleasure. I am acquainted with my personal history; and I have it in my power to assure you that you never can advance my welfare by such means. You may, perhaps, have abandoned this project a long time. If so, excuse my giving you unnecessary trouble. If not, I entreat you, on the assurance I have given you, henceforth to lay it aside. I beg you to do this, for my peace."

"I am bound to confess," said Mr. Guppy, "that you express yourself, miss, with that good sense and right feeling for which I gave you credit. Nothing can be more satisfactory than such right feeling, and if I mistook any intentions on your part just now, I am prepared to tender a full apology. I should wish to be understood, miss, as hereby offering that apology—limiting it, as your own good sense and right feeling will point out the necessity of, to the present proceedings."

I must say for Mr. Guppy that the shuffling manner he had had upon him improved very much. He seemed truly glad to be able to do something I asked, and he looked ashamed.

"If you will allow me to finish what I have to say at once, so that I may have no occasion to resume," I went on, seeing him about to speak, "you will do me a kindness, sir. I come to you as privately as possible, because you announced this impression of yours to me in a confidence which I have really wished to respect—and which I always have respected, as you remember. I have mentioned my illness. There really is no reason why I should hesitate to say that I know very well that any little delicacy I might have had in making a request to you, is quite removed. Therefore I make the entreaty I have now preferred; and I hope you will have sufficient consideration for me, to accede to it."

I must do Mr. Guppy the further justice of saying that he had looked more and more ashamed, and that he looked most ashamed, and very earnest, when he now replied with a burning face:

"Upon my word and honour, upon my life, upon my soul, Miss Summerson, as I am a living man, I'll act according to your wish! I'll never go another step in opposition to it. I'll take my oath to it, if it will be any satisfaction to you. In what I promise at this present time touching the matters now in question," continued Mr. Guppy, rapidly, as if he were repeating a familiar form of words. "I speak the truth, the whole truth, and nothing but the truth, so——"

"I am quite satisfied," said I, rising at this point, "and I thank you very much. Caddy, my dear, I am ready!"

Mr. Guppy's mother returned with Caddy (now making me the recipient of her silent laughter and her nudges), and we took our leave. Mr. Guppy saw us to the door with the air of one who was either imperfectly awake or walking in his sleep; and we left him there, staring.

But in a minute he came after us down the street without any hat, and with his long hair all blown about, and stopped us, saying fervently:

"Miss Summerson, upon my honour and soul, you may depend upon me!"

"I do," said I, "quite confidently."

"I beg your pardon, miss," said Mr. Guppy, going with one leg and staying with the other, "but this lady being present—your own witness—it might be a satisfaction to your mind (which I should wish to set at rest) if you was to repeat those admissions."

"Well, Caddy," said I, turning to her, "perhaps you will not be surprised when I tell you, my dear, that there never has been any engagement—"

"No proposal or promise of marriage whatsoever," suggested Mr. Guppy.

"No proposal or promise of marriage whatsoever," said I, "between this gentleman—"

"William Guppy of Penton Place, Pentonville, in the county of Middlesex," he murmured.

"Between this gentleman, Mr. William Guppy, of Penton Place, Pentonville, in the county of Middlesex, and myself."

"Thank you, miss," said Mr. Guppy. "Very full,—er—excuse me —lady's name, Christian and surname both?"

I gave them.

"Married woman, I believe?" said Mr. Guppy. "Married woman. Thank you. Formerly Caroline Jellyby, spinster, then of Thavies Inn, within the city of London, but extra-parochial;[5] now of Newman Street, Oxford Street. Much obliged."

He ran home and came running back again.

"Touching that matter, you know, I really and truly am very sorry that my arrangements in life, combined with circumstances over which I have no control, should prevent a renewal of what was wholly terminated some time back," said Mr. Guppy to me, forlornly and despondently, "but it couldn't be. Now *could* it, you know! I only put it to you."

I replied it certainly could not. The subject did not admit of a doubt. He thanked me, and ran to his mother's again—and back again.

"It's very honourable of you, miss, I am sure," said Mr. Guppy. "If an altar could be erected in the bowers of friendship—but, upon my soul, you may rely upon me in every respect, save and except the tender passion only!"

The struggle in Mr. Guppy's breast, and the numerous oscillations it occasioned him between his mother's door and us, were sufficiently conspicuous in the windy street (particularly as his hair wanted cutting), to make us hurry away. I did so with a lightened heart; but when we last looked back, Mr. Guppy was still oscillating in the same troubled state of mind.

Chapter XXXIX

ATTORNEY AND CLIENT

The name of MR. VHOLES, preceded by the legend GROUND FLOOR, is inscribed upon a door-post in Symond's Inn, Chancery Lane; a little, pale, wall-eyed, woe-begone inn, like a large dust-binn of two compartments and a sifter.[1] It looks as if Symond were a sparing man in his day, and constructed his inn of old building

5. Some Inns were exempt from paying taxes to the district in which they were located and were hence outside the authority of their parish.

1. A *dust-binn* was a box, fitted with doored compartments, for depositing ashes and rubbish. On top was a *sifter*, a wooden tray with high edges, fitted with a wire mesh to strain ashes from coal. For a lawyer's account of a similar dingy office, see Eugene Wrayburn in *Our Mutual Friend* (ch. III): "There are four of us, with our names painted on a door-post in right of one black hole called a set of chambers."

materials, which took kindly to the dry rot and to dirt and all things decaying and dismal, and perpetuated Symond's memory with congenial shabbiness. Quartered in this dingy hatchment[2] commemorative of Symond, are the legal bearings of Mr. Vholes.

Mr. Vholes's office, in disposition retiring and in situation retired, is squeezed up in a corner, and blinks at a dead wall. Three feet of knotty floored dark passage bring the client to Mr. Vholes's jet black door, in an angle profoundly dark on the brightest midsummer morning, and encumbered by a black bulkhead of cellarage staircase, against which belated civilians generally strike their brows. Mr. Vholes's chambers are on so small a scale, that one clerk can open the door without getting off his stool, while the other who elbows him at the same desk has equal facilities for poking the fire. A smell as of unwholesome sheep, blending with the smell of must and dust, is referable to the nightly (and often daily) consumption of mutton fat in candles, and to the fretting of parchment forms and skins in greasy drawers. The atmosphere is otherwise stale and close. The place was last painted or whitewashed beyond the memory of man, and the two chimneys smoke, and there is a loose outer surface of soot everywhere, and the dull cracked windows in their heavy frames have but one piece of character in them, which is a determination to be always dirty, and always shut, unless coerced. This accounts for the phenomenon of the weaker of the two usually having a bundle of firewood thrust between its jaws in hot weather.

Mr. Vholes is a very respectable man. He has not a large business, but he is a very respectable man. He is allowed by the greater attorneys who have made good fortunes, or are making them, to be a most respectable man. He never misses a chance in his practice; which is a mark of respectability. He never takes any pleasure; which is another mark of respectability. He is reserved and serious, which is another mark of respectability. His digestion is impaired, which is highly respectable. And he is making hay of the grass which is flesh,[3] for his three daughters. And his father is dependent on him in the Vale of Taunton.

The one great principle of the English law is, to make business for itself. There is no other principle distinctly, certainly, and consistently maintained through all its narrow turnings. Viewed by this light it becomes a coherent scheme, and not the monstrous maze the laity are apt to think it. Let them but once clearly perceive that its grand principle is to make business for itself at their expense, and surely they will cease to grumble.

But, not perceiving this quite plainly—only seeing it by halves in

2. Memorial to a man's achievement, usually a panel featuring his coat of arms and often a motto called, in heraldry, his *bearings*.

3. "For all flesh is as grass. . . . The grass withereth, and the flower thereof falleth away" (I Peter 1:24).

a confused way—the laity sometimes suffer in peace and pocket, with a bad grace, and *do* grumble very much. Then this respectability of Mr. Vholes is brought into powerful play against them. "Repeal this statute, my good sir?" says Mr. Kenge, to a smarting client, "repeal it, my dear sir? Never, with my consent. Alter this law, sir, and what will be the effect of your rash proceeding on a class of practitioners very worthily represented, allow me to say to you, by the opposite attorney in the case, Mr. Vholes? Sir, that class of practitioners would be swept from the face of the earth. Now you cannot afford—I would say, the social system cannot afford—to lose an order of men like Mr. Vholes. Diligent, persevering, steady, acute in business.[4] My dear sir, I understand your present feelings against the existing state of things, which I grant to be a little hard in your case; but I can never raise my voice for the demolition of a class of men like Mr. Vholes." The respectability of Mr. Vholes has even been cited with crushing effect before Parliamentary committees, as in the following blue minutes[5] of a distinguished attorney's evidence. "Question (number five hundred and seventeen thousand eight hundred and sixty-nine). If I understand you, these forms of practice indisputably occasion delay? Answer. Yes, some delay. Question. And great expense? Answer. Most assuredly they cannot be gone through for nothing. Question. And unspeakable vexation? Answer. I am not prepared to say that. They have never given *me* any vexation; quite the contrary. Question. But you think that their abolition would damage a class of practitioners? Answer. I have no doubt of it. Question. Can you instance any type of that class? Answer. Yes. I would unhesitatingly mention Mr. Vholes. He would be ruined. Question. Mr. Vholes is considered, in the profession, a respectable man? Answer"—which proved fatal to the inquiry for ten years—"Mr. Vholes is considered, in the profession, a *most* respectable man."

So in familiar conversation, private authorities no less disinterested will remark that they don't know what this age is coming to; that we are plunging down precipices; that now here is something else gone; and these changes are death to people like Vholes; a man of undoubted respectability, with a father in the Vale of Taunton, and three daughters at home. Take a few steps more in this direction, say they, and what is to become of Vholes's father? Is he to perish? And of Vholes's daughters? Are they to be shirt-makers or governesses? As though, Mr. Vholes and his relations being minor cannibal chiefs, and it being proposed to abolish cannibalism, indignant champions were to put the case thus: Make man-eating unlawful, and you starve the Vholeses!

In a word, Mr. Vholes, with his three daughters and his father in

4. See Romans 12:11 and Proverbs 22:29.

5. Minutes recorded on blue paper used for official documents.

the Vale of Taunton, is continually doing duty, like a piece of timber, to shore up some decayed foundation that has become a pitfall and a nuisance. And with a great many people in a great many instances, the question is never one of a change from Wrong to Right (which is quite an extraneous consideration), but is always one of injury or advantage to that eminently respectable legion, Vholes.

The Chancellor is, within these ten minutes, "up" for the long vacation. Mr. Vholes, and his young client, and several blue bags hastily stuffed, out of all regularity of form, as the larger sort of serpents are in their first gorged state, have returned to the official den. Mr. Vholes, quiet and unmoved, as a man of so much respectability ought to be, takes off his close black gloves as if he were skinning his hands, lifts off his tight hat as if he were scalping himself, and sits down at his desk. The client throws his hat and gloves upon the ground—tosses them anywhere, without looking after them or caring where they go; flings himself into a chair, half sighing and halt groaning; rests his aching head upon his hand, and looks the portrait of Young Despair.

"Again nothing done!" says Richard. "Nothing, nothing done!"

"Don't say nothing done, sir," returns the placid Vholes. "That is scarcely fair, sir, scarcely fair!"

"Why, what *is* done?" says Richard, turning gloomily upon him.

"That may not be the whole question," returns Vholes. "The question may branch off into what is doing, what is doing?"

"And what is doing?" asks the moody client.

Vholes, sitting with his arms on the desk, quietly bringing the tips of his five right fingers to meet the tips of his five left fingers, and quietly separating them again, and fixedly and slowly looking at his client, replies:

"A good deal is doing, sir. We have put our shoulders to the wheel, Mr. Carstone, and the wheel is going round."

"Yes, with Ixion[6] on it. How am I to get through the next four or five accursed months?" exclaims the young man, rising from his chair and walking about the room.

"Mr. C," returns Vholes, following him close with his eyes wherever he goes, "your spirits are hasty, and I am sorry for it on your account. Excuse me if I recommend you not to chafe so much, not to be so impetuous, not to wear yourself out so. You should have more patience. You should sustain yourself better."

"I ought to imitate you, in fact, Mr. Vholes?" says Richard, sitting down again with an impatient laugh, and beating the Devil's Tattoo[7] with his boot on the patternless carpet.

6. A king whose punishment for crimes was to be eternally bound in Hades to an ever-revolving wheel of fire.

7. A tapping or drumming signifying impatience.

"Sir," returns Vholes, always looking at the client, as if he were making a lingering meal of him with his eyes as well as with his professional appetite. "Sir," returns Vholes, with his inward manner of speech and his bloodless quietude; "I should not have had the presumption to propose myself as a model, for your imitation or any man's. Let me but leave a good name to my three daughters, and that is enough for me; I am not a self-seeker. But, since you mention me so pointedly, I will acknowledge that I should like to impart to you a little of my—come, sir, you are disposed to call it insensibility, and I am sure I have no objection—say insensibility—a little of my insensibility."

"Mr. Vholes," explains the client, somewhat abashed, "I had no intention to accuse you of insensibility."

"I think you had, sir, without knowing it," returns the equable Vholes. "Very naturally. It is my duty to attend to your interests with a cool head, and I can quite understand that to your excited feelings I may appear, at such times as the present, insensible. My daughters may know me better; my aged father may know me better. But they have known me much longer than you have, and the confiding eye of affection is not the distrustful eye of business. Not that I complain, sir, of the eye of business being distrustful; quite the contrary. In attending to your interests, I wish to have all possible checks upon me; it is right that I should have them; I court inquiry. But your interests demand that I should be cool and methodical, Mr. Carstone; and I cannot be otherwise—no, sir, not even to please you."

Mr. Vholes, after glancing at the official cat who is patiently watching a mouse's hole, fixes his charmed gaze again on his young client, and proceeds in his buttoned-up half-audible voice as if there were an unclean spirit[8] in him that will neither come out nor speak out:

"What are you to do, sir, you inquire, during the vacation. I should hope you gentlemen of the army may find many means of amusing yourselves, if you give your minds to it. If you had asked me what *I* was to do, during the vacation, I could have answered you more readily. I am to attend to your interests. I am to be found here day by day, attending to your interests. That is my duty, Mr. C; and term-time or vacation makes no difference to me. If you wish to consult me as to your interests, you will find me here at all times alike. Other professional men go out of town. I don't. Not that I blame them for going; I merely say, I don't go. This desk is your rock,[9] sir!"

Mr. Vholes gives it a rap, and it sounds as hollow as a coffin. Not

8. See the "Baptism" service in *The Book of Common Prayer*: "I command thee, unclean spirit . . . that thou come out, and depart from these infants."

9. See Matthew 7:24–25.

to Richard, though. There is encouragement in the sound to him. Perhaps Mr. Vholes knows there is.

"I am perfectly aware, Mr. Vholes," says Richard, more familiarly and good-humouredly, "that you are the most reliable fellow in the world; and that to have to do with you, is to have to do with a man of business who is not to be hoodwinked. But put yourself in my case, dragging on this dislocated life, sinking deeper and deeper into difficulty every day, continually hoping and continually disappointed, conscious of change upon change for the worse in myself, and of no change for the better in anything else; and you will find it a dark-looking case sometimes, as I do."

"You know," says Mr. Vholes, "that I never give hopes, sir. I told you from the first, Mr. C, that I never give hopes. Particularly in a case like this, where the greater part of the costs comes out of the estate, I should not be considerate of my good name, if I gave hopes. It might seem as if costs were my object. Still, when you say there is no change for the better, I must, as a bare matter of fact, deny that."

"Aye?" returns Richard, brightening. "But how do you make it out?"

"Mr. Carstone, you are represented by——"

"You said just now—a rock."

"Yes, sir," says Mr. Vholes, gently shaking his head and rapping the hollow desk, with a sound as if ashes were falling on ashes, and dust on dust,[1] a rock."That's something. You are separately represented, and no longer hidden and lost in the interests of others. *That's* something. The suit does not sleep; we wake it up, we air it, we walk it about. *That's* something. It's not all Jarndyce,[2] in fact as well as in name. *That's* something. Nobody has it all his own way now, sir. And *that's* something, surely."

Richard, his face flushing suddenly, strikes the desk with his clenched hand.

"Mr. Vholes! If any man had told me, when I first went to John Jarndyce's house, that he was anything but the disinterested friend he seemed—that he was what he has gradually turned out to be—I could have found no words strong enough to repel the slander; I could not have defended him too ardently. So little did I know of the world! Whereas, now, I do declare to you that he becomes to me the embodiment of the suit; that, in place of its being an abstraction, it is John Jarndyce; that the more I suffer, the more

1. See the "Burial of the Dead" ceremony in *The Book of Common Prayer*: "we therefore commit his body to the ground: earth to earth, ashes to ashes, dust to dust."

2. I.e., the suit is no longer exclusively concerned with Jarndyce because Carstone is now part of it. Vholes also seems to be drawing on the analogy (especially evident in British pronunciation) between *Jarndyce* and *jaundice*.

indignant I am with him; that every new delay, and every new disappointment, is only a new injury from John Jarndyce's hand."

"No, no," says Vholes. "Don't say so. We ought to have patience, all of us. Besides, I never disparage, sir, I never disparage."

"Mr. Vholes," returns the angry client. "You know as well as I, that he would have strangled the suit if he could."

"He was not active in it," Mr. Vholes admits, with an appearance of reluctance. "He certainly was not active in it. But however, but however, he might have had amiable intentions. Who can read the heart, Mr. C?"

"You can," returns Richard.

"I, Mr. C?"

"Well enough to know what his intentions were. Are, or are not, our interests conflicting? Tell—me—that?" says Richard, accompanying his last three words with three raps on his rock of trust.

"Mr. C," returns Vholes, immovable in attitude and never winking his hungry eyes, "I should be wanting in my duty as your professional adviser, I should be departing from my fidelity to your interests, if I represented those interests as identical with the interests of Mr. Jarndyce. They are no such thing, sir. I never impute motives; I both have, and am, a father, and I never impute motives. But I must not shrink from a professional duty, even if it sows dissension in families. I understand you to be now consulting me professionally, as to your interests? You are so? I reply then, they are not identical with those of Mr. Jarndyce."

"Of course they are not!" cries Richard. "You found that out, long ago."

"Mr. C," returns Vholes, "I wish to say no more of any third party than is necessary. I wish to leave my good name unsullied, together with any little property of which I may become possessed through industry and perseverance, to my daughters Emma, Jane, and Caroline. I also desire to live in amity with my professional brethren. When Mr. Skimpole did me the honour, sir—I will not say the very high honour, for I never stoop to flattery—of bringing us together in this room, I mentioned to you that I could offer no opinion or advice as to your interests, while those interests were intrusted to another member of the profession. And I spoke in such terms as I was bound to speak, of Kenge and Carboy's office, which stands high. You, sir, thought fit to withdraw your interests from that keeping nevertheless, and to offer them to me. You brought them with clean hands, sir, and I accepted them with clean hands. Those interests are now paramount in this office. My digestive functions, as you may have heard me mention, are not in a good state, and rest might improve them; but I shall not rest, sir, while I am your representative. Whenever you want me, you will find me here.

Summon me anywhere, and I will come. During the long vacation, sir, I shall devote my leisure to studying your interests more and more closely, and to making arrangements for moving heaven and earth (including, of course, the Chancellor) after Michaelmas term; and when I ultimately congratulate you, sir," says Mr. Vholes, with the severity of a determined man, "when I ultimately congratulate you, sir, with all my heart, on your accession to fortune—which, but that I never give hopes, I might say something further about—you will owe me nothing beyond whatever little balance may be then outstanding of the costs as between solicitor and client, not included in the taxed costs allowed out of the estate. I pretend to no claim upon you, Mr. C, but for the zealous and active discharge—not the languid and routine discharge, sir: that much credit I stipulate for—of my professional duty. My duty prosperously ended, all between us is ended."

Vholes finally adds, by way of rider to this declaration of his principles, that as Mr. Carstone is about to rejoin his regiment, perhaps Mr. C will favour him with an order on his agent for twenty pounds on account.

"For there have been many little consultations and attendances of late, sir," observes Vholes, turning over the leaves of his Diary, "and these things mount up, and I don't profess to be a man of capital. When we first entered on our present relations, I stated to you openly—it is a principle of mine that there never can be too much openness between solicitor and client—that I was not a man of capital; and that if capital was your object, you had better leave your papers in Kenge's office. No, Mr. C, you will find none of the advantages, or disadvantages, of capital here, sir. This," Vholes gives the desk one hollow blow again, "is your rock; it pretends to be nothing more."

The client, with his dejection insensibly relieved, and his vague hopes rekindled, takes pen and ink and writes the draft; not without perplexed consideration and calculation of the date it may bear, implying scant effects in the agent's hands. All the while, Vholes, buttoned up in body and mind, looks at him attentively. All the while, Vholes's official cat watches the mouse's hole.

Lastly, the client, shaking hands, beseeches Mr. Vholes, for Heaven's sake and Earth's sake, to do his utmost to "pull him through" the Court of Chancery. Mr. Vholes, who never gives hopes, lays his palm upon the client's shoulder, and answers with a smile, "Always here, sir. Personally, or by letter, you will always find me here, sir, with my shoulder to the wheel." Thus they part; and Vholes, left alone, employs himself in carrying sundry little matters out of his Diary and into his draft book, for the ultimate behoof of his three daughters. So might an industrious fox, or bear, make up his account of chickens or stray travellers with an eye to his cubs; not to disparage by that word the three raw-visaged, lank, and buttoned-up maidens, who dwell with the parent Vholes in an earthy cottage situated in a damp garden at Kennington.

Richard, emerging from the heavy shade of Symond's Inn into the sunshine of Chancery Lane—for there happens to be sunshine there to-day—walks thoughtfully on, and turns into Lincoln's Inn, and passes under the shadow of the Lincoln's Inn trees. On many such loungers have the speckled shadows of those trees often fallen; on the like bent head, the bitten nail, the lowering eye, the lingering step, the purposeless and dreamy air, the good consuming and consumed, the life turned sour. This lounger is not shabby yet, but that may come. Chancery, which knows no wisdom but in Precedent, is very rich in such Precedents; and why should one be different from ten thousand?

Yet the time is so short since his depreciation began, that as he saunters away, reluctant to leave the spot for some long months together, though he hates it, Richard himself may feel his own case as if it were a startling one. While his heart is heavy with corroding care, suspense, distrust, and doubt, it may have room for some sorrowful wonder when he recalls how different his first visit there, how different he, how different all the colours of his mind. But injustice breeds injustice; the fighting with shadows and being defeated by them, necessitates the setting up of substances to combat; from the impalpable suit which no man alive can understand, the time for that being long gone by, it has become a gloomy relief to turn to the palpable figure of the friend who would have saved him from this ruin, and make *him* his enemy. Richard has told Vholes the truth. Is he in a hardened or a softened mood, he still lays his injuries equally at that door; he was thwarted, in that quarter, of a set putpose, and that purpose could only originate in the one subject that is resolving his existence into itself; besides it is a justification to him in his own eyes to have an embodied antagonist and oppressor.

Is Richard a monster in all this,—or would Chancery be found rich in such Precedents too, if they could be got for citation from the Recording Angel?

Two pairs of eyes not unused to such people look after him, as, biting his nails and brooding, he crosses the square, and is swallowed up by the shadow of the southern gateway. Mr. Guppy and Mr. Weevle are the possessors of those eyes, and they have been leaning in conversation against the low stone parapet under the trees. He passed close by them, seeing nothing but the ground.

"William," says Mr. Weevle, adjusting his whiskers; "there's combustion going on there! It's not a case of Spontaneous, but it's smouldering combustion it is."

"Ah!" says Mr. Guppy, "he wouldn't keep out of Jarndyce, and I suppose he's over head and ears in debt. I never knew much of him. He was as high as the Monument[3] when he was on trial at our place. A good riddance to me, whether as clerk or client! Well, Tony, that, as I was mentioning, is what they're up to."

Mr. Guppy, refolding his arms, resettles himself against the parapet, as resuming a conversation of interest.

"They are still up to it, sir," says Mr. Guppy, "still taking stock, still examining papers, still going over the heaps and heaps of rubbish. At this rate they'll be at it these seven years."

"And Small is helping?"

"Small left us at a week's notice. Told Kenge, his grandfather's business was too much for the old gentleman, and he could better himself by undertaking it. There had been a coolness between myself and Small on account of his being so close. But he said you and I began it; and as he had me there—for we did—I put our acquaintance on the old footing. That's how I come to know what they're up to."

"You haven't looked in at all?"

"Tony," says Mr. Guppy, a little disconcerted, "to be unreserved with you, I don't greatly relish the house, except in your company, and therefore I have not; and therefore I proposed this little appointment for our fetching away your things. There goes the hour by the clock! Tony"; Mr. Guppy becomes mysteriously and tenderly eloquent; "it is necessary that I should impress upon your mind once more, that circumstances over which I have no control, have made a melancholy alteration in my most cherished plans, and in that unrequited image which I formerly mentioned to you as a friend. That image is shattered, and that idol is laid low. My only wish now, in connexion with the objects which I had an idea of carrying out in the court, with your aid as a friend, is to let 'em alone and bury 'em in oblivion. Do you think it possible, do you think it at all likely (I put it to you, Tony, as a friend), from your knowledge of the ways of that capricious and deep old character who fell a prey to the—Spontaneous element; do you, Tony, think it at all likely that, on second thoughts, he put those letters away anywhere, after you saw him alive, and that they were not destroyed that night?"

Mr. Weevle reflects for some time. Shakes his head. Decidedly thinks not.

"Tony," says Mr. Guppy, as they walk towards the court, "once again understand me, as a friend. Without entering into further explanations, I may repeat that the idol is down. I have no purpose to serve now, but burial in oblivion. To that I have pledged myself.

3. A high stone column erected in the 1670's to commemorate the Great Fire that had destroyed the center of London.

I owe it to myself, and I owe it to the shattered image, as also to the circumstances over which I have no control. If you was to express to me by a gesture, by a wink, that you saw lying anywhere in your late lodgings, any papers that so much as looked like the papers in question, I would pitch them into the fire, sir, on my own responsibility."

Mr. Weevle nods. Mr. Guppy, much elevated in his own opinion by having delivered these observations, with an air in part forensic and in part romantic—this gentleman having a passion for conducting anything in the form of an examination, or delivering anything in the form of a summing up or a speech—accompanies his friend with dignity to the court.

Never, since it has been a court, has it had such a Fortunatus's[4] purse of gossip as in the proceedings at the rag and bottle shop. Regularly, every morning at eight, is the elder Mr. Smallweed brought down to the corner and carried in, accompanied by Mrs. Smallweed, Judy, and Bart; and regularly, all day, do they all remain there until nine at night, solaced by gipsy dinners, not abundant in quantity, from the cook's shop; rummaging and searching, digging, delving, and diving among the treasures of the late lamented. What those treasures are, they keep so secret, that the court is maddened. In its delirium it imagines guineas pouring out of teapots, crown-pieces overflowing punch-bowls, old chairs and mattresses stuffed with Bank of England notes. It possesses itself of the sixpenny history (with highly-coloured folding frontispiece) of Mr. Daniel Dancer and his sister, and also of Mr. Elwes, of Suffolk, and transfers all the facts from those authentic narratives[5] to Mr. Krook. Twice when the dustman is called in to carry off a cartload of old paper, ashes, and broken bottles, the whole court assembles and pries into the baskets as they come forth. Many times the two gentlemen who write with the ravenous little pens on the tissue paper are seen prowling in the neighbourhood—shy of each other—their late partnership being dissolved. The Sol skilfully carries a vein of the prevailing interest through the Harmonic nights. Little Swills, in what are professionally known as "patter" allusions to the subject, is received with loud applause; and the same vocalist "gags" in the regular business like a man inspired. Even Miss M. Melvilleson, in the revived Caledonian melody of "We're a' nodding,"[6] points

4. Hero of a sixteenth-century romance who acquired a magic purse containing inexhaustible supplies of money.

5. Pamphlets telling the sensational stories of two misers, Daniel Dancer (1716–94) and John Elwes (1714–89). Both men had lived in squalor like Krook, and both left vast fortunes at the time of their deaths.

6. "We're A' Noddin," an old Scottish song, adapted by Robert Burns, includes a stanza: "Cats like milk,/ And dogs like broo [i.e., broth]; Lads like lasses weel,/ And lasses lads too." The chorus refers to everyone at our home being joyous: "We're a' noddin,/ Nid nid noddin,/ We're a' noddin/ At our house at hame!"

the sentiment that "the dogs love broo" (whatever the nature of that refreshment may be) with such archness, and such a turn of the head towards next door, that she is immediately understood to mean, Mr. Smallweed loves to find money, and is nightly honoured with a double encore. For all this, the court discovers nothing; and, as Mrs. Piper and Mrs. Perkins now communicate to the late lodger whose appearance is the signal for a general rally, it is in one continued ferment to discover everything, and more.

Mr. Weevle and Mr. Guppy, with every eye in the court's head upon them, knock at the closed door of the late lamented's house, in a high state of popularity. But, being contrary to the court's expectation admitted, they immediately become unpopular, and are considered to mean no good.

The shutters are more or less closed all over the house, and the ground-floor is sufficiently dark to require candles. Introduced into the back shop by Mr. Smallweed the younger, they, fresh from the sunlight, can at first see nothing save darkness and shadows; but they gradually discern the elder Mr. Smallweed, seated in his chair upon the brink of a well or grave of waste paper; the virtuous Judy groping therein, like a female sexton; and Mrs. Smallweed on the level ground in the vicinity, dirtily snowed up in a heap of paper fragments, print and manuscript, which would appear to be the accumulated compliments that have been sent flying at her in the course of the day. The whole party, Small included, are blackened with dust and dirt, and present a fiendish appearance not relieved by the general aspect of the room. There is more litter and lumber in it than of old, and it is dirtier if possible; likewise, it is ghostly with traces of its dead inhabitant, and even with his chalked writing on the wall.

On the entrance of visitors, Mr. Smallweed and Judy simultaneously fold their arms and stop in their researches.

"Aha!" croaks the old gentleman. "How de do, gentlemen, how de do! Come to fetch your property, Mr. Weevle? That's well, that's well. Ha! ha! We should have been forced to sell you up, sir, to pay your warehouse room, if you had left it here much longer. You feel quite at home here, again, I dare say? Glad to see you, glad to see you!"

Mr. Weevle, thanking him, casts an eye about. Mr. Guppy's eye follows Mr. Weevle's eye. Mr. Weevle's eye comes back without any new intelligence in it. Mr. Guppy's eye comes back, and meets Mr. Smallweed's eye. That engaging old gentleman is still murmuring, like some wound-up instrument running down. "How de do, sir—how de—how——" And then having run down, he lapses into grinning silence, as Mr. Guppy starts at seeing Mr. Tulkinghorn standing in the darkness opposite, with his hands behind him.

"Gentleman so kind as to act as my solicitor," says Grandfather

Smallweed. "I am not the sort of client for a gentleman of such note; but he is so good!"

Mr. Guppy slightly nudging his friend to take another look, makes a shuffling bow to Mr. Tulkinghorn, who returns it with an easy nod. Mr. Tulkinghorn is looking on as if he had nothing else to do, and were rather amused by the novelty.

"A good deal of property here, sir, I should say," Mr. Guppy observes to Mr. Smallweed.

"Principally rags and rubbish, my dear friend! rags and rubbish! Me and Bart, and my grand-daughter Judy, are endeavouring to make out an inventory of what's worth anything to sell. But we haven't come to much as yet, we—haven't—come—to—hah!"

Mr. Smallweed has run down again; while Mr. Weevle's eye, attended by Mr. Guppy's eye, has again gone round the room and come back.

"Well, sir," says Mr. Weevle. "We won't intrude any longer, if you'll allow us to go up-stairs."

"Anywhere, my dear sir, anywhere! You're at home. Make yourself so, pray!"

As they go up-stairs, Mr. Guppy lifts his eyebrows inquiringly, and looks at Tony. Tony shakes his head. They find the old room very dull and dismal, with the ashes of the fire that was burning on that memorable night yet in the discoloured grate. They have a great disinclination to touch any object, and carefully blow the dust from it first. Nor are they desirous to prolong their visit; packing the few moveables with all possible speed, and never speaking above a whisper.

"Look here," says Tony, recoiling. "Here's that horrible cat coming in!"

Mr. Guppy retreats behind a chair. "Small told me of her. She went leaping and bounding and tearing about, that night, like a Dragon, and got out on the house-tops, and roamed about up there for a fortnight, and then came tumbling down the chimney very thin. Did you ever see such a brute? Looks as if she knew all about it, don't she? Almost looks as if she was Krook. Shoohoo! Get out, you goblin!"

Lady Jane in the doorway, with her tiger-snarl from ear to ear, and her club of a tail, shows no intention of obeying; but Mr. Tulkinghorn stumbling over her, she spits at his rusty legs, and swearing wrathfully, takes her arched back up-stairs. Possibly to roam the house-tops again, and return by the chimney.

"Mr. Guppy," says Mr. Tulkinghorn, "could I have a word with you?"

Mr. Guppy is engaged in collecting the Galaxy Gallery of British Beauty from the wall, and depositing those works of art in their old ignoble bandbox. "Sir," he returns, reddening, "I wish to act with courtesy towards every member of the profession, and especially, I am sure, towards a member of it so well known as yourself—I will truly add, sir, so distinguished as yourself. Still, Mr. Tulkinghorn, sir, I must stipulate that if you have any word with me, that word is spoken in the presence of my friend."

"Oh, indeed?" says Mr. Tulkinghorn.

"Yes, sir. My reasons are not of a personal nature at all; but they are amply sufficient for myself."

"No doubt, no doubt." Mr. Tulkinghorn is as imperturbable as the hearthstone to which he has quietly walked. "The matter is not of that consequence that I need put you to the trouble of making any conditions, Mr. Guppy." He pauses here to smile, and his smile is as dull and rusty as his pantaloons.[7] "You are to be congratulated, Mr. Guppy; you are a fortunate young man, sir."

"Pretty well so, Mr. Tulkinghorn; I don't complain."

"Complain? High friends, free admission to great houses, and access to elegant ladies! Why, Mr. Guppy, there are people in London who would give their ears to be you."

Mr. Guppy, looking as if he would give his own reddening and still reddening ears to be one of those people at present instead of himself, replies, "Sir, if I attend to my profession, and do what is right by Kenge and Carboy, my friends and acquaintances are of no consequence to them, nor to any member of the profession, not excepting Mr. Tulkinghorn of the Fields. I am not under any obligation to explain myself further; and with all respect for you, sir, and without offence—I repeat, without offence——"

"O, certainly!"

"—I don't intend to do it."

"Quite so," says Mr. Tulkinghorn, with a calm nod. "Very good: I see by these portraits that you take a strong interest in the fashionable great, sir?"

He addresses this to the astounded Tony, who admits the soft impeachment.[8]

"A virtue in which few Englishmen are deficient," observes Mr. Tulkinghorn. He has been standing on the hearthstone, with his back to the smoked chimney-piece, and now turns round, with his glasses to his eyes. "Who is this? 'Lady Dedlock.' Ha! A very good likeness in its way, but it wants force of character. Good day to you, gentlemen; good day!"

When he has walked out, Mr. Guppy in a great perspiration, nerves himself to the hasty completion of the taking down of the Galaxy Gallery, concluding with Lady Dedlock.

"Tony," he says hurriedly to his astonished companion, "let us be quick in putting the things together, and in getting out of this

7. Breeches.
8. See Sheridan's *The Rivals* (V.iii): "I own the soft impeachment."

place. It were in vain longer to conceal from you, Tony, that between myself and one of the members of a swanlike aristocracy whom I now hold in my hand, there has been undivulged communication and association. The time might have been, when I might have revealed it to you. It never will be more. It is due alike to the oath I have taken, alike to the shattered idol, and alike to circumstances over which I have no control, that the ole should be buried in oblivion. I charge you as a friend, by the interest you have ever testified in the fashionable intelligence, and by any little advances with which I may have been able to accommodate you, so to bury it without a word of inquiry!"

This charge Mr. Guppy delivers in a state little short of forensic lunacy, while his friend shows a dazed mind in his whole head of hair, and even in his cultivated whiskers.

Chapter XL

NATIONAL AND DOMESTIC

England has been in a dreadful state for some weeks. Lord Coodle would go out, Sir Thomas Doodle wouldn't come in, and there being nobody in Great Britain (to speak of) except Coodle and Doodle, there has been no Government. It is a mercy that the hostile meeting between those two great men, which at one time seemed inevitable, did not come off; because if both pistols had taken effect, and Coodle and Doodle had killed each other, it is to be presumed that England must have waited to be governed until young Coodle and young Doodle, now in frocks and long stockings, were grown up. This stupendous national calamity, however, was averted by Lord Coodle's making the timely discovery, that if in the heat of debate he had said that he scorned and despised the whole ignoble career of Sir Thomas Doodle, he had merely meant to say that party differences should never induce him to withhold from it the tribute of his warmest admiration; while it as opportunely turned out, on the other hand, that Sir Thomas Doodle had in his own bosom expressly booked Lord Coodle to go down to posterity as the mirror of virtue and honour. Still England has been for some weeks in the dismal strait of having no pilot (as was well observed by Sir Leicester Dedlock) to weather the storm;[1] and the marvellous part of the matter is, that England has not appeared to

1. "The Pilot That Weathered the Storm" was the title of a verse-tribute to Prime Minister William Pitt, written by George Canning in 1802 (Canning himself became Prime Minister in 1827). See Wendy Hine, *George Canning* (1973), p. 109. Canning's later career in Parliament has some curious parallels with Sir Thomas Doodle's, including a duel and later a violent exchange of insults in the House in which he and his opponent, Henry Brougham, only avoided being committed to custody of the Sergeant-at-Arms by making ludicrously round-about apologies. This incident was used by Dickens in the first chapter of *Pickwick Papers.*

care very much about it, but has gone on eating and drinking and marrying and giving in marriage, as the old world did in the days before the flood.[2] But Coodle knew the danger, and Doodle knew the danger, and all their followers and hangers-on had the clearest perception of the danger. At last Sir Thomas Doodle has not only condescended to come in, but has done it handsomely, bringing in with him all his nephews, all his male cousins, and all his brothers-in-law. So there is hope for the old ship yet.

Doodle has found that he must throw himself upon the country—chiefly in the form of sovereigns and beer.[3] In this metamorphosed state he is available in a good many places simultaneously, and can throw himself upon a considerable portion of the country at one time. Britannia being much occupied in pocketing Doodle in the form of sovereigns, and swallowing Doodle in the form of beer, and in swearing herself black in the face that she does neither—plainly to the advancement of her glory and morality—the London season[4] comes to a sudden end, through all the Doodleites and Coodleites dispersing to assist Britannia in those religious exercises.

Hence Mrs. Rouncewell, housekeeper at Chesney Wold, foresees, though no instructions have yet come down, that the family may shortly be expected, together with a pretty large accession of cousins and others who can in any way assist the great Constitutional work. And hence the stately old dame, taking Time by the forelock,[5] leads him up and down the staircases, and along the galleries and passages, and through the rooms, to witness before he grows any older that everything is ready; that floors are rubbed bright, carpets spread, curtains shaken out, beds puffed and patted, still-room[6] and kitchen cleared for action,—all things prepared as beseems the Dedlock dignity.

This present summer evening, as the sun goes down, the preparations are complete. Dreary and solemn the old house looks, with so many appliances of habitation, and with no inhabitants except the pictured forms upon the walls. So did these come and go, a Dedlock in possession might have ruminated passing along; so did they see this gallery hushed and quiet, as I see it now; so think, as I think, of the gap that they would make in this domain when they were gone; so find it, as I find it, difficult to believe that it could be, without them; so pass from my world, as I pass from theirs, now

2. See Genesis 6:7.
3. Buying votes with gold coins and free drinks.
4. Chiefly the months of May, June, and July, when the country gentry visited London.
5. As T. W. Hill notes, Time, as traditionally represented, is a bald-headed old man with a long forelock of hair. To take him by the forelock is to seize the chance of controlling a future event. As the proverb has it: "Take Time by the forelock for he is bald behind."
6. Room in which homemade liqueurs were distilled and tea and coffee prepared.

Sunset in the long Drawing-room at Chesney Wold.

closing the reverberating door; so leave no blank to miss them, and so die.

Through some of the fiery windows, beautiful from without, and set, at this sunset hour, not in dull grey stone, but in a glorious house of gold, the light excluded at other windows pours in, rich, lavish, overflowing like the summer plenty in the land. Then do the frozen Dedlocks thaw. Strange movements come upon their features, as the shadows of leaves play there. A dense Justice in a corner is beguiled into a wink. A staring Baronet, with a truncheon, gets a dimple in his chin. Down into the bosom of a stony shepherdess there steals a fleck of light and warmth, that would have done it good, a hundred years ago. One ancestress of Volumnia, in high-heeled shoes, very like her—casting the shadow of that virgin event before[7] her full two centuries—shoots out into a halo and becomes a saint. A maid of honour to the court of Charles the Second, with large round eyes (and other charms to correspond), seems to bathe in glowing water, and it ripples as it glows.

But the fire of the sun is dying. Even now the floor is dusky, and shadow slowly mounts the walls, bringing the Dedlocks down like age and death. And now, upon my Lady's picture over the great chimney-piece, a weird shade falls from some old tree, that turns it pale, and flutters it, and looks as if a great arm held a veil or hood, watching an opportunity to draw it over her. Higher and darker rises shadow on the wall—now a red gloom on the ceiling—now the fire is out.

All that prospect, which from the terrace looked so near, has moved solemnly away, and changed—not the first nor the last of beautiful things that look so near and will so change—into a distant phantom. Light mists arise, and the dew falls, and all the sweet scents in the garden are heavy in the air. Now, the woods settle into great masses as if they were each one profound tree. And now the moon rises, to separate them, and to glimmer here and there in horizontal lines behind their stems, and to make the avenue a pavement of light among high cathedral arches fantastically broken.

Now, the moon is high; and the great house, needing habitation more than ever, is like a body without life. Now, it is even awful, stealing through it, to think of the live people who have slept in the solitary bedrooms; to say nothing of the dead. Now is the time for shadow, when every corner is a cavern, and every downward step a pit, when the stained glass is reflected in pale and faded hues upon the floors, when anything and everything can be made of the heavy staircase beams excepting their own proper shapes, when the armour has dull lights upon it not easily to be distinguished from stealthy

7. Cf. Thomas Campbell, *Lochiel's Warning* (line 46): "And coming events cast their shadows before."

movement, and when barred helmets are frightfully suggestive of heads inside. But, of all the shadows in Chesney Wold, the shadow in the long drawing-room upon my Lady's picture is the first to come, the last to be disturbed. At this hour and by this light it changes into threatening hands raised up, and menacing the handsome face with every breath that stirs.

"She is not well, ma'am," says a groom in Mrs. Rouncewell's audience-chamber.

"My Lady not well! What's the matter?"

"Why, my Lady has been but poorly, ma'am, since she was last here—I don't mean with the family, ma'am, but when she was here as a bird of passage-like. My Lady has not been out much for her, and has kept her room a good deal."

"Chesney Wold, Thomas," rejoins the housekeeper, with proud complacency, "will set my Lady up! There is no finer air, and no healthier soil, in the world!"

Thomas may have his own personal opinions on this subject; probably hints them, in his manner of smoothing his sleek head from the nape of his neck to his temples; but he forbears to express them further, and retires to the servants' hall to regale on cold meat-pie and ale.

This groom is the pilot-fish[8] before the nobler shark. Next evening, down come Sir Leicester and my Lady with their largest retinue, and down come the cousins and others from all the points in the compass. Thenceforth for some weeks, backward and forward rush mysterious men with no names, who fly about all those particular parts of the country on which Doodle is at present throwing himself in an auriferous[9] and malty shower, but who are merely persons of a restless disposition and never do anything anywhere.

On these national occasions, Sir Leicester finds the cousins useful. A better man than the Honourable Bob Stables to meet the Hunt at dinner, there could not possibly be. Better got up gentlemen than the other cousins, to ride over to polling-booths and hustings[1] here and there, and show themselves on the side of England, it would be hard to find. Volumnia is a little dim, but she is of the true descent; and there are many who appreciate her sprightly conversation, her French conundrums so old as to have become in the cycles of time almost new again, the honour of taking the fair Dedlock in to dinner, or even the privilege of her hand in the dance. On these national occasions, dancing may be a patriotic service; and Volumnia is constantly seen hopping about, for the good of an ungrateful and unpensioning country.

8. A small mackerel which is reputed to lead sharks to food.
9. Golden.

1. Temporary platforms for speakers seeking election to Parliament.

My Lady takes no great pains to entertain the numerous guests, and, being still unwell, rarely appears until late in the day. But, at all the dismal dinners, leaden lunches, basilisk[2] balls, and other melancholy pageants, her mere appearance is a relief. As to Sir Leicester, he conceives it utterly impossible that anything can be wanting, in any direction, by any one who has the good fortune to be received under that roof; and in a state of sublime satisfaction, he moves among the company, a magnificent refrigerator.

Daily the cousins trot through dust, and canter over roadside turf, away to hustings and polling-booths (with leather gloves and hunting-whips for the counties, and kid gloves and riding-canes for the boroughs), and daily bring back reports on which Sir Leicester holds forth after dinner. Daily the restless men who have no occupation in life, present the appearance of being rather busy. Daily, Volumnia has a little cousinly talk with Sir Leicester on the state of the nation, from which Sir Leicester is disposed to conclude that Volumnia is a more reflecting woman than he had thought her.

"How are we getting on?" says Miss Volumnia, clasping her hands. "*Are* we safe?"

The mighty business is nearly over by this time, and Doodle will throw himself off the country in a few days more. Sir Leicester has just appeared in the long drawing-room after dinner; a bright particular star,[3] surrounded by clouds of cousins.

"Volumnia," replies Sir Leicester, who has a list in his hand, "we are doing tolerably!"

"Only tolerably!"

Although it is summer weather, Sir Leicester always has his own particular fire in the evening. He takes his usual screened seat near it, and repeats, with much firmness and a little displeasure, as who should say, I am not a common man, and when I say tolerably, it must not be understood as a common expression; "Volumnia, we are doing tolerably."

"At least there is no opposition to *you*," Volumnia asserts with confidence.

"No, Volumnia. This distracted country has lost its senses in many respects, I grieve to say, but——"

"It is not so mad as that. I am glad to hear it!"

Volumnia's finishing the sentence restores her to favour. Sir Leicester, with a gracious inclination of his head, seems to say to himself, "A sensible woman this, on the whole, though occasionally precipitate."

In fact, as to this question of opposition, the fair Dedlock's obser-

2. A fabulous reptile reputedly able to kill persons by looking at them.

3. See *All's Well That Ends Well* (I.i.97–99): "'Twere all one/ That I should love a bright particular star,/ And think to wed it." (Noted by Norman Page.)

vation was superfluous: Sir Leicester, on these occasions, always delivering in his own candidateship, as a kind of handsome wholesale order to be promptly executed. Two other little seats that belong to him, he treats as retail orders of less importance; merely sending down the men, and signifying to the tradespeople, "You will have the goodness to make these materials into two members of parliament, and to send them home when done."

"I regret to say, Volumnia, that in many places the people have shown a bad spirit, and that their opposition to the Government has been of a most determined and most implacable description."

"W-r-retches!" says Volumnia.

"Even," proceeds Sir Leicester, glancing at the circumjacent cousins on sofas and ottomans, "even in many—in fact, in most—of those places in which the Government has carried it against a faction—"

(Note, by the way, that the Coodleites are always a faction with the Doodleites, and that the Doodleites occupy exactly the same position towards the Coodleites.)

"—Even in them I am shocked, for the credit of Englishmen, to be constrained to inform you that the Party has not triumphed without being put to an enormous expense. Hundreds," says Sir Leicester, eyeing the cousins with increasing dignity and swelling indignation, "hundreds of thousands of pounds!"

If Volumnia have a fault, it is the fault of being a trifle too innocent; seeing that the innocence which would go extremely well with a sash and tucker,[4] is a little out of keeping with the rouge and pearl necklace. Howbeit, impelled by innocence, she asks.

"What for?"

"Volumnia," remonstrates Sir Leicester, with his utmost severity. "Volumnia!"

"No, no, I don't mean what for," cries Volumnia, with her favourite little scream. "How stupid I am! I mean what a pity!"

"I am glad," returns Sir Leicester, "that you *do* mean what a pity."

Volumnia hastens to express her opinion that the shocking people ought to be tried as traitors, and made to support the Party.

"I am glad, Volumnia," repeats Sir Leicester, unmindful of these mollifying sentiments, "that you *do* mean what a pity. It is disgraceful to the electors. But as you, though inadvertently, and without intending so unreasonable a question, asked me 'what for?' let me reply to you. For necessary expenses. And I trust to your good sense, Volumnia, not to pursue the subject, here or elsewhere."

Sir Leicester feels it incumbent on him to observe a crushing aspect towards Volumnia, because it is whispered abroad that these

4. Neckpiece of lace or other cloth worn by women, especially by schoolgirls.

necessary expenses will, in some two hundred election petitions, be unpleasantly connected with the word bribery; and because some graceless jokers have consequently suggested the omission from the Church service of the ordinary supplication in behalf of the High Court of Parliament,[5] and have recommended instead that the prayers of the congregation be requested for six hundred and fifty-eight gentlemen in a very unhealthy state.[6]

"I suppose," observes Volumnia, having taken a little time to recover her spirits after her late castigation, "I suppose Mr. Tulkinghorn has been worked to death."

"I don't know," says Sir Leicester, opening his eyes, "why Mr. Tulkinghorn should be worked to death. I don't know what Mr. Tulkinghorn's engagements may be. He is not a candidate."

Volumnia had thought he might have been employed. Sir Leicester could desire to know by whom, and what for? Volumnia, abashed again, suggests, by Somebody—to advise and make arrangements. Sir Leicester is not aware that any client of Mr. Tulkinghorn has been in need of his assistance.

Lady Dedlock, seated at an open window with her arms upon its cushioned ledge and looking out at the evening shadows falling on the park, has seemed to attend since the lawyer's name was mentioned.

A languid cousin with a moustache, in a state of extreme debility, now observes from his couch, that—man told him ya'as'dy that Tulkinghorn had gone down t' that iron place t' give legal 'pinion 'bout something; and that, contest being over t' day, 'twould be highly jawlly thing if Tulkinghorn should pear with news that Coodle man was floored.

Mercury in attendance with coffee informs Sir Leicester, hereupon, that Mr. Tulkinghorn has arrived, and is taking dinner. My Lady turns her head inward for the moment, then looks out again as before.

Volumnia is charmed to hear that her Delight is come. He is so original, such a stolid creature, such an immense being for knowing all sorts of things and never telling them! Volumnia is persuaded that he must be a Freemason. Is sure he is at the head of a lodge, and wears short aprons, and is made a perfect Idol of, with candlesticks and trowels. These lively remarks the fair Dedlock delivers in her youthful manner, while making a purse.

"He has not been here once," she adds, "since I came. I really had some thought of breaking my heart for the inconstant creature. I had almost made up my mind that he was dead."

5. *The Book of Common Prayer* includes "A Prayer for the High Court of Parliament, to be read during their Sessions."

6. Members of the House of Commons such as Sir Leicester.

It may be the gathering gloom of evening, or it may be the darker gloom within herself, but a shade is on my Lady's face, as if she thought, "I would he were!"

"Mr. Tulkinghorn," says Sir Leicester, "is always welcome here, and always discreet wheresoever he is. A very valuable person, and deservedly respected."

The debilitated cousin supposes he is, " 'normously rich fler."

"He has a stake in the country," says Sir Leicester, "I have no doubt. He is, of course, handsomely paid, and he associates almost on a footing of equality with the highest society."

Everybody starts. For a gun is fired close by.

"Good gracious, what's that?" cries Volumnia, with her little withered scream.

"A rat," says my Lady. "And they have shot him."[7]

Enter Mr. Tulkinghorn, followed by Mercuries with lamps and candles.

"No, no," says Sir Leicester, "I think not. My Lady, do you object to the twilight?"

On the contrary, my Lady prefers it.

"Volumnia?"

O! nothing is so delicious to Volumnia, as to sit and talk in the dark.

"Then take them away," says Sir Leicester. "Tulkinghorn, I beg your pardon. How do you do?"

Mr. Tulkinghorn with his usual leisurely ease advances, renders his passing homage to my Lady, shakes Sir Leicester's hand, and subsides into the chair proper to him when he has anything to communicate, on the opposite side of the Baronet's little newspaper-table. Sir Leicester is apprehensive that my Lady, not being very well, will take cold at that open window. My Lady is obliged to him, but would rather sit there, for the air. Sir Leicester rises, adjusts her scarf about her, and returns to his seat. Mr. Tulkinghorn in the meanwhile takes a pinch of snuff.

"Now," says Sir Leicester. "How has that contest gone?"

"Oh, hollow from the beginning. Not a chance. They have brought in both their people. You are beaten out of all reason. Three to one."

It is a part of Mr. Tulkinghorn's policy and mastery to have no political opinions; indeed, *no* opinions. Therefore he says "you" are beaten, and not "we."

Sir Leicester is majestically wroth. Volumnia never heard of such a thing. The debilitated cousin holds that it's—sort of thing that's sure tapn slongs votes—giv'n—Mob.

7. Cf. the scene of the slaying of the counselor, Polonius: "How now! A rat? Dead, for a ducat, dead!" (*Hamlet*, III.iv.23–24).

"It's the place, you know," Mr. Tulkinghorn goes on to say in the fast increasing darkness, when there is silence again, "where they wanted to put up Mrs. Rouncewell's son."

"A proposal which, as you correctly informed me at the time, he had the becoming taste and perception," observes Sir Leicester, "to decline. I cannot say that I by any means approve of the sentiments expressed by Mr. Rouncewell, when he was here for some half-hour, in this room; but there was a sense of propriety in his decision which I am glad to acknowledge."

"Ha!" says Mr. Tulkinghorn. "It did not prevent him from being very active in this election, though."

Sir Leicester is distinctly heard to gasp before speaking. "Did I understand you? Did you say that Mr. Rouncewell had been very active in this election?"

"Uncommonly active."

"Against——"

"O dear yes, against you. He is a very good speaker. Plain and emphatic. He made a damaging effect, and has great influence. In the business-part of the proceedings he carried all before him."

It is evident to the whole company, though nobody can see him, that Sir Leicester is staring majestically.

"And throughout he was much assisted," says Mr. Tulkinghorn, as a wind-up, "by his son."

"By his son, sir?" repeats Sir Leicester, with awful politeness.

"By his son."

"The son who wished to marry the young woman in my Lady's service?"

"That son. He has but one."

"Then upon my honour," says Sir Leicester, after a terrific pause, during which he has been heard to snort and felt to stare; "then upon my honour, upon my life, upon my reputation and principles, the floodgates of society are burst open, and the waters have—a—obliterated the landmarks of the framework of the cohesion by which things are held together!"

General burst of cousinly indignation. Volumnia thinks it is really high time, you know, for somebody in power to step in and do something strong. Debilitated cousin thinks—Country's going—DAYVLE—steeple-chase pace.

"I beg," says Sir Leicester, in a breathless condition, "that we may not comment further on this circumstance. Comment is superfluous. My Lady, let me suggest in reference to that young woman——"

"I have no intention," observes my Lady from her window, in a low but decided tone, "of parting with her."

"That was not my meaning," returns Sir Leicester. "I am glad to hear you say so. I would suggest that as you think her worthy of your patronage you should exert your influence to keep her from these dangerous hands. You might show her what violence would be done, in such association, to her duties and principles; and you might preserve her for a better fate. You might point out to her that she probably would, in good time, find a husband at Chesney Wold by whom she would not be—" Sir Leicester adds, after a moment's consideration, "dragged from the altars of her forefathers."

These remarks he offers with his unvarying politeness and deference when he addresses himself to his wife. She merely moves her head in reply. The moon is rising; and where she sits there is a little stream of cold pale light, in which her head is seen.

"It is worthy of remark," says Mr. Tulkinghorn, "however, that these people are, in their way, very proud."

"Proud?" Sir Leicester doubts his hearing.

"I should not be surprised if they all voluntarily abandoned the girl—yes, lover and all—instead of her abandoning them, supposing she remained at Chesney Wold under such circumstances."

"Well!" says Sir Leicester, tremulously. "Well! You should know, Mr. Tulkinghorn. You have been among them."

"Really, Sir Leicester," returns the lawyer, "I state the fact. Why, I could tell you a story—with Lady Dedlock's permission."

Her head concedes it, and Volumnia is enchanted. A story! O he is going to tell something at last! A ghost in it, Volumnia hopes!

"No. Real flesh and blood." Mr. Tulkinghorn stops for an instant, and repeats, with some little emphasis grafted upon his usual monotony, "Real flesh and blood, Miss Dedlock. Sir Leicester, these particulars have only lately become known to me. They are very brief. They exemplify what I have said. I suppress names for the present. Lady Dedlock will not think me ill-bred, I hope?"

By the light of the fire, which is low, he can be seen looking towards the moonlight. By the light of the moon Lady Dedlock can be seen, perfectly still.

"A townsman of this Mr. Rouncewell, a man in exactly parallel circumstances as I am told, had the good fortune to have a daughter who attracted the notice of a great lady. I speak of really a great lady; not merely great to him, but married to a gentleman of your condition, Sir Leicester.

Sir Leicester condescendingly says, "Yes, Mr. Tulkinghorn"; implying that then she must have appeared of very considerable moral dimensions indeed, in the eyes of an ironmaster.

"The lady was wealthy and beautiful, and had a liking for the girl, and treated her with great kindness, and kept her always near her. Now this lady preserved a secret under all her greatness, which she had preserved for many years. In fact, she had in early life been engaged to marry a young rake—he was a captain in the army—nothing connected with whom came to any good. She never did marry him, but she gave birth to a child of which he was the father."

By the light of the fire he can be seen looking towards the moonlight. By the moonlight, Lady Dedlock can be seen in profile, perfectly still.

"The captain in the army being dead, she believed herself safe; but a train of circumstances with which I need not trouble you, led to discovery. As I received the story, they began in an imprudence on her own part one day, when she was taken by surprise; which shows how difficult it is for the firmest of us (she was very firm) to be always guarded. There was great domestic trouble and amazement, you may suppose; I leave you to imagine, Sir Leicester, the husband's grief. But that is not the present point. When Mr. Rouncewell's townsman heard of the disclosure, he no more allowed the girl to be patronised and honoured, than he would have suffered her to be trodden underfoot before his eyes. Such was his pride, that he indignantly took her away, as if from reproach and disgrace. He had no sense of the honour done him and his daughter by the lady's condescension; not the least. He resented the girl's position, as if the lady had been the commonest of commoners. That is the story. I hope Lady Dedlock will excuse its painful nature."

There are various opinions on the merits, more or less conflicting with Volumnia's. That fair young creature cannot believe there ever was any such lady, and rejects the whole history on the threshold. The majority incline to the debilitated cousin's sentiment, which is in few words—"no business—Rouncewell's fernal townsman." Sir Leicester generally refers back in his mind to Wat Tyler,[8] and arranges a sequence of events on a plan of his own.

There is not much conversation in all, for late hours have been kept at Chesney Wold since the necessary expenses elsewhere began, and this is the first night in many on which the family have been alone. It is past ten, when Sir Leicester begs Mr. Tulkinghorn to ring for candles. Then the stream of moonlight has swelled into a lake, and then Lady Dedlock for the first time moves, and rises, and comes forward to a table for a glass of water. Winking cousins, bat-like in the candle glare, crowd round to give it; Volumnia (always ready for something better if procurable) takes another, a very mild sip of which contents her; Lady Dedlock, graceful, self-possessed, looked after by admiring eyes, passes away slowly down the long perspective by the side of the Nymph, not at all improving her as a question of contrast.

8. See p. 79, note 7.

Chapter XLI

IN MR. TULKINGHORN'S ROOM

Mr. Tulkinghorn arrives in his turret-room, a little breathed by the journey up, though leisurely performed. There is an expression on his face as if he had discharged his mind of some grave matter, and were, in his close way, satisfied. To say of a man so severely and strictly self-repressed that he is triumphant would be to do him as great an injustice as to suppose him troubled with love or sentiment, or any romantic weakness. He is sedately satisfied. Perhaps there is a rather increased sense of power upon him, as he loosely grasps one of his veinous wrists with his other hand, and holding it behind his back walks noiselessly up and down.

There is a capacious writing-table in the room, on which is a pretty large accumulation of papers. The green lamp is lighted, his reading-glasses lie upon the desk, the easy-chair is wheeled up to it, and it would seem as though he had intended to bestow an hour or so upon these claims on his attention before going to bed. But he happens not to be in a business mind. After a glance at the documents awaiting his notice—with his head bent low over the table, the old man's sight for print or writing being defective at night—he opens the French window and steps out upon the leads. There he again walks slowly up and down, in the same attitude; subsiding, if a man so cool may have any need to subside, from the story he has related down-stairs.

The time was once, when men as knowing as Mr. Tulkinghorn would walk on turret-tops in the star-light, and look up into the sky to read their fortunes there. Hosts of stars are visible to-night, though their brilliancy is eclipsed by the splendour of the moon. If he be seeking his own stars, as he methodically turns and turns upon the leads, it should be but a pale one to be so rustily represented below. If he be tracing out his destiny, that may be written in other characters nearer to his hand.

As he paces the leads, with his eyes most probably as high above his thoughts as they are high above the earth, he is suddenly stopped in passing the window by two eyes that meet his own. The ceiling of his room is rather low; and the upper part of the door, which is opposite the window, is of glass. There is an inner baize door, too, but the night being warm he did not close it when he came up-stairs. These eyes that meet his own, are looking in through the glass from the corridor outside. He knows them well. The blood has not flushed into his face so suddenly and redly for many a long year, as when he recognises Lady Dedlock.

He steps into the room, and she comes in too, closing both the doors behind her. There is a wild disturbance—is it fear or anger?—in her eyes. In her carriage and all else, she looks as she looked down-stairs two hours ago.

Is it fear, or is it anger, now? He cannot be sure. Both might be as pale, both as intent.

"Lady Dedlock?"

She does not speak at first, nor even when she has slowly dropped into the easy-chair by the table. They look at each other, like two pictures.

"Why have you told my story to so many persons?"

"Lady Dedlock, it was necessary for me to inform you that I knew it."

"How long have you known it?"

"I have suspected it a long while—fully known it, a little while."

"Months?"

"Days."

He stands before her, with one hand on a chair-back and the other in his old-fashioned waistcoat and shirt-frill, exactly as he has stood before her at any time since her marriage. The same formal politeness, the same composed deference that might as well be defiance; the whole man the same dark, cold object, at the same distance, which nothing has ever diminished.

"Is this true concerning the poor girl?"

He slightly inclines and advances his head, as not quite understanding the question.

"You know what you related. Is it true? Do her friends know my story also? Is it the town-talk yet? Is it chalked upon the walls and cried in the streets?"

So! Anger, and fear, and shame. All three contending. What power this woman has to keep these raging passions down! Mr. Tulkinghorn's thoughts take such form as he looks at her, with his ragged grey eyebrows a hair's-breadth more contracted than usual, under her gaze.

"No, Lady Dedlock. That was a hypothetical case, arising out of Sir Leicester's unconsciously carrying the matter with so high a hand. But it would be a real case if they knew—what we know."

"Then they do not know it yet?"

"No."

"Can I save the poor girl from injury before they know it?"

"Really, Lady Dedlock," Mr. Tulkinghorn replies, "I cannot give a satisfactory opinion on that point."

And he thinks, with the interest of attentive curiosity, as he watches the struggle in her breast, "The power and force of this woman are astonishing!"

"Sir," she says, for the moment obliged to set her lips with all the energy she has, that she may speak distinctly, "I will make it plainer. I do not dispute your hypothetical case. I anticipated it, and felt its truth as strongly as you can do, when I saw Mr. Rouncewell here. I knew very well that if he could have had the power of seeing me as I was, he would consider the poor girl tarnished by having for a moment been, although most innocently, the subject of my great and distinguished patronage. But I have an interest in her; or I should rather say—no longer belonging to this place—I *had*; and if you can find so much consideration for the woman under your foot as to remember that, she will be very sensible of your mercy."

Mr. Tulkinghorn, profoundly attentive, throws this off with a shrug of self-depreciation, and contracts his eyebrows a little more.

"You have prepared me for my exposure, and I thank you for that too. Is there anything that you require of me? Is there any claim that I can release, or any charge or trouble that I can spare my husband in obtaining *his* release, by certifying to the exactness of your discovery? I will write anything, here and now, that you will dictate. I am ready to do it."

And she would do it! thinks the lawyer, watchful of the firm hand with which she takes the pen!

"I will not trouble you, Lady Dedlock. Pray spare yourself."

"I have long expected this, as you know. I neither wish to spare myself, nor to be spared. You can do nothing worse to me than you have done. Do what remains, now."

"Lady Dedlock, there is nothing to be done. I will take leave to say a few words, when you have finished."

Their need for watching one another should be over now, but they do it all this time, and the stars watch them both through the opened window. Away in the moonlight lie the woodland fields at rest, and the wide house is as quiet as the narrow one. The narrow one! Where are the digger and the spade, this peaceful night, destined to add the last great secret to the many secrets of the Tulkinghorn existence? Is the man born yet, is the spade wrought yet? Curious questions to consider, more curious perhaps not to consider, under the watching stars upon a summer night.

"Of repentance or remorse, or any feeling of mine," Lady Dedlock presently proceeds, "I say not a word. If I were not dumb, you would be deaf. Let that go by. It is not for your ears."

He makes a feint of offering a protest, but she sweeps it away with her disdainful hand.

"Of other and very different things I come to speak to you. My jewels are all in their proper places of keeping. They will be found there. So, my dresses. So, all the valuables I have. Some ready money I had with me, please to say, but no large amount. I did not wear my own dress, in order that I might avoid observation. I went, to be henceforward lost. Make this known. I leave no other charge with you."

"Excuse me, Lady Dedlock," says Mr. Tulkinghorn, quite unmoved. "I am not sure that I understand you. You went?—"

"To be lost to all here. I leave Chesney Wold to-night. I go this hour."

Mr. Tulkinghorn shakes his head. She rises; but he, without removing hand from chair-back or from old-fashioned waistcoat and shirt-frill, shakes his head.

"What? Not go as I have said?"

"No, Lady Dedlock," he very calmly replies.

"Do you know the relief that my disappearance will be? Have you forgotten the stain and blot upon this place, and where it is, and who it is?"

"No, Lady Dedlock, not by any means."

Without deigning to rejoin, she moves to the inner door and has it in her hand, when he says to her, without himself stirring hand or foot, or raising his voice:

"Lady Dedlock, have the goodness to stop and hear me, or before you reach the staircase I shall ring the alarm-bell and rouse the house. And then I must speak out, before every guest and servant, every man and woman, in it."

He has conquered her. She falters, trembles, and puts her hand confusedly to her head. Slight tokens these in any one else; but when so practised an eye as Mr. Tulkinghorn's sees indecision for a moment in such a subject, he thoroughly knows its value.

He promptly says again, "Have the goodness to hear me, Lady Dedlock," and motions to the chair from which she has risen. She hesitates, but he motions again, and she sits down.

"The relations between us are of an unfortunate description, Lady Dedlock; but as they are not of my making, I will not apologise for them. The position I hold in reference to Sir Leicester is so well known to you, I can hardly imagine but that I must long have appeared in your eyes the natural person to make this discovery."

"Sir," she returns without looking up from the ground, on which her eyes are now fixed, "I had better have gone. It would have been far better not to have detained me. I have no more to say."

"Excuse me, Lady Dedlock, if I add, a little more to hear."

"I wish to hear it at the window, then. I can't breathe where I am."

His jealous glance as she walks that way, betrays an instant's misgiving that she may have it in her thoughts to leap over, and dashing against ledge and cornice, strike her life out upon the terrace below. But a moment's observation of her figure as she stands in the window without any support, looking out at the stars—not up—

gloomily out at those stars which are low in the heavens—reassures him. By facing round as she has moved, he stands a little behind her.

"Lady Dedlock, I have not yet been able to come to a decision satisfactory to myself, on the course before me. I am not clear what to do, or how to act next. I must request you, in the meantime, to keep your secret as you have kept it so long, and not to wonder that I keep it too."

He pauses, but she makes no reply.

"Pardon me, Lady Dedlock. This is an important subject. You are honouring me with your attention?"

"I am."

"Thank you. I might have known it, from what I have seen of your strength of character. I ought not to have asked the question, but I have the habit of making sure of my ground, step by step, as I go on. The sole consideration in this unhappy case is Sir Leicester."

"Then why," she asks in a low voice, and without removing her gloomy look from those distant stars, "do you detain me in his house?"

"Because he *is* the consideration. Lady Dedlock, I have no occasion to tell you that Sir Leicester is a very proud man; that his reliance upon you is implicit; that the fall of that moon out of the sky, would not amaze him more than your fall from your high position as his wife."

She breathes quickly and heavily, but she stands as unflinchingly as ever he has seen her in the midst of her grandest company.

"I declare to you, Lady Dedlock, that with anything short of this case that I have, I would as soon have hoped to root up, by means of my own strength and my own hands, the oldest tree on this estate, as to shake your hold upon Sir Leicester, and Sir Leicester's trust and confidence in you. And even now, with this case, I hesitate. Not that he could doubt (that, even with him, is impossible), but that nothing can prepare him for the blow."

"Not my flight?" she returns. "Think of it again."

"Your flight, Lady Dedlock, would spread the whole truth, and a hundred times the whole truth, far and wide. It would be impossible to save the family credit for a day. It is not to be thought of."

There is a quiet decision in his reply, which admits of no remonstrance.

"When I speak of Sir Leicester being the sole consideration, he and the family credit are one. Sir Leicester and the baronetcy, Sir Leicester and Chesney Wold, Sir Leicester and his ancestors and his patrimony"; Mr. Tulkinghorn very dry here; "are, I need not say to you, Lady Dedlock, inseparable."

"Go on!"

"Therefore," says Mr. Tulkinghorn, pursuing his case in his jog-trot style, "I have much to consider. This is to be hushed up, if it can be. How can it be, if Sir Leicester is driven out of his wits, or laid upon a death-bed? If I inflicted this shock upon him to-morrow morning, how could the immediate change in him be accounted for? What could have caused it? What could have divided you? Lady Dedlock, the wall-chalking and the street-crying would come on directly; and you are to remember that it would not affect you merely (whom I cannot at all consider in this business), but your husband, Lady Dedlock, your husband."

He gets plainer as he gets on, but not an atom more emphatic or animated.

"There is another point of view," he continues, "in which the case presents itself. Sir Leicester is devoted to you almost to infatuation. He might not be able to overcome that infatuation, even knowing what we know. I am putting an extreme case, but it might be so. If so, it were better that he knew nothing. Better for common sense, better for him, better for me. I must take all this into account, and it combines to render a decision very difficult."

She stands looking out at the same stars without a word. They are beginning to pale, and she looks as if their coldness froze her.

"My experience teaches me," says Mr. Tulkinghorn, who has by this time got his hands in his pockets, and is going on in his business consideration of the matter, like a machine. "My experience teaches me, Lady Dedlock, that most of the people I know would do far better to leave marriage alone. It is at the bottom of three-fourths of their troubles. So I thought when Sir Leicester married, and so I always have thought since. No more about that. I must now be guided by circumstances. In the meanwhile I must beg you to keep your own counsel, and I will keep mine."

"I am to drag my present life on, holding its pains at your pleasure, day by day. Am I?" she asks, still looking at the distant sky.

"Yes, I am afraid so, Lady Dedlock."

"It is necessary, you think, that I should be so tied to the stake?"

"I am sure that what I recommend is necessary."

"I am to remain on this gaudy platform, on which my miserable deception has been so long acted, and it is to fall beneath me when you give the signal?" she says slowly.

"Not without notice, Lady Dedlock. I shall take no step without forewarning you."

She asks all her questions as if she were repeating them from memory, or calling them over in her sleep.

"We are to meet as usual?"

"Precisely as usual, if you please."

"And I am to hide my guilt, as I have done so many years?"

"As you have done so many years. I should not have made that reference myself, Lady Dedlock, but I may now remind you that your secret can be no heavier to you than it was, and is no worse and no better than it was. *I* know it certainly, but I believe we have never wholly trusted each other."

She stands absorbed in the same frozen way for some little time before asking:

"Is there anything more to be said to-night?"

"Why," Mr. Tulkinghorn returns methodically, as he softly rubs his hands, "I should like to be assured of your acquiescence in my arrangements, Lady Dedlock."

"You may be assured of it."

"Good. And I would wish in conclusion to remind you, as a business precaution, in case it should be necessary to recall the fact in any communication with Sir Leicester, that throughout our interview I have expressly stated my sole consideration to be Sir Leicester's feelings and honour, and the family reputation. I should have been happy to have made Lady Dedlock a prominent consideration, too, if the case had admitted of it; but unfortunately it does not!"

"I can attest your fidelity, sir."

Both before and after saying it she remains absorbed, but at length moves, and turns, unshaken in her natural and acquired presence, towards the door. Mr. Tulkinghorn opens both the doors exactly as he would have done yesterday, or as he would have done ten years ago, and makes his old-fashioned bow as she passes out. It is not an ordinary look that he receives from the handsome face as it goes into the darkness, and it is not an ordinary movement, though a very slight one, that acknowledges his courtesy. But, as he reflects when he is left alone, the woman has been putting no common constraint upon herself.

He would know it all the better, if he saw the woman pacing her own rooms with her hair wildly thrown from her flung back face, her hands clasped behind her head, her figure twisted as if by pain. He would think so all the more if he saw the woman thus hurrying up and down for hours, without fatigue, without intermission, followed by the faithful step upon the Ghost's Walk. But he shuts out the now chilled air, draws the window-curtain, goes to bed, and falls asleep. And truly when the stars go out and the wan day peeps into the turret-chamber, finding him at his oldest, he looks as if the digger and the spade were both commissioned, and would soon be digging.

The same wan day peeps in at Sir Leicester pardoning the repentant country in a magnificently condescending dream; and at the cousins entering on various public employments, principally receipt of salary; and at the chaste Volumnia, bestowing a dower of fifty thousand pounds upon a hideous old General, with a mouth of false teeth like a pianoforte too full of keys, long the admiration of Bath and the terror of every other community. Also into rooms high in the roof, and into offices in court-yards and over stables, where humbler ambition dreams of bliss, in keepers' lodges, and in holy matrimony with Will or Sally. Up comes the bright sun, drawing everything up with it—the Wills and Sallys, the latent vapour in the earth, the drooping leaves and flowers, the birds and beasts and creeping things,[1] the gardeners to sweep the dewy turf and unfold emerald velvet where the roller passes, the smoke of the great kitchen fire wreathing itself straight and high into the lightsome air. Lastly, up comes the flag over Mr. Tulkinghorn's unconscious head, cheerfully proclaiming that Sir Leicester and Lady Dedlock are in their happy home, and that there is hospitality at the place in Lincolnshire.

Chapter XLII

IN MR. TULKINGHORN'S CHAMBERS

From the verdant undulations and the spreading oaks of the Dedlock property, Mr. Tulkinghorn transfers himself to the stale heat and dust of London. His manner of coming and going between the two places, is one of his impenetrabilities. He walks into Chesney Wold as if it were next door to his chambers, and returns to his chambers as if he had never been out of Lincoln's Inn Fields. He neither changes his dress before the journey, nor talks of it afterwards. He melted out of his turret-room this morning, just as now, in the late twilight, he melts into his own square.

Like a dingy London bird among the birds at roost in these pleasant fields, where the sheep are all made into parchment, the goats into wigs, and the pasture into chaff, the lawyer, smoke-dried and faded, dwelling among mankind but not consorting with them, aged without experience of genial youth, and so long used to make his cramped nest in holes and corners of human nature that he has forgotten its broader and better range, comes sauntering home. In the oven made by the hot pavements and hot buildings, he has baked himself dryer than usual; and he has, in his thirsty mind, his mellowed port-wine half a century old.

The lamplighter is skipping up and down his ladder on Mr. Tulkinghorn's side of the Fields, when that high-priest of noble mysteries arrives at his own dull court-yard. He ascends the door-steps, and is gliding into the dusky hall, when he encounters, on the top step, a bowing and propitiatory little man.

"Is that Snagsby?"

1. "Birds, and four-footed beasts, and creeping things" (Romans 1:23).

"Yes sir. I hope you are well sir. I was just giving you up, sir, and going home."

"Aye? What is it? What do you want with me?"

"Well, sir," says Mr. Snagsby, holding his hat at the side of his head, in his deference towards his best customer, "I was wishful to say a word to you sir."

"Can you say it here?"

"Perfectly sir."

"Say it then." The lawyer turns, leans his arms on the iron railing at the top of the steps, and looks at the lamplighter lighting the court-yard.

"It is relating," says Mr. Snagsby, in a mysterious low voice: "it is relating—not to put too fine a point upon it—to the foreigner sir."

Mr. Tulkinghorn eyes him with some surprise. "What foreigner?"

"The foreign female sir. French, if I don't mistake? I am not acquainted with that language myself, but I should judge from her manners and appearance that she was French; anyways, certainly foreign. Her that was up-stairs sir, when Mr. Bucket and me had the honour of waiting upon you with the sweeping-boy that night."

"Oh! yes, yes. Mademoiselle Hortense."

"Indeed sir?" Mr. Snagsby coughs his cough of submission behind his hat. "I am not acquainted myself with the names of foreigners in general, but I have no doubt it *would* be that." Mr. Snagsby appears to have set out in this reply with some desperate design of repeating the name; but on reflection coughs again to excuse himself.

"And what can you have to say, Snagsby," demands Mr. Tulkinghorn, "about her?"

"Well sir," returns the stationer, shading his communication with his hat, "it falls a little hard upon me. My domestic happiness is very great—at least, it's as great as can be expected, I'm sure—but my little woman is rather given to jealousy. Not to put too fine a point upon it, she is very much given to jealousy. And you see, a foreign female of that genteel appearance coming into the shop, and hovering—I should be the last to make use of a strong expression, if I could avoid it, but hovering sir—in the court—you know it is—now ain't it? I only put it to yourself sir."

Mr. Snagsby having said this in a very plaintive manner, throws in a cough of general application to fill up all the blanks.

"Why, what do you mean?" asks Mr. Tulkinghorn.

"Just so sir," returns Mr. Snagsby; "I was sure you would feel it yourself, and would excuse the reasonableness of *my* feelings when coupled with the known excitableness of my little woman. You see, the foreign female—which you mentioned her name just now, with quite a native sound I am sure—caught up the word Snagsby that night, being uncommon quick, and made inquiry, and got the direction and come at dinner-time. Now Guster, our young woman, is timid and has fits, and she, taking fright at the foreigner's looks—which are fierce—and at a grinding manner that she has of speaking—which is calculated to alarm a weak mind—gave way to it, instead of bearing up against it, and tumbled down the kitchen stairs out of one into another, such fits as I do sometimes think are never gone into, or come out of, in any house but ours. Consequently there was by good fortune ample occupation for my little woman, and only me to answer the shop. When she *did* say that Mr. Tulkinghorn, being always denied to her by his Employer (which I had no doubts at the time was a foreign mode of viewing a clerk) she would do herself the pleasure of continually calling at my place until she was let in here. Since then she has been, as I began by saying, hovering—Hovering sir," Mr. Snagsby repeats the word with pathetic emphasis, "in the court. The effects of which movement it is impossible to calculate. I shouldn't wonder if it might have already given rise to the painfullest mistakes even in the neighbours' minds, not mentioning (if such a thing was possible) my little woman. Whereas, Goodness knows," says Mr. Snagsby, shaking his head, "I never had an idea of a foreign female, except as being formerly connected with a bunch of brooms and a baby, or at the present time with a tamborine and ear-rings.[1] I never had, I do assure you sir."

Mr. Tulkinghorn has listened gravely to this complaint, and inquires, when the stationer has finished, "And that's all, is it, Snagsby?"

"Why yes sir, that's all," says Mr. Snagsby, ending with a cough that plainly adds, "and it's enough too—for me."

"I don't know what Mademoiselle Hortense may want or mean, unless she is mad," says the lawyer.

"Even if she was, you know sir," Mr. Snagsby pleads, "it wouldn't be a consolation to have some weapon or another in the form of a foreign dagger, planted in the family."

"No," says the other. "Well, well! This shall be stopped. I am sorry you have been inconvenienced. If she comes again, send her here."

Mr. Snagsby, with much bowing and short apologetic coughing,

1. In early nineteenth-century London, brooms were sold in the streets by "Buy a Broom" girls, chiefly from Flanders and Germany. The allusion to the baby is unidentified, but the tambourine suggests a gypsy broom-peddler as described in Louis Hayes' *Reminiscences of Manchester from 1840*: "a dark-skinned gypsy, with black glossy hair, who dressed in the gayest of colours and danced and sang her quaint little songs, whilst her little white wooden broom . . had always a ready sale."

takes his leave, lightened in heart. Mr. Tulkinghorn goes up-stairs, saying to himself, "These women were created to give trouble, the whole earth over. The Mistress not being enough to deal with, here's the maid now! But I will be short with *this* jade at least!"

So saying, he unlocks his door, gropes his way into his murky rooms, lights his candles, and looks about him. It is too dark to see much of allegory over-head there; but that importunate Roman, who is for ever toppling out of the clouds and pointing, is at his old work pretty distinctly. Not honouring him with much attention, Mr. Tulkinghorn takes a small key from his pocket, unlocks a drawer in which there is another key, which unlocks a chest in which there is another, and so comes to the cellar-key, with which he prepares to descend to the regions of old wine. He is going towards the door with a candle in his hand, when a knock comes.

"Who's this?—Aye, aye, mistress, it's you, is it? You appear at a good time. I have just been hearing of you. Now! What do *you* want?"

He stands the candle on the chimney-piece in the clerk's hall, and taps his dry cheek with the key, as he addresses these words of welcome to Mademoiselle Hortense. That feline personage, with her lips tightly shut, and her eyes looking out at him sideways, softly closes the door before replying.

"I have had great deal of trouble to find you, sir."

"*Have* you!"

"I have been here very often, sir. It has always been said to me, he is not at home, he is engage, he is this and that, he is not for you."

"Quite right, and quite true."

"Not true. Lies!"

At times, there is a suddenness in the manner of Mademoiselle Hortense so like a bodily spring upon the subject of it, that such subject involuntarily starts and falls back. It is Mr. Tulkinghorn's case at present, though Mademoiselle Hortense, with her eyes almost shut up (but still looking out sideways), is only smiling contemptuously and shaking her head.

"Now, mistress," says the lawyer, tapping the key hastily upon the chimney-piece. "If you have anything to say, say it, say it."

"Sir, you have not use me well. You have been mean and shabby."

"Mean and shabby, eh?" returns the lawyer, rubbing his nose with the key.

"Yes. What is it that I tell you? You know you have. You have attrapped me—catched me—to give you information; you have asked me to show you the dress of mine my Lady must have wore that night, you have prayed me to come in it here to meet that boy—Say! Is it not?" Mademoiselle Hortense makes another spring.

"You are a vixen, a vixen!" Mr. Tulkinghorn seems to meditate, as he looks distrustfully at her; then he replies, "Well, wench, well. I paid you."

"You paid me!" she repeats, with fierce disdain. "Two sovereign! I have not change them, I ref-use them, I des-pise them, I throw them from me!" Which she literally does, taking them out of her bosom as she speaks, and flinging them with such violence on the floor, that they jerk up again into the light before they roll away into corners, and slowly settle down there after spinning vehemently.

"Now!" says Mademoiselle Hortense, darkening her large eyes again. "You have paid me? Eh my God, O yes!"

Mr. Tulkinghorn rubs his head with the key, while she entertains herself with a sarcastic laugh.

"You must be rich, my fair friend," he composedly observes, "to throw money about in that way!"

"I *am* rich," she returns, "I am very rich in hate. I hate my Lady, of all my heart. You know that."

"Know it? How should I know it?"

"Because you have known it perfectly, before you prayed me to give you that information. Because you have known perfectly that I was en-r-r-r-raged!" It appears impossible for Mademoiselle to roll the letter r sufficiently in this word, notwithstanding that she assists her energetic delivery, by clenching both her hands, and setting all her teeth.

"Oh! I knew that, did I?" says Mr. Tulkinghorn, examining the wards of the key.

"Yes, without doubt. I am not blind. You have made sure of me because you knew that. You had reason! I det-est her." Mademoiselle folds her arms, and throws this last remark at him over one of her shoulders.

"Having said this, have you anything else to say, Mademoiselle?"

"I am not yet placed. Place me well. Find me a good condition! If you cannot, or do not choose to do that, employ me to pursue her, to chase her, to disgrace and to dishonour her. I will help you well, and with a good will. It is what *you* do. Do I not know that?"

"You appear to know a good deal," Mr. Tulkinghorn retorts.

"Do I not? Is it that I am so weak as to believe, like a child, that I come here in that dress to rec-eive that boy, only to decide a little bet, a wager?—Eh my God, O yes!" In this reply, down to the word "wager" inclusive, Mademoiselle has been ironically polite and tender; then, as suddenly dashed into the bitterest and most defiant scorn, with her black eyes in one and the same moment very nearly shut, and staringly wide open.

"Now, let us see," says Mr. Tulkinghorn, tapping his chin with the key, and looking imperturbably at her, "how this matter stands."

"Ah! Let us see," Mademoiselle assents, with many angry and tight nods of her head.

"You come here to make a remarkably modest demand, which you have just stated, and it not being conceded, you will come again."

"And again," says Mademoiselle, with more tight and angry nods. "And yet again. And yet again. And many times again. In effect, for ever!"

"And not only here, but you will go to Mr. Snagsby's, too, perhaps? That visit not succeeding either, you will go again perhaps?"

"And again," repeats Mademoiselle, cataleptic with determination. "And yet again. And yet again. And many times again. In effect, for ever!"

"Very well. Now Mademoiselle Hortense, let me recommend you to take the candle and pick up that money of yours. I think you will find it behind the clerk's partition in the corner yonder."

She merely throws a laugh over her shoulder, and stands her ground with folded arms.

"You will not, eh?"

"No, I will not!"

"So much the poorer you; so much the richer I! Look, mistress, this is the key of my wine-cellar. It is a large key, but the keys of prisons are larger. In this city, there are houses of correction (where the treadmills are, for women) the gates of which are very strong and heavy, and no doubt the keys too. I am afraid a lady of your spirit and activity would find it an inconvenience to have one of those keys turned upon her for any length of time. What do you think?"

"I think," Mademoiselle replies, without any action, and in a clear obliging voice, "that you are a miserable wretch."

"Probably," returns Mr. Tulkinghorn, quietly blowing his nose. "But I don't ask what you think of myself; I ask what you think of the prison."

"Nothing. What does it matter to me?"

"Why it matters this much, mistress," says the lawyer, deliberately putting away his handkerchief, and adjusting his frill, "the law is so despotic here, that it interposes to prevent any of our good English citizens from being troubled, even by a lady's visits, against his desire. And, on his complaining that he is so troubled, it takes hold of the troublesome lady, and shuts her up in prison under hard discipline. Turns the key upon her, mistress." Illustrating with the cellar-key.

"Truly?" returns Mademoiselle, in the same pleasant voice.

"That is droll! But—my faith!—still what does it matter to me?"

"My fair friend," says Mr. Tulkinghorn, "make another visit here, or at Mr. Snagsby's, and you shall learn."

"In that case you will send Me to the prison, perhaps?"

"Perhaps."

It would be contradictory for one in Mademoiselle's state of agreeable jocularity to foam at the mouth, otherwise a tigerish expansion thereabouts might look as if a very little more would make her do it.

"In a word, mistress," says Mr. Tulkinghorn, "I am sorry to be unpolite, but if you ever present yourself uninvited here——or there——again, I will give you over to the police. Their gallantry is great, but they carry troublesome people through the streets in an ignominious manner; strapped down on a board, my good wench."

"I will prove you," whispers Mademoiselle, stretching out her hand, "I will try if you dare to do it!"

"And if," pursues the lawyer, without minding her, "I place you in that good condition of being locked up in jail, it will be some time before you find yourself at liberty again."

"I will prove you," repeats Mademoiselle in her former whisper.

"And now," proceeds the lawyer, still without minding her, "you had better go. Think twice, before you come here again."

"Think you," she answers, "twice two hundred times!"

"You were dismissed by your lady, you know," Mr. Tulkinghorn observes, following her out upon the staircase, "as the most implacable and unmanageable of women. Now turn over a new leaf, and take warning by what I say to you. For what I say, I mean; and what I threaten, I will do, mistress."

She goes down without answering or looking behind her. When she is gone, he goes down too; and returning with his cobweb-covered bottle, devotes himself to a leisurely enjoyment of its contents; now and then, as he throws his head back in his chair, catching sight of the pertinacious Roman pointing from the ceiling.

Chapter XLIII

ESTHER'S NARRATIVE

It matters little now, how much I thought of my living mother who had told me evermore to consider her dead. I could not venture to approach her, or to communicate with her in writing, for my sense of the peril in which her life was passed was only to be equalled by my fears of increasing it. Knowing that my mere existence as a living creature was an unforeseen danger in her way, I could not always conquer that terror of myself which had seized me when I first knew the secret. At no time did I dare to utter her name. I felt as if I did not even dare to hear it. If the conversation anywhere, when I was present, took that direction, as it sometimes naturally did, I tried not to hear—I mentally counted, repeated something that I knew, or went out of the room. I am conscious now, that I often did these things when there can have been no danger of her being spoken of; but I did them in the dread I had of hearing anything that might lead to her betrayal, and to her betrayal through me.

It matters little now how often I recalled the tones of my mother's voice, wondered whether I should ever hear it again as I so longed to do, and thought how strange and desolate it was that it should be so new to me. It matters little that I watched for every public mention of my mother's name; that I passed and repassed the door of her house in town, loving it, but afraid to look at it; that I once sat in the theatre when my mother was there and saw me, and when we were so wide asunder, before the great company of all degrees, that any link or confidence between us seemed a dream. It is all, all over. My lot has been so blest that I can relate little of myself which is not a story of goodness and generosity in others. I may well pass that little, and go on.

When we were settled at home again, Ada and I had many conversations with my guardian, of which Richard was the theme. My dear girl was deeply grieved that he should do their kind cousin so much wrong; but she was so faithful to Richard, that she could not bear to blame him, even for that. My guardian was assured of it, and never coupled his name with a word of reproof. "Rick is mistaken, my dear," he would say to her. "Well, well! we have all been mistaken over and over again. We must trust to you and time to set him right."

We knew afterwards what we suspected then; that he did not trust to time until he had often tried to open Richard's eyes. That he had written to him, gone to him, talked with him, tried every gentle and persuasive art his kindness could devise. Our poor devoted Richard was deaf and blind to all. If he were wrong, he would make amends when the Chancery suit was over. If he were groping in the dark, he could not do better than do his utmost to clear away those clouds in which so much was confused and obscured. Suspicion and misunderstanding were the fault of the suit? Then let him work the suit out, and come through it to his right mind. This was his unvarying reply. Jarndyce and Jarndyce had obtained such possession of his whole nature, that it was impossible to place any consideration before him which he did not—with a distorted kind of reason—make a new argument in favour of his doing what he did. "So that it is even more mischievous," said my guardian once to me, "to remonstrate with the poor dear fellow, than to leave him alone."

I took one of these opportunities of mentioning my doubts of Mr. Skimpole as a good adviser for Richard.

"Adviser!" returned my guardian, laughing. "My dear, who would advise with Skimpole?"

"Encourager would perhaps have been a better word," said I.

"Encourager!" returned my guardian again. "Who could be encouraged by Skimpole?"

"Not Richard?" I asked.

"No," he replied. "Such an unworldly, uncalculating, gossamer creature, is a relief to him, and an amusement. But as to advising or encouraging, or occupying a serious station towards anybody or anything, it is simply not to be thought of in such a child as Skimpole."

"Pray, cousin John," said Ada, who had just joined us, and now looked over my shoulder, "what made him such a child?"

"What made him such a child?" inquired my guardian, rubbing his head, a little at a loss.

"Yes, cousin John."

"Why," he slowly replied, roughening his head more and more, "he is all sentiment, and—susceptibility, and—and sensibility—and—and imagination. And these qualities are not regulated in him, somehow. I suppose the people who admired him for them in his youth, attached too much importance to them, and too little to any training that would have balanced and adjusted them; and so he became what he is. Hey?" said my guardian, stopping short, and looking at us hopefully. "What do you think, you two?"

Ada, glancing at me, said she thought it was a pity he should be an expense to Richard.

"So it is, so it is," returned my guardian, hurriedly. "That must not be. We must arrange that. I must prevent it. That will never do."

And I said I thought it was to be regretted that he had ever introduced Richard to Mr. Vholes, for a present of five pounds.

"Did he?" said my guardian, with a passing shade of vexation on his face. "But there you have the man. There you have the man! There is nothing mercenary in that, with him. He has no idea of the value of money. He introduces Rick; and then he is good friends with Mr. Vholes, and borrows five pounds of him. He means nothing by it, and thinks nothing of it. He told you himself, I'll be bound, my dear?"

"Oh yes!" said I.

"Exactly!" cried my guardian, quite triumphant. "There you have the man! If he had meant any harm by it, or was conscious of any harm in it, he wouldn't tell it. He tells it as he does it, in mere simplicity. But you shall see him in his own home, and then you'll understand him better. We must pay a visit to Harold Skimpole, and caution him on these points. Lord bless you, my dears, an infant, an infant!"

In pursuance of this plan, we went into London on an early day, and presented ourselves at Mr. Skimpole's door.

He lived in a place called the Polygon,[1] in Somers Town, where there were at that time a number of poor Spanish refugees[2] walking about in cloaks, smoking little paper cigars.[3] Whether he was a better tenant than one might have supposed, in consequence of his friend Somebody always paying his rent at last, or whether his inaptitude for business rendered it particularly difficult to turn him out, I don't know; but he had occupied the same house some years. It was in a state of dilapidation quite equal to our expectation. Two or three of the area railings were gone; the water-butt was broken; the knocker was loose; the bell-handle had been pulled off a long time, to judge from the rusty state of the wire; and dirty footprints on the steps were the only signs of its being inhabited.

A slatternly full-blown girl, who seemed to be bursting out at the rents in her gown and the cracks in her shoes, like an over-ripe berry, answered our knock by opening the door a very little way, and stopping up the gap with her figure. As she knew Mr. Jarndyce (indeed Ada and I both thought that she evidently associated him with the receipt of her wages), she immediately relented and allowed us to pass in. The lock of the door being in a disabled condition, she then applied herself to securing it with the chain, which was not in good action either, and said would we go up-stairs?

We went up-stairs to the first floor, still seeing no other furniture than the dirty footprints. Mr. Jarndyce, without further ceremony, entered a room there, and we followed. It was dingy enough, and not at all clean; but furnished with an odd kind of shabby luxury, with a large footstool, a sofa, and plenty of cushions, an easy-chair, and plenty of pillows, a piano, books, drawing materials, music, newspapers, and a few sketches and pictures. A broken pane of glass in one of the dirty windows was papered and wafered over; but there was a little plate of hothouse nectarines on the table, and there was another of grapes, and another of sponge-cakes, and there was a bottle of light wine. Mr. Skimpole himself reclined

1. A ring of houses built in the late eighteenth century.

2. A band of exiles seeking to overthrow the Spanish government who settled in this section of London in the late 1820's. This group, under General Torrijos, perished in 1831 during an unsuccessful landing in Spain. Since they were succeeded by later waves of political exiles from Spain and other countries who settled in London, it is not justifiable to date the action of the novel only by the appearance of the Torrijos exiles (as some authorities have done).

3. Cigarettes.

upon the sofa, in a dressing gown, drinking some fragrant coffee from an old china cup—it was then about mid-day—and looking at a collection of wallflowers in the balcony.

He was not in the least disconcerted by our appearance, but rose and received us in his usual airy manner.

"Here I am, you see!" he said, when we were seated: not without some little difficulty, the greater part of the chairs being broken. "Here I am! This is my frugal breakfast. Some men want legs of beef and mutton for breakfast; *I* don't. Give my my peach, my cup of coffee, and my claret; I am content. I don't want them for themselves, but they remind me of the sun. There's nothing solar about legs of beef and mutton. Mere animal satisfaction!"

"This is our friend's consulting room (or would be, if he ever prescribed), his sanctum, his studio," said my guardian to us.

"Yes," said Mr. Skimpole, turning his bright face about, "this is the bird's cage. This is where the bird lives and sings. They pluck his feathers now and then, and clip his wings; but he sings, he sings!"

He handed us the grapes, repeating in his radiant way, "he sings! Not an ambitious note, but still he sings."

"These are very fine," said my guardian. "A present?"

"No," he answered. "No! Some amiable gardener sells them. His man wanted to know, when he brought them last evening, whether he should wait for the money. 'Really, my friend,' I said, 'I think not—if your time is of any value to you.' I suppose it was, for he went away."

My guardian looked at us with a smile, as though he asked us, "Is it possible to be worldly with this baby?"

"This is a day," said Mr. Skimpole, gaily taking a little claret in a tumbler, "that will ever be remembered here. We shall call it the Saint Clare and Saint Summerson day. You must see my daughters. I have a blue-eyed daughter who is my Beauty daughter, I have a Sentiment daughter, and I have a Comedy daughter. You must see them all. They'll be enchanted."

He was going to summon them, when my guardian interposed, and asked him to pause a moment, as he wished to say a word to him first. "My dear Jarndyce," he cheerfully replied, going back to his sofa, "as many moments as you please. Time is no object here. We never know what o'clock it is, and we never care. Not the way to get on in life, you'll tell me? Certainly. But we *don't* get on in life. We don't pretend to do it."

My guardian looked at us again, plainly saying, "You hear him?"

"Now Harold," he began, "the word I have to say, relates to Rick."

"The dearest friend I have!" returned Mr. Skimpole, cordially. "I suppose he ought not to be my dearest friend, as he is not on terms with you. But he is, I can't help it; he is full of youthful poetry, and I love him. If you don't like it, I can't help it. I love him."

The engaging frankness with which he made this declaration, really had a disinterested appearance, and captivated my guardian; if not, for the moment, Ada too.

"You are welcome to love him as much as you like," returned Mr. Jarndyce, "but we must save his pocket, Harold."

"Oh!" said Mr. Skimpole. "His pocket! Now, you are coming to what I don't understand." Taking a little more claret, and dipping one of the cakes in it, he shook his head, and smiled at Ada and me with an ingenuous foreboding that he never could be made to understand.

"If you go with him here or there," said my guardian, plainly, "you must not let him pay for both."

"My dear Jarndyce," returned Mr. Skimpole, his genial face irradiated by the comicality of this idea, "what am I to do? If he takes me anywhere, I must go. And how can *I* pay? I never have any money. If I had any money, I don't know anything about it. Suppose I say to a man, how much? Suppose the man says to me seven and sixpence? *I* know nothing about seven and sixpence. It is impossible for me to pursue the subject, with any consideration for the man. I don't go about asking busy people what seven and sixpence is in Moorish—which I don't understand. Why should I go about asking them what seven and sixpence is in Money—which I don't understand?"

"Well," said my guardian, by no means displeased with this artless reply, "if you come to any kind of journeying with Rick, you must borrow the money of me (never breathing the least allusion to that circumstance), and leave the calculation to him."

"My dear Jarndyce," returned Mr. Skimpole, "I will do anything to give you pleasure, but it seems an idle form—a superstition. Besides, I give you my word, Miss Clare and my dear Miss Summerson, I thought Mr. Carstone was immensely rich. I thought he had only to make over something, or to sign a bond, or a draft, or a cheque, or a bill, or to put something on a file somewhere, to bring down a shower of money."

"Indeed it is not so, sir," said Ada. "He is poor."

"No, really?" returned Mr. Skimpole, with his bright smile, "you surprise me."

"And not being the richer for trusting in a rotten reed," said my guardian, laying his hand emphatically on the sleeve of Mr. Skimpole's dressing-gown, "be you very careful not to encourage him in that reliance, Harold."

"My dear good friend," returned Mr. Skimpole, "and my dear Miss Summerson, and my dear Miss Clare, how can I do that? It's business, and I don't know business. It is he who encourages me. He emerges from great feats of business, presents the brightest prospects before me as their result, and calls upon me to admire them. I *do* admire them—as bright prospects. But I know no more about them, and I tell him so."

The helpless kind of candour with which he presented this before us, the light-hearted manner in which he was amused by his innocence, the fantastic way in which he took himself under his own protection and argued about that curious person, combined with the delightful ease of everything he said exactly to make out my guardian's case. The more I saw of him, the more unlikely it seemed to me, when he was present, that he could design, conceal, or influence anything; and yet the less likely that appeared when he was not present, and the less agreeable it was to think of his having anything to do with any one for whom I cared.

Hearing that his examination (as he called it) was now over, Mr. Skimpole left the room with a radiant face to fetch his daughters (his sons had run away at various times), leaving my guardian quite delighted by the manner in which he had vindicated his childish character. He soon came back, bringing with him the three young ladies and Mrs. Skimpole, who had once been a beauty, but was now a delicate high-nosed invalid, suffering under a complication of disorders.

"This," said Mr. Skimpole, "is my Beauty daughter, Arethusa—plays and sings odds and ends like her father. This is my Sentiment daughter, Laura—plays a little but don't sing. This is my Comedy daughter, Kitty—sings a little but don't play. We all draw a little, and compose a little, and none of us have any idea of time or money."

Mrs. Skimpole sighed, I thought, as if she would have been glad to strike out this item in the family attainments. I also thought that she rather impressed her sigh upon my guardian, and that she took every opportunity of throwing in another.

"It is pleasant," said Mr. Skimpole, turning his sprightly eyes from one to the other of us, "and it is whimsically interesting, to trace peculiarities in families. In this family we are all children, and I am the youngest."

The daughters, who appeared to be very fond of him, were amused by this droll fact; particularly the Comedy daughter.

"My dears, it is true," said Mr. Skimpole, "is it not? So it is, and so it must be, because, like the dogs in the hymn, 'it is our nature to.'[4] Now, here is Miss Summerson with a fine administrative

4. From *The Divine Songs* (1715) of Isaac Watts (1674–1748): "Let dogs delight to bark and bite,/ For God hath made them so;/ Let bears and lions growl and fight,/ For 'tis their nature to."

capacity, and a knowledge of details perfectly surprising. It will sound very strange in Miss Summerson's ears, I dare say, that we know nothing about chops in this house. But we don't; not the least. We can't cook anything whatever. A needle and thread we don't know how to use. We admire the people who possess the practical wisdom we want; but we don't quarrel with them. Then why should they quarrel with us? Live, and let live, we say to them. Live upon your practical wisdom, and let us live upon you!"

He laughed, but, as usual, seemed quite candid, and really to mean what he said.

"We have sympathy, my roses," said Mr. Skimpole, "sympathy for everything. Have we not?"

"O yes, papa!" cried the three daughters.

"In fact, that is our family department," said Mr. Skimpole, "in this hurly-burly of life. We are capable of looking on and of being interested, and we *do* look on, and we *are* interested. What more can we do? Here is my Beauty daughter, married these three years. Now, I dare say her marrying another child, and having two more, was all wrong in point of political economy; but it was very agreeable. We had our little festivities on those occasions, and exchanged social ideas. She brought her young husband home one day, and they and their young fledgelings have their nest up-stairs. I dare say, at some time or other, Sentiment and Comedy will bring *their* husbands home, and have *their* nests up-stairs too. So we get on, we don't know how, but somehow."

She looked very young, indeed, to be the mother of two children; and I could not help pitying both her and them. It was evident that the three daughters had grown up as they could, and had had just as little hap-hazard instruction as qualified them to be their father's playthings in his idlest hours. His pictorial tastes were consulted, I observed, in their respective styles of wearing their hair; the Beauty daughter being in the classic manner; the Sentiment daughter luxuriant and flowing; and the Comedy daugher in the arch style, with a good deal of sprightly forehead, and vivacious little curls dotted about the corners of her eyes. They were dressed to correspond, though in a most untidy and negligent way.

Ada and I conversed with these young ladies, and found them wonderfully like their father. In the meanwhile Mr. Jarndyce (who had been rubbing his head to a great extent, and hinting at a change in the wind) talked with Mrs. Skimpole in a corner, where we could not help hearing the chink of money. Mr. Skimpole had previously volunteered to go home with us, and had withdrawn to dress himself for the purpose.

"My roses," he said, when he came back, "take care of mamma. She is poorly to-day. By going home with Mr. Jarndyce for a day or two, I shall hear the larks sing, and preserve my amiability. It has been tried, you know, and would be tried again if I remained at home."

"That bad man!" said the Comedy daughter.

"At the very time when he knew papa was lying down by his wall-flowers, looking at the blue sky," Laura complained.

"And when the smell of hay was in the air!" said Arethusa.

"It showed a want of poetry in the man," Mr. Skimpole assented; but with perfect good-humour. "It was coarse. There was an absence of the finer touches of humanity in it! My daughters have taken great offence," he explained to us, "at an honest man——"

"Not honest, papa. Impossible!" they all three protested.

"At a rough kind of fellow—a sort of human hedgehog rolled up," said Mr. Skimpole, "who is a baker in this neighbourhood, and from whom we borrowed a couple of arm-chairs. We wanted a couple of arm-chairs, and we hadn't got them, and therefore of course we looked to a man who *had* got them, to lend them. Well! this morose person lent them, and we wore them out. When they were worn out, he wanted them back. He had them back. He was contented, you will say. Not at all. He objected to their being worn. I reasoned with him, and pointed out his mistake. I said, 'Can you, at your time of life, be so headstrong, my friend, as to persist that an arm-chair is a thing to put upon a shelf and look at? That it is an object to contemplate, to survey from a distance, to consider from a point of sight? Don't you *know* that these arm-chairs were borrowed to be sat upon?' He was unreasonable and unpersuadable, and used intemperate language. Being as patient as I am at this minute, I addressed another appeal to him. I said, 'Now, my good man, however our business capacities may vary, we are all children of one great mother, Nature. On this blooming summer morning here you see me' (I was on the sofa) 'with flowers before me, fruit upon the table, the cloudless sky above me, the air full of fragrance, contemplating Nature. I entreat you, by our common brotherhood, not to interpose between me and a subject so sublime, the absurd figure of an angry baker!' But he did," said Mr. Skimpole, raising his laughing eyebrows in playful astonishment; "he did interpose that ridiculous figure, and he does, and he will again. And therefore I am very glad to get out of his way, and to go home with my friend Jarndyce."

It seemed to escape his consideration that Mrs. Skimpole and the daughters remained behind to encounter the baker; but this was so old a story to all of them that it had become a matter of course. He took leave of his family with a tenderness as airy and graceful as any other aspect in which he showed himself, and rode away with us in perfect harmony of mind. We had an opportunity of seeing through some open doors, as we went down-stairs, that his own apartment was a palace to the rest of the house.

I could have no anticipation, and I had none, that something very startling to me at the moment, and ever memorable to me in what ensued from it, was to happen before this day was out. Our guest was in such spirits on the way home, that I could do nothing but listen to him and wonder at him; nor was I alone in this, for Ada yielded to the same fascination. As to my guardian, the wind, which had threatened to become fixed in the east when we left Somers Town, veered completely round, before we were a couple of miles from it.

Whether of questionable childishness or not, in any other matters, Mr. Skimpole had a child's enjoyment of change and bright weather. In no way wearied by his sallies on the road, he was in the drawing-room before any of us; and I heard him at the piano while I was yet looking after my housekeeping, singing refrains of barcaroles and drinking songs, Italian and German, by the score.

We were all assembled shortly before dinner, and he was still at the piano idly picking out in his luxurious way little strains of music, and talking between whiles of finishing some sketches of the ruined old Verulam wall,[5] to-morrow, which he had begun a year or two ago and had got tired of; when a card was brought in, and my guardian read aloud in a surprised voice:

"Sir Leicester Dedlock!"

The visitor was in the room while it was yet turning round with me, and before I had the power to stir. If I had had it, I should have hurried away. I had not even the presence of mind, in my giddiness, to retire to Ada in the window, or to see the window, or to know where it was. I heard my name, and found that my guardian was presenting me, before I could move to a chair.

"Pray be seated, Sir Leicester."

"Mr. Jarndyce," said Sir Leicester in reply, as he bowed and seated himself, "I do myself the honour of calling here—"

"You do *me* the honour, Sir Leicester."

"Thank you—of calling here on my road from Lincolnshire, to express my regret that any cause of complaint, however strong, that I may have against a gentleman who—who is known to you and has been your host, and to whom therefore I will make no further reference, should have prevented you, still more ladies under your escort and charge, from seeing whatever little there may be to gratify a polite and refined taste, at my house, Chesney Wold."

"You are exceedingly obliging, Sir Leicester, and on behalf of

5. Remains of the walls of a city called, in Roman times, Verulamium. Its site, in the vicinity of St. Albans, is now called Old Verulam.

those ladies (who are present) and for myself, I thank you very much."

"It is possible, Mr. Jarndyce, that the gentleman to whom, for the reasons I have mentioned, I refrain from making further allusion—it is possible, Mr. Jarndyce, that that gentleman may have done me the honour so far to misapprehend my character, as to induce you to believe that you would not have been received by my local establishment in Lincolnshire with that urbanity, that courtesy, which its members are instructed to show to all ladies and gentlemen who present themselves at that house. I merely beg to observe, sir, that the fact is the reverse."

My guardian delicately dismissed this remark without making any verbal answer.

"It has given me pain, Mr. Jarndyce," Sir Leicester weightily proceeded. "I assure you, sir, it has given—Me—pain—to learn from the housekeeper at Chesney Wold, that a gentleman who was in your company in that part of the county, and who would appear to possess a cultivated taste for the Fine Arts, was likewise deterred, by some such cause, from examining the family pictures with that leisure, that attention, that care, which he might have desired to bestow upon them, and which some of them might possibly have repaid." Here he produced a card, and read, with much gravity and a little trouble, through his eye-glass, "Mr. Hirrold,—Herald—Harold—Skampling—Skumpling—I beg your pardon,—Skimpole."

"This is Mr. Harold Skimpole," said my guardian, evidently surprised.

"Oh!" exclaimed Sir Leicester, "I am happy to meet Mr. Skimpole, and to have the opportunity of tendering my personal regrets. I hope, sir, that when you again find yourself in my part of the county, you will be under no similar sense of restraint."

"You are very obliging, Sir Leicester Dedlock. So encouraged, I shall certainly give myself the pleasure and advantage of another visit to your beautiful house. The owners of such places as Chesney Wold," said Mr. Skimpole, with his usual happy and easy air, "are public benefactors. They are good enough to maintain a number of delightful objects for the admiration and pleasure of us poor men; and not to reap all the admiration and pleasure that they yield, is to be ungrateful to our benefactors."

Sir Leicester seemed to approve of this sentiment highly. "An artist, sir?"

"No," returned Mr. Skimpole. "A perfectly idle man. A mere amateur."

Sir Leicester seemed to approve of this even more. He hoped he might have the good fortune to be at Chesney Wold when Mr.

Skimpole next came down into Lincolnshire. Mr. Skimpole professed himself much flattered and honoured.

"Mr. Skimpole mentioned," pursued Sir Leicester, addressing himself again to my guardian; "mentioned to the housekeeper, who, as he may have observed, is an old and attached retainer of the family——"

("That is, when I walked through the house the other day, on the occasion of my going down to visit Miss Summerson and Miss Clare," Mr. Skimpole airily explained to us.)

"That the friend with whom he had formerly been staying there, was Mr. Jarndyce." Sir Leicester bowed to the bearer of that name. "And hence I became aware of the circumstance for which I have professed my regret. That this should have occurred to any gentleman, Mr. Jarndyce, but especially a gentleman formerly known to Lady Dedlock, and indeed claiming some distant connexion with her, and for whom (as I learn from my Lady herself) she entertains a high respect, does, I assure you, give—Me—pain."

"Pray say no more about it, Sir Leicester," returned my guardian. "I am very sensible, as I am sure we all are, of your consideration. Indeed the mistake was mine, and I ought to apologise for it."

I had not once looked up. I had not seen the visitor, and had not even appeared to myself to hear the conversation. It surprises me to find that I can recall it, for it seemed to make no impression on me as it passed. I heard them speaking, but my mind was so confused, and my instinctive avoidance of this gentleman made his presence so distressing to me, that I thought I understood nothing, through the rushing in my head and the beating of my heart.

"I mentioned the subject to Lady Dedlock," said Sir Leicester, rising, "and my Lady informed me that she had had the pleasure of exchanging a few words with Mr. Jarndyce and his wards, on the occasion of an accidental meeting during their sojourn in the vicinity. Permit me, Mr. Jarndyce, to repeat to yourself, and to these ladies, the assurance I have already tendered to Mr. Skimpole. Circumstances undoubtedly prevent my saying that it would afford me any gratification to hear that Mr. Boythorn had favoured my house with his presence; but those circumstances are confined to that gentleman himself, and do not extend beyond him."

"You know my old opinion of him," said Mr. Skimpole, lightly appealing to us. "An amiable bull, who is determined to make every colour scarlet!"

Sir Leicester Dedlock coughed, as if he could not possibly hear another word in reference to such an individual; and took his leave with great ceremony and politeness. I got to my own room with all possible speed, and remained there until I had recovered my self-command. It had been very much disturbed; but I was thankful to find, when I went down-stairs again, that they only rallied me for having been shy and mute before the great Lincolnshire baronet.

By that time I had made up my mind that the period was come when I must tell my guardian what I knew. The possibility of my being brought into contact with my mother, of my being taken to her house,—even of Mr. Skimpole's, however distantly associated with me, receiving kindnesses and obligations from her husband,—was so painful, that I felt I could no longer guide myself without his assistance.

When we had retired for the night, and Ada and I had had our usual talk in our pretty room, I went out at my door again, and sought my guardian among his books. I knew he always read at that hour; and as I drew near, I saw the light shining out into the passage from his reading-lamp.

"May I come in, guardian?"

"Surely, little woman. What's the matter?"

"Nothing is the matter. I thought I would like to take this quiet time of saying a word to you about myself."

He put a chair for me, shut his book, and put it by, and turned his kind attentive face towards me. I could not help observing that it wore that curious expression I had observed in it once before—on that night when he had said that he was in no trouble which I could readily understand.

"What concerns you, my dear Esther," said he, "concerns us all. You cannot be more ready to speak than I am to hear."

"I know that, guardian. But I have such need of your advice and support. O! you don't know how much need I have to-night."

He looked unprepared for my being so earnest, and even a little alarmed.

"Or how anxious I have been to speak to you," said I, "ever since the visitor was here to-day."

"The visitor, my dear! Sir Leicester Dedlock?"

"Yes."

He folded his arms, and sat looking at me with an air of the profoundest astonishment, awaiting what I should say next. I did not know how to prepare him.

"Why, Esther," said he, breaking into a smile, "our visitor and you are the two last persons on earth I should have thought of connecting together!"

"O yes, guardian, I know it. And I too, but a little while ago."

The smile passed from his face, and he became graver than before. He crossed to the door to see that it was shut (but I had seen to that), and resumed his seat before me.

"Guardian," said I, "do you remember, when we were overtaken by the thunderstorm, Lady Dedlock's speaking to you of her sister?"

"Of course. Of course I do."

"And reminding you that she and her sister had differed; had 'gone their several ways'?"

"Of course."

"Why did they separate, Guardian?"

His face quite altered as he looked at me. "My child, what questions are these! I never knew. No one but themselves ever did know, I believe. Who could tell what the secrets of those two handsome and proud women were! You have seen Lady Dedlock. If you had ever seen her sister, you would know her to have been as resolute and haughty as she."

"O guardian, I have seen her many and many a time!"

"Seen her?"

He paused a little, biting his lip. "Then, Esther, when you spoke to me long ago of Boythorn, and when I told you that he was all but married once, and that the lady did not die, but died to him, and that that time had had its influence on his later life—did you know it all, and know who the lady was?"

"No, guardian," I returned, fearful of the light that dimly broke upon me. "Nor do I know yet."

"Lady Dedlock's sister."

"And why," I could scarcely ask him, "why, guardian, pray tell me why were *they* parted?"

"It was her act, and she kept its motives in her inflexible heart. He afterwards did conjecture (but it was mere conjecture), that some injury which her haughty spirit had received in her cause of quarrel with her sister, had wounded her beyond all reason; but she wrote him that from the date of that letter she died to him—as in literal truth she did—and that the resolution was exacted from her by her knowledge of his proud temper and his strained sense of honour, which were both her nature too. In consideration for those master points in him, and even in consideration for them in herself, she made the sacrifice, she said, and would live in it and die in it. She did both, I fear; certainly he never saw her, never heard of her from that hour. Nor did any one."

"O guardian, what have I done!" I cried, giving way to my grief; "what sorrow have I innocently caused!"

"You caused, Esther?"

"Yes, guardian. Innocently, but most surely. That secluded sister is my first remembrance."

"No, no!" he cried, starting.

"Yes, guardian, yes! And *her* sister is my mother!"

I would have told him all my mother's letter, but he would not hear it then. He spoke so tenderly and wisely to me, and he put so plainly before me all I had myself imperfectly thought and hoped in my better state of mind, that, penetrated as I had been with fervent gratitude towards him through so many years, I believed I had never loved him so dearly, never thanked him in my heart so fully, as I did that night. And when he had taken me to my room and kissed me at the door, and when at last I lay down to sleep, my thought was how could I ever be busy enough, how could I ever be good enough, how in my little way could I ever hope to be forgetful enough of myself, devoted enough to him, and useful enough to others, to show him how I blessed and honoured him.

Chapter XLIV

THE LETTER AND THE ANSWER

My guardian called me into his room next morning, and then I told him what had been left untold on the previous night. There was nothing to be done, he said, but to keep the secret, and to avoid another such encounter as that of yesterday. He understood my feeling, and entirely shared it. He charged himself even with restraining Mr. Skimpole from improving his opportunity. One person whom he need not name to me, it was not now possible for him to advise or help. He wished it were; but no such thing could be. If her mistrust of the lawyer whom she had mentioned were well-founded, which he scarcely doubted, he dreaded discovery. He knew something of him, both by sight and by reputation, and it was certain that he was a dangerous man. Whatever happened, he repeatedly impressed upon me with anxious affection and kindness, I was as innocent of, as himself; and as unable to influence.

"Nor do I understand," said he, "that any doubts tend towards you, my dear. Much suspicion may exist without that connexion."

"With the lawyer," I returned. "But two other persons have come into my mind since I have been anxious." Then I told him all about Mr. Guppy, who I feared might have had his vague surmises when I little understood his meaning, but in whose silence after our last interview I expressed perfect confidence.

"Well," said my guardian. "Then we may dismiss him for the present. Who is the other?"

I called to his recollection the French maid, and the eager offer of herself she had made to me.

"Ha!" he returned, thoughtfully, "that is a more alarming person than the clerk. But after all, my dear, it was but seeking for a new service. She had seen you and Ada a little while before, and it was natural that you should come into her head. She merely proposed herself for your maid, you know. She did nothing more."

"Her manner was strange," said I.

"Yes, and her manner was strange when she took her shoes off, and showed that cool relish for a walk that might have ended in her death-bed," said my guardian. "It would be useless self-distress and torment to reckon up such chances and possibilities. There are very few harmless circumstances that would not seem full of perilous meaning, so considered. Be hopeful, little woman. You can be nothing better than yourself; be that, through this knowledge, as you were before you had it. It is the best you can do for everybody's sake. I sharing the secret with you——"

"And lightening it, guardian, so much," said I.

"—Will be attentive to what passes in that family, so far as I can observe it from my distance. And if the time should come when I can stretch out a hand to render the least service to one whom it is better not to name even here, I will not fail to do it for her dear daughter's sake."

I thanked him with my whole heart. What could I ever do but thank him! I was going out at the door, when he asked me to stay a moment. Quickly turning round, I saw that same expression on his face again; and all at once, I don't know how, it flashed upon me as a new and far off possibility that I understood it.

"My dear Esther," said my guardian, "I have long had something in my thoughts that I have wished to say to you."

"Indeed?"

"I have had some difficulty in approaching it, and I still have. I should wish it to be so deliberately said, and so deliberately considered. Would you object to my writing it?"

"Dear guardian, how could I object to your writing anything for *me* to read?"

"Then see, my love," said he, with his cheery smile; "am I at this moment quite as plain and easy—do I seem as open, as honest and old-fashioned, as I am at any time?"

I answered in all earnestness, "Quite." With the strictest truth, for his momentary hesitation was gone (it had not lasted a minute), and his fine, sensible, cordial, sterling manner was restored.

"Do I look as if I suppressed anything, meant anything but what I said, had any reservation at all, no matter what?" said he, with his bright clear eyes on mine.

I answered, most assuredly he did not.

"Can you fully trust me, and thoroughly rely on what I profess, Esther?"

"Most thoroughly," said I with my whole heart.

"My dear girl," returned my guardian, "give me your hand."

He took it in his, holding me lightly with his arm, and, looking down into my face with the same genuine freshness and faithfulness of manner—the old protecting manner which had made that house my home in a moment—said, "You have wrought changes in me, little woman, since the winter day in the stagecoach. First and last you have done me a world of good, since that time."

"Ah, guardian, what have you done for me since that time!"

"But," said he, "that is not to be remembered now."

"It never can be forgotten."

"Yes, Esther," said he, with a gentle seriousness, "it is to be forgotten now; to be forgotten for a while. You are only to remember now, that nothing can change me as you know me. Can you feel quite assured of that, my dear?"

"I can, and I do," I said.

"That's much," he answered. "That's everything. But I must not take that, at a word. I will not write this something in my thoughts, until you have quite resolved within yourself that nothing can change me as you know me. If you doubt that in the least degree, I will never write it. If you are sure of that, on good consideration, send Charley to me this night week—'for the letter.' But if you are not quite certain, never send. Mind, I trust to your truth, in this thing as in everything. If you are not quite certain on that one point, never send!"

"Guardian," said I, "I am already certain. I can no more be changed in that conviction, than you can be changed towards me. I shall send Charley for the letter."

He shook my hand and said no more. Nor was any more said in reference to this conversation, either by him or me, through the whole week. When the appointed night came, I said to Charley as soon as I was alone, "Go and knock at Mr. Jarndyce's door, Charley, and say you have come from me—'for the letter.'" Charley went up the stairs, and down the stairs, and along the passages—the zig-zag way about the old-fashioned house seemed very long in my listening ears that night—and so came back, along the passages, and down the stairs, and up the stairs, and brought the letter. "Lay it on the table, Charley," said I. So Charley laid it on the table and went to bed, and I sat looking at it without taking it up, thinking of many things.

I began with my overshadowed childhood, and passed through those timid days to the heavy time when my aunt lay dead, with her resolute face so cold and set; and when I was more solitary with

Mrs. Rachael, than if I had had no one in the world to speak to or to look at. I passed to the altered days when I was so blest as to find friends in all around me, and to be beloved. I came to the time when I first saw my dear girl, and was received into that sisterly affection which was the grace and beauty of my life. I recalled the first bright gleam of welcome which had shone out of those very windows upon our expectant faces on that cold bright night, and which had never paled. I lived my happy life there over again, I went through my illness and recovery, I thought of myself so altered and of those around me so unchanged; and all this happiness shone like a light from one central figure, represented before me by the letter on the table.

I opened it and read it. It was so impressive in its love for me, and in the unselfish caution it gave me, and the consideration it showed for me in every word, that my eyes were too often blinded to read much at a time. But I read it through three times, before I laid it down. I had thought beforehand that I knew its purport, and I did. It asked me, would I be the mistress of Bleak House?

It was not a love letter though it expressed so much love, but was written just as he would at any time have spoken to me. I saw his face, and heard his voice, and felt the influence of his kind protecting manner, in every line. It addressed me as if our places were reversed; as if all the good deeds had been mine, and all the feelings they had awakened, his. It dwelt on my being young, and he past the prime of life; on his having attained a ripe age, while I was a child; on his writing to me with a silvered head, and knowing all this so well as to set it in full before me for mature deliberation. It told me that I would gain nothing by such a marriage, and lose nothing by rejecting it; for no new relation could enhance the tenderness in which he held me, and whatever my decision was, he was certain it would be right. But he had considered this step anew, since our late confidence, and had decided on taking it; if it only served to show me, through one poor instance, that the whole world would readily unite to falsify the stern prediction of my childhood. I was the last to know what happiness I could bestow upon him, but of that he said no more; for I was always to remember that I owed him nothing, and that he was my debtor, and for very much. He had often thought of our future; and, foreseeing that the time must come, and fearing that it might come soon, when Ada (now very nearly of age) would leave us, and when our present mode of life must be broken up, had become accustomed to reflect on this proposal. Thus he made it. If I felt that I could ever give him the best right he could have to be my protector, and if I felt that I could happily and justly become the dear companion of his remaining life, superior to all lighter chances and changes than Death, even then he could not have me bind myself irrevocably, while this letter was yet so new to me; but, even then, I must have ample times for reconsideration. In that case, or in the opposite case, let him be unchanged in his old relation, in his old manner, in the old name by which I called him. And as to his bright Dame Durden and little housekeeper, she would ever be the same, he knew.

This was the substance of the letter; written throughout with a justice and a dignity, as if he were indeed my responsible guardian, impartially representing the proposal of a friend against whom in his integrity he stated the full case.

But he did not hint to me, that when I had been better-looking, he had had this same proceeding in his thoughts, and had refrained from it. That when my old face was gone from me, and I had no attractions, he could love me just as well as in my fairer days. That the discovery of my birth gave him no shock. That his generosity rose above my disfigurement, and my inheritance of shame. That the more I stood in need of such fidelity, the more firmly I must trust in him to the last.

But *I* knew it, I knew it well now. It came upon me as the close of the benignant history I had been pursuing, and I felt that I had but one thing to do. To devote my life to his happiness was to thank him poorly, and what had I wished for only the other night but some new means of thanking him?

Still I cried very much; not only in the fulness of my heart after reading the letter, not only in the strangeness of the prospect—for it was strange though I had expected the contents—but as if something for which there was no name or distinct idea were indefinitely lost to me. I was very happy, very thankful, very hopeful; but I cried very much.

By-and-by I went to my old glass. My eyes were red and swollen, and I said, "O Esther, Esther, can that be you!" I am afraid the face in the glass was going to cry again at this reproach, but I held up my finger at it, and it stopped.

"That is more like the composed look you comforted me with, my dear, when you showed me such a change!" said I, beginning to let down my hair. "When you are mistress of Bleak House, you are to be as cheerful as a bird. In fact, you are always to be cheerful; so let us begin for once and for all."

I went on with my hair now, quite comfortably. I sobbed a little still, but that was because I had been crying; not because I was crying then.

"And so, Esther, my dear, you are happy for life. Happy with your best friends, happy in your old home, happy in the power of doing a great deal of good, and happy in the undeserved love of the best of men."

I thought, all at once, if my guardian had married some one else, how should I have felt, and what should I have done! That would have been a change indeed. It presented my life in such a new and blank form, that I rang my housekeeping keys and gave them a kiss before I laid them down in their basket again.

Then I went on to think, as I dressed my hair before the glass, how often had I considered within myself that the deep traces of my illness, and the circumstances of my birth, were only new reasons why I should be busy, busy, busy—useful, amiable, serviceable, in all honest, unpretending ways. This was a good time, to be sure, to sit down morbidly and cry! As to its seeming at all strange to me at first (if that were any excuse for crying, which it was not) that I was one day to be the mistress of Bleak House, why should it seem strange? Other people had thought of such things, if I had not. "Don't you remember, my plain dear," I asked myself, looking at the glass, "what Mrs. Woodcourt said before those scars were there, about your marrying——"

Perhaps the name brought them to my remembrance. The dried remains of the flowers. It would be better not to keep them now. They had only been preserved in memory of something wholly past and gone, but it would be better not to keep them now.

They were in a book, and it happened to be in the next room—our sitting-room, dividing Ada's chamber from mine. I took a candle, and went softly in to fetch it from its shelf. After I had it in my hand, I saw my beautiful darling, through the open door, lying asleep, and I stole in to kiss her.

It was weak in me, I know, and I could have no reason for crying; but I dropped a tear upon her dear face, and another, and another. Weaker than that, I took the withered flowers out, and put them for a moment to her lips. I thought about her love for Richard; though, indeed, the flowers had nothing to do with that. Then I took them into my own room, and burned them at the candle, and they were dust in an instant.

On entering the breakfast-room next morning, I found my guardian just as usual; quite as frank, as open, and free. There being not the least constraint in his manner, there was none (or I think there was none) in mine. I was with him several times in the course of the morning, in and out, when there was no one there; and I thought it not unlikely that he might speak to me about the letter; but he did not say a word.

So on the next morning, and the next, and for at least a week; over which time Mr. Skimpole prolonged his stay. I expected, every day, that my guardian might speak to me about the letter; but he never did.

I thought then, growing uneasy, that I ought to write an answer. I tried over and over again in my own room at night, but I could not write an answer that at all began like a good answer; so I thought each night I would wait one more day. And I waited seven more days, and he never said a word.

At last Mr. Skimpole having departed, we three were one afternoon going out for a ride; and I being dressed before Ada, and going down, came upon my guardian, with his back towards me, standing at the drawing-room window looking out.

He turned on my coming in, and said, smiling, "Aye, it's you, little woman, is it?" and looked out again.

I had made up my mind to speak to him now. In short, I had come down on purpose. "Guardian," I said, rather hesitating and trembling, "when would you like to have the answer to the letter Charley came for?"

"When it's ready, my dear," he replied.

"I think it is ready," said I.

"Is Charley to bring it?" he asked, pleasantly.

"No. I have brought it myself, guardian," I returned.

I put my two arms round his neck and kissed him; and he said was this the mistress of Bleak House; and I said yes; and it made no difference presently, and we all went out together, and I said nothing to my precious pet about it.

Chapter XLV

IN TRUST

One morning when I had done jingling about with my baskets of keys, as my beauty and I were walking round and round the garden I happened to turn my eyes towards the house, and saw a long thin shadow going in which looked like Mr. Vholes. Ada had been telling me only that morning, of her hopes that Richard might exhaust his ardour in the Chancery suit by being so very earnest in it; and therefore, not to damp my dear girl's spirits, I said nothing about Mr. Vholes's shadow.

Presently came Charley, lightly winding among the bushes, and tripping along the paths, as rosy and pretty as one of Flora's attendants, instead of my maid, saying, "O if you please, miss, would you step and speak to Mr. Jarndyce!"

It was one of Charley's peculiarities, that whenever she was charged with a message she always began to deliver it as soon as she beheld, at any distance, the person for whom it was intended. Therefore I saw Charley, asking me in her usual form of words, to "step and speak" to Mr. Jarndyce, long before I heard her. And when I did hear her, she had said it so often that she was out of breath.

I told Ada I would make haste back, and inquired of Charley, as we went in, whether there was not a gentleman with Mr. Jarndyce? To which Charley, whose grammar, I confess to my shame, never did any credit to my educational powers, replied, "Yes, miss. Him as come down in the country with Mr. Richard."

A more complete contrast than my guardian and Mr. Vholes, I suppose there could not be. I found them looking at one another across a table; the one so open, and the other so close; the one so broad and upright, and the other so narrow and stooping; the one giving out what he had to say in such a rich ringing voice, and the other keeping it in such a cold-blooded, gasping, fish-like manner; that I thought I never had seen two people so unmatched.

"You know Mr. Vholes, my dear," said my guardian. Not with the greatest urbanity, I must say.

Mr. Vholes rose, gloved and buttoned up as usual, and seated himself again, just as he had seated himself beside Richard in the gig. Not having Richard to look at, he looked straight before him.

"Mr. Vholes," said my guardian, eyeing his black figure, as if he were a bird of ill-omen, "has brought an ugly report of our most unfortunate Rick." Laying a marked emphasis on most unfortunate, as if the words were rather descriptive of his connexion with Mr. Vholes.

I sat down between them; Mr. Vholes remained immoveable, except that he secretly picked at one of the red pimples on his yellow face with his black glove.

"And as Rick and you are happily good friends, I should like to know," said my guardian, "what you think, my dear. Would you be so good as to—as to speak up, Mr. Vholes?"

Doing anything but that, Mr. Vholes observed:

"I have been saying that I have reason to know, Miss Summerson, as Mr. C's professional adviser, that Mr. C's circumstances are at the present moment in an embarrassed state. Not so much in point of amount, as owing to the peculiar and pressing nature of liabilities Mr. C has incurred, and the means he has of liquidating or meeting the same. I have staved off many little matters for Mr. C; but there is a limit to staving off, and we have reached it. I have made some advances out of pocket to accommodate these unpleasantnesses, but I necessarily look to being repaid, for I do not pretend to be a man of capital, and I have a father to support in the Vale of Taunton, besides striving to realise some little independence for three dear girls at home. My apprehension is, Mr. C's circumstances being such, lest it should end in his obtaining leave to part with his commission; which at all events is desirable to be made known to his connexions."

Mr. Vholes, who had looked at me while speaking, here merged into the silence he could hardly be said to have broken, so stifled was his tone; and looked before him again.

"Imagine the poor fellow without even his present resource," said my guardian to me. "Yet what can I do? You know him, Esther. He would never accept of help from me, now. To offer it, or hint at it, would be to drive him to an extremity, if nothing else did."

Mr. Vholes hereupon addressed me again.

"What Mr. Jarndyce remarks, miss, is no doubt the case, and is the difficulty. I do not see that anything is to be done. I do not say that anything is to be done. Far from it. I merely come down here under the seal of confidence and mention it, in order that everything may be openly carried on, and that it may not be said afterwards that everything was not openly carried on. My wish is that everything should be openly carried on. I desire to leave a good name behind me. If I consulted merely my own interests with Mr. C, I should not be here. So insurmountable, as you must well know, would be his objections. This is not a professional attendance. This can be charged to nobody. I have no interest in it, except as a member of society and a father—*and* a son," said Mr. Vholes, who had nearly forgotten that point.

It appeared to us that Mr. Vholes said neither more nor less than the truth, in intimating that he sought to divide the responsibility, such as it was, of knowing Richard's situation. I could only suggest that I should go down to Deal, where Richard was then stationed, and see him, and try if it were possible to avert the worst. Without consulting Mr. Vholes on this point, I took my guardian aside to propose it, while Mr. Vholes gauntly stalked to the fire, and warmed his funeral gloves.

The fatigue of the journey formed an immediate objection on my guardian's part; but as I saw he had no other, and as I was only too happy to go, I got his consent. We had then merely to dispose of Mr. Vholes.

"Well, sir," said Mr. Jarndyce, "Miss Summerson will communicate with Mr. Carstone, and we can only hope that his position may be yet retrievable. You will allow me to order you lunch after your journey, sir."

"I thank you, Mr. Jarndyce," said Mr. Vholes, putting out his long black sleeve, to check the ringing of the bell, "not any. I thank you, no, not a morsel. My digestion is much impaired, and I am but a poor knife and fork at any time. If I was to partake of solid food at this period of the day, I don't know what the consequences might be. Everything having been openly carried on, sir, I will now with your permission take my leave."

"And I would that you could take your leave, and we could all take our leave, Mr. Vholes," returned my guardian, bitterly, "of a Cause you know of."

Mr. Vholes, whose black dye was so deep from head to foot that it had quite steamed before the fire, diffusing a very unpleasant perfume, made a short one-sided inclination of his head from the neck, and slowly shook it.

"We whose ambition it is to be looked upon in the light of respectable practitioners, sir, can but put our shoulders to the wheel. We do it, sir. At least, I do it myself; and I wish to think well of my professional brethren, one and all. You are sensible of an obligation not to refer to me, miss, in communicating with Mr. C?"

I said I would be careful not to do it.

"Just so, miss. Good morning. Mr. Jarndyce, good morning, sir." Mr. Vholes put his dead glove, which scarcely seemed to have any hand in it, on my fingers, and then on my guardian's fingers, and took his long thin shadow away. I thought of it on the outside of the coach, passing over all the sunny landscape between us and London, chilling the seed in the ground as it glided along.

Of course it became necessary to tell Ada where I was going and why I was going; and of course she was anxious and distressed. But she was too true to Richard to say anything but words of pity and words of excuse; and in a more loving spirit still—my dear devoted girl!—she wrote him a long letter, of which I took charge.

Charley was to be my travelling companion, though I am sure I wanted none, and would willingly have left her at home. We all went to London that afternoon, and finding two places in the mail, secured them. At our usual bed-time, Charley and I were rolling away seaward, with the Kentish letters.

It was a night's journey in those coach times;[1] but we had the mail to ourselves, and did not find the night very tedious. It passed with me as I suppose it would with most people under such circumstances. At one while, my journey looked hopeful, and at another hopeless. Now I thought I should do some good, and now I wondered how I could ever have supposed so. Now it seemed one of the most reasonable things in the world that I should have come, and now one of the most unreasonable. In what state I should find Richard, what I should say to him, and what he would say to me,

1. It took nine hours by coach to travel the seventy-five miles from London to the seaport of Deal.

occupied my mind by turns with these two states of feeling; and the wheels seemed to play one tune (to which the burden of my guardian's letter set itself) over and over again all night.

At last we came into the narrow streets of Deal: and very gloomy they were, upon a raw misty morning. The long flat beach, with its little irregular houses, wooden and brick, and its litter of capstans, and great boats, and sheds, and bare upright poles with tackle and blocks, and loose gravelly waste places overgrown with grass and weeds, wore as dull an appearance as any place I ever saw. The sea was heaving under a thick white fog; and nothing else was moving but a few early ropemakers, who, with the yarn twisted round their bodies, looked as if, tired of their present state of existence, they were spinning themselves into cordage.

But when we got into a warm room in an excellent hotel, and sat down, comfortably washed and dressed, to an early breakfast (for it was too late to think of going to bed), Deal began to look more cheerful. Our little room was like a ship's cabin, and that delighted Charley very much. Then the fog began to rise like a curtain; and numbers of ships, that we had no idea were near, appeared. I don't know how many sail the waiter told us were then lying in the Downs. Some of these vessels were of grand size: one was a large Indiaman just come home: and when the sun shone through the clouds, making silvery pools in the dark sea, the way in which these ships brightened, and shadowed, and changed, amid a bustle of boats pulling off from the shore to them and from them to the shore, and a general life and motion in themselves and everything around them, was most beautiful.

The large Indiaman was our great attraction, because she had come into the Downs in the night. She was surrounded by boats; and we said how glad the people on board of her must be to come ashore. Charley was curious, too, about the voyage, and about the heat in India, and the serpents and the tigers; and as she picked up such information much faster than grammar, I told her what I knew on those points. I told her, too, how people in such voyages were sometimes wrecked and cast on rocks, where they were saved by the intrepidity and humanity of one man. And Charley asking how that could be, I told her how we knew at home of such a case.

I had thought of sending Richard a note, saying I was there, but it seemed so much better to go to him without preparation. As he lived in barracks I was a little doubtful whether this was feasible, but we went out to reconnoitre. Peeping in at the gate of the barrack-yard, we found everything very quiet at that time in the morning; and I asked a serjeant standing on the guardhouse-steps, where he lived. He sent a man before to show me, who went up some bare stairs, and knocked with his knuckles at a door, and left us.

"Now then!" cried Richard from within. So I left Charley in the little passage, and going on to the half-open door, said "Can I come in, Richard? It's only Dame Durden."

He was writing at a table, with a great confusion of clothes, tin cases, books, boots, brushes, and portmanteaus, strewn all about the floor. He was only half-dressed—in plain clothes, I observed, not in uniform—and his hair was unbrushed, and he looked as wild as his room. All this I saw after he had heartily welcomed me, and I was seated near him, for he started upon hearing my voice, and caught me in his arms in a moment. Dear Richard! He was ever the same to me. Down to—ah, poor poor fellow!—to the end, he never received me but with something of his old merry boyish manner.

"Good Heaven, my dear little woman," said he, "how do you come here? Who could have thought of seeing you? Nothing the matter? Ada is well?"

"Quite well. Lovelier than ever, Richard!"

"Ah!" he said, leaning back in his chair. "My poor cousin! I was writing to you, Esther."

So worn and haggard as he looked, even in the fulness of his handsome youth, leaning back in his chair, and crushing the closely written sheet of paper in his hand!

"Have you been at the trouble of writing all that, and am I not to read it after all?" I asked.

"Oh, my dear," he returned, with a hopeless gesture. "You may read it in the whole room. It is all over here."

I mildly entreated him not to be despondent. I told him that I had heard by chance of his being in difficulty, and had come to consult with him what could best be done.

"Like you, Esther, but useless, and so *not* like you!" said he, with a melancholy smile. "I am away on leave this day—should have been gone in another hour—and that is to smooth it over, for my selling out. Well! Let bygones be bygones. So this calling follows the rest. I only want to have been in the church, to have made the round of all the professions."

"Richard," I urged, "it is not so hopeless as that?"

"Esther," he returned, "it is indeed. I am just so near disgrace as that those who are put in authority over me (as the catechism goes)[2] would far rather be without me than with me. And they are right. Apart from debts and duns, and all such drawbacks, I am not fit even for this employment. I have no care, no mind, no heart, no soul, but for one thing. Why, if this bubble hadn't broken now," he said, tearing the letter he had written into fragments, and moodily casting them away, by driblets, "how could I have gone abroad?

2. See in the Anglican catechism: "My duty . . . is . . . To honour and obey the Queen, and all that are put in authority under her."

I must have been ordered abroad; but how could I have gone? How could I, with my experience of that thing, trust even Vholes unless I was at his back!"

I suppose he knew by my face what I was about to say, but he caught the hand I had laid upon his arm, and touched my own lips with it to prevent me from going on.

"No, Dame Durden! Two subjects I forbid—must forbid. The first is John Jarndyce. The second, you know what. Call it madness, and I tell you I can't help it now, and can't be sane. But it is no such thing; it is the one object I have to pursue. It is a pity I ever was prevailed upon to turn out of my road for any other. It would be wisdom to abandon it now, after all the time, anxiety, and pains I have bestowed upon it! O yes, true wisdom. It would be very agreeable, too, to some people; but I never will."

He was in that mood in which I thought it best not to increase his determination (if anything could increase it) by opposing him. I took out Ada's letter, and put it in his hand.

"Am I to read it now?" he asked.

As I told him yes, he laid it on the table, and, resting his head upon his hand, began. He had not read far, when he rested his head upon his two hands—to hide his face from me. In a little while he rose as if the light were bad, and went to the window. He finished reading it there, with his back towards me; and, after he had finished and had folded it up, stood there for some minutes with the letter in his hand. When he came back to his chair, I saw tears in his eyes.

"Of course, Esther, you know what she says here?" He spoke in a softened voice, and kissed the letter as he asked me.

"Yes, Richard."

"Offers me," he went on, tapping his foot upon the floor, "the little inheritance she is certain of so soon—just as little and as much as I have wasted—and begs and prays me to take it, set myself right with it, and remain in the service."

"I know your welfare to be the dearest wish of her heart," said I. "And oh, my dear Richard, Ada's is a noble heart."

"I am sure it is. I—I wish I was dead!"

He went back to the window, and laying his arm across it, leaned his head down on his arm. It greatly affected me to see him so; but I hoped he might become more yielding, and I remained silent. My experience was very limited; I was not at all prepared for his rousing himself out of this emotion to a new sense of injury.

"And this is the heart that the same John Jarndyce, who is not otherwise to be mentioned between us, stepped in to estrange from me," said he, indignantly. "And the dear girl makes me this generous offer from under the same John Jarndyce's roof and with the same John Jarndyce's gracious consent and connivance, I dare say, as a new means of buying me off."

"Richard!" I cried out, rising hastily, "I will not hear you say such shameful words!" I was very angry with him indeed, for the first time in my life; but it only lasted a moment. When I saw his worn young face looking at me as if he were sorry, I put my hand on his shoulder, and said, "If you please, my dear Richard, do not speak in such a tone to me. Consider!"

He blamed himself exceedingly; and told me in the most generous manner, that he had been very wrong, and that he begged my pardon a thousand times. At that I laughed, but trembled a little too, for I was rather fluttered after being so fiery.

"To accept this offer, my dear Esther," said he, sitting down beside me, and resuming our conversation—"once more, pray, pray forgive me; I am deeply grieved—to accept my dearest cousin's offer is, I need not say, impossible. Besides, I have letters and papers that I could show you, which would convince you it is all over here. I have done with the red coat, believe me. But it is some satisfaction, in the midst of my troubles and perplexities, to know that I am pressing Ada's interests in pressing my own. Vholes has his shoulder to the wheel, and he cannot help urging it on as much for her as for me, thank God!"

His sanguine hopes were rising within him, and lighting up his features, but they made his face more sad to me than it had been before.

"No, no!" cried Richard, exultingly. "If every farthing of Ada's little fortune were mine, no part of it should be spent in retaining me in what I am not fit for, can take no interest in, and am weary of. It should be devoted to what promises a better return, and should be used where she has a larger stake. Don't be uneasy for me! I shall now have only one thing on my mind, and Vholes and I will work it. I shall not be without means. Free of my commission, I shall be able to compound with some small usurers, who will hear of nothing but their bond now—Vholes says so. I should have a balance in my favour anyway, but that will swell it. Come, come! You shall carry a letter to Ada from me, Esther, and you must both of you be more hopeful of me, and not believe that I am quite cast away just yet, my dear."

I will not repeat what I said to Richard. I know it was tiresome, and nobody is to suppose for a moment that it was at all wise. It only came from my heart. He heard it patiently and feelingly; but I saw that on the two subjects he had reserved, it was at present hopeless to make any representation to him. I saw too, and had experienced in this very interview, the sense of my guardian's remark that it was even more mischievous to use persuasion with him than to leave him as he was.

Therefore I was driven at last to asking Richard if he would mind convincing me that it really was all over there, as he had said, and that it was not his mere impression. He showed me without hesitation a correspondence making it quite plain that his retirement was arranged. I found, from what he told me, that Mr. Vholes had copies of these papers, and had been in consultation with him throughout. Beyond ascertaining this, and having been the bearer of Ada's letter, and being (as I was going to be) Richard's companion back to London, I had done no good by coming down. Admitting this to myself with a reluctant heart, I said I would return to the hotel and wait until he joined me there; so he threw a cloak over his shoulders and saw me to the gate, and Charley and I went back along the beach.

There was a concourse of people in one spot, surrounding some naval officers who were landing from a boat, and pressing about them with unusual interest. I said to Charley this would be one of the great Indiaman's boats now, and we stopped to look.

The gentlemen came slowly up from the waterside, speaking good-humouredly to each other and to the people around, and glancing about them as if they were glad to be in England again. "Charley, Charley!" said I, "come away!" And I hurried on so swiftly that my little maid was surprised.

It was not until we were shut up in our cabin-room, and I had had time to take breath, that I began to think why I had made such haste. In one of the sun-burnt faces I had recognised Mr. Allan Woodcourt, and I had been afraid of his recognising me. I had been unwilling that he should see my altered looks. I had been taken by surprise, and my courage had quite failed me.

But I knew this would not do, and I now said to myself, "My dear, there is no reason—there is and there can be no reason at all—why it should be worse for you now, than it ever has been. What you were last month, you are to-day; you are no worse, you are no better. This is not your resolution; call it up, Esther, call it up!" I was in a great tremble—with running—and at first was quite unable to calm myself; but I got better, and I was very glad to know it.

The party came to the hotel. I heard them speaking on the staircase. I was sure it was the same gentlemen because I knew their voices again—I mean I knew Mr. Woodcourt's. It would still have been a great relief to me to have gone away without making myself known, but I was determined not to do so. "No, my dear, no. No, no, no!"

I untied my bonnet, and put my veil half up—I think I mean

half down, but it matters very little—and wrote on one of my cards that I happened to be there with Mr. Richard Carstone; and I sent it in to Mr. Woodcourt. He came immediately. I told him I was rejoiced to be by chance among the first to welcome him home to England. And I saw that he was very sorry for me.

"You have been in shipwreck and peril since you left us, Mr. Woodcourt," said I, "but we can hardly call that a misfortune which enabled you to be so useful and so brave. We read of it with the truest interest. It first came to my knowledge through your old patient, poor Miss Flite, when I was recovering from my severe illness."

"Ah! little Miss Flite!" he said. "She lives the same life yet?"

"Just the same."

I was so comfortable with myself now, as not to mind the veil, and to be able to put it aside.

"Her gratitude to you, Mr. Woodcourt, is delightful. She is a most affectionate creature, as I have reason to say."

"You—you have found her so?" he returned. "I—I am glad of that." He was so very sorry for me that he could scarcely speak.

"I assure you," said I, "that I was deeply touched by her sympathy and pleasure at the time I have referred to."

"I was grieved to hear that you had been very ill."

"I was very ill."

"But you have quite recovered?"

"I have quite recovered my health and my cheerfulness," said I. "You know how good my guardian is, and what a happy life we lead; and I have everything to be thankful for, and nothing in the world to desire."

I felt as if he had greater commiseration for me than I had ever had for myself. It inspired me with new fortitude, and new calmness, to find that it was I who was under the necessity of reassuring him. I spoke to him of his voyage out and home, and of his future plans, and of his probable return to India. He said that was very doubtful. He had not found himself more favoured by fortune there, than here. He had gone out a poor ship's surgeon, and had come home nothing better. While we were talking, and when I was glad to believe that I had alleviated (if I may use such a term) the shock he had had in seeing me, Richard came in. He had heard down-stairs who was with me, and they met with cordial pleasure.

I saw that after their first greetings were over, and when they spoke of Richard's career, Mr. Woodcourt had a perception that all was not going well with him. He frequently glanced at his face, as if there were something in it that gave him pain; and more than once he looked towards me, as though he sought to ascertain whether I knew what the truth was. Yet Richard was in one of his sanguine states, and in good spirits; and was thoroughly pleased to see Mr. Woodcourt again, whom he had always liked.

Richard proposed that we all should go to London together; but Mr. Woodcourt, having to remain by his ship a little longer, could not join us. He dined with us, however, at an early hour; and became so much more like what he used to be, that I was still more at peace to think I had been able to soften his regrets. Yet his mind was not relieved of Richard. When the coach was almost ready, and Richard ran down to look after his luggage, he spoke to me about him.

I was not sure that I had a right to lay his whole story open; but I referred in a few words to his estrangement from Mr. Jarndyce, and to his being entangled in the ill-fated Chancery suit. Mr. Woodcourt listened with interest and expressed his regret.

"I saw you observe him rather closely," said I. "Do you think him so changed?"

"He is changed," he returned, shaking his head.

I felt the blood rush into my face for the first time, but it was only an instantaneous emotion. I turned my head aside, and it was gone.

"It is not," said Mr. Woodcourt, "his being so much younger or older, or thinner or fatter, or paler or ruddier, as there being upon his face such a singular expression. I never saw so remarkable a look in a young person. One cannot say that it is all anxiety, or all weariness; yet it is both, and like ungrown despair."

"You do not think he is ill?" said I.

No. He looked robust in body.

"That he cannot be at peace in mind, we have too much reason to know," I proceeded. "Mr. Woodcourt, you are going to London?"

"To-morrow or the next day."

"There is nothing Richard wants so much, as a friend. He always liked you. Pray see him when you get there. Pray help him sometimes with your companionship, if you can. You do not know of what service it might be. You cannot think how Ada, and Mr. Jarndyce, and even I—how we should all thank you, Mr. Woodcourt!"

"Miss Summerson," he said, more moved than he had been from the first, "before Heaven, I will be a true friend to him! I will accept him as a trust, and it shall be a sacred one!"

"God bless you," said I, with my eyes filling fast; but I thought they might, when it was not for myself. "Ada loves him—we all love him, but Ada loves him as we cannot. I will tell her what you say. Thank you, and God bless you, in her name!"

Richard came back as we finished exchanging these hurried words, and gave me his arm to take me to the coach.

"Woodcourt," he said, unconscious with what application, "pray let us meet in London!"

"Meet?" returned the other. "I have scarcely a friend there, now, but you. Where shall I find you?"

"Why, I must get a lodging of some sort," said Richard, pondering. "Say at Vholes's, Symond's Inn."

"Good! Without loss of time."

They shook hands heartily. When I was seated in the coach, and Richard was yet standing in the street, Mr. Woodcourt laid his friendly hand on Richard's shoulder, and looked at me. I understood him, and waved mine in thanks.

And in his last look as we drove away, I saw that he was very sorry for me. I was glad to see it. I felt for my old self as the dead may feel if they ever revisit these scenes. I was glad to be tenderly remembered, to be gently pitied, not to be quite forgotten.

Chapter XLVI

STOP HIM!

Darkness rests upon Tom-all-Alone's. Dilating and dilating since the sun went down last night, it has gradually swelled until it fills every void in the place. For a time there were some dungeon lights[1] burning, as the lamp of Life burns in Tom-all-Alone's, heavily, heavily, in the nauseous air, and winking—as that lamp, too, winks in Tom-all-Alone's—at many horrible things. But they are blotted out. The moon has eyed Tom with a dull cold stare, as admitting some puny emulation of herself in his desert region unfit for life and blasted by volcanic fires; but she has passed on, and is gone. The blackest nightmare in the infernal stables[2] grazes on Tom-all-Alone's, and Tom is fast asleep.

Much mighty speech-making there has been, both in and out of Parliament, concerning Tom, and much wrathful disputation how Tom shall be got right. Whether he shall be put into the main road by constables, or by beadles, or by bell-ringing, or by force of figures, or by correct principles of taste, or by high church, or by low church, or by no church; whether he shall be set to splitting trusses of polemical straws with the crooked knife of his mind,[3] or whether he shall be put to stone-breaking instead. In the midst of

1. Unidentified as a name for special lighting fixtures but probably referring to the small iron lamps called *crusie* or grease lamps commonly used in prisons, in which cheap fish oils or grease-drippings provided a flickering light and nauseous odor.

2. *Nightmare* means night-spirit not night-horse. Dickens' pun may have been inspired by "Witches, and Other Night Fears," an essay in which Charles Lamb spoke of keeping a "stud" full of nightmares.

3. The allusion or quotation here has not been identified.

Tom-all-alone's.

which dust and noise, there is but one thing perfectly clear, to wit, that Tom only may and can, or shall and will, be reclaimed according to somebody's theory but nobody's practice. And in the hopeful meantime, Tom goes to perdition head foremost in his old determined spirit.

But he has his revenge. Even the winds are his messengers,[4] and they serve him in these hours of darkness. There is not a drop of Tom's corrupted blood but propagates infection and contagion somewhere. It shall pollute, this very night, the choice stream (in which chemists on analysis would find the genuine nobility) of a Norman house, and his Grace shall not be able to say Nay to the infamous alliance. There is not an atom of Tom's slime, not a cubic inch of any pestilential gas in which he lives, not one obscenity or degradation about him, not an ignorance, not a wickedness, not a brutality of his committing, but shall work its retribution, through every order of society, up to the proudest of the proud, and to the highest of the high. Verily, what with tainting, plundering, and spoiling, Tom has his revenge.[5]

It is a moot point whether Tom-all-Alone's be uglier by day or by night; but on the argument that the more that is seen of it the more shocking it must be, and that no part of it left to the imagination is at all likely to be made so bad as the reality, day carries it. The day begins to break now; and in truth it might be better for the national glory even that the sun should sometimes set upon the British dominions,[6] than that it should ever rise upon so vile a wonder as Tom.

A brown sunburnt gentleman, who appears in some inaptitude for sleep to be wandering abroad rather than counting the hours on a restless pillow, strolls hitherward at this quiet time. Attracted by curiosity, he often pauses and looks about him, up and down the miserable byways. Nor is he merely curious, for in his bright dark eye there is compassionate interest; and as he looks here and there, he seems to understand such wretchedness, and to have studied it before.

On the banks of the stagnant channel of mud which is the main street of Tom-all-Alone's, nothing is to be seen but the crazy houses, shut up and silent. No waking creature save himself appears, except in one direction, where he sees the solitary figure of a woman

4. In the revised version of the Bible, published in 1885, fifteen years after Dickens' death, this expression appears: "who makest the winds thy messengers" (Psalms 104:4). In the version of the Bible known in Dickens' lifetime, it does not appear, and we have been unable to trace it elsewhere.

5. As indicated in an article by Stephen Gill, this expression combines two sentences from the Bible: "Verily, I say unto you, They have their reward" (Matthew 6:16), and "Vengeance is mine; I will repay, saith the Lord" (Romans 12:19).

6. The saying that an Empire is one "on which the sun never sets" is of uncertain origin. It was applied to the empires of Rome and Spain as well as to that of Great Britain.

sitting on a door-step. He walks that way. Approaching, he observes that she has journeyed a long distance, and is footsore and travel-stained. She sits on the door-step in the manner of one who is waiting, with her elbow on her knee and her head upon her hand. Beside her is a canvas bag, or bundle, she has carried. She is dozing probably, for she gives no heed to his steps as he comes toward her.

The broken footway is so narrow, that when Allan Woodcourt comes to where the woman sits, he has to turn into the road to pass her. Looking down at her face, his eye meets hers, and he stops.

"What is the matter?"

"Nothing, sir."

"Can't you make them hear? Do you want to be let in?"

"I'm waiting till they get up at another house—a lodging-house —not here," the woman patiently returns. "I'm waiting here because there will be sun here presently to warm me."

"I am afraid you are tired. I am sorry to see you sitting in the street."

"Thank you, sir. It don't matter."

A habit in him of speaking to the poor, and of avoiding patronage or condescension, or childishness (which is the favourite device, many people deeming it quite a subtlety to talk to them like little spelling books), has put him on good terms with the woman easily.

"Let me look at your forehead," he says, bending down. "I am a doctor. Don't be afraid. I wouldn't hurt you for the world."

He knows that by touching her with his skilful and accustomed hand, he can soothe her yet more readily. She makes a slight objection, saying, "It's nothing"; but he has scarcely laid his fingers on the wounded place when she lifts it up to the light.

"Aye! A bad bruise, and the skin sadly broken. This must be very sore."

"It do ache a little, sir," returns the woman, with a started tear upon her cheek.

"Let me try to make it more comfortable. My handkerchief won't hurt you."

"O dear no, sir, I'm sure of that!"

He cleanses the injured place and dries it; and having carefully examined it and gently pressed it with the palm of his hand, takes a small case from his pocket, dresses it, and binds it up. While he is thus employed, he says, after laughing at his establishing a surgery in the street;

"And so your husband is a brickmaker?"

"How do you know that, sir?" asks the woman, astonished.

"Why, I suppose so, from the colour of the clay upon your bag and on your dress. And I know brickmakers go about working at piecework in different places. And I am sorry to say I have known them cruel to their wives too."

The woman hastily lifts up her eyes as if she would deny that her injury is referable to such a cause. But feeling the hand upon her forehead, and seeing his busy and composed face, she quietly drops them again.

"Where is he now?" asks the surgeon.

"He got into trouble last night, sir; but he'll look for me at the lodging-house."

"He will get into worse trouble if he often misuses his large and heavy hand as he has misused it here. But you forgive him, brutal as he is, and I say no more of him, except that I wish he deserved it. You have no young child?"

The woman shakes her head. "One as I calls mine, sir, but it's Liz's."

"Your own is dead. I see! Poor little thing!"

By this time he has finished, and is putting up his case. "I suppose you have some settled home. Is it far from here?" he asks, good-humouredly making light of what he has done, as she gets up and curtseys.

"It's a good two or three-and-twenty mile from here, sir. At Saint Albans. You know Saint Albans, sir? I thought you gave a start like, as if you did?"

"Yes, I know something of it. And now I will ask you a question in return. Have you money for your lodging?"

"Yes, sir," she says, "really and truly." And she shows it. He tells her, in acknowledgment of her many subdued thanks, that she is very welcome, gives her good day, and walks away. Tom-all-Alone's is still asleep, and nothing is astir.

Yes, something is! As he retraces his way to the point from which he descried the woman at a distance sitting on the step, he sees a ragged figure coming very cautiously along, crouching close to the soiled walls—which the wretchedest figure might as well avoid—and furtively thrusting a hand before it. It is the figure of a youth, whose face is hollow, and whose eyes have an emaciated glare. He is so intent on getting along unseen, that even the apparition of a stranger in whole garments does not tempt him to look back. He shades his face with his ragged elbow as he passes on the other side of the way, and goes shrinking and creeping on, with his anxious hand before him, and his shapeless clothes hanging in shreds. Clothes made for what purpose, or of what material, it would be impossible to say. They look, in colour and in substance, like a bundle of rank leaves of swampy growth, that rotted long ago.

Allan Woodcourt pauses to look after him and note all this, with a shadowy belief that he has seen the boy before. He cannot recall how, or where; but there is some association in his mind with such a form. He imagines that he must have seen it in some hospital or refuge; still, cannot make out why it comes with any special force on his remembrance.

He is gradually emerging from Tom-all-Alone's in the morning light, thinking about it, when he hears running feet behind him; and looking round, sees the boy scouring towards him at great speed, followed by the woman.

"Stop him, stop him!" cries the woman, almost breathless. "Stop him, sir!"

He darts across the road into the boy's path, but the boy is quicker than he—makes a curve—ducks—dives under his hands—comes up half-a-dozen yards beyond him, and scours away again. Still, the woman follows, crying, "Stop him, sir, pray stop him!" Allan, not knowing but that he has just robbed her of her money, follows in chase, and runs so hard, that he runs the boy down a dozen times; but each time he repeats the curve, the duck, the dive, and scours away again. To strike at him, on any of these occasions, would be to fell and disable him; but the pursuer cannot resolve to do that; and so the grimly ridiculous pursuit continues. At last the fugitive, hard-pressed, takes to a narrow passage, and a court which has no thoroughfare. Here, against a hoarding of decaying timber, he is brought to bay, and tumbles down, lying gasping at his pursuer, who stands and gasps at him until the woman comes up.

"O you Jo!" cries the woman. "What? I have found you at last!"

"Jo," repeats Allan, looking at him with attention, "Jo! Stay. To be sure! I recollect this lad some time ago being brought before the Coroner."

"Yes, I see you once afore at the Inkwhich," whimpers Jo. "What of that? Can't you never let such an unfortnet as me alone? An't I unfortnet enough for you yet? How unfortnet do you want me fur to be? I've been a chivied and a chivied, fust by one on you and nixt by another on you, till I'm worrited to skins and bones. The Inkwhich warn't my fault. I done nothink. He wos wery good to me, he wos; he was the only one I knowed to speak to, as ever come across my crossing. It an't wery likely I should want him to be Inkwhich'd. I only wish I wos, myself. I don't know why I don't go and make a hole in the water, I'm sure I don't."

He says it with such a pitiable air, and his grimy tears appear so real, and he lies in the corner up against the hoarding so like a growth of fungus or any unwholesome excrescence produced there in neglect and impurity, that Allan Woodcourt is softened towards him. He says to the woman, "Miserable creature, what has he done?"

To which she only replies, shaking her head at the prostrate figure more amazedly than angrily: "O you Jo, you Jo. I have found you at last!"

"What has he done?" says Allan. "Has he robbed you?"

"No, sir, no. Robbed me? He did nothing but what was kind-hearted by me, and that's the wonder of it."

Allan looks from Jo to the woman, and from the woman to Jo, waiting for one of them to unravel the riddle.

"But he was along with me, sir," says the woman,—"O you Jo!—he was along with me, sir; down at Saint Albans, ill, and a young lady Lord bless her for a good friend to me took pity on him when I durstn't, and took him home——"

Allan shrinks back from him with a sudden horror.

"Yes, sir, yes. Took him home, and made him comfortable, and like a thankless monster he ran away in the night, and never has been seen or heard of since, till I set eyes on him just now. And that young lady that was such a pretty dear, caught his illness, lost her beautiful looks, and wouldn't hardly be known for the same young lady now, if it wasn't for her angel temper, and her pretty shape, and her sweet voice. Do you know it? You ungrateful wretch, do you know that this is all along of you and of her goodness to you?" demands the woman, beginning to rage at him as she recalls it, and breaking into passionate tears.

The boy, in rough sort stunned by what he hears, falls to smearing his dirty forehead with his dirty palm, and to staring at the ground, and to shaking from head to foot until the crazy hoarding against which he leans, rattles.

Allan restrains the woman, merely by a quiet gesture, but effectually.

"Richard told me," he falters,—"I mean, I have heard of this—don't mind me for a moment, I will speak presently."

He turns away, and stands for a while looking out at the covered passage. When he comes back, he has recovered his composure; except that he contends against an avoidance of the boy, which is so very remarkable, that it absorbs the woman's attention.

"You hear what she says. But get up, get up!"

Jo, shaking and chattering, slowly rises, and stands, after the manner of his tribe in a difficulty, sideways against the hoarding, resting one of his high shoulders against it, and covertly rubbing his right hand over his left, and his left foot over his right.

"You hear what she says, and I know it's true. Have you been here ever since?"

"Wishermaydie if I seen Tom-all-Alone's till this blessed morning," replies Jo hoarsely.

"Why have you come here now?"

Jo looks all round the confined court, looks at his questioner, no higher than the knees, and finally answers;

"I don't know how to do nothink, and I can't get nothink to do. I'm wery poor and ill, and I thought I'd come back here when there warn't nobody about, and lay down and hide somewheres as I knows on till arter dark, and then go and beg a trifle of Mr. Sangsby. He wos allus willin fur to give me somethink, he wos, though Mrs. Sangsby she wos allus a chivying on me—like everybody everywheres."

"Where have you come from?"

Jo looks all round the court again, looks at his questioner's knees again, and concludes by laying his profile against the hoarding in a sort of resignation.

"Did you hear me ask you where you have come from?"

"Tramp then," says Jo.

"Now, tell me," proceeds Allan, making a strong effort to overcome his repugnance, going very near to him, and leaning over him with an expression of confidence, "tell me how it came about that you left that house, when the good young lady had been so unfortunate as to pity you, and take you home."

Jo suddenly comes out of his resignation, and excitedly declares, addressing the woman, that he never known about the young lady, that he never heern about it, that he never went fur to hurt her, that he would sooner have hurt his own self, that he'd sooner have had his unfortnet ed chopped off than ever gone a-nigh her, and that she wos wery good to him, she wos. Conducting himself throughout as if in his poor fashion he really meant it, and winding up with some very miserable sobs.

Allan Woodcourt sees that this is not a sham. He constrains himself to touch him. "Come, Jo. Tell me."

"No. I dustn't," says Jo, relapsing into the profile state. "I dustn't, or I would."

"But I must know," returns the other, "all the same. Come, Jo."

After two or three such adjurations, Jo lifts up his head again, looks round the court again, and says in a low voice, "Well, I'll tell you somethink. I was took away. There!"

"Took away? In the night?"

"Ah!" Very apprehensive of being overheard, Jo looks about him, and even glances up some ten feet at the top of the hoarding, and through the cracks in it, lest the object of his distrust should be looking over, or hidden on the other side.

"Who took you away?"

"I dustn't name him," says Jo. "I dustn't do it, sir."

"But I want, in the young lady's name, to know. You may trust me. No one else shall hear."

"Ah, but I don't know," replies Jo, shaking his head fearfully, "as he *don't* hear."

"Why, he is not in this place."

"Oh, ain't he though?" says Jo. "He is in all manner of places, all at wunst."

Allan looks at him in perplexity, but discovers some real meaning and good faith at the bottom of this bewildering reply. He patiently awaits an explicit answer; and Jo, more baffled by his patience than by anything else, at last desperately whispers a name in his ear.

"Aye!" says Allan. "Why, what had you been doing?"

"Nothink, sir. Never done nothink to get myself into no trouble, 'cept in not moving on and the Inkwhich. But I'm a moving on now. I'm a moving on to the berryin ground—that's the move as I'm up to."

"No, no, we will try to prevent that. But what did he do with you?"

"Put me in a horsepittle," replied Jo, whispering, "till I wos discharged, then give me a little money—four half bulls, wot you may call half-crowns—and ses 'Hook it! Nobody wants you here,' he ses. 'You hook it. You go and tramp,' he ses. 'You move on,' he ses. 'Don't let me ever see you nowheres within forty mile of London, or you'll repent it.' So I shall, if ever he does see me, and he'll see me if I'm above ground," concludes Jo, nervously repeating all his former precautions and investigations.

Allan considers a little; then remarks, turning to the woman, but keeping an encouraging eye on Jo: "He is not so ungrateful as you supposed. He had a reason for going away, though it was an insufficient one."

"Thank'ee, sir, thank'ee!" exclaims Jo. "There now! See how hard you wos upon me. But only you tell the young lady wot the genlmn ses, and it's all right. For *you* wos wery good to me too, and I knows it."

"Now, Jo," says Allan, keeping his eye upon him, "come with me, and I will find you a better place than this to lie down and hide in. If I take one side of the way and you the other to avoid observation, you will not run away, I know very well, if you make me a promise."

"I won't, not unless I wos to see *him* a-coming, sir."

"Very well. I take your word. Half the town is getting up by this time, and the whole town will be broad awake in another hour. Come along. Good day again, my good woman."

"Good day again, sir, and I thank you kindly many times again."

She has been sitting on her bag, deeply attentive, and now rises and takes it up. Jo, repeating, "Ony you tell the young lady as I never went fur to hurt her and wot the genlmn ses!" nods and shambles and shivers, and smears and blinks, and half laughs and half cries, a farewell to her, and takes his creeping way along after Allan Woodcourt, close to the houses on the opposite side of the street. In this order, the two come up out of Tom-all-Alone's into the broad rays of the sunlight and the purer air.

Chapter XLVII

JO'S WILL

As Allan Woodcourt and Jo proceed along the streets, where the high church spires and the distances are so near and clear in the morning light that the city itself seems renewed by rest, Allan revolves in his mind how and where he shall bestow his companion. "It surely is a strange fact," he considers, "that in the heart of a civilised world this creature in human form should be more difficult to dispose of than an unowned dog." But it is none the less a fact because of its strangeness, and the difficulty remains.

At first, he looks behind him often, to assure himself that Jo is still really following. But look where he will, he still beholds him close to the opposite houses, making his way with his wary hand from brick to brick and from door to door, and often, as he creeps along, glancing over at him, watchfully. Soon satisfied that the last thing in his thoughts is to give him the slip, Allan goes on; considering with a less divided attention what he shall do.

A breakfast-stall at a street corner suggests the first thing to be done. He stops there, looks round, and beckons Jo. Jo crosses, and comes halting and shuffling up, slowly scooping the knuckles of his right hand round and round in the hollowed palm of his left—kneading dirt with a natural pestle and mortar. What is a dainty repast to Jo is then set before him, and he begins to gulp the coffee, and to gnaw the bread-and-butter; looking anxiously about him in all directions as he eats and drinks, like a scared animal.

But he is so sick and miserable, that even hunger has abandoned him. "I thought I was amost a-starvin, sir," says Jo, soon putting down his food; "but I don't know nothink—not even that. I don't care for eating wittles nor yet for drinking on em." And Jo stands shivering, and looking at the breakfast wonderingly.

Allan Woodcourt lays his hand upon his pulse, and on his chest. "Draw breath, Jo!" "It draws," says Jo, "as heavy as a cart." He might add, "and rattles like it"; but he only mutters, "I'm a moving on, sir."

Allan looks about for an apothecary's shop. There is none at hand, but a tavern does as well or better. He obtains a little measure of wine, and gives the lad a portion of it very carefully. He begins to revive, almost as soon as it passes his lips. "We may repeat that dose, Jo," observes Allan, after watching him with his attentive face. "So! Now we will take five minutes' rest, and then go on again."

Leaving the boy sitting on the bench of the breakfast-stall, with his back against an iron railing, Allan Woodcourt paces up and down in the early sunshine, casting an occasional look towards him without appearing to watch him. It requires no discernment to perceive that he is warmed and refreshed. If a face so shaded can brighten, his face brightens somewhat; and, by little and little, he eats the slice of bread he had so hopelessly laid down. Observant of these signs of improvement, Allan engages him in conversation; and elicits to his no small wonder the adventure of the lady in the veil, with all its consequences. Jo slowly munches, as he slowly tells it. When he has finished his story and his bread, they go on again.

Intending to refer his difficulty in finding a temporary place of refuge for the boy, to his old patient, zealous little Miss Flite, Allan leads the way to the court where he and Jo first foregathered. But all is changed at the rag and bottle shop; Miss Flite no longer lodges there; it is shut up; and a hard-featured female, much obscured by dust, whose age is a problem—but who is indeed no other than the interesting Judy—is tart and spare in her replies. These sufficing, however, to inform the visitor that Miss Flite and her birds are domiciled with a Mrs. Blinder, in Bell Yard, he repairs to that neighbouring place; where Miss Flite (who rises early that she may be punctual at the Divan[1] of justice held by her excellent friend the Chancellor) comes running down-stairs, with tears of welcome and with open arms.

"My dear physician!" cries Miss Flite. "My meritorious, distinguished, honourable officer!" She uses some odd expressions, but is as cordial and full of heart as sanity itself can be—more so than it often is. Allan, very patient with her, waits until she has no more raptures to express; then points out Jo, trembling in a door-way, and tells her how he comes there.

"Where can I lodge him hereabouts for the present? Now you have a fund of knowledge and good sense, and can advise me."

Miss Flite, mighty proud of the compliment, sets herself to consider; but it is long before a bright thought occurs to her. Mrs. Blinder is entirely let, and she herself occupies poor Gridley's room. "Gridley!" exclaims Miss Flite, clapping her hands, after a twentieth repetition of this remark. "Gridley! To be sure! of course! My dear physician! General George will help us out."

It is hopeless to ask for any information about General George, and would be, though Miss Flite had not already run up-stairs to put on her pinched bonnet and her poor little shawl, and to arm herself with her reticule of documents. But as she informs her physician, in her disjointed manner, on coming down in full array, that

1. A Turkish term for a courtroom.

General George, whom she often calls upon, knows her dear Fitz-Jarndyce, and takes a great interest in all connected with her, Allan is induced to think that they may be in the right way. So he tells Jo, for his encouragement, that this walking about will soon be over now; and they repair to the General's. Fortunately it is not far.

From the exterior of George's Shooting Gallery, and the long entry, and the bare perspective beyond it, Allan Woodcourt augurs well. He also descries promise in the figure of Mr. George himself, striding towards them in his morning exercise with his pipe in his mouth, no stock on, and his muscular arms developed by broad-sword and dumb-bell, weightily asserting themselves through his light shirt-sleeves.

"Your servant, sir," says Mr. George, with a military salute. Good-humouredly smiling all over his broad forehead up into his crisp hair, he then defers to Miss Flite, as, with great stateliness and at some length, she performs the courtly ceremony of presentation. He winds it up with another "Your servant, sir!" and another salute.

"Excuse me, sir. A sailor, I believe?" says Mr. George.

"I am proud to find I have the air of one," returns Allan; "but I am only a sea-going doctor."

"Indeed, sir! I should have thought you was a regular blue-jacket, myself."

Allan hopes Mr. George will forgive his intrusion the more readily on that account, and particularly that he will not lay aside his pipe, which, in his politeness, he has testified some intention of doing. "You are very good, sir," returns the trooper. "As I know, by experience, that it's not disagreeable to Miss Flite, and since it's equally agreeable to yourself——" and finishes the sentence by putting it between his lips again. Allan proceeds to tell him all he knows about Jo; unto which the trooper listens with a grave face.

"And that's the lad, sir, is it?" he inquires, looking along the entry to where Jo stands staring up at the great letters on the white-washed front, which have no meaning in his eyes.

"That's he," says Allan. "And, Mr. George, I am in this difficulty about him. I am unwilling to place him in a hospital, even if I could procure him immediate admission, because I foresee that he would not stay there many hours, if he could be so much as got there. The same objection applies to a workhouse; supposing I had the patience to be evaded and shirked, and handed about from post to pillar in trying to get him into one—which is a system that I don't take kindly to."

"No man does, sir," returns Mr. George.

"I am convinced that he would not remain in either place, because he is possessed by an extraordinary terror of this person who ordered him to keep out of the way; in his ignorance he believes this person to be everywhere, and cognisant of everything."

"I ask your pardon, sir," says Mr. George. "But you have not mentioned that party's name. Is it a secret, sir?"

"The boy makes it one. But his name is Bucket."

"Bucket the Detective, sir?"

"The same man."

"The man is known to me, sir," returns the trooper, after blowing out a cloud of smoke, and squaring his chest; "and the boy is so far correct that he undoubtedly is a—rum customer."[2] Mr. George smokes with a profound meaning after this, and surveys Miss Flite in silence.

"Now, I wish Mr. Jarndyce and Miss Summerson at least to know that this Jo, who tells so strange a story, has re-appeared; and to have it in their power to speak with him, if they should desire to do so. Therefore I want to get him, for the present moment, into any poor lodging kept by decent people, where he would be admitted. Decent people and Jo, Mr. George," says Allan, following the direction of the trooper's eyes along the entry, "have not been much acquainted, as you see. Hence the difficulty. Do you happen to know any one in this neighbourhood, who would receive him for a while, on my paying for him beforehand?"

As he puts the question, he becomes aware of a dirty-faced little man, standing at the trooper's elbow, and looking up, with an oddly twisted figure and countenance, into the trooper's face. After a few more puffs at his pipe, the trooper looks down askant at the little man, and the little man winks up at the trooper.

"Well, sir," says Mr. George, "I can assure you that I would willingly be knocked on the head at any time, if it would be at all agreeable to Miss Summerson; and consequently I esteem it a privilege to do that young lady any service, however small. We are naturally in the vagabond way here, sir, both myself and Phil. You see what the place is. You are welcome to a quiet corner of it for the boy, if the same would meet your views. No charge made, except for rations. We are not in a flourishing state of circumstances here, sir. We are liable to be tumbled out neck and crop, at a moment's notice. However, sir, such as the place is, and so long as it lasts, here it is at your service."

With a comprehensive wave of his pipe, Mr. George places the whole building at his visitor's disposal.

"I take it for granted, sir," he adds, "you being one of the medical staff, that there is no present infection about this unfortunate subject?"

Allan is quite sure of it.

2. An odd or queer person.

"Because, sir," says Mr. George, shaking his head sorrowfully, "we have had enough of that."

His tone is no less sorrowfully echoed by his new acquaintance. "Still I am bound to tell you," observes Allan, after repeating his former assurance, "that the boy is deplorably low and reduced; and that he may be—I do not say that he is—too far gone to recover."

"Do you consider him in present danger, sir?" inquires the trooper.

"Yes, I fear so."

"Then, sir," returns the trooper, in a decisive manner, "it appears to me—being naturally in the vagabond way myself—that the sooner he comes out of the street, the better. You Phil! Bring him in!"

Mr. Squod tacks out, all on one side, to execute the word of command; and the trooper, having smoked his pipe, lays it by. Jo is brought in. He is not one of Mrs. Pardiggle's Tockahoopo Indians; he is not one of Mrs. Jellyby's lambs, being wholly unconnected with Borrioboola-Gha; he is not softened by distance and unfamiliarity; he is not a genuine foreign-grown savage; he is the ordinary home-made article. Dirty, ugly, disagreeable to all the senses, in body a common creature of the common streets, only in soul a heathen. Homely filth begrimes him, homely parasites devour him, homely sores are in him, homely rags are on him: native ignorance, the growth of English soil and climate, sinks his immortal nature lower than the beasts that perish. Stand forth, Jo, in uncompromising colours! From the sole of thy foot to the crown of thy head, there is nothing interesting about thee.

He shuffles slowly into Mr. George's gallery, and stands huddled together in a bundle, looking all about the floor. He seems to know that they have an inclination to shrink from him, partly for what he is, and partly for what he has caused. He, too, shrinks from them. He is not of the same order of things, not of the same place in creation. He is of no order and no place; neither of the beasts, nor of humanity.

"Look here, Jo!" says Allan. "This is Mr. George."

Jo searches the floor for some time longer, then looks up for a moment, and then down again.

"He is a kind friend to you, for he is going to give you lodging room here."

Jo makes a scoop with one hand, which is supposed to be a bow. After a little more consideration, and some backing and changing of the foot on which he rests, he mutters that he is "wery thankful."

"You are quite safe here. All you have to do at present is to be obedient, and get strong. And mind you tell us the truth here, whatever you do, Jo."

"Wishermaydie if I don't, sir," says Jo, reverting to his favourite declaration. "I never done nothink yit, but wot you knows on, to get myself into no trouble. I never was in no other trouble at all, sir —'sept not knowin' nothink and starwation."

"I believe it. Now attend to Mr. George. I see he is going to speak to you."

"My intention merely was, sir," observes Mr. George, amazingly broad and upright, "to point out to him where he can lie down, and get a thorough good dose of sleep. Now, look here." As the trooper speaks he conducts them to the other end of the gallery, and opens one of the little cabins. "There you are, you see! Here is a mattress, and here you may rest, on good behaviour, as long as Mr., I ask your pardon, sir"; he refers apologetically to the card Allan has given him; "Mr. Woodcourt pleases. Don't you be alarmed if you hear shots; they'll be aimed at the target, and not you. Now, there's another thing I would recommend, sir," says the trooper, turning to his visitor. "Phil, come here!"

Phil bears down upon them, according to his usual tactics.

"Here is a man, sir, who was found, when a baby, in the gutter. Consequently, it is to be expected that he takes a natural interest in this poor creature. You do, don't you, Phil?"

"Certainly and surely I do, guv'ner," is Phil's reply.

"Now I was thinking, sir," says Mr. George, in a martial sort of confidence, as if he were giving his opinion in a council of war at a drum-head,[3] that if this man was to take him to a bath, and was to lay out a few shillings in getting him one or two coarse articles——"

"Mr. George, my considerate friend," returns Allan, taking out his purse, "it is the very favour I would have asked."

Phil Squod and Jo are sent out immediately on this work of improvement. Miss Flite, quite enraptured by her success, makes the best of her way to Court; having great fears that otherwise her friend the Chancellor may be uneasy about her, or may give the judgment she has so long expected, in her absence; and observing, "which you know, my dear physician, and general, after so many years, would be too absurdly unfortunate!" Allan takes the opportunity of going out to procure some restorative medicines; and obtaining them near at hand, soon returns, to find the trooper walking up and down the gallery, and to fall into step and walk with him.

"I take it, sir," says Mr. George, "that you know Miss Summerson pretty well?"

Yes, it appears.

"Not related to her, sir?"

No, it appears.

"Excuse the apparent curiosity," says Mr. George. "It seemed to me probable that you might take more than a common interest in

3. A battlefield court-martial or council at which a drum serves as a table.

this poor creature, because Miss Summerson had taken that unfortunate interest in him. 'Tis *my* case, sir, I assure you."

"And mine, Mr. George."

The trooper looks sideways at Allan's sun-burnt cheek and bright dark eye, rapidly measures his height and build, and seems to approve of him.

"Since you have been out, sir, I have been thinking that I unquestionably know the rooms in Lincoln's Inn Fields, where Bucket took the lad, according to his account. Though he is not acquainted with the name, I can help you to it. It's Tulkinghorn. That's what it is."

Allan looks at him inquiringly, repeating the name.

"Tulkinghorn. That's the name, sir. I know the man; and know him to have been in communication with Bucket before, respecting a deceased person who had given him offence. *I* know the man, sir. To my sorrow."

Allan naturally asks what kind of man he is?

"What kind of man! Do you mean to look at?"

"I think I know that much of him. I mean to deal with. Generally, what kind of man?"

"Why, then I'll tell you, sir," returns the trooper, stopping short, and folding his arms on his square chest, so angrily, that his face fires and flushes all over; "he is a confoundedly bad kind of man. He is a slow-torturing kind of man. He is no more like flesh and blood, than a rusty old carbine is. He is a kind of man—by George!—that has caused me more restlessness, and more uneasiness, and more dissatisfaction with myself, than all other men put together. That's the kind of man Mr. Tulkinghorn is!"

"I am sorry," says Allan, "to have touched so sore a place."

"Sore?" The trooper plants his legs wider apart, wets the palm of his broad right hand, and lays it on his imaginary moustache. "It's no fault of yours, sir; but you shall judge. He has got a power over me. He is the man I spoke of just now, as being able to tumble me out of this place neck and crop. He keeps me on a constant see-saw. He won't hold off, and he won't come on. If I have a payment to make him, or time to ask him for, or anything to go to him about, he don't see me, don't hear me—passes me on to Melchisedech's in Clifford's Inn, Melchisedech's in Clifford's Inn passes me back again to him—he keeps me prowling and dangling about him, as if I was made of the same stone as himself. Why, I spend half my life now, pretty well, loitering and dodging about his door. What does he care? Nothing. Just as much as the rusty old carbine I have compared him to. He chafes and goads me, till—Bah! nonsense—I am forgetting myself. Mr. Woodcourt"; the trooper resumes his march; "all I say is, he is an old man; but I am glad I shall never have the chance of setting spurs to my horse, and riding at him in a fair field. For if I had that chance, in one of the humours he drives me into—he'd go down, sir!"

Mr. George has been so excited, that he finds it necessary to wipe his forehead on his shirt-sleeve. Even while he whistles his impetuosity away with the National Anthem, some involuntary shakings of his head and heavings of his chest still linger behind; not to mention an occasional hasty adjustment with both hands of his open shirt-collar, as if it were scarcely open enough to prevent his being troubled by a choking sensation. In short, Allan Woodcourt has not much doubt about the going down of Mr. Tulkinghorn on the field referred to.

Jo and his conductor presently return, and Jo is assisted to his mattress by the careful Phil; to whom, after due administration of medicine by his own hands, Allan confides all needful means and instructions. The morning is by this time getting on apace. He repairs to his lodgings to dress and breakfast; and then, without seeking rest, goes away to Mr. Jarndyce to communicate his discovery.

With him Mr. Jarndyce returns alone, confidentially telling him that there are reasons for keeping this matter very quiet indeed; and showing a serious interest in it. To Mr. Jarndyce, Jo repeats in substance what he said in the morning; without any material variation. Only, that cart of his is heavier to draw, and draws with a hollower sound.

"Let me lay here quiet, and not be chivied no more," falters Jo; "and be so kind any person as is a passin' nigh where I used fur to sweep, as jist to say to Mr. Sangsby that Jo, wot he known once, is a moving on right forards with his duty, and I'll be wery thankful. I'd be more thankful than I am aready, if it wos any ways possible for an unfortnet to be it."

He makes so many of these references to the law-stationer in the course of a day or two, that Allan, after conferring with Mr. Jarndyce, good-naturedly resolves to call in Cook's Court; the rather, as the cart seems to be breaking down.

To Cook's Court, therefore, he repairs. Mr. Snagsby is behind his counter in his grey coat and sleeves, inspecting an Indenture of several skins[4] which has just come in from the engrosser's; an immense desert of law-hand and parchment, with here and there a resting-place of a few large letters, to break the awful monotony, and save the traveller from despair. Mr. Snagsby puts up at one of these inky wells, and greets the stranger with his cough of general preparation for business.

"You don't remember me, Mr. Snagsby?"

4. Deeds written on parchment.

The stationer's heart begins to thump heavily, for his old apprehensions have never abated. It is as much as he can do to answer, "No, sir, I can't say I do. I should have considered—not to put too fine a point upon it—that I never saw you before, sir."

"Twice before," says Allan Woodcourt. "Once at a poor bedside, and once—"

"It's come at last!" thinks the afflicted stationer, as recollection breaks upon him. "It's got to a head now, and is going to burst!" But, he has sufficient presence of mind to conduct his visitor into the little counting-house, and to shut the door.

"Are you a married man, sir?"

"No, I am not."

"Would you make the attempt, though single," says Mr. Snagsby, in a melancholy whisper, "to speak as low as you can? For my little woman is a listening somewheres, or I'll forfeit the business and five hundred pound!"

In deep dejection Mr. Snagsby sits down on his stool, with his back against his desk, protesting:

"I never had a secret of my own, sir. I can't charge my memory with ever having once attempted to deceive my little woman on my own account, since she named the day. I wouldn't have done it, I dursn't have done it. Whereas, and nevertheless, I find myself wrapped round with secrecy and mystery, till my life is a burden to me."

His visitor professes his regret to hear it, and asks him does he remember Jo? Mr. Snagsby answers with a suppressed groan, O don't he!

"You couldn't name an individual human being—except myself—that my little woman is more set and determined against than Jo," says Mr. Snagsby.

Allan asks why?

"Why?" repeats Mr. Snagsby, in his desperation clutching at the clump of hair at the back of his bald head. "How should *I* know why? But you are a single person, sir, and may you long be spared to ask a married person such a question!"

With this beneficent wish, Mr. Snagsby coughs a cough of dismal resignation, and submits himself to hear what the visitor has to communicate.

"There again!" says Mr. Snagsby, who, between the earnestness of his feelings, and the suppressed tones of his voice, is discoloured in the face. "At it again, in a new direction! A certain person charges me, in the solemnest way, not to talk of Jo to any one, even my little woman. Then comes another certain person, in the person of yourself, and charges me, in an equally solemn way, not to mention Jo to that other certain person above all other persons. Why, this a private asylum! Why, not to put too fine a point upon it, this is Bedlam, sir!" says Mr. Snagsby.

But it is better than he expected, after all; being no explosion of the mine below him, or deepening of the pit into which he has fallen. And being tender-hearted, and affected by the account he hears of Jo's condition, he readily engages to "look around" as early in the evening as he can manage it quietly. He looks round very quietly, when the evening comes; but it may turn out that Mrs. Snagsby is as quiet a manager as he.

Jo is very glad to see his old friend; and says, when they are left alone, that he takes it uncommon kind as Mr. Sangsby should come so far out of his way on accounts of sich as him. Mr. Snagsby, touched by the spectacle before him, immediately lays upon the table half-a-crown: that magic balsam of his for all kinds of wounds.

"And how do you find yourself, my poor lad?" inquires the stationer, with his cough of sympathy.

"I am in luck, Mr. Sangsby, I am," returns Jo, "and don't want for nothink. I'm more cumfbler nor you can't think. Mr. Sangsby! I'm wery sorry that I done it, but I didn't go fur to do it, sir."

The stationer softly lays down another half-crown, and asks him what it is that he is sorry for having done?

"Mr. Sangsby," says Jo, "I went and giv a illness to the lady as wos and yit as warn't the t'other lady, and none of 'em never says nothink to me fur having done it, on accounts of their being ser good and my having been s'unfortnet. The lady come herself and see me yesday, and she ses, 'Ah, Jo!' she ses. 'We thought we'd lost you, Jo!' she ses. And she sits down a smilin so quiet, and don't pass a word nor yit a look upon me for having done it, she don't, and I turns agin the wall, I doos, Mr. Sangsby. And Mr. Jarnders, I see him a forced to turn away his own self. And Mr. Woodcot, he come fur to give me somethink fur to ease me, wot he's allus a doin on day and night, and wen he come a bendin over me and a speakin up so bold, I see his tears a fallin, Mr. Sangsby."

The softened stationer deposits another half-crown on the table. Nothing less than a repetition of that infallible remedy will relieve his feelings.

"Wot I wos a thinkin on, Mr. Sangsby," proceeds Jo, "wos, as you wos able to write wery large, p'raps?"

"Yes, Jo, please God," returns the stationer.

"Uncommon precious large, p'raps?" says Jo, with eagerness.

"Yes, my poor boy."

Jo laughs with pleasure. "Wot I wos a thinkin on then, Mr. Sangsby, wos, that wen I moved on as fur as ever I could go and and couldn't be moved no furder, whether you might be so good p'raps, as to write out, wery large so that any one could see it anywheres, as that I wos wery truly hearty sorry that I done it and that I never went fur to do it; and that though I didn't know nothink at all, I knowd as Mr. Woodcot once cried over it and wos allus grieved over it, and that I hoped as he'd be able to forgiv me in his mind. If the writin could be made to say it wery large, he might."

"It shall say it, Jo. Very large."

Jo laughs again. "Thank'ee, Mr. Sangsby. It's wery kind of you, sir, and it makes me more cumfbler nor I was afore."

The meek little stationer, with a broken and unfinished cough, slips down his fourth half-crown—he has never been so close to a case requiring so many—and is fain to depart. And Jo and he, upon this little earth, shall meet no more. No more.

For the cart so hard to draw, is near its journey's end, and drags over stony ground. All round the clock it labours up the broken steeps, shattered and worn. Not many times can the sun rise, and behold it still upon its weary road.

Phil Squod, with his smoky gunpowder visage, at once acts as nurse and works as armourer at his little table in a corner; often looking round, and saying with a nod of his green baize cap, and an encouraging elevation of his one eyebrow, "Hold up, my boy! Hold up!" There, too, is Mr. Jarndyce many a time, and Allan Woodcourt almost always; both thinking, much, how strangely Fate has entangled this rough outcast in the web of very different lives. There, too, the trooper is a frequent visitor, filling the doorway with his athletic figure, and, from his superfluity of life and strength, seeming to shed down temporary vigour upon Jo, who never fails to speak more robustly in answer to his cheerful words.

Jo is in a sleep or in a stupor to-day, and Allan Woodcourt, newly arrived, stands by him, looking down upon his wasted form. After a while, he softly seats himself upon the bedside with his face towards him—just as he sat in the law-writer's room—and touches his chest and heart. The cart had very nearly given up, but labours on a little more.

The trooper stands in the doorway, still and silent. Phil has stopped in a low clinking noise, with his little hammer in his hand. Mr. Woodcourt looks round with that grave professional interest and attention on his face, and, glancing significantly at the trooper, signs to Phil to carry his table out. When the little hammer is next used, there will be a speck of rust upon it.

"Well, Jo! What is the matter? Don't be frightened."

"I thought," says Jo, who has started, and is looking round, "I thought I wos in Tom-all-Alone's agin. An't there nobody here but you, Mr. Woodcot?"

"Nobody."

"And I ain't took back to Tom-all-Alone's. Am I, sir?"

"No." Jo closes his eyes, muttering, "I'm wery thankful."

After watching him closely a little while, Allan puts his mouth very near his ear, and says to him a low, distinct voice:

"Jo! Did you ever know a prayer?"

"Never know'd nothink, sir."

"Not so much as one short prayer?"

"No, sir. Nothink at all. Mr Chadbands he wos a prayin wunst at Mr. Sangsby's and I heerd him, but he sounded as if he wos a speakin' to his-self, and not to me. He prayed a lot, but *I* couldn't make out nothink on it. Different times, there wos other genlmen come down Tom-all-Alone's a prayin, but they all mostly sed as the t'other wuns prayed wrong, and all mostly sounded to be a talking to theirselves, or a passing blame on the t'others, and not a talkin to us. *We* never knowd nothink. *I* never knowd what it wos all about."

It takes him a long time to say this; and few but an experienced and attentive listener could hear, or hearing, understand him. After a short relapse into sleep or stupor, he makes, of a sudden, a strong effort to get out of bed.

"Stay, Jo! What now?"

"It's time fur me to go to that there berryin ground, sir," he returns, with a wild look.

"Lie down, and tell me. What burying ground, Jo?"

"Where they laid him as wos wery good to me, wery good to me indeed, he wos. It's time fur me to go down to that there berryin ground, sir, and ask to be put along with him. I wants to go there and be berried. He used fur to say to me, 'I am as poor as you to-day, Jo,' he ses. I wants to tell him that I am as poor as him now, and have come there to be laid along with him."

"Bye and bye, Jo. Bye and bye."

"Ah! P'raps they wouldn't do it if I wos to go myself. But will you promise to have me took there, sir, and laid along with him?"

"I will, indeed."

"Thank'ee, sir. Thank'ee, sir. They'll have to get the key of the gate afore they can take me in, for it's allus locked. And there's a step there, as I used fur to clean with my broom.—It's turned wery dark, sir. Is there any light a comin?"

"It is coming fast, Jo."

Fast. The cart is shaken all to pieces, and the rugged road is very near its end.

"Jo, my poor fellow!"

"I hear you, sir, in the dark, but I'm a gropin—a gropin—let me catch hold of your hand."

"Jo, can you say what I say?"

"I'll say anythink as you say, sir, for I knows it's good."

"OUR FATHER."

"Our Father!—yes, that's wery good, sir."

"WHICH ART IN HEAVEN."

"Art in Heaven—is the light a comin, sir?"

"It is close at hand. HALLOWED BE THY NAME!"

"Hallowed be—thy——"

The light is come upon the dark benighted way. Dead!

Dead, your Majesty. Dead, my lords and gentlemen. Dead, Right Reverends and Wrong Reverends of every order. Dead, men and women, born with Heavenly compassion in your hearts. And dying thus around us every day.

Chapter XLVIII

CLOSING IN

The place in Lincolnshire has shut its many eyes again, and the house in town is awake. In Lincolnshire, the Dedlocks of the past doze in their picture-frames, and the low wind murmurs through the long drawing-room as if they were breathing pretty regularly. In town, the Dedlocks of the present rattle in their fire-eyed carriages through the darkness of the night, and the Dedlock Mercuries, with ashes (or hair-powder) on their heads, symptomatic of their great humility, loll away the drowsy mornings in the little windows of the hall. The fashionable world—tremendous orb, nearly five miles round—is in full swing, and the solar system works respectfully at its appointed distances.

Where the throng is thickest, where the lights are brightest, where all the senses are ministered to with the greatest delicacy and refinement, Lady Dedlock is. From the shining heights she has scaled and taken, she is never absent. Though the belief she of old reposed in herself, as one able to reserve whatsoever she would under her mantle of pride, is beaten down; though she has no assurance that what she is to those around her, she will remain another day; it is not in her nature, when envious eyes are looking on, to yield or to droop. They say of her, that she has lately grown more handsome and more haughty. The debilitated cousin says of her that she's beauty nough—tsetup Shopofwomen—but rather larming kind—remindingmanfact—inconvenient woman[1]—who *will* getoutofbedandbawthstablishment—Shakspeare.

Mr. Tulkinghorn says nothing; looks nothing. Now, as heretofore, he is to be found in doorways of rooms, with his limp white cravat loosely twisted into its old-fashioned tie, receiving patronage from

1. Lady Macbeth (*Macbeth*, V.i).

the Peerage, and making no sign. Of all men he is still the last who might be supposed to have any influence upon my Lady. Of all women she is still the last who might be supposed to have any dread of him.

One thing has been much on her mind since their late interview in his turret-room at Chesney Wold. She is now decided, and prepared to throw it off.

It is morning in the great world; afternoon according to the little sun. The Mercuries, exhausted by looking out of window, are reposing in the hall; and hang their heavy heads, the gorgeous creatures, like overblown sunflowers. Like them, too, they seem to run to a deal of seed in their tags and trimmings. Sir Leicester, in the library, has fallen asleep for the good of the country, over the report of a Parliamentary committee. My Lady sits in the room in which she gave audience to the young man of the name of Guppy. Rosa is with her, and has been writing for her and reading to her. Rosa is now at work upon embroidery, or some such pretty thing; and as she bends her head over it my Lady watches her in silence. Not for the first time to-day.

"Rosa."

The pretty village face looks brightly up. Then, seeing how serious my Lady is, looks puzzled and surprised.

"See to the door. Is it shut?"

Yes. She goes to it and returns, and looks yet more surprised.

"I am about to place confidence in you, child, for I know I may trust your attachment, if not your judgment. In what I am going to do, I will not disguise myself to you at least. But I confide in you. Say nothing to any one of what passes between us."

The timid little beauty promises in all earnestness to be trustworthy.

"Do you know," Lady Dedlock asks her, signing to her to bring her chair nearer; "do you know, Rosa, that I am different to you from what I am to any one?"

"Yes, my Lady. Much kinder. But then I often think I know you as you really are."

"You often think you know me as I really am? Poor child, poor child!"

She says it with a kind of scorn—though not of Rosa—and sits brooding, looking dreamily at her.

"Do you think, Rosa, you are any relief or comfort to me? Do you suppose your being young and natural, and fond of me and grateful to me, makes it any pleasure to me to have you near me?"

"I don't know, my Lady; I can scarcely hope so. But, with all my heart, I wish it was so."

"It is so, little one."

The pretty face is checked in its flush of pleasure, by the dark expression on the handsome face before it. It looks timidly for an explanation.

"And if I were to say to-day, Go! Leave me! I should say what would give me great pain and disquiet, child, and what would leave me very solitary."

"My Lady! Have I offended you?"

"In nothing. Come here."

Rosa bends down on the footstool at my Lady's feet. My Lady, with that motherly touch of the famous Ironmaster night, lays her hand upon her dark hair, and gently keeps it there.

"I told you, Rosa, that I wished you to be happy, and that I would make you so if I could make anybody happy on this earth. I can not. There are reasons now known to me, reasons in which you have no part, rendering it far better for you that you should not remain here. You must not remain here. I have determined that you shall not. I have written to the father of your lover, and he will be here to-day. All this I have done for your sake."

The weeping girl covers her hand with kisses, and says what shall she do, what shall she do, when they are separated! Her mistress kisses her on the cheek, and makes no other answer.

"Now, be happy, child, under better circumstances. Be beloved and happy!"

"Ah, my Lady, I have sometimes thought—forgive my being so free—that *you* are not happy."

"I!"

"Will you be more so, when you have sent me away? Pray, pray, think again. Let me stay a little while!"

"I have said, my child, that what I do, I do for your sake, not my own. It is done. What I am towards you, Rosa, is what I am now—not what I shall be a little while hence. Remember this, and keep my confidence. Do so much for my sake, and thus all ends between us!"

She detaches herself from her simple-hearted companion, and leaves the room. Late in the afternoon, when she next appears upon the staircase, she is in her haughtiest and coldest state. As indifferent as if all passion, feeling, and interest, had been worn out in the earlier ages of the world, and had perished from its surface with its other departed monsters.

Mercury has announced Mr. Rouncewell, which is the cause of her appearance. Mr. Rouncewell is not in the library; but she repairs to the library. Sir Leicester is there, and she wishes to speak to him first.

"Sir Leicester, I am desirous—but you are engaged."

O dear no! Not at all. Only Mr. Tulkinghorn.

Always at hand. Haunting every place. No relief or security from him for a moment.

"I beg your pardon, Lady Dedlock. Will you allow me to retire?"

With a look that plainly says, "You know you have the power to remain if you will," she tells him it is not necessary, and moves towards a chair. Mr. Tulkinghorn brings it a little forward for her with his clumsy bow, and retires into a window opposite. Interposed between her and the fading light of day in the now quiet street, his shadow falls upon her, and he darkens all before her. Even so does he darken her life.

It is a dull street under the best conditions; where the two long rows of houses stare at each other with that severity, that half-a-dozen of its greatest mansions seem to have been slowly stared into stone, rather than originally built in that material. It is a street of such dismal grandeur, so determined not to condescend to liveliness, that the doors and windows hold a gloomy state of their own in black paint and dust, and the echoing mews[2] behind have a dry and massive appearance, as if they were reserved to stable the stone chargers of noble statues. Complicated garnish of iron-work entwines itself over the flights of steps in this awful street; and, from these petrified bowers, extinguishers for obsolete flambeaux gasp at the upstart gas. Here and there a weak little iron hoop, through which bold boys aspire to throw their friends' caps (its only present use), retains its place among the rusty foliage, sacred to the memory of departed oil. Nay, even oil itself, yet lingering at long intervals in a little absurd glass pot, with a knob in the bottom like an oyster, blinks and sulks at newer lights every night, like its high and dry master in the House of Lords.[3]

Therefore there is not much that Lady Dedlock, seated in her chair, could wish to see through the window in which Mr. Tulkinghorn stands. And yet—and yet—she sends a look in that direction, as if it were her heart's desire to have that figure removed out of the way.

Sir Leicester begs his Lady's pardon. She was about to say?

"Only that Mr. Rouncewell is here (he has called by my appointment), and that we had better make an end of the question of that girl. I am tired to death of the matter."

2. Carriage-houses often built in rows along an alley, like garages, and usually with living quarters for coachmen and servants on the floor above the stables.

3. Entrances to fashionable houses in the eighteenth century had been dimly illuminated by oil lamps consisting of a small pan of oil (with a floating wick) inside a glass pot. Such pots were suspended from a *hoop* at the top of an elaborate wrought-iron lamp-post. The introduction of gas lighting in the first half of the nineteenth century rendered these structures obsolete, although some aristocratic house-owners continued to oppose gas. *Extinguishers* were iron cones, attached to the lamp-post, in which footmen formerly used to smother the torches (*flambeaux*) they carried when escorting ladies from their carriages into a house.

"What can I do—to—assist?" demands Sir Leicester, in some considerable doubt.

"Let us see him here, and have done with it. Will you tell them to send him up?"

"Mr. Tulkinghorn, be so good as to ring. Thank you. Request," says Sir Leicester, to Mercury, not immediately remembering the business term, "request the iron gentleman to walk this way."

Mercury departs in search of the iron gentleman, finds, and produces him. Sir Leicester receives that ferruginous person, graciously.

"I hope you are well, Mr. Rouncewell. Be seated. (My solicitor, Mr. Tulkinghorn.) My Lady was desirous, Mr. Rouncewell," Sir Leicester skilfully transfers him with a solemn wave of his hand, "was desirous to speak with you. Hem!"

"I shall be very happy," returns the iron gentleman, "to give my best attention to anything Lady Dedlock does me the honour to say."

As he turns towards her, he finds that the impression she makes upon him is less agreeable than on the former occasion. A distant supercilious air makes a cold atmosphere about her; and there is nothing in her bearing, as there was before, to encourage openness.

"Pray, sir," says Lady Dedlock, listlessly, "may I be allowed to inquire whether anything has passed between you and your son, respecting your son's fancy?"

It is almost too troublesome to her languid eyes to bestow a look upon him, as she asks this question.

"If my memory serves me, Lady Dedlock, I said, when I had the pleasure of seeing you before, that I should seriously advise my son to conquer that—fancy." The ironmaster repeats her expression with a little emphasis.

"And did you?"

"O! of course I did."

Sir Leicester gives a nod, approving and confirmatory. Very proper. The iron gentleman having said that he would do it, was bound to do it. No difference in this respect between the base metals and the precious. Highly proper.

"And pray has he done so?"

"Really, Lady Dedlock, I cannot make you a definite reply. I fear not. Probably not yet. In our condition of life, we sometimes couple an intention with our—our fancies, which renders them not altogether easy to throw off. I think it is rather our way to be in earnest."

Sir Leicester has a misgiving that there may be a hidden Wat Tylerish[4] meaning in this expression, and fumes a little. Mr.

4. See p. 79, note 7.

Rouncewell is perfectly good-humoured and polite; but, within such limits, evidently adapts his tone to his reception.

"Because," proceeds my Lady, "I have been thinking of the subject—which is tiresome to me."

"I am very sorry, I am sure."

"And also of what Sir Leicester said upon it, in which I quite concur"; Sir Leicester flattered; "and if you cannot give us the assurance that this fancy is at an end, I have come to the conclusion that the girl had better leave me."

"I can give no such assurance, Lady Dedlock. Nothing of the kind."

"Then she had better go."

"Excuse me, my Lady," Sir Leicester considerately interposes, "but perhaps this may be doing an injury to the young woman, which she has not merited. Here is a young woman," says Sir Leicester, magnificently laying out the matter with his right hand, like a service of plate, "whose good fortune it is to have attracted the notice and favour of an eminent lady, and to live, under the protection of that eminent lady, surrounded by the various advantages which such a position confers, and which are unquestionably very great—I believe unquestionably very great, sir—for a young woman in that station of life. The question then arises, should that young woman be deprived of these many advantages and that good fortune, simply because she has"; Sir Leicester, with an apologetic but dignified inclination of his head towards the ironmaster, winds up his sentence; "has attracted the notice of Mr. Rouncewell's son? Now, has she deserved this punishment? Is this just towards her? Is this our previous understanding?"

"I beg your pardon," interposes Mr. Rouncewell's son's father. "Sir Leicester, will you allow me? I think I may shorten the subject. Pray dismiss that from your consideration. If you remembered anything so unimportant—which is not to be expected—you would recollect that my first thought in the affair was directly opposed to her remaining here."

Dismiss the Dedlock patronage from consideration? O! Sir Leicester is bound to believe a pair of ears that have been handed down to him through such a family, or he really might have mistrusted their report of the iron gentleman's observations.

"It is not necessary," observes my Lady, in her coldest manner, before he can do anything but breathe amazedly, "to enter into these matters on either side. The girl is a very good girl; I have nothing whatever to say against her; but she is so far insensible to her many advantages and her good fortune, that she is in love—or supposes she is, poor little fool—and unable to appreciate them."

Sir Leicester begs to observe, that wholly alters the case. He might have been sure that my Lady had the best grounds and reasons in support of her view. He entirely agrees with my Lady. The young woman had better go.

"As Sir Leicester observed, Mr. Rouncewell, on the last occasion, when we were fatigued by this business," Lady Dedlock languidly proceeds, "we cannot make conditions with you. Without conditions, and under present circumstances, the girl is quite misplaced here, and had better go. I have told her so. Would you wish to have her sent back to the village, or would you like to take her with you, or what would you prefer?"

"Lady Dedlock, if I may speak plainly——"

"By all means."

"—I should prefer the course which will the soonest relieve you of the incumbrance, and remove her from her present position."

"And to speak as plainly," she returns, with the same studied carelessness, "so should I. Do I understand that you will take her with you?"

The iron gentleman makes an iron bow.

"Sir Leicester, will you ring?" Mr. Tulkinghorn steps forward from his window and pulls the bell. "I had forgotten you. Thank you." He makes his usual bow, and goes quietly back again. Mercury, swift-responsive, appears, receives instructions whom to produce, skims away, produces the aforesaid, and departs.

Rosa has been crying, and is yet in distress. On her coming in, the ironmaster leaves his chair, takes her arm in his, and remains with her near the door ready to depart.

"You are taken charge of, you see," says my Lady, in her weary manner, "and are going away well protected. I have mentioned that you are a very good girl, and you have nothing to cry for."

"She seems after all," observes Mr. Tulkinghorn, loitering a little forward with his hands behind him, "as if she were crying at going away."

"Why, she is not well-bred, you see," returns Mr. Rouncewell with some quickness in his manner, as if he were glad to have the lawyer to retort upon; "and she is an inexperienced little thing, and knows no better. If she had remained here, sir, she would have improved, no doubt."

"No doubt," is Mr. Tulkinghorn's composed reply.

Rosa sobs out that she is very sorry to leave my Lady, and that she was happy at Chesney Wold, and has been happy with my Lady, and that she thanks my Lady over and over again. "Out, you silly little puss!" says the ironmaster, checking her in a low voice, though not angrily; "have a spirit, if you're fond of Wat!" My Lady merely waves her off with indifference, saying, "There, there, child!

You are a good girl. Go away!" Sir Leicester has magnificently disengaged himself from the subject, and retired into the sanctuary of his blue coat. Mr. Tulkinghorn, an indistinct form against the dark street now dotted with lamps, looms in my Lady's view, bigger and blacker than before.

"Sir Leicester and Lady Dedlock," says Mr. Rouncewell, after a pause of a few moments, "I beg to take my leave, with an apology for having again troubled you, though not of my own act, on this tiresome subject. I can very well understand, I assure you, how tiresome so small a matter must have become to Lady Dedlock. If I am doubtful of my dealing with it, it is only because I did not at first quietly exert my influence to take my young friend here away, without troubling you at all. But it appeared to me—I dare say magnifying the importance of the thing—that it was respectful to explain to you how the matter stood, and candid to consult your wishes and convenience. I hope you will excuse my want of acquaintance with the polite world."

Sir Leicester considers himself evoked out of the sanctuary by these remarks. "Mr. Rouncewell," he returns, "do not mention it. Justifications are unnecessary, I hope, on either side."

"I am glad to hear it, Sir Leicester; and if I may, by way of a last word, revert to what I said before of my mother's long connexion with the family, and the worth it bespeaks on both sides, I would point out this little instance here on my arm, who shows herself so affectionate and faithful in parting, and in whom my mother, I dare say, has done something to awaken such feelings—though of course Lady Dedlock, by her heartfelt interest and her genial condescension, has done much more."

If he mean this ironically, it may be truer than he thinks. He points it, however, by no deviation from his straightforward manner of speech, though in saying it he turns towards that part of the dim room where my Lady sits. Sir Leicester stands to return his parting salutation, Mr. Tulkinghorn again rings, Mercury takes another flight, and Mr. Rouncwell and Rosa leave the house.

Then lights are brought in, discovering Mr. Tulkinghorn still standing in his window with his hands behind him, and my Lady still sitting with his figure before her, closing up her view of the night as well as of the day. She is very pale. Mr. Tulkinghorn observing it as she rises to retire, thinks, "Well she may be! The power of this woman is astonishing. She has been acting a part the whole time." But he can act a part too—his one unchanging character—and as he holds the door open for this woman, fifty pairs of eyes, each fifty times sharper than Sir Leicester's pair, should find no flaw in him.

Lady Dedlock dines alone in her own room to-day. Sir Leicester is whipped in to the rescue of the Doodle Party, and the discomfiture of the Coodle Faction. Lady Dedlock asks, on sitting down to dinner, still deadly pale (and quite an illustration of the debilitated cousin's text), whether he is gone out? Yes. Whether Mr. Tulkinghorn is gone yet? No. Presently she asks again, is he gone *yet*? No. What is he doing? Mercury thinks he is writing letters in the library. Would my Lady wish to see him? Anything but that.

But he wishes to see my Lady. Within a few more minutes he is reported as sending his respects, and could my Lady please to receive him for a word or two after her dinner? My Lady will receive him now. He comes now, apologising for intruding, even by her permission, while she is at table. When they are alone, my Lady waves her hand to dispense with such mockeries.

"What do you want, sir?"

"Why, Lady Dedlock," says the lawyer, taking a chair at a little distance from her, and slowly rubbing his rusty legs up and down, up and down, up and down; "I am rather surprised by the course you have taken."

"Indeed?"

"Yes, decidedly. I was not prepared for it. I consider it a departure from our agreement and your promise. It puts us in a new position, Lady Dedlock. I feel myself under the necessity of saying that I don't approve of it."

He stops in his rubbing, and looks at her, with his hands on his knees. Imperturbable and unchangeable as he is, there is still an indefinable freedom in his manner, which is new, and which does not escape this woman's observation.

"I do not quite understand you."

"O yes you do, I think. I think you do. Come, come, Lady Dedlock, we must not fence and parry now. You know you like this girl."

"Well, sir?"

"And you know—and I know—that you have not sent her away for the reasons you have assigned, but for the purpose of separating her as much as possible from—excuse my mentioning it as a matter of business—any reproach and exposure that impend over yourself."

"Well, sir?"

"Well, Lady Dedlock," returns the lawyer, crossing his legs, and nursing the uppermost knee. "I object to that. I consider that a dangerous proceeding. I know it to be unnecessary, and calculated to awaken speculation, doubt, rumour, I don't know what, in the house. Besides, it is a violation of our agreement. You were to be exactly what you were before. Whereas, it must be evident to yourself, as it is to me, that you have been this evening very different from what you were before. Why, bless my soul, Lady Dedlock, transparently so!"

"If, sir," she begins, "in my knowledge of my secret—" But he interrupts her.

"Now Lady Dedlock, this is a matter of business, and in a matter of business the ground cannot be kept too clear. It is no longer your secret. Excuse me. That is just the mistake. It is my secret, in trust for Sir Leicester and the family. If it were your secret, Lady Dedlock, we should not be here, holding this conversation."

"That is very true. If, in my knowledge of *the* secret, I do what I can to spare an innocent girl (especially, remembering your own reference to her when you told my story to the assembled guests at Chesney Wold) from the taint of my impending shame, I act upon a resolution I have taken. Nothing in the world, and no one in the world, could shake it, or could move me." This she says with great deliberation and distinctness, and with no more outward passion than himself. As for him, he methodically discusses his matter of business, as if she were any insensible instrument used in business.

"Really? Then you see, Lady Dedlock," he returns, "you are not to be trusted. You have put the case in a perfectly plain way, and according to the literal fact; and, that being the case, you are not to be trusted."

"Perhaps you may remember that I expressed some anxiety on this same point, when we spoke at night at Chesney Wold?"

"Yes," says Mr. Tulkinghorn, coolly getting up and standing on the hearth. "Yes. I recollect, Lady Dedlock, that you certainly referred to the girl; but that was before we came to our arrangement, and both the letter and the spirit of our arrangement altogether precluded any action on your part, founded upon my discovery. There can be no doubt about that. As to sparing the girl, of what importance or value is she? Spare! Lady Dedlock, here is a family name compromised. One might have supposed that the course was straight on—over everything, neither to the right nor to the left, regardless of all considerations in the way, sparing nothing, treading everything under foot."

She has been looking at the table. She lifts up her eyes, and looks at him. There is a stern expression on her face, and a part of her lower lip is compressed under her teeth. "This woman understands me," Mr. Tulkinghorn thinks, as she lets her glance fall again. "*She* cannot be spared. Why should she spare others?"

For a little while they are silent. Lady Dedlock has eaten no dinner, but has twice or thrice poured out water with a steady hand and drunk it. She rises from table, takes a lounging-chair, and reclines in it, shading her face. There is nothing in her manner to express weakness or excite compassion. It is thoughtful, gloomy, concentrated. "This woman," thinks Mr. Tulkinghorn, standing on the hearth, again a dark object closing up her view, "is a study."

He studies her at his leisure, not speaking for a time. She too studies something at her leisure. She is not the first to speak; appearing indeed so unlikely to be so, though he stood there until midnight, that even he is driven upon breaking silence.

"Lady Dedlock, the most disagreeable part of this business interview remains; but it is business. Our agreement is broken. A lady of your sense and strength of character will be prepared for my now declaring it void, and taking my own course."

"I am quite prepared."

Mr. Tulkinghorn inclines his head. "That is all I have to trouble you with, Lady Dedlock."

She stops him as he is moving out of the room, by asking, "This is the notice I was to receive? I wish not to misapprehend you."

"Not exactly the notice you were to receive, Lady Dedlock, because the contemplated notice supposed the agreement to have been observed. But virtually the same, virtually the same. The difference is merely in a lawyer's mind."

"You intend to give me no other notice?"

"You are right. No."

"Do you contemplate undeceiving Sir Leicester to-night?"

"A home question!" says Mr. Tulkinghorn, with a slight smile, and cautiously shaking his head at the shaded face. "No, not to-night."

"To-morrow?"

"All things considered, I had better decline answering that question, Lady Dedlock. If I were to say I don't know when, exactly, you would not believe me, and it would answer no purpose. It may be to-morrow. I would rather say no more. You are prepared, and I hold out no expectations which circumstances might fail to justify. I wish you good evening."

She removes her hand, turns her pale face towards him as he walks silently to the door, and stops him once again as he is about to open it.

"Do you intend to remain in the house any time? I heard you were writing in the library. Are you going to return there?"

"Only for my hat. I am going home."

She bows her eyes rather than her head, the movement is so slight and curious; and he withdraws. Clear of the room he looks at his watch, but is inclined to doubt it by a minute or thereabouts. There is a splendid clock upon the staircase, famous, as splendid clocks not often are, for its accuracy. "And what do *you* say?" Mr. Tulkinghorn inquires, referring to it. "What do you say?"

If it said now, "Don't go home!" What a famous clock, hereafter, if it said to-night of all the nights that it has counted off, to this old man of all the young and old men who have ever stood before it, "Don't go home!" With its sharp clear bell, it strikes three-quarters after seven, and ticks on again. "Why, you are worse than I thought you," says Mr. Tulkinghorn, muttering reproof to his watch. "Two minutes wrong? At this rate you won't last my time." What a watch to return good for evil, if it ticked in answer, "Don't go home!"

He passes out into the streets, and walks on, with his hands behind him, under the shadow of the lofty houses, many of whose mysteries, difficulties, mortgages, delicate affairs of all kinds, are treasured up within his old black satin waistcoat. He is in the confidence of the very bricks and mortar. The high chimney-stacks telegraph family secrets to him. Yet there is not a voice in a mile of them to whisper, "Don't go home!"

Through the stir and motion of the commoner streets; through the roar and jar of many vehicles, many feet, many voices; with the blazing shop-lights lighting him on, the west wind blowing him on, and the crowd pressing him on; he is pitilessly urged upon his way, and nothing meets him, murmuring, "Don't go home!" Arrived at last in his dull room, to light his candles, and look round and up, and see the Roman pointing from the ceiling, there is no new significance in the Roman's hand to-night, or in the flutter of the attendant groupes, to give him the late warning, "Don't come here!"

It is a moonlight night; but the moon, being past the full, is only now rising over the great wilderness of London. The stars are shining as they shone above the turret-leads at Chesney Wold. This woman, as he has of late been so accustomed to call her, looks out upon them. Her soul is turbulent within her; she is sick at heart, and restless. The large rooms are too cramped and close. She cannot endure their restraint, and will walk alone in a neighbouring garden.

Too capricious and imperious in all she does, to be the cause of much surprise in those about her as to anything she does, this woman, loosely muffled, goes out into the moonlight. Mercury attends with the key. Having opened the garden-gate, he delivers the key[5] into his Lady's hand at her request, and is bidden to go back. She will walk there some time, to ease her aching head. She may be an hour; she may be more. She needs no further escort. The gate shuts upon its spring with a clash, and he leaves her, passing on into the dark shade of some trees.

A fine night, and a bright large moon, and multitudes of stars. Mr. Tulkinghorn, in repairing to his cellar, and in opening and shutting those resounding doors, has to cross a little prison-like

5. Residents in London's West End often have access to large gardens adjacent to their houses. The gardens are fenced, with locked gates for which only nearby residents have keys.

yard. He looks up casually, thinking what a fine night, what a bright large moon, what multitudes of stars! A quiet night, too.

A very quiet night. When the moon shines very brilliantly, a solitude and stillness seem to proceed from her, that influence even crowded places full of life. Not only is it a still night on dusty high roads and on hill-summits, whence a wide expanse of country may be seen in repose, quieter and quieter as it spreads away into a fringe of trees against the sky, with the grey ghost of a bloom upon them; not only is it a still night in gardens and in woods, and on the river where the water-meadows are fresh and green, and the stream sparkles on among pleasant islands, murmuring weirs, and whispering rushes; not only does the stillness attend it as it flows where houses cluster thick, where many bridges are reflected in it, where wharves and shipping make it black and awful, where it winds away from these disfigurements through marshes whose grim beacons stand like skeletons washed ashore, where it expands through the bolder region of rising grounds, rich in corn-field windmill and steeple, and where it mingles with the ever-heaving sea; not only is it a still night on the deep, and on the shore where the watcher stands to see the ship with her spread wings cross the path of light that appears to be presented to only him; but even on this stranger's wilderness of London there is some rest. Its steeples and towers, and its one great dome, grow more ethereal; its smoky housetops lose their grossness, in the pale effulgence; the noises that arise from the streets are fewer and are softened, and the footsteps on the pavements pass more tranquilly away. In these fields of Mr. Tulkinghorn's inhabiting, where the shepherds play on Chancery pipes that have no stop,[6] and keep their sheep in the fold by hook and by crook until they have shorn them exceeding close, every noise is merged, this moonlight night, into a distant ringing hum, as if the city were a vast glass, vibrating.

What's that? Who fired a gun or pistol? Where was it?

The few foot-passengers start, stop, and stare about them. Some windows and doors are opened, and people come out to look. It was a loud report, and echoed and rattled heavily. It shook one house, or so a man says who was passing. It has aroused all the dogs in the neighbourhood, who bark vehemently. Terrified cats scamper across the road. While the dogs are yet barking and howling—there is one dog howling like a demon—the church-clocks, as if they were startled too, begin to strike. The hum from the streets, likewise, seems to swell into a shout. But it is soon over. Before the last clock begins to strike ten, there is a lull. When it has ceased, the fine

6. Traditional shepherds' pipes contain holes or *stops*; the Chancery lawyers' pipes, having no stop, would produce a monotonous serenade and also, by pun, an unceasing one.

night, the bright large moon, and multitudes of stars, are left at peace again.

Has Mr. Tulkinghorn been disturbed? His windows are dark and quiet, and his door is shut. It must be something unusual indeed, to bring *him* out of his shell. Nothing is heard of him, nothing is seen of him. What power of cannon might it take to shake that rusty old man out of his immoveable composure?

For many years, the persistent Roman has been pointing, with no particular meaning, from that ceiling. It is not likely that he has any new meaning in him to-night. Once pointing, always pointing—like any Roman, or even Briton, with a single idea. There he is, no doubt, in his impossible attitude, pointing unavailingly, all night long. Moonlight, darkness, dawn, sunrise, day. There he is still, eagerly pointing, and no one minds him.

But, a little after the coming of the day, come people to clean the rooms. And either the Roman has some new meaning in him, not expressed before, or the foremost of them goes wild; for, looking up at his outstretched hand, and looking down at what is below it, that person shrieks and flies. The others, looking in as the first one looked, shriek and fly too, and there is an alarm in the street.

What does it mean? No light is admitted into the darkened chamber, and people unaccustomed to it, enter, and, treading softly, but heavily, carry a weight into the bedroom, and lay it down. There is whispering and wandering all day, strict search of every corner, careful tracing of steps, and careful noting of the disposition of every article of furniture. All eyes look up at the Roman, and all voices murmur, "If he could only tell what he saw!"

He is pointing at a table, with a bottle (nearly full of wine) and a glass upon it, and two candles that were blown out suddenly, soon after being lighted. He is pointing at an empty chair, and at a stain upon the ground before it that might be almost covered with a hand. These objects lie directly within his range. An excited imagination might suppose that there was something in them so terrific, as to drive the rest of the composition, not only the attendant big-legged boys, but the clouds and flowers and pillars too—in short the very body and soul of Allegory, and all the brains it has—stark mad. It happens surely, that every one who comes into the darkened room and looks at these things, looks up at the Roman, and that he is invested in all eyes with mystery and awe, as if he were a paralysed dumb witness.

So, it shall happen surely, through many years to come, that ghostly stories shall be told of the stain upon the floor, so easy to be covered, so hard to be got out; and that the Roman, pointing from the ceiling, shall point, so long as dust and damp and spiders spare him, with far greater significance than he ever had in Mr. Tulking-

A new meaning in the Roman.

horn's time, and with a deadly meaning. For, Mr. Tulkinghorn's time is over for evermore; and the Roman pointed at the murderous hand uplifted against his life, and pointed helplessly at him, from night to morning lying face downward on the floor, shot through the heart.

Chapter XLIX

DUTIFUL FRIENDSHIP

A great annual occasion has come round in the establishment of Mr. Joseph Bagnet, otherwise Lignum Vitae, ex-artilleryman and present bassoon-player. An occasion of feasting and festival. The celebration of a birthday in the family.

It is not Mr. Bagnet's birthday. Mr. Bagnet merely distinguishes that epoch in the musical instrument business, by kissing the children with an extra smack before breakfast, smoking an additional pipe after dinner, and wondering towards evening what his poor old mother is thinking about it,—a subject of infinite speculation, and rendered so by his mother having departed this life, twenty years. Some men rarely revert to their father, but seem, in the bank-books of their remembrance, to have transferred all their stock of filial affection into their mother's name. Mr. Bagnet is one of these. Perhaps his exalted appreciation of the merits of the old girl, causes him usually to make the noun-substantive, Goodness, of the feminine gender.

It is not the birthday of one of the three children. Those occasions are kept with some marks of distinction, but they rarely overleap the bounds of happy returns and a pudding. On young Woolwich's last birthday, Mr. Bagnet certainly did, after observing upon his growth and general advancement, proceed in a moment of profound reflection on the changes wrought by time, to examine him in the catechism; accomplishing with extreme accuracy the questions number one and two, What is your name? and Who gave you that name? but there failing in the exact precision of his memory, and substituting for number three,[1] the question And how do you like that name? which he propounded with a sense of its importance, in itself so edifying and improving, as to give it quite an orthodox air. This, however, was a speciality on that particular birthday, and not a generic solemnity.

It is the old girl's birthday; and that is the greatest holiday and reddest-letter day in Mr. Bagnet's calendar. The auspicious event is always commemorated according to certain forms, settled and pre-

1. The third question reads: "What did your Godfathers and Godmothers then for you?"

scribed by Mr. Bagnet some years since. Mr. Bagnet being deeply convinced that to have a pair of fowls for dinner is to attain the highest pitch of imperial luxury, invariably goes forth himself very early in the morning of this day to buy a pair; he is, as invariably, taken in by the vendor, and installed in the possession of the oldest inhabitants of any coop in Europe. Returning with these triumphs of toughness tied up in a clean blue and white cotton handkerchief (essential to the arrangements), he in a casual manner invites Mrs. Bagnet to declare at breakfast what she would like for dinner. Mrs. Bagnet, by a coincidence never known to fail, replying Fowls, Mr. Bagnet instantly produces his bundle from a place of concealment, amidst general amazement and rejoicing. He further requires that the old girl shall do nothing all day long, but sit in her very best gown, and be served by himself and the young people. As he is not illustrious for his cookery, this may be supposed to be a matter of state rather than of enjoyment on the old girl's part; but she keeps her state with all imaginable cheerfulness.

On this present birthday, Mr. Bagnet has accomplished the usual preliminaries. He has bought two specimens of poultry, which, if there be any truth in adages, were certainly not caught with chaff,[2] to be prepared for the spit; he has amazed and rejoiced the family by their unlooked-for production; he is himself directing the roasting of the poultry; and Mrs. Bagnet, with her wholesome brown fingers itching to prevent what she sees going wrong, sits in her gown of ceremony, an honoured guest.

Quebec and Malta lay the cloth for dinner, while Woolwich, serving, as beseems him, under his father, keeps the fowls revolving. To these young scullions, Mrs. Bagnet occasionally imparts a wink, or a shake of the head, or a crooked face, as they make mistakes.

"At half-after one." Says Mr. Bagnet. "To the minute. They'll be done."

Mrs. Bagnet, with anguish, beholds one of them at a stand-still before the fire, and beginning to burn.

"You shall have a dinner, old girl," says Mr. Bagnet. "Fit for a queen."

Mrs. Bagnet shows her white teeth cheerfully, but to the perception of her son, betrays so much uneasiness of spirit, that he is impelled by the dictates of affection to ask her, with his eyes, what is the matter?—thus standing, with his eyes wide open, more oblivious of the fowls than before, and not affording the least hope of a return to consciousness. Fortunately, his elder sister perceives the cause of the agitation in Mrs. Bagnet's breast, and with an admoni-

2. See *Don Quixote* (I.iv.5): "You must not think, sir, to catch old birds with chaff."

tory poke recalls him. The stopped fowls going round again, Mrs. Bagnet closes her eyes, in the intensity of her relief.

"George will look us up," says Mr. Bagnet. "At half-after four. To the moment. How many years, old girl. Has George looked us up. This afternoon?"

"Ah, Lignum, Lignum, as many as make an old woman of a young one, I begin to think. Just about that, and no less," returns Mrs. Bagnet, laughing, and shaking her head.

"Old girl," says Mr. Bagnet. "Never mind. You'd be as young as ever you was. If you wasn't younger. Which you are. As everybody knows."

Quebec and Malta here exclaim, with clapping of hands, that Bluffy is sure to bring mother something, and begin to speculate on what it will be.

"Do you know, Lignum," says Mrs. Bagnet, casting a glance on the table-cloth, and winking, "salt!" at Malta with her right eye, and shaking the pepper away from Quebec with her head; "I begin to think George is in the roving way again."

"George," returns Mr. Bagnet, "will never desert. And leave his old comrade. In the lurch. Don't be afraid of it."

"No, Lignum. No. I don't say he will. I don't think he will. But if he could get over this money-trouble of his, I believe he would be off."

Mr. Bagnet asks why?

"Well," returns his wife, considering. "George seems to me to be getting not a little impatient and restless. I don't say but what he's as free as ever. Of course he must be free, or he wouldn't be George; but he smarts, and seems put out."

"He's extra-drilled," says Mr. Bagnet. "By a lawyer. Who would put the devil out."

"There's something in that," his wife assents; "but so it is, Lignum."

Further conversation is prevented, for the time, by the necessity under which Mr. Bagnet finds himself of directing the whole force of his mind to the dinner, which is a little endangered by the dry humour of the fowls in not yielding any gravy, and also by the made-gravy acquiring no flavour, and turning out of a flaxen complexion. With a similar perverseness, the potatoes crumble off forks in the process of peeling, upheaving from their centres in every direction, as if they were subject to earthquakes. The legs of the fowls, too, are longer than could be desired, and extremely scaly. Overcoming these disadvantages to the best of his ability, Mr. Bagnet at last dishes, and they sit down at table; Mrs. Bagnet occupying the guest's place at his right hand.

It is well for the old girl that she has but one birthday in a year, for two such indulgences in poultry might be injurious. Every kind of finer tendon and ligament that it is in the nature of poultry to possess, is developed in these specimens in the singular form of guitar-strings. Their limbs appear to have struck roots into their breasts and bodies, as aged trees strike roots into the earth. Their legs are so hard, as to encourage the idea that they must have devoted the greater part of their long and arduous lives to pedestrian exercises, and the walking of matches. But Mr. Bagnet, unconscious of these little defects, sets his heart on Mrs. Bagnet eating a most severe quantity of the delicacies before her; and as that good old girl would not cause him a moment's disappointment on any day, least of all on such a day, for any consideration, she imperils her digestion fearfully. How young Woolwich cleans the drum-sticks without being of ostrich descent, his anxious mother is at a loss to understand.

The old girl has another trial to undergo after the conclusion of the repast, in sitting in state to see the room cleared, the hearth swept, and the dinner-service washed up and polished in the back yard. The great delight and energy with which the two young ladies apply themselves to these duties, turning up their skirts in imitation of their mother, and skating in and out on little scaffolds of pattens, inspire the highest hopes for the future, but some anxiety for the present. The same causes lead to a confusion of tongues,[3] a clattering of crockery, a rattling of tin mugs, a whisking of brooms, and an expenditure of water, all in excess; while the saturation of the young ladies themselves is almost too moving a spectacle for Mrs. Bagnet to look upon, with the calmness proper to her position. At last the various cleansing processes are triumphantly completed; Quebec and Malta appear in fresh attire, smiling and dry; pipes, tobacco, and something to drink, are placed upon the table; and the old girl enjoys the first peace of mind she ever knows on the day of this delightful entertainment.

When Mr. Bagnet takes his usual seat, the hands of the clock are very near to half-past four; as they mark it accurately, Mr. Bagnet announces,

"George! Military time."

It is George; and he has hearty congratulations for the old girl (whom he kisses on the great occasion), and for the children, and for Mr. Bagnet. "Happy returns to all!" says Mr. George.

"But, George, old man!" cries Mrs. Bagnet, looking at him curiously. "What's come to you?"

"Come to me?"

3. Cf. Genesis 11:7–9.

"Ah! you are so white, George—for you—and look so shocked. Now don't he, Lignum?"

"George," says Mr. Bagnet, "tell the old girl. What's the matter."

"I didn't know I looked white," says the trooper, passing his hands over his brow, "and I didn't know I looked shocked, and I'm sorry I do. But the truth is, that boy who was taken in at my place died yesterday afternoon, and it has rather knocked me over."

"Poor creetur!" says Mrs. Bagnet, with a mother's pity. "Is he gone? Dear, dear!"

"I didn't mean to say anything about it, for it's not birthday talk, but you have got it out of me, you see, before I sit down. I should have roused up in a minute," says the trooper, making himself speak more gaily, "but you're so quick, Mrs. Bagnet."

"You're right. The old girl," says Mr. Bagnet. "Is as quick. As powder."[4]

"And what's more, she's the subject of the day, and we'll stick to her," cries Mr. George. "See here, I have brought a little brooch along with me. It's a poor thing, you know, but it's a keepsake. That's all the good it is, Mrs. Bagnet."

Mr. George produces his present, which is greeted with admiring leapings and clappings by the young family, and with a species of reverential admiration by Mr. Bagnet. "Old girl," says Mr. Bagnet. "Tell him my opinion of it."

"Why, it's a wonder, George!" Mrs. Bagnet exclaims. "It's the beautifullest thing that ever was seen!"

"Good!" says Mr. Bagnet. "My opinion."

"It's so pretty, George," cries Mrs. Bagnet, turning it on all sides, and holding it out at arm's length, "that it seems too choice for me."

"Bad!" says Mr. Bagnet. "Not my opinion."

"But whatever it is, a hundred thousand thanks, old fellow," says Mrs. Bagnet, her eyes sparkling with pleasure, and her hand stretched out to him; "and though I have been a cross-grained soldier's wife to you sometimes, George, we are as strong friends, I am sure, in reality, as ever can be. Now you shall fasten it on yourself, for good luck, if you will, George."

The children close up to see it done, and Mr. Bagnet looks over young Woolwich's head to see it done, with an interest so maturely wooden, yet so pleasantly childish, that Mrs. Bagnet cannot help laughing in her airy way, and saying, "O Lignum, Lignum, what a precious old chap you are!" But the trooper fails to fasten the brooch. His hand shakes, he is nervous, and it falls off. "Would

4. Gunpowder.

any one believe this?" says he, catching it as it drops, and looking round. "I am so out of sorts that I bungle at an easy job like this!"

Mrs. Bagnet concludes that for such a case there is no remedy like a pipe; and fastening the brooch herself in a twinkling, causes the trooper to be inducted into his usual snug place, and the pipes to be got into action. "If that don't bring you round, George," says she, "just throw your eye across here at your present now and then, and the two together *must* do it."

"You ought to do it of yourself," George answers; "I know that very well, Mrs. Bagnet. I'll tell you how, one way and another, the blues have got to be too many for me. Here was this poor lad. 'Twas dull work to see him dying as he did, and not be able to help him."

"What do you mean, George? You did help him. You took him under your roof."

"I helped him so far, but that's little. I mean, Mrs. Bagnet, there he was, dying without ever having been taught much more than to know his right hand from his left. And he was too far gone to be helped out of that."

"Ah, poor creetur!" says Mrs. Bagnet.

"Then," says the trooper, not yet lighting his pipe, and passing his heavy hand over his hair, "that brought up Gridley in a man's mind. His was a bad case too, in a different way. Then the two got mixed up in a man's mind with a flinty old rascal who had to do with both. And to think of that rusty carbine, stock and barrel, standing up on end in his corner, hard, indifferent, taking everything so evenly—it made flesh and blood tingle, I do assure you."

"My advice to you," returns Mrs. Bagnet, "is to light your pipe, and tingle that way. It's wholesomer and comfortabler, and better for the health altogether."

"You're right," says the trooper, "and I'll do it."

So he does it: though still with an indignant gravity that impresses the young Bagnets, and even causes Mr. Bagnet to defer the ceremony of drinking Mrs. Bagnet's health; always given by himself, on these occasions, in a speech of exemplary terseness. But the young ladies having composed what Mr. Bagnet is in the habit of calling "the mixtur," and George's pipe being now in a glow, Mr. Bagnet considers it his duty to proceed to the toast of the evening. He addresses the assembled company in the following terms.

"George. Woolwich. Quebec. Malta. This is her birthday. Take a day's march. And you won't find such another.[5] Here's towards her!"

The toast having been drunk with enthusiasm, Mrs. Bagnet

5. See the proverb: "You won't find such another in a day's march," i.e., within fifteen or twenty miles.

returns thanks in a neat address of corresponding brevity. This model composition is limited to the three words "And wishing yours!" which the old girl follows up with a nod at everybody in succession, and a well-regulated swig of the mixture. This she again follows up, on the present occasion, by the wholly unexpected exclamation, "Here's a man!"

Here *is* a man, much to the astonishment of the little company, looking in at the parlour-door. He is a sharp-eyed man—a quick keen man—and he takes in everybody's look at him, all at once, individually and collectively, in a manner that stamps him a remarkable man.

"George," says the man, nodding, "how do you find yourself?"

"Why, it's Bucket!" cries Mr. George.

"Yes," says the man, coming in and closing the door. "I was going down the street here, when I happened to stop and look in at the musical instruments in the shop-window—a friend of mine is in wants of a second-hand wiolinceller, of a good tone—and I saw a party enjoying themselves, and I thought it was you in the corner; I thought I couldn't be mistaken. How goes the world with you, George, at the present moment? Pretty smooth? And with you, ma'am? And with you, governor? And Lord!" says Mr. Bucket, opening his arms, "here's children too! You may do anything with me, if you only show me children. Give us a kiss, my pets. No occasion to inquire who *your* father and mother is. Never saw such a likeness in my life!"

Mr. Bucket, not unwelcome, has sat himself down next to Mr. George, and taken Quebec and Malta on his knees. "You pretty dears," says Mr. Bucket, "give us another kiss; it's the only thing I'm greedy in. Lord bless you, how healthy you look! And what may be the ages of these two, ma'am? I should put 'em down at the figures of about eight and ten."

"You're very near, sir," says Mrs. Bagnet.

"I generally am near," returns Mr. Bucket, "being so fond of children. A friend of mine has had nineteen of 'em, ma'am, all by one mother, and she's still as fresh and rosy as the morning. Not so much so as yourself, but, upon my soul, she comes near you! And what do you call these, my darling?" pursues Mr. Bucket, pinching Malta's cheeks. "These are peaches, these are. Bless your heart! And what do you think about father? Do you think father could recommend a second-hand wiolinceller of a good tone for Mr. Bucket's friend, my dear? My name's Bucket. Ain't that a funny name?"

These blandishments have entirely won the family heart. Mrs. Bagnet forgets the day to the extent of filling a pipe and a glass for Mr. Bucket, and waiting upon him hospitably. She would be glad to receive so pleasant a character under any circumstances, but she tells him that as a friend of George's she is particularly glad to see him this evening, for George has not been in his usual spirits.

"Not in his usual spirits?" exclaims Mr. Bucket. "Why, I never heard of such a thing! What's the matter, George? You don't intend to tell me you've been out of spirits. What should you be out of spirits for? You haven't got anything on your mind, you know."

"Nothing particular," returns the trooper.

"*I* should think not," rejoins Mr. Bucket. "What could you have on your mind, you know! And have these pets got anything on *their* minds, eh? Not they; but they'll be upon the minds of some of the young fellows, some of these days, and make 'em precious low-spirited. I ain't much of a prophet, but I can tell you that, ma'am."

Mrs. Bagnet, quite charmed, hopes Mr. Bucket has a family of his own.

"There, ma'am!" says Mr. Bucket. "Would you believe it? No, I haven't. My wife, and a lodger, constitute my family. Mrs. Bucket is as fond of children as myself, and as wishful to have 'em; but no. So it is. Worldly goods are divided unequally, and man must not repine. What a very nice back yard, ma'am! Any way out of that yard, now?"

There is no way out of that yard.

"Ain't there really?" says Mr. Bucket. "I should have thought there might have been. Well, I don't know as I ever saw a back yard that took my fancy more. Would you allow me to look at it? Thank you. No, I see there's no way out. But what a very good-proportioned yard it is!"

Having cast his sharp eye all about it, Mr. Bucket returns to his chair next his friend Mr. George, and pats Mr. George affectionately on the shoulder.

"How are your spirits, now, George?"

"All right now," returns the trooper.

"That's your sort!" says Mr. Bucket. "Why should you ever have been otherwise? A man of your fine figure and constitution has no right to be out of spirits. That ain't a chest to be out of spirits, is it, ma'am? And you haven't got anything on your mind, you know, George; what could you have on your mind!"

Somewhat harping on this phrase, considering the extent and variety of his conversational powers, Mr. Bucket twice or thrice repeats it to the pipe he lights, and with a listening face that is particularly his own. But the sun of his sociality soon recovers from this brief eclipse, and shines again.

"And this is brother, is it, my dears?" says Mr. Bucket, referring to Quebec and Malta for information on the subject of young Woolwich. "And a nice brother he is—half brother, I mean to say. For he's too old to be your boy, ma'am."

"I can certify at all events that he is not anybody else's," returns Mrs. Bagnet, laughing.

"Well, you do surprise me! Yet he's like you, there's no denying. Lord, he's wonderfully like you! But about what you may call the brow, you know, *there* his father comes out!" Mr. Bucket compares the faces with one eye shut up, while Mr. Bagnet smokes in stolid satisfaction.

This is an opportunity for Mrs. Bagnet to inform him, that the boy is George's godson.

"George's godson, is he?" rejoins Mr. Bucket, with extreme cordiality. "I must shake hands over again with George's godson. Godfather and godson do credit to one another. And what do you intend to make of him, ma'am? Does he show any turn for any musical instrument?"

Mr. Bagnet suddenly interposes, "Plays the Fife. Beautiful."

"Would you believe it, governor," says Mr. Bucket, struck by the coincidence, "that when I was a boy I played the fife myself? Not in a scientific way, as I expect he does, but by ear. Lord bless you! British Grenadiers—there's a tune to warm an Englishman up! *Could* you give us British Grenadiers, my fine fellow?"

Nothing could be more acceptable to the little circle than this call upon young Woolwich, who immediately fetches his fife and performs the stirring melody; during which performance Mr. Bucket, much enlivened, beats time, and never fails to come in sharp with the burden, "Brit Ish Gra-a-anadeers!"[6] In short, he shows so much musical taste, that Mr. Bagnet actually takes his pipe from his lips to express his conviction that he is a singer. Mr. Bucket receives the harmonious impeachment so modestly: confessing how that he did once chaunt a little, for the expression of the feelings of his own bosom, and with no presumptuous idea of entertaining his friends: that he is asked to sing. Not to be behind-hand in the sociality of the evening, he complies, and gives them "Believe me if all those endearing young charms."[7] This ballad, he informs Mrs. Bagnet, he considers to have been his most powerful ally in moving the heart of Mrs. Bucket when a maiden, and inducing her to approach the altar—Mr. Bucket's own words are, to come up to the scratch.[8]

This sparkling stranger is such a new and agreeable feature in the evening, that Mr. George, who testified no great emotions of pleasure on his entrance, begins, in spite of himself, to be rather proud of him. He is so friendly, is a man of so many resources, and so easy to get on with, that it is something to have made him known there.

6. Chorus lines of the regimental song of the Grenadier Guards: "But of all the world's brave heroes there's none that can compare/ With a tow row row row row row row, To the British Grenadiers."

7. A popular love song from the *Irish Melodies* of Thomas Moore (1779–1852).

8. Up to scratch: a prize-fighting term. See p. 235, note 1.

Mr. Bagnet becomes, after another pipe, so sensible of the value of his acquaintance, that he solicits the honour of his company on the old girl's next birthday. If anything can more closely cement and consolidate the esteem which Mr. Bucket has formed for the family, it is the discovery of the nature of the occasion. He drinks to Mrs. Bagnet with a warmth approaching to rapture, engages himself for that day twelvemonth more than thankfully, makes a memorandum of the day in a large black pocket-book with a girdle to it, and breathes a hope that Mrs. Bucket and Mrs. Bagnet may before then become, in a manner, sisters. As he says himself, what is public life without private ties? He is in his humble way a public man, but it is not in that sphere that he finds happiness. No, it must be sought within the confines of domestic bliss.

It is natural, under these circumstances, that he, in his turn, should remember the friend to whom he is indebted for so promising an acquaintance. And he does. He keeps very close to him. Whatever the subject of the conversation, he keeps a tender eye upon him. He waits to walk home with him. He is interested in his very boots; and observes even them attentively, as Mr. George sits smoking cross-legged in the chimney-corner.

At length, Mr. George rises to depart. At the same moment Mr. Bucket, with the secret sympathy of friendship, also rises. He dotes upon the children to the last, and remembers the commission he has undertaken for an absent friend.

"Respecting that second-hand wiolinceller, governor—could you recommend me such a thing?"

"Scores," says Mr. Bagnet.

"I am obliged to you," returns Mr. Bucket, squeezing his hand. "You're a friend in need. A good tone, mind you! My friend is a regular dab at it. Ecod, he saws away at Mo-zart and Handel, and the rest of the big-wigs, like a thorough workman. And you needn't," says Mr. Bucket, in a considerate and private voice, "you needn't commit yourself to too low a figure, governor. I don't want to pay too large a price for my friend; but I want you to have your proper percentage, and be remunerated for your loss of time. That is but fair. Every man must live, and ought to it."

Mr. Bagnet shakes his head at the old girl, to the effect that they have found a jewel of price.

"Suppose I was to give you a look in, say at half arter ten to-morrow morning. Perhaps you could name the figures of a few wiolincellers of a good tone?" says Mr. Bucket.

Nothing easier. Mr. and Mrs. Bagnet both engage to have the requisite information ready, and even hint to each other at the practicability of having a small stock collected there for approval.

"Thank you," says Mr. Bucket, "thank you. Good night, ma'am.

Good night, governor. Good night, darlings. I am much obliged to you for one of the pleasantest evenings I ever spent in my life."

They, on the contrary, are much obliged to him for the pleasure he has given them in his company; and so they part with many expressions of good-will on both sides. "Now, George, old boy," says Mr. Bucket, taking his arm at the shop-door, "come along!" As they go down the little street, and the Bagnets pause for a minute looking after them, Mrs. Bagnet remarks to the worthy Lignum that Mr. Bucket "almost clings to George like, and seems to be really fond of him."

The neighbouring streets being narrow and ill paved, it is a little inconvenient to walk there two abreast and arm in arm. Mr. George therefore soon proposes to walk singly. But Mr. Bucket, who cannot make up his mind to relinquish his friendly hold, replies, "Wait half a minute, George. I should wish to speak to you first." Immediately afterwards, he twists him into a public-house, and into a parlour, where he confronts him, and claps his own back against the door.

"Now, George," says Mr. Bucket. "Duty is duty, and friendship is friendship. I never want the two to clash, if I can help it. I have endeavoured to make things pleasant to-night, and I put it to you whether I have done it or not. You must consider yourself in custody, George."

"Custody? What for?" returns the trooper, thunderstruck.

"Now, George," says Mr. Bucket, urging a sensible view of the case upon him with his fat forefinger, "duty, as you know very well, is one thing, and conversation is another. It's my duty to inform you that any observations you may make will be liable to be used against you. Therefore, George, be careful what you say. You don't happen to have heard of a murder?"

"Murder!"

"Now, George," says Mr. Bucket, keeping his forefinger in an impressive state of action, "bear in mind what I've said to you. I ask you nothing. You've been in low spirits this afternoon. I say, you don't happen to have heard of a murder?"

"No. Where has there been a murder?"

"Now, George," says Mr. Bucket, "don't you go and commit yourself. I'm a going to tell you what I want you for. There has been a murder in Lincoln's Inn Fields—gentleman of the name of Tulkinghorn. He was shot last night. I want you for that."

The trooper sinks upon a seat behind him, and great drops start out upon his forehead, and a deadly pallor overspreads his face.

"Bucket! It's not possible that Mr. Tulkinghorn has been killed, and that you suspect *me*?"

"George," returns Mr. Bucket, keeping his forefinger going, "it is certainly possible, because it's the case. This deed was done last night at ten o'clock. Now, you know where you were last night at ten o'clock, and you'll be able to prove it, no doubt."

"Last night! Last night?" repeats the trooper, thoughtfully. Then it flashes upon him. "Why, great Heaven, I was there last night!"

"So I have understood, George," returns Mr. Bucket, with great deliberation. "So I have understood. Likewise you've been very often there. You've been seen hanging about the place, and you've been heard more than once in a wrangle with him, and it's possible —I don't say it's certainly so, mind you, but it's possible—that he may have been heard to call you a threatening, murdering, dangerous fellow."

The trooper gasps as if he would admit it all, if he could speak.

"Now, George," continues Mr. Bucket, putting his hat upon the table, with an air of business rather in the upholstery way than otherwise, "my wish is, as it has been all the evening, to make things pleasant. I tell you plainly there's a reward out, of a hundred guineas, offered by Sir Leicester Dedlock, Baronet. You and me have always been pleasant together; but I have got a duty to discharge; and if that hundred guineas is to be made, it may as well be made by me as by another man. On all of which accounts, I should hope it was clear to you that I must have you, and that I'm damned if I don't have you. Am I to call in any assistance, or is the trick done?"

Mr. George has recovered himself, and stands up like a soldier. "Come," he says; "I am ready."

"George," continues Mr. Bucket, "wait a bit!" With his upholsterer manner, as if the trooper were a window to be fitted up, he takes from his pocket a pair of handcuffs. "This is a serious charge, George, and such is my duty."

The trooper flushes angrily, and hesitates a moment; but holds out his hands, clasped together, and says, "There! Put them on!"

Mr. Bucket adjusts them in a moment. "How do you find them? Are they comfortable? If not, say so, for I wish to make things as pleasant as is consistent with my duty, and I've got another pair in my pocket." This remark he offers like a most respectable tradesman, anxious to execute an order neatly, and to the perfect satisfaction of his customer. "They'll do as they are? Very well! Now, you see, George;" he takes a cloak from a corner, and begins adjusting it about the trooper's neck; "I was mindful of your feelings when I come out, and brought this on purpose. There! Who's the wiser?"

"Only I," returns the trooper; "but, as I know it, do me one more good turn, and pull my hat over my eyes."

"Really, though! Do you mean it? Ain't it a pity? It looks so."

"I can't look chance men in the face with these things on," Mr. George hurriedly replies. "Do, for God's sake, pull my hat forward."

So strongly entreated, Mr. Bucket complies, puts his own hat on, and conducts his prize into the streets; the trooper marching on as steadily as usual, though with his head less erect; and Mr. Bucket steering him with his elbow over the crossings and up the turnings.

Chapter L

ESTHER'S NARRATIVE

It happened that when I came home from Deal, I found a note from Caddy Jellyby (as we always continued to call her), informing me that her health, which had been for some time very delicate, was worse, and that she would be more glad than she could tell me if I would go to see her. It was a note of a few lines, written from the couch on which she lay, and enclosed to me in another from her husband, in which he seconded her entreaty with much solicitude. Caddy was now the mother, and I the godmother, of such a poor little baby—such a tiny old-faced mite, with a countenance that seemed to be scarcely anything but cap-border,[1] and a little lean, long-fingered hand, always clenched under its chin. It would lie in this attitude all day, with its bright specks of eyes open, wondering (as I used to imagine) how it came to be so small and weak. Whenever it was moved it cried; but at all other times it was so patient, that the sole desire of its life appeared to be, to lie quiet, and think. It had curious little dark veins in its face, and curious little dark marks under its eyes, like faint remembrances of poor Caddy's inky days; and altogether, to those who were not used to it, it was quite a piteous little sight.

But it was enough for Caddy that *she* was used to it. The projects with which she beguiled her illness, for little Esther's education, and little Esther's marriage, and even for her own old age, as the grandmother of little Esther's little Esthers, was so prettily expressive of devotion to this pride of her life, that I should be tempted to recall some of them, but for the timely remembrance that I am getting on irregularly as it is.

To return to the letter. Caddy had a superstition about me, which had been strengthening in her mind ever since that night long ago, when she had lain asleep with her head in my lap. She almost—I think I must say quite—believed that I did her good whenever I was near her. Now, although this was such a fancy of the affectionate girl's that I am almost ashamed to mention it, still it might have all the force of a fact when she was really ill. Therefore I set off to Caddy, with my guardian's consent, post-haste; and she

1. Lace frill on a baby's bonnet.

and Prince made so much of me, that there never was anything like it.

Next day I went again to sit with her, and next day I went again. It was a very easy journey; for I had only to rise a little earlier in the morning, and keep my accounts, and attend to housekeeping matters before leaving home. But when I had made these three visits, my guardian said to me, on my return at night:

"Now, little woman, little woman, this will never do. Constant dropping will wear away a stone, and constant coaching will wear out a Dame Durden. We will go to London for a while, and take possession of our old lodgings."

"Not for me, dear guardian," said I, "for I never feel tired"; which was strictly true. I was only too happy to be in such request.

"For me then," returned my guardian; "or for Ada, or for both of us. It is somebody's birthday to-morrow, I think."

"Truly I think it is," said I, kissing my darling who would be twenty-one to-morrow.

"Well," observed my guardian, half pleasantly, half seriously, "that's a great occasion, and will give my fair cousin some necessary business to transact in assertion of her independence, and will make London a more convenient place for all of us. So to London we will go. That being settled, there is another thing—how have you left Caddy?"

"Very unwell, guardian. I fear it will be some time before she regains her health and strength."

"What do you call some time, now?" asked my guardian, thoughtfully.

"Some weeks, I am afraid."

"Ah!" He began to walk about the room with his hands in his pockets, showing that he had been thinking as much. "Now what do you say about her doctor? Is he a good doctor, my love?"

I felt obliged to confess that I knew nothing to the contrary; but that Prince and I had agreed only that evening, that we would like his opinion to be confirmed by some one.

"Well, you know," returned my guardian, quickly, "there's Woodcourt."

I had not meant that, and was rather taken by surprise. For a moment, all that I had had in my mind in connexion with Mr. Woodcourt seemed to come back and confuse me.

"You don't object to him, little woman?"

"Object to him, guardian? Oh no!"

"And you don't think the patient would object to him?"

So far from that, I had no doubt of her being prepared to have a great reliance on him, and to like him very much. I said that he was no stranger to her personally, for she had seen him often in his kind attendance on Miss Flite.

"Very good," said my guardian. "He has been here to-day, my dear, and I will see him about it to-morrow."

I felt, in this short conversation—though I did not know how, for she was quiet, and we interchanged no look—that my dear girl well remembered how merrily she had clasped me round the waist when no other hands than Caddy's had brought me the little parting token. This caused me to feel that I ought to tell her, and Caddy too, that I was going to be the mistress of Bleak House; and that if I avoided that disclosure any longer, I might become less worthy in my own eyes of its master's love. Therefore, when we went up-stairs, and had waited listening until the clock struck twelve, in order that only I might be the first to wish my darling all good wishes on her birthday, and to take her to my heart, I set before her, just as I had set before myself, the goodness and honour of her cousin John, and the happy life that was in store for me. If ever my darling were fonder of me at one time than at another in all our intercourse, she was surely fondest of me that night. And I was so rejoiced to know it, and so comforted by the sense of having done right, in casting this last idle reservation away, that I was ten times happier than I had been before. I had scarcely thought it a reservation a few hours ago; but now that it was gone, I felt as if I understood its nature better.

Next day we went to London. We found our old lodging vacant, and in half an hour were quietly established there, as if we had never gone away. Mr. Woodcourt dined with us to celebrate my darling's birthday; and we were as pleasant as we could be with the great blank among us that Richard's absence naturally made on such an occasion. After that day I was for some weeks—eight or nine as I remember—very much with Caddy; and thus it fell out that I saw less of Ada at this time than any other since we had first come together, except the time of my own illness. She often came to Caddy's; but our function there was to amuse and cheer her, and we did not talk in our usual confidential manner. Whenever I went home at night, we were together; but Caddy's rest was broken by pain, and I often remained to nurse her.

With her husband and her poor little mite of a baby to love, and their home to strive for, what a good creature Caddy was! So self-denying, so uncomplaining, so anxious to get well on their account, so afraid of giving trouble, and so thoughtful of the unassisted labours of her husband and the comforts of old Mr. Turveydrop; I had never known the best of her until now. And it seemed so curious that her pale face and helpless figure should be lying there day after day, where dancing was the business of life; where the kit and the apprentices began early every morning in the ball-room, and where the untidy little boy waltzed by himself in the kitchen all the afternoon.

At Caddy's request, I took the supreme direction of her apartment, trimmed it up, and pushed her, couch and all, into a lighter and more airy and more cheerful corner than she had yet occupied; then, every day, when we were in our neatest array, I used to lay my small small namesake in her arms, and sit down to chat or work, or read to her. It was at one of the first of these quiet times that I told Caddy about Bleak House.

We had other visitors besides Ada. First of all we had Prince, who in his hurried intervals of teaching used to come softly in and sit softly down, with a face of loving anxiety for Caddy and the very little child. Whatever Caddy's condition really was, she never failed to declare to Prince that she was all but well—which I, Heaven forgive me, never failed to confirm. This would put Prince in such good spirits, that he would sometimes take the kit from his pocket and play a chord or two to astonish the baby—which I never knew it to do in the least degree, for my tiny namesake never noticed it at all.

Then there was Mrs. Jellyby. She would come occasionally with her usual distraught manner, and sit calmly looking miles beyond her grandchild, as if her attention were absorbed by a young Borrioboolan on its native shores. As bright-eyed as ever, as serene, and as untidy, she would say, "Well, Caddy, child, and how do you do today?" And then would sit amiably smiling, and taking no notice of the reply; or would sweetly glide off into a calculation of the number of letters she had lately received and answered, or of the coffee-bearing power of Borrioboola-Gha. This she would always do with a serene contempt for our limited sphere of action, not to be disguised.

Then there was old Mr. Turveydrop, who was from morning to night and from night to morning the subject of innumerable precautions. If the baby cried, it was nearly stifled lest the noise should make him uncomfortable. If the fire wanted stirring in the night, it was surreptitiously done lest his rest should be broken. If Caddy required any little comfort that the house contained, she first carefully discussed whether he was likely to require it too. In return for this consideration, he would come into the room once a day, all but blessing it—showing a condescension, and a patronage, and a grace of manner, in dispensing the light of his high-shouldered presence, from which I might have supposed him (if I had not known better) to have been the benefactor of Caddy's life.

"My Caroline," he would say, making the nearest approach that he could to bending over her. "Tell me that you are better to-day."

"O much better, thank you, Mr. Turveydrop," Caddy would reply.

"Delighted! Enchanted! And our dear Miss Summerson. She is not quite prostrated by fatigue?" Here he would crease up his eyelids, and kiss his fingers to me; though I am happy to say he had ceased to be particular in his attentions, since I had been so altered.

"Not at all," I would assure him.

"Charming! We must take care of our dear Caroline, Miss Summerson. We must spare nothing that will restore her. We must nourish her. My dear Caroline;" he would turn to his daughter-in-law with infinite generosity and protection; "want for nothing, my love. Frame a wish and gratify it, my daughter. Everything this house contains, everything my room contains, is at your service, my dear. Do not," he would sometimes add, in a burst of Deportment, "even allow my simple requirements to be considered, if they should at any time interfere with your own, my Caroline. Your necessities are greater than mine."[2]

He had established such a long prescriptive right to this Deportment (his son's inheritance from his mother), that I several times knew both Caddy and her husband to be melted to tears by these affectionate self-sacrifices.

"Nay, my dears," he would remonstrate; and when I saw Caddy's thin arm about his fat neck as he said it, I would be melted too, though not by the same process; "Nay, nay! I have promised never to leave ye. Be dutiful and affectionate towards me, and I ask no other return. Now, bless ye! I am going to the Park."

He would take the air there, presently, and get an appetite for his hotel dinner. I hope I do old Mr. Turveydrop no wrong; but I never saw any better traits in him than these I faithfully record, except that he certainly conceived a liking for Peepy, and would take the child out walking with great pomp—always, on those occasions, sending him home before he went to dinner himself, and occasionally with a halfpenny in his pocket. But even this disinterestedness was attended with no inconsiderable cost, to my knowledge; for before Peepy was sufficiently decorated to walk hand in hand with the professor of Deportment, he had to be newly dressed, at the expense of Caddy and her husband, from top to toe.

Last of our visitors, there was Mr. Jellyby. Really when he used to come in of an evening, and ask Caddy in his meek voice how she was, and then sit down with his head against the wall, and make no attempt to say anything more, I liked him very much. If he found me bustling about, doing any little thing, he sometimes half took his coat off, as if with an intention of helping by a great exertion;

2. Cf. the dying words of Sir Philip Sidney: "Thy needs are greater than mine."

but he never got any further. His sole occupation was to sit with his head against the wall, looking hard at the thoughtful baby; and I could not quite divest my mind of a fancy that they understood one another.

I have not counted Mr. Woodcourt among our visitors, because he was now Caddy's regular attendant. She soon began to improve under his care; but he was so gentle, so skilful, so unwearying in the pains he took, that it is not to be wondered at, I am sure. I saw a good deal of Mr. Woodcourt during this time, though not so much as might be supposed; for, knowing Caddy to be safe in his hands, I often slipped home at about the hours when he was expected. We frequently met, notwithstanding. I was quite reconciled to myself now; but I still felt glad to think that he was sorry for me, and he still *was* sorry for me I believed. He helped Mr. Badger in his professional engagements, which were numerous; and had as yet no settled projects for the future.

It was when Caddy began to recover, that I began to notice a change in my dear girl. I cannot say how it first presented itself to me; because I observed it in many slight particulars, which were nothing in themselves, and only became something when they were pieced together. But I made it out, by putting them together, that Ada was not so frankly cheerful with me as she used to be. Her tenderness for me was as loving and true as ever; I did not for a moment doubt that; but there was a quiet sorrow about her which she did not confide to me, and in which I traced some hidden regret.

Now I could not understand this; and I was so anxious for the happiness of my own pet, that it caused me some uneasiness, and set me thinking often. At length, feeling sure that Ada suppressed this something from me, lest it should make me unhappy too, it came into my head that she was a little grieved—for me—by what I had told her about Bleak House.

How I persuaded myself that this was likely, I don't know. I had no idea that there was any selfish reference in my doing so. I was not grieved for myself: I was quite contented and quite happy. Still, that Ada might be thinking—for me, though I had abandoned all such thoughts—of what once was, but was now all changed, seemed so easy to believe, that I believed it.

What could I do to reassure my darling (I considered then) and show her that I had no such feelings? Well! I could only be as brisk and busy as possible; and that I had tried to be all along. However, as Caddy's illness had certainly interfered, more or less, with my home duties—though I had always been there in the morning to make my guardian's breakfast, and he had a hundred times laughed, and said there must be two little women, for his little woman was never missing—I resolved to be doubly diligent and gay. So I went about the house, humming all the tunes I knew; and I sat working and working in a desperate manner, and I talked and talked, morning, noon, and night.

And still there was the same shade between me and my darling.

"So, Dame Trot," observed my guardian, shutting up his book, one night when we were all three together; "so Woodcourt has restored Caddy Jellyby to the full enjoyment of life again?"

"Yes," I said; "and to be repaid by such gratitude as hers, is to be made rich, guardian."

"I wish it was," he returned, "with all my heart."

So did I too, for that matter. I said so.

"Aye! We would make him as rich as a Jew, if we knew how. Would we not, little woman?"

I laughed as I worked, and replied that I was not sure about that, for it might spoil him, and he might not be so useful, and there might be many who could ill spare him. As, Miss Flite, and Caddy herself, and many others.

"True," said my guardian. "I had forgotten that. But we would agree to make him rich enough to live, I suppose? Rich enough to work with tolerable peace of mind? Rich enough to have his own happy home, and his own household gods—and household goddess, too, perhaps?"

That was quite another thing, I said. We must all agree in that.

"To be sure," said my guardian. "All of us. I have a great regard for Woodcourt, a high esteem for him; and I have been sounding him delicately about his plans. It is difficult to offer aid to an independent man, with that just kind of pride which he possesses. And yet I would be glad to do it if I might, or if I knew how. He seems half inclined for another voyage. But that appears like casting such a man away."

"It might open a new world to him," said I.

"So it might, little woman," my guardian assented. "I doubt if he expects much of the old world. Do you know I have fancied that he sometimes feels some particular disappointment, or misfortune, encountered in it. You never heard of anything of that sort?"

I shook my head.

"Humph," said my guardian. "I am mistaken, I dare say."

As there was a little pause here, which I thought, for my dear girl's satisfaction, had better be filled up, I hummed an air as I worked which was a favourite with my guardian.

"And do you think Mr. Woodcourt will make another voyage?" I asked him, when I had hummed it quietly all through.

"I don't quite know what to think, my dear, but I should say it was likely at present that he will give a long trial to another country."

"I am sure he will take the best wishes of all our hearts with him wherever he goes," said I; "and though they are not riches, he will never be the poorer for them, guardian, at least."

"Never, little woman," he replied.

I was sitting in my usual place, which was now beside my guardian's chair. That had not been my usual place before the letter, but it was now. I looked up at Ada, who was sitting opposite; and I saw, as she looked at me, that her eyes were filled with tears, and that tears were falling down her face. I felt that I had only to be placid and merry, once for all to undeceive my dear, and set her loving heart at rest. I really was so, and I had nothing to do but to be myself.

So I made my sweet girl lean upon my shoulder—how little thinking what was heavy on her mind!—and I said she was not quite well, and put my arm about her, and took her up-stairs. When we were in our own room, and when she might perhaps have told me what I was so unprepared to hear, I gave her no encouragement to confide in me; I never thought she stood in need of it.

"O my dear good Esther," said Ada, "if I could only make up my mind to speak to you and my cousin John, when you are together!"

"Why, my love?" I remonstrated. "Ada? why should you not speak to us?"

Ada only drooped her head and pressed me closer to her heart.

"You surely don't forget, my beauty," said I, smiling, "what quiet, old-fashioned people we are, and how I have settled down to be the discreetest of dames? You don't forget how happily and peacefully my life is all marked out for me, and by whom? I am certain that you don't forget by what a noble character, Ada. That can never be."

"No, never, Esther."

"Why, then, my dear," said I, "there can be nothing amiss—and why should you not speak to us?"

"Nothing amiss, Esther?" returned Ada. "O when I think of all these years, and of his fatherly care and kindness, and of the old relations among us, and of you, what shall I do, what shall I do!"

I looked at my child in some wonder, but I thought it better not to answer, otherwise than by cheering her; and so I turned off into many little recollections of our life together, and prevented her from saying more. When she lay down to sleep, and not before, I returned to my guardian to say good night; and then I came back to Ada, and sat near her for a little while.

She was asleep, and I thought as I looked at her that she was a little changed. I had thought so, more than once lately. I could not decide, even looking at her while she was unconscious, how she was changed; but something in the familiar beauty of her face looked different to me. My guardian's old hopes of her and Richard arose sorrowfully in my mind, and I said to myself, "she has been anxious about him," and I wondered how that love would end.

When I had come home from Caddy's while she was ill, I had often found Ada at work, and she had always put her work away, and I had never known what it was. Some of it now lay in a drawer near her, which was not quite closed. I did not open the drawer; but I still rather wondered what the work could be, for it was evidently nothing for herself.

And I noticed as I kissed my dear, that she lay with one hand under her pillow so that it was hidden.

How much less amiable I must have been than they thought me, how much less amiable than I thought myself, to be so pre-occupied with my own cheerfulness and contentment, as to think that it only rested with me to put my dear girl right, and set her mind at peace!

But I lay down, self-deceived, in that belief. And I awoke in it next day, to find that there was still the same shade between me and my darling.

Chapter LI

ENLIGHTENED

When Mr. Woodcourt arrived in London, he went, that very same day, to Mr. Vholes's in Symond's Inn. For he never once, from the moment when I entreated him to be a friend to Richard, neglected or forgot his promise. He had told me that he accepted the charge as a sacred trust, and he was ever true to it in that spirit.

He found Mr. Vholes in his office, and informed Mr. Vholes of his agreement with Richard, that he should call there to learn his address.

"Just so, sir," said Mr. Vholes. "Mr. C's address is not a hundred miles from here, sir, Mr. C's address is not a hundred miles from here. Would you take a seat, sir?"

Mr. Woodcourt thanked Mr. Vholes, but he had no business with him beyond what he had mentioned.

"Just so, sir. I believe, sir," said Mr. Vholes, still quietly insisting on the seat by not giving the address, "that you have influence with Mr. C. Indeed I am aware that you have."

"I was not aware of it myself," returned Mr. Woodcourt; "but I suppose you know best."

"Sir," rejoined Mr. Vholes, self-contained, as usual, voice and all, "it is a part of my professional duty to know best. It is a part of my professional duty to study and to understand a gentleman who confides his interests to me. In my professional duty I shall not be wanting, sir, if I know it. I may, with the best intention, be wanting in it without knowing it; but not if I know it, sir."

Mr. Woodcourt again mentioned the address.

"Give me leave, sir," said Mr. Vholes. "Bear with me for a moment. Sir, Mr. C is playing for a considerable stake, and cannot play without—need I say what?"

"Money, I presume?"

"Sir," said Mr. Vholes, "to be honest with you (honesty being my golden rule, whether I gain by it or lose, and I find that I generally lose), money is the word. Now, sir, upon the chances of Mr. C's game I express to you no opinion, *no* opinion. It might be highly impolitic in Mr. C, after playing so long and so high, to leave off; it might be the reverse. I say nothing. No, sir," said Mr. Vholes, bringing his hand flat down upon his desk, in a positive manner, "nothing."

"You seem to forget," returned Mr. Woodcourt, "that I ask you to say nothing, and have no interest in anything you say."

"Pardon me, sir!" retorted Mr. Vholes, "you do yourself an injustice. No sir! Pardon me! You shall not—shall not in my office, if I know it—do yourself an injustice. You are interested in anything, and in everything, that relates to your friend. I know human nature much better, sir, than to admit for an instant that a gentleman of your appearance is not interested in whatever concerns his friend."

"Well," replied Mr. Woodcourt, "that may be. I am particularly interested in his address."

("The number, sir,") said Mr. Vholes, parenthetically, ("I believe I have already mentioned). If Mr. C is to continue to play for this considerable stake, sir, he must have funds. Understand me! There are funds in hand at present. I ask for nothing; there are funds in hand. But, for the onward play, more funds must be provided; unless Mr. C is to throw away what he has already ventured—which is wholly and solely a point for his consideration. This, sir, I take the opportunity of stating openly to you, as the friend of Mr. C. Without funds, I shall always be happy to appear and act for Mr. C, to the extent of all such costs as are safe to be allowed out of the estate: not beyond that. I could not go beyond that, sir, without wronging some one. I must either wrong my three dear girls; or my venerable father, who is entirely dependent on me—in the Vale of Taunton; or some one. Whereas, sir, my resolution is (call it weakness or folly if you please) to wrong no one."

Mr. Woodcourt rather sternly rejoined that he was glad to hear it.

"I wish, sir," said Mr. Vholes, "to leave a good name behind me.

Therefore, I take every opportunity of openly stating to a friend of Mr. C, how Mr. C is situated. As to myself, sir, the labourer is worthy of his hire. If I undertake to put my shoulder to the wheel, I do it, and I earn what I get. I am here for that purpose. My name is painted on the door outside with that object."

"And Mr. Carstone's address, Mr. Vholes?"

"Sir," returned Mr. Vholes, "as I believe I have already mentioned, it is next door. On the second story you will find Mr. C's apartments. Mr. C desires to be near his professional adviser; and I am far from objecting, for I court inquiry."

Upon this, Mr. Woodcourt wished Mr. Vholes good day, and went in search of Richard, the change in whose appearance he began to understand now but too well.

He found him in a dull room, fadedly furnished; much as I had found him in his barrack-room but a little while before, except that he was not writing, but was sitting with a book before him, from which his eyes and thoughts were far astray. As the door chanced to be standing open, Mr. Woodcourt was in his presence for some moments without being perceived; and he told me that he never could forget the haggardness of his face, and the dejection of his manner, before he was aroused from his dream.

"Woodcourt, my dear fellow!" cried Richard, starting up with extended hands, "you come upon my vision like a ghost."

"A friendly one," he replied, "and only waiting, as they say ghosts do, to be addressed. How does the mortal world go?" They were seated now, near together.

"Badly enough and slowly enough," said Richard; "speaking at least for my part of it."

"What part is that?"

"The Chancery part."

"I never heard," returned Mr. Woodcourt, shaking his head, "of its going well yet."

"Nor I," said Richard, moodily. "Who ever did?"

He brightened again in a moment, and said, with his natural openness:

"Woodcourt, I should be sorry to be misunderstood by you, even if I gained by it in your estimation. You must know that I have done no good this long time. I have not intended to do much harm, but I seem to have been capable of nothing else. It may be that I should have done better by keeping out of the net into which my destiny has worked me; but I think not, though I dare say you will soon hear, if you have not already heard, a very different opinion. To make short of a long story, I am afraid I have wanted an object; but I have an object now—or it has me—and it is too late to discuss it. Take me as I am, and make the best of me."

"A bargain," said Mr. Woodcourt. "Do as much by me in return."

"Oh! You," returned Richard, "you can pursue your art for its own sake; and can put your hand upon the plough, and never turn; and can strike a purpose out of anything. You, and I, are very different creatures."

He spoke regretfully, and lapsed for a moment into his weary condition.

"Well, well!" he cried, shaking it off, "everything has an end. We shall see! So you will take me as I am, and make the best of me?"

"Aye! indeed I will." They shook hands upon it laughingly, but in deep earnestness. I can answer, for one of them, with my heart of hearts.

"You come as a godsend," said Richard, "for I have seen nobody here yet but Vholes. Woodcourt, there is one subject I should like to mention, for once and for all, in the beginning of our treaty. You can hardly make the best of me if I don't. You know, I dare say, that I have an attachment to my cousin Ada?"

Mr. Woodcourt replied that I had hinted as much to him.

"Now pray," returned Richard, "don't think me a heap of selfishness. Don't suppose that I am splitting my head and half breaking my heart over this miserable Chancery suit, for my own rights and interests alone. Ada's are bound up with mine: they can't be separated; Vholes works for both of us. Do think of that!"

He was so very solicitous on this head, that Mr. Woodcourt gave him the strongest assurances that he did him no injustice.

"You see," said Richard, with something pathetic in his manner of lingering on the point, though it was off-hand and unstudied, "to an upright fellow like you, bringing a friendly face like yours here, I cannot bear the thought of appearing selfish and mean. I want to see Ada righted, Woodcourt, as well as myself; I want to do my utmost to right her, as well as myself; I venture what I can scrape together to extricate her, as well as myself. Do, I beseech you, think of that!"

Afterwards, when Mr. Woodcourt came to reflect on what had passed, he was so very much impressed by the strength of Richard's anxiety on this point, that in telling me generally of his first visit to Symond's Inn, he particularly dwelt upon it. It revived a fear I had had before, that my dear girl's little property would be absorbed by Mr. Vholes, and that Richard's justification to himself would be sincerely this. It was just as I began to take care of Caddy that the interview took place; and I now return to the time when Caddy had recovered, and the shade was still between me and my darling.

I proposed to Ada, that morning, that we should go and see

Richard. It a little surprised me to find that she hesitated, and was not so radiantly willing as I had expected.

"My dear," said I, "you have not had any difference with Richard since I have been so much away?"

"No, Esther."

"Not heard of him, perhaps?" said I.

"Yes, I have heard of him," said Ada.

Such tears in her eyes, and such love in her face. I could not make my darling out. Should I go to Richard's by myself? I said. No, Ada thought I had better not go by myself. Would she go with me? Yes, Ada thought she had better go with me. Should we go now? Yes, let us go now. Well, I could not understand my darling, with the tears in her eyes and the love in her face!

We were soon equipped, and went out. It was a sombre day, and drops of chill rain fell at intervals. It was one of those colourless days when everything looks heavy and harsh. The houses frowned at us, the dust rose at us, the smoke swooped at us, nothing made any compromise about itself, or wore a softened aspect. I fancied my beautiful girl quite out of place in the rugged streets; and I thought there were more funerals passing along the dismal pavements, than I had seen before.

We had first to find out Symond's Inn. We were going to inquire in a shop, when Ada said she thought it was near Chancery Lane. "We are not likely to be far out, my love, if we go in that direction," said I. So to Chancery Lane we went; and there, sure enough, we saw it written up. Symond's Inn.

We had next to find out the number. "Or Mr. Vholes's office will do," I recollected, "for Mr. Vholes's office is next door." Upon which Ada said, perhaps that was Mr. Vholes's office in the corner there. And it really was.

Then came the question, which of the two next doors? I was for going to the one, and my darling was for going to the other; and my darling was right again. So up we went to the second story, when we came to Richard's name in great white letters on a hearse-like panel.

I should have knocked, but Ada said perhaps we had better turn the handle and go in. Thus we came to Richard, poring over a table covered with dusty bundles of papers which seemed to me like dusty mirrors reflecting his own mind. Wherever I looked, I saw the ominous words that ran in it, repeated. Jarndyce and Jarndyce.

He received us very affectionately, and we sat down. "If you had come a little earlier," he said, "you would have found Woodcourt here. There never was such a good fellow as Woodcourt is. He finds time to look in between whiles, when anybody else with half his work to do would be thinking about not being able to come. And he is so cheery, so fresh, so sensible, so earnest, so—everything that I am not, that the place brightens whenever he comes, and darkens whenever he goes again."

"God bless him," I thought, "for his truth to me!"

"He is not so sanguine, Ada," continued Richard, casting his dejected look over the bundles of papers, "as Vholes and I are usually; but he is only an outsider, and is not in the mysteries. We have gone into them, and he has not. He can't be expected to know much of such a labyrinth."

As his look wandered over the papers again, and he passed his two hands over his head, I noticed how sunken and how large his eyes appeared, how dry his lips were, and how his finger-nails were all bitten away.

"Is this a healthy place to live in, Richard, do you think?" said I.

"Why, my dear Minerva," answered Richard, with his old gay laugh, "it is neither a rural nor a cheerful place; and when the sun shines here, you may lay a pretty heavy wager that it is shining brightly in an open spot. But it's well enough for the time. It's near the offices, and near Vholes."

"Perhaps," I hinted, "a change from both——"

"—Might do me good?" said Richard, forcing a laugh as he finished the sentence. "I shouldn't wonder! But it can only come in one way now—in one of two ways, I should rather say. Either the suit must be ended, Esther, or the suitor. But it shall be the suit, the suit, my dear girl!"

These latter words were addressed to Ada, who was sitting nearest to him. Her face being turned away from me and towards him, I could not see it.

"We are doing very well," pursued Richard. "Vholes will tell you so. We are really spinning along. Ask Vholes. We are giving them no rest. Vholes knows all their windings and turnings, and we are upon them everywhere. We have astonished them already. We shall rouse up that nest of sleepers, mark my words!"

His hopefulness had long been more painful to me than his despondency; it was so unlike hopefulness, had something so fierce in its determination to be it, was so hungry and eager, and yet so conscious of being forced and unsustainable, that it had long touched me to the heart. But the commentary upon it now indelibly written in his handsome face, made it far more distressing than it used to be. I say indelibly; for I felt persuaded that if the fatal cause could have been for ever terminated, according to his brightest visions, in that same hour, the traces of the premature anxiety, self-reproach, and disappointment it had occasioned him, would have remained upon his features to the hour of his death.

"The sight of our dear little woman," said Richard: Ada still remaining silent and quiet: "is so natural to me, and her compassionate face is so like the face of old days——"

Ah! No, no. I smiled and shook my head.

"—So exactly like the face of old days," said Richard in his cordial voice, and taking my hand with the brotherly regard which nothing ever changed, "that I can't make pretences with her. I fluctuate a little; that's the truth. Sometimes I hope, my dear, and sometimes I—don't quite despair, but nearly. I get," said Richard, relinquishing my hand gently, and walking across the room, "so tired!"

He took a few turns up and down, and sunk upon the sofa. "I get," he repeated gloomily, "so tired. It is such weary weary work!"

He was leaning on his arm, saying these words in a meditative voice, and looking at the ground, when my darling rose, put off her bonnet, kneeled down beside him with her golden hair falling like sunlight on his head, clasped her two arms round his neck, and turned her face to me. O, what a loving and devoted face I saw!

"Esther, dear," she said very quietly, "I am not going home again."

A light shone in upon me all at once.

"Never any more. I am going to stay with my dear husband. We have been married above two months. Go home without me, my own Esther; I shall never go home any more!" With those words my darling drew his head down on her breast, and held it there. And if ever in my life I saw a love that nothing but death could change, I saw it then before me.

"Speak to Esther, my dearest," said Richard, breaking the silence presently. "Tell her how it was."

I met her before she could come to me, and folded her in my arms. We neither of us spoke; but with her cheek against my own, I wanted to hear nothing. "My pet," said I. "My love. My poor, poor girl!" I pitied her so much. I was very fond of Richard, but the impulse that I had upon me was to pity her so much.

"Esther, will you forgive me? Will my cousin John forgive me?"

"My dear," said I, "to doubt it for a moment is to do him a great wrong. And as to me!"—why, as to me, what had *I* to forgive!

I dried my sobbing darling's eyes, and sat beside her on the sofa, and Richard sat on my other side; and while I was reminded of that so different night when they had first taken me into their confidence, and had gone on in their own wild happy way, they told me between them how it was.

"All I had, was Richard's," Ada said; "and Richard would not take it, Esther, and what could I do but be his wife when I loved him dearly!"

"And you were so fully and so kindly occupied, excellent Dame

Durden," said Richard, "that how could we speak to you at such a time! And besides, it was not a long-considered step. We went out one morning and were married."

"And when it was done, Esther," said my darling, "I was always thinking how to tell you, and what to do for the best. And sometimes I thought you ought to know it directly; and sometimes I thought you ought not to know it, and keep it from my cousin John; and I could not tell what to do and I fretted very much."

How selfish I must have been, not to have thought of this before! I don't know what I said now. I was so sorry, and yet I was so fond of them, and so glad that they were fond of me; I pitied them so much, and yet I felt a kind of pride in their loving one another. I never had experienced such painful and pleasurable emotion at one time; and in my own heart I did not know which predominated. But I was not there to darken their way; I did not do that.

When I was less foolish and more composed, my darling took her wedding ring from her bosom, and kissed it, and put it on. Then I remembered last night, and told Richard that ever since her marriage she had worn it at night when there was no one to see. Then Ada blushingly asked me how did I know that, my dear? Then I told Ada how I had seen her hand concealed under her pillow, and had little thought why, my dear. Then they began telling me how it was, all over again; and I began to be sorry and glad again, and foolish again, and to hide my plain old face as much as I could, lest I should put them out of heart.

Thus the time went on, until it became necessary for me to think of returning. When that time arrived it was the worst of all, for then my darling completely broke down. She clung round my neck, calling me by every dear name she could think of, and saying what should she do without me! Nor was Richard much better; and as for me, I should have been the worst of the three, if I had not severely said to myself, "Now, Esther, if you do, I'll never speak to you again!"

"Why, I declare," said I, "I never saw such a wife. I don't think she loves her husband at all. Here, Richard, take my child, for goodness' sake." But I held her tight all the while, and could have wept over her I don't know how long.

"I give this dear young couple notice," said I, "that I am only going away to come back to-morrow; and that I shall be always coming backwards and forwards, until Symond's Inn is tired of the sight of me. So I shall not say good bye, Richard. For what would be the use of that, you know, when I am coming back so soon!"

I had given my darling to him now, and I meant to go; but I lingered for one more look of the precious face, which it seemed to rive my heart to turn from.

So I said (in a merry bustling manner) that unless they gave me some encouragement to come back, I was not sure that I could take that liberty; upon which my dear girl looked up, faintly smiling through her tears, and I folded her lovely face between my hands, and gave it one last kiss, and laughed, and ran away.

And when I got down-stairs, O how I cried! It almost seemed to me that I had lost my Ada for ever. I was so lonely, and so blank without her, and it was so desolate to be going home with no hope of seeing her there, that I could get no comfort for a little while, as I walked up and down in a dim corner, sobbing and crying.

I came to myself by-and-by, after a little scolding, and took a coach home. The poor boy whom I had found at St. Albans had reappeared a short time before, and was lying at the point of death; indeed, was then dead, though I did not know it. My guardian had gone out to inquire about him, and did not return to dinner. Being quite alone, I cried a little again; though, on the whole, I don't think I behaved so very, very ill.

It was only natural that I should not be quite accustomed to the loss of my darling yet. Three or four hours were not a long time, after years. But my mind dwelt so much upon the uncongenial scene in which I had left her, and I pictured it as such an over-shadowed stony-hearted one, and I so longed to be near her, and taking some sort of care of her, that I determined to go back in the evening, only to look up at her windows.

It was foolish, I dare say; but it did not then seem at all so to me, and it does not seem quite so even now. I took Charley into my confidence, and we went out at dusk. It was dark when we came to the new strange home of my dear girl, and there was a light behind the yellow blinds. We walked past cautiously three or four times, looking up; and narrowly missed encountering Mr. Vholes, who came out of his office while we were there, and turned his head to look up too, before going home. The sight of his lank black figure, and the lonesome air of that nook in the dark, were favourable to the state of my mind. I thought of the youth and love and beauty of my dear girl, shut up in such an ill-assorted refuge, almost as if it were a cruel place.

It was very solitary and very dull, and I did not doubt that I might safely steal up-stairs. I left Charley below, and went up with a light foot, not distressed by any glare from the feeble oil lanterns on the way. I listened for a few moments; and in the musty rotting silence of the house, believed that I could hear the murmur of their young voices. I put my lips to the hearse-like panel of the door, as a kiss for my dear, and came quietly down again, thinking that one of these days I would confess to the visit.

And it really did me good; for, though nobody but Charley and I knew anything about it, I somehow felt as if it had diminished the separation between Ada and me, and had brought us together again for those moments. I went back, not quite accustomed yet to the change, but all the better for that hovering about my darling.

My guardian had come home, and was standing thoughtfully by the dark window. When I went in, his face cleared and he came to his seat; but he caught the light upon my face, as I took mine.

"Little woman," said he. "You have been crying."

"Why, yes, guardian," said I, "I am afraid I have been, a little. Ada has been in such distress, and is so very sorry, guardian."

I put my arm on the back of his chair; and I saw in his glance that my words, and my look at her empty place, had prepared him.

"Is she married, my dear?"

I told him all about it, and how her first entreaties had referred to his forgiveness.

"She has no need of it," said he. "Heaven bless her, and her husband!" But just as my first impulse had been to pity her, so was his. "Poor girl, poor girl! Poor Rick! Poor Ada!"

Neither of us spoke after that; until he said with a sigh, "Well, well, my dear! Bleak House is thinning fast."

"But its mistress remains, guardian." Though I was timid about saying it, I ventured because of the sorrowful tone in which he had spoken. "She will do all she can to make it happy," said I.

"She will succeed, my love!"

The letter had made no difference between us, except that the seat by his side had come to be mine; it made none now. He turned his old bright fatherly look upon me, laid his hand on my hand in his old way, and said again, "She will succeed, my dear. Nevertheless, Bleak House is thinning fast, O little woman!"

I was sorry presently that this was all we said about that. I was rather disappointed. I feared I might not quite have been all I had meant to be, since the letter and the answer.

Chapter LII

OBSTINACY

But one other day had intervened, when, early in the morning as we were going to breakfast, Mr. Woodcourt came in haste with the astounding news that a terrible murder had been committed, for which Mr. George had been apprehended and was in custody. When he told us that a large reward was offered by Sir Leicester Dedlock for the murderer's apprehension, I did not in my first consternation understand why; but a few more words explained to me that the murdered person was Sir Leicester's lawyer, and immediately my mother's dread of him rushed into my remembrance.

This unforeseen and violent removal of one whom she had long watched and distrusted, and who had long watched and distrusted her; one for whom she could have had few intervals of kindness, always dreading in him a dangerous and secret enemy, appeared so awful, that my first thoughts were of her. How appalling to hear of such a death, and be able to feel no pity! How dreadful to remember, perhaps, that she had sometimes even wished the old man away, who was so swiftly hurried out of life!

Such crowding reflections, increasing the distress and fear I always felt when the name was mentioned, made me so agitated that I could scarcely hold my place at the table. I was quite unable to follow the conversation, until I had had a little time to recover. But when I came to myself, and saw how shocked my guardian was; and found that they were earnestly speaking of the suspected man, and recalling every favourable impression we had formed of him, out of the good we had known of him; my interest and my fears were so strongly aroused in his behalf that I was quite set up again.

"Guardian, you don't think it possible that he is justly accused?"

"My dear, I *can't* think so. This man whom we have seen so open-hearted and compassionate; who, with the might of a giant, has the gentleness of a child; who looks as brave a fellow as ever lived, and is so simple and quiet with it; this man justly accused of such a crime? I can't believe it. It's not that I don't or I won't. I can't!"

"And I can't," said Mr. Woodcourt. "Still, whatever we believe or know of him, we had better not forget that some appearances are against him. He bore an animosity towards the deceased gentleman. He has openly mentioned it in many places. He is said to have expressed himself violently towards him, and he certainly did about him, to my knowledge. He admits that he was alone, on the scene of the murder, within a few minutes of its commission. I sincerely believe him to be as innocent of any participation in it, as I am; but these are all reasons for suspicion falling upon him."

"True," said my guardian; and he added, turning to me, "it would be doing him a very bad service, my dear, to shut our eyes to the truth in any of these respects."

I felt, of course, that we must admit, not only to ourselves but to others, the full force of the circumstances against him. Yet I knew withal (I could not help saying) that their weight would not induce us to desert him in his need.

"Heaven forbid!" returned my guardian. "We will stand by him, as he himself stood by the two poor creatures who are gone." He meant Mr. Gridley and the boy, to both of whom Mr. George had given shelter.

Mr. Woodcourt then told us that the trooper's man had been

with him before day, after wandering about the streets all night like a distracted creature. That one of the trooper's first anxieties was that we should not suppose him guilty. That he had charged his messenger to represent his perfect innocence, with every solemn assurance he could send us. That Mr. Woodcourt had only quieted the man by undertaking to come to our house very early in the morning, with these representations. He added that he was now upon his way to see the prisoner himself.

My guardian said, directly, he would go too. Now, besides that I liked the retired soldier very much, and that he liked me, I had that secret interest in what had happened, which was only known to my guardian. I felt as if it came close and near to me. It seemed to become personally important to myself that the truth should be discovered, and that no innocent people should be suspected; for suspicion, once run wild, might run wilder.

In a word, I felt as if it were my duty and obligation to go with them. My guardian did not seek to dissuade me, and I went.

It was a large prison, with many courts and passages so like one another, and so uniformly paved, that I seemed to gain a new comprehension, as I passed along, of the fondness that solitary prisoners, shut up among the same staring walls from year to year, have had—as I have read—for a weed, or a stray blade of grass. In an arched room by himself, like a cellar up-stairs: with walls so glaringly white, that they made the massive iron window-bars and iron-bound door even more profoundly black than they were: we found the trooper standing in a corner. He had been sitting on a bench there, and had risen when he heard the locks and bolts turn.

When he saw us, he came forward a step with his usual heavy tread, and there stopped and made a slight bow. But as I still advanced, putting out my hand to him, he understood us in a moment.

"This is a load off my mind, I do assure you, miss and gentlemen," said he, saluting us with great heartiness and drawing a long breath. "And now I don't so much care how it ends."

He scarcely seemed to be the prisoner. What with his coolness and his soldierly bearing, he looked far more like the prison guard.

"This is even a rougher place than my gallery to receive a lady in," said Mr. George, "but I know Miss Summerson will make the best of it." As he handed me to the bench on which he had been sitting, I sat down; which seemed to give him great satisfaction.

"I thank you, miss," said he.

"Now, George," observed my guardian, "as we require no new assurances on your part, so I believe we need give you none on ours."

"Not at all, sir. I thank you with all my heart. If I was not innocent of this crime, I couldn't look at you and keep my secret to myself, under the condescension of the present visit. I feel the present visit very much. I am not one of the eloquent sort, but I feel it, Miss Summerson and gentlemen, deeply."

He laid his hand for a moment on his broad chest, and bent his head to us. Although he squared himself again directly, he expressed a great amount of natural emotion by these simple means.

"First," said my guardian, "can we do anything for your personal comfort, George?"

"For which, sir?" he inquired, clearing his throat.

"For your personal comfort. Is there anything you want, that would lessen the hardship of this confinement?"

"Well, sir," replied Mr. George, after a little cogitation, "I am equally obliged to you; but tobacco being against the rules, I can't say that there is."

"You will think of many little things, perhaps, by-and-by. Whenever you do, George, let us know."

"Thank you, sir. Howsoever," observed Mr. George, with one of his sunburnt smiles, "a man who has been knocking about the world in a vagabond kind of way as long as I have, gets on well enough in a place like the present, so far as that goes."

"Next, as to your case," observed my guardian.

"Exactly so, sir," returned Mr. George, folding his arms upon his breast with perfect self-possession and a little curiosity.

"How does it stand now?"

"Why, sir, it is under remand[1] at present. Bucket gives me to understand that he will probably apply for a series of remands from time to time, until the case is more complete. How it is to be made more complete I don't myself see; but I dare say Bucket will manage it somehow."

"Why, Heaven save us, man!" exclaimed my guardian, surprised into his old oddity and vehemence, "you talk of yourself as if you were somebody else!"

"No offence, sir," said Mr. George. "I am very sensible of your kindness. But I don't see how an innocent man is to make up his mind to this kind of thing without knocking his head against the walls, unless he takes it in that point of view."

"That is true enough, to a certain extent," returned my guardian, softened. "But my good fellow, even an innocent man must take ordinary precautions to defend himself."

"Certainly, sir. And I have done so. I have stated to the magistrates, 'Gentlemen, I am as innocent of this charge as yourselves; what has been stated against me in the way of facts, is perfectly

1. Sent back to court for instructions about proceedings and hence effecting a postponement of the case coming to trial.

true; I know no more about it.' I intend to continue stating that, sir. What more can I do? It's the truth."

"But the mere truth won't do," rejoined my guardian.

"Won't it, indeed, sir? Rather a bad look-out for me!" Mr. George good-humouredly observed.

"You must have a lawyer," pursued my guardian. "We must engage a good one for you."

"I ask your pardon, sir," said Mr. George, with a step backward. "I am equally obliged. But I must decidedly beg to be excused from anything of that sort."

"You won't have a lawyer?"

"No, sir." Mr. George shook his head in the most emphatic manner. "I thank you all the same, sir, but—no lawyer!"

"Why not?"

"I don't take kindly to the breed," said Mr. George. "Gridley didn't. And—if you'll excuse my saying so much—I should hardly have thought you did yourself, sir."

"That's Equity,"[2] my guardian explained, a little at a loss; "that's Equity, George."

"Is it, indeed, sir?" returned the trooper, in his off-hand manner. "I am not acquainted with those shades of names myself, but in a general way I object to the breed."

Unfolding his arms, and changing his position, he stood with one massive hand upon the table, and the other on his hip, as complete a picture of a man who was not to be moved from a fixed purpose as ever I saw. It was in vain that we all three talked to him, and endeavoured to persuade him; he listened with that gentleness which went so well with his bluff bearing, but was evidently no more shaken by our representations than his place of confinement was.

"Pray think, once more, Mr. George," said I. "Have you no wish, in reference to your case?"

"I certainly could wish it to be tried, miss," he returned, "by court-martial; but that is out of the question, as I am well aware. If you will be so good as to favour me with your attention for a couple of minutes, miss, not more, I'll endeavour to explain myself as clearly as I can."

He looked at us all three in turn, shook his head a little as if he were adjusting it in the stock and collar of a tight uniform, and after a moment's reflection went on.

"You see, miss, I have been hand-cuffed and taken into custody, and brought here. I am a marked and disgraced man, and here I

2. The cases of Gridley and Jarndyce came under the jurisdiction of Chancery, the Court of Equity. The charge of murder against George would be tried in one of the courts of Common Law. See the Introductory Note on Law Courts.

am. My shooting-gallery is rummaged, high and low, by Bucket; such property as I have—'tis small—is turned this way and that, till it don't know itself; and (as aforesaid) here I am! I don't particular complain of that. Though I am in these present quarters through no immediately preceding fault of mine, I can very well understand that if I hadn't gone into the vagabond way in my youth, this wouldn't have happened. It *has* happened. Then comes the question, how to meet it."

He rubbed his swarthy forehead for a moment, with a good-humoured look, and said apologetically, "I am such a short-winded talker that I must think a bit." Having thought a bit, he looked up again, and resumed.

"How to meet it. Now, the unfortunate deceased was himself a lawyer, and had a pretty tight hold of me. I don't wish to rake up his ashes, but he had, what I should call if he was living, a Devil of a tight hold of me. I don't like his trade the better for that. If I had kept clear of his trade, I should have kept outside this place. But that's not what I mean. Now, suppose I had killed him. Suppose I really had discharged into his body any one of those pistols recently fired off, that Bucket has found at my place, and, dear me! might have found there any day since it has been my place. What should I have done as soon as I was hard and fast here? Got a lawyer."

He stopped on hearing some one at the locks and bolts, and did not resume until the door had been opened and was shut again. For what purpose opened, I will mention presently.

"I should have got a lawyer, and he would have said (as I have often read in the newspapers), 'my client says nothing, my client reserves his defence—my client this, that, and t'other.' Well, 'tis not the custom of that breed to go straight, according to my opinion, or to think that other men do. Say, I am innocent, and I get a lawyer. He would be as likely to believe me guilty as not; perhaps more. What would he do, whether or no? Act as if I was;—shut my mouth up, tell me not to commit myself, keep circumstances back, chop the evidence small, quibble, and get me off perhaps! But, Miss Summerson, do I care for getting off in that way; or would I rather be hanged in my own way—if you'll excuse my mentioning anything so disagreeable to a lady?"

He had warmed into his subject now, and was under no further necessity to wait a bit.

"I would rather be hanged in my own way. And I mean to be! I don't intend to say," looking round upon us, with his powerful arms akimbo and his dark eyebrows raised, "that I am more partial to being hanged than another man. What I say is, I must come off clear and full or not at all. Therefore, when I hear stated against me what is true, I say it's true; and when they tell me, 'whatever you say will be used,' I tell them I don't mind that; I mean it to be used. If they can't make me innocent out of the whole truth, they are not likely to do it out of anything less, or anything else. And if they are, it's worth nothing to me."

Taking a pace or two over the stone floor, he came back to the table, and finished what he had to say.

"I thank you, miss, and gentlemen both, many times for your attention, and many times more for your interest. That's the plain state of the matter, as it points itself out to a mere trooper with a blunt broadsword kind of a mind. I have never done well in life, beyond my duty as a soldier; and if the worst comes after all, I shall reap pretty much as I have sown.[3] When I got over the first crash of being seized as a murderer—it don't take a rover, who has knocked about so much as myself, so very long to recover from a crash—I worked my way round to what you find me now. As such, I shall remain. No relations will be disgraced by me, or made unhappy for me, and—and that's all I've got to say."

The door had been opened to admit another soldierly-looking man of less prepossessing appearance at first sight, and a weather-tanned, bright-eyed wholesome woman with a basket, who, from her entrance, had been exceedingly attentive to all Mr. George had said. Mr. George had received them with a familiar nod and a friendly look, but without any more particular greeting in the midst of his address. He now shook them cordially by the hand, and said, "Miss Summerson and gentlemen, this an old comrade of mine, Joseph Bagnet. And this is his wife, Mrs. Bagnet."

Mr. Bagnet made us a stiff military bow, and Mrs. Bagnet dropped us a curtsey.

"Real good friends of mine they are," said Mr. George. "It was at their house I was taken."

"With a second-hand wiolinceller," Mr. Bagnet put in, twitching his head angrily. "Of a good tone. For a friend. That money was no object to."

"Mat," said Mr. George, "you have heard pretty well all I have been saying to this lady and these two gentlemen. I know it meets your approval?"

Mr. Bagnet, after considering, referred the point to his wife. "Old girl," said he. "Tell him. Whether or not. It meets my approval."

"Why, George," exclaimed Mrs. Bagnet, who had been unpacking her basket, in which there was a piece of cold pickled pork, a little tea and sugar, and a brown loaf, "you ought to know it don't. You ought to know it's enough to drive a person wild to hear you. You won't be got off this way, and you won't be got off that way—

3. See Galatians 6:7: "for whatsoever a man soweth, that shall he also reap."

what do you mean by such picking and choosing? It's stuff and nonsense, George."

"Don't be severe upon me in my misfortunes, Mrs. Bagnet," said the trooper lightly.

"Oh! Bother your misfortunes!" cried Mrs. Bagnet, "if they don't make you more reasonable than that comes to. I never was so ashamed in my life to hear a man talk folly, as I have been to hear you talk this day to the present company. Lawyers? Why, what but too many cooks should hinder you from having a dozen lawyers, if the gentleman recommended them to you?"

"This is a very sensible woman," said my guardian. "I hope you will persuade him, Mrs. Bagnet."

"Persuade him, sir?" she returned. "Lord bless you, no. You don't know George. Now there!" Mrs. Bagnet left her basket to point out with both her bare brown hands. "There he stands! As self-willed and as determined a man, in the wrong way, as ever put a human creature under Heaven, out of patience! You could as soon take up and shoulder an eight-and-forty pounder[4] by your own strength, as turn that man, when he has got a thing into his head, and fixed it there. Why, don't I know him!" cried Mrs. Bagnet. "Don't I know you, George! You don't mean to set up for a new character with *me*, after all these years, I hope?"

Her friendly indignation had an exemplary effect upon her husband, who shook his head at the trooper several times, as a silent recommendation to him to yield. Betweenwhiles, Mrs. Bagnet looked at me; and I understood, from the play of her eyes, that she wished me to do something, though I did not comprehend what.

"But I have given up talking to you, old fellow, years and years," said Mrs. Bagnet, as she blew a little dust off the pickled pork, looking at me again; "and when ladies and gentlemen know you as well as I do, they'll give up talking to you too. If you are not too headstrong to accept of a bit of dinner, here it is."

"I accept it with many thanks," returned the trooper.

"Do you though, indeed?" said Mrs. Bagnet, continuing to grumble on good-humouredly. "I'm sure I'm surprised at that. I wonder you don't starve in your own way also. It would only be like you. Perhaps you'll set your mind upon *that*, next." Here she again looked at me; and I now perceived from her glances at the door and at me, by turns, that she wished us to retire, and to await her following us, outside the prison. Communicating this by similar means to my guardian and Mr. Woodcourt, I rose.

"We hope you will think better of it, Mr. George," said I; "and we shall come to see you again, trusting to find you more reasonable."

4. Cannon firing a forty-eight-pound missile.

"More grateful, Miss Summerson, you can't find me," he returned.

"But more persuadable we can, I hope," said I. "And let me entreat you to consider that the clearing up of this mystery, and the discovery of the real perpetrator of this deed, may be of the last importance to others besides yourself."

He heard me respectfully, but without much heeding these words, which I spoke, a little turned from him, already on my way to the door; he was observing (this they afterwards told me) my height and figure, which seemed to catch his attention all at once.

" 'Tis curious," said he. "And yet I thought so at the time!"

My guardian asked him what he meant.

"Why, sir," he answered, "when my ill-fortune took me to the dead man's staircase on the night of his murder, I saw a shape so like Miss Summerson's go by me in the dark, that I had half a mind to speak to it."

For an instant I felt such a shudder as I never felt before or since, and hope I shall never feel again.

"It came down-stairs as I went up," said the trooper, "and crossed the moonlighted window with a loose black mantle on; I noticed a deep fringe to it. However, it has nothing to do with the present subject, excepting that Miss Summerson looked so like it at the moment, that it came into my head."

I cannot separate and define the feelings that arose in me after this: it is enough that the vague duty and obligation I had felt upon me from the first of following the investigation, was, without my distinctly daring to ask myself any question, increased; and that I was indignantly sure of there being no possibility of a reason for my being afraid.

We three went out of the prison, and walked up and down at some short distance from the gate, which was in a retired place. We had not waited long, when Mr. and Mrs. Bagnet came out too, and quickly joined us.

There was a tear in each of Mrs. Bagnet's eyes, and her face was flushed and hurried. "I didn't let George see what I thought about it, you know, miss," was her first remark when she came up; "but he's in a bad way, poor old fellow!"

"Not with care and prudence, and good help," said my guardian.

"A gentleman like you ought to know best, sir," returned Mrs. Bagnet, hurriedly drying her eyes on the hem of her grey cloak; "but I am uneasy for him. He has been so careless, and said so much that he never meant. The gentlemen of the juries might not understand him as Lignum and me do. And then such a number of circumstances have happened bad for him, and such a number of people will be brought forward to speak against him, and Bucket is so deep."

"With a second-hand wiolinceller. And said he played the fife. When a boy." Mr. Bagnet added, with great solemnity.

"Now, I tell you, miss," said Mrs. Bagnet; "and when I say miss, I mean all! Just come into the corner of the wall, and I'll tell you!"

Mrs. Bagnet hurried us into a more secluded place, and was at first too breathless to proceed; occasioning Mr. Bagnet to say, "Old girl! Tell 'em!"

"Why, then, miss," the old girl proceeded, untying the strings of her bonnet for more air, "you could as soon move Dover Castle as move George on this point, unless you had got a new power to move him with. And I have got it!"

"You are a jewel of a woman," said my guardian. "Go on!"

"Now, I tell you, miss," she proceeded, clapping her hands in her hurry and agitation a dozen times in every sentence, "that what he says concerning no relations is all bosh. They don't know of him, but he does know of them. He has said more to me at odd times than to anybody else, and it warn't for nothing that he once spoke to my Woolwich about whitening and wrinkling mother's heads. For fifty pounds he had seen his mother that day. She's alive, and must be brought here straight!"

Instantly Mrs. Bagnet put some pins into her mouth and began pinning up her skirts all round, a little higher than the level of her grey cloak; which she accomplished with surprising dispatch and dexterity.

"Lignum," said Mrs. Bagnet, "you take care of the children, old man, and give me the umbrella! I'm away to Lincolnshire, to bring that old lady here."

"But, bless the woman!" cried my guardian, with his hand in his pocket, "how is she going? What money has she got?"

Mrs. Bagnet made another application to her skirts, and brought forth a leathern purse in which she hastily counted over a few shillings, and which she then shut up with perfect satisfaction.

"Never you mind for me, miss. I'm a soldier's wife, and accustomed to travelling in my own way. Lignum, old boy," kissing him, "one for yourself; three for the children. Now, I'm away into Lincolnshire after George's mother!"

And she actually set off while we three stood looking at one another, lost in amazement. She actually trudged away in her grey cloak at a sturdy pace, and turned the corner, and was gone.

"Mr. Bagnet," said my guardian. "Do you mean to let her go in that way?"

"Can't help it," he returned. "Made her way home once. From

another quarter of the world. With the same grey cloak. And same umbrella. Whatever the old girl says, do. Do it! Whenever the old girl says, *I*'ll do it. She does it."

"Then she is as honest and genuine as she looks," rejoined my guardian, "and it is impossible to say more for her."

"She's Colour-Serjeant of the Nonpareil battalion," said Mr. Bagnet, looking at us over his shoulder, as he went his way also. "And there's not such another. But I never own to it before her. Discipline must be maintained."

Chapter LIII

THE TRACK

Mr. Bucket and his fat forefinger are much in consultation together under existing circumstances. When Mr. Bucket has a matter of this pressing interest under his consideration, the fat forefinger seems to rise to the dignity of a familiar demon. He puts it to his ears, and it whispers information; he puts it to his lips, and it enjoins him to secrecy; he rubs it over his nose, and it sharpens his scent; he shakes it before a guilty man, and it charms him to destruction. The Augurs[1] of the Detective Temple invariably predict, that when Mr. Bucket and that finger are much in conference, a terrible avenger will be heard of before long.

Otherwise mildly studious in his observation of human nature, on the whole a benignant philosopher not disposed to be severe upon the follies of mankind, Mr. Bucket pervades a vast number of houses, and strolls about an infinity of streets: to outward appearance rather languishing for want of an object. He is in the friendliest condition towards his species, and will drink with most of them. He is free with his money, affable in his manners, innocent in his conversation—but, through the placid stream of his life, there glides an under-current of forefinger.

Time and place cannot bind Mr. Bucket. Like man in the abstract, he is here to-day and gone to-morrow—but, very unlike man indeed, he is here again the next day. This evening he will be casually looking into the iron extinguishers[2] at the door of Sir Leicester Dedlock's house in town; and to-morrow morning he will be walking on the leads at Chesney Wold, where erst the old man walked whose ghost is propitiated with a hundred guineas. Drawers, desks, pockets, all things belonging to him, Mr. Bucket examines. A few hours afterwards, he and the Roman will be alone together, comparing forefingers.

1. Roman prophets appointed to make predictions of future events.

2. See p. 575, note 3.

It is likely that these occupations are irreconcilable with home enjoyment, but it is certain that Mr. Bucket at present does not go home. Though in general he highly appreciates the society of Mrs. Bucket—a lady of a natural detective genius, which if it had been improved by professional exercise, might have done great things, but which has paused at the level of a clever amateur—he holds himself aloof from that dear solace. Mrs. Bucket is dependent on their lodger (fortunately an amiable lady in whom she takes an interest) for companionship and conversation.

A great crowd assembles in Lincoln's Inn Fields on the day of the funeral. Sir Leicester Dedlock attends the ceremony in person; strictly speaking, there are only three other human followers, that is to say, Lord Doodle, William Buffy, and the debilitated cousin (thrown in as a make-weight), but the amount of inconsolable carriages is immense. The Peerage contributes more four-wheeled affliction than has ever been seen in that neighbourhood. Such is the assemblage of armorial bearings on coach panels, that the Heralds' College[3] might be supposed to have lost its father and mother at a blow. The Duke of Foodle sends a splendid pile of dust and ashes, with silver wheel-boxes, patent axles, all the last improvements, and three bereaved worms,[4] six feet high, holding on behind, in a bunch of woe. All the state coachmen in London seem plunged into mourning; and if that dead old man of the rusty garb be not beyond a taste in horse-flesh (which appears impossible), it must be highly gratified this day.

Quiet among the undertakers and the equipages, and the calves of so many legs all steeped in grief, Mr. Bucket sits concealed in one of the inconsolable carriages, and at his ease surveys the crowd through the lattice blinds. He has a keen eye for a crowd—as for what not?—and looking here and there, now from this side of the carriage, now from the other, now up at the house windows, now along the people's heads, nothing escapes him.

"And there you are, my partner, eh?" says Mr. Bucket to himself, apostrophising Mrs. Bucket, stationed, by his favour, on the steps of the deceased's house. "And so you are. And so you are! And very well indeed you are looking, Mrs. Bucket!"

The procession has not started yet, but is waiting for the cause of its assemblage to be brought out. Mr. Bucket, in the foremost emblazoned carriage, uses his two fat forefingers to hold the lattice a hair's breadth open while he looks.

And it says a great deal for his attachment, as a husband, that he is still occupied with Mrs. B. "There you are, my partner, eh?" he murmuringly repeats. "And our lodger with you. I'm taking notice

3. A royal corporation instituted to supervise the use of coats of arms.

4. Footmen posing as mourners.

of you, Mrs. Bucket; I hope you're all right in your health, my dear!"

Not another word does Mr. Bucket say; but sits with most attentive eyes until the sacked depository[5] of noble secrets is brought down—Where are all those secrets now? Does he keep them yet? Did they fly with him on that sudden journey?—and until the procession moves, and Mr. Bucket's view is changed. After which he composes himself for an easy ride; and takes note of the fittings of the carriage, in case he should ever find such knowledge useful.

Contrast enough between Mr. Tulkinghorn shut up in his dark carriage, and Mr. Bucket shut up in *his*. Between the immeasurable track of space beyond the little wound that has thrown the one into the fixed sleep which jolts so heavily over the stones of the streets, and the narrow track of blood which keeps the other in the watchful state expressed in every hair of his head! But it is all one to both; neither is troubled about that.

Mr. Bucket sits out the procession in his own easy manner, and glides from the carriage when the opportunity he has settled with himself arrives. He makes for Sir Leicester Dedlock's, which is at present a sort of home to him, where he comes and goes as he likes at all hours, where he is always welcome and made much of, where he knows the whole establishment, and walks in an atmosphere of mysterious greatness.

No knocking or ringing for Mr. Bucket. He has caused himself to be provided with a key, and can pass in at his pleasure. As he is crossing the hall, Mercury informs him, "Here's another letter for you, Mr. Bucket, come by post," and gives it him.

"Another one, eh?" says Mr. Bucket.

If Mercury should chance to be possessed by any lingering curiosity as to Mr. Bucket's letters, that wary person is not the man to gratify it. Mr. Bucket looks at him, as if his face were a vista of some miles in length, and he were leisurely contemplating the same.

"Do you happen to carry a box?" says Mr. Bucket.

Unfortunately Mercury is no snuff-taker.

"Could you fetch me a pinch from anywheres?" says Mr. Bucket. "Thankee. It don't matter what it is; I'm not particular as to the kind. Thankee!"

Having leisurely helped himself from a canister borrowed from somebody down-stairs for the purpose, and having made a considerable show of tasting it, first with one side of his nose and then with the other, Mr. Bucket, with much deliberation, pronounces it of the right sort, and goes on, letter in hand.

Now, although Mr. Bucket walks up-stairs to the little library

5. The body wrapped in its burial shroud. Cf. p. 14: "the silent depository" of "noble secrets."

within the larger one, with the face of a man who receives some scores of letters every day, it happens that much correspondence is not incidental to his life. He is no great scribe; rather handling his pen like the pocket-staff he carries about with him always convenient to his grasp; and discourages correspondence with himself in others, as being too artless and direct a way of doing delicate business. Further, he often sees damaging letters produced in evidence, and has occasion to reflect that it was a green thing to write them. For these reasons he has very little to do with letters, either as sender or receiver. And yet he has received a round half-dozen, within the last twenty-four hours.

"And this," says Mr. Bucket, spreading it out on the table, "is in the same hand, and consists of the same two words."

What two words?

He turns the key in the door, ungirdles his black pocket-book (book of fate to many), lays another letter by it, and reads, boldly written in each, "LADY DEDLOCK."

"Yes, yes," says Mr. Bucket. "But I could have made the money without this anonymous information."

Having put the letters in his book of Fate, and girdled it up again, he unlocks the door just in time to admit his dinner, which is brought upon a goodly tray, with a decanter of sherry. Mr. Bucket frequently observes, in friendly circles where there is no restraint, that he likes a toothful of your fine old brown East Inder sherry better than anything you can offer him. Consequently he fills and empties his glass, with a smack of his lips; and is proceeding with his refreshment, when an idea enters his mind.

Mr. Bucket softly opens the door of communication between that room and the next, and looks in. The library is deserted, and the fire is sinking low. Mr. Bucket's eye, after taking a pigeon-flight round the room, alights upon a table where letters are usually put as they arrive. Several letters for Sir Leicester are upon it. Mr. Bucket draws near, and examines the directions. "No," he says, "there's none in that hand. It's only me as is written to. I can break it to Sir Leicester Dedlock, Baronet, to-morrow."

With that he returns to finish his dinner with a good appetite; and after a light nap, is summoned into the drawing-room. Sir Leicester has received him there these several evenings past, to know whether he has anything to report. The debilitated cousin (much exhausted by the funeral), and Volumnia, are in attendance.

Mr. Bucket makes three distinctly different bows to these three people. A bow of homage to Sir Leicester, a bow of gallantry to Volumnia, and a bow of recognition to the debilitated cousin; to whom it airily says, "You are a swell about town, and you know me, and I know you." Having distributed these little specimens of his tact, Mr. Bucket rubs his hands.

"Have you anything new to communicate, officer?" inquires Sir Leicester. "Do you wish to hold any conversation with me in private?"

"Why—not to-night, Sir Leicester Dedlock, Baronet."

"Because my time," pursues Sir Leicester, "is wholly at your disposal, with a view to the vindication of the outraged majesty of the law."

Mr. Bucket coughs, and glances at Volumnia, rouged and necklaced, as though he would respectfully observe, "I do assure you, you're a pretty creetur. I've seen hundreds worse-looking at your time of life, I have indeed."

The fair Volumnia, not quite unconscious perhaps of the humanising influence of her charms, pauses in the writing of cocked-hat notes,[6] and meditatively adjusts the pearl necklace. Mr. Bucket prices that decoration in his mind, and thinks it as likely as not that Volumnia is writing poetry.

"If I have not," pursues Sir Leicester, "in the most emphatic manner, adjured you, officer, to exercise your utmost skill in this atrocious case, I particularly desire to take the present opportunity of rectifying any omission I may have made. Let no expense be a consideration. I am prepared to defray all charges. You can incur none, in pursuit of the object you have undertaken, that I shall hesitate for a moment to bear."

Mr. Bucket makes Sir Leicester's bow again, as a response to this liberality.

"My mind," Sir Leicester adds, with generous warmth, "has not, as may be easily supposed, recovered its tone since the late diabolical occurrence. It is not likely ever to recover its tone. But it is full of indignation to-night, after undergoing the ordeal of consigning to the tomb the remains of a faithful, a zealous, a devoted adherent."

Sir Leicester's voice trembles, and his grey hair stirs upon his head. Tears are in his eyes; the best part of his nature is aroused.

"I declare," he says, "I solemnly declare, that until this crime is discovered and, in the course of justice, punished, I almost feel as if there were a stain upon my name. A gentleman who has devoted a large portion of his life to me, a gentleman who has devoted the last day of his life to me, a gentleman who has constantly sat at my table and slept under my roof, goes from my house to his own, and is struck down within a hour of his leaving my house. I cannot say but that he may have been followed from my house, watched at my house, even first marked because of his association with my house —which may have suggested his possessing greater wealth, and being altogether of greater importance than his own retiring

6. Notes folded in the three-cornered shape of a cocked hat.

demeanour would have indicated. If I cannot, with my means, and my influence, and my position, bring all the perpetrators of such a crime to light, I fail in the assertion of my respect for that gentleman's memory, and of my fidelity towards one who was ever faithful to me."

While he makes this protestation with great emotion and earnestness, looking round the room as if he were addressing an assembly, Mr. Bucket glances at him with an observant gravity in which there might be, but for the audacity of the thought, a touch of compassion.

"The ceremony of to-day," continues Sir Leicester, "strikingly illustrative of the respect in which my deceased friend"; he lays a stress upon the word, for death levels all distinctions; "was held by the flower of the land, has, I say, aggravated the shock I have received from this most horrible and audacious crime. If it were my brother who had committed it, I would not spare him."

Mr. Bucket looks very grave. Volumnia remarks of the deceased that he was the trustiest and dearest person!

"You must feel it as a deprivation to you, miss," replies Mr. Bucket, soothingly, "no doubt. He was calculated to *be* a deprivation, I'm sure he was."

Volumnia gives Mr. Bucket to understand, in reply, that her sensitive mind is fully made up never to get the better of it as long as she lives; that her nerves are unstrung for ever; and that she has not the least expectation of ever smiling again. Meanwhile she folds up a cocked hat for that redoubtable old general at Bath, descriptive of her melancholy condition.

"It gives a start to a delicate female," says Mr. Bucket, sympathetically, "but it'll wear off."

Volumnia wishes of all things to know what is doing? Whether they are going to convict, or whatever it is, that dreadful soldier? Whether he had any accomplices, or whatever the thing is called in the law? And a great deal more to the like artless purpose.

"Why, you see, miss," returns Mr. Bucket, bringing the finger into persuasive action—and such is his natural gallantry, that he had almost said, my dear; "it ain't easy to answer those questions at the present moment. Not at the present moment. I've kept myself on this case, Sir Leicester Dedlock, Baronet," whom Mr. Bucket takes into the conversation in right of his importance, "morning, noon, and night. But for a glass or two of sherry, I don't think I could have had my mind so much upon the stretch as it has been. I *could* answer your questions, miss, but duty forbids it. Sir Leicester Dedlock, Baronet, will very soon be made acquainted with all that has been traced. And I hope that he may find it"; Mr. Bucket again looks grave; "to his satisfaction."

The debilitated cousin only hopes some fler'll be executed—zample. Thinks more interest's wanted—get man hanged presentime—than get man place ten thousand a year. Hasn't a doubt—zample—far better hang wrong fler than no fler.

"*You* know life, you know, sir," says Mr. Bucket, with a complimentary twinkle of his eye and crook of his finger, "and you can confirm what I've mentioned to this lady. *You* don't want to be told, that, from information I have received, I have gone to work. You're up to what a lady can't be expected to be up to. Lord! especially in your elevated station of society, miss," says Mr. Bucket, quite reddening at another narrow escape from my dear.

"The officer, Volumnia," observes Sir Leicester, "is faithful to his duty, and perfectly right."

Mr. Bucket murmurs, "Glad to have the honour of your approbation, Sir Leicester Dedlock, Baronet."

"In fact, Volumnia," proceeds Sir Leicester, "it is not holding up a good model for imitation, to ask the officer any such questions as you have put to him. He is the best judge of his own responsibility; he acts upon his responsibility. And it does not become us, who assist in making the laws, to impede or interfere with those who carry them into execution. Or," says Sir Leicester, somewhat sternly, for Volumnia was going to cut in before he had rounded his sentence; "or who vindicate their outraged majesty."

Volumnia with all humility explains that she has not merely the plea of curiosity to urge (in common with the giddy youth of her sex in general), but that she is perfectly dying with regret and interest for the darling man whose loss they all deplore.

"Very well, Volumnia," returns Sir Leicester. "Then you cannot be too discreet."

Mr. Bucket takes the opportunity of a pause to be heard again.

"Sir Leicester Dedlock, Baronet, I have no objections to telling this lady, with your leave and among ourselves, that I look upon the case as pretty well complete. It is a beautiful case—a beautiful case—and what little is wanting to complete it, I expect to be able to supply in a few hours."

"I am very glad indeed to hear it," says Sir Leicester. "Highly creditable to you."

"Sir Leicester Dedlock, Baronet," returns Mr. Bucket, very seriously, "I hope it may at one and the same time do me credit, and prove satisfactory to all. When I depict it as a beautiful case, you see, miss," Mr. Bucket goes on, glancing gravely at Sir Leicester, "I mean from my point of view. As considered from other points of view, such cases will always involve more or less unpleasantness. Very strange things comes to our knowledge in families, miss; bless your heart, what you would think to be phenomonons, quite."

Volumnia, with her innocent little scream, supposes so.

"Aye, and even in gen-teel families, in high families, in great families," says Mr. Bucket, again gravely eyeing Sir Leicester aside. "I have had the honour of being employed in high families before; and you have no idea—come, I'll go so far as to say not even *you* have any idea, sir," this to the debilitated cousin, "what games goes on!"

The cousin, who has been casting sofa-pillows on his head, in a prostration of boredom, yawns, "Vayli"—being the used-up for "very likely."

Sir Leicester, deeming it time to dismiss the officer, here majestically interposes with the words, "Very good. Thank you!" and also with a wave of his hand, implying not only that there is an end to the discourse, but that if high families fall into low habits they must take the consequences. "You will not forget, officer," he adds, with condescension, "that I am at your disposal when you please."

Mr. Bucket (still grave) inquires if to-morrow morning, now, would suit, in case he should be as for'ard as he expects to be? Sir Leicester replies, "All times are alike to me." Mr. Bucket makes his three bows, and is withdrawing, when a forgotten point occurs to him.

"Might I ask, by-the-bye," he says, in a low voice, cautiously returning, "who posted the Reward-bill on the staircase."

"*I* ordered it to be put up there," replies Sir Leicester.

"Would it be considered a liberty, Sir Leicester Dedlock, Baronet, if I was to ask you why?"

"Not at all. I chose it as a conspicuous part of the house. I think it cannot be too prominently kept before the whole establishment. I wish my people to be impressed with the enormity of the crime, the determination to punish it, and the hopelessness of escape. At the same time, officer, if you in your better knowledge of the subject see any objection——"

Mr. Bucket sees none now; the bill having been put up, had better not be taken down. Repeating his three bows he withdraws: closing the door on Volumnia's little scream, which is a preliminary to her remarking that that charmingly horrible person is a perfect Blue Chamber.[7]

In his fondness for society, and his adaptability to all grades, Mr. Bucket is presently standing before the hall-fire—bright and warm on the early winter night—admiring Mercury.

"Why, you're six foot two, I suppose?" says Mr. Bucket.

"Three," says Mercury.

"Are you so much? But then, you see, you're broad in proportion,

7. In one of the versions of a story by Charles Perrault (1628–1703), the Blue Chamber was a locked room which Bluebeard forbade his wives to investigate because it contained the bodies of former wives he had murdered.

and don't look it. You're not one of the weak-legged ones, you ain't. Was you ever modelled now?" Mr. Bucket asks, conveying the expression of an artist into the turn of his eye and head.

Mercury never was modelled.

"Then you ought to be, you know," says Mr. Bucket; "and a friend of mine that you'll hear of one day as a Royal Academy Sculptor, would stand something handsome to make a drawing of your proportions for the marble. My Lady's out, ain't she?"

"Out to dinner."

"Goes out pretty well every day, don't she?"

"Yes."

"Not to be wondered at!" says Mr. Bucket. "Such a fine woman as her, so handsome and so graceful and so elegant, is like a fresh lemon on a dinner-table, ornamental wherever she goes. Was your father in the same way of life as yourself?"

Answer in the negative.

"Mine was," says Mr. Bucket. "My father was first a page, then a footman, then a butler, then a steward, then a innkeeper. Lived universally respected, and died lamented. Said with his last breath that he considered service the most honourable part of his career, and so it was. I've a brother in service, *and* a brother-in-law. My Lady a good temper?"

Mercury replies, "As good as you can expect."

"Ah!" says Mr. Bucket, "a little spoilt? A little capricious? Lord! What can you anticipate when they're so handsome as that? And we like 'em all the better for it, don't we?"

Mercury, with his hands in the pockets of his bright peach-blossom small-clothes, stretches his symmetrical silk legs with the air of a man of gallantry, and can't deny it. Come the roll of wheels and a violent ringing at the bell. "Talk of the Angels," says Mr. Bucket. "Here she is!"

The doors are thrown open, and she passes through the hall. Still very pale, she is dressed in slight mourning, and wears two beautiful bracelets. Either their beauty, or the beauty of her arms, is particularly attractive to Mr. Bucket. He looks at them with an eager eye, and rattles something in his pocket—halfpence perhaps.

Noticing him at his distance, she turns an inquiring look on the other Mercury who has brought her home.

"Mr. Bucket, my Lady."

Mr. Bucket makes a leg,[8] and comes forward, passing his familiar demon over the region of his mouth.

"Are you waiting to see Sir Leicester?"

"No, my Lady, I've seen him!"

"Have you anything to say to me?"

"Not just at present, my Lady."

8. A kind of bowing in which one leg is drawn back and the other bent.

"Have you made any new discoveries?"

"A few, my Lady."

This is merely in passing. She scarcely makes a stop, and sweeps up-stairs alone. Mr. Bucket, moving towards the staircase-foot, watches her as she goes up the steps the old man came down to his grave; past murderous groups of statuary, repeated with their shadowy weapons on the wall; past the printed bill, which she looks at going by; out of view.

"She's a lovely woman, too, she really is," says Mr. Bucket, coming back to Mercury. "Don't look quite healthy though."

Is not quite healthy, Mercury informs him. Suffers much from headaches.

Really? That's a pity! Walking, Mr. Bucket would recommend for that. Well, she tries walking, Mercury rejoins. Walks sometimes for two hours, when she has them bad. By night, too.

"Are you sure you're quite so much as six foot three?" asks Mr. Bucket, "begging your pardon for interrupting you a moment."

Not a doubt about it.

"You're so well put together that I shouldn't have thought it. But the household troops, though considered fine men, are built so straggling.—Walks by night, does she? When it's moonlight, though?"

O yes. When it's moonlight! Of course. O, of course! Conversational and acquiescent on both sides.

"I suppose you ain't in the habit of walking, yourself?" says Mr. Bucket. "Not much time for it, I should say?"

Besides which, Mercury don't like it. Prefers carriage exercise.

"To be sure," says Mr. Bucket. "That makes a difference. Now I think of it," says Mr. Bucket, warming his hands, and looking pleasantly at the blaze, "she went out walking, the very night of this business."

"To be sure she did! I let her into the garden over the way."

"And left her there. Certainly you did. I saw you doing it."

"I didn't see *you*," says Mercury.

"I was rather in a hurry," returns Mr. Bucket, "for I was going to visit a aunt of mine that lives at Chelsea—next door but two to the old original Bun House[9]—ninety year old the old lady is, a single woman, and got a little property. Yes, I chanced to be passing at the time. Let's see. What time might it be? It wasn't ten."

"Half-past nine."

"You're right. So it was. And if I don't deceive myself, my Lady was muffled in a loose black mantle, with a deep fringe to it?"

"Of course she was."

Of course she was. Mr. Bucket must return to a little work he has

9. A popular bakery shop and museum. The "original" establishment, well over a century old, was demolished in 1839.

to get on with up-stairs; but he must shake hands with Mercury in acknowledgement of his agreeable conversation, and will he—this is all he asks—will he, when he has a leisure half-hour, think of bestowing it on that Royal Academy sculptor, for the advantage of both parties?

Chapter LIV

SPRINGING A MINE

Refreshed by sleep, Mr. Bucket rises betimes in the morning, and prepares for a field-day. Smartened up by the aid of a clean shirt and a wet hair-brush, with which instrument, on occasions of ceremony, he lubricates such thin locks as remain to him after his life of severe study, Mr. Bucket lays in a breakfast of two mutton chops as a foundation to work upon, together with tea, eggs, toast, and marmalade, on a corresponding scale. Having much enjoyed these strengthening matters, and having held subtle conference with his familiar demon, he confidently instructs Mercury "just to mention quietly to Sir Leicester Dedlock, Baronet, that whenever he's ready for me, I'm ready for him." A gracious message being returned, that Sir Leicester will expedite his dressing and join Mr. Bucket in the library within ten minutes, Mr. Bucket repairs to that apartment; and stands before the fire, with his finger on his chin, looking at the blazing coals.

Thoughtful Mr. Bucket is; as a man may be, with weighty work to do; but composed, sure, confident. From the expression of his face, he might be a famous whist-player for a large stake—say a hundred guineas certain—with the game in his hand, but with a high reputation involved in his playing his hand out to the last card, in a masterly way. Not in the least anxious or disturbed is Mr. Bucket, when Sir Leicester appears; but he eyes the baronet aside as he comes slowly to his easy-chair, with that observant gravity of yesterday, in which there might have been yesterday, but for the audacity of the idea, a touch of compassion.

"I am sorry to have kept you waiting, officer, but I am rather later than my usual hour this morning. I am not well. The agitation, and the indignation from which I have recently suffered, have been too much for me. I am subject to—gout"; Sir Leicester was going to say indisposition, and would have said it to anybody else, but Mr. Bucket palpably knows all about it; "and recent circumstances have brought it on."

As he takes his seat with some difficulty, and with an air of pain, Mr. Bucket draws a little nearer, standing with one of his large hands on the library-table.

"I am not aware, officer," Sir Leicester observes, raising his eyes to his face, "whether you wish us to be alone; but that is entirely as you please. If you do, well and good. If not, Miss Dedlock would be interested——"

"Why, Sir Leicester Dedlock, Baronet," returns Mr. Bucket, with his head persuasively on one side, and his forefinger pendant at one ear like an ear-ring, "we can't be too private, just at present. You will presently see that we can't be too private. A lady, under any circumstances, and especially in Miss Dedlock's elevated station of society, can't but be agreeable to me; but speaking without a view to myself, I will take the liberty of assuring you that I know we can't be too private."

"That is enough."

"So much so, Sir Leicester Dedlock, Baronet," Mr. Bucket resumes, "that I was on the point of asking your permission to turn the key in the door."

"By all means." Mr. Bucket skilfully and softly takes that precaution; stooping on his knee for a moment, from mere force of habit, so to adjust the key in the lock as that no one shall peep in from the outerside.

"Sir Leicester Dedlock, Baronet, I mentioned yesterday evening, that I wanted but a very little to complete this case. I have now completed it, and collected proof against the person who did this crime."

"Against the soldier?"

"No, Sir Leicester Dedlock; not the soldier."

Sir Leicester looks astounded, and inquires, "Is the man in custody?"

Mr. Bucket tells him, after a pause, "It was a woman."

Sir Leicester leans back in his chair, and breathlessly ejaculates, "Good Heaven!"

"Now, Sir Leicester Dedlock, Baronet," Mr. Bucket then begins, standing over him with one hand spread out on the library-table, and the forefinger of the other in impressive use, "it's my duty to prepare you for a train of circumstances that may, and I go so far as to say that will, give you a shock. But, Sir Leicester Dedlock, Baronet, you are a gentleman; and I know what a gentleman is, and what a gentleman is capable of. A gentleman can bear a shock, when it must come, boldly and steadily. A gentleman can make up his mind to stand up against almost any blow. Why, take yourself, Sir Leicester Dedlock, Baronet. If there's a blow to be inflicted on you, you naturally think of your family. You ask yourself, how would all them ancestors of yours, away to Julius Cæsar—not to go beyond him at present—have borne that blow; you remember scores of them that would have borne it well; and you bear it well on their accounts, and to maintain the family credit. That's the way you argue, and that's the way you act, Sir Leicester Dedlock, Baronet."

Sir Leicester, leaning back in his chair, and grasping the elbows, sits looking at him with a stony face.

"Now, Sir Leicester Dedlock," proceeds Mr. Bucket, "thus preparing you, let me beg of you not to trouble your mind, for a moment, as to anything having come to *my* knowledge. I know so much about so many characters, high and low, that a piece of information more or less, don't signify a straw. I don't suppose there's a move on the board that would surprise *me*; and as to this or that move having taken place, why my knowing it is no odds at all; any possible move whatever (provided it's in a wrong direction) being a probable move according to my experience. Therefore, what I say to you, Sir Leicester Dedlock, Baronet, is, don't you go and let yourself be put out of the way, because of my knowing anything of your family affairs."

"I thank you for your preparation," returns Sir Leicester, after a silence, without moving hand, foot, or feature; "which I hope is not necessary, though I give it credit for being well intended. Be so good as to go on. Also"; Sir Leicester seems to shrink in the shadow of his figure; "also, to take a seat, if you have no objection."

None at all. Mr. Bucket brings a chair, and diminishes his shadow. "Now, Sir Leicester Dedlock, Baronet, with this short preface I come to the point. Lady Dedlock——"

Sir Leicester raises himself in his seat, and stares at him fiercely. Mr. Bucket brings the finger into play as an emollient.

"Lady Dedlock, you see she's universally admired. That's what her Ladyship is; she's universally admired," says Mr. Bucket.

"I would greatly prefer, officer," Sir Leicester returns, stiffly, "my Lady's name being entirely omitted from this discussion."

"So would I, Sir Leicester Dedlock, Baronet, but—it's impossible."

"Impossible?"

Mr. Bucket shakes his relentless head.

"Sir Leicester Dedlock, Baronet, it's altogether impossible. What I have got to say, is about her Ladyship. She is the pivot it all turns on."

"Officer," retorts Sir Leicester, with a fiery eye, and a quivering lip, "you know your duty. Do your duty; but be careful not to overstep it. I would not suffer it. I would not endure it. You bring my Lady's name into this communication, upon your responsibility—upon your responsibility. My Lady's name is not a name for common persons to trifle with!"

"Sir Leicester Dedlock, Baronet, I say what I must say, and no more."

"I hope it may prove so. Very well. Go on. Go on, sir!"

Glancing at the angry eyes which now avoid him, and at the angry figure trembling from head to foot, yet striving to be still, Mr. Bucket feels his way with his forefinger, and in a low voice proceeds.

"Sir Leicester Dedlock, Baronet, it becomes my duty to tell you that the deceased Mr. Tulkinghorn long entertained mistrusts and suspicions of Lady Dedlock."

"If he had dared to breathe them to me, sir—which he never did—I would have killed him myself!" exclaims Sir Leicester, striking his hand upon the table. But, in the very heat and fury of the act, he stops, fixed by the knowing eyes of Mr. Bucket, whose forefinger is slowly going, and who, with mingled confidence and patience, shakes his head.

"Sir Leicester Dedlock, the deceased Mr. Tulkinghorn was deep and close; and what he fully had in his mind in the very beginning, I can't quite take upon myself to say. But I know from his lips, that he long ago suspected Lady Dedlock of having discovered, through the sight of some handwriting—in this very house, and when you yourself, Sir Leicester Dedlock, were present—the existence, in great poverty, of a certain person, who had been her lover before you courted her, and who ought to have been her husband"; Mr. Bucket stops, and deliberately repeats, "ought to have been her husband; not a doubt about it. I know from his lips, that when that person soon afterwards died, he suspected Lady Dedlock of visiting his wretched lodging, and his wretcheder grave, alone and in secret. I know from my own inquiries, and through my eyes and ears, that Lady Dedlock did make such visit, in the dress of her own maid; for the deceased Mr. Tulkinghorn employed me to reckon up her Ladyship—if you'll excuse my making use of the term we commonly employ—and I reckoned her up, so far, completely. I confronted the maid, in the chambers in Lincoln's Inn Fields, with a witness who had been Lady Dedlock's guide; and there couldn't be the shadow of a doubt that she had worn the young woman's dress, unknown to her. Sir Leicester Dedlock, Baronet, I did endeavour to pave the way a little towards these unpleasant disclosures, yesterday, by saying that very strange things happened even in high families sometimes. All this, and more, has happened in your own family, and to and through your own Lady. It's my belief that the deceased Mr. Tulkinghorn followed up these inquiries to the hour of his death; and that he and Lady Dedlock even had bad blood between them upon the matter, that very night. Now, only you put that to Lady Dedlock, Sir Leicester Dedlock, Baronet; and ask her Ladyship whether, even after he had left here, she didn't go down to his chambers with the intention of saying something further to him, dressed in a loose black mantle with a deep fringe to it."

Sir Leicester sits like a statue, gazing at the cruel finger that is probing the life-blood of his heart.

"You put that to her Ladyship, Sir Leicester Dedlock, Baronet, from me, Inspector Bucket of the Detective. And if her Ladyship makes any difficulty about admitting of it, you tell her that it's no use; that Inspector Bucket knows it, and knows that she passed the soldier as you called him (though he's not in the army now), and knows that she knows she passed him, on the staircase. Now, Sir Leicester Dedlock, Baronet, why do I relate all this?"

Sir Leicester, who has covered his face with his hands, uttering a single groan, requests him to pause for a moment. By and by, he takes his hands away; and so preserves his dignity and outward calmness, though there is no more colour in his face than in his white hair, that Mr. Bucket is a little awed by him. Something frozen and fixed is upon his manner, over and above its usual shell of haughtiness; and Mr. Bucket soon detects an unusual slowness in his speech, with now and then a curious trouble in beginning, which occasions him to utter inarticulate sounds. With such sounds, he now breaks silence; soon, however, controlling himself to say, that he does not comprehend why a gentleman so faithful and zealous as the late Mr. Tulkinghorn should have communicated to him nothing of this painful, this distressing, this unlooked-for, this overwhelming, this incredible intelligence.

"Again Sir Leicester Dedlock, Baronet," returns Mr. Bucket, "put it to her Ladyship to clear that up. Put it to her Ladyship, if you think it right, from Inspector Bucket of the Detective. You'll find, or I'm much mistaken, that the deceased Mr. Tulkinghorn had the intention of communicating the whole to you, as soon as he considered it ripe; and further, that he had given her Ladyship so to understand. Why, he might have been going to reveal it on the very morning when *I* examined the body! You don't know what I'm going to say and do, five minutes from this present time, Sir Leicester Dedlock, Baronet; and supposing I was to be picked off now, you might wonder why I hadn't done it, don't you see?"

True. Sir Leicester, avoiding, with some trouble, those obtrusive sounds, says "True." At this juncture, a considerable noise of voices is heard in the hall. Mr. Bucket, after listening, goes to the library-door, softly unlocks and opens it, and listens again. Then he draws in his head, and whispers, hurriedly, but composedly, "Sir Leicester Dedlock, Baronet, this unfortunate family affair has taken air, as I expected it might; the deceased Mr. Tulkinghorn being cut down so sudden. The chance to hush it, is to let in these people now in a wrangle with your footmen. Would you mind sitting quiet—on the family account—while I reckon 'em up? And would you just throw in a nod, when I seem to ask you for it?"

Sir Leicester indistinctly answers, "Officer. The best you can, the best you can!" and Mr. Bucket, with a nod and a sagacious crook of the forefinger, slips down into the hall, where the voices quickly die away. He is not long in returning, a few paces ahead of Mercury, and a brother deity also powdered and in peach-blossom smalls,[1] who bear between them a chair in which is an incapable old man. Another man and two women come behind. Directing the pitching of the chair, in an affable and easy manner, Mr. Bucket dismisses the Mercuries, and locks the door again. Sir Leicester looks on at this invasion of the sacred precincts with an icy stare.

"Now, perhaps you may know me, ladies and gentlemen," says Mr. Bucket, in a confidential voice. "I am Inspector Bucket of the Detective, I am; and this," producing the tip of his convenient little staff from his breast-pocket, "is my authority. Now, you wanted to see Sir Leicester Dedlock, Baronet. Well! You do see him; and, mind you, it ain't every one as is admitted to that honour. Your name, old gentleman, is Smallweed; that's what your name is; I know it well."

"Well, and you never heard any harm of it!" cries Mr. Smallweed, in a shrill loud voice.

"You don't happen to know why they killed the pig, do you?" retorts Mr. Bucket, with a steadfast look, but without loss of temper.

"No!"

"Why, they killed him," says Mr. Bucket, "on account of his having so much cheek. Don't *you* get into the same position, because it isn't worthy of you. You ain't in the habit of conversing with a deaf person, are you?"

"Yes," snarls Mr. Smallweed, "my wife's deaf."

"That accounts for your pitching your voice so high. But as she ain't here, just pitch it an octave or two lower, will you, and I'll not only be obliged to you, but it'll do you more credit," says Mr. Bucket. "This other gentleman is in the preaching line, I think?"

"Name of Chadband," Mr. Smallweed puts in, speaking henceforth in a much lower key.

"Once had a friend and brother serjeant of the same name," says Mr. Bucket, offering his hand, "and consequently feel a liking for it. Mrs. Chadband, no doubt?"

"And Mrs. Snagsby," Mr. Smallweed introduces.

"Husband a law-stationer, and a friend of my own," says Mr. Bucket. "Love him like a brother!—Now, what's up?"

1. Knee-breeches.

"Do you mean what business have we come upon?" Mr. Smallweed asks, a little dashed by the suddenness of this turn.

"Ah! You know what I mean. Let us hear what it's all about in presence of Sir Leicester Dedlock, Baronet. Come."

Mr. Smallweed, beckoning Mr. Chadband, takes a moment's counsel with him in a whisper. Mr. Chadband, expressing a considerable amount of oil from the pores of his forehead and the palms of his hands, says aloud, "Yes. You first!" and retires to his former place.

"I was the client and friend of Mr. Tulkinghorn," pipes Grandfather Smallweed, then; "I did business with him. I was useful to him, and he was useful to me. Krook, dead and gone, was my brother-in-law. He was own brother to a brimstone magpie—leastways Mrs. Smallweed. I come into Krook's property. I examined all his papers and all his effects. They was all dug out under my eyes. There was a bundle of letters belonging to a dead and gone lodger, as was hid away at the back of a shelf in the side of Lady Jane's bed—his cat's bed. He hid all manner of things away, everywheres. Mr. Tulkinghorn wanted 'em and got 'em, but I looked 'em over first. I'm a man of business, and I took a squint at 'em. They was letters from the lodger's sweetheart, and she signed Honoria. Dear me, that's not a common name, Honoria, is it? There's no lady in this house that signs Honoria, is there? O no, I don't think so! O no, I don't think so! And not in the same hand, perhaps? O no, I don't think so!"

Here Mr. Smallweed, seized with a fit of coughing in the midst of his triumph, breaks off to ejaculate, "O dear me! O Lord! I'm shaken all to pieces!"

"Now, when you're ready," says Mr. Bucket, after awaiting his recovery, "to come to anything that concerns Sir Leicester Dedlock, Baronet, here the gentleman sits, you know."

"Haven't I come to it, Mr. Bucket?" cries Grandfather Smallweed. "Isn't the gentleman concerned yet? Not with Captain Hawdon, and his ever affectionate Honoria, and their child into the bargain? Come, then, I want to know where those letters are. That concerns me, if it don't concern Sir Leicester Dedlock. I will know where they are. I won't have 'em disappear so quietly. I handed 'em over to my friend and solicitor, Mr. Tulkinghorn; not to anybody else."

"Why he paid you for them, you know, and handsome too," says Mr. Bucket.

"I don't care for that. I want to know who's got 'em. And I tell you what we want—what we all here want, Mr. Bucket. We want more pains-taking and search-making into this murder. We know where the interest and the motive was, and you have not done enough. If George the vagabond dragoon had any hand in it, he was only an accomplice, and was set on. You know what I mean as well as any man."

"Now, I tell you what," says Mr. Bucket, instantaneously altering his manner, coming close to him, and communicating an extraordinary fascination to the forefinger, "I am damned if I am a going to have my case spoilt, or interfered with, or anticipated by so much as half a second of time, by any human being in creation. *You* want more pains-taking and search-making? *You* do? Do you see this hand, and do you think that *I* don't know the right time to stretch it out, and put it on the arm that fired that shot?"

Such is the dread power of the man, and so terribly evident it is that he makes no idle boast, that Mr. Smallweed begins to apologise. Mr. Bucket, dismissing his sudden anger, checks him.

"The advice I give you, is, don't you trouble your head about the murder. That's my affair. You keep half an eye on the newspapers; and I shouldn't wonder if you was to read something about it before long, if you look sharp. I know my business, and that's all I've got to say to you on that subject. Now about those letters. You want to know who's got 'em. I don't mind telling you. *I* have got 'em. Is that the packet?"

Mr. Smallweed looks, with greedy eyes, at the little bundle Mr. Bucket produces from a mysterious part of his coat, and identifies it as the same.

"What have you got to say next?" asks Mr. Bucket. "Now, don't open your mouth too wide, because you don't look handsome when you do it."

"I want five hundred pound."

"No, you don't; you mean fifty," says Mr. Bucket, humorously.

It appears, however, that Mr. Smallweed means five hundred.

"That is, I am deputed by Sir Leicester Dedlock, Baronet, to consider (without admitting or promising anything) this bit of business," says Mr. Bucket; Sir Leicester mechanically bows his head; "and you ask me to consider a proposal of five hundred pounds. Why, it's an unreasonable proposal! Two fifty would be bad enough, but better than that. Hadn't you better say two fifty?"

Mr. Smallweed is quite clear that he had better not.

"Then," says Mr. Bucket, "let's hear Mr. Chadband. Lord! Many a time I've heard my old fellow-serjeant of that name; and a moderate man he was in all respects, as ever I come across!"

Thus invited, Mr. Chadband steps forth, and after a little sleek smiling and a little oil-grinding with the palms of his hands, delivers himself as follows:

"My friends, we are now—Rachael my wife, and I—in the mansions of the rich and great. Why are we now in the mansions of the rich and great, my friends? Is it because we are invited? Because we are bidden to feast with them, because we are bidden to rejoice with them, because we are bidden to play the lute with them, because we are bidden to dance with them? No. Then why are we here, my friends? Air we in possession of a sinful secret, and doe we require corn, and wine, and oil—or, what is much the same thing, money—for the keeping thereof? Probably so, my friends."

"You're a man of business, you are," returns Mr. Bucket, very attentive; "and consequently you're going on to mention what the nature of your secret is. You are right. You couldn't do better."

"Let us then, my brother, in a spirit of love," says Mr. Chadband, with a cunning eye, "proceed untoe it. Rachael, my wife, advance!"

Mrs. Chadband, more than ready, so advances as to jostle her husband into the background, and confronts Mr. Bucket with a hard frowning smile.

"Since you want to know what we know," says she, "I'll tell you. I helped to bring up Miss Hawdon, her Ladyship's daughter. I was in the service of her Ladyship's sister, who was very sensitive to the disgrace her Ladyship brought upon her, and gave out, even to her Ladyship, that the child was dead—she *was* very nearly so—when she was born. But she's alive, and I know her." With these words, and a laugh, and laying a bitter stress on the word "Ladyship," Mrs. Chadband folds her arms, and looks implacably at Mr. Bucket.

"I suppose now," returns that officer, "*you* will be expecting a twenty-pound note, or a present of about that figure?"

Mrs. Chadband merely laughs, and contemptuously tells him he can "offer" twenty pence.

"My friend the law-stationer's good lady, over there," says Mr. Bucket, luring Mrs. Snagsby forward with the finger. "What may *your* game be, ma'am?"

Mrs. Snagsby is at first prevented, by tears and lamentations, from stating the nature of her game: but by degrees it confusedly comes to light, that she is a woman overwhelmed with injuries and wrongs, whom Mr. Snagsby has habitually deceived, abandoned, and sought to keep in darkness, and whose chief comfort, under her afflictions, has been the sympathy of the late Mr. Tulkinghorn; who showed so much commiseration for her, on one occasion of his calling in Cook's Court in the absence of her perjured husband, that she has of late habitually carried to him all her woes. Everybody, it appears, the present company excepted, has plotted against Mrs. Snagsby's peace. There is Mr. Guppy, clerk to Kenge and Carboy, who was at first as open as the sun at noon, but who suddenly shut up as close as midnight, under the influence—no doubt—of Mr. Snagsby's suborning and tampering. There is Mr. Weevle, friend of Mr. Guppy, who lived mysteriously up a court, owing to the like coherent causes. There was Krook, deceased; there was Nimrod, deceased; and there was Jo, deceased; and they were "all in it." In what, Mrs. Snagsby does not with particularity express; but she knows that Jo was Mr. Snagsby's son, "as well as if a trumpet had spoken it," and she followed Mr. Snagsby when he went on his last visit to the boy, and if he was not his son why did he go? The one occupation of her life has been, for some time back, to follow Mr. Snagsby to and fro, and up and down, and to piece suspicious circumstances together—and every circumstance that has happened has been most suspicious; and in this way she has pursued her object of detecting and confounding her false husband, night and day. Thus did it come to pass that she brought the Chadbands and Mr. Tulkinghorn together, and conferred with Mr. Tulkinghorn on the change in Mr. Guppy, and helped to turn up the circumstances in which the present company are interested, casually, by the wayside; being still, and ever, on the great high road that is to terminate in Mr. Snagsby's full exposure and a matrimonial separation. All this, Mrs. Snagsby, as an injured woman, and the friend of Mrs. Chadband, and the follower of Mr. Chadband, and the mourner of the late Mr. Tulkinghorn, is here to certify under the seal of confidence, with every possible confusion and involvement possible and impossible; having no pecuniary motive whatever, no scheme or project but the one mentioned; and bringing here, and taking everywhere, her own dense atmosphere of dust, arising from the ceaseless working of her mill of jealousy.

While this exordium is in hand—and it takes some time—Mr. Bucket, who has seen through the transparency of Mrs. Snagsby's vinegar at a glance, confers with his familiar demon, and bestows his shrewd attention on the Chadbands and Mr. Smallweed. Sir Leicester Dedlock remains immovable, with the same icy surface upon him; except that he once or twice looks towards Mr. Bucket, as relying on that officer alone of all mankind.

"Very good," says Mr. Bucket. "Now I understand you, you know; and, being deputed by Sir Leicester Dedlock, Baronet, to look into this little matter," again Sir Leicester mechanically bows in confirmation of the statement, "can give it my fair and full attention. Now, I won't allude to conspiring to extort money, or anything of that sort, because we are men and women of the world here, and our object is to make things pleasant. But I tell you what I *do* wonder at; I am surprised that you should think of making a noise below in the hall. It was so opposed to your interests. That's what I look at."

"We wanted to get in," pleads Mr. Smallweed.

"Why, of course, you wanted to get in," Mr. Bucket assents with cheerfulness; "but for a old gentleman at your time of life—what I call truly venerable, mind you!—with his wits sharpened, as I have no doubt they are, by the loss of the use of his limbs, which occasions all his animation to mount up into his head—not to consider, that if he don't keep such a business as the present as close as possible it can't be worth a mag[2] to him, is so curious! You see your temper got the better of you; that's where you lost ground," says Mr. Bucket in an argumentative and friendly way.

"I only said I wouldn't go, without one of the servants came up to Sir Leicester Dedlock," returns Mr. Smallweed.

"That's it! That's where your temper got the better of you. Now, you keep it under another time, and you'll make money by it. Shall I ring for them to carry you down?"

"When are we to hear more of this?" Mrs. Chadband sternly demands.

"Bless your heart for a true woman! Always curious, your delightful sex is!" replies Mr. Bucket, with gallantry. "I shall have the pleasure of giving you a call to-morrow or next day—not forgetting Mr. Smallweed and his proposal of two fifty."

"Five hundred!" exclaims Mr. Smallweed.

"All right! Nominally five hundred"; Mr. Bucket has his hand on the bell-rope; "*shall* I wish you good day for the present, on the part of myself and the gentleman of the house?" he asks, in an insinuating tone.

Nobody having the hardihood to object to his doing so, he does it, and the party retire as they came up. Mr. Bucket follows them to the door; and returning, says with an air of serious business:

"Sir Leicester Dedlock, Baronet, it's for you to consider whether or not to buy this up. I should recommend, on the whole, it's being bought up myself; and I think it may be bought pretty cheap. You see, that little pickled cowcumber of a Mrs. Snagsby had been used by all sides of the speculation, and has done a deal more harm in bringing odds and ends together than if she had meant it. Mr. Tulkinghorn, deceased, he held all these horses in his hand, and could have drove 'em his own way, I haven't a doubt; but he was fetched off the box head-foremost, and now they have got their legs over the traces, and are all dragging and pulling their own ways. So it is, and such is life. The cat's away, and the mice they play; the frost breaks up, and the water runs. Now, with regard to the party to be apprehended."

Sir Leicester seems to wake, though his eyes have been wide open; and he looks intently at Mr. Bucket, as Mr. Bucket refers to his watch.

"The party to be apprehended is now in this house," proceeds Mr. Bucket, putting up his watch with a steady hand, and with rising spirits, "and I'm about to take her into custody in your presence. Sir Leicester Dedlock, Baronet, don't you say a word, nor yet stir. There'll be no noise, and no disturbance at all. I'll come back in the course of the evening, if agreeable to you, and endeavour to

2. Halfpenny.

meet your wishes respecting this unfortunate family matter, and the nobbiest[3] way of keeping it quiet. Now, Sir Leicester Dedlock, Baronet, don't you be nervous on account of the apprehension at present coming off. You shall see the whole case clear, from first to last."

Mr. Bucket rings, goes to the door, briefly whispers Mercury, shuts the door, and stands behind it with his arms folded. After a suspense of a minute or two, the door slowly opens, and a French woman enters. Mademoiselle Hortense.

The moment she is in the room, Mr. Bucket claps the door to, and puts his back against it. The suddenness of the noise occasions her to turn; and then, for the first time, she sees Sir Leicester Dedlock in his chair.

"I ask you pardon," she mutters hurriedly. "They tell me there was no one here."

Her step towards the door brings her front to front with Mr. Bucket. Suddenly a spasm shoots across her face, and she turns deadly pale.

"This is my lodger, Sir Leicester Dedlock," says Mr. Bucket, nodding at her. "This foreign young woman has been my lodger for some weeks back."

"What do Sir Leicester care for that, you think, my angel?" returns Mademoiselle, in a jocular strain.

"Why, my angel," returns Mr. Bucket, "we shall see."

Mademoiselle Hortense eyes him with a scowl upon her tight face, which gradually changes into a smile of scorn. "You are very mysterious. Are you drunk?"

"Tolerable sober, my angel," returns Mr. Bucket.

"I come from arriving at this so detestable house with your wife. Your wife have left me, since some minutes. They tell me downstairs that your wife is here. I come here, and your wife is not here. What is the intention of this fool's play, say then?" Mademoiselle demands, with her arms composedly crossed, but with something in her dark cheek beating like a clock.

Mr. Bucket merely shakes the finger at her.

"Ah, my God, you are an unhappy idiot!" cries Mademoiselle, with a toss of her head and a laugh.—"Leave me to pass downstairs, great pig." With a stamp of her foot, and a menace.

"Now, Mademoiselle," says Mr. Bucket, in a cool determined way, "you go and sit down upon that sofy."

"I will not sit down upon nothing," she replies, with a shower of nods.

"Now, Mademoiselle," repeats Mr. Bucket, making no demonstration, except with the finger; "you sit down upon that sofy."

"Why?"

3. Smartest or best possible.

"Because I take you into custody on a charge of murder, and you don't need to be told it. Now, I want to be polite to one of your sex and a foreigner, if I can. If I can't, I must be rough; and there's rougher ones outside. What I am to be, depends on you. So I recommend you, as a friend, afore another half a blessed moment has passed over your head, to go and sit down upon that sofy."

Mademoiselle complies, saying in a concentrated voice, while that something in her cheek beats fast and hard, "You are a Devil."

"Now, you see," Mr. Bucket proceeds approvingly, "you're comfortable, and conducting yourself as I should expect a foreign young woman of your sense to do. So I'll give you a piece of advice, and it's this, Don't you talk too much. You're not expected to say anything here, and you can't keep too quiet a tongue in your head. In short, the less you Parlay, the better you know." Mr. Bucket is very complacent over this French explanation.

Mademoiselle, with that tigerish expansion of the mouth, and her black eyes darting fire upon him, sits upright on the sofa in a rigid state, with her hands clenched—and her feet too, one might suppose—muttering, "O, you Bucket, you are a Devil!"

"Now, Sir Leicester Dedlock, Baronet," says Mr. Bucket, and from this time forth the finger never rests, "this young woman, my lodger, was her Ladyship's maid at the time I have mentioned to you; and this young woman, besides being extraordinary vehement and passionate against her Ladyship after being discharged——"

"Lie!" cries Mademoiselle. "I discharge myself."

"Now, why don't you take my advice?" returns Mr. Bucket, in an impressive, almost in an imploring tone. "I'm surprised at the indiscreetness you commit. You'll say something that'll be used against you, you know. You're sure to come to it. Never you mind what I say till it's given in evidence. It's not addressed to you."

"Discharge, too!" cries Mademoiselle, furiously, "by her Ladyship! Eh, my faith, a pretty Ladyship! Why, I r-r-r-ruin my character by remaining with a Ladyship so infame!"

"Upon my soul I wonder at you!" Mr. Bucket remonstrates. "I thought the French were a polite nation, I did, really. Yet to hear a female going on like that, before Sir Leicester Dedlock, Baronet!"

"He is a poor abused!" cries Mademoiselle. "I spit upon his house, upon his name, upon his imbecility," all of which she makes the carpet represent. "Oh, that he is a great man! O yes, superb! O Heaven! Bah!"

"Well, Sir Leicester Dedlock," proceeds Mr. Bucket, "this intemperate foreigner also angrily took it into her head that she had established a claim upon Mr. Tulkinghorn, deceased, by attending on the occasion I told you of, at his chambers; though she was liberally paid for her time and trouble."

"Lie!" cries Mademoiselle. "I ref-use his money alltogezzer."

("If you *will* Parlay, you know," says Mr. Bucket, parenthetically, "you must take the consequences.) Now, whether she became my lodger, Sir Leicester Dedlock, with any deliberate intention then of doing this deed and blinding me, I give no opinion on; but she lived in my house, in that capacity, at the time that she was hovering about the chambers of the deceased Mr. Tulkinghorn with a view to a wrangle, and likewise persecuting and half frightening the life out of an unfortunate stationer."

"Lie!" cries Mademoiselle. "All lie!"

"The murder was committed, Sir Leicester Dedlock, Baronet, and you know under what circumstances. Now, I beg of you to follow me close with your attention for a minute or two. I was sent for, and the case was entrusted to me. I examined the place, and the body, and the papers, and everything. From information I received (from a clerk in the same house) I took George into custody, as having been seen hanging about there, on the night, and at very nigh the time, of the murder; also, as having been overheard in high words with the deceased on former occasions—even threatening him, as the witness made out. If you ask me, Sir Leicester Dedlock, whether from the first I believed George to be the murderer, I tell you candidly No; but he might be, notwithstanding; and there was enough against him to make it my duty to take him, and get him kept under remand. Now, observe!"

As Mr. Bucket bends forward in some excitement—for him—and inaugurates what he is going to say with one ghostly beat of his forefinger in the air, Mademoiselle Hortense fixes her black eyes upon him with a dark frown, and sets her dry lips closely and firmly together.

"I went home, Sir Leicester Dedlock, Baronet, at night, and found this young woman having supper with my wife, Mrs. Bucket. She had made a mighty show of being fond of Mrs. Bucket from her first offering herself as our lodger, but that night she made more than ever—in fact, overdid it. Likewise she overdid her respect, and all that, for the lamented memory of the deceased Mr. Tulkinghorn. By the living Lord it flashed upon me, as I sat opposite to her at the table and saw her with a knife in her hand, that she had done it!"

Mademoiselle is hardly audible, in straining through her teeth and lips the words, "You are a Devil."

"Now where," pursues Mr. Bucket, "had she been on the night of the murder? She had been to the theayter. (She really was there, I have since found, both before the deed and after it.) I knew I had an artful customer to deal with, and that proof would be very difficult; and I laid a trap for her—such a trap as I never laid yet, and such a ventur as I never made yet. I worked it out in my mind while I was talking to her at supper. When I went up-stairs to bed, our house being small and this young woman's eyes sharp, I stuffed the sheet into Mrs. Bucket's mouth that she shouldn't say a word of surprise, and told her all about it.—My dear, don't you give your mind to that again, or I shall link your feet together at the ankles." Mr. Bucket, breaking off, has made a noiseless descent upon Mademoiselle, and laid his heavy hand upon her shoulder.

"What is the matter with you now?" she asks him.

"Don't you think any more," returns Mr. Bucket, with admonitory finger, "of throwing yourself out of window. That's about what's the matter with me. Come! Just take my arm. You needn't get up; I'll sit down by you. Now take my arm, will you? I'm a married man, you know; you're acquainted with my wife. Just take my arm."

Vainly endeavouring to moisten those dry lips, with a painful sound, she struggles with herself and complies.

"Now we're all right again. Sir Leicester Dedlock, Baronet, this case could never have been the case it is, but for Mrs. Bucket, who is a woman in fifty thousand—in a hundred and fifty thousand! To throw this young woman off her guard, I have never set foot in our house since; though I've communicated with Mrs. Bucket, in the baker's loaves and in the milk, as often as required. My whispered words to Mrs. Bucket, when she had the sheet in her mouth, were, 'My dear, can you throw her off continually with natural accounts of my suspicions against George, and this, and that, and t'other? Can you do without rest, and keep watch upon her, night and day? Can you undertake to say, She shall do nothing without my knowledge, she shall be my prisoner without suspecting it, she shall no more escape from me than from death, and her life shall be my life, and her soul my soul, till I have got her, if she did this murder?' Mrs. Bucket says to me, as well as she could speak, on account of the sheet, 'Bucket, I can!' And she has acted up to it glorious!"

"Lies!" Mademoiselle interposes. "All lies, my friend!"

"Sir Leicester Dedlock, Baronet, how did my calculations come out under these circumstances! When I calculated that this impetuous young woman would overdo it in new directions, was I wrong or right? I was right. What does she try to do? Don't let it give you a turn! To throw the murder on her Ladyship!"

Sir Leicester rises from his chair, and staggers down again.

"And she got encouragement in it from hearing that I was always here, which was done a'purpose. Now, open that pocket-book of mine, Sir Leicester Dedlock, if I may take the liberty of throwing it towards you, and look at the letters sent to me, each with the two words, LADY DEDLOCK, in it. Open the one directed to yourself, which I stopped this very morning, and read the three words, LADY DEDLOCK, MURDERESS, in it. These letters have been falling about like a shower of lady-birds. What do you say now to Mrs. Bucket, from her spy-place, having seen them all written by this young woman? What do you say to Mrs. Bucket having, within this half-hour, secured the corresponding ink and paper, fellow half-sheets and what not? What do you say to Mrs. Bucket having watched the posting of 'em every one by this young woman, Sir Leicester Dedlock, Baronet?" Mr. Bucket asks, triumphant in his admiration of his lady's genius.

Two things are especially observable, as Mr. Bucket proceeds to a conclusion. First, that he seems imperceptibly to establish a dreadful right of property in Mademoiselle. Secondly, that the very atmosphere she breathes seems to narrow and contract about her, as if a close net, or a pall, were being drawn nearer and yet nearer around her breathless figure.

"There is no doubt that her Ladyship was on the spot at the eventful period," says Mr. Bucket; "and my foreign friend here saw her, I believe, from the upper part of the staircase. Her Ladyship and George and my foreign friend were all pretty close on one another's heels. But that don't signify any more, so I'll not go into it. I found the wadding of the pistol with which the deceased Mr. Tulkinghorn was shot. It was a bit of the printed description of your home at Chesney Wold. Not much in that, you'll say, Sir Leicester Dedlock, Baronet. No. But when my foreign friend here is so thoroughly off her guard as to think it a safe time to tear up the rest of that leaf, and when Mrs. Bucket puts the pieces together and finds the wadding wanting, it begins to look like Queer Street."[4]

"These are very long lies," Mademoiselle interposes. "You prose great deal. Is it that you have almost all finished, or are you speaking always?"

"Sir Leicester Dedlock, Baronet," proceeds Mr. Bucket, who delights in a full title, and does violence to himself when he dispenses with any fragment of it, "the last point in the case which I am now going to mention, shows the necessity of patience in our business, and never doing a thing in a hurry. I watched this young woman yesterday, without her knowledge, when she was looking at the funeral, in company with my wife, who planned to take her there; and I had so much to convict her, and I saw such an expression in her face, and my mind so rose against her malice towards her Ladyship, and the time was altogether such a time for bringing down what you may call retribution upon her, that if I had been a younger hand with less experience, I should have taken her, certain. Equally, last night, when her Ladyship, as is so universally admired I am sure, come home, looking—why, Lord! a man might almost

4. A legendary street where people in difficulties are supposed to reside.

say like Venus rising from the ocean, it was so unpleasant and inconsistent to think of her being charged with a murder of which she was innocent, that I felt quite to want to put an end to the job. What should I have lost? Sir Leicester Dedlock, Baronet, I should have lost the weapon. My prisoner here proposed to Mrs. Bucket, after the departure of the funeral, that they should go, per bus, a little ways into the country, and take tea at a very decent house of entertainment. Now, near that house of entertainment there's a piece of water. At tea, my prisoner got up to fetch her pocket-handkercher from the bed-room where the bonnets was; she was rather a long time gone, and came back a little out of wind. As soon as they came home this was reported to me by Mrs. Bucket, along with her observations and suspicions. I had the piece of water dragged by moonlight, in presence of a couple of our men, and the pocket-pistol was brought up before it had been there half-a-dozen hours. Now, my dear, put your arm a little further through mine, and hold it steady, and I sha'n't hurt you!"

In a trice Mr. Bucket snaps a handcuff on her wrist. "That's one," says Mr. Bucket. "Now the other, darling. Two, and all told!"

He rises; she rises too. "Where," she asks him, darkening her large eyes until their drooping lids almost conceal them—and yet they stare, "where is your false, your treacherous and cursed wife?"

"She's gone forrard to the Police Office," returns Mr. Bucket. "You'll see her there, my dear."

"I would like to kiss her!" exclaims Mademoiselle Hortense panting tigress-like.

"You'd bite her, I suspect," says Mr. Bucket.

"I would!" making her eyes very large. "I would love to tear her, limb from limb."

"Bless you, darling," says Mr. Bucket, with the greatest composure; "I'm fully prepared to hear that. Your sex have such a surprising animosity against one another, when you do differ. You don't mind me half so much, do you?"

"No. Though you are a Devil still."

"Angel and devil by turns, eh?" cries Mr. Bucket. "But I am in my regular employment, you must consider. Here! Let me put your shawl tidy. I've been lady's maid to a good many before now. Anything wanting to the bonnet? There's a cab at the door."

Mademoiselle Hortense, casting an indignant eye at the glass, shakes herself perfectly neat in one shake, and looks, to do her justice, uncommonly genteel.

"Listen then, my angel," says she, after several sarcastic nods. "You are very spiritual. But can you re-store him back to life?"

Mr. Bucket answers "Not exactly."

"That is droll. Listen yet one time. You are very spiritual. Can you make a honourable lady of Her?"

"Don't be so malicious," says Mr. Bucket.

"Or a haughty gentleman of *Him?*" cries Mademoiselle, referring to Sir Leicester with ineffable disdain. "Eh! O then regard him! The poor infant! Ha! ha! ha!"

"Come, come, why this is worse Parlaying than the other," says Mr. Bucket. "Come along!"

"You cannot do these things? Then you can do as you please with me. It is but the death, it is all the same. Let us go, my angel. Adieu you old man, grey. I pity you, and I des-pise you!"

With these last words, she snaps her teeth together, as if her mouth closed with a spring. It is impossible to describe how Mr. Bucket gets her out, but he accomplishes that feat in a manner peculiar to himself; enfolding and pervading her like a cloud, and hovering away with her as if he were a homely Jupiter,[5] and she the object of his affections.

Sir Leicester, left alone, remains in the same attitude as though he were still listening, and his attention were still occupied. At length he gazes round the empty room, and finding it deserted, rises unsteadily to his feet, pushes back his chair, and walks a few steps, supporting himself by the table. Then he stops; and, with more of those inarticulate sounds, lifts up his eyes and seems to stare at something.

Heaven knows what he sees. The green, green woods of Chesney Wold, the noble house, the pictures of his forefathers, strangers defacing them, officers of police coarsely handling his most precious heir-looms, thousands of fingers pointing at him, thousands of faces sneering at him. But if such shadows flit before him to his bewilderment, there is one other shadow which he can name with something like distinctness even yet, and to which alone he addresses his tearing of his white hair, and his extended arms.

It is she, in association with whom, saving that she has been for years a main fibre of the root of his dignity and pride, he has never had a selfish thought. It is she whom he has loved, admired, honoured, and set up for the world to respect. It is she who, at the core of all the constrained formalities and conventionalities of his life, has been a stock of living tenderness and love, susceptible as nothing else is of being struck with the agony he feels. He sees her, almost to the exclusion of himself; and cannot bear to look upon her cast down from the high place she has graced so well.

5. Identified with Zeus, the Greek god of the heavens, who assumed various guises in pursuing *objects of his affections* such as the maiden Io, whom he visited in the form of a dark *cloud*.

And, even to the point of his sinking on the ground, oblivious of his suffering, he can yet pronounce her name with something like distinctness in the midst of those intrusive sounds, and in a tone of mourning and compassion rather than reproach.

Chapter LV

FLIGHT

Inspector Bucket of the Detective has not yet struck his great blow, as just now chronicled, but is yet refreshing himself with sleep preparatory to his field-day, when, through the night and along the freezing wintry roads, a chaise and pair comes out of Lincolnshire, making its way towards London.

Railroads shall soon traverse all this country, and with a rattle and a glare the engine and train shall shoot like a meteor over the wide night-landscape, turning the moon paler; but, as yet,[1] such things are non-existent in these parts, though not wholly unexpected. Preparations are afoot, measurements are made, ground is staked out. Bridges are begun, and their not yet united piers desolately look at one another over roads and streams, like brick and mortar couples with an obstacle to their union; fragments of embankments are thrown up, and left as precipices with torrents of rusty carts and barrows tumbling over them; tripods of tall poles appear on hilltops, where there are rumours of tunnels; everything looks chaotic, and abandoned in fell hopelessness. Along the freezing roads, and through the night, the post-chaise makes its way without a railroad on its mind.

Mrs. Rouncewell, so many years housekeeper at Chesney Wold, sits within the chaise; and by her side sits Mrs. Bagnet with her grey cloak and umbrella. The old girl would prefer the bar in front, as being exposed to the weather, and a primitive sort of perch more in accordance with her usual course of travelling; but Mrs. Rouncewell is too thoughtful of her comfort to admit of her proposing it. The old lady cannot make enough of the old girl. She sits, in her stately manner, holding her hand, and, regardless of its roughness, puts it often to her lips, "You are a mother, my dear soul," says she many times, "and you found out my George's mother!"

"Why, George," returns Mrs. Bagnet, "was always free with me, ma'am, and when he said at our house to my Woolwich, that of all the things my Woolwich could have to think of when he grew to be a man, the comfortablest would be that he had never brought a sorrowful line to his mother's face, or turned a hair of her head

1. According to T. W. Hill, these details suggest that the story is set in the late 1830's just before the development of railways in Lincolnshire in the 1840's.

grey, then I felt sure, from his way, that something fresh had brought his own mother into his mind. I had often known him to say to me, in past times, that he had behaved bad to her."

"Never, my dear!" returns Mrs. Rouncewell, bursting into tears. "My blessing on him, never! He was always fond of me, and loving to me, was my George! But he had a bold spirit, and he ran a little wild, and went for a soldier. And I know he waited at first, in letting us know about himself, till he should rise to be an officer; and when he didn't rise, I know he considered himself beneath us, and wouldn't be a disgrace to us. For he had a lion heart, had my George, always from a baby!"

The old lady's hands stray about her as of yore, while she recalls, all in a tremble, what a likely lad, what a fine lad, what a gay good-humoured clever lad he was; how they all took to him, down at Chesney Wold; how Sir Leicester took to him when he was a young gentleman; how the dogs took to him; how even the people, who had been angry with him, forgave him the moment he was gone, poor boy. And now to see him after all, and in a prison too! And the broad stomacher[2] heaves, and the quaint upright old-fashioned figure bends under its load of affectionate distress.

Mrs. Bagnet, with the instinctive skill of a good warm heart, leaves the old housekeeper to her emotions for a little while—not without passing the back of her hand across her own motherly eyes—and presently chirps up in her cheery manner:

"So I says to George when I goes to call him in to tea (he pretended to be smoking his pipe outside), 'What ails you this afternoon, George, for gracious sake? I have seen all sorts, and I have seen you pretty often in season and out of season, abroad and at home, and I never see you so melancholly penitent.' 'Why, Mrs. Bagnet,' says George, 'it's because I *am* melancholly and penitent both, this afternoon, that you see me so,' 'What have you done, old fellow?' I says. 'Why, Mrs. Bagnet,' says George, shaking his head, 'what I have done has been done this many a long year, and is best not tried to be undone now. If I ever get to Heaven, it won't be for being a good son to a widowed mother; I say no more.' Now, ma'am, when George says to me that it's best not tried to be undone now, I have my thoughts as I have often had before, and I draw it out of George how he comes to have such things on him that afternoon. Then George tells me that he has seen by chance, at the lawyer's office, a fine old lady that has brought his mother plain before him; and he runs on about that old lady till he quite forgets himself, and paints her picter to me as she used to be, years upon years back. So I says to George when he has done, who is this

2. Ornamental vest covering chest and stomach.

old lady he has seen? And George tell me it's Mrs. Rouncewell, housekeeper for more than half a century to the Dedlock family down at Chesney Wold in Lincolnshire. George has frequently told me before that he's a Lincolnshire man, and I says to my old Lignum that night, 'Lignum, that's his mother for five-and-for-ty pound!' "

All this Mrs. Bagnet now relates for the twentieth time at least within the last four hours. Trilling it out, like a kind of bird; with a pretty high note, that it may be audible to the deaf old lady above the hum of the wheels.

"Bless you, and thank you," says Mrs. Rouncewell. "Bless you and thank you, my worthy soul!"

"Dear heart!" cries Mrs. Bagnet, in the most natural manner. "No thanks to me, I am sure. Thanks to yourself, ma'am, for being so ready to pay 'em! And mind once more, ma'am, what you had best do on finding George to be your own son, is, to make him—for your sake—have every sort of help to put himself in the right, and clear himself of a charge of which he is as innocent as you or me. It won't do to have truth and justice on his side; he must have law and lawyers," exclaims the old girl, apparently persuaded that the latter form a separate establishment, and have dissolved partnership with truth and justice for ever and a day.

"He shall have," says Mrs. Rouncewell, "all the help that can be got for him in the world, my dear. I will spend all I have, and thankfully, to procure it. Sir Leicester will do his best, the whole family will do their best. I—I know something, my dear; and will make my own appeal, as his mother parted from him all these years, and finding him in a jail at last."

The extreme disquietude of the old housekeeper's manner in saying this, her broken words, and her wringing of her hands, make a powerful impression on Mrs. Bagnet, and would astonish her but that she refers them all to her sorrow for her son's condition. And yet Mrs. Bagnet wonders, too, why Mrs. Rouncewell should murmur so distractedly, "My Lady, my Lady, my Lady!" over and over again.

The frosty night wears away, and the dawn breaks, and the post-chaise comes rolling on through the early mist, like the ghost of a chaise departed. It has plenty of spectral company, in ghosts of trees and hedges, slowly vanishing and giving place to the realities of day. London reached, the travellers alight; the old housekeeper in great tribulation and confusion; Mrs. Bagnet, quite fresh and collected—as she would be, if her next point, with no new equipage and outfit, were the Cape of Good Hope, the Island of Ascension, Hong Kong, or any other military station.

But when they set out for the prison where the trooper is confined, the old lady has managed to draw about her, with her lavender-coloured dress, much of the staid calmness which is its usual accompaniment. A wonderfully grave, precise, and handsome piece of old china she looks; though her heart beats fast, and her stomacher is ruffled, more than even the remembrance of this wayward son has ruffled it these many years.

Approaching the cell, they find the door opening and a warder in the act of coming out. The old girl promptly makes a sign of entreaty to him to say nothing; assenting, with a nod, he suffers them to enter as he shuts the door.

So George, who is writing at his table, supposing himself to be alone, does not raise his eyes, but remains absorbed. The old housekeeper looks at him, and those wandering hands of hers are quite enough for Mrs. Bagnet's confirmation; even if she could see the mother and the son together, knowing what she knows, and doubt their relationship.

Not a rustle of the housekeeper's dress, not a gesture, not a word betrays her. She stands looking at him as he writes on, all unconscious, and only her fluttering hands give utterance to her emotions. But they are eloquent; very, very eloquent. Mrs. Bagnet understands them. They speak of gratitude, of joy, of grief, of hope; of inextinguishable affection, cherished with no return since this stalwart man was a stripling; of a better son loved less, and this son loved so fondly and so proudly; and they speak in such touching language, that Mrs. Bagnet's eyes brim up with tears, and they run glistening down her sun-browned face.

"George Rouncewell! O, my dear child, turn and look at me!"

The trooper starts up, clasps his mother round the neck, and falls down on his knees before her. Whether in a late repentance, whether in the first association that comes back upon him, he puts his hands together as a child does when it says its prayers, and raising them towards her breast, bows down his head, and cries.

"My George, my dearest son! Always my favourite, and my favourite still, where have you been these cruel years and years? Grown such a man too, grown such a fine strong man. Grown so like what I knew he must be, if it pleased God he was alive!"

She can ask, and he can answer, nothing connected for a time. All that time the old girl, turned away, leans one arm against the whitened wall, leans her honest forehead upon it, wipes her eyes with her serviceable grey cloak, and quite enjoys herself like the best of old girls as she is.

"Mother," says the trooper, when they are more composed; "forgive me first of all, for I know my need of it."

Forgive him! She does it with all her heart and soul. She always has done it. She tells him how she has had it written in her will, these many years, that he was her beloved son George. She has never believed any ill of him, never. If she had died without this happiness—and she is an old woman now, and can't look to live very long—she would have blessed him with her last breath, if she had had her senses, as her beloved son George.

"Mother, I have been an undutiful trouble to you, and I have my reward; but of late years I have had a kind of a glimmering of a purpose in me, too. When I left home I didn't care much, mother—I am afraid not a great deal—for leaving; and went away and 'listed, harum-scarum, making believe to think that I cared for nobody, no not I, and that nobody cared for me."[3]

The trooper has dried his eyes, and put away his handkerchief; but there is an extraordinary contrast between his habitual manner of expressing himself and carrying himself, and the softened tone in which he speaks, interrupted occasionally by a half-stifled sob.

"So I wrote a line home, mother, as you too well know, to say I had 'listed under another name, and I went abroad. Abroad, at one time I thought I would write home next year, when I might be better off; and when that year was out, I thought I would write home next year, when I might be better off; and when that year was out again, perhaps I didn't think much about it. So on, from year to year, through a service of ten years, till I began to get older, and to ask myself why should I ever write?"

"I don't find any fault, child—but not to ease my mind, George? Not a word to your loving mother, who was growing older, too?"

This almost overturns the trooper afresh; but he sets himself up with a great, rough, sounding clearance of his throat.

"Heaven forgive me, mother, but I thought there would be small consolation then in hearing anything about *me*. There were you, respected and esteemed. There was my brother, as I read in chance north-country papers now and then, rising to be prosperous and famous. There was I, a dragoon, roving, unsettled, not self-made like him, but self-unmade—all my earlier advantages thrown away, all my little learning unlearnt, nothing picked up but what unfitted me for most things that I could think of. What business had *I* to make myself known? After letting all that time go by me, what good could come of it? The worst was past with you, mother. I knew by that time (being a man) how you had mourned for me, and wept for me, and prayed for me; and the pain was over, or was softened down, and I was better in your mind as it was."

The old lady sorrowfully shakes her head; and taking one of his powerful hands, lays it lovingly upon her shoulder.

3. From "The Miller of the Dee," a song in Isaac Bickerstaff's musical comedy *Love in a Village* (1763).

"No, I don't say that it was so, mother, but that I made it out to be so. I said just now what good could come of it? Well, my dear mother, some good might have come of it to myself—and there was the meanness of it. You would have sought me out; you would have purchased my discharge; you would have taken me down to Chesney Wold; you would have brought me and my brother and my brother's family together; you would all have considered anxiously how to do something for me, and set me up as a respectable civilian. But how could any of you feel sure of me, when I couldn't so much as feel sure of myself? How could you help regarding as an incumbrance and a discredit to you, an idle dragooning chap, who was an incumbrance and a discredit to himself, excepting under discipline? How could I look my brother's children in the face, and pretend to set them an example—I, the vagabond boy, who had run away from home, and been the grief and unhappiness of my mother's life? 'No, George.' Such were my words, mother, when I passed this in review before me: 'You have made your bed. Now lie upon it.' "

Mrs. Rouncewell, drawing up her stately form, shakes her head at the old girl with a swelling pride upon her, as much as to say, "I told you so!" The old girl relieves her feelings, and testifies her interest in the conversation, by giving the trooper a great poke between the shoulders with her umbrella; this action she afterwards repeats, at intervals, in a species of affectionate lunacy: never failing, after the administration of each of these remonstrances, to resort to the whitened wall and the grey cloak again.

"This was the way I brought myself to think, mother, that my best amends was to lie upon that bed I had made, and die upon it. And I should have done it (though I have been to see you more than once down at Chesney Wold, when you little thought of me), but for my old comrade's wife here, who I find has been too many for me. But I thank her for it. I thank you for it, Mrs. Bagnet, with all my heart and might."

To which Mrs. Bagnet responds with two pokes.

And now the old lady impresses upon her son George, her own dear recovered boy, her joy and pride, the light of her eyes, the happy close of her life, and every fond name she can think of, that he must be governed by the best advice obtainable by money and influence; that he must yield up his case to the greatest lawyers that can be got; that he must act, in this serious plight, as he shall be advised to act; and must not be self-willed, however right, but must promise to think only of his poor old mother's anxiety and suffering until he is released, or he will break her heart.

"Mother, 'tis little enough to consent to," returns the trooper, stopping her with a kiss; "tell me what I shall do, and I'll make a late beginning, and do it. Mrs. Bagnet, you'll take care of my mother, I know?"

A very hard poke from the old girl's umbrella.

"If you'll bring her acquainted with Mr. Jarndyce and Miss Summerson, she will find them of her way of thinking, and they will give her the best advice and assistance."

"And, George," says the old lady, "we must send with all haste for your brother. He is a sensible sound man as they tell me—out in the world beyond Chesney Wold, my dear, though I don't know much of it myself—and will be of great service."

"Mother," returns the trooper, "is it too soon to ask a favour?"

"Surely not, my dear."

"Then grant me this one great favour. Don't let my brother know."

"Not know what, my dear?"

"Not know of me. In fact, mother, I can't bear it; I can't make up my mind to it. He has proved himself so different from me, and has done so much to raise himself while I've been soldiering, that I haven't brass enough in my composition, to see him in this place and under this charge. How could a man like him be expected to have any pleasure in such a discovery? It's impossible. No, keep my secret from him, mother; do me a greater kindness than I deserve, and keep my secret from my brother, of all men."

"But not always, dear George?"

"Why, mother, perhaps not for good and all—though I may come to ask that too—but keep it now, I do entreat you. If it's ever broke to him that his Rip of a brother[4] has turned up, I could wish," says the trooper, shaking his head very doubtfully, "to break it myself; and be governed, as to advancing or retreating, by the way in which he seems to take it."

As he evidently has a rooted feeling on this point, and as the depth of it is recognised in Mrs. Bagnet's face, his mother yields her implicit assent to what he asks. For this he thanks her heartily.

"In all other respects, my dear mother, I'll be as tractable and obedient as you can wish; on this one alone, I stand out. So now I am ready even for the lawyers. I have been drawing up," he glances at his writing on the table, "an exact account of what I knew of the deceased, and how I came to be involved in this unfortunate affair. It's entered, plain and regular, like an orderly-book; not a word in it but what's wanted for the facts. I did intend to read it, straight on end, whensoever I was called upon to say anything in my defence. I

4. Cf. Irving's story, *Rip Van Winkle*.

hope I may be let to do it still; but I have no longer a will of my own in this case, and whatever is said or done, I give my promise not to have any."

Matters being brought to this so far satisfactory pass, and time being on the wane, Mrs. Bagnet proposes a departure. Again and again the old lady hangs upon her son's neck, and again and again the trooper holds her to his broad chest.

"Where are you going to take my mother, Mrs. Bagnet?"

"I am going to the town house, George, the family house. I have some business there, that must be looked to directly," Mrs. Rouncewell answers.

"Will you see my mother safe there, in a coach, Mrs. Bagnet? But of course I know you will. Why should I ask it!"

Why indeed, Mrs. Bagnet expresses with the umbrella.

"Take her, my old friend, and take my gratitude along with you. Kisses to Quebec and Malta, love to my godson, a hearty shake of the hand to Lignum, and this for yourself, and I wish it was ten thousand pound in gold, my dear!" So saying, the trooper puts his lips to the old girl's tanned forehead, and the door shuts upon him in his cell.

No entreaties on the part of the good old housekeeper will induce Mrs. Bagnet to retain the coach for her own conveyance home. Jumping out cheerfully at the door of the Dedlock mansion, and handing Mrs. Rouncewell up the steps, the old girl shakes hands and trudges off; arriving soon afterwards in the bosom of the Bagnet family, and falling to washing the greens, as if nothing had happened.

My Lady is in that room in which she held her last conference with the murdered man, and is sitting where she sat that night, and is looking at the spot where he stood upon the hearth, studying her so leisurely, when a tap comes at the door. Who is it? Mrs. Rouncewell. What has brought Mrs. Rouncewell to town so unexpectedly?

"Trouble, my Lady. Sad trouble. O, my Lady, may I beg a word with you?"

What new occurrence is it that makes this tranquil old woman tremble so? Far happier than her Lady, as her Lady has often thought, why does she falter in this manner, and look at her with such strange mistrust?

"What is the matter? Sit down and take your breath."

"O, my Lady, my Lady. I have found my son—my youngest, who went away for a soldier so long ago. And he is in prison."

"For debt?"

"O no, my Lady; I would have paid any debt, and joyful."

"For what is he in prison then?"

"Charged with a murder, my Lady, of which he is as innocent as—as I am. Accused of the murder of Mr. Tulkinghorn."

What does she mean by this look and this imploring gesture? Why does she come so close? What is the letter that she holds?

"Lady Dedlock, my dear Lady, my good Lady, my kind Lady! You must have a heart to feel for me, you must have a heart to forgive me. I was in this family before you were born. I am devoted to it. But think of my dear son wrongfully accused."

"*I* do not accuse him."

"No, my Lady, no. But others do, and he is in prison and in danger. O Lady Dedlock, if you can say but a word to help to clear him, say it!"

What delusion can this be? What power does she suppose is in the person she petitions, to avert this unjust suspicion, if it be unjust? Her Lady's handsome eyes regard her with astonishment, almost with fear.

"My Lady, I came away last night from Chesney Wold to find my son in my old age, and the step upon the Ghost's Walk was so constant and so solemn that I never heard the like in all these years. Night after night, as it has fallen dark, the sound has echoed through your rooms, but last night it was awfullest. And as it fell dark last night, my Lady, I got this letter."

"What letter is it?"

"Hush! Hush!" The housekeeper looks round, and answers in a frightened whisper: "My Lady, I have not breathed a word of it, I don't believe what's written in it, I know it can't be true, I am sure and certain that it is not true. But my son is in danger, and you must have a heart to pity me. If you know of anything that is not known to others, if you have any suspicion, if you have any clue at all, and any reason for keeping it in your own breast, O my dear Lady, think of me, and conquer that reason, and let it be known! This is the most I consider possible. I know you are not a hard lady, but you go your own way always without help, and you are not familiar with your friends; and all who admire you—and all do—as a beautiful and elegant lady, know you to be one far away from themselves, who can't be approached close. My Lady, you may have some proud or angry reasons for disdaining to utter something that you know; if so, pray, O pray, think of a faithful servant whose whole life has been passed in this family which she dearly loves, and relent, and help to clear my son! My Lady, my good Lady," the old housekeeper pleads with genuine simplicity, "I am so humble in my place, and you are by nature so high and distant, that you may not think what I feel for my child; but I feel so much, that I have come here to make so bold as to beg and pray you not to be scornful of us, if you can do us any right or justice at this fearful time!"

Lady Dedlock raises her without one word, until she takes the letter from her hand.

"Am I to read this?"

"When I am gone, my Lady, if you please; and then remembering the most that I consider possible."

"I know of nothing I can do. I know of nothing I reserve, that can affect your son. I have never accused him."

"My Lady, you may pity him the more, under a false accusation, after reading the letter."

The old housekeeper leaves her with the letter in her hand. In truth she is not a hard lady naturally; and the time has been when the sight of the venerable figure sueing to her with such strong earnestness would have moved her to great compassion. But so long accustomed to suppress emotion, and keep down reality; so long schooled for her own purposes, in that destructive school which shuts up the natural feelings of the heart, like flies in amber, and spreads one uniform and dreary gloss over the good and bad, the feeling and the unfeeling, the sensible and the senseless; she has subdued even her wonder until now.

She opens the letter. Spread out upon the paper is a printed account of the discovery of the body, as it lay face downward on the floor, shot through the heart; and underneath is written her own name, with the word Murderess attached.

It falls out of her hand. How long it may have lain upon the ground, she knows not; but it lies where it fell, when a servant stands before her announcing the young man of the name of Guppy. The words have probably been repeated several times, for they are ringing in her head before she begins to understand them.

"Let him come in!"

He comes in. Holding the letter in her hand, which she has taken from the floor, she tries to collect her thoughts. In the eyes of Mr. Guppy she is the same Lady Dedlock, holding the same prepared, proud, chilling state.

"Your Ladyship may not be at first disposed to excuse this visit from one who has never been very welcome to your Ladyship—which he don't complain of, for he is bound to confess that there never has been any particular reason on the face of things, why he should be; but I hope when I mention my motives to your Ladyship, you will not find fault with me," says Mr. Guppy.

"Do so."

"Thank your Ladyship. I ought first to explain to your Ladyship," Mr. Guppy sits on the edge of a chair, and puts his hat on the carpet at his feet, "that Miss Summerson, whose image, as I formerly mentioned to your Ladyship, was at one period of my life imprinted on my art until erased by circumstances over which I had no control, communicated to me, after I had the pleasure of waiting on your Ladyship last, that she particularly wished me to take no steps whatever in any matter at all relating to her. And Miss Summerson's wishes being to me a law (except as connected with circumstances over which I have no control), I consequently never expected to have the distinguished honour of waiting on your Ladyship again."

And yet he is here now, Lady Dedlock moodily reminds him.

"And yet I am here now," Mr. Guppy admits. "My object being to communicate to your Ladyship, under the seal of confidence, why I am here."

He cannot do so, she tells him, too plainly or too briefly.

"Nor can I," Mr. Guppy returns with a sense of injury upon him, "too particularly request your Ladyship to take particular notice that it's no personal affair of mine that brings me here. I have no interested views of my own to serve in coming here. If it was not for my promise to Miss Summerson, and my keeping of it sacred,—I, in point of fact, shouldn't have darkened these doors again, but should have seen 'em further first."

Mr. Guppy considers this a favourable moment for sticking up his hair with both hands.

"Your Ladyship will remember when I mention it, that the last time I was here, I run against a party very eminent in our profession, and whose loss we all deplore. That party certainly did from that time apply himself to cutting in against me in a way that I will call sharp practice, and did make it, at every turn and point, extremely difficult for me to be sure that I hadn't inadvertently led up to something contrairy to Miss Summerson's wishes. Self-praise is no recommendation; but I may say for myself that I am not so bad a man of business neither."

Lady Dedlock looks at him in stern inquiry. Mr. Guppy immediately withdraws his eyes from her face, and looks anywhere else.

"Indeed, it has been made so hard," he goes on, "to have any idea what that party was up to in combination with others, that until the loss which we all deplore, I was gravelled—an expression which your Ladyship, moving in the higher circles, will be so good as to consider tantamount to knocked over. Small likewise—a name by which I refer to another party, a friend of mine that your Ladyship is not acquainted with—got to be so close and double-faced that at times it wasn't easy to keep one's hands off his ed. However, what with the exertion of my humble abilities, and what with the help of a mutual friend by the name of Mr. Tony Weevle (who is of a high aristocratic turn, and has your Ladyship's portrait always hanging up in his room), I have now reasons for an apprehension, as to which I come to put your Ladyship upon your guard. First, will your Ladyship allow me to ask you whether you have had any strange visitors this morning? I don't mean fashionable visitors, but such visitors, for instance, as Miss Barbary's old servant, or as a person without the use of his lower extremities, carried up-stairs similarly to a Guy?"[5]

"No!"

"Then I assure your Ladyship that such visitors have been here, and have been received here. Because I saw them at the door, and waited at the corner of the square till they came out, and took half-an-hour's turn afterwards to avoid them."

"What have I to do with that, or what have you? I do not understand you. What do you mean?"

"Your Ladyship, I come to put you on your guard. There may be no occasion for it. Very well. Then I have only done my best to keep my promise to Miss Summerson. I strongly suspect (from what Small has dropped, and from what we have corkscrewed out of him) that those letters I was to have brought to your Ladyship were not destroyed when I supposed they were. That if there was anything to be blown upon, it *is* blown upon. That the visitors I have alluded to have been here this morning to make money of it. And that the money is made, or making."

Mr. Guppy picks up his hat and rises.

"Your Ladyship, you know best, whether there's anything in what I say, or whether there's nothing. Something or nothing, I have acted up to Miss Summerson's wishes in letting things alone, and in undoing what I had begun to do, as far as possible; that's sufficient for me. In case I should be taking a liberty in putting your Ladyship on your guard when there's no necessity for it, you will endeavour, I should hope, to outlive my presumption, and I shall endeavour to outlive your disapprobation. I now take my farewell of your Ladyship, and assure you that there's no danger of your ever being waited on by me again."

She scarcely acknowledges these parting words by any look; but when he has been gone a little while, she rings her bell.

"Where is Sir Leicester?"

Mercury reports that he is at present shut up in the library, alone.

"Has Sir Leicester had any visitors this morning?"

Several, on business. Mercury proceeds to a description of them, which has been anticipated by Mr. Guppy. Enough; he may go.

So! All is broken down. Her name is in these many mouths, her husband knows his wrongs, her shame will be published—may be spreading while she thinks about it—and in addition to the thunderbolt so long foreseen by her, so unforeseen by him, she is denounced by an invisible accuser as the murderess of her enemy.

5. See p. 329, note 7.

Her enemy he was, and she has often, often, often, wished him dead. Her enemy he is, even in his grave. This dreadful accusation comes upon her, like a new torment at his lifeless hand. And when she recalls how she was secretly at his door that night, and how she may be represented to have sent her favourite girl away, so soon before, merely to release herself from observation, she shudders as if the hangman's hands were at her neck.

She has thrown herself upon the floor, and lies with her hair all wildly scattered, and her face buried in the cushions of a couch. She rises up, hurries to and fro, flings herself down again, and rocks and moans. The horror that is upon her, is unutterable. If she really were the murderess, it could hardly be, for the moment, more intense.

For as her murderous perspective, before the doing of the deed, however subtle the precautions for its commission, would have been closed up by a gigantic dilation of the hateful figure, preventing her from seeing any consequences beyond it; and as those consequences would have rushed in, in an unimagined flood, the moment the figure was laid low—which always happens when a murder is done; so now she sees that when he used to be on the watch before her, and she used to think, "if some mortal stroke would but fall on this old man and take him from my way!" it was but wishing that all he held against her in his hand might be flung to the winds, and chance-sown in many places. So, too, with the wicked relief she has felt in his death. What was his death but the key-stone of a gloomy arch removed, and now the arch begins to fall in a thousand fragments, each crushing and mangling piecemeal!

Thus, a terrible impression steals upon and overshadows her, that from this pursuer, living or dead—obdurate and imperturbable before her in his well-remembered shape, or not more obdurate and imperturbable in his coffin-bed,—there is no escape but in death. Hunted, she flies. The complication of her shame, her dread, remorse, and misery, overwhelms her at its height; and even her strength of self-reliance is overturned and whirled away, like a leaf before a mighty wind.

She hurriedly addresses these lines to her husband, seals, and leaves them on her table.

> "If I am sought for, or accused of, his murder, believe that I am wholly innocent. Believe no other good of me, for I am innocent of nothing else that you have heard, or will hear, laid to my charge. He prepared me, on that fatal night, for his disclosure of my guilt to you. After he had left me, I went out, on pretence of walking in the garden where I sometimes walk, but really to follow him, and make one last petition that he would not protract the dreadful suspense on which I had been racked by him,

you do not know how long, but would mercifully strike next morning.

"I found his house dark and silent. I rang twice at his door, but there was no reply, and I came home.

"I have no home left. I will encumber you no more. May you, in your just resentment, be able to forget the unworthy woman on whom you have wasted a most generous devotion—who avoids you, only with a deeper shame than that with which she hurries from herself—and who writes this last adieu!"

She veils and dresses quickly, leaves all her jewels and her money, listens, goes down-stairs at a moment when the hall is empty, opens and shuts the great door; flutters away in the shrill frosty wind.

Chapter LVI

PURSUIT

Impassive, as behoves its high breeding, the Dedlock town house stares at the other houses in the street of dismal grandeur, and gives no outward sign of anything going wrong within. Carriages rattle, doors are battered at, the world exchanges calls; ancient charmers with skeleton throats, and peachy cheeks that have a rather ghastly bloom upon them seen by daylight, when indeed these fascinating creatures look like Death and the Lady[1] fused together, dazzle the eyes of men. Forth from the frigid Mews[2] come easily swinging carriages guided by short-legged coachmen in flaxen wigs, deep sunk into downy hammer-cloths;[3] and up behind mount luscious Mercuries, bearing sticks of state,[4] and wearing cocked hats broadwise: a spectacle for the Angels.

The Dedlock town house changes not externally, and hours pass before its exalted dulness is disturbed within. But Volumnia the fair, being subject to the prevalent complaint of boredom, and finding that disorder attacking her spirits with some virulence, ventures at length to repair to the library for change of scene. Her gentle tapping at the door producing no response, she opens it and peeps in; seeing no one there, takes possession.

The sprightly Dedlock is reputed, in that grass-grown city of the ancients, Bath, to be stimulated by an urgent curiosity, which impels her on all convenient and inconvenient occasions to sidle about with a golden glass at her eye, peering into objects of every description. Certain it is that she avails herself of the present opportunity of hovering over her kinsman's letters and papers, like a bird;

1. Title of a ballad (often illustrated with woodcuts) popular in the eighteenth century, in which a rich lady pleads with Death to spare her from his summons.
2. See p. 575, note 2.
3. Cloth coverings for the coachman's seat on a well-equipped carriage.
4. Long staffs carried by footmen to protect their employers and for ceremonial purposes.

taking a short peck at this document, and a blink with her head on one side at that document, and hopping about from table to table, with her glass at her eye in an inquisitive and restless manner. In the course of these researches, she stumbles over something; and turning her glass in that direction, sees her kinsman lying on the ground like a felled tree.

Volumnia's pet little scream acquires a considerable augmentation of reality from this surprise, and the house is quickly in commotion. Servants tear up and down stairs, bells are violently rung, doctors are sent for, and Lady Dedlock is sought in all directions, but not found. Nobody has seen or heard her since she last rang her bell. Her letter to Sir Leicester is discovered on her table;—but it is doubtful yet whether he has not received another missive from another world, requiring to be personally answered; and all the living languages, and all the dead, are as one to him.

They lay him down upon his bed, and chafe, and rub, and fan, and put ice to his head, and try every means of restoration. Howbeit, the day has ebbed away, and it is night in his room, before his stertorous breathing lulls, or his fixed eyes show any consciousness of the candle that is occasionally passed before them. But when this change begins, it goes on; and by and by he nods, or moves his eyes, or even his hand, in token that he hears and comprehends.

He fell down, this morning, a handsome stately gentleman; somewhat infirm, but of a fine presence, and with a well-filled face. He lies upon his bed, an aged man with sunken cheeks, the decrepit shadow of himself. His voice was rich and mellow; and he had so long been thoroughly persuaded of the weight and import to mankind of any word he said, that his words really had come to sound as if there were something in them. But now he can only whisper; and what he whispers sounds like what it is—mere jumble and jargon.

His favourite and faithful housekeeper stands at his bedside. It is the first fact he notices, and he clearly derives pleasure from it. After vainly trying to make himself understood in speech, he makes signs for a pencil. So inexpressively, that they cannot at first understand him; it is his old housekeeper who makes out what he wants, and brings him a slate.

After pausing for some time, he slowly scrawls upon it, in a hand that is not his, "Chesney Wold?"

No, she tells him; he is in London. He was taken ill in the library, this morning. Right thankful she is that she happened to come to London, and is able to attend upon him.

"It is not an illness of any serious consequence, Sir Leicester. You will be much better to-morrow, Sir Leicester. All the gentlemen say so." This, with the tears coursing down her fair old face.

After making a survey of the room, and looking with particular attention all round the bed where the doctors stand, he writes, "My Lady."

"My Lady went out, Sir Leicester, before you were taken ill, and don't know of your illness yet."

He points again, in great agitation, at the two words. They all try to quiet him, but he points again with increased agitation. On their looking at one another, not knowing what to say, he takes the slate once more, and writes, "My Lady. For God's sake, where?" And makes an imploring moan.

It is thought better that his old housekeeper should give him Lady Dedlock's letter, the contents of which no one knows or can surmise. She opens it for him, and puts it out for his perusal. Having read it twice by a great effort, he turns it down so that it shall not be seen, and lies moaning. He passes into a kind of relapse, or into a swoon; and it is an hour before he opens his eyes, reclining on his faithful and attached old servant's arm. The doctors know that he is best with her; and, when not actively engaged about him, stand aloof.

The slate comes into requisition again; but the word he wants to write, he cannot remember. His anxiety, his eagerness, and affliction at this pass, are pitiable to behold. It seems as if he must go mad, in the necessity he feels for haste, and the inability under which he labours of expressing to do what, or to fetch whom. He has written the letter B., and there stopped. Of a sudden, in the height of his misery, he puts Mr. before it. The old housekeeper suggests Bucket. Thank Heaven! That's his meaning.

Mr. Bucket is found to be down-stairs, by appointment. Shall he come up?

There is no possibility of misconstruing Sir Leicester's burning wish to see him, or the desire he signifies to have the room cleared of every one but the housekeeper. It is speedily done; and Mr. Bucket appears. Of all men upon earth, Sir Leicester seems fallen from his high estate to place his sole trust and reliance upon this man.

"Sir Leicester Dedlock, Baronet, I'm sorry to see you like this. I hope you'll cheer up. I'm sure you will, on account of the family credit."

Sir Leicester puts her letter in his hand and looks intently in his face while he reads it. A new intelligence comes into Mr. Bucket's eye, as he reads on; with one hook of his finger, while that eye is still glancing over the words, he indicates, "Sir Leicester Dedlock, Baronet, I understand you."

Sir Leicester writes upon the slate. "Full forgiveness. Find——" Mr. Bucket stops his hand.

"Sir Leicester Dedlock, Baronet, I'll find her. But my search after her must be begun out of hand. Not a minute must be lost."

With the quickness of thought, he follows Sir Leicester Dedlock's look towards a little box upon a table.

"Bring it here, Sir Leicester Dedlock, Baronet? Certainly. Open it with one of these here keys? Certainly. The littlest key? *To* be sure. Take the notes out? So I will. Count 'em? That's soon done. Twenty and thirty's fifty, and twenty's seventy, and fifty's one twenty, and forty's one sixty. Take 'em for expenses? That I'll do, and render an account of course. Don't spare money? No, I won't."

The velocity and certainty of Mr. Bucket's interpretation on all these heads is little short of miraculous. Mrs. Rouncewell, who holds the light, is giddy with the swiftness of his eyes and hands, as he starts up, furnished for his journey.

"You're George's mother, old lady; that's about what you are, I believe?" says Mr. Bucket, aside, with his hat already on, and buttoning his coat.

"Yes, sir, I am his distressed mother."

"So I thought, according to what he mentioned to me just now. Well, then, I'll tell you something. You needn't be distressed no more. Your son's all right. Now, don't you begin a-crying; because what you've got to do is to take care of Sir Leicester Dedlock, Baronet, and you won't do that by crying. As to your son, he's all right, I tell you; and he sends his loving duty, and hoping you're the same. He's discharged honourable; that's about what *he* is; with no more imputation on his character than there is on yours, and yours is a tidy one, *I*'ll bet a pound. You may trust me, for I took your son. He conducted himself in a game way, too, on that occasion; and he's a fine-made man, and you're a fine-made old lady, and you're a mother and son, the pair of you, as might be showed for models in a caravan.[5] Sir Leicester Dedlock, Baronet, what you've trusted to me I'll go through with. Don't you be afraid of my turning out of my way, right or left; or taking a sleep, or a wash, or a shave, till I have found what I go in search of. Say everything as is kind and forgiving on your part? Sir Leicester Dedlock, Baronet, I will. And I wish you better, and these family affairs smoothed over—as, Lord! many other such family affairs equally has been, and equally will be, to the end of time."

With this peroration, Mr. Bucket, buttoned up, goes quietly out, looking steadily before him as if he were already piercing the night, in quest of the fugitive.

His first step is to take himself to Lady Dedlock's rooms, and look all over them for any trifling indication that may help him.

5. Wax-work models of eminent persons, carried in caravans, exhibited at travelling shows.

The rooms are in darkness now; and to see Mr. Bucket with a wax-light in his hand, holding it above his head, and taking a sharp mental inventory of the many delicate objects so curiously at variance with himself, would be to see a sight—which nobody *does* see, as he is particular to lock himself in.

"A spicy boudoir this," says Mr. Bucket, who feels in a manner furbished up in his French by the blow of the morning. "Must have cost a sight of money. Rum articles to cut away from, these; she must have been hard put to it!"

Opening and shutting table-drawers, and looking into caskets and jewel-cases, he sees the reflection of himself in various mirrors, and moralises thereon.

"One might suppose I was a moving in the fashionable circles, and getting myself up for Almack's,"[6] says Mr. Bucket. "I begin to think I must be a swell in the Guards, without knowing it."

Ever looking about, he has opened a dainty little chest in an inner drawer. His great hand, turning over some gloves which it can scarcely feel, they are so light and soft within it, comes upon a white handkerchief.

"Hum! Let's have a look at *you*," says Mr. Bucket, putting down the light. "What should *you* be kept by yourself for? What's *your* motive? Are you her Ladyship's property, or somebody else's? You've got a mark upon you, somewheres or another, I suppose?"

He finds it as he speaks, "Esther Summerson."

"Oh!" says Mr. Bucket, pausing, with his finger at his ear. "Come, I'll take *you*."

He completes his observations as quietly and carefully as he has carried them on, leaves everything else precisely as he found it, glides away after some five minutes in all, and passes into the street. With a glance upward at the dimly lighted windows of Sir Leicester's room, he sets off, full swing, to the nearest coach-stand, picks out the horse for his money and directs to be driven to the Shooting Gallery. Mr. Bucket does not claim to be a scientific judge of horses; but he lays out a little money on the principal events in that line, and generally sums up his knowledge of the subject in the remark, that when he sees a horse as can go, he knows him.

His knowledge is not at fault in the present instance. Clattering over the stones at a dangerous pace, yet thoughtfully bringing his keen eyes to bear on every slinking creature whom he passes in the midnight streets, and even on the lights in upper windows where people are going or gone to bed, and on all the turnings that he rattles by, and alike on the heavy sky, and on the earth where the snow lies thin—for something may present itself to assist him any-

6. The most exclusive fashionable establishment in London, where high-society balls were held throughout the Season.

where—he dashes to his destination at such a speed, that when he stops, the horse half smothers him in a cloud of steam.

"Unbear him[7] half a moment to freshen him up, and I'll be back."

He runs up the long wooden entry, and finds the trooper smoking his pipe.

"I thought I should, George, after what you have gone through, my lad. I haven't a word to spare. Now, honour! All to save a woman. Miss Summerson that was here when Gridley died—that was the name, I know—all right!—where does she live?"

The trooper has come from there, and gives him the address near Oxford Street.

"You won't repent it, George. Good night!"

He is off again, with an impression of having seen Phil sitting by the frosty fire, staring at him open-mouthed; and gallops away again, and gets out in a cloud of steam again.

Mr. Jarndyce, the only person up in the house, is just going to bed; rises from his book, on hearing the rapid ringing at the bell; and comes down to the door in his dressing-gown.

"Don't be alarmed sir." In a moment his visitor is confidential with him in the hall, has shut the door, and stands with his hand upon the lock. "I've had the pleasure of seeing you before. Inspector Bucket. Look at that handkerchief, sir, Miss Esther Summerson's. Found it myself put away in a drawer of Lady Dedlock's, quarter of an hour ago. Not a moment to lose. Matter of life or death. You know Lady Dedlock?"

"Yes."

"There has been a discovery there, to-day. Family affairs have come out. Sir Leicester Dedlock, Baronet, has had a fit—apoplexy or paralysis—and couldn't be brought to, and precious time has been lost. Lady Dedlock disappeared this afternoon, and left a letter for him that looks bad. Run your eye over it. Here it is!"

Mr. Jarndyce having read it, asks him what he thinks?

"I don't know. It looks like suicide. Anyways, there's more and more danger, every minute, of its drawing to that. I'd give a hundred pound an hour to have got the start of the present time. Now, Mr. Jarndyce, I am employed by Sir Leicester Dedlock, Baronet, to follow her and find her—to save her, and take her his forgiveness. I have money and full power, but I want something else. I want Miss Summerson."

Mr. Jarndyce, in a troubled voice, repeats "Miss Summerson?"

"Now, Mr. Jarndyce"; Mr. Bucket has read his face with the greatest attention all along: "I speak to you as a gentleman of a

7. Loosen the harness that holds the horse's head up.

humane heart, and under such pressing circumstances as don't often happen. If ever delay was dangerous, it's dangerous now; and if ever you couldn't afterwards forgive yourself for causing it, this is the time. Eight or ten hours, worth, as I tell you, a hundred pound a-piece at least, have been lost since Lady Dedlock disappeared. I am charged to find her. I am Inspector Bucket. Besides all the rest that's heavy on her, she has upon her, as she believes, suspicion of murder. If I follow her alone, she, being in ignorance of what Sir Leicester Dedlock, Baronet, has communicated to me, may be driven to desperation. But if I follow her in company with a young lady, answering to the description of a young lady that she has a tenderness for—I ask no question, and I say no more than that—she will give me credit for being friendly. Let me come up with her, and be able to have the hold upon her of putting that young lady for'ard, and I'll save her and prevail with her if she is alive. Let me come up with her alone—a harder matter—and I'll do my best; but I don't answer for what the best may be. Time flies; it's getting on for one o'clock. When one strikes, there's another hour gone; and it's worth a thousand pound now, instead of a hundred."

This is all true, and the pressing nature of the case cannot be questioned. Mr. Jarndyce begs him to remain there, while he speaks to Miss Summerson. Mr. Bucket says he will; but acting on his usual principle, does no such thing—following up-stairs instead, and keeping his man in sight. So he remains, dodging and lurking about in the gloom of the staircase while they confer. In a very little time, Mr. Jarndyce comes down, and tells him that Miss Summerson will join him directly, and place herself under his protection, to accompany him where he pleases. Mr. Bucket, satisfied, expresses high approval; and awaits her coming, at the door.

There, he mounts a high tower in his mind, and looks out far and wide. Many solitary figures he perceives, creeping through the streets; many solitary figures out on heaths, and roads, and lying under haystacks. But the figure that he seeks is not among them. Other solitaries he perceives, in nooks of bridges, looking over; and in shadowed places down by the river's level; and a dark, dark, shapeless object drifting with the tide, more solitary than all, clings with a drowning hold on his attention.

Where is she? Living or dead, where is she? If, as he folds the handkerchief and carefully puts it up, it were able, with an enchanted power, to bring before him the place where she found it, and the night landscape near the cottage where it covered the little child, would he descry her there? On the waste, where the brick-kilns are burning with a pale blue flare; where the straw-roofs of the wretched huts in which the bricks are made, are being scattered by the wind; where the clay and water are hard frozen, and the mill in which the gaunt blind horse goes round all day, looks like an instrument of human torture;—traversing this deserted blighted spot, there is a lonely figure with the sad world to itself, pelted by the snow and driven by the wind, and cast out, it would seem, from all companionship. It is the figure of a woman, too; but it is miserably dressed, and no such clothes ever came through the hall, and out at the great door, of the Dedlock mansion.

Chapter LVII

ESTHER'S NARRATIVE

I had gone to bed and fallen asleep, when my guardian knocked at the door of my room and begged me to get up directly. On my hurrying to speak to him and learn what had happened, he told me, after a word or two of preparation, that there had been a discovery at Sir Leicester Dedlock's. That my mother had fled; that a person was now at our door who was empowered to convey to her the fullest assurances of affectionate protection and forgiveness, if he could possibly find her; and that I was sought for to accompany him, in the hope that my entreaties might prevail upon her, if his failed. Something to this general purpose I made out; but I was thrown into such a tumult of alarm, and hurry and distress, that, in spite of every effort I could make to subdue my agitation, I did not seem, to myself, fully to recover my right mind until hours had passed.

But I dressed and wrapped up expeditiously without waking Charley, or any one; and went down to Mr. Bucket, who was the person entrusted with the secret. In taking me to him my guardian told me this, and also explained how it was that he had come to think of me. Mr. Bucket, in a low voice, by the light of my guardian's candle, read to me, in the hall, a letter that my mother had left upon her table; and, I suppose within ten minutes of my having been aroused, I was sitting beside him rolling swiftly through the streets.

His manner was very keen, and yet considerate when he explained to me that a great deal might depend on my being able to answer, without confusion, a few questions that he wished to ask me. These were, chiefly, whether I had had much communication with my mother (to whom he only referred as Lady Dedlock); when and where I had spoken with her last; and how she had become possessed of my handkerchief. When I had satisfied him on these points, he asked me particularly to consider—taking time to think—whether, within my knowledge, there was any one, no matter where, in whom she might be at all likely to confide, under circumstances of the last necessity. I could think of no one but my guardian. But, by and by, I mentioned Mr. Boythorn. He came into my mind, as connected with his old chivalrous manner of mentioning my mother's name; and with what my guardian had informed me of his engagement to her sister, and his unconscious connexion with her unhappy story.

My companion had stopped the driver while we held this conversation, that we might the better hear each other. He now told him to go on again; and said to me, after considering within himself for a few moments, that he had made up his mind how to proceed. He was quite willing to tell me what his plan was: but I did not feel clear enough to understand it.

We had not driven very far from our lodgings, when we stopped in a bye-street, at a public-looking place lighted up with gas. Mr. Bucket took me in and sat me in an arm-chair, by a bright fire. It was now past one, as I saw by the clock against the wall. Two police officers, looking in their perfectly neat uniform not at all like people who were up all night, were quietly writing at a desk; and the place seemed very quiet altogether, except for some beating and calling out at distant doors underground, to which nobody paid any attention.

A third man in uniform, whom Mr. Bucket called and to whom he whispered his instructions, went out; and then the two others advised together, while one wrote from Mr. Bucket's subdued dictation. It was a description of my mother that they were busy with; for Mr. Bucket brought it to me when it was done, and read it in a whisper. It was very accurate indeed.

The second officer, who had attended to it closely, then copied it out, and called in another man in uniform (there were several in an outer room) who took it up and went away with it. All this was done with the greatest dispatch, and without the waste of a moment; yet nobody was at all hurried. As soon as the paper was sent out upon its travels, the two officers resumed their former quiet work of writing with neatness and care. Mr. Bucket thoughtfully came and warmed the soles of his boots, first one and then the other, at the fire.

"Are you well wrapped up, Miss Summerson?" he asked me, as his eyes met mine. "It's a desperate sharp night for a young lady to be out in."

I told him I cared for no weather, and was warmly clothed.

"It may be a long job," he observed; "but so that it ends well, never mind, miss."

"I pray to Heaven it may end well!" said I.

He nodded comfortingly. "You see, whatever you do, don't you go and fret yourself. You keep yourself cool, and equally ready for anything that may happen; and it'll be the better for you, the better for me, the better for Lady Dedlock, and the better for Sir Leicester Dedlock, Baronet."

He was really very kind and gentle; and as he stood before the fire warming his boots, and rubbing his face with his forefinger, I felt a confidence in his sagacity which re-assured me. It was not yet a quarter to two, when I heard horses' feet and wheels outside. "Now, Miss Summerson," said he, "we are off, if you please!"

He gave me his arm, and the two officers courteously bowed me out, and we found at the door a phaeton or barouche, with a postilion and post horses. Mr. Bucket handed me in, and took his own seat on the box. The man in uniform whom he had sent to fetch this equipage, then handed him up a dark lantern at his request; and when he had given a few directions to the driver, we rattled away.

I was far from sure that I was not in a dream. We rattled with great rapidity through such a labyrinth of streets, that I soon lost all idea where we were; except that we had crossed and re-crossed the river, and still seemed to be traversing a low-lying, water-side, dense neighbourhood of narrow thoroughfares, chequered by docks and basins, high piles of warehouses, swing-bridges, and masts of ships. At length we stopped at the corner of a little slimy turning, which the wind from the river, rushing up it, did not purify; and I saw my companion, by the light of his lantern, in conference with several men, who looked like a mixture of police and sailors. Against the mouldering wall by which they stood, there was a bill, on which I could discern the words, "Found Drowned"; and this, and an inscription about Drags, possessed me with the awful suspicion shadowed forth in our visit to that place.

I had no need to remind myself that I was not there, by the indulgence of any feeling of mine, to increase the difficulties of the search, or to lessen its hopes, or enhance its delays. I remained quiet; but what I suffered in that dreadful spot I never can forget. And still it was like the horror of a dream. A man yet dank and muddy, in long swollen sodden boots and a hat like them, was called out of a boat, and whispered with Mr. Bucket, who went away with him down some slippery steps—as if to look at something secret that he had to show. They came back, wiping their hands upon their coats, after turning over something wet; but thank God it was not what I feared!

After some further conference, Mr. Bucket (whom everybody seemed to know and defer to) went in with the others at a door, and left me in the carriage; while the driver walked up and down by his horses, to warm himself. The tide was coming in, as I judged from the sound it made; and I could hear it break at the end of the alley, with a little rush towards me. It never did so—and I thought

The Night.

it did so, hundreds of times, in what can have been at the most a quarter of an hour, and probably was less—but the thought shuddered through me that it would cast my mother at the horses' feet.

Mr. Bucket came out again, exhorting the others to be vigilant, darkened his lantern, and once more took his seat. "Don't you be alarmed, Miss Summerson, on account of our coming down here," he said, turning to me. "I only want to have everything in train, and to know that it is in train by looking after it myself. Get on, my lad!"

We appeared to retrace the way we had come. Not that I had taken note of any particular objects in my perturbed state of mind, but judging from the general character of the streets. We called at another office or station for a minute, and crossed the river again. During the whole of this time, and during the whole search, my companion, wrapped up on the box, never relaxed in his vigilance a single moment; but when we crossed the bridge he seemed, if possible, to be more on the alert than before. He stood up to look over the parapet; he alighted, and went back after a shadowy female figure that flitted past us; and he gazed into the profound black pit of water, with a face that made my heart die within me. The river had a fearful look, so overcast and secret, creeping away so fast between the low flat lines of shore: so heavy with indistinct and awful shapes, both of substance and shadow: so deathlike and mysterious. I have seen it many times since then, by sunlight and by moonlight, but never free from the impressions of that journey. In my memory, the lights upon the bridge are always burning dim; the cutting wind is eddying round the homeless woman whom we pass; the monotonous wheels are whirling on; and the light of the carriage-lamps reflected back, looks palely in upon me—a face, rising out of the dreaded water.

Clattering and clattering through the empty streets, we came at length from the pavement on to dark smooth roads, and began to leave the houses behind us. After a while, I recognised the familiar way to Saint Albans. At Barnet, fresh horses were ready for us, and we changed and went on. It was very cold indeed; and the open country was white with snow, though none was falling then.

"An old acquaintance of yours, this road, Miss Summerson," said Mr. Bucket, cheerfully.

"Yes," I returned. "Have you gathered any intelligence?"

"None that can be quite depended on as yet," he answered; "but it's early times as yet."

He had gone into every late or early public-house where there was a light (they were not a few at that time, the road being then much frequented by drovers), and had got down to talk to the turnpike-keepers. I had heard him ordering drink, and clinking money, and making himself agreeable and merry everywhere; but whenever he took his seat upon the box again, his face resumed its watchful steady look, and he always said to the driver in the same business tone. "Get on, my lad!"

With all these stoppages, it was between five and six o'clock and we were yet a few miles short of Saint Albans, when he came out of one of these houses and handed me in a cup of tea.

"Drink it, Miss Summerson, it'll do you good. You're beginning to get more yourself now, ain't you?"

I thanked him, and said I hoped so.

"You was what you may call stunned at first," he returned; "and Lord! no wonder. Don't speak loud, my dear. It's all right. She's on ahead."

I don't know what joyful exclamation I made, or was going to make, but he put up his finger, and I stopped myself.

"Passed through here on foot, this evening, about eight or nine. I heard of her first at the archway toll, over at Highgate, but couldn't make quite sure. Traced her all along, on and off. Picked her up at one place, and dropped her at another; but she's before us now, safe. Take hold of this cup and saucer, Ostler. Now, if you wasn't brought up to the butter trade, look out and see if you can catch half-a-crown in your t'other hand. One, two, three, and there you are! Now, my lad, try a gallop!"

We were soon in Saint Albans, and alighted a little before day, when I was just beginning to arrange and comprehend the occurrences of the night, and really to believe that they were not a dream. Leaving the carriage at the posting-house and ordering fresh horses to be ready, my companion gave me his arm, and we went towards home.

"As this is your regular abode, Miss Summerson, you see," he observed, "I should like to know whether you've been asked for by any stranger answering the description, or whether Mr. Jarndyce has. I don't much expect it, but it might be."

As we ascended the hill, he looked about him with a sharp eye—the day was now breaking—and reminded me that I had come down it one night, as I had reason for remembering, with my little servant and poor Jo: whom he called Toughey.

I wondered how he knew that.

"When you passed a man upon the road, just yonder, you know," said Mr. Bucket.

Yes, I remembered that too, very well.

"That was me," said Mr. Bucket.

Seeing my surprise, he went on:

"I drove down in a gig that afternoon, to look after that boy. You might have heard my wheels when you came out to look after him yourself, for I was aware of you and your little maid going up, when I was walking the horse down. Making an inquiry or two about him in the town, I soon heard what company he was in; and was coming among the brick-fields to look for him, when I observed you bringing him home here."

"Had he committed any crime?" I asked.

"None was charged against him," said Mr. Bucket, coolly lifting off his hat; "but I suppose he wasn't over-particular. No. What I wanted him for, was in connextion with keeping this very matter of Lady Dedlock quiet. He had been making his tongue more free than welcome, as to a small accidental service he had been paid for by the deceased Mr. Tulkinghorn; and it wouldn't do, at any sort of price, to have him playing those games. So having warned him out of London, I made an afternoon of it to warn him to keep out of it now he *was* away, and go farther from it, and maintain a bright look out that I didn't catch him coming back again."

"Poor creature!" said I.

"Poor enough," assented Mr. Bucket, "and trouble enough, and well enough away from London, or anywhere else. I was regularly turned on my back when I found him taken up by your establishment, I do assure you."

I asked him why? "Why, my dear?" said Mr. Bucket. "Naturally there was no end to his tongue then. He might as well have been born with a yard and a half of it, and a remnant over."

Although I remember this conversation now, my head was in confusion at the time, and my power of attention hardly did more than enable me to understand that he entered into these particulars to divert me. With the same kind intention, manifestly, he often spoke to me of indifferent things, while his face was busy with the one object that we had in view. He still pursued this subject, as we turned in at the garden gate.

"Ah!" said Mr. Bucket. "Here we are, and a nice retired place it is. Puts a man in mind of the country house in the Woodpecker-tapping, that was known by the smoke which so gracefully curled.[1] They're early with the kitchen fire, and that denotes good servants. But what you've always got to be careful of with servants, is, who comes to see 'em; you never know what they're up to, if you don't know that. And another thing, my dear. Whenever you find a young man behind the kitchen door, you give that young man in charge on suspicion of being secreted in a dwelling-house with an unlawful purpose."

1. A song written in America by Thomas Moore (1779–1852): "I knew by the smoke so gracefully curled/ Above the green elms, that a cottage was near, . . ./ Every leaf was at rest, and I heard not a sound,/ But the woodpecker tapping the hollow beech tree."

We were now in front of the house; he looked attentively and closely at the gravel for footprints, before he raised his eyes to the windows.

"Do you generally put that elderly young gentleman in the same room, when he's on a visit here, Miss Summerson?" he inquired, glancing at Mr. Skimpole's usual chamber.

"You know Mr. Skimpole!" said I.

"What do you call him again?" returned Mr. Bucket, bending down his ear. "Skimpole, is it? I've often wondered what his name might be. Skimpole. Not John. I should say, nor yet Jacob!"

"Harold," I told him.

"Harold. Yes. He's a queer bird is Harold," said Mr. Bucket, eyeing me with great expression.

"He's a singular character," said I.

"No idea of money," observed Mr. Bucket.—"He takes it though!"

I involuntarily returned for answer, that I perceived Mr. Bucket knew him.

"Why, now I'll tell you, Miss Summerson," he rejoined. "Your mind will be all the better for not running on one point too continually, and I'll tell you for a change. It was him as pointed out to me where Toughey was. I made up my mind, that night, to come to the door and ask for Toughey, if that was all; but, willing to try a move or so first, if any such was on the board, I just pitched up a morsel of gravel at that window where I saw a shadow. As soon as Harold opens it and I have had a look at him, thinks I, you're the man for me. So I smoothed him down a bit, about not wanting to disturb the family after they was gone to bed, and about its being a thing to be regretted that charitable young ladies should harbour vagrants; and then, when I pretty well understood his ways, I said, I should consider a fypunnote well bestowed if I could relieve the premises of Toughey without causing any noise or trouble. Then says he, lifting up his eyebrows in the gayest way, 'it's no use mentioning a fypunnote to me, my friend, because I'm a mere child in such matters, and have no idea of money.' Of course I understood what his taking it so easy meant; and being now quite sure he was the man for me, I wrapped the note round a little stone and threw it up to him. Well! He laughs and beams, and looks as innocent as you like, and says, 'But I don't know the value of these things. What am I to *do* with this?' 'Spend it, sir,' says I. 'But I shall be taken in,' he says 'they won't give me the right change, I shall lose it, it's no use to me.' Lord, you never saw such a face as he carried it with! Of course he told me where to find Toughey, and I found him."

I regarded this as very treacherous on the part of Mr. Skimpole towards my guardian, and as passing the usual bounds of his childish innocence.

"Bounds, my dear?" returned Mr. Bucket. "Bounds? Now, Miss Summerson, I'll give you a piece of advice that your husband will find useful when you are happily married and have got a family about you. Whenever a person says to you that they are as innocent as lambs in all concerning money, look well after your own money, for they are dead certain to collar it, if they can. Whenever a person proclaims to you 'In worldly matters I'm a child,' you consider that that person is only a crying off from being held accountable, and that you have got that person's number, and it's Number One.[2] Now, I am not a poetical man myself, except in a vocal way, when it goes round a company, but I'm a practical one, and that's my experience. So's this rule. Fast and loose in one thing, Fast and loose in everything. I never knew it fail. No more will you. Nor no one. With which caution to the unwary, my dear, I take the liberty of pulling this here bell, and so go back to our business."

I believe it had not been for a moment out of his mind, any more than it had been out of my mind, or out of his face. The whole household were amazed to see me, without any notice, at that time in the morning, and so accompanied; and their surprise was not diminished by my inquiries. No one, however, had been there. It could not be doubted that this was the truth.

"Then, Miss Summerson," said my companion, "we can't be too soon at the cottage where those brickmakers are to be found. Most inquiries there I leave to you, if you'll be so good as to make 'em. The naturalest way is the best way, and the naturalest way is your own way."

We set off again immediately. On arriving at the cottage, we found it shut up, and apparently deserted: but one of the neighbours who knew me, and who came out when I was trying to make some one hear, informed me that the two women and their husbands now lived together in another house, made of loose rough bricks, which stood on the margin of the piece of ground where the kilns were, and where the long rows of bricks were drying. We lost no time in repairing to this place, which was within a few hundred yards; and as the door stood ajar, I pushed it open.

There were only three of them sitting at breakfast; the child lying asleep on a bed in the corner. It was Jenny, the mother of the dead child, who was absent. The other woman rose on seeing me; and the men, though they were, as usual, sulky and silent, each gave me

2. As noted by T. Yamamoto, the expression is also used in *Oliver Twist,* ch. XLIII: "it's your object to take care of number one . . . meaning yourself."

a morose nod of recognition. A look passed between them when Mr. Bucket followed me in, and I was surprised to see that the woman evidently knew him.

I had asked leave to enter, of course. Liz (the only name by which I knew her) rose to give me her own chair, but I sat down on a stool near the fire, and Mr. Bucket took a corner of the bedstead. Now that I had to speak, and was among people with whom I was not familiar, I became conscious of being hurried and giddy. It was very difficult to begin, and I could not help bursting into tears.

"Liz," said I, "I have come a long way in the night and through the snow, to inquire after a lady——"

"Who has been here, you know," Mr. Bucket struck in, addressing the whole group, with a composed propitiatory face; "that's the lady the young lady means. The lady that was here last night, you know."

"And who told *you* as there was anybody here?" inquired Jenny's husband, who had made a surly stop in his eating, to listen, and now measured him with his eye.

"A person of the name of Michael Jackson, with a blue velveteen waistcoat with a double row of mother of pearl buttons," Mr. Bucket immediately answered.

"He had as good mind his own business, whoever he is," growled the man.

"He's out of employment, I believe," said Mr. Bucket, apologetically for Michael Jackson, "and so gets talking."

The woman had not resumed her chair, but stood faltering with her hand upon its broken back, looking at me. I thought she would have spoken to me privately, if she had dared. She was still in this attitude of uncertainty, when her husband, who was eating with a lump of bread and fat in one hand, and his clasp-knife in the other, struck the handle of his knife violently on the table, and told her with an oath to mind *her* business at any rate, and sit down.

"I should like to have seen Jenny very much," said I, "for I am sure she would have told me all she could about this lady, whom I am very anxious indeed—you cannot think how anxious—to overtake. Will Jenny be here soon? Where is she?"

The woman had a great desire to answer, but the man, with another oath, openly kicked at her foot with his heavy boot. He left it to Jenny's husband to say what he chose, and after a dogged silence the latter turned his shaggy head towards me.

"I'm not partial to gentlefolks coming into my place, as you've heerd me say afore now, I think, miss. I let their places be, and it's curious they can't let my place be. There'd be a pretty shine made if I was to go a wisitin *them,* I think. Howsever, I don't so much complain of you as of some others; and I'm agreeable to make you a civil answer, though I give notice that I'm not a going to be drawed like a badger. Will Jenny be here soon? No, she won't. Where is she? She's gone up to Lunnun."

"Did she go last night?" I asked.

"Did she go last night? Ah, she went last night," he answered, with a sulky jerk of his head.

"But was she here when the lady came? And what did the lady say to her? And where is the lady gone? I beg and pray you to be so kind as to tell me," said I, "for I am in great distress to know."

"If my master would let me speak, and not say a word of harm —" the woman timidly began.

"Your master," said her husband, muttering an imprecation with slow emphasis, "will break your neck, if you meddle with wot don't concern you."

After another silence, the husband of the absent woman, turning to me again, answered me with his usual grumbling unwillingness.

"Wos Jenny here when the lady come? Yes, she wos here when the lady come. Wot did the lady say to her? Well, I'll tell you wot the lady said to her. She said, 'You remember me as come one time to talk to you about the young lady as had been a wisiting of you? You remember me as give you somethink handsome for a hankecher wot she had left?' Ah, she remembered. So we all did. Well, then, wos that young lady up at the house now? No, she warn't up at the house now. Well, then, lookee here. The lady was upon a journey all alone, strange as we might think it, and could she rest herself where you're a setten, for a hour or so. Yes, she could, and so she did. Then she went—it might be at twenty minutes past eleven, and it might be at twenty minutes past twelve; we ain't got no watches here to know the time by, nor yet clocks. Where did she go? I don't know where she go'd. She went one way, and Jenny went another; one went right to Lunnun, and t'other went right from it. That's all about it. Ask this man. He heerd it all, and see it all. He knows."

The other man repeated, "That's all about it."

"Was the lady crying?" I inquired.

"Devil a bit," returned the first man. "Her shoes was the worse, and her clothes was the worse, but she warn't—not as I see."

The woman sat with her arms crossed, and her eyes upon the ground. Her husband had turned his seat a little, so as to face her; and kept his hammer-like hand upon the table, as if it were in readiness to execute his threat if she disobeyed him.

"I hope you will not object to my asking your wife," said I, "how the lady looked?"

"Come, then!" he gruffly cried to her. "You hear wot she says. Cut it short, and tell her."

"Bad," replied the woman. "Pale and exhausted. Very bad."

"Did she speak much?"

"Not much, but her voice was hoarse."

She answered, looking all the while at her husband for leave.

"Was she faint?" said I. "Did she eat or drink here?"

"Go on!" said the husband, in answer to her look. "Tell her and cut it short."

"She had a little water, miss, and Jenny fetched her some bread and tea. But she hardly touched it."

"And when she went from here"—I was proceeding, when Jenny's husband impatiently took me up.

"When she went from here, she went right away Nor'ard by the high road. Ask on the road if you doubt me, and see if it warn't so. Now, there's the end. That's all about it."

I glanced at my companion; and finding that he had already risen and was ready to depart, thanked them for what they had told me, and took my leave. The woman looked full at Mr. Bucket as he went out, and he looked full at her.

"Now, Miss Summerson," he said to me, as we walked quickly away. "They've got her ladyship's watch among 'em. That's a positive fact."

"You saw it?" I exclaimed.

"Just as good as saw it," he returned. "Else why should he talk about his 'twenty minutes past,' and about his having no watch to tell the time by? Twenty minutes! He don't usually cut his time so fine as that. If he comes to half-hours, it's as much as *he* does. Now, you see, either her ladyship gave him that watch, or he took it. I think she gave it him. Now, what should she give it him for? What should she give it him for?"

He repeated this question to himself several times, as we hurried on; appearing to balance between a variety of answers that arose in his mind.

"If time could be spared," said Mr. Bucket—"which is the only thing that can't be spared in this case—I might get it out of that woman; but it's too doubtful a chance to trust to, under present circumstances. They are up to keeping a close eye upon her, and any fool knows that a poor creetur like her, beaten and kicked and scarred and bruised from head to foot, will stand by the husband that ill uses her, through thick and thin. There's something kept back. It's a pity but what we had seen the other woman."

I regretted it exceedingly; for she was very grateful, and I felt sure would have resisted no entreaty of mine.

"It's possible, Miss Summerson," said Mr. Bucket, pondering on it, "that her ladyship sent her up to London with some word for you, and it's possible that her husband got the watch to let her go. It don't come out altogether so plain as to please me, but it's on the cards. Now, I don't take kindly to laying out the money of Sir Leicester Dedlock, Baronet, on these Roughs, and I don't see my way to the usefulness of it at present. No! So far, our road, Miss Summerson, is for'ard—straight ahead—and keeping everything quiet!"

We called at home once more, that I might send a hasty note to my guardian, and then we hurried back to where we had left the carriage. The horses were brought out as soon as we were seen coming, and we were on the road again in a few minutes.

It had set in snowing at daybreak, and it now snowed hard. The air was so thick with the darkness of the day, and the density of the fall, that we could see but a very little way in any direction. Although it was extremely cold, the snow was but partially frozen, and it churned—with a sound as if it were a beach of small shells—under the hoofs of the horses, into mire and water. They sometimes slipped and floundered for a mile together, and we were obliged to come to a standstill to rest them. One horse fell three times in this first stage, and trembled so, and was so shaken, that the driver had to dismount from his saddle and lead him at last.

I could eat nothing, and could not sleep; and I grew so nervous under those delays, and the slow pace at which we travelled, that I had an unreasonable desire upon me to get out and walk. Yielding to my companion's better sense, however, I remained where I was. All this time, kept fresh by a certain enjoyment of the work in which he was engaged, he was up and down at every house we came to; addressing people whom he had never beheld before, as old acquaintances; running in to warm himself at every fire he saw; talking and drinking and shaking hands at every bar and tap; friendly with every waggoner, wheelwright, blacksmith, and toll-taker; yet never seeming to lose time, and always mounting to the box again with his watchful, steady face, and his business-like "Get on, my lad!"

When we were changing horses the next time, he came from the stable yard, with the wet snow encrusted upon him, and dropping off him—plashing and crashing through it to his wet knees, as he had been doing frequently since we left Saint Albans—and spoke to me at the carriage side.

"Keep up your spirits. It's certainly true that she came on here, Miss Summerson. There's not a doubt of the dress by this time, and the dress has been seen here."

"Still on foot?" said I.

"Still on foot. I think the gentleman you mentioned must be the point she's aiming at; and yet I don't like his living down in her own part of the country, neither."

"I know so little," said I. "There may be some one else nearer here, of whom I never heard."

"That's true. But whatever you do, don't you fall a crying, my dear; and don't you worry yourself no more than you can help. Get on, my lad!"

The sleet fell all that day unceasingly, a thick mist came on early, and it never rose or lightened for a moment. Such roads I had never seen. I sometimes feared we had missed the way and got into the ploughed grounds, or the marshes. If I ever thought of the time I had been out, it presented itself as an indefinite period of great duration; and I seemed, in a strange way, never to have been free from the anxiety under which I then laboured.

As we advanced, I began to feel misgivings that my companion lost confidence. He was the same as before with all the roadside people, but he looked graver when he sat by himself on the box. I saw his finger uneasily going across and across his mouth, during the whole of one long weary stage. I overheard that he began to ask the drivers of coaches and other vehicles coming towards us, what passengers they had seen in other coaches and vehicles that were in advance. Their replies did not encourage him. He always gave me a re-assuring beck of his finger, and lift of his eyelid, as he got upon the box again; but he seemed perplexed now, when he said, "Get on, my lad!"

At last, when we were changing, he told me that he had lost the track of the dress so long that he began to be surprised. It was nothing, he said, to lose such a track for one while, and to take it up for another while, and so on; but it had disappeared here in an unaccountable manner, and we had not come upon it since. This corroborated the apprehensions I had formed when he began to look at direction-posts, and to leave the carriage at cross roads for a quarter of an hour at a time while he explored them. But I was not to be down-hearted, he told me; for it was as likely as not that the next stage might set us right again.

The next stage, however, ended as that one ended; we had no new clue. There was a spacious inn here, solitary, but a comfortable substantial building, and as we drove in under a large gateway before I knew it, where a landlady and her pretty daughters came to the carriage-door, entreating me to alight and refresh myself while the horses were making ready, I thought it would be uncharitable to refuse. They took me up-stairs to a warm room, and left me there.

It was at the corner of the house, I remember, looking two ways. On one side, to a stable-yard open to a bye-road, where the ostlers were unharnessing the splashed and tired horses from the muddy carriage; and beyond that, to the bye-road itself, across which the sign was heavily swinging: on the other side, to a wood of dark pine-trees. Their branches were encumbered with snow, and it silently dropped off in wet heaps while I stood at the window. Night was setting in, and its bleakness was enhanced by the contrast of the pictured fire glowing and gleaming in the window-pane. As I looked among the stems of the trees, and followed the discoloured marks in the snow where the thaw was sinking into it and undermining it, I thought of the motherly face brightly set off by daughters that had just now welcomed me, and of *my* mother lying down in such a wood to die.

I was frightened when I found them all about me, but I remembered that before I fainted I tried very hard not to do it; and that was some little comfort. They cushioned me up, on a large sofa by the fire; and then the comely landlady told me that I must travel no further to-night, but must go to bed. But this put me into such a tremble lest they should detain me there, that she soon recalled her words, and compromised for a rest of half-an-hour.

A good endearing creature she was. She, and her three fair girls all so busy about me. I was to take hot soup and broiled fowl, while Mr. Bucket dried himself and dined elsewhere; but I could not do it when a snug round table was presently spread by the fireside, though I was very unwilling to disappoint them. However, I could take some toast and some hot negus;[3] and as I really enjoyed that refreshment, it made some recompense.

Punctual to the time, at the half-hour's end the carriage came rumbling under the gateway, and they took me down, warmed, refreshed, comforted by kindness, and safe (I assured them) not to faint any more. After I had got in and had taken a grateful leave of them all, the youngest daughter—a blooming girl of nineteen, who was to be the first married, they had told me—got upon the carriage step, reached in, and kissed me. I have never seen her, from that hour, but I think of her to this hour as my friend.

The transparent windows with the fire and light, looking so bright and warm from the cold darkness out of doors, were soon gone, and again we were crushing and churning the loose snow. We went on with toil enough; but the dismal roads were not much worse than they had been, and the stage was only nine miles. My companion smoking on the box—I had thought at the last inn of begging him to do so, when I saw him standing at a great fire in a comfortable cloud of tobacco—was as vigilant as ever; and as quickly down and up again, when we came to any human abode or any human creature. He had lighted his little dark lantern, which seemed to be a favourite with him, for we had lamps to the car-

3. Mixture of port wine, boiling water, and sliced lemons.

riage; and every now and then he turned it upon me, to see that I was doing well. There was a folding-window to the carriage-head, but I never closed it, for it seemed like shutting out hope.

We came to the end of the stage, and still the lost trace was not recovered. I looked at him anxiously when we stopped to change; but I knew by his yet graver face, as he stood watching the ostlers, that he had heard nothing. Almost in an instant afterwards, as I leaned back in my seat, he looked in, with his lighted lantern in his hand, an excited and quite different man.

"What is it?" said I, starting. "Is she here?"

"No, no. Don't deceive yourself, my dear. Nobody's here. But I've got it!"

The crystallised snow was in his eyelashes, in his hair, lying in ridges on his dress. He had to shake it from his face, and get his breath before he spoke to me.

"Now, Miss Summerson," said he, beating his finger on the apron, "don't you be disappointed at what I'm a going to do. You know me. I'm Inspector Bucket, and you can trust me. We've come a long way; never mind. Four horses out there for the next stage up! Quick!"

There was a commotion in the yard, and a man came running out of the stables to know "if he meant up or down?"

"Up, I tell you! Up! Ain't it English? Up!"

"Up?" said I, astonished. "To London! Are we going back?"

"Miss Summerson," he answered, "back. Straight back as a die. You know me. Don't be afraid. I'll follow the other, by G—."

"The other?" I repeated. "Who?"

"You called her Jenny, didn't you? I'll follow her. Bring those two pair out here, for a crown a man. Wake up, some of you!"

"You will not desert this lady we are in search of; you will not abandon her on such a night, and in such a state of mind as I know her to be in!" said I, in an agony, and grasping his hand.

"You are right, my dear, I won't. But I'll follow the other. Look alive here with them horses. Send a man for'ard in the saddle to the next stage, and let him send another for'ard again, and order four on, up, right through. My darling, don't you be afraid!"

These orders, and the way in which he ran about the yard, urging them, caused a general excitement that was scarcely less bewildering to me than the sudden change. But in the height of the confusion, a mounted man galloped away to order the relays, and our horses were put to with great speed.

"My dear," said Mr. Bucket, jumping up to his seat, and looking in again—"you'll excuse me if I'm too familiar—don't you fret and worry yourself no more than you can help. I say nothing else at present; but you know me, my dear; now, don't you?"

I endeavoured to say that I knew he was far more capable than I of deciding what we ought to do; but was he sure that this was right? Could I not go forward by myself in search of——I grasped his hand again in my distress, and whispered it to him—of my own mother.

"My dear," he answered, "I know, I know, and would I put you wrong, do you think? Inspector Bucket. Now you know me, don't you?"

What could I say but yes!

"Then you keep up as good a heart as you can, and you rely upon me for standing by you, no less than by Sir Leicester Dedlock, Baronet. Now, are you right there?"

"All right, sir!"

"Off she goes, then. And get on, my lads!"

We were again upon the melancholy road by which we had come; tearing up the miry sleet and thawing snow, as if they were torn up by a waterwheel.

Chapter LVIII

A WINTRY DAY AND NIGHT

Still impassive, as behoves its breeding, the Dedlock town house carries itself as usual towards the street of dismal grandeur. There are powdered heads from time to time in the little windows of the hall, looking out at the untaxed powder[1] falling all day from the sky; and, in the same conservatory, there is peach blossom[2] turning itself exotically to the great hall fire from the nipping weather out of doors. It is given out that my Lady has gone down into Lincolnshire, but is expected to return presently.

Rumour, busy overmuch, however, will not go down into Lincolnshire. It persists in flitting and chattering about town. It knows that that poor unfortunate man, Sir Leicester, has been sadly used. It hears, my dear child, all sorts of shocking things. It makes the world of five miles round, quite merry. Not to know that there is something wrong at the Dedlocks' is to augur[3] yourself unknown. One of the peachy-cheeked charmers with the skeleton throats, is already apprised of all the principal circumstances that will come out before the Lords, on Sir Leicester's application for a bill of divorce.

At Blaze and Sparkle's the jewellers, and at Sheen and Gloss's the

1. The snow is contrasted with hair-powder, as used for the "powdered heads" of the footmen, which was subject to tax.
2. The colored costumes of the footmen.
3. According to Stephen Gill, *augur* should be *argue*, and hence the allusion is to Satan's speech to the angels who did not recognize him: "Not to know me argues yourselves unknown/ The lowest of your throng." (*Paradise Lost,* IV.830–31.) The manuscript and proofs clearly indicate that Dickens wrote *augur*.

mercers, it is and will be for several hours the topic of the age, the feature of the century. The patronesses of those establishments, albeit so loftily inscrutable, being as nicely weighed and measured there as any other article of the stock-in-trade, are perfectly understood in this new fashion by the rawest hand before the counter. "Our people, Mr. Jones," said Blaze and Sparkle to the hand in question on engaging him, "our people, sir, are sheep—mere sheep. Where two or three marked ones go, all the rest follow. Keep those two or three in your eye, Mr. Jones, and you have the flock." So, likewise, Sheen and Gloss to *their* Jones, in reference to knowing where to have the fashionable people, and how to bring what they (Sheen and Gloss) choose, into fashion. On similar unerring principles, Mr. Sladdery the librarian, and indeed the great farmer of gorgeous sheep,[4] admits this very day, "Why yes, sir, there certainly *are* reports concerning Lady Dedlock, very current indeed among my high connexion, sir. You see, my high connexion must talk about something, sir; and it's only to get a subject into vogue with one or two ladies I could name, to make it go down with the whole. Just what I should have done with those ladies, sir, in the case of any novelty you had left to me to bring in, they have done of themselves in this case through knowing Lady Dedlock, and being perhaps a little innocently jealous of her too, sir. You'll find, sir, that this topic will be very popular among my high connexion. If it had been a speculation, sir, it would have brought money. And when I say so, you may trust to my being right, sir; for I have made it my business to study my high connexion, and to be able to wind it up like a clock, sir."

Thus rumour thrives in the capital, and will not go down into Lincolnshire. By half-past five, post meridian, Horse Guards' time,[5] it has even elicited a new remark from the Honourable Mr. Stables, which bids fair to outshine the old one, on which he has so long rested his colloquial reputation. This sparkling sally is to the effect that, although he always knew she was the best-groomed woman in the stud, he had no idea she was a bolter. It is immensely received in turf-circles.

At feasts and festivals also: in firmaments she has often graced, and among constellations she outshone but yesterday, she is still the prevalent subject. What is it? Who is it? When was it? Where was it? How was it? She is discussed by her dear friends with all the genteelest slang in vogue, with the last new word, the last new manner, the last new drawl, and the perfection of polite indiffer-

4. On Sladdery's pre-eminence in controlling his flock of aristocratic clients, see p. 15.

5. A clock on a turret over the entrance to the Horse Guards Parade. According to John Timbs, it was regarded by residents of London as infallibly accurate (*Curiosities of London*, 1855, p. 378).

ence. A remarkable feature of the theme is, that it is found to be so inspiring that several people come out upon it who never came out before—positively say things! William Buffy carries one of these smartnesses from the place where he dines, down to the House, where the Whip for his party hands it about with his snuff-box, to keep men together who want to be off, with such effect that the Speaker (who has had it privately insinuated into his own ear under the corner of his wig) cries "Order at the bar!" three times without making an impression.

And not the least amazing circumstance connected with her being vaguely the town talk, is, that people hovering on the confines of Mr. Sladdery's high connexion, people who know nothing and ever did know nothing about her, think it essential to their reputation to pretend that she is their topic too; and to retail her at second-hand with the last new word and the last new manner, and the last new drawl, and the last new polite indifference, and all the rest of it, all at second-hand but considered equal to new, in inferior systems and to fainter stars. If there be any man of letters, art, or science among these little dealers, how noble in him to support the feeble sisters on such majestic crutches!

So goes the wintry day outside the Dedlock mansion. How within it?

Sir Leicester lying in his bed can speak a little, though with difficulty and indistinctness. He is enjoined to silence and to rest, and they have given him some opiate to lull his pain; for his old enemy is very hard with him. He is never asleep, though sometimes he seems to fall into a dull waking doze. He caused his bedstead to be moved out nearer to the window, when he heard it was such inclement weather; and his head to be so adjusted, that he could see the driving snow and sleet. He watches it as it falls, throughout the whole wintry day.

Upon the least noise in the house, which is kept hushed, his hand is at the pencil. The old housekeeper, sitting by him, knows what he would write, and whispers, "No, he has not come back yet, Sir Leicester. It was late last night when he went. He has been but a little time gone yet."

He withdraws his hand, and falls to looking at the sleet and snow again, until they seem, by being long looked at, to fall so thick and fast, that he is obliged to close his eyes for a minute on the giddy whirl of white flakes and icy blots.

He began to look at them as soon as it was light. The day is not yet far spent, when he conceives it to be necessary that her rooms should be prepared for her. It is very cold and wet. Let there be good fires. Let them know that she is expected. Please see to it yourself. He writes to this purpose on his slate, and Mrs. Rouncewell with a heavy heart obeys.

"For I dread, George," the old lady says to her son, who waits below to keep her company when she has a little leisure; "I dread, my dear, that my Lady will never more set foot within these walls."

"That's a bad presentiment, mother."

"Nor yet within the walls of Chesney Wold, my dear."

"That's worse. But why, mother?"

"When I saw my Lady yesterday, George, she looked to me—and I may say at me too—as if the step on the Ghost's Walk had almost walked her down."

"Come, come! You alarm yourself with old-story fears, mother."

"No, I don't, my dear. No, I don't. It's going on for sixty year that I have been in this family, and I never had any fear for it before. But it's breaking up, my dear; the great old Dedlock family is breaking up."

"I hope not, mother."

"I am thankful I have lived long enough to be with Sir Leicester in this illness and trouble; for I know I am not too old, nor too useless, to be a welcomer sight to him than anybody else in my place would be. But the step on the Ghost's Walk will walk my Lady down, George; it has been many a day behind her, and now it will pass her, and go on."

"Well, mother dear, I say again, I hope not."

"Ah, so do I, George," the old lady returns, shaking her head, and parting her folded hands. "But if my fears come true, and he has to know it, who will tell him!"

"Are these her rooms?"

"These are my Lady's rooms, just as she left them."

"Why now," says the trooper, glancing round him, and speaking in a lower voice, "I begin to understand how you come to think as you do think, mother. Rooms get an awful look about them when they are fitted up, like these, for one person you are used to see in them, and that person is away under any shadow: let alone being God knows where."

He is not far out. As all partings foreshadow the great final one,—so, empty rooms, bereft of a familiar presence, mournfully whisper what your room and what mine must one day be. My Lady's state has a hollow look, thus gloomy and abandoned; and in the inner apartment, where Mr. Bucket last night made his secret perquisition, the traces of her dresses and her ornaments, even the mirrors accustomed to reflect them when they were a portion of herself, have a desolate and vacant air. Dark and cold as the wintry day is, it is darker and colder in these deserted chambers than in many a hut that will barely exclude the weather; and though the servants heap fires in the grates, and set the couches and chairs within the warm glass screens that let the ruddy light shoot through to the furthest corners, there is a heavy cloud upon the rooms which no light will dispel.

The old housekeeper and her son remain until the preparations are complete, and then she returns up-stairs. Volumnia has taken Mrs. Rouncewell's place in the meantime: though pearl necklaces and rouge pots, however calculated to embellish Bath, are but indifferent comforts to the invalid under present circumstances. Volumnia not being supposed to know (and indeed not knowing) what is the matter, has found it a ticklish task to offer appropriate observations; and consequently has supplied their place with distracting smoothings of the bed-linen, elaborate locomotion on tiptoe, vigilant peeping at her kinsman's eyes, and one exasperating whisper to herself of "He is asleep." In disproof of which superfluous remark, Sir Leicester has indignantly written on the slate, "I am not."

Yielding, therefore, the chair at the bedside to the quaint old housekeeper, Volumnia sits at a table a little removed, sympathetically sighing. Sir Leicester watches the sleet and snow, and listens for the returning steps that he expects. In the ears of his old servant, looking as if she had stepped out of an old picture-frame to attend a summoned Dedlock to another world, the silence is fraught with echoes of her own words, "Who will tell him!"

He has been under his valet's hands this morning, to be made presentable; and is as well got up as the circumstances will allow. He is propped with pillows, his grey hair is brushed in its usual manner, his linen is arranged to a nicety, and he is wrapped in a responsible dressing-gown. His eye-glass and his watch are ready to his hand. It is necessary—less to his own dignity now perhaps, than for her sake—that he should be seen as little disturbed, and as much himself, as may be. Women will talk, and Volumnia, though a Dedlock, is no exceptional case. He keeps her here, there is little doubt, to prevent her talking somewhere else. He is very ill: but he makes his present stand against distress of mind and body, most courageously.

The fair Volumnia being one of those sprightly girls who cannot long continue silent without imminent peril of seizure by the dragon Boredom, soon indicates the approach of that monster with a series of undisguisable yawns. Finding it impossible to suppress those yawns by any other process than conversation, she compliments Mrs. Rouncewell on her son; declaring that he positively is one of the finest figures she ever saw, and as soldierly a looking person she should think, as what's his name, her favourite Life

Guardsman—the man she doats on—the dearest of creatures—who was killed at Waterloo.[6]

Sir Leicester hears this tribute with so much surprise, and stares about him in such a confused way, that Mrs. Rouncewell feels it necessary to explain.

"Miss Dedlock don't speak of my eldest son, Sir Leicester, but my youngest. I have found him. He has come home."

Sir Leicester breaks silence with a harsh cry. "George? Your son George come home, Mrs. Rouncewell?"

The old housekeeper wipes her eyes. "Thank God. Yes, Sir Leicester."

Does this discovery of some one lost, this return of some one so long gone, come upon him as a strong confirmation of his hopes? Does he think, "Shall I not, with the aid I have, recall her safely after this; there being fewer hours in her case than there are years in his?"

It is of no use entreating him; he is determined to speak now, and he does. In a thick crowd of sounds, but still intelligibly enough to be understood.

"Why did you not tell me, Mrs. Rouncewell?"

"It happened only yesterday, Sir Leicester, and I doubted your being well enough to be talked to of such things."

Besides, the giddy Volumnia now remembers with her little scream that nobody was to have known of his being Mrs. Rouncewell's son, and that she was not to have told. But Mrs. Rouncewell protests, with warmth enough to swell the stomacher, that of course she would have told Sir Leicester as soon as he got better.

"Where is your son George, Mrs. Rouncewell?" asks Sir Leicester.

Mrs. Rouncewell, not a little alarmed by his disregard of the doctor's injunctions, replies, in London.

"Where in London?"

Mrs. Rouncewell is constrained to admit that he is in the house.

"Bring him here to my room. Bring him directly."

The old lady can do nothing but go in search of him. Sir Leicester, with such power of movement as he has, arranges himself a little, to receive him. When he has done so, he looks out again at the falling sleet and snow, and listens again for the returning steps. A quantity of straw has been tumbled down in the street to deaden

6. Probably alluding to Lance-Corporal John Shaw (1789–1815), a prize-fighter whose "Herculean" physique made him a favorite model for painters. Shaw became famous for his exploits as a Lifeguardsman at the battle of Waterloo where he reputedly killed ten French lancers, afterwards dying himself of wounds. See p. 312, note 8. Volumnia's enthusiasm here for military exploits is one instance in which she resembles her namesake, the Roman matron, in Shakespeare's *Coriolanus*.

the noises there, and she might be driven to the door perhaps without his hearing wheels.

He is lying thus, apparently forgetful of his newer and minor surprise, when the housekeeper returns, accompanied by her trooper son. Mr. George approaches softly to the bedside, makes his bow, squares his chest, and stands, with his face flushed, very heartily ashamed of himself.

"Good Heaven, and it is really George Rouncewell!" exclaims Sir Leicester. "Do you remember me, George?"

The trooper needs to look at him, and to separate this sound from that sound, before he knows what he has said: but doing this, and being a little helped by his mother, he replies:

"I must have a very bad memory, indeed, Sir Leicester, if I failed to remember you."

"When I look at you, George Rouncewell," Sir Leicester observes with difficulty, "I see something of a boy at Chesney Wold—I remember well—very well."

He looks at the trooper until tears come into his eyes, and then he looks at the sleet and snow again.

"I ask your pardon, Sir Leicester," says the trooper, "but would you accept of my arms to raise you up? You would lie easier, Sir Leicester, if you would allow me to move you."

"If you please, George Rouncewell; if you will be so good."

The trooper takes him in his arms like a child, lightly raises him, and turns him with his face more towards the window. "Thank you. You have your mother's gentleness," returns Sir Leicester, "and your own strength. Thank you."

He signs to him with his hand not to go away. George quietly remains at the bedside, waiting to be spoken to.

"Why did you wish for secrecy?" It takes Sir Leicester some time to ask this.

"Truly I am not much to boast of, Sir Leicester, and I—I should still, Sir Leicester, if you was not so indisposed—which I hope you will not be long—I should still hope for the favour of being allowed to remain unknown in general. That involves explanations not very hard to be guessed at, not very well timed here, and not very creditable to myself. However opinions may differ on a variety of subjects, I should think it would be universally agreed, Sir Leicester, that I am not much to boast of."

"You have been a soldier," observes Sir Leicester, "and a faithful one."

George makes his military bow. "As far as that goes, Sir Leicester, I have done my duty under discipline, and it was the least I could do."

"You find me," says Sir Leicester, whose eyes are much attracted towards him, "far from well, George Rouncewell."

"I am very sorry both to hear it and to see it, Sir Leicester."

"I am sure you are. No. In addition to my older malady, I have had a sudden and bad attack. Something that deadens—"making an endeavour to pass one hand down one side; "and confuses—" touching his lips.

George, with a look of assent and sympathy, makes another bow. The different times when they were both young men (the trooper much the younger of the two), and looked at one another down at Chesney Wold, arise before them both, and soften both.

Sir Leicester, evidently with a great determination to say, in his own manner, something that is on his mind before relapsing into silence, tries to raise himself among his pillows a little more. George, observant of the action, takes him in his arms again and places him as he desires to be. "Thank you, George. You are another self to me. You have often carried my spare gun at Chesney Wold, George. You are familiar to me in these strange circumstances, very familiar." He has put Sir Leicester's sounder arm over his shoulder in lifting him up, and Sir Leicester is slow in drawing it away again, as he says these words.

"I was about to add," he presently goes on, "I was about to add, respecting this attack, that it was unfortunately simultaneous with a slight misunderstanding between my Lady and myself. I do not mean that there was any difference between us (for there has been none), but that there was a misunderstanding of certain circumstances important only to ourselves, which deprives me, for a little while, of my Lady's society. She has found it necessary to make a journey,—I trust will shortly return. Volumnia, do I make myself intelligible? The words are not quite under my command, in the manner of pronouncing them."

Volumnia understands him perfectly; and in truth he delivers himself with far greater plainness than could have been supposed possible a minute ago. The effort by which he does so, is written in the anxious and labouring expression of his face. Nothing but the strength of his purpose enables him to make it.

"Therefore, Volumnia, I desire to say in your presence—and in the presence of my old retainer and friend, Mrs. Rouncewell, whose truth and fidelity no one can question—and in the presence of her son, George, who comes back like a familiar recollection of my youth in the home of my ancestors at Chesney Wold—in case I should relapse, in case I should not recover, in case I should lose both my speech and the power of writing, though I hope for better things——"

The old housekeeper weeping silently; Volumnia in the greatest agitation, with the freshest bloom on her cheeks; the trooper with his arms folded and his head a little bent, respectfully attentive.

"Therefore I desire to say, and to call you all to witness—beginning, Volumnia, with yourself, most solemnly—that I am on unaltered terms with Lady Dedlock. That I assert no cause whatever of complaint against her. That I have ever had the strongest affection for her, and that I retain it undiminished. Say this to herself, and to every one. If you ever say less than this, you will be guilty of deliberate falsehood to me."

Volumnia tremblingly protests that she will observe his injunctions to the letter.

"My lady is too high in position, too handsome, too accomplished, too superior in most respects to the best of those by whom she is surrounded, not to have her enemies and traducers, I dare say. Let it be known to them, as I make it known to you, that being of sound mind, memory, and understanding, I revoke no disposition I have made in her favour. I abridge nothing I have ever bestowed upon her. I am on unaltered terms with her, and I recall—having the full power to do it if I were so disposed, as you see—no act I have done for her advantage and happiness."

His formal array of words might have at any other time, as it has often had, something ludicrous in it; but at this time it is serious and affecting. His noble earnestness, his fidelity, his gallant shielding of her, his generous conquest of his own wrong and his own pride for her sake, are simply honourable, manly, and true. Nothing less worthy can be seen through the lustre of such qualities in the commonest mechanic, nothing less worthy can be seen in the best-born gentleman. In such a light both aspire alike, both rise alike, both children of the dust shine equally.

Overpowered by his exertions, he lays his head back on his pillows, and closes his eyes; for not more than a minute; when he again resumes his watching of the weather, and his attention to the muffled sounds. In the rendering of those little services, and in the manner of their acceptance, the trooper has become installed as necessary to him. Nothing had been said, but it is quite understood. He falls a step or two backward to be out of sight, and mounts guard a little behind his mother's chair.

The day is now beginning to decline. The mist, and the sleet into which the snow has all resolved itself, are darker, and the blaze begins to tell more vividly upon the room walls and furniture. The gloom augments; the bright gas springs up in the streets; and the pertinacious oil lamps which yet hold their ground here, with their source of life half frozen and half thawed, twinkle gaspingly, like fiery fish out of water—as they are.[7] The world, which has been rumbling over the straw and pulling at the bell, "to inquire," begins to go home, begins to dress, to dine, to discuss its dear friend, with all the last new modes, as already mentioned.

Now, does Sir Leicester become worse; restless, uneasy, and in great pain. Volumnia lighting a candle (with a predestined aptitude for doing something objectionable) is bidden to put it out again, for it is not yet dark enough. Yet it is very dark too; as dark as it will be all night. By and by she tries again. No! Put it out. It is not dark enough yet.

His old housekeeper is the first to understand that he is striving to uphold the fiction with himself that it is not growing late.

"Dear Sir Leicester, my honoured master," she softly whispers, "I must, for your own good, and my duty, take the freedom of begging and praying that you will not lie here in the lone darkness, watching and waiting, and dragging through the time. Let me draw the curtains and light the candles, and make things more comfortable about you. The church-clocks will strike the hours just the same, Sir Leicester, and the night will pass away just the same. My Lady will come back, just the same."

"I know it, Mrs. Rouncewell, but I am weak—and he has been so long gone."

"Not so very long, Sir Leicester. Not twenty-four hours yet."

"But that is a long time. O it is a long time!"

He says it with a groan that wrings her heart.

She knows that this is not a period for bringing the rough light upon him; she thinks his tears too sacred to be seen, even by her. Therefore, she sits in the darkness for a while, without a word; then gently begins to move about; now stirring the fire, now standing at the dark window looking out. Finally he tells her, with recovered self-command, "As you say, Mrs. Rouncewell, it is no worse for being confessed. It is getting late, and they are not come. Light the room!" When it is lighted, and the weather shut out, it is only left to him to listen.

But they find that, however dejected and ill he is, he brightens when a quiet pretence is made of looking at the fires in her rooms, and being sure that everything is ready to receive her. Poor pretence as it is, these allusions to her being expected keep up hope within him.

Midnight comes, and with it the same blank. The carriages in the streets are few, and other late sounds in that neighbourhood there are none, unless a man so very nomadically drunk as to stray into the frigid zone goes brawling and bellowing along the pavement.

7. Such lamps used whale oil. See p. 575, note 3.

Upon this wintry night it is so still, that listening to the intense silence is like looking at intense darkness. If any distant sound be audible in this case, it departs through the gloom like a feeble light in that, and all is heavier than before.

The corporation of servants are dismissed to bed (not unwilling to go, for they were up all last night), and only Mrs. Rouncewell and George keep watch in Sir Leicester's room. As the night lags tardily on—or rather when it seems to stop altogether, at between two and three o'clock—they find a restless craving on him to know more about the weather, now he cannot see it. Hence George, patrolling regularly every half hour to the rooms so carefully looked after, extends his march to the hall-door, looks about him, and brings back the best report he can make of the worst of nights; the sleet still falling, and even the stone footways lying ankle-deep in icy sludge.

Volumnia, in her room up a retired landing on the staircase—the second turning past the end of the carving and gilding—a cousinly room containing a fearful abortion of a portrait of Sir Leicester, banished for its crimes, and commanding in the day a solemn yard, planted with dried-up shrubs like antediluvian specimens of black tea—is a prey to horrors of many kinds. Not last nor least among them, possibly, is a horror of what may befall her little income, in the event, as she expresses it, "of anything happening" to Sir Leicester. Anything, in this sense, meaning one thing only, and that the last thing that can happen to the consciousness of any baronet in the known world.

An effect of these horrors is, that Volumnia finds she cannot go to bed in her own room, or sit by the fire in her own room, but must come forth with her fair head tied up in a profusion of shawl, and her fair form enrobed in drapery, and parade the mansion like a ghost: particularly haunting the rooms, warm and luxurious, prepared for one who still does not return. Solitude under such circumstances being not to be thought of, Volumnia is attended by her maid, who, impressed from her own bed for that purpose, extremely cold, very sleepy, and generally an injured maid as condemned by circumstances to take office with a cousin, when she had resolved to be maid to nothing less than ten thousand a year, has not a sweet expression of countenance.

The periodical visits of the trooper to these rooms, however, in the course of his patrolling, is an assurance of protection and company, both to mistress and maid, which renders them very acceptable in the small hours of the night. Whenever he is heard advancing, they both make some little decorative preparation to receive him; at other times, they divide their watches into short scraps of oblivion, and dialogues, not wholly free from acerbity, as to whether

Miss Dedlock, sitting with her feet upon the fender, was or was not falling into the fire when rescued (to her great displeasure) by her guardian genius the maid.

"How is Sir Leicester now, Mr. George?" inquires Volumnia, adjusting her cowl over her head.

"Why, Sir Leicester is much the same, miss. He is very low and ill, and he even wanders a little sometimes."

"Has he asked for me?" inquires Volumnia tenderly.

"Why, no, I can't say he has, miss. Not within my hearing, that is to say."

"This is a truly sad time, Mr. George."

"It is indeed, miss. Hadn't you better go to bed?"

"You had a deal better go to bed, Miss Dedlock," quoth the maid, sharply.

But Volumnia answers No! No! She may be asked for, she may be wanted at a moment's notice. She never should forgive herself "if anything was to happen" and she was not on the spot. She declines to enter on the question, mooted by the maid, how the spot comes to be there, and not in her own room (which is nearer to Sir Leicester's); but staunchly declares that on the spot she will remain. Volumnia further makes a merit of not having "closed an eye"—as if she had twenty or thirty—though it is hard to reconcile this statement with her having most indisputably opened two within five minutes.

But when it comes to four o'clock, and still the same blank, Volumnia's constancy begins to fail her, or rather it begins to strengthen; for she now considers that it is her duty to be ready for the morrow, when much may be expected of her; that, in fact, howsoever anxious to remain upon the spot, it may be required of her, as an act of self-devotion, to desert the spot. So, when the trooper reappears with his "Hadn't you better go to bed, miss?" and when the maid protests, more sharply than before, "You had a deal better go to bed, Miss Dedlock!" she meekly rises and says, "Do with me what you think best!"

Mr. George undoubtedly thinks it best to escort her on his arm to the door of her cousinly chamber, and the maid as undoubtedly thinks it best to hustle her into bed with mighty little ceremony. Accordingly, these steps are taken; and now the trooper, in his rounds, has the house to himself.

There is no improvement in the weather. From the portico, from the eaves, from the parapet, from every ledge and post and pillar, drips the thawed snow. It has crept, as if for shelter, into the lintels of the great door—under it, into the corners of the windows, into every chink and crevice of retreat, and there wastes and dies. It is falling still; upon the roof, upon the skylight; even through the skylight, and drip, drip, drip, with the regularity of the Ghost's Walk, on the stone floor below.

The trooper, his old recollections awakened by the solitary grandeur of a great house—no novelty to him once at Chesney Wold—goes up the stairs and through the chief rooms, holding up his light at arm's length. Thinking of his varied fortunes within the last few weeks, and of his rustic boyhood, and of the two periods of his life so strangely brought together across the wide intermediate space; thinking of the murdered man whose image is fresh in his mind; thinking of the lady who has disappeared from these very rooms, and the tokens of whose recent presence are all here; thinking of the master of the house up-stairs, and of the foreboding "Who will tell him?" he looks here and looks there, and reflects how he *might* see something now, which it would tax his boldness to walk up to, lay his hand upon, and prove to be a fancy. But it is all blank; blank as the darkness above and below, while he goes up the great staircase again; blank as the oppressive silence.

"All is still in readiness, George Rouncewell?"

"Quite orderly and right, Sir Leicester."

"No word of any kind?"

The trooper shakes his head.

"No letter that can possibly have been overlooked?"

But he knows there is no such hope as that, and lays his head down without looking for an answer.

Very familiar to him, as he said himself some hours ago, George Rouncewell lifts him into easier positions through the long remainder of the blank wintry night; and, equally familiar with his unexpressed wish, extinguishes the light, and undraws the curtains at the first late break of day. The day comes like a phantom. Cold, colourless, and vague, it sends a warning streak before it of a deathlike hue, as if it cried out, "Look what I am bringing you, who watch there! Who will tell him?"

Chapter LIX

ESTHER'S NARRATIVE

It was three o'clock in the morning when the houses outside London did at last begin to exclude the country, and to close us in with streets. We had made our way along roads in a far worse condition than when we had traversed them by daylight, both the fall and the thaw having lasted ever since; but the energy of my companion had never slackened. It had only been, as I thought, of less assistance than the horses in getting us on, and it had often aided them. They had stopped exhausted, halfway up hills, they had been driven through streams of turbulent water, they had slipped down and become entangled with the harness; but he and his little lantern had been always ready, and when the mishap was set right, I had never heard any variation in his cool, "Get on, my lads!"

The steadiness and confidence with which he had directed our journey back, I could not account for. Never wavering, he never even stopped to make an inquiry until we were within a few miles of London. A very few words, here and there, were then enough for him; and thus we came, at between three and four o'clock in the morning, into Islington.

I will not dwell on the suspense and anxiety with which I reflected all this time, that we were leaving my mother farther and farther behind every minute. I think I had some strong hope that he must be right, and could not fail to have a satisfactory object in following this woman; but I tormented myself with questioning it, and discussing it, during the whole journey. What was to ensue when we found her, and what could compensate us for this loss of time, were questions also that I could not possibly dismiss; my mind was quite tortured by long dwelling on such reflections, when we stopped.

We stopped in a high-street, where there was a coach-stand. My companion paid our two drivers, who were as completely covered with splashes as if they had been dragged along the roads like the carriage itself; and giving them some brief direction where to take it, lifted me out of it, and into a hackney-coach he had chosen from the rest.

"Why, my dear!" he said, as he did this. "How wet you are!"

I had not been conscious of it. But the melted snow had found its way into the carriage; and I had got out two or three times when a fallen horse was plunging and had to be got up; and the wet had penetrated my dress. I assured him it was no matter; but the driver, who knew him, would not be dissuaded by me from running down the street to his stable, whence he brought an armful of clean dry straw. They shook it out and strewed it well about me, and I found it warm and comfortable.

"Now, my dear," said Mr. Bucket, with his head in at the window after I was shut up. "We're a going to mark this person down. It may take a little time, but you don't mind that. You're pretty sure that I've got a motive. Ain't you?"

I little thought what it was—little thought in how short a time I should understand it better; but I assured him that I had confidence in him.

"So you may have, my dear," he returned. "And I tell you what!

If you only repose half as much confidence in me as I repose in you, after what I've experienced of you, that'll do. Lord! you're no trouble at all. I never see a young woman in any station of society—and I've seen many elevated ones too—conduct herself like you have conducted yourself, since you was called out of your bed. You're a pattern, you know, that's what you are," said Mr. Bucket, warmly; "you're a pattern."

I told him I was very glad, as indeed I was, to have been no hindrance to him; and that I hoped I should be none now.

"My dear," he returned, "when a young lady is as mild as she's game, and as game as she's mild, that's all I ask, and more than I expect. She then becomes a Queen, and that's about what you are yourself."

With these encouraging words—they really were encouraging to me under those lonely and anxious circumstances—he got upon the box, and we once more drove away. Where we drove, I neither knew then, nor have ever known since; but we appeared to seek out the narrowest and worst streets in London. Whenever I saw him directing the driver, I was prepared for our descending into a deeper complication of such streets, and we never failed to do so.

Sometimes we emerged upon a wider thoroughfare, or came to a larger building than the generality, well lighted. Then we stopped at offices like those we had visited when we began our journey, and I saw him in consultation with others. Sometimes he would get down by an archway, or at a street corner, and mysteriously show the light of his little lantern. This would attract similar lights from various dark quarters, like so many insects, and a fresh consultation would be held. By degrees we appeared to contract our search within narrower and easier limits. Single police officers on duty could now tell Mr. Bucket what he wanted to know, and point to him where to go. At last we stopped for a rather long conversation between him and one of these men, which I supposed to be satisfactory from his manner of nodding from time to time. When it was finished he came to me, looking very busy and attentive.

"Now, Miss Summerson," he said to me, "you won't be alarmed whatever comes off, I know. It's not necessary for me to give you any further caution, than to tell you that we have marked this person down, and that you may be of use to me before I know it myself. I don't like to ask such a thing, my dear, but would you walk a little way?"

Of course I got out directly, and took his arm.

"It ain't so easy to keep your feet," said Mr. Bucket; "but take time."

Although I looked about me confusedly and hurriedly, as we

crossed the street, I thought I knew the place. "Are we in Holborn?" I asked him.

"Yes," said Mr. Bucket. "Do you know this turning?"

"It looks like Chancery Lane."

"And was christened so, my dear," said Mr. Bucket.

We turned down it, and as we went, shuffling through the sleet, I heard the clocks strike half-past five. We passed on in silence, and as quickly as we could with such a foothold, when some one coming towards us on the narrow pavement, wrapped in a cloak, stopped and stood aside to give me room. In the same moment I heard an exclamation of wonder, and my own name, from Mr. Woodcourt. I knew his voice very well.

It was so unexpected, and so—I don't know what to call it, whether pleasant or painful—to come upon it after my feverish wandering journey, and in the midst of the night, that I could not keep back the tears from my eyes. It was like hearing his voice in a strange country.

"My dear Miss Summerson, that you should be out at this hour, and in such weather!"

He had heard from my guardian of my having been called away on some uncommon business, and said so to dispense with any explanation. I told him that we had but just left a coach, and were going—but then I was obliged to look at my companion.

"Why, you see, Mr. Woodcourt"; he had caught the name from me; "we are a going at present into the next street.—Inspector Bucket."

Mr. Woodcourt, disregarding my remonstrances, had hurriedly taken off his cloak, and was putting it about me. "That's a good move, too," said Mr. Bucket, assisting, "a very good move."

"May I go with you?" said Mr. Woodcourt. I don't know whether to me or my companion.

"Why, Lord!" exclaimed Mr. Bucket, taking the answer on himself. "Of course you may."

It was all said in a moment, and they took me between them, wrapped in the cloak.

"I have just left Richard," said Mr. Woodcourt. "I have been sitting with him since ten o'clock last night.

"O dear me, he is ill!"

"No, no, believe me; not ill, but not quite well. He was depressed and faint—you know he gets so worried and so worn sometimes—and Ada sent to me of course, and when I came home I found her note, and came straight here. Well! Richard revived so much after a little while, and Ada was so happy, and so convinced of its being my doing, though God knows I had little enough to do with it, that

I remained with him until he had been fast asleep some hours. As fast asleep as she is now, I hope!"

His friendly and familiar way of speaking of them, his unaffected devotion to them, the grateful confidence with which I knew he had inspired my darling, and the comfort he was to her; could I separate all this from his promise to me? How thankless I must have been if it had not recalled the words he said to me, when he was so moved by the change in my appearance. "I will accept him as a trust, and it shall be a sacred one!"

We now turned into another narrow street. "Mr. Woodcourt," said Mr. Bucket, who had eyed him closely as we came along, "our business takes us to a law-stationer's here; a certain Mr. Snagsby's. What, you know him, do you?" He was so quick that he saw it in an instant.

"Yes, I know a little of him, and have called upon him at this place."

"Indeed, sir?" said Mr. Bucket. "Then will you be so good as to let me leave Miss Summerson with you for a moment, while I go and have half a word with him?"

The last police officer with whom he had conferred was standing silently behind us. I was not aware of it until he struck in, on my saying I heard some one crying.

"Don't be alarmed, miss," he returned. "It's Snagsby's servant."

"Why, you see," said Mr. Bucket, "the girl's subject to fits, and has 'em bad upon her to-night. A most contrairy circumstance it is, for I want certain information out of that girl, and she must be brought to reason somehow."

"At all events, they wouldn't be up yet, if it wasn't for her, Mr. Bucket," said the other man. "She's been at it pretty well all night, sir."

"Well, that's true," he returned. "My light's burnt out. Show your's a moment."

All this passed in a whisper, a door or two from the house in which I could faintly hear crying and moaning. In the little round of light produced for the purpose, Mr. Bucket went up to the door and knocked. The door was opened, after he had knocked twice; and he went in, leaving us standing in the street.

"Miss Summerson," said Mr. Woodcourt; "if, without obtruding myself on your confidence, I may remain near you, pray let me do so."

"You are truly kind," I answered. "I need wish to keep no secret of my own from you; if I keep any, it is another's."

"I quite understand. Trust me, I will remain near you only so long as I can fully respect it."

"I trust implicitly to you," I said. "I know and deeply feel how sacredly you keep your promise."

After a short time the little round of light shone out again, and Mr. Bucket advanced towards us in it with his earnest face. "Please to come in, Miss Summerson," he said, "and sit down by the fire. Mr. Woodcourt, from information I have received I understand you're a medical man. Would you look to this girl and see if anything can be done to bring her round? She has a letter somewhere that I particularly want. It's not in her box, and I think it must be about her; but she is so twisted and clenched up, that she is difficult to handle without hurting."

We all three went into the house together; although it was cold and raw, it smelt close too from being up all night. In the passage behind the door, stood a scared, sorrowful-looking little man in a grey coat, who seemed to have a naturally polite manner, and spoke meekly.

"Down-stairs, if you please, Mr. Bucket," said he. "The lady will excuse the front kitchen; we use it as our workaday sitting-room. The back is Guster's bedroom, and in it she's a carrying on, poor thing, to a frightful extent!"

We went down-stairs, followed by Mr. Snagsby, as I soon found the little man to be. In the front kitchen, sitting by the fire, was Mrs. Snagsby, with very red eyes and a very severe expression of face.

"My little woman," said Mr. Snagsby, entering behind us, "to wave—not to put too fine a point upon it, my dear—hostilities, for one single moment, in the course of this prolonged night, here is Inspector Bucket, Mr. Woodcourt, and a lady."

She looked very much astonished, as she had reason for doing, and looking particularly hard at me.

"My little woman," said Mr. Snagsby, sitting down in the remotest corner by the door, as if he were taking a liberty, "it is not unlikely that you may inquire of me why Inspector Bucket, Mr. Woodcourt, and a lady, call upon us in Cook's Court, Cursitor Street, at the present hour. I don't know. I have not the least idea. If I was to be informed, I should despair of understanding, and I'd rather not be told."

He appeared so miserable, sitting with his head upon his hand, and I appeared so unwelcome, that I was going to offer an apology, when Mr. Bucket took the matter on himself.

"Now, Mr. Snagsby," said he, "the best thing you can do, is to go along with Mr. Woodcourt to look after your Guster——"

"My Guster, Mr. Bucket!" cried Mr. Snagsby. "Go on, sir, go on. I shall be charged with that next."

"And to hold the candle," pursued Mr. Bucket without correcting himself, "or hold her, or make yourself useful in any way you're asked. Which there's not a man alive more ready to do; for you're a man of urbanity and suavity, you know, and you've got the sort of heart that can feel for another. (Mr. Woodcourt, would you be so good as see to her, and if you can get that letter from her, to let me have it as soon as ever you can?)"

As they went out, Mr. Bucket made me sit down in a corner by the fire, and take off my wet shoes, which he turned up to dry upon the fender; talking all the time.

"Don't you be at all put out, miss, by the want of a hospitable look from Mrs. Snagsby there, because she's under a mistake altogether. She'll find that out, sooner than will be agreeable to a lady of her generally correct manner of forming her thoughts, because I'm a going to explain it to her." Here, standing on the hearth with his wet hat and shawls in his hand, himself a pile of wet, he turned to Mrs. Snagsby. "Now, the first thing that I say to you, as a married woman, possessing what you may call charms, you know—'Believe me, if all those endearing, and cetrer'—you're well acquainted with the song, because it's in vain for you to tell me that you and good society are strangers—charms—attractions, mind you, that ought to give you confidence in yourself—is, that you've done it."

Mrs. Snagsby looked rather alarmed, relented a little, and faltered, what did Mr. Bucket mean?

"What does Mr. Bucket mean?" he repeated; and I saw by his face, that all the time he talked he was listening for the discovery of the letter—to my own great agitation; for I knew then how important it must be; "I'll tell you what he means, ma'am. Go and see Othello acted. That's the tragedy for you."

Mrs. Snagsby consciously asked why.

"Why?" said Mr. Bucket. "Because you'll come to that, if you don't look out. Why, at the very moment while I speak, I know what your mind's not wholly free from, respecting this young lady. But shall I tell you who this young lady is? Now, come, you're what I call an intellectual woman—with your soul too large for your body, if you come to that, and chafing it—and you know me, and you recollect where you saw me last, and what was talked of in that circle. Don't you? Yes! Very well. This young lady is that young lady."

Mrs. Snagsby appeared to understand the reference better than I did at the time.

"And Toughey—him as you call Jo—was mixed up in the same business, and no other; and the law-writer that you know of, was mixed up in the same business, and no other; and your husband, with no more knowledge of it than your great grandfather, was mixed up (by Mr. Tulkinghorn, deceased, his best customer) in the same business, and no other; and the whole bileing[1] of people was mixed up in the same business, and no other. And yet a married woman, possessing your attractions, shuts her eyes (and sparklers too), and goes and runs her delicate-formed head against a wall. Why, I am ashamed of you! (I expected Mr. Woodcourt might have got it by this time.)"

Mrs. Snagsby shook her head, and put her handkerchief to her eyes.

"Is that all?" said Mr. Bucket, excitedly. "No. See what happens. Another person mixed up in that business and no other, a person in a wretched state, comes here to-night, and is seen a speaking to your maid-servant; and between her and your maid-servant there passes a paper that I would give a hundred pound for, down. What do you do? You hide and you watch 'em, and you pounce upon that maid-servant—knowing what she's subject to, and what a little thing will bring 'em on—in that surprising manner, and with that severity, that, by the Lord, she goes off and keeps off, when a Life may be hanging upon that girl's words!"

He so thoroughly meant what he said now, that I involuntarily clasped my hands, and felt the room turning away from me. But it stopped. Mr. Woodcourt came in, put a paper into his hand, and went away again.

"Now Mrs. Snagsby, the only amends you can make," said Mr. Bucket, rapidly glancing at it, "is to let me speak a word to this young lady in private here. And if you know of any help that you can give to that gentleman in the next kitchen there, or can think of any one thing that's likelier than another to bring the girl round, do your swiftest and best!" In an instant she was gone, and he had shut the door. "Now, my dear, you're steady, and quite sure of yourself?"

"Quite," said I.

"Whose writing is that?"

It was my mother's. A pencil-writing, on a crushed and torn piece of paper, blotted with wet. Folded roughly like a letter, and directed to me at my guardian's.

"You know the hand," he said, "and if you are firm enough to read it to me, do! But be particular to a word."

It had been written in portions, at different times. I read as follows:

"I came to the cottage with two objects. First, to see the dear one, if I could, once more—but only to see her—not to speak to

1. A full load of laundry to be boiled in one pot made up a *whole boiling,* i.e., here *the whole lot.*

her, or let her know that I was near. The other object, to elude pursuit, and to be lost. Do not blame the mother for her share. The assistance that she rendered me, she rendered on my strongest assurance that it was for the dear one's good. You remember her dead child. The men's consent I bought, but her help was freely given."

" 'I came.' That was written," said my companion, "when she rested there. It bears out what I made of it. I was right."

The next was written at another time.

> "I have wandered a long distance, and for many hours, and I know that I must soon die. These streets! I have no purpose but to die. When I left I had a worse; but I am saved from adding that guilt to the rest. Cold, wet, and fatigue, are sufficient causes for my being found dead; but I shall die of others, though I suffer from these. It was right that all that had sustained me should give way at once, and that I should die of terror and my conscience."

"Take courage," said Mr. Bucket. "There's only a few words more."

Those, too, were written at another time. To all appearance, almost in the dark.

> "I have done all I could to be lost. I shall be soon forgotten so, and shall disgrace him least. I have nothing about me by which I can be recognised. This paper I part with now. The place where I shall lie down, if I can yet get so far, has been often in my mind. Farewell. Forgive."

Mr. Bucket, supporting me with his arm, lowered me gently into my chair. "Cheer up! Don't think me hard with you, my dear, but as soon as ever you feel equal to it, get your shoes on and be ready."

I did as he required; but I was left there a long time, praying for my unhappy mother. They were all occupied with the poor girl, and I heard Mr. Woodcourt directing them and speaking to her often. At length he came in with Mr. Bucket; and said that as it was important to address her gently, he thought it best that I should ask her for whatever information we desired to obtain. There was no doubt that she could now reply to questions, if she were soothed, and not alarmed. The questions, Mr. Bucket said, were, how she came by the letter, what passed between her and the person who gave her the letter, and where the person went. Holding my mind as steadily as I could to these points, I went into the next room with them. Mr. Woodcourt would have remained outside, but at my solicitation went in with us.

The poor girl was sitting on the floor where they had laid her down. They stood around her though at a little distance, that she might have air. She was not pretty, and looked weak and poor; but she had a plaintive and a good face, though it was still a little wild. I kneeled on the ground beside her, and put her poor head on my shoulder; whereupon she drew her arm round my neck, and burst into tears.

"My poor girl," said I, laying my face against her forehead; for indeed I was crying too, and trembling; "it seems cruel to trouble you now, but more depends on our knowing something about this letter, than I could tell you in an hour."

She began piteously declaring that she didn't mean any harm, she didn't mean any harm, Mrs. Snagsby.

"We are all sure of that," said I. "But pray tell me how you got it."

"Yes, dear lady, I will, and tell you true. I'll tell true, indeed, Mrs. Snagsby."

"I am sure of that," said I. "And how was it?"

"I had been out on an errand, dear lady—long after it was dark—quite late; and when I came home, I found a common-looking person, all wet and muddy, looking up at our house. When she saw me coming in at the door, she called me back, and said did I live here? and I said yes, and she said she knew only one or two places about here, but had lost her way, and couldn't find them. O what shall I do, what shall I do! They won't believe me! She didn't say any harm to me, and I didn't say any harm to her, indeed, Mrs. Snagsby!"

It was necessary for her mistress to comfort her; which she did, I must say, with a good deal of contrition: before she could be got beyond this.

"She could not find those places," said I.

"No!" cried the girl, shaking her head. "No! Couldn't find them. And she was so faint, and lame, and miserable, O so wretched! that if you had seen her, Mr. Snagsby, you'd have given her half-a-crown, I know!"

"Well, Guster, my girl," said he, at first not knowing what to say. "I hope I should."

"And yet she was so well spoken," said the girl, looking at me with wide-open eyes, "that it made a person's heart bleed. And so she said to me, did I know the way to the burying-ground? And I asked her which burying-ground? And she said, the poor burying-ground. And so I told her I had been a poor child myself, and it was according to parishes. But she said she meant a poor burying-ground not very far from here, where there was an archway, and a step, and an iron gate."

As I watched her face, and soothed her to go on, I saw that Mr. Bucket received this with a look which I could not separate from one of alarm.

"O dear, dear!" cried the girl, pressing her hair back with her hands, "what shall I do, what shall I do! She meant the burying-ground where the man was buried that took the sleeping-stuff—that you came home and told us of, Mr. Snagsby—that frightened me so, Mrs. Snagsby. O I am frightened again. Hold me!"

"You are so much better now," said I. "Pray, pray tell me more."

"Yes I will, yes I will! But don't be angry with me, that's a dear lady, because I have been so ill."

Angry with her, poor soul!

"There! Now I will, now I will. So she said, could I tell her how to find it, and I said yes, and I told her; and she looked at me with eyes like almost as if she was blind, and herself all waving back. And so she took out the letter, and showed it me, and said if she was to put that in the post-office, it would be rubbed out and not minded and never sent; and would I take it from her, and send it, and the messenger would be paid at the house? And so I said yes, if it was no harm, and she said no—no harm. And so I took it from her, and she said she had nothing to give me, and I said I was poor myself, and consequently wanted nothing. And so she said God bless you! and went."

"And did she go——?"

"Yes," cried the girl, anticipating the inquiry, "yes! she went the way I had shown her. Then I came in, and Mrs. Snagsby came behind me from somewhere, and laid hold of me, and I was frightened."

Mr. Woodcourt took her kindly from me. Mr. Bucket wrapped me up, and immediately we were in the street. Mr. Woodcourt hesitated, but I said, "Don't leave me now!" and Mr. Bucket added, "You'll be better with us, we may want you; don't lose time."

I have the most confused impressions of that walk. I recollect that it was neither night nor day; that morning was dawning, but the street-lamps were not yet put out; that the sleet was still falling, and that all the ways were deep with it. I recollect a few chilled people passing in the streets. I recollect the wet house-tops, the clogged and bursting gutters and water-spouts, the mounds of blackened ice and snow over which we passed, the narrowness of the courts by which we went. At the same time I remember, that the poor girl seemed to be yet telling her story audibly and plainly in my hearing; that I could feel her resting on my arm; that the stained house fronts put on human shapes and looked at me; that great water-gates seemed to be opening and closing in my head, or in the air; and that the unreal things were more substantial than the real.

At last we stood under a dark and miserable covered way, where one lamp was burning over an iron gate, and where the morning faintly struggled in. The gate was closed. Beyond it, was a burial-ground—a dreadful spot in which the night was very slowly stirring; but where I could dimly see heaps of dishonoured graves and stones, hemmed in by filthy houses, with a few dull lights in their windows, and on whose walls a thick humidity broke out like a disease. On the step at the gate, drenched in the fearful wet of such a place, which oozed and splashed down everywhere, I saw, with a cry of pity and horror, a woman lying—Jenny, the mother of the dead child.

I ran forward, but they stopped me, and Mr. Woodcourt entreated me, with the greatest earnestness, even with tears, before I went up to the figure to listen for an instant to what Mr. Bucket said. I did so, as I thought. I did so, as I am sure.

"Miss Summerson, you'll understand me, if you think a moment. They changed clothes at the cottage."

They changed clothes at the cottage. I could repeat the words in my mind, and I knew what they meant of themselves; but I attached no meaning to them in any other connexion.

"And one returned," said Mr. Bucket, "and one went on. And the one that went on, only went on a certain way agreed upon to deceive, and then turned across country, and went home. Think a moment!"

I could repeat this in my mind too, but I had not the least idea what it meant. I saw before me, lying on the step, the mother of the dead child. She lay there, with one arm creeping round a bar of the iron gate, and seeming to embrace it. She lay there, who had so lately spoken to my mother. She lay there, a distressed, unsheltered, senseless creature. She who had brought my mother's letter, who could give me the only clue to where my mother was; she who was to guide us to rescue and save her whom we had sought so far, who had come to this condition by some means connected with my mother that I could not follow, and might be passing beyond our reach and help at that moment; she lay there, and they stopped me! I saw, but did not comprehend, the solemn and compassionate look in Mr. Woodcourt's face. I saw, but did not comprehend, his touching the other on the breast to keep him back. I saw him stand uncovered in the bitter air, with a reverence for something. But my understanding for all this was gone.

I even heard it said between them:

"Shall she go?"

"She had better go. Her hands should be the first to touch her. They have a higher right than ours."

I passed on to the gate, and stooped down. I lifted the heavy head, put the long dank hair aside, and turned the face. And it was my mother, cold and dead.

Chapter LX

PERSPECTIVE

I proceed to other passages of my narrative. From the goodness of all about me, I derived such consolation as I can never think of unmoved. I have already said so much of myself, and so much still remains, that I will not dwell upon my sorrow. I had an illness, but it was not a long one; and I would avoid even this mention of it, if I could quite keep down the recollection of their sympathy.

I proceed to other passages of my narrative.

During the time of my illness, we were still in London, where Mrs. Woodcourt had come, on my guardian's invitation, to stay with us. When my guardian thought me well and cheerful enough to talk with him in our old way—though I could have done that sooner, if he would have believed me—I resumed my work, and my chair beside his. He had appointed the time himself, and we were alone.

"Dame Trot," said he, receiving me with a kiss, "welcome to the Growlery again, my dear. I have a scheme to develop, little woman. I purpose to remain here, perhaps for six months, perhaps for a longer time—as it may be. Quite to settle here for a while, in short."

"And in the meanwhile leave Bleak House?" said I.

"Aye, my dear! Bleak House," he returned, "must learn to take care of itself."

I thought his tone sounded sorrowful; but, looking at him, I saw his kind face lighted up by its pleasantest smile.

"Bleak House," he repeated; and his tone did *not* sound sorrowful, I found, "must learn to take care of itself. It is a long way from Ada, my dear, and Ada stands much in need of you."

"It is like you, guardian," said I, "to have been taking that into consideration, for a happy surprise to both of us."

"Not so disinterested either, my dear, if you mean to extol me for that virtue; since, if you were generally on the road, you could be seldom with me. And besides, I wish to hear as much and as often of Ada as I can, in this condition of estrangement from poor Rick. Not of her alone, but of him too, poor fellow."

"Have you seen Mr. Woodcourt this morning, guardian?"

"I see Mr. Woodcourt every morning, Dame Durden."

"Does he still say the same of Richard?"

"Just the same. He knows of no direct bodily illness that he has; on the contrary, he believes that he has none. Yet he is not easy about him; who *can* be?"

My dear girl had been to see us lately, every day; sometimes twice in a day. But we had foreseen, all along, that this would only last until I was quite myself. We knew full well that her fervent heart was as full of affection and gratitude towards her cousin John as it had ever been, and we acquitted Richard of laying any injunctions upon her to stay away; but we knew, on the other hand, that she felt it a part of her duty to him, to be sparing of her visits at our house. My guardian's delicacy had soon perceived this, and had tried to convey to her that he thought she was right.

"Dear, unfortunate, mistaken Richard," said I. "When will he awake from his delusion!"

"He is not in the way to do so now, my dear," replied my guardian. "The more he suffers, the more averse he will be to me: having made me the principal representative of the great occasion of his suffering."

I could not help adding, "So unreasonably!"

"Ah, Dame Trot, Dame Trot!" returned my guardian, "what shall we find reasonable in Jarndyce and Jarndyce! Unreason and injustice at the top, unreason and injustice at the heart and at the bottom, unreason and injustice from beginning to end—if it ever has an end—how should poor Rick, always hovering near it, pluck reason out of it? He no more gathers grapes from thorns, or figs from thistles,[1] than older men did, in old times."

His gentleness and consideration for Richard, whenever we spoke of him, touched me so, that I was always silent on this subject very soon.

"I suppose the Lord Chancellor, and the Vice Chancellors, and the whole Chancery battery of great guns, would be infinitely astonished by such unreason and injustice in one of their suitors," pursued my guardian. "When those learned gentlemen begin to raise moss-roses from the powder they sow in their wigs, I shall begin to be astonished too!"

He checked himself in glancing towards the window to look where the wind was, and leaned on the back of my chair instead.

"Well, well, little woman! To go on, my dear. This rock we must leave to time, chance, and hopeful circumstance. We must not shipwreck Ada upon it. She cannot afford, and he cannot afford, the remotest chance of another separation from a friend. Therefore, I

1. See Matthew 7:16: "Ye shall know them by their fruits. Do men gather grapes of thorns, or figs of thistles?"

have particularly begged of Woodcourt, and I now particularly beg of you, my dear, not to move this subject with Rick. Let it rest. Next week, next month, next year, sooner or later, he will see me with clearer eyes. I can wait."

But I had already discussed it with him, I confessed; and so, I thought, had Mr. Woodcourt.

"So he tells me," returned my guardian. "Very good. He has made his protest, and Dame Durden has made hers, and there is nothing more to be said about it. Now, I come to Mrs. Woodcourt. How do you like her, my dear?"

In answer to this question, which was oddly abrupt, I said I liked her very much, and thought she was more agreeable than she used to be.

"I think so too," said my guardian. "Less pedigree? Not so much of Morgan-ap—what's his name?"

That was what I meant, I acknowledged; though he was a very harmless person, even when we had had more of him.

"Still, upon the whole, he is as well in his native mountains," said my guardian. "I agree with you. Then, little woman, can I do better for a time than retain Mrs. Woodcourt here?"

No. And yet——

My guardian looked at me, waiting for what I had to say.

I had nothing to say. At least I had nothing in my mind that I could say. I had an undefined impression that it might have been better if we had had some other inmate, but I could hardly have explained why, even to myself. Or, if to myself, certainly not to anybody else.

"You see," said my guardian, "our neighbourhood is in Woodcourt's way, and he can come here to see her as often as he likes, which is agreeable to them both; and she is familiar to us, and fond of you."

Yes. That was undeniable. I had nothing to say against it. I could not have suggested a better arrangement; but I was not quite easy in my mind. Esther, Esther, why not? Esther, think!

"It is a very good plan indeed, dear guardian, and we could not do better."

"Sure, little woman?"

Quite sure. I had had a moment's time to think, since I had urged that duty on myself, and I was quite sure.

"Good," said my guardian. "It shall be done. Carried unanimously."

"Carried unanimously," I repeated, going on with my work.

It was a cover for his book-table that I happened to be ornamenting. It had been laid by on the night preceding my sad journey, and never resumed. I showed it to him now, and he admired it highly. After I had explained the pattern to him, and all the great effects that were to come out by-and-by, I thought I would go back to our last theme.

"You said, dear guardian, when we spoke of Mr. Woodcourt before Ada left us, that you thought he would give a long trial to another country. Have you been advising him since?"

"Yes, little woman; pretty often."

"Has he decided to do so?"

"I rather think not."

"Some other prospect has opened to him, perhaps?" said I.

"Why—yes—perhaps," returned my guardian, beginning his answer in a very deliberate manner. "About half a year hence or so, there is a medical attendant for the poor to be appointed at a certain place in Yorkshire. It is a thriving place, pleasantly situated; streams and streets, town and country, mill and moor; and seems to present an opening for such a man. I mean, a man whose hopes and aims may sometimes lie (as most men's sometimes do, I dare say) above the ordinary level, but to whom the ordinary level will be high enough after all, if it should prove to be a way of usefulness and good service leading to no other. All generous spirits are ambitious, I suppose; but the ambition that calmly trusts itself to such a road, instead of spasmodically trying to fly over it, is of the kind I care for. It is Woodcourt's kind."

"And will he get this appointment?" I asked.

"Why, little woman," returned my guardian, smiling, "not being an oracle, I cannot confidently say; but I think so. His reputation stands very high; there were people from that part of the country in the shipwreck; and, strange to say, I believe the best man has the best chance. You must not suppose it to be a fine endowment. It is a very, very commonplace affair, my dear; an appointment to a great amount of work and a small amount of pay; but better things will gather about it, it may be fairly hoped."

"The poor of that place will have reason to bless the choice, if it falls on Mr. Woodcourt, guardian."

"You are right, little woman; that I am sure they will."

We said no more about it, nor did he say a word about the future of Bleak House. But it was the first time I had taken my seat at his side in my mourning dress, and that accounted for it I considered.

I now began to visit my dear girl every day, in the dull dark corner where she lived. The morning was my usual time; but whenever I found I had an hour or so to spare, I put on my bonnet and bustled off to Chancery Lane. They were both so glad to see me at all hours, and used to brighten up so when they heard me opening the door and coming in (being quite at home, I never knocked), that I had no fear of becoming troublesome just yet.

On these occasions I frequently found Richard absent. At other times he would be writing, or reading papers in the Cause, at that table of his, so covered with papers, which was never disturbed. Sometimes I would come upon him, lingering at the door of Mr. Vholes's office. Sometimes I would meet him in the neighbourhood, lounging about, and biting his nails. I often met him wandering in Lincoln's Inn, near the place where I had first seen him, O how different, how different!

That the money Ada brought him was melting away with the candles I used to see burning after dark in Mr. Vholes's office, I knew very well. It was not a large amount in the beginning; he had married in debt; and I could not fail to understand, by this time, what was meant by Mr. Vholes's shoulder being at the wheel—as I still heard it was. My dear made the best of housekeepers, and tried hard to save; but I knew that they were getting poorer and poorer every day.

She shone in the miserable corner like a beautiful star. She adorned and graced it so, that it became another place. Paler than she had been at home, and a little quieter than I had thought natural to her she was yet so cheerful and hopeful, her face was so unshadowed, that I half believed she was blinded by her love for Richard to his ruinous career.

I went one day to dine with them, while I was under this impression. As I turned into Symond's Inn, I met little Miss Flite coming out. She had been to make a stately call upon the wards in Jarndyce, as she still called them, and had derived the highest gratification from that ceremony. Ada had already told me that she called every Monday at five o'clock, with one little extra white bow in her bonnet, which never appeared there at any other time, and with her largest reticule of documents on her arm.

"My dear!" she began. "So delighted! How do you do! So glad to see you. And you are going to visit our interesting Jarndyce wards? *To* be sure! Our beauty is at home, my dear, and will be charmed to see you."

"Then Richard is not come in yet?" said I. "I am glad of that, for I was afraid of being a little late."

"No, he is not come in," returned Miss Flite. "He has had a long day in Court. I left him there, with Vholes. You don't like Vholes, I hope? *Don't* like Vholes. Dan-gerous man!"

"I am afraid you see Richard oftener than ever now?" said I.

"My dearest," returned Miss Flite, "daily and hourly. You know what I told you of the attraction on the Chancellor's table? My dear, next to myself he is the most constant suitor in Court. He begins quite to amuse our little party. Ve-ry friendly little party, are we not?"

It was miserable to hear this from her poor mad lips, though it was no surprise.

"In short, my valued friend," pursued Miss Flite, advancing her lips to my ear, with an air of equal patronage and mystery, "I must tell you a secret. I have made him my executor. Nominated, constituted, and appointed him. In my will. Ye-es."

"Indeed?" said I.

"Ye-es," repeated Miss Flite, in her most genteel accents, "my executor, administrator, and assign. (Our Chancery phrases, my love.) I have reflected that if I should wear out, he will be able to watch that judgment. Being so very regular in his attendance."

It made me sigh to think of him.

"I did at one time mean," said Miss Flite, echoing the sigh, "to nominate, constitute, and appoint poor Gridley. Also very regular, my charming girl. I assure you, most exemplary! But he wore out, poor man, so I have appointed his successor. Don't mention it. This is in confidence."

She carefully opened her reticule a little way, and showed me a folded piece of paper inside, as the appointment of which she spoke.

"Another secret, my dear. I have added to my collection of birds."

"Really, Miss Flite?" said I, knowing how it pleased her to have her confidence received with an appearance of interest.

She nodded several times, and her face became overcast and gloomy. "Two more. I call them the Wards in Jarndyce. They are caged up with all the others. With Hope, Joy, Youth, Peace, Rest, Life, Dust, Ashes, Waste, Want, Ruin, Despair, Madness, Death, Cunning, Folly, Words, Wigs, Rags, Sheepskin, Plunder, Precedent, Jargon, Gammon, and Spinach!"

The poor soul kissed me, with the most troubled look I had ever seen in her; and went her way. Her manner of running over the names of her birds, as if she were afraid of hearing them even from her own lips, quite chilled me.

This was not a cheering preparation for my visit, and I could have dispensed with the company of Mr. Vholes, when Richard (who arrived within a minute or two after me) brought him to share our dinner. Although it was a very plain one, Ada and Richard were for some minutes both out of the room together, helping to get ready what we were to eat and drink. Mr. Vholes took that opportunity of holding a little conversation in a low voice with me. He came to the window where I was sitting, and began upon Symond's Inn.

"A dull place, Miss Summerson, for a life that is not an official one," said Mr. Vholes, smearing the glass with his black glove to make it clearer for me.

"There is not much to see here," said I.

"Nor to hear, miss," returned Mr. Vholes. "A little music does occasionally stray in; but we are not musical in the law, and soon eject it. I hope Mr. Jarndyce is as well as his friends could wish him?"

I thanked Mr. Vholes, and said he was quite well.

"I have not the pleasure to be admitted among the number of his friends myself," said Mr. Vholes, "and I am aware that the gentlemen of our profession are sometimes regarded in such quarters with an unfavourable eye. Our plain course, however, under good report and evil report, and all kinds of prejudice (we are the victims of prejudice), is to have everything openly carried on. How do you find Mr. C looking, Miss Summerson?"

"He looks very ill. Dreadfully anxious."

"Just so," said Mr. Vholes.

He stood behind me, with his long black figure reaching nearly to the ceiling of those low rooms; feeling the pimples on his face as if they were ornaments, and speaking inwardly and evenly as though there were not a human passion or emotion in his nature.

"Mr. Woodcourt is in attendance upon Mr. C, I believe?" he resumed.

"Mr. Woodcourt is his disinterested friend," I answered.

"But I mean in professional attendance, medical attendance."

"That can do little for an unhappy mind," said I.

"Just so," said Mr. Vholes.

So slow, so eager, so bloodless and gaunt, I felt as if Richard were wasting away beneath the eyes of this adviser, and there were something of the Vampire in him.

"Miss Summerson," said Mr. Vholes, very slowly rubbing his gloved hands, as if, to his cold sense of touch, they were much the same in black kid or out of it, "this was an ill-advised marriage of Mr. C's."

I begged he would excuse me from discussing it. They had been engaged when they were both very young, I told him (a little indignantly), and when the prospect before them was much fairer and brighter. When Richard had not yielded himself to the unhappy influence which now darkened his life.

"Just so," assented Mr. Vholes again. "Still, with a view to everything being openly carried on, I will, with your permission, Miss Summerson, observe to you that I consider this a very ill-advised marriage indeed. I owe the opinion, not only to Mr. C's connexions, against whom I should naturally wish to protect myself, but also to my own reputation—dear to myself, as a professional man aiming to keep respectable; dear to my three girls at home, for whom I am striving to realise some little independence; dear, I will even say, to my aged father, whom it is my privilege to support."

"It would become a very different marriage, a much happier and better marriage, another marriage altogether, Mr. Vholes," said I, "if Richard were persuaded to turn his back on the fatal pursuit in which you are engaged with him."

Mr. Vholes, with a noiseless cough—or rather gasp—into one of his black gloves, inclined his head as if he did not wholly dispute even that.

"Miss Summerson," he said, "it may be so; and I freely admit that the young lady who has taken Mr. C's name upon herself in so ill-advised a manner—you will I am sure not quarrel with me for throwing out that remark again, as a duty I owe to Mr. C's connexions—is a highly genteel young lady. Business has prevented me from mixing much with general society, in any but a professional character; still I trust I am competent to perceive that she is a highly genteel young lady. As to beauty, I am not a judge of that myself, and I never did give much attention to it from a boy; but I dare say the young lady is equally eligible, in that point of view. She is considered so (I have heard) among the clerks in the Inn, and it is a point more in their way than in mine. In reference to Mr. C's pursuit of his interests——"

"O! His interests, Mr. Vholes!"

"Pardon me," returned Mr. Vholes, going on in exactly the same inward and dispassionate manner, "Mr. C takes certain interests under certain wills disputed in the suit. It is a term we use. In reference to Mr. C's pursuit of his interests, I mentioned to you, Miss Summerson, the first time I had the pleasure of seeing you, in my desire that everything should be openly carried on—I used those words, for I happened afterwards to note them in my diary, which is producible at any time—I mentioned to you that Mr. C had laid down the principle of watching his own interests; and that when a client of mine laid down a principle which was not of an immoral (that is to say, unlawful) nature, it devolved upon me to carry it out. I *have* carried it out; I *do* carry it out. But I will not smooth things over, to any connexion of Mr. C's, on any account. As open as I was to Mr. Jarndyce, I am to you. I regard it in the light of a professional duty to be so, though it can be charged to no one. I openly say, unpalatable as it may be, that I consider Mr. C's affairs in a very bad way, that I consider Mr. C himself in a very bad way, and that I regard this as an exceedingly ill-advised marriage.—Am I here, sir? Yes, I thank you; I am here, Mr. C, and enjoying the pleasure of some agreeable conversation with Miss Summerson, for which I have to thank you very much, sir!"

He broke off thus, in answer to Richard, who addressed him as he came into the room. By this time, I too well understood Mr.

Vholes's scrupulous way of saving himself and his respectability, not to feel that our worst fears did but keep pace with his client's progress.

We sat down to dinner, and I had an opportunity of observing Richard, anxiously. I was not disturbed by Mr. Vholes (who took off his gloves to dine), though he sat opposite to me at the small table; for I doubt if, looking up at all, he once removed his eyes from his host's face. I found Richard thin and languid, slovenly in his dress, abstracted in his manner, forcing his spirits now and then, and at other intervals relapsing into a dull thoughtfulness. About his large bright eyes that used to be so merry, there was a wanness and a restlessness that changed them altogether. I cannot use the expression that he looked old. There is a ruin of youth which is not like age; and into such a ruin Richard's youth and youthful beauty had all fallen away.

He ate little and seemed indifferent what it was; showed himself to be much more impatient than he used to be; and was quick, even with Ada. I thought, at first, that his old light-hearted manner was all gone; but it shone out of him sometimes, as I had occasionally known little momentary glimpses of my own old face to look out upon me from the glass. His laugh had not quite left him either; but it was like the echo of a joyful sound, and that is always sorrowful.

Yet he was as glad as ever, in his old affectionate way, to have me there; and we talked of the old times pleasantly. These did not appear to be interesting to Mr. Vholes, though he occasionally made a gasp, which I believe was his smile. He rose shortly after dinner, and said that with the permission of the ladies he would retire to his office.

"Always devoted to business, Vholes!" cried Richard.

"Yes, Mr. C," he returned, "the interests of clients are never to be neglected, sir. They are paramount in the thoughts of a professional man like myself, who wishes to preserve a good name among his fellow practitioners and society at large. My denying myself the pleasure of the present agreeable conversation, may not be wholly irrespective of your own interests, Mr. C."

Richard expressed himself quite sure of that, and lighted Mr. Vholes out. On his return he told us, more than once, that Vholes was a good fellow, a safe fellow, a man who did what he pretended to do, a very good fellow indeed! He was so defiant about it, that it struck me he had begun to doubt Mr. Vholes.

Then he threw himself on the sofa, tired out; and Ada and I put things to rights, for they had no other servant than the woman who attended to the chambers. My dear girl had a cottage piano there, and quietly sat down to sing some of Richard's favourites; the lamp being first removed into the next room, as he complained of its hurting his eyes.

I sat between them, at my dear girl's side, and felt very melancholy listening to her sweet voice. I think Richard did too; I think he darkened the room for that reason. She had been singing some time, rising between whiles to bend over him and speak to him; when Mr. Woodcourt came in. Then he sat down by Richard; and half playfully, half earnestly, quite naturally and easily, found out how he felt, and where he had been all day. Presently he proposed to accompany him in a short walk on one of the bridges, as it was a moonlight airy night; and Richard readily consenting, they went out together.

They left my dear girl still sitting at the piano, and me still sitting beside her. When they were gone out, I drew my arm round her waist. She put her left hand in mine (I was sitting on that side), but kept her right upon the keys—going over and over them, without striking any note.

"Esther, my dearest," she said, breaking silence, "Richard is never so well, and I am never so easy about him, as when he is with Allan Woodcourt. We have to thank you for that."

I pointed out to my darling how this could scarcely be, because Mr. Woodcourt had come to her cousin John's house, and had known us all there; and because he had always liked Richard, and Richard had always liked him, and—and so forth.

"All true," said Ada; "but that he is such a devoted friend to us, we owe to you."

I thought it best to let my dear girl have her way, and to say no more about it. So I said as much. I said it lightly, because I felt her trembling.

"Esther, my dearest, I want to be a good wife, a very, very good wife indeed. You shall teach me."

I teach! I said no more; for I noticed the hand that was fluttering over the keys, and I knew that it was not I who ought to speak; that it was she who had something to say to me.

"When I married Richard, I was not insensible to what was before him. I had been perfectly happy for a long time with you, and I had never known any trouble or anxiety, so loved and cared for; but I understood the danger he was in, dear Esther."

"I know, I know, my darling."

"When we were married, I had some little hope that I might be able to convince him of his mistake; that he might come to regard it in a new way as my husband, and not pursue it all the more desperately for my sake—as he does. But if I had not had that hope, I would have married him just the same, Esther. Just the same!"

In the momentary firmness of the hand that was never still—a firmness inspired by the utterance of these last words, and dying away with them—I saw the confirmation of her earnest tones.

"You are not to think, my dearest Esther, that I fail to see what you see, and fear what you fear. No one can understand him better than I do. The greatest wisdom that ever lived in the world could scarcely know Richard better than my love does."

She spoke so modestly and softly, and her trembling hand expressed such agitation, as it moved to and fro upon the silent notes! My dear, dear girl!

"I see him at his worst, every day. I watch him in his sleep. I know every change of his face. But when I married Richard, I was quite determined, Esther, if Heaven would help me, never to show him that I grieved for what he did, and so to make him more unhappy. I want him, when he comes home, to find no trouble in my face. I want him, when he looks at me, to see what he loved in me. I married him to do this, and this supports me."

I felt her trembling more. I waited for what was yet to come; and I now thought I began to know what it was.

"And something else supports me, Esther."

She stopped a minute. Stopped speaking only; her fluttering hand was still in motion.

"I look forward a little while, and I don't know what great aid may come to me. When Richard turns his eyes upon me then, there may be something lying on my breast more eloquent than I have been, with greater power than mine to show him his true course, and win him back."

Her hand stopped now. She clasped me in her arms, and I clasped her in mine.

"If that little creature should fail too, Esther, I still look forward. I look forward a long while, through years and years, and think that then, when I am growing old, or when I am dead perhaps, a beautiful woman, his daughter, happily married, may be proud of him and a blessing to him. Or that a generous brave man, as handsome as he used to be, as hopeful, and far more happy, may walk in the sunshine with him, honouring his grey head, and saying to himself, 'I thank God this is my father! ruined by a fatal inheritance, and restored through me!' "

O, my sweet girl, what a heart was that which beat so fast against me!

"These hopes uphold me, my dear Esther, and I know they will. Though sometimes even they depart from me, before a dread that arises when I look at Richard."

I tried to cheer my darling, and asked her what it was? Sobbing and weeping, she replied:

"That he may not live to see his child."

Chapter LXI

A DISCOVERY

The days when I frequented that miserable corner which my dear girl brightened, can never fade in my remembrance. I never see it, and I never wish to see it, now; I have been there only once since; but in my memory there is a mournful glory shining on the place, which will shine for ever.

Not a day passed without my going there, of course. At first I found Mr. Skimpole there, on two or three occasions, idly playing the piano, and talking in his usual vivacious strain. Now, besides my very much mistrusting the probability of his being there without making Richard poorer, I felt as if there were something in his careless gaiety, too inconsistent with what I knew of the depths of Ada's life. I clearly perceived, too, that Ada shared my feelings. I therefore resolved, after much thinking of it, to make a private visit to Mr. Skimpole, and try delicately to explain myself. My dear girl was the great consideration that made me bold.

I set off one morning, accompanied by Charley, for Somers Town. As I approached the house, I was strongly inclined to turn back, for I felt what a desperate attempt it was to make an impression on Mr. Skimpole, and how extremely likely it was that he would signally defeat me. However, I thought that being there, I would go through with it. I knocked with a trembling hand at Mr. Skimpole's door—literally with a hand, for the knocker was gone—and after a long parley gained admission from an Irishwoman, who was in the area when I knocked, breaking up the lid of the water-butt with a poker, to light the fire with.

Mr. Skimpole, lying on the sofa in his room, playing the flute a little, was enchanted to see me. Now, who should receive me, he asked? Who would I prefer for mistress of the ceremonies? Would I have his Comedy daughter, his Beauty daughter, or his Sentiment daughter? Or would I have all the daughters at once, in a perfect nosegay?

I replied, half defeated already, that I wished to speak to himself only, if he would give me leave.

"My dear Miss Summerson, most joyfully! Of course," he said, bringing his chair near mine, and breaking into his fascinating smile, "of course it's not business. Then it's pleasure!"

I said it certainly was not business that I came upon, but it was not quite a pleasant matter.

"Then, my dear Miss Summerson," said he, with the frankest gaiety, "don't allude to it. Why should you allude to anything that is *not* a pleasant matter? *I* never do. And you are a much pleasanter creature, in every point of view, than I. You are perfectly pleasant; I am imperfectly pleasant; then, if I never allude to an unpleasant matter, how much less should you! So that's disposed of, and we will talk of something else."

Although I was embarrassed, I took courage to intimate that I still wished to pursue the subject.

"I should think it a mistake," said Mr. Skimpole, with his airy laugh, "if I thought Miss Summerson capable of making one. But I don't!"

"Mr. Skimpole," said I, raising my eyes to his, "I have so often heard you say that you are unacquainted with the common affairs of life——"

"Meaning our three banking-house friends, L, S, and who's the junior partner? D?"[1] said Mr. Skimpole, brightly. "Not an idea of them!"

"—That, perhaps," I went on, "you will excuse my boldness on that account. I think you ought most seriously to know that Richard is poorer than he was."

"Dear me!" said Mr. Skimpole. "So am I, they tell me."

"And in very embarrassed circumstances."

"Parallel case, exactly!" said Mr. Skimpole, with a delighted countenance.

"This at present naturally causes Ada much secret anxiety; and as I think she is less anxious when no claims are made upon her by visitors, and as Richard has one uneasiness always heavy on his mind, it has occurred to me to take the liberty of saying that—if you would—not——"

I was coming to the point with great difficulty, when he took me by both hands, and, with a radiant face and in the liveliest way, anticipated it.

"Not go there? Certainly not, my dear Miss Summerson, most assuredly not. Why *should* I go there? When I go anywhere, I go for pleasure. I don't go anywhere for pain, because I was made for pleasure. Pain comes to *me* when it wants me. Now, I have had very little pleasure at our dear Richard's lately, and your practical sagacity demonstrates why. Our young friends, losing the youthful poetry which was once so captivating in them, begin to think, 'this is a man who wants pounds.' So I am; I always want pounds: not for myself, but because tradespeople always want them of me. Next, our young friends begin to think, becoming mercenary, 'this is the man who *had* pounds,—who borrowed them'; which I did. I always borrow pounds. So our young friends, reduced to prose (which is much to be regretted), degenerate in their power of imparting pleasure to me. Why should I go to see them, therefore? Absurd!"

Through the beaming smile with which he regarded me, as he

1. Abbreviation for Pounds, Shillings, and Pence, derived from the Latin forms for this coinage: *Librae, Solidi, Denarii.*

reasoned thus, there now broke forth a look of disinterested benevolence quite astonishing.

"Besides," he said, pursuing his argument, in his tone of light-hearted conviction, "if I don't go anywhere for pain—which would be a perversion of the intention of my being, and a monstrous thing to do—why should I go anywhere to be the cause of pain? If I went to see our young friends in their present ill-regulated state of mind, I should give them pain. The associations with me would be disagreeable. They might say, 'this is the man who had pounds, and who can't pay pounds,' which I can't, of course; nothing could be more out of the question! Then, kindness requires that I shouldn't go near them—and I won't."

He finished by genially kissing my hand, and thanking me. Nothing but Miss Summerson's fine tact, he said, would have found this out for him.

I was much disconcerted; but I reflected that if the main point were gained, it mattered little how strangely he perverted everything leading to it. I had determined to mention something else, however, and I thought I was not to be put off in that.

"Mr. Skimpole," said I, "I must take the liberty of saying, before I conclude my visit, that I was much surprised to learn, on the best authority, some little time ago, that you knew with whom that poor boy left Bleak House, and that you accepted a present on that occasion. I have not mentioned it to my guardian, for I fear it would hurt him unnecessarily; but I may say to you that I was much surprised."

"No? Really surprised, my dear Miss Summerson?" he returned, inquiringly, raising his pleasant eyebrows.

"Greatly surprised."

He thought about it for a little while, with a highly agreeable and whimsical expression of face; then quite gave it up, and said, in his most engaging manner:

"You know what a child I am. Why surprised?"

I was reluctant to enter minutely into that question; but as he begged I would, for he was really curious to know, I gave him to understand, in the gentlest words I could use, that his conduct seemed to involve a disregard of several moral obligations. He was much amused and interested when he heard this, and said "No, really?" with ingenuous simplicity.

"You know I don't pretend to be responsible. I never could do it. Responsibility is a thing that has always been above me—or below me," said Mr. Skimpole, "I don't even know which; but, as I understand the way in which my dear Miss Summerson (always remarkable for her practical good sense and clearness) puts this case, I should imagine it was chiefly a question of money, do you know?"

I incautiously gave a qualified assent to this.

"Ah! Then you see," said Mr. Skimpole, shaking his head, "I am hopeless of understanding it."

I suggested, as I rose to go, that it was not right to betray my guardian's confidence for a bribe.

"My dear Miss Summerson," he returned, with a candid hilarity that was all his own, "I can't be bribed."

"Not by Mr. Bucket?" said I.

"No," said he. "Not by anybody. I don't attach any value to money. I don't care about it, I don't know about it, I don't want it. I don't keep it—it goes away from me directly. How can *I* be bribed?"

I showed that I was of a different opinion, though I had not the capacity for arguing the question.

"On the contrary," said Mr. Skimpole, "I am exactly the man to be placed in a superior position, in such a case as that. I am above the rest of mankind, in such a case as that. I can act with philosophy, in such a case as that. I am not warped by prejudices, as an Italian baby is by bandages.[2] I am as free as the air. I feel myself as far above suspicion as Caesar's wife."[3]

Anything to equal the lightness of his manner, and the playful impartiality with which he seemed to convince himself, as he tossed the matter about like a ball of feathers, was surely never seen in anybody else!

"Observe the case, my dear Miss Summerson. Here is a boy received into the house and put to bed, in a state that I strongly object to. The boy being in bed, a man arrives—like the house that Jack built. Here is the man who demands the boy who is received into the house and put to bed in a state that I strongly object to.[4] Here is a bank-note produced by the man who demands the boy who is received into the house and put to bed in a state that I strongly object to. Here is the Skimpole who accepts the bank-note produced by the man who demands the boy who is received into the house and put to bed in a state that I strongly object to. Those are the facts. Very well. Should the Skimpole have refused the note? *Why* should the Skimpole have refused the note? Skimpole protests to Bucket; 'what's this for? I don't understand it, it is of no use to me, take it away.' Bucket still entreats Skimpole to accept it. Are there reasons why Skimpole, not being warped by prejudices, should accept it? Yes. Skimpole perceives them. What are they? Skimpole reasons with himself, this is a tamed lynx, an active

2. Swaddling of infants (i.e., wrapping them tightly in a long roll of bandages) persisted in continental countries long after the practice had been largely abandoned in England.

3. According to Plutarch's *Lives*, Julius Caesar justified divorcing his wife without knowing whether or not she was guilty of the accusations made against her: "Because I will not that my wife be so much as suspected."

4. Cf. the nursery rhyme: "This is the Cat that killed the Rat,/ That ate the malt/ That lay in the House that Jack built."

police-officer, an intelligent man, a person of a peculiarly directed energy and great subtlety both of conception and execution, who discovers our friends and enemies for us when they run away, recovers our property for us when we are robbed, avenges us comfortably when we are murdered. This active police-officer and intelligent man has acquired, in the exercise of his art, a strong faith in money; he finds it very useful to him, and he makes it very useful to society. Shall I shake that faith in Bucket, because I want it myself; shall I deliberately blunt one of Bucket's weapons; shall I possibly paralyse Bucket in his next detective operation? And again. If it is blameable in Skimpole to take the note, it is blameable in Bucket to offer the note—much more blameable in Bucket, because he is the knowing man. Now, Skimpole wishes to think well of Bucket; Skimpole deems it essential, in its little place, to the general cohesion of things, that he *should* think well of Bucket. The State expressly asks him to trust to Bucket. And he does. And that's all he does!"

I had nothing to offer in reply to this exposition, and therefore took my leave. Mr. Skimpole, however, who was in excellent spirits, would not hear of my returning home attended only by "Little Coavinses," and accompanied me himself. He entertained me, on the way, with a variety of delightful conversation; and assured me, at parting, that he should never forget the fine tact with which I had found that out for him about our young friends.

As it so happened that I never saw Mr. Skimpole again, I may at once finish what I know of his history. A coolness arose between him and my guardian, based principally on the foregoing grounds, and on his having heartlessly disregarded my guardian's entreaties (as we afterwards learned from Ada) in reference to Richard. His being heavily in my guardian's debt, had nothing to do with their separation. He died some five years afterwards, and left a diary behind him, with letters and other materials towards his Life; which was published, and which showed him to have been the victim of a combination on the part of mankind against an amiable child. It was considered very pleasant reading, but I never read more of it myself than the sentence on which I chanced to light on opening the book. It was this. "Jarndyce, in common with most other men I have known, is the Incarnation of Selfishness."

And now I come to a part of my story, touching myself very nearly indeed, and for which I was quite unprepared when the circumstances occurred. Whatever little lingerings may have now and then revived in my mind, associated with my poor old face, had only revived as belonging to a part of my life that was gone—gone like my infancy or my childhood. I have suppressed none of my many weaknesses on that subject, but have written them as faithfully as my memory has recalled them. And I hope to do, and mean to do, the same down to the last words of these pages; which I see now, not so very very far before me.

The months were gliding away; and my dear girl, sustained by the hopes she had confided to me, was the same beautiful star in the miserable corner. Richard, more worn and haggard, haunted the Court day after day; listlessly sat there the whole day long, when he knew there was no remote chance of the suit being mentioned; and became one of the stock sights of the place. I wonder whether any of the gentlemen remembered him as he was when he first went there.

So completely was he absorbed in his fixed idea, that he used to avow in his cheerful moments, that he should never have breathed the fresh air now "but for Woodcourt." It was only Mr. Woodcourt who could occasionally divert his attention, for a few hours at a time; and rouse him, even when he sunk into a lethargy of mind and body that alarmed us greatly, and the returns of which became more frequent as the months went on. My dear girl was right in saying that he only pursued his errors the more desperately for her sake. I have no doubt that his desire to retrieve what he had lost, was rendered the more intense by his grief for his young wife, and became like the madness of a gamester.

I was there, as I have mentioned, at all hours. When I was there at night, I generally went home with Charley in a coach; sometimes my guardian would meet me in the neighbourhood, and we would walk home together. One evening he had arranged to meet me at eight o'clock. I could not leave, as I usually did, quite punctually to the time, for I was working for my dear girl, and had a few stitches more to do, to finish what I was about; but it was within a few minutes past the hour, when I bundled up my little work-basket, gave my darling my last kiss for the night, and hurried down-stairs. Mr. Woodcourt went with me, as it was dusk.

When we came to the usual place of meeting—it was close by, and Mr. Woodcourt had often accompanied me before—my guardian was not there. We waited half an hour, walking up and down; but there were no signs of him. We agreed that he was either prevented from coming, or that he had come, and gone away; and Mr. Woodcourt proposed to walk home with me.

It was the first walk we had ever taken together, except that very short one to the usual place of meeting. We spoke of Richard and Ada the whole way. I did not thank him, in words, for what he had done—my appreciation of it had risen above all words then—but I hoped he might not be without some understanding of what I felt so strongly.

Arriving at home and going up-stairs, we found that my guardian was out, and that Mrs. Woodcourt was out too. We were in the very same room into which I had brought my blushing girl, when her youthful lover, now her so altered husband, was the choice of her young heart; the very same room, from which my guardian and I had watched them going away through the sunlight, in the fresh bloom of their hope and promise.

We were standing by the opened window, looking down into the street, when Mr. Woodcourt spoke to me. I learned in a moment that he loved me. I learned in a moment that my scarred face was all unchanged to him. I learned in a moment that what I had thought was pity and compassion, was devoted, generous, faithful love. O, too late to know it now, too late, too late. That was the first ungrateful thought I had. Too late.

"When I returned," he told me, "when I came back, no richer than I went away, and found you newly risen from a sick bed, yet so inspired by sweet consideration for others, and so free from a selfish thought——"

"O, Mr. Woodcourt, forbear, forbear!" I entreated him. "I do not deserve your high praise. I had many selfish thoughts at that time, many!"

"Heaven knows, beloved of my life," said he, "that my praise is not a lover's praise, but the truth. You do not know what all around you see in Esther Summerson, how many hearts she touches and awakens, what sacred admiration and what love she wins."

"O, Mr. Woodcourt," cried I, "it is a great thing to win love, it is a great thing to win love! I am proud of it, and honoured by it; and the hearing of it causes me to shed these tears of mingled joy and sorrow—joy that I have won it, sorrow that I have not deserved it better; but I am not free to think of yours."

I said it with a stronger heart; for when he praised me thus, and when I heard his voice thrill with his belief that what he said was true, I aspired to be more worthy of it. It was not too late for that. Although I closed this unforeseen page in my life to-night, I could be worthier of it all through my life. And it was a comfort to me, and an impulse to me, and I felt a dignity rise up within me that was derived from him, when I thought so.

He broke the silence.

"I should poorly show the trust that I have in the dear one who will evermore be as dear to me as now," and the deep earnestness with which he said it, at once strengthened me and made me weep, "if, after her assurance that she is not free to think of my love, I urged it. Dear Esther, let me only tell you that the fond idea of you which I took abroad, was exalted to the Heavens when I came home. I have always hoped, in the first hour when I seemed to stand in any ray of good fortune, to tell you this. I have always feared that I should tell it you in vain. My hopes and fears are both fulfilled to-night. I distress you. I have said enough."

Something seemed to pass into my place that was like the Angel he thought me, and I felt so sorrowful for the loss he had sustained! I wished to help him in his trouble, as I had wished to do when he showed that first commiseration for me.

"Dear Mr. Woodcourt," said I, "before we part to-night, something is left for me to say. I never could say it as I wish—I never shall—but——"

I had to think again of being more deserving of his love, and his affliction, before I could go on.

"—I am deeply sensible of your generosity, and I shall treasure its remembrance to my dying hour. I know full well how changed I am, I know you are not unacquainted with my history, and I know what a noble love that is which is so faithful. What you have said to me, could have affected me so much from no other lips; for there are none that could give it such a value to me. It shall not be lost. It shall make me better."

He covered his eyes with his hand, and turned away his head. How could I ever be worthy of those tears?

"If, in the unchanged intercourse we shall have together—in tending Richard and Ada; and I hope in many happier scenes of life—you ever find anything in me which you can honestly think is better than it used to be, believe that it will have sprung up from to-night, and that I shall owe it to you. And never believe, dear dear Mr. Woodcourt, never believe that I forget this night; or that while my heart beats, it can be insensible to the pride and joy of having been beloved by you."

He took my hand, and kissed it. He was like himself again, and I felt still more encouraged.

"I am induced, by what you said just now," said I, "to hope that you have succeeded in your endeavour?"

"I have," he answered. "With such help from Mr. Jarndyce as you who know him so well can imagine him to have rendered me, I have succeeded."

"Heaven bless him for it," said I, giving him my hand; "and Heaven bless you in all you do!"

"I shall do it better for the wish," he answered; "it will make me enter on these new duties, as on another sacred trust from you."

"Ah! Richard!" I exclaimed involuntarily, "what will he do when you are gone?"

"I am not required to go yet; I would not desert him, dear Miss Summerson, even if I were."

One other thing I felt it needful to touch upon, before he left me. I knew that I should not be worthier of the love I could not take, if I reserved it.

"Mr. Woodcourt," said I, "you will be glad to know from my lips before I say Good night, that in the future, which is clear and bright before me, I am most happy, most fortunate, have nothing to regret or to desire."

It was indeed a glad hearing to him, he replied.

"From my childhood I have been," said I, "the object of the untiring goodness of the best of human beings; to whom I am so bound by every tie of attachment, gratitude, and love, that nothing I could do in the compass of a life could express the feelings of a single day."

"I share those feelings," he returned. "You speak of Mr. Jarndyce."

"You know his virtues well," said I, "but few can know the greatness of his character as I know it. All its highest and best qualities have been revealed to me in nothing more brightly than in the shaping out of that future in which I am so happy. And if your highest homage and respect had not been his already,—which I know they are,—they would have been his, I think, on this assurance, and in the feeling it would have awakened in you towards him for my sake."

He fervently replied, that indeed indeed they would have been. I gave him my hand again.

"Good night," I said; "good-bye."

"The first, until we meet to-morrow; the second, as a farewell to this theme between us for ever?"

"Yes."

"Good night; good-bye!"

He left me, and I stood at the dark window watching the street. His love, in all its constancy and generosity, had come so suddenly upon me, that he had not left me a minute when my fortitude gave way again, and the street was blotted out by my rushing tears.

But they were not tears of regret and sorrow. No. He had called me the beloved of his life, and had said I would be evermore as dear to him as I was then; and I felt as if my heart would not hold the triumph of having heard those words. My first wild thought had died away. It was not too late to hear them, for it was not too late to be animated by them to be good, true, grateful, and contented. How easy my path; now much easier than his!

Chapter LXII

ANOTHER DISCOVERY

I had not the courage to see any one that night. I had not even the courage to see myself, for I was afraid that my tears might a little reproach me. I went up to my room in the dark, and prayed in the dark, and lay down in the dark to sleep. I had no need of any light to read my guardian's letter by, for I knew it by heart. I took it from the place where I kept it, and repeated its contents by its own light of integrity and love, and went to sleep with it on my pillow.

I was up very early in the morning, and called Charley to come for a walk. We bought flowers for the breakfast-table, and came back and arranged them, and were as busy as possible. We were so early, that I had good time still for Charley's lesson, before breakfast; Charley (who was not in the least improved in the old defective article of grammar) came through it with great applause; and we were altogether very notable. When my guardian appeared, he said, "Why, little woman, you look fresher than your flowers!" And Mrs. Woodcourt repeated and translated a passage from the Mewlinwillinwodd, expressive of my being like a mountain with the sun upon it.

This was all so pleasant, that I hope it made me still more like the mountain than I had been before. After breakfast, I waited my opportunity, and peeped about a little, until I saw my guardian in his own room—the room of last night—by himself. Then I made an excuse to go in with my housekeeping keys, shutting the door after me.

"Well, Dame Durden?" said my guardian; the post had brought him several letters, and he was writing. "You want money?"

"No, indeed, I have plenty in hand."

"There never was such a Dame Durden," said my guardian, "for making money last."

He had laid down his pen, and leaned back in his chair looking at me. I have often spoken of his bright face, but I thought I had never seen it look so bright and good. There was a high happiness upon it, which made me think, "he has been doing some great kindness this morning."

"There never was," said my guardian, musing as he smiled upon me, "such a Dame Durden for making money last."

He had never yet altered his old manner. I loved it, and him, so much, that when I now went up to him and took my usual chair, which was always put at his side—for sometimes I read to him, and sometimes I talked to him, and sometimes I silently worked by him—I hardly liked to disturb it by laying my hand on his breast. But I found I did not disturb it at all.

"Dear guardian," said I, "I want to speak to you. Have I been remiss in anything?"

"Remiss in anything, my dear!"

"Have I not been what I have meant to be, since—I brought the answer to your letter, guardian?"

"You have been everything I could desire, my love."

"I am very glad indeed to hear that," I returned. "You know, you said to me, was this the mistress of Bleak House? And I said, yes."

"Yes," said my guardian, nodding his head. He had put his arm about me, as if there were something to protect me from; and looked in my face, smiling.

"Since then," said I, "we have never spoken on the subject except once."

"And then I said, Bleak House was thinning fast; and so it was, my dear."

"And *I* said," I timidly reminded him, "but its mistress remained."

He still held me, in the same protecting manner, and with the same bright goodness in his face.

"Dear guardian," said I, "I know how you have felt all that has happened, and how considerate you have been. As so much time has passed, and as you spoke only this morning of my being so well again, perhaps you expect me to renew the subject. Perhaps I ought to do so. I will be the mistress of Bleak House when you please."

"See," he returned gaily, "what a sympathy there must be between us! I have had nothing else, poor Rick excepted—it's a large exception—in my mind. When you came in, I was full of it. When shall we give Bleak House its mistress, little woman?"

"When you please."

"Next month?"

"Next month, dear guardian."

"The day on which I take the happiest and best step of my life —the day on which I shall be a man more exulting and more enviable than any other man in the world—the day on which I give Bleak House its little mistress—shall be next month, then," said my guardian.

I put my arms round his neck and kissed him, just as I had done on the day when I brought my answer.

A servant came to the door to announce Mr. Bucket, which was quite unnecessary, for Mr. Bucket was already looking in over the servant's shoulder. "Mr. Jarndyce and Miss Summerson," said he, rather out of breath, "with all apologies for intruding, *will* you allow me to order up a person that's on the stairs, and that objects to being left there in case of becoming the subject of observations in his absence? Thank you. Be so good as chair that there Member[1] in this direction, will you?" said Mr. Bucket, beckoning over the banisters.

This singular request produced an old man in a black skull-cap,

1. To celebrate a candidate's victory in being elected as a Member of Parliament, his followers would carry him through the streets of his constituency in a chair. (Noted by Norman Page.)

unable to walk, who was carried up by a couple of bearers, and deposited in the room near the door. Mr. Bucket immediately got rid of the bearers, mysteriously shut the door, and bolted it.

"Now you see, Mr. Jarndyce," he then began, putting down his hat, and opening his subject with a flourish of his well-remembered finger, "you know me, and Miss Summerson knows me. This gentleman likewise knows me, and his name is Smallweed. The discounting line is his line principally, and he's what you may call a dealer in bills. That's about what *you* are, you know, ain't you?" said Mr. Bucket, stopping a little to address the gentleman in question, who was exceedingly suspicious of him.

He seemed about to dispute this designation of himself, when he was seized with a violent fit of coughing.

"Now, Moral, you know!" said Mr. Bucket, improving the accident. "Don't you contradict when there ain't no occasion, and you won't be took in that way. Now, Mr. Jarndyce, I address myself to you. I've been negotiating with this gentleman on behalf of Sir Leicester Dedlock, Baronet; and one way and another I've been in and out and about his premises a deal. His premises are the premises formerly occupied by Krook, Marine Store Dealer—a relation of this gentleman's, that you saw in his lifetime, if I don't mistake?"

My guardian replied "Yes."

"Well! You are to understand," said Mr. Bucket, "that this gentleman he come into Krook's property, and a good deal of Magpie property there was. Vast lots of waste paper among the rest. Lord bless you, of no use to nobody!"

The cunning of Mr. Bucket's eye, and the masterly manner in which he contrived, without a look or a word against which his watchful auditor could protest, to let us know that he stated the case according to previous agreement, and could say much more of Mr. Smallweed if he thought it advisable, deprived us of any merit in quite understanding him. His difficulty was increased by Mr. Smallweed's being deaf as well as suspicious, and watching his face with the closest attention.

"Among them odd heaps of old papers, this gentleman, when he comes into the property, naturally begins to rummage, don't you see?" said Mr. Bucket.

"To which? Say that again," cried Mr. Smallweed, in a shrill, sharp voice.

"To rummage," repeated Mr. Bucket. "Being a prudent man, and accustomed to take care of your own affairs, you begin to rummage among the papers as you have come into; don't you?"

"Of course I do," cried Mr. Smallweed.

"Of course you do," said Mr. Bucket, conversationally, "and much to blame you would be if you didn't. And so you chance to find, you know," Mr. Bucket went on, stooping over him with an air of cheerful raillery which Mr. Smallweed by no means reciprocated, "and so you chance to find, you know, a paper, with the signature of Jarndyce to it. Don't you?"

Mr. Smallweed glanced with a troubled eye at us, and grudgingly nodded assent.

"And coming to look at that paper, at your full leisure and convenience—all in good time, for you're not curious to read it, and why should you be?—what do you find it to be but a Will, you see. That's the drollery of it," said Mr. Bucket, with the same lively air of recalling a joke for the enjoyment of Mr. Smallweed, who still had the same crest-fallen appearance of not enjoying it at all; "what do you find it to be, but a Will?"

"I don't know that it's good as a will, or as anything else," snarled Mr. Smallweed.

Mr. Bucket eyed the old man for a moment—he had slipped and shrunk down in his chair into a mere bundle—as if he were much disposed to pounce upon him; nevertheless, he continued to bend over him with the same agreeable air, keeping the corner of one of his eyes upon us.

"Notwithstanding which," said Mr. Bucket, "you get a little doubtful and uncomfortable in your mind about it, having a very tender mind of your own."

"Eh? What do you say I have got of my own?" asked Mr. Smallweed, with his hand to his ear.

"A very tender mind."

"Ho! Well, go on," said Mr. Smallweed.

"And as you've heard a good deal mentioned regarding a celebrated Chancery will case, of the same name; and as you know what a card Krook was for buying all manner of old pieces of furniter, and books, and papers, and what not, and never liking to part with 'em, and always a going to teach himself to read; you begin to think—and you never was more correct in your born days—'Ecod, if I don't look about me, I may get into trouble regarding this will.' "

"Now, mind how you put it, Bucket," cried the old man anxiously, with his hand at his ear. "Speak up; none of your brimstone tricks. Pick me up; I want to hear better. O Lord, I am shaken to bits!"

Mr. Bucket had certainly picked him up at a dart. However, as soon as he could be heard through Mr. Smallweed's coughing, and his vicious ejaculations of "O my bones! O dear! I've no breath in my body! I'm worse than the chattering, clattering, brimstone pig at home!" Mr. Bucket proceeded in the same convivial manner as before.

"So, as I happen to be in the habit of coming about your premises, you take me into your confidence, don't you?"

I think it would be impossible to make an admission with more ill-will, and a worse grace, than Mr. Smallweed displayed when he admitted this; rendering it perfectly evident that Mr. Bucket was the very last person he would have thought of taking into his confidence, if he could by any possibility have kept him out of it.

"And I go into the business with you,—very pleasant we are over it; and I confirm you in your well-founded fears, that you will-get-yourself-in-to-a-most precious line if you don't come out with that there will," said Mr. Bucket, emphatically; "and accordingly you arrange with me that it shall be delivered up to this present Mr. Jarndyce, on no conditions. If it should prove to be valuable, you trusting yourself to him for your reward; that's about where it is, ain't it?"

"That's what was agreed," Mr. Smallweed assented, with the same bad grace.

"In consequence of which," said Mr. Bucket, dismissing his agreeable manner all at once, and becoming strictly business-like, "you've got that will upon your person at the present time; and the only thing that remains for you to do is, just to Out with it!"

Having given us one glance out of the watching corner of his eye, and having given his nose one triumphant rub with his forefinger, Mr. Bucket stood with his eyes fastened on his confidential friend, and his hand stretched forth ready to take the paper and present it to my guardian. It was not produced without much reluctance, and many declarations on the part of Mr. Smallweed that he was a poor industrious man, and that he left it to Mr. Jarndyce's honour not to let him lose by his honesty. Little by little he very slowly took from a breast-pocket a stained discoloured paper, which was much singed upon the outside, and a little burnt at the edges, as if it had long ago been thrown upon a fire, and hastily snatched off again. Mr. Bucket lost no time in transferring this paper, with the dexterity of a conjurer, from Mr. Smallweed to Mr. Jarndyce. As he gave it to my guardian, he whispered behind his fingers:

"Hadn't settled how to make their market of it. Quarrelled and hinted about it. I laid out twenty pound upon it. First, the avaricious grandchildren split upon him, on account of their objections to his living so unreasonably long, and then they split on one another. Lord! there ain't one of the family that wouldn't sell the other for a pound or two, except the old lady—and she's only out of it because she's too weak in her mind to drive a bargain."

"Mr. Bucket," said my guardian aloud, "whatever the worth of this paper may be to any one, my obligations are great to you; and if it be of any worth, I hold myself bound to see Mr. Smallweed remunerated accordingly."

"Not according to your merits you know," said Mr. Bucket, in friendly explanation to Mr. Smallweed. "Don't you be afraid of that. According to its value."

"That is what I mean," said my guardian. "You may observe, Mr. Bucket, that I abstain from examining this paper myself. The plain truth is, I have forsworn and abjured the whole business these many years, and my soul is sick of it. But Miss Summerson and I will immediately place the paper in the hands of my solicitor in the cause, and its existence shall be made known without delay to all other parties interested."

"Mr. Jarndyce can't say fairer than that, you understand," observed Mr. Bucket, to his fellow visitor. "And it being now made clear to you that nobody's a going to be wronged—which must be a great relief to *your* mind—we may proceed with the ceremony of chairing you home again."

He unbolted the door, called in the bearers, wished us good morning, and with a look full of meaning, and a crook of his finger at parting, went his way.

We went our way too, which was to Lincoln's Inn, as quickly as possible. Mr. Kenge was disengaged; and we found him at his table in his dusty room, with the inexpressive-looking books, and the piles of papers. Chairs having been placed for us by Mr. Guppy, Mr. Kenge expressed the surprise and gratification he felt at the unusual sight of Mr. Jarndyce in his office. He turned over his double eye-glass as he spoke, and was more Conversation Kenge than ever.

"I hope," said Mr. Kenge, "that the genial influence of Miss Summerson," he bowed to me, "may have induced Mr. Jarndyce," he bowed to him, "to forego some little of his animosity towards a Cause and towards a Court which are—shall I say, which take their place in the stately vista of the pillars of our profession?"

"I am inclined to think," returned my guardian, "that Miss Summerson has seen too much of the effects of the Court and the Cause to exert any influence in their favour. Nevertheless, they are a part of the occasion of my being here. Mr. Kenge, before I lay this paper on your desk, and have done with it, let me tell you how it has come into my hands."

He did so shortly and distinctly. "It could not, sir," said Mr. Kenge, "have been stated more plainly and to the purpose, if it had been a case at law." "Did you ever know English law, or equity either, plain and to the purpose?" said my guardian. "O fie!" said Mr. Kenge.

At first he had not seemed to attach much importance to the paper, but when he saw it he appeared more interested, and when he had opened and read a little of it through his eye-glass, he became amazed. "Mr. Jarndyce," he said, looking off it, "you have perused this?"

"Not I!" returned my guardian.

"But, my dear sir," said Mr. Kenge, "it is a Will of later date than any in the suit. It appears to be all in the Testator's handwriting. It is duly executed and attested. And even if intended to be cancelled, as might possibly be supposed to be denoted by these marks of fire, it is *not* cancelled. Here it is, a perfect instrument!"

"Well!" said my guardian. "What is that to me?"

"Mr. Guppy!" cried Mr. Kenge, raising his voice.—"I beg your pardon, Mr. Jarndyce."

"Sir."

"Mr. Vholes of Symond's Inn. My compliments. Jarndyce and Jarndyce. Glad to speak with him."

Mr. Guppy disappeared.

"You ask me what is this to you, Mr. Jarndyce. If you had perused this document, you would have seen that it reduces your interest considerably, though still leaving it a very handsome one, still leaving it a very handsome one," said Mr. Kenge, waving his hand persuasively and blandly. "You would further have seen, that the interests of Mr. Richard Carstone and Miss Ada Clare, now Mrs. Richard Carstone, are very materially advanced by it."

"Kenge," said my guardian, "if all the flourishing wealth that the suit brought into this vile Court of Chancery could fall to my two young cousins, I should be well contented. But do you ask *me* to believe that any good is to come of Jarndyce and Jarndyce?"

"O really, Mr. Jarndyce! Prejudice, prejudice. My dear sir, this is a very great country, a very great country. Its system of equity is a very great system, a very great system. Really, really!"

My guardian said no more, and Mr. Vholes arrived. He was modestly impressed by Mr. Kenge's professional eminence.

"How do you do, Mr. Vholes? Will you be so good as to take a chair here by me, and look over this paper?"

Mr. Vholes did as he was asked, and seemed to read it every word. He was not excited by it; but he was not excited by anything. When he had well examined it, he retired with Mr. Kenge into a window, and shading his mouth with his black glove, spoke to him at some length. I was not surprised to observe Mr. Kenge inclined to dispute what he said before he had said much, for I knew that no two people ever did agree about anything in Jarndyce and Jarndyce. But he seemed to get the better of Mr. Kenge too, in a conversation that sounded as if it were almost composed of the words, "Receiver-General," "Accountant-General," "Report," "Estate," and "Costs." When they had finished, they came back to Mr. Kenge's table, and spoke aloud.

"Well! But this is a very remarkable document, Mr. Vholes?" said Mr. Kenge.

Mr. Vholes said, "Very much so."

"And a very important document, Mr. Vholes?" said Mr. Kenge.

Again Mr. Vholes said, "Very much so."

"And as you say, Mr. Vholes, when the Cause is in the paper next Term, this document will be an unexpected and interesting feature in it," said Mr. Kenge, looking loftily at my guardian.

Mr. Vholes was gratified, as a smaller practitioner striving to keep respectable, to be confirmed in any opinion of his own by such an authority.

"And when," asked my guardian, rising after a pause, during which Mr. Kenge had rattled his money, and Mr. Vholes had picked his pimples, "when is next Term?"

"Next Term, Mr. Jarndyce, will be next month," said Mr. Kenge. "Of course we shall at once proceed to do what is necessary with this document, and to collect the necessary evidence concerning it; and of course you will receive our usual notification of the Cause being in the paper."

"To which I shall pay, of course, my usual attention."

"Still bent, my dear sir," said Mr. Kenge, showing us through the outer office to the door, "still bent, even with your enlarged mind, on echoing a popular prejudice? We are a prosperous community, Mr. Jarndyce, a very prosperous community. We are a great country, Mr. Jarndyce, we are a very great country. This is a great system, Mr. Jarndyce, and would you wish a great country to have a little system? Now, really, really!"

He said this at the stair-head, gently moving his right hand as if it were a silver trowel, with which to spread the cement of his words on the structure of the system, and consolidate it for a thousand ages.

Chapter LXIII

STEEL AND IRON

George's shooting-gallery is to let, and the stock is sold off, and George himself is at Chesney Wold, attending on Sir Leicester in his rides, and riding very near his bridle-rein, because of the uncertain hand with which he guides his horse. But not to-day is George so occupied. He is journeying to-day into the iron country farther north, to look about him.

As he comes into the iron country farther north, such fresh green woods as those of Chesney Wold are left behind; and coalpits and ashes, high chimneys and red bricks, blighted verdure, scorching fires, and a heavy never-lightening cloud of smoke, become the features of the scenery. Among such objects rides the trooper, looking about him, and always looking for something he has come to find.

At last, on the black canal bridge of a busy town, with a clang of iron in it, and more fires and more smoke than he has seen yet, the trooper, swart with the dust of the coal roads, checks his horse and asks a workman does he know the name of Rouncewell thereabouts?

"Why, master," quoth the workman, "do I know my own name?"

" 'Tis so well known here, is it, comrade?" asks the trooper.

"Rouncewells? Ah! you're right."

"And where might it be now?" asks the trooper, with a glance before him.

"The bank, the factory, or the house?" the workman wants to know.

"Hum! Rouncewells is so great apparently," mutters the trooper, stroking his chin, "that I have as good as half a mind to go back again. Why, I don't know which I want. Should I find Mr. Rouncewell at the factory, do you think?"

" 'Tain't easy to say where you'd find him—at this time of the day you might find either him or his son there, if he's in town; but his contracts take him away."

And which is the factory? Why, he sees those chimneys—the tallest ones! Yes, he sees *them*. Well! let him keep his eye on those chimneys, going on as straight as ever he can, and presently he'll see 'em down a turning on the left, shut in by a great brick wall which forms one side of the street. That's Rouncewells.

The trooper thanks his informant, and rides slowly on, looking about him. He does not turn back, but puts up his horse (and is much disposed to groom him too) at a public-house where some of Rouncewell's hands are dining, as the ostler tells him. Some of Rouncewell's hands have just knocked off for dinner time, and seem to be invading the whole town. They are very sinewy and strong, are Rouncewell's hands—a little sooty too.

He comes to a gateway in the brick wall, looks in, and sees a great perplexity of iron lying about, in every stage, and in a vast variety of shapes; in bars, in wedges, in sheets; in tanks, in boilers, in axles, in wheels, in cogs, in cranks, in rails; twisted and wrenched into eccentric and perverse forms, as separate parts of machinery; mountains of it broken-up, and rusty in its age; distant furnaces of it glowing and bubbling in its youth; bright fireworks of it showering about, under the blows of the steam hammer; red-hot iron, white-hot iron, cold-black iron; an iron taste, an iron smell, and a Babel of iron sounds.

"This is a place to make a man's head ache, too!" says the trooper, looking about him confusedly for a counting-house. "Who comes here? This is very like me before I was set up. This ought to be my nephew, if likenesses run in families. Your servant, sir."

"Yours, sir. Are you looking for any one?"

"Excuse me. Young Mr. Rouncewell, I believe?"

"Yes."

"I was looking for your father, sir. I wished to have a word with him."

The young man, telling him he is fortunate in his choice of a time, for his father is there, leads the way to the office where he is to be found. "Very like me before I was set up—devilish like me!" thinks the trooper, as he follows. They come to a building in the yard; with an office on an upper floor. At sight of the gentleman in the office, Mr. George turns very red.

"What name shall I say to my father?" asks the young man.

George, full of the idea of iron, in desperation answers "Steel," and is so presented. He is left alone with the gentleman in the office, who sits at a table with account-books before him, and some sheets of paper, blotted with hosts of figures and drawings of cunning shapes. It is a bare office, with bare windows, looking on the iron view below. Tumbled together on the table are some pieces of iron, purposely broken to be tested, at various periods of their service, in various capacities. There is iron-dust on everything; and the smoke is seen, through the windows, rolling heavily out of the tall chimneys, to mingle with the smoke from a vaporous Babylon of other chimneys.

"I am at your service, Mr. Steel," says the gentleman, when his visitor has taken a rusty chair.

"Well, Mr. Rouncewell," George replies, leaning forward with his left arm on his knee, and his hat in his hand; and very chary of meeting his brother's eye; "I am not without my expectations, that in the present visit I may prove to be more free than welcome. I have served as a Dragoon in my day; and a comrade of mine that I was once rather partial to, was, if I don't deceive myself, a brother of yours. I believe you had a brother who gave his family some trouble, and ran away, and never did any good but in keeping away?"

"Are you quite sure," returns the ironmaster, in an altered voice, "that your name is Steel?"

The trooper falters, and looks at him. His brother starts up, calls him by his name, and grasps him by both hands.

"You are too quick for me!" cries the trooper, with the tears springing out of his eyes. "How do you do, my dear old fellow? I never could have thought you would have been half so glad to see me as all this. How do you do, my dear old fellow, how do you do!"

They shake hands, and embrace each other, over and over again; the trooper still coupling his "How do you do, my dear old fellow!" with his protestation that he never could have thought his brother would have been half so glad to see him as all this!

"So far from it," he declares, at the end of a full account of what has preceded his arrival there, "I had very little idea of making myself known. I thought, if you took by any means forgivingly to my name, I might gradually get myself up to the point of writing a letter. But I should not have been surprised, brother, if you had considered it anything but welcome news to hear of me."

"We will show you at home what kind of news we think it, George," returns his brother. "This is a great day at home, and you could not have arrived, you bronzed old soldier, on a better. I make an agreement with my son Watt to-day, that on this day twelvemonth he shall marry as pretty and as good a girl as you have seen in all your travels. She goes to Germany to-morrow with one of your nieces, for a little polishing up in her education. We make a feast of the event, and you will be made the hero of it."

Mr. George is so entirely overcome at first by this prospect, that he resists the proposed honour with great earnestness. Being overborne, however, by his brother and his nephew—concerning whom he renews his protestations that he never could have thought they would have been half so glad to see him—he is taken home to an elegant house, in all the arrangements of which there is to be observed a pleasant mixture of the originally simple habits of the father and mother, with such as are suited to their altered station and the higher fortunes of their children. Here Mr. George is much dismayed by the graces and accomplishments of his nieces that are; and by the beauty of Rosa, his niece that is to be; and by the affectionate salutations of these young ladies, which he receives in a sort of dream. He is sorely taken aback, too, by the dutiful behaviour of his nephew; and has a woful consciousness upon him of being a scapegrace. However, there is great rejoicing, and a very hearty company, and infinite enjoyment: and Mr. George comes bluffly and martially through it all; and his pledge to be present at the marriage and give away the bride, is received with universal favour. A whirling head has Mr. George that night when he lies down in the state-bed of his brother's house, to think of all these things, and to see the images of his nieces (awful all the evening in their floating muslins), waltzing, after the German manner, over his counterpane.

The brothers are closeted next morning in the ironmaster's room; where the elder is proceeding, in his clear sensible way, to show how he thinks he may best dispose of George in his business, when George squeezes his hand and stops him.

"Brother, I thank you a million times for your more than brotherly welcome, and a million times more to that for your more than brotherly intentions. But my plans are made. Before I say a word as to them, I wish to consult you upon one family point. How," says the trooper, folding his arms, and looking with indomitable firmness at his brother, "how is my mother to be got to scratch me?"

"I am not sure that I understand you, George," replies the ironmaster.

"I say, brother, how is my mother to be got to scratch me? She must be got to do it, somehow."

"Scratch you out of her will, I think you mean?"

"O course I do. In short," says the trooper, folding his arms more resolutely yet, "I mean—*to*—scratch me!"

"My dear George," returns his brother, "is it so indispensable that you should undergo that process?"

"Quite! Absolutely! I couldn't be guilty of the meanness of coming back without it. I should never be safe not to be off again. I have not sneaked home to rob your children, if not yourself, brother, of your rights. I, who forfeited mine long ago! If I am to remain, and hold up my head, I must be scratched. Come. You are a man of celebrated penetration and intelligence, and you can tell me how it's to be brought about."

"I can tell you, George," replies the ironmaster, deliberately, "how it is not to be brought about, which I hope may answer the purpose as well. Look at our mother, think of her, recall her emotion when she recovered you. Do you believe there is a consideration in the world that would induce her to take such a step against her favourite son? Do you believe there is any chance of her consent, to balance against the outrage it would be to her (loving dear old lady!) to propose it? If you do, you are wrong. No, George! You must make up your mind to remain *un*scratched. I think," there is an amused smile on the ironmaster's face, as he watches his brother, who is pondering, deeply disappointed; "I think you may manage almost as well as if the thing were done, though."

"How, brother?"

"Being bent upon it, you can dispose by will of anything you have the misfortune to inherit, in any way you like, you know."

"That's true!" says the trooper, pondering again. Then he wistfully asks, with his hand on his brother's knee, "Would you mind mentioning that, brother, to your wife and family?"

"Not at all."

"Thank you. You wouldn't object to say, perhaps, that although an undoubted vagabond, I am a vagabond of the harum scarum order, and not of the mean sort?"

The ironmaster, repressing his amused smile, assents.

"Thank you. Thank you. It's a weight off my mind," says the trooper, with a heave of his chest as he unfolds his arms, and puts a hand on each leg; "though I had set my heart on being scratched, too!"

The brothers are very like each other, sitting face to face; but a certain massive simplicity, and absence of usage in the ways of the world, is all on the trooper's side.

"Well," he proceeds, throwing off his disappointment, "next and last, those plans of mine. You have been so brotherly as to propose to me to fall in here, and take my place among the products of your perseverance and sense. I thank you heartily. It's more than brotherly, as I said before; and I thank you heartily for it," shaking him a long time by the hand. "But the truth is, brother, I am a—I am a kind of a Weed, and it's too late to plant me in a regular garden."

"My dear George," returns the elder, concentrating his strong steady brow upon him, and smiling confidently; "leave that to me, and let me try."

George shakes his head. "You could do it, I have not a doubt, if anybody could; but it's not to be done. Not to be done, sir! Whereas it so falls out, on the other hand, that I am able to be of some trifle of use to Sir Leicester Dedlock since his illness—brought on by family sorrows; and that he would rather have that help from our mother's son than from anybody else."

"Well, my dear George," returns the other, with a very slight shade upon his open face, "if you prefer to serve in Sir Leicester Dedlock's household brigade——"

"There it is, brother!" cries the trooper, checking him, with his hand upon his knee again: "there it is! You don't take kindly to that idea; I don't mind it. You are not used to being officered; I am. Everything about you is in perfect order and discipline; everything about me requires to be kept so. We are not accustomed to carry things with the same hand, or to look at 'em from the same point. I don't say much about my garrison manners, because I found myself pretty well at my ease last night, and they wouldn't be noticed here, I dare say, once and away.[1] But I shall get on best at Chesney Wold—where there's more room for a Weed than there is here; and the dear old lady will be made happy besides. Therefore I accept of Sir Leicester Dedlock's proposals. When I come over next year to give away the bride, or whenever I come, I shall have the sense to keep the household brigade in ambuscade, and not to manœuvre it on your ground. I thank you heartily again, and am proud to think of the Rouncewells as they'll be founded by you."

"You know yourself, George," says the elder brother, returning the grip of his hand, "and perhaps you know me better than I know myself. Take your way. So that we don't quite lose one another again, take your way."

"No fear of that!" returns the trooper. "Now, before I turn my horse's head homeards, brother, I will ask you—if you'll be so good—to look over a letter for me. I brought it with me to send from these parts, as Chesney Wold might be a painful name just now to the person it's written to. I am not much accustomed to corre-

1. Except on rare occasions.

spondence myself, and I am particular respecting this present letter, because I want it to be both straightforward and delicate."

Herewith he hands a letter, closely written in somewhat pale ink but in a neat round hand, to the ironmaster, who reads as follows:

"MISS ESTHER SUMMERSON,

"A communication having been made to me by Inspector Bucket of a letter to myself being found among the papers of a certain person, I take the liberty to make known to you that it was but a few lines of instruction from abroad, when, where, and how to deliver an enclosed letter to a young and beautiful lady, then unmarried in England. I duly observed the same.

"I further take the liberty to make known to you, that it was got from me as proof of hand-writing only, and that otherwise I would not have given it up as appearing to be the most harmless in my possession, without being previously shot through the heart.

"I further take the liberty to mention, that if I could have supposed a certain unfortunate gentleman to have been in existence, I never could and never would have rested until I had discovered his retreat, and shared my last farthing with him, as my duty and my inclination would have equally been. But he was (officially) reported drowned, and assuredly went over the side of a transport-ship at night in an Irish harbour, within a few hours of her arrival from the West Indies, as I have myself heard both from officers and men on board, and know to have been (officially) confirmed.

"I further take the liberty to state that in my humble quality as one of the rank and file, I am, and shall ever continue to be, your thoroughly devoted and admiring servant, and that I esteem the qualities you possess above all others, far beyond the limits of the present dispatch.

"I have the honour to be,

"GEORGE."

"A little formal," observes the elder brother, refolding it with a puzzled face.

"But nothing that might not be sent to a pattern young lady?" asks the younger.

"Nothing at all."

Therefore it is sealed, and deposited for posting among the iron correspondence of the day. This done, Mr. George takes a hearty farewell of the family party, and prepares to saddle and mount. His brother, however, unwilling to part with him so soon, proposes to ride with him in a light open carriage to the place where he will bait[2] for the night, and there remain with him until morning: a servant riding, for so much of the journey, on the thorough-bred old

2. Rest at an inn.

grey from Chesney Wold. The offer being gladly accepted, is followed by a pleasant ride, a pleasant dinner, and a pleasant breakfast, all in brotherly communion. Then they once more shake hands long and heartily, and part; the ironmaster turning his face to the smoke and fires, and the trooper to the green country. Early in the afternoon, the subdued sound of his heavy military trot is heard on the turf in the avenue as he rides on with imaginary clank and jingle of accoutrements under the old elm trees.

Chapter LXIV

ESTHER'S NARRATIVE

Soon after I had had that conversation with my guardian, he put a sealed paper in my hand one morning, and said, "This is for next month, my dear." I found in it two hundred pounds.

I now began very quietly to make such preparations as I thought were necessary. Regulating my purchases by my guardian's taste, which I knew very well, of course, I arranged my wardrobe to please him, and hoped I should be highly successful. I did it all so quietly, because I was not quite free from my old apprehension that Ada would be rather sorry, and because my guardian was so quiet himself. I had no doubt that under all the circumstances we should be married in the most private and simple manner. Perhaps I should only have to say to Ada, "Would you like to come and see me married to-morrow, my pet?" Perhaps our wedding might even be as unpretending as her own, and I might not find it necessary to say anything about it until it was over. I thought that if I were to choose, I would like this best.

The only exception I made was Mrs. Woodcourt. I told her that I was going to be married to my guardian, and that we had been engaged some time. She highly approved. She could never do enough for me; and was remarkably softened now, in comparison with what she had been when we first knew her. There was no trouble she would not have taken to have been of use to me; but I need hardly say that I only allowed her to take as little as gratified her kindness without tasking it.

Of course this was not a time to neglect my guardian; and of course it was not a time for neglecting my darling. So I had plenty of occupation—which I was glad of; and as to Charley, she was absolutely not to be seen for needlework. To surround herself with great heaps of it—baskets full and tables full—and do a little, and spend a great deal of time in staring with her round eyes at what there was to do, and persuade herself that she was going to do it, were Charley's great dignities and delights.

Meanwhile, I must say, I could not agree with my guardian on the subject of the Will, and I had some sanguine hopes of Jarndyce and Jarndyce. Which of us was right will soon appear, but I certainly did encourage expectations. In Richard, the discovery gave occasion for a burst of business and agitation that buoyed him up for a little time; but he had lost the elasticity even of hope now, and seemed to me to retain only its feverish anxieties. From something my guardian said one day, when we were talking about this, I understood that my marriage would not take place until after the Term-time we had been told to look forward to; and I thought the more, for that, how rejoiced I should be if I could be married when Richard and Ada were a little more prosperous.

The Term was very near indeed, when my guardian was called out of town, and went down into Yorkshire on Mr. Woodcourt's business. He had told me beforehand that his presence there would be necessary. I had just come in one night from my dear girl's, and was sitting in the midst of all my new clothes, looking at them all around me, and thinking, when a letter from my guardian was brought to me. It asked me to join him in the country; and mentioned by what stage-coach my place was taken, and at what time in the morning I should have to leave town. It added in a postscript that I would not be many hours from Ada.

I expected few things less than a journey at that time, but I was ready for it in half-an-hour, and set off as appointed early next morning. I travelled all day, wondering all day what I could be wanted for at such a distance; now I thought it might be for this purpose, and now I thought it might be for that purpose; but I was never, never, never near the truth.

It was night when I came to my journey's end, and found my guardian waiting for me. This was a great relief, for towards evening I had begun to fear (the more so as his letter was a very short one) that he might be ill. However, there he was, as well as it was possible to be; and when I saw his genial face again at its brightest and best, I said to myself he has been doing some other great kindness. Not that it required much penetration to say that, because I knew that his being there at all was an act of kindness.

Supper was ready at the hotel, and when we were alone at table he said:

"Full of curiosity, no doubt, little woman, to know why I have brought you here?"

"Well, guardian," said I, "without thinking myself a Fatima,[1] or you a Blue Beard, I am a little curious about it."

1. In one of the versions of a story by Charles Perrault (1628–1703), Fatima, the seventh wife of Bluebeard, is overcome with curiosity to discover what is in a locked room which her husband has forbidden her to enter (it contains the murdered bodies of his six previous wives).

"Then to ensure your night's rest, my love," he returned, gaily, "I won't wait until to-morrow to tell you. I have very much wished to express to Woodcourt, somehow, my sense of his humanity to poor unfortunate Jo, his inestimable services to my young cousins, and his value to us all. When it was decided that he should settle here, it came into my head that I might ask his acceptance of some unpretending and suitable little place, to lay his own head in. I therefore caused such a place to be looked out for, and such a place was found on very easy terms, and I have been touching it up for him and making it habitable. However, when I walked over it the day before yesterday, and it was reported ready, I found that I was not housekeeper enough to know whether things were all as they ought to be. So I sent off for the best little housekeeper that could possibly be got, to come and give me her advice and opinion. And here she is," said my guardian, "laughing and crying both together!"

Because he was so dear, so good, so admirable. I tried to tell him what I thought of him, but I could not articulate a word.

"Tut, tut!" said my guardian. "You make too much of it, little woman. Why how you sob, Dame Durden, how you sob!"

"It is with exquisite pleasure, guardian—with a heart full of thanks."

"Well, well," said he. "I am delighted that you approve. I thought you would. I meant it as a pleasant surprise for the little mistress of Bleak House."

I kissed him, and dried my eyes. "I know now!" said I. "I have seen this in your face a long while!"

"No; have you really, my dear?" said he. "What a Dame Durden it is to read a face!"

He was so quaintly cheerful that I could not long be otherwise, and was almost ashamed of having been otherwise at all. When I went to bed, I cried. I am bound to confess that I cried; but I hope it was with pleasure, though I am not quite sure it was with pleasure. I repeated every word of the letter twice over.

A most beautiful summer morning succeeded; and after breakfast we went out arm in arm, to see the house of which I was to give my mighty housekeeping opinion. We entered a flower-garden by a gate in a side wall, of which he had the key; and the first thing I saw, was, that the beds and flowers were all laid out according to the manner of my beds and flowers at home.

"You see, my dear," observed my guardian, standing still, with a delighted face, to watch my looks; "knowing there could be no better plan, I borrowed yours."

We went on by a pretty little orchard, where the cherries were nestling among the green leaves, and the shadows of the apple-trees were sporting on the grass, to the house itself,—a cottage, quite a rustic cottage of doll's rooms; but such a lovely place, so tranquil and so beautiful, with such a rich and smiling country spread around it; with water sparkling away into the distance, here all overhung with summer-growth, there turning a humming mill; at its nearest point glancing through a meadow by the cheerful town, where cricket-players were assembling in bright groups, and a flag was flying from a white tent that rippled in the sweet west wind. And still, as we went through the pretty rooms, out at the little rustic verandah doors, and underneath the tiny wooden colonnades, garlanded with woodbine, jasmine, and honeysuckle, I saw, in the papering on the walls, in the colours of the furniture, in the arrangement of all the pretty objects, *my* little tastes and fancies, *my* little methods and inventions which they used to laugh at while they praised them, my odd ways everywhere.

I could not say enough in admiration of what was all so beautiful, but one secret doubt arose in my mind, when I saw this. I thought, O would he be the happier for it! Would it not have been better for his peace that I should not have been so brought before him? Because, although I was not what he thought me, still he loved me very dearly, and it might remind him mournfully of what he believed he had lost. I did not wish him to forget me,—perhaps he might not have done so, without these aids to his memory,—but my way was easier than his, and I could have reconciled myself even to that, so that he had been the happier for it.

"And now, little woman," said my guardian, whom I had never seen so proud and joyful as in showing me these things, and watching my appreciation of them, "now, last of all, for the name of this house."

"What is it called, dear guardian?"

"My child," said he, "come and see."

He took me to the porch, which he had hitherto avoided, and said, pausing before we went out:

"My dear child, don't you guess the name?"

"No!" said I.

We went out of the porch; and he showed me written over it, BLEAK HOUSE.

He lead me to a seat among the leaves close by, and sitting down beside me, and taking my hand in his, spoke to me thus:

"My darling girl, in what there has been between us, I have, I hope, been really solicitous for your happiness. When I wrote you the letter to which you brought the answer," smiling as he referred to it, "I had my own too much in view; but I had yours too. Whether, under different circumstances, I might ever have renewed the old dream I sometimes dreamed when you were very young, of making you my wife one day, I need not ask myself. I did renew it; and I wrote my letter, and you brought your answer. You are following what I say, my child?"

I was cold, and I trembled violently; but not a word he uttered was lost. As I sat looking fixedly at him, and the sun's rays descended, softly shining through the leaves, upon his bare head, I felt as if the brightness on him must be like the brightness of the Angels.

"Hear me, my love, but do not speak. It is for me to speak now. When it was that I began to doubt whether what I had done would really make you happy, is no matter. Woodcourt came home, and I soon had no doubt at all."

I clasped him round the neck, and hung my head upon his breast, and wept. "Lie lightly, confidently, here, my child," said he, pressing me gently to him. "I am your guardian and your father now. Rest confidently here."

Soothingly, like the gentle rustling of the leaves; and genially, like the ripening weather; and radiantly and beneficently, like the sunshine; he went on.

"Understand me, my dear girl. I had no doubt of your being contented and happy with me, being so dutiful and so devoted; but I saw with whom you would be happier. That I penetrated his secret when Dame Durden was blind to it, is no wonder; for I knew the good that could never change in her, better far than she did. Well! I have long been in Allan Woodcourt's confidence, although he was not, until yesterday, a few hours before you came here, in mine. But I would not have my Esther's bright example lost; I would not have a jot of my dear girl's virtues unobserved and unhonoured; I would not have her admitted on sufferance into the line of Morgan ap Kerrig, no, not for the weight in gold of all the mountains in Wales!"

He stopped to kiss me on the forehead, and I sobbed and wept afresh. For I felt as if I could not bear the painful delight of his praise.

"Hush, little woman! Don't cry; this is to be a day of joy. I have looked forward to it," he said, exultingly, "for months on months! A few words more, Dame Trot, and I have said my say. Determined not to throw away one atom of my Esther's worth, I took Mrs. Woodcourt into a separate confidence. 'Now madam,' said I, 'I clearly perceive—and indeed I know, to boot—that your son loves my ward. I am further very sure that my ward loves your son, but will sacrifice her love to a sense of duty and affection, and will sacrifice it so completely, so entirely, so religiously, that you should never suspect it though you watched her night and day.' Then I told her all our story—ours—yours and mine. 'Now, madam,' said

I, 'come you, knowing this, and live with us. Come you, and see my child from hour to hour; set what you see, against her pedigree, which is this, and this'—for I scorned to mince it—'and tell me what is the true legitimacy, when you shall have quite made up your mind on that subject.' Why, honour to her old Welsh blood, my dear!" cried my guardian, with enthusiasm, "I believe the heart it animates beats no less warmly, no less admiringly, no less lovingly, towards Dame Durden, than my own!"

He tenderly raised my head, and as I clung to him, kissed me in his old fatherly way again and again. What a light, now, on the protecting manner I had thought about!

"One more last word. When Allan Woodcourt spoke to you, my dear, he spoke with my knowledge and consent—but I gave him no encouragement, not I, for these surprises were my great reward, and I was too miserly to part with a scrap of it. He was to come, and tell me all that passed; and he did. I have no more to say. My dearest, Allan Woodcourt stood beside your father when he lay dead—stood beside your mother. This is Bleak House. This day I give this house its little mistress; and before God, it is the brightest day in all my life!"

He rose, and raised me with him. We were no longer alone. My husband—I have called him by that name full seven happy years now—stood at my side.

"Allan," said my guardian, "take from me, a willing gift, the best wife that ever a man had. What more can I say for you, than that I know you deserve her! Take with her the little home she brings you. You know what she will make it, Allan; you know what she had made its namesake. Let me share its felicity sometimes, and what do I sacrifice? Nothing, nothing."

He kissed me once again; and now the tears were in his eyes, as he said more softly;

"Esther, my dearest, after so many years, there is a kind of parting in this too. I know that my mistake has caused you some distress. Forgive your old guardian, in restoring him to his old place in your affections; and blot it out of your memory. Allan, take my dear."

He moved away from under the green roof of leaves, and stopping in the sunlight outside, and turning cheerfully towards us, said:

"I shall be found about here somewhere. It's a West wind, little woman, due west! Let no one thank me any more; for I am going to revert to my bachelor habits, and if anybody disregards this warning, I'll run away, and never come back!"

What happiness was ours that day, what joy, what rest, what

hope, what gratitude, what bliss! We were to be married before the month was out; but when we were to come and take possession of our own house, was to depend on Richard and Ada.

We all three went home together next day. As soon as we arrived in town, Allan went straight to see Richard, and to carry our joyful news to him and my darling. Late as it was, I meant to go to her for a few minutes before lying down to sleep: but I went home with my guardian first, to make his tea for him, and to occupy the old chair by his side; for I did not like to think of its being empty so soon.

When we came home, we found that a young man had called three times in the course of that one day, to see me; and that, having been told, on the occasion of his third call, that I was not expected to return before ten o'clock at night, he had left word, "that he would call again about then." He had left his card three times. Mr. Guppy.

As I naturally speculated on the object of these visits, and as I always associated something ludicrous with the visitor, it fell out that in laughing about Mr. Guppy I told my guardian of his old proposal, and his subsequent retractation. "After that," said my guardian, "we will certainly receive this hero." So instructions were given that Mr. Guppy should be shown in when he came again; and they were scarcely given when he did come again.

He was embarrassed when he found my guardian with me, but recovered himself, and said, "How de do, sir?"

"How do you do, sir?" returned my guardian.

"Thank you, sir, I am tolerable," returned Mr. Guppy. "Will you allow me to introduce my mother, Mrs. Guppy of the Old Street Road, and my particular friend, Mr. Weevle? That is to say, my friend has gone by the name of Weevle, but his name is really and truly Jobling."

My guardian begged them to be seated, and they all sat down.

"Tony," said Mr. Guppy to his friend, after an awkward silence. "Will you open the case?"

"Do it yourself," returned the friend, rather tartly.

"Well, Mr. Jarndyce, sir," Mr. Guppy, after a moment's consideration, began; to the great diversion of his mother, which she displayed by nudging Mr. Jobling with her elbow, and winking at me in a most remarkable manner; "I had an idea that I should see Miss Summerson by herself, and was not quite prepared for your esteemed presence. But Miss Summerson has mentioned to you, perhaps, that something has passed between us on former occasions?"

"Miss Summerson," returned my guardian smiling, "has made a communication to that effect to me."

"That," said Mr. Guppy, "makes matters easier. Sir, I have come out of my articles at Kenge and Carboy's, and I believe with satisfaction to all parties. I am now admitted (after undergoing an examination that's enough to badger a man blue, touching a pack of nonsense that he don't want to know) on the roll of attorneys, and have taken out my certificate, if it would be any satisfaction to you to see it."

"Thank you, Mr. Guppy," returned my guardian. "I am quite willing—I believe I use a legal phrase—to admit the certificate."

Mr. Guppy therefore desisted from taking something out of his pocket, and proceeded without it.

"I have no capital myself, but my mother has a little property which takes the form of an annuity"; here Mr. Guppy's mother rolled her head as if she never could sufficiently enjoy the observation, and put her handkerchief to her mouth, and again winked at me; "and a few pound for expenses out of pocket in conducting business, will never be wanting, free of interest, which is an advantage, you know," said Mr. Guppy, feelingly.

"Certainly an advantage," returned my guardian.

"I *have* some connexion," pursued Mr. Guppy, "and it lays in the direction of Walcot Square, Lambeth. I have therefore taken a ouse in that locality, which, in the opinion of my friends, is a hollow bargain (taxes ridiculous, and use of fixtures included in the rent), and intend setting up professionally for myself there, forthwith."

Here Mr. Guppy's mother fell into an extraordinary passion of rolling her head, and smiling waggishly at anybody who would look at her.

"It's a six-roomer, exclusive of kitchens," said Mr. Guppy, "and in the opinion of my friends, a commodious tenement. When I mention my friends, I refer principally to my friend Jobling, who I believe has known me," Mr. Guppy looked at him with a sentimental air, "from boyhood's hour?"

Mr. Jobling confirmed this with a sliding movement of his legs.

"My friend Jobling will render me his assistance in the capacity of clerk, and will live in the ouse," said Mr. Guppy. "My mother will likewise live in the ouse, when her present quarter in the Old Street Road shall have ceased and expired; and consequently there will be no want of society. My friend Jobling is naturally aristocratic by taste; and besides being acquainted with the movements of the upper circles, fully backs me in the intentions I am now developing."

Mr. Jobling said "certainly," and withdrew a little from the elbow of Mr. Guppy's mother.

"Now, I have no occasion to mention to you, sir, you being in the confidence of Miss Summerson," said Mr. Guppy, "(mother, I wish you'd be so good as to keep still), that Miss Summerson's image was formerly inprinted on my art, and that I made her a proposal of marriage."

"That I have heard," returned my guardian.

"Circumstances," pursued Mr. Guppy, "over which I had no control but quite the contrary, weakened the impression of that image for a time. At which time Miss Summerson's conduct was highly genteel; I may even add, magnanimous."

My guardian patted me on the shoulder, and seemed much amused.

"Now, sir," said Mr. Guppy, "I have got into that state of mind myself, that I wish for a reciprocity of magnanimous behaviour. I wish to prove to Miss Summerson that I can rise to a heigth, of which perhaps she hardly thought me capable. I find that the image which I did suppose had been eradicated from my art, is *not* eradicated. Its influence over me is still tremenjous; and yielding to it I am willing to overlook the circumstances over which none of us have had any control, and to renew those proposals to Miss Summerson which I had the honour to make at a former period. I beg to lay the ouse in Walcot Square, the business, and myself, before Miss Summerson for her acceptance."

"Very magnanimous indeed, sir," observed my guardian.

"Well, sir," replied Mr. Guppy, with candour, "my wish is to *be* magnanimous. I do not consider that in making this offer to Miss Summerson, I am by any means throwing myself away; neither is that the opinion of my friends. Still, there are circumstances which I submit may be taken into account as a set-off against any little drawbacks of mine, and so a fair and equitable balance arrived at."

"I take upon myself, sir," said my guardian, laughing as he rang the bell, "to reply to your proposals on behalf of Miss Summerson. She is very sensible of your handsome intentions, and wishes you good evening, and wishes you well."

"Oh!" said Mr. Guppy, with a blank look. "Is that tantamount, sir, to acceptance, or rejection, or consideration?"

"To decided rejection, if you please!" returned my guardian.

Mr. Guppy looked incredulously at his friend, and at his mother who suddenly turned very angry, and at the floor, and at the ceiling.

"Indeed?" said he. "Then, Jobling, if you was the friend you represent yourself, I should think you might hand my mother out of the gangway, instead of allowing her to remain where she ain't wanted."

But Mrs. Guppy positively refused to come out of the gangway. She wouldn't hear of it. "Why, get along with you," said she to my guardian, "what do you mean? Ain't my son good enough for you? You ought to be ashamed of yourself. Get out with you!"

"My good lady!" returned my guardian, "it is hardly reasonable to ask me to get out of my own room."

"I don't care for that," said Mrs. Guppy. "Get out with you. If we ain't good enough for you, go and procure somebody that is good enough. Go along and find 'em."

I was quite unprepared for the rapid manner in which Mrs. Guppy's power of jocularity merged into a power of taking the profoundest offence.

"Go along and find somebody that's good enough for you," repeated Mrs. Guppy. "Get out!" Nothing seemed to astonish Mr. Guppy's mother so much, and to make her so very indignant, as our not getting out. "Why don't you get out?" said Mrs. Guppy. "What are you stopping here for?"

"Mother," interposed her son, always getting before her, and pushing her back with one shoulder, as she sidled at my guardian, "*will* you hold your tongue?"

"No, William," she returned; "I won't! Not unless he gets out, I won't!"

However, Mr. Guppy and Mr. Jobling together closed on Mr. Guppy's mother (who began to be quite abusive), and took her, very much against her will, down-stairs; her voice rising a stair higher every time her figure got a stair lower, and insisting that we should immediately go and find somebody who was good enough for us, and above all things that we should get out.

Chapter LXV

BEGINNING THE WORLD

The term had commenced, and my guardian found an intimation from Mr. Kenge that the Cause would come on in two days. As I had sufficient hopes of the will to be in a flutter about it, Allan and I agreed to go down to the Court that morning. Richard was extremely agitated, and was so weak and low, though his illness was still of the mind, that my dear girl indeed had sore occasion to be supported. But she looked forward—a very little way now—to the help that was to come to her, and never drooped.

It was at Westminster that the Cause was to come on. It had come on there, I dare say, a hundred times before, but I could not divest myself of an idea that it *might* lead to some result now. We left home directly after breakfast, to be at Westminster Hall in good time; and walked down there through the lively streets—so happily and strangely it seemed!—together.

As we were going along, planning what we should do for Richard and Ada, I heard somebody calling "Esther! My dear Esther! Esther!" And there was Caddy Jellyby, with her head out of the window of a little carriage which she hired now to go about in to her pupils (she had so many), as if she wanted to embrace me at a hundred yards' distance. I had written her a note to tell her of all that my guardian had done, but had not had a moment to go and see her. Of course we turned back; and the affectionate girl was in that state of rapture, and was so overjoyed to talk about the night when she brought me the flowers, and was so determined to squeeze my face (bonnet and all) between her hands, and go on in a wild manner altogether, calling me all kinds of precious names, and telling Allan I had done I don't know what for her, that I was just obliged to get into the little carriage and calm her down, by letting her say and do exactly what she liked. Allan, standing at the window, was as pleased as Caddy; and I was as pleased as either of them; and I wonder that I got away as I did, rather than that I came off, laughing, and red, and anything but tidy, and looking after Caddy, who looked after us out of the coach-window as long as she could see us.

This made us some quarter of an hour late, and when we came to Westminster Hall, we found that the day's business was begun. Worse than that, we found such an unusual crowd in the Court of Chancery that it was full to the door, and we could neither see nor hear what was passing within. It appeared to be something droll, for occasionally there was a laugh, and a cry of "Silence!" It appeared to be something interesting, for every one was pushing and striving to get nearer. It appeared to be something that made the professional gentlemen very merry, for there were several young counsellors in wigs and whiskers on the outside of the crowd, and when one of them told the others about it, they put their hands in their pockets, and quite doubled themselves up with laughter, and went stamping about the pavement of the hall.

We asked a gentleman by us, if he knew what cause was on? He told us Jarndyce and Jarndyce. We asked him if he knew what was doing in it? He said, really no he did not, nobody ever did; but as well as he could make out, it was over. Over for the day? we asked him. No, he said; over for good.

Over for good!

When we heard this unaccountable answer, we looked at one another quite lost in amazement. Could it be possible that the Will had set things right at last, and that Richard and Ada were going to be rich? It seemed too good to be true. Alas, it was!

Our suspense was short; for a break up soon took place in the crowd, and the people came streaming out looking flushed and hot, and bringing a quantity of bad air with them. Still they were all exceedingly amused, and were more like people coming out from a Farce or a Juggler than from a court of Justice. We stood aside, watching for any countenance we knew; and presently great bundles of papers began to be carried out—bundles in bags, bundles too large to be got into any bags, immense masses of papers of all shapes and no shapes, which the bearers staggered under, and threw down for the time being, anyhow, on the Hall pavement, while they went back to bring out more. Even these clerks were laughing. We glanced at the papers, and seeing Jarndyce and Jarndyce everywhere, asked an official-looking person who was standing in the midst of them, whether the cause was over. "Yes," he said; "it was all up with it at last!" and burst out laughing too.

At this juncture, we perceived Mr. Kenge coming out of Court with an affable dignity upon him, listening to Mr. Vholes, who was deferential, and carried his own bag. Mr. Vholes was the first to see us. "Here is Miss Summerson, sir," he said. "And Mr. Woodcourt."

"O indeed! Yes. Truly!" said Mr. Kenge, raising his hat to me with polished politeness. "How do you do? Glad to see you. Mr. Jarndyce is not here?"

No. He never came there, I reminded him.

"Really," returned Mr. Kenge, "it is as well that he is *not* here to-day, for his—shall I say, in my good friend's absence, his indomitable singularity of opinion?—might have been strengthened, perhaps; not reasonably, but might have been strengthened."

"Pray what has been done to-day?" asked Allan.

"I beg your pardon?" said Mr. Kenge, with excessive urbanity.

"What has been done to-day?"

"What has been done," repeated Mr. Kenge. "Quite so. Yes. Why, not much has been done; not much. We have been checked—brought up suddenly, I would say—upon the—shall I term it threshold?"

"Is this Will considered a genuine document, sir?" said Allan; "will you tell us that?"

"Most certainly, if I could," said Mr. Kenge; "but we have not gone into that, we have not gone into that."

"We have not gone into that," repeated Mr. Vholes, as if his low inward voice were an echo.

"You are to reflect, Mr. Woodcourt," observed Mr. Kenge, using his silver trowel, persuasively and smoothingly, "that this has been a great cause, that this has been a protracted cause, that this has been a complex cause. Jarndyce and Jarndyce has been termed, not inaptly, a Monument of Chancery practice."

"And Patience[1] has sat upon it a long time," said Allan.

"Very well indeed, sir," returned Mr. Kenge, with a certain condescending laugh he had. "Very well! You are further to reflect, Mr. Woodcourt," becoming dignified almost to severity, "that on

1. See *Twelfth Night* (II.iv.115–18).

the numerous difficulties, contingencies, masterly fictions, and forms of procedure in this great cause, there has been expended study, ability, eloquence, knowledge, intellect, Mr. Woodcourt, high intellect. For many years, the—a—I would say the flower of the Bar, and the—a—I would presume to add, the matured autumnal fruits of the Woolsack[2]—have been lavished upon Jarndyce and Jarndyce. If the public have the benefit, and if the country have the adornment, of this great Grasp, it must be paid for in money or money's worth, sir."

"Mr. Kenge," said Allan, appearing enlightened all in a moment. "Excuse me, our time presses. Do I understand that the whole estate is found to have been absorbed in costs?"

"Hem! I believe so," returned Mr. Kenge. "Mr. Vholes, what do *you* say?"

"I believe so," said Mr. Vholes.

"And that thus the suit lapses and melts away?"

"Probably," returned Mr. Kenge. "Mr. Vholes?"

"Probably," said Mr. Vholes.

"My dearest life," whispered Allan, taking me hurriedly from them, "this will break Richard's heart!"

There was such a shock of apprehension in his face, and he knew Richard so perfectly, and I too had seen so much of his gradual decay, that what my dear girl had said to me in the fulness of her foreboding love, sounded like a knell in my ears.

"In case you should be wanting Mr. C, sir," said Mr. Vholes, coming after us, "you'll find him in Court. I left him there resting himself a little. Good day, sir; good day, Miss Summerson." As he gave me that slowly devouring look of his, while twisting up the strings of his bag, before he hastened with it after Mr. Kenge, the benignant shadow of whose conversational presence he seemed afraid to leave, he gave one gasp as if he had swallowed the last morsel of this client, and his black buttoned-up unwholesome figure glided away to the low door at the end of the Hall.

"My dear love," said Allan, "leave to me, for a little while, the charge you gave me. Go home with this intelligence, and come to Ada's by-and-by!"

I would not let him take me to a coach, but entreated him to go to Richard without a moment's delay, and leave me to do as he wished. Hurrying home, I found my guardian, and told him gradually with what news I had returned. "Little woman," said he, quite unmoved for himself, "to have done with the suit on any terms is a greater blessing than I had looked for. But my poor young cousins!"

2. A seat, cushioned with wool, used by the Lord Chancellor on ceremonial occasions.

We talked about them all the morning, and discussed what it was possible to do. In the afternoon, my guardian walked with me to Symond's Inn, and left me at the door. I went up-stairs. When my darling heard my footsteps, she came out into the small passage and threw her arms round my neck; but she composed herself directly, and said that Richard had asked for me several times. Allan had found him sitting in a corner of the court, she told me, like a stone figure. On being roused, he had broken away, and made as if he would have spoken in a fierce voice to the judge. He was stopped by his mouth being full of blood, and Allan had brought him home.

He was lying on the sofa with his eyes closed, when I went in. There were restoratives on the table; the room was made as airy as possible, and was darkened, and was very orderly and quiet. Allan stood behind him, watching him gravely. His face appeared to me to be quite destitute of colour, and now that I saw him without his seeing me I fully saw, for the first time, how worn away he was. But he looked handsomer than I had seen him look for many a day.

I sat down by his side in silence. Opening his eyes by-and-by, he said, in a weak voice, but with his old smile, "Dame Durden, kiss me, my dear!"

It was a great comfort and surprise to me, to find him in his low state cheerful and looking forward. He was happier, he said, in our intended marriage, than he could find words to tell me. My husband had been a guardian angel to him and Ada, and he blessed us both, and wished us all the joy that life could yield us. I almost felt as if my own heart would have broken, when I saw him take my husband's hand, and hold it to his breast.

We spoke of the future as much as possible, and he said several times that he must be present at our marriage if he could stand upon his feet. Ada would contrive to take him, somehow, he said. "Yes, surely, dearest Richard!" But as my darling answered him thus hopefully, so serene and beautiful, with the help that was to come to her so near,—I knew—I knew!

It was not good for him to talk too much; and when he was silent, we were silent too. Sitting beside him, I made a pretence of working for my dear, as he had always been used to joke about my being busy. Ada leaned upon his pillow, holding his head upon her arm. He dozed often; and whenever he awoke without seeing him, said, first of all, "Where is Woodcourt?"

Evening had come on, when I lifted up my eyes, and saw my guardian standing in the little hall. "Who is that, Dame Durden?" Richard asked me. The door was behind him, but he had observed in my face that some one was there.

I looked to Allan for advice, and as he nodded "Yes," bent over Richard and told him. My guardian saw what passed, came softly by me in a moment, and laid his hand on Richard's. "O sir," said Richard, "you are a good man, you are a good man!" and burst into tears for the first time.

My guardian, the picture of a good man, sat down in my place, keeping his hand on Richard's.

"My dear Rick," said he, "the clouds have cleared away, and it is bright now. We can see now. We were all bewildered, Rick, more or less. What matters! And how are you, my dear boy?"

"I am very weak, sir, but I hope I shall be stronger. I have to begin the world."

"Aye, truly; well said!" cried my guardian.

"I will not begin it in the old way now," said Richard, with a sad smile. "I have learned a lesson now, sir. It was a hard one; but you shall be assured, indeed, that I have learned it."

"Well, well," said my guardian, comforting him; "well, well, well, dear boy!"

"I was thinking, sir," resumed Richard, "that there is nothing on earth I should so much like to see as their house—Dame Durden's and Woodcourt's house. If I could be removed there when I begin to recover my strength, I feel as if I should get well there, sooner than anywhere."

"Why, so have I been thinking too, Rick," said my guardian, "and our little woman likewise; she and I have been talking of it, this very day. I dare say her husband won't object. What do you think?"

Richard smiled; and lifted up his arm to touch him, as he stood behind the head of his couch.

"I say nothing of Ada," said Richard, "but I think of her, and have thought of her very much. Look at her! see her here, sir, bending over this pillow when she has so much need to rest upon it herself, my dear love, my poor girl!"

He clasped her in his arms, and none of us spoke. He gradually released her; and she looked upon us, and looked up to Heaven, and moved her lips.

"When I get down to Bleak House," said Richard, "I shall have much to tell you, sir, and you will have much to show me. You will go, won't you?"

"Undoubtedly, dear Rick."

"Thank you; like you, like you," said Richard. "But it's all like you. They have been telling me how you planned it, and how you remembered all Esther's familiar tastes and ways. It will be like coming to the old Bleak House again."

"And you will come there too, I hope, Rick. I am a solitary man now, you know, and it will be a charity to come to me. A charity to come to me, my love!" he repeated to Ada, as he gently passed his hand over her golden hair, and put a lock of it to his lips. (I think he vowed within himself to cherish her if she were left alone.)

"It was all a troubled dream?" said Richard, clasping both my guardian's hands eagerly.

"Nothing more, Rick; nothing more."

"And you, being a good man, can pass it as such, and forgive and pity the dreamer, and be lenient and encouraging when he wakes?"

"Indeed I can. What am I but another dreamer, Rick?"

"I will begin the world!" said Richard, with a light in his eyes.

My husband drew a little nearer towards Ada, and I saw him solemnly lift up his hand to warn my guardian.

"When shall I go from this place, to that pleasant country where the old times are, where I shall have strength to tell what Ada has been to me, where I shall be able to recall my many faults and blindnesses, where I shall prepare myself to be a guide to my unborn child?" said Richard. "When shall I go?"

"Dear Rick, when you are strong enough," returned my guardian.

"Ada, my darling!"

He sought to raise himself a little. Allan raised him so that she could hold him on her bosom: which was what he wanted.

"I have done you many wrongs, my own. I have fallen like a poor stray shadow on your way, I have married you to poverty and trouble, I have scattered your means to the winds. You will forgive me all this, my Ada, before I begin the world?"

A smile irradiated his face, as she bent to kiss him. He slowly laid his face down upon her bosom, drew his arms closer round her neck, and with one parting sob began the world. Not this world, O not this! The world that sets this right.

When all was still, at a late hour, poor crazed Miss Flite came weeping to me, and told me she had given her birds their liberty.

Chapter LXVI

DOWN IN LINCOLNSHIRE

There is a hush upon Chesney Wold in these altered days, as there is upon a portion of the family history. The story goes, that Sir Leicester paid some who could have spoken out, to hold their peace; but it is a lame story, feebly whispering and creeping about, and any brighter spark of life it shows soon dies away. It is known for certain that the handsome Lady Dedlock lies in the mausoleum in the park, where the trees arch darkly overhead, and the owl is heard at night making the woods ring; but whence she was brought home, to be laid among the echoes of that solitary place, or how she died, is all mystery. Some of her old friends, principally to be found among the peachy-cheeked charmers with the skeleton throats, did once occasionally say, as they toyed in a ghastly manner with large fans—like charmers reduced to flirting with grim Death,[1] after losing all their other beaux—did once occasionally say, when the World assembled together, that they wondered the ashes of the Dedlocks, entombed in the mausoleum, never rose against the profanation of her company. But the dead-and-gone Dedlocks take it very calmly, and have never been known to object.

Up from among the fern in the hollow, and winding by the bridle-road among the trees, comes sometimes to this lonely spot the sound of horses' hoofs. Then may be seen Sir Leicester—invalided, bent, and almost blind, but of a worthy presence yet—riding with a stalwart man beside him, constant to his bridle-rein. When they come to a certain spot before the mausoleum door, Sir Leicester's accustomed horse stops of his own accord, and Sir Leicester, pulling off his hat, is still for a few moments before they ride away.

War rages yet with the audacious Boythorn, though at uncertain intervals, and now hotly, and now coolly; flickering like an unsteady fire. The truth is said to be, that when Sir Leicester came down to Lincolnshire for good, Mr. Boythorn showed a manifest desire to abandon his right of way, and do whatever Sir Leicester would: which Sir Leicester, conceiving to be a condescension to his illness or misfortune, took in such high dudgeon, and was so magnificently aggrieved by, that Mr. Boythorn found himself under the necessity of committing a flagrant trespass to restore his neighbour to himself. Similarly Mr. Boythorn continues to post tremendous placards on the disputed thoroughfare, and (with his bird upon his head) to hold forth vehemently against Sir Leicester in the sanctuary of his own home; similarly, also, he defies him as of old in the little church, by testifying a bland unconsciousness of his existence. But it is whispered that when he is most ferocious towards his old foe, he is really most considerate; and that Sir Leicester, in the dignity of being implacable, little supposes how much he is humoured. As little does he think how near together he and his antagonist have suffered, in the fortunes of two sisters; and his antagonist, who knows it now, is not the man to tell him. So the quarrel goes on to the satisfaction of both.

In one of the lodges of the park; that lodge within sight of the house where, once upon a time, when the waters were out down in Lincolnshire, my Lady used to see the Keeper's child; the stalwart man, the trooper formerly, is housed. Some relics of his old calling hang upon the walls, and these it is the chosen recreation of a little lame man about the stable-yard to keep gleaming bright. A busy little man he always is, in the polishing at harness-house doors, of

1. See p. 667, note 1.

stirrup-irons, bits, curb-chains, harness-bosses, anything in the way of a stable-yard that will take a polish: leading a life of friction. A shaggy little damaged man, withal, not unlike an old dog of some mongrel breed, who has been considerably knocked about. He answers to the name of Phil.

A goodly sight it is to see the grand old housekeeper (harder of hearing now) going to church on the arm of her son, and to observe—which few do, for the house is scant of company in these times—the relations of both towards Sir Leicester, and his towards them. They have visitors in the high summer weather, when a grey cloak and umbrella, unknown to Chesney Wold at other periods, are seen among the leaves; when two young ladies are occasionally found gambolling, in sequestered saw-pits and such nooks of the park; and when the smoke of two pipes wreathes away into the fragrant evening air, from the trooper's door. Then is a fife heard trolling within the lodge, on the inspiring topic of the British Grenadiers; and, as the evening closes in, a gruff inflexible voice is heard to say, while two men pace together up and down, "But I never own to it before the old girl. Discipline must be maintained."

The greater part of the house is shut up, and it is a show-house no longer; yet Sir Leicester holds his shrunken state in the long drawing-room for all that, and reposes in his old place before my Lady's picture. Closed in by night with broad screens, and illumined only in that part, the light of the drawing-room seems gradually contracting and dwindling until it shall be no more. A little more, in truth, and it will be extinguished for Sir Leicester; and the damp door in the mausoleum which shuts so tight, and looks so obdurate, will have opened and received him.

Volumnia, growing with the flight of time pinker as to the red in her face, and yellower as to the white, reads to Sir Leicester in the long evenings, and is driven to various artifices to conceal her yawns: of which the chief and most efficacious is the insertion of the pearl necklace between her rosy lips. Long-winded treatises on the Buffy and Boodle question, showing how Buffy is immaculate and Boodle villainous, and how the country is lost by being all Boodle and no Buffy, or saved by being all Buffy and no Boodle (it must be one of the two, and can never be anything else), are the staple of her reading. Sir Leicester is not particular what it is, and does not appear to follow it very closely; further than that he always comes broad awake the moment Volumnia ventures to leave off, and sonorously repeating her last word, begs with some displeasure to know if she finds herself fatigued? However, Volumnia, in the course of her bird-like hopping about and pecking at papers, has alighted on a memorandum concerning herself, in the event of "anything happening" to her kinsman, which is handsome compensation for an extensive course of reading, and holds even the dragon Boredom at bay.

The cousins generally are rather shy of Chesney Wold in its dulness, but take to it a little in the shooting season, when guns are heard in the plantations, and a few scattered beaters and keepers wait at the old places of appointment, for low spirited twos and threes of cousins. The debilitated cousin, more debilitated by the dreariness of the place, gets into a fearful state of depression, groaning under penitential sofa-pillows in his gunless hours, and protesting that such fernal old jail's—nough t'sew fler up[2]—frever.

The only great occasions for Volumnia, in this changed aspect of the place in Lincolnshire, are those occasions, rare and widely-separated, when something is to be done for the county, or the country, in the way of gracing a public ball. Then, indeed, does the tuckered sylph come out in fairy form, and proceed with joy under cousinly escort to the exhausted old assembly-room, fourteen heavy miles off; which, during three hundred and sixty-four days and nights of every ordinary year, is a kind of Antipodean lumber-room, full of old chairs and tables, upside down. Then, indeed, does she captivate all hearts by her condescension, by her girlish vivacity, and by her skipping about as in the days when the hideous old general with the mouth too full of teeth, had not cut one of them at two guineas each. Then does she twirl and twine, a pastoral nymph of good family, through the mazes of the dance. Then do the swains appear with tea, with lemonade, with sandwiches, with homage. Then is she kind and cruel, stately and unassuming, various, beautifully wilful. Then is there a singular kind of parallel between her and the little glass chandeliers of another age, embellishing that assembly-room; which, with their meagre stems, their spare little drops, their disappointing knobs where no drops are, their bare little stalks from which knobs and drops have both departed, and their little feeble prismatic twinkling, all seem Volumnias.

For the rest, Lincolnshire life to Volumnia is a vast blank of overgrown house looking out upon trees, sighing, wringing their hands, bowing their heads, and casting their tears upon the window-panes in monotonous depression. A labyrinth of grandeur, less the property of an old family of human beings and their ghostly likenesses, than of an old family of echoings and thunderings which start out of their hundred graves at every sound, and go resounding through the building. A waste of unused passages and staircases, in which to drop a comb upon a bedroom floor at night is to send a stealthy footfall on an errand through the house. A place where few people care to go about alone; where a maid screams if an ash drops from the fire, takes to crying at all times and seasons,

2. I.e., enough to exhaust a feller.

becomes the victim of a low disorder of the spirits, and gives warning and departs.

Thus Chesney Wold. With so much of itself abandoned to darkness and vacancy; with so little change under the summer shining or the wintry lowering; so sombre and motionless always—no flag flying now by day, no rows of lights sparkling by night; with no family to come and go, no visitors to be the souls of pale cold shapes of rooms, no stir of life about it;—passion and pride, even to the stranger's eye, have died away from the place in Lincolnshire, and yielded it to dull repose.

Chapter LXVII

THE CLOSE OF ESTHER'S NARRATIVE

Full seven happy years I have been the mistress of Bleak House. The few words that I have to add to what I have written, are soon penned; then I, and the unknown friend to whom I write, will part for ever. Not without much dear remembrance on my side. Not without some, I hope, on his or hers.

They gave my darling into my arms, and through many weeks I never left her. The little child who was to have done so much, was born before the turf was planted on its father's grave. It was a boy; and I, my husband, and my guardian, gave him his father's name.

The help that my dear counted on, did come to her; though it came, in the Eternal wisdom, for another purpose. Though to bless and restore his mother, not his father, was the errand of this baby, its power was mighty to do it. When I saw the strength of the weak little hand, and how its touch could heal my darling's heart, and raise up hope within her, I felt a new sense of the goodness and the tenderness of God.

They throve; and by degrees I saw my dear girl pass into my country garden, and walk there with her infant in her arms. I was married then. I was the happiest of the happy.

It was at this time that my guardian joined us, and asked Ada when she would come home?

"Both houses are your home, my dear," said he, "but the older Bleak House claims priority. When you and my boy are strong enough to do it, come and take possession of your home."

Ada called him "her dearest cousin, John." But he said, No, it must be guardian now. He was her guardian henceforth, and the boy's; and he had an old association with the name. So she called him guardian, and has called him guardian ever since. The children know him by no other name.—I say the children; I have two little daughters.

It is difficult to believe that Charley (round-eyed still, and not at all grammatical) is married to a miller in our neighbourhood; yet so it is; and even now, looking up from my desk as I write, early in the morning at my summer window, I see the very mill beginning to go round. I hope the miller will not spoil Charley; but he is very fond of her, and Charley is rather vain of such a match—for he is well to do, and was in great request. So far as my small maid is concerned, I might suppose Time to have stood for seven years as still as the mill did half an hour ago; since little Emma, Charley's sister, is exactly what Charley used to be. As to Tom, Charley's brother, I am really afraid to say what he did at school in cyphering, but I think it was Decimals. He is apprenticed to the miller, whatever it was; and is a good bashful fellow, always falling in love with somebody, and being ashamed of it.

Caddy Jellyby passed her very last holidays with us, and was a dearer creature than ever; perpetually dancing in and out of the house with the children, as if she had never given a dancing-lesson in her life. Caddy keeps her own little carriage now, instead of hiring one, and lives full two miles further westward than Newman Street. She works very hard, her husband (an excellent one) being lame, and able to do very little. Still, she is more than contented, and does all she has to do with all her heart. Mr. Jellyby spends his evenings at her new house with his head against the wall, as he used to do in her old one. I have heard that Mrs. Jellyby was understood to suffer great mortification, from her daughter's ignoble marriage and pursuits; but I hope she got over it in time. She has been disappointed in Borrioboola-Gha, which turned out a failure in consequence of the King of Borrioboola wanting to sell everybody—who survived the climate—for Rum; but she has taken up with the rights of women to sit in Parliament, and Caddy tells me it is a mission involving more correspondence than the old one. I had almost forgotten Caddy's poor little girl. She is not such a mite now; but she is deaf and dumb. I believe there never was a better mother than Caddy, who learns, in her scanty intervals of leisure, innumerable deaf and dumb arts, to soften the affliction of her child.

As if I were never to have done with Caddy, I am reminded here of Peepy and old Mr. Turveydrop. Peepy is in the Custom-House, and doing extremely well. Old Mr. Turveydrop, very apoplectic, still exhibits his Deportment about town; still enjoys himself in the old manner; is still believed in, in the old way. He is constant in his patronage of Peepy, and is understood to have bequeathed him a favourite French clock in his dressing-room—which is not his property.

With the first money we saved at home, we added to our pretty house by throwing out a little Growlery expressly for my guardian; which we inaugurated with great splendour the next time he came down to see us. I try to write all this lightly, because my heart is full in drawing to an end; but when I write of him, my tears will have their way.

I never look at him, but I hear our poor dear Richard calling him a good man. To Ada and her pretty boy, he is the fondest father; to me, he is what he has ever been, and what name can I give to that? He is my husband's best and dearest friend, he is our children's darling, he is the object of our deepest love and veneration. Yet while I feel towards him as if he were a superior being, I am so familiar with him, and so easy with him, that I almost wonder at myself. I have never lost my old names, nor has he lost his; nor do I ever, when he is with us, sit in any other place than in my old chair at his side. Dame Trot, Dame Durden, Little Woman!—all just the same as ever; and I answer, Yes, dear guardian! just the same.

I have never known the wind to be in the East for a single moment, since the day when he took me to the porch to read the name. I remarked to him once, that the wind seemed never in the East now: and he said, No, truly; it had finally departed from that quarter on that very day.

I think my darling girl is more beautiful than ever. The sorrow that has been in her face—for it is not there now—seems to have purified even its innocent expression, and to have given it a diviner quality. Sometimes, when I raise my eyes and see her, in the black dress that she still wears, teaching my Richard, I feel—it is difficult to express—as if it were so good to know that she remembers her dear Esther in her prayers.

I call him my Richard! But he says that he has two mamas, and I am one.

We are not rich in the bank, but we have always prospered, and we have quite enough. I never walk out with my husband, but I hear the people bless him. I never go into a house of any degree, but I hear his praises, or see them in grateful eyes. I never lie down at night, but I know that in the course of that day he has alleviated pain, and soothed some fellow-creature in a time of need. I know that from the beds of those who were past recovery, thanks have often, often gone up, in the last hour, for his patient ministration. Is not this to be rich?

The people even praise Me as the doctor's wife. The people even like Me as I go about, and make so much of me that I am quite abashed. I owe it all to him, my love, my pride! They like me for his sake, as I do everything I do in life for his sake.

A night or two ago, after bustling about preparing for my darling and my guardian and little Richard, who are coming to-morrow, I was sitting out in the porch of all places, that dearly memorable porch, when Allan came home. So he said, "My precious little woman, what are you doing here?" And I said, "The moon is shining so brightly, Allan, and the night is so delicious, that I have been sitting here, thinking."

"What have you been thinking about, my dear?" said Allan then.

"How curious you are!" said I. "I am almost ashamed to tell you, but I will. I have been thinking about my old looks—such as they were."

"And what have you been thinking about *them*, my busy bee?" said Allan.

"I have been thinking, that I thought it was impossible that you *could* have loved me any better, even if I had retained them."

"—Such as they were?" said Allan, laughing.

"Such as they were, of course."

"My dear Dame Durden," said Allan, drawing my arm through his, "do you ever look in the glass?"

"You know I do; you see me do it."

"And don't you know that you are prettier than you ever were?"

I did not know that; I am not certain that I know it now. But I know that my dearest little pets are very pretty, and that my darling is very beautiful, and that my husband is very handsome, and that my guardian has the brightest and most benevolent face that ever was seen; and that they can very well do without much beauty in me—even supposing——

THE END

No. II. APRIL. Price 1s.

BLEAK HOUSE

BY

CHARLES DICKENS.

WITH ILLUSTRATIONS BY H. K. BROWNE.

LONDON: BRADBURY & EVANS, BOUVERIE STREET.

AGENTS: J. MENZIES, EDINBURGH; MURRAY AND SON, GLASGOW; J. M'GLASHAN, DUBLIN.

☞ NOTICE is hereby given that the Author of "BLEAK HOUSE" reserves to himself the right of publishing a Translation in France.

Cover for a monthly number of *Bleak House* (April, 1852)

A Note on the Text

Bleak House, Charles Dickens' ninth novel, was first published in nineteen monthly installments, beginning in March, 1852, and ending in September, 1853. Each installment was written shortly before publication.

The textual history of the novel is richly documented. In addition to some comments in the author's correspondence, especially with his friend John Forster, who quoted from it in his *Life of Dickens,* students have at their disposal the writer's working plans, his complete manuscript (MS), and his corrected proofs (CP). After the first edition in book form (1853), whose text is identical with that of the monthly parts, Dickens more or less sanctioned three later editions during his lifetime. Every stage of the textual history is discussed below and taken into account in the textual notes.

But, before dealing with the manuscript, it is necessary to reproduce the evidence concerning the earliest phases of Dickens' labor on *Bleak House.*

Title

The first item in the *Bleak House* MS at the Victoria and Albert Museum is a series of ten slips—half-sheets of Dickens' usual writing paper—recording his search for a suitable title for his new novel. They are reproduced below, with numbers showing the order in which they have been preserved in the first volume of the bound MS, and with all the underscorings, cancellations, and alternatives introduced by Dickens. A series of two or three short parallel lines under a phrase was his constant way—exemplified in all his chapter headings—of pointing to an item that was to be printed in capitals.

1

Tom-All-Alone's

The Ruined House

2

Tom-All-Alone's

The Solitary House

~~That never knew happiness~~

That was always shut up

Bleak House Academy

The East Wind

3

Tom-All-Alone's

Building
Factory
Mill

The Ruined House

That got into Chancery

and never got out

4

Tom-All-Alone's

The Solitary House

where the grass grew

5

Tom-All-Alone's

The Solitary House

That was always shut up

never lighted

6

Tom-All-Alone's,

The Ruined Mill,

That got into Chancery

and never got out.

7

Tom-All-Alone's

The Solitary House

Where the Wind howled

8

Tom-All-Alone's

House

The Ruined ~~Mill~~

That got into Chancery

and never got out.

9

Tom-All-Alone's

The Ruined House

~~In Chancery~~

That got into Chancery

and never got out.

10

Bleak House

and The East Wind

How they both got into Chancery

and never got out

Bleak House.

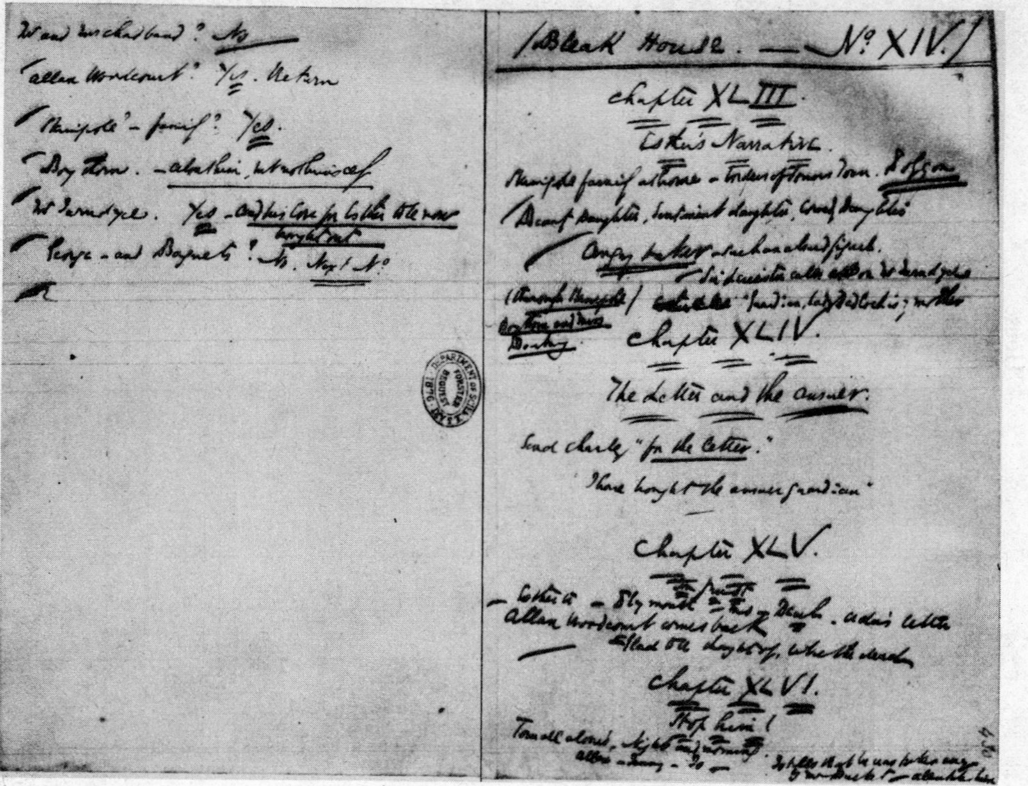

Woodcourt unclaimed? No

Allan Woodcourt? Yes. Return

Skimpole?—finish? Yes.

Boythorn.—already in, but not himself

Mr Jarndyce. Yes—And his love for Esther. Tell it now [illegible]

George—and Bagnets? No. Next No.

/ Bleak House. —— No. XIV. /

Chapter XLIII.

Esther's Narrative.

Skimpole's family at home—[illegible] Somers Town. Polygon

Beauty daughter, Sentiment daughter, Comedy daughter

Angry baker [illegible]

Sir Leicester [illegible] guardian, Lady Dedlock; mother

(Through Skimpole) [illegible] Bucket [illegible]

Chapter XLIV.

The Letter and the answer.

Send Charley "for the letter."

"I have brought the answer guardian."

Chapter XLV.

In Trust

Esther's—Deal—Ada's letter

Allan Woodcourt comes back

[illegible]

Chapter XLVI.

Stop him!

Tom all alone's. Night and morning. [illegible]

[illegible] Jo—

[illegible]

Dickens' *Mems.* for N° XIV of *Bleak House* (COURTESY OF THE VICTORIA AND ALBERT MUSEUM)

Dickens' Working Plans

From the time of his writing *Dombey and Son* (1846–48), it became Dickens' practice to jot down on loose sheets of paper a series of briefly worded suggestions, for his own guidance, about the novel he was engaged in writing—suggestions about its plot and theme, about names of characters, and, in particular, about how his story might best be divided into parts for publication. He presumably kept one or more of these sheets on his desk while he was writing his story.

The MS of *Bleak House* thus contains one sheet of working memoranda —or *Mems.* as Dickens was fond of calling them—for each of the nineteen monthly installments. They are bound inside the MS volumes, each at the head of the relevant installment. Each sheet was folded down the center to provide for two columns of entries; since two pages (the left-hand pages for N° I and N° VIII) are blank, the *Mems.* for our novel consist of thirty-six pages.

In general, Dickens seems to have used the left-hand side of each sheet for one kind of note and the right-hand side for another kind. On the left-hand side are lists of incidents, key phrases, and queries (not always chronologically arranged) that look like the raw material of the "number" in the making. On the right-hand side this material is more methodically divided into chapters, and it may be inferred that the right-hand side therefore represents in great part a later stage of Dickens' planning. Some points, however, are by no means clear, and one among the many questions raised by the *Mems.* is whether their function was purely prospective. Was it not, also, and at the same time, retrospective?

It is, in fact, not unlikely that Dickens sometimes added to both sides of his sheet while already at work on the current number, for two kinds of ink, or two different pens, have occasionally been used on the same page, thus pointing to the composition of the *Mems.* in at least two stages. The answers given by Dickens to his own queries often, and not surprisingly, seem to be of later date than the questions themselves. The chapter headings, likewise, must have been introduced later than the chapter numbers. It would seem that the first stage, on the right-hand side, was the division of the number and of the *Mems.* page into chapters (normally three; occasionally four, or more); in the first and ninth installments the allocation of space is seen to have been revised; and an occasional overcrowding of the space reserved in the *Mems.* for one chapter occurs when the chapter turns out to require an unusual amount of preliminary-jotting down.

Since it was out of the question to print complete facsimiles of the *Mems.*—they would be too difficult to read—we are unable to reproduce all their peculiarities, such as the size and thickness of each letter or line, but we carefully show the location of each entry on the page, and we preserve Dickens' cancellations. There remains a slight uncertainty in a few cases about capital initials, which are not always distinguishable from lowercase letters on the MS.

[Nº I—*right-hand side*]

(Bleak House ~~and the East Wind~~ Nº I)

Chapter I.

In Chancery

The great cause of Jarndyce and Jarndyce

Chapter II.

In ~~the fashionable world~~ fashion

Lady Dedlock. Open country house picture

Law writer.

Chapter III Sir Leicester Dedlock

Mr. Tulkinghorn

moment

work up from this

A Progress.

Esther Summerson.

Lady Dedlock's child.

Chapter ~~III~~. IV.

Telescopic Philanthropy

The two wards, the subjects of the unhappy story of

Jarndyce and Jarndyce

Richard Carstone

Ada

Mrs. Jellyby. Her daughter Caddy Jellyby. The children & household

[Nº II——*left-hand side*]

Introduce the old Marine store Dealer who has the papers

2
Bleak House and John Jarndyce.

Leonard Skimpole

3
Foreshadowing Legend of the country house

Mrs. Rouncewell—two sons

Grandson Watt

Rosa

[Nº II——*right-hand side*]

(Bleak House and The East Wind————Nº II.)

Chapter V.

A Morning Adventure.

Chapter VI.

Quite at home.

Chapter VII.

The Ghost's Walk.

[Nº III——*left-hand side*]

mems.

Richard and Ada—love. Yes. Slightly
Miss Jellyby? No
Nemo? Yes
New people—Mrs. Pardiggle—New traits in Richard
yes Yes—slightly
Coavinses? No.

[Nº III——*right-hand side*]

(Bleak House————Nº III.)

Chapter VIII.

Covering a Multitude of Sins.

Chapter IX.

Signs and Tokens.

Chapter X.

The Law-Writer

[Nº IV——*left-hand side*]

Coroner's Inquest. Harmonic Meeting-room
Little Cheeks } the comic
Swills } vocalist

Beadle — Boy. Jo.

Coroner

~~Picture~~ churchyard & broom

Chesney Wold

Rosa & Watt? Yes. Slightly. ~~Carry on~~ Carry on

Esther.

Miss Jellyby? No.

[Nº IV—*right-hand side*]

Bleak House——Nº IV.)

Chapter XI.

Our dear brother.

Chapter XII.

On the Watch

country house—clear, cold day

riding from Paris home

Brilliant and distinguished circle

Boodle

French Lady's maid. and

Buffy

Mr. Tulkinghorn and Lady Dedlock. Each watching the other.

Open that interest and

leave them so.

Chapter III.

Esther's Narrative.

[Nº V—*left-hand side*]

Richard. No.

Miss Jellyby? Yes. Dancing Master's son.

~~Joe~~ Jo? Yes

Snagsby? No

The Brickmaker's Family? No
Allan Woodcourt.
John
Coavinses? Yes. George
Miles
Edmund
Leonard

Skimpole and Boythorn brought together? Next time

Miss Flite's friends?—Her birds? Yes slightly. The birds. Not the friends.

Old Turveydrop—Pathetic too—blesses people—My son! &c

"I have forgotten to mention again—at least, I have not mentioned—"

[N° V——*right-hand side*]

(Bleak House————N° V.)

Chapter XIV.

Deportment.

Mr. Turveydrop. Prince Turveydrop
George the Fourth, Old Turveydrop's model of
Deportment

Chapter XV.

Bell Yard

Skimpole – Coavinses –
Charley, working for the rest
"only a follerer"

Gridley, the man from Shropshire
Skimpole delighted. Employed Coavinses.

Chapter XVI

Tom-All-Alone's

Tom-All-Alone's the ruined property in Jarndyce & Jarndyce. already described by Mr. Jarndyce.

The Dedlock gout—family gout

Jo. Shadowing forth of Lady Dedlock at the churchyard.

Pointing hand of Allegory—consecrated ground
"Is it Blessed?"

[Nº VI——*left-hand side*]

Bayham Badgers? Yes. To introduce Richard's unreliability

Richard? Yes. Carry through, his character—developing itself.

Boythorn and Skimpole. Yes. Not much

Rosa ~~& Ir~~ and Watt? Slightly

Mrs. Rouncewell? No

My lady's maid? Slightly

Mr. Guppy? Yes.

Snagsby? Yes. Carry through.

[Nº VI——*right-hand side*]

(Bleak House————Nº VI.)

Chapter XVII.

Esther's Narrative.

Captain Swosser of the Royal Navy, & Professor Dingo
Geological hammer

Richard "O! It's all right enough. Let us talk about something else"

Allan Woodcourt

Esther

The flowers. Does it look like that sort of thing?"

Chapter XVIII "Why, rather like" my dear

Lady Dedlock

Down at Boythorn's in the high summertime

old garden wall

The little church in the Park—Lady Dedlock & Esther

storm. Esther supposed to speak—but Lady Dedlock
Hortense. walking barefoot home

Chapter XIX

Moving on

The great remedy for Jo, and all such as he. Move on!
Mr. and Mrs. Chadband (Mistress Rachael). Can we fly my friends? We cannot. And why can we not fly my friends?" &c &c
—a man with a good deal of train oil in his composition
—Closing picture on the bridge
Golden Cross of St Pauls
—so high up—so far off—

[N° VII——*left-hand side*]

Mems.

Mr. Guppy—His mother? Not yet
Mr. Krook Yes

The Turveydrops. No. Next time
Tom-All-Alone's. D°. Yes.

Miss Flite—Her friend? Not yet
The Brickmaker's family? Slightly
Gridley? Very slightly
Mr. Tulkinghorn? Carry on

mems: for future

Mr. Tulkinghorn finds Joe—hearing from Mr. Snagsby what he said there—and gets him to identify Lady Dedlock
Tony Jobling in his lodging, mistaken for the dead lodger
Has Lady Dedlock's picture among the Galaxy Gallery

[N° VII——*right-hand side*]

(Bleak House——————N° VII.)

Chapter XX.

A New Lodger

Mr. Guppy's friend who went over Chesney Wold with him, gets established at Krook's.

Tony Jobling.—Assumed name Owen. Weevle.

Mr. Smallweed (Ancient Office-lad)

Slap-Bang Dinner

"There are chords-" Thank you Guppy, I dont know but what I will take a—" &c —

Krook getting on

Chapter XXI

The Smallweed Family

No childhood—no amusements.

old man—old-woman—old grandchildren

Cushion. You're a brimstone chatterer.

Trooper. Shooting Gallery

Phil Squod.

Chapter XXII

Mr. Bucket

Mr. Snagsby—Detective officer

Frenchwoman / Jo.

"That there's the wale, the bonnet, and the gownd."

[Nº VIII——*right-hand side*]

(Bleak House————Nº VIII.)

Chapter XXIII.

Esther's Narrative

French Maid— ~~co~~

Richard. Downward Progress. Jarndyce & Jarndyce
The Army

Caddy Jellyby's engagement—Mr. Turveydrop—"My children you will always live with me"—meaning, I shall always live with you Mrs. Jellyby.

Charley—Esther's maid

Chapter XXIV.

An Appeal Case.

Richard. Engagement off.

Gridley taken refuge with the trooper.

Gridley's death Bucket.

The shadow of Miss Flite on Richard

Chapter XXV.

Mrs. Snagsby sees it all.

Mrs. Snagsby becomes jealous—Mr. Snagsby must be that boy's father.

Sets herself to watch him at all times

Let all concerned in any secresy, Beware!

(Guster pities Jo—so like him in the first part of her fortunes)

[Nº IX—*left-hand side*]

Mems.

Boythorn?
Skimpole?
Hortense?
Sir Leicester?
Lady Dedlock?
Mr. Guppy?
Mr. Weevle?
The Smallweeds
Mrs. Rouncewell's other son, or Watt, or Rosa?—Yes.

[Nº IX——*right-hand side*]

(Bleak House————Nº IX.)

Chapter XXVI.

Sharpshooters

Shooting Gallery. George washing—and Phil

Visitors—Mr. Smallweed and Judy

Your Brimstone Grandmother

For any writing of Captain Hawdon's

So to Mr. Tulkinghorn's

Chapter XXVII.

More old Soldiers than one.

Mr. Tulkinghorn's room

George and the boxes. Strong box.

Matthew Bagnet. Mrs. Bagnet. Quebec and Malta, and Young Woolwich

Discipline must be maintained—Tell him my opinion, old girl a threatening, murderous, dangerous fellow.

Chapter XXVIII.

The Ironmaster

Chesney Wold and the cousins

Mrs. Rouncewell's other son. Watt and Rosa.

Chapter XXIX.

The Young Man.

Mr. Guppy waits on Lady Dedlock. She finds that Esther is her child.

Guppy to bring ~~Kro~~ Krook's papers from the old portmanteau

[Nº X——*left-hand side*]

Richard?—No

Caddy Jellyby's marriage? Yes.

Brickmaker's family?

Charley's illness Yes.

Dawn of Esther's

Krook's death? Yes

Miss Flite? Yes. Carry Allan Woodcourt through, by her

Connect Esther & Jo? Yes.

——— ——— Mrs. Snagsby?

Esther's love must be kept in view, to make the coming trial the greater ~~as~~ and the victory the more meritorious.

[Nº X——right-hand side]

(Bleak House————Nº X.)

Chapter XXX.

Esther's Narrative.

Mrs. Woodcourt.

Caddy Jellyby's marriage.

No East Wind with the little Woman

Chapter XXXI.

Nurse and Patient.

JO begin the illnesses from him. His disappearance

Then, Charley ill

Then, Esther

Ada

~~Kee~~ "She will try to make her way into the room. Keep her out!"

"For I cannot see you Charley—I am blind"

Chapter XXXII.

The appointed time.

Weevle uneasiness

Snagsby

Guppy and Weevle—soot—oil from the window

all Injustice, and wrong—"Spontaneous Combustion and no other death."

[Nº XI——*left-hand side*]

Richard—No.

Mrs. Bucket No.

Smallweed progress—Tulkinghorn—George & Bagnet.

Yes

Hortense and Tulkinghorn? No

[Nº *XI——right-hand side*]

(Bleak House————Nº XI.)

Chapter XXXIII.

Interlopers.

The Court, under the excitement

Krook Mrs. Smallweed's brother. Smallweeds take possession

Lady Dedlock—the young man—and the old man.

Chapter XXXIV.

A turn of the Screw

By old Smallweed & Mr. Tulkinghorn

The Bagnets

Mr. George sees his mother.

Young Woolwich

Chapter XXXV.

Esther's Narrative.

Her illness and gradual recovery

Necklace and the beads ——————

Looking glass taken away.

Chapter XXXVI.

Work in Richard and the love

"And now I must tell the little secret."

[Nº *XII—left-hand side*]

Bring out Skimpole? Yes

Lady Dedlock. To begin with?—Yes.

[*Nº XII—right-hand side*]

(Bleak House——Nº XII.)

Chapter XXXVI.

Chesney Wold.

Esther & Charley at Mr. Boythorn's.

Interview with her mother

The Ghost's Walk

Meeting with Ada.

Chapter XXXVII.

Jarndyce and Jarndyce.

Richard's progress — distrust of Mr. Jarndyce naturally engendered by the suit.

Mr. Vholes—~~supp~~ Emma, Jane, and Caroline Vholes—Supports aged father in the Vale of Taunton

Driving away to Jarndyce & Jarndyce

Chapter XXXVIII. Close with that

A Struggle

Dancing apprentices. — remind Caddy of "the Sweeps"

— Mr. Guppy's mother's

"You wouldn't object to admit that, Miss, perhaps?"

Mr. Guppy's contention with his legal and illegal angels

[*Nº XIII—left-hand side*]

Krook's cat. Yes.

The Smallweeds, in connexion with the house in the Court. Yes

Sir Leicester Dedlock?—And the cousins? Yes

Lady Dedlock? Yes

Finds that Mr. Tulkinghorn has discovered her secret? Yes.

Their interview at night, at Chesney Wold? Yes

Wind up with Esther's Narrative?

No. French woman. Lay that ground.

[*Nº XIII——right-hand side*]

(Bleak House——————Nº XIII.)

Chapter XXXIX.

Attorney and client.

Vholes—Symond's Inn

The respectability of the Vholes legion. Make man-eating unlawful, and you starve the Vholeses.

Richard's decline—Carry on.

Guppy and Tony—Court—Smallweeds in possession.

Carry on to next.

Chapter XL.

National and Domestic.

Coodle and Doodle. No Gov^{t} without Coodle or Doodle only two men in the country.

Volumnia. Debilitated cousin. Country house

—Electioneering. Sir Leicester—658 gentlemen in a bad way.

Carry through Rouncewell and Rosa, to Tulkinghorn's story. So to next.

Chapter XLI.

In Mr. Tulkinghorn's Room.

~~Tul~~ Tulkinghorn's room at night. Lady Dedlock comes to him there.

Begin grim shadow on him

Chapter XLII.

In Mr. Tulkinghorn's chambers.

Lincoln's Inn Fields—Tulkinghorn coming back at night—London bird.

Begin with Snagsby, and

work up to

Frenchwoman.

[N° XIV——*left-hand side*]

Mr. and Mrs. Chadband? No

Allan Woodcourt? Yes. Return

Skimpole—family? Yes.

Boythorn.—about him, but not himself

Mr. Jarndyce. Yes—And his love for Esther to be now brought out

George—and Bagnets? No. Next N°

[N° XIV——*right-hand side*]

(Bleak House.————N° XIV.)

Chapter XLIII.

Esther's Narrative.

Skimpole family at home—borders of Somers Town Polygon

Beauty Daughter, Sentiment Daughter, Comedy Daughter

Angry baker—such an absurd figure.

Sir Leicester calls ~~at~~ on Mr. Jarndyce.

~~Esther takes~~ "Guardian, Lady Dedlock is my mother.

(through Skimpole Boythorn and Miss Barbary)

Chapter XLIV.

The Letter and the Answer.

Send Charley "for the letter."

I have brought the answer Guardian."

Chapter XLV.

In trust

Esther to—Plymouth—no—Deal. Ada's letter.

Allan Woodcourt comes back

Glad to be thought of like the dead

Chapter XLVI.

Stop him!

Tom-All-Alone's. Night and morning.

Allan—Jenny—Jo—

Jo tells that he was taken away by Mr. Bucket —Allan takes him

[Nº XV——*left-hand side*]

Mr. Tulkinghorn to be shot. Pointing Roman

George to be taken by Bucket. Yes.

Jo? Yes. Kill him.

Allan?—and Richard? Not Richard

Mr. Guppy? No.

Smallweeds? No.

Lead up to murder through Chesney Wold? No. Through house in town.

Mrs. Bucket? No

Snagbys? Mr. Slightly

Chadbands? Not yet.

[Nº XV——*right-hand side*]

(Bleak House.————Nº XV.)

Chapter XLVII

Jo's Will

Esther.

"If it could be written wery large as I didn't go to do it—"

Our father

Dead my Lords and gentlemen

Chapter XLVIII

Closing in

Gather up Ironmaster and Rosa

Lady Dedlock and Mr. Tulkinghorn

If it said now, Don't go home! High and mighty street.

Shot.

Pointing Roman

Chapter XLIX

Dutiful Friendship

The old girl's birthday.

George

Mr. Bucket

Making things pleasant

Hundred Pound reward—Sir Leicester—

George taken

Handcuffs—and hat over his eyes

[Nº XVI——*left-hand side*]

Ada and Richard? Yes married

Esther and Allan? Yes. Carry on gently

Lady Dedlock? dº

Mr. George. Yes.

Sir Leicester? Very little. reserve for next time. Hold him in.

Boythorn? In connexion with Lady Dedlock?

No.

[Nº XVI——*right-hand side*]

(Bleak House.————Nº XVI.)

Chapter L.

Esther's Narrative.

Caddy Jellyby—Ill

and a poor little child

Esther there constantly—Work in Woodcourt

observes Ada changing

"Still the same shadow on my darling"

Chapter LI.

Enlightened.

Allan Woodcourt. Vholes

Richard living in—Cursitor Street? Carey Street? Dyer's Buildings? Symond's Inn

Not going home, my dear, any more. Richard is my dear husband!

Esther "Bleak House is thinning fast Little Woman!"

Chapter LII.

Obstinacy.

Mr. George in prison

object to the breed Sir

old girl and Mrs. Rouncewell

Chapter LIII.

The Track

Disconsolate coaches

Bucket & Sir Leicester—Volumnia & debilitated cousin.

Bucket & Mercury.

[Nº XVII—*left-hand side*]

Guppy? Yes.

And Weevle? No.

Smallweeds? Grandfather.

The Chadbands? Yes.

[Nº XVII——*right-hand side*]

(Bleak House————Nº XVII.)

Chapter LIV.

Springing a Mine.

Bucket & Sir Leicester.

So to the Chadbands, Smallweed, Mrs. Snagsby

Disclosure of the murder. Madlle Hortense taken.

"My Lodger." all in Bucket's hands

Sir Leicester swoons—compassionate and sorrowful. not angry.

Chapter LV.

Flight.

Mrs. Rouncewell & the old girl.

George and his mother. His brother.

Mrs. Rouncewell & Lady Dedlock. Mr. Guppy

"My enemy alive and dead"—Hunted, she flies

Chapter LVI.

Pursuit.

Sir Leicester ill. To him, Mr. Bucket. "Save her."

Hurry, in pursuit. Handkerchief. Takes Esther

with him. Hurry, hurry!

[Nº XVIII——*left-hand side*]

All Esther's Narrative? No.

Pursuit interest sustained throughout

Ending with the churchyard gate, and Lady Dedlock lying dead upon the step.

Mr. Bucket and Esther.

Snagsby's and Guster? Yes.

Mr. Boythorn? No.

Allan Woodcourt? Yes.

Explain the change of clothes or leave it? Explain it at the last.

[Nº XVIII——*right-hand side*]

(Bleak House.————Nº XVIII.)

Chapter LVII.

Esther's Narrative.

Journey through the snow. Beginning with the water-side.

Thaw coming on.

Mr. Bucket got Jo away, by bribing Mr. Skimpole. "No idea of money. But he Takes it though."

Brickmakers

Inn picture.

Lady Dedlock has changed clothes with Jenny—to avoid being traced—has got her to go on, certain miles—has herself returned to London.

Mr. Bucket~~'s excitement~~ "I have got it by the Lord!"

Chapter LVIII.

A Wintry day and night.

Carry on suspense

Impassive House in Town.

Bring Sir Leicester and George together. old youthful feeling of Chesney Wold. "Who will tell him"

Night picture—Volumnia and maid—Volumnia's room. George. solitary house

Chapter LIX.

Esther's Narrative.

Mr. Bucket
and Mrs. Snagsby

Take up from first chapter

Allan Woodcourt.

Guster causes delay "Bring her round somehow in the Lord's name!"

"And it was my mother cold and dead."

[Nos *XIX and XX—left-hand side*]

Richard's death.

Vholes and Conversation Kenge at the end of the suit.

Grandfather Smallweed and the will?

George and his brother. Betrothal day

Esther and Allan Woodcourt

Her father. The letter of instructions George gave Mr. Tulkinghorn

Sir Leicester, in connexion with
Boythorn
Mrs. Rouncewell
Volumnia

The old girl and
the Bagnet family

Debilitated Cousin

Mr. Snagsby. No George

Mr. Guppy's handsome proposal—His mother. Tony Jobling

Jellybys and Turveydrops—Deportment

Chesney Wold picture. Sir Leicester and George. Boythorn obliged to pretend to be still in opposition—Lady Dedlock

Charley ✓ in the Mausoleum—without being found very much to disturb the deceased Dedlocks.

Miss Flite and her birds—Mr. Skimpole ✓

[*Nos XIX and XX——right-hand side*]

(Bleak House.——Nos XIX and XX.)

Chapter LX.

Perspective.

Mrs. Woodcourt and Allan. Prepare the way.

Ada and Richard—Prepare the way. Vholes, the evil genius

Ada's secret—"~~The~~ And something else upholds me Esther."

—"That he may not live to see the child who is to do so much

Chapter LXI.

A discovery

Mr. Skimpole. Life afterwards written. "Jarndyce Incarnation of selfishness."

Allan Woodcourt's declaration

Chapter LXII.

Another Discovery

Mr. Bucket and the will

Smallweed

Esther and Mr. Jarndyce

Chapter LXIII.

Steel and Iron.

George and his brother's family

His letter to Esther about the paper

Chapter LXIV

Esther's Narrative

Mistress of Bleak House

Mr. Guppy's magnanimity

Chapter LXV.

Beginning the world.

Richard's death.

Chapter LXVI.

Down in Lincolnshire

Mr. Boythorn—

~~Chesney Wold~~ Mausoleum

Peace.

Chapter LXVII.

The Close of Esther's Narrative.

Wind up. End [?]

The Running Headlines

The early editions of *Bleak House* carried no running headlines; these appeared for the first time in the Charles Dickens Edition. Since it was our privilege to have access to the copy of the Cheap Edition (1866) in which Dickens inserted most of them in his own hand, we can assert that the running headlines were a deliberate addition on his part. Unsensational they are, but not uninteresting to us, and certainly not uninteresting to Dickens, who appears to have taken pains over them. The Library Edition ran to 516 pages, and thus provided opportunity for 257 running headlines (one to each right-hand page except the first). Dickens in fact forgot, or omitted, to supply a running headline for page 507, and inserted only 256. But the Charles Dickens Edition for which they were intended ran to 540 pages, thus carrying 269 running headlines; 2 of the original ones had been cancelled, 51 altered wholly or in part, and 15 entirely new ones introduced. As they stand, the running headlines are a combination of straightforward summary, ironical commentary, and moral judgment.

What follows is a list of the running headlines as they appear in the Charles Dickens Edition, chapter by chapter (chapter numbers being given in parentheses *before* the relevant entries). It will be seen that, because of the new distribution of the chapters over the pages, a running headline referring to the end of one chapter has occasionally been replaced by one concerning the beginning of the next, and vice versa. All the headlines identical with the MS insertions in Dickens' copy of the Library Edition are here printed in ordinary type. Headlines in italics are those altered from MS version (this being added between brackets). Headlines in small capitals are those that did not appear at all in MS. The two headlines printed between brackets are the two that were cancelled.

(I) Jarndyce and Jarndyce. (II) My Lady Dedlock down at "her Place"; Mr. Tulkinghorn; Lady Dedlock bored to death. (III) Esther's childhood; Mr. Kenge, of Kenge and Carboy; Greenleaf; *A Farewell to Old Friends* [Kenge and Carboy's young gentleman]; The Wards in Chancery. (IV) Mrs. Jellyby; Borrioboola-Gha; For the benefit of the Natives; *Cousin Jarndyce* [Caddy Jellyby]. (V) A WALK BEFORE BREAKFAST; Mr. Krook; "A little—M—you know"; Superior to Chancery. (VI) Welcome to Bleak House; An old-fashioned House; Esther appointed Housekeeper; Mr. Skimpole; Coavinses; The east wind rises. (VII) Chesney Wold; Company to see the House; The Legend of the Ghost's Walk. (VIII) More at home in Bleak House; A Will—and no way; *Wiglomeration* [The genteel side of begging letter-writing]; *A Visitor's Lady and Family* [A visiting lady and family]; Mrs. Pardiggle's patronage; True womanly sympathy. (IX) Dame Durden; Mr. Boythorn; The Boythorn and Dedlock wars; *Mr. Guppy* [Mr. Guppy "without prejudice"]; MR. GUPPY DECLARES HIMSELF. (X) Mr. Snagsby, Law-Stationer; [Mr. Snagsby's Romance]; A Visitor to Mr. Snagsby; A *Copying-clerk's Lodgings* [Nemo at home]. (XI) Too much opium; *About Nemo or Nimrod* [The Court Circular]; The Coroner's Inquest; A *depraved Witness* [Little Swills's friends rally round him]; A GRAVE-YARD AND ITS VISITOR. (XII) Sir Leicester and Lady Dedlock; Rosa; Boodle and Buffy; Diamond cut Diamond. (XIII) What is Richard to be?; Under the eye of Guppy; Mrs. Bayham Badger's three; A pair of lovers; Some one else. (XIV) A Woman and a sister; Young Mr. Turveydrop and old Mr. Ditto; Deportment; Mr. Turveydrop Senior blesses his son; Miss Flite and her Doctor; Mr. Krook's Noble and Learned Brother. (XV) *Quale-worship* [No idea of money]; *As to Boythorn and the Coavinses* [Neckett's children]; Little Charley; Gridley's case; *The Man from Shropshire* [Great Family Inheritances]. (XVI) Jo; Jo and the jolly servant; GRAVEYARD VISITORS. (XVII) Experiences of Mrs. Bayham Badger; An Anchor wanted; The Virtues of the Mothers; Mr. Woodcourt, and the Mewlinnwillinwodd. (XVIII) Richard's way of making money; Concerning Sir Arrogant Numskull; Mr. Boythorn's Earnestness; As the Poles asunder; Esther's pictures of herself. (XIX) The Long Vacation; Mr. and Mrs. Chadband; This boy; Mrs. Chadband cross-examined. (XX) Mr. Guppy's Rival; A Slap-bang Dinner; A chance for Jobling; An application to the Lord Chancellor; Mr. Krook's lodger takes possession.

(XXI) Ill weeds don't always grow apace; Grandfather Smallweed; Mr. George; About Captain Hawdon; *The Captain's Friends and Enemies* [George's Shooting-Gallery]; *Phil's Marks* [Mr. Snagsby "runs over" a little evidence]. (XXII) *Only Mr. Bucket* [On the way to Tom-All-Alone's]; Only a job for Jo; CONDUCTED TO LINCOLN'S INN FIELDS. (XXIII) Mademoiselle Hortense; Richard sinking into a Chancery Suitor; Put not your trust in Chancery; Deportment droops; The real original African Break-Down; A model Mother. (XXIV) A friendly Difference; An estrangement; No hurry whatever; Gridley in hiding; Gridley's Retreat; Gridley's last Refuge. (XXV) Mr. Chadband discourses on a Gentile; Mr. Chadband inquires concerning Terewth; MRS. SNAGSBY WATCHFUL. (XXVI) Mr. George and his man Phil; Phil at the Commander's disposal; Now for a pipe!; The Papers pocketed. (XXVII) The Trooper not responsive; Washing Greens; The old girl; The Trooper in the same mind. (XXVIII) Company at Chesney Wold; The right Ironmaster in the wrong place; *Sir Leicester Dedlock astonished* [Lady Dedlock softened]. (XXIX) The Young Man of the name of Guppy; The Young Man on dangerous ground; A *little Girl's real name* [The young man may bring the papers]. (XXX) Mrs. Woodcourt's wheedling; FORTUNE-TELLING; Preparations for Caddy Jellyby's Marriage; Preparations continued; Caddy Jellyby married. (XXXI) Charley's Education; Two of them?; Or three of them?; The Patient gone; Charley and Charley's Nurse. (XXXII) Another member of the Court Circular; All in the Downs; The soot is falling, surely; A Horrible House. (XXXIII) The Court excited; A difference between friends; *The Patriarch appears* [Mrs. Smallweed as a Pig-headed Jackdaw]; *The Court upon its mettle* [Sensational memory of the late Mr. Krook]; *Mr. Guppy is shown the door* [A letter for Mr. George]. (XXXIV) *Phil offers several remarks* [Mrs. Bagnet mistrusts Mr. George]; *A Bit of Mrs. Bagnet's Mind* [Discipline must be maintained]; *The Unfortunate George* [Referred to Mr. Smallweed's Lawyer]; *Taken in hand by Tulkinghorn* [A dry subject]; THE TROOPER'S COUNSEL. (XXV) *The Old Face gone* [Esther's illness]; *Poor Rick* [Warped by Chancery]; A Visit from Miss Flite; A baleful attraction. (XXXVI) Esther in the country; Not a pretty lady now; Esther's Mother; Her letter to her daughter; Ada coming. (XXXVII) An interview with Richard; Jarndyce and Jarndyce a blight; Richard justifies himself; Ada's letter to Richard; Mr. Vholes; *Did she keep her Word?* [At Caddy Turveydrop's]. (XXXVIII) Apprentices to the Dancing Business; Nobility of Mr. Guppy's nature; *Mr. Guppy again and again* [Mr. Vholes's office]. (XXXIX) *Questions and Answers* [What is doing?]; *Mr. Vholes never gives Hopes* [Mr. Vholes's hands are clean]; [About those letters?]; *A New Entry for the Recording Angel* [Mr. Tulkinghorn congratulates Mr. Guppy. (XL) THE BACK-SHOP; Coodle and Doodle; *Shadows* [The Party]; *Volumnia is too innocent* [The Party beaten by a Faction]; *The Pride of the Lower Classes* [Bed-Time]. (XLI) THE ICE BREAKS; Lady Dedlock and Mr. Tulkinghorn; Tied to the stake. (XLII) Relating to the Foreign Female; Defiance on the part of the Foreign Female. (XLIII) *Rick is mistaken* [The Lawyer not a man of gallantry]; Mr. Skimpole at Home; Mr. Skimpole's Family; Sir Leicester Dedlock has been pained; Lady Dedlock's Sister. (XLIV) Esther's Guardian speaks to her; Esther happy for life. (XLV) Mr. Vholes calls; Esther at Deal; Only one thing on Richard's mind; Mr. Woodcourt a friend to Richard. (XLVI) Allan Woodcourt in Tom-All-Alone's; Unfortunate Jo; *Jo's Declaration* [Jo moving on, at last]. (XLVII) GENERAL GEORGE TO THE RESCUE; An Asylum for Jo; Phil Squod takes charge of Jo; Mr. Snagsby *finds it better than he expects* [beset by Bedlam]; Jo's Death. (XLIII) Lady Dedlock and Rosa; The Iron Gentleman; A matter of business with Lady Dedlock; Don't go home!; Shot through the heart. (XLIX) The Old Girl's Birthday; Mr. Bucket joins the company; Mr. Bucket and the second-hand Violoncello; Mr. Bucket must have Mr. George. (L) Caddy and Caddy's child; Caddy cured. (LI) Mr. Vholes's professional Duty; Richard's object; Richard and Ada married; Bleak House *thinning fast* [thins fast]. (LII) Mr. George in Prison; Mr. George states his case; *The Old Girl lectures on an old subject* [Mrs. Bagnet discovers a new power]. (LIII) Mr. Bucket looks out; Mr. Bucket at Sir Leicester Dedlock's; *The Debilitated Cousin on Capital Punishment* [Mr. Bucket is a perfect Blue Chamber]; *Opinions on Beauty* [Mr. Bucket's Field Day]. (LIV) Mr. Bucket does his duty; THE CRUEL FINGER; Mr. Bucket wishes to know "what's up"; Mr. Bucket and Mrs. Snagsby's "game"; Mr. Bucket presents his Lodger; Mr. Bucket *presents his evidence* [offers his arm to a lady]; Mr. Bucket appropriates the Foreign Female. (LV) The Old Girl and the Old Housekeeper; The Prodigal Son; An Old Servant's Appeal; Mr. Guppy puts my Lady on her guard. (LVI) Sir Leicester Dedlock falls; Mr. Bucket pursues his investigations; Time is everything to Mr. Bucket. (LVII) Esther starts with Mr. Bucket; Mr. Bucket retrospective; Mr. Bucket quotes one Michael Jackson; Mr. Bucket follows the one; *The end of the Stage* [Mr. Bucket follows the other]. (LVIII) A Topic for Society; *Hollow State* [The Lost found]; The Heart and Soul of a Gentleman; Mr. George keeps watch. (LIX) *Back to London* [Mr. Bucket very near his object]; *Chancery Lane* [Mr. Snagsby has no idea of anything]; *Mr. Bucket's Advice* [Mr. Bucket presses onward]; THE POOR GIRL'S STORY. (LX) *Welcome to the Growlery* [Mr. Bucket achieves his purpose]; A very good Plan indeed; Miss

Flite reverts to the baleful attraction; Mr. C's interests and affairs; Ada looks far forward. (LXI) No, really?; Mr. Woodcourt's love for Esther; Goodnight; good-bye! (LXII) Magpie Property; More Conversation Kenge than ever; "A *great country, Mr. Jarndyce*" [The Trooper's nephew]. (LXIII) The Brothers; *George's Letter* [Wedding-Purchases]. (LXIV) Another Bleak House; *The Guardian bestows a great gift* [The Wind due West]; MR. GUPPY IS MAGNANIMOUS [no MS headline ins. on p. 507]. (LXV) THE DECISION IN JARNDYCE V. JARNDYCE; Nothing left but costs; *Beginning the World* [The suit passes to the Court of Appeal]. (LXVI) The altered place in Lincolnshire. (LVII) Drawing to an end.

In the above list, the somewhat erratic policy of the Charles Dickens Edition with regard to capital initials has been adhered to. In the same edition nearly all, but not quite all, the running headlines were printed with a period at the end. We have made no attempt to record Dickens' hesitations and deletions while he was writing the headlines; his deletions are seldom decipherable. (The words "Goodnight; good-bye!" form one headline, not two, at the end of chapter LXI.)

Textual History

The complete manuscript of *Bleak House*, preserved in two bound volumes in the Forster Collection at the Victoria and Albert Museum in London, shares the usual characteristics of most of Dickens' manuscripts, though it is in some respects worse—i.e., harder to read—than many of them. Its pages are often crowded, and there are numerous deletions, corrections, and insertions almost throughout. Besides, some of the later chapters were written in unusually pale ink. Admittedly, most of our editorial work has been done on microfilm copies of both manuscript and corrected proofs, but the difficulties encountered seem to have been simply enhanced, not created, by this circumstance.

For each monthly part, the novelist aimed at providing, as exactly as possible, copy for thirty-two pages of fifty lines each, and he appears to have trained himself to make his manuscript pages contain as much matter as the printed pages. In any case, seventeen of the installments of *Bleak House* take up between twenty-nine and thirty-two pages of manuscript each. The first part, because of Dickens' usual hesitation and difficulty when beginning a new work of fiction, has many cancellations and five sheets numbered A through E have been added to its thirty-two normal pages; it thus runs to thirty-seven pages in all. As for the final issue, improperly called "double number" or "Numbers XIX & XX," it was of more flexible length than the others, for Dickens always allowed himself some elbowroom to wind up a complex story without leaving any loose ends. However, it was never twice the size of the other numbers, but only about one third longer; the final installment of *Bleak House* takes up forty-three manuscript and forty-eight printed pages.

Dickens himself carefully numbered his MS pages in clear numerals writ-

A page from the original manuscript of *Bleak House* (Chapter XXX, page 7) (COURTESY OF THE VICTORIA AND ALBERT MUSEUM)

ten at the top center of the page. He began every monthly installment with a fresh page 1. The MS pages have however been renumbered—possibly not by Dickens—consecutively throughout each of the two bound volumes (in the top right-hand corner) and again throughout the whole MS (at the back of the pages).

The difficulty of reading Dickens' handwriting will be sufficiently apparent from our textual notes. His compositors were often baffled. It is not our purpose here to invite compassion for our editorial labors, which were fully as fascinating as they were sometimes excruciating. But a few particulars must be mentioned, as accounting for the few remaining uncertainties. Dickens did not always clearly distinguish between a capital initial and the corresponding lowercase letter; his version of *my* consists of a thin horizontal line followed by a thinner vertical one; the adverbial ending *-ly* he reduced to a vertical bar, sometimes so very thin as to be almost—or quite—imperceptible; his possessive cases are often difficult to identify because the apostrophe is missing or placed above the final *s;* his punctuation was very incompletely shown on his MS, and he strove hard to establish it—according to his own idiosyncratic system—at the proof stage.

There are some inconsistencies—and a few downright errors—in Dickens' MS spelling as well as in others of his procedures. His chapter headings, for instance, are usually written on the MS, but sometimes only inserted in proof, and in a few baffling cases they have been inserted in proof although they also legibly appear on the MS.

Each of the compositors employed by Dickens' printers and publishers—Bradbury and Evans in 1852–53—wrote his name on the manuscript at the beginning of the portion he had been assigned to set up. This practice, however, seems to have been discontinued or the names rubbed out, halfway through the novel. Few significant inferences can be drawn from the lists thus collated. The only interesting facts that can be pointed out are that as there are over forty different names for the first thirty-two chapters of *Bleak House,* it would appear that Bradbury and Evans gave permanent or part-time employment to a considerable staff. The normal stint for one man was about one page of MS, and rarely, if ever, exceeded two pages. The best hands, trained presumably in deciphering Dickens' handwriting, like Brown, Lachore (or Lochore), Morris, Roger (or Rogers), Samwell, Snowsill, and Trenor (or Trevor) did between ten and eighteen portions of those chapters, and often took two separate sections of the same chapter; Snowsill even did three stints of chapter XX. Other names occur but once or twice; one Jackson, for instance, tried his hand, with disastrous results, on chapter XXV only. In a few cases, at the end of a monthly number, there seems to have been unusual hurry, and the MS has been cut up into smaller fragments of a few lines each. The fragments appear to have been quite literally cut up, and pasted together again later.

As will appear from the textual notes, the corrected proofs of *Bleak House* preserved at the Victoria and Albert Museum are of considerable textual interest, though the collection is obviously far from complete. There is at least one set for each chapter or monthly part, sometimes two, and occasionally a fragment of a third set. Where a single set has been preserved, there usually is evidence of earlier and/or later revision done by

Dickens on another set, or other sets, unfortunately missing. The end of the novel seems to have been more perfunctorily attended to than the rest, both by author and printer: the compositional errors grow more numerous and escape correction more frequently, as if Dickens had failed to check the proofs against his own MS.

The first edition appeared in two forms, whose texts are identical: the nineteen monthly installments and the one-volume edition of 1853, which was made up of parts bound together without their green covers (see illustration showing the cover of the monthly number for April, 1852), but with all the illustrations (by "Phiz," i.e., Hablôt K. Browne). The novelties of the one-volume edition were a dedication,[1] a preface, a Table of Contents, a List of Plates, and a brief but interesting list of Errata.

The following chart sums up the characteristics of *Bleak House* in MS, monthly parts, and first edition.

Date	Number of Part	Chapters	Number of MS pages	Pages in 1st edition
March, 1852	I	I–IV	37	1–32
April, 1852	II	V–VII	32	33–64
May, 1852	III	VIII–X	29½	65–96
June, 1852	IV	XI–XIII	30	97–118
July, 1852	V	XIV–XVI	29	119–160
August, 1852	VI	XVII–XIX	31	161–192
Sept. 1852	VII	XX–XXII	31	193–224
Oct., 1852	VIII	XXIII–XXV	30	225–256
Nov., 1852	IX	XXVI–XXIX	29	257–288
Dec., 1852	X	XXX–XXXII	31	289–320
Jan., 1853	XI	XXXIII–XXXV	29½	321–352
Feb., 1853	XII	XXXVI–XXXVIII	31	353–384
March, 1853	XIII	XXXIX–XLII	29½	385–416
April, 1853	XIV	XLIII–XLVI	29	417–448
May, 1853	XV	XLVII–XLIX	31	449–480
June, 1853	XVI	L–LIII	30	481–512
July, 1853	XVII	LIV–LVI	30	513–544
August, 1853	XVIII	LVII–LIX	29	545–576
Sept., 1853	XIX–XX	LX–LXVII	43	577–624

The three other editions of *Bleak House* published in Dickens' lifetime appeared as parts of as many collected editions of his works.

The Cheap Edition (C) of 1858 was issued by Bradbury and Evans. Its one-volume, double-column *Bleak House*—advertised as "uniform with the Cheap Edition of former works published by Chapman and Hall"—sold for five shillings. The main innovation was a slightly revised or updated preface; this and its other textual characteristics are discussed below and illustrated in the textual notes.

The Library Edition (L) of 1859, now published jointly by Messrs.

1. DEDICATED/ AS A REMEMBRANCE OF OUR FRIENDLY UNION/ TO MY COMPANIONS/ IN THE/ GUILD OF LITERATURE AND ART This dedication was preserved in C, but omitted in L and CD. We have not restored it because of its purely topical interest.

Chapman and Hall and Bradbury and Evans, was issued at the rate of one six-shilling volume per month; *Bleak House* filled two volumes—single column—which came out in June and July of 1859. The Library Edition is an almost servile reproduction of the Cheap Edition. It contains no significant innovations. Like the Cheap Edition, it is discussed below and taken into account in the textual notes.

It should be noted that neither Dickens himself nor anyone else, outside of the publisher's advertisements, ever seems to have claimed that the text of these editions had been revised by the author.

Not so the one-volume Charles Dickens Edition (CD) of 1868 (Chapman and Hall), which is currently regarded as providing an authoritative text because it is said to embody the author's final revisions (see *New Cambridge Bibliography of English Literature*, vol. III, 1969, p. 783). No such claim is made within the *Bleak House* volume itself, though the Charles Dickens Edition of another novel—*Great Expectations*— advertises itself as "printed from the edition that was carefully revised by the author in 1867 and 1868." We cannot pronounce on the truth of this assertion in the case of *Great Expectations*, but in those of *Hard Times* (see our Norton Critical Edition, 1966) and *Bleak House* (see below) there is no definitive evidence of authorial revision—let alone *careful* revision—beyond the insertion of the running headlines and one fresh footnote in the preface.

Of course, no edition of *Bleak House* later than the Charles Dickens was controlled by the author; none, therefore, has the slightest textual relevance.

Our Text

Our choice of the first (1853) edition as our copy-text is in accordance with the principles set forth by the best authorities in the valuable MLA pamphlet *Statement of Editorial Principles. A Working Manual for Editing Nineteenth Century American Texts* (1967). This 1853 text we have slightly amended. For instance, we do not print it "warts and all," since it has not seemed to us sensible to preserve its dozen or so misprints, but we believe it to be demonstrably superior to any other form *Bleak House* has ever appeared in. The original manuscript is too uncertain, inconsistent, unfinished, to serve as a copy-text. That is self-evident. But the unsuitability of the Cheap, Library, and Charles Dickens Editions for the purposes of a copy-text still needs to be vigorously—and, we hope, finally—exposed. Our demonstration rests on the following steps: we made a word-by-word comparison between 1853 and CD. This resulted in a list of 462 passages showing differences between the two (most of them are individual substantive differences, but others constitute a fair sampling of accidentals); the 462 relevant passages were then checked in C and L. The textual notes embody our findings for all substantive variations. There may have been other temporary deviations from 1853 in C and L, unspotted by us because they have not survived in CD. We do not claim to have examined them; we have, in fact, quite deliberately treated them as textually irrelevant.

We are left, then, with 462 differences between 1853 and CD; 451 of them have, on their first appearance, come to stay, and thus present a clear view of the evolution of the text; of these 451, C is responsible for 160, L for 26, and CD for 265. If we now break up our figures differently, again into three categories, i.e., acceptable changes (mostly of accidentals), indifferent changes (that are neither improvements nor deteriorations), and deplorable changes, we find that the 160 innovations in C comprise 74 acceptable, 15 indifferent, and 70 deplorable changes (plus one doubtful case); for the 26 L novelties, the corresponding figures are 24, one, and one; and for the 265 CD changes 72, 42, and 148 (plus three doubtful cases).

Thus, we have very little evidence that Dickens revised the text of *Bleak House* for the Charles Dickens Edition. The external evidence, in fact, is of a negative kind: the copy of C used for the insertion of running headlines bears not a single other correction.[2] It is improbable, and certainly not proved, that he used another copy of the same or another early edition for another type of revision. And if he did, the least one can say is that he made very poor use of it. What seems most likely is that, if Dickens really did revise the text of *Bleak House* for CD, he must have done so very perfunctorily in proof. This conjecture cannot be entirely ruled out, for there are a few clusters of two or three changes in one page (usually of the "indifferent" kind) that *may* not be due to compositors' oversights. In any case, CD sanctions 70 errors introduced into C and one created by L, and adds 148 fresh ones. Our final impression, then, is that CD is the worst, not the best, edition of *Bleak House* published during the author's life.

Bad as it is, the CD edition is however responsible for some of the emendations introduced into our text. The nine mistakes listed in Dickens' errata (he had written *Gusher* for *Quale* four times, *Leonard* for *Harold*—Skimpole—four times also, and *swollen* for *swelled* once) were all corrected in C and the corrected forms preserved in L and CD. The twelve major misprints of 1853—a remarkably and enviably small number for a book of that length—were similarly eliminated (ten in C, one in L, and the last in CD).[3] Eleven other changes seem to be for the better, because they improve the sense or the style (seven), increase the consistency of Jo's speech (two), or restore manuscript spellings (two); of these eleven improvements, three occur for the first time in C, one in L, and seven in CD. The four doubtful cases (one from C and three from CD) are of words or phrases that seem unlikely to have been altered through mere compositional negligence. All the other "acceptable" changes are of accidentals: punctuation, hyphenation and word division, capitalization, and mostly spelling. In addition to the variations studied in separate sections below (*shew/show*, *-or/-our*, etc.), they concern such things as the substitution of *-able* for *-eable* (in words like *immovable*), of *-eys* for *-ies* (in *chimneys*, *attorneys*, etc.), of *recall* for *recal*, of *secrecy* for *secresy*, of *steadfast* for *stedfast*, of *wagon* for *waggon*, and the normalization of some possessive cases, such as the replacement of *your's* by *yours* and the like. Most of these changes were gradual. Many of them had in fact begun within the 1853 edition, and all of them were pursued, unsystematically enough, in C,

2. Dr. Michael Slater kindly examined *every* page of that copy for us.

3. It is astonishing that *tremulouslessly* for *tremulously* should have survived in C, but so it did.

L, and CD.[4] Obviously, they were not matters in which Dickens himself took strong interest or to which he devoted much attention or energy. They would perhaps come under the heading of house style and were the printer's and publisher's rather than the author's concern.

Yet we have not felt justified in rejecting the CD spellings where they appear to represent a tendency towards normalization or modernization; in other words, we could not aim at making the spelling of our text either more modern or more obsolete than Dickens and his printers thought fit in 1868. To be precise, where the 1853 and CD texts agree, we adhere to their common version and do not further modernize (e.g., in the case of *up-stairs*). Where they disagree, we make individual decisions on the clear principle that the later (i.e., CD) spellings, when consistent, are to be preferred.

With regard to the CD variants of the "indifferent" kind, we have not accepted them as emendations even though they had no damaging effects on the text. They consist mainly—in forty-one cases—of the omission, addition, or substitution of one or two tool-words; or again of an altered word order (seven cases). Our principle has been, in such cases, that the evidence of Dickens having had anything to do with them is too slight to give us the assurance that he would have preferred the later version to what he had written in his manuscript and sanctioned in one or more sets of proofs. For instance, several paragraphs are broken up in CD alone without any apparent reason or advantage, and all too probably for practical or technical, not literary, purposes. And of course we reject any C or CD change that runs counter to the author's explicit directions on the 1853 proofs.

Besides, the bulk of the C and CD innovations are by no means harmless, or helpful, or creditable. They consist of many different categories (after each of which the number of relevant cases is given in parentheses: minor alterations like de-italicization of one word or shifting of the italics to the wrong word (four); cancellation or addition of a capital initial (seven);[5] substitutions of singular for plural (two) or plural for singular (six); slight changes affecting one word (nine); and significant changes in punctuation (seven).[6] The more serious kinds are ordinary misprints (only two of them: *Chanceller*, and *sandled* for *sandalled*); the introduction of new contracted forms, whereas Dickens for some reason had sedulously eliminated them from the speech of most of his characters in the proofs in 1853 (five); the weakening of picturesque speech, mostly in the case of Jo (twenty-eight, of which fifteen occur in C, one in L, and six in CD; Jo's *Sangsby* becomes *Snagsby* four times in C and twice more in CD); the omission of one or more significant words (twenty-three, of which twenty-one are in CD alone); the change of verbal tense (thirty; thirteen of these—

4. In one case 53 *gypsey* becomes *gypsy* in C, and *gipsy* in L and CD. And one *wagons* of 1853 becomes *waggons* in C, reverts to *wagons* in L, but is *waggons* once more in CD.

5. The alternation between *will* and *Will* in chapters LXII and LXV, over which Dickens took great but baffling pains in proof, remains bewildering. As for the alternation between *guardian* in narrative and *Guardian* in Esther's speech as a mode of address to Mr. Jarndyce, it was only gradually introduced into the first edition, and became more systematic later.

6. One 1853 comma becomes a question mark in C, but is again a comma in L, and finally—and erroneously—a question mark in CD.

six from C and seven from CD—are preterites for presents, due to the impersonal narrator's constant resort to the latter); and finally eighty-eight downright errors, of which it may be useful to present a brief selection here: C changes *confusedly* to *confessedly*, *oddest* to *oldest*, and *grave kind voice* to *grave kind of voice*; CD changes *dragoon* to *dragon*, *state* to *taste*, *apartment* to *department*, *generic* to *general*, *merged* to *emerged*, *steeps* to *steps* (up which a cart is said to be laboring), *I was for going to* to *I was going for*, *fell* to *full*, *fact* to *act*, *pretend* to *intend*, and *surprising* to *surpassing*.

We hope it will henceforth be clear that by taking CD as their copy-text for *Bleak House*, editors would needlessly increase their labors and/or jeopardize the accuracy of their results.

Our treatment of the original manuscript and adoption of eighty-three emendations from its pages are again based on the above-quoted MLA *Editorial Principles*, and mainly on the admirable rule that "The editor's intent is to achieve the text which the author would approve" (op. cit., p. 8). Yet the way in which this general rule can be applied is by no means always clear. We have often been held back by the feeling that it would be arrogant on our part to decide that Dickens "would approve" a better text than the one he seemed to approve to the extent of having it printed and extensively circulated. On the other hand, nobody, to the best of our knowledge, had as yet undertaken a minute, word-by-word comparison of the original manuscript and all the later relevant forms of the text of *Bleak House*; and when we say that nobody had done that, we *do* mean not even Dickens himself. We have therefore had to decide, in a number of cases—not without striving hard, through mature deliberation, to achieve firm conviction—that it was both our right and our duty to be kinder to Dickens than he seemed to demand, or perhaps deserve, from his editors. To be precise once more, we must explain what we have done in that respect, and why. Our eighty-three retrievals of hitherto ignored manuscript readings result from the elimination of a slightly larger number of similar possibilities, i.e., of other cases where the manuscript had also been misread by the compositor and where Dickens had also failed to restore his original version in proof. Our rule was to retrieve only such forms as we feel certain Dickens would have preferred if he had had time to give his whole mind to the choice, because they make the text better, sometimes slightly, but always unquestionably. When a compositor went wrong, one of three things happened: either (1) Dickens set things right (such incidents are not normally recorded in our textual notes—there are over 650 of them, and as many as 41 in a single chapter—besides the few that we *have* recorded in order to give some idea of the problems involved in Dickens' collaboration with his printers and of the pitfalls that threatened both); or (2) Dickens altered his original version (sometimes because he did not check proof against manuscript, sometimes because he availed himself of the opportunity to reduce ambiguity or obscurity—he seems to have been sensitive to compositors' misreadings when he spotted them); or (3) Dickens left the misreading untouched. In cases (1) and (2), in spite of great temptation, and with one or two exceptions only, we have accepted the 1853 readings. But in case (3), where there is strong reason to believe that the misreading was not deliberately preferred and sanctioned (i.e., when the sense is ruined, the expression impoverished, or the consistency reduced), we have felt justified in retrieving the manuscript version. In many cases, our conviction was strengthened by seeing the state of the manuscript, by realizing how sorely tried the compositors must have been, how natural their mistakes were (like most of us, they would tend to read, even in legible passages, what they expected to find, while Dickens tended to write in the most unexpected manner), and by the occurrence of several unspotted misreadings in chapters where Dickens had spotted and eliminated scores of others.

Textual Notes

The textual notes of this edition record every kind of variant for one specimen chapter; Chapter V was found particularly suitable for that purpose, because the history of its text is fully documented. The reader will thus be able to observe, for instance, the kind of work that Dickens did on his punctuation, and the evolution of his spelling. But for the other sixty-six chapters, some variants have had to be omitted in order to save space, and also because certain types of accidental changes are of little intrinsic interest and make for tediousness by their recurrence; the exhaustive recording of accidentals did not seem justified by the kind of edition we were aiming at. We have therefore left out most changes in punctuation and spelling, the elimination of contracted forms (*it is* for *it's*, *I will* for *I'll*, *ain't* for *an't*), the late italicization or romanization of pronouns (in which respect no edition is consistent), paragraphing, word division, capitalization, and also, more arbitrarily no doubt, the insertion and cancellations of *and* and *that*. Besides, as explained above, we have had to decide that compositors' mistakes, when duly corrected by the author in proof, were only incidentally part of the textual history and could thus be economically discarded. Yet a separate section at the end of the present note is meant to give some idea of the kind of results to be achieved by examining certain categories of minor variants unrecorded in the textual notes (mostly in the matter of spelling).

With all these deliberate and, we hope, reasonable omissions, we are left with nearly four thousand textual notes, including all the substantive CD variants (the date of whose first appearance is indicated, for many of them originated in C, and a few in L); all manuscript peculiarities and errors; all corrections in proof, either established or inferable; all the passages cancelled in proof, and a few significant ones at manuscript stage.

The textual notes are identified by chapter-, page-, and line-numbers. Before the notes concerning each chapter, a brief headnote lists the material available for that chapter and its specific characteristics, if any. Textual notes not signposted by asterisks in the text itself tend to be longer, because they need more words to make identification of passage and variant easier; but the text is thus made cleaner and the notes more interesting, even for consecutive independent reading by the student.

A NOTE ON SOME PECULIARITIES OF SPELLING

This section is intended to save space by giving here a summary description of some of the material that has been omitted from the textual notes. As explained above, there are a number of words (*secrecy*, *recall*, and the like) whose spelling was more or less systematically modernized in 1868, or even earlier; the full textual notes given for Chapter V provide a sampling of the changes made in that respect as in every other. But two or three categories deserve separate treatment here, as showing—or shewing—how uncertain and arbitrary Dickens and his printers—like many of their contemporaries, of course—were in matters of spelling.

SHEW/SHOW. Dickens consistently used the *e* spelling for *shew, shews, shewed, shewing,* with the single exception of the word *Show-House* (in Chapter LXVI). The Cheap, Library, and Charles Dickens editions consistently used the *o* spelling. But in between the two extremes there was considerable hesitation. In twenty chapters manuscript *shew* is set up in proof as *show,* and left uncorrected. In ten chapters manuscript *shew* is set us as *shew* in proof and printed as *shew* in the first edition. In seven chapters manuscript *shew* is alternately preserved and changed to *show* in the first edition.

-OR/-OUR. Dickens' preference for the *-or* over the *-our* ending is well known, and he justified it as late as 1856 in a letter to Miss Burdett-Coutts;[7] the reasons he gave were interesting, but he was wrong in assuming that *-or* was the "modern" spelling and that it was then gaining ground in Britain. As a rule, then, one expects to find *-or* in manuscript and early editions, replaced by *-our* in the Charles Dickens Edition only. And that is more or less what happens, but only more or less. Of the twenty-three relevant words used in *Bleak House* Dickens normally spelled sixteen with *-or* and seven with *-our*; for thirteen words—seven of the *-or*, six of the *-our* variety—he achieved consistency of a kind, but these are mostly words employed only between one and four times (*clangor, rigor, vigor,* but *armour, behaviour, demeanour*). For the other ten words, and especially for the most common ones (*favor, honor,* and *labor*; and *humour* and *neighbour*), the variations are astonishing; the *u* in them is seen to appear for the first time at every possible stage from manuscript to Charles Dickens Edition; spellings used in proof were altered in first edition without having been corrected by Dickens; and in at least twenty chapters the same word or words are printed with the two spellings in the 1853 text, or in proof, or in both.

AN'T/AIN'T. Dickens used both these forms, not without discrimination, in his manuscript. He seems to have believed that at a certain, fairly low, social level, people would say *an't* as the contracted negative of *am, is, are,* and *ain't* as the contracted negative of *have* or *has.* This idiosyncratic distinction understandably disconcerted his compositors; nor did Dickens insist on preserving it, so that the *an't* used mostly by Bucket and Jo, though occasionally also by Guppy, Jobling, the Smallweeds, and the Bagnets, was set up as *ain't* in some twelve chapters; it was set up as *an't* in proof, but printed as *ain't* in the 1853 text in six other chapters; the remaining *ants*', with very few exceptions (there are some in Chapters XXI–XXII of the Charles Dickens Edition) went by the board in the Cheap Edition.

The other peculiarities and the evolution of Dickens' spelling will be sufficiently apparent from the textual notes and from our comments on the

7. See *The Heart of Charles Dickens*, ed. Edgar Johnson (New York: Duell, Sloan & Pearce; Boston: Little, Brown & Co., 1952), p. 322.

Cheap, Library, and Charles Dickens editions above and need not be examined in detail here. The only useful remarks that suggest themselves at this point are (a) that Dickens fancied some already old-fashioned spellings (like *mattrass* for *mattress*); (b) that there must have been a separate set of proofs for each monthly part, not seen by Dickens, reserved for technical and "house style" corrections.

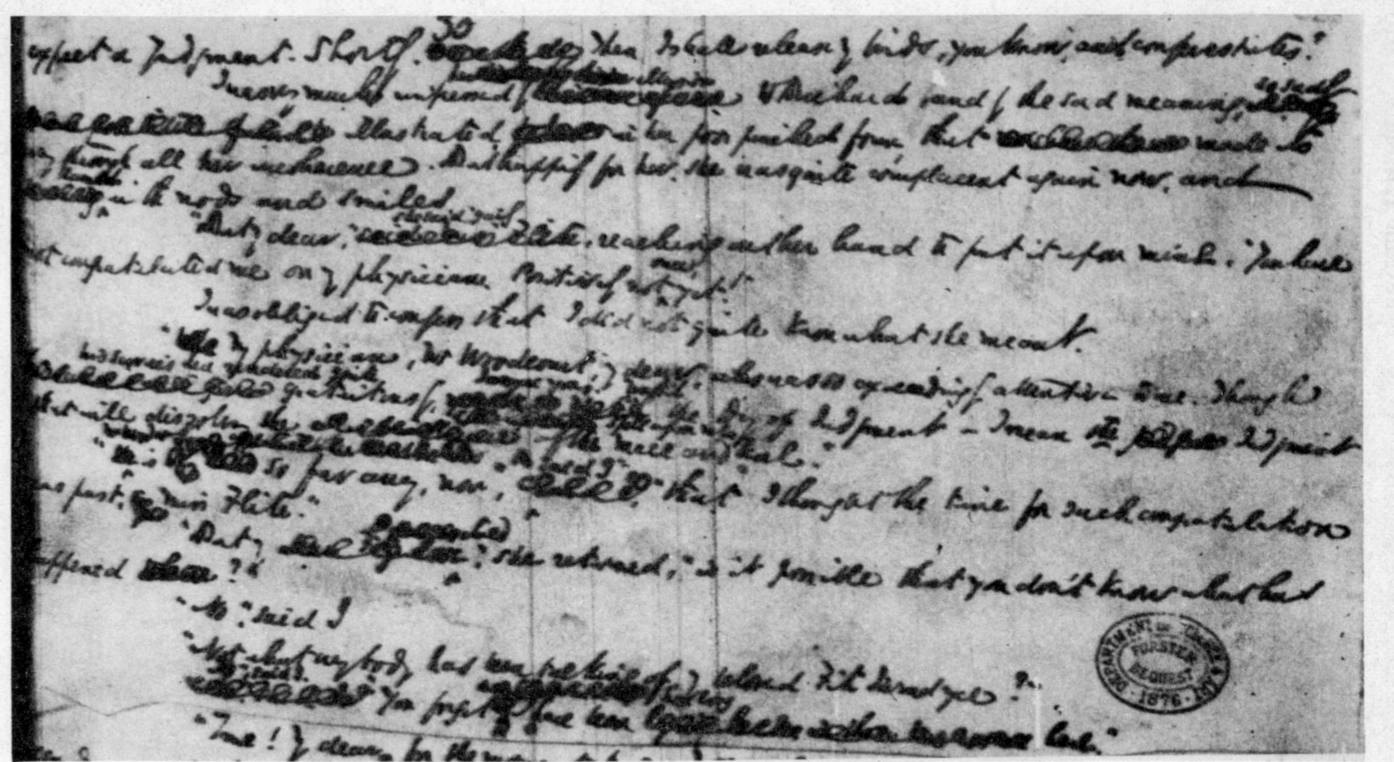

A passage from the original manuscript which was misread by the compositor and hitherto uncorrected (Chapter XXXV, page 20). (COURTESY OF THE VICTORIA AND ALBERT MUSEUM)

Textual Notes

Abbreviations Used

MS = original manuscript
CP = corrected proofs (CP1, CP2, CP3, when there are more than one set)
53 = first edition in volume form (1853)
C = Cheap Edition (1858)
L = Library Edition (1859)
CD = Charles Dickens Edition (1868)
p.t. = present text
(?) = doubtful word
punct. = punctuation
corr. = corrected
n.c. = not corrected
canc. = canceled
ins. = inserted
em. ad = emendation adopted
D = Charles Dickens

When a note begins with a fragment of text followed by "corr. on CP to" this implies that CP adequately reproduced MS (and that D was thus correcting himself), whereas notes beginning with "CP:" imply that CP text was different from MS (and that D was correcting compositor). Notes beginning with "MS:" usually draw attention to some peculiarity to be found in MS alone. Our other procedures we hope will be understood without difficulty.

Preface MS of Preface placed at end of MS volumes; two sets of CP, presumably CPI and CP3—latter identical with 53 text—CP2 apparently missing

3.1 MS–53: *A few months ago, on a public occasion, a Chancery Judge* C–CD: *A Chancery Judge once* [em. ad.—like other changes in this Preface—as corresponding to D's wishes for later editions]

3.4 *subject of a rather general popular prejudice* corr. on CP1 to *subject of much popular prejudice*

3.21 CP1: *Dip me* corr. to *Pity me* [as in MS]

3.24 *in no essential whatever altered* corr. on CP1 to *in no essential altered*

3.28 MS–53: *present moment there is*; asterisk, not figure in C–L C–CD: *present moment[1] there is* [footnote in C–CD]

4.2 MS: *and my friend* n.c. on CP1 CP3–CD: *and my good friend*

4.4 MS: *by all good authorities)* n.c. on CP1 CP3–CD: *by all authorities)*

4.19–20 MS: *higher court, his sentence was revised, and he was acquitted, expressly because* n.c. on CP1 CP3–CD: *higher court, he was acquitted, because*

4.24–25 MS–53: *at page 329,* [no footnote in 53] C: *at page 275* [no footnote] L: *at page 27, vol. II* [no footnote] CD: *at page 27, vol. II;* [but CD is in one vol., and the reference should be to page 288; footnote in CD only]

4.31 MS: *of familiar things. I believe I have never had so many readers as in this book. May we meet again! My labor of love is, so far, ended. LONDON August, 1853. My labor . . . ended.* canc. on CP1 Thus in CP3–53. C–CD: *of familiar things.*

Chapter I MS, one set of CP, obviously CP2; CP1 missing

5.6 MS: *lizzard* (?) CP–CD: *lizard*
5.6 MS: *chimney-tops,* CP–CD: *chimney-pots,*
5.8 MS: *one might suppose,* CP–CD: *one might imagine,*
5.14 MS–53: *(if the day* C–CD: *(if this day)*
5.15 MS: *at those points to* CP–CD: *at those points tenaciously to*
5.15–16 MS: *to the pavement, as layers upon layers of barnacles stick to the keel of a ship, and accumulating* CP–CD: p.t.
5.18 MS: *meadows—full sponges at present from which the hop of a sparrow would squeeze out superabundant moisture; fog down* CP–CD: *meadows; fog down*
5.21 MS: *into the coppers of the cabooses* CP–CD: *into the cabooses*
5.28 MS: *over the clammy parapets* CP–CD: *over the parapets*
5.30 MS: *hanging in misty space.* CP–CD: *hanging in the misty clouds.*
5.32 MS: *as the bleared and blurred sun may,* CP–CD: *as the sun may,*
5.32 MS: *from the marshy fields,* CP–CD: *from the spongey fields,*
5.34 MS: *and unwilling look. Nothing has any defined outline. Passengers, vehicles, horses, and houses, all ghosts together.* CP–CD: *and unwilling look.*
6.26–27 *mountains of nonsense,* corr. on CP to *mountains of costly nonsense,*
7.7 MS: *give—the admonition.* CP–CD: *give—the warning.*
7.25–26 MS: *carries something in a reticule* CP–CD: *carries some small litter in her reticule*
7.26–27 MS: *her documents, but they are principally paper* CP–CD: *her documents, principally consisting of paper*
7.30–31 MS: *accounts of which he never had any* CP–CD: *accounts of which it is not pretended that he had ever any*
7.42 MS: *scarecrow of a cause* CP–CD: *scarecrow of a suit*
8.11 MS: *and ridden away into* CP–CD: *and trotted away into*
8.23 MS: *Very good things* CP–CD: *Good things*
8.24 MS: *by certain bulbous-shoed old* CP–CD: *by blue-nosed, bulbous-shoed old*
8.31 MS: *maces, petty bags, and privy purses.* CP–CD: *maces, bags, and purses.*
8.33 MS: *its withered hand* CP–CD: *its unwholesome hand*
8.39 MS–53: *has been made the better* C–CD: *has been made better*
8.41 *influences that never come* corr. on CP to *influences that can never come*
8.42 MS: *the weary suitors* CP–CD: *the wretched suitors*
9.8 MS: *in all their infinite varieties,* CP–CD: *in all their many varieties,*
10.8 MS: *with a bass voice,* CP–CD: *with a terrific bass voice,*

Chapter II MS, one set of CP, presumably CP1; CP2 apparently missing; D wrote at top of first page of CP *Inserted in proof*; corresponding MS pages numbered A through E instead of in ordinary numerals; see Number Plan I

10.35 *Rip Van Winkle, who had* corr. on CP to *Rip Van Winkles, who have*
11.5 *come to the void* corr. on CP to *come to the brink of the void*
11.11 *the growth thereof sometimes* corr. on CP to *its growth sometimes* 53–CD: *its growth is sometimes*
11.27–30 *The shot . . . falling rain.* [whole sentence added on back of MS page]
11.28 *loses its sharp ring* corr. on CP to *loses its sharpness*
11.34 MS–CP: *time out of mind,* 53–CD: *from old time,*
11.39 MS–CP: *the light of the fire* 53–CD: *the light of a fire*
11.40 MS–CP: *and the smoke* 53–CD: *and smoke*
12.4 *seemed to turn pale and vanish* corr. on CP to *seemed to vanish*
12.7–8 *like the fiend, omniscient* corr. on CP to *like the fiend, is omniscient*
12.25 *with his white hair* corr. on CP to *with his light grey hair*
13.1 *mentioned. Lady Dedlock,* corr. on CP to *mentioned. My Lady Dedlock,*
13.2–3 *but rather the freezing* corr. on CP to *but rather into the freezing*
14.4 *Talkinghorn* corr. on CP to *Tulkinghorn* here and through this chapter [MS spelling not always clear, but seems to be *Tulkinghorn*]
14.11–12 MS: *sometimes at home, at corners* CP: *sometimes quite at home, at corners* corr. to *sometimes speechless but quite at home, at corners*
14.16 *gravity* ins. on CP in blank left by compositor [*gravity* not in MS (?)]
14.19 MS: *Tulkinghorn* [quite legible here]
14.32 *knows her class weaknesses,* corr. on CP to *knows her weaknesses,*
15.1 MS: *Lulliput.*
15.4 *with the various public;* corr. on CP to *with the general public;*
15.10, 12, 13, 15 *of my connexion,* corr. on CP to *of my high connexion,*
15.29 MS–CP [n.c.]: *says Mr. Tulkinghorn.* 53–CD: *replies Mr. Tulkinghorn.*
15.36–37 *is a ridiculous accident.* corr. on CP to *is a most ridiculous accident.*
16.22 *and prolixity,* corr. on CP to *and prolixities,*
16.30 *and unusual tone.* corr. on CP to *and her unusual tone.*
16.32 MS–CP (?): *playing with her screen.* 53–CD: *toying with her screen.*
16.34 MS–L: *legal character it has,* CD: *legal character which it has.*
16.40 MS–L: *who has risen* CD: *who had risen*
16.42–43 MS–CP [n.c.]: *only that; but like* 53–CD: *only that; but it is like*
16.43 *Ring for Marie, and take* corr. on CP to *Ring, and take*

17.5 *read to him.* corr. on CP to *read to him alone.*

Chapter III MS and one set of CP—presumably CP2; CP1 and CP3 missing

7.13–14 MS: *not clever, you know, and you* CP–CD: *not clever, you know very well, and you*
17.14 MS: *must be very patient* CP–CD: *must be patient*
17.32 MS: *O, she was a good* CP [n.c.]: *Oh, she was a good* 53–CD: *She was a good*
18.22–23 MS: *Summersun* (?)
19.11 MS–53: *I had caught hold* C–CD: *I caught hold*
19.23 *no one but a woman* corr. on CP to *no one save a woman*
20.4–5 MS–53: *confusedly* C–CD: *confessedly*
20.24 *and was gliding* corr. on CP to *and I was gliding*
20.27–28 *a white cravat, his hair brushed off his forehead, large gold* corr. on CP to *a white cravat, large gold*
20.24–29 *Sitting with her . . . his little finger.* [whole passage ins. on separate slip pasted on to back of MS page]
20.31 MS: *in her natural stern way* CP–CD: *in her naturally stern way*
20.36 MS: *"I see"* CP–CD: *"Ah!"*
20.42 MS–CP [n.c.]: *my aunt and I* 53–CD: *my godmother and I*
21.25 *Kinge,* (?) corr. on CP to *Kenge,*
21.33 MS–L: *"It really is* CD: *"It is really*
23.4–5 MS: *first-class establishment;* CP–CD: *first-rate establishment;*
23.19 *the—a—"* corr. on CP to *the—a—so forth."*
23.25 *worth telling.* corr. on CP to *worth the telling.*
24.12 MS: *skaiters*
24.19 MS: *when a very gruff and boisterous voice* CP–CD: *when a voice*
24.34 MS: *"Why are you crying?"* CP–CD: *"And what are you crying for?"*
24.42–43 MS: *at the sides of his head,* CP–CD: *at the side of his head,*
25.1 MS–CP [n.c.]: *"D——n Mrs. Rachael!"* CP–CD: *"Con-found Mrs. Rachael!"*
26.6–7 MS–L: *the uncertain and unreal air* CD: *the uncertain and the unreal air*
26.11 MS–L: *rather than to have really* CD: *rather than really*
26.41 MS–CP [n.c.]: *happy and most grateful;* 53–CD: *happy and grateful;*
27.1–2 MS–L: *how regularly my accounts* CD: *how regular my accounts*
27.9 MS–CP [n.c.]: *will very soon fall* 53–CD: *will soon fall*
27.18 MS: *client* CP–CD: *clt*
27.18 MS: *about* CP–CD: *abt*
27.19 MS: *in this case,* CP–CD: *in this cause,*
27.20 MS: *eligible* CP–CD: *elgble*
28.20–21 *in that country),* corr. on CP to *in all that country),*
28.23–24 *"Thank God! thank God!"* corr. on CP to *"O, I am so thankful, I am so thankful!"*
29.32 MS–L: *the stranger for its being* CD: *the stranger from its being*
29.32–33 MS–L: *the day-time, and the candles* CD: *the day-time, the candles*
27.37 MS: *to see that it was* CP–CD: *to see if it was*
30.40 *seventeen* corr. on CP to *eighteen* then *eighteen* canc. and corr. to *nineteen*
31.7 MS: *in ten minutes;* CP–CD: *in five minutes;*
31.24–27 *It touched me . . . pride of parents.* [whole passage ins. on separate slip pasted on to back of MS page]
31.31–32 *"A dreary name," said the Lord Chancellor. "But* [n.c.] *far from being a dreary place, my lord," said Mr. Kenge.* ins. on CP 53: p.t.
32.4–5 MS: *and with a slight smile.* CP–CD: *and with a smile.*
32.11 *"No, my lord."* ins. on CP.
32.32 MS: *we all went out together,* CP–CD: *we all went out,*
33.32–33 MS: *she was still curtseying and smiling there and saying,* CP–CD: *she was still there, saying, still with a curtsey and a smile between every little sentence,*
33.34–35 MS: *Kenge! Pray accept* CP–CD: *Kenge! Ha! Pray accept*

Chapter IV MS and one set of CP—presumably CP2; CP1 and CP3 missing

35.8 MS–CP [n.c.]: *devotes herself to a variety* 53–CD: *devotes herself to an extensive variety*
35.9 MS–CP [n.c.]: *at present devoted* 53–CD: *at present (until something else attracts her) devoted*
35.9–10 MS: *who has devoted herself to the colonnization* [sic] *of Africa; with a view* CP–CD: *who devotes herself entirely . . . the subject of Africa; with a view* [p.t.]
35.18 MS: *said Mr. Kenge, feeling his chin, "is* CP–CD: *said Mr. Kenge, "is*
35.21 MS: *"A nonentity, perhaps, sir?"* CP–CD: *"A nonentity, sir?"*
35.35–36 MS: *yes, they had been, and that a coach* CP–CD: *yes, they had been sent round and a coach*
36.5 MS: *"We shall just twist up* CP–CD: *"We just twist up*
36.10 MS: *very thick,* CP–CD: *very dense,*
36.11 MS: *though, miss, I'm sure,"* CP–CD: *though, I'm sure,"*
36.12–13 MS: *do you good, judging* CP–CD: *do you good, miss, judging*
36.13 *from appearances."* corr. on CP to *from your appearance."*
37.11–12 MS: *whom it is difficult* CP–CD: *whom it was difficult*
37.17 MS: *recorded its progress* CP–CD: *recorded its passage*
37.19–20 MS–CP [n.c.]: *a pretty, diminutive,* 53–CD: *a pretty, very diminutive,*
37.20 MS–CP [n.c.]: *with black handsome* 53–CD: *with handsome*

37.36 MS: *and was nearly filled* CP–CD: *and nearly filled*
38.5–6 MS: *or in its right place.* CP–CD: *or its right place.*
38.11–12 MS: *My African project* CP–CD: *The African project*
38.12 *employs* corr. on CP to *at present employs*
38.13 MS–CP [n.c.]: *and private individuals* 53–CD: *and with private individuals*
38.14 *anxious for the welfare of their species* not in MS–CP
38.15 MS: *I hope by this time* CP–CD: *We hope by this time*
38.16 MS–CP [n.c.]: *two hundred manufacturing families* 53–CD: *two hundred healthy families*
38.17 MS: *natives at Borrioboola-Gha,* CP–CD: *natives of Borrioboola-Gha,*
38.32 MS: *into Holborn,* CP: *into Holborn, you know,* corr. to *into Holborn,*
38.37 MS: *look over my remarks* CP–CD: *look over some remarks*
39.13–14 MS: *and I interrupted* CP–CD: *and as I interrupted*
39.26 MS: *I know, I am so much* CP–CD: *I know, being so much*
39.37–38 MS: *"if there* is *any."* CP–CD: *"the question is, if there* is *any."*
40.19 MS: *choking* CP–CD: *choaking*
40.24 MS: *washed in a dish-pie,* CP–CD: *washed his hands in a dish-pie,*
40.30 *a beautiful piece of beef,* corr. on CP to *a piece of roast beef,*
41.2–3 MS–CP [n.c.]: *proceedings of committees, or resolutions of meetings,* 53–CD: *proceedings of ladies' committees, or resolutions of ladies' meetings,*
41.4 MS–CP [n.c.]: *people who were anxious to cultivate* 53–CD: *people excited in various ways about the cultivation of*
41.4–5 MS: *of coffee, others* CP–CD: *of coffee, and natives, others*
41.9–10 MS: *a mild gentleman in spectacles, of a large heavy figure, was* CP–CD: *a mild bald gentleman in spectacles was*
41.11–12 MS: *seemed placidly to submit* CP–CD: *seemed passively to submit*
41.28 MS–CP [n.c.]: *letters in a single day,* 53–CD: *letters respecting Africa in a single day,*
41.34 MS: *subject to low spirits and never spoke.* CP–CD: *subject to low spirits.*
42.5 MS–L: *like a dragoon,* CD: *like a dragon,*
42.11–12 MS: *I knew perfectly well that I had* CP–CD: *I knew that I had*
42.22 MS–CP [n.c.]: *the benefit of others —* 53–CD: *the benefit of Natives—*
42.37 MS–L: *Shaking back her* CD: *Shaking her*
42.38–39 *partly at her laugh,* corr. on CP to *partly at her beauty,*
43.29 MS: *middle figure* CP–CD: *middle finger*
43.29–30 MS: *smearing it all over her face;* CP–CD: *smearing it over the ink stains on her face;*
43.36 MS: *and I was very sorry.* CP–CD: *and I was sorry.*
43.37 MS: *and smoothed her forehead,* CP–CD: *and touched her forehead,*
44.5 MS: *wonder you were not* CP–CD: *wonder you two were not*
44.7 MS: *you call yourselves* CP–CD: *you think yourselves*
44.40 MS: *and wept bitterly.* CP–CD: *and wept.*
44.41 MS: *but she said, No, no, no;* CP–CD: *but she cried, No, no;*
44.42 MS: *she only wanted to stay* CP–CD: *she wanted to stay*
45.5 MS: *rest upon my lap,* CP–CD: *rest on my lap,*
45.8 MS: *amidst the scenes* CP–CD: *among the scenes*
45.11–12 *so lately parted.* corr. on CP to *so recently parted.*
45.13 MS: *some one at Bleak House.* CP–CD: *some one in authority at Bleak House.*
45.14 MS: *I was no one, too.* CP–CD: *I was no one.*
45.15 MS: *The benumbed day* CP–CD: *The purblind day*
45.15 MS: *struggling with the darkness and the fog,* CP–CD: *struggling with the fog,*

Chapter V MS and two sets of CP—this chapter has been selected to provide a sample of complete record of *all* variants

45.20 *was clammy and raw,* corr. on CP1 to *was raw,*
45.20–21 *seemed very heavy—*corr. on CP1 to *seemed heavy—*
45.28 MS: *daudle* (?) CP1: *dandle* corr. to *dawdle*
45.31 *any overnight.* corr. on CP1 to *any, overnight.*
45.33 *Miss Summerson, and* corr. on CP1 to *Miss Summerson; and*
45.37 CP1: *"then I'll get* corr. to *"I'll get* [as in MS]
45.39 *Ada, looking like the sleeping beauty just awake, said* corr. on CP1 [which had *awoke* for *awake*] to *Ada said*
46.1–2 *possible, staring* corr. on CP1 to *possible; staring*
46.6 MS: *taking this liberty,* CP1: *taking the liberty,* corr. to *taking such a liberty,*
46.11 CP1: *waiting-room,* corr. to *writing-room,* [as in MS]
46.11–12 MS–L: *parlor* CD: *parlour*
46.14 MS–L: *Below stairs* CD: *Below-stairs*
46.18–19 *out of a public-house with a hackney-coachman, wiping* corr. on CP1 to *out of a public-house wiping* and on CP2 to *out of a public-house, wiping*
46.20 MS: *oflock* [this is what D's handwriting of this word always makes it look like]
46.22 *CP1: Thavie's* corr. to *Thavies* [as in MS]
46.24 CP1: *Ada and Miss Jellyby,* corr. to *Ada, and Miss Jellyby* [punct. not legible in MS]

46.29 MS&L: *my dear,"* C&D: *my dear?"*
46.31 CP1: *"Let's go* corr. to *"Let us go* [as in MS]
46.31–32 Between *at any rate," said I,* and *She then walked me* the following passage has been canc. on CP1: *"You needn't laugh, Miss Summerson; you wouldn't like it yourself; you call yourself very good-tempered—" "Really I don't, my dear," said I. "You do. You know you do, Miss Summerson. Don't say you don't; you do!—I beg your pardon, I mean you* are,*" she said with quick, and yet grudging, concession. "Don't be angry with me, dear! I am so pro-voked!"*
46.33 *"Now you are* corr. on CP1 to *"Now, you are*
46.35 MS–53: *night after night till* C–CD: *night after night, till*
46.36 MS: *Methusaleh,* (?)
46.38 *remonstrated in* corr. on CP1 to *remonstrated, in*
46.41 *"Oh!* corr. on CP1 to *"O!*
47.1 *all made over* corr. on CP1 to *All made over* [as in MS]
47.2 MS: *shew* CP–CD: *show*
47.4 *shocked too,* corr. on CP1 to *shocked too;*
47.4 *both shocked and* corr. on CP1 to *both shocked, and*
47.12–13 CP1: *Ma's management."* corr. to *Ma's management!"* [MS punct. not clear]
47.19 *at my side, while* corr. on CP1 to *at my side; while*
47.22 CP1: *windows, and* corr. to *windows and* [as in MS]
47.25–26 *Richard, behind me.* corr. on CP1 to *Richard to Ada, behind me.*
47.29–30 MS–53: *curtseying and smiling,* C–CD: *curtseying, and smiling,*
47.30 *saying with* corr. on CP1 to *saying, with*
47.32 MS: *curtsyed* (?) CP1–53: *curtsied* C–CD: *curtseyed*
47.41 MS–L: *honor* CD: *honour*
47.42 CP1: *regularly, with* corr. to *regularly. With* [as in MS]
47.44 CP1: *lady recovering* corr. to *lady, recovering* [as in MS]
48.5 CP1: *Oh dear,* corr. to *O dear,* [as in MS]
48.7 *The birds* corr. on CP1 to *Where the birds*
48.8 CP1: *here, in contemplation* corr. to *here. In contemplation* [as in MS]
48.13 *fulfilled, and* corr. on CP1 to *fulfilled; and*
48.24 *time with much* corr. on CP1 to *time, with much*
48.26 MS: *humouring* CP1–L: *humoring* CD: *humouring*
48.29 MS: *of the Inn,* CP1–L: *of the inn,* CD: *of the Inn,*
48.31–32 CP1: *—RAG AND* corr. to *RAG AND* [as in MS]
48.33 CP1: *—DEALER IN* corr. to *DEALER IN* [as in MS]
48.38 MS: *GENTLEMENS'* (?)
48.39 MS: *nothing sold there.* CP–CD: *nothing to be sold there.*
48.40 MS: *bottles—* CP1: *bottles,* corr. to *bottles:*
48.41–42 MS: *ink bottles.* CP1: *ink bottles;* (?) corr. to *ink bottles:*
49.2 *and, as it were,* corr. on CP1 to *and of being, as it were,*
49.11 *and dispatch* corr. on CP2 to *and dispatch:*
49.13 MS: *shop-door,* CP1–L: *shop door,* CD: *shop-door,*
49.13 MS: *were heaps of* CP1: *heaps of* corr. to *lay heaps of*
49.14 MS: *discolored* CP1–CP2 [n.c.]: *discoloured* 53–L: *discolored* CD: *discoloured*
49.14 MS: *dogs'-eared* CP–CD: *dog's-eared*
49.16 *thousands* corr. on CP1 to *hundreds*
49.18 *rags still tumbled* corr. on CP2 to *rags tumbled*
49.20 *gowns chopped small,* corr. on CP1 to *gowns torn up.*
49.22 MS: *yonder great heaps of bones, picked very clean* CP1: *heap* corr. to *pile* and *in a corner* ins. CP2: passage further corr. to *yonder bones in a corner, piled together and picked very clean,*
49.27 MS: *lantorn* (?)
49.31 CP1: *as if he was* corr. to *as if he were* [as in MS]
49.32 *white stubble,* corr. on CP2 to *white hairs,*
49.33 MS–53: *looked, from* C–CD: *looked from*
49.34 *upwards,* corr. on CP1 to *upward,*
49.38 MS: *house-door* CP1–L: *house door* CD: *house-door*
49.39 MS: *now said, that as* CP–CD: *now said that, as*
49.42–50.1 MS–CP1: *we would "walk up,"* corr. on CP2 to *we would walk up,*
50.1 *apartments* corr. on CP1 to *apartment*
50.1 *for an instant,* corr. on CP1 to *for an instant;*
50.2–3 CP1: *she desired, that I* corr. to *she desired; that I* [no punct. in MS]
50.4–5 MS: *curious:at any rate* (?) CP1: *curious at any rate* corr. to *curious;—at any rate*
50.7–8 CP1: *We all went* corr. to *we all went* [as in MS]
50.19 *true enough!"* corr. on CP1 to *true enough,"*
50.25 MS: *lovely hair! I buy hair.* CP1: *lovely hair! Strong hair. Strong hair.* canc.
50.26 MS: *color and* corr. on CP1 to *color, and* thus in CP2–L CD: *colour, and*
50.31 *look, that even* corr. on CP1 to *look, which even*
50.32 MS–53: *Ada, who, startled* C–CD: *Ada, who startled*
50.38 *and all as the* corr. on CP1 to *and all, as the* thus in 53 C–CD: *and all as the*
50.39 *nothing) wasting* corr. on CP1 to *nothing), wasting*

51.2 CP1: *I don't* corr. to I *don't* [as in MS]
51.3 *every day when* corr. on CP1 to *every day, when*
51.8 MS: *shew* CP–CD: *show*
51.8 CP1: *you can scratch.* corr. to *you scratch.* [as in MS]
51.13 CP1: *and this was* corr. to *and hers was* [as in MS]
51.14 *It was a very* corr. on CP1 to *It's a very*
51.28 *the old man in* corr. on CP1 to *the old man, in*
51.29 *"Think of that!"* corr. on CP1 to *"Think of it!"*
51.39 *forefinger, and* corr. on CP1 to *forefinger; and*
52.2 MS: *"Yes.* CP1: *"Yes,* corr. to *"Yes!*
52.4 CP1: *slightly to his* corr. to *slightly at his* [as in MS]
52.4 *lodger, "Tom* corr. on CP2 to *lodger; "Tom*
52.10 *it's being driven mad by inches.* corr. on CP1 to *it's going mad by grains.*
52.11 CP1: *himself just* corr. to *himself, just* [as in MS]
52.17 MS: *certainty sooner* CP1–53: *certainty, sooner* C–CD: *certainty sooner*
52.21 CP1: *judgment* corr. to *Judgment* [as in MS] C–CD: *judgment*
52.22 CP1: *alone, and* corr. to *alone; and* [MS punct. not clear]
52.24 *Chancery) and* corr. on CP1 to *Chancery-lane); and* Thus in 53–L CD: *Chancery Lane); and*
52.30–31 *The old man . . . lantern up.* [whole sentence written on separate slip pasted on to back of MS page]
52.33 CP1: *into the court* corr. to *into court* [as in MS]
52.34 *Hi! How my* corr. on CP1 to *How my*
52.36–37 *or had* corr. on CP1 to *or as if they had*
52.37 CP1: *Oh dear* corr. to *O dear* [as in MS]
52.37 *do with it if they* corr. on CP1 to *do with it, if they*
52.39 MS–L: *color* CD: *colour*
52.44 CP1: *uneasiness in the* corr. to *uneasiness, in the* [as in MS]
53.2 MS–C: *upstairs* L: *up-stairs* [end of line] CD: *up-stairs*
53.2 CP1: *again, informing* corr. to *again; informing* [no legible punct. in MS]
53.2 CP1: *us with* corr. to *us, with* [as in MS]
53.5 CP1: *the house in a* corr. to *the house, in a* [as in MS]
53.6 MS–L: *glimpse of the roof of Lincoln's* CD: *glimpse of Lincoln's*
53.8 CP1: *there, she* corr. to *there. She* [as in MS]
53.8–9 *in the night—(especially* corr. on CP1 to *in the night: especially*
53.11 CP1: *from books of* corr. to *from books, of* [as in MS]
53.13 *documents" as* corr. on CP1 to *documents," as*
53.17–18 CP1: *I thought, as I* corr. to *I thought as I* [as in MS]
53.19 MS–L: *honored,* CD: *honoured,*
53.22 *situation, in* corr. on PC1 to *situation. In*
53.27 MS: *Judgment*
53.39 CP1: *liberty, when* corr. to *liberty. When* [as in MS]
53.39 MS: *Judgment*
53.40 *in prison though.* corr. on CP1 to *in prison, though.*
53.41 CP1: *that one by one,* corr. to *that; one by one,* [as in MS]
53.45 *a question she never* corr. on CP1 to *a question, she never*
54.1 *a reply, but* corr. on CP1 to *a reply; but*
54.4 *matters being* corr. on CP1 to *while matters are*
54.5 *prevailing,* corr. on CP1 to *prevails,*
54.5 *I may* corr. on CP1 to I *may*
54.5 CP1: *found stark* corr. to *found lying stark* [as in MS]
54.13 *singing while I* corr. on CP1 to *singing, while I*
54.13 MS–L: *court.* CD: *Court.*
54.16 MS–L: *honor* CD: *honour*
54.16–17 CP1: *of "youth," a smile and curtsey; "hope," a smile and curtsey; and "beauty,"* corr. to *of youth," a smile and curtsey; "hope," a smile and curtsey; "and beauty,"* [as in MS] CP2 still has *of "youth,"* n.c. but 53 has *of youth,"*
54.18 CP1: *There!* corr. to *"There!* [as in MS]
54.20 CP1: *old lady–the* corr. to *old lady; the* [as in MS]
54.21 CP1: *for it—"because* corr. to *for it; "because* [no punct. in MS]
54.21 CP1: *thec at* corr. to *the cat* [as in MS]
54.22 MS: *downstairs—* CP1–C: *down stairs—* L–CD: *down-stairs—*
54.23 *in the parapet* corr. on CP1 to *on the parapet*
54.23 *outside for* corr. on CP1 to *outside, for* thus in 53 CD: *outside for*
54.26 CP1: *shortly being given* corr. to *being shortly given* [as in MS]
54.27 MS: *malice: I half* CP1: *malice, I half* corr. to *malice. I half*
54.28 *wolf, of the old* corr. on CP1 to *wolf of the old*
54.30 *bells reminding* corr. on CP1 to *bells, reminding*
54.34 MS–L: *court?* CD: *Court?*
54.36 MS: *downstairs.* CP1–C: *down stairs.* L–CD: *down-stairs.*
54.41 *tell us in a* corr. on CP1 to *tell us, in a*
54.41 *whisper as we* corr. on CP1 to *whisper, as we*
54.43 MS–L: *to sell—in* CD: *to sell, in*
55.3–4 MS: *explanation: "a law-writer.* CP1: *explanation, "a law-writer.* corr. to *explanation; "a law-writer.*
55.13 *waste paper in a* corr. on CP1 to *waste paper, in a*
55.17 MS: *panneling* CP1–CP2 [n.c.]: *paneling* 53–CD: *panelling*
55.18 *old lady had* corr. on CP1 to *old lady, had*
55.20 *stop me,* corr. on CP1 to *stay me,*

55.20 CP1: *the letter* J corr. to *the letter J* [as in MS]
55.28 CP1: "J." corr. to "*J.*" [as in MS]
55.30 CP1: *an* a *in its place* corr. to *an a in its place* [as in MS]
55.32 CP1: *the letter* r, corr. to *the letter r,* [as in MS]
55.33 *quickly until* corr. on CP1 to *quickly, until*
55.40 MS: *the two words* CP1–CD: *the words* [MS reading restored here, as having been inadvertently overlooked by compositor]
55.40 *This,* corr. on CP2 to *These,*
56.3 *his cat upon her shelf above him looked* corr. on CP1 to *his cat looked*
56.3 MS: *looked so wicked staring at me,* CP1: *looked so wicked,* corr. to *looked so wickedly at me,*
56.4 MS–C: *upstairs,* L–CD: *up-stairs,*
56.16 CP1: *upon one side* corr. to *up on one side* [as in MS]
56.19–20 CP1: *returned Ada,* corr. to *returned Ada.* and *run on* written twice by D in margin of following canc. passage: "*I am sure.*"/ "*To me too,*" *said Richard thoughtfully.*/ "*If the Lord Chancellor would decide against my interest as far as that is concerned, or at least would say I was only entitled to—how much could you and I live upon, Esther?*" *said Ada, blushing.*/ "*No!*" *cried Richard,* "*he had better decide against me. I can go anywhere—go for a soldier, if that's all, and never be missed. I would sell my best chance, if I could, on the shortest notice and the lowest terms.*"/ "*And go abroad?*" *said Ada.*/ "*Yes!*"/ "*India, perhaps?*" [MS had "*To India, perhaps?*"]/ "*Why yes, I think so,*" *returned Richard.* "*What do you think?*"/ "*I have not thought about it,*" *said Ada.*
56.20 *only sorry* corr. on CP1 to *grieved*
56.21 *others, and* corr. on CP1 to *others; and*
56.22 *they are—and* corr. on CP1 to *they are; and*
56.23 *another without* corr. on CP1 to *another, without*
56.27 CP1: *all this war of* corr. to *all this wasteful* [as in MS]
56.29 CP1: *serene,* corr. to *serenely,* [MS not legible]
56.31–32 CP1 *happened if men* corr. to *happened, if men* [MS punct. not legible]
56.32 CP1: *rascals, and* corr. to *rascals; and* [as in MS]
56.33–34 CP1: *call you Ada.*" corr. to *call you Ada?*" [as in MS]
56.36 MS–L: "*At all events, Ada, Chancery* CD: "*At all events, Chancery*
56.36–37 MS–L: *bad influence on* CD: *bad influences on*
56.43 *appeared, and* corr. on CP1 to *appeared; and*
57.3 *breakfast, for* corr. on CP1 to *breakfast; for*
57.7 CP1: *Billy* corr. to *Peepy* [as in MS]
57.10 *absence and* corr. on CP1 to *absence, and*
57.10 CP1: *circle surprised* corr. to *circle, surprised* [as in MS]
57.14 MS: *oflock* (?) [see note on 46.20 above]
57.18 CP1: *steps, Peepy,* corr. to *steps; Peepy,* [as in MS]
57.22 CP1: *Thavie's* corr. to *Thavies* [as in MS]

Chapter VI MS and two sets of CP; apparently no CP missing; unusually high number of alterations and cancellations in this chapter seems due: (a) to attempt to tone down resemblance to Leigh Hunt in Skimpole's portrait; (b) to need to shorten an overwritten chapter

57.26 *the great extent* corr. on CP1 to *the extent*
57.28 *the vast amount of traffic* corr. on CP1 to *the great traffic*
57.33, 36, 58.13 MS: *wagon(s)* but *waggoner* (58.7) and *waggon* (58.18)
58.13 *respectively delivered to each of us,* corr. on CP1 to p.t.
58.23–27 D wrote on CP2: *Printer. Put this letter in the type, in which Little Emily's letters are printed in Copperfieid* [CP1–CP2 have the letter in ordinary type, 53 in smaller type]
59.13–14 *we had got* corr. on CP1 to *we got*
59.27 MS: *heigtened*
59.39 *pointed gables* corr. on CP1 to *peaks in the roof*
59.39–40 MS: *a broad circular sweep* CP1–CD: *a circular sweep* [MS reading restored here, as having been inadvertently overlooked by compositor]
61.18–19 MS–CP1: *said Mr. Jarndyce.* "*But come, come! Come and see your rooms!*" corr. on CP2 to *said Mr. Jarndyce.*
62.10 *boldly saying,* corr. on CP1 to *boldly said,*
62.12 *given me,*" *kissed him.* corr. on CP1 to *given me.*"
62.22 *find older* corr. on CP1 to *find still older*
62.26 MS–53: *all round* C–CD: *all around*
62.29 *looking out* corr. on CP1 to *looking down*
62.30 *belong to Ada.* corr. on CP1 to *belong to Ada and me.*
62.41 *an unexpected and surprising manner* corr. on CP1 to *an unexpected manner*
62.43–44 MS: *a Native-Hindoo chair that turned into a sofa,* CP1: *a Native-Hindoo that turned into a chair and* corr. to *a Native-Hindoo chair that was also* CP2: *that* corr. to *which*
62.45 *a skeleton* corr. on CP1 to *a bamboo skeleton*
63.2 *came, without at all expecting it, on* corr. on CP1 to *came on*
63.6–7 *any furniture in* corr. on CP1 to *any furniture standing in*
63.10 *horses being cleaned,* corr. on CP1 to *horses being rubbed down,*
63.11 MS: *and to Get over,* CP1–CD: *and Get over,*

63.19 *chairs, that stood* corr. on CP1 to *chairs, which stood*

63.22–23 *a real trout,* corr. on CP1 to *a real trout in a case,*

63.26–27 MS: *lady's hay-making,*

63.32 MS–C: *boddice* L–CD: *bodice*

63.33 *still-room.* corr. on CP1 to *breakfast-room.*

63.34 *taking a heavy gentleman* corr. on CP1 to *taking a complacent gentleman*

64.1 *wherever* corr. on CP1 to *wheresoever*

64.13 *barely an hour* corr. on CP1 to *barely half an hour*

64.17 *said Mr. Jarndyce;* corr. on CP1 to *pursued Mr. Jarndyce;*

64.22–24 MS–CP1: *"He knows everybody in short, who is engaged in efforts for the amelioration of—anything.* corr. on CP2 to *"He is a musical man; an Amateur, but might have been a Professional. He is an artist, too; an Amateur, but might have been a Professional.*

64.38 *Leonard Skimpole's* corr. on CP1 to *Harold Skimpole's*

64.39 MS–CP1: *or other. Nobody knows how. The wind's* corr. on CP2 to *or other.—The wind's*

65.3–4 *a bunch of keys* corr. on CP1 to *two bunches of keys*

65.24–25 MS: *He had a refined delicate face, was a little bright creature, with a rather large head; but* ins. on CP1 *refined* canc. on CP2

65.29 *a fairer complexion,* corr. on CP1 to *a richer complexion,*

65.29–30 *darker hair,* corr. on CP1 to *browner hair,*

65.32 *a graceful easy negligence* corr. on CP1 to *an easy negligence*

65.33 MS–CP1: *disposed, his shirt-collar wavy, and his* corr. on CP2 to *disposed, and his*

66.4–5 MS: *in bed, reading fairy-tales,* CP1: *-tales,* corr. to *-stories,* CP2: *fairy-stories* corr. to *the newspapers* and *or making fancy sketches in pencil* ins.

66.9 MS–CP1: *and married on that income,* corr. on CP2 to *and married,*

66.13 MS–53: *two of the oddest* C–CD: *two of the oldest*

66.17 *Well! He said so* corr. on CP1 to *Well! So*

66.17–19 MS: *He was very fond of fairy-tales, very fond of poetry, very fond of nature,* CP1: *-tales,* corr. to *-stories,* and *poetry,* to *verses,* CP2: whole sentence corr. to p.t.

66.21 MS–CP1: *Give him books,* corr. on CP2 to *Give him the papers,*

66.22 *fruit in season;* corr. on CP1 to *fruit in the season;*

66.22 MS–CP1: *a few prints,* corr. on CP2 to *a few sheets of Bristol-board,*

66.27 *any object you prefer to chase;* corr. on CP1 to *any object you prefer;*

66.27 *Leonard Skimpole* corr. on CP1 to *Harold Skimpole*

66.38–39 *he was so clear* corr. on CP1 to *he was very clear*

66.42–67.1 *I can sketch it, and alter it. I can set it to music.* ins. on CP2

67.4 MS: *a bright-eyed, loveable, embraceable woman, embraceable* canc. on CP1 and *loveable* on CP2

67.12 MS–CP1: *silence, and the dense* corr. on CP2 to *silence, and sketching the dense*

67.14 MS: *do it thoroughly. There is a great breathing active principle of desire to crush what is false and wrong, and to set up what is right and tender* [CP1: *under* corr. to *tender*] *which we recognize and admire by* [*by* omitted by compositor; restored on CP1] *the name of Jarndyce! I can sympathize with that, in the same way.* Whole passage canc. on CP2.

67.15 *Leonard Skimpole* corr. on CP1 to *Harold Skimpole*

67.16–17 MS–CP1: *of astute, multiplication-table, business habits,* corr. on CP2 to *of business habits,*

67.22 MS–CP2: *creatures of the world, whom* 53–CD: *creatures, whom*

67.32–33 *leads to consequences that augment the total of the Beautiful?* CP1: *beautiful* corr. to *Beautiful* CP2: passage corr. to *leads to such pleasant consequences?* [apparently not in D's hand; possibly in John Forster's]

67.34 CP1: *(playful still,* corr. to *(playful,* [MS illegible]

68.1 MS: *fancifully and gaily* CP1: *powerfully and gaily* corr. to *gaily*

68.2–3 MS: *his genial way of* CP1–CD: *his genial ways of*

68.17 after *mistake her for it.* following passage canc. on CP1: *"When I saw her yesterday for the first time—" I was going to answer./"For the first time only yesterday! This is delightful!" he cried with enthusiasm. "We are escaping from the counting-house world into the happy golden age. Cold forms are vanishing. I am growing young again!"/ "Indeed," said I, "it is very pleasant to think how sure the influence of such beauty and such gentleness together—"/ "Yes," he repeated, with the happy tears in his eyes, "together."/ "— How sure their influence is. Yesterday seems to me quite a long time ago. If we were to be separated to-morrow, I should feel, I think, as if I had to contend with the impressions of years instead of hours. I hope," I added, suddenly remembering how clever he was, "that it is not foolish to say so."/ He kissed my hand with quite a child's gallantry, and replied with such fervor and earnestness, and was so familiarly eloquent upon youth, and grace, and loveliness, and upon their influences expanding like circles in the water, or sounds in the air, that I could have listened for an hour.* [*Run on* written by D after *for it.*]

68.17–18 *We will not," he added, "call* corr. on CP1 to *We will not call*

68.24 *"I don't* corr. on CP1 to *"O! I don't*

68.24 *said Mr. Skimpole,* corr. on CP1 to *cried Mr. Skimpole,*

68.25 *I do,"* corr. on CP1 to *I do know,"*

68.30 *with dewy roses;* corr. on CP2 to *with roses;*

68.30 *through sunny bowers,* corr. on CP2 to *through bowers,*

69.14–16 MS–CP1: beginning of this paragraph stands as follows: *Mr. Skimpole had not much voice for singing, but what he had was agreeable, and he sang with taste.* corr. on CP2 to p.t.

69.38 MS–L: *on a sofa,* CD: *on the sofa,*

70.10 MS–CP1: *mentioned; but you know my infirmity—no idea of money!"* corr. on CP2 to *mentioned."*

70.16 MS–53: *lift him up out* C–CD: *lift him out*

70.21 *Mr. Skimpole.* corr. on CP1 to *Mr. Skimpole, smiling.*

70.23 MS: *should prefer* CP1–CD: *would prefer*

70.30 *"Jail. Or,"* corr. on CP1 to *"Jail,"*

70.31 *"Coavinses."* corr. on CP1 to *"Or Coavinses."*

70.39 MS–CP1: *suggested, in his amiable, airy way, as if* corr. on CP2 to *suggested, as if*

71.4 MS–CP1: *returned Skimpole, with his beautiful, refined smile. "That* corr. on CP2 to *returned Mr. Skimpole. "That*

71.9–10 *, as he made . . . of a book* ins. on CP2

71.20–21 *, as he looked . . . on one side* ins. on CP2

71.21–22 MS: *utterly incable*

71.22 MS–CP1: *helping myself—you know my infirmities—and entirely* corr. on CP2 to *helping myself, and entirely*

71.23 between *to be free.* and *The butterflies* MS–CP1 have following passage: *That's not much. I only ask to walk tomorrow morning among the fallen leaves, and hear them rustle at my feet, instead of pacing across and across the parlor of our friend's friends* [corr. on CP1 to *friend's friend's* MS had *friends friends*] *Coavinses—however worthy Coavins may be; and I have no doubt that Coavins is a worthy man, and loves his children. Mine are inexpensive pleasures;* [*and*—not in MS—canc. on CP1] *it is not a costly pursuit to walk among the fallen leaves, and hear them rustle;* [*and* canc. on CP1] *I ask no more!* canc. on CP2 Then this, canc. on CP1: *This small sum (or small sum as it somehow seems to sound to me, though I am no authority, I know) is the only impediment in my path, the only cloud in my horizon. That removed, my way is clear—my sky unbroken.*

71.24 *Leonard Skimpole* corr. on CP1 to *Harold Skimpole*

71.40–41 *the abstract contemplation* corr. on CP1 to *the contemplation*

71.41 *affected his sensitive mind.* corr. on CP2 to *affected him.*

71.45–46 after *delighted Mr. Skimpole.* following paragraph canc. on CP1: *"It refreshes a helpless creature like me, my dear Miss Summerson," he said, standing with his back to the fire, looking towards me, as I sat at the table, with pen and ink and banknotes, "to see that womanly aptitude for bringing down an airy film of generosity from the skies, and stamping it with the earthly form and shape that makes it current here. I sympathize with it, and admire it. I can't do more, but I do that. It charms me! I can't regret being the child I am, when I am blessed with such a power of appreciating the practical wisdom that our common mother teaches to some favored creatures!"*

72.5 *"Coavinses,"* corr. on CP2 to *"My friend,"*

72.5–6 *standing with his back to the fire,* ins. on CP1 and *after giving up the sketch when it was half finished,* on CP2

72.8 *I think Coavinses reply* corr. on CP2 to *I think the reply*

72.15 between *proceeded Mr. Skimpole,* and *"it was a fine day.* following passage was canc. on CP1: *"In a gig, perhaps?"/ "Shay," said Coavinses./ "Well! Chaise," proceeded Mr. Skimpole, "you —"/ "How could I come in two on 'em" retorted Coavinses, with scorn. "You don't suppose one shay warn't enough? —Talk of shays!"/ Mr. Skimpole laughed gaily at us, and nodded soothingly at Coavinses./ "True!" he said. "Never mind that; it's not the point. When you came down here,* [*Run on* written by D in margin of CP1]

72.22 CP1: *"What* corr. to *"Wot* [as in MS] CP2: *"Who* corr. to *"Wot*

72.27 *Leonard Skimpole* corr. on CP1 to *Harold Skimpole*

72.27–29 *Leonard* corr. on CP1 to *Harold Harold Skimpole loves* corr. on CP2 to *loves* [both changes made three times]

72.30 CP1: *seem to me a* [*very* ins.] *violence to this bright Shakspearian sort of all-entrancing* [corr. to *all-embracing* as in MS] *day that I am* CP2: *seem to me any violence . . . all-embracing day* canc.

72.30 *Leonard Skimpole* corr. on CP1 to *Harold Skimpole*

72.36 *with a nod that* corr. on CP1 to *with a jerk that*

72.39 *said Mr. Skimpole.* corr. on CP1 to *said Mr. Skimpole, thoughtfully.*

72.39 *"Thank you, Coavinses."* corr. on CP2 to *"Thank you, my friend."*

73.3 in *very fond of the game, very* canc. by D in MS, but printed in CP1 and not canc. later

73.7–8 MS–CP1: *when Mr. Skimpole accompanied himself in a variety of sentimental and classical songs;* corr. on CP2 to *when Mr. Skimpole played some fragments of his own compositions;*

73.8 *at the piano, and at our* corr. on CP2 to *at the piano and the violincello, and at our*

73.13–14 *it was eleven* corr. on CP1 to *at eleven*

73.14–15 MS–CP1: *sang, hilariously,* corr. on CP2 to *rattled, hilariously,*

73.18 *if he had thought fit,* corr. on CP1 to *if he had seen fit,*

73.25 *How did you* corr. on CP1 to *How could you*

73.38 CP1: *winking again* corr. to *walking again* [as in MS]

73.43 *in difficulties," said Mr. Jarndyce, still walking up and down, in the same restless and whimsical manner.* corr. on CP1 to *in difficulties."*

74.3 *that I feel bound to keep* corr. on CP1 to *that I ought to keep*

74.5 *shall tell you* corr. on CP1 to *will tell you*

74.10 *really, you, both of you, know—eh—to get* corr. on CP1 to *really—to get*

74.15 *rubbing them over* corr. on CP1 to *rubbing them all over*

74.31 *Leonard Skimpole* corr. on CP1 to *Harold Skimpole*

74.33–34 MS: *bright face clear away,* CP1–CD: *bright face clearing,* [MS reading restored here, as somewhat better than compositor's misreading]

75.1 MS–CP1: your *having the money! Hasn't a notion of the value of money; if it had* corr. on CP2 to your *having the money! If it had*

75.6–7 *Esther, and even you, Ada, for I don't know that your little purse (spangles, beads, or some such pretty claptraps, I'll be bound) is safe* corr. on CP1 to p.t.

75.22 *went away humming* corr. on CP1 to *went away singing*

75.38 *and the confidence* corr. on CP1 to *and with the confidence*

76.6 *thankful* corr. on CP1 to *grateful*

76.7 *my two little baskets* corr. on CP2 to *my little basket*

Chapter VII MS and two sets of CP; apparently no CP missing

76.32 *whose stall is* corr. on CP1 to *whose place is*

76.37 CP1: *startled* corr. to *stabled* [as in MS]

77.2 *beguile the tediousness of the time* corr. on CP1 to *beguile the time*

77.15 *he may say* corr. on CP1 to *he may growl*

77.18 CP1: *as on the pack,* corr. to *across the park* [as in MS]

77.20 *been obstinate* corr. on CP1 to *been very obstinate*

77.26 *plants to bite.* corr. on CP2 to *plants to gnaw.*

77.27 *troubled always with* corr. on CP1 to *always troubled with*

77.30 *The very goose,* corr. on CP1 to *The discontented goose,*

78.11 *reposes, shut-up, on* corr. on CP1 to *reposes on*

78.17 *Ask her, this rainy day,* corr. on CP1 to *Ask her how long, this rainy day,*

78.28 MS: *supersedle* (?)

79.5 *made a steward* corr. on CP1 to *made steward*

79.11 MS: *great unhappiness.* CP1–CD: *great uneasiness.*

79.13 *she knew* corr. on CP1 to *well knowing*

79.14 *any aptitude* corr. on CP1 to *an aptitude*

79.19 after *to the baronet.* following passage was canc. on CP1 and *run on* written by D in margin: *Sir Leicester stood confounded. If (he said) the boy could not settle down at Chesney Wold, in itself the most astonishing circumstance in the world, could he not serve his country in the ranks of her defenders, as his brother had done? Must he rush to her destruction, at his early age, and with his paricidal* [*sic* on CP1 but *parricidal* in MS] *hand strike at her?" However,*

79.23 *these unhappy tendencies."* corr. on CP1 to *these deplorable tendencies."* *deplorable* canc. on CP2

79.27 *as a portion of some odd* corr. on CP1 to *as one of a body of some odd*

79.34 MS–53: *preparation* C–CD: *preparations*

79.37–38 between *see you, Watt!* and *And, once again,* following passage canc. on CP1: *—Sir Leicester once remarked, in a moment of inspiration, that he considered the coincidence between the Christian name of his rock ahead the arch-rebel Tyler and the surname of the instructor* [corr. to *inventor* as in MS] *of the steam-engine* [*to* ins. as in MS] *have meaning in it—*

80.10 *"O, quite."* corr. on CP1 to *"Quite."*

80.15 *of the best company* corr. on CP1 to *of good company*

80.17–18 between *just now.* and *You called her* following passage was canc. on CP1 and *run on* written by D in margin: "/ *"She is more than pretty, Watt. She is good."/ "I have no doubt of that—and I am sure of the other.*

80.19 MS: *Daughter of* [*She is* first written, but canc. in MS] CP1–CD: *She is daughter of* [MS reading restored here, as more satisfactory than compositor's apparent and understandable misreading]

80.35 CP1: *rested on* corr. to *beaten on* [as in MS]

81.25 *his wet outer coat* corr. on CP1 to *his wet dreadnought*

81.33 MS: *forlorn depression* CP1–CD: *profound depression* [MS reading restored here, as better than compositor's apparent misreading]

81.40–41 *and prettier for being so.* corr. on CP1 to *and prettier.*

82.3 MS: *anything whatever to* CP1–CD: *anything to*

82.25 *of those potentates.* corr. on CP1 to *of those magnates.*

82.28 *"if I don't believe I must* CP1–CD: *"if I don't think I must*

82.28 *that picture!"* corr. on CP1 to *that picture, you know!"*

82.38 *elegant and costly,* corr. on CP1 to *elegant,*

82.41 *tired of as soon as* corr. on CP1 to *tired of before*

83.1 *Mr. Guppy; "what's* corr. on CP1 to *Mr. Guppy, greedily curious; "what's*

83.4 *a great deal shyer than ever now.* corr. on CP1 to *shyer than ever.*

83.10 *the better I know it,* corr. on CP1 to

the better I seem to know it seem to canc. on CP2

83.10–11 MS: *without knowing how I know it!"* CP1 [n.c.]: *without knowing I know it!" how* ins. on CP2

83.12 *It has nothing* corr. on CP1 to *The story has nothing*

83.9 *by a window,* corr. on CP1 to *by the fast-darkening window,*

83.9 *tells them thus:* corr. on CP1 to *tells them:*

83.21 *of the conspirators* corr. on CP1 to *of the rebels*

83.25 *very likely though indeed."* corr. on CP1 to *very likely indeed."*

83.26–27 *thinks a family of that antiquity* corr. on CP1 to *considers that a family of such antiquity*

83.27–28 *She considers a ghost one* corr. on CP1 to *She regards a ghost as one*

83.29 *have no pretension.* corr. on CP1 to *have no claim.*

83.37 *was ever nearer* corr. on CP1 to *was always nearer*

83.38 *footstep coming along* corr. on CP1 to *footstep passing along*

83.40 *draws closer to* corr. on CP1 to *draws nearer to*

84.5 *a young boy,* corr. on CP1 to *a young gentleman,*

84.6 *(it is said, by Sir Morbury's* corr. on CP1 to *(by Sir Morbury's*

84.7 *hated the very race* corr. on CP1 to *hated the race*

84.12 *into the stable where* corr. on CP1 to *into the stall where*

84.12–13 *his own horse* corr. on CP1 to *his own favorite horse*

84.14–15 *and striking out,* corr. on CP1 to *and lashing out,*

84.17 MS–L: *to little more* CD: *to a little more*

84.22–23 *with the balustrade and with a stick,* corr. on CP1 to *with the help of the stone balustrade and with the help of a stick,* thus in CP2–53 C–L: *and with the help of a stick, and with the help of the stone balustrade,* CD: *with the help of the stone balustrade,*

84.24 *with greater difficulty and greater pain* corr. on CP1 to *with greater difficulty*

84.27 *saw her sink* corr. on CP1 to *saw her drop*

84.29 *steadily and coldly,* corr. on CP1 to *fixedly and coldly,*

84.30–31 MS–CP1: *I will walk here as I list, until* corr. on CP2 to *I will walk here, until*

84.38 *heard at night,* corr. on CP1 to *heard after dark,*

85.3 *must be heard in the night,* corr. on CP1 to *must be heard.*

85.5 *(placed here, 'a purpose)* ins. on CP1

85.8 CP1: *I believe."* corr. to *I think."* [as in MS]

85.9 *sets it going."* corr. on CP1 to *"set it a going."*

85.12 *it's late enough* corr. on CP1 to *it is dark enough*

85.14 *and all?"* corr. on CP1 to *and everything?"*

85.15 MS: *"Some singular reverberation —but I certainly can!"* CP1: *"Some singular reverberation—that I certainly can!"* corr. to *"I certainly can!"*

Chapter VIII MS and one set of CP: no other set missing

85 chapter-heading ins. on CP [but is in MS]

85.22–23 *like my own memory* corr. on CP to *like my memory*

85.26 *to expand* corr. on CP to *to enlarge*

85.30 *shone fair and bright* corr. on CP to *shone bright*

85.31 *in which the Abbey Church* corr. on CP to *in which the* [*ancient* canc.] *old Abbey Church*

85.35 before *Every part of the house* following passage canc. on CP: *I was in such a flutter about my two bunches of keys that I had been dreaming for an hour before I got up. that the more I tried to open a variety of locks with them, the more determined they were not to fit any. No dream could have been less prophetic.*

85.36 *I had actually no trouble* corr. on CP to *I had no trouble*

85.36 *with my two bunches of keys:* ins. on CP

86.10 *to lean out at me,* corr. on CP to *to smile out at me,*

86.17 *she came tripping out* corr. on CP to *she came out*

86.24 *the overweening boastful assumptions* corr. on CP to *the overweening assumptions*

86.31 MS–L: *insupportable* CD: *unsupportable*

86.37 *"You must excuse* corr. on CP to *"You will excuse*

87.9 *I had been away some* corr. on CP to *They had occupied me for some*

87.9 *and was passing* corr. on CP to *and I was passing*

87.26–27 *I spoke a word. He was agitated, and* corr. on CP to *I spoke. He was disconcerted, and*

88.6 *shook my head in a most emphatic manner.* corr. on CP to *shook my head.*

88.9 *of the case seem to have disappeared* corr. on CP to *of the case have long disappeared*

88.15 *equitably* ins. on CP [MS not legible]

88.15 *waltzing ourselves to* corr. on CP to *waltzing ourselves off to* [MS not legible]

88.24–25 *such a hopeless condition* corr. on CP to *such a miserable condition*

88.25–26 *condition that they had far better have had nothing left them at all;* corr. on CP to p.t.

88.32 *reams of paper* corr. on CP to *cartloads of papers* [*paper* written at very edge of MS sheet]

88.33 *which is the same thing,* corr. on CP to *which is the usual course,*

88.35 *and fees, as was* corr. on CP to *and*

fees and nonsense and corruption, as was

88.38 *Law can't do* corr. on CP to *Law finds it can't do*

88.38 *Equity can't do* corr. on CP to *Equity finds it can't do*

89.1 *again, and never ending anywhere.* corr. on CP to *again, and nothing never ends.* 53–CD: *again, and nothing ever ends.*

89.2–3 *for we* must be corr. on CP to *for we are made parties to it, and* must be

89.14 *bring it somehow to* corr. on CP to *bring it to*

89.15 *the neglected place became* corr. on CP to *the place became*

89.17 *When I, a young man, brought* corr. on CP to *When I brought*

89.27 *at this day as Bleak House* corr. on CP to *at this day what Bleak House*

89.30 *or know it* corr. on CP to *or will ever know it*

89.33 MS: *bared blank shutters* CP: *barred blank shutters* corr. to *bare blank shutters*

89.36 *door like Death's* corr. on CP to *door might be Death's*

90.2 *looking hard at me,* corr. on CP to *looking seriously at me,*

90.10 *in a more determined* corr. on CP to *in a still more determined*

90.11 *looked at him as calmly and quietly as I could by the utmost force of my resolution.* corr. on CP to *looked at him quietly.*

90.15–16 *not the courage to* corr. on CP to *not the honesty to*

90.22–23 *our lives here,"* corr. on CP to *our lives here, my dear,"*

90.23 *gaily;* corr. on CP to *playfully;*

90.28 *I foresee, that one* corr. on CP to *Esther, that one*

91.3 MS–L: *in his pockets* CD: *into his pockets*

91.10–11 *of used up legal Sexton,* corr. on CP to *of ridiculous Sexton,*

91.11 *merits of cases* corr. on CP to *merits of causes*

91.12 CP1: *Charity Court,* corr. to *Quality Court,* [as in MS]

91.16–17 *ceremonious, vastly* corr. on CP to *vastly ceremonious,* [MS order not clear]

91.17 *unsatisfactory,* ins. on CP

91.20 *but so it is."* corr. on CP to *so it is."*

92.2 CP1: *only a scolding* corr. to *only a concluding* [MS illegible]

92.3 *word for once and for good. Esther,* corr. on CP to *word. Esther,*

92.26 *I think they were more* corr. on CP to *I think they were even more*

92.30 *dealing subscription-cards* corr. on CP to *dealing out subscription-cards*

92.37–38 *debts on buildings,* corr. on CP to *debts on old buildings,*

92.42 *whose devotion* corr. on CP to *whose deep devotion*

93.2 *to a silver tea-service.*corr. on CP to *to a silver teapot.*

93.8 *by millions,* corr. on CP to *by tens of thousands,*

93.8–9 *their candidate* corr. on CP to *their candidates*

93.10 *how feverish they must be.* corr. on CP to *what feverish lives they must lead.*

93.11 *for their rapacious* corr. on CP to *for this rapacious*

93.15–21 *We observed that . . . no noise at all.* whole sentence written on separate slip pasted on to back of MS page

93.22 *the latter class;* corr. on CP to *the former class;*

93.25 *who took up a great deal of room. Not that her figure was very large, but she had the effect* corr. on CP to *who had the effect*

93.34 *the boy who gave his* corr. on CP to *the boy who sent out his*

93.38 MS: *(nine), one-and-* CP: *(nine), gave one-and-* [n.c.] 53–CD: *(nine), one-and-*

93.38 *sixpence-halfpenny to the Preservation of Perpetual Peace;* corr. on CP to *sixpence-halfpenny to the Timbuctoo Conference;* 53–CD: *sixpence-halfpenny;*

93.39 MS: *(seven), eightpence* CP: *(seven), gave eightpence* corr. to *(seven), eightpence*

93.41 *never to use* corr. on CP to *never, through life, to use*

94.2 MS–53: *weazen* C–CD: *weazened*

94.4 *the Tockahoopos,* corr. on CP to *the Tockahoopo Indians,*

94.10 CP: *utterly miserable.*corr. to *evenly miserable.* [as in MS]

94.15 *loud tone,* corr. on CP to *loud, hard tone,*

94.16–17 *take the same opportunity of* corr. on CP to *take the opportunity of*

95.11 *as if he never could smile more, and never could, or would, forgive* corr. on CP to *as if he never could, or would, forgive*

95.20 *Mr. Pardiggle (who is in the law) brings up* corr. on CP to *Mr. Pardiggle brings up*

95.33 *Mr. Gush?"* corr. on CP to *Mr. Gusher?"*

95.34–35 *Mr. Gush's* corr. on CP to *Mr. Gusher's*

96.2 CP: *as to the quiet nature* corr. to *as to the guilty nature* [as in MS]

96.6 MS: *it is so prominent* CP–CD: *it is so prominent*

96.8 *I freely admit, I am a woman of business.* ins. on CP

96.12 MS–L: *why it was* CD: *what it was*

96.13 MS–L: *but this was what* CD: *but this is what*

96.26 *of fatigue, I am* corr. on CP to *of fatigue, my good friend, I am*

96.39 *could teach fathers and mothers and old people,* corr. on CP to *could teach others,*

96.43 *expand.* corr. on CP to *expand itself.*

96.43 *All this I said, because I sincerely felt that I could not assume an authority to which I might be able to establish no pretension; and I said it with anything*

corr. on CP to *All this I said, with anything*
97.8 *looks of enquiry, and,* corr. on CP to *looks, and,*
97.27–28 *when the alleged boner was his parent* corr. on CP to *in connexion with his parent*
97.31 *What do you mean by calling it* corr. on CP to *Why do you call it*
97.32 *and never letting* corr. on CP to *and never let*
97.36 *upon my toes whenever he could.* corr. on CP to *upon my toes.*
97.38 *was in fact* corr. on CP to *stood in fact*
97.43–44 *of being rational.* corr. on CP to *of being natural.*
98.7 *men and women, very dirty and indifferent, lounged* corr. on CP to *men and women lounged*
98.20 *powerful youth of eighteen,* corr. on CP to *powerful young man,*
98.21 *a strong collar* corr. on CP to *a collar*
98.24 *bruised eye, but nobody* corr. on CP to *bruised eye; nobody*
98.26–27 *and systematic* ins. on CP
98.38–39 MS: *of the young man* CP–53: *of the young men* C–CD: *of the young man* [em. ad.]
99.1 MS: *draw'd* CP: *chained* corr. to *drawed*
99.2 MS: *accordin to* CP–CD: *according to*
99.3 CP: *to be arter!* corr. to *to be up to.* [as in MS]
99.3 *got no call* corr. on CP to *got no occasion*
99.7–8 *it's onwholesome too,* corr. on CP to *it's nat'rally onwholesome,*
99.9 MS: *dead wen Infants,* CP: *dead when Infants,* corr. to *dead Infants,*
99.26 *took the family* corr. on CP to *took the whole family*
99.31 *had not been such a woman of business, with such* corr. on CP to *had not had such*
99.32 *stared about them;* corr. on CP to *stared;*
99.40 *so much less bustle.* corr. on CP to *so much tact.*
100.18 *else (unconsciously, I have no doubt) a show* corr. on CP to *else, a show*
100.19–20 *and of dealing in it to a large extent.* ins. on CP
100.24 *She only shook her head and looked* corr. on CP to *She only looked*
100.26 *with one hand,* corr. on CP to *with her hand,*
100.27 *of noise* corr. on CP to *with noise*
100.34 *a sight like this* corr. on CP to *a sight so pitiful as this*
100.35 *such pity,* corr. on CP to *such compassion,*
100.36 *weeping over the waxen form, and* corr. on CP to *weeping, and*
100.42 *we told her* corr. on CP to *we whispered to her*
101.12 *tears fell fast,* corr. on CP to *tears fell,*
101.15 *It was very affecting to see* corr. on CP to *I thought it very touching to see*
101.32 after *changed directly.* whole following paragraph canc. on CP: *"Excellent people, you know," he said, beginning to walk about, "Mrs. Pardiggle and all the rest of 'em. Excellent people! Do a deal of good, and mean to do a good deal more. But they want one pattern out of all varieties of Looms, they must be in extremes, they will knock in tintacks with a sledge hammer, they make such a bustle and noise, and they are so confoundedly indefatigable!—O Lord, yes, I feel the wind all over me!"*
101.38 *His sister* corr. on CP to *The sister*
101.45–102.1 *watching for* corr. on CP to *a watching for*
102.5 *had her child* corr. on CP to *had the child*
102.7 MS–53: *we went softly* C–CD: *she went softly*
102.10 *calm figure,* corr. on CP to *waxen form,*
102.24 *and saw a halo* corr. on CP to *and seemed to see a halo*
102.25 *from Ada's golden* corr. on CP to *through Ada's drooping*
102.27–28 *peaceful baby breast!* corr. on CP to *peaceful breast!*
102.28–29 *child was not all* corr. on CP to *child might not be all*
102.30 CP: *of her penalty, when* corr. to *of her presently, when* [as in MS]

CHAPTER IX MS and one set of CP, presumably CP1, as there seems to have been further slight revision on missing CP2

103.6 *bright* corr. on CP to *bright-winged*
103.12 *found them out—O quite soon.* corr. on CP to *found them out quite soon.*
103.23 *"Our little old* corr. on CP to *"Our dear little old*
103.23 *a capital little old* corr. on CP to *a capital old*
103.26–27 CP: *dry grinding* corr. to *day—grinding* [as in MS]
103.27 MS–CP [n.c.]: *at those slates and* 53–CD: *at these books and*
103.29–30 MS–CP [n.c.]: *our comfortable Mrs. Bountiful,* 53–CD: *our comfortable friend,*
103.36 *Ah! Richard* corr. on CP to *Ah! Perhaps Richard*
103.37–38 *now, and the inclination of his childhood for the sea was to be gratified at last. He was to enter the Navy very soon, and was to be made a Midshipman, and* corr. on CP to *now, and there was some talk of gratifying the inclination of his childhood for the sea.*
103.40 *favor;* corr. on CP to *favor, generally;*
103.41 *advance the interests* corr. on CP to *advance the prospects*
103.43 *not probable* corr. on CP to *not at all probable*

104.2 *do his duty in that* corr. on CP to *do his duty in any*
104.3 *had devoted himself.* corr. on CP to *might devote himself.*
104.6 *have done it too.* corr. on CP to *have done it.*
104.8 *the Lord Chancellor* corr. on CP to *the Chancellor*
104.39 *drew upon it over and over again.* corr. on CP to *drew upon it.*
104.45 *I believe Richard Carstone's was* corr. on CP to *I believe Richard's was*
105.6 *and always (though there was already an indefinite shadow of separation upon us) so happy, and* corr. on CP to *and always so happy, sanguine, and*
105.39 *the heart of the man,* corr. on CP to *the warm heart of the man,*
106.5 MS: *Graythorn* [n.c. here; corr. elsewhere to *Baythorn,* then *Boythorn*]
106.18–19 MS–L: *ever to have had such* CD: *ever to have such*
106.19 MS–L: *I would have that* CD: *I would have had that*
107.16 *a lion face* corr. on CP to *a fine composure of face*
107.16 *when silent,* ins. on CP
107.18 *he was never at rest,* corr. on CP to *he gave it no rest,*
108.1–2 *I would take* corr. on CP to *I would seize*
108.3 *shake him till* corr. on CP to *shake him until*
108.8 *"I thank you,* corr. on CP to *"I thank you, Lawrence,*
108.8–9 *at present, Lawrence,"* corr. on CP to *at present,"*
108.9 *Mr. Jarndyce, "that* corr. on CP to *Mr. Jarndyce, laughing, "that*
108.38 *pardon very earnestly,"* Corr. on CP to *pardon,"*
109.5–6 *stewed down into one,* corr. on CP to *melted into one,*
109.26 *the most insupportable* corr. on CP to *the insupportable*
109.32 *the fiercest of* corr. on CP to *the angriest of*
109.40 *"here he softened in a moment."* ins. on CP
110.11–12 *You may rely* corr. on CP to *Jarndyce, you may rely*
110.22 *and thought some* corr. on CP to *and I thought some*
110.27 *mild and agreeable* corr. on CP to *agreeable*
110.33 *"But engaged to* corr. on CP to *"But he meant to*
111.5 *you have told me."* corr. on CP to *you have told me so."*
111.20 *of my life. But the occasions were very rare indeed, when, dreaming at all, I dreamed of any other time.* corr. on CP to *of my life.*
112.1 *but found him* corr. on CP to *but I found him*
112.13 MS: *Then my lunch was(?)* CP–CD: *The lunch was*
112.17 *evidently firing* corr. on CP to *evidently blowing*
112.38–39 MS–L: *every thing I can* CD: *everything that I can*
113.9 *"I am quite at a loss,* corr. on CP to *"I am at a loss,*
113.12 MS: *sufficient; I"* CP–CD: *sufficient."*
113.13–14 *either planing his forehead with his handkerchief, or* ins. on CP
113.15 MS: *"You. If you would* CP–CD: *"If you would*
113.31 *although unassuming* corr. on CP to *though unassuming*
113.38 CP: *healthiest* corr. to *'ealthiest* [MS not clear, but looks like *healthiest* corr. to *'elthiest*]
113.39–40 *I adore you and I make an offer!"* corr. on CP to p.t.
114.3 MS: *looked at me piteously,* corr. to *looked piteous,*(?) CP–CD: *looked piteously,*
114.23–24 *interests, turning round upon your injurers, and pushing* corr. on CP to *interests, and pushing*
114.29 *I begged him,* corr. on CP to *I requested him,*
114.35 *hackney-coach.* corr. on CP to *'ackney-coach.*
114.41 *speak of your interest,* corr. on CP to *speak of interest,*
115.4 *to me the greatest proof* corr. on CP to *to me a proof*
115.5 *opinion that it is in your power to offer,* corr. on CP to *opinion,*
115.5–6 *to thank you. I do thank you. I have* corr. on CP to *to thank you. I have*
115.6–7 *little reason for pride, and I feel none.* corr. on CP to *little reason to be proud, and I am not proud.*
115.16 *can never change—* corr. on CP to *can never alter—*
115.18 *or anything),* corr. on CP to *or anything of that sort),*
115.24 *passed the door, and in a manner that reminded me, I well remembered afterwards, of a person studying a likeness in a picture.* corr. on CP to *passed the door.*
115.32 *felt that an old* corr. on CP to *felt as if an old*

Chapter X MS and one set of CP, presumably CP1, as one or two further corrections seem to imply existence of missing CP2

116.13 *he has lain* corr. on CP to *he has been recumbent*
116.14 MS–L: *wagons* CD: *waggons* [em.ad.]
116.29, 117.21 CP: *Cook's-Courters* corr. to *Cook's-Courtiers* [as in MS]
116.36 *this gossamer report* corr. on CP to *this frothy report*
117.23–24 *stormy and fitful character.* corr. on CP to *stormy character.*
117.32–33 *really aged three or four and twenty, but looking a round ten years older,* ins. on CP
117.33 *drawback;* corr. on CP to *drawback of fits;*
117.37 *to be uppermost at* corr. on CP to *to be near her at*

118.8 MS–L: *and of Coavins's* CD: *and of Coavinses'* [em.ad.]
118.14–24 *Mr. Snagsby refers . . . behaviour and Mrs. Snagsby's.* whole passage written on separate slip pasted on to back of MS page
118.30 *in reality do look down* corr. on CP to *in reality look down*
118.33 *as an instrument of correction* ins. on CP
119.2 *what time Turnstile* corr. on CP to *when Turnstile*
119.3–4 *out of it, that* corr. on CP to *out of this, that*
119.5–10 *The day is closing . . . Lincoln's Inn Fields.* whole paragraph written on separate slip pasted on to back of MS page
119.8 MS–L: *over the leaden slice* CD: *over the slice*
119.17–18 *to be its object* corr. on CP to *to be Allegory's object*
119.19 CP–L: *transcendant* CD: *transcendent* [em. ad.; MS not clear, possibly *transcendent*]
119.22 *whom no man can* corr. on CP to *whom nobody can*
119.23–24 *in the dusk of the present afternoon* ins. on CP
119.25 CP: *Long broad-backed* corr. to *Heavy broad-backed* [MS: *High broad-backed*]
120.3 *must sweep them* corr. on CP to *must gather them*
120.4–5 *with Allegory staring at* corr. on CP to *with foreshortened Allegory staring down at*
120.5 *as if it meant to swoop upon him,* ins. on CP
120.11 MS: *Draughts that* CP–CD: *Drafts that*
120.14 MS–53: *made at the stationer's,* C–L: *made at the stationers,* CD: *made at the stationers',*
120.16 *the crossing-sweeper at the corner.* corr. on CP to *any crossing-sweeper in Holborn.*
120.21 MS: *puts on his head,* CP–CD: *puts on his hat,*
120.31 *about one,* corr. on CP to *at half-past one,*
120.34,42 *"Is he at home?"* corr. on CP to *"Master at home?"*
120.40 *the dull admiration* corr. on CP to *the unprofitable admiration*
120.43 *He is at home,* corr. on CP to *Master is at home,*
120.44 *glad on the whole to get* corr. on CP to *glad to get*
121.6 *"I want a word* corr. on CP to *"I want half a word*
121.9 *changed in a moment from inertness to alacrity.* corr. on CP to *brightened in a moment.*
121.15–17 *Mr. Snagsby, as a timid man, . . to save words.* ins. on CP
121.26 *"Who copied it,* corr. on CP to *"Who copied this,*
121.33 MS–53: *which seems to have* C–CD: *which seemed to have*
122.2 *, with his deferential cough* ins. on CP
122.2 MS: *That's the person's name.* CP: *A person's name.* corr. to *It is a person's name.* [MS reading restored here, as much better than D's own correction due to compositor's misreading]
122.7 *addresses a cough* corr. on CP to *addresses an explanatory cough*
122.12 *he sticks up at* corr. on CP to *he sticks up down at*
122.13 *Chambers, and that.* corr. on CP to *Chambers, and so forth.*
122.16 MS–L: *of Coavins's,* CD: *of Coavinses'* [em. ad.; same change made wherever the name occurs in this chapter]
122.16 *where lights are* corr. on CP to *where lights shine*
123.7 MS–53: *and attornies* C–CD: *and attorneys* [em. ad.]
123.9 *the wisdom* corr. on CP to *to the forensic wisdom*
123.28 *goes a little way,* corr. on CP to *goes a short way,*
123.40 *"Hi! It's what* corr. on CP to *"It's what*
123.41 *if he'd come!"* corr. on CP to *if he'd come, sir!"*
123.43–44 MS–CP [n.c.]: *Mr. Krook, with his cat's tail feather in his cap, stands* 53–CD: *Mr. Krook, with his cat beside him, stands*
124.4 *"Lady Jane!"* corr. on CP to *"Order, Lady Jane!*
124.4 *Behave yourself, my lady!* corr. on CP to *Behave yourself to visitors, my lady!*
124.7 *"Not I, my friend, What do they say* corr. on CP to *"What do they say*
124.8 *sold himself to the Devil;* corr. on CP to *sold himself to the Enemy;*
124.10–11 *that bargain as not.* corr. on CP to *that bargain as any other.*
124.11 *my advice to you!"* corr. on CP to *my advice!"*
124.14 *and puts his candle out by accident* corr. on CP to *and accidentally extinguishes his candle*
124.19–20 *a wilderness bespattered with* corr. on CP to *a wilderness marked with*
124.21 *serves for a cabinet* corr. on CP to *serves for cabinet*
124.25 *the darkness,* corr. on CP to *the darkness of the night,*
124.33 *its wick has doubled over, burning still,* corr. on CP to *its wick (still burning) has doubled over,*
124.37 MS–L: *filthy as the air,* CD: *as the air is,*
124.40 *the vapid taste* corr. on CP to *the bitter, vapid taste*
125.1 *has awakened him.* corr. on CP to *has awakened his friend.*

Chapter XI MS and one set of CP, possibly CP2, as a few variants between MS and CP, and between CP and 53, seem to point to existence of missing CP1 and CP3

125 chapter-heading ins. on CP [but is in MS]
125.7–8 CP: *in the death room,* corr. to *in the dark room,* [as in MS]
125.14 *bends over the red* corr. on CP to *stoops over the red*
125.24–25 *shaking his head and lifting his eyebrows* ins. on CP
125.34 *Call for Maggie* corr. on CP to *Call for Miss* [*Flighty* canc.] *Flite*
125.35 *for Maggie,* corr. on CP to *for* [*Flighty* canc.] *Flite,*
125.38–39 *Maggie, Maggie!* corr. on CP to *Miss Flite! Flite!*
125.39 *Maggie!"* corr. on CP to *Flite!"*
126.1 *"Run, Maggie,* corr. on CP to *"Run, Flite,*
126.10–11 *he has been dead* corr. on CP to *he wull have been dead*
126.17 CP: *tak' my departure,"* corr. to *tak' my depairture,"* [as in MS]
126.20 *takes the candle, passes it* corr. on CP to *passes the candle*
126.26–27 *, taking the candle from the surgeon's outstretched hand* ins. on CP
126.27 *told me once, that was* corr. on CP to *told me once, I was*
126.35 *"Ah!" Krook* corr. on CP to *"Yes!" Krook*
126.43 CP: *circumstances* corr. to *circumstarnces* [as in MS] thus in 53 C–CD: *circumstances*
126.45 *"Six weeks. Going on for seven."* corr. on CP to *"Six weeks."*
127.1–2 MS: *"Well!" says the young man, resuming his examination,"* he *will never pay it.* CP: *"Well!"* corr. to *"Ah!"* [no other corrections] 53–CD *"He will never pay it!" says the young man, resuming his examination."*
127.6 *towards the other face,* corr. on CP to *towards that other face,*
127.8 *wild as it was,* corr. on CP to *uncouth as it was,*
127.13 *I know no more, sir."* corr. on CP to *I know no more of him."*
127.16 *from both kinds of interest* corr. on CP to *from all three kinds of interest*
127.17 MS: *the young surgeon's professional* CP: *surgeon's* ins. in blank left by compositor
128.13–15 *to help him out./ "About that, sir!" says Mr. Snagsby./ A pause.* corr. on CP to *to help him out./ A pause.*
128.28 CP: *he was in want of* corr. to *he was in wants of* [as in MS] thus in 53–L CD: *he was in want of*
128.31 CP: *a sort of apishness at frankness,* corr. to *a sort of argumentative frankness,* [as in MS, but MS almost illegible]
128.42 *"why didn't you* corr. on CP to *"Mr. Snagsby, why didn't you*
128.44 MS: *gradiwally* CP–CD: *gradually*
129.3 *on the Thursday night,* corr. on CP to *on the Wednesday night,*
129.4 *on the Friday morning.* corr. on CP to *on the Thursday morning.*
129.11 MS: *with a grin.* CP–CD: *with a sudden grin.*
129.20 *he is standing close* corr. on CP to *he is standing so close*
129.24 *Maggie peeps* corr. on CP to *Miss* [*Flighty* canc.] *Flite peeps*
129.27 MS–C: *neck-kerchief* L–CD: *neckerchief* [em. ad.]
131.1,2 MS: *Mrs. Jolly's* CP: *Mrs. Jelly's* corr. to *Mrs. Green's*
131.10 CP–53: *choruses fragments* C–CD: *chorusses fragments* [MS illegible]
131.11–12 *into soup.* corr. on CP to *into soup for the workhouse.*
131.16 CP: *policeman (to drink a little* corr. to *policeman (to whom a little* [MS not clear, but probably *whom*]
131.21 *for anything within the range between* corr. on CP to *for anything between*
131.25 MS–L: *nothing is rightly spelt* CD: *nothing rightly spelt*
131.30 *new to look at,* corr. on CP to *new to stare at,*
131.34 CP: *figure on the lid,* corr. to *figure on the bed,* [as in MS]
131.39 *with that lady.* corr. on CP to *with that excellent woman.*
132.1 *Meetings come off* corr. on CP to *Meetings take place*
132.2 *the chair is taken* corr. on CP to *the chair is filled*
132.18 *awful shapes—this being another aspect of the wisdom to which we are indebted for our Chancery and many other blessings.* corr. on CP to *awful shapes.*
133.28 *Mrs. Piper is pushed* corr. on CP to *Mrs. Piper pushed*
133.28 *Mrs. Piper is sworn.* corr. on CP to *Mrs. Piper sworn.*
133.29 MS: *Anastatia* CP–CD: *Anastasia*
133.31 CP: *in parentheses* corr. to *in parenthesis* [as in MS] thus in 53–L CD: *in parentheses*
133.33 MS: *is a Divon-turner)* (?) CP–CD: *is a cabinet-maker)*
133.35–36 *Alexander James Piper is aged* corr. to *Alexander James Piper aged* [MS not clear]
133.37 *the suffering of that child* corr. on CP to *the sufferings gentlemen of that child*
134.2 MS: *to go about as Mrs. Perkins was sitivated being* CP: *sitivated* corr. to *sitiwated,* then whole phrase corr. to *to go about some children being*
134.3 *she may be* corr. on CP to *Mrs. Perkins may be*
134.3 *perduced* corr. on CP to *brought forward*
134.6 *especially if of* corr. on CP to *specially if of*
134.16–17 *been seen speaking* corr. on CP to *been seen a speaking*
134.35 *something very bad* corr. on CP to *something wery bad*
134.14–15 *(whom he knew* corr. on CP to *(whom he recognized*
135.30 *heerd me tell him how I thanked*

him for it. corr. on CP to *heerd me tell him so.*

135.33 *puts a shilling* corr. on CP to *puts a half-crown*

135.34 MS: *—meaning a lady—* CP–CD: *—I mean a lady—*

135.37 *The exceptional nature of the occasion has so unsettled them, that half-a-dozen* corr. on CP to *In the sequel, half-a-dozen*

135.37 *fade into a cloud* corr. on CP to *are caught up in a cloud*

135.38 *pipe-smoke in the parlor* corr. on CP to *pipe-smoke that pervades the parlor*

136.12 *(not the least in the world like him)* ins. on CP

136.12–13 *outdoes himself in describing the Inquest,* corr. on CP to *describes the Inquest,*

136.13–14 *pianoforte, accompanying the* corr. on CP to *pianoforte accompaniment to the*

136.23 *to which it lifted itself,* corr. on CP to *to which it crept,*

136.24–25 CP: *the non-extinguished fire* corr. to *the now-extinguished fire* [as in MS]

136.28 *for there Guster murders* corr. on CP to *where Guster murders*

136.35–36 *Dutch-cheese and bread-basket,* corr. on CP to *Dutch-cheese,*

136.36 MS: *and fell head foremost into a fit* CP: *and fell head forward into a fit* corr. to *and fell into a fit*

136.37–38 *a chain or rosary of fits,* corr. on CP to *a chain of fits,*

136.42 between *and go to bed.* and *Hence, Mr. Snagsby,* following sentence canc. on CP: *These attacks have been treated through the night with such astonishing quantities of vinegar (occasioning the house to smell as if Guster were pickled salmon), coupled with such remarkable applications to the patient's nose, and so much general distraction, that morning has seemed put off indefinitely.*

137.6 *be of any use to him,* corr. on CP to *be of any moment to him,*

137.13 *sisters not departed;* corr. on CP to *sisters who have not*

137.17 *a Caffre shudder at,* corr. on CP to *a Caffre would shudder at,*

137.27 *for ye cannot come* corr. on CP to *for you cannot come*

137.29 *and ye who do* corr. on CP to *and you who do*

137.35 *It holds it* corr. on CP to *It holds the gate*

138.3–4 *a dim ray of light* corr. on CP to *a distant ray of light*

Chapter XII MS and one set of CP; no earlier CP presumably missing; 3 minor divergences between CP and 53 are probably misprints

138 chapter-heading ins. on CP [but is in MS]

138.29–30 *with my Lady's woman, and Sir Leicester's man, affectionate in the rumble,* corr. on CP to *(my Lady's woman and Sir Leicester's man affectionate in the rumble),*

139.2–3 *off to the Place* corr. on CP to *off by the Place*

139.12–14 *of our Lady to say a word or two within flare of a flame of gas, by little trips at the base of a pillar* corr. on CP to *of our Lady, to say a word or two at the base of a pillar, within flare of a rusty little gridiron-full of gusty little tapers—* [*tapers* was the MS word misread as *trips* by compositor]

139.16 *billiard, card, and domino playing,* corr. on CP to *billiard card and domino playing,* [this eccentric punct., preserved in 53–CD, is quite deliberate and later editors not justified in restoring commas]

139.19–20 *for being evidently pleased.* corr. on CP to *for being in spirits.*

139.21 *Weariness of spirit* corr. on CP to *Weariness of soul*

139.29 *in a plain with two dark* corr. on CP to *in a plain: two dark*

139.33–34 *so inexhaustible a subject for reflection.* corr. on CP to *so inexhaustible a subject.*

140.21 MS–L: *unmistakeable* CD: *unmistakable* [em. ad.]

140.44 *like the smallest fry.* corr. on CP to *like the small fry.*

140.44 CP: *particularly hard* corr. to *habitually hard* [as in MS]

141.4 *At least, through the same* corr. on CP to *Through the same*

141.7 *by an angry pile of fire* corr. on CP to *by a pile of fire*

141.12 MS: *malecontents*

141.14 CP: *debate, united by one* corr. to *debate, incited by one* [as in MS]

141.27 *is looking charming,"* corr. on CP to *is looking charmingly well,"*

141.32–33 MS: *whatsoever else she may* CP–CD: *whatever else she may*

141.44 *"Well! Take care* corr. on CP to *"Take care*

142.27 *—or so much as hear—* corr. on CP to *—nor so much as to hear—*

143.1–2 MS–CP [n.c.]: *"because I—because I have an inexpressible desire* 53–CD: *"because I have an inexpressible desire* [*because I—* restored here as expressing clear authorial intention and likely to have been inadvertently lost]

143.8–9 *from the southern* corr. on CP to *from somewhere in the southern*

143.9 *between Avignon and* corr. on CP to *about Avignon and*

143.19 *She-Wolf.* corr. on CP to *She-Wolf imperfectly tamed.*

143.22 *words with which to belabour* corr. on CP to *words to shower upon*

143.23 *she showers them* corr. on CP to *she pours them*

143.24–25 *is quite relieved* corr. on CP to *is rather relieved*

143.30 MS: *Ha ha ha!* corr. to *Ha ha!* CP: *Ha, ha!* corr. to *Ha, ha, ha!*

144.4 *from their presentation at* corr. on CP to *from their breaking cover at*

144.5 *to their presentation at the Court of*

Death. corr. on CP to *to their being run down to Death.*

144.20–21 *no jack-towel* corr. on CP to *no clear-starched, jack-towel*

144.26 *or who goes to see all the executions,* ins. on CP

144.31–33 after *its own digestion,* MS has **see back* and *to which no rational . . . disguised. There are* written at back of MS page

144.33–34 *There* are./ *At Chesney Wold, this January week, are some* corr. on CP to *There* are, *at Chesney Wold, this January week, some*

145.3–4 *picturesque and charming,* corr. on CP to *picturesque and faithful,*

145.8 *and keep down* corr. on CP to *and to keep down*

145.12 *walking backwards* corr. on CP to *walking backward*

145.13–14 *of past ages,* corr. on CP to *of past generations,*

145.15 *from the passing time.* corr. on CP to *from the moving age.*

145.34 *(as is manifest* corr. on CP to *(as is made manifest*

145.37 *the Honorable* corr. on CP to *the Right Honorable*

145.39–40 MS: *only the manner that* CP: *only the measure of it that* corr. to *only the manner of it that*

145.40 *arises out of Cuffy.* corr. on CP to *is attributable to Cuffy.*

146.6 *being as you are,* corr. on CP to *being as you now are,*

146.7 MS: *and as to minor* CP: *and also some minor* corr. to *and as to some minor*

146,9 *is in question under the generic name of country but* corr. on CP to *is in question but*

146.19 *than is good for the brilliant* corr. on CP to *than the brilliant*

146.19–20 *distinguished circle.* corr. on CP to *distinguished circle will find good for itself in the long run.*

146.22 *will be found in active* corr. on CP to *may be seen in active*

146.31 *his retiring habit* corr. on CP to *his quiet habit*

146.38 *when he is down here,* ins. on CP

146.42 *glances round the table* corr. on CP to *glances down the table*

147.6–7 *sees her brooding face* corr. on CP to *sees her own brooding face*

147.14–15 MS–CP [n.c.]: *the bright groupes* 53–CD: *the bright groups*

147.16 *dispersed about the house,* corr. on CP to *dispersed,*

147.23 *is his secret.* corr. on CP to *is his personal secret.*

147.32–33 *Gracious observation.* corr. on CP to *A gracious observation.*

148.8 *any little minor point."* corr. on CP to *any minor point."*

148.24 *of a burthen,* corr. on CP to *of a burden,*

148.25–26 *the next effectual thing* corr. on CP to *the next satisfactory thing*

148.29–30 *addresses Mr. Tulkinghorn in her unimpassioned manner for the* corr. on CP to *addresses Mr. Tulkinghorn for the*

148.44 MS: *panneled*

149.6 *He looks across his arm at my Lady.* ins. on CP

149.9–10 *Lady Dedlock anticipates.* corr. on CP to *Lady Dedlock languidly anticipates.*

149.12 *"Lord bless me!" exclaims* corr. on CP to *"O dear me!" remonstrates* 53–CD: *remonstrated* [*remonstrates* restored here]

149.19 *"For it is quite* corr. on CP to *"It is quite*

149.30–31 *the lawyer, calmly,* corr. on CP to *the lawyer, with undisturbed calmness,*

150.1 *what he called himself,* corr. on CP to *what he had called himself,*

150.14–15 *renews his protest,* corr. on CP to *renews his stately protest,*

150.15 *and says, that* corr. on CP to *saying, that*

150.17 MS: *to hear no about* CP–CD: *to hear no more about*

150.22 *does so with a bow,* corr. on CP to *does so with deference,*

150.34–35 *each would sacrifice to know* corr. on CP to *each would give to know*

150.35 *—is hidden* corr. on CP to *—all this is hidden*

150.36 *for the present,* corr. on CP to *for the time,*

Chapter XIII MS and one set of CP, which is clearly CP2, with CP1 missing

150.39 *we seemed to me to make* corr. on CP to *we seemed to make*

151.11–12 *engendered in him* corr. on CP to *engendered or confirmed in him*

151.30 *varied his education* corr. on CP to *enlarged his education*

151.30–31 *forgetting the accomplishment.* corr. on CP to *forgetting how to do it.*

151.37–38 *classic Rome made* corr. on CP to *classic Rome or Greece made*

152.9 *He had chosen* corr. on CP to *He said he had chosen*

152.9 *his profession, and there was nothing more to be said about it. The more* corr. on CP to *his profession, and the more*

152.10 *was clear, and that the art* corr. on CP to *was clear; the art*

152.17 *was a special case.* corr. on CP to *was a solitary case.*

152.37 *cried Mr. Boythorn.* corr. on CP to *cried Mr. Boythorn, firmly.*

153.3–4 *the acceptance of their clerks,* corr. on CP to *the acceptance of clerks.*

153.15 MS–L: *expired; and as he still* CD: *expired; and he still*

153.32 MS: *his youth has been passed,* CP [n.c.]–CD: *his youth had been passed,* [*has* restored as required by context]

153.35 CP: *more eminently poetical field* corr. to *more eminently practical field* [as in MS]

155.10 MS: *a general limpness and feebleness* CP–CD: *a general feebleness*
155.28 MS: *expence*
156.5 MS: *against the post looking up, and evidently* CP–CD: *against the post, and evidently*
156.40–41 MS: *has had three husbands?"* CP–CD: *has had two former husbands?"*
157.42 MS: *Swosser was.* CP–CD: *Swosser pre-eminently was.*
158.37 MS: *where he fell—where he fell raked* CP–CD: *where he fell—raked*
159.5 MS–L: *both of whom seemed to have* CD: *both of whom seem to have*
159.22 MS: *cried Ada.* CP–CD: *murmured Ada.*
159.26–33 MS has only: *"O Esther you would never guess! It's about my cousin Richard!"*
159.42 MS: *with a fresh burst* CP–CD: *with a burst*
160.1–2 MS: *and laugh, and cry again, was so* CP–CD: *and laugh, was so*
160.6–14 between *I don't know how long!"* and *"No?" said I.* MS had only: *"But that's not the worst of it, Esther dear!" cried Ada, trembling, holding me tighter, and laying down her head again upon my breast.* CP–CD: p.t.
160.15 MS: *not even then that!"* CP–CD: *not even that!"*
160.40–41 MS: *a little while—indeed I enjoyed it very much, myself—and then* CP–CD: p.t.
160.45 MS: *their duty with each other,* CP–CD: *their duty to each other,*
161.4 MS: *all sorts of sensible names,* CP–CD: *all sorts of endearing and sensible names,*
161.14 MS–53: *secresy* C–CD: *secrecy* [em.ad.]
161.15 MS: *What is it, housekeeper?"* CP–CD: *what is it, Esther?"*
161.16–17 MS–L: *when we first came* CD: *when first we came*
161.20–23 MS: *that I did so. "Because," said I, "Ada and Richard* CP–CD: p.t.
161.28 MS: *"The deuce you did, Mrs. Shipton!"* CP–CD: *"The deuce you did!"*
161.35–36 MS: *relations between us which* CP–CD: *relations between us four which*
161.40 MS: *reasons making it desirable.* CP–CD: *reasons to make it desirable.*
162.2 MS: *a chain of iron.* CP–CD: *a chain of lead.*
162.4 MS: *three or four years hence,* CP–CD: *a few years hence,*
162.27–28 MS: *the abilities of all the great men ever on the earth, you could do* CP–CD: *the abilities of all the great men, past and present, you could do*
162.29 MS: *without thoroughly meaning it,* CP–CD: *without sincerely meaning it,*
162.31–32 MS: *from Fortune carelessly, or by fits* CP–CD: *from Fortune by fits*
162.39 MS: *make her miserable—* CP–CD: *make her unhappy—*
162.42 MS: *Love her truly, Rick,* CP–CD: *Love her, Rick,*
163.1 MS: *all* must *go ill.* CP–CD: *all will go ill.*
163.2 MS: *better go out for a walk."* CP–CD: *better take a walk."*
163.19 MS: *"He may gain,* CP–CD: *"Rick may gain,*
163.20 MS: *Mr. Jarndyce.* CP–CD: *Mr. Jarndyce, shaking his head.*
163.21–22 MS: *and counsellor.* CP–CD: *and counsellor always near.*
163.29–31 MS: *what Esther never will,—that there is a little woman of the name of Esther to be held in remembrance above all other little women!"* CP–CD: *what Esther never will,—that the little woman is to be held in remembrance above all other people!"*
163.31–32 between *all other people!"* and *I have omitted* CP has a blank line [no blank line in MS or 53–CD]
163.34 MS: *—a surgeon.* CP–CD: *—a young surgeon.*
163.35 MS: *thought him sensible* CP–CD: *thought him very sensible*

Chapter XIV MS and one set of CP, presumably CP2; missing: CP1 (8 substantive divergences between MS and CP2) and CP3 (40 substantive divergences between CP2 and 53)

163.38–39 *to my charge with all the fervent words that his love for her, and his trust in me inspired.* corr. on CP to *to my charge with great love for her, and great trust in me.*
164.1 MS–L: *was to write to Richard* CD: *was to write Richard*
164.8 *"And if the Chancery suit* corr. on CP to *"And if the suit*
164.11 MS–53: *asked Richard, pausing, "why* C–L: *asked Richard pausing, "why* CD: *asked Richard, "why*
164.18 MS–CP [n.c.]: *it goes on, sweet cousin,* 53–CD: *it goes on, dear cousin,*
164.24 *"We know Chancery better* corr. on CP to *"We know it better*
164.26 *It is, by solemn* corr. on CP to *The Court is, by solemn*
164.31 MS–CP [n.c.]: *We consign the suit to* 53–CD: *We consign the whole thing to*
164.38–39 *as would fortify the great wall* corr. on CP to *as would man the great wall*
164.43–44 MS–CP [n.c.]: *somewhere, to a large African tea-drinking, in the West of England, and had* 53–CD: *somewhere, to a tea-drinking, and had*
164.44 MS–CP [n.c.]: *For, besides the* 53–CD: *Besides the*
164.44–165.2 MS–CP [n.c.]: *there was to be a Conference, and after the Conference Mrs. Jellyby was to travel to certain places to stimulate certain people who were flagging a little, as to the pecuniary part of the great Borrioboolan question.*

All this involved, 53–CD: p.t. *[there was to be some considerable . . . of Borrioboola Gha. All this involved,]*

165.3–4 MS–CP [n.c.]: *part in the excursion* 53–CD: *part in the proceedings*

165.7–8 MS–CP [n.c.]: *after breakfast, to enrol some Borrioboolan candidates attached to the East London Branch* 53–CD: *after breakfast, on some Borrioboolan business, arising out of a society called the East London Branch*

165.26 MS–CP [n.c.]: *the little boxing-gloves of* 53–CD: *the little gloves of*

165.35 *very much improved* corr. on CP to *unaccountably improved*

165.39 MS: *at us, in a way that we could not but pity.* CP–CD: *at us.*

166.13 MS–CP [n.c.]: *—a man and a brother!"* 53–CD: *—man and a brother!"*

167.3–4 MS–CP [n.c.]: *if he could, when every tradesman sends in any stuff he likes,* 53–CD: *if he could. When all our tradesmen send into our house any stuff they like.*

167.7 *If I was Pa,* corr. on CP to *I declare if I was Pa,*

167.19 *I won't be an African slave* corr. on CP to *I won't be a slave*

167.25 *how much bitterly* corr. on CP to *how much of bitterly*

167.33 MS–CP [n.c.]: *another, divining that there was something more to come.* 53–CD: *another, foreseeing something more.*

168.4 MS–CP [n.c.]: *and cried so over* 53–CD: *and cried so much over*

168.8–9 MS–L: *his place in my lap,* CD: *his place on my lap,*

168.13 MS–L: *were not yet equal to* CD: *were not equal to*

168.14–15 *by the leg,* corr. on CP to *by one leg.*

168.21–22 *wasn't in sight, and put it off, and kept me at the desk; but I was* corr. on CP to *wasn't in sight; but I was*

168.31–32 MS–CP [n.c.]: *she retorted," but I am* 53–CD: *she retorted a little anxiously, "but I am*

168.43 *the unfortunate child* corr. on CP to *the afflicted child*

168.44 MS–CP [n.c.]: *with a dismal noise.* 53–CD: *with a very low-spirited noise.*

169.14 *for his Deportment. He used to teach it."* corr. on CP to *for his Deportment."*

169.15 *"What does he teach now?"* corr. on CP to *"What does he teach?"* 53–CD: *"Does he teach?"*

169.16 *in particular, now,"* corr. on CP to *in particular,"*

169.22 MS–CP [n.c.]: *and frequently* 53–CD: *and that she frequently*

169.24 MS–CP [n.c.]: *few minutes, and Miss Flite, of course, was always present. "I go there,* 53–CD: *few minutes. "I go there,*

169.34 MS–CP [n.c.]: *—I am sure,* 53–CD: *—at least, I am sure,*

170.16–17 *looking rather rakish* corr. on CP to *looking rakish*

170.43 MS: *to fear," that with timid* CP–CD: *to fear," with timid*

171.23–24 MS: *of white gloves in his hand, with which* CP–CD: *of white gloves, with which*

171.28–29 MS–L: *he was like nothing in the world but* CD: *he was not like anything in the world but* [em. ad.]

171.32 MS: *And really, as he bowed* CP–CD: *As he bowed*

171.34 MS: *with a most affecting* CP: *with the most affecting* corr. to *with quite an affecting*

171.38–39 *"Go on!"* corr. on CP to *"Go on, my son!"*

171.43 MS: *breath he could command,* CP–CD: *breath he could spare,*

171.45–173.1 MS: *His illustrious father* CP–CD: *His distinguished father*

173.9 MS–CP [n.c.]: *—even shabby,* 53–CD: *—almost shabby.*

173.12 MS–CP [n.c.]: *concerning this distinguished person.* 53–CD: *concerning this person.*

173.18 MS–CP [n.c.]: *inquisitive, I have no doubt. The old lady,* 53–CD: *inquisitive. The old lady,*

173.26 MS: *to his fame.* (?) CP: *to his fancy.* corr. to *to his position.*

173.29 *and idle resort;* corr. on CP to *and lounging resort;*

173.30 *lead a lounging life* corr. on CP to *lead an idle life*

173.31 MS–CP [n.c.]: *For this,* 53–CD: *To enable him to do this,*

173.33 *labored on to that hour,* corr. on CP to *labored on that hour,* [an obvious—though very unusual—mistake made by D on CP] 53: *labored to that hour,*

174.7 *being amused by all this, though* corr. on CP to *being amused, though*

174.27 MS–CP [n.c.]: *on the sofa.* 53–CD: *on the sofa. And really he did look very like it.*

174.29 CP: *gently flattening his fingers.* corr. to *gently fluttering his fingers.* [as in MS (?)]

174.34 *"Are we not?"* corr. on CP to *"Are we not, sir?"*

174.37 *develops vulgarity most confoundedly.* corr. on CP to *develops vulgarity.* [MS had *con-foundedly.]*

174.38 MS–CP [n.c.]: *partiality, but I am not a bad witness.* 53–CD: *partiality.*

174.40 MS–CP [n.c.]: *Prince Regent once did me* 53–CD: *Prince Regent did me*

175.25 *his cravat. "My Son!"* corr. on CP to *his cravat.*

176.10–11 *I think, in the Opera* corr. on CP to *I think, at the French house, in the Opera*

176.20–21 *of his simple, cheerful, almost childish* corr. on CP to *of his childish* 53–CD: *of his almost childish*

176.24–25 *that really made me almost as irate with his father as* corr. on CP to *that made me scarcely less irate with his father than*

176.25 MS–CP [n.c.]: *old lady herself.* 53–CD: *old lady.*

177.1 MS–53: *with the best intentions,"* C–CD: *with the best intention,"*

177.38–39 MS–CP [n.c.]: *through them if we can."* 53–CD: *through them."*
178.4 MS–CP [n.c.]: *Miss Flite had so secretly* 53–CD: *Miss Flite had secretly*
178.7 *and even fear.* corr. on CP to *and even dread.*
178.12 MS–CP [n.c.]: *while a gentleman* 53–CD: *while a medical gentleman*
178.37 MS–53: *in a grave kind voice,* C–CD: *in a grave kind of voice,*
178.40 MS: *occurence*
179.5 *a compassionate smile,* corr. on CP to *an observant smile,*
179.23 *smiled mildly at me* corr. on CP to *smiled at me*
180.10–11 *Might I take* corr. on CP to *Mightn't I take*
180.17 *as soon go elsewhere."* corr. on CP to *sooner go somewhere else."*
180.36 *by my very noble* corr. on CP to *by my noble*
180.41 *—which it never will—* corr. on CP to *—which it won't—*
180.41 *never been in Chancery* corr. on CP to *never been caged*
181.2 *"it's there* corr. on CP to *"I think it's there*
181.8 MS–CP [n.c.]: *linked to him, hand to hand, he could* 53–CD: *linked to him, he could*
181.12 MS–CP [n.c.]: *sometimes held him back,* 53–CD: *sometimes detained him,*
181.19 MS–CP [n.c.]: *was extraordinary.* 53–CD: *was incessant.*
181.21 MS–CP [n.c.]: *looked back constantly.* 53–CD: *looked back.*
181.22–23 MS–CP [n.c.]: *open mouth, and* 53–CD: *open mouth, with a curious expression of a sense of power, and*
181.23–24 MS: *screwing up his eyes,* CP–CD: *turning up his eyes,*
181.25 MS–CP [n.c.]: *of his face with an engrossing interest.* 53–CD: *of his face.*
182.26 MS–CP [n.c.]: *Or, that my Guardian invited* 53–CD: *Or, that Mr. Jarndyce invited*

Chapter XV MS and one set of CP, presumably CP2; missing: CP1 (3 divergences between MS and CP), CP3 (37 divergences between CP and 53)

182.32 MS–CP [n.c.]: *my Guardian was* 53–CD: *Mr. Jarndyce was*
183.1 *power of admiration.* corr. on CP to *power of indiscriminate admiration.*
183.5 MS: *devotion. But I soon* CP–CD: *devotion. I soon*
184.12 *bilious, and he had* corr. on CP to *bilious, and therefore he had*
184.42 MS–CP [n.c.]: *amazed at the question,* 53–CD: *amazed by the question,*
185.13 MS–CP [n.c.]: *"Too boisterous,* 53–CD: *"A little too boisterous,*
185.15 MS–CP [n.c.]: *But a sledge-hammering* 53–CD: *But, I grant a sledge-hammering*
185.26 *angels to help him:* corr. on CP to *angels to guard him:*
185.40–41 *in possession, he calls it.* corr. on CP to *in possession, I think he calls it.*
186.4 MS–L: *"That Coavinses* CD: *"The Coavinses*
186.12–13 MS–CP [n.c.]: *upon the notes* 53–CD: *upon the keys*
186.21 MS–CP [n.c.]: *or our want* 53–CD: *or by our want*
186.31–32 *so new and refreshing,* corr. on CP to *so new and so refreshing,*
186.35 *which he said was* corr. on CP to *which he called*
186.43 *said the boy. "There was."* corr. on CP to *said the boy. "Well?"*
187.15–16 *shop, and in it a* corr. on CP to *shop. In it, was a*
187.19–20 MS–L: *opposite the top of the stairs."* CD: *opposite the stairs."*
187.20 MS–L: *handed me a key* CD: *handed me the key*
187.34 MS–CP [n.c.]: *abruptly and even fiercely.* 53–CD: *abruptly and fiercely.*
187.36 *and great prominent eyes.* corr. on CP to *and prominent eyes.*
188.13 MS–CP [n.c.]: *limp nankeen bonnet* 53–CD: *limp bonnet*
188.16 *a washing, mum,"* corr. on CP to *a washing,"*
188.29 MS–CP [n.c.]: *all the haste she could upstairs.* 53–CD: *all the haste she could.*
189.4 *and tenderly.* corr. on CP to *and mournfully.*
190.7 *saw the silent tears* corr. on CP to *saw two silent tears*
190.14 MS–CP [n.c.]: *"O, it's not much* 53–CD: *"It's not much*
190.26 CP: *he was a dying then!—"* corr. to *he was a lying there—"* [*a* not canc.] 53–CD: *he was lying there—"*
190.31 MS–L: *but a follerer.* CD: *but a follower.*
190.34 MS–CP [n.c.]: *It wasn't liked by* 53–CD: *It wasn't approved by*
190.40 MS–CP [n.c.]: *I was in doubts of doing right.* 53–CD: *I was in doubts.*
191.3–4 MS–CP [n.c.]: *gave his consent gruffly—* 53–CD: *gave his consent gruff—*
191.32 MS: *over the groupe,* CP–CD: *over the group,*
191.35 MS–CP [n.c.]: *noticed this, and* 53–CD: *noticed it, and*
192.2 *anything of the Courts* corr. on CP to *anything of Courts*
192.5–6 *his wrath. "I beg* corr. on CP to *his wrath." If so, I beg*
192.21 *should go down right mad!* corr. on CP to *be driven mad!*
192.22 MS–CP [n.c.]: *by revenging of them* 53–CD: *by revenging them*
192.37 MS: *three hundred pound* CP–CD: *three hundred pounds*
192.43 MS–CP [n.c.]: *three hundred pound* 53–CD: *three hundred pounds*
192.44 MS–CP [n.c.]: *that question, I was* 53–CD: *that question, my brother filing a bill, I was*
193.1–2 MS: *made defendants* CP [n.c.]: *made dependants* 53–CD: *made defendants*
193.6 MS–CP [n.c.]: *—mind you, there were* 53–CD: *—remember, there were*

193.7 MS–CP [n.c.]: *seventeen!—but* 53–CD: *seventeen as yet!—but*
193.13 MS–CP [n.c.]: *I stand, this day!** and at bottom of same page **Nothing thus stated in these* [*passages* corr. to] *pages of the Court of Chancery is imaginary. This is an actual case.* 53–CD: *I stand, this day!* [no footnote]
193.22 *"It's the system!* corr. on CP to *"The system!*
193.26–27 *It's the system.* corr. on CP to *He sits there to administer the system.*
193.31 MS–CP [n.c.]: *out of some one for my money,* 53–CD: *out of some one for my ruin,*
193.34–35 MS–CP [n.c.]: *of that system, face* 53–CD: *of that system against me, face*
193.36 MS–CP [n.c.]: *was quite fearful.* 53–CD: *was fearful.*
193.38 *"I have!"* corr. on CP to *"I have done!"*
193.42–43 *and sometimes go* corr. on CP to *and sometimes I go* 53–CD: *and I sometimes go*
193.43–44 MS–CP [n.c.]: *though it's amusing,* 53–CD: *though they have found it amusing,*
193.45 MS–CP [n.c.]: *and all that—it's the next best thing to a play.* 53–CD: *and all that.*
194.5 MS–CP [n.c.]: *could hold my brains* 53–CD: *could hold my wits*
194.10–11 MS–CP [n.c.]: *and it is the past that drives me* 53–CD: *and the past drives me*
194.11 MS: *fiercely out once more,* CP–CD: *fiercely out,*
194.15–16 *many a time.* corr. on CP to *many and many a time.*
194.33 *Mr. Skimpole then began* corr. on CP to *Upon that, Mr. Skimpole began*
195.3–4 MS–CP [n.c.]: *politician, attacking his opponents in the most reckless manner, but,* 53–CD: *politician, dealing in all sorts of parliamentary rhetoric; but,*
195.6 *was the worse,* corr. on CP to *was much the worse,*
195.9 MS–CP [n.c.]: *illustrated the same thing!* 53–CD: *illustrated the same principle!*
195.12 *If he had been* corr. on CP to *There had been times when, if he had been*
195.18 MS: *ennabling*
195.25–26 MS–CP [n.c.]: *beside the graver childhood* 53–CD: *by the side of the graver childhood*
195.26–27 MS–CP [n.c.]: *made my Guardian a smile* 53–CD: *made my Guardian smile*

Chapter XVI MS and one set of CP, presumably a late set (CP2?) uncorrected; missing: CP1 (25 divergences between MS and CP) and CP3(?)

196.29–30 MS: *shining in, adown the long* CP–CD: *shining in, down the long*
197.7 MS: *of his acquaintance accustomed* CP–CD: *of his acquaintance also accustomed*
197.14 MS: *that distinct* (?) *ray of light* CP–CD: *that distant ray of light*
197.15 MS: *the churchyard step, because the dead man had been "wery good to me"?* CP–CD: *the churchyard step?*
197.20 MS: *his mental condition, usually, when asked* CP–CD: *his mental condition, when asked*
197.27 MS: *avoided of all decent people;* CP–CD: *avoided by all decent people;*
198.7 MS: *plaintiff or defendant; or whether* CP–CD: *plaintiff or defendant in Jarndyce and Jarndyce; or whether*
198.18 MS: *people read as they ride by, and to see* CP–CD: *people read, and to see*
198.41 MS: *His way lying by Lincoln's Inn Fields,* CP–CD: *His way lying through many streets,*
199.18–19 MS: *up and down Holborn,* CP–CD: *up and down the street,*
199.23 MS: *mouthfulls*
199.30–31 MS: *in a very few years they will lose* CP–CD: *in a very few years they will so degenerate that they will lose*
199.39 MS: *to close in: wet, dirty, and dejected.* CP–CD: *to close in.*
199.43 MS: *ill-condition fellow* CP–CD: *ill-conditioned fellow*
200.3–4 MS–53: *for such no-reason,* C–CD: *for such no reason,* [hyphen restored, as clearly intended by D, and making sentence less obscure]
200.4–5 MS: *pointing there? So he don't.* CP–CD: *pointing there? So he does not look out of window.*
200.22 MS: *plys* CP–CD: *plies*
200.27–28 MS–53: *she asks behind her veil.* C–CD: *she asked behind her veil.*
200.29 MS: *staring at the veil,* CP–CD: *staring moodily at the veil,*
200.32 MS: *nothink about no Ink—where* CP–CD: *nothink about no—where*
200.40 MS: *Did he looked.*
201.4–5 MS: *he has got at that suspicion.* CP–CD: *he has got at the suspicion of her being a lady.*
201.16 MS: *"Now, go before* CP–CD: *"Go before*
201.22 MS–L: *"I am fly,"* CD: *"I'm fly,"*
201.24 MS–CP [n.c.]: *recoiling from him as if he were a noxious animal.* 53–CD: *recoiling from him.*
201.26 MS: *Go on!* CP–CD: *Go on before!*
202.5 MS–53: *sticking to the terms imposed* C–CD: *sticking to the forms imposed*
202.14 MS: *if the gate wos open.* CP–CD: *if the gate was open.* [MS reading restored as likely to have been inadvertently overlooked]
202.16–17 MS: *he goes! Into the* CP–CD: *he goes! Ho! Into the*
204.1 MS: *yellow—that it is gold.* CP–CD: *yellow—gold.*
204.9 MS: *and three balls.* CP–CD: *and three or four balls.*

204.14 MS: *to stay on the other side* CP–CD: *to try the other side*
204.17 MS: *more distinct!"* CP–CD: *more distinct than it is to-night!"*

Chapter XVII MS and two sets of CP, presumably CP1 and CP2; 3 divergences between CP2 and 53 may imply existence of CP3, missing

204.25 *as it addressed* corr. on CP1 to *as it had addressed*
204.30 MS–L: *They were great qualities* CD: *They were good qualities*
204.35 *these opinions, in my prosing little way, not because* corr. on CP1 to *these opinions, not because*
204.40 *the incalculable uncertainties* corr. on CP1 to *the uncertainties*
205.2 MS–CP2 [n.c.]: *came to see us one afternoon,* 53–CD: *coming one afternoon,*
205.17–18 MS–53: *"you'll excuse my calling* C–CD: *"you'll excuse me calling*
205.30 *I can assure you.* corr. on CP1 to *I assure you.*
206.22–23 *not that interest* corr. on CP1 to *not that positive interest*
206.26 MS–53: *who take to it from* C–CD: *who take it from*
206.39 *is that—in short, it is* corr. on CP1 to *is—in short, is*
208.11–12 *I think Richard right."* corr. on CP1 to *I think Richard is right."*
208.24 MS: *proceededed,*
208.41 MS–L: *how much more so did it* CD: *how much more did it*
209.32 *worth while, but* corr. on CP1 to *worth while to undo what had been done, but*
209.32–33 *must be done.* corr. on CP1 to *must be undone.*
210.14 *our saying over again,* corr. on CP1 to *our saying again,*
210.26 *impatient and headlong kind,* corr. on CP1 to *impatient and fitful kind,*
210.38 MS: *should mistaken* CP–CD: *should be mistaken*
211.8 *I swear," he added, pinching her cheek.* corr. on CP1 to *I swear!"*
211.27–28 *which followed it* corr. on CP1 to *which now followed it*
211.43–212.1 *in the glass, crying.* corr. on CP1 to *in the glass, almost crying.*
212.2 MS: *to make you happy, you ungrateful heart!"* CP1: *to make happy your ungrateful heart!"* corr. to *to make happy, you ungrateful heart!"* CP2: CP1 text corr. to *to make you happy, ungrateful heart!"* 53–CD: *to make you happy, you ungrateful heart!"*
212.8–9 *in that work—it was quite a sum—and I resolved* corr. on CP1 to *in that work, and I resolved*
212.11 *left some worsted* corr. on CP1 to *left some silk*
212.40 *that* I *could readily understand!"* corr. on CP1 to *that* I *could understand!"*
213.20 *to him alone I owed* corr. on CP1 to *to him I owed*
213.25 *from a maiden lady living* corr. on CP1 to *from a lady living*
213.30 *a girl then twelve* corr. on CP1 to *an orphan girl then twelve*
213.40 *the terrible religion* corr. on CP1 to *the distorted religion*
213.41 *of the dread need there was* corr. on CP1 to *of the need there was*
214.4 MS: *Mr. Kenge. To him, the lady said,* CP–CD: *Mr. Kenge. The lady said,* [MS reading restored as likely to have been inadvertently overlooked]
214.10 *I kissed his hand again and held it for a little while.* corr. on CP1 to *I held his hand for a little while in mine.*
214.17 *I saw his former* corr. on CP1 to *At the word Father, I saw his former*
214.18–19 *but it passed across him, and so swiftly* corr. on CP1 to *but it had been there, and it had come so swiftly*
214.20 *given hin some shock.* corr. on CP1 to *given him a shock.*
214.43 *hoped to fight through* corr. on CP1 to *hoped to contend through*
215.13 CP1: *Crumlinwalliniver* corr. to *Crumlinwallinwer* [as in MS]
215.15 CP: *Mewlinnwallinwodd.* corr. to *Mewlinnwillinwodd.* [as in MS]
215.19 *She admonished him that* corr. on CP1 to *She told him that*
215.27–28 *he was too considerate of her to let her see* corr. on CP2 to *he was too considerate to let her see*
215.29 *to make his acknowledgments* corr. on CP1 to *to making his acknowledgments*
215.30–31 *happy hours—I remember that he called them* corr. on CP1 to *happy hours—he called them*
216.8–11 MS: *two lovers!"* see back* and next three lines *["What? . . . her cheek.]* written on separate slip pasted on to back of MS page
216.13 MS: *her affianced would be* CP–CD: *Prince would be*
216.17 *put them in my breast.* corr. on CP1 to *put them in my dress.*
216.27 *left them on purpose!"* corr. on CP1 to *left them on purpose!"*
216.27–28 between *on purpose!"* and *"Do they look* MS has: *(a white line here)*
216.31 CP2 is followed by another set of proofs for this chapter with *Go through very carefully* written, not in D's hand (?) at the top of p. 161, but not corr.

Chapter XVIII MS and two sets of CP; presumably no missing link

216 chapter-heading ins. on CP1 [but is in MS]
217.4 *These vacillations* corr. on CP1 to *His vacillations*
217.7 *he took considerable credit* corr. on CP1 to *he took great credit*
217.13 MS–53: *to sticking in the east;* C–CD: *to stick in the east;*
217.34 *neat waistcoat or two* corr. on CP1 to *neat waistcoat and buttons*
218.3 *down there yet by any means!"* corr. on CP1 to *down there yet!"*
218.7 MS–L: *as often as* CD: *so often as*

218.9 MS: *unncessary*
219.8 *"Good," said I,* corr. on CP1 to *"Very well," said I,*
219.14–15 *Eastern in it—* corr. on CP1 to *Eastern about it—*
219.19 *you are a man* corr. on CP1 to *you say you are a man*
219.34 *full of wild roses,* corr. on CP1 to *full of wild flowers,*
220.3 *with great alacrity, as we drove up.* corr. on CP1 to *with great alacrity.*
220.11 *Six-and-twenty minutes!"* corr. on CP1 to *Twenty-six minutes!"*
220.24 CP1: *or horse's useless foot of mine,* corr. to *or horse's foot of mine,* [MS not clear]
221.31 *gambolled swiftly,* corr. on CP1 to *travelled swiftly,*
222.2 *rested all around it.* corr. on CP1 to *rested on all around it.* then on CP2 to *rested all around it.* thus in 53–L CD: *rested on all around it.*
222.10 *a young man sitting* corr. on CP1 to *a young gentleman sitting*
222.30–31 *venerable red wall* corr. on CP1 to *venerable wall*
222.33 *like a green cloister,* corr. on CP1 to *like green cloisters,* [MS had *like a green cloisters,*]
223.3 *and a scrap of list* corr. on CP1 to *and scrap of list*
223.4–5 MS–L: *it was easier to fancy that . . . than that they had* CD: *it was easy to fancy that . . . and that they had*
223.13 *to ring a bell* corr. on CP1 to *to ring a large bell*
224.3 *already in their seats in the chancel,* corr. on CP1 to *already in their seats,*
224.4 *stately footmen (ridiculously out of keeping with the place),* corr. on CP1 to *stately footmen;*
224.7 at the top of p. 177 of CP1 *1, July 14* is written in left-hand corner
224.18 *glance round the church,* corr. on CP1 to *glance over the church,*
224.21 *faces round me* corr. on CP1 to *faces around me*
224.24 *ringer with one foot in a stirrup was working* corr. on CP1 to *ringer was working*
224.24 *inestimably bright and precious,* corr. on CP1 to *inestimably bright.*
224.32,33 *Can I ever forget* corr. on CP1 to *Shall I ever forget*
225.8 *met her beautiful eyes;* corr. on CP1 to *met her eyes;*
225.26–27 *agitation of mind, that I* corr. on CP1 to *agitation, that I*
225.38 MS–L: *much state and gallantry* CD: *much taste and gallantry*
225.42–43 *great delight),* corr. on CP1 to *infinite delight),*
226.12–13 MS: *with-hold*
226.18–19 *my points outwards.* corr. on CP1 to *my points outward.*
226.19–20 *my silver lining to the moon like Milton's* corr. on CP1 to *my silver lining outward like Milton's*
226.22 *"Suppose you went down* corr. on CP2 to *"But suppose you went down*
226.23–24 *or of this fellow, as we started from Sir Leicester. How then?"* corr. on CP2 to *or of this fellow—How then?"*
226.39–40 *as principle, Harold* corr. on CP1 to *as principle, Mr. Harold*
227.5 *and lay no claim* corr. on CP1 *and I lay no claim*
227.5 *and don't want* corr. on CP1 to *and I don't want*
227.17 *or singing scraps* corr. on CP1 to *or to singing scraps*
227.25–26 MS: *Mercenary creatures may ask,* CP1–CD: *Mercenary creatures ask,* [MS reading restored as likely to have been inadvertently overlooked]
228.10 *we heard it thunder in* corr. on CP1 to *we heard thunder muttering in*
228.21 *this lodge in a deep* corr. on CP1 to *this lodge standing in a deep*
228.38 *said Ada.* corr. on CP1 to *said Ada, quietly.*
229.4 *It was not fright.* corr. on CP1 to *No. It was not fright.*
230.21–22 between *could not be helped."* and *Lady Dedlock again sat* following passage canc. on CP1: *Did you know her, afterwards?"/ He shook his head./ "You never met her?"/ "Never."/ You are, of course, aware that she is dead?"/ "Yes," he said, "I heard of it some time ago. She lived so retired, that I heard of it by mere accident."*
230.22–23 *The storm had by this time passed upon* corr. on CP1 to *The storm soon began to pass*
230.23 *The shower had greatly abated,* corr. on CP1 to *The shower greatly abated,*
230.23–24 *the lightning had ceased,* corr. on CP1 to *the lightning ceased,*
231.2–3 *his offered arm,* corr. on CP1 to *his proffered arm,*
231.15–16 *deliberately after it through the wet grass.* corr. on CP1 to *deliberately in the same direction, through the wettest of the wet grass.*
231.17 *"Is the woman mad?"* corr. on CP1 to *"Is that young woman mad?"*
231.32 *but singing strongly,* corr. on CP1 to *but singing sweetly,* then correction canc.
231.34 *carriage made of burnished silver.* corr. on CP1 to *carriage made of silver.*
231.35 *a peaceful figure in the* corr. on CP1 to *a peaceful figure too in the*

Chapter XIX MS and one complete set of CP CP2 plus 2 pages of beginning of another set CP1; the few trifling divergences between MS and CP and between CP and 53 do not conclusively point to existence of any missing CP

231.39 MS: *brazened-face, and not* CP–53: *brazened-faced, and not* C–CD: *brazen-faced, and not*
232.21 MS–53: *could only see him now!* C–CD: *could see him now!*
232.38–233.1 MS: *a French watering-place.* see back* following sentence *(The learned . . . six weeks.)* written on back of MS page

233.1–2 *the natural heat of his more than auburn whiskers and his gingery complexion* corr. on CP to *the natural heat of his gingery complexion*
233.11 *If such a shipwrecked member of the bar* corr. on CP to *If such a lonely member of the bar*
233.21 MS–53: *All the blind mens dogs* C–CD: *All the blind men's dogs* [em.ad.]
233.38 after *of the most fastidious mind.* CP1 stops and CP2 takes over; what served as CP1 for beginning of this chapter was the continuation of the set used as CP1 for ch. XVIII; most of the corrections are made on continuation of what served as CP2 for ch. XVIII; in first two pages of this CP2 the two corrections of CP1 have been made but there are no further corrections
234.3 *He has leisure for more musing* corr. on CP to *He has more leisure for musing*
234.5 *and says to the two* corr. on CP to *and he says to the two*
234.5–6 *in such weather* corr. on CP to *in such hot weather*
234.17 *nothing so very particular* corr. on CP to *nothing so very remarkable*
234.18–19 *to render his volunteering at all necessary;* corr. on CP to *to render his volunteering, on his own account, at all incumbent on his conscience;*
234.20–21 *by this vessel,* corr. on CP to *by the vessel,*
234.26 *who she knows is endowed* corr. on CP to *whom she knows to be endowed*
235.23–24 CP: *I meantersay,* corr. to *Imeantersay,* [as in MS]
235.28 *severe-looking woman, of whom the eye or ear of this history seems to have some previous knowledge.* corr. on CP to *severe-looking, silent woman.*
236.13–14,18,23 MS–53: *thousing seven hunderd and* C–CD: *thousing seven hundred and*
236.22 *Speak, child!"* corr. on CP to *Speak, maiden!"*
236.29 CP: *to give a shilling in indignation,* corr. to *to grow shrill in indignation,* [as in MS]
237.1 MS: *stalks to the tea-table,* CP–CD: *stalks to the table,*
237.14 *we are called upon to walk?* corr. on CP to *we are calculated to walk?*
237.26 *Chadband's being able to pile verbose flights* corr. on CP to *Chadband's piling verbose flights*
237.32 MS–L: *at Mrs. Snagsby's table,* CD: *at Mr. Snagsby's table,*
238.2–3 MS–53: *at this period of* C–CD: *at which period of*
238.22 *"O my eyes!* corr. on CP to *"O my eye!*
238.26 *an impassive shake.* corr. on CP to *a passionless shake.*
238.30 *"O! Well! Really,* corr. on CP to *"Well! Really,*
238.32 *does seem the question.* corr. on CP to *does seem a question.*
238.34–239.2 at back of MS page there is an earlier tentative version of what follows: *is to move on."/ By this time, Mr. and Mrs. Chadband, and Mrs. Snagsby, hearing the altercation, have come down the stairs, while Guster has come up stairs*
238.40–41 end of this paragraph *(You are by no means . . . Move on!")* ins. on CP
239.11 *Pray have patience,* corr. on CP to *Pray have a moment's patience,*
239.40 *I am, sir,* corr. on CP to *I am indeed, sir,*
239.44 MS: *Mr. Sangsby,* CP: *Mr. Snagsby,* corr. to *Mr. Sangsby,* thus in 53 C–CD: *Mr. Snagsby,*
240.23 *you really must move on,"* corr. on CP to *you really must do it,"*
241.7–9 *Mrs. Snagsby feels that it lifts them higher in* corr. on CP to *Mrs. Snagsby feels, not only that it gratifies her inquisitive disposition, but that it lifts her husband's establishment higher in*
241.12–13 MS–CP [n.c.]: *cobler's-wax,* 53–CD: *cobbler's-wax,*
241.17 MS–CP [n.c.]: *"Oh! For years!"* 53–CD: *"For years!"*
241.18–19 *Mrs. Snagsby explains* corr. on CP to *Mrs. Snagsby triumphantly explains*
241.36 *or a gentleman of your* corr. on CP to *or was it a gentleman of your*
241.37 *come to it in time.* corr. on CP to *come to it presently.*
241.39 *"Oh! A child, then!"* corr. on CP to *"Oh! A child!"*
241.40 *the regular professional eye* corr. on CP to *the regular acute professional eye*
242.6 MS: *no Missing of the girl* CP–CD: *no Miss-ing of the girl*
242.14–15 *and rises.* corr. on CP to *and rises, with a smoking head, which he dabs at with his pocket-handkerchief.*
242.36 *How glorious to be* corr. on CP to *O glorious to be*
243.1 *And do you now cool yourself* corr. on CP to *And do you cool yourself*
243.5–6 *Let us inquire."* corr. on CP to *Let us, in a spirit of love, inquire."*
243.11–12 MS: *folding itself up into its fat smile again,* CP–CD: *folding itself into its fat smile again* [*up* restored, because *again* refers back to 236.21, where *up* is used]
243.12 *smile again, "it is* corr. on CP to *smile again as he looks around, "it is*
243.43 *in his eyes, but the crowning* corr. on CP to *in his eyes, the crowning*

Chapter XX MS and one set of CP; the few trifling divergences between MS and CP are not enough to imply existence of missing earlier CP; there seems to have been unusual hurry in the setting of this chapter, or its end, MS being cut up into smaller fragments than was customary, these being distributed among a larger group of compositors

244 chapter-heading ins. on CP [is in MS,

but written with a different pen from rest of chapter]

244.22 MS: *off a lobster and lettuces,* CP–CD: *off a lobster and lettuce,*

244.25 *Mr. Guppy is a gentleman whose professional duty it is to be suspicious. He suspects* corr. on CP to *Mr. Guppy suspects*

244.33–34 *to Mr. Guppy to find the newcomer* corr. on CP to *to Mr. Guppy, therefore, to find the newcomer*

244.39 *Whether Young Smallweed was ever a boy* corr. on CP to *Whether Young Smallweed*

244.39–245.1 *called Chick Weed,* corr. on CP to *called Small, and eke Chick Weed,*

245.1 *as it were to express* corr. on CP to *as it were jocularly to express*

245.1–2 MS: *fledgling) was ever a boy is unknown in* CP: *fledgling) is unknown* corr. to *fledgling) was ever a boy is much doubted in*

245.3 *He is understood* corr. on CP to *He is facetiously understood*

245.10 *he is much patronized),* corr. on CP to *he is patronized),*

245.24 *and mortar, and the begrimed casements, Mr. Guppy* corr. on CP to *and mortar, Mr. Guppy*

245.38–39 *got one to spare," says Jobling, persuasively. "I want* corr. on CP to *got one to spare. I want*

246.25 *Which notification to all* corr. on CP to *This notification to all*

246.27–28 MS: *inform his patrons* CP–CD: *informs his patron*

247.2–3 CP: *a kind of fossil chip,* corr. to *a kind of fossil Imp,* [as in MS, but MS very difficult to read]

248.34–35 *"about pastry?"* corr. on CP to *"what would you recommend about pastry?"*

248.37 *archly.* corr. on CP to *with an arch look.*

248.38 MS–L: *Thank you, Guppy,* CD: *Thank you, Mr. Guppy,*

249.4–5 *—you don't mind Smallweed, I know!"* corr. on CP to *—you don't mind Smallweed?"*

249.8 *"Sir, you do me proud."* corr. on CP to *"Sir, to you!"*

249.30–31 *Mr. Guppy observes.* corr. on CP to *remonstrates Mr. Guppy.*

249.38 *"I had very confident* corr. on CP to *"I had confident*

250.2 *any new connexion,* corr. on CP to *any new professional connexion,*

250.4 MS: *when you have got any money?* CP–CD: *when you have got no money?*

250.9–10 *fashion and whiskers and horseflesh have been my three weaknesses,* corr. on CP to *fashion and whiskers have been my weaknesses,*

250.39 *Now, as it is Mr. Guppy's* corr. on CP to *As it is Mr. Guppy's*

250.41 MS: *the trenchant severity* CP: *the triumphant severity* corr. to *that trenchant severity*

250.43 *by both remaining silent.* corr. on CP to *by remaining silent.*

251.7 *"Now, gentlemen,"* corr. on CP to *"Now, gentlemen of the jury,"*

251.18 *examination-tone,* corr. on CP to *cross-examination-tone,*

251.32 *if you choose,* corr. on CP to *if you chose.*

251.32–33 MS–L: *I'll tell you another* CD: *I tell you another*

252.1–2 *heard me remark, on more than one occasion, that* corr. on CP to *heard me remark, that*

252.3 *"Rather!"* corr. on CP to *"A few!"*

252.12 MS: *a sort of a knowledge of him.* CP–CD: *a sort of knowledge of him* [MS reading restored as likely to have been inadvertently overlooked and agreeing with D's usual practice in similar contexts]

252.13 *everything else suits well."* corr. on CP to *everything else suits."*

252.28 *says with emotion,* corr. on CP to *says with feeling,* then correction canc.

252.31–32 *shake hands in a fervent manner, and Mr. Jobling adds,* corr. on CP to *shake hands, and Mr. Jobling adds in a feeling manner,*

252.37 *don't mind that, of course."* corr. on CP to *don't mind that?"*

252.43 *I dare say!" with other fragmentary grumblings to a similar purpose.* corr. on CP to *I dare say!"* [MS had *purport.*]

253.2 MS: *negociation* CP–CD: *negotiations*

253.8 *go and see him, Tony.* corr. on CP to *go and see him.*

253.14 CP: *and six heads* corr. to *and six breads* [as in MS]

253.16–17 *Half a sovereign, Polly,* corr. on CP to *Eight and six in half a sovereign, Polly,*

253.27 CP: *breathing stentoriously* corr. to *breathing stertorously* [as in MS]

253.38–39 *returns Jobling, "it'll last* corr. on CP to *returns Jobling, rather alarmed, "it'll last*

254.10 *He still sits,* corr. on CP to *The old man still sits,*

254.27–28 *says Krook.* corr. on CP to *says the suspicious Krook.*

254.29 *says Mr. Guppy.* corr. on CP to *Mr. Guppy explains.*

254.34 *"We found it so,"* corr. on CP to *"I assure you we found it so,"*

255.12 *name of Mr. Owen,* corr. on CP to *Mr. Manger,* (?) then to *Mr. Weevle,*

255.16 *see the room, sir?"* corr. on CP to *see the room, young man?"*

255.27 *Mr. Owen* corr. on CP to *Mr. Weevle* [same change made consistently through end of chapter, wherever the name occurs]

255.33 *he would gladly terminate* corr. on CP to *he would terminate*

256.10–11 *these magnificent works,* corr. on CP to *these magnificent portraits,*

256.11 *confined in a box* corr. on CP to *confined in a band-box*

256.13 *Beauty, though a strong family likeness may be observed in it, wears* corr. on CP to *Beauty wears*

256.13 *every variety of dress,* corr. on CP to *every variety of fancy-dress,*
256.15–16 *every variety of terrace-balustrade,* corr. on CP to *every variety of flower-pot and balustrade,*
256.22 *did the brilliant* corr. on CP to *accomplished the brilliant*
256.40 *is inclined to offer* corr. on CP to *is impelled to offer*

Chapter XXI MS and one set of CP, presumably CP1; no conclusive evidence of existence of earlier CP; CP2 missing

257 chapter-heading ins. on CP [not in MS]
257.9–10 *in an always solitary,* corr. on CP to *in a little narrow street, always solitary,*
257.10–11 *shady, grave bye-street, closely bricked in* corr. on CP to *shady, and sad, closely bricked in*
257.11–12 *of one old forest tree,* corr. on CP to *of an old forest tree,* [MS not clear]
257.16 *grandmother became weak* corr. on CP to *grandmother, now living, became weak*
257.17 *into what is called a childish state.* corr. on CP to *into a childish state.*
257.23–24 *as to his lower limbs;* corr. on CP to *as to his lower, and nearly so as to his upper, limbs;*
257.26–27 *In respect of imagination, wonder, and other such capacities,* corr. on CP to *In respect to ideality, reverence, wonder, and other such phrenological attributes,*
257.32–33 *horny-skinned, money-getting species* corr. on CP to *horny-skinned, two-legged, money-getting species*
257.36–37 *enterprise he broke* corr. on CP to *enterprise in which all the loss was intended to have been strictly* (?) *on the other side, he broke* [*strictly* not in 53–CD]
257.38–258.1 *his existence; it couldn't* corr. on CP to *his existence; therefore it couldn't*
258.1–5 last sentence of paragraph (*As his character . . . failure of education.*) marked in margin of CP: *Leave this in, or not, as you think best. C.D.* This note is struck out, possibly by John Forster, and the sentence left in.
258.22–23 MS: *with something sad upon their minds.* CP: *with something and upon their minds.* corr. to *with something depressing upon their minds.*
258.27–28 *an allegorical representation* corr. on CP to *no bad allegorical representation*
258.30 MS: *wile away* CP: *while away* corr. to *wile away* thus in 53–CD
258.32 *Mr. Smallweed's usual* corr. on CP to *Grandfather Smallweed's usual*
258.34 *when in action.* corr. on CP to *when it is in action*
259.6 *to say it wants?"* corr. on CP to *to say it wants then?"*
259.13 *and says, like a horrible* corr. on CP to *and screeches, like a horrible*
259.13–14 *old parrot, "Ten* corr. on CP to *old parrot without any plumage, "Ten*
259.22–23 *at such times,* corr. on CP to *at these times,*
259.28–29 MS–L: *again sit fronting* CP: *again fronting*
259.44–260.1 *instinctive fear on both* corr. on CP to *instinctive repugnance on both*
260.21, 23 *"Charley, you mean?"* corr. on CP to *"Charley, do you mean?"*
260.24–25 *Grandmother Smallweed, chuckling,* corr. on CP to *This touches a spring in Grandmother Smallweed, who, chuckling,*
260.25 *cries a great many times in succession—"Over the water!* corr. on CP to *cries—"Over the water!*
261.6 *back room, mum," replies* corr. on CP to *back room, miss," replies*
261.19, 21 MS: *expence*
262.30 *such a fool* corr. on CP to *such a confounded fool*
262.32–33 *an old pig. Confound you, you are* corr. on CP to *an old pig. You are*
263.11 CP [n.c.]: *have that girl into her tea.* 53: *have that girl in to her tea.* [as in MS]
263.32 *some further difficulty* corr. on CP to *some more difficulty*
263.41 *Without further announcement* corr. on CP to *Without other announcement*
263.42 *comes striding in.* corr. on CP to *walks in.*
264.7 *I have the honor of knowing;* corr. on CP to *I have had the honor of seeing before;*
264.9–10 MS–CP [n.c.]: *han't seen him* 53–CD: *ha'n't seen him* [3 pages later *ha'n't* in CP for *han't* in MS]
264.17 MS–L: *a swarthy browned man* CD: *a swarthy brown man*
264.17–18 MS: *stoutly-built, tall and good-looking,* CP [n.c.]: *stoutly built, and good-looking,* 53–CD: *well made, and good-looking,*
265.2 *become at least two sizes larger.* corr. on CP to *become two sizes larger.*
265.10 MS–L: *her poor chair all in a muddle.* CD: *her poor hair all in a muddle.* [em. ad.]
265.14 *"Truly, I suppose* corr. on CP to *"I suppose*
265.14–15 MS: *the old man only* [or *slily*?] *hints,* 53–CD: *the old man hints,*
265.18 *astonished at that."* corr. on CP to *astonished at it."*
265.25 *the three months' interest!* corr. on CP to *the two months' interest!*
265.26–27 *the three months' money,* corr. on CP to *the two months' interest-money,*
265.42–43 *so mercenary as that.* corr. on CP to *so mercenary as that, sir.*
266.21 *The old man nods "I hear you."* corr. on CP to *"I hear you."*
267.8 *a sweltering old toad.* corr. on CP to *a sweltering toad.*

267.19 *that he winks with* corr. on CP to *that the old man winks with*
267.33–34 *at Mr. Smallweed sideways with grave* corr. on CP to *at Mr. Smallweed with grave*
267.41 MS: *I can't afford to.* corr. to *I can't afford to it.* CP: *I can't afford to it.* corr. to *I can't afford to do it.*
268.7 MS: *"Down be down-hearted,*
268.12 *make you an advance* corr. on CP to *make you a further advance*
269.4,9 MS: *I' the name of* CP: *I the name of* corr. to *In the name of*
269.16 *Mr. Hawcott (Captain Hawcott,* corr. on CP to *Mr. Hawdon (Captain Hawdon,*
269.25–26 *have throttled him than* corr. on CP to *have strangled him than*
269.27–28 *to throttle him now."* corr. on CP to *to strangle him now."*
269.33 *to the bowl which* corr. on CP to *to the pipe-bowl which*
269.38–39 *he had a pistol at his head."* corr. on CP to *he held a pistol to his head."*
270.3 MS–CP [n.c.]: *says the old man.* 53–CD: *snarls the old man.*
270.11 *I tell you he went over* corr. on CP to *He went over*
270.19–20 *for a quarter,* corr. on CP to *for two months,*
270.23 *"You think your friend* corr. on CP to *"So you think your friend*
270.37 CP: *while away* corr. to *wile away* [as in MS] thus in 53–CD
270.40–41 *a grave enough face, seeming to think of several things.* corr. on CP to *a grave enough face.*
271.2 MS: *the feats of the strength;* CP–CD: *the feats of strength;*
271.4 MS–CP [n.c.]: *swordmanship,* 53–CD: *swordsmanship,*
271.22 MS–L: *exercises are being pursued* CD: *exercises being pursued*
271.33 MS: *to have blown up,* CP–CD: *to have been blown up,*
271.36 MS–CP [n.c.]: *scrambling up.* 53–CD: *scrambling to his feet.*
271.40 *"Shut up shop!"* corr. on CP to *"Shut up shop, Phil!"*
272.16–17 *makes his own, and Phil* corr. on CP to *makes his own bed, and Phil*
272.25 *"Good night, sir."* corr. on CP to *"Good night, guv'ner."*

Chapter XXII MS and one set of CP, presumably CP1; the few divergences between MS and CP seem to be all compositors' misreadings; 4 divergences between CP and 53 may point to existence of CP2, missing

272 chapter-heading ins. on CP [not in MS]
273.6 MS: *one of its trusty* CP–CD: *one of its trustiest*
273.11–12 MS–CP [n.c.]: *old port. For, though a hard-grained* 53–CD: *old port. Though a hard-grained*
273.18 MS: *heralded a remote* CP–CD: *heralded by a remote*
273.23 *So Mr. Tulkinghorn, sitting* corr. on CP to *Mr. Tulkinghorn, sitting*
273.38 *but with his chair* corr. on CP to *though with his chair*
273.39 MS–53: *drawn a little away from it,* C–CD: *drawn a little way from it,*
274.30 MS–53: *too fine a point upon it—* C–CD: *too fine a point on it—*
275.12 MS: *a hat and stick in his hands,* CP–CD: *a hat and stick in his hand,*
275.18 MS–CP [n.c.]: *He is a steady-looking,* 53–CD: *He is a stoutly built, steady-looking,*
275.28–29 *he is very useful* corr. on CP to *he is very intelligent*
275.38 *to stand on end. "Dear me!"* corr. on CP to *to stand on end.*
275.42–43 *Bucket dives down* corr. on CP to *Bucket dips down*
276.15 MS–L: *"That's what you are,* CD: *"That's what* you *are,*
276.15 *"Very good. Now it an't* corr. on CP to *"Now it an't*
276.22 MS–CP [n.c.]: *returns the stationer.* 53–CD: *returns the other.*
276.38–39 *"You're right!—on account* corr. on CP to *"You're right," returns Mr. Bucket, shaking hands with him quite affectionately, "on account*
276.41 *Tom-All-Alone's, now, and to keep* corr. on CP to *Tom-All-Alone's, and to keep*
277.31 MS–53: *When they come at last* C–CD: *When they came at last*
277.35 MS–L: *a villanous street,* CD: *a villainous street,* [em. ad.]
277.37 *such vile smells* corr. on CP to *such smells*
277.43–278.1 *as a sort of shabby* corr. on CP to *as a kind of shabby*
278.2 *"Here's fever coming* corr. on CP to *"Here's the fever coming*
278.24 MS: *stationery,* CP–CD: *stationary,*
278.32 MS–CP [n.c.]: *—a drunken, fiery face* 53–CD: *—a drunken face*
280.5 MS–53: *look round you,* C–CD: *look around you,*
280.6 *Look there";* corr. on CP to *Look at them":*
280.9 MS: *that you* see *grow up, master!"* CP: *that you, master,* see *grow up!"* corr. to *that you* see *grow up!"*
280.11 *look arter you* corr. on CP to *look after you*
280.13 MS: *"I mean to try,"* (?) CP–CD: *"I mean to try hard,"*
280.22 *as Jenny's child did."* corr. on CP to *as Jenny's child died."*
280.28–29 *walking up and down,* corr. on CP to *walking up and down as she nurses,*
280.32 MS: *what fortun' would* CP–CD: *what fortune would*
281.27 *he has got the key* corr. on CP to *he has the key*
282.35–36 MS: *nor yit her rings, nor yit her woice.* CP–CD: *nor yet her rings, nor yet her woice.* [MS reading restored, as

clearly deliberate, and inadvertently overlooked]

282.35–36 MS–53: *it's her heigth* C–CD: *it's her height*

282.43 *tilts the coins* corr. on CP to *tells the coins*

283.11 *this wager."* corr. on CP to *this little wager."*

283.17,19,20 MS: *Madamoiselle*

283.36, 284.1 *Bucket,* corr. on CP to *Mr. Bucket,*

284.9 MS: *unchallengable*

284.11–12 *of his being made away with,* corr. on CP to *of her husband's being made away with,*

284.12 *and, within the last* corr. on CP to *and who, within the last*

Chapter XXIII MS, CP1 and 3 pages of CP2; several divergences between CP1 and 53 point to further corrections on missing pages of CP2

284.21 *and several* corr. on CP to *and, although several*

284.21 *but her face* corr. on CP to *her face*

285.17 MS–L: *I will say not a word* CD: *I will not say a word*

285.21 MS–CP [n.c.]: *to find a service* 53–CD: *to find service*

285.36 *one devoted to you!* corr. on CP to *one so devoted to you!*

285.40–41 *half afraid of her.* corr. on CP to *almost afraid of her.*

286.3 *figure to yourself how.* corr. on CP to *figure to yourself now.*

286.23 *keep it faithfuller.* corr. on CP to *keep it faithfully.*

286.31 *coming to Bleak House every Saturday* corr. on CP to *coming every Saturday*

286.43 MS: *what a great "if"* CP–CD: *what a great* if

287.27 *my dear Richard," I suggested.* corr. on CP to *my dear Richard."*

287.28 *eh?" said Richard. "Well!* corr. on CP to *eh? Well!*

287.31–32 MS–CP [n.c.] *emphasizing* 53–CD: *strongly emphasizing*

287.32 *were the difficulty;* corr. on CP to *expressed the difficulty;*

288.1 *to be systematic* corr. on CP to *to be steady and systematic*

288.17–18 *with the consciousness that I am* corr. on CP to *conscious sometimes that I am*

288.21 *so moved or so despondent.* corr. on CP to *so moved.*

288.24 *my giving way a little now,* corr. on CP to *my being a little soft now,*

289.11–12 CP [n.c.]: *the best think* thus in 53 C–CD: *the best thing* [as in MS; em. ad.]

289.13 *The Chancery proceedings* corr. on CP to *These proceedings*

289.36–37 MS: *sorely and, I thought, how could this end, when* CP: *sorely; and, I thought, how would this, how could this end, when* corr. to *sorely. For, I thought, how would this end, how could this end, when*

289.42 *any trust in Chancery, which no one trusted, and which was held in universal dread, contempt, and horror; I entreated him to regard it as something so flagrant and bad, that nothing short* [MS: *little short*] *of a miracle could bring any good out of it to any one. To all I said,* corr. on CP2 to *any trust in Chancery. To all I said,*

290.1 *to that in substance, let me say what I would.* corr. on CP to *to that in substance.*

290.12 *affectionately patting* corr. on CP to *affectionately squeezing*

290.33 *in a good humour with myself and everybody else.* corr. on CP to *in a good humour.*

291.6 *he is so very considerate* corr. on CP to *he is so considerate*

291.8 *be dreadfully overcome* corr. on CP to *be very much overcome*

291.22 *laughing heartily, with her* corr. on CP to *laughing, with her*

291.42 MS: *a entirely new pair* [*entirely* ins. and *a* n.c.]

291.44–45 *took me to* corr. on CP to *we went to*

292.36 CP: *the Model, aghast,* corr. to *the Model, pale and aghast,* 53–CD: *the model, pale and aghast,*

292.41 *reclining gracefully upon* corr. on CP to *reclining on*

293.36–37 *resist you.* corr. on CP to *resist your prayer.*

294.10 *God only knows how long* corr. on CP to *it is impossible to say how long*

294.20 *points of a deportment* corr. on CP to *points of Deportment*

294.21–22 *originated in this imperfect sphere—you may* corr. on CP to *originated—you may*

294.30 *depend upon I will* corr. on CP to *depend I will*

294.36 some *light;* corr. on CP to some *ray of light,—*

294.40 MS: *if were to go* CP–CD: *if we were to go*

295.2 MS–CP [n.c.]: *and looked dirtier* 53–CD: *and it looked dirtier*

295.37 *began Caddy, her eyes filling.* corr. on CP to *began Caddy.*

295.42–43 *be a drudging clerk* corr. on CP to *be a mere drudge*

296.2 *Drudging clerk?* corr. on CP to *A mere drudge?*

296.15 *far away at Africa* corr. on CP to *far away into Africa*

296.20 *to see Miss Summerson, my dear,"* corr. on CP to *to see Miss Summerson,"*

296.26 MS: *I don't how),* CP: *I don't see how),* corr. to *I don't know how),*

296.31 *her bonnet, covered her eyes with her hand, took* corr. on CP to *her bonnet, took*

296.34 MS: *"Oh, you ridiculous* CP–CD: *"O, you ridiculous*

297.3,6 MS–53: *Mr. Gusher* C–CD: *Mr. Quale* [em. ad., as suggested by D's own Errata]

297.8 *no doubt you did, and it is well for*

him that you did. corr. on CP to *no doubt you did.*
297.29 *of this sort,"* corr. on CP to *of this kind,"*
297.34 *in my work, you weakest of creatures, but* corr. on CP to *in my work, but*
298.2–3 *Good-bye! Fifty-eight* corr. on CP to *Good-bye! When I tell you that I have fifty-eight*
298.4–5 *this morning!"* corr. on CP to *this morning, I need not apologise for having very little leisure."*
298.22 *throwing himself out whenever* corr. on CP to *throwing himself into the area whenever*
298.30 *wiser? So* I *did not wish* corr. on CP to *wiser? I did not wish*
298.34–35 *in my small way, and gradually found my heart filling so full that I was obliged to ring my bunch of keys a little.* corr. on CP to *in my small way.*
298.38 *a way of making* corr. on CP to *a method of making*
298.38–39 *Everybody, from* corr. on CP to *Everybody in the house, from*
298.40 *spoke so cheerfully,* corr. on CP to *spoke so cheerily,*
298.45 *prosing, O for hours!* corr. on CP to *prosing, for a length of time.*
299.6 *stooping down and* corr. on CP to *stooping down in astonishment, and*
299.15 *says Charley, with* corr. on CP to *says Charley, clapping her hands, with*
299.39 *Then Charley dried* corr. on CP to *Charley dried*

Chapter XXIV MS, CP1, CP2 with first 3 pages missing; no conclusive evidence of any earlier or later CP missing

300 chapter-heading ins. on CP [not in MS]
300.31 MS: *entred* (?)
301.9 *were waiting impatiently,* corr. on CP1 to *were sitting,*
301.16 *kindnesses of late that I* corr. on CP1 to *kindnesses that I*
301.35 *Now do you give* corr. on CP1 to *Do you give*
301.36–37 *My dear girl, Ada,"* corr. on CP1 to *My dear girl,"*
302.24–25 *I go further.* corr. on CP1 to *I must go further.*
303.4–5 *Come! Be ready. Each of you* corr. on CP1 to *Come! Each of you*
303.12–13 MS: *not right! I must not* CP–CD: *not right, and I must not*
303.16 *Richard then gave* corr. on CP1 to *Richard gave*
303.40 *her hand,* corr. on CP1 to *her trembling hand,*
303.44 *same doubts of him* corr. on CP1 to *same opinion of him*
304.11 *he would in very recklessness* corr. on CP1 to *he would recklessly*
304.13 MS: *and became* (?) CP1: *and become* corr. to *and would become*
304.19–20 *these conversations of ours,* corr. on CP1 to *these conversations,*
304.38 *you have quite a large* corr. on CP1 to *you have a large*
305.5 *he has got something* corr. on CP1 to *he has something*
306.20 MS–53: *a sort of a friendship."* C–CD: *a sort of friendship."*
306.31 *for what he called* corr. on CP1 to *of what he called*
306.38–39 *has got Gridley* corr. on CP1 to *has got this Gridley*
307.27 *attending much to* corr. on CP1 to *paying much attention to*
307.29 MS: *resting on hand:* CP–CD: *resting on his hand;*
307.31 MS: *in groupes;*
307.40 *under him, wigged and unwigged, looking* corr. on CP1 to *under him, looking*
307.42–43 *universal dread, contempt,* corr. on CP1 to *universal horror, contempt,*
307.43–308.2 *something so flagrant . . . to any one.* identical with passage canc. on CP2 of ch. XXIII
308.18 *to any kind of result.* corr. on CP1 to *to any result.*
308.39–40 *his handsome youthful face.* corr. on CP1 to *his handsome young face.*
309.5 *Mrs. Rachel* corr. on CP1 to *Mrs. Rachael*
309.13 *Mrs. Rachel!" said I.* corr. on CP1 to *Mrs. Rachael!" I remonstrated.*
309.15 *and hope you'll* corr. on CP2 to *and I hope you'll*
309.18 *Mrs. Rachel's* corr. on CP1 to *Mrs. Rachael's*
309.21–22 MS: *Richard and I were making our own way* CP–CD: *Richard and I were making our way* [MS reading restored as clearer and likely to have been inadvertently overlooked]
309.31 MS: *when we are out* CP–CD: *when we were out*
310.7 *one hand into his breast,* corr. on CP1 to *one hand in his breast,*
310.10 *as celebrated here as* corr. on CP1 to *as celebrated as*
310.25–26 *and said,* corr. on CP1 to *and as she too said,*
310.36 MS: *apologized,* CP–CD: *apologised,*
310.40–41 *with a large* corr. on CP1 to *and carrying a large*
310.41 *cane, and a bunch of watch-seals, addressed* corr. on CP1 to *cane, addressed*
311.1–2 *letters overhead in which* corr. on CP1 to *letters in which*
311.39–40 MS: *round this gallery like that";* CP–CD: *round the gallery like that";* [MS reading restored as agreeing better with Bucket's usual style]
311.42 *won't have it. I'll split your head open in half a minute."* corr. on CP1 to *won't have it."*
312.12–13 *that it's square between* corr. on CP1 to *that it's honorable between*
312.22 *a fifty-pound note* corr. on CP1 to *a fifty-pun note* 53–CD: *a fifty-pun' note*
313.1 *he slightingly observed,* corr. on CP1 to *he slightly observed,*

313.7 *enclosed at the sides,* corr. on CP1 to *enclosed the sides,*
313.11 MS: *canvass-covered*
313.12–13 *that I saw no likeness in his colorless face at first to* corr. on CP1 to *that I recognised no likeness in his colorless face at first to* corr. on CP2 to p.t. (*that at first I recognised . . . face to*)
313.14 *and dwelling* corr. on CP2 to *and still dwelling*
313.23–24 *man from Shropshire we had* corr. on CP1 to *man from Shropshire whom we had*
313.31 *shock hands very earnestly,* corr. on CP1 to *shook hands earnestly,*
313.42–43 *look upon us—look upon us!"* corr. on CP1 to *Look at us—look at us!"* [new paragraph here in MS only]
314.4 *Miss Flite, with tears.* corr. on CP1 to *Miss Flite, in tears.*
314.9–11 *How long my heart has given way, I don't know; it seemed to go in an hour.* corr. on CP1 to *How long I have been wearing out, I don't know; I seemed to break down in an hour.*
314.11–12 *I charge every body here, to lead them* corr. on CP2 to *I hope every body, here, will lead them*
314.31 *asked Mr. George,* corr. on CP1 to *asked George,*
314.37 *like being worn out, is it?* corr. on CP1 to *like being worn out.*
315.6 *returned Bucket.* corr. on CP1 to *returned Bucket, anxiously.*
315.14 after *so many years!"* MS has: *(white line here)*
315.18–19 *darkness of the night. And through his farewell words* corr. on CP1 to *darkness of the darkest night. And through Richard's farewell words*

Chapter XXV MS and one set of CP; no other CP missing; many mistakes on CP made by one compositor—named Jackson—new to the task

315.30 *Tom-All-Alone's and* corr. on CP to *For Tom-All-Alone's and*
316.9 *the trying peculiarity* corr. on CP to *the fearful peculiarity*
316.45 *by the wrong end, likely to engender confusion.* corr. on CP to *by the wrong end.*
320.19–20 *a mover on* corr. on CP to *a mover-on* [D wrote in margin, in addition to ordinary correction signs, mover-on *one word*]
320.23 MS: *will throw him a back-fall* CP: *will show him a back-fall* corr. to *will throw him an argumentative back-fall*
320.26 *and precious stones.* corr. on CP to *and of precious stones.*
320.31 *greatly posed by* corr. on CP to *greatly perplexed by*
320.45 *and pauses. Mr. Snagsby* corr. on CP to *and pauses, but Mr. Snagsby*
322.4–5 *to conquer,—when* corr. on CP to *to conquer, for his sake—when*
322.14–15 *down stairs," if* corr. on CP to *down stairs for the purpose," if*
322.24 MS–L: *says Chadband,* CD: *said Chadband,*
322.32–33 *Cook's Court echoes* corr. on CP to *Cook's Court re-echoes*
322.44 CP: *a revengeful air,* corr. to *a remorseful air,* [as in MS]
323.12 *talk five minutes.* corr. on CP to *talk for five minutes.*
323.13 MS: *"Mr. Sangsby* CP: *"Mr. Snagsby* corr. to *"Mr. Sangsby* thus in 53 C–CD: *"Mr. Snagsby*
323.20 *to eat, boy,"* corr. on CP to *to eat, poor boy,"*
323.35 MS: *Mr. Sangsby!"* CP: *Mr. Snagsby!"* corr. to *Mr. Sangsby!"* thus in 53 C–CD: *Mr. Snagsby!"*
323.40–41 MS: *"I am fly, master." And good night.* CP: *"I am fly, master! And good night."* corr. to *"I am fly, master!" And so, good night.*
324.3 *let all concerned beware, for* corr. on CP to *let all concerned in the secresy beware! For*

Chapter XXVI MS and one set of CP; at least one divergence between CP and 53 may point to existence of later CP, missing

324 chapter-heading ins. on CP: *Sharpshooters* (?) canc. *The Shooting-Gallery* canc. *Sharpshooters* [not in MS]
324.6 *with dull eye and* corr. on CP to *with dull eyes and*
325.27 MS–L: *says Phil,* CD: *said Phil,*
325.29 MS–L: *"On accounts of* CD: *"On account of*
325.32 *says Phil doubtfully.* corr. on CP to *says Phil.*
325.35 *the setting of very* corr. on CP to *the setting forth of very*
325.44 *on his knees. Whether he does this in* corr. on CP to *on his knees. Either in*
325.45 *manner of eating, does not appear.* corr. on CP to *manner of eating.*
326.21 *couldn't climb still,* corr. on CP to *couldn't climb yet,*
326.24 MS: *"Aye!* CP–CD: *"Ay!*
326.28 MS: *Let her be in peace,* CP–CD: *Let her rest in peace,*
327.3–4 MS: *to himself wery comfortable,* CP: *to himself,* corr. to *to himself very comfortable,*
327.18 *took the bis'ness.* corr. on CP to *took the business.*
327.34 *I was so young,* corr. on CP to *I was young,*
327.40–41 *forge, sitivated below low-water mark, where* corr. on CP to *forge, where*
328.10–13 MS: *a nightcap—"*see back* next two lines (*"And hobbling . . . sticks. When—"*) written on separate slip pasted on to back of MS page
328.38 *express entire devotion* corr. on CP to *express devotion*
329.14 CP: *to immediately recite* corr. to *immediately to recite* [in MS *immediately* ins. above line; caret placed first first before *to*, then canc. and placed after *to*]
330.3–4 CP: *withdraws at first his* corr. to *withdraws adjusting his* [as in MS]

330.24 *retires cynically.* corr. on CP to *retires.*
331.1 *O Lord!* corr. on CP to *O dear me!*
331.13 MS: *faced about towards* CP: *faced about towards* corr. to *faced-about towards* [in addition to usual correction signs, D wrote in margin: *one word* faced-about] thus in 53 C–CD: *faced about towards*
331.14 *please God?"* corr. on CP to *please the Powers?"*
331.20 *looks horrid gleaming* corr. on CP to *looks awfully gleaming* 53–CD: *looks awful gleaming*
331.24 MS–L: *paying off all scores* CD: *paying off old scores*
331.26 CP: *he'd have her head off."* corr. to *he'd shave her head off."* [as in MS]
332.10 *Hoo, ho!* corr. on CP to *Ho, ho!*
332.12 *tell you what it is,"* corr. on CP to *tell you what,"*
332.19 *that he can breathe freely as yet.* corr. on CP to *that he is not smothered yet.*
332.20 MS–CP [n.c.]: *a friendly call," says* 53–CD: *a friendly call," continues*
332.28 *eyes on Judy,* corr. on CP to *eyes musingly fixed on Judy,*
332.32 *looking for* corr. on CP to *looking unconsciously for*
334.15 *squeezing his black velvet cap* corr. on CP to *squeezing up his velvet cap*
334.19 MS: *of paper in that* CP–CD: *or paper that*
334.34 *a hard-headed old silver watch,* corr. on CP to *a lean old silver watch,*
334.34–35 MS–L: *like the legs of a skeleton.* CD: *like the leg of a skeleton.*
335.4 MS: *"Aye!* CP–CD: *"Ay!*

Chapter XXVII MS, one set of CP, and two fragments of another identical set, n.c.; a few minor divergences between CP and 53 seem to point to possible existence of missing CP2

335 chapter-heading ins. on CP [not in MS]
336.1 *seen him too, in my younger days, I think.* corr. on CP to *seen him too, I think.*
336.27 *As usual rustily drest,* corr. on CP to *Rustily drest,*
336.44–45 *he could in more senses than one)* corr. on CP to *he can in two senses)*
337.11 *"Now, George!—* corr. on CP to *"Well, George?—*
337.42 MS–CP [n.c.]: *I should prefer to keep it."* 53–CD: *I should prefer to have it."*
337.43–338.1 MS–L: *same attitude, looks at the ground, looks at the painted* CD: *same attitude, looks at the painted*
338.12 *Tulkinghorn, handing him* corr. on CP to *Tulkinghorn, suddenly handing him*
338.29 MS: *nee'r-do-weele.*
338.41 *pointed adjective* corr. on CP to *favorite adjective*
339.3–4 MS: *utters such occasional sentences as* CP–CD: *utters an occasional sentence, as* [MS reading restored as definitely better and likely to have been misread by compositor]
339.24 MS: *"Aye!* CP–CD: *"Ay!*
339.41 MS–L: *with a final answer* CD: *with the final answer*
340.3 *"If I wasn't bodily as weak* corr. on CP to *"If I wasn't as weak*
340.20–21 CP [n.c.]: *I have been periodically* 53: *I have him periodically* [as in MS]
340.41 MS–CP [n.c.]: *glance at Rapier-Lane and Hanging-Sword Alley, which seem* 53–CD: *glance at Hanging-Sword Alley, which would seem*
341.3 CP–L: *centering in* CD: *centreing in* [as in MS]
341.5 *stronger iron monster, ready* corr. on CP to *stronger iron monster than he, ready*
342.9 *widder* corr. on CP to *widow*
342.13 *respectable civilian now.* corr. on CP to *respectable man now.*
342.13 *widder* corr. on CP to *widow*
342.14 *there was something in—and* corr. on CP to *there was something in her—and*
342.23 MS–L: *into that apartment.* CD: *into that department.*
342.37 *play the fife."* corr. on CP to *play the fife in a military piece."*
342.38 *my godson, Young Woolwich!" cries* corr. on CP to *my godson!" cries*
342.42–43 *young 'uns growing up.* corr. on CP to *children growing up.*
343.16–17 *of a drummer.* corr. on CP to *of a young drummer.*
343.30 *says the old girl,* corr. on CP to *the old girl says,*
343.34 *"be damned. What college* corr. on CP to *"What college*
344.4–5 *before her. It was* corr. on CP to *before her. Discipline must be maintained. It was* [ins. sentence had been canc. on MS]
344.18 *they rock up* (?) corr. on CP to *they walk up*
344.23 *Mr. Bagnet developes* corr. on CP to *Mrs. Bagnet developes*
344.41 *involve some pattening* corr. on CP to *involve much pattening*
345.6 *to Mr. Bagnet solely, but having an eye on* corr. on CP to *to Mr. Bagnet, but having an eye solely on*
345.12 MS: *"You mean to act* CP: *"You really mean to act* corr. to *"You act*
345.24 *and have a talk* corr. on CP to *and to have a talk*
345.24–25 MS–CP [n.c.]: *over all times* 53–CD: *over old times*
345.29–30 *expected at the theatre;* corr. on CP to *expected by a British public at the theatre;*
345.32 *the pocket of Young Woolwich,* corr. on CP to *the pocket of his godson,*
345.40 *gypsey fashion more or less.* corr. on CP to *gypsey fashion.* thus in 53 C: *gypsy* L–CD: *gipsy* [em. ad.]

346.3 CP: [as in MS] *bell-handle to open* corr. to *bell-handle or to open* [as in MS]
346.13 *knows well enough.* corr. on CP to *knows well enough at a glance.*
346.19 *"What then?"* corr. on CP to *"What then, sir?"*
346.22 *that man. A threatening,* corr. on CP to *that man. Gridley? A threatening,*
346.33 *five minutes following he is* corr. on CP to *five minutes he is*

Chapter XXVIII MS and one set of CP; an unusually high proportion of the unusually few corrections are of compositors' misreadings of MS; one substantive divergence between CP and 53 is not enough to infer existence of missing CP2

347.25–26 *so go through life—high life.* corr. on CP to *so go through high life.*
347.32 CP–53: *counsinship* C–CD: *cousinship* [em. ad.]
348.20 MS–L: *these were not times* CD: *these were not the times*
349.7 *repeats to somebody,* corr. on CP to *repeats to some chosen person,*
350.23 MS: *"I ne-ver heard* CP–CD: *"I never heard* [MS reading restored as likely to have been inadvertently overlooked]
350.24 MS–L: *exclaims Volumnia.* CD: *exclaimed Volumnia.*
352.27 *what you do mean."* corr. on CP to *what you mean."*
353.19–20 MS–L: *than we had ourselves,* CD: *than we have had ourselves,*
353.34 MS–L: *quite sure that you are* CD: *quite sure you are*
354.37 *honored by my Lady's notice* corr. on CP to *honored with my Lady's notice*
355.27–28 *says smilingly:* corr. on CP to *says smiling:*
356.20 MS–CP [n.c.]: *but is indignant,* 53–CD: *but is really indignant,*

Chapter XXIX MS and one set of CP; 3 substantive divergences between CP and 53 may point to existence of CP2, missing; few corrections in that chapter, which seems to have been hurriedly corrected, the "overmatter" having been absorbed, not canc.

357.5 MS–L: *smell of the little church,* CD: *smell of a little church,*
357.22 MS: *miscellaneous article* CP–CD: *miscellaneous articles*
357.38–39 MS–53: *only give him the greater zest for what he is set upon, and make him* C–L: *only gives him . . . and make him* CD: *only gives him the greater zest for what he is set upon, and makes him*
357.39 *the more dogged and the more steady, in it.* corr. on CP to *the more inflexible in it.*
358.7 MS: *Sir Leicester's sits*
359.2 MS: *"It is quite right.* CP–CD: *"It's quite right.* [MS reading restored, the compositor's misreading being understandable but deplorable]
359.13 MS–CP [n.c.]: *Mr. Guppy, much embarrassed.* 53–CD: *Mr. Guppy, embarrassed.*
359.22 CP: *strangely unfortunate.* corr. to *strangely importunate.* [as in MS]
361.35 MS–CP [n.c.]: *—which I again mention* 53–CD: *—which I mention*
361.37 CP: *on my heart.* corr. to *on my art.* [as in MS]
362.5 MS: *the principle* CP–CD: *the principal*
362.23 MS: *these interrogoraties,*
363.9 *some time ago, within a twelvemonth, a law-writer* corr. on CP to *some time ago, a law-writer*
363.29 after *holds the screen. My* rest of chapter printed on CP as *Matter over the two sheets* in an additional page of 59 lines numbered 289; but page 289 is the first page of ch. XXX in CP–53; all the pages in that number have 53 or 54 lines instead of the usual 50 or 51.
363.33 MS–53: *could possibly be* C–CD: *could be possibly*
364.1–2 MS–C: *both those names* L–CD: *both these names*
364.13–14 *or do they hide as much as they reveal?* corr. on CP to *or, if not, what do they hide?*
364.19 MS–CP [n.c.]: *says Mr. Guppy.* 53–CD: *says Mr. Guppy, a little injured.*
364.27 MS–L: *accept of anything* CD: *accept anything*

Chapter XXX MS and one set of CP; numerous corrections of punct. in this chapter made in paler ink than other corrections seem to result from separate reading

365.2 MS: *a widow lady.* (?) CP–CD: *an elderly lady.*
365.10 *I knew, to be* corr. on CP to *I knew very well, to be*
365.11 *it was very unreasonable;* corr. on CP to *it was unreasonable;*
366.18 *of him, no doubt, to recollect* corr. on CP to *of him, I dare say, to recollect*
366.25 *an opinion on—"* corr. on CP to *an opinion—"*
366.29 MS: *and added "He seemed* CP: *and added, he seemed* corr. to *and added that he seemed*
367.16 *and will have* corr. on CP to *and as he will have*
367.36–37 *so busy, and so prudent, and so neat,* corr. on CP to *so busy, and so neat,*
367.41–42 *of the night quite wretched.* corr. on CP to *of that night quite uncomfortable.* thus in 53–L CD: *of that night uncomfortable.*
368.8 *things she said to me, if it were only pleasant to her to say them?* corr. on CP to *things she said to me?*
368.16 *account for, or at least,* corr. on CP to *account for. At least,*
368.33 *as if it were a tunnel or something*

of that kind,—with corr. on CP to *as if it were a tunnel—with*

370.16–17 *which beyond all doubt it was.* corr. on CP to *which I am afraid it was.*

370.22 MS: *reparing,*

370.24–25 *being at least as pleased with the idea as she was herself,* corr. on CP to *being as pleased with the idea as Caddy was,*

370.36 *help crying a little,* corr. on CP to *help reddening a little,*

371.22 *a pale boy* corr. on CP to *an unwholesome boy*

371.27 *The pale boy,* corr. on CP to *The unwholesome boy,*

371.39 MS: *confine our greater efforts* CP–CD: *confine our greatest efforts*

372.2–3 *the pale boy* corr. on CP to *the unwholesome boy*

372.20–21 *somehow.* corr. on CP to *somewhere.*

373.7–8 *nothing which* corr. on CP to *no domestic object which*

373.16 MS: *—old bits of mouldy pie,* CP–CD: *—bits of mouldy pie,*

373.20 *butter sticking to them,* corr. on CP to *butter sticking to the binding,*

373.23–24 MS–L: *he came in regularly* CD: *he came regularly*

373.27 *on the evening before* corr. on CP to *on the night before*

373.32 *don't drink. If we happen to get a sober one, she begins to drink almost as soon as she comes. Ma's ruinous* corr. on CP to *don't drink. Ma's ruinous*

374.5–6 *opened his mouth a great many times now,* corr. on CP to *opened his mouth now, a great many times,*

374.30–31 *Caddy wept to think* corr. on CP to *Caddy cried to think*

375.4,28 MS–53: *Mr. Gusher,* C–CD: *Mr. Quale,* [em. ad., as suggested by D's own Errata]

375.10–11 *was to be incessantly moving resolutions at* corr. on CP to *was to be always moving declaratory resolutions about things in general at*

375.19 *to be on bad terms with* corr. on CP to *to be on terms of coolness with*

375.33–34 *that there was no hope for the world but in the emancipation* corr. on CP to *that the only practical thing for the world was the emancipation*

376.1 *manner was decidedly grim,* corr. on CP to *manner was grim,*

376.2 *proceedings with* corr. on CP to *proceedings, as part of Woman's wrongs, with*

376.19 *A more ungenial company there could hardly have been; but my guardian* corr. on CP to *My guardian*

376.20–21 *something agreeable out of such material.* corr. on CP to *something agreeable even out of the ungenial company.*

376.40 MS–53: *not in the least angry* C–CD: *not the least angry*

376.41 MS: *before I go away?"* CP–CD: *before I go away, Ma?"*

377.13 *"God bless you, father!"* corr. on CP to *"Thank you over and over again, father!"*

377.35 MS: *in your own room,* CP–CD: *in your own bedroom,*

377.37 *with an air as if he were giving him ten thousand pounds.* corr. on CP to *with a great air.*

377.40 *Well! They drove away;* corr. on CP to *They drove away;*

378.15 *It was only their love* corr. on CP to *Well, it was only their love* 53–CD: *Well! It was only their love*

Chapter XXXI MS and one set of CP; no conclusive evidence of earlier proof missing; 3 substantive divergences between CP and 53 seem to point to existence of missing CP2

378 no chapter-heading on CP though it is in MS

378.24 *power at all over* corr. on CP to *power over*

378.26 *like a donkey.* corr. on CP to *like a saddle-donkey.*

378.27 MS–L: *young hand made;* CD: *young hand had made;*

379.45 MS: *folded so close* CP–CD: *folded so closely*

380.9 *in the damp wind.* corr. on CP to *in the wind.*

380.15 *into it sullen lines* corr. on CP to *into it long sullen lines*

380.22 *I am very sure—* corr. on CP to *I am quite sure—*

380.23 *happen to me, dating from that night.* corr. on CP to *happen to me.*

380.44 *closer, and had* corr. on CP to *closer than before, and had*

381.7 *"I won't go to* corr. on CP to *"I won't go no more to*

381.15 MS–53: *berrying ground.* C–CD: *berryin ground.* [em. ad. as being more usual in Jo's speech]

381.33 MS: *I s'pose* CP–CD: *I 'spose* [MS reading restored as more natural]

381.42 *found him resting at* corr. on CP to *found him at*

382.2 *as if he were speaking to himself, or were half awake.* corr. on CP to *as if he were half awake.*

382.9 MS–53: *Mrs. Sangsby,* C–CD: *Mrs. Snagsby,*

382.29 *it was time for him to be going.* corr. on CP to *he was expected to be going.*

382.32 *doing it, in* corr. on CP to *doing all this, in*

382.42 MS: *she had running,*

383.1 *oblivious, thankful,* corr. on CP to *oblivious, half-thankful,*

383.9 *drunken husband who was stumbling homeward.* corr. on CP to *drunken husband.*

383.16 *some little bundle* corr. on CP to *some small bundle*

383.24 MS: *sheter*

383.28 MS: *dies anywheres,"* CP: *dies anywhere,"* corr. to *dies everywheres,"*

383.37–38 *the hill. I doubted* corr. on CP to *the hill. We passed but one man. I doubted*
383.38 *got there without* corr. on CP to *got home without*
383.39 MS–CP [n.c.]: *his steps were* 53–CD: *the boy's steps were*
383.42 MS–L: *shrunk into a corner* CD: *shrunk into the corner*
383.43–44 MS–L: *that could scarcely* CD: *that scarcely could*
384.10, 387.10, 11 MS–53: *Leonard* C–CD: *Harold* [em. ad. as suggested by D's own Errata]
384.19–20 *as we stood by him.* corr. on CP to *as we stood by.*
384.35 *were a prisoner,* corr. on CP to *were a convicted prisoner,*
384.44 *"Our young friend, you know, is not* corr. on CP to *"Our young friend is not*
385.5 MS: *such another child on earth as you are."* CP–CD: *such another child on earth as yourself."* [MS reading restored as better than compositor's inadvertently uncorr. misreading]
385.10 *health, has an excellent* corr. on CP to *health, he has an excellent*
385.19 *of romance too; and* corr. on CP to *of romance; and*
385.24 *said Mr. Skimpole, "as* corr. on CP to *said Mr. Skimpole cheerfully, "as*
386.2 *though he never* corr. on CP to *for he never*
386.8 *recommendations.* corr. on CP to *recommendation.*
386.14 *what was done too, as if* corr. on CP to *what was done, as if* [MS not clear]
386.16 CP–L: *we soon get* CD: *we soon got* [em. ad. as required by context; MS not clear, looks like *get* but may be *got*]
386.35–36 *he sung one* corr. on CP to *he sang one*
387.1–2 *"for it made him chirp,"* corr. on CP to *"for he absolutely chirped,"*
387.2–3 *"to think by what* corr. on CP to *"when he thought by what*
387.21–22 *among the sympathisers* corr. on CP to *among the active sympathisers* [MS had *sympathizers*]
387.33 *an unoccupied cart-house* corr. on CP to *an empty cart-house*
388.21 MS: *I think I am ill."* CP–CD: *I think I'm ill."* [MS reading restored as more consistent with D's usual policy]
388.35–36 *wrote her a letter,* corr. on CP to *wrote her a long letter,*
388.40 CP: *clear sweet voice* corr. on CP to *dear sweet voice* [as in MS—(?)]
389.17–18 *my little sister* corr. on CP to *this little sister*
389.24 MS: *she would lie quiet* CP–CD: *she would be quiet* [MS reading restored as better than compositor's inadvertently uncorr. misreading]
389.38–39 *he might be raised up likewise,* corr. on CP to *he likewise might be raised up,*
389.42 *would show* corr. on CP to *would I show* [MS had *shew*]
389.44 MS–L: *restored in Heaven!* CD: *restored to Heaven!*
390.3 *and the higher trust* corr. on CP to *and the last higher trust*
390.17 MS–L: *what I had felt* CD: *what I felt*
390.33–34 *in my face; and came* corr. on CP to *in my face; and she came*
390.39 *quiet and resigned* corr. on CP to *quiet and composed*
391.1 *said Charley.* corr. on CP to *said Charley, quietly.*
391.3 *"It's very little* corr. on CP to *"It is very little* thus in 53–L CD: *"It's very little*
391.13–14 *wished to ask him, relative* corr. on CP to *wished to ask, relative*
391.16 *and day melting* corr. on CP to *and of day melting*
391.36 MS: *for a little while, and speak to me a little.* CP: *a little.* canc. 53–CD: *for a little while, and touch me with your hand.*

Chapter XXXII MS and one set of CP; no conclusive evidence of any earlier CP missing; clear evidence of extant CP being the latest set

392.7 MS: *In a dirty upper casements,* CP: *In a dirty upper casement,* corr. to *In dirty upper casements*
392.7–8 *a hazy little patch* corr. on CP to *hazy little patches*
392.8 *reveals where* corr. on CP to *reveal where*
392.14 *the Chancellor* corr. on CP to *the Lord Chancellor* thus in 53–L CD: *the Lord Chanceller*
392.23 MS–53: *"continual in liquor,"* C–CD: *"continually in liquor,"*
393.1–2 *the entertainment.* corr. on CP to *the entertainments.*
393.6 *(and Mrs. Perkins's)* corr. on CP to *(and, by implication, Mrs. Perkins's)*
393.18 *a close dull night,* corr. on CP to *a close night,*
393.18–19 *the damp is searching, too—what they call in the court a muggy night—and there is* corr. on CP to *the damp cold is searching too; and there is*
393.27 *shut up shop,* corr. on CP to *shut up his shop,*
393.46 *to be got; and what* corr. on CP to *to be got here; and what*
394.4 *taste a little;* corr. on CP to *taste the air a little;*
394.10 CP: *—chopseh?"* corr. to *—Chops, eh?"* [MS does look like *—chopseh?"*]
394.21 *"Do you, indeed? Then you see you* corr. on CP to *"Then, you see, you*
394.35 MS–L: *find the rent high,* CD: *find the rent too high,*
395.12 CP–53: *a kind of proprietor-shop* C–CD: *a kind of proprietorship* [em. ad. though MS looks like *-shop*]
395.12 *with Mr. Weevle,* corr. on CP to *in Mr. Weevle,*
395.13 *Brewer's houses* corr. on CP to *Brewers' houses*

395.19 *"Seems a kind of Fate* corr. on CP to *"Seems a Fate*
396.6–7 *blessed-looking candle for you!"* corr. on CP to *blessed-looking candle!"*
396.17 *room, I think—and old* corr. on CP to *room—and old*
396.17–18 *Boguey down stairs."* corr. on CP to *Boguey down stairs, I suppose."*
396.18 MS–53: *snuffer-tray* C–CD: *snuffers-tray*
396.24 MS–L: *"Yes, and be—* CD: *"Yes, and he—*
396.33 *we needn't have more* corr. on CP to *we couldn't have more*
396.34 *affects to laugh,* corr. on CP to *affects to smile;*
397.21–22 *who has an image* corr. on CP to *who has an unrequited image*
397.24 *possess all that* corr. on CP to *possess in yourself all that*
397.27 *garden, if I may so express myself, is open* corr. on CP to *garden is open*
397.32 *have begun it,* corr. on CP to *have taken it up,*
397.44 *Never forgets* corr. on CP to *He never forgets*
398.1 *helped him shut up* corr. on CP to *helped him to shut up*
398.2 *got 'em then* corr. on CP to *got the letters then*
398.3–5 *shewed 'em me. I heard him* corr. on CP to *shewed 'em me. When the shop was closed, he took them out of his cap, hung his cap on the chair-back, and stood turning them over before the fire. I heard him*
398.6 *singing, like* corr. on CP to *humming, like*
398.8 *a old rat* corr. on CP to *an old rat*
398.16 *he knows 'em* corr. on CP to *he knows most of them*
398.28 *"A woman's. I'd bet fifty to one* corr. on CP to *"A woman's. Fifty to one*
398.30 *been voraciously biting* corr. on CP to *been biting*
398.32–33 *at his coat-sleeve.* corr. on CP to *at his coat-sleeve. It takes his attention. He stares at it, aghast.*
398.38 MS: *Con-found the stuff,* CP–CD: *Confound the stuff,* [MS reading restored as clearly deliberate and inadvertently overlooked]
399.5 MS–L: *at his coat-sleeve,* CD: *at the coat-sleeve,*
399.5 *as they continue their* corr. on CP to *as they pursue their*
399.8 *from the lodger's* corr. on CP to *from his lodger's*
399.31 *is almost five hundred* corr. on CP to *is about five hundred* [MS illegible]
399.35 *forces us to it—but he knows better—they'll be* corr. on CP to *forces us to it, they'll be*
399.36–38 MS: *won't they?"/ "Ye-es," is the unwilling reply of Mr. Weevle as he rubs his chin./ "Why, Tony,"* CP: *won't they?"/ "Why, Tony,"* corr. to *won't they?"/ "Ye-es," is Mr. Weevle's reluctant admission./ "Why, Tony,"*
400.9–10 MS: *to the onor of* CP: *to the honor of*
400.10 *calculated, possibly, to serve* corr. on CP to *calculated to serve*
400.29–30 *in the very room where* corr. on CP to *in the room where*
400.36 *"Yes, but in most* corr. on CP to *"I know there have; but in most*
401.22–23 *of documents of value.* corr. on CP to *of documents.*
401.26 *suggests, after* corr. on CP to *suggests with an eye shut, after*
401.28 *may have correctly got it* corr. on CP to *may have got it*
401.30 *they were worth* corr. on CP to *they are worth*
401.32 *by staring at* corr. on CP to *by long staring at*
401.33–34 *about the Chancellor's* corr. on CP to *about the Lord Chancellor's*
401.46 *out of window for Heaven's sake?"* corr. on CP to *out of window?"*
402.16 *it is his right.* corr. on CP to *it is his right hand.*
402.23 *calls loudly,* corr. on CP to *asks loudly,*
402.27 MS: *he is* not *there!"* CP–CD: *he is not there!"—* [MS italics restored as demanded by tone of this chapter]
402.27 *He ends this* corr. on CP to *Tony ends this*
402.32 MS–L: *There is very little fire* CD: *There is a very little fire*
402.37–403.7 between *cap and coat.* and *They advance slowly* long passage (*"Look!" whispers . . . in this evil place."*) ins. on CP [end of a number underwritten by about half a page]
403.12–13 *here is tinder from burnt paper,* corr. on CP to *here is the tinder from a little bundle of burnt paper,*
403.14–15 *a little charred and broken* corr. on CP to *a small charred and broken*
403.16 MS: *he* is *here!* CP: *he is here!* corr. to *he* IS *here!* [*small caps* written by D in margin]
403.19 *for God's sake!* corr. on CP to *for Heaven's sake!*
403.20–21 *Chancellor in that Court,* corr. on CP to *Chancellor of that Court,*
403.28 *no other death of all* corr. on CP to *none other of all*

Chapter XXXIII MS and two sets of CP; no conclusive evidence of any earlier set missing; slight but clear evidence of further revision, possibly on CP3, missing

403.33 *by Mooney, the active* corr. on CP2 to *by the active*
404.24 *hadn't a note* corr. on CP2 to *hadn't a single note*
404.28 *the disgusting effluvia,* corr. on CP2 to *the foetid effluvia,* [D seems to have written *faetid*]
404.30 *All these and a great* corr. on CP1 to *All this and a great*
404.33–34 CP–53: *the Sol's Arm's* C–CD: *the Sol's Arms* [em. ad. as in MS]
405.4–6 *aloft on the West of England, and holding on with all his might,* corr. on CP1 to *aloft on the Phoenix, and holding*

on to that fabulous creature with all his might,
405.9 MS–L: *been likewise left* CD: *likewise been left*
405.38 MS: *phisiognomy*
406.3–4 *what it is, sir.* corr. on CP1 to *what it is.*
406.5–6 *says Mr. Snagsby, "I was* corr. on CP1 to *says Mr. Snagsby, somewhat promptly backed away, "I was*
406.10 *next door.* corr. on CP1 to *next door then.*
406.32 *aside to a cask.* [no paragraph] corr. on CP1 to *aside to an adjacent cask.* [paragraph]
407.3 *combusting any person?"* corr. on CP1 to *combusting any person, my dear?"*
407.8–9 *that is incomprehensible,* corr. on CP1 to *that is mysterious,*
407.18 *the aged party* corr. on CP1 to *the venerable party*
407.25 MS–CP2 [n.c.]: *severe and scornful smile,* 53–CD: *severe and sinister smile,*
407.43 *as many dark cobwebs* corr. on CP1 to *as many of the dark cobwebs*
408.4 MS–53: *William G!"* C–CD: *William G.!"*
408.27–28 *cutting him short." If I made a mistake, there's an end of it. Say what* corr. on CP1 to *cutting him short. "Say what*
408.28 MS–CP2 [n.c.]: *got to say. Get on with your barrow!"* 53–CD: *got to say!"*
408.37–41 *this unfortunate old—gentleman?"/ "What facts* corr. on CP1 to *this unfortunate old Mo—gentleman?" (Mr. Guppy was going to say, Mogul, but thinks gentleman better suited to the circumstances.)/ "What facts?*
409.2 MS–53: *for twelve o'clock* C–CD: *at twelve o'clock*
409.10 *says Mr. Guppy.* corr. on CP1 to *says the injured Guppy.*
409.35 *the appetite of disappointment.* corr. on CP1 to *the appetite of vexation.*
409.36 MS: *"Weigh with me?" he replies. "If, when I muster up courage enough to go into the house to take away my clothes, I find a morsel of that soot in one of my boxes, I'll burn every individual rag I possess, except the clothes I stand in—and I hate and detest even these." Mr. Guppy glances at his raw* (?) *gloom* (?) *, and they both shudder. "Talk in that* corr. to *"Certainly not. Talk in that*
410.22 *Ask for one* corr. on CP1 to *Ask me for a*
410.23 *penny more, and I'll summons you before the clock strikes twelve!* corr. on CP1 to *penny more, and I'll have my lawful revenge upon you.*
411.14 *says Grandfather* corr. on CP1 to *whines Grandfather*
411.21 *on terms. He was eccentric—* corr. on CP1 to *on terms. He was not fond of us. He was eccentric—*
411.22–23 *not likely)* corr. on CP1 to *not at all likely)*
411.30 *about him yourselves that* corr. on CP1 to *about him that*
411.35 MS–53: *observes Small;* C–CD: *observed Small;*
411.42 *as my solicitor, though I am not a Nob, and grass* corr. on CP1 to *as my solicitor; and grass*
412.3 *Mrs. Smallweed, as if she were a mechanical figure, and some spring in her had been touched, instantly begins* corr. on CP1 to *Mrs. Smallweed instantly begins*
412.11 *you dog. Yes! That's what you are. You're a Brimstone* corr. on CP1 to *you dog, you brimstone*
412.16, 18 *Pick me up,* corr. on CP1 to *Shake me up,*
412.31–32 MS: *is responsible for* CP1–CD: *is answerable for*
412.35–36 *carried into the next house,* corr. on CP1 to *carried on a visit of sentiment into the next house,*
413.4–5 *puts up* KING corr. on CP1 to *puts up "The popular song of* KING
413.8 CP2: *exra expence,* corr. to *extra expence,* [as in MS] 53–CD: *extra expense,*
413.15 *orders to prepare* corr. on CP1 to *orders to construct*
413.23–414.2 MS: *has ever imagined.** *see back* *The less the court understands* long passage *(Some of these authorities . . . offensive.)* written on separate slip pasted on to back of MS page
413.23 *authorities hold* corr. on CP1 to *authorities (of course the wisest) hold*
413.27–28 *Transactions; and likewise* corr. on CP1 to *Transactions; and also of a book not quite unknown, on English Medical Jurisprudence; and likewise*
413.31–32 *in his time, as rather a wise man; and also* corr. on CP1 to *in his time, as having gleams of reason in him; and also*
413.32 *of the writings of* corr. on CP2 to *of the testimony of*
414.4 *it has in the Sol's* corr. on CP1 to *it has in the stock in trade of the Sol's*
414.7 MS–L: *meeting at Manchester,—* CD: *meeting in Manchester,—*
414.13 *perfectly enchanted.* corr. on CP1 to *particularly charmed.*
414.26 *that he is hustled about and moved on,* corr. on CP1 to *that he is moved on,*
414.29 *to be thrust out.* corr. on CP1 to *to be shut out.*
414.39 *at the door; he wants to see the lady too.* corr. on CP1 to *at the door; but he wants to see my Lady too.*
415.32–33 *did not put him away,* corr. on CP1 to *did not utterly put him away,*
415.35 *"Is that all?" says* corr. on CP1 to *"Is this all you have to say?" enquires*
416.1 MS: *of the name of Tulking-*

horn's. CP1–CD: *of the name of Tulkinghorn.*

416.14–15 *and hopes Mr. Tulkinghorn* corr. on CP1 to *and cringingly hopes that Mr. Tulkinghorn*

416.20 *"To be sure. Thank you,* corr. on CP1 to *"To be sure. Why, thank you,*

Chapter XXXIV MS and two sets of CP, presumably CP1 and CP2; no conclusive evidence of any earlier or later CP missing

417.8 MS–L: *handle of his brush.* CD: *handle of the brush.*

417.10 *guv'ner,* corr. on CP1 to *commander,*

417.13 MS–CP1 [n.c.]: *Mr. Joseph Bagnet* CP2–CD: *Mr. Matthew Bagnet*

417.21 CP1: *mischievous* corr. to *mischeevious* [as in MS]

417.24–25 *I may say, double this principal in interest."* corr. on CP1 to *I may say, half as much again as this principal, in interest and one thing and another."*

417.26–27 *a very extraordinary wrench* corr. on CP2 to *a very unaccountable wrench*

417.33 *to a end at last, guv'ner."* corr. on CP1 to *to a end at last."*

417.38 *and a vice* corr. on CP1 to *and a wice*

418.2 MS–L: *he must and he will* CD: *he must and will*

418.6 *Ah! I wish I could."* corr. on CP1 to *I wish I could."*

419.8 *"Well, George,"* corr. on CP2 to *"Well, George, old fellow,"*

419.14 *folds her arms,* corr. on CP1 to *crosses her arms,*

419.19 MS–L: *says Mrs. Bagnet,* CD: *said Mrs. Bagnet,*

419.19–20 *Number Seventy-Four and myself,"* corr. on CP2 to *Lignum and myself,"*

419.20 *she generally speaks* corr. on CP2 to *she often speaks*

419.20–22 *her husband as Number Seventy-Four, which is supposed to have been his old regimental number* corr. on CP2 to *her husband by this appellation, on account, as it is supposed, of Lignum Vitae having been his old regimental nickname*

419.22–23 *acquainted;* corr. on CP2 to *acquainted, in compliment to the extreme hardness and toughness of his physiognomy;*

419.24 *looked in, to make* corr. on CP2 to *looked in, we have, to make*

419.31 *For Seventy-Four,* corr. on CP2 to *For Lignum,*

419.37 MS–53: *Her quick bright eye* C–CD: *Her bright quick eye*

419.39 *of Seventy-Four's!* corr. on CP2 to *of Lignum's!*

419.41 *a troubled face.* corr. on CP1 to *a troubled visage.*

420.1–2 *of Seventy-Four's,* corr. on CP2 to *of Lignum's,*

420.8 MS: *uneasiness and anxiety* (?) *at* CP1: *uneasiness and sympathy at* corr. to *great uneasiness at*

420.14 *to lie down on.* corr. on CP1 to *to lie upon.*

420.22–23 *looks alternately at him and the grey* corr. on CP1 to *looks distressfully at the grey*

420.24–25 *but looking at his* corr. on CP1 to *but still looking at his*

420.32–33 *as kindly as* corr. on CP1 to *as forgivingly as*

420.37 *"Why didn't he* corr. on CP2 to *"Oh! Why didn't he*

421.5–6 *piece of lumber."* corr. on CP1 to *piece of old stores."*

421.21–22 *hanging over us.* corr. on CP1 to *hanging over our heads.*

421.22 *There! Forget* corr. on CP1 to *Come! Forget*

421.31 *it isn't—in short, it isn't* corr. on CP1 to *it's not—in short, it's not*

421.38–39 *as if he were immediately going* corr. on CP1 to *as if he had made a final confession, and were immediately going*

422.6 *"I trust Seventy-Four* corr. on CP2 to *"I trust my old Lignum*

422.8–9 will *bring him* corr. on CP2 to will *bring Lignum*

422.10 *umbrella, returns,* corr. on CP1 to *umbrella, goes home,*

422.13 *people in the whole great city of London, and within ten miles around, less likely* corr. on CP1 to *people in England less likely*

422.30 MS–L: *returns the trooper.* CD: *says the trooper.*

422.39 MS–C: *"and that true to* L–CD: *"and true to*

422.43 *bless her open face,* corr. on CP1 to *bless her,*

423.10 *circumstances* corr. on CP1 to *circumstance*

423.13 *his feet embarrassed in the drawer* corr. on CP1 to *his feet in the drawer*

423.13–14 CP1: *a paper foot-path,* corr. to *a paper foot-bath* [as in MS]

423.16 *"My dear friends,"* corr. on CP2 to *"My dear friend,"*

423.16–17 *two affectionate hands* corr. on CP1 to *two lean, affectionate arms*

423.24–25 *Military air!"* corr. on CP1 to *Military air, sir!"*

424.20 *arrange the matter* corr. on CP2 to *arrange the affair*

424.29 MS–L: *proceeds in this soldierly* CD: *proceeds in his soldierly*

424.43 *to arrange all this* corr. on CP1 to *to arrange this*

425.1 MS: *his family's minds,* CP1–CD: *his family's mind,*

425.4–5 CP1: *bound to silence when* corr. to *found to be silent when* [MS had *found to silent when*]

425.18 MS–CP2 [n.c.]: *now has attained* 53–CD: *has now attained*

425.35 *lawyer. What do you* corr. on CP1 to *lawyer. Now, what do you*

427.33 MS–C: *should we be melancholly boys?'* L: *melancholy boys?'* CD: *should we be melancholy, boys?'*

428.16–17 *not in my course* corr. on CP1 to *not at all in my course*
428.30 *implicated—nominally,* corr. on CP1 to *implicated in this unfortunate affair—nominally,*
429.11–12 *answers, "I must* corr. on CP1 to *answers with a long breath, "I must*
429.15–16 MS: *and who now puts his hand* CP1–CD: *and who puts his hand* [MS reading restored as likely to have been inadvertently overlooked and rather better than compositor's omission]
429.20 *"It's only a letter* corr. on CP1 to *" 'Tis only a letter*
429.39 *their Bluffy* corr. on CP1 to *their existing Bluffy*
429.42 *He remains clouded* corr. on CP1 to *He remains in close order, clouded*
430.9 *Mrs. Bagnet, threading* corr. on CP1 to *Mrs. Bagnet, quietly threading*
430.11 *"Ain't I good company? I am afraid* corr. on CP1 to *"Am I? Not good company? Well, I am afraid* [MS had *An't I*]
430.14 *like Bluffy, ain't it?"* corr. on CP1 to *like Bluffy, too!"* [MS had *an't it*]
430.16 *"true, for all that!"* corr. on CP1 to *"true, I am afraid. These little 'uns are always right."* CP2: *little 'uns* corr. to *little ones*
430.18 *stupid soldier's wife—* corr. on CP1 to *stupid old soldier's wife—* CP2: *stupid* corr. to *shrill*
430.20–21 *shouldn't do to you."* corr. on CP1 to *shouldn't say to you now."*
430.22–23 *"Not a bit of it."* corr. on CP1 to *"Not a morsel of it."*
430.26 *I trusted Seventy-Four* corr. on CP2 to *I trusted Lignum*
431.1–2 *think when you're a man,* corr. on CP 1 to *think of when you are a man,*
431.3 *sitting the boy* corr. on CP1 to *seating the boy*

Chapter XXXV MS and one set of CP; 3 substantive divergences between CP and 53 may imply existence of CP2 missing

431.13 MS–CP [n.c.]: *crossed a dark ocean,* 53–CD: *crossed a dark lake,*
431.23–24 *time were lost and became* corr. on CP to *time became*
432.10 MS-L: *might be better able* CD: *might be the better able*
432.17 *and knew with* corr. on CP to *and I knew with*
432.41 CP: *was greatly sorry for,* corr. to *was quietly sorry for,* [MS adverb illegible but cannot be *quietly*]
433.11 *pretty tea-board with* corr. on CP to *pretty tea-table with*
433.14 *ready on the little table at the bedside,* corr. on CP to *ready at the bedside,*
434.6 *even kinder to me* corr. on CP to *even fonder of me*
434.15–16 *for the best. Everything she does is for the best, and of the best. But here* corr. on CP to *for the best. But here*
434.29 *he writes to me under* corr. on CP to *he wrote to me under*
434.34 *worse, many and many a time.* corr. on CP to *worse, many a time.*
435.26–27 *friends, and not distrustful foes, and we* corr. on CP to *friends, instead of distrustful foes, and that we* [MS had *and that we*]
435.42 MS: *procratisnates,*
436.35 CP: *such precious vows* corr. to *such ferocious vows* [as in MS]
437.3–4 *should write him a letter* corr. on CP to *should send him a letter*
437.5 MS–53: *for of all the places* C–CD: *for all the places*
437.9 MS: *tired to soon;* CP–CD: *tired too soon;*
437.22–23 *fall gently on my mind with a good influence.* corr. on CP to *fall like a gentle lesson on my mind at that time.*
437.33–34 MS–L: *and to do some good* CD: *and to do good*
437.38 *these mercies?* corr. on CP to *those mercies?*
438.31 *said she, in her* corr. on CP to *said she to me, in her*
439.42 CP [n.c.]–53: *donbtful if* C–CD: *doubtful if* [em. ad., as in MS]
440.28 *felt them drawing* corr. on CP to *felt them even drawing*
440.30 *She touched me* corr. on CP to *She tapped me*
440.43 CP: *swiftly drawn to* corr. to *drawn —swiftly—to* [as in MS]
441.5 MS: *in this delivery of which* CP–CD: *in the delivery of which*
441.29 *I was very much impressed* corr. on CP to *I was much impressed*
441.33 MS: *reaching out her hand* CP–CD: *reaching another hand* [MS reading restored, for obvious reasons]
441.39–40 MS–CP [n.c.]: *gratuitously, I assure you!* 53–CD: *gratuitously. Until*
442.28 *fallen down at his feet* corr. on CP to *fallen at his feet*
442.45 *when they were distinguished by the* corr. on CP to *when they consisted of the*
443.4 *of every kind,* corr. on CP to *of every sort,*
443.4 MS–CP [n.c.]: *are among its nobility!* 53–CD: *are added to its nobility!*
443.9 after *very mad indeed.* white line ins. on CP [*white line here* written by D in margin; no white line shown in MS]
443.10 *with a little secret* corr. on CP to *with the little secret*

Chapter XXXVI MS and two sets of CP; no conclusive evidence of any other set or sets missing

443.32 *road. And every* corr. on CP1 to *road. And I found every* and on CP2 to *road. I found every*
443.34 *in nature was more beautiful* corr. on CP1 to *in nature, more beautiful*
443.35 *than it had ever been.* corr. on CP1 to *than I had ever found it yet.*
443.37 *full of pleasure* corr. on CP1 to *full of delight*

444.7–8 *sat down and cried, a dozen times,* corr. on CP1 to *sat down, overcome, a dozen times,*
444.14 *you are sensible enough* corr. on CP1 to *you are quite sensible enough*
444.31–32 CP1: *I said, "Esther, alone, now, in your room, if you are* corr. to *I said now, alone in my own room, "Esther, if you are* [MS had *I said, now in my own room.*]
444.35–36 *and read a little while.* corr. on CP1 to *and thought a little more.*
444.42 *I put it aside,* corr. on CP1 to *I put my hair aside,*
444.43 *in the mirror. I was encouraged* corr. on CP1 to *in the mirror; encouraged*
445.1 *before my eyes and started* corr. on CP1 to *before it and started*
445.2–3 MS: *I knew the extent of the alteration in it even better* CP1–CD: *I knew the extent of the alteration in it better* [MS reading restored as likely to have been inadvertently overlooked and yet better than misreading]
445.10 *quite tranquilly and thankfully.* corr. on CP1 to *quite thankfully.*
445.17 CP1: *to him, because—though in the secret* corr. to *to him, even in the secret* [MS had *to him, though in the secret*]
445.18 *know—I could* corr. on CP1 to *know, because I could*
445.34 *wishing very much to be fully* corr. on CP1 to *wishing to be fully*
446.2 *and his mane all over* corr. on CP1 to *and a mane all over*
446.12 *laugh at him with such* corr. on CP1 to *laugh with such*
446.14 *his own rough coat.* corr. on CP1 to *his rough coat.*
446.20–21 *came to the conclusion that* corr. on CP1 to *came to the decision that*
446.33–34 *many of them before,* corr. on CP1 to *many of the grown people before,*
446.38 *on its hinges like the flap of a table, it shut up* corr. on CP1 to *on its hinges, it shut up*
447.1 *to Africa, and from Africa* corr. on CP1 to *To America, and from America*
447.5–6 *going on invitation into so many* corr. on CP2 to *sitting on invitation in so many*
447.6 *cottages, and writing* corr. on CP1 to *cottages, going on with Charley's education, and writing* CP2: *writing to Ada* corr. to *writing long letters to Ada*
447.9–10 *forget it or be reconciled to it. I felt* corr. on CP1 to *forget it. I felt*
447.16–17 CP1: *inferiority. I happened* corr. to *inferiority. One of these particularly touched me. I happened* [as in MS, except for *of these*]
447.28 *I thought,* corr. on CP1 to *I thought with shame,* and on CP2 to *I thought,*
448.2 *flowers for my room, she took* corr. on CP1 to *flowers, she took*
448.7 *uninterested; on* corr. on CP1 to *uninterested about the building; on*
448.8–9 *ranged inside, and whether* corr. on CP1 to *ranged, and whether*
448.15 MS: *did. For whatsoever reason* CP1: *did; for whatsoever reason* corr. to *did. For whatever reason*
448.25 *and little, however, it revealed* corr. on CP1 to *and little, it revealed*
448.33 *outstretched arms,* corr. on CP1 to *outstretched hands,*
448.35 *that I had dreamed of* corr. on CP1 to *that I had pined for and dreamed of*
448.37 MS–CP2 [n.c.]: *in her's before.* 53–CD: *in hers before.*
449.3 *in my thoughts.* corr. on CP1 to *in my whirling thoughts.*
449.10 *home, my dear, and I will* corr. on CP1 to *home, and I will*
449.12–13 *bonnet, which was all disordered, and went* corr. on CP1 to *bonnet, and went*
449.26–27 *gratitude to God* corr. on CP1 to *gratitude to the Providence of God*
449.28–29 CP1: *could look at me* corr. to *could ever now look at me* [MS had *could ever look at me*]
449.32 *for, over and above the trouble* corr. on CP1 to *for, besides the trouble*
449.37 *or could ever change.* corr. on CP1 to *or could change.*
449.44 *two troubled hearts* corr. on CP1 to *two troubled minds*
449.45 *said my mother,* corr. on CP1 to *groaned my mother,*
450.1 MS: *I must traverse* CP1–CD: *I must travel*
450.6–7 *she cast it off again directly.* corr. on CP1 to *she soon cast it off again.*
450.12 *than any shriek could have been.* corr. on CP1 to *than any shriek.*
450.13 CP1: *were willing* corr. to *were unwilling* [as in MS]
450.20 *nearly mad.* corr. on CP1 to *nearly frantic.*
450.41 *to-morrow, next day, any day."* corr. on CP1 to *to-morrow, any day."*
450.44 *kissing my hand.* corr. on CP1 to *kissing my hands.* [MS not clear]
451.1 *to be either; and I dread that. He's* corr. on CP1 to *to be either. He is*
451.3 *profitable privilege,* corr. on CP1 to *profit, privilege,*
451.11 *"He has none. He is perfectly indifferent* corr. on CP1 to *"He has none, and no passion. He is indifferent* CP2: *passion* corr. to *anger*
451.21 *resolved. In the hollowness of my empty heart I have outbidden* corr. on CP1 to *resolved. I have long outbidden*
451.23 *many more, will outlive* corr. on CP1 to *many more. I will outlive*
451.26 *is still the same.* corr. on CP1 to *is the same.*
451.34 *who till this time* corr. on CP1 to *who until this time*
451.36 *"You may confide fully* corr. on CP1 to *"Confide fully*
452.6 *my child!" she said passionately.* corr. on CP1 to *my child!" she said.*
452.7 CP1: *upon thy neck* corr. to *upon my neck* [as in MS]
452.8 *no more. The name of the master of this place, whom I have wronged beyond reparation, must be saved from public*

reproach and discredit, if it can be saved. To hope corr. on CP1 to *no more. To hope*

452.8–9 *to do that, I must* corr. on CP1 to *to do what I seek to do, I must*

452.16 *We embraced one another* corr. on CP1 to *We held one another*

452.21 *such repose* corr. on CP1 to *such complete repose*

452.30–31 *restrain tears of the wildest grief;* corr. on CP1 to *restrain bursts of grief;*

453.4–5 *here. It has* corr. on CP1 to *here; for it has* and on CP2 to *here. It has*

453.7–8 *or bad, that I* corr. on CP1 to *or bad in me, that I*

453.11 *had an absolute terror* corr. on CP1 to *had a terror*

453.30 *the same feelings.* corr. on CP1 to *the same distress.*

453.32 *bats, that* corr. on CP1 to *bats, which*

453.41 *the moss and ivy* corr. on CP1 to *the trained moss and ivy*

453.41 *about them, and the old* corr. on CP1 to *about them, and around the old*

453.42 *sun-dial, and were trained to keep their bounds; and I heard* corr. on CP1 to *sun-dial; and I heard*

454.1 *at the night over the family escutcheons* corr. on CP1 to *at the gloom over the family escutcheons* and on CP2 to *at the evening gloom over the escutcheons*

454.26 *thankless and unreasonable this state* corr. on CP1 to *thankless this state*

454.40–41 *never have had such* corr. on CP1 to *never have been reserved for such*

455.10 *through the day better* corr. on CP1 to *through the intermediate time better*

455.10–11 MS: *talking a long walk*

455.20–21 *my darling so dearly that* corr. on CP1 to *my darling so well that*

455.26 *look for Esther,* corr. on CP1 to *look for her old Esther,*

455.33 *I could quite* corr. on CP1 to *could I quite*

456.15 *nothing—as she fell upon my neck!* corr. on CP1 to *nothing!*

456.19 *like an infant,* corr. on CP1 to *like a child,*

Chapter XXXVII MS, one incomplete and two complete sets of CP; CP1 for first five pages, then CP2, have most of the usual corrections; CP3 used mainly for altering end of chapter

456.29 *at any other time;* corr. on CP1 to *at another time;*

456.37 *was very great.* corr. on CP1 to *was great.*

457.28 *That was W. Grubble,* corr. on CP1 to *It was W. Grubble,*

457.34 MS: *a beau-tiful woman,* CP1–CD: *a beautiful woman,* [MS reading restored as intentional, and only inadvertently overlooked]

458.9 MS–L: *from the ceiling.* CD: *from his ceiling.*

458.11–12 *comfortably dressed* corr. on CP1 to *cosily dressed*

458.37 *said I, "to understand* corr. on CP1 to *said I, shaking my head, "to understand*

459.3 *I want to walk quietly into* corr. on CP1 to *I want to come quietly into* and on CP2 to *I want to appear quietly in*

459.34 *he called him—* corr. on CP1 to *he called Mr. Skimpole—*

459.35–36 *he would come to see* corr. on CP1 to *he was bent on coming to see*

459.38 MS: *expences*

460.5 *a pink silk stocking.* corr. on CP1 to *a silk stocking.*

460.25 *some steady principles and purposes,* corr. on CP1 to *some right principle and purpose,*

460.31 *Mr. Skimpole's open avowal* corr. on CP1 to *Mr. Skimpole's avowal*

460.36 *I walked quietly in* corr. on CP1 to *I walked softly in*

461.1 MS: *I had a worrying idea that* CP1: *I had a worrying idea lest* corr. to *I had a tormenting idea that*

461.2 *his truth* corr. on CP2 to *his best truth*

461.23 MS: *looking beamingly round upon us over a glass of wine-and-water,* CP1: *looking beamingly over a glass of wine-and-water round upon us,* corr. to *looking beamingly at us over a glass of wine-and-water,*

461.30–31 *to wait for him very long,* corr. on CP1 to *to wait for him long,*

462.6 *why not, Esther," said Richard. "If you* corr. on CP1 to *why not, Esther. If you*

462.16 no CP1 preserved after that point, but CP2 seems to take over, i.e., serve as CP1: further corrections made on a later set, called CP3 in following notes

463.43 *without one offended* corr. on CP2 to *without an offended*

464.30 *afraid of that,"* corr. on CP2 to *afraid for me,"*

464.31 *blessed girl, to return to whom is like walking out of a weary dream; but you* corr. on CP2 to *blessed girl; but you*

465.22–23 *flying reports* corr. on CP2 to *flying rumours*

465.23–24 *imprudent; because, on the* corr. on CP2 to *imprudent; on the*

465.40 MS: *character were not dyed* CP2: *character was not dyed* corr. to *character were not being dyed*

465.42–43 *"I don't know who may not,* [the phrase would make better sense without *not,* but *not* is in MS–CD]

465.44 MS–CP3: *settled life."* 53: *setted life."* C–CD: *settled life."* [em. ad., as *setted* is an obvious 53 misprint]

466.23–24 *a far greater* corr. on CP2 to *a far, far greater*

466.25–26 *and presently wrote* corr. on CP3 to *and she presently wrote*

466.27 text of letter had been set up in ordinary type on CP; D wrote *PRINTER. Set up this letter in smaller type, as in Copperfield;* letter is in smaller type on CP3

466.28 *to repeat for myself* corr. on CP2 to *to repeat most earnestly for myself*

466.42 *with me for this.* corr. on CP2 to *with me for saying this.*
467.3 *love better* corr. on CP2 to *love much better*
467.3 *than the object of your first fancy.* corr. on CP3 to *than your first fancy.*
467.4–5 *that she would much prefer* corr. on CP2 to *that the object of your choice would greatly prefer*
467.9–10 *and of indifference* corr. on CP2 to *and of your indifference*
467.15 *in him, even for the time, if any.* corr. on CP2 to *in him, if any.*
467.35 MS: *a handfull*
468.10 *he had just then.* corr. on CP2 to *he entertained just then.*
468.15 *wouldn't, I feel convinced;* corr. on CP2 to *wouldn't, I know;*
468.17 MS: *It was very unfortunate for Richard, I said.* CP–CD: *"It was very unfortunate for Richard," I said.* [MS reading restored because *was* seems to imply reported speech and thus preclude inverted commas]
468.20 *—excellent man—good deal* corr. on CP2 to *—an excellent man—a good deal*
468.41–42 CP2: *their flocks serenely* corr. to *their flocks severely* [as in MS]
468.42 MS: *sticking-plaister*
469.2 *The whole line* corr. on CP2 to *The whole race*
469.39 MS–L: *hastily presenting* CD: *hastily representing*
470.3 *in the paper,* corr. on CP2 to *in the Chancellor's paper,*
470.11 *post town inn,* corr. on CP3 to *post town in,*
470.18 MS–L: *while I am gone?"* CD: *when I am gone?"*
470.29 CP2: *it is not ruinous,* corr. to *it is not immoral,* [as in MS]
470.36 *"Indeed, miss," said* corr. on CP2 to *"Indeed?" said*
471.12 *daughters, miss," he said.* corr. on CP2 to *daughters," he said.*
471.19 MS–L: *as he ever replied* CD: *as he had ever replied*
471.19–20 *to anything—"It is all the same* corr. on CP3 to *to anything—"You will drive me, will you, sir? It is all the same*
471.27–28 *were gone. We were both surprised, on our rising to accompany Richard to the little inn, that he rather objected to our going./ "Why, the fact is," he at length explained, with a hearty burst of laughter,—"it's very ridiculous, but since it must come out,—there's nothing kept here; there was nothing to be got, but a mourning-coach that happens to be waiting to be taken back; and I am going to drive Mr. Vholes over in that."/ Ada turned pale, and was quite distressed.* [*distressed.* corr. on CP to *shocked.*] *I must say that I too felt uncomfortable, and was not relieved by the great applicability of the carriage to Mr. Vholes. But Richard's high spirits carried everything away, and we all went out* corr. on CP3 to *were gone./ Richard's high spirits carrying everything before them, we all went out*
471.29 *the hill, where* corr. on CP2 to *the hill above the village, where*
471.30 *ordered the coach* corr. on CP3 to *ordered a gig*
471.31 *at the heads of the grey horses that had been* corr. on CP3 to *at the head of the gaunt pale horse that had been*
471.33 *those two seated on the box in* corr. on CP3 to *those two seated side by side in*
471.38–40 *high trees, and those two driving away* corr. on CP3 to *high trees, the gaunt pale horse with his ears pricked up, and the driving away*
471.41 *that night, that Richard's* corr. on CP2 to *that night, how Richard's*
472.1–2 *give him. He thought* corr. on CP2 to *give him; how he thought*
472.7–8 *the distance shortens and the goal is visible;* corr. on CP2 to *the distance already shortens and the journey's end is growing visible;*
472.9–10 MS–L: *it casts ashore,* CD: *it cast ashore,*

Chapter XXXVII MS and two sets of CP; no other CP missing; CP2 has corrections mainly of passages ins. on CP1

472 chapter-heading ins. on CP1 [but is in MS]
472.18 *all I have got to say* corr. on CP1 to *all I have to say*
472.22 MS: *journies*
472.25 *when my fussy arrangements* corr. on CP1 to *when these arrangements*
472.36–473.1 *fear she would make her husband jealous of me.* corr. on CP1 to *fear I should make her husband jealous.*
473.15 *We are quite good friends,* corr. on CP1 to *We are good friends,*
474.13 MS: *expence,*
474.19 *have a tolerably good ear* corr. on CP1 to *have a very good ear*
474.28 *my heart. I conscientiously* corr. on CP1 to *my heart. For I conscientiously*
474.31 *perseverance which was* corr. on CP2 to *perseverance that was*
475.5–6 *one little limp girl, in a dirty gauzy dress.* corr. on CP1 to *one dirty little limp girl, in a gauzy dress.*
475.8 MS: *sandaled* CP1–L: *sandalled* CD: *sandled*
475.18 *to be a kind of enjoyment* corr. on CP1 to *to be some sense of enjoyment*
475.36 *little gauzy girl,* corr. on CP2 to *little gauzy child,*
475.38 *the cloudy bonnet* corr. on CP1 to *the dowdy bonnet*
476.21–22 *of the pleasantest of oddities, surely!* corr. on CP1 to *of the pleasantest of oddities.*
476.24 *next to my having* corr. on CP1 to *next to having*
476.36 *the very gentleman who* corr. on CP1 to *the gentleman who*
476.38 *to be the proper person* corr. on CP1 to *to be naturally the person*

477.11 *will you put* corr. on CP1 to *will you be so good as to put*
477.20 MS–L: *acknowledged its receipt* CD: *acknowledged the receipt*
477.22 *was so highly delighted that she* corr. on CP1 to *was so diverted that she*
477.26 MS–C: *mother now,* L: *mother, now,* CD: *mother just now,*
477.30 *unspeakably diverted* corr. on CP1 to *unspeakably entertained*
477.35 *highly irritating* corr. on CP1 to *highly exasperating*
477.38–39 *when I put up* corr. on CP1 to *when I now put up*
478.2–3 *amazement and uneasiness.* corr. on CP1 to *amazement and apprehension.*
478.4 *said Mr. Guppy,* corr. on CP1 to *stammered Mr. Guppy,*
478.12 CP1–53: *"A kind of a giddy* C–CD: *"A kind of giddy*
478.11–18 MS: *and fluttered his papers./ "My intention was* CP1: *and fluttered his fingers./ "My intention was* corr. to p.t.
478.21 *to admit that at once. Though* corr. on CP1 to *to admit that? Though*
478.22–23 *satisfaction to your mind—if you made that* corr. on CP1 to *satisfaction to—to your mind—if you was to put in that*
478.24 *"Surely there can be* corr. on CP1 to *"There can be*
478.31–32 *such declaration was final,* corr. on CP1 to *such declaration on my part was final,*
478.33 *"No doubt," said I.* corr. on CP1 to *"I quite understand that," said I.*
478.34 *"Perhaps—it may* corr. on CP1 to *"Perhaps—er—it may*
478.39 *I quite regret that* corr. on CP1 to *I regret that*
478.42 *it will always be* corr. on CP1 to *it will ever be*
478.42 *entwined with* corr. on CP1 to *entwined—er—with*
479.4 *and excellent feeling,* corr. on CP1 to *and right feeling,*
479.4–5 *will keep you square—that* corr. on CP1 to *will keep you as square as possible—that*
479.19 MS–53: *thought of it most, lately—* C–CD: *thought of it most lately*
479.20 *I decided* corr. on CP1 to *I have decided* [MS not clear]
479.33 *gave you credit, and for which any person acquainted with you would give you credit likewise, I am sure. Nothing* corr. on CP2 to *gave you credit. Nothing*
479.30–39 *for my peace."/ I must say for Mr. Guppy* corr. on CP1 to p.t. [*"I am bound to confess . . . present proceedings."* ins.]
479.44 *a kindness, Mr. Guppy.* corr. on CP2 to *a kindness, sir.*
480.16–18 *in question, I speak* corr. on CP1 to *in question," continued Mr. Guppy, rapidly, as if he were repeating a familiar form of words, "I speak*
481.9 *Oxford-street, in the county of Middlesex, aforesaid. Much obliged."* corr. on CP2 to *Oxford-street. Much obliged."*
480.32–481.10 *"I do," said I, quite confidently./ He ran home* corr. on CP1 to p.t. [about two thirds of a page ins.; the insert being too long for bottom of proof page, after *suggested Mr. Guppy.* D wrote *Over. Next page* and on next page *Insertion continued from previous page.*]
481.11 *"Touching that other matter,* corr. on CP1 to *"Touching that matter,*
481.14–15 *Mr. Guppy to me, in a forlorn manner, "but* corr. on CP2 to *Mr. Guppy to me, forlornly and despondently, "but*
481.23 *tender passion, you may indeed!"* corr. on CP1 to *tender passion only!"*
481.27–29 *hurry away, which I did with a lightened heart.* corr. on CP1 to *hurry away. I did so with a lightened heart; but when we last looked back, Mr. Guppy was still oscillating in the same troubled state of mind, only that he now neither got to us nor got to his mother's, but in his distraction turned and turned midway.* CP2: end of sentence canc. from *only that he* so that p.t. stops at *troubled state of mind.*

Chapter XXXIX MS and one set of CP; 4 uncorrected divergences between MS and CP seem to be compositors' misreadings like the score of corrected ones; the 5 slight divergences between CP and 53 do not definitely imply D's own work on a later set of CP

481 chapter-heading ins. on CP [not in MS]: *The Pilgrim's Progress* canc. *Attorney and Client*
481.34 MS–L: *sparing man in his day,* CD: *sparing man in his way,*
482.3 *Quartered, as aforesaid, in this* corr. on CP to *Quartered in this*
482.4 CP [n.c.]: *legal learnings* 53–CD: *legal bearings* [as in MS]
482.6 *is mewed up* corr. on CP to *is squeezed up*
482.8 *door, squeezed into an angle* corr. on CP to *door, in an angle*
482.19 MS: *chimnies*
482.24–25 *in the hot weather.* corr. on CP to *in hot weather.*
482.41 MS: *expence,*
483.10 MS–L: *I would say,* CD: *I will say,*
483.17–18 *of an eminent attorney's* corr. on CP to *of a distinguished attorney's*
483.38–39 *He must perish.* corr. on CP to *Is he to perish?*
483.39 *Why, they must be* corr. on CP to *Are they to be*
484.33 *"How am I* corr. on CP to *"Yes, with Ixion on it. How am I*
484.40 *more fortitude.* corr. on CP to *more patience.*
484.41 CP [n.c.]: *said Richard,* 53–CD: *says Richard,* [as in MS]
485.6 MS–53: *leave a good name* C–CD: *leave the good name*

485.36 *more in detail.* corr. on CP to *more readily.*
486.19 *brightening afresh. "But* corr. on CP to *brightening. "But*
486.29 *has it his own way* corr. on CP to *has it all his own way*
486.37 *too enthusiastically.* corr. on CP to *too ardently.*
487.5–6 *as well as I do, that* corr. on CP to *as well as I, that*
487.22–23 *MS–L: it sows dissension* CD: *it sows dissensions*
487.24 *I reply they are* corr. on CP to *I reply then, they are*
487.44 *I shall never rest,* corr. on CP to *I shall not rest,*
488.16 *this explicit declaration* corr. on CP to *this declaration*
488.42 *find me here, sir."* corr. on CP to *find me here, sir, with my shoulder to the wheel."*
489.19 MS: *suspence,*
489.19–20 *room for a little sorrowful wonder* corr. on CP to *room for some sorrowful wonder*
490.4 MS: *that, as I was mentioning, is what* CP–CD: *that as I was mentioning is what* [MS punct. restored as likely to have been overlooked though expressing better sense in better language than compositor's version]
490.10 *is helping, eh?"* corr. on CP to *is helping?"*
490.25 MS: *controul,*
490.32–33 MS: *from your knowledge of the ways of that capricious and deep old character* CP: *from your knowledge of the things of that* corr. to *from your knowledge of that* [MS reading restored in spite of D's failure to do so himself, probably through haste or carelessness rather than change of mind]
490.38–39 *head. Thinks not.* corr. on CP to *head. Decidedly thinks not.*
490.40 *as they slowly walk* corr. on CP to *as they walk*
491.2 MS: *controul.*
491.5–6 CP: *on your responsibility."* corr. to *on my own responsibility."* [as in MS]
491.26 *Elwes, of Northamptonshire,* corr. on CP to *Elwes, of Suffolk,*
491.29–30 MS–CP [n.c]: *and prys into* 53–CD: *and pries into*
491.38 CP: *the revived melody of "we're a nodding,"* corr. to *the revived Caledonian melody of "we're a' nodding,"* [*Caledonian* not in MS; MS not clear for *a* or *a'*]
492.21 MS: *dirtily snowed up in* CP–CD: *snowed up in* [*dirtily* restored as introducing intentional contrast and likely to have been inadvertently overlooked by compositor]
492.25 *a demoniacal appearance* corr. on CP to *a fiendish appearance*
492.27 *otherwise, it is ghostly* corr. on CP to *likewise, it is ghostly*
493.6 *to do at the moment, and were* corr. on CP to *to do, and were*
493.32 MS: *got out on the house-tops,* CP–CD: *got out on the house-top,* [MS reading restored because of back-reference at end of following paragraph]
495.3–4 CP: *undisguised communication* corr. to *undivulged communication* [as in MS]
495.7 MS: *controul,*
495.7 MS: *that the ole should be* CP: *whole* corr. to *ole* 53: *ole* C–CD: *whole*
495.11 *without a syllable* corr. on CP to *without a word*

Chapter XL MS and one set of CP; same type of textual problems as in XXXIX; chapter very poorly set up by compositors and not very conscientiously checked against MS by D

495 chapter-heading ins. on CP [not in MS]
495.19 *those gentlemen, which* corr. on CP to *those two great men, which*
495.23 *and stockings,* corr. on CP to *and long stockings,*
495.27 *he had meant* corr. on CP to *he had merely meant*
495.28 MS: *with-hold*
495.32–33 MS: *been for some weeks* CP–CD: *been some weeks* [MS reading restored as likely to have been inadvertently overlooked by compositor]
496.1 *much about the pilot; but* corr. on CP to *much about it; but*
496.23–24 *work in hand. And* corr. on CP to *work. And*
498.6 *in the land, and wakes all the latent brightness in its ray. Then do* corr. on CP to *in the land. Then do*
498.9 CP: *into a nun.* (?) corr. to *into a wink.* [as in MS]
498.10 MS: *stoney*
498.12 *An ancestress* corr. on CP to *One ancestress*
498.36 *without life in its silence and immobility. Now,* corr. on CP to *without life. Now,*
498.40 MS: *in such pale and faded hues* CP: *in such pale and faded lines* corr. to *in pale and faded hues*
498.42 *staircase balustrades and beams* corr. on CP to *staircase beams*
499.24–25 MS–53: *points in the compass.* C–CD: *points of the compass.*
499.40 *occasions, even dancing may* corr. on CP to *occasions, dancing may*
499.41 [MS unclear] CP: *is seen constantly swimming about,* corr. to *is seen constantly hopping about,* 53–CD: *is constantly seen hopping about,*
500.3 MS: *stately balls,* CP: *state balls,* corr. to *basilisk balls,*
500.4 *pageants, however haughty and indifferent her manner, her mere appearance* corr. on CP to *pageants, her mere appearance*
500.17 *Volumnia is really a more* corr. on CP to *Volumnia is a more*
500.17 *than he thought her.* corr. on CP to *than he had thought her.*
501.8 CP: *"Forgot to say,* corr. to *"I regret to say,* [as in MS]
501.9 MS: *that their opposition to* CP–

CD: *that this opposition to* [MS reading restored as agreeing better with context and likely to have been inadvertently overlooked]

501.14–15 *against a hireling faction—"* corr. on CP to *against a faction—"*

501.16 *always a hireling faction,* corr. on CP to *always a faction,*

501.20 *the Government has not* corr. on CP to *the Party has not*

501.21 MS: *expence.*

501.26–27 *the rouge and the pearl* corr. on CP to *the rouge and pearl*

501.33,38 MS: *"that you* do *mean* CP–CD: *"that you do mean* [MS italics restored as clearly intentional and understandably overlooked by compositor]

501.36 *support the Government.* corr. on CP to *support the Party.*

501.41–502.1 MS: *expences*

502.11 *says Sir Leicester, "why* corr. on CP to *says Sir Leicester, opening his eyes, "why*

502.24 *that a man told him* corr. on CP to *that—man told him*

502.25 CP–L: *gone down to t'that* CD: *gone down t'that* [em. ad. as in MS]

502.34 *solid creature,* corr. on CP to *stolid creature,*

502.38 *trowels; which lively remarks* corr. on CP to *trowels. These lively remarks*

502.41–42 *my heart. I had* corr. on CP to *my heart for the inconstant creature. I had*

503.21 *Oh! nothing is so charming to* corr. on CP to *O! nothing is so delicious to*

503.28 MS: *on the empty side of* CP: *on the opposite of* corr. to *on the opposite side of*

503.35 *"Oh, a hollow thing from* corr. on CP to *"Oh, hollow from*

503.42 MS: *it's sort of thing* CP: *it's a sort of thing* corr. to *it's—sort of thing*

504.22 MS: *"And throughout he was much assisted* CP–CD: *"And he was much assisted* [*throughout* restored as clearly intentional and likely to have been inadvertently overlooked]

504.24 MS: *"By his son?" repeats* CP: *"By his son?" repeated* corr. to *"By his son, sir?" repeats*

504.38 *—DEVIL—* corr. on CP to *—DAYVLE—*

504.44 *but very decided* corr. on CP to *but decided*

505.2 *you might exert* corr. on CP to *you should exert*

505.20 CP–C: *tremulouslessly* L–CD: *tremulously* [em. ad. as in MS]

505.43–44 *for this girl,* corr. on CP to *for the girl,*

505.44 *and had her* corr. on CP to *and kept her*

506.6–7 *towards the moonlight, as if to correct his remembrance. By the moonlight,* corr. on CP to *towards the moonlight. By the moonlight,*

506.13–14 *firmest of us to be* corr. on CP to *firmest of us (she was very firm) to be*

506.14 *sore domestic trouble* corr. on CP to *great domestic trouble*

506.16 *my present point.* corr. on CP to *the present point.*

506.24 after *nature."* D began insert with *Lady D* then canc. this and wrote in blank space at bottom of CP page—only 28 lines long, instead of usual 50—*Printer. Manage to bring this down, as I would rather not write more in. It can be easily done by bringing the previous chapter over, a little. C.D.*

506.27 MS–CP [n.c.]: *thresh-hold.* 53–CD: *threshold.*

506.33 MS: *expences*

506.40–41 *a meek sip* corr. on CP to *a very mild sip*

506.42–43 *slowly, by the side of that Nymph down the long perspective, not at all* corr. on CP to *slowly down the long perspective by the side of that Nymph, not at all*

Chapter XLI MS and one set of CP; same type of textual problems as in XXXIX and XL

507 chapter-heading ins. on CP [not in MS] *Face to Face* canc. *In Mr. Tulkinghorn's Room*

507.4 *close way, well satisfied.* corr. on CP to *close way, satisfied.*

507.11–12 *there is (as there usually is) a pretty large* corr. on CP to *is a pretty large*

507.17 *head stooped low* corr. on CP to *head bent low*

507.28–29 *represented. If he be* corr. on CP to *represented below. If he be*

507.31 MS: *As he regularly paces* CP–CD: *As he paces*

508.21 *dark, steady object,* corr. on CP to *dark, cold object,*

508.33 *her kindling gaze.* corr. on CP to *her gaze.*

508.35–36 *with too high a hand.* corr. on CP to *with so high a hand.*

509.8 MS: *to this place—I* had; CP–CD: *to this place—I had;* [MS italics restored as clearly intentional and understandably overlooked]

509.13 *self-disparagement,* corr. on CP to *self-depreciation,*

509.20 *And so she would* corr. on CP to *And she would*

509.23 *as you well know.* corr. on CP to *as you know.*

509.32–33 *that shall add* corr. on CP to *destined to add*

509.34 *born, is the spade wrought?* corr. on CP to *born yet, is the spade wrought yet?*

510.1 CP: *wear your dress,* corr. to *wear my own dress,* [as in MS]

510.8–9 MS–L: *without removing hand* CD: *without moving hand*

510.15 *who it is?" she passionately asks him.* corr. on CP to *who it is?"*

510.26 *so shrewd an eye* corr. on CP to *so practised an eye*

510.32 *of my making or of my seeking, I will* corr. on CP to *of my making, I will*

510.40 *at the window.* corr. on CP to *at the window, then.*
511.23 *amaze him so much as your fall* corr. on CP to *amaze him more than your fall*
511.25 *breathes very quickly* corr. on CP to *breathes quickly*
511.25 *unfalteringly* corr. on CP to *unflinchingly*
511.28–29 CP: *of your strength and my own hands,* corr. to *of my own strength and my own hands,*
511.34 MS: *my flight?" she returns.* CP–CD: *my flight?" she returned.* [MS reading restored for obvious reasons]
511.37 *for a single day.* corr. on CP to *for a day.*
511.43–44 *need not say to Lady Dedlock,* corr. on CP to *need not say to you, Lady Dedlock,*
512.5–6 *divided you? Why, Lady Dedlock,* corr. on CP to *divided you? Lady Dedlock,*
512.18 *it helps to render* corr. on CP to *it combines to render*
512.20 *coldness fixed and froze her.* corr. on CP to *coldness froze her.*
512.27 *since, and so no more* corr. on CP to *since. No more*
512.31 MS: *day by day, Am I?"* CP–CD: *day by day?"* [MS reading restored as more satisfactory and appearing to have been inadvertently overlooked]
512.35 *platform, upon which* corr. on CP to *platform, on which*
512.37 MS–L: *she says slowly.* CD: *she said slowly.*
512.41 *in her sleep, mechanically looking away at the stars the whole time.* corr. on CP to *in her sleep.*
513.8 *he slowly rubs* corr. on CP to *he softly rubs*
513.14 *with Sir Leicester—though it may not be—that* corr. on CP to *with Sir Leicester, that*
513.32 *as if by violent pain.* corr. on CP to *as if by pain.*
513.36 *draws the curtain,* corr. on CP to *draws the window-curtain,*
513.41 *peeps at* corr. on CP to *peeps in at*
513.42 CP: *in some magnificently condescending* corr. to *in a magnificently condescending* [as in MS] 53–CD: *in a majestically condescending* [MS adverb restored, as likely to have been inadvertently altered when line was reset]
514.5 *with Joe or Sally.* corr. on CP to *with Will or Sally.*
514.6 *up with it—the latent* corr. on CP to *up with it—the Wills and Sallys, the latent*
514.9 *the roller goes, the Joes and Sallys, the smoke* corr. on CP to *the roller passes, the smoke*

Chapter XLII MS and one set of CP; same type of textual characteristics as in three preceding chapters

514 chapter-heading ins. on CP [not in MS]

514.20–21 *He never changes* corr. on CP to *He neither changes*
514.21 *journey, or talks* corr. on CP to *journey, nor talks*
515.32 *upon me, sir.* corr. on CP to *upon me.*
515.40 MS: *Poor Mr. Snagsby having* CP: *Now, Mr. Snagsby having* corr. to *Mr. Snagsby having*
516.6 *which are, not to put too fine a point upon it, fierce,* corr. on CP to *which are fierce—*
516.14 MS–53: *no doubts at the time* C–CD: *no doubt at the time*
517.2 *muttering to himself,* corr. on CP to *saying to himself,*
517.7 MS–L: *much of Allegory* CD: *much of the Allegory*
517.17–18 MS: *do you want?"* CP–CD: *do you want?"* [MS italics restored as expressing clear and useful intention]
517.19 CP–L: *in the clerks' hall,* CD: *in the clerk's hall,* [em. ad. though MS not clear, because Mr. Tulkinghorn had only one clerk]
518.7 CP [n.c.]: *I re-fuse them,* 53–CD: *I ref-use them,* [as in MS]
518.23 *you have then known* corr. on CP to *you have known*
518.26 *her hands, stamping one of her feet, and setting* corr. on CP to *her hands, and setting*
518.35 *a good position!* corr. on CP to *a good condition!*
518.43–44 *and even tender;* corr. on CP to *and tender;*
519.9 *with the former angry nods.* corr. on CP to *with more tight and angry nods.*
519.19 MS–CP [n.c.]: *the clerk's partition* 53–C: *the clerks' partition* L–CD: *the clerk's partition* [em. ad., see 517.19]
519.21 *with her folded arms.* corr. on CP to *with folded arms.*
519.24–25 *Mistress, this is* corr. on CP to *Look, Mistress, this is* 53–CD: *Look, mistress, this is*
519.40 MS: *it interposes to prevent* CP–CD: *it interferes to prevent* [*interposes* restored as better than compositor's overlooked misreading]
520.12–13 *police, whose gallantry is great, but who carry* corr. on CP to *police. Their gallantry is great, but they carry*
520.18 *that good position* corr. on CP to *that good condition*
520.19 *find herself free* corr. on CP to *find yourself at liberty*
520.20 *in a whisper.* corr. on CP to *in her former whisper.*
520.24 *by your lady,"* corr. on CP to *by your lady, you know,"*

Chapter XLIII MS and one set of CP, presumably CP1; 6 minor divergences between MS and CP do not provide conclusive evidence of earlier CP missing; 5 substantive divergences between CP and 53 point to further revision by D, presumably on CP2, missing

521.6–7 *there was no danger* corr. on CP to *there can have been no danger*
521.8 *hearing something* corr. on CP to *hearing anything*
521.10,13 *Little does it matter* corr. on CP to *It matters little*
521.25 *Richard, in her loving heart, that* corr. on CP to *Richard, that*
521.27 *word of reproach.* corr. on CP to *word of reproof.*
521.31 *Ah! well, we knew* corr. on CP to *We knew*
522.5–6 *My dear Dame Durden, who would* corr. on CP to *My dear, who would*
522.11 *replied. "No, my dear. Such an* corr. on CP to *replied. Such an*
522.22 *—and refinement—* corr. on CP to *—and sensibility—*
522.30 MS: *expence*
522.32 *must quietly prevent* corr. on CP to *must prevent*
523.3 *We will pay* corr. on CP to *We must pay*
523.15 MS: *to our expectations.* CP–CD: *to our expectation.*
523.21 *like a sort of over-ripe* corr. on CP to *like an over-ripe*
524.9 MS: *breakfast;* I *don't.* CP–CD: *breakfast; I don't.* [MS italics restored as clearly intentional and inadvertently overlooked]
524.13–14 MS–CP [n.c.]: *"This is our friend's room, sanctum, studio,"* 53–CD: p.t.
524.30–31 MS–L: *call it the Saint Clare* CD: *call it Saint Clare*
525.21 MS: I *know nothing* CP–CD: *I know nothing* [MS italics restored as clearly intentional and inadvertently overlooked]
525.32 *a mere superstition.* corr. on CP to *a superstition.*
526.3 *before me, and calls* corr. on CP to *before me as their result, and calls*
526.3–4 MS: *I* do *admire them*— CP–CD: *I do admire them*— [MS italics restored as clearly intentional and inadvertently overlooked]
526.4 *know nothing more* corr. on CP to *know no more*
526.16 *his catechism* corr. on CP to *his examination*
526.17–18 *daughters, leaving* corr. on CP to *daughters (his sons had run away at various times), leaving*
526.24–25 MS–CP [n.c]: *Beauty daughter, Juliet—a remembrance of Shakespeare —plays* 53–CD: *Beauty daughter, Arethusa–plays*
526.26 MS–CP [n.c.]: *Laura—a remembrance of Petrarch—plays a little* 53–CD: *Laura–plays a little*
526.26–27 MS–CP [n.c.]: *Comedy daughter, Susannah—a remembrance of Beaumarchais—sings* 53–CD: *Comedy daughter, Kitty—sings*
527.23–24 MS: *Sentiment and Comedy will bring* their *husbands home, I dare say, at some time or other, and have* CP–CD: p.t.
527.24 *nests up-stairs.* corr. on CP to *nests up-stairs too.*
527.39 MS–L: *and hinting at* CD: *and hinted at*
527.44 MS–L: *care of mamma.* CD: *care of mama.*
528.1 *I shall escape vexation, hear the larks* corr. on CP to *I shall hear the larks*
528.5 MS–L: *papa was lying down by* CD: *papa was lying ill by*
528.7 MS–CP [n.c.]: *said Juliet.* 53–CD: *said Arethusa.*
528.20 *back. Ha! He was* corr. on CP to *back. He was*
528.26 *these chairs* corr. on CP to *these arm-chairs*
528.31 *of our great mother,* corr. on CP to *of one great mother,*
528.37 MS–L: *laughing eyebrows* CD: *laughing eyes*
529.22 MS: *Old* (?) *Verulam wall,* CP–CD: *old Verulam wall,*
529.31 *to a chair, and feel that I was stunned.* corr. on CP to *to a chair.*
529.39–40 CP–CD: *farther reference,* [*farther* corr. to *further* though MS is not clear, in accordance with usage adhered to when phrase is repeated in 530.4
530.6 MS–L: *so far to misapprehend* CD: *so far as to misapprehend*
530.14 CP: *Sir Leicester gately* [blank left by disconcerted compositor] corr. to *Sir Leicester weightily* [as in MS but misreading excusable]
530.23 MS: *—Hirald—* (?) CP: *—Hirald* — (?) corr. to *—Herald—*
533.16 CP: *"Seen her! No!* corr. to *"Seen her?"* [as in MS; what had been mistaken for *No* was D's usual sign for a new paragraph]
533.26 *tell me—were* they corr. on CP to *tell me why were* they
533.27 *her act, little woman, and she* corr. on CP to *her act, and she*
533.36 *sacrifice, and would* corr. on CP to *sacrifice, she said, and would*

Chapter XLIV MS and one set of CP; nothing missing
534.16 *he said, after a few days, but to keep* corr. on CP to *he said, but to keep*
534.20–21 *possible to advise* corr. on CP to *possible for him to advise*
534.23 *dreaded her discovery.* corr. on CP to *dreaded discovery.*
534.30 CP: *"I trust the lawyer,"* corr. to *"With the lawyer,"* [as in MS]
534.37 *maid who had put off her shoes to walk through the wet grass, and the eager* corr. on CP to *maid, and the eager*
534.38 *she had afterwards made* corr. on CP to *she had made*
534.39 *"that tigress is a more* corr. on CP to *"that is a more*
535.11 *Be cheerful,* corr. on CP to *Be hopeful,*
535.17 *time should arise when* corr. on CP to *time should come when*

535.19–20 *I shall not fail to do it for her daughter's sake."* corr. on CP to *I will not fail to do it for her dear daughter's sake."*
535.34 *"There, see,* corr. on CP to *"Then see,*
535.43 *eyes full on mine.* corr. on CP to *eyes on mine.*
536.10 *world of softening good,* corr. on CP to *world of good,*
536.19 *he answered heartily.* corr. on CP to *he answered.*
536.25–26 *your truth, Dame Durden, in this thing* corr. on CP to *your truth, in this thing*
536.44 *to the waste time* corr. on CP to *to the heavy time*
537.14 *the unselfish advice* corr. on CP to *the unselfish caution*
538.8 *and dignity,* corr. on CP to *and a dignity,*
538.8 *my guardian,* corr. on CP to *my responsible guardian,*
538.20 *of that benignant* corr. on CP to *of the benignant*
538.22 MS: *wished for only the other night* CP–CD: *wished for the other night* [*only* restored as useful to sense and likely to have been inadvertently overlooked]
538.25 *of this prospect—* corr. on CP to *of the prospect—*
538.39–40 *sobbed now and then, but* corr. on CP to *sobbed a little still, but*
538.41 *crying at all then.* corr. on CP to *crying then.*
538.42 *my dear," I thought, "you are* corr. on CP to *my dear, you are*
539.10 *ways, to make some amends. This was* corr. on CP to *ways. This was*
539.33 after *in an instant.* D wrote on MS *Printer. A white line here.*
539.35–36 *not the least alteration* corr. on CP to *not the least constraint*
539.36–37 *(or I hope and believe there was* corr. on CP to *(or I think there was*
540.10 MS: *said smilingly,* (?) CP–CD: *said, smiling,*

Chapter XLV MS and one set of CP; no earlier set missing; at least one divergence between CP and 53 may point to further revision done by D, presumably, on CP2, missing

540 chapter-heading ins. on CP but is in MS
541.36 *amount, so far as I know, as owing* corr. on CP to *amount, as owing*
541.36–37 *the pressing nature of the liabilities* corr. on CP to *the peculiar and pressing nature of liabilities*
542.1 MS: *least it should* CP–CD: *lest it should*
542.4–5 MS–L: *here merged into* CD: *here emerged into*
542.32 *funereal gloves.* corr. on CP to *funeral gloves.*
542.33 *The length and fatigue of* corr. on CP to *The fatigue of*
543.1 *consequence* corr. on CP to *consequences*
543.4 *I would to God you could* corr. on CP to *I would that you could*
543.17 *I said I should* corr. on CP to *I said I would*
544.1 *with those two* corr. on CP to *with these two*
544.2–3 MS–CP [n.c.]: *to play one tune over and over* 53–CD: *to play one tune (to which the burden of my guardian's letter set itself) over and over*
544.3 *all night long.* corr. on CP to *all night.*
544.14 *in a good hotel,* corr. on CP to *in an excellent hotel,*
544.31–32 *the heat out there,* corr. on CP to *the heat in India,*
544.32 *the serpents and tigers;* corr. on CP to *the serpents and the tigers;*
544.40 *this was possible,* corr. on CP to *this was feasible,*
544.43 *asked a sergeant where* corr. on CP to *asked a sergeant standing on the guard-house steps, where*
545.11 *to the last he never* corr. on CP to *to the end, he never*
545.25 *all over with me here."* corr. on CP to *all over here."*
545.29 CP: *"Esther, like you, but useless and* corr. to *"Like you, Esther; but useless, and* [MS not clear]
545.30 *with a smile.* corr. on CP to *with a melancholy smile.*
545.39 *all such devilries,* corr. on CP to *all such drawbacks,*
545.42–43 *and dropping them by* corr. on CP to *and moodily casting them away, by*
546.13 *upon it! True* corr. on CP to *upon it! O yes, true*
546.19 *on his table,* corr. on CP to *on the table,*
547.5 *angry indeed,* corr. on CP to *angry with him indeed,*
547.12 MS: *I laughed at that,* CP–CD: *At that I laughed,*
547.12–13 *but cried a little too, at the same time, for I was* corr. on CP to *but trembled a little too, for I was*
547.21 *There's Vholes with his shoulder* corr. on CP to *Vholes has his shoulder*
547.36 MS–L: *that will swell it.* CD: *that would swell it*
548.19 *unusual excitement.* corr. on CP to *unusual interest.*
548.25 *was quite surprised.* corr. on CP to *was surprised.*
548.43 *not to do it.* corr. on CP to *not to do so.*
548.43 *my dear, no," I said, "no,* [MS: *"No.*] corr. to *my dear, no. No,*
549.8–9 *with great interest.* corr. on CP to *with the truest interest*
549.24 *"But have quite* corr. on CP to *"But you have quite*
549.27–28 *nothing more in the world* corr. on CP to *nothing in the world*
549.36 *talking thus,and when I* corr. on CP to *talking, and when I*

549.41 *had a clear perception* corr. on CP to *had a perception*
549.42 *not going on well* corr. on CP to *not going well*
550.13 *immeshed in the ill-fated* corr. on CP to *entangled in the ill-fated*
550.24–25 MS: *weariness; it is like ungrown* CP: *weariness; it is like ingrown* corr. to *weariness; yet it is both, and like ungrown*
550.37 *he said, and seemed more moved* corr. on CP to *he said, more moved*
551.1–2 *"let us meet* corr. on CP to *"pray let us meet*
551.3–4 *there, but you.* corr. on CP to *there, now, but you.*
551.9–10 *laid his hand upon his* corr. on CP to *laid his friendly hand upon Richard's*
551.12–13 *was sorry* corr. on CP to *was very sorry*
551.15 two lines canc. at end of chapter in MS: *If a friend rose up for Richard out of what was past and gone, that would be a new cause for gratitude and a new reason for all things happening as they had. I was*

Chapter XLVI MS and one set of CP, presumably CP1; no earlier CP missing; two substantive divergences between CP and 53 may point to further revision done by D presumably on CP2, missing

551 chapter-heading ins. on CP, but is in MS, apparently as a late addition
551.17 MS–53: *it has gradually swollen* C–CD: *it has gradually swelled* [em. ad., in accordance with D's own Errata]
551.27 CP: *nightly speech-making* corr. to *mighty speech-making* [as in MS]
551.30–31 after *force of figures,* MS has *see back* and at back of page *or by correct principles of taste,*
553.18 *Tom is mighty for evil and has* corr. on CP to *Tom has*
553.31 MS: *byeways.*
553.31–32 *for his bright dark eye is softened by compassionate* corr. on CP to *for in his bright dark eye there is compassionate*
554.5 MS: *canvass bag,*
554.6 MS–53: *towards her.* C–CD: *toward her.*
554.13,14 *"I'm a waiting* corr. on CP to *"I'm waiting*
554.18 *"Thankee, sir.* corr. on CP to *"Thank you, sir.*
554.29 MS–CP [n.c.]: *the skin broken.* 53–CD: *the skin sadly broken.*
554.42 MS–53: *asks the woman,* C–CD: *asked the woman,*
555.2 *to their wives besides."* corr. on CP to *to their wives too."*
555.18 *some home.* corr. on CP to *some settled home.*
555.21 *two-and-twenty* corr. on CP to *two or three-and-twenty*
555.25 *Have you got money* corr. on CP to *Have you money*
556.12 *Thus urged, he darts* corr. on CP to *He darts*
556.17–18 MS: *down half a dozen times;* (?) CP [n.c.]: *down nearly a dozen times;* 53–CD: *down a dozen times;*
556.30 *says Jo.* corr. on CP to *whimpers Jo.*
556.34 MS: *worritted* CP: *worritted* corr. to *worrited* thus in 53 C–CD: *worritted*
556.42–43 *produced in neglect* corr. on CP to *produced there in neglect*
557.15 *he run away* corr. on CP to *he ran away*
557.19–20 *her angel's temper, and her pretty figure,* corr. on CP to *her angel temper, and her pretty shape,*
557.30 *"—I mean, I know something—* corr. on CP to *"—I mean, I have heard of this—*
557.35 *woman's whole attention.* corr. on CP to *woman's attention.*
557.38 *of his race in* corr. on CP to *of his tribe in*
558.5–6 *somewheres till* corr. on CP to *somewheres as I knows on till*
558.7,8 MS–L: *Sangsby* CD: *Snagsby*
558.22 *he never knowd* corr. on CP to *he never known*
558.24–25 *he'd better have had* corr. on CP to *he'd sooner have had*
558.32 *I would, sir."* corr. on CP to *I would."*
558.44 *in the good young lady's* corr. on CP to *in the young lady's*
559.5 MS–53: *all at wunst."* C–CD: *all at wanst."*
559.12–13 *moving on now, sir," says Jo. "I'm a moving on* corr. on CP to *moving on now. I'm a moving on*
559.17 MS: *"Till I wos* CP–CD: *"till I was* [*wos* restored as presumably deliberate]
559.26–27 *you naturally supposed.* corr. on CP to *you supposed.*
559.36 MS–CP [n.c.]: *you will not 'hook it,' I know* 53–CD: *you will not run away, I know*
559.42 *and thank you* corr. on CP to *and I thank you*
559.44–45 *that I never* corr. on CP to *as I never*
560.1 *shambles, and smears* corr. on CP to *shambles and shivers, and smears*
560.3–4 *opposite side.* corr. on CP to *opposite side of the street.*

Chapter XLVII MS and one set of CP; divergences between MS and CP seem due to compositors' misreadings, 20 of which were corrected; slight evidence of further revision, presumably on CP2, missing

560.9 *bestow his miserable companion* corr. on CP to *bestow his companion*
560.11 *creature in the human form* corr. on CP to *creature in human form*
560.13 *remains the same.* corr. on CP to *remains.*
560.31–32 CP: *soon pulling down his*

frock; corr. to *soon putting down his food;* [as in MS]

561.13 MS: *has* (?) *finished both his story* CP: *had finished with his story* corr. to *has finished his story*

561.20 *and dry in her spare replies.* corr. on CP to *and spare in her replies.*

561.34 *fund of good sense,* corr. on CP to *fund of knowledge and good sense,*

561.37 *she herself has* corr. on CP to *she herself occupies*

561.39 MS: *of this disconsolate remark.* CP: *of this desolate remark.* corr. to *of this remark.*

562.1 *already knows her dear* corr. on CP to *knows her dear*

562.5 *now, and repair* corr. on CP to *now; and they repair*

562.25 *will no means lay aside* corr. on CP to *will not lay aside*

562.38–39 *as got there at all.* corr. on CP to *as got there.*

563.1–2 CP: *out of the way, and who, in his ignorance, he seems to believe is everywhere,* corr. to *out of the way; and who he seems, in his ignorance, to believe is everywhere,* [as in MS] 53–CD: *out of the way; in his ignorance, he believes this person to be everywhere,*

563.3 *"I beg your pardon,* corr. on CP to *"I ask your pardon,*

563.15 *to speak to him,* corr. on CP to *to speak with him,*

563.36 *The fact is, we are liable* corr. on CP to *We are liable*

564.1 *shaking his head feeling* [MS: *feelingly*] *and sorrowfully,* corr. on CP to *shaking his head sorrowfully,*

564.4 *he observes,* corr. on CP to *observes Allan,*

564.15–27 MS: this section (*and the trooper, . . . about thee.*) written on slip of paper pasted on over what seems to have been earlier version of same passage

564.16 CP [n.c.]: *Mrs. Pardiggles'* 53–CD: *Mrs. Pardiggle's* [MS had no apostrophe]

564.18–19 *unfamiliarness* [MS: *unfamiliarity*]; *he is not a comfort or convenience to anyone, as a pretence afar off for leaving evil things at hand alone;* corr. on CP to *unfamiliarity;*

564.28–29 *gathered together* corr. on CP to *huddled together*

564.32 *For he is not of the same* corr. on CP to *He is not of the same*

564.46 *"Upon my soul I will, sir,"* corr. on CP to *"Wishermaydie if I don't, sir,"*

565.4 *"Well! I believe it.* corr. on CP to *"I believe it.*

565.6–7 *CP: amazing broad* corr. to *amazingly broad* [MS almost illegible; perhaps *towering broad*]

565.10–11 *Here's a mattrass,* corr. on CP to *Here is a mattrass,* 53–CD: *Here is a mattress,*

565.41 *"Yes."* corr. on CP to *Yes, it appears.*

565.43 *"No."* corr. on CP to *No, it appears.*

565.44–45 *"It appeared to me* corr. on CP to *"It seemed to me*

566.23 *a damned bad* corr. on CP to *a confoundedly bad*

566.31 MS–L: *lays it on his imaginary* CD: *lays it on the imaginary*

566.36 *or if I have time* corr. on CP to *or time*

566.38–39 MS: *pass me back again* CP–CD: *passes me back again*

566.43 *goads me with his indifference, till* corr. on CP to *goads me, till*

567.11–12 *on* [MS: *in*] *the hypothetical case referred to.* corr. on CP to *on the field referred to.*

567.22 *a grave and serious interest* corr. on CP to *a serious interest*

567.30 MS–53 *if it was* C–CD *if it wos* [em. ad. as more consistent]

567.33 *after taking counsel with* corr. on CP to *after conferring with*

567.41 *from madness.* corr. on CP to *from despair.*

568.4 *before."* corr. on CP to *before, sir."*

568.11 *a married man, sir?" he inquires in a melancholy whisper.* corr. on CP to *a married man, sir?"*

568.13–14 *though single, to speak* corr. on CP to *though single," says Mr. Snagsby in a melancholy whisper," to speak*

568.19 *of my own.* corr. on CP to *of my own, sir.*

568.20 *with having* corr. on CP to *with ever having*

568.21 *since ever she named* corr. on CP to *since she named*

568.32 MS–CP [n.c.]: *desperation actually clutching* 53–CD: *desperation clutching*

568.33 *clump of black hair* corr. on CP to *clump of hair*

568.38 *to communicate. Which he accordingly tells him.* corr. on CP to *to communicate.*

568.40–41 *livid in the face.* corr. on CP to *discolored in the face.*

568.45 *to that certain person* corr. on CP to *to that other certain person*

567.19–20 *can't think—I say! I'm werry* corr. on CP to *can't think, Mr. Sangsby! I'm werry* 53–CD: *can't think, Mr. Sangsby. I'm werry*

567.20 *do it, Mr. Snagsby."* corr. on CP to *do it, sir."*

567.25 MS: *fur having done it,* CP–CD: *for having done it,* [*fur* restored for greater consistency]

567.32 MS: *always* CP: *allas* corr. to *allus*

569.33 CP: *a benden* corr. to *a bendin* [MS not clear]

570.5 MS–53: *forgiv me* C–CD: *forgive me*

570.9 *makes me much more* corr. on CP to *makes me more*

570.15 MS: *stoney*

570.15–16 MS–L: *broken steeps,* CD: *broken steps.*

570.18 *visage, acts* corr. on CP to *visage, at once acts*

570.19–20 *corner, ever and anon looking* corr. on CP to *corner; often looking*

570.21 MS: *"You hold up,* CP–CD: *"Hold up.*

570.27 *shed down some temporary vigor* corr. on CP to *shed down temporary vigor*
571.2 *"No, no."* corr. on CP to *"No."*
571.4 *in a slow,* corr. on CP to *in a low,*
571.6 MS–53: *"Never know'd* C–CD: *"Never knowd*
571.21 MS: *"Stay, Jo, stay!* CP–CD: *"Stay, Jo!*
571.22 MS: *"It's time fur me* CP–CD: *"It's time for me* [*fur* restored for greater consistency; D himself made same correction at least twice in this chapter though he overlooked it twice also]
571.24 *tell me. There! What* corr. on CP to *tell me. What*
572.7 CP: *be—thy—name!"* corr. to *be thy —"* 53–CD: *be—thy—"*
572.11 *Heavenly pity and compassion* corr. on CP to *Heavenly compassion*

Chapter XLVIII MS and one set of CP; no definite evidence of earlier CP missing; 5 substantive differences between CP and 53 may point to existence of later set of CP, missing

572.30 *she will be suffered to remain* corr. on CP to *she will remain*
572.34 MS: *—t'setup* CP: *—setup* corr. to *—tsetup*
573.11–12 CP: *Like them they seem to run to a good deal* [MS: *to a deal*] *of seed, too, in their bags* [MS: *tags*] *and* corr. to *Like them too, they seem to run to a deal of seed, in their tags and*
573.17 MS–CP [n.c.]: *embroidering,* 53–CD: *embroidery,*
574.6 *leave me solitary."* corr. on CP to *leave me very solitary."*
574.12–13 *and would make* corr. on CP to *and that I would make*
574.15 *no part whatever,* corr. on CP to *no part,*
574.22 MS: *"Now, my (?) happy child, in better* CP: *"Now, my happy child, better* corr. to *"Now, be happy, child, under better*
574.30 *What I really am* corr. on CP to *What I am*
574.32 MS–CP [n.c.]: *and so all ends* 53.–CD: *and thus all ends*
574.44 *"Sir Leicester, I—but you* corr. on CP to *"Sir Leicester, I am desirous—but you*
575.10 *darken her existence.* corr. on CP to *darken her life.*
575.11 MS–CP [n.c.]: *under the best of circumstances;* 53–CD: *under the best conditions;*
575.32 MS–L: *that figure removed* CD: *that figure moved*
575.36 *that I think we had better* corr. on CP to *that we had better*
576.28 *that—that fancy."* corr. on CP to *that—fancy."*
576.34–35 *the basest metals* corr. on CP to *the base metals*
577.7 *Sir Leicester highly flattered;* corr. on CP to *Sir Leicester flattered;*
577.16 *laying out* corr. on CP to *magnificently laying out*
577.26 *"attracted* corr. on CP to *"has attracted*
577.31 MS–53: *If you remembered* C–CD: *If you remember*
578.3 *her view of the case.* corr. on CP to *her view.*
578.25 *yet in much distress.* corr. on CP to *yet in distress.*
578.28 *"There! You are taken charge of,"* corr. on CP to *"You are taken charge of, you see,"*
578.32–33 *at going away really."* corr. on CP to *at going away."*
579.11 *it is because* corr. on CP to *it is only because*
579.14 *it was only respectful* corr. on CP to *it was respectful*
579.15 *and only candid* corr. on CP to *and candid*
579.18 *invoked* corr. on CP to *evoked*
579.31 *he turns his broad forehead towards* corr. on CP to *he turns towards*
580.20 *"Yes, indeed.* corr. on CP to *"Yes, decidedly.*
580.24–25 MS–CP [n.c.]: *on his knees and his head on one side.* 53–CD: *on his knees.*
580.29 *Yes, yes, you do.* corr. on CP to *I think you do.*
580.36 *that may come upon yourself."* corr. on CP to *that impend over yourself."*
581.5 *your secret. That is* corr. on CP to *your secret. Excuse me! That is* [53–CD: *Excuse me.*]
581.12 *I have made.* corr. on CP to *I have taken.*
581.17 *"Then you see,* corr. on CP to *"Really? Then you see,*
581.29 *or value was she?* corr. on CP to *or value is she?*
581.34 *She now lifts up* corr. on CP to *She lifts up*
581.35 CP: *a stormy expression* corr. to *a stern expression* [as in MS]
581.38 *should anybody be spared?"* corr. on CP to *should she spare others?"*
581.46 *for a while.* corr. on CP to *for a time.*
582.5 *it is business, and must be done.* corr. on CP to *it is business.*
582.5 *Therefore a lady* corr. on CP to *A lady*
582.6–7 *my declaring* corr. on CP to *my now declaring*
582.20 *with a smile,* corr. on CP to *with a slight smile,*
582.21 *"But, not* corr. on CP to *"No, not*
582.28 MS–CP [n.c.]: *fail to fulfil.* 53–CD: *fail to justify.*
582.29 *Permit me to wish you* corr. on CP to *I wish you*
583.4 MS: *O what a watch* CP–CD: *What a watch*
583.21 CP: *groups,* corr. to *groupes,* [as in MS] thus in 53–L CD: *groups,*
583.34 *opened the gate,* corr. on CP to *opened the garden gate,*

583.35 MS–L: *his Lady's hand* CD: *his Lady's hands*
583.37 *needs no escort home.* corr. on CP to *needs no further escort.*
583.42–584.1 MS: *prison-like paved yard, and he* CP–CD: *prison-like yard. He*
584.14–15 MS: *where it winds away from* CP–CD: *where it winds from* [*away* restored as useful and likely to have been inadvertently overlooked]
585.6 *cannon, now, might it* corr. on CP to *cannon might it*
585.24 MS: *wandering in the room there all day,* CP: *wandering there all day,* corr. to *wandering all day,*
585.25 *careful noting* corr. on CP to *careful tracing of steps, and careful noting*
585.26 *Several eyes* corr. on CP to *All eyes*
585.26–27 *several voices* corr. on CP to *all voices*
585.36 MS: *all the spare* (?) *brains* CP–CD: *all the brains*
585.37 *It surely happens,* corr. on CP to *It happens surely,*
585.41 *shall surely happen,* corr. on CP to *shall happen surely,*
585.42–43 *that stain on the floor, so easily covered,* corr. on CP to *that stain upon the floor, so easy to be covered,*

Chapter XLIX MS and one set of CP, presumably CP2, there being abundant evidence of both earlier and later revisions, pointing to probable existence of CP1 and CP3, both missing
587.17 MS–53: *all their stock* C–CD: *all the stock*
587.25–26 MS–L: *observing upon his growth* CD: *observing on his growth*
587.33–34 MS–CP [n.c.]: *as to give it quite the air of a Fortieth Article.* 53–CD: *as to give it quite an orthodox air.*
587.35 MS–L: *a generic solemnity.* CD: *a general solemnity.*
588.14–15 *not remarkable for* corr. on CP to *not illustrious for*
588.32 *with anguish unspeakable, beholds* corr. on CP to *with anguish, beholds*
590.3 MS–L: *that it is in the nature* CD: *that is in the nature*
590.20 *delight and consequent energy* corr. on CP to *delight and energy*
590.24 MS–L: *lead to a confusion* CD: *lead to confusion*
590.34 MS: *the hands of the Dutch clock* CP–CD: *the hands of the clock*
590.40 *says Mr. George. "Your wife that —and your mother, children—she is happiness itself; that's what she is."* corr. on CP to *says Mr. George.*
590.41 MS–CP [n.c.]: *says Mrs. Bagnet,* 53–CD: *cries Mrs. Bagnet,*
591.6 MS–CP [n.c.]: *I look shocked,* 53–CD: *I looked shocked,*
591.29–30 MS: *too good me."* CP: *too good for me."* corr. to *too choice for me."*
591.40 MS–L: *yet so pleasantly* CD: *yet pleasantly*
592.11–12 *poor lad, you know. 'Twas* corr. on CP to *poor lad. 'Twas*
592.23 MS–CP [n.c.]: *bad case too.* 53–CD: *bad case too, in a different way.*
592.26–27 MS–CP [n.c.]: *everything so easy—* 53–CD: *everything so evenly—*
592.28 MS: *is to you light your* CP–CD: *is to light your*
592.43 *with great enthusiasm,* corr. on CP to *with enthusiasm,*
593.8 *looking stealthily in* corr. on CP to *looking in*
593.14 MS–CP [n.c.]: *coming in.* 53–CD: *coming in and closing the door.*
593.16–17 MS–L: *is in wants of* CD: *is in want of*
593.26 *not unwelcome already, has set himself* corr. on CP to *not unwelcome, has sat himself* [MS had *sat*]
593.36 *she's very near it!* corr. on CP to *she comes near it!* 53–CD: *she comes near you!*
593.38 MS–L: *Malta's cheek.* CD: *Malta's cheeks.* [em. ad.]
593.43 MS–CP [n.c.]: *a pipe and glass* 53–CD: *a pipe and a glass*
594.26 MS: *no way out of it.* CP–CD: *no way out.*
594.32 *"Oh, I am all right* corr. on CP to *"All right*
594.46 MS–CP [n.c.]: *to be your's,* 53–CD: *to be your boy,*
595.18 *by ear, you know. Lord* corr. on CP to *by ear. Lord*
595.20 *fine little fellow?"* corr. on CP to *fine fellow?"*
595.33 *he afterwards informs* corr. on CP to *he informs*
595.34 MS–CP [n.c.]: *Mrs. Bagnet, in confidence, he* 53–CD: *Mrs. Bagnet, he*
596.32 MS–CP [n.c.]: *and private tone,* 53–CD: *and private voice,*
596.34 MS: *too pay too large*
596.35 MS–CP [n.c.]: *be paid for* 53–CD: *be remunerated for*
597.15 MS: *half a moment,* CP–CD: *half a minute,*
597.16–17 MS: *into a little parlor,* CP–53: *into a parlor,*
597.17 MS–CP [n.c.]: *claps his back* 53–CD: *claps his own back*
597.21 MS–CP [n.c.]: *make things pleasant,* 53–CD: *make things pleasant tonight,*
597.28 MS: *you may make to me will be* CP–CD: *you may make will be*
597.31 MS: *"A murder!"* CP–CD: *"Murder!"*
597.43–44 MS: *is killed, and* CP–CD: *has been killed, and*
598.6–7 MS: *with deliberation.* CP–CD: *with great deliberation.*
598.15 *in the upholstering way* corr. on CP to *in the upholstery way*
598.17 MS: *that there's already a reward out,* CP–CD: *that there's a reward out,*
598.21 MS–L: *by me as by another* CD: *by me as any other*
598.34 *as consistent with* corr. on CP to *as is consistent with*
598.41 MS–CP [n.c.]: *"but, as I am,* 53–CD: *"but, as I know it,*

598.44–45 *Mr. George replies.* corr. on CP to *Mr. George hurriedly replies.*
599.4 MS–CP [n.c.]: *guiding him with* 53–CD: *steering him with*

Chapter L MS and one set of CP; two divergences between CP and 53 may point to existence of CP2, missing

599.6 *Jellyby, informing* corr. on CP to *Jellyby (as we always continued to call her), informing*
599.15 *hand, that was always* corr. on CP to *hand, always*
599.17 *so small.* corr. on CP to *so small and weak.*
599.21 *weak remembrances* corr. on CP to *faint remembrances*
599.37–38 *So I set off* corr. on CP to *Therefore I set off*
600.7 *to me, in his own kind way, on my return* corr. on CP to *to me, on my return*
600.9 *constant fatigue will* corr. on CP to *constant coaching will*
600.24 *a long time before* corr. on CP to *some time before*
600.26 *call a long time,* corr. on CP to *call some time,*
600.31 *doctor, my dear?"* corr. on CP to *doctor, my love?"*
600.35 *"Well!"* corr. on CP to *"Well, you know!"*
601.13 MS–53: *the clocks struck* C–CD: *the clock struck*
601.18 MS–L: *than at another in* CD: *than another in*
601.20 *so blest to know* corr. on CP to *so rejoiced to know*
601.30–31 *seven or eight* corr. on CP to *eight or nine*
601.33 MS: *than at any other since* CP–CD: *than any other since*
601.34–35 *and therefore we did not talk* corr. on CP to *and we did not talk*
601.39–40 *self-denying and uncomplaining,* corr. on CP to *self-denying, so uncomplaining,*
602.3 CP: *little boy walked* corr. to *little boy waltzed* [as in MS]
602.27 *no notice whatever of* corr. on CP to *no notice of*
602.31 *a good-natured contempt* corr. on CP to *a serene contempt*
603.17 *with your own, Caroline.* corr. on CP to *with your own, my Caroline.*
603.19–20 *this Deportment (dating from before his son's birth, and his son's inheritance* corr. on CP to *this Deportment (his son's inheritance*
603.26 *Be affectionate* corr. on CP to *Be dutiful and affectionate*
603.26–27 *no further return.* corr. on CP to *no other return.*
603.28–29 *his tavern dinner.* corr. on CP to *his hotel dinner.*
603.32 *walking with him—* corr. on CP to *walking with great pomp—*
603.33–34 *and sometimes with* corr. on CP to *and occasionally with*
603.35 MS–CP [n.c.]: *no inconsiderable expence,* 53–CD: *no inconsiderable cost,*
604.7 *his care; he was so gentle, so skilful, and so unwearying* corr. on CP to *his care; but he was so gentle, so skilful, so unwearying*
604.11 MS: *often went home at about* CP: *often went home about* corr. to *often slipped home at about*
604.26 *regret or reserve.* corr. on CP to *regret.*
604.37 *such thoughts myself—of what once might have been, but was* corr. on CP to *such thoughts—of what once was, but was*
605.4 *in a most desperate manner,* corr. on CP to *in a desperate manner,*
605.6 *that same shade* corr. on CP to *the same shade*
605.7 *said my guardian,* corr. on CP to *observed my guardian,*
605.10 *"Yes," I returned,* corr. on CP to *"Yes," I said,*
605.12 *he said,* corr. on CP to *he returned,*
605.21 *to live?* corr. on CP to *to live, I suppose?*
605.23 MS–CP [n.c.]: *houseless goddess,* 53–CD: *household goddess,*
605.28 *about such matters.* corr. on CP to *about his plans.*
605.35 *old world. I have* corr. on CP to *old world. Do you know I have*
605.42 *a favorite of my guardian's.* corr. on CP to *a favorite with my guardian.*
606.10 MS–L: *looked up at Ada,* CD: *looked up to Ada,*
606.26 MS: *Ada only drooped her head* CP: *dropped* corr. to *drooped* thus in 53–L CD: *dropped*
606.33 *"No, never, never, Esther."* corr. on CP to *"No, never, Esther."*
606.34 MS: *"there is nothing* CP–CD: *"there can be nothing*
606.36 *returned Ada, weeping bitterly.* corr. on CP to *returned Ada.*
607.16 *less amiable even than* corr. on CP to *less amiable than*

Chapter LI MS and one set of CP; nothing missing

607.23–24 *he never, from* corr. on CP to *he never once, from*
607.40 *"Well, sir," rejoined* corr. on CP to *"Sir," rejoined*
608.19 *no personal interest* corr. on CP to *no interest*
609.4–5 *My name is on the door* corr. on CP to *My name is painted outside*
609.19–20 *never should forget* corr. on CP to *never could forget*
609.29 *is that, just now?"* corr. on CP to *is that?"*
610.7–8 *his weary state.* corr. on CP to *his weary condition.*
610.21 *"Well," returned* corr. on CP to *"Now pray," returned*
611.14 *a sombre dark day,* corr. on CP to *a sombre day,*
611.29–30 *in the corner.* corr. on CP to *in the corner there.*

611.31–32 MS–L: *I was for going to the one, and my darling was for going to the other;* CD: *I was going for the one, and my darling was going for the other;*
611.35 MS: *pannel.*
612.1 *so sensible, so—* corr. on CP to *so sensible, so earnest, so—*
612.24–25 MS–L: *the suit, the suit,* CD: *the suit, my dear girl, the suit,*
612.30 *We are spinning* corr. on CP to *We are really spinning*
612.38–39 *now written indelibly in* corr. on CP to *now indelibly written in*
613.3 *I smiled* corr. on CP to *Ah! No, no. I smiled*
613.6 *make false pretences* corr. on CP to *make pretences*
613.20 *I could not answer her. A light shone* corr. on CP to *A light shone*
613.40 *and gone on* corr. on CP to *and had gone on*
614.9 *Ah, how selfish* corr. on CP to *How selfish*
614.12 *a kind of joy* corr. on CP to *a kind of pride*
614.15 *their way; I only know I did not* corr. on CP to *their way; I did not*
614.18–19 *told Richard she had always worn it* corr. on CP to *told Richard that ever since her marriage she had worn it*
614.30 *should she ever do* corr. on CP to *should she do*
615.39 *any glare of light from the feeble* corr. on CP to *any glare from the feeble*
615.42 MS: *pannel*
616.19 *with a good-humored* [MS: *-humoured*] *sigh,* corr. on CP to *with a sigh,*
616.27 *his hand on mine* corr. on CP to *his hand on my hand*

Chapter LII MS and one set of CP; the few divergences between MS and CP do not point conclusively to existence of earlier CP missing; at least 3 substantive divergences between CP and 53 show that further revision was done by D, presumably on CP2 missing

617.3 *had no intervals* corr. on CP to *had few intervals*
617.11 *scarcely keep my place* corr. on CP to *scarcely hold my place*
617.34 *"Right,"* corr. on CP to *"True,"*
617.38–39 *But I knew withal (I said) that* corr. on CP to *Yet I knew withal (I could not help saying) that*
617.41 *"God forbid!"* corr. on CP to *"Heaven forbid!"*
618.15 *grow wilder.* corr. on CP to *run wilder.*
618.16 *as if I had some duty* corr. on CP to *as if it were my duty*
618.19 *I seemed to acquire* corr. on CP to *I seemed to gain*
618.29 *made a bow.* corr. on CP to *made a slight bow.*
618.33–34 *taking a long breath.* corr. on CP to *drawing a long breath.*
618.42 *said my guardian,* corr. on CP to *observed my guardian,*
618.43 MS–CP [n.c.]: *part, I believe* 53–CD: *part, so I believe* [this is part of 3 lines set up at bottom of CP page 497, but transferred in 53 to top of p. 498, marked *Over* on CP, not in D's handwriting]
619.7 *natural and affecting emotion* corr. on CP to *natural emotion*
619.16 *some little things* corr. on CP to *many little things*
619.20 MS: *vagabond kind of way* CP–CD: *vagabond kind of a way* [MS reading restored as likely to have been inadvertently overlooked]
619.23 *"That's the point, sir,"* corr. on CP to *"Exactly so, sir,"*
619.31–32 *my guardian, with his old* corr. on CP to *my guardian, surprised into his old*
620.8 *said Mr. George,* corr. on CP to *said Mr. George, with a step backward.*
620.16–17 *should hardly think you* corr. on CP to *should hardly have thought you*
620.22 *to the breed altogether."* corr. on CP to *to the breed."*
620.42 *marked and suspected man,* corr. on CP to *marked and disgraced man,*
621.20–21 *and might have found* corr. on CP to *and, dear me! might have found*
621.30 *other men do. I am* corr. on CP to *other men do. Say, I am*
621.34 *quibble about everything, and get* corr. on CP to *quibble, and get*
622.9–10 *with a broadsword kind* corr. on CP to *with a blunt broadsword kind*
622.17 *and—and that's all* corr. to *and—that's all* 53–CD: *and—and that's all*
622.18–19 MS: *soldierly-looking man* CP–CD: *soldier-looking man* [MS reading restored as better English than compositor's understandable misreading]
622.24 *shook them by the hand,* corr on CP to *shook them cordially by the hand,*
622.37 *Mr. Bagnet referred* corr. on CP to *Mr. Bagnet, after considering, referred*
622.43 *won't get off* corr. on CP to *won't be got off*
623.9 MS: *too many cooks spoiling* (?) *the broth should hinder* CP: *cooks stirring the broth should* corr. to *cooks should*
623.17 MS: *creetur* CP–CD: *creature*
623.19 *when he had once got* corr. on CP to *when he has got*
623.26 *I now understood,* corr. on CP to *I understood,*
623.36 CP: *in your own way too.* corr. to *in your own way likewise.* 53–CD: *in your own way also.*
624.5 *of this crime,* corr. on CP to *of this deed,*
624.20–21 *with a black mantle on. However,* corr. on CP to *with a loose black mantle on; I noticed a deep fringe to it. However,*
624.26–27 *without distinctly asking myself* corr. on CP to *without my distinctly daring to ask myself*
624.42–43 MS: *mightn't understand* CP–CD: *might not understand*
624.43–44 MS–CP [n.c.]: *such a many circumstances* 53–CD: *such a number of circumstances*

625.2 *so deep and artful."* corr. on CP to *so deep."*
625.6 *all! Here! Just come* corr. on CP to *all! Just come*
625.15 *beating her hands together in* corr. on CP to *clapping her hands in*
625.18 *he do know* corr. on CP to *he does know*
625.19 *he spoke* corr. on CP to *he once spoke*
625.20 MS: *mothers' heads.* CP [n.c.]–53: *mother's heads.* C–CD: *mothers' heads.* [em. ad]
625.21 MS: *fifty pound* CP–CD: *fifty pounds*
625.25 MS–L: *with surprising dispatch* CD: *with surpassing dispatch*
625.30 *"But Lord bless the* corr. on CP to *"But, bless the*
625.36 MS–L: *to travelling in my own way.* CD: *to travel my own way.*
625.44 *returned. "Trust her fully. Made her way* corr. on CP to *returned. "Made her way*
626.6 *"She leads the Nonpareil* corr. on CP to *"She's Color-Sergeant to the Nonpareil*
626.6–7 MS–CP [n.c.]: *Mr. Bagnet, going his way* 53–CD: *Mr. Bagnet, looking at us over his shoulder, as he went his way*
626.8 *own it* corr. on CP to *own to it*

Chapter LIII MS and one set of CP; no evidence of earlier set missing; 3 substantive divergences between CP and 53 may point to existence of CP2, missing; further revision would be rendered necessary by the many lengthy MS inserts on CP1 and the ingenious printer's devices to spread out the text and thus eke out an underwritten number

626.15–16 *sharpens his intelligence;* corr. on CP to *sharpens his scent;*
626.18 MS–L: *are much in conference* CD: *are in much conference*
626.31 *This present evening* corr. on CP to *This evening*
627.2–3 *never goes home.* corr. on CP to *does not go home.*
627.5 *would have done* corr. on CP to *might have done*
627.8 *a lady in whom* corr. on CP to *an amiable lady in whom*
627.12 *human mourners,* corr. on CP to *human followers,*
627.13 CP: *William Duffy,* corr. to *William Buffy,* [MS had *Buffy,* and *Boodle* (?)]
627.17 MS: *coach-pannels,* CP–CD: *coach panels,*
627.22–23 MS–L: *seem plunged* CD: *seemed plunged*
627.23 *that old man* corr. on CP to *that dead old man*
627.35–36 *very well you are* corr. on CP to *very well indeed you are*
628.17–18 *and slips from* corr. on CP to *and glides from*
628.28 *says Mr. Bucket. "Thankee!"* corr. on CP to *says Mr. Bucket* [at this point CP has *Take in "A,"* referring to MS fragment added to CP and called *Insertions in the No; A* is the passage from *If Mercury should chance to letter in hand.*]
628.38 MS insert on CP: *cannister*
629.4–5 *convenient to his hand;* corr. on CP to *convenient to his grasp;*
629.40 *and the fair Volumnia,* corr. on CP to *and Volumnia,*
630.6 MS–CP [n.c.]: *Dedlock."* 53–CD: *Dedlock, Baronet."*
630.13 after *I have indeed."* CP has *Take in B,* referring to second MS insert; *B* is the passage from *The fair Volumnia, not quite* to *a touch of compassion.*
630.22 MS [ins. on CP]: *expence* 53–CD: *expense*
630.26 MS [ins. on CP]–53: *Mr. Bucket makes* C–CD: *Mr. Bucket made*
631.1–2 MS–L: *means, and my influence,* CD: *means and influence,*
631.13 *distinctions—"in which my deceased friend was held* corr. on CP to *distinctions; "was held*
631.14 *has aggravated* corr. on CP to *has, I say, aggravated*
631.17 *looks grave and shakes his head.* corr. on CP to *looks very grave.*
631.18 *dearest creature!* corr. on CP to *dearest person!*
631.21 after *sure he was."* CP has *Take in C,* referring to third MS insert on CP; *C* is the passage from *Volumnia gives* to *it'll wear off."*
631.28 MS [ins. on CP]: *"It's a start for* 53–CD: *"It gives a start to*
631.30 *But Volumnia wishes* corr. on CP to *Volumnia wishes*
631.33 *deal more.* corr. on CP to *deal more to the like artless purpose.*
631.40 MS: *glass of two of*
632.4–5 *complimentary crook* corr. on CP to *complimentary twinkle of his eye and crook*
632.21–22 *rounded the sentence;* corr. on CP to *rounded his sentence;*
632.38 *hope it will at the same time* corr. on CP to *hope it may at one and the same time*
632.44 MS–53: *phenomonons* C–CD: *phenomenons*
633.7–8 *in extreme dejection, yawns,* corr. on CP to *in a prostration of boredom, yawns,*
633.11–12 *and with a wave* corr. on CP to *and also with a wave*
633.13 *but also that if high* corr. on CP to *but that if high*
633.26 *chose it as an unusual and remarkable place.* corr. on CP to *chose it as a conspicuous part of the house.*
633.42 *then you're broad* corr. on CP to *then, you see, you're broad*
634.1 *don't look it on that account.* corr. on CP to *don't look it.*
634.18 MS–53: *a innkeeper.* C–CD: *an innkeeper.*
634.27–28 MS–CP [n.c.]: *of his flaming orange-colored small-clothes,* 53–CD: *of his bright peach-blossom small-clothes,*

634.9 CP: *my Lady." He advances, and she asks him:* corr. to *my Lady."* CP then has *Take in D,* referring to fourth MS insert; *D* is passage from *Mr. Bucket makes a leg,* to *at present, my Lady."*

635.6 *past the groups* corr. on CP to *past murderous groups*

635.19 *that I couldn't* corr. on CP to *that I shouldn't*

635.24 after *on both sides* CP has *Take in E,* referring to fifth MS insert; *E* is passage from *"I suppose you ain't* to *makes a difference.* [at end of insert D wrote *(Printer. Then run on.)*]

635.30 MS: *walking on the very night* CP–CD: *walking, the very night*

635.42 *in a black mantle,* corr. on CP to *in a loose black mantle,*

636 Number stopped on CP at page 510; with the five inserts and the new lines created by printer's devices two pages have been added

Chapter LIV MS and one set of CP; no conclusive evidence of earlier or later CP missing; MS especially difficult to read, hence some 50 compositors' mistakes, a few of which are recorded below

636 chapter-heading ins. on CP [not in D's handwriting; no heading in MS]

636.13–14 *his familiar finger,* corr. on CP to *his familiar demon,*

637.1–2 *that is as you please. If you do, well.* corr. on CP to *that is entirely as you please. If you do, well and good.*

637.7–8 MS–L: *under any circumstances,* CD: *under the circumstances,*

637.13–14 *Mr. Bucket pursues,* corr. on CP to *Mr. Bucket resumes,*

637.30 *"Good God!"* corr. on CP to *"Good Heaven!"*

637.31 MS: *Mr. Bucket then begins,* CP–CD: *Mr. Bucket begins,* [MS reading restored as better than text hitherto printed and likely to have been inadvertently overlooked]

637.32 *with one hand on* corr. on CP to *with one hand spread out on*

637.40 *Dedlock.* corr. on CP to *Dedlock, Baronet.* [*Baronet* had been first written, then canc. in MS]

637.43 *beyond him, have borne* corr. on CP to *beyond him at present—have borne*

638.8–9 CP: *a piece of infamy* corr. to *a piece of information* [as in MS]

638.22–23 *bright a chair.* corr. on CP to *brings a chair, and diminishes his shadow.*

639.6 *it's my duty* corr. on CP to *it becomes my duty*

639.7 *Mr. Tulkinghorn entertained* corr. on CP to *Mr. Tulkinghorn long entertained*

639.21 CP: *in great part,* corr. to *in great poverty,* [as in MS]

639.23 MS: *stops and repeats,* (?) CP: *stops and reflects,* corr. to *stops and deliberately repeats,*

639.24 MS: *not a doubt of it.* CP–CD: *not a doubt about it.*

639.26 MS–L: *his wretcheder grave,* CD: *his wretched grave,*

639.30 MS: *excuse me making use* CP–CD: *excuse my making use*

639.38 *All this has* corr. on CP to *All this, and more, has*

640.3–4 *that is feeling the tenderest recesses of his heart.* corr. on CP to *that is probing the life-blood of his heart.*

640.21 MS: *controuling*

640.27–28 MS–L: *if you think right,* CD: *if you think it right,* [em. ad.]

640.28–29 *Then you'll find* corr. on CP to *You'll find*

640.32–33 MS–L: *reveal it on the very* CD: *reveal it the very*

640.43 *being took away so* corr. on CP to *being cut down so*

640.44 *to hush it up, is* corr. on CP to *to hush it, is*

641.7 MS–L: *peach-blossom smalls,* CD: *peach-blossomed smalls,*

641.15 *Detective, and this,"* corr. on CP to *Detective, I am; and this,"*

641.17 *Baronet. You do see* corr. on CP to *Baronet. Well! You do see*

641.23 *killed the celebrated pig,* corr. on CP to *killed the pig,*

641.33 *here, pitch it* corr. on CP to *here, just pitch it*

642.7 *oil through the pores* corr. on CP to *oil from the pores*

642.14 MS–53: *I come in to Krook's property.* C–CD: *I come into Krook's property.* [em ad.]

642.17 *hid away in the side* corr. on CP to *hid away at the back of a shelf in the side*

642.22 CP: *that's a common name,* corr. to *that's not a common name,* [MS not clear]

642.29 *Mr. Bucket coolly, after* corr. on CP to *Mr. Bucket, after*

642.40–41 *says Mr. Bucket, quietly putting his hands into his pockets.* corr. to *says Mr. Bucket.*

643.5 MS: *If I'm going* CP: *if I am going* corr. to *if I am a going*

643.45 *rich and great?* corr. on CP to *rich and great, my friends?*

644.10 CP: *Rachel* corr. to *Rachael* [MS not clear but looks like *Rachel*]

644.22 *looks impenetrably and obdurately at* corr. on CP to *looks implacably at*

644.43 CP: *salooning and tampering.* corr. to *suborning and tampering.* [as in MS]

645.1 *doesn't with any particularity* corr. on CP to *does not with particularity*

645.4 *if he were not* corr. on CP to *if he was not*

645.33 *into this matter,"* corr. on CP to *into this little matter,"*

645.39 *to your own interests.* corr. on CP to *to your interests.*

645.42 MS–L: *Bucket assents* CD: *Bucket asserts*

645.44 *call venerable,* corr. on CP to *call truly venerable,*

646.2 *worth a single mag* corr. on CP to *worth a mag*

646.5 *without they came up* corr. on CP to *without one of the servants came up*
646.13 *with arch gallantry.* corr. on CP to *with gallantry.*
646.21 *Nobody objecting* corr. on CP to *Nobody having the hardihood to object*
646.31 *have driven 'em* corr. on CP to *have drove 'em*
646.41 *putting it up* corr. on CP to *putting up his watch*
647.1 *the unfortunate* corr. on CP to *this unfortunate*
647.8 MS: *suspence*
647.17 *A spasm* corr. on CP to *Suddenly a spasm*
647.19–20 *nodding at her with his folded arms.* corr. on CP to *nodding at her.*
647.32 *fool's play?"* corr. on CP to *fool's play, say then?"*
648.4 MS: *depends upon you.* CP–CD: *depends on you.*
648.7 *complies, and says, in* corr. on CP to *complies, saying in*
648.11 *your good sense* corr. on CP to *your sense*
648.15 CP: *this peculiar explanation.* corr. to *this french explanation.* [as in MS] 53–C: *french* L–CD: *French* [em. ad.]
648.34 *says Mr. Bucket.* corr. on CP to *Mr. Bucket remonstrates.*
648.42 *took it in her head* corr. on CP to *took it into her head*
649.1 CP: *parley,"* corr. to *Parley,"* [MS: *parlay,"*]
649.9 *"All lies!"* corr. on CP to *"All lie!"*
649.11 *you know exactly under* corr. on CP to *you know under*
649.31 *a considerable show* corr. on CP to *a mighty show*
649.45 CP: *such a venter* corr. to *such a ventur* [MS not clear]
650.9–10 MS: *That's about what's* CP–CD: *That's what's* [MS reading restored as agreeing with Bucket's usual speech]
650.16 *all right.* corr. on CP to *all right again.*
650.22 CP: *she had the secret in keeping,* corr. to *she had the sheet in her mouth,* [as in MS]
650.23–24 *accounts of George,* corr. on CP to *accounts of my suspicions against George,*
650.29 *got her?* corr. on CP to *got her, if she did this murder?*
650.32 MS: *"All lies, my angel!"* CP: *"He's my angel!"* corr. to *"All lies, my friend!"*
650.43 *DEDLOCK.* corr. on CP to *DEDLOCK, in it.*
651.1–2 *all written?* corr. on CP to *all written by this young woman?*
651.4 MS: *seized* CP–CD: *secured*
651.6 *every one,* corr. on CP to *every one by this young woman,*
651.24 *so put off her guard* corr. on CP to *so thoroughly off her guard*
651.25 *and Mrs. Bucket* corr. on CP to *and when Mrs. Bucket*
651.32 *in the full title,* corr. on CP to *in a full title,*
652.12–13 *with her suspicions,* corr. on CP to *with her observations and suspicions.*
652.25 *"I should like* corr. on CP to *"I would like*
652.31–32 *such an animosity* corr. on CP to *such a surprising animosity*
652.36 MS: *employment anyhow. Here! Let me put* CP: *employment anyhow. Let me put* corr. to *employment, you must consider. Let me put* [*Here!* restored as a useful transition seeming to have been inadvertently overlooked]
652.43 MS: *Can you* CP: *Can't you* corr. to *But can you*
652.43 MS–53: *res-tore* C: *re-store* [end of line] L–CD: *restore*
653.5 *O my God regard* corr. on CP to *O then regard*
653.14–15 MS–L: *manner . peculiar* CD: *manner so peculiar*
653.21 *and makes a few steps,* corr. on CP to *and walks a few steps,*
653.29–30 *bewilderment and dread,* corr. on CP to *bewilderment,*
653.34 *the main fibre* corr. on CP to *a main fibre*
653.39–40 *sees her, not himself,* corr. on CP to *sees her, almost to the exclusion of himself,*
654.3 MS: *those unmeaning sounds,* CP: *those numerous sounds,* corr. to *those intrusive sounds,*

Chapter LV MS and one set of CP; same textual characteristics as LIV; 39 compositors' misreadings

654 chapter-heading ins. on CP [not in MS]
654.18 *as abrupt precipices* corr. on CP to *as precipices*
654.19 MS: *carts and horses* (?) CP–CD: *carts and barrows*
654.20 CP: *remains of tunnels;* corr. to *rumours of tunnels;* [as in MS]
654.21 MS–L: *fell hopelessness.* CD: *full hopelessness.*
654.21–22 *Over the freezing* corr. on CP to *Along the freezing*
654.25 *within it;* corr. on CP to *within the chaise;*
654.29 MS: *is far too thoughtful* C–CD: *is too thoughtful*
654.33 *George's mother, my noble boy!"* corr. on CP to *George's mother!"*
655.3 *say to me that he had* corr. on CP to *say to me, in past times, that he had*
655.7 *I am sure he waited* corr. on CP to *I know he waited*
655.23 *her motherly eyes—* corr. on CP to *her own motherly eyes—*
655.24 *her own cheery manner:* corr. on CP to *her cheery manner:*
655.29,30 MS–L: *melanchally* CD: *melancholy*
655.38 *such things heavy on him* corr. on CP to *such things on him*
655.42 MS–53: *paints her picter* C–CD: *paints her picture*
655.43 *years ago.* corr. on CP to *years back.*

656.9 MS: *audible to the deaf old lady* CP–CD: *audible to the old lady* [*deaf* restored as part of the deliberate contrast seeming to have been inadvertently overlooked]
656.20–21 *that they form quite a separate* corr. on CP to *that the latter form a separate*
656.23 "*every help* corr. on CP to "*all the help*
656.30 *her broken lamentations,* corr. on CP to *her broken words,*
656.34 *murmur in a kind of distraction,* corr. on CP to *murmur so distractedly,*
657.1–2 *with the lavender-colored shawl,* corr. on CP to *with her lavender-colored dress,*
657.2 *calmness and deportment which* corr. on CP to *calmness which*
657.20 MS: *But they are eloquent; very, very eloquent.* CP–CD: *But they are very eloquent; very, very eloquent.* [MS reading restored as likely to have been inadvertently altered]
657.24 *speak of it all in such* corr. on CP to *speak in such*
657.26 CP: *sun-tanned face.* corr. to *sun-browned face.* [as in MS] thus in 53 C–CD: *sun-brown face.*
657.33 MS: *my dearest, dearest son!* CP–CD: *my dearest son!*
657.39 MS: *upon it, dries* CP: *upon it, and dries* corr. to *upon it, wipes*
658.7 CP: *a kind of glimmering* corr. to *a kind of a glimmering* [as in MS] thus in 53 C–CD: *a kind of glimmering*
658.26 *the trooper again,* corr. on CP to *the trooper afresh,*
658.29 MS: *anything about* me. CP–CD: *anything about me.* [MS italics restored as appearing to have been inadvertently overlooked]
658.40 *in your mind dead than living.*" corr. on CP to *in your mind as it was.*"
658.42 *hands between her own, lays it* corr. on CP to *hands, lays it*
658.42 MS: *upon her heart.* CP–CD: *upon her shoulder.*
659.1 "*I don't say* corr. on CP to "*No, I don't say*
659.9 MS: *I shouldn't* (?) CP–CD: *I couldn't*
659.21–22 *her strong interest* corr. on CP to *her interest*
659.29–31 *done it, but for my old* corr. on CP to *done it (though I have been to see you more than once down at Chesney Wold, when you little thought of me) but for my old*
659.31 *who, I see* corr. on CP to *who, I find*
659.32 *thank her for it, mother.* corr. on CP to *thank her for it.*
659.44 *it's little* corr. on CP to *'tis little*
660.4 *the old girl.* corr. on CP to *the old girl's umbrella.*
660.8 *we'll send* corr. on CP to *we must send*
660.14 *great favor," says the trooper, kissing her hand." Don't* corr. on CP to *great favor. Don't*
660.19–20 *I haven't the least of a face to see him* corr. on CP to *I haven't enough brass in my composition to see him*
660.25 MS: *my dear George?*" C:–CD: *dear George?*"
660.28 *rip of a brother* corr. on CP to *Rip of a brother*
660.34 MS: *thanks her heartily.* CP–CD: *thanks her kindly.* [MS reading restored as better than probably inadvertent alteration]
660.36 *I stand out firm.* corr. on CP to *I stand out.*
660.37 *drawing out,* corr. on CP to *drawing up,*
660.40 *entered up, plain* corr. on CP to *entered, plain*
661.7 *broad chest with his great tears rolling down his face.* corr. on CP to *broad chest.*
661.9 MS: *to the town house, George,* CP: *to the town house, my son,* corr. to *to the town house, my dear,* [MS reading restored as better than either misreading or correction]
661.22 *the coach to take her home.* corr. on CP to *the coach for her own conveyance home.*
661.26–27 *as if she had never been away.* corr. on CP to *as if nothing had happened.*
661.36–37 *often thought her, why* corr. on CP to *often thought, why*
662.4 *so close and kneel?* corr. on CP to *so close?*
662.24–25 *in an agitated whisper:* corr. on CP to *in a frightened whisper:*
662.44 *pray you on my knees not to be* corr. on CP to *pray you not to be*
663.25 *the ground, how long she may have been unconscious, she knows* corr. on CP to *the ground, she knows*
663.28 *she understands them.* corr. on CP to *she begins to understand them.*
663.35 MS–L: *been very welcome* CD: *been welcome*
663.40 "*Please to do so.*" corr. on CP to "*Do so.*"
663.41 *I should first explain* corr. on CP to *I ought first to explain*
664.3 MS–L: *in any matter* CD: *in any manner*
664.5 *I had no* corr. on CP to *I have no*
664.17–18 *sacred—I, in point* corr. on CP to *sacred, I—in point* 53–CD: *sacred—I, in point*
664.25 *that I call* corr. on CP to *that I will call*
664.28 CP: *contrary* corr. to *contrairy* [as in MS] thus in 53 C–CD: *contrary*
664.29 *say of myself* corr. on CP to *say for myself*
664.40 CP: *off his ears.* corr. to *off his ed.* [as in MS]
665.4 CP: *to a jug?*" corr. to *to a Guy?*" [as in MS]
665.15–16 *twisted out of him)* corr. on CP to *corkscrewed out of him)*
665.18 *it is now blown upon.* corr. on CP to *it is blown upon.*
665.22–24 "*Your Ladyship, I don't want*

to say a word more, and I don't want to hear a word more. I have acted corr. on CP to *"Your Ladyship, you know best, whether there's anything in what I say, or whether there's nothing. Something or nothing, I have acted*

665.29 *I now beg to take farewell* corr. on CP to *I now take my farewell*

665.30 *and to assure* corr. on CP to *and assure*

665.32 *any look or sign,* corr. on CP to *any look,*

665.33 *rings the bell.* corr. on CP to *rings her bell.*

665.40 *All is broken* corr. on CP to *So! All is broken*

666.1 *often, often, wished* corr. on CP to *often, often, often, wished*

666.3 *a new torture* corr. on CP to *a new torment*

666.16 MS–53: *dilation* C–CD: *dilatation*

666.18 MS: *rushed in an* CP–CD: *rushed in, in an*

666.21 *if a mortal stroke* corr. on CP to *if some mortal stroke*

666.21–22 *fall upon this man* corr. on CP to *fall on this old man*

666.24–25 *she felt* corr. on CP to *she has felt*

666.26–27 *fragments, crushing* corr. on CP to *fragments, each crushing*

666.30 *well-remembered guise,* corr. on CP to *well-remembered shape,*

666.34 *of reliance* corr. on CP to *of self-reliance*

666.34 *whirled before it like* corr. on CP to *whirled away like*

666.45 *I have been racked* corr. on CP to *I had been racked by him* thus in 53 C–CD: *I have been racked by him*

667.5 MS: *I encumber you* CP–CD: *I will encumber you*

667.7 *you wasted* corr. on CP to *you have wasted*

Chapter LVI MS and one set of CP, presumably CP1; most of the corrections, apparently not, or not all, in D's hand, are of compositors' mistakes (23 of them); MS extremely difficult to read, as in LIV–LV; clear evidence of further revision, done, presumably, on CP2, missing

668.32–33 CP: *It is the first party* corr. to *It is the first fact* [as in MS] thus in 53–L CD: *It is the first act*

668.37 MS–L: *brings him a slate.* CD: *brings in a slate.*

669.39 MS–L: *in his hand,* CD: *in his hands,*

669.44 CP: *"Fall, forgiveness.* corr. to *"Full forgiveness.* [as in MS]

670.30–31 MS: *in a carawan.* CP–CD: *in a caravan.*

670.36–37 MS: *as many other such family affairs* CP: *as many other family affairs* corr. to *as, Lord! many other family affairs* [*such* restored as useful and likely to have been inadvertently overlooked]

672.28–29 MS–CP [n.c.]: *had come out.* 53–CD: *have come out.*

673.16 MS–L:*—a harder matter—* CD:*—a hard matter—*

673.42 CP: *On the waste, where* corr. to *On the wastes, where* 53–CD: *On the waste, where*

Chapter LVII MS and one set of CP; no definite evidence of earlier or later CP missing; a very poorly set-up chapter; over 40 compositors' misreadings corrected by D, at least 7 not corr.

674.30 *very keen and intent,* corr. on CP to *very keen,*

675.31 *at all hurried, or made any kind of show.* corr. on CP to *at all hurried.*

675.33 *with great neatness* corr. on CP to *with neatness*

675.44–45 MS: *cool, and equally ready for anything* CP–CD: *cool, and equal for anything* [MS reading restored as better and seeming to have been accidentally overlooked]

676.19–20 MS: *docks, basins,* CP–CD: *docks and basins,*

676.29 CP: *nobody to remind myself* corr. to *no need to remind myself* [as in MS]

676.33–34 MS: *yet dank and muddy,* CP–CD: *yet dark and muddy,* [MS reading restored as obviously what D intended]

676.41 *with all the others* corr. on CP to *with the others*

677.6 *our coming here,"* corr. on CP to *our coming down here,"*

679.11 *at first, you see,"* corr. on CP to *at first,"*

680.1 *your maid* corr. on CP to *your little maid*

680.20 *thrown upon my back* corr. on CP to *turned on my back*

680.24 MS: *born with twenty yards of it,* CP: *born within twenty yards of it,* corr. to *born with a yard and a half of it,*

680.28 *to divert and entertain me.* corr. on CP to *to divert me.*

681.17 MS: *perceived that Mr. Bucket* CP–CD: *perceived Mr. Bucket*

681.26–27 *you're about the man* corr. on CP to *you're the man*

681.30 CP: *understood his wigs,* corr. to *understood his ways,* [as in MS]

682.2–3 *bounds of his looseness of principle.* corr. on CP to *bounds of his childish innocence.*

682.7–8 MS: *as innocent as lambs in all* CP–CD: *as innocent as can be in all* [MS reading restored as more picturesque and Bucket-like than compositor's inadvertent misreading]

682.11 *that person's just a crying* corr. on CP to *that person is only a crying*

682.15 *my practical experience.* corr. on CP to *my experience.*

682.26 *them brickmakers* corr. on CP to *those brickmakers*

682.27 MS: *so good as make 'em.* CP–CD: *so good as to make 'em.*

682.28–29 CP: *naturalest is your own* corr. to *naturalest way is your own* [as in MS]
683.26 *gets talking, you see."* corr. on CP to *gets talking."*
683.32 *upon the table,* corr. on CP to *on the table,*
683.33 MS–L: her *business* CD: her *own business*
683.39 *kicked at her with* corr. on CP to *kicked at her foot with*
684.1 CP: *Housever,* (?) corr. to *Howsever,* [as in MS] thus in 53 C–CD: *Howsoever,*
684.23 MS–53: *hankecher* C–CD: *handkercher*
684.30 MS: *we an't got* (?) CP: *we arn't got* corr. to *we ain't got*
685.1 MS–53: *wot she says.* C–CD: *what she says.*
685.28 CP: *comes wharf hours,* corr. to *comes to half hours,* [as in MS]
685.37–38 *circumstances, for they are up to* corr. on CP to *circumstances. They are up to*
685.38–39 *and, besides, any fool* corr. on CP to *and any fool*
686.7 *is on for'ard—* corr. on CP to *is for'ard—*
687.36 *But the next stage ended,* corr. on CP to *The next stage, however, ended,*
687.40 *and warm myself* corr. on CP to *and refresh myself*
687.42 *a cheerful room,* corr. on CP to *a warm room,*
687.44 MS: *the hostlers*
688.12 *about me—I sitting on the floor, crying—but I* corr. on CP to *about me, but I*
689.6 MS: *the hostlers,*
689.23 MS: *english?* CP–CD: *English?*
689.29 CP: *a crown a mare.* corr. to *a crown a man.* [as in MS]
689.39 CP: *this sudden change.* corr. to *the sudden change.* [MS illegible]
689.42 MS: *jumping up to his seat,* CP–CD: *jumping to his seat,* [MS reading restored as better and likely to have been inadvertently overlooked]
689.44 *I say no more at* corr. on CP to *I say nothing else at*
690.9 CP: *keep us as good heart* corr. to *keep up as good a heart* [MS had *keep up a good heart* with *as* ins. above *a* and a caret misplaced between *up* and *a*]

Chapter LVIII MS and one set of CP; no evidence of earlier or later CP missing; compositors unusually inefficient: over 25 misreadings corr. by D

691.5 CP: *the hand behind* corr. to *the rawest hand behind* [as in MS; compositor had left blank for difficult word]
692.1 *is, it is found* corr. on CP to *is, that it is found*
692.3 *William Doodle* corr. on CP to *William Buffy*
692.14–15 *retail her with the last* corr. on CP to *retail her at second-hand with the last*
692.16 *new indifference,* corr. on CP to *new polite indifference,*
692.16–17 *the rest of it, in inferior* corr. on CP to *the rest of it, all at second-hand but considered equal to new, in inferior*
692.19 *among these, how noble* corr. on CP to *among these little dealers, how noble*
692.27 MS–L: *he seem to fall* CD: *he seems to fall* [em. ad.]
692.30–31 *through the whole* corr. on CP to *throughout the whole*
692.23 after *it will pass* MS has *see back* and on separate slip pasted on to back of page text from *her, and go on."* to *will tell him!"*
693.38–39 CP: *My Lady's stall* corr. to *My Lady's state* [as in MS]
693.39 MS: *thus gloomily abandoned;* CP–CD: *thus gloomy and abandoned;*
694.2 *heap great fires in the grates,* corr. on CP to *heap fires in the grates,*
694.3 MS: *let the ruddy light* CP–CD: *let their ruddy light* [MS reading restored as more adequate—the light is not the light of the screens—and seeming to have been inadvertently altered]
694.4–5 *no light dispels.* corr. on CP to *no light will dispel.*
694.11 *not accurately knowing)* corr. on CP to *not knowing)*
694.28 *nicety, he is* corr. on CP to *nicety, and he is*
694.29 *dressing-gown, and wears his signet-ring.* corr. on CP to *dressing-gown.*
694.41–42 *she abruptly compliments* corr. on CP to *she compliments*
695.20 *tell me this,* corr. on CP to *tell me,*
696.6 *squares himself* corr. on CP to *squares his chest*
696.7 *ashamed.* corr. on CP to *ashamed of himself.*
696.16–17 *I remember him well—* corr. on CP to *I remember well—*
696.20 *says George,* corr. on CP to *says the trooper,*
696.31 *to ask.* corr. on CP to *to ask this.*
696.33 *wasn't indisposed—* corr. on CP to *was not so indisposed—*
696.37 *But, however* corr. on CP to *However*
697.5 *a sudden attack, a bad attack.* corr. on CP to *a sudden and bad attack.*
697.22 *he goes on,* corr. on CP to *he presently goes on,*
697.33 MS: *plainnes*
697.40 *who has come back* corr. on CP to *who comes back*
698.36 *it is understood.* corr. on CP to *it is quite understood.*
699.12–13 between *not growing late.* and *"Dear Sir Leicester,* following passage is canc. on CP: *"George," she whispers softly, when Volumnia has gone down to dinner, "Sir Leicester don't like the thought of shutting out my Lady for another night. Go away a little while, my dear. I'll speak to him."/ The trooper retires, and Mrs. Rouncewell takes her*

chair at the bedside./ "Sir Leicester."/ "That's Mrs. Rouncewell?"/ "Surely, yes, Sir Leicester."/ "I was afraid you had left me."/ His hand is lying close beside her. She kisses it./ "It's the dull one," says Sir Leicester. "But I feel that, Mrs. Rouncewell."/ It is too dark to see him; she thinks, however, that he puts his other hand before his eyes./ "Where is your son George? He is not gone? I want him here. I want only you and him; I would rather have no one else to-night."/ "He hoped he might be of some use, and he is not gone, Sir Leicester."/"I thank him!"

699.13 *master," the old housekeeper pursues,* corr. on CP to *master," she softly whispers,*

699.20 *just the same, too."* corr. on CP to *just the same."*

699.24 *that's a long time. Oh, it's* corr. on CP to *that is a long time. O it is* [MS had *that's* and *it's* but *O*]

699.29–30 *at the window* corr. on CP to *at the dark window*

699.37 *to receive her. Many a time, consequently, the old housekeeper trots downstairs to see, as she tells George, with her own eyes, that nothing is neglected. Poor pretence* corr. on CP to *to receive her. Poor pretence*

699.38 *as it is, it is very plain that these allusions* corr. on CP to *as it is, these allusions*

700.13–14 *the worst of nights. The mist still brooding, the sleet* corr. on CP to *the worst of nights; the sleet*

700.20 MS: *antedulivian* (?)

700.23 *she usually expresses it,* corr. on CP to *she expresses it,*

701.18–19 *the question, how the spot* corr. on CP to the *question, mooted by the maid, how the spot*

701.19 MS–L: *in her own room* CD: *in her room*

701.45–702.1 *through the skylight now,* corr. on CP to *through the skylight.*

702.2 *on the stone below.* corr. on CP to *on the stone floor below.*

702.8–9 *and of the two so brought* corr. on CP to *and of the two periods of his life so strangely brought*

702.8–9 *space of his life; thinking* corr. on CP to *space; thinking*

702.9 *image is so fresh* corr. on CP to *image so fresh*

702.13 *and thinks how he* might corr. on CP to *and reflects how he* might

702.16 *and below as he goes* corr. on CP to *and below, while he goes*

702.24 *down dejectedly without* corr. on CP to *down without*

702.25 *Quite familiar* corr. on CP to *very familiar*

702.27 CP: *blank of the wintry night;* corr. to *blank wintry night;* [MS: *blank of wintry night;* (?)]

702.28 CP: *and even draws* corr. to *and undraws* [as in MS]

702.29 *the day confronts them like* corr. on CP to *The day comes like*

Chapter LIX MS and one set of CP; no earlier or later set missing

702.37–38 MS–L: *companion had never slackened.* CD: *companion never slackened.*

703.28 MS: *"how wet* CP: *"Now wet* corr. to *"How wet*

703.30 *its way in; and* corr. on CP to *its way into the carriage; and*

703.31–32 *the wet had clung to me.* corr. on CP to *the wet had penetrated my dress.*

703.42 *understand it; but I* corr. on CP to *understand it better; but I*

703.44 *"Now I tell you* corr. on CP to *"And I tell you*

704.1 *half so much* corr. on CP to *half as much*

704.4 *elewated ones* corr. on CP to *elevated ones*

705.15 *midst of very night,* corr. on CP to *midst of the night,*

705.29 *"a very good move it is."* corr. on CP to *"a very good move."*

705.30 *go there with you?"* corr. on CP to *go with you?"*

706.6–7 *should I have been* corr. on CP to *I must have been*

706.11–12 *our little business* corr. on CP to *our business*

706.17 *"Will you be* corr. on CP to *"Then will you be*

706.24–25 *and she's got 'em bad* corr. on CP to *and has 'em bad*

706.25 CP: *contrary* corr. to *contrairy* [as in MS] thus in 53–L CD: *contrary*

706.27 *to reason somehow or other."* corr. on CP to *to reason somehow."*

707.4 *with an earnest face.* corr. on CP to *with his earnest face.*

707.5–6 MS: *understand you're a* CP–CD: *understand you are a* [MS reading restored, Bucket being one of the few characters from whose speech contracted forms have not been deliberately eliminated by D]

707.8 *She's got a letter* corr. on CP to *She has a letter*

707.9–10 *must be somewhere about her;* corr. on CP to *must be about her;*

707.10–11 *she is so difficult to handle without hurting, twisted and clenched up."* corr. on CP to *she is so twisted and clenched up, that she is difficult to handle without hurting."*

707.13 *from being shut up* corr. on CP to *from being up*

707.26 *to put a fine upon it—* corr. on CP to *to put too fine a point upon it—*

707.29 *as she had good reason* corr. on CP to *as she had reason*

707.40 *took the matter to himself.* corr. on CP to *took the matter on himself.*

708.3 CP: *Which there ain't a man* corr. to *Which there's not a man* [MS had *there an't*]

708.12 *from Mrs. Snagsby, because* corr. on CP to *from Mrs. Snagsby there, because*

708.14 CP: *manner of framing* corr. on CP

to *manner of forming* [MS not clear, but looks rather like *framing*]

708.32 *Now at the very* corr. on CP to *Why, at the very*

708.37–38 *in that elevated circle.* corr. on CP to *in that circle.*

709.10 *said Mr. Bucket.* corr. on CP to *said Mr. Bucket, excitedly.*

709.15 MS: *you hide and watch* CP–CD: *you hide and you watch*

709.24 *"Now the only amends you can make, Mrs. Snagsby,"* corr. on CP to *"Now Mrs. Snagsby, the only amends you can make,"*

709.27–28 *think of anything* corr. on CP to *think of any one thing*

709.42 MS: *to this cottage* CP–CD: *to the cottage*

710.6 paragraph ending with *was freely given."* set up in ordinary type on CP D wrote in margin: *This in the type formerly used for letters*

710.10 *"I have now wandered* corr. on CP to *"I have wandered*

710.17 paragraph ending with *and my conscience."* set up in ordinary type on CP D wrote in margin *This in the letter type*

710.22 *done what I could* corr. on CP to *done all I could*

710.25 MS–L: *can yet get* CD: *can get*

710.26 paragraph ending with *Farewell. Forgive."* set up in ordinary type on CP D wrote in margin: *This in the letter type*

710.29 *as soon as you feel* corr. on CP to *as soon as ever you feel*

710.30 *but I sat there* corr. on CP to *but I was left there*

711.4–5 MS–L: *on my shoulder;* CD: *upon my shoulder;*

711.13 *all sure of that now,"* corr. on CP to *all sure of that,"*

711.20–21 *when she see me* corr. on CP to *when she saw me*

711.37 *so well spoken, dear lady,"* corr. on CP to *so well spoken,"*

712.8 *frightened now again, dear lady. Hold me!"* corr. on CP to *frightened again. Hold me!"*

712.9 *But pray, pray tell* corr. on CP to *Pray, pray tell*

712.10 MS: *don't me angry*

713.3 MS: *miserable archway, where* CP: *miserable arching, where* corr. to *miserable covered way, where*

713.7 *dimly see a heap of* corr. on CP to *dimly see heaps of*

713.8–9 *houses, where dull lights burnt, and on whose* corr. on CP to *houses, with a few dull lights in their windows, and on whose*

713.10 *steeped in the fearful wet* corr. on CP to *drenched in the fearful wet*

713.16 *went up to that figure,* corr. on CP to *went up to the figure,*

713.20 *Well! They changed* corr. on CP to *They changed*

Chapter LX MS and one set of CP; no evidence of earlier or later CP missing

714.6 *narrative. The goodness* corr. on CP to *narrative. From the goodness*

714.7 *such sympathy and consolation* corr. on CP to *such consolation*

714.7–8 *think of with dry eyes.* corr. on CP to *think of unmoved.*

714.9 *upon my sorrows.* corr. on CP to *upon my sorrow.*

714.11 *recollection of their tenderness and love.* corr. on CP to *recollection of their sympathy.*

714.22 *I propose to remain* corr. on CP to *I purpose to remain* thus in 53–L CD: *I propose to remain*

714.33 MS–L: *"It is like you,* CD: *"It's like you,*

714.39 CP: *not of her, but* corr. to *not of her alone, but* [MS had *Not only of her, but*]

715.15–16 *will he wake from* corr. on CP to *will he awake from*

715.19 MS: *the foremost representative* CP: *the previous representative* corr. to *the principal representative*

715.22–23 *returned my guardian, shaking his head, "shall we* corr. on CP to *returned my guardian, "what shall we*

715.28 MS: *in old time."* CP–CD: *in old times."*

716.2 *this subject with him.* corr. on CP to *this subject with Rick.*

716.19 *said my guardian, laughing.* corr. on CP to *said my guardian.*

716.24 MS: *impression there that it* CP: *impression then that it* corr. to *impression that it*

716.32 *That was all undeniable.* corr. on CP to *That was undeniable.*

716.45 *never resumed since.* corr. on CP to *never resumed.*

717.13 MS: *a thriving rising place,* CP–CD: *a thriving place,*

717.22 *Woodcourt's kind, I am well assured."* corr. on CP to *Woodcourt's kind."*

717.26–27 MS: *in the wreck:* CP: *in the wreek;* corr. to *in the shipwreck;*

718.1 MS: *papers in the cause,* CP: *papers in the corner,* corr. to *papers in the Cause,*

718.6–7 *how different, O how* corr. on CP to *how different, how*

718.13 *My pet made* corr. on CP to *My dear made*

718.17 *it seemed another* corr. on CP to *it became another*

718.18–19 MS: *natural to her, she was yet* CP–CD: *natural when she was yet* [MS reading restored as obviously better then compositor's uncorr. misreading]

718.26 *My pet had already* corr. on CP to *Ada had already*

718.30 CP: *"My dear Fitz-Jarndyce!" she begun.* corr. to *"My dear!" she began.* [MS had *Fitz-Jarndyce* but *began*]

718.30 CP: *"How do you do!* corr. to *How do you do!* [D wrote *not Ital* in margin of CP; MS had: How *do you do!*]

718.30–31 *Glad to see you.* corr. on CP to *So glad to see you.*
718.36 *"My dear Fitz-Jarndyce, no, he is not* corr. on CP to *"No, he is not*
718.40 *"My dearest Fitz-Jarndyce,"* corr. on CP to *"My dearest,"*
719.10 *to think of him, and it brought the tears into my eyes.* corr. on CP to *to think of him.*
719.12–13 *very regular, Fitz-Jarndyce.* corr. on CP to *very regular, my charming girl.*
719.25 *caged up now, with* corr. on CP to *caged up with*
719.32 *her own lips, chilled me.* corr. on CP to *her own lips, quite chilled me.*
720.23,36 *"Quite so,"* corr. on CP to *"Just so,"*
720.31 MS: *excuse me from discussing it.* CP–CD: *excuse me for discussing it.*
720.36 *"But still, with a view* corr. on CP to *"Still, with a view*
720.43–44 CP: *independence; and dear, I will ever say,* corr. to *independence; dear, I will even say* [MS had *and* but *even*]
721.17–18 *It is considered so* corr. on CP to *She is considered so*
721.19–20 *it is more in their way* corr. on CP to *it is a point more in their way*
721.43–44 *addressed him cheerfully as he* corr. on CP to *addressed him as he*
722.16 *He ate very little,* corr. on CP to *He ate little,*
722.25 *They did not* corr. on CP to *These did not* [MS not clear]
723.1 *being first moved* corr. on CP to *being first removed*
724.5–6 *could not know Richard* corr. on CP to *could scarcely know Richard*
724.20–21 MS: *her fluttering hand was* CP–CD: *her hand was* [MS reading restored as better than compositor's probable oversight]
724.40 MS: *my own dear Esther,* CP–CD: *my dear Esther,*
724.45 *to see his child—the child who is to do so much!"* corr. on CP to *to see his child."*
724.45 for the first time in this novel, next chapter begins in middle of MS page, not on a separate page, the final monthly number being of more flexible length than the others.

Chapter LXI MS and one set of CP; no definite evidence of earlier or later set missing; of the 9 divergences between MS and CP, 2 may be deliberate emendations, the others being apparent oversights

725.24–25 MS: *the lid of the water-butt* CP–CD: *the lid of a water-butt* [MS reading restored as likely to have been inadvertently overlooked and more damaging to the status of the Skimpole house]
725.32–33 MS: *to speak himself only,*
725.35 MS–L: *his chair near mine,* CD: *his chair nearer mine,*
726.33 MS: *when he wants me.* CP–CD: *when it wants me.*
726.44 *beaming smiles* corr. on CP to *beaming smile*
727.10 *and can't pay* corr. on CP to *and who can't pay*
727.22 *you knew at the time with whom* corr. on CP to *you knew with whom*
727.40 MS–L: *I don't pretend* CD: *I don't intend*
729.9–10 MS–L: *shall I possibly paralyse* [MS: *paralyze*] CD: *shall I positively paralyse*
729.16 MS: *to trust to Bucket and to confide in Bucket.* CP–CD: *to trust to Bucket.*
729.27 MS–L: *based chiefly on* CD: *based principally on* [em. ad. because unlikely to be accidental]
729.28 *having very heartlessly* corr. on CP to *having heartlessly*
729.41 *occurred. I am sure of that. Whatever* corr. on CP to *occurred. Whatever*
730.2 MS–53: *not so very very far* C–CD: *not so very far*
730.4 MS–L: *confided to me,* CD: *confided in me,*
730.11–12 *to avow himself in his* corr. on CP to *to avow in his*
730.26–27 MS–L: *punctually to the time,* CD: *punctually at the time,*
730.28–29 MS: *minutes past the hour,* CP–CD: *minutes of the hour,* [MS reading restored as making better sense than compositor's apparent misreading]
731.12–13 MS–L: *no richer than I went* CD: *no richer than when I went*
731.20 *the unadorned truth.* corr. on CP to *the truth.*
732.3 MS: *comisseration*
732.36 *those new duties* corr. on CP to *these new duties*
732.39 MS: *"I am not not required*
733.2 MS–L: *or to desire."* CD: *or desire."*
733.11 *no one can know* corr. on CP to *few can know*
733.14 *so eminently happy.* corr. on CP to *so happy.*
733.32 *and my heart* corr. on CP to *and I felt as if my heart*

Chapter LXII MS and one set of CP; no evidence of earlier or later set missing

734.1 *by heart every word.* corr. on CP to *by heart.*
734.3 *integrity and tenderness,* corr. on CP to *integrity and love,*
734.7 *as busy as bees, if not as useful.* corr. on CP to *as busy as possible.*
734.28 *bright benevolent face,* corr. on CP to *bright face,*
734.38–39 MS: *I found that I did not* CP: *I found that did not* corr. to *I found I did not*
735.29 *its best mistress—* corr. on CP to *its little mistress—*
735.32–33 *my answer; just as on that day, it would have made no difference in a*

minute, even supposing that no one had come to the room door./ It was a servant to announce corr. on CP to *my answer./ A servant came to the door to announce*
736.9 *That's what* corr. on CP to *That's about what*
736.14 "*Moral,* corr. on CP to "*Now, Moral,*
736.19 *his premises a good deal.* corr. on CP to *his premises a deal.*
736.30 *previous agreement between them, and* corr. on CP to *previous agreement, and*
736.35 MS: "*Among these odd heaps,* CP: "*Among the odd heaps* corr. to "*Among them odd heaps*
737.13 *as a Will,* corr. on CP to *as a will,* thus in 53–L CD: *as a Will,*
737.28,33, 738.8 MS–L: *will* CD: *Will*
737.34 MS: "*Eh! now, mind* (?) CP: "*Oh, now, mind* corr. to "*Now, mind*
737.39 MS: *could be heard through* CP: *could he heard though* corr. to *could be heard though* thus in 53 C–CD: *could be heard through* [em.ad.]
738.17 *Will* corr. on CP to *will* thus in 53–L CD: *Will*
738.22–23 *and hand it to* corr. on CP to *and present it to*
738.42 *bound in honor to see* corr. on CP to *bound to see*
739.45 *will* corr. on CP to *Will* 53: *will* C–CD: *Will*
740.13 *considerably, still leaving* corr. on CP to *considerably, though still leaving*
741.5 *opinion of his by* corr. on CP to *opinion of his own by*
741.26 MS of Chapter LXIII begins on same page, immediately after end of LXII

Chapter LXIII MS and one set of CP; no conclusive evidence of any earlier or later set missing; the 9 substantive divergences between MS and CP probably due to compositors' misreadings, like the twenty errors corr. by D

742.15 *find him; you might at this time* corr. on CP to *find him—at this time*
742.41 MS: *looking about him confusedly for* CP–CD: *looking about him for* [*confusedly* restored as its loss seems both inadvertent and deplorable]
743.1 MS–L: *I wished to have* CD: *I wish to have*
743.12 MS: *account-books about him,* CP–CD: *account-books before him,*
743.31 "*Are you sure,*" corr. on CP to "*Are you quite sure,*"
743.44 MS: *that he never could have thought* CP–CD: *that he never thought* [*could have* restored because this is a repetition of phrase used in preceding paragraph]
744.1 *I could not have been* corr. on CP to *I should not have been*
744.11 MS: *Mr. George's modesty is so entirely overcome* CP–CD: *Mr. George is so entirely overcome*
744.22 *of those young ladies,* corr. on CP to *of these young ladies,*
744.26–27 MS: *bluffly and martially* CP–CD: *bluff and martial* [adverbs restored as more satisfactory; *-ly* ending often and understandably missed by compositors in D's MSS]
744.40 *my plans, such as they are, are made.* corr. on CP to *my plans are made.*
745.3 MS: "*To scratch you* CP–CD: "*Scratch you*
745.14 MS: *to be be brought about.*"
745.16 *which I hope will answer* corr. on CP to *which I hope may answer*
745.18–19 MS: *there is any consideration* (?) CP–CD: *there is a consideration*
745.21–22 CP: *dear old body!)* corr. to *dear old lady!)* [MS not clear; possibly *body*]
745.31 MS: *his hand on his brother's knee,* CP–CD: *his hand on his brother's,* [*knee* restored as making George's gesture more natural and characteristic; such a short word could easily be overlooked by compositor]
745.35 CP: *an uneducated vagabond,* corr. to *an undoubted vagabond,* [as in MS]
745.38 *It's a considerable weight off* corr. on CP to *It's a weight off*
746.6 MS: *in any regular garden.*" CP–CD: *in a regular garden.*"
746.38 *take your own way.*" corr. on CP to *take your way.*"
746.40 MS: *home'ards,* CP–L: *homeards,* CD: *homewards,*
747.9–10 MS: *where and when and how* CP–CD: *where, when and how*
747.29 *devoted servant,* corr. on CP to *devoted and admiring servant,*
747.33 whole letter set up in smaller type on CP though MS carries no direction to that effect

Chapter LXIV MS and one set of CP; no definite evidence of any earlier or later set missing

748.16 *my old apprehensions* corr. on CP to *my old apprehension*
749.2 MS: *some dawning hopes* CP: *some deceiving hopes* corr. to *some sanguine hopes*
749.22 *that I should not be* corr. on CP to *that I would not be*
749.25 CP: *I trembled all day, wondered all day, what* corr. to *I travelled all day, wondering all day, what* [MS had *travelled* and *wondered*]
749.36 *of kindness in itself.* corr. on CP to *of kindness.*
750.1 "*There to secure* corr. on CP to "*Then to ensure*
750.11 *reported to me ready,* corr. on CP to *reported ready,*
750.33 *not quite satisfied it was* corr. on CP to *not quite sure it was* [MS: *not quite sure that it* (?)]
751.3 MS: *with a rich and* CP–CD: *with such a rich and*
751.7 MS: *groupes,*

751.15 MS: my *odd ways* CP: *my odd things* corr. to *my odd ways*
751.17 *as I saw this;* corr. on CP to *when I saw this.*
751.23 *done so, even without* corr. on CP to *done so, without*
751.24–25 *reconciled myself to that,* corr. on CP to *reconciled myself even to that,*
753.16–17 *My dear, Allan* corr. on CP to *My dearest, Allan*
753.24–25 MS: *the best and dearest wife that* CP–CD: *the best wife that*
753.25 MS–L: *ever a man had.* CD: *ever man had.*
753.34–35 *to his old place and blot* corr. on CP to *to his old place in your affections; and blot*
753.43 after *come back!"* MS has *(Printer. White line here)*
754.6 *news to my darling.* corr. on CP to *news to him and my darling.*
754.14 *at night, had left* corr. on CP to *at night, he had left*
754.15 MS: *call again about* CP–CD: *call about* [*again* restored as abundantly justified by context and likely to have been inadvertently overlooked]
754.18 *it naturally fell out* corr. on CP to *it fell out*
755.16 MS: *a few pound* CP–CD: *a few pounds* [*pound* restored as probably deliberate and overlooked by compositor]
755.31–32 *Jobling, who has known* corr. on CP to *Jobling, who I believe has known*
756.9 *genteel; I will add,* corr. on CP to *genteel, I may even add,*
756.14 MS: *heigth,* CP–CD: *heighth,* [MS spelling restored in accordance with D's practise elsewhere]
756.18–19 CP: *none of us had any* corr. to *none of us have had any* [MS not clear but looks like *none of us here had any*]

Chapter LXV MS and one set of CP; no other set missing

757.27 *the Will* corr. on CP to *the will* thus in 53–L CD: *the Will* [see also 758.38; in this chapter *court* and *cause* often but not always corr. on CP to *Court* and *Cause*; further capitalizations of *Court* occur in CD only]
758.38 *the will* corr. on CP to *the Will*
759.29 MS: *thresh-hold?"* CP–CD: *thres hold?"*
759.32 *"Most willingly, if* corr. on CP to *"Most certainly, if*
759.44 MS–L: *dignified to severity,* CD: *dignified almost to severity,* [em. ad. because addition of *almost* seems unlikely to be compositor's initiative]
760.13–14 *"Mr. Vholes?"* corr. on CP to *"Mr. Vholes, what do you say?"*
760.19–20 MS: *whispered Allan, taking me hurriedly from them, "this will* CP–CD: *whispered Allan, "this will* [MS reading restored as alone making scene fully intelligible; words overlooked by CP compositor were written apart from text and relevant caret almost concealed by another insert]
760.32 CP: *morsel of his client,* corr. to *morsel of this client,* [as in MS] *this* in 53–L CD: *his*
761.7 MS–L: *sitting in a corner* CD: *sitting in the corner*
761.11 MS–L: *on the sofa* CD: *on a sofa*
761.11–12 *went in. The room* corr. on CP to *went in. There were restoratives on the table; the room*
761.31–32 *answered thus* corr. on CP to *answered him thus*
762.27 *behind his bed's head.* corr. on CP to *behind the head of his couch.* thus in 53–L CD: *of the couch.*
763.3 MS–L: *"It was all a* CD: *"It was a*
763.3–4 *both his hands* corr. on CP to *both my guardian's hands*
763.5 MS: *"No more, Rick; no more."* CP–CD: *"Nothing more, Rick; nothing more."*

Chapter LXVI MS and one set of CP; no other set missing

763.31 MS: *a hush on* CP–CD: *a hush upon*
763.40 *all vague mystery.* corr. on CP to *all mystery.*
764.1 *peachey-cheeked* corr. on CP to *peachy-cheeked*
764.12 MS–53: *of a worthy presence* C–CD: *of worthy presence*
764.22 MS–53: *to be a concession to* C–CD: *to be a condescension to* [em. ad. as the change makes sense and is not certainly a compositor's invention]
764.25 *committing a trespass* corr. on CP to *committing a flagrant trespass*
764.33 MS: *how he is humoured.* CP–CD: *how much he is humoured.*
765.17 CP: *a gentle inflexible voice* corr. to *a gruff inflexible voice* [as in MS]
765.18 MS: *to say, as two men* CP: *to say, as the two men* corr. to *to say, while the two men*
765.25 *contracting and perishing out until* corr. on CP to *contracting and dwindling until*
765.27–28 CP: *shuts so tight and obdurate shall have* corr. to *shuts so tight, and looks so obdurate, will have* [MS had *tightly* (?) *and looks* and *shall*]
765.28 MS: *opened to receive him.* CP: *opened and relieved him.* corr. to *opened and recieved him.* 53–CD: *relieved* [*received* introduced here as making better sense and being D's intention expressed both in MS and—however inefficiently—on CP]
765.33–34 MS: *Long-winded orations or treatises on the Buffy* CP: *Long-winded critics on treatises on Buffy* corr. to *Long-winded treatises on the Buffy*
765.35 MS: *villainnous* (?)
765.37 MS: *can never be* CP–CD: *cannot be* [MS reading restored as better than compositor's misreading]
766.26 CP: *kind and comely,* corr. to *kind and cruel,* [as in MS]

766.34 CP: *house looking upon the sighing trees wringing* corr. to *house looking out upon the trees, sighing, wringing* [MS had *looking upon sighing trees wringing*]

767.10 Chapter LXVII begins on same MS page as end of LXVI

Chapter LXVII MS and one set of CP; no other set missing

767.20–21 MS: *did come to her, though it came, in the Eternal* CP: *did come to her through it, in the Eternal* corr. to *did come to her; though it came, in the Eternal*

767.34 *of your own."* corr. on CP to *of your home."*

767.41 CP: *believe Aunt Charley* corr. to *believe that Charley* [as in MS]

768.12 *a good-looking bashful* corr. on CP to *a good bashful*

768.19–20 *Prince (an excellent husband to her) being lame,* corr. on CP to *her husband (an excellent one) being lame,*

768.28–29 *rights of women, and Caddy* corr. on CP to *rights of women to sit in Parliament, and Caddy*

768.34 CP: *the affection of her child.* corr. to *the affliction of her child.* [as in MS]

768.37 *doing very well.* corr. on CP to *doing extremely well.*

768.40 *to have left him* corr. on CP to *to have bequeathed him*

768.44 CP: *a little fowlery* corr. to *a little Growlery* [as in MS]

769.5–6 *to me, what he has* corr. on CP to *to me, he is what he has*

769.12 *other place but in* corr. on CP to *other place than in*

769.25 *as if I were so glad to know* corr. on CP to *as if it were so good to know*

769.27 *call him Richard!* corr. on CP to *call him my Richard!*

769.29 *not at all rich,* corr. on CP to *not rich in the bank,*

769.30–31 *but I know the people* corr. on CP to *but I hear the people*

769.34 MS: *in a time of need.* CP–CD: *in the time of need.* [*a* restored as better than compositor's alternative]

769.35–36 *have often gone up,* corr. on CP to *have often, often gone up,*

769.36 *his gentle ministration.* corr. on CP to *his patient ministration.*

769.41 *everything in life* corr. on CP to *everything I do in life*

770.24 MS–53–L: *THE END* C–CD: this has been canc.

770 at the end of MS is a separate slip in D's handwriting: *Last page, third and fourth lines from top/* For *He has two mammas, and am one/* Read *He has two mammas and I am one* This note must have been sent by D to the printer's after he has returned CP, but the *I* is in CP, and the comma has not been canc.

The Genesis and Composition of Bleak House

Chronology: 1850-53

October, 1850	Final number of *David Copperfield* published. Residing at Devonshire Place in London. Engaged in amateur theater productions.
January, 1851	Plays staged at Rockingham Castle. Begins writing (by dictation) *A Child's History of England.*
March, 1851	Death of Dickens' father. *The Times* initiating campaign for Chancery reforms.
April, 1851	Death of Dickens' infant daughter, Dora. Publishes article on police in *Household Words.*
May, 1851	Speech to Metropolitan Sanitary Association.
June, 1851	Moves out of Devonshire Place to seaside at Broadstairs.
August, 1851	Planning new novel. Visits Stroud Valley.
September, 1851	Visits Chatsworth, estate of Duke of Devonshire.
October, 1851	Returns from seaside to new house in London, Tavistock.
November, 1851	Begins writing *Bleak House.* Visits Walter S. Landor at Bath.
December, 1851	Family Christmas at Tavistock House.
February, 1852	Fall of Lord John Russell's government, succeeded by the Conservatives under Lord Derby and Benjamin Disraeli. Dickens' fortieth birthday.
March, 1852	First number of *Bleak House* published as monthly installment.
April, 1852	Bills in Parliament for reform of Chancery, sanitation, and against bribery in elections.
May, 1852	Third number (Chapters VIII–X) published; fourth number written.
June, 1852	Declines to run for Parliament. Visits St. Albans for backgrounds for *Bleak House.*

July, 1852	Summer residence at Dover (until October).
August, 1852	Heavy rains and severe floodings in Midlands.
September, 1852	*Bleak House* attacked by Lord Denman, former Lord Chancellor, for its allegedly irresponsible social criticism.
October, 1852	Returns from seaside to Tavistock House.
December, 1852	Derby-Disraeli government falls; succeeded by two-party coalition under Lord Aberdeen.
January, 1853	Visits London slums to inspect sites for model housing.
June, 1853	Moves to Boulogne with family for the summer.
August, 1853	Final "double number" of *Bleak House* written (published in September).

Dickens' Letters on the Composition of *Bleak House*†

On February 21, 1851, about two months after the final number of *David Copperfield* had been published, Dickens remarked in a letter to Mary Boyle about "the first shadows of a new story hovering in a ghostly way about me (as they usually begin to do, when I have finished an old one)." Some six months later, while he was living at Broadstairs, these shadows apparently began to take firmer shape. On August 17, 1851, he wrote to Angela Burdett-Coutts: "I begin to be pondering afar off, a new book. Violent restlessness, and vague ideas of going I don't know where, I don't know why, are the present symptoms of the disorder."[1] To other correspondents he also reported, at this time, that he proposed to visit a beautiful valley in Gloucestershire, apparently to inspect scenery that might be used in the new novel, and in September he did make the journey there. Although these latter letters have not been published, the substance of them can be reconstituted in an account by his friend and biographer, John Forster, who visited him at Broadstairs in August:

> But now his own restlessness with fancies for a new book had risen beyond bounds, and for the time he was eager to open it in that prettiest quaintest bit of English landscape, Strood[2] valley, which reminded him always of a Swiss scene. I had not left him many days when these lines followed me. 'I very nearly packed up a portmanteau and went away * * * into the mountains of Switzerland, alone! Still the victim of an intolerable restlessness * * * * I sit down between whiles to think of a new story, and as it begins to grow, such a torment of a desire to be anywhere but where I am * * * takes hold of me, that it is like being *driven away*.' * * * * It was not until the end of November * * * that the book was begun.

[From Letter to F. M. Evans, September 26, 1851]

I find my new house so remarkable for nothing as for its Drainage—which is of a most powerful description. * * * Wait till I get rid of my workmen and get to my work, and see if we don't raise the (East) wind!

† The letters here reprinted are from Walter Dexter, ed., *The Letters of Charles Dickens*, vols. 10–12 of *The Nonesuch Dickens* (Bloomsbury: The Nonesuch Press, 1937–38), with the exception of the letters to Angela Burdett-Coutts, which (unless otherwise noted) are from Edgar Johnson, ed., *The Heart of Charles Dickens* (New York: Duell, Sloan and Pearce, 1952).

1. From *Letters of Charles Dickens to Baroness Burdett-Coutts*, edited by Charles B. Osborne (1931), pp. 108–09. Reprinted by permission of John Murray (Publishers) Ltd.

2. Forster's spelling here is misleading. Dickens was referring to Stroud Valley in Gloucestershire, not to Strood in Kent.

[From Letter to the Duke of Devonshire, September 28, 1851, from Broadstairs]

I am in the first throes of a new book, and am spasmodically altering and arranging a new house besides,—and am walking by the sea every day, endeavouring to think of both sets of distraction to some practical end.

[From Letter to Henry Austin, October 7, 1851]

Oh! if this were to last long;[3] the distraction of the new book, the whirling of the story through one's mind, escorted by workmen, the imbecility, the wild necessity of beginning to write, the not being able to do so, the O! I should go—O!

[From Letter to Angela Burdett-Coutts, October 9, 1851]

I am three parts distracted and the fourth part wretched in the agonies of getting into a new house—Tavistock House, Tavistock Square. Pending which desirable consummation of my troubles, I *can not* work at my new book—having all my notions of order turned completely topsy-turvy.

[From Letter to F. M. Evans, October 12, 1851]

As I never get a moment's respite from the convulsions incident to my present severe attack of Tavistock House * * * I can by no means get to work. But I hope by vigorous exertions to get settled in three weeks or so, and then go at it Ding Dong.

[From Letter to Mr. Eeles, a decorator, October 22, 1851]

I send you the list I have made for the book-backs.[4] I should like the History of a Short Chancery Suit to come at the bottom of one recess, and the Catalogue of Statues of the Duke of Wellington at the bottom of the other.

[From Letter to F. M. Evans, December 7, 1851]

You will be glad to hear that I have only the last short chapter to do, to complete No. 1.

[From Letter to W. H. Wills, December 8, 1851]

I am obliged to you for the Chancery information. I had got to that Number of Solicitors—by a sort of instinct I suppose—but had modestly limited my costs to from forty to fifty thousand pounds.

[From Letter to George Hogarth, March 4, 1852]

I was very much pleased * * * to find that you think so highly of No. 1. It has been a very great success, and is blazing away merrily.

3. Written from his new house in London, which was being redecorated.

4. A shelf of imitation books installed in Dickens' library, with titles on the backs making jokes on various aspects of Victorian life such as Chancery delays and the proliferation of statues honoring Wellington (who was to die the following year).

[From Letter to John Forster, March 7, 1852[5]]

Wild ideas are upon me of going to Paris—Rouen—Switzerland—somewhere—and writing the remaining two thirds of the next No. aloft in some queer inn room. I have been hanging over it, and have got restless. Want a change I think. Stupid. We were at 30,000 when I last heard. * * * I enclose proofs of No. 2. Browne[6] has done Skimpole, and helped to make him singularly unlike the great original. Look it over, and say what occurs to you.

[From Letter to John Forster, March 18, 1852]

I have gone over every part of it very carefully, and I think I have made it much less like. I have also changed Leonard to Harold. I have no right to give Hunt pain, and I am so bent upon not doing it that I wish you would look at all the proof once more, and indicate any particular place in which you feel it particularly like. Whereupon I will alter that place.

[From Letter to W. F. de Cerjat, May 8, 1852]

I hope you will like Bleak House better and better as you go on. It is a most enormous success; all the prestige of Copperfield (which was very great) falling upon it, and raising its circulation above all my other books. I am very much interested, having just written No. IV.

[From Letter to Angela Burdett-Coutts, June 1, 1852]

I am afraid I cannot get out in the middle of the day on Thursday, for I am hard at work with No. 5, and anxious to get it done. And if I let myself out of my room under such circumstances, I have lost my power over myself for the day.

[From Letter to Rev. Henry Christopherson,[7] July 9, 1852]

If you think the balance between the home mission and the foreign mission justly held in the present time, I do not. * * * Indeed I have very grave doubts whether a great commercial country, holding communication with all parts of the world, can better Christianise the benighted portions of it than by the bestowal of its wealth and energy on the making of good Christians at home, and on the utter removal of neglected and untaught childhood from its streets, before it wanders elsewhere.

5. After a visit to the cemetery where his infant daughter, Dora, was buried.

6. H. K. Browne, who drew the illustrations for *Bleak House*. Modifications of his illustrations and of Dickens' text (see the following letter) were aimed at reducing the resemblance between Skimpole and Leigh Hunt. See below, "A Dictionary of *Bleak House* Originals."

7. Christopherson had written a letter protesting about the scene of Jo on the steps of the Missionary Society headquarters (ch. XVI).

[From Letter to Mary Boyle, July 22, 1852]

To let you into a secret, I am not quite sure that I ever did like, or ever shall like, anything quite so well as Copperfield. But I foresee, I think, some very good things in Bleak House * * * * This is one of what I call my wandering days before I fall to work. I seem to be always looking at such times for something I have not found in life, but may possibly come to a few thousands of years hence, in some other part of some other system. God knows.

[From Letter to Angela Burdett-Coutts, November 19, 1852]

I came home yesterday in time to write an article for the next No of *Household Words* * * * objecting to the whole State Funeral, and showing why. * * * * I have been so busy, leading up to the great turning idea of the Bleak House, that I have lived the last week or ten days in a perpetual scald and boil.[8]

[From Letter to Mrs. Richard Watson, November 22, 1852]

You ask * * * about Bleak House. Its circulation is half as large again as Copperfield![9] I have just now come to the point I have beeen patiently working up to in the writing, and I hope it will suggest to you a pretty and affecting thing.

[From Letter to W. H. Wills, from Boulogne, June 18, 1853]

Thank God I have done half the No. with great ease, and hope to finish on Thursday or Friday next. O * * * what a relief to get the No. out! * * * *I don't think* * * * I shall come to London until after the completion of Bleak House No. 18—the No. after this now in hand.

[From Letter to Hablôt K. Browne, June 29, 1853]

I send the subjects for the next No.: will you let me see the sketches here by post. * * * I am now ready with all four subjects for the concluding double No. and will post them to you tomorrow.

[From Letter to W. H. Wills, August 7, 1853 (with Wills' replies in brackets)]

Will you make at once an enquiry into the Day Chancery cause, as

1. When was it instituted? [About 1834 as near as I know]
2. How much nearer is it now to its completion? [As far off as ever]

8. The State Funeral was for the Duke of Wellington. The section of *Bleak House* referred to, according to Edgar Johnson, was chapters XXVI–XXIX.

9. A forthcoming study by Robert L. Patten, *Charles Dickens and His Publishers,* provides a full-scale account of the financial success of *Bleak House* in parts. Sales of monthly numbers held above 30,000 copies, and Dickens' earnings therefrom totaled about £500 a number.

3. What has been spent in costs? [At least £70,000]

4. How many Counsel appear—about—whenever the Court is moved? [Formerly always 17, sometimes 30 or 40; it used to be said the whole Bar. The number has been much reduced]

[From Letter to Mrs. Richard Watson, August 27, 1853]

I like the conclusion very much, and think it very *pretty indeed.* * * * I never had so many readers.

A Dictionary of *Bleak House* Originals: Persons and Places

Bleak House, like *Pickwick Papers,* is one of Dickens' novels that has prompted a remarkable number of articles devoted to showing that the inspiration for creating some of his characters and settings derived from his knowledge of actual persons and places, and that these real-life "originals" served as models for him in various sections of his novel. Some readers find such investigations offensive; they contend that to identify a prototype is somehow to cast a slur on the artist's imaginative capacities and his originality. Such readers are advised to by-pass the following compilation. On the other hand, those who enjoy inquiries into the relations between fact and fiction can argue that to identify a prototype casts no slur upon an artist. Instead, such identifications harmlessly provide materials for interesting comparisons that can offer glimpses into the shaping power of a novelist's creative imagination. Dickens himself remarked in a letter of September 7, 1852, while he was writing *Bleak House,* that "most writers of fiction write, partly from their experience, and partly from their imagination, and * * * in the work to which you refer I have had recourse to both sources."

At times, the resemblances between prototypes and fictional creations in *Bleak House* are strong and unmistakable, such as the similarities between Harold Skimpole and the poet, Leigh Hunt, or between Chesney Wold and the estate of Rockingham Castle. At other times, the suggested resemblances are faint and seem far-fetched or pointless. In what follows, examples of the second category have been kept to the minimum; otherwise, we have not been concerned primarily with evaluation.

The compilation of notes and articles has had to be highly selective, but in most instances the articles cited refer to what has been previously written on the topic so that any reader interested in exploring the question in greater depth can thereby locate the earlier sources.

Bleak House. Reputed original: a house in St. Albans in Hertfordshire now bearing a plaque "Bleak House." It would be more accurate to say that Dickens was inspired by the surroundings of the whole St. Albans region rather than by any particular house that has so far been identified. In an unpublished letter (June 17, 1852) Dickens speaks of having visited St. Albans to get on-the-spot impressions of settings for *Bleak House*. See also Trevor Blount on "The Importance of Place in *Bleak House,*" *Dickensian,* LXI (1965), 140–49.

Blowers, Mr. The name of this lawyer, appearing in chapter I, may have been inspired by a Chancery lawyer, Mr. Joseph Blower, who testified in a lawsuit of 1826, in the case of *Stevens* vs. *Guppy*. (Noted by Robert Newsom in a forthcoming book on *Bleak House*).

Boythorn, Lawrence. Original: Walter Savage Landor (1775–1864), poet, essayist and friend of Dickens. Landor's hearty outspokenness was proverbial. As a landowner, after posting a sign warning a neighbor to keep off his property, he had been sued for libel. Dickens visited him at the time he began composing *Bleak House* and reported in a letter (Nov. 13, 1851): "I saw old Landor at Bath * * * When he was last in town, 'Kenyon drove him about, by God, half the morning, under a most damnable pretence of taking him to where Walter [his godson, Walter Landor Dickens] was at school, and they never found the confounded house!' " Dickens later stated that Boythorn was "a most exact portrait" of his friend. See T. Sturge Cotterell, in *Dickensian*, XLIV (1948), 209–16; and R. H. Super, *Walter Savage Landor* (New York, 1954), pp. 405–6.

Bucket, Inspector. Reputed original: Inspector Charles Frederick Field of the London Metropolitan Police. In 1850–51, Dickens wrote several articles on Field and the police force for *Household Words*. In one article he described the Inspector (here called "Wield") as "a middle-aged man of a portly presence, with a large, moist, knowing eye, a husky voice, and a habit of emphasising his conversation by the aid of a corpulent fore-finger, which is constantly in juxtaposition with his eyes or nose" (*Household Words*, July 27, 1850, p. 409). On September 18, 1853, Dickens wrote a letter to *The Times* denying that Bucket had been modeled on Field. See his *Reprinted Pieces*, and *Uncollected Writings from Household Words*, ed. Harry Stone (1968), 253–73. See also Philip Collins, *Dickens and Crime* (1962/68), 196–219; and Michael Steig in *Papers of the Michigan Academy*, L (1965), 575–84.

Chesney Wold. Original: Rockingham Castle in Northamptonshire, located about twenty miles south of the city of Leicester, an estate where Dickens had often been a guest. In 1853 he wrote to his hosts:

> In some of the descriptions of Chesney Wold, I have taken many bits, chiefly about trees and shadows, from observations made at Rockingham. I wonder whether you have ever thought so!

See Leslie Staples, in *Dickensian*, XLI (1945), 80–81.

Dedlock, Sir Leicester. In at least one particular (his reliance upon his servants, Mrs. Rouncewell and George), he has been said to resemble the sixth Duke of Devonshire (1790–1858) who entertained Dickens at his estate at Chatsworth in September, 1851. See T. W. Hill, *Dickensian*, XL (1944), 43. Concerning the Dedlock cousins and Disraeli's "Young England" political movement, see Trevor Blount, *Nineteenth-Century Fiction*, XXI (1966), 149–65.

Flite, Miss. Reputed original: "Miss R—", a notorious eccentric of the 1830's described in *Oddities of London Life* (1838) as "a little sharp-featured woman, bearing an enormous bag" who presented herself in Chancery court "demanding an instant investigation into the documents she was prepared to produce in support of her alleged rights." See John Butt, "*Bleak House* Once More," *Critical Quarterly*, I (1959), 302–7, and Trevor Blount, *Dickens Studies*, I (1965), 112–14.

Gridley. Reputed original, as Dickens states in his Preface, a case described in a pamphlet by W. Challinor, *The Court of Chancery: Its Inherent Defects as Exhibited in Its System of Procedure and of Fees* (1849). The pamphlet has not been reprinted. In general see

Trevor Blount, "The Documentary Symbolism of Chancery in *Bleak House*," *Dickensian*, LXII (1966), 47–52, 106–11, 167–74.

Guster. Reputed original: any maltreated child from Drouet's orphanage at Tooting. See note to p. 117, and also A. W. C. Brice and K. J. Fielding, in *Victorian Studies*, XII (1968), 227–44; and Philip Collins on apprenticed servants in *Nineteenth-Century Fiction*, XIV (1960), 345–49.

Hortense. Reputed original: Maria Manning, a Belgian woman who, previous to marriage, had served in England as a maid to Lady Blantyre, daughter of the Duchess of Sutherland. In 1849 she was convicted (with her husband) of murdering a man, her weapon having been a pistol. The *Chronicles of Newgate* record that after her sentencing she vehemently cursed judge and jury, and she had to be removed from court in handcuffs. "Her favourite and most often-repeated expression was 'Damn seize you all.' " See Edwin Pugh, *The Dickens Originals* (1912), p. 258. Before her execution she attempted to commit suicide. A handsome woman, usually dressed in black satin, Mrs. Manning made a striking impression on the spectators of her execution, at which Dickens himself was present, as also was Herman Melville. Especially striking, *The Times* reported, was her "diabolical self-possession." According to B. B. Valentine, Dickens has "reproduced with wonderful exactness the broken English, impatient gestures and volubility" of Mrs. Manning. See *Dickensian, XIX* (1923), 21–22; and also LXVII (1970), 12–15 (article by James A. Davies).

Jellyby, Mrs. Reputed original: Mrs. Caroline Chisholm (1807–77), whose work in organizing the Family Colonization Loan Society was supported by Dickens but whose housekeeping prompted his comment in a letter (March 4, 1850): "I dream of Mrs. Chisholm, and her housekeeping. The dirty faces of her children are my continual companions." See Philip Collins, in *Nineteenth-Century Fiction*, XIV (1960), 345–49; and *Uncollected Writings from Household Words*, pp. 85–86 and Appendix C. Mrs. Jellyby's Borrioboola-Gha project was reputedly modeled on an ill-fated expedition of 1841 to establish a colony on the banks of the Niger, about which Dickens wrote an article. See John Butt and Kathleen Tillotson, *Dickens at Work* (1957), pp. 194–95, where Dickens' letter defending his portrait is cited:

> Mrs. Jellyby gives offence merely because the word "Africa," is unfortunately associated with her wild Hobby. No kind of reference to Slavery is made or intended, in that connexion. It must be obvious to anyone who reads about her. [December 22, 1852]

Jo. Reputed original: George Ruby, a fourteen-year old crossing-sweep whose appearance as a witness was reported in Dickens' *Household Narrative*, in 1850. See "Cross-Examination of a Witness at an Inquest" in the Backgrounds section in the present volume, and also articles by W. V. Harris, *Dickensian*, LXIV (1968), 48–49; and K. J. Fielding and A. W. Brice, *Dickensian*, LXIV (1968), 131–40, and LXV (1969), 35–41. Associated with Jo is the burial ground pictured in chapters XI and XVI. Its reputed original was the churchyard grounds of St. Martins-in-the-Fields off Drury Lane. In 1868, responding to an enquiry from a woman in America, Dickens indicated the location which had provided his model sixteen years earlier:

> Walk through the centre avenue of Covent Garden Market * * * Keep straight on along the side of the Drury Lane Theatre, and about halfway down * * * is a closely hemmed-in grave-yard—happily long disused and closed by the Law. I do not remember that the grave-yard is accessible from the street now, but when I was a boy it was to be got at by a low covered passage under a house, and was guarded by a rusty iron gate. In that churchyard I long afterwards buried the "Nemo" of Bleak House.

See Fielding and Brice in *Dickens the Craftsman*, ed. Robert Patlow (1970), pp. 115–39.

Kenge, Conversation. The name, at least, may have been suggested by Richard Sharp (1759–1835), a Member of Parliament and celebrated talker who was known as "Conversation Sharp."

Krook. No specific rag-and-bottle dealer has been proposed as a prototype for Krook, but his death by spontaneous combustion is supposed to have been based on several historic instances, as Dickens himself stated in his Preface and in chapter XXXIII as well as in a letter of February 7, 1853, to Dr. John Elliotson, who had sent him a paper on the topic:

> Before writing that chapter of Bleak House, I had looked up all the more famous cases you quote * * * but three or four * * * are new to me * * * * It is inconceivable to me how people can reject such evidence.

See Gordon Haight, in *Nineteenth-Century Fiction*, X (1955), 53–63; and Elizabeth Wiley, in *Dickensian*, LVIII (1962), 120–25; George Perkins, *Dickensian*, LX (1964), 57–64; Trevor Blount, in *Dickens Studies Annual* (1970), 183–212; and E. Gaskell, in *Dickensian*, LXIX (1973), 25–35.

Neckett, Charlie. Reputed original in her role as maidservant to the Smallweeds (ch. XXI): Jane Wilbred, a sixteen-year-old pauper who was starved and maltreated by a lawyer, George Sloane, and his wife. The Sloanes were sentenced to two years in prison in 1850, their case having been extensively reported in the press, including Dickens' own news summary, *Household Narrative* (1850), p. 271 and 1851, pp. 11, 38, 199). See Trevor Blount, in *Dickens Studies*, III (1967), 63–67. A similar case of maltreatment, in which the maidservant died, was reported in *Illustrated London News*, Feb. 15, 1851, p. 139; and see also May 31, 1851, p. 501 for a report on a new law for the protection of servants.

Rouncewell, Mrs. Reputed original: Elizabeth Ball Dickens (1745–1824), grandmother of Charles Dickens and housekeeper at Crewe Hall in Cheshire; one of her sons was a success in business, and the other (Dickens' father) suffered from "idleness and general incapacity." See A. T. Butler, "The Dickens Ancestry," in *Dickensian*, XLV (1949), 64–73.

Skimpole, Harold. Original: Leigh Hunt (1784–1859), a poet and essayist whose sense of financial responsibility was casual. In a letter of Sept. 25, 1853, Dickens commented about Skimpole:

> I suppose he is the most exact portrait that was ever painted in words! * * * It is so awfully true that I made a bargain with myself "never to do so any more." * * * It is an absolute reproduction of a real man. Of course I have been careful to keep

> the outward figure away from the fact; but in all else it is the life itself.[1]

Earlier letters indicate, however, that under pressure from admirers of Hunt, Dickens had sought to tone down the similarities between his portrait and its prototype. The textual notes to chapter VI in the present edition, recording changes made by Dickens in proof, will be found to bear this out. One such change involved Skimpole's name. It has been alleged that Dickens originally called him *Leonard Horner*—where the initials would have been a clear give-away to Hunt's identity—but nowhere in the texts does the name *Horner* appear. The first name, *Leonard,* however, is clearly present in proof, at which point it was changed to *Harold*. Another modification (see Textual Notes to chapter XLIII) was to change the names of Skimpole's daughters. They were originally called *Juliet* and *Susannah* (which was clearly too reminiscent of *Julia* and *Jacintha,* the names of Hunt's daughters), and in proof they became *Arethusa* and *Kitty*. Later, Dickens made further amends by tributes to what he called Skimpole's "great original" in articles published after the novel had appeared. See John Forster's life of Dickens (VI, ch. 7); Louis Landré's *Leigh Hunt* (Paris, 1935), 269–74; and K. J. Fielding, in *Dickensian,* LXIV (1968), 5–9.

Summerson, Esther. Reputed original: Georgina Hogarth (1827–1917), Dickens' sister-in-law, who excelled in the management of his household. See Arthur Adrian, *Georgina Hogarth* (1957), 33–34. It is reported by Leslie Staples that Miss Hogarth herself, late in her life, remarked that although she strongly disliked to be identified with the character Agnes in *David Copperfield,* she did not object to being likened to Esther in *Bleak House*.

Tom-All-Alone's. Reputed original: The house of Thomas Clarke, a recluse of whom Dickens learned in his childhood. See George H. Ford, in *Dickensian,* LXV (1969), 84–89.

Turveydrop, Mr. Reputed original: John Henry Skelton (born ca. 1775), author of *The Anatomy of Conduct*. See Lionel Stevenson in *Dickensian,* LXIV (1947), 39–41, and also XLII (1966), 39–40. It has also been suggested that his name may derive from a children's song: "Turvey, turvey, clothed in black / With silver buttons upon your back." See *Dickensian,* XLV (1969), 111.

1. *Harper's Monthly Magazine,* CXII (April, 1906), 717–18.

[illegible] outside [illegible] from the first [illegible] all [illegible] it is the [illegible].

[illegible] quite [illegible] Dickens had [illegible] between [illegible] the [illegible] in chapter VI [illegible] present edition [illegible] changes made by Dickens [illegible] found [illegible]. It has been alleged that [illegible] originally called [illegible] [illegible] [illegible]. The first name, [illegible], however, is clearly present [illegible] [illegible]. Another modification [illegible] [illegible] change the names [illegible] [illegible]. They were originally called [illegible] [illegible] which was [illegible] [illegible] the names [illegible] became [illegible] and [illegible]. Later [illegible] [illegible] [illegible] [illegible] after the novel had appeared [illegible] [illegible] and [illegible] Fielding [illegible] [illegible].

[illegible]. Reputed original [illegible] [illegible] who [illegible] in the [illegible] of his house [illegible] [illegible] [illegible] that [illegible] [illegible] [illegible] [illegible] [illegible] [illegible] [illegible] [illegible] [illegible] [illegible] [illegible].

[illegible]. Reputed original [illegible] the house of Thomas [illegible] [illegible] which Dickens [illegible] [illegible] [illegible] [illegible].

[illegible]. Reputed original [illegible] [illegible] [illegible] [illegible] [illegible] [illegible] [illegible] [illegible] [illegible] [illegible] [illegible] [illegible] [illegible] with silver buttons [illegible]. See [illegible].

1. [illegible] 1940, [illegible].

Backgrounds

As the prefaces to his novels indicate, Dickens considered the recording of social history an important aspect of the art of novel writing, and *Bleak House* provides an especially striking example of how contemporary events and topics are prominently featured in his fictional world. The topicality of *Bleak House* is of two kinds. Some of the references to the contemporary scene involve topics that are so recurrently represented in the novel as to make them of central importance; these are pollution, government, and the law. The following selections are therefore restricted to these three topics. A word should be said, however, about the less important topical references, those which, however newsworthy, are treated in the novel only in passing. Thus when Boythorn declaims against the low salaries paid to surgeons (Chapter XIII) he is re-airing an issue prominently featured in newspapers of the 1840's but only peripherally treated in the novel. Similar are the allusions to the special kind of religious zeal represented by Mrs. Pardiggle's High Church attitudes. Although historical scholars have demonstrated convincingly that Mrs. Pardiggle's attitudes relate to one of the most touchy questions of the period—the role Catholicism might play in England (a topic that was being bitterly argued following the Pope's establishment of an English Roman Catholic hierarchy in 1850)[1]—yet these Catholic and Anglo-Catholic controversies are, topically, of minor significance in *Bleak House*. Dickens' novel is fascinatingly full of interesting passing allusions of this kind. Even some of the descriptions of weather might have impressed his early readers as having contemporary reference: the sodden landscapes at Chesney Wold are curiously anticipatory of the severe flooding of the English midlands caused by the record-breaking rainfall of 1852.

For such events or topics that play a minor role in *Bleak House* we have not had space to offer separate units of background documents, but under the heading "A Dictionary of *Bleak House* Originals," in the preceding section, we have included several illustrations of a related kind of small-scale allusions to the Victorian scene. These occur when Dickens has modeled a character on some living contemporary, as, for example, when the woman philanthropist, Mrs. Chisholm, served him as the prototype for Mrs. Jellyby and her Borrioboola-Gha mission, or when some event, such as the cholera epidemic at Tooting, inspired his commentary, in the novel, on the mistreatment of orphans.

1. John Butt and Kathleen Tillotson, *Dickens at Work* (1957), p. 180.

Pollution

"In all my writings, I hope I have taken every available opportunity of showing the want of sanitary improvements in the neglected dwellings of the poor"—so wrote Dickens in a preface to *Martin Chuzzlewit* in November, 1849. Like all of his contemporaries, Dickens had good cause to regard pollution and sanitation as problems of the highest importance. A year earlier England had been afflicted with a cholera plague. In fifteen months 30,000 persons were stricken in London alone, of whom 14,600 had died.[1] And in 1853 it was reported in Parliament that mortality from smallpox was greater than in any country in Europe.[2] Such ravages, it became recognized, were occasioned by pollution of air and water and food. Some forms of pollution had of course always been a feature of communal life, but others were novel or were newly accentuated by the crowded conditions of modern urban life and by developments in commerce and industry. By some it was assumed that disease was spread by pollution of the air, as Dickens represents it at times in *Bleak House* ("the winds are his messengers" he writes of Tom-All-Alone's and its fevers). By others it was attributed to pollution of supplies of drinking water and food, as contended in a medical report of 1849 cited below. About such issues Dickens himself was exceptionally well informed. Early in 1849 his interest had been sharpened by an incident at a scandalously overcrowded orphanage at Tooting in which an outbreak of cholera carried off 180 children—a disaster about which he wrote four articles and to which he alludes in Chapter X of *Bleak House*. On the larger-scale aspects of pollution, it is known that he had studied reports, formal and informal, and that his speech on sanitation in 1851 was based on this considerable knowledge.

In this speech he mentions that his knowledge of sanitary problems had been reinforced by using his own eyes and nose. The smells to which he alludes were a remarkable mélange. As foreign visitors remarked, the vast number of horses and cattle passing through its streets made London smell like a stable, an aroma not noxious but distinctive. More offensive was the presence of coal smoke, a form of pollution that occasioned the remarkable brown fog—the "London particular" as Guppy calls it. Most offensive was the odor from overcrowded city cemeteries such as the one attached to the church of St. Martins-in-the-Fields, which served as Dickens' model in picturing Nemo's last resting place. And if pollution of air seemed an ever-pressing problem, the pollution of water, attributable to a long-outmoded system of sewage disposal, was even more pressing and dangerous.

Despite the seeming insurmountability of the problems, Dickens and many of his contemporaries were eager to confront the challenge, and, through exposure of abuses, to work towards correction through legislation.

1. *Annual Register*, 1849, Chron., pp. 422–30.

2. *Annual Register*, 1853, History, p. 208.

The variety of writings employed to this end range from reports of official committees to those of individual investigators such as Mayhew and Gavin and the journalists who contributed sober editorials or jocular news stories to *Punch* and *Household Words*.[3] One thing that is striking about these reports is their gruesome frankness. The reputed squeamishness of the Victorians has always been stressed by later generations, but if we are to judge from what they wrote on pollution, it is evident that they could be remarkably unsqueamish—stronger-stomached, in fact, than their successors.

THOMAS MILLER

A London Fog†

Such of our country readers as have never been in town about this season of the year, can scarcely imagine what it is to grope their way through a downright thorough London Fog. It is something like being imbedded in a dilution of yellow peas-pudding, just thick enough to get through it without being wholly choked or completely suffocated. You can just see through the yard of it which, at the next stride, you are doomed to swallow, and that is all. It is a kind of meat and drink, and very sorry sustenance for those who are asthmatical, as you may tell by hearing one old cough answering to another from opposite sides of the street, and which, although you cannot see the passengers, you can tell, from their grumbling, that they do not like the fare at all. You have the same soft-soapy atmosphere served up at breakfast, dinner, tea, and supper; every time you open your mouth you partake of it, and all day long you are compelled to burn lights, and, in addition to the fog, inhale the fumes from gas, candle, or lamp, which have no more chance of escape than you have, so burn on dim, yellow, and sulkily, as if the very lights needed all the warmth they could obtain, and thus confine themselves to illuminating the smallest possible space. The whole city seems covered with a crust, and all the light you can see beneath it appears as if struggling through the huge yellow basin it overspreads. You fancy that all the smoke which had ascended for years from the thousands of London chimneys, had fallen down all at once, after having rotted somewhere above the clouds; smelling as if it had been kept too long, and making you wheeze and sneeze, as if all the colds in the world were rushing into your head for warmth, and did not care a straw about killing a few thousands of people, so long as they could but lodge comfortably for a few hours anywhere. You blow like a grampus in a quicksand, with the keel of

3. For additional articles on pollution, see, in *Household Words,* "Health by Act of Parliament" (August 10, 1850) and "King Dirt" (March 27, 1852).

† From *Illustrated London News, Christmas Supplement* (1849), p. 419.

a seventy-four on his back, and get about as much fresh air as if you were in his situation: a pair of bellows with a hole in the side, through which you might cram your double fist, would make perfect music, when blown, compared to the noise of your own breathing. You seem as if you had swallowed six broken-winded horses; that they were inside of you alive and kicking; and, for the soul of you, you cannot get rid of one. * * *

Although a real Londoner looks upon a dense December fog as a common occurrence, and lights up his premises with as little ceremony as he would do at the close of the day, yet, to one unused to such a scene, there is something startling in the appearance of a vast city wrapt in a kind of darkness which seems neither to belong to the day nor the night, at the mid-noon hour, while the gas is burning in the windows of long miles of streets. The greatest marvel, after all, is that so few accidents happen in this dim, unnatural light, in the midst of which business seems to go on as usual, and would do, we believe, were the whole of London buried in midnight darkness at noonday, which would only be looked upon as a further deepening of the overhanging gloom. The number of lighted torches which are carried and waved at the corners and crossings of the streets add greatly to the wild and picturesque effect of the scene, as they flash redly upon the countenances of the passengers, and, in the distance, have the effect of a city enveloped in a dense mass of smoke, through which the smouldering flames endeavour in vain to penetrate.

During a heavy fog many accidents occur on the river, through barges running foul of each other, or vessels coming athwart the bridges—for there is no seeing the opening arch from the rock-like buttress, as the whole river looks like one huge bed of dense stagnant smoke, through which no human eye can penetrate. If you lean over the balustrades of the bridge, you cannot see the vessel which may at that moment be passing beneath, so heavy is the cloudy curtain which covers the water. At such times the steamboats cease running, and rest quietly at their moorings, for the man at the wheel would be unable to see half the length of his vessel. Sometimes a steamer, coming up the river, takes a fancy to a shorter cut, by trying to clear Blackwall Reach, and come overland through the Marshes below Greenwich, or by running her head into the Isle of Dogs, where she lies aground until the next tide.

HENRY MAYHEW

Of the Horse-Dung of the Streets of London†

"Familiarity with streets of crowded traffic deadens the senses to the perception of their actual condition. Strangers coming from the country frequently describe the streets of London as smelling of dung like a stable-yard."

Such is one of the statements in a Report submitted to Parliament, and there is no reason to doubt the fact. Every English visitor to a French city, for instance, must have detected street-odours of which the inhabitants were utterly unconscious. In a work which between 20 and 30 years ago was deservedly popular, Mathews's "Diary of an Invalid," it is mentioned that an English lady complaining of the villainous rankness of the air in the first French town she entered—Calais, if I remember rightly—received the comfortable assurance, "It is the smell of the Continent, ma'am." Even in Cologne, itself, the "most stinking city of Europe," as it has been termed, the citizens are insensible to the foul airs of their streets, and yet possess great skill in manufacturing perfumed and distilled waters for the toilet, pluming themselves on the delicacy and discrimination of their nasal organs. What we perceive in other cities, as strangers, those who visit London detect in our streets—that they smell of dung like stable-yards. It is idle for London denizens, because they are unconscious of the fact, to deny the existence of any such effluvia. I have met with nightmen who have told me that there was "nothing particular" in the smell of the cesspools they were emptying; they "hardly perceived it." One man said, "Why, it's like the sort of stuff I've smelt in them ladies' smelling-bottles." An eminent tallow-melter said, in the course of his evidence before Parliament during a sanitary inquiry, that the smell from the tallow-melting on his premises was not only healthful and reviving—for invalids came to inhale it—but agreeable. I mention these facts to meet the scepticism which the official assertion as to the stable-like odour of the streets may, perhaps, provoke. When, however, I state the *quantity* of horse-dung and "cattle-droppings" voided in the streets, all incredulity, I doubt not, will be removed.

"It has been ascertained," says the Report of the National Philanthropic Association, "that four-fifths of the street-dirt consist of horse and cattle-droppings."

Let us, therefore, endeavour to arrive at definite notions as to the absolute quantity of this element of street-dirt. * * *

A series of experiments in this department of equine physiology * * * were carefully conducted under the superintendence of Professor Varnell. The food, drink, and voidances of several horses, kept in stable all day long, were separately weighed and measured; and

† From *London Labour and the London Poor*, II (1851), 193–96.

the following were the results with an animal of medium size and sound health:—

" 'Royal Veterinary College,
Sept. 29, 1849

" 'Brown horse of middle size ate in 24 hours, of hay, 16 lbs.; oats, 10 lbs.; chaff, 4 lbs.; in all .... 30 lbs.
Drank of water, in 24 hours, 6 gallons, or .... 48 lbs.
Total .... 78 lbs.
Voided in the form of fæces .... 49 lbs.
Allowance for nutrition, supply of waste in system, perspiration, and urine .... 29 lbs.

(Signed)
" 'George Varnell,
" 'Demonstrator of Anatomy.' "

Here we find the excretions to be 11 lbs. more than those of the French horse experimented upon by M. Boussingault; but then the solid food given to the English horse was 4 lbs. more, and the liquid upwards of 7 lbs. extra.

We may then, perhaps, assume, without fear of erring, that the excrements voided by horses in the course of 24 hours, weigh, at the least, 45 lbs.

Hence the gross quantity of dung produced by the 7,300,000 horses which traverse the London streets in the course of the twelvemonth will be 7,300,000 × 45, or 328,500,000 lbs., which is upwards of 146,651 tons. But these horses cannot be said to be at work above six hours each day; we must, therefore, divide the above quantity by four, and thus we find that there are 36,662 tons of horse-dung annually dropped in the streets of London.

I am informed, on good authority, that the evacuations of an ox, in 24 hours, will, on the average, exceed those of a horse in weight by about a fifteenth, while, if the ox be disturbed by being driven, the excretions will exceed the horse's by about a twelfth. As the oxen are not driven in the streets, or detained in the market for so long a period as horses are out at work, it may be fair to compute that their droppings are about the same, individually, as those of the horses.

Hence as there are 224,000 horned cattle yearly brought to London, we have 224,000 × 45 lbs. = 10,080,000 lbs., or 4500 tons, for the gross quantity of ordure dropped by this number of animals in the course of 24 hours, so that, dividing by 4, as before, we find that there are 1125 tons of ordure annually dropped by the "horned cattle" in the streets of London.

Concerning the sheep, I am told that it may be computed that the ordure of five sheep is about equal in weight to that of two oxen. As regards the other animals it may be said that their "droppings" are insignificant, the pigs and calves being very generally carted to and from the market, as, indeed, are some of the fatter and more valuable sheep and lambs. All these facts being taken into consideration, I am told by a regular frequenter of Smithfield market, that it will be best to calculate the droppings of each of the 1,617,300 sheep, calves, and pigs yearly coming to the metropolis at about one-fourth of those of the horned cattle; so that multiplying 1,617,300 by 10, instead of 45, we have 16,173,000 lbs., or 7220 tons, for the weight of ordure deposited by the entire number of sheep, calves, and pigs annually brought to the metropolis, and then dividing this by 4, as usual, we find that the droppings of the calves, sheep, and pigs in the streets of London amount to 1805 tons per annum.

Now putting together all the preceding items we obtain the following results:—

Gross Weight of the Horse-Dung and Cattle-Droppings annually deposited in the Streets of London:—

	Tons.
Horse-dung	36,662
Droppings of horned cattle	1,125
Droppings of sheep, calves, and pigs	1,805
	39,592

Hence we perceive that the gross weight of animal excretions dropped in the public thoroughfares of the metropolis is about 40,000 tons per annum, or, in round numbers, 770 tons every week-day—say 100 tons a day. * * *

The next question becomes—what is done with this vast amount of filth?

The Board of Health is a much better guide upon this point than upon the matter of quantity: "Much of the horse-dung dropped in the London streets, under ordinary circumstances," we are told, "dries and is pulverized, and with the common soil is carried into houses as dust, and dirties clothes and furniture. The odour arising from the surface evaporation of the streets when they are wet is chiefly from horse-dung. Susceptible persons often feel this evaporation, after partial wetting, to be highly oppressive. The surface-water discharged into sewers from the streets and roofs of houses is found to contain as much filth as the soil-water from the house-drains."

Here, then, we perceive that the whole of the animal manure let fall in the streets is worse than wasted, and yet we are assured that it is an article, which, if properly collected, is of considerable value.

The Spa-Fields Burial Ground†

The repeated complaints and representations of the Committee of the inhabitants of Clerkenwell have at length attracted the attention of the Home Secretary to the existing nuisance and malprac-

† From *The Times*, March 5, 1845, p. 7.

tices that have so long prevailed in the neighborhood of Exmouth-street, Spa-fields. A communication was made by Sir J. Graham to the Police Commissioners on Saturday, and Captain Hay, the Assistant Commissioner, on that day inspected the Spa-fields burial ground, accompanied by Mr. Watt, the chairman, Mr. Clarke, the secretary, and several other respectable householders. The stench arising from decomposed human bodies was declared by Captain Hay to be insufferable, and the Committee were directed to forward such information as they could collect (reduced into writing) for the guidance of Sir J. Graham. * * * It appears that the manner in which this extraordinary and revolting work of demolition was first discovered is this:—Reuben Room, a gravedigger at the burial ground, had a child interred some time since, and upon his discharge, he insisted on removing the body, asserting that he well knew after he left that the coffin would be burnt, the body and limbs severed, and deposited elsewhere. Police constable Henry Webb, O 106, and Martin 144, were called in to prevent Room opening the grave, upon which he took the two officers to an out-house, where they saw the lids of several coffins being consumed over a fierce fire, and pieces of "human flesh" (to use the officers' own words) "were attached to the coffins the size of their hands." The following is a copy of the written depositions that have been transmitted to Sir James Graham:

"Reuben Room examined—I was in the employ of Mr. F. Green, as grave-digger in 1837, and continued in his employ for about six years. Our mode of working the ground was not commencing at one end and working to the other, but digging wherever it was ordered, totally regardless whether the ground was full or not; for instance, to dig a grave seven feet deep at a particular spot, I have often disturbed and mutilated seven or eight bodies; that is, I have severed heads, arms, legs, or whatever came in my way with a crowbar, pick-axe, chopper, and saw. Of the bodies, some were quite fresh and some decomposed. I have had as much as 1-1/2 cwt. of human flesh on what we term the "beef-board" at the foot of the grave at one time. I have often put a rope round the neck of the corpse to drag it out of the coffin, fastening one end of the rope to a tombstone so as to keep the corpse upright to get at the coffin from underneath, to make room for the flesh of other bodies. The coffins were taken away and burnt with pieces of decomposed flesh adhering thereto. I have taken up half a ton of wood out of one grave, because I had to take out two tiers of coffins, some of which were quite fresh, and we used to cut them up for struts, used for shoring up the graves. We had as many as 50 or 60 sides of coffins always in use to keep the ground from falling in when digging. We have buried as many as 45 bodies in one day, besides still-borns. I and Tom Smith kept an account one year; we buried 2,017 bodies besides still-borns, which are generally enclosed in deal coffins. We have taken them up when they have been in the ground only two days, and used them to light fires with. I have been up to my knees in human flesh by jumping on the bodies so as to cram them into the least possible space at the bottom of the graves in which fresh bodies were afterwards placed. We covered over the flesh at the bottom by a small layer of mould. I have ruptured myself in dragging a heavy corpse out of the coffin. It was a very heavy one. It slipped from my hold lifting it by the shoulders. The corpse was quite fresh. These occurrences took place every day.

"Robert Watt examined—I live at No. 14 Exmouth-street, Spa-fields. I have been an inhabitant for ten years during which time I have been disgusted with the mode of conducting the ground. * * * I have seen the spot opened and re-opened during the last ten years, and bodies continually placed therein. I have remarked this to the officiating minister, when he replied that it was not injurious to the inhabitants, and no business of his. I have frequently heard and seen the grave-diggers employed in destroying the coffins. * * * *

"John Lynn—I live at No. 4 Exmouth-street; am landlord of the whole of the northern row, which contains 11 houses, all of which abut on the east side of the Spa-fields burial-ground. I have been landlord of the above for seven years; during the whole of which period I have heard complaints made by the various tenants of most shocking sights in the above ground, and have often been applied to come and behold them with my own eyes—the breaking up of coffins and disturbing the contents. On one occasion, when repairing the roofs of the houses, I saw what appeared a mash, which seemed to me to be the bowels of a corpse, which the grave-digger attempted to gather up in a shovel, and place in a barrow; and, after several attempts failing, he was obliged to put it in the earth. The smell from the graveyard, arising from the continual disturbing of the earth and keeping graves continually open (averaging 30 per week) is so intolerable that the majority of tenants are continually shifting. The smell, even in cold weather, especially at night, is quite unbearable. I have been an eye-witness to the removal of parts of coffins in all states of preservation, at all times in the fore part of the day.

"Ann Mitchell—I live at 8-1/2, Garden-walk, Spa-fields. I entered on the 3d of February 1844. I have been subject to illness ever since and so have my husband and children. Within ten days after taking the above cottage my two children fell ill; they were covered with watery blisters all over the body—symptoms constantly in the vicinity. My house is at the back of the bone-house. I have heard noises nightly, knocking from 2 till 5 in the morning. My room sweats, the paper is spoiled, and I have a nasty, coppery taste in my mouth.

"Harriet Woods—I live at No. 13, Northampton-row. Went to my house in 1842. Saw Thomas Smith with a little blue coffin quite new. He broke it to pieces with a pickaxe, mangled the contents and mixed it with the earth. Saw him look around to see if any one was watching. Have seen him continually wheel away wood and return ashes from the bone-house. Once saw him hold up what appeared to be the head of a woman by the hair. Mrs. Gill, a lodger, also witnessed it. On another occasion I called to him, and he used threatening language; he said he should have my old bones before long. Have seen this sort of thing constantly. I have lost five children out of eight; two on one day by a malignant fever. Have seen Tom Smith jump on the coffins.

"William Penny, Inspector of the O division, stated as follows:—In December, 1843, a petition was presented to the magistrates at Clerkenwell Police court, signed by about 150 inhabitants. The magistrate gave me the petition, and desired me to see to it. I did so; and went immediately to a one-story erection in the burial ground, called a 'bone-house,' where I found a large fire on the floor and in the grate. The fire consisted of coffin-boards of full grown people and children broken up; some were quite sound with pieces of black cloth and handles and plates, and pieces of shrouds were flying about. The smell was indescribable. I have visited the ground many times since and I have found it in the same state. Have repeated experience in my nightly rounds of the horrible stench from the burial ground.

"John Newman, an inhabitant near the spot, confirms the principal points of the foregoing statements and adds, that the burials averaged from 15 to 30 on a Sunday, and from 6 to 12 on Mondays."

The greatest excitement continues to prevail throughout the parish, and it is understood that a Parliamentary inquiry will be forthwith instituted into these serious charges against the managers of the ground.

W. H. WILLS AND GEORGE HOGARTH

Heathen and Christian Burial†

If, from the heights of our boasted civilisation, we take * * * a survey of other nations—savage nations included,—we shall, with humiliation, be forced to acknowledge that in no age and in no country have the dead been disposed of so prejudicially to the living

† From *Household Words: Conducted by Charles Dickens*, April 6, 1850, pp. 43–48.

as in Great Britain. Consigning mortal remains to closely-packed burial-grounds in crowded cities; covering—scarcely interring them * * * while the exhalations of putrefaction always vitiate the air, is a custom which prejudice has preserved the longest to this land. A calculation * * * quoted by the Board of Health in their admirable report on Burials, estimates the amount of noxious gases evolved annually from the metropolitan grave-yards alone at 55,261 cubic feet per acre. * * *

The Mahommedans again show much better taste than Christians in their Mausoleums and burial-places—they never bury in their temples or within the walls of a town. * * *

Among the Caffres, Hottentots, and other savage tribes of Southern Africa * * * it seems to have been customary to expose aged and helpless people in desert places, and leave them to die, because of a superstition against any one expiring in a hut. Intercourse with civilization is mitigating this and other barbarities.

It appears extraordinary, that amidst the advance which has been made in social and sanitary science, Great Britain should be the last to give up the unwholesome custom of continuing the dead as near neighbors to the quick. * * *

At last, however, we have good reason to hope that intramural burials, with all their attendant evils, will speedily be themselves buried with the barbarous relics of the past.

R. H. HORNE

[A Visit with the River-God, Father Thames]†

"Do not think me ungrateful," said I, "nor by any means insensible of the honour you do me; but the truth is, that, although I drink more tea than most men, probably than any other gentleman in London, I am rather scrupulous as to the water I make it with."

"Indeed!" exclaimed the River-god; "then come with me, and I will show you the magnificent broad stream from which my urn is constantly filled."

A great torch flashed before my eyes!—then another!—then three or four!—then a dozen were dancing round me, and waving me onward, and along with them—now this way, now that, now up, now descending slippery steps—till I found myself seated in a huge dark barge, with Father Thames, and floating slowly down the stream by torchlight.

† "Father Thames," from *Household Words: Conducted by Charles Dickens*, Feb. 1, 1851, p. 446.

"How black and solid stands the forest of shipping on each side!—how large and black lie their shadows on the water!—how the lights glance from the windows on the shore!—how fast the current runs! Commerce—commerce!—but, what is that floating by?—pah! it's a dead dog, or something—'a sort of not-of-the-newest poor-john!' How very thick the water is hereabouts, Father Thames; and, pray, may I inquire what that black, sluggish stream may be which I see pouring into you from a wide, bricked archway, yonder?"

"Oh, that's one of my sewers," replied the Father of Rivers, without turning his head, "my Blackfriars sewer outlet; and a fine, generous, open fellow, he is."

"So he seems," said I; "have you any more of them?"

"Oh, yes: one generally near every bridge, with here and there another, and another, just as the quantity of sewerage in a neighbourhood has determined. They all come to me. I have, in fact, a hundred and forty-one sewers between Battersea and London Bridge. All come to me, sir." * * *

I was silent for some time, as well I might be, after such a dose of "information for the people;" and during this pause in the conversation, I had unconsciously dangled one arm over the side of the barge, till presently my hand, by a swell of the current, was immersed above the wrist. I drew it up, and found it covered—coated, I may say—with a thick, dingy, slimy liquid of an offensive odour. Gazing on the water around, as we proceeded, I saw that we were surrounded by whole acres of it. I looked at the imperturbable countenance of Father Thames.

"What in the world is all this?" said I.

"The mess we are passing through?" responded the giant coolly;—"oh, it's only a little scum derived from barges, and lime-works, and colliers, and the shipping around us, and bone-grinders, and tar-works, and dredging-machines, and steamers, and back-gardens, and floating remains of creatures from knackers' yards, and rotting vegetables, and what not."

"And what *not*, indeed, Father Thames!" cried I, starting up, quite unable to endure it any longer; "is *this* the water you make your tea with?"

"And do all my cooking with," continued Old Thames, taking no sort of notice of my dismay and excitement; "and all my washing. I have done so, you must know very well, for years and years—my water being in just the same state as you now see it. * * * So now—about barge—we'll return home to Somerset House to tea!"

"Father Thames," said I, firmly, though with every respect; "Father Thames, if I drink a single cup of your tea, then—to quote the words of the immortal Falstaff, who knew a trick worth two of it—'fillip me with a three-man beetle.' "

THOMAS CARLYLE

[Typhus-Fever in Edinburgh]†

One of Dr. Alison's Scotch facts struck us much. A poor Irish Widow, her husband having died in one of the Lanes of Edinburgh, went forth with her three children, bare of all resource, to solicit help from the Charitable Establishments of that City. At this Charitable Establishment and then at that she was refused; referred from one to the other, helped by none;—till she had exhausted them all; till her strength and heart failed her: she sank down in typhus-fever; died, and infected her Lane with fever, so that 'seventeen other persons' died of fever there in consequence. The humane Physician asks thereupon, as with a heart too full for speaking, Would it not have been *economy* to help this poor Widow? She took typhus-fever, and killed seventeen of you!—Very curious. The forlorn Irish Widow applies to her fellow-creatures, as if saying, "Behold I am sinking, bare of help: ye must help me! I am your sister, bone of your bone; one God made us; ye must help me!" They answer, "No; impossible: thou art no sister of ours." But she proves her sisterhood; her typhus-fever kills *them*: they actually were her brothers, though denying it! Had man ever to go lower for a proof?

For, as indeed was very natural in such case, all government of the Poor by the Rich has long ago been given over to Supply-and-demand Laissez-faire and such like, and universally declared to be 'impossible.' "You are no sister of ours; what shadow of proof is there? Here are our parchments, our padlocks, proving indisputably our money-safes to be *ours*, and you to have no business with them. Depart! It is impossible!"—Nay, what wouldst thou thyself have us do? cry indignant readers. Nothing, my friends—till you have got a soul for yourselves again. Till then all things are 'impossible.' Till then I cannot even bid you buy, as the old Spartans would have done, two-pence worth of powder and lead, and compendiously shoot to death this poor Irish Widow: even that is 'impossible' for you. Nothing is left but that she prove her sisterhood by dying, and infecting you with typhus. Seventeen of you lying dead will not deny such proof that she *was* flesh of your flesh; and perhaps some of the living may lay it to heart.

'Impossible: of a certain two-legged animal with feathers, it is said if you draw a distinct chalk-circle round him, he sits imprisoned, as if girt with the iron ring of Fate; and will die there, though within sight of victuals,—or sit in sick misery there, and be fatted

† From *Past and Present*, III (1843), ch. 2.

to death. The name of this poor two-legged animal is—Goose; and they make of him, when well fattened, *Pâté de foie gras*, much prized by some!

HECTOR GAVIN, M.D.

[Sanitation in a London Suburb]†

In this *most dirty street* * * * a person named Baker, lately dead, here found a receptacle for every kind of manure * * * in every stage of offensive and disgusting decomposition; the manure is piled to a considerable height, and is left to dry in the sun; but beside this table mountain of manure, extensive and deep lakes of putrefying *night soil* are dammed up with the more solid dung, and refuse, forming together, mountain and lake, a scene of the most disgusting character. * * * If foul privies, and overflowing cesspools are justly considered sources of disease and death,—if they are correctly termed insidious and fatal poisons * * * how shall we regard those who supinely and apathetically submit their fellow beings to its lethal operation. * * * The decomposing organic particles which are ever being set free from the putrescent mass, are wafted by each wind that blows, over a population to whom they bring disease and death, as surely as, though more insidiously than, the deadly simoon. * * *

At the end of the street, and abutting on a brick-field, the road is in a muddy state, and resembles a stagnant pool covered with green slime.

[Report on a Meeting of the Westminster Medical Society to Discuss How Cholera Is Spread]‡

The interest regarding the discussion on cholera continues unabated. The rooms of the Society, this evening, were crowded to excess. * * * The discussion on Dr. Webster's paper was postponed, by consent, until Dr. Snow had read his paper 'On the Pathology and Mode of Communication of Cholera.' He said that he had been led, contrary to the usual opinion, to consider cholera as being * * * a local affection of the mucous membrane of the alimentary canal, and not an affection of the whole system, depending on a poison in the blood. * * * The recent discovery of peculiar microscopic cells, believed to be of a vegetable character, in great abun-

† From *Sanitary Ramblings* (1848), pp. 9, 29.

‡ From *The Lancet: A Journal of* * * * *Medical and Chemical Science*, Oct. 13, 1849, pp. 431-33.

dance, in the cholera discharges, tended to confirm this view of the nature of cholera. An attentive examination of the history of cholera, as an epidemic, showed that it was communicable by human intercourse; and although there were many facts opposed to the theory of cholera being contagious, in the same way that the eruptive fevers were believed to be, yet, in the sequel, these facts would afford the strongest evidence of the communication of the disease. If the alimentary canal were the seat of cholera, and the disease were communicable, it was clear that it must be conveyed by something which passed from the mucous membrane of the stomach and intestines of one patient to that of another, which it could only do by being swallowed. * * * * One important medium of the conveyance of the cholera poison from one patient to another was the drinking-water, when it became contaminated by the evacuations, either by their permeating the ground and getting into wells, or by their being conveyed by sewers into a river. Since he (Dr. Snow) first published his views on this point, Dr. William Budd had found the microscopic bodies before alluded to in such drinking-water of cholera districts as received the contents of sewers. Dr. Snow then related a number of instances where, as in Albion-terrace, Wandsworth-road, there was a very high mortality from cholera in connexion with the contamination of the water with discharges from the patients. He attributed the high mortality on the south side of the Thames to three causes—viz., the drinking from certain tidal ditches, which prevails to so great extent in Rotherhithe and Bermondsey; the water supplied by the water-works in this part of London, which is generally procured from the Thames in the midst of sewers; and to the contamination of a number of the wells by the contents of the cesspools, which are often as deep as the wells. The low elevation of the ground had no connexion with cholera, except when combined with infected water. Westminster had the same elevation as the Borough, and yet the mortality from cholera was not half so great. Bethlem Hospital and the Queen's Prison had all but escaped cholera, situated in a low level, but having pure water of their own. * * *

Dr. Brittan had found microscopic bodies in the atmosphere, which he considered to be the same as those existing in the alimentary canal. He (Dr. Snow) understood that others had not succeeded in finding them in the air, and he was of opinion, that if they should be generally found in the atmosphere, even of infected districts, they could not be the real cause of cholera, for all the evidence he had collected was opposed to the idea that the cause of cholera existed in the air.

Mr. Walshe explained why, in districts where the water in open tidal ditches was too offensive to use in any way, cholera was less prevalent than where that fluid was somewhat more pure; for in one the people refrained from drinking it, while in the other, as about "Jacob's Island," in Rotherhithe, it was no uncommon thing to see the people making use of the necessaries over the stream from which they fetched their supply of water. He spoke of the value of house-to-house visitation as likely to form a supply of valuable materials respecting the cause of the disease and its mode of propagation.

CHARLES DICKENS

[Speech to the Metropolitan Sanitary Association]†

May 10, 1851

That no one can estimate the amount of mischief which is grown in dirt; that no one can say, here it stops, or there it stops, either in its physical or its moral results, when both begin in the cradle and are not at rest in the obscene grave [*hear, hear*], is now as certain as it is that the air from Gin Lane will be carried, when the wind is Easterly, into May Fair, and that if you once have a vigorous pestilence raging furiously in Saint Giles's, no mortal list of Lady Patronesses can keep it out of Almack's. [*Hear, hear.*]

Twelve or fifteen years ago, some of the first valuable reports of Mr. Chadwick and of Dr. Southwood Smith[1] strengthening and much enlarging my previous imperfect knowledge of this truth, made me, in my sphere, earnest in the Sanitary Cause. And I can honestly declare tonight, that all the use I have since made of my eyes—or nose [*laughter*]—that all the information I have since been able to acquire through any of my senses, has strengthened me in the conviction that Searching Sanitary Reform must precede all other social remedies [*cheers*] and that even Education and Religion can do nothing where they are most needed, until the way is paved for their ministrations by Cleanliness and Decency. [*Hear.*] * * * What avails it to send a Missionary to me, a miserable man or woman living in a foetid Court where every sense bestowed upon me for my delight becomes a torment, and every minute of my life is new mire added to the heap under which I lie degraded? To what natural feeling within me is he to address himself? * * * But, give me my first glimpse of Heaven through a little of its light and air —give me water—help me to be clean—lighten this heavy atmos-

† From *The Speeches of Charles Dickens*, ed. K. J. Fielding (1960), 128–30.

1. Edwin Chadwick (1800–90) and Southwood Smith (1788–1861) were pioneer reformers advocating improvements in sanitation and slum conditions in the 1830's and 1840's.

phere in which my spirit droops and I become the indifferent and callous creature that you see me—gently and kindly take the body of my dead relation out of the small room where I grow to be so familiar with the awful change that even *its* sanctity is lost to me—and, Teacher, then I'll hear, you know how willingly, of Him whose thoughts were so much with the Poor, and who had compassion for all human sorrow! [*Applause.*]

I am now, gentlemen, to propose to you as a toast a public Body without whose efficient aid this preparation so much to be desired, for Christianity at home, cannot be effected; and, by whom, if we earnestly desire such preparation, we must stand, giving them all the support it is in our power to render. I mean, the Board of Health.[2]

2. The Board of Health, established in 1848, had recommended various reforms for the supply of pure water, but according to Dickens (later in his speech) the Board had been unable to implement their proposals because of opposition from "a few noisy little landlords interested in the maintenance of abuses" and because of indifference on the part of the Government.

Government

Most of Dickens' contemporaries were convinced, and with considerable cause, that parliamentary democratic institutions were working effectively to further human progress. Dickens himself, as editor of *Household Words*, if not as a novelist, could sometimes share this sense of satisfaction. When a French political writer predicted that England was doomed to decline, a reply appeared in *Household Words* (July 6, 1850) by Dickens' sub-editor. The reply makes mincemeat of the prediction by citing statistics proving the extraordinary success of the English economy in solving the challenging problems that had confronted the country throughout the so-called Hungry Forties. A year later Dickens himself contributed an article contrasting English achievements, as represented by the Great Exhibition, with the stagnant and backward culture of China (July 5, 1851). The mid-Victorian mood of self-confidence has been summed up in the comment of a twentieth-century historian, G. M. Young: "Of all the decades in our history, a wise man would choose the eighteen-fifties to be young in."

This self-congratulatory mood was nevertheless not shared in all quarters. Most outspoken in the vein that it was the worst of times rather than the best of times was Thomas Carlyle, whose apocalyptic *Latter-Day Pamphlets* are represented below. Dickens profoundly admired Carlyle's writings and shared many of his views of society, especially the elder writer's impatience with the ineptitudes of Parliamentary government. Some events in the 1850's, alluded to in *Bleak House*, reinforced Dickens' sense of impatience and dissatisfaction. One was the scandal about bribery in elections which led to a bill being introduced in Parliament in April, 1852, to correct such abuses as those referred to in Chapter XL of *Bleak House*, of which there had recently been an especially flagrant example at St. Albans, one of the settings for Dickens' novel. The Parliament of 1852 was known, in fact, as the Bribery Parliament. Even more important to Dickens were the ominous signs of instability in the whole party system. Votes of no confidence throughout 1852 led to short-lived governments and a shuffling of cabinets culminating, in December, with the formation of a coalition government having Lord Aberdeen as Prime Minister. Although the real flaws in the political scene did not become fully exposed until the country had drifted into war with Russia in 1853, Dickens did not wait for such specific evidence. His Coodle-Doodle figures are represented in the same spirit of ridicule as Carlyle's Parliamentary leaders, the Honourable Felix Parvulus and the Right Honourable Felicissimus Zero.

Similarities between the anatomy of social and political life in *Bleak House* and *Latter-Day Pamphlets* are also marked in Carlyle's picture of England as a kind of polluted dung-heap, an Augean stable desperately in need of cleansing—a figure offering a nice example of how two topics treated in *Bleak House*, pollution and government, overlap each other.

THOMAS CARLYLE

Downing Street†

From all corners of the wide British Dominion there rises one complaint against the ineffectuality of what are nicknamed our 'red-tape' establishments, our Government Offices, Colonial Office, Foreign Office and the others, in Downing Street and the neighbourhood. * * * Every one may remark what a hope animates the eyes of any circle, when it is reported * * * that Sir Robert Peel[1] has in his mind privately resolved to go, one day, into that stable of King Augias, which appals human hearts, so rich is it, high-piled with the droppings of two hundred years; and Hercules-like to load a thousand night-wagons from it, and turn running water into it, and swash and shovel at it, and never leave till the antique pavement, and real basis of the matter, show itself clean again! In any intelligent circle such a rumour, like the first break of day to men in darkness, enlightens all eyes. * * *

The State itself, not in Downing Street alone but in every department of it, has altered much from what it was in past times; and it will again have to alter very much, to alter I think from top to bottom, if it means to continue existing in the times that are now coming and come!

The State, left to shape itself by dim pedantries and traditions, without distinctness of conviction, or purpose beyond that of helping itself over the difficulty of the hour, has become, instead of a luminous vitality permeating with its light all provinces of our affairs, a most monstrous agglomerate of inanities, as little adapted for the actual wants of a modern community as the worst citizen need wish. The thing it is doing is by no means the thing we want to have done. What we want! Let the dullest British man endeavour to raise in his mind this question, and ask himself in sincerity what the British Nation wants at this time. Is it to have, with endless jargoning, debating, motioning and counter-motioning, a settlement effected between the Honourable Mr. This and the Honourable Mr. That, as to their respective pretensions to ride the high horse? Really it is unimportant which of them ride it. Going upon past experience long continued now, I should say with brevity, 'Either of them—Neither of them.' If our Government is to be a No-Government, what is the matter who administers it? Fling an orange-skin into St. James's Street; let the man it hits be your man. He, if you breed him a little to it, and tie the due official bladders to his ankles, will do as well as another this sublime problem of bal-

† From *Latter-Day Pamphlets*, Nos. 3–4 (1850).

1. Peel (1788–1850), who had been Prime Minister in the mid-1840's, was admired by Carlyle as a strong leader, a statesman of a different stamp from the inept politicians pictured elsewhere throughout Carlyle's pamphlet.

ancing himself upon the vortexes, with the long loaded-pole in his hands; and will, with straddling painful gestures, float hither and thither, walking the waters in that singular manner for a little while, as well as his foregoers did, till he also capsize, and be left floating feet uppermost; after which you choose another.

What an immense pother, by parliamenting and palavering in all corners of your empire, to decide such a question as that! * * *

A mighty question indeed! Who shall be Premier, and take in hand the 'rudder of government,' otherwise called the 'spigot of taxation;' shall it be the Honourable Felix Parvulus, or the Right Honourable Felicissimus Zero? By our electioneerings and Hansard Debatings, and ever-enduring tempest of jargon that goes on everywhere, we manage to settle that; to have it declared, with no bloodshed except insignificant blood from the nose in hustings-time, but with immense beershed and inkshed and explosion of nonsense, which darkens all the air, that the Right Honourable Zero is to be the man. That we firmly settle; Zero, all shivering with rapture and with terror, mounts into the high saddle; cramps himself on, with knees, heels, hands and feet; and the horse gallops—whither it lists. That the Right Honourable Zero should attempt controlling the horse—Alas, alas, he, sticking on with beak and claws, is too happy if the horse will only gallop anywhither, and not throw him. Measure, polity, plan or scheme of public good or evil, is not in the head of Felicissimus; except, if he could but devise it, some measure that would please his horse for the moment, and encourage him to go with softer paces, godward or devilward as it might be, and save Felicissimus's leather, which is fast wearing. This is what we call a Government in England, for nearly two centuries now. * * *

Abler men in Downing Street, abler men to govern us: yes, that, sure enough, would gradually remove the dung-mountains, however high they are; that would be the way, nor is there any other way, to remedy whatsoever has gone wrong in Downing Street and in the wide regions, spiritual and temporal, which Downing Street presides over! * * *

England with the largest mass of real living interests ever intrusted to a Nation; and with a mass of extinct imaginary and quite dead interests piled upon it to the very Heavens, and encumbering it from shore to shore,—does reel and stagger ominously in these years; urged by the Divine Silences and the Eternal Laws to take practical hold of its living interests and manage them: and clutching blindly into its venerable extinct and imaginary interests, as if that were still the way to do it. England must contrive to manage its living interests, and quit its dead ones and their methods, or else depart from its place in this world. Surely England is called as no Nation ever was, to summon-out its *kings*, and set them to that high work!—Huge inorganic England, nigh choked under the exuviae of a thousand years, and blindly sprawling amid chartisms, ballot-boxes, prevenient graces, and bishops' nightmares, must, as the preliminary and commencement of organisation, learn to *breathe* again,—get 'lungs' for herself again, as we defined it. That is imperative upon her: she too will die, otherwise, and cough her last upon the streets some day;—how can she continue living? To enfranchise whatsoever of Wisdom is born in England, and set that to the sacred task of coercing and amending what of Folly is born in England: Heaven's blessing is purchasable by that; by not that, only Heaven's curse is purchasable. The reform contemplated, my liberal friends perceive, is a truly radical one; no ballot-box ever went so deep into the roots: a radical, most painful, slow and difficult, but most indispensable reform of reforms.

[On Parliament and National Prosperity: An Editorial on the Opening of Parliament] †

The British Legislature has commenced its ordinary session under circumstances that render its meeting of more than usual interest and importance. The Parliament of the world has opened. Constitutional liberty, in the only great country in Europe where it is either understood or permitted, is about to give the neighbouring nations a new example of its effective working. We may be assured that those nations will watch with curiosity, not unmixed with a deeper feeling, the deliberations of an assembly so illustrious, and, unfortunately for the interests of humanity and civilisation, so unrivalled.

The meeting of a new British Parliament, and its probable results, are always to be considered under a twofold aspect. How will its constitution affect home politics? and what influence will its deliberations exercise upon the general policy of Europe, and of the world? At the present time both of these questions are of a complexity seldom seen, and of an importance seldom exceeded in history.

The "condition of England" question, that a few short years ago was of such painful interest, is now most cheering. If the observer or commentator takes his stand upon a platform high above the bustle and jostle of warring factions, and of the fragments of dismembered parties that exist in and out of the Legislature, he will have much reason to rejoice at the position of his country, and the most satisfactory grounds for hoping that England will more than ever be the example and the guide of less favoured nations, and the friend and mainstay elsewhere of those principles of rational liberty

† From *Illustrated London News*, Nov. 6, 1852, pp. 369–70.

and moderate statesmanship which have made her what she is. Formerly, * * * the condition of the people of England was one upon which no statesman could reflect without misgivings for the future. The repeal of the Corn-laws, and the emancipation of industry from the impediments and trammels of a tax upon food, has happily either altogether removed or greatly diminished this anxiety. With cheap food and steady employment, the people once believed and felt to be so dangerous, are happy and contented. The jails and the workhouses are empty; the manufacturers' labourers have wages to spare, not only for comforts and luxuries, but for provident investment; and the farmers' labourers, formerly the least paid, the most hopeless and dispirited of all labourers, find, to their comfort, that they are no longer a drag and an incumbrance upon the soil, but that they are valuable for their thews and their sinews, for their skill and for their good conduct. They have at last been raised above the daily dread of the workhouse that formerly beset them. We are aware that it is not alone to the repeal of the Corn and Navigation-laws, and to the gradual remission of taxes that impeded the extension of trade and manufactures, that all these favourable results are to be attributed. The discovery of the gold of California and Australia, and the pre-existent causes which led to what is called the "Exodus" of the Irish, and what may as justly, in regard to Australia, be called the "Exodus" of the English people, have no doubt contributed to raise the value of labour, both skilled and unskilled, in every part of the country; * * * The circumstances of Great Britain have been vastly altered by the operation of both these causes; and it will be the greatest of the duties that will devolve upon the Parliament of 1852 to prepare a financial policy in accordance with these new and favourable facts, and to settle thereby upon a still more solid and permanent basis the prosperity of the country. * * * We cannot doubt for a moment of the progression and triumph of those true principles of trade and fiscal policy, which allow a great people to thrive and to be happy, and to stand first in wealth, in enterprise, and in industry, among the nations of the world.

As regards foreign politics, it must be confessed that the New Parliament will enter upon its existence at a critical period. The omens of impending trouble and confusion, if not of strife and calamity, are many, and they thicken around Europe as we write. Everywhere we behold the elements of change and disorder. Mighty armies are marshalled, and no one knows against what enemy or what country they will be led forth in battle array. * * * Everywhere in Continental Europe we see the unhappy spectacle of nations that desire freedom, but do not understand it; of nations that both love and understand, but cannot attain it; and of nations that are the slavish, and even contented victims of unrelenting despotism. In all the darkness of Europe there is but one bright spot, and that is in our own island. Although there are many questions in abeyance—that may well cause uneasiness, among ourselves, such as unhappy theological disputes, the fierce polemics of Ireland, the state of the Church of England, and other points of difference, minor perhaps, but still of grave significancy—the New Parliament of this country may well be proud of the position it will hold, and thankful for the privilege of legislating for so great and so advancing a people. Representative Government, elsewhere discredited, has its abiding place and sanctuary here; and, whatever the chances and changes of factions and parties amongst us may be, we may confidently indulge the hope that the cause of constitutional liberty throughout the world will not suffer through any act or deed of the British Legislature.

[Speech from the Throne on National Progress]†

August 20, 1853

Her Majesty contemplates with grateful satisfaction and thankfulness to Almighty God the tranquility which prevails throughout her dominions; together with that peaceful industry and obedience to the laws which insure the welfare of all classes of her subjects. It is the first desire of Her Majesty to promote the advance of every social improvement, and, with the aid of your wisdom, still further to extend the prosperity and happiness of her people.

† From *Annual Register*, 1853, History, p. 209.

Law Courts, Inquests, and Police

In addition to documents relating to Chancery practice, about which Dickens' magazine, *Household Words*, kept up a running battle,[1] the following selections include a report of an inquest resembling the inquest attended by Jo in *Bleak House* and also a selection from one of Dickens' several articles about the police forces and the detective officers who were said to have provided models for his Inspector Bucket. Because much of *Bleak House* treats of the ineptitudes of the legal system, it is appropriate to have a reminder of one branch of the law that is presented, both in the novel and in Dickens' journalism, not as faultless but at least as efficient.

The account of his 1851 visit to a London slum, under police escort, may be compared with his similar experience in 1842, when he was accompanied by the painter Daniel Maclise and the poet Henry W. Longfellow. Maclise, on this occasion, like Mr. Snagsby in the novel (Chapter XXII), was so nauseated by the spectacle that he became ill.[2]

SUTTON SHARPE

[Testimony of a Barrister Concerning Chancery Costs and Delays]†

. . . Perhaps the Committee will allow me to mention three Causes which have come under my Observation lately which will illustrate what I have been saying; in Two of them I was personally concerned, the other has been furnished to me. One is the Cause of Bankes v. De Spencer. The Bill in this Case was filed in the Year 1832; the Cause was set down for hearing in Trinity Term 1834; as in this Stage it could be heard as a short Cause, it was heard in December 1834. A Reference was made to the Master to take certain Accounts; the Master made his Report on the 11th of June 1836, and the Cause was set down for hearing, on further Directions, in Michaelmas 1836. It did not get into the regular Paper for hearing till July 1839. During that Time an Event occurred, the Birth of a Child, which rendered it necessary for the Plaintiff to file

1. E.g., "The Martyrs of Chancery" (Dec. 7, 1850, and Feb. 15, 1851).
2. See *The Letters of Charles Dickens*, Pilgrim Edition, III (1974), p. 343.
† Presented by Sutton Sharpe (1840) before the Lords' Select Committee on Administration of Justice. From *English Historical Documents*, ed. G. M. Young, London (1956), XII, 525–27.

a Supplemental Bill, which was filed in the Month of January 1838; this would not have been necessary if the Cause had been heard in Michaelmas Term 1836, when it was ready for hearing: this Supplemental Bill necessarily occasioned a considerable Expense. On the 30th of July 1839 the Cause was again on the Paper for hearing, as it was also on the 31st of that Month; it then went out of the Paper, and did not come in again before the Vacation. In Michaelmas Term 1839 a special Application was made to the Vice Chancellor to let the Cause stand at the Head of the Paper the First Day of Causes after Term, which was ordered; it accordingly stood on the Paper on the 3rd of December. It was in the Paper again on the 4th of December, and on the 5th; then it went out of the Paper, and did not come in again till the 18th of December; it was in the Paper again on the 29th of January, the 30th of January, the 12th of February, the 13th, the 15th, the 17th, the 18th, the 19th, the 20th, the 21st, the 24th, the 25th, the 26th, the 27th, the 28th, the 29th, the 2nd of March, the 3rd and 4th of March, without being touched, and on the 5th of March it was called on and partially heard, and again partially heard on the 6th; it came on again on the 9th, but was not then touched, and on the 10th it was finally heard and disposed of.

Q. Have the Solicitors a Fee upon each of those days that the Cause is in the Paper?

They have.

Q. Every Party?

Yes; besides the Refreshers that were given to Counsel each Term the Cause was in the Paper.

A Chancery Bone of Contention†

Our newspaper contemporaries ought really to engage an efficient staff of first-rate writers of romance to do justice to the reports of the proceedings in the Courts of Chancery. A mere matter-of-fact style becomes 'pale' and ineffective in dealing with subjects that surpass in extravagance the wildest and most exciting matters of fiction.

What might not a feverish imagination make of the following 'little affair' that came off the other day in the Court of Sir R. T. Kindersley? The question in the case was whether an old lady, who died in 1827 (only twenty-five years ago, which is nothing in the age of a Chancery suit), had by her will executed a power of appointment, reserved to her by her marriage settlement.

One would imagine the question would be simple enough, and easily answered; but sixteen counsel were employed in arguing that

† From *Punch*, 22 (June, 1852), p. 255.

she had, and that she hadn't * * * * It is wonderful how so apparently small a bone of contention can give employment to the jaws of no less than sixteen barristers.

This, however, is not all, for in a Chancery suit it is not sufficient to have a standing army of standing counsel on both sides, but there is a neutral position to be taken up by somebody, and on this occasion it was filled by Mr. Follett and Mr. Busk, who 'appeared for the Trustees,' who had no interest in the result one way or the other. No wonder 'his Honour' said, that 'after the number of cases that had been cited he should reserve his judgment.' We defy anyone to have any judicial faculty left after listening to eighteen barristers on one point, and we would lay a wager * * * that however simple the question, the amount of 'learning' employed upon it must have reduced it to a mass of inextricable confusion. Happily for the sanity of Chancery suitors in general, they are usually dead before it comes to their turn to have the matters in which they are interested brought before the Court, and the survivors entitled to the 'fund' have been born to consider the 'fund' as the sport of the law, so that they are really in the position fallaciously ascribed to the eels, and have become, by use, hardened to the process of skinning.

[A Review of *Bleak House* on Chancery]†

The great centre, around which the events and characters revolve, and a glimpse of which is afforded in the opening chapter, is the Court of Chancery, that tomb into which the fortunes and hopes of so many thousands have slowly descended. A very fruitful theme. Perhaps it would have been well if Mr. Dickens had given an earlier exposition of it. Had his present work appeared twenty years ago, it would have been a revelation of strange mysteries to the public, and might now be looked upon as having contributed to promote the beneficial changes effected, or on the way to be effected, by recent legislation. As it is, he is rather late. He only exhibits in a stronger and more romantic light what has been pretty well made known before through the earnest prose of plainer men. In this respect, he reminds us of a fact which has often struck us in regard to the sparkling writers who, in many things, profess to lead the age. They are no prophets. *Punch* deals severe blows at abuses, on which the public eye is fixed, but seldom deserves the credit of discovering them. We have generally noticed that he has followed in the track of the less imaginative *Times*; and even the conductors of the 'leading journal' derive their inspiration, not from their own genius, but

† Review of *Bleak House* in *Eclectic Review*, Dec. 1853, pp. 666–67.

from the communications of nameless men of business, who, brought into contact with the evils which still have their roots among us, snatch a few minutes from their ordinary avocations, and relieve their irritated feelings by sending an account of their wrongs to Printing-House-square.

[Cross-Examination of a Witness at an Inquest]†

We recently commented upon a case of exclusion of evidence. Another has occurred hardly less remarkable in its way. A boy of fourteen years of age was put in the witness-box at Guildhall, in evidence of a savage assault on a police officer. The report states,

He looked quite astonished upon taking hold of the book.

Alderman Humphrey: Well, do you know what you are about. Do you know what an oath is?

Boy: No.

Alderman Humphrey: Do you know what a Testament is?

Boy: No.

Alderman Humphrey: Can you read?

Boy: No.

Alderman Humphrey: Do you ever say your prayers?

Boy: No; never.

Alderman Humphrey: Do you know what prayers are?

Boy: No.

Alderman Humphrey: Do you know what God is?

Boy: No.

Alderman Humphrey: Do you know what the Devil is?

Boy: No. I've heard of the Devil, but I don't know him.

Alderman Humphrey: What do you know my poor fellow?

Boy: I knows how to sweep the crossing.

Alderman Humphrey: And that's all?

Boy: That's all. I sweeps the crossing.

The Alderman said, that in all his experience he had never met with anything like the deplorable ignorance of the unfortunate child in the witness-box. He, of course, could not take the evidence of a creature *who knew nothing whatever of the obligation to tell the truth.*

Now, it is to be remarked that the boy's answers, though they discover ignorance the most brutal and lamentable, denote at the same time a strict fidelity to truth. He could not but have perceived

† From "Exclusion of Evidence," in the *Examiner*, Jan. 12, 1850. The author may have been Dickens. See K. J. Fielding and Alec W. Brice, "Charles Dickens on 'The Exclusion of Evidence,'" *Dickensian*, Sept. 1968, pp. 131–40.

that the ignorance he was displaying was disgraceful, the magistrate's reception of his replies sufficiently expressed that fact; but nevertheless he continued to answer directly and truly to the questions, not attempting any dissimulation, subterfuge, or false pretences. He professed to know nothing out of the world or in the world except to sweep the crossing.

There are many things which an alderman does not know, but would an alderman, put to the question, have been as strictly veracious as the boy in confessing his ignorance, especially if it were an ignorance to which any shame attached? Let us suppose the alderman under examination:

Q. Do you know what a logarithm is?

Q. Can you construe an ode of Horace?

Q. Can you read Greek?

Q. Do you ever say anything which anybody thinks worth hearing or repeating?

Q. Do you know what chlorine is?

Q. What do you know? my poor alderman.

A. I know how to eat a city feast.

Does any one believe that an alderman would have answered these interrogatories as directly and honestly as the boy answered the questions put to him? There would have been some shuffling, some evasion of the confession of ignorance. Molière had a thorough understanding of the false shame which makes the generality of people prefer a falsity to an avowal of ignorance; and when one of his characters is asked whether he understands Latin, he makes him reply confidently that he does, but proceeds to say, 'But pray talk to me as if I did not understand it'. In every society we see the shifts to which people will have recourse to conceal their deficiencies of knowledge. This boy Ruby, however, was naked and not ashamed, and amongst the many things he did not know was to feign that he did know. He was a truthful witness against himself, as society had to its shame suffered him to be; and for the very evidence of his adherence to truth most faithfully, the magistrate puts him aside as not to be trusted as a witness. Now, we will venture to say that amongst boys thoroughly well schooled in the Catechism, and who would furnish Alderman Humphrey with the exactest particulars respecting the Devil, there is not one in a dozen who would have answered questions touching on their deficiencies so frankly and ingenuously. They would probably have explained the obligation of an oath unexceptionably, but without observing with equal strictness the laws of veracity. It may happen occasionally, as in the case of this neglected, unfortunate boy Ruby, that falsehood has been as little learnt as the nature of an oath.

CHARLES DICKENS

[A Police-Conducted Tour of a Slum]†

Saint Giles's clock strikes nine. We are punctual. Where is Inspector Field? Assistant Commissioner of Police is already here, enwrapped in oil-skin cloak, and standing in the shadow of Saint Giles's steeple. Detective Serjeant, weary of speaking French all day to foreigners unpacking at the Great Exhibition, is already here. Where is Inspector Field?

Inspector Field is, to-night, the guardian genius of the British Museum. He is bringing his shrewd eye to bear on every corner of its solitary galleries, before he reports 'all right.' * * * All is quiet, and Inspector Field goes warily on, making little outward show of attending to anything in particular, just recognising the Ichthyosaurus as a familiar acquaintance, and wondering, perhaps, how the detectives did it in the days before the Flood. * * *

Inspector Field comes in, wiping his forehead, for he is of a burly figure, and has come fast from * * * the Sculptures of Nineveh, and from the traces of an elder world, when these were not. Is Rogers ready? Rogers is ready, strapped and great-coated, with a flaming eye in the middle of his waist, like a deformed Cyclops. Lead on, Rogers, to Rats' Castle!

How many people may there be in London, who, if we had brought them deviously and blindfold, to this street, fifty paces from the Station House, and within call of Saint Giles's church, would know it for a not remote part of the city in which their lives are passed? How many, who amidst this compound of sickening smells, these heaps of filth, these tumbling houses, with all their vile contents, animate and inanimate, slimily overflowing into the black road, would believe that they breathe *this* air? How much Red Tape may there be, that could look round on the faces which now hem us in—for our appearance here has caused a rush from all points to a common centre—the lowering foreheads, the sallow cheeks, the brutal eyes, the matted hair, the infected, vermin-haunted heaps of rags—and say "I have thought of this. I have not dismissed the thing. I have neither blustered it away, nor frozen it away, nor tied it up and put it away, nor smoothly said pooh, pooh! to it, when it has been shown to me"?

This is not what Rogers wants to know, however. What Rogers wants to know, is, whether you *will* clear the way here, some of you, or whether you won't; because if you don't do it right on end, he'll lock you up! * * *

† From "On Duty with Inspector Field," *Household Words*, June 14, 1851, pp. 265–67.

Clear the street here, half a thousand of you! Cut it, Mrs. Stalker—none of that—we don't want you! Rogers of the flaming eye, lead on to the tramps' lodging-house!

A dream of baleful faces attends to the door. Now, stand back all of you! In the rear, Detective Serjeant plants himself, composedly whistling, with his strong right arm across the narrow passage. Mrs. Stalker, I am something'd that need not be written here, if you won't get yourself into trouble, in about half a minute, if I see that face of yours again!

Saint Giles's church clock, striking eleven, hums through our hand from the dilapidated door of a dark outhouse as we open it, and are stricken back by the pestilent breath that issues from within. Rogers, to the front with the light, and let us look!

Ten, twenty, thirty—who can count them? Men, women, children, for the most part naked, heaped upon the floor like maggots in a cheese! Ho! In that dark corner yonder! Does any body lie there? Me Sir, Irish me, a widder, with six children. And yonder? Me Sir, Irish me, with me wife and eight poor babes. And to the left there? Me Sir, Irish me, along with two more Irish boys as is me friends. And to the right there? Me Sir and the Murphy fam'ly, numbering five blessed souls. And what's this, coiling, now, about my foot? Another Irish me, pitifully in want of shaving, whom I have awakened from sleep—and across my other foot lies his wife—and by the shoes of Inspector Field lie their three eldest—and their three youngest are at present squeezed between the open door and the wall. * * *

They are all awake now, the children excepted, and most of them sit up, to stare. Wheresoever Mr. Rogers turns the flaming eye, there is a spectral figure rising, unshrouded, from a grave of rags. Who is the landlord here?—I am, Mr. Field, says a bundle of ribs and parchment against the wall, scratching itself.—Will you spend this money fairly, in the morning, to buy coffee for 'em all?—Yes Sir, I will!—O he'll do it Sir, he'll do it fair. He's honest! cry the spectres. And with thanks and Good Night sink into their graves again.

Thus, we make our New Oxford Streets, and our other new streets, never heeding, never asking where the wretches whom we clear out, crowd. With such scenes at our doors, with all the plagues of Egypt tied up with bits of cobweb in kennels so near our homes, we timorously make our Nuisance Bills and Boards of Health, nonentities, and think to keep away the Wolves of Crime and Filth, by our electioneering ducking to little vestry-men, and our gentlemanly handling of Red Tape!

Criticism

The number of essays attempting to identify the distinctive qualities of *Bleak House*, many of them being criticism of first quality, makes the task of selection exceptionally difficult. In trying to provide a representative sampling we have been made frustratingly aware of how many valuable essays we have not been able to include. Many of these are listed in the Bibliography or in footnotes throughout the present volume. It will be noted that studies of the historical backgrounds and topography of *Bleak House* are excluded from the following section; these are referred to instead in parts of the sections headed "Backgrounds" and "Genesis and Composition," especially in the sub-section "A Dictionary of *Bleak House* Originals" (pp. 891–895).

GEORGE BRIMLEY

[A Review of *Bleak House* in the *Spectator*]†

"I believe I have never had so many readers," says Mr. Dickens in the preface to *Bleak House*, "as in this book." We have no doubt that he has the pleasantest evidence of the truth of this conviction in the balance-sheet of his publishing-account; and, without any more accurate knowledge of the statistics of his circulation than the indications furnished by limited personal observation, we should not be surprised to find that *Punch* and the *Times* newspaper were his only rivals in this respect. Whatever such a fact may not prove, it does prove incontestably that Mr. Dickens has a greater power of amusing the book-buying public of England than any other living writer; and moreover establishes, what we should scarcely have thought probable, that his power of amusing is not weakened now that the novelty of his style has passed away, nor his public wearied by the repetition of effects in which truth of nature and sobriety of thought are largely sacrificed to mannerism and point. Author and public react upon each other; and it is no wonder that a writer, who finds that his peculiar genius and his method of exhibiting it secure him an extensive and sustained popularity, should be deaf to the remonstrances of critics when they warn him of defects that his public does not care for, or urge him to a change of method which might very probably thin his audience for the immediate present, and substitute the quiet approval of the judicious for the noisy and profitable applause of crowded pit and gallery. Intellectual habits, too, become strengthened by use, and a period comes in the life of a man of genius when it is hopeless to expect from him growth of faculty or correction of faults.

Bleak House is, even more than any of its predecessors, chargeable with not simply faults, but absolute want of construc-

† Sept. 24, 1853, pp. 923–25.

tion. A novelist may invent an extravagant or an uninteresting plot—may fail to balance his masses, to distribute his light and shade—may prevent his story from marching, by episode and discursion: but Mr. Dickens discards plot, while he persists in adopting a form for his thoughts to which plot is essential, and where the absence of a coherent story is fatal to continuous interest. In *Bleak House,* the series of incidents which form the outward life of the actors and talkers has no close and necessary connexion; nor have they that higher interest that attaches to circumstances which powerfully aid in modifying and developing the original elements of human character. The great Chancery suit of Jarndyce and Jarndyce, which serves to introduce a crowd of persons as suitors, lawyers, law-writers, law-stationers, and general spectators of Chancery business, has positively not the smallest influence on the character of any one person concerned; nor has it any interest of itself. Mr. Richard Carstone is not made reckless and unsteady by his interest in the great suit, but simply expends his recklessness and unsteadiness on it, as he would on something else if it were non-existent. This great suit is lugged in by the head and shoulders, and kept prominently before the reader, solely to give Mr. Dickens the opportunity of indulging in stale and commonplace satire upon the length and expense of Chancery proceedings, and exercises absolutely no influence on the characters and destinies of any one person concerned in it. The centre of the arch has nothing to do in keeping the arch together. * * * And not only is this story both meagre and melodramatic, and disagreeably reminiscent of that vilest of modern books Reynolds's *Mysteries of London,* but it is so unskilfully managed that the daughter is in no way influenced either in character or destiny by her mother's history; and the mother, her husband, the prying solicitor, the French maid, and the whole Dedlock set, might be eliminated from the book without damage to the great Chancery suit, or perceptible effect upon the remaining characters. We should then have less crowd, and no story; and the book might be called "Bleak House, or the Odd Folks that have to do with a long Chancery Suit." * * *

The love of strong effect, and the habit of seizing peculiarities and presenting them instead of characters, pervade Mr. Dickens's gravest and most amiable portraits, as well as those expressly intended to be ridiculous and grotesque. His heroine in *Bleak House* is a model of unconscious goodness; sowing love and reaping it wherever she goes, diffusing round her an atmosphere of happiness and a sweet perfume of a pure and kindly nature. Her unconsciousness and sweet humility of disposition are so profound that scarcely a page of her autobiography is free from a record of these admirable qualities. With delightful naïveté she writes down the praises that are showered upon her on all hands; and it is impossible to doubt the simplicity of her nature, because she never omits to assert it with emphasis. This is not only coarse portraiture, but utterly untrue and inconsistent. Such a girl would not write her own memoirs, and certainly would not bore one with her goodness till a wicked wish arises that she would either do something very "spicy," or confine herself to superintending the jam-pots at Bleak House. Old Jarndyce himself, too, is so dreadfully amiable and supernaturally benevolent, that it has been a common opinion during the progress of the book, that he would turn out as great a rascal as Skimpole; and the fox on the symbolical cover with his nose turned to the East wind has been conjectured by subtile intellects to be intended for his double. We rejoice to find that those misanthropical anticipations were unfounded; but there must have been something false to general nature in the portrait that suggested them—some observed peculiarity of an individual presented too exclusively, or an abstract conception of gentleness and forbearance worked out to form a sharp contrast to the loud, self-assertive, vehement, but generous and tender Boythorne. This gentleman is one of the most original and happiest conceptions of the book, a humourist study of the highest merit. Mr. Tulkinghorn, the Dedlock confidential solicitor, is an admirable study of mere outward characteristics of a class; but his motives and character are quite incomprehensible, and we strongly suspect that Mr. Dickens had him shot out of the way as the only possible method of avoiding an enigma of his own setting which he could not solve. Tulkinghorn's fate excites precisely the same emotion as the death of a noxious brute. He is a capital instance of an old trick of Mr. Dickens, by which the supposed tendencies and influences of a trade or profession are made incarnate in a man, and not only is "the dyer's hand subdued to what it works in," but the dyer is altogether eliminated, and his powers of motion, his shape, speech, and bodily functions, are translated into the dye-tub. This gives the effect of what some critics call marvellous individuality. It gives distinctness at any rate, and is telling; though it may be questionable whether it is not a more fatal mistake in art than the careless and unobservant habit which many writers have of omitting to mark the effect of occupations upon the development and exhibition of the universal passions and affections. Conversation Kenge and Vholes, solicitors in the great Jarndyce case, have each their little characteristic set of phrases, and are well marked specimens of the genus lawyer; but as they only appear in their professional capacity, we are not entitled to question them as to their qualities as men.

The allied families of Jellyby and Turveydrop are in Dickens's happiest vein, though Mrs. Jellyby is a coarse exaggeration of an existing folly. They may, we think, stand beside the Micawbers. Mrs. Jellyby's daughter Caddy is the only female in the book we thoroughly relish: there is a blending of pathos and fun in the description of her under the tyranny of Borrioboola Gha, that is irresistible; and her rapid transformation from a sulky, morose, overgrown child, to a graceful and amiable young woman, under the genial influence of Esther Summerson, is quite Cinderella-like, and as charming as any fairy tale. Inspector Bucket, of the Detective Force, bears evidence of the careful study of this admirable department of our Police by the editor of *Household Words*; and, as in the case of Kenge and Vholes, the professional capacity is here the object, and we do not require a portraiture of the man and his affections. Poor Joe, the street-sweeping urchin, is drawn with a skill that is never more effectively exercised than when the outcasts of humanity are its subjects; a skill which seems to depart in proportion as the author rises in the scale of society depicted. Dickens has never yet succeeded in catching a tolerable likeness of man or woman whose lot is cast among the high-born and wealthy. Whether it is that the lives of such present less that is outwardly funny or grotesque, less that strikes the eye of a man on the lookout for oddity and point, or that he knows nothing of their lives, certain it is that his people of station are the vilest daubs; and Sir Leicester Dedlock, Baronet, with his wife and family circle, are no exceptions.

If Mr. Dickens were now for the first time before the public, we should have found our space fully occupied in drawing attention to his wit, his invention, his eye for common life, for common men and women, for the everyday aspect of streets and houses, his tendency to delineate the affections and the humours rather than the passions of mankind; and his defects would have served but to shade and modify the praises that flow forth willingly at the appearance among us of a true and original genius. And had his genius gone on growing and maturing, clearing itself of extravagance, acquiring art by study and reflection, it would not be easy to limit the admiration and homage he might by this time have won from his countrymen. As it is, he must be content with the praise of amusing the idle hours of the greatest number of readers; not, we may hope, without improvement to their hearts, but certainly without profoundly affecting their intellects or deeply stirring their emotions. Clever he undoubtedly is: many of his portraits excite pity, and suggest the existence of crying social sins; but of almost all we are obliged to say that they border on and frequently reach caricature, of which the essence is to catch a striking likeness by exclusively selecting and exaggerating a peculiarity that marks the man but does not represent him. Dickens belongs in literature to the same class as his illustrator, Hablot Browne, in design, though he far surpasses the illustrator in range and power.

[Anonymous Review of *Bleak House* in the *Examiner*]†

The addition of another to the list of elaborate works upon which Mr. Dickens rests his claim to be remembered in future times, forms always an event in contemporary literature; and *Bleak House* being finished, opinions upon it are now freely exchanged on all sides. Some find in it occasion to feel sorely aggrieved because Mr. Dickens is not so inhuman as to be absolutely faultless. Some suggest modifications, and point out how they would have planned it if it had been their's to write. Some are in raptures over one part, some over another, and some very particular fellows are carping at every part. The judgments on *Bleak House* are, in short, as various as judgments are apt to be upon a man whose failings it is thought a subtle test of criticism to discover, for the very reason that all the world admires and likes him, and his books are bought and read by everybody.

That this latest of his books has filled the fancies of its readers with new groups of people as familiar and real as any that in life they may have known; that it overflows with inimitable grace and tenderness; that it is stored with the most subtle wit, and with a humour, hearty and true, that sets always instinctively at work our pleasantest and kindliest emotions; that mirth and pathos abound in it, that its satire is always just and manly, and that it is full of generous indignation against social usages that create wrong and perpetuate suffering among us,—is simply in other words to say that it is a book written by Mr. Dickens. That it has also faults is to say that it is not quite a miracle, even though written by him. Many faults truly may be found with it, and such as properly accompany great qualities. In the whole line of immortals throughout the history of literature, there will be discovered few writers indeed who have produced unexceptionable books. Books become everlasting by the genius that is in them, and by their unquestionable elevation above the products of men having only ordinary power. Their accompanying defects are but tokens of a true humanity, and perhaps scarcely detract from the enjoyment we derive from them. * * *

Upon this high ground we must stand if we would properly discuss *Bleak House*. It touches and amuses us, but it is destined to draw tears and smiles also from our children's children. Mr. Dickens

† Oct. 8, 1853, p. 643.

has a large public in the present, and we do not hesitate to declare our belief that he will have one hardly less large in the future. The world will grow wiser than it is, the abuses attacked by this greatest of humorists and kindliest of satirists will disappear—but the spirit in which he writes, and to which he appeals, is indestructible; and the emotions he awakens are not more fresh and true to us than they will be to future generations.

The first remark we are disposed to make on *Bleak House* has relation to its plot. The conduct of the story appears to us singularly skilful. Not without justice has it been objected that the habit of writing a story in monthly parts is apt to lead to a greater concern for the part than for the whole, and to interfere with the steady and continuous working of every event up to the final issue. But let us in the present instance with no less justice remark, that the habit of reading a story in parts is equally apt to prevent many readers from noticing how thoroughly a work so presented to them is calculated for perusal as a whole. The studied and elaborate care bestowed upon the construction of *Bleak House* is very manifest. Event leads to event; and chance words, or the deeds of chance people, that seem perfectly irrelevant, are seen everywhere, precisely as in real life, exerting a direct and powerful bearing on the course taken by a train of incidents whereof the issue is one of life or death, of happiness or misery, to men and women perfectly unknown to them. Taking the mere surface view of such treatment, it would of course be easy to exhibit its apparent want of connection and design, and to display in the attempt only our own very real want of sagacity. This subtle linking together of the deeds and interests of many people, so far as they bear on the progress of one given set of incidents, is in fact truer to nature, infinitely truer, than the common plan of representing half a dozen men and women acting and re-acting on each other exclusively, as if they were fenced out from the surrounding world. Its drawback is that it compels the use of a large number of characters which come and go during the progress of the story; and, as their purpose in the narrative is not always evident until the reader can look back from the journey's end over the ground he has traversed, they may now and then cause some confusion in the reader's mind, and produce an effect like that of an over-crowded picture. But the art rather than the artist is there in fault.

Be this as it may, never in any former work has Mr. Dickens made use of a plot so evidently planned before-hand with minute consideration, or throughout so elaborately studied. Even the fits of the little law-stationer's servant aid directly in the chain of little things that lead indirectly to the catastrophe of Lady Dedlock's death. So dexterously indeed are the many little incidents of this kind leading to great results managed throughout *Bleak House*, that we can hardly feel surprise if the results should by not very careful readers be received as substantive and independent facts, and the small precedent details held altogether separable from them, as a mere cloud of isolated incidents. A novel may have its too superficial readers, as life has its too hasty observers.

At the close of his preface Mr. Dickens marks incidentally the general character of the tale by the intimation that in it he has purposely dwelt upon the romantic side of familiar things. Marvellous is the skill with which, towards this intention, the great Chancery suit on which the plot hinges, and on incidents connected with which, important or trivial, all the passion and suffering turns, is worked into every part of the book. Whenever the occasion arises, or the art of the story-teller requires, the thick atmosphere of law that rises out of Jarndyce *v.* Jarndyce is made to cling like a fog about the people in the story. It may be more or less, but there it is. Either as a thick cloud or a light mist, it is to be seen everywhere. Lawyers of many grades, law clerks of all kinds, the copyist, the law-stationer, the usurer, suitors of every description, haunters of the law courts and their victims, live and move round about the life of the chief persons in the tale, and exercise almost insensibly, but very certainly, a continual influence upon them. Compare this with what a commonplace writer would have preferred, and a congenial critic recommended, and you will understand what the power of a man of genius really is. To have made the plot itself a connected story of a Chancery suit would have been (except for the merest commonplace) one of the clumsiest and most impracticable designs conceivable. Mr. Dickens knew better what he was about, and the use made of Jarndyce *v.* Jarndyce in *Bleak House* is always complete and masterly.

The other grand feature of the tale, connected also closely yet quite naturally with this, is the Dedlock household. It is brought out with equal power, with the same thoughtful elaboration, and with as perfect a result. Not only have we Sir Leicester, a true gentleman with all his weaknesses; and Lady Dedlock, the supercilious woman of fashion, with a busy heart painfully throbbing beneath that hard and quiet outside; but Volumnia and the cousins, the town house and the footmen, the country house and its good old-fashioned housekeeper, all are worked out with the finish of a master. From the first glimpse of the assembled Dedlock household, discussing the Doodles and Foodles and Cuffys and Buffys in which they believe politics to consist, down to the last chapters that concern them—chapters, including the flight and pursuit of the unhappy Lady Dedlock, which are in conception and construction absolutely wonderful—the power and care spent upon the group are unceasingly exerted (yet so successfully as to bear no trace of effort) to keep it throughout in that central position towards which the other sections of the tale may be seen gradually and surely to converge.

Taking the story piecemeal, as a mere gallery of pictures and persons, we are disposed to think that there are particular groups in *Bleak House* finer than anything that even Mr. Dickens has yet produced in the same way. Exquisitely true and tender as are his descriptions of the suffering classes in former writings, we can remember none by which we have been touched so deeply, or that has been graced by so much of the very finest writing, as the entire tale of the street-wandering Joe as it may be gathered from the pages of the book before us. In the trooper George, the Bagnets, and their humble household, we have another of those fine, broad, hearty exemplifications of humour in which Mr. Dickens delights, in which all the ludicrous features of every object or incident are intensely enjoyed and made prominent, yet with a most genuine and charming sentiment at the same time underlying it all. Nothing is repulsive; everything is large, laughable, and true; and the most homely and ungainly figures become radiant with the spirit of goodness. The character of Esther Summerson has been much elaborated, and the early portions of her narrative are as charming as anything Mr. Dickens has ever written—indeed some of the best things in the book may be found throughout it, full as it is of noble fancies, and delicate and graceful thoughts; but we suspect that Mr. Dickens undertook more than man could accomplish when he resolved to make her the *naïve* revealer of her own good qualities. We cannot help detecting in some passages an artificial tone, which, if not self-consciousness, is at any rate not such a tone as would be used in her narrative by a person of the character depicted. Yet the graces and virtues of Esther have won so many hearts that we do not care to dwell on our objection to his method of displaying them; and as to the one or two other characters of the book which we might have wished away, these are quite lost in that crowd of fresh and ever real creations that will live while the language continues. Mrs. Jellyby and her despondent husband, her daughter Caddy and the Turveydrops, the trooper George and his man Phil, the brickmakers' wives and the dead infant, the law-stationer and his little woman, Boythorn and Skimpole, Mr. Chadband and the Coavinses, the mother of Mr. Guppy, the inscrutable and impassable Tulkinghorn, to say nothing of poor Miss Flite or the immortal Bucket, and a dozen others, have been added here to the long list of ideal people with whom Mr. Dickens has made his countrymen intimately and permanently acquainted.

Mr. Dickens's characters, as all the world knows, pass their names into our language, and become types. It is an evidence of his possession of the highest power that the best of them are thus made each to embody some characteristic feature, to personify some main idea, which are ever after found universally applicable. Such has been the aim of the highest class of dramatists and novelists since the beginning of all literature. They know little how much there is in any one man's head or heart, who expect to have every character in a tale laid bare before them as on a psychological dissecting table, and demonstrated minutely. We see nobody minutely in real life. The rough estimates we form of character are on the whole (if we possess any tact) correct; but men touch and interfere with one another by the contact of their extremes, and it is the prominences, the sharp angles, that are most likely to appear in a tale really worth the telling. Hence it is therefore, as well as for other reasons, that the dramatist or novelist is concerned chiefly with the display of salient points in each one of his characters. The rest of the sketch is filled up by the reader or spectator instinctively (and sufficiently) out of his own experience. Squire Allworthy, Blifil, Philosopher Square, Parson Adams, Trulliber, and all the rest of Fielding's characters were formed upon this plan; nor was it thought unjust or unnatural by the great novelist to give distinctness to the picture in each case, by just so much of genial strength and breadth of colouring as should prevent his idea from being impressed too faintly on the public mind.

It is for the most part much more easy than correct to cry out—exaggeration. We may be only betraying our ignorance after all. There is an eastern saying to the effect that there is in the world precisely what the eye can find in it, and let us not suppose that what limits our view in any particular direction, should of necessity be an equal restriction to the view of a man of genius. Of Mr. Dickens it is to be said, if of any one, that his main strength has lain in the ability to concentrate his thoughts on objects external to himself. If his mere personality were at every turn set up as the limit and bound to his perceptions, if it were still his recurring habit to take his own character as the infallible test of all other characters, he would in each fresh essay be always retracing only the old weary ground. But ready and eager at all times, with genial warmth and fulness, to enter in all the peculiarities of others, we have him continually throughout his books apprehending and interpreting new forms of character and truth, and carrying with each new achievement of his genius new pleasure and delight into thousands of homes—because his genius is his fellow-feeling with his race. * * *

G. K. CHESTERTON

[Characters in *Bleak House*]†

A picaresque novel is only a very eventful biography; but the opening of *Bleak House* is quite another business altogether. It is admirable in quite another way. The description of the fog in the first chapter of *Bleak House* is good in itself; but it is not merely good in itself, like the description of the wind in the opening of *Martin Chuzzlewit*; it is also good in the sense that Maeterlinck is good; it is what the modern people call an atmosphere. Dickens begins in the Chancery fog because he means to end in the Chancery fog. He did not begin in the Chuzzlewit wind because he meant to end in it; he began in it because it was a good beginning. This is perhaps the best short way of stating the peculiarity of the position of *Bleak House*. In this *Bleak House* beginning we have the feeling that it is not only a beginning; we have the feeling that the author sees the conclusion and the whole. The beginning is alpha and omega: the beginning and the end. He means that all the characters and all the events shall be read through the smoky colours of that sinister and unnatural vapour.

The same is true throughout the whole tale; the whole tale is symbolic and crowded with symbols. Miss Flite is a funny character, like Miss La Creevy, but Miss La Creevy means only Miss La Creevy. Miss Flite means Chancery. The rag-and-bone man, Krook, is a powerful grotesque; so is Quilp; but in the story Quilp only means Quilp; Krook means Chancery. Rick Carstone is a kind and tragic figure like Sidney Carton; but Sidney Carton only means the tragedy of human nature; Rick Carstone means the tragedy of Chancery. Little Jo dies pathetically like Little Paul; but for the death of Little Paul we can only blame Dickens; for the death of Little Jo we blame Chancery. Thus the artistic unity of the book, compared to all the author's earlier novels, is satisfying, almost suffocating. There is the *motif*, and again the *motif*. Almost everything is calculated to assert and re-assert the savage morality of Dickens's protest against a particular social evil. The whole theme is that which another Englishman as jovial as Dickens defined shortly and finally as the law's delay. The fog of the first chapter never lifts.

In this twilight he traced wonderful shapes. Those people who fancy that Dickens was a mere clown; that he could not describe anything delicate or deadly in the human character,—those who fancy this are mostly people whose position is explicable in many

† From G. K. Chesterton, *Appreciations and Criticisms of the Works of Charles Dickens*, published in the United States by E. P. Dutton & Co., Inc., and from *Introduction to Bleak House*, Everyman's Library series, published by J. M. Dent & Sons Ltd. Reprinted by permission.

easy ways. The vast majority of the fastidious critics have, in the quite strict and solid sense of the words, never read Dickens at all; hence their opposition is due to and inspired by a hearty innocence which will certainly make them enthusiastic Dickensians if they ever, by some accident, happen to read him. In other cases it is due to a certain habit of reading books under the eye of a conventional critic, admiring what we expect to admire, regretting what we are told to regret, waiting for Mr. Bumble to admire him, waiting for Little Nell to despise her. Yet again, of course, it is sometimes due to that basest of all artistic indulgences (certainly far baser than the pleasure of absinthe or the pleasure of opium), the pleasure of appreciating works of art which ordinary men cannot appreciate. Surely the vilest point of human vanity is exactly that; to ask to be admired for admiring what your admirers do not admire. But whatever be the reason, whether rude or subtle, which has prevented any particular man from personally admiring Dickens, there is in connection with a book like *Bleak House* something that may be called a solid and impressive challenge. Let anyone who thinks that Dickens could not describe the semi-tones and the abrupt instincts of real human nature simply take the trouble to read the stretch of chapters which detail the way in which Carstone's mind grew gradually morbid about his chances in Chancery. Let him note the manner in which the mere masculinity of Carstone is caught; how as he grows more mad he grows more logical, nay, more rational. Good women who love him come to him, and point out the fact that Jarndyce is a good man, a fact to them solid like an object of the senses. In answer he asks them to understand his position. He does not say this; he does not say that. He only urges that Jarndyce may have become cynical in the affair in the same sense that he himself may have become cynical in the affair. He is always a man; that is to say, he is always unanswerable, always wrong. The passionate certainty of the woman beats itself like battering waves against the thin smooth wall of his insane consistency. I repeat: let any one who thinks that Dickens was a gross and indelicate artist read that part of the book. If Dickens had been the clumsy journalist that such people represent, he never could have written such an episode at all. A clumsy journalist would have made Rick Carstone in his mad career cast off Esther and Ada and the others. The great artist knew better. He knew that even if all the good in a man is dying, the last sense that dies is the sense that knows a good woman from a bad; it is like the scent of a noble hound.

The clumsy journalist would have made Rick Carstone turn on John Jarndyce with an explosion of hatred, as of one who had made an exposure—who had found out what low people call "a false friend" in what they call "his true colours." The great artist knew better; he knew that a good man going wrong tries to salve his soul to the last with the sense of generosity and intellectual justice. He will try to love his enemy if only out of mere love of himself. As the wolf dies fighting, the good man gone wrong dies arguing. This is what constitutes the true and real tragedy of Richard Carstone. It is strictly the one and only great tragedy that Dickens wrote. It is like the tragedy of Hamlet. The others are not tragedies because they deal almost with dead men. The tragedy of old Dorrit is merely the sad spectacle of a dotard dragged about Europe in his last childhood. The tragedy of Steerforth is only that of one who dies suddenly; the tragedy of old Dombey only that of one who was dead all the time. But Rick is a real tragedy, for he is still alive when the quicksand sucks him down.

It is impossible to avoid putting in the first place this pall of smoke which Dickens has deliberately spread over the story. It is quite true that the country underneath is clear enough to contain any number of unconscious comedians or of merry monsters such as he was in the custom of introducing into the carnival of his tales. But he meant us to take the smoky atmosphere seriously. Charles Dickens, who was, like all men who are really funny about funny things, horribly serious about serious things, certainly meant us to read this story in terms of his protest and his insurrection against the emptiness and arrogance of law, against the folly and the pride of judges. Everything else that there is in this story entered into it through the unconscious or accidental energy of his genius, which broke in at every gap. But it was the tragedy of Richard Carstone that he meant, not the comedy of Harold Skimpole. He could not help being amusing; but he meant to be depressing.

Another case might be taken as testing the greater seriousness of this tale. The passages about Mrs. Jellyby and her philanthropic schemes show Dickens at his best in his old and more familiar satiric manner. But in the midst of the Jellyby pandemonium, which is in itself described with the same *abandon* and irrelevance as the boarding-house of Mrs. Todgers or the travelling theatre of Mr. Crummles, the elder Dickens introduced another piece of pure truth and even tenderness. I mean the account of Caddy Jellyby. If Carstone is a truly masculine study of how a man goes wrong, Caddy is a perfectly feminine study of how a girl goes right. Nowhere else perhaps in fiction, and certainly nowhere else in Dickens, is the mere female paradox so well epitomised, the unjust use of words covering so much capacity for a justice of ultimate estimate; the seeming irresponsibility in language concealing such a fixed and pitiless sense of responsibility about things; the air of being always at daggers-drawn with her own kindred, yet the confession of incurable kinship implied in pride and shame; and, above all, that thirst for order and beauty as for something physical; that strange female power of hating ugliness and waste as good men can only hate sin and bad men virtue. Every touch in her is true, from her first bewildering outbursts of hating people because she likes them, down to the sudden quietude and good sense which announces that she has slipped into her natural place as a woman. Miss Clare is a figure-head, Miss Summerson in some ways a failure; but Miss Caddy Jellyby is by far the greatest, the most human, and the most really dignified of all the heroines of Dickens.

With one or two exceptions, all the effects in this story are of this somewhat quieter kind, though none of them are so subtly successful as Rick Carstone and Caddy. Harold Skimpole begins as a sketch drawn with a pencil almost as airy and fanciful as his own. The humour of the earlier scenes is delightful—the scenes in which Skimpole looks on at other people paying his debts with the air of a kindly outsider, and suggests in formless legal phraseology that they might "sign something" or "make over something," or the scene in which he tries to explain the advantages of accepting everything to the apoplectic Mr. Boythorn. But it was one of the defects of Dickens as a novelist that his characters always became coarser and clumsier as they passed through the practical events of a story, and this would necessarily be so with Skimpole, whose position was conceivable even to himself only on the assumption that he was a mere spectator of life. Poor Skimpole only asked to be kept out of the business of this world, and Dickens ought to have kept him out of the business of *Bleak House*. By the end of the tale he has brought Skimpole to doing acts of mere low villainy. This altogether spoils the ironical daintiness of the original notion. Skimpole was meant to end with a note of interrogation. As it is, he ends with a big, black, unmistakable blot. Speaking purely artistically, we may say that this is as great a collapse or vulgarisation as if Richard Carstone had turned into a common blackguard and wife-beater, or Caddy Jellyby into a comic and illiterate landlady. Upon the whole it may, I think, be said that the character of Skimpole is rather a piece of brilliant moralising than of pure observation or creation. Dickens had a singularly just mind. He was wild in his caricatures, but very sane in his impressions. Many of his books were devoted, and this book is partly devoted, to a denunciation of aristocracy—of the idle class that lives easily upon the toil of nations. But he was fairer than many modern revolutionists, and he insisted on satirising also those who prey on society not in the name of rank or law, but in the name of intellect and beauty. Sir Leicester Dedlock and Mr. Harold Skimpole are alike in accepting with a royal unconsciousness the anomaly and evil of their position. But the idleness and insolence of the aristocrat is human and humble compared to the idleness and insolence of the artist.

With the exception of a few fine freaks, such as Turveydrop and Chadband, all the figures in this book are touched more delicately, even more faintly, than is common with Dickens. But if the figures are touched more faintly, it is partly because they are figures in a fog—the fog of Chancery. Dickens meant that twilight to be oppressive; for it was the symbol of oppression. Deliberately he did not dispel the darkness at the end of this book, as he does dispel it at the end of most of his books. Pickwick gets out of the Fleet Prison; Carstone never gets out of Chancery but by death. This tyranny, Dickens said, shall not be lifted by the light subterfuge of a fiction. This tyranny shall never be lifted till all Englishmen lift it together.

GEORGE FORD

[A Note on *Bleak House* and Kafka]†

That Kafka, like Dostoevsky, was directly indebted to Dickens we know from the testimony of his diary. He could be critical of Dickens' faults, and it is interesting that his complaints might be applied equally well to the work of Lawrence. He refers to "Dickens' opulence and great, careless prodigality, but in consequence passages of awful insipidity in which he wearily works over effects he has already achieved. Gives one a barbaric impression . . . that I . . . thanks to my weakness . . . have been able to avoid." If Kafka's novels resemble those of Dickens, it is not in any overflowing Lawrence-like vitalism. He himself speaks of valuing Dickens' "method." The opening chapter of his novel *America* he describes as "a sheer imitation of Dickens. . . ." Although Kafka's reputation in England may have passed its peak, there must still be many readers for whom these words would be a potent recommendation for a reexploration of Dickens' "method."

One way of pointing up the parallels very briefly is to consider three novels which are concerned with the Law. James G. Cozzens' *The Just and the Unjust* contains several scenes in which the nature of the Law is discussed as it is also discussed in the interview between Richard Carstone and Mr. Vholes in *Bleak House* and between Joseph K. and the chaplain in Kafka's *The Trial*. But the similarity is one of situation only, for if Mr. Cozzens' scenes are examined more closely, we become aware of an immense gap. His scenes are admirable examples of conventional realism. We get from them a wise and sensible report concerning various difficulties in the administration of justice. The novelist is aware of these

† From George Ford, *Dickens and His Readers* (Princeton, 1955). Reprinted by permission of Princeton University Press.

difficulties, but he is never really bewildered by them for a moment. Neither is his reader. *The Just and the Unjust* thus consists of straightforward narrative without a trace of incongruous humor, or of poetry, or of any kind of symbolical overtones. In *Bleak House* we have the same *kind* of feeling in listening to Mr. Vholes as we have in listening to Kafka's priest or to the lawyers who reply to K.'s enquiries. There is a sense of endlessly bewildering muddle, a muddle so immense that it becomes painfully funny. It is in this sense that *Bleak House* and *The Trial* obviously belong in one category, and *The Just and the Unjust* in another.

On the other hand, because Kafka is primarily concerned with the apparent muddle of Divine Law, and Dickens with the actual muddle of human law, there are also inevitable differences in their methods. Kafka's method is closer to allegory, and hence his law courts are further removed from the law courts in Mr. Cozzens' novel than are those of Dickens. What is symbolical is always literally true, and the symbolical significance can be passed over if the reader wishes (the fog in *Bleak House* is real fog, and the snow in Joyce's story "The Dead" is real snow; as such they are typical symbols). What is allegorical may be more convincing or vivid as a nightmare is convincing or vivid, but literal correspondence to ordinary experience is not required, and the reader can hardly escape the realization that the narrative is moving on two levels (at least two levels). A *Christmas Carol* might be cited as a kind of Dickensian allegory, but his usual preference is for the symbolical. With Kafka, the preference is reversed. Although *The Castle* is more sophisticated than *Pilgrim's Progress,* it is evident that its method is much closer to Bunyan's than Dickens ever came. *Bleak House* therefore represents a mid-point between the method of *Pilgrim's Progress* at one extreme and *The Just and the Unjust* at the other.[1]

J. HILLIS MILLER

[The World of *Bleak House*]†

* * *

> It is a dull street under the best conditions; where the two long rows of houses stare at each other with that severity, that half-a-dozen of its greatest mansions seem to have been slowly stared into stone, rather than originally built in that material. (48)

1. For further studies of Dickens and Kafka, see Murray Krieger's *The Tragic Vision* (New York, 1960), pp. 138–40; Mark Spilka, *Dickens and Kafka* (Bloomington, Ind., 1963); and John Carey, *The Violent Effigy* (London, 1973), pp. 174–75.

† From J. Hillis Miller, *Charles Dickens: The World of His Novels* (Cambridge, Mass.: Harvard University Press). Copyright © 1958 by the President and Fellows of Harvard College. Reprinted by permission. Numbers in parentheses refer to chapter numbers in *Bleak House.*

> The Temple, Chancery Lane, Serjeants' Inn, and Lincoln's Inn even unto the Fields, are like tidal harbours at low water; where stranded proceedings, offices at anchor, idle clerks lounging on lopsided stools that will not recover their perpendicular until the current of Term sets in, lie high and dry upon the ooze of the long vacation. (19)

Though the world of *Bleak House* is not, we discover, the sheer atomistic chaos it at first appears to be, the connection, by repetition, of successive moments in isolated locations does not organize this chaos. It does not seem that a truly human existence is possible here—no organization of time into a lived duration, no relation between people making possible significant communication. But we come to see that the inhuman fixity and paralysis which seems to possess things and men in *Bleak House* is not a permanent condition. It is not now in the same stasis it has always maintained. The houses were not originally stone. They were "slowly stared into stone." And the ooze and idleness of the long vacation is merely the motionless end point of a progressive withdrawal of the tide of human action and life. Prior to the timeless paralysis of things there was a long process of deceleration and decay. It is impossible to stop the forward movement of things in time. Both an attempt to freeze the present as a repetition of a past time and the eternally repeated moment of expectation which awaits some definitive event in the future are essentially a denial of the proper human relation to time and to the objective world. Both are cut off from the "moving age." But man cannot cut himself off from time and the world. If he is not related authentically to them, if he does not command them, they will command him. He will be assimilated into the inhuman world and become part of a mechanical concatenation of causes and effects which is a horrible parody of historical continuity. In the absence of human intervention things will take matters into their own hands, and initiate a long natural process of decay and disintegration in which man will become unwittingly involved. The world possesses an immanent tendency toward decomposition which only the most delicately and resolutely applied constructive force can counteract. And it is just this force which is almost totally absent in *Bleak House*.

The world of the novel is already, when the story begins, a kind of junk heap of broken things. This is especially apparent in the great number of disorderly, dirty, broken-down interiors in the novel. The Jellyby household is "nothing but bills, dirt, waste, noise, tumbles down-stairs, confusion, and wretchedness" (14). At the time of the preparations for Caddy Jellyby's marriage "nothing belonging to the family, which it had been possible to break, was unbroken . . . ; nothing which it had been possible to spoil in any way, was unspoilt; . . . no domestic object which was capable of collecting dirt, from a dear child's knee to the door-plate, was without as much dirt as could well accumulate upon it" (30). The Jellyby house is perhaps the extreme case, but Skimpole's home too is "in a state of dilapidation" (43), Symond's Inn, where Richard Carstone's lawyer, Vholes, lives, has been made "of old building materials, which took kindly to the dry rot and to dirt and all things decaying and dismal" (39), and Richard himself lives in a room which is full of "a great confusion of clothes, tin cases, books, boots, brushes, and portmanteaus, strewn all about the floor" (45). The "dusty bundles of papers" in his room seem to Esther "like dusty mirrors reflecting his own mind" (51).

These present states of disorder are not simply inorganic formlessness; they are the terminal point of an organically interconnected series of stages which led naturally and inevitably from one to another. The present stage of rottenness is the result of an inverted process of growth, "like [that] of fungus or any unwholesome excrescence produced . . . in neglect and impurity" (46). Such a process escapes from the discontinuous, but only to replace it with a mode of continuity which is apparently an irreversible growth toward death. This death will be defined as the putrefaction of every organic form and as the pulverization of every structured inorganic thing. There is here no Spencerian constructive law immanent in nature and guaranteeing, through the impersonal operation of causality, the creation of ever finer and more discriminated forms of life. Rather, it is as though the generative cause and immanent principle of growth had been withdrawn altogether, leaving things to fall back to their primal disorder.

Sometimes this process appears, not as a certain stage which it has now reached, but in the very midst of its happening. Although the participles in the opening paragraphs of the novel suggested the present activity of inanimate objects, participial forms can also express the falling away and disintegration from moment to moment of things which are collapsing into chaos. Thus, Esther is painfully aware of "the musty *rotting* silence of the house" where Ada and Richard are living (51), and in Nemo's room, "one old mat, trodden to shreds of rope-yarn, lies *perishing* upon the hearth" (10). A description of the beach at Deal shows it as a kind of wasteland of disunity, and ends with the apparent metamorphosis of the inhabitants into a lower form of existence. The heterogeneity gives way at last to a single substance into which the men seem to be transforming themselves, just as the litter of the beach dissolves into the sea and the fog: "The long flat beach, with its little irregular houses, wooden and brick, and its litter of capstans, and great boats, and sheds, and bare upright poles with tackle and blocks, and loose gravelly waste places overgrown with grass and weeds, wore as dull an appearance as any place I ever saw. The sea was heaving under a thick white fog; and nothing else was moving but a few early ropemakers, who, with the yarn twisted round their bodies, looked as if, tired of their present state of existence, they were spinning themselves into cordage" (45). Perhaps the best example of this disintegration is the initial description of Tom-all-Alone's, which makes an elaborate use of present participles to express an active process of decomposition matching the forward movement of time: "It is a street of perishing blind houses, with their eyes stoned out; without a pane of glass, without so much as a window-frame, with the bare blank shutters tumbling from their hinges and falling asunder; the iron rails peeling away in flakes of rust; the chimneys sinking in; the stone steps to every door (and every door might be Death's Door) turning stagnant green; the very crutches on which the ruins are propped, decaying" (8).

One might plot the curve of this approach to maximum entropy by a series of crucial points. There was once evidently, long ago in the past, a time when things were orderly, when everything fitted into its place in an organic structure, and when each individual object was itself a formal unity. From that point things passed eventually to a stage in which they were simply collections of broken objects thrown pell-mell together. Things are then like the wreckage left behind after the destruction of a civilization. Each fragmentary form once had a use and a purpose, but is now merely debris. Such collections form the contents of Krook's rag and bottle shop or of the closets of the Jellyby house:

> In all parts of the window, were quantities of dirty bottles: blacking bottles, medicine bottles, ginger-beer and soda-water bottles, pickle bottles, wine bottles, ink bottles. . . . A little way within the shop-door, lay heaps of old crackled parchment scrolls, and discoloured and dog's-eared law-papers. I could have fancied that all the rusty keys, of which there must have been hundreds huddled together as old iron, had once belonged to doors of rooms or strong chests in lawyers' offices. The litter of rags . . . might have been counsellors' bands and gowns torn up. One had only to fancy . . . that yonder bones in a corner, piled together and picked very clean, were the bones of clients, to make the picture complete. (5)
>
> But such wonderful things came tumbling out of the closets when they were opened—bits of mouldy pie, sour bottles, Mrs. Jellyby's caps, letters, tea, forks, odd boots and shoes of children, firewood, wafers, saucepan-lids, damp sugar in odds and ends of paper bags, footstools, blacklead brushes, bread, Mrs. Jellyby's bonnets, books with butter sticking to the binding, guttered candle-ends put out by being turned upside down in broken candle-

sticks, nutshells, heads and tails of shrimps, dinner-mats, gloves, coffee-grounds, umbrellas. . . . (30)

Not only are things moving in the direction of increasing disorder, they are also moving further and further beyond the limits of human intelligence. Whatever human meaning and order there may have been originally is now obliterated in complexity which defies comprehension: "This scarecrow of a suit has, in course of time, become so complicated, that no man alive knows what it means" (1). Even if there were some intelligible purpose in the original impetus which set the case in motion, that purpose has been utterly lost in its own self-proliferating complexity. Now the case runs automatically, without any direction from the thousands of people, suitors and lawyers, who are mere parties to it, mere instruments of its autonomous activity: "It's about a Will, and the trusts under a Will—or it was, once. It's about nothing but Costs, now. We are . . . equitably waltzing ourselves off to dusty death, about Costs. That's the great question. All the rest, by some extraordinary means, has melted away" (8).

But in the end even this kind of structure, a structure so elaborate that it cannot be understood by the human mind, yields to complete heterogeneity. And a world of complete heterogeneity is, paradoxically, a world of complete homogeneity. Since nothing has any relation to anything else and cannot therefore be understood in terms of a contrast to anything else, everything is, finally, the equivalent of everything else. The contents of Krook's rag and bone shop, like everything involved in Chancery, are transformed at last to mere undifferentiated dust, another form of the fog and mud which dominate the opening scene of the novel. Everything there is "wasting away and going to rack and ruin," turning into "rust and must and cobwebs" (5). The final product is made up of thousands of distinct particles, but each particle is, in the end, no more than another example of the general pulverization. So Tom-all-Alone's is at one stage of its decay like the ruined body of a man half dead and crawling with vermin: "these tumbling tenements contain, by night, a swarm of misery. As, on the ruined human wretch, vermin parasites appear, so, these ruined shelters have bred a crowd of foul existence that crawls in and out of gaps in walls and boards; and coils itself to sleep, in maggot numbers, where the rain drips in . . ." (16). But later on even this semblance of life disappears from the scene and Tom-all-Alone's is like the cold and lifeless moon, a "desert region unfit for life and blasted by volcanic fires" (46), with a "stagnant channel of mud" for a main street (46). In the end, any organic entity, whether human or material, which gets caught up in the process of decomposition becomes nothing but a powdery or pasty substance, without form or life. This process can be either a physical or a spiritual disintegration, either the destruction of the individual through his absorption in the impersonal institution of "law and equity," or the dissolution of all solid material form in "that kindred mystery, the street mud, which is made of nobody knows what, and collects about us nobody knows whence or how" (10). One of the basic symbolic equations of the novel is the suggested parallel between these two forms of disintegration.

The mud and fog of the opening paragraphs of the novel are not, we can see now, the primeval stuff out of which all highly developed forms evolve. They are the symptoms of a general return to the primal slime, a return to chaos which is going on everywhere in the novel and is already nearing its final end when the novel begins.

The human condition of the characters of *Bleak House* is, then, to be thrown into a world which is neither fresh and new nor already highly organized, but is a world which has already gone bad. From the very first moment in which they are aware of themselves at all, the characters find themselves involved in this world. Their dereliction is to be already a suitor in a case which began long before they were born, or already tainted with the quasi-sin of illegitimacy. Their mode of being in the world is to be already committed to a situation which they have not chosen.

This dereliction will never end, as long as the character is alive. It is the permanent condition of human existence in *Bleak House*. The fact that almost all of the characters in the novel are in one way or another engaged in an endless suit in Chancery is much more than a mere device of narrative unity. To be involved in an endless case, a case which can only be concluded by the total using up of both suit and suitor, becomes a symbol in the novel of what it is to be in the world at all. It is because a person is part of a process, because he is born into a case which is going on at his birth and remains unfinished throughout his life, that he cannot settle down, cannot find some definitive formulation of his identity and of his place in the world. But to be unfinished, to be open toward the future, to be evermore about to be, is, for Dickens, to be human. Richard suffers the human situation itself and defines the state of all the characters when he describes himself as living permanently in a "temporary condition" (23): ". . . I am a very unfortunate dog not to be more settled, but how *can* I be more settled? If you lived in an unfinished house, you couldn't settle down in it; if you were condemned to leave everything you undertook, unfinished, you would find it hard to apply yourself to anything; and yet that's my unhappy case. I was born into this unfinished contention with all its chances and changes, and it began to unsettle me before I quite knew the difference between a suit at law and a suit of clothes; and it has gone on unsettling me ever since" (23). Richard's error is not to understand that his case can never be finished, to live in the expectation of an end which will settle his life in a permanent form: "it can't last for ever. We shall come on for a final hearing, and get judgment in our favour. . . . These proceedings will come to a termination, and then I am provided for" (23). But the nature of these proceedings is precisely to be interminable, as long as the character is alive.

For many of the characters the determining cause which has made of their situations what they irrevocably are, occurred so long before their birth that it assumes a quasi-mythical character. They attempt to trace the series of effects and causes from the present moment back retrogressively to the first cause, only to be lost in the mists and confusions of the past. Long, long ago in the past, so long ago that no one now has any direct contact with what happened then, the chain of causes and effects which has brought things to their present pass was initiated. Such characters seem to be involved in a kind of original sin for which they must innocently suffer: "How mankind ever came to be afflicted with Wiglomeration, or for whose sins these young people ever fell into a pit of it, I don't know; so it is" (8).

But for other characters the definitive event which has determined their lives is prior to the beginning of the novel but not prior to their birth. As in Faulkner's novels, we are presented with characters who are when we first meet them already doomed by something which happened long ago in their own lives, something which they hide carefully from the world, but on which their conscious attention is permanently fixed in a kind of retrospective fascination. All their lives are spent attempting unsuccessfully to escape from this determining moment. It is a constantly reënacted failure which only makes their lives all the more permanently attached to a past from which they cannot separate themselves, and which irrevocably defines them as what they are. The secretly obsessed quality of many of the characters in *Bleak House* makes this novel very different from *Martin Chuzzlewit*. In the earlier novel the characters either had no inner lives at all as distinct from their environments, or had subjectivities which were anonymous and empty, mere pure and vivid vision, existing only in the present. In *Bleak House*, some characters are seen as possessing, not this anonymous lucidity, but a concentrated awareness of their pasts and of their destinies. Such consciousnesses are not yet shown from the inside, as they will be in *Little Dorrit*, but their presence is unmistakably implied by the actions of the characters and revealed in occasional glimpses of their interior worlds. Of the tragedy of Boythorn's projected marriage, Jarndyce says: "That time has had its influence on all his later life" (9, and see 43). And Nemo was living, we realize, in the constant suffering of the tragedy of his relations to Lady Dedlock, just as George Rouncewell's bluff exterior hides a secret remorse for having run away from home, and just as Tulkinghorn lives in a state of quiet desperation. He is shown for one moment as he is for himself, remembering a friend of his, obviously a surrogate for himself, a "man of the same mould," who "lived the same kind of life until he was seventy-five years old," and then hanged himself (22). But Lady Dedlock is, of course, the chief example of this theme. Her boredom hides an intense concentration on her own past, and all her attempts to cease to be the lover of Captain Hawdon only carry her more irresistibly toward her final reaffirmation of her past self. Her tragedy, like that of Racine's characters, of Hardy's, or of Faulkner's, is the tragedy of the irrevocable. Her fate is to be the doomed victim of her own past, a past which continues itself ineluctably into her present state as long as she lives.

But the determining cause which makes impotent victims of all these characters does not exist solely as a kind of mythical event occurring so long ago that no direct contact with it is possible, nor does it exist solely as an impersonal force which imposes itself from the outside on people and warps or destroys them. It may be both of these, but in its most powerful form it is immanent, present in the contemporary spiritual condition of the characters, although they may not even be consciously aware of it. It is able to get inside its victims, and inhabit them as a destructive force. It then no longer needs to exist as an exterior power, and can withdraw and disappear, leaving the possessed character to his isolated doom. Everywhere in *Bleak House* we can see the intrusion into the present of a fatally determining past from which the characters can in no way free themselves because it has become part of the very substance of their beings. In *Bleak House* the present is not really something isolated and without engagement in the past, but is the preservation of the past and its continuation in the present. Inhabited by immanent determining forces tending irreversibly toward their dissolution, the characters disintegrate, just as Grandfather Smallweed collapses "like some wound-up instrument running down" (39), and just as his daughter "dwindled away like touchwood" (21).

The self-enclosed life of the characters of *Bleak House* is, then, not a mechanical repetition. It is a clock that runs down, something organic which has died and decays, the entropy of an enclosed system approaching the maximum equilibrium of its forces. As in the "circumscribed universe" of Poe,[1] since there is no influx of life, energy, air, or novelty from the outside, there is a gradual

1. See Georges Poulet, "L'Univers circonscrit d'Edgar Poe," *Les Temps Modernes,* CXIV, CXV (1955), 2179–2204.

exhaustion of the forces inside, a disaggregation of all solid forms, as all diversity is slowly transformed into a bland and motionless homogeneity. Such an enclosed system will, like a case in Chancery, eventually "die out of its own vapidity" (24), or "lapse and melt away" (65). Beneath a carapace of solitude the will, the strength, the life of these characters exhausts itself, consumes itself in its own internal activity. So Richard, "the good consuming and consumed, the life turned sour," is slowly transformed into "the one subject that is resolving his existence into itself" (39). Wholly enclosed within his own obsession, such a character experiences a steady decomposition of his life, an acceleration toward the ultimate disorder and lifelessness of dust and mud:

> My whole estate . . . has gone in costs. The suit, still undecided, has fallen into rack, and ruin, and despair, with everything else . . . (15)

> In the meantime [while Tom Jarndyce became absorbed in his suit], the place became dilapidated, the wind whistled through the cracked walls, the rain fell through the broken roof, the weeds choked the passage to the rotting door. (8)

> His voice had faded, with the old expression of his face, with his strength, with his anger, with his resistance to the wrongs that had at last subdued him. The faintest shadow of an object full of form and colour, is such a picture of it, as he was of the man from Shropshire whom we had spoken with before. (24)

> . . . it is the same death eternally—inborn, inbred, engendered in the corrupted humours of the vicious body itself, and that only —Spontaneous Combustion, and none other of all the deaths that can be died. (32)

Krook's death by spontaneous combustion, described in the last quotation, is of course the most notorious example of this return to homogeneity in *Bleak House*. Krook is transformed into the basic elements of the world of the novel, fog and mud. The heavy odor in the air, as if bad pork chops were frying, and the "thick yellow liquor" which forms on the window sill as Krook burns into the circumambient atmosphere, are particularly horrible versions of these elements.

But if the deterioration of the characters in *Bleak House* can appear as the inescapable fulfillment of an inner principle of corruption, it can also appear as a destiny which draws the characters from some prospective point toward their doom. Instead of being pushed from behind or from within, the characters may be attracted from the future. This may appear in the sudden collapse or dissolution of some object or person which has long been secretly mined from within by decay, and goes to pieces in a moment when some artificial foundation or sustaining principle gives way. So the houses in Tom-all-Alone's collapse (16); so the man from Shropshire "break[s] down in an hour" (24); and so the death of Tulkinghorn seems to Lady Dedlock "but the key-stone of a gloomy arch removed, and now the arch begins to fall in a thousand fragments, each crushing and mangling piecemeal!" (55). "It was right," she says, "that all that had sustained me should give way at once, and that I should die of terror and my conscience"(59). Indeed the spontaneous combustion of Krook is just such a rapid fulfillment of a process which has been preparing itself invisibly for a long time, just as the stroke which paralyzes Sir Leicester makes him physically what he spiritually has been all along, a frozen and outmoded form of life, speaking "mere jumble and jargon" (56).

In all these cases, it is as though a hidden orientation suddenly revealed itself when, all restraint gone, the character yields at last to a destiny which has been attracting him with ever-increasing intensity. As Bucket says, "the frost breaks up, and the water runs" (54). It does not run randomly, however, but toward a center which has all along been exerting its gravitational pull. This pull does not now commence, but only now manifests itself. And so Miss Flite can speak of the Court of Chancery not as a first cause, but as a final cause drawing men to their ruin by means of its irresistible magnetic attraction:

> "There's a cruel attraction in the place. You *can't* leave it. And you *must* expect. . . . It's the Mace and Seal upon the table."
>
> What could they do, did she think? I mildly asked her.
>
> "Draw," returned Miss Flite. "Draw people on, my dear. Draw peace out of them. Sense out of them. Good looks out of them. Good qualities out of them. I have felt them even drawing my rest away in the night. Cold and glittering devils!" (35)

For many characters their disintegration is not so much the working out of a chain of causes and effects begun long in the past as it is the fatal convergence of their inner lives and their external situations toward a point where both will coincide at their death. Richard had mistakenly believed that "either the suit must be ended, . . . or the suitor" (51). But he is slowly consumed by his vampire-like lawyer, Vholes, just as the case of Jarndyce and Jarndyce is entirely consumed in costs. When both processes are finally complete, Vholes gives "one gasp as if he had swallowed the last morsel of his client" (65). The termination of the interminable case coincides necessarily with the exhaustion of all the money involved in it, and with the simultaneous death of Richard. All of these events inevitably occur together as the vanishing point toward which all the parallel motions have been converging, as toward their final cause. This temporal progression is glimpsed by Esther in a momentary scene which prognosticates Richard's fate. It is a good example of the way scenes in Dickens which are initially merely narrative realism are transformed into symbolic expressions of the entire destiny of a character: "I shall never forget those two seated side by side in the lantern's light; Richard, all flush and fire and laughter, with the reins in his hand; Mr. Vholes, quite still, black-gloved, and buttoned up, looking at him as if he were looking at his prey and charming it. I have before me the whole picture of the warm dark night, the summer lightning, the dusty track of road closed in by hedgerows and high trees, the gaunt pale horse with his ears pricked up, and the driving away at speed to Jarndyce and Jarndyce" (37).

In the same way the life and death of Jo the crossing sweeper are made symbolic. During his life Jo has been continually forced to "move on." His death is imaged as the "breaking down" of a cart that as it disintegrates approaches closer and closer to an end point which will be its total fragmentation: "For the cart so hard to draw, is near its journey's end, and drags over stony ground. All round the clock it labours up the broken steps,[2] shattered and worn. Not many times can the sun rise, and behold it still upon its weary road" (47). And so the death of Lady Dedlock is described as a journey which is the slow closing in of her destiny: "When I saw my Lady yesterday, . . . she looked to me . . . as if the step on the Ghost's Walk had almost walked her down" (58). Like Richard's future, the prospect before and beside the road which she is journeying is getting narrower and narrower. The end point will be her death, the complete extinction of all possibility of choice or movement: "The dark road I have trodden for so many years will end where it will. I follow it alone to the end, whatever the end be. . . . [Danger] has closed around me, almost as awfully as if these woods of Chesney Wold had closed around the house; but my course through it is the same" (36).

But this sudden break-up of things when the keystone of the arch has been removed may be imaged not as a narrowing, but as a descent deeper and deeper into the pit of the dark and unformed. When the fragile foundations which have been precariously upholding things give way, there is a sudden drop vertically into infernal depths. The Chancery suit is a "dead sea" (37), and Richard "sink[s] deeper and deeper into difficulty every day, continually hoping and continually disappointed, conscious of change upon change for the worse in [himself]" (39). Mr. Snagsby, being led by Bucket and his colleagues into the heart of Tom-all-Alone's,

2. *Steeps* rather than *steps* in Norton text [*Editors*].

"feels as if he were going, every moment deeper and deeper down, into the infernal gulf" (22). What he sees is like a vision of hell itself. Not the least horrible part of this visionary experience is the way the human dwellers in Tom-all-Alone's seem to have been transformed into the elements they live in, the fog and mud: ". . . Mr. Snagsby passes along the middle of a villainous street, undrained, unventilated, deep in black mud and corrupt water. . . . [The] crowd flows round, and from its squalid depths obsequious advice heaves up to Mr. Bucket. Whenever they move, and the angry bull's-eyes glare, it fades away, and flits about them up the alleys, and in the ruins, and behind the walls . . ." (22).

But it is Lady Dedlock's journey to death, after the murder of Tulkinghorn has revealed her secret, which is the most elaborate dramatization of this kind of disintegration. The chase after Lady Dedlock by Bucket and Esther is not simply a Victorian melodrama. It is a subtly symbolic dramatization of the destiny of Lady Dedlock and of her relation to her daughter. Once her "freezing mood" is melted, she rapidly becomes, like Poe's mesmerized man when his trance is broken, what she has really been all along: dead. The thawing snow, the change of direction from a centrifugal flight outward from the city to a return to the center of disintegration and corruption where her dead lover lies buried, her disguise in the dress of a brickmaker's wife whose baby has died, all these function symbolically. Here, more intensely than for any other character, we experience the descent into formlessness which follows inevitably the failure to achieve a proper relation to the onward motion of time.

Bucket's chase after Lady Dedlock is presented through Esther's eyes. All that happens has for her a visionary, dream-like quality: "I was far from sure that I was not in a dream" (57); ". . . the stained house fronts put on human shapes and looked at me; . . . great water-gates seemed to be opening and closing in my head, or in the air; . . . the unreal things were more substantial than the real" (59). The dominant symbol of the whole sequence is contained here in the image of water-gates opening and closing. The process of Lady Dedlock's dying after her freezing mood has broken is mirrored in nature itself in the melting snow which lies everywhere that night: "From the portico, from the eaves, from the parapet, from every ledge and post and pillar, drips the thawed snow. It has crept, as if for shelter, into the lintels of the great door—under it, into the corners of the windows, into every chink and crevice of retreat, and there wastes and dies" (58).

At the center of all this melting is perhaps the river, which is reached by a "labyrinth of streets" (57). There, Bucket fears, Lady Dedlock may be found; ". . . he gazed into the profound black pit of water, with a face that made my heart die within me. The river had a fearful look, so overcast and secret, creeping away so fast between the low flat lines of shore: so heavy with indistinct and awful shapes, both of substance and shadow: so deathlike and mysterious" (57). But the real center, reached by "descending into a deeper complication of such streets" (59), is the pauper graveyard, the low point into which all things are resolving, the center of anonymity, putrefaction, and formlessness, the point at which Lady Dedlock at last becomes herself at the very moment of her death: "The gate was closed. Beyond it, was a burial-ground—a dreadful spot in which the night was very slowly stirring; but where I could dimly see heaps of dishonoured graves and stones, hemmed in by filthy houses, with a few dull lights in their windows, and on whose walls a thick humidity broke out like a disease. On the step at the gate, drenched in the fearful wet of such a place, which oozed and splashed down everywhere, I saw, with a cry of pity and horror, a woman lying—Jenny, the mother of the dead child" (59). But the woman is, of course, really Lady Dedlock, herself the mother of a dead child, the child Esther might have been. That Lady Dedlock's death is in a way a liberation is suggested by her contrary movements during her flight out from the city and then back toward its dark center. At the extremity of her outward flight she sends her surrogate, the brickmaker's wife, on out into the open country to lead her pursuers astray. This woman, in her movement toward freedom and openness, is Lady Dedlock's representative only because Lady Dedlock herself voluntarily chooses to return to her destined death at Nemo's grave, or, rather, to her death at a place where she is still shut off by one final symbolic barrier, the closed gate, from union with her dead lover. In assuming at last the self she has been fleeing for so long, Lady Dedlock achieves the only kind of freedom possible in Dickens' world, the freedom to be one's destined self, the Kierkegaardian freedom to will to accept oneself as what one already irrevocably is.

But for most of the characters, even such a narrow freedom is not possible. Their decomposition happens to them, rather than being chosen, and the image for their final end is not even permitted the hint of life-giving regeneration suggested by Lady Dedlock's melting from her frozen state. Their lives are single cases of a vast process of disintegration into dust, and the entire world of the novel is being transformed into "ashes . . . falling on ashes, and dust on dust" (39):

> In his lowering magazine of dust, the universal article into which his papers and himself, and all his clients, and all things of earth, animate and inanimate, are resolving, Mr. Tulkinghorn sits at one of the open windows. . . . (22)

A. O. J. COCKSHUT

[Order and Madness in *Bleak House*]†

Bleak House begins, as everyone knows, in a fog. And probably most readers have felt that this was important. There is an obvious and explicit connection between this fog and the mental fog of the law courts. But there is also something more. The world of *Bleak House* is a world in which no problem is really faced, in which nothing is understood, in which the meaning of words has decayed. Hints of this come early: "Another ruined suitor, who periodically appears from Shropshire, and breaks out into efforts to address the Chancellor at the close of the day's business, and who can by no means be made to understand that the Chancellor is legally ignorant of his existence after making it desolate for a quarter of a century. . . ."

They are all in the same boat. Normal distinctions of judgment, intelligence, even of sanity, break down. The Lord Chancellor does not understand. Jo, the crossing sweeper, does not understand. The mad Miss Flite doesn't understand. Even the excellent Jarndyce completely mistakes the character of Harold Skimpole.

It is this universal threat of uncertainty, of course, that surrounds with an aura of horror the people who are generally agreed to be crazy. Miss Flite, with her "judgment on the Day of Judgment," Krook, with his insane parody of the Lord Chancellor, are, in a sense, right. They estimate the probable working of the legal system more accurately than do the sensible men. Their madness can be seen as a window upon a strange world of sanity. Yet it is madness all the same. We are reminded of the mad characters in Jacobean plays. There is hardly a parallel in the Victorian period.

Yet all this was achieved without any sacrifice of that marvellous vividness in the presentation of physical objects and of peculiarities of behaviour, which Dickens had possessed from the first. The fog is at once the most actual and the most symbolical of all fogs.

By making some of the bitterest opponents of the legal system crazy, Dickens extended the range of his social criticism. He was very prone to fits of impotent irritation and superficial reforming zeal. Temperamentally, he may have been inclined to condemn all the abuses and anomalies of law in a lump as manifestly absurd. But in *Bleak House* he has passed beyond this point. In a world of such uncertainty even law courts may be suspected of having some positive value. However, this is revealed only gradually.

† From A. O. J. Cockshut, *The Imagination of Charles Dickens*, © 1961 by A. O. J. Cockshut. Reprinted by permission of New York University Press and Collins Publishers, London.

The point at which Dickens most obviously emerges from his habit of condemning authority and order without reservation is in the character of Skimpole. Skimpole is the answer to the question, which the younger Dickens would never have thought of asking: "What would Pickwick be like if he had no money?" Skimpole is portrayed with all the bitterness of personal disillusionment. Skimpole had, as it were, taken in Dickens himself, for he was peculiarly susceptible to the cant of a false generosity, as are most men, who, like him, are avaricious and ashamed of being avaricious. So Skimpole's talk has that peculiar note of being just too convincing to be true.

> He had no objection to honey, he said, but he protested against the overweening assumptions of Bees. He didn't at all see why the busy Bee should be proposed as a model to him; he supposed that the Bee liked to make honey, or he wouldn't do it—nobody asked him. It was not necessary for the Bee to make such a merit of his tastes. If every confectioner went buzzing about the world, banging against everything that came in his way, egotistically calling upon everybody to take notice that he was going to his work and must not be interrupted, the world would be quite an insupportable place.

This passage comes in Chapter 8, which is called "Covering a Multitude of Sins." It is a packed and fascinating chapter, containing Mr. Jarndyce's attack on Wiglomeration and a study of the slow, self-righteous workings of official charity. The chapter achieves an extraordinary balance. It contains in miniature the forces which prevent the book as a whole from being just a cheap attack on the legal system. It is as if truth lay undetected in the midst of three kinds of error—official justice, official charity, and the bogus, informal good will of Skimpole, which can appear to the unwary eye so very like a viable alternative to the other horrors.

Skimpole's "good nature" is a kind of mirror-image of Jarndyce's. And it is significant that Jarndyce cannot see through him, while Esther easily does so. Skimpole stands as a monument to the hard-won fairness of mind of a man naturally prejudiced, the creation of a natural individualist unwillingly convinced of the need for routine, order and restraint. And this conviction came to its full development just when he was attacking the most absurd of all embodiments of these venerable ideas, the Court of Chancery. And on the opposite side, there is a moving, though much less noticeable monument to the same new feelings—the figure of Neckett, the bailiff, whom Skimpole named Coavinses. Skimpole airily tells Jarndyce of his death: Coavinses has been arrested by the great Bailiff. He will never do violence to the sunshine any more." Jarndyce goes to inquire about Neckett's orphaned children, and asks a local boy whether

Neckett was industrious. " 'Was Neckett?' said the boy. 'Yes, wery much so. He was never tired of watching. He'd set upon a post at a street corner, eight or ten hours at a stretch, if he undertook to do it.' " And Jarndyce comments, "He might have done worse, he might have undertaken to do it, and not done it."

Neckett represents routine, law and order in their basest, but still genuine form, just as the Jarndyce case itself shows them at their most pompous and absurd. And behind Neckett stands his family ("Three children. No mother. And that Coavinses' profession. Being unpopular. The rising Coavinses. Were at a considerable disadtage."), and the unexpected forces of a more spontaneous life. It takes a big man to think of such things in the middle of an angry attack on legal forms. In view of all this even Mr. Kenge's fantastic justification of the Chancery system acquires a certain hollow dignity.

Neckett gives a hint of an important moment in Dickens's development. Even in *Oliver Twist* and in the early chapters of *David Copperfield* written not long before, evil had remained mainly an external threat. The lost solitary fugitive, hemmed in by dark powers, is (along with his fantastic humour) Dickens's main contribution to the mythology of literature. By this I mean the ideas which an author's name suggests to people who have hardly read him. But in *Bleak House* we get something new, only faintly foreshadowed in a few scenes of *The Old Curiosity Shop* and *Barnaby Rudge*. The evil without does not only threaten and pursue; it now calls out to the evil within, and sometimes finds a ready answer. Consequently, a new value is seen to reside in the "undickensian" ideas of order, restraint, convention of which Neckett is the lowest and dullest, and therefore the most impressive representative. The correspondence of outer and inner evil appears first casually in tiny details:

"Although the morning was raw, and although the fog still seemed heavy—I say seemed, for the windows were so encrusted with dirt, that they would have made midsummer sunshine dim ——" It occurs more strikingly in Chapter 14, where incurable delusion is placed squarely beside monstrous oppression. On one side are Miss Flite's birds, with their terrifying list of names, representing the practices and victims of Chancery—"Hope, Joy, Youth, Peace, Rest, Life, Dust, Ashes, Waste, Want, Ruin, Despair, Madness, Death, Cunning, Folly, Words, Wigs, Rags, Sheepskin, Plunder, Precedent, Jargon, Gammon and Spinach." (This has some claim to be called the best list in literature.) But in the same chapter and in the same house is Krook, the sham Chancellor, who won't allow himself to be taught to read, because someone might teach him wrong and "I'd rather trust my own self than another." Dickens had always been aware of obsessions, but usually in the past he had been concerned with their superficial humorous side. If we compare Mr. Dick's obsession with Krook's, the difference will be obvious. The satirical attack on the legal system is strengthened rather than weakened by this new balance, and new respect for order.

W. J. HARVEY

[The Double Narrative of *Bleak House*]†

* * * *Bleak House* is for Dickens a unique and elaborate experiment in narration and plot composition. It is divided into two intermingled and roughly concurrent stories; Esther Summerson's first-person narrative and an omniscient narrative told consistently in the historic present. The latter takes up thirty-four chapters; Esther has one less. Her story, however, occupies a good deal more than half the novel. The reader who checks the distribution of these two narratives against the original part issues will hardly discern any significant pattern or correlation. Most parts contain a mixture of the two stories; one part is narrated entirely by Esther and five parts entirely by the omniscient author. Such a check does, however, support the view that Dickens did not, as is sometimes supposed, use serial publication in the interest of crude suspense. A sensational novelist, for example, might well have ended a part issue with Chapter 31; Dickens subdues the drama by adding another chapter to the number. The obvious exception to this only proves the rule; in the final double number the suspense of Bucket's search for Lady Dedlock is heightened by cutting back to the omniscient narrative and the stricken Sir Leicester. In general, however, Dickens's control of the double narrative is far richer and subtler than this. Through this technique, as I shall try to show, he controls the immense, turbulent and potentially confusing material of his novel. Indeed, the narrative method seems to me to be part of the very substance of *Bleak House*, expressive of what, in the widest and deepest sense, the novel is about.

Let us first examine the structural functions of Esther Summerson and her narrative. Esther has generally been dismissed as insipid, one of Dickens's flat, non-comic good characters, innocent of imaginative life, more of a moral signpost than a person. Even if we accept this general judgment we may still find good reaons why Dickens had necessarily to sacrifice vitality or complexity here in

† From W. J. Harvey, *Character and the Novel*, © W. J. Harvey 1965. Reprinted by permission of Cornell University Press, Mrs. M. A. Harvey, and Chatto and Windus Ltd.

order to elaborate or intensify other parts of his novel. If Dickens, far from failing to create a lively Esther, is deliberately suppressing his natural exuberance in order to create a flat Esther, then we may properly consider one of Esther's functions to be that of a brake, controlling the runaway tendency of Dickens's imagination—controlling, in other words, the impulse to episodic intensification.

Can we possibly accept this view? The contrasting styles of the two narratives, while they offer the reader relief and variety, also seem to me evidence of Dickens's control in making Esther what she is, even at the risk of insipidity and dullness. The omniscient style has all the liveliness, fantastication and poetic density of texture that we typically associate with Dickens. Esther's narrative is plain, matter-of-fact, conscientiously plodding. Only very rarely does her style slip and allow us to glimpse Dickens guiding her pen—as when, for instance, she observes "Mr. Kenge, standing with his back to the fire, and casting his eyes over the dusty hearthrug as if it were Mrs. Jellyby's biography" (Chapter 4), or when, as Turveydrop bows to her, she could "almost believe I saw creases come into the white of his eyes" (Chapter 14). Here one may glimpse Dickens chafing at his self-imposed discipline. Such moments apart, any stylistic vivacity or idiosyncrasy in Esther's prose comes from the oddities and foibles of other characters. Dickens imagines them; Esther merely reports them. Even when, at moments of emotional stress, her prose strays into the purple patch, one still feels that this is the rhetoric of an amateur, not to be compared, for instance, with the controlled crescendo of Jo's death. Similarly, whenever the straightforward flow of Esther's narratives falters—as in her over-casual mention of Allan Woodcourt at the end of Chapter 14—we prefer to see this as appropriate to her character rather than to spot Dickens signalling a new relationship to us behind her back. That, of course, is precisely what he is doing, but the disguise of style persuades us to focus on Esther and not on her creator. (There is, I think, a corresponding and quite remarkable impersonality about the omniscient narrative. The general impression is of a vast, collective choric voice brilliantly mimicking the varied life it describes, yet able to generalize and comment without lapsing into the idiom of one man, of Dickens himself. Obviously the style exploits and manipulates our sympathies; yet surprisingly rarely do we feel that Dickens is directly buttonholing us.)

As I have said, the two narratives are *roughly* concurrent. Deliberately so; Dickens juggles the two chronologies by keeping the details sufficiently vague. Only rarely do we feel any awkwardness in this temporal matching together and any obvious discontinuity generally has a specific narrative or dramatic point. Esther's tale, taken in isolation, plods forward in the simplest kind of sequence. Yet, being autobiographical, it is retrospective and was written, so we are told, at the very end, seven years after the main events. This simplicity is rarely disturbed; only occasionally does Esther sound the note of "If I had known then what I know now"; only occasionally does she throw an anticipatory light forward into the shadowy future of her tale as, for example, she does at the end of Chapter 37. The reason is that, despite the retrospective nature of her story, Esther must *seem* to be living in a dramatic present, ignorant of the plot's ramifications. Dickens is *really* omniscient in the other narrative; godlike he surveys time as though it were an eternal present and Esther must seem to belong to that present. It is a convention most readers readily accept.

In what ways does Esther's tale throw light on its teller? During his later period Dickens showed considerable interest in the possibilities of the first-person narrative. In some cases—*David Copperfield, Great Expectations*—the adult narrator judges implicitly or explicitly, his growth towards maturity. Esther is clearly not in this category; she swiftly advances from child to woman and scarcely changes at all. We feel that she was "born old"—a feeling reflected in the nicknames given her, though in fact she is little older than Ada Clare. On the other hand, she cannot be classed with Miss Wade, of *Little Dorrit,* whose story is taken by some critics as an early exercise in that kind of point-of-view technique which dramatizes a limited or crippled consciousness so that what is conveyed to the reader differs radically from the intention of the narrator. Clearly, we are meant to take Esther on trust. If what she tells us is wrong or limited this signifies no moral blindspot in her, no flaw in her sensibility but only her necessary innocence of the full ramifications of the plot. Dickens's treatment of Esther is devoid of irony. We have only to imagine what narrative would have resulted if the teller had been Skimpole—or even Richard Carstone—to see that Esther's responses, attitudes, and actions are never qualified or criticized. She is, in short, thoroughly idealized.

One result of the idealizing process is the static nature of Esther's character, the essentials of which we quickly come to know. These never change; her story merely exhibits them in a variety of situations in which she is generally the patient rather than the agent. That is, Esther *does* very little in the sense of initiating a chain of actions by a deliberate choice. Things are done to her or because of her rather than by her. Devastating things happen to Esther from the moment of her birth, but she generally emerges with her usual placidity and acceptance of duty. Indeed, at times Dickens takes care to subdue the effect on the reader of these crises through which Esther as patient must pass. The chapter which deals, for example, with the recognition scene between Esther and her mother closes in fact with Esther's reunion with Ada. The curious thing is the feelings aroused by the Esther–Ada relationship seem more intense—and intensely rendered—than those aroused by the Esther–Lady Dedlock encounter.

Esther then is static, consistent, passive. She is also good. The difficulties of combining these qualities to produce a compelling character are so immense that we should wonder not that Dickens fails, but that his failure is so slight. Still, he does fail. The exigencies of the narrative force him to reveal Esther's goodness in a coy and repellent manner; she is, for instance, continually imputing to others qualities which the author transparently wishes us to transfer to her. Esther's goodness is most acceptable when she is least conscious of its effects radiating out to impinge on others. Similarly, her narrative is most acceptable when she is pushed from the centre of the stage by the typical inhabitants of the Dickens world. Happily, this is usually so. In other words, Dickens has to reconcile in Esther the demands of a narrator and a main character and he chooses to subdue Esther as a character in the interests of her narrative function. We do not, so to speak, look *at* Esther; we look *through* her at the teeming Dickensian world. This viewpoint is no Jamesian dramatization of a particular consciousness; Esther is as lucid and neutral as a clear window. We look through at a human landscape but we are not, as with James, constantly aware that the window is limited by its frame or that it has a scratch here and an opaque spot there. The penalty Dickens pays for this is the insipidity of Esther's character. But then, *Bleak House* is a thickly populated novel; each character claims his own share of attention and all are connected by a complicated series of interlocking actions. There is no single centre, no Jamesian *disponible*; rather we have a complex field of force, of interacting stresses and strains. Given this complication it would be too much to ask of the reader that he concentrate on the perceiver as well as the perceived. Were Esther to be complicated the novel would have to be correspondingly simplified and the Dickens world depopulated. Who would wish it so? If the real subject-matter of a novel is a subtly dramatized consciousness then the objects of that consciousness will tend to the sparse refinements of the closet drama. Dickens is the opposite of this; he is to Shakespeare as James is to Racine.

While this, I hope, explains the necessary limitations of Esther's character, it only pushes the real problem one stage further back. Why was it necessary to have a narrator of this kind at all? Any adequate answer must also take into account the omniscient narrative as well. The two narratives are the systole and diastole of the novel and between them they produce the distinctive effect of *Bleak House*; something that I can only call, in a crudely impressionistic manner, the effect of *pulsation*, of constant expansion and contraction, radiation and convergence.

The famous first chapter of *Bleak House* has had more than its fair share of critical attention; at the risk of tedium, therefore, I wish to isolate two striking features of Dickens's method. The omniscient eye which surveys the scene is like the lens of a film camera in its mobility. It may encompass a large panoramic view or, within a sentence, it may swoop down to a close scrutiny of some character or local detail. Closely related to this mobility is the constant expansion and contraction from the omniscient eye to Esther's single viewpoint. Closely related again is the constant expansion and contraction of the total narrative; now concentrating at great length on some episode, now hustling the plot along with a rapid parade of characters. Dickens's narrative skill is nowhere more evident than in his control of tempo.

All this I mean by *pulsation*. But Chapter 1 displays yet another related effect. The scene contracts to the Court of Chancery at the heart of the fog, but suddenly this process is reversed; Chancery monstrously expands to encompass the whole country:

> This is the Court of Chancery; which has its decaying houses and its blighted lands in every shire; which has its worn-out lunatic in every madhouse, and its dead in every churchyard. . . .

The heart of Chancery in this respect is Tom All Alone's the breeding-ground of disease (again the radiation of infection). The two are appropriately linked, for Chancery *is* a disease and is constantly described in these terms.

This theme is, of course, abundantly worked out in the novel—in Miss Flite, in Gridley, and above all, in Richard Carstone. The idea of corruption radiating out from a rotten centre (Chancery *and* Tom All Alone's) is reflected, in geographical terms, in the constant to-and-fro movement betweeen London, Bleak House, and Chesney Wold. But this idea is counterpointed, in plot terms, by the sense one has of convergence, especially the sense of something closing-in on Lady Dedlock. Geography and plot coalesce in the final constriction of the chase and the discovery of Lady Dedlock dead near her lover's tomb.

This pulsation, this interaction of radiation and convergence, is also temporal. The case of Jarndyce and Jarndyce does not merely fan out in the present to enmesh innocent and remote people; it also has a terrible history:

> Innumerable children have been born into the cause; innumerable young people have married into it; innumerable old people have died out of it. Scores of persons have deliriously found

themselves made parties in Jarndyce and Jarndyce, without knowing how or why; whole families have inherited legendary hatreds with the suit.

Diverse pressures from the past converge to mould the present; Jarndyce and Jarndyce bears down on Richard Carstone; the past catches up with Esther and finally with her mother. This temporal convergence is reflected in the structure of the novel as a whole and locally, in its parts. Thus the first chapter given to Esther (Chapter 3) quickly brings us from her childhood back to the dramatic present already described in the omniscient first chapter. Sometimes the dramatic present is illuminated by a shaft driven back into the past; thus both Boythorn and Miss Barbary are in some sense enlarged by the revelation of their abortive love long ago. Or again, the dramatic present will be left unexplained until time has passed and many pages have been turned; thus, on a small scale, the mystery of Jo's disappearance from Bleak House or, on a large scale, Bucket's uncovering of Tulkinghorn's murderess.

Granted the extremely complicated tangle of effects I have labelled *pulsation*, the desirability of a simple, lucid, straightforward narrative such as Esther's should be obvious. It offers us stability, a point of rest in a flickering and bewildering world, the promise of some guidance through the labyrinth. The usual novel may be compared to a pebble thrown into a pool; we watch the ripples spread. But in *Bleak House* Dickens has thrown in a whole handful of pebbles and what we have to discern is the immensely complicated tracery of half-a-dozen circles expanding, meeting, interacting. Esther —to change the metaphor—has the stability of a gyroscope; by her we chart our way.

She is, of course, much more than this. She is, as well, a moral touchstone; her judgments are rarely emphatic but we accept them. She can see Richard more clearly than Ada; through her Skimpole is revealed in his true colours and the Growlery becomes a sign of Jarndyce's obtuseness. She is also the known constant by which we judge all the other variables of character. Through her we can see the horrifyingly vivid notation of decay and infection that signals the slow process of Richard's destruction. (Among other things, the intertwining of the two narratives enables Dickens, drastically to foreshorten and mould the *apparent* time sequence here.) Again, by her consistency Esther contributes to the wonderfully skilful characterization of Sir Leicester and Guppy, who change by fits and starts throughout the novel. Because these characters demand very different reactions from us at different times we impute complexity and development to them. In fact they are not so much complex as discontinuous. Dickens's art lies in masking this discontinuity and Esther in large part provides a convincing façade; because she is a simple unity we are conjured into believing that the heterogeneity of Guppy or Sir Leicester is a unified complexity.

Finally—and perhaps most important—by intertwining the two narratives Dickens compels us to a double vision of the teeming, fantastic world of *Bleak House*. We—and Esther—are within; we—and the omniscient author—are outside. This double perspective forces us as readers to make connections which as I have said, because *we* make them have more validity than if Dickens had made them for us. The most crucial instance is Esther's ignorance of so much that surrounds her. What she sees she sees clearly; but she cannot see more than a fraction of the whole. In this she is not alone; one of the triumphs of the novel is the delicacy with which Dickens handles the knowledge, suspicions, guesses, and mistakes of the various characters. Some of them are limited to one or other of the narrative streams; Esther is never seen by the omniscient eye, nor does Tulkinghorn ever appear personally in Esther's narrative. This corresponds to their limited knowledge; Tulkinghorn, for all his plotting, never knows of Esther's relation to Lady Dedlock while there is no substantial evidence that Esther knows anything of her father until after her mother's death.

Granted this, the opportunities for dramatic irony are clearly enormous and it is to Dickens's credit as an artist that with great tact he refuses many of the chances for irony offered by the interlocking narratives. How close—all unknowing—is Esther to meeting her father during her first visit to Krook's? Yet we scarcely perceive this, even on a re-reading of the novel. A lesser artist would have wrung dry the irony of such an incident, but Dickens is sound in his refusal to do so. For the novel, as it stands, is so taut, so potentially explosive, that to expatiate on, or to underline, its implications would make it quite intolerable. Of course the irony is there but it is kept latent and, so to speak, subcritical; it does not explode in the reader's conscious attention. In this, of course, its effect is almost the opposite of that which I tried to analyse in *Death in Venice*. Mann's story depends largely on its insistently schematic nature, whereas Dickens's problem—like that of most novelists—is to avoid over-schematization, to control the complex and manifold life of the novel without drawing too much attention to the art involved. In this he is again helped by his chosen mode of narration. Through the double narrative Dickens refracts, reflects, varies, distorts, reiterates his major themes, and the disturbing resonance thus set up is expressive of his deepest sense of what life is like. *Bleak House* is so dense with examples of this process that I will quote only one, very minor example. In Chapter 25, Mrs. Snagsby is suspicious:

> Mrs. Snagsby screws a watchful glance on Jo, as he is brought into the little drawing-room by Guster. He looks at Mr. Snagsby the moment he comes in. Aha! Why does he look at Mr. Snagsby? Mr. Snagsby looks at him. Why should he do that, but that Mrs. Snagsby sees it all? Why else should that look pass between them; why else should Mr. Snagsby be confused, and cough a signal cough behind his hand. It is as clear as crystal that Mr. Snagsby is that boy's father.

Mrs. Snagsby's magnificent illogicality is a comic analogue, a parody of the dominant atmosphere of the book, that of hints, guesses, suspicions, conspiracies. It is also a distorted echo of one of the novel's major themes, that of parents and children. Even here, in an insignificant corner of the book, its major concerns are repeated and echoed in a different key; this abundance of doubling, paralleling, contrasting, this constant modulation from sinister to pathetic or comic, serves to create a density of life providing a context for those vivid scenes of episodic intensification. We accept these, take them on trust as more than brilliant but isolated moments, because we know they mesh with that complicated web of human affairs which entangles all the characters, even the most trivial. We weave this web, this pattern, as the tale shuttles to and fro between its two tellers and, of course, it is a pattern which gradually and continuously develops and emerges.[1]

H. M. DALESKI

[Transformation in a Sick Society]†

* * *

How radical, then, is Dickens's attack on mid-Victorian England? Commenting on the symbolism of Krook's death, Edgar Johnson says "the injustices of an unjust society" are no longer seen as "subjects for local cure or even amputation": "Nothing will do short of the complete annihilation that they will ultimately provide by blowing up of their own corruption";[1] while Monroe Engel (also in relation to Krook's "[dissolving] of spontaneous combustion") maintains that "a kind of inevitable dissolution is the hope", though "it is clear that Dickens has grave doubts that enough will happen by

1. See Bibliography (p. 986) for a list of essays discussing the effectiveness of Esther's role in what Harvey calls "the double narrative." [*Editors.*]

† From H. M. Daleski, *Dickens and the Art of Analogy*, copyright © 1970 by H. M. Daleski. Reprinted by permission of Shocken Books Inc., and Faber and Faber.

1. *Charles Dickens*, II, 782.

peaceful process."[2] It seems to me, however, that at this stage of his career (and *Bleak House* should be regarded as his first major attempt to come to grips with the society in which he lived) Dickens was neither as radical nor as pessimistic as these pronouncements suggest. Though it is true that the novel presents an image of possible social collapse—presenting it not alone through the death of Krook but through the equally representative deaths of Richard and Lady Dedlock and though the pervasive disease imagery—the collapse is neither prescribed nor hoped for. It is presented as a warning, a prophetic warning of what will inevitably come to pass if a stiff-necked people refuses to change its ways. But the way to change, to peaceful recuperation, as it were, is throughout presented as both clear and accessible.

Since the two major factors in the diagnosis of what has caused the corruption of Tom's blood are shown to be parasitism and the evasion of responsibility by properly constituted authority, it would seem to follow that all that is required in such a society is a readiness to make one's own way and to accept responsibility. Such, at any rate, is the cure apparently propounded in *Bleak House*. Anticipating Samuel Smiles, Dickens sets against the horde of parasites, as George H. Ford has pointed out,[3] some representative exemplars of self-help: the young Turveydrop, Rouncewell the ironmaster, Allan Woodcourt, and of course Esther Summerson. And against widespread dereliction he places the ubiquitous benevolence of Mr. Jarndyce. Since these characters epitomize qualities that Dickens may be taken to recommend, it is a drawback that they are not presented with greater imaginative vitality; Woodcourt, for instance, remaining pale for all his goodness, and the more robust presence of Mr. Jarndyce being a little too benign for ordinary flesh and blood. It is a further drawback that goodness should sometimes appear as the mask of the prig, as all too often in the case of Esther, or of smugness, as in the case of Rouncewell. Dickens, it seems, like so many artists, is more at home in the mud and mire and fog than in the pure empyrean. Nevertheless, the virtue of these characters, especially that of Mr. Jarndyce and Esther, has an important function in the novel.

Mr. Jarndyce is viewed as a kind of natural guardian (as other men are natural athletes), and he is called Guardian not alone by Esther but also by Ada (after Richard's death and at his insistence) and by Esther's children, who "know him by no other name" (67).[4] He is viewed, that is, as performing functions on a personal

2. *The Maturity of Dickens* (Cambridge, Mass., 1959), p. 122.
3. "Self-Help and the Helpless in *Bleak House*," *From Jane Austen to Joseph Conrad*, ed. Robert C. Rathburn and Martin Steinman (Minneapolis, 1958), pp. 97–100.
4. Quotations are identified by chapter numbers, supplied by the editors, rather than by the page numbers used by Mr. Daleski. [*Editors.*]

level that are supposedly fulfilled by institutions (such as Chancery and Parliament) on a national level. Characteristically, he takes responsibility for all the weak and the needy with whom he comes in contact, though the typical object of his attentions (the symbolic object) is the orphan. Thus it is that he successively takes responsibility for Esther, for Ada and Richard, for Charley and Coavinses' other children, and for Jo. And he does so, of course, without in any way neglecting other responsibilities, being strongly differentiated from Mrs. Jellyby, whose assumption of responsibility in regard to the families of those who are to cultivate coffee and educate the natives of Borrioboola-Gha covers a multitude of evasions in regard to her own family; and from Mrs. Pardiggle, who arms herself with uplifting tracts and "[pounces] upon the poor . . . applying benevolence to them like a strait-waistcoat" (30) while their children (as in the case of Jenny's baby) die round her; and he is equally differentiated from Harold Skimpole, who is only "a mere child in the world".

Mr. Jarndyce, moreover, typically helps those in need by enabling them to help themselves. "Trust in nothing but in Providence and your own efforts," he tells Richard (13); and it is in this spirit that he providentially offers his services to others—as in the case of Esther, the representative instance. He is no sooner aware of the predicament of the unknown orphan than he willingly assumes responsibility for her, but with the "expectation" that Conversation Kenge (inimitably) details:

> "Mr. Jarndyce," he pursued, "being aware of the—I would say, desolate—position of our young friend, offers to place her at a first-rate establishment; where her education shall be completed, where her comfort shall be secured, where her reasonable wants shall be anticipated, where she shall be eminently qualified to discharge her duty in that station of life unto which it has pleased—shall I say Providence?—to call her." . . .
>
> "Mr. Jarndyce," he went on, "makes no condition, beyond expressing his expectation that our young friend will not at any time remove herself from the establishment in question without his knowledge and concurrence. That she will faithfully apply herself to the acquisition of those accomplishments, upon the exercise of which she will be ultimately dependent. That she will tread in the paths of virtue and honour, and—the—a—so forth." (3)

What Mr. Jarndyce requires of Esther, we see, is quite simply that she keep faith with him, the expectation (and demonstration) of fidelity being as much a concomitant of the assumption of responsibility as betrayal is shown to be a consequence of its evasion. Having kept faith, Esther is rewarded not only by being given the chance to stand on her own feet but by being delegated her own area of responsibility: on becoming housekeeper at Bleak House, she stands looking at the basket of keys—the keys of office, as it were—with which she has been presented, "quite lost in the magnitude of [her] trust" (6).

Esther consolidates her position at Bleak House, becoming, as Skimpole puts it, "the very touchstone of responsibility":

> "Now when you mention responsibility," he resumed, "I am disposed to say, that I never had the happiness of knowing any one whom I should consider so refreshingly responsible as yourself. You appear to me to be the very touchstone of responsibility. When I see you, my dear Miss Summerson, intent upon the perfect working of the whole little orderly system of which you are the centre, I feel inclined to say to myself—in fact I do say to myself, very often—*that's* responsibility!" (37)

Skimpole's evasive pleasantry should not be taken to invalidate the truth of his description of Esther's position. His account of her achievement, indeed, suggests how central (from yet another point of view) Esther's role in the novel is. If her success at Bleak House (a success which is capped, if not crowned, by Mr. Jarndyce's proposal of marriage to her) sets her as far apart as her social class from Jo, the abandoned orphan of the slums who is lower than a drover's dog; we cannot help reflecting that it is to Tom-all-Alone's—or thereabouts—that she would certainly have gone on the death of Miss Barbary if not for the grace of Mr. Jarndyce. Esther's success (with Mr. Jarndyce's aid), that is, is meant to be representative of what can be done through a combination of effort and due assumption of responsibility. Moreover, having achieved "the perfect working of the whole little orderly system" of which she is the centre, and having achieved it through assuming responsibility in her turn, Esther also in effect demonstrates what is required for the efficient running of the "great country" and the "great system" of which Conversation Kenge boasts to Mr. Jarndyce, and of which Parliament and Chancery are the centres. Dickens, in other words, far from being a revolutionary, is calling in *Bleak House* for nothing more subversive than a change of housekeepers.

It is now clear, I think, why Dickens hesitated between a variant of Tom-all-Alone's and of Bleak House in choosing his title. Ruin and perfect system, disease and health—the question is which shall be bequeathed to the children of England. The choice of Bleak House as the title, the name of the house redeemed by Mr. Jarndyce from the ravages of Chancery, must be taken to point to the author's faith in the possibility of renovation, to his hope that a Jo, having made his way from Tom-all-Alone's to Bleak House, will find his permanent home there. Such a hope, of course, ignores the presence—even in a Bleak House—of a Skimpole. The Skimpoles remain impervious even to a Jarndyce; they are not willing to keep faith. It is only when Dickens perceives the limitations of Mr. Jarndyce's position, perceives the limits of his redemptive capacity, that he begins to think in terms of transformation rather than rehabilitation. In the closing pages of the novel we are given some idea of the kind of transformation he will steadily come to envisage: Esther reports that, despite the loss of her "old looks", her husband thinks she is "prettier" than she ever was (67). If it is Mr. Jarndyce's benevolence that counteracts the blight of her childhood, it is Woodcourt's love, we see, that transforms the blight of Chancery.

IAN OUSBY

The Broken Glass: Vision and Comprehension in *Bleak House*†

After the first glance, there were slight features in the midst of this crowd of objects, which sprung out from the mass without any reason, as it were, and took hold of the attention whether the spectator would or no. Thus, the revolving chimney-pots on one great stack of buildings seemed to be turning gravely to each other every now and then, and whispering the result of their separate observation of what was going on below. Others, of a crook-backed shape, appeared to be maliciously holding themselves askew, that they might shut the prospect out and baffle Todgers's. The man who was mending a pen at an upper window over the way, became of paramount importance in the scene, and made a blank in it, ridiculously disproportionate in its extent, when he retired. The gambols of a piece of cloth upon the dyer's pole had far more interest for the moment than all the changing motion of the crowd. Yet even while the looker-on felt angry with himself for this, and wondered how it was, the tumult swelled into a roar; the hosts of objects seemed to thicken and expand a hundredfold; and after gazing round him, quite scared, he turned into Todgers's again, much more rapidly than he came out; and ten to one he told M. Todgers afterwards that if he hadn't done so, he would certainly have come into the street by the shortest cut; that is to say, head-foremost.

Martin Chuzzlewit, "Town and Todgers's"

In classic pieces of Dickens criticism, both Dorothy Van Ghent

† From *Nineteenth-Century Fiction*, vol. 29, No. 4 (March, 1975), pp. 381–392. © 1975 by The Regents of the University of California. Reprinted by permission of The Regents and the author.

and J. Hillis Miller have singled out this passage from *Martin Chuzzlewit*—it describes the view from the roof of Todgers's, the boardinghouse where Mr. Pecksniff and his daughters stay in London—as crucial to Dickens' view of the relation between the observer and the scene that he attempts to comprehend.[1] The physical world, especially that complex and crowded urban world of which the Todgers's roof affords a bird's-eye view, poses disquieting problems of perception. Rather than presenting itself to the eye in a passive and orderly manner it takes on a fractious and menacing life of its own. The spectator quickly abandons any attempt to view the scene as a continuous and ordered whole, becomes fascinated by separate and unrelated details, and finally falls victim to a rising hysteria. As Miss Van Ghent and Miller suggest, these difficulties of perception recur throughout Dickens' work; the present essay will examine their role in *Bleak House*.

From the beginning, the narrative of *Bleak House* presupposes a correspondence between the external appearance of things and their inner condition. The physical muddle which the book's opening paragraphs evoke so powerfully is the outward manifestation of a deeper, moral disorder: a loss of coherence, vitality and connection. The characters' struggles to understand this disordered environment —and these form perhaps the book's central theme—are thus continually expressed through acts of perception in the simplest sense: they try to see the world clearly and to see it whole.

In this effort they are largely unsuccessful, for the world abounds in impediments to clear vision. In the opening description it is shrouded in fog and unnatural darkness. The soot-blackened landscape, the narrator remarks in the first of a sequence of apocalyptic images, appears to be in mourning "for the death of the sun"; even the gas lamps have "a haggard and unwilling look." The end of the second paragraph presents a vignette which typifies the condition of the characters, with their partial and inadequate view of their surroundings: "Chance people on the bridges peeping over the parapets into a nether sky of fog, with fog all round them, as if they were up in a balloon, and hanging in the misty clouds."

This evocation moves quickly from the general to the particular, from a description of nameless but typical inhabitants of London to the Court of Chancery, at once emblem and cause of the pervading malaise. Here, in a striking image, the Lord High Chancellor is seen, "addressed by a large advocate with great whiskers, a little

1. Dorothy Van Ghent, "The Dickens World: A View from Todgers's," *Sewanee Review*, 58 (1950), 419–38; and J. Hillis Miller, *Charles Dickens: The World of His Novels* (Cambridge, Mass.: Harvard Univ. Press, 1958), 116–18.

voice, and an interminable brief, and outwardly directing his contemplation to the lantern in the roof, where he can see nothing but fog" (1).[2] This obviously echoes, on smaller scale, the earlier image of a world deprived of the sun's light, and it aptly hints at that view of Chancery which the book is quick to develop in more explicit terms; for the Court's labyrinthine activities lack any guiding light, and they obscure rather than illuminate the subjects of their proceedings. This motif of defective vision reappears later in connection with the Court. At the opening of chapter 32, for example, the narrator notes of Lincoln's Inn: "From tiers of staircase windows, clogged lamps like the eyes of Equity, bleared Argus with a fathomless pocket for every eye and an eye upon it, dimly blink at the stars." The law has, moreover, the knack of reducing everything it touches to a similar state of sightlessness. Tom-All-Alone's, the property of Jarndyce versus Jarndyce, is, as Mr. Jarndyce describes it to Esther, "a street of perishing blind houses, with their eyes stoned out" (8).

The novel's second chapter follows the same structure as the first. It moves from an evocation of a typically deadened and debilitated landscape—this time the country seat of the Dedlocks, Chesney Wold—to a description of the dilemma of its inhabitants.[3] Here, as before, the link is accomplished by a description of the difficulties encountered by the characters in viewing their environment. After a marvelously rich and detailed account of the dank and gloomy family estate, the narrative shifts adroitly to Lady Dedlock's viewpoint: "The view from my Lady Dedlock's own windows is alternately a lead-coloured view, and a view in Indian ink" (2). A few sentences later the scene that Lady Dedlock observes is described in some detail:

> My Lady Dedlock (who is childless), looking out in the early twilight from her boudoir at a keeper's lodge, and seeing the light of a fire upon the latticed panes, and smoke rising from the chimney, and a child, chased by a woman, running out into the rain to meet the shining figure of a wrapped-up man coming through the gate, has been put quite out of temper. (2)

When the reader encounters this passage for the first time the parenthetical phrase serves adequately to account for her apparent detachment and her concealed chagrin. Childless herself, she can only be a silent and distant spectator of such domestic scenes. But when the passage is read in the light of the novel's denouement it

2. Quotations are identified by chapter numbers, supplied by the editors, rather than page numbers used by Mr. Ousby. [*Editors.*]

3. Compare my analysis of this scene with that offered by C. B. Cox, "A Dickens Landscape," *Critical Quarterly,* 2 (1960), 58–60. Cox argues that the decaying park of Chesney Wold and Lady Dedlock's distant prospect of it are emblems of her inner condition, "a sophisticated boredom which has lost all real contact with life."

takes on a more precise reference to her fate. The spectacle of the child "chased by a woman" recalls Lady Dedlock's separation from her illegitimate daughter, Esther Summerson. One further notes in chapter 18 that the lodge is actually the scene of Lady Dedlock's first interview with Esther.

If the lodgekeeper and his family form a suggestive tableau, its significance is increased by the fact that to Lady Dedlock it remains merely a tableau. She is separated from it by the window, and what she sees is in fact a picture, a "view in Indian ink." It is described in terms that make it the verbal counterpart of those dark and brooding plates with which "Phiz," the illustrator, punctuates the text. And if the modern reader is quick to see the scene as a visual symbol, it would to a Victorian audience have been strongly reminiscent of those popular narrative paintings—works like Arthur Hughes's "The Tryst" or Augustus Egg's "Past and Present"—which tell a melodramatic or sentimental story by means of small visual hints. Lady Dedlock, as her manner of frozen detachment would suggest, has become an outsider in her own life, merely a passive and helpless observer of her own fate.

Many of the other characters live, like Lady Dedlock, in attempted denial of their responsibilities; and in their case, too, this attitude is signified by their visual relation to the world around them. Mrs. Jellyby, full of charity towards misery abroad but indifferent towards misery at home, is, as the title of the chapter which introduces her warns, an exponent of "Telescopic Philanthropy." Esther notes at their first meeting:

> She was a pretty, very diminutive, plump woman, of from forty to fifty, with handsome eyes, though they had a curious habit of seeming to look a long way off. As if—I am quoting Richard again—they could see nothing nearer than Africa! (4)

Harold Skimpole, the eternally irresponsible child, is even more detached from his immediate environment. He continually withdraws from the messy entanglements of his personal life—his downtrodden family and his string of debts—to the dreamy contemplation of imagined scenes. His attitude to misery abroad is far more disturbing than Mrs. Jellyby's bossy philanthropy, for Skimpole views his imaginary scenes solely as objects of aesthetic appreciation:

> "Take the case of the Slaves on American plantations. I dare say they are worked hard, I dare say they don't altogether like it, I dare say theirs is an unpleasant experience on the whole; but they people the landscape for me, they give it a poetry for me, and perhaps that is one of the pleasanter objects of their existence." (18)

Commonly, however, people do not enjoy such detachment: they are irrevocably trapped in the thick of things. "I admired," Esther says of her first walk through London, "the long successions and varieties of streets, the quantity of people already going to and fro, the number of vehicles passing and repassing, the busy preparations in the setting forth of shop windows and the sweeping out of shops, and the extraordinary creatures in rags, secretly groping among the swept-out rubbish for pins and other refuse" (5). Obviously here "admire," to judge from Esther's tone, retains much of its secondary meaning of "to wonder at." For the physical world of *Bleak House*, like the view from the roof of Todgers's, is of a disordered variety which quickly bewilders the visual sense: Esther's first impression of the streets of London is that they are "in such a distracting state of confusion that I wondered how the people kept their senses" (3). Krook's shop is an apt emblem for the physical condition of things: an ill-lit assortment of items, hopelessly unrelated and disordered.

The characters can rarely attempt to view this dense "crowd of objects" clearly or completely. Like the "chance people on bridges" in the opening chapter, they are reduced to "peeping." In fact, the word "peep" echoes through the book, neatly conveying the partial and fragmented view of things which people usually achieve. Esther, for example, after her arrival at Bleak House, watches the dawn prospect from her window change "at every new peep" (8) and then decides to "take a peep at the garden" (8). Mrs. Snagsby, curious about Tulkinghorn's business with her husband (the lawyer is trying to find out where Nemo lives), "peeps at them through the window-blind" (10); and, shortly afterwards, at Nemo's death-bed, Miss Flite "peeps and trembles just within the door" (11). It is obviously no coincidence that the youngest member of the Jellyby family, a relentlessly curious and peripatetic child, should be named "Peepy."

The term "peep" suggests a childish inquisitiveness, or a timid and old-maidish activity. But in *Bleak House* curiosity can quickly take less innocuous forms. Krook, for example, leads an endlessly watchful life, casting rapacious glances on his visitors, Esther and the wards of Chancery, like the glances that his cat bestows on Miss Flite's birds. Similarly, Mademoiselle Hortense, Lady Dedlock's maid, has "a watchful way of looking out of the corners of her eyes without turning her head, which could be pleasantly dispensed with—especially when she is in ill-humour and near knives" (12). But this watchfulness bears scant results. In Hortense's case it is merely self-destructive; becoming embroiled in the mystery of Lady Dedlock's past, she first kills Tulkinghorn and then is herself trapped by the police detective, Inspector Bucket. Krook, for all his vigilance, can never make sense of this rubbish-heap of possessions. He cannot even learn to read the vital letters between Nemo and Lady Dedlock which he owns. Like the man on the roof at Todgers's, he can view individual details clearly enough, but can never understand the whole. Tony Jobling reports to Guppy: "He can make all the letters separately, and he knows most of them separately when he sees them; . . . but he can't put them together" (32).

The world of objects does not remain passive and inanimate under people's watchful gaze. As in the scene from *Martin Chuzzlewit*, it assumes a life of its own and becomes in its turn watchful. The family portraits in the Dedlock mansion, for example, are presented not simply as furniture or background but as a silent audience to the human drama. At times they share the well-bred but bewildered curiosity of the living Dedlocks themselves: "A staring old Dedlock in a panel, as large as life and as dull, looks as if he didn't know what to make of it—which was probably his general state of mind in the days of Queen Elizabeth" (12).[4] In a similar fashion the fire in the Lord Chancellor's room is described as a witness to the first meeting between Esther and the wards of Chancery, Richard Carstone and Ada Clare: "Our all three coming together for the first time, in such an unusual place, was a thing to talk about; and we talked about it; and the fire, which had left off roaring, winked its red eyes at us—as Richard said—like a drowsy old Chancery lion" (3). The image adds a nicely disquieting touch to an already ominous occasion. More obviously sinister is the way that the idea of the inanimate world assuming eyes is used in the scene where Tulkinghorn discovers Nemo's body: "No curtain veils the darkness of the night, but the discoloured shutters are drawn together; and through the two gaunt holes pierced in them, famine might be staring in—the Banshee of the man upon the bed" (10).

At this point the world of things seems to form a silent conspiracy, possibly hostile but at least indifferent to the fate of its human inhabitants. The sense that landscapes, especially the landscape of the city, represent an alien and baffling system pervades the book. The spectator is continually presented with a labyrinth to which he has lost—if indeed he ever possessed—the clue. In this respect Jo, the book's naked unaccommodated man, suffers from an extreme form of a problem which plagues most of the other characters. Jo's illiteracy makes him utterly unable to detect any meaning or order in the surrounding world, let alone any benevolent relation to himself:

> It must be a strange state to be like Jo! To shuffle through the streets, unfamiliar with the shapes, and in utter darkness as to the meaning, of those mysterious symbols, so abundant over the

4. Compare J. R. Harvey's useful account of the role played by pictures in *Bleak House* in *Victorian Novelists and Their Illustrators* (London: Sidgwick and Jackson, 1970), pp. 156–57.

> shops, and at the corners of streets, and on the doors, and in the windows! To see people read, and to see people write, and to see the postman deliver letters, and not to have the least idea of all that language—to be, to every scrap of it, stone blind and dumb! (25)

Shortly after this passage the narrator, still implicitly reconstructing Jo's outlook, speaks of the bewildering and hectic activity of the city in a significant image: "The town awakes; the great tee-totum is set up for its daily spin and whirl; all that unaccountable reading and writing, which has been suspended for a few hours, recommences" (25). Very often unaccountable visual spectacles present themselves to the looker-on as a whirling circular motion; the effect is to create giddiness, much as the view from the roof of Todgers's produced vertigo. In chapter 56, for example, Inspector Bucket makes a number of rapid deductions about the paralyzed Sir Leicester Dedlock's wishes concerning the missing Lady Dedlock and proceeds equally quickly to act upon them. His behavior is incomprehensible to Mrs. Rouncewell, the Dedlock family housekeeper: "Mrs. Rouncewell, who holds the light, is giddy with the swiftness of his eyes and hands, as he starts up, furnished for his journey." The same idea is repeated a little later in describing the confusion and helplessness of Sir Leicester after his wife's disappearance: "He withdraws his hand, and falls to looking at the sleet and snow again, until they seem, by being long looked at, to fall so thick and fast, that he is obliged to close his eyes for a minute on the giddy whirl of white flakes and icy blots" (58).

Esther Summerson, the novel's heroine, experiences a similar "hallucinatory incoherence"[5] as she falls asleep on the evening after her arrival in London:

> At first I was painfully awake, and vainly tried to lose myself, with my eyes closed, among the scenes of the day. At length, by slow degrees, they became indistinct and mingled. I began to lose the identity of the sleeper [Caddy Jellyby] resting on me. Now it was Ada; now, one of my old Reading friends from whom I could not believe I had so recently parted. Now, it was the little mad woman worn out with curtseying and smiling; now, some one in authority at Bleak House. Lastly, it was no one, and I was no one. (4)

Of course, this has much of the after-supper dream about it: it is a kaleidoscopic version of the visual impressions left by Esther's first day in London. But, in a deeper sense, it also reflects the confusion and ignorance about her identity and her surroundings from which Esther suffers, and which are especially relevant at this point in her

5. The phrase is used by Miller, p. 163, in connection with the description of fog which begins the book.

life. She has been brought up in ignorance of her real parentage by her aunt, Miss Barbary, and she is now passing through London on her way to meet for the first time her guardian, Mr. Jarndyce, and to become the housekeeper of Bleak House.

The growth of Esther's understanding of herself and her past is one of the book's main movements. Dickens' preoccupation with how his characters see their surroundings plays a crucial role in his description of her *Bildung*: Esther's development is signified by moments of progressively clear vision of the world around her. If she begins with a muddled and unclear view of her surroundings, typical of the characters in the novel, she quickly begins to transcend this condition. At the end of the book the inner and outer disorder of the world still remains, but Esther herself has become a testament to the power of the individual to achieve a clear-sightedness which is at once literal and metaphorical.

Shortly after the moment of "hallucinatory incoherence" mentioned above, Esther moves from London and the Jellyby household to Bleak House. The change wrought by her establishment in this friendly and life-giving atmosphere is neatly imaged in an account of the view from her bedroom window which greets her when she wakens at Bleak House for the first time:

> It was interesting when I dressed before daylight, to peep out of window, where my candles were reflected in the black panes like two beacons, and, finding all beyond still enshrouded in the indistinctness of last night, to watch how it turned out when the day came on. As the prospect gradually revealed itself, and disclosed the scene over which the wind had wandered in the dark, like my memory over my life; I had a pleasure in discovering the unknown objects that had been around me in my sleep. At first they were faintly discernible in the mist, and above them the later stars still glimmered. That pale interval over, the picture began to enlarge and fill up so fast, that, at every new peep, I could have found enough to look at for an hour. Imperceptibly, my candles became the only incongruous part of the morning, the dark places in my room all melted away, and the day shone bright upon a cheerful landscape, prominent in which the old Abbey Church, with its massive tower, threw a softer train of shadow on the view than seemed compatible with its rugged character. (8)

Inevitably, the scene is reminiscent of that first view of Lady Dedlock looking out on the park of Chesney Wold. However, Esther and Lady Dedlock have very different perceptions of the world outside their windows. The prospect before Lady Dedlock exists merely as a set of static, frozen vignettes. Esther, by contrast, looks out upon a landscape in a process of continual and orderly change—a change, moreover, which continually enlarges and clarifies her view. Where Lady Dedlock remains a detached and distant observer, Esther, immediately after the quoted passage, is shown going out to explore and to become a part of the landscape she has seen from a distance.

Of course, her development is far from complete at this point, for she has yet to learn the identity of her parents. The solution to that mystery begins to emerge during her visit to Boythorn when she sees Lady Dedlock in the local church. Esther's response is a semi-conscious recognition of Lady Dedlock's resemblance to herself and to Miss Barbary: "But why her face should be, in a confused way, like a broken glass to me, in which I saw scraps of old remembrances . . . I could not think" (18). Shortly after this she falls ill of the disease unwittingly brought to Bleak House by Jo. As is common in Dickens' fiction, the illness signifies an important crisis in the sufferer's life: Esther emerges from it tested and matured, ready for her recognition scene with Lady Dedlock.

After her recovery the smallpox scars are the visible symbol of how much Esther has changed; but while the illness runs its course its main effect is to make her blind. It is quite literally a dark night of the soul. Esther is separated from contact with her usual surroundings and deprived of her bearings:

> Before I had been confined to it [her sickroom] many days, everything else seemed to have retired into a remote distance, where there was little or no separation between the various stages of my life which had been really divided by years. In falling ill, I seemed to have crossed a dark lake, and to have left all my experiences, mingled together by the great distance, on the healthy shore. (35)

In her blindness she experiences dreams rather like that kaleidoscope of impressions quoted earlier. Here, however, the dreaming is a vital and necessary contact with her imagination: shut off from the physical world, she inhabits a "pure culture" in which she can work out the problem of her relation with Lady Dedlock.

Two visual images dominate her dreams. The first, that of the staircase, signifies her own laborious progress towards the truth about her identity. The second is more complex:

> Dare I hint at that worse time when, strung together somewhere in great black space, there was a flaming necklace, or ring, or starry circle of some kind, of which *I* was one of the beads! And when my only prayer was to be taken off from the rest, and when it was such inexplicable agony and misery to be a part of the dreadful thing? (35)

From her first appearance Lady Dedlock has been associated with imagery of stars and of jewelry. The world of fashion to which she belongs is, the narrator suggests when he first describes it, "a world wrapped up in too much jeweller's cotton and fine wool, and cannot hear the rushing of the larger worlds, and cannot see them as they circle round the sun" (2). The idea of the necklace and its component beads, moreover, suggests that notion of vital interrelation implied by the denouement of the Esther Summerson–Lady Dedlock plot and explicitly enforced by the novel's larger theme of social responsibility.

The idea of blindness, then, and of visually symbolic dreams is essential to Esther's realization of her true identity. This process, however, is not complete until near the end of the book when, after the long coach journey with Inspector Bucket, she is brought to see the body of her mother at the graveyard where her father, Nemo, is buried. During this journey Esther's incomprehension of her situation is repeatedly indicated through her visual relation to her surroundings. The experience seems like a dream to her and, just as she had earlier gone blind, she here lapses into a confused and partial perception of the city landscape through which she is traveling:

> We rattled with great rapidity through such a labyrinth of streets, that I soon lost all idea where we were; except that we had crossed and recrossed the river, and still seemed to be traversing a low-lying, waterside, dense neighbourhood of narrow thoroughfares, chequered by docks and basins, high piles of warehouses, swing-bridges, and masts of ships. (57)

Inspector Bucket, the police detective who leads the search for Lady Dedlock and who accompanies Esther on the coach ride, is an ideal guide, and not merely because of the ready sympathy he shows for her suffering. Almost alone among the characters in the book, he is clear and confident in his perceptions of the world around him. The confused and variegated spectacle of the city holds no terrors for him, as this description of his behavior at Tulkinghorn's funeral shows: "He has a keen eye for a crowd—as for what not?—and looking here and there, now from this side of the carriage, now from the other, now up at the house windows, now along the people's heads, nothing escapes him" (53). Bucket, indeed, can transcend the partial viewpoint to which most of the characters are limited and see the world from a godlike eminence like that enjoyed by the third-person narrator. His speculations about the whereabouts of Lady Dedlock are described in a significant image:

> He mounts a high tower in his mind, and looks out far and wide. Many solitary figures he perceives, creeping through the streets; many solitary figures out on heaths, and roads, and lying under

> haystacks. But the figure that he seeks is not among them. Other solitaries he perceives, in nooks of bridges, looking over; and in shadowed places down by the river's level; and a dark, dark, shapeless object drifting with the tide, more solitary than all, clings with a drowning hold on his attention. (56)

Bucket, then, is Esther's guide in metaphorical as well as literal ways: he is her mentor in the last stage of her progress towards self-realization. For what he leads her to at the end of the tortuous journey through London is a picture, or *tableau mort*, for her to look at and understand: "I saw before me, lying on the step, the mother of the dead child. She lay there, with one arm creeping round a bar of the iron gate, and seeming to embrace it" (59). This is obviously a counterpart to that earlier tableau of the lodgekeeper, his wife and child which Lady Dedlock had viewed from her window at Chesney Wold. Like the earlier scene, the scene at the graveyard tells a story: it shows Lady Dedlock vainly trying to break through the barrier that separates her from her dead lover. Even the minor appurtenances of the scene are heavily symbolic: the night is just beginning to yield to the dawn, and the ice (Lady Dedlock's frozen detachment)[6] is beginning to melt. The tableau represents a moment of clarity and order amidst confusion, and it completes Esther's education. It symbolizes her family history which, once properly understood, loses its sinister and destructive power over the present. For Esther, indeed, the scene holds a promise indicated by the title of a later chapter in the book: "Beginning the World."

6. See Miller, pp. 203–4, for a useful discussion of the images of freezing and melting associated with Lady Dedlock.

Bibliography

I

The Dickens section of *The New Cambridge Bibliography of English Literature* (1969), compiled by Philip Collins, provides a comprehensive list of various kinds of writings about Dickens. For an assessment of such writings, see Ada Nisbet's survey in *Victorian Fiction: A Guide to Research* (ed. Lionel Stevenson, 1964, pp. 44–153), and for writings since 1962 see the forthcoming survey by Philip Collins in *Victorian Fiction: A Second Guide to Research* (ed. George Ford). See also *A Bibliography of Dickensian Criticism, 1836–1975* (ed. R. C. Churchill, 1975). For checklists of recent studies, since 1970, see *Dickens Studies Newsletter.*

II

The two most important full-scale biographies are John Forster's *Charles Dickens* (with annotations by J. W. T. Ley, 1928), and Edgar Johnson's *Charles Dickens* (1952). Angus Wilson's *The World of Charles Dickens* (1970) combines a pictorial biography with a critical study. For a special aspect of Dickens' character, see Fred Kaplan, *Dickens and Mesmerism* (1975). Also informative are *The Speeches of Charles Dickens* (ed. K. J. Fielding, 1960); *Uncollected Writings from "Household Words"* (ed. Harry Stone, 1968); and *Charles Dickens: The Public Readings* (ed. Philip Collins, 1975). The Pilgrim edition of Dickens' letters (eds. Madeline House, Graham Storey, and Kathleen Tillotson) will eventually comprise twelve volumes. Already three have been published (1965, 1970, 1974).

III

From the large store of general critical studies of Dickens' novels, the following chronological listing represents only a selective sampling, and it omits books that have been cited elsewhere in the present edition, such as H. M. Daleski's *Dickens and the Art of Analogy.*

G. K. Chesterton, *Charles Dickens* (1906); Edmund Wilson, *The Wound and the Bow* (1941); Humphry House, *The Dickens World* (1941); George Orwell, *Dickens, Dali and Others* (1946); John Butt and Kathleen Tillotson, *Dickens at Work* (1957); Monroe Engel, *The Maturity of Dickens* (1959); John Gross and Gabriel Pearson, eds., *Dickens and the Twentieth Century* (1962); Philip Collins, *Dickens and Crime* (1962); Robert Garis, *The Dickens Theatre* (1965); Taylor Stoehr, *Dickens: The Dreamer's Stance* (1965); K. J. Fielding, *Charles Dickens: A Critical Introduction* (1965); Archibald Coolidge, Jr., *Charles Dickens as Serial Novelist* (1967); Barbara Hardy, *Dickens: The Later Novels* (1968); Sylvère Monod, *Dickens the Novelist* (1968); F. R. and Q. D. Leavis, *Dickens the Novelist* (1970); Michael Slater, ed., *Dickens and Fame: 1870–1970* (Centenary Number of *Dickensian*, May, 1970); Philip Collins, ed., *Dickens: The Critical Heritage* (1971); Ada Nisbet and Blake Nevius, eds., *Dickens Centennial Essays* (1971); Alexander Welsh, *The City of Dickens* (1971); Philip Hobsbaum, *A Reader's Guide to Charles Dickens* (1972); Garrett Stewart, *Dickens and the Trials of Imagination* (1974); Alfred B. Harbage, *A Kind of Power: The Shakespeare-Dickens Analogy* (1975); Albert J. Guerard, *The Triumph of the Novel: Dickens, Dostoevsky, Faulkner* (1976).

IV

For discussions of *Bleak House* itself, see, in the present volume, essays by Miller and others. These titles are not repeated in the following list, and articles cited in the Backgrounds section are also excluded here. Studies of Esther Summerson are listed separately in the final section below.

Morton W. Zabel, "*Bleak House*" (1956) in *The Dickens Critics*, eds. George Ford and Lauriat Lane (1961), 325–48; Louis Crampton, "Satire and Symbolism in *Bleak House*," *Nineteenth-Century Fiction* (1958), 284–303; George H. Ford, "Self-Help and the Helpless in *Bleak House*," in *From Jane Austen to Joseph Conrad*, eds. R. S. Rathburn and Martin Steinmann (1958); John Butt, "*Bleak House* Once More," *Critical Quarterly* (1959), 302–7; Leonard Deen, "Style and Unity in *Bleak House*," *Criticism* (1961), 206–18; Robert Donovan, "Structure and Idea in *Bleak House*," *English Literary History* (June, 1962), 175–201; Joseph Fradin, "Will and Society in *Bleak House*," *PMLA* (1966), 95–109; Trevor Blount, "Sir Leicester Dedlock and 'Deportment' Turveydrop: Some Aspects of Dickens's Use of Parallelism," *Nineteenth-Century Fiction* (1966), 149–65; Ann Wilkinson, "*Bleak House:* From Faraday to Judgment Day," *English Literary History* (1967), 225–47; Stephen C. Gill, "Allusion in *Bleak House*," *Nineteenth-Century Fiction* (1967), 145–54; William F. Axton, "Religious and Scientific Imagery in *Bleak House*," *Nineteenth-Century Fiction* (1968), 349–59; Jacob Korg, ed., *Twentieth-Century Interpretations of "Bleak House"* (1968); A. E. Dyson, ed., *Dickens: "Bleak House": A Casebook* (1969); R. D. McMaster, "Dickens: The Dandy and the Savage," *Studies in the Novel* (1969), 133–46; Michael Steig, "Dickens' Excremental Vision," *Victorian Studies* (1970), 339–54; Trevor Blount, "Dickens and Mr. Krook's Spontaneous Combustion," *Dickens Studies Annual* (1970), 205–11; Michael Steig and F. A. C. Wilson, "Hortense versus Bucket: The Ambiguity of Order in *Bleak House*," *Modern Language Quarterly* (1972), 289–98; Grahame Smith, *Bleak House* (1974); D. W. Jefferson, "The Artistry of *Bleak House*," *Essays and Studies of the English Association* (1974), 37–51; Susan Shatto, "New Notes on *Bleak House*," *Dickens Studies Newsletter* (1975), 78–82, 108–15; Michael Wilkins, "Dickens's Portrayal of the Dedlocks," *Dickensian* (May, 1976), 67–74.

V

The effectiveness of Esther's role in what W. J. Harvey calls "the double narrative" has been extensively discussed by critics. See M. E. Grenander, "The Mystery and the Moral," *Nineteenth-Century Fiction* (1956), 301–5; K. Sorensen, "Subjective Narration in *Bleak House*," *English Studies* (1959), 431–39; William Axton, "The Trouble with Esther," *Modern Language Quarterly* (1965), 545–57; R. J. Dunn, "Esther's Role in *Bleak House*," *Dickensian* (1966), 163–66; Doris Delespinasse, "The Significance of Dual Point of View in *Bleak House*," *Nineteenth-Century Fiction* (1968), 253–64; Martha Rosso, "Dickens and Esther," *Dickensian* (1969), 90–94; Sylvère Monod, "Esther Summerson, Charles Dickens and the Reader of *Bleak House*," *Dickens Studies* (1969), 5–24; A. E. Dyson, "*Bleak House:* Esther Better Not Born?" in his edition *"Bleak House": A Casebook* (1969); Mary Daehler Smith, "The Thematic Function of Esther Summerson," *Victorian Newsletter* (Fall, 1970), 14–18; Philip Collins, *A Critical Commentary on "Bleak House"* (1971), 29–33; Ellen Moers, "*Bleak House*: The Agitating Women," *Dickensian* (1973), 13–24; Alex Zwerdling, "Esther Summerson Rehabilitated," *PMLA* (1973), 429–39; Crawford Kilian, "In Defence of Esther Summerson," *Dalhousie Review* (1974), 318–28.

NORTON CRITICAL EDITIONS

AUSTEN *Emma* edited by Stephen M. Parrish
AUSTEN *Pride and Prejudice* edited by Donald J. Gray
Beowulf (the Donaldson translation) edited by Joseph M. Tuso
Blake's Poetry and Designs selected and edited by Mary Lynn Johnson and John E. Grant
BOCCACCIO *The Decameron* selected, translated, and edited by Mark Musa and Peter E. Bondanella
BRONTË, CHARLOTTE *Jane Eyre* edited by Richard J. Dunn
BRONTË, EMILY *Wuthering Heights* edited by William M. Sale, Jr. *Second Edition*
Robert Browning's Poetry selected and edited by James F. Loucks
Byron's Poetry selected and edited by Frank D. McConnell
CARROLL *Alice in Wonderland* selected and edited by Donald J. Gray
CERVANTES *Don Quixote* (the Ormsby translation, substantially revised) edited by Joseph R. Jones and Kenneth Douglas
Anton Chekhov's Plays translated and edited by Eugene K. Bristow
Anton Chekhov's Short Stories selected and edited by Ralph E. Matlaw
CHOPIN *The Awakening* edited by Margaret Culley
CLEMENS *Adventures of Huckleberry Finn* edited by Sculley Bradley, Richmond Croom Beatty, E. Hudson Long, and Thomas Cooley *Second Edition*
CLEMENS *A Connecticut Yankee in King Arthur's Court* edited by Allison R. Ensor
CLEMENS *Pudd'nhead Wilson* and *Those Extraordinary Twins* edited by Sidney E. Berger
CONRAD *Heart of Darkness* edited by Robert Kimbrough *Second Edition*
CONRAD *Lord Jim* edited by Thomas Moser
CONRAD *The Nigger of the "Narcissus"* edited by Robert Kimbrough
CRANE *Maggie: A Girl of the Streets* edited by Thomas A. Gullason
CRANE *The Red Badge of Courage* edited by Sculley Bradley, Richmond Croom Beatty, E. Hudson Long, and Donald Pizer *Second Edition*
Darwin edited by Philip Appleman *Second Edition*
DEFOE *Moll Flanders* edited by Edward Kelly
DEFOE *Robinson Crusoe* edited by Michael Shinagel
DICKENS *Bleak House* edited by George Ford and Sylvère Monod
DICKENS *Hard Times* edited by George Ford and Sylvère Monod
John Donne's Poetry selected and edited by A. L. Clements
DOSTOEVSKY *Crime and Punishment* (the Coulson translation) edited by George Gibian *Second Edition*
DOSTOEVSKY *The Brothers Karamazov* (the Garnett translation revised by Ralph E. Matlaw) edited by Ralph E. Matlaw
DREISER *Sister Carrie* edited by Donald Pizer
ELIOT *Middlemarch* edited by Bert G. Hornback
FIELDING *Tom Jones* edited by Sheridan Baker
FLAUBERT *Madame Bovary* edited with a substantially new translation by Paul de Man
GOETHE *Faust* translated by Walter Arndt and edited by Cyrus Hamlin
HARDY *Jude the Obscure* edited by Norman Page
HARDY *The Mayor of Casterbridge* edited by James K. Robinson
HARDY *The Return of the Native* edited by James Gindin
HARDY *Tess of the d'Urbervilles* edited by Scott Elledge *Second Edition*
HAWTHORNE *The Blithedale Romance* edited by Seymour Gross and Rosalie Murphy
HAWTHORNE *The House of the Seven Gables* edited by Seymour Gross
HAWTHORNE *The Scarlet Letter* edited by Sculley Bradley, Richmond Croom Beatty, E. Hudson Long, and Seymour Gross *Second Edition*
George Herbert and the Seventeenth-Century Religious Poets selected and edited by Mario A. Di Cesare

HOMER *The Odyssey* translated and edited by Albert Cook
HOWELLS *The Rise of Silas Lapham* edited by Don L. Cook
IBSEN *The Wild Duck* translated and edited by Dounia B. Christiani
JAMES *The Ambassadors* edited by S. P. Rosenbaum
JAMES *The American* edited by James A. Tuttleton
JAMES *The Portrait of a Lady* edited by Robert D. Bamberg
JAMES *The Turn of the Screw* edited by Robert Kimbrough
JAMES *The Wings of the Dove* edited by J. Donald Crowley and Richard A. Hocks
Ben Jonson and the Cavalier Poets selected and edited by Hugh Maclean
Ben Jonson's Plays and Masques selected and edited by Robert M. Adams
MACHIAVELLI *The Prince* translated and edited by Robert M. Adams
MALTHUS *An Essay on the Principle of Population* edited by Philip Appleman
MELVILLE *The Confidence-Man* edited by Hershel Parker
MELVILLE *Moby-Dick* edited by Harrison Hayford and Hershel Parker
MEREDITH *The Egoist* edited by Robert M. Adams
MILL *On Liberty* edited by David Spitz
MILTON *Paradise Lost* edited by Scott Elledge
MORE *Utopia* translated and edited by Robert M. Adams
NEWMAN *Apologia Pro Vita Sua* edited by David J. DeLaura
NORRIS *McTeague* edited by Donald Pizer
Adrienne Rich's Poetry selected and edited by Barbara Charlesworth Gelpi and Albert Gelpi
The Writings of St. Paul edited by Wayne A. Meeks
SHAKESPEARE *Hamlet* edited by Cyrus Hoy
SHAKESPEARE *Henry IV, Part I* edited by James J. Sanderson *Second Edition*
Bernard Shaw's Plays selected and edited by Warren Sylvester Smith
Shelley's Poetry and Prose edited by Donald H. Reiman and Sharon B. Powers
SOPHOCLES *Oedipus Tyrannus* translated and edited by Luci Berkowitz and Theodore F. Brunner
SPENSER *Edmund Spenser's Poetry* selected and edited by Hugh Maclean *Second Edition*
STENDHAL *Red and Black* translated and edited by Robert M. Adams
STERNE *Tristram Shandy* edited by Howard Anderson
SWIFT *Gulliver's Travels* edited by Robert A. Greenberg *Revised Edition*
The Writings of Jonathan Swift edited by Robert A. Greenberg and William B. Piper
TENNYSON *In Memoriam* edited by Robert Ross
Tennyson's Poetry selected and edited by Robert W. Hill, Jr.
THOREAU *Walden and Civil Disobedience* edited by Owen Thomas
TOLSTOY *Anna Karenina* (the Maude translation) edited by George Gibian
TOLSTOY *War and Peace* (the Maude translation) edited by George Gibian
TURGENEV *Fathers and Sons* edited with a substantially new translation by Ralph E. Matlaw
VOLTAIRE *Candide* translated and edited by Robert M. Adams
WATSON *The Double Helix* edited by Gunther S. Stent
WHITMAN *Leaves of Grass* edited by Sculley Bradley and Harold W. Blodgett
WOLLSTONECRAFT *A Vindication of the Rights of Woman* edited by Carol H. Poston
WORDSWORTH *The Prelude: 1799, 1805, 1850* edited by Jonathan Wordsworth, M. H. Abrams, and Stephen Gill
Middle English Lyrics selected and edited by Maxwell S. Luria and Richard L. Hoffman
Modern Drama edited by Anthony Caputi
Restoration and Eighteenth-Century Comedy edited by Scott McMillin

arration-
891 - roman a' clef 1) problem of identy
multi-plot novel - 2) cause of J + J
1/2 = ester, 1/2 = 3rd person
result - presentation of mystery + effects, probability working, doesn't violate sensibility.
3rd person omn - 5
repeating - 22, 28, 29, 30, 31, 96 = well
style - 234, 8, 115, 88, 92, 246, 237, 318, 116
232, 39, 59
Bleak house - west = good, rich
east = dirt, bad, poor
realism vs romance - 3, 4
passion - L. Ded vs maid
chancery - crook =
deportment - Turveydrop 171 vs 174 - to son
vs Sir Ded. \ to society
> both have same dangerous characteristics
charity & lanthropy - Mrs. Jellyby - 42, 46
Mrs. Pardiggle - 98
vs 100
vs 183
church vs society - 198

* Central Problems
- parliment to exist for betterment of society, but are only concerned w/ whats abroad

* Responsibility to society not upheld

The Deadlocks - 690, 452, 663, 713, 571, = Mrs
78, 668, 698, 551, 570.

Mr. Tulkinghorn - 146, 10, 13, 514, 583

Dehuminization of characters

Smallweed - 257, 259

Vhole - 488, 485, 541, 720

Mad. Hortense - 224, 517

Esther's growth - 19, ch. 3, 25, 391, 380, 431,
529, 532, 538, 674, 676, 703

Web - 570, 257